J2.66

Pocket
Dictionary

Second Edition

Oxford University Press

Oxford University Press, Great Clarendon Street, Oxford OX2 6DP

Oxford New York
Athens Auckland Bangkok Bogota Bombay
Buenos Aires Calcutta Cape Town Dar es Salaam
Delhi Florence Hong Kong Istanbul Karachi
Kuala Lumpur Madras Madrid Melbourne
Mexico City Nairobi Paris Singapore
Taipei Tokyo Toronto

and associated companies in
Berlin Ibadan

OXFORD *and* OXFORD ENGLISH *are trade marks of Oxford University Press*

© *Oxford University Press 1980, 1983, 1991*

First published 1983 (ten impressions)
Second Edition 1991
Eighth impression 1997

(Originally published as Oxford Keys English Dictionary, 1980)

ISBN 0 19 431282 8

Chief Compiler
Martin H. Manser
with assistance from
Fergus McGauran

Text capture and processing by Oxford University Press.
Phototypesetting by Pindar Graphics Origination, Scarborough, N. Yorks.
Printed in Hong Kong.

Contents

Using the dictionary

Headwords

The headwords are shown in **bold type**:

dance
table

When two headwords have the same spelling but different meanings they are numbered

head¹
head²

Compound words and derivatives

Compound words are made up of two or more words joined together (e.g. *housework*). Derivatives are words formed from other words (e.g. *hugely* from *huge*). These types of words appear in **bold type** at the end of the entry:

huge /hju:dʒ/ *adj* very large. **hugely** *adv* very much.

house¹ /haʊs/ *n* [C] ... '**housework** *n* [U] work done in a house, eg cleaning and cooking.

Idioms and phrasal verbs

One of the major difficulties for any person learning English is understanding idiomatic expressions and phrasal verbs whose meanings are not clear from the meaning of the headword. In this dictionary idioms and phrasal verbs are shown in **bold type**, and are clearly defined with examples to show how they are used:

hook /hʊk/ *n* [C] **1** curved piece of metal, plastic, etc used for catching hold of sth or for hanging sth on. **2** (in boxing) short blow with the elbow bent. **3** (idm) **off the 'hook** (a) (of a telephone receiver) not resting on the main part of the telephone. (b) (*infml*) no longer in a difficult situation: *let/get sb off the ~*.

Nouns

Nouns which can be used in the singular (*a dog*) and/or plural (*some dogs*) are marked [C] (countable):

label /'leɪbl/ *n* [C]

Nouns which do not have a plural form (*sugar, milk*) are marked [U] (uncountable). These nouns are used with *some, much, a lot of, enough*, etc:

linen /'lɪnɪn/ *n* [U]

Some nouns can be used as either countable or uncountable. They are marked [C, U]. For example **coffee** is [C] as in *Two coffees please*, and [U] as in *Have we got any coffee left?* Most nouns in English have regular plurals, formed by adding *s* to the noun e.g. *dog – dogs*, or by adding *es* if the noun ends in s, z, x, ch or sh e.g. *church – churches*. If a noun does not have a regular plural, the irregular form is shown in the dictionary:

man[1] /mæn/ *n* (*pl* **men** /men/)
lady /'leɪdɪ/ *n* [C] (*pl* **-ies**)
life /laɪf/ *n* (*pl* **lives** /laɪvz/)

Adjectives

All adjectives of one syllable ending in a consonant (e.g. *kind, green*) make the comparative and superlative forms by adding *-er, -est* to the end of the adjective. Adjectives with one or two syllables which do not follow this pattern, but add *-r, -st, -ier, -iest* are shown in the dictionary:

free /friː/ *adj* (~**r** /-ə(r)/, ~**st**)
gentle /'dʒentl/ *adj* (~**r** /-lə(r)/, ~**st** /-lɪst/)
happy /'hæpɪ/ *adj* (**-ier, -iest**)

Verbs

When the spelling and pronunciation of the past tense (*pt*) and past participle (*pp*) of a verb are irregular, these forms are shown at the beginning of the entry for the verb:

know /nəʊ/ *v* (*pt* **knew** /njuː; *US* nuː/, *pp* ~**n** /nəʊn/)
rise[1] /raɪz/ *v* (*pt* **rose** /rəʊz/, *pt* ~**n** /'rɪzn/)

Doubled consonants. Many verbs that end in a single consonant have this letter repeated to make the past tense, past participle or present participle (e.g. *stop – stopped – stopping*). Some adjectives repeat the final consonant in the same way (e.g. *hot – hotter – hottest*). These are shown in the dictionary:

rot /rɒt/ *v* (**-tt-**)
sad /sæd/ *adj* (~**der**, ~**dest**)

Prepositions after verbs, adjectives and nouns

Many verbs, adjectives and nouns are regularly followed by a particular preposition and many of the most common of these are shown in the dictionary. Prepositions given in brackets are those which often occur following the word; those not in brackets always follow it:

familiarize /fəˈmɪlɪəraɪz/ v [T] *with*||
sensitive /ˈsensətɪv/ *adj* 1 (*to*)||

The circle ○

This is used to separate two examples in the same entry:

have[1] ... *1 ~* /I've finished. ○ *She has/she's gone.*

The tilde ~

The symbol ~ is used in place of the headword in examples:

fight /faɪt/ v (*pt, pp* **fought** /fɔːt/) 1 [I, T] use force with the hands or weapons against (sb): (*fig*) *~ against poverty.*

It also replaces the full headword when plural forms are given. A hyphen (-) stands for part of the headword:

tomato /təˈmɑːtəʊ; *US* -meɪt-/ n [C] (*pl* **~es**)
fifty /ˈfɪftɪ/ *pron, adj, n* [C] (*pl* **-ies**)

The slant mark /

The slant mark / is used to show choice in a phrase. For example:

at first/second hand means that both *at first hand* and *at second hand* are possible expressions in English.

Brackets ( )

Brackets ( ) are used to show that words may be omitted from a phrase or sentence. For example:

get sth over (with) means that *get sth over* and *get sth over with* are both possible expressions.

The arrow ⇨

The arrow ⇨ is used to show a cross-reference. It guides you to another part of the dictionary where you will find more information:

make[1] ... **make up ground** ⇨ GROUND[1].

A a

A, a[1] /eɪ/ n [C] (pl **A's, a's** /eɪz/) the first letter of the English alphabet. **A level** n [C] (Brit) examination in a particular subject at about the age of 18 and necessary for entrance to a university.

A[2] abbr ampere(s).

a /ə; strong form eɪ/ (also an /ən; strong form æn/) indefinite article (an is used before a vowel sound) **1** one: a book ○ a teacher ○ a million pounds. **2** (used of number, quantity, groups, etc): a lot of money. **3** each: 70 miles an hour.

aback /əˈbæk/ adv (phr v) **take sb aback** ⇔ TAKE[1].

abacus /ˈæbəkəs/ n [C] frame with beads which slide on rods, used for counting.

abandon /əˈbændən/ v [T] **1** go away from completely. **2** give up: ~ an idea. **3** (fml) ~ oneself to yield completely to a feeling. **abandoned** adj **1** no longer used. **2** (of behaviour) wild. **abandonment** n [U].

abashed /əˈbæʃt/ adj embarrassed; ashamed.

abate /əˈbeɪt/ v [I] (fml) (esp of wind or pain) become less strong. **abatement** n [U]: noise ~ment.

abattoir /ˈæbətwɑː(r)/; US ˌæbəˈtwɑːr/ n [C] place where animals are killed for food.

abbess /ˈæbes/ n [C] woman who is the head of a convent.

abbey /ˈæbi/ n [C] building in which monks or nuns live(d).

abbot /ˈæbət/ n [C] man who is the head of a monastery.

abbreviate /əˈbriːvɪeɪt/ v [T] make (a word, phrase, etc) shorter. **abbreviation** /əˌbriːvɪˈeɪʃn/ n [C] short form of a word or phrase.

abdicate /ˈæbdɪkeɪt/ v [I, T] give up (a high position, responsibility, etc). **abdication** /ˌæbdɪˈkeɪʃn/ n [U].

abdomen /ˈæbdəmən/ n [C] part of the body containing the stomach. **abdominal** /æbˈdɒmɪnl/ adj.

abduct /əbˈdʌkt, æb-/ v [T] take (sb) away illegally, using force. **abduction** /əbˈdʌkʃn, æb-/ n [U, C].

aberration /ˌæbəˈreɪʃn/ n [C, U] action or way of behaving that is not normal.

abet /əˈbet/ v (-tt-) (idm) **aid and abet** ⇔ AID.

abhor /əbˈhɔː(r)/ v (-rr-) [T] (fml)

hate very much. **abhorrence** /əbˈhɒrəns/ n [U]. **abhorrent** /-ənt/ adj.

abide /əˈbaɪd/ v **1** [T] tolerate: She can't ~ that man. **2** [I] by// keep or obey a law, promise, etc. **abiding** adj lasting or enduring.

ability /əˈbɪlətɪ/ n [C, U] (pl -ies) skill or power.

abject /ˈæbdʒekt/ adj (fml) **1** (of conditions) poor, miserable: ~ poverty. **2** not having self-respect. **abjectly** adv.

ablaze /əˈbleɪz/ adj **1** burning; on fire. **2** (fig) shining brightly.

able /ˈeɪbl/ adj (~r, ~st) **1** to// having the power, means or opportunity to do sth: Are you ~ to come with us? **2** clever; skilled. **able-bodied** adj physically strong. **ably** adv.

abnormal /æbˈnɔːml/ adj not normal; unusual. **abnormality** /ˌæbnɔːˈmælətɪ/ n [C, U] (pl -ies). **abnormally** adv.

aboard /əˈbɔːd/ adv, prep on or into a ship, aircraft or train or a bus.

abode /əˈbəʊd/ n [sing] (fml) **1** house or home. **2** (idm) (of) ,no fixed a'bode (having) no permanent place to live.

abolish /əˈbɒlɪʃ/ v [T] put an end to: ~ taxes. **abolition** /ˌæbəˈlɪʃn/ n [U].

abominable /əˈbɒmɪnəbl/; US -mən-/ adj **1** (infml) very unpleasant: ~ weather. **2** (fml) causing hatred and disgust: ~ behaviour. **abominably** adv.

aboriginal /ˌæbəˈrɪdʒənl/ adj (of a person or animal) existing in a region from earliest times. **aboriginal** (also **Aboriginal**) n [C] aboriginal inhabitant of Australia.

Aborigine /ˌæbəˈrɪdʒənɪ/ n [C] aboriginal inhabitant of Australia.

abort /əˈbɔːt/ v [I, T] **1** (cause sb to) end a pregnancy before the foetus is fully developed. **2** end (sth) before it is completed: ~ a space flight. **abortion** /əˈbɔːʃn/ n [C, U] (instance of) aborting(1). **abortive** adj unsuccessful.

abound /əˈbaʊnd/ v [I] (in/with//) have or exist in large numbers or quantities.

about[1] /əˈbaʊt/ prep **1** on the subject of: a book ~ flowers. **2** in many directions in: walking ~ the town. **3** concerned or occupied with: And while you're ~ it, . . . , ie while you are doing that. **4** (idm) **be about to do sth** be going to do sth immediately. **how/what about . . . ?** (a) (used when making a suggestion): *How ~ some more tea?* (b) (used when asking for information): *What ~ the money – do we have enough?*

about² /əˈbaʊt/ *adv* **1** a little more or less than: *It costs ~ £100.* **2** in many different directions: *The children were rushing ~.* **3** here and there: *papers lying ~ in the room.* **4** moving around: *There was no one ~.* **a, bout 'turn** *n* [C] complete change of position or opinion.

above¹ /əˈbʌv/ *prep* **1** higher than: *fly ~ the clouds.* **2** greater in number, price, weight, etc than. **3** too good, respected, etc for: *be ~ stealing/suspicion.* **4** (idm) above 'all most important of all. above one's 'head ⇒ HEAD¹.

above² /əˈbʌv/ *adv* **1** at or to a higher point: *the shelf ~.* **2** earlier in a book, etc: *See ~, page 16.*

abrasion /əˈbreɪʒn/ *n* **1** [U] scraping or rubbing. **2** [C] injury where the skin has been scraped.

abrasive /əˈbreɪsɪv/ *adj* **1** that scrapes or rubs sth away; rough. **2** (*fig*) rude and harsh: *an ~ manner.*

abreast /əˈbrest/ *adv* **1** side by side. **2** (idm) be/keep abreast of sth be/remain well-informed about sth.

abridge /əˈbrɪdʒ/ *v* [T] make (a book, etc) shorter. **abridgement** *n* [C, U].

abroad /əˈbrɔːd/ *adv* in or to another country: *travel ~.*

abrupt /əˈbrʌpt/ *adj* **1** sudden and unexpected: *an ~ stop.* **2** (of behaviour) rough and unfriendly. **abruptly** *adv.* **abruptness** *n* [U].

abscess /ˈæbses/ *n* [C] painful swelling in the body, containing pus.

abscond /əbˈskɒnd/ *v* [I] (*fml*) go away suddenly and secretly.

absence /ˈæbsəns/ *n* **1** [U] (occasion or period of) being away: *~ from school.* **2** [sing] non-existence: *the ~ of information.*

absent¹ /ˈæbsənt/ *adj* (*from*)// not present at a place. **absent-'minded** *adj* with one's mind on other things; forgetful.

absent² /æbˈsent/ *v* (*fml*) ~ oneself (from) stay away from a place.

absentee /ˌæbsənˈtiː/ *n* [C] person who is absent.

absolute /ˈæbsəluːt/ *adj* **1** complete; total: *~ trust.* **2** certain; undoubted: *~ proof.* **3** having unlimited power: *an ~ ruler.* **4** not measured in relation to other things: *an ~ standard.* **absolutely** *adv* **1** completely. **2**

/ˌæbsəˈluːtlɪ/ (*infml*) (used for expressing agreement).

absolve /əbˈsɒlv/ *v* [T] *from/of//* (*fml*) declare (sb) to be free from blame, a duty, etc.

absorb /əbˈsɔːb/ *v* [T] **1** take in (a liquid, heat, light, etc). **2** hold the interest and attention of: *~ed in her work.* **absorbent** *adj* that absorbs liquid easily. **absorption** /əbˈsɔːpʃn/ *n* [U].

abstain /əbˈsteɪn/ *v* [I] **1** (*from*)// keep oneself from drinking, etc. **2** vote neither for nor against a proposal.

abstemious /əbˈstiːmɪəs/ *adj* not eating or drinking a lot; moderate.

abstention /əbˈstenʃn/ *n* [C, U] instance of abstaining(2).

abstinence /ˈæbstɪnəns/ *n* [U] practice of abstaining(1), esp from alcoholic drink.

abstract /ˈæbstrækt/ *adj* **1** existing as an idea, rather than having a physical or practical existence: *Beauty is ~.* **2** (of art) not showing objects in a realistic way. **3** (of a noun) that refers to an abstract quality or state, eg *freedom.* **abstract** *n* [C] short account of a book; summary.

absurd /əbˈsɜːd/ *adj* unreasonable; ridiculous. **absurdity** *n* [U, C] (*pl* **-ies**). **absurdly** *adv.*

abundance /əˈbʌndəns/ *n* [U, sing] quantity that is more than enough. **abundant** /-dənt/ *adj.* **abundantly** *adv.*

abuse¹ /əˈbjuːz/ *v* [T] **1** make bad or wrong use of. **2** treat cruelly. **3** say rude things to or about.

abuse² /əˈbjuːs/ *n* **1** [U] rude or cruel words: *hurl ~ at sb.* **2** [C, U] wrong or bad use: *the ~ of power.* **abusive** *adj* using rude or cruel words.

abysmal /əˈbɪzməl/ *adj* very bad: *an ~ failure.* **abysmally** *adv.*

abyss /əˈbɪs/ *n* [C] hole so deep that it seems to have no bottom.

academic /ˌækəˈdemɪk/ *adj* **1** of (teaching or learning in) schools, colleges, etc. **2** theoretical; not practical. **academic** *n* [C] teacher at a university, college, etc. **academically** /-klɪ/ *adv.*

academy /əˈkædəmɪ/ *n* [C] (*pl* **-ies**) **1** school for special training: *a music ~.* **2** society for people interested in the arts, etc.

accede /əkˈsiːd/ *v* [I] (*to*)// (*fml*) agree to a request, suggestion, etc.

accelerate /əkˈseləreɪt/ *v* [I, T] move faster. **acceleration** /əkˌseləˈreɪʃn/ *n* [U]. **accelerator** *n* [C] pedal in a car, etc that is pressed with the foot to increase the car's speed.

accent /ˈæksənt, ˈæksənt/ n [C] 1 individual, local or national way of speaking. 2 mark written over or under a letter, eg the symbol on the *e* in *café*. 3 special emphasis or force given to sth. **accent** /ækˈsent/ v [T] put emphasis on (a syllable or word).

accentuate /əkˈsentʃʊeɪt/ v [T] give more importance or emphasis to: *The tight shirt ~d his fat stomach.*

accept /əkˈsept/ v 1 [I, T] agree to take (sth offered); say yes to (an offer, etc): ~ *a present.* 2 [T] agree to; recognize or believe: ~ *the truth.* **acceptable** *adj* worth accepting; welcome or tolerable. **acceptance** n [U, C].

access /ˈækses/ n [U] (*to*) 1 way into a place. 2 opportunity or right to use sth. **access** v [T] get information from (a computer). **accessible** *adj* easy to reach, use, etc.

accession /ækˈseʃn/ n [U] reaching a high position: *the King's ~ to the throne.*

accessory /əkˈsesərɪ/ n [C] 1 thing that is useful but not essential: *car accessories.* 2 (also **accessary**) (*law*) person who helps another in a crime.

accident /ˈæksɪdənt/ n 1 [C] event that happens unexpectedly, esp causing injury or damage. 2 (idm) **by accident** as a result of chance. **accidental** /ˌæksɪˈdentl/ *adj.* **accidentally** /-təlɪ/ *adv.*

acclaim /əˈkleɪm/ v [T] (*fml*) greet or welcome with strong approval. **acclaim** n [U] (*fml*) enthusiastic welcome or approval.

acclimatize /əˈklaɪmətaɪz/ v [I, T] (*to*) (get oneself) used to a new climate or new conditions.

accolade /ˈækəleɪd; US ˌækəˈleɪd/ n [C] (*fml*) praise or approval.

accommodate /əˈkɒmədeɪt/ v [T] 1 provide (sb) with a place to live. 2 do a favour to; oblige. **accommodating** *adj* helpful. **accommodation** /əˌkɒməˈdeɪʃn/ n [U] room(s), esp for living in.

accompaniment /əˈkʌmpənɪmənt/ n [C] 1 thing that usually goes with another thing. 2 music played to support a singer or another instrument.

accompanist /əˈkʌmpənɪst/ n [C] person who plays a musical accompaniment.

accompany /əˈkʌmpənɪ/ v (*pt, pp* -ied) [T] 1 go (somewhere) with (sb). 2 be present or occur at the same time as: *wind accompanied by rain.* 3 play a musical accom-

paniment to.

accomplice /əˈkʌmplɪs; US əˈkɒm-/ n [C] person who helps another do sth wrong.

accomplish /əˈkʌmplɪʃ; US əˈkɒm-/ v [T] succeed in doing. **accomplished** *adj* skilled. **accomplishment** n 1 [U] successful completion. 2 [C] thing well done; skill: *Ability to play the piano well is quite an ~.*

accord /əˈkɔːd/ n (idm) **in accord (with sth/sb)** agreeing with sth/sb. **of one's own ac'cord** without being asked or forced; willingly. **accord** v [I] (*with*) (*fml*) agree with sth.

accordance /əˈkɔːdəns/ n (idm) **in accordance with sth** in agreement with sth.

accordingly /əˈkɔːdɪŋlɪ/ *adv* because of sth just mentioned; for that reason.

according to /əˈkɔːdɪŋ tu:/ *prep* 1 as stated by or in: *A ~ to a recent report, people in Britain don't take enough exercise.* ○ *A ~ to my doctor, I ought to go on a diet.* 2 in a way that agrees with: *act ~ to one's principles.* 3 in proportion to: *arranged ~ to size.*

accordion /əˈkɔːdɪən/ n [C] musical instrument with bellows and a keyboard.

accost /əˈkɒst; US əˈkɔːst/ v [T] go up to and speak to (esp a stranger).

account¹ /əˈkaʊnt/ n 1 [C] report: *give an ~ of the meeting.* 2 [C] money kept in a bank: *open a bank ~.* 3 accounts [pl] detailed record of money spent and received. 4 [U] of great, no, etc ac'count of great, no, etc importance. **on ac'count of sth** because of sth. **on no account** not for any reason. **take ac'count of sth, take sth into ac'count** include sth in one's thinking; consider.

account² /əˈkaʊnt/ v (phr v) **account for sth** (a) be an explanation of sth: *This ~ s for his behaviour.* (b) give an explanation of how (money) is spent. **accountable** *adj* responsible.

accountant /əˈkaʊntənt/ n [C] person whose job is to keep or examine financial accounts. **accountancy** /-tənsɪ/ n [U] profession of an accountant. **accounting** n [U] work of an accountant.

accredited /əˈkredɪtɪd/ *adj* officially recognized: *our ~ representative.*

accrue /əˈkruː/ v [I] (*fml*) come as an (esp financial) increase.

accumulate /əˈkjuːmjʊleɪt/ v [I, T] become or make greater in quantity. **accumulation**

/ə,kju:mju'leɪʃn/ n [C, U].

accurate /'ækjərət/ adj exact; correct. **accuracy** /-rəsɪ/ n [U]. **accurately** adv.

accusation /,ækju:'zeɪʃn/ n [C] statement accusing sb of having done wrong.

accuse /ə'kju:z/ v [T] (of) say that (sb) has done wrong: ~ sb of theft. **the accused** person accused of a crime. **accuser** n [C].

accustom /ə'kʌstəm/ v [T] make (oneself, sb or sth) used to sth. **accustomed** adj usual.

ace /eɪs/ n [C] 1 playing card with a large single spot on it. 2 (infml) person who is extremely skilled: an ~ footballer.

ache /eɪk/ n [C] (often in compounds) continuous dull pain: 'headache. **ache** v [I] 1 suffer from an ache: My head ~s. 2 for/to// want sth very much: He is aching for home. ○ ~ to go home.

achieve /ə'tʃiːv/ v [T] gain or reach by effort; get (sth) done: ~ one's aim. **achievement** n [C, U].

Achilles /ə'kɪliːz/ n (idm) **Achilles' heel** weak or vulnerable point in sb's character. **Achilles' tendon** n [C] tendon joining the muscles at the back of the leg to the heel.

acid /'æsɪd/ n 1 [U, C] (chemistry) substance that contains hydrogen and which may burn holes. 2 (idm) the **'acid test** test of the true value of sth. **acid** adj 1 sour. 2 (fig) very unkind. **,acid 'rain** n [U] rain containing acid substances that kills trees, crops, etc.

acknowledge /ək'nɒlɪdʒ/ v [T] 1 accept the truth of; admit: I ~ my mistake. 2 report that one has received (eg a letter). 3 show that one has noticed (sb). 4 show that one is thankful for. **acknowledgement** (also **acknowledgment**) n [C, U].

acne /'æknɪ/ n [U] spots on the face and neck.

acorn /'eɪkɔːn/ n [C] fruit of the oak tree.

acoustic /ə'kuːstɪk/ adj of sound. **acoustics** n 1 [pl] qualities that make a room good or bad for hearing music or speeches in. 2 [U] study of sound.

acquaint /ə'kweɪnt/ v [T] with// make (sb/oneself) familiar with sth. **acquaintance** n 1 [C] person whom one knows slightly. 2 [U] (with//) (esp slight) knowledge of sb/sth. 3 (idm) **make sb's acquaintance** (idm) to get to know sb; meet personally. **acquainted** adj (with//) knowing sb personally.

acquiesce /,ækwɪ'es/ v [I] (in)// (fml) accept sth without protest. **acquiescence** n [U].

acquire /ə'kwaɪə(r)/ v [T] gain by one's own ability, efforts, etc; obtain. **acquisition** /,ækwɪ'zɪʃn/ n 1 [C] something acquired. 2 [U] action of acquiring. **acquisitive** /ə'kwɪzətɪv/ adj fond of acquiring things.

acquit /ə'kwɪt/ v (-tt-) 1 [T] declare that (sb) is not guilty. 2 ~ **oneself** behave in the way that is stated: He ~ed himself very well. **acquittal** n [C].

acre /'eɪkə(r)/ n [C] measure of land; 4840 square yards (about 4050 square metres). **acreage** /'eɪkərɪdʒ/ n [U] area measured in acres.

acrid /'ækrɪd/ adj (esp of smell or taste) sharp or bitter.

acrimonious /,ækrɪ'məʊniəs/ adj (fml) (esp of quarrels) bitter. **acrimony** /'ækrɪmənɪ; US -məʊnɪ/ n [U].

acrobat /'ækrəbæt/ n [C] person who can do skilful physical acts, eg walking on a rope, esp at a circus. **acrobatic** /,ækrə'bætɪk/ adj. **acrobatics** n [pl].

acronym /'ækrənɪm/ n [C] word formed from the first letters of a name, eg NATO.

across /ə'krɒs; US ə'krɔːs/ adv, prep 1 from one side to the other side: swim ~ the lake. 2 on the other side (of): My house is just ~ the street.

acrylic /ə'krɪlɪk/ adj synthetic material made from chemicals and used for making clothes.

act¹ /ækt/ v 1 [I] do sth; behave: We must ~ quickly. 2 [I, T] perform (a part) in a play or film. 3 (phr v) **act as sb/sth** perform the function of sb/sth. **acting** n [U] (skill or work of) performing in plays, etc. **acting** adj doing the duties of another person for a short time: the ~ing manager.

act² /ækt/ n [C] 1 something done: an ~ of kindness. 2 process of doing sth: caught in the ~ of stealing. 3 law made by a government: an A~ of Parliament. 4 main division of a play. 5 one of a series of short performances: a circus ~. 6 (infml) pretended way of behaviour: put on an ~. 7 (idm) an **act of 'God** event caused by uncontrollable natural forces.

action /'ækʃn/ n 1 [U] process of doing sth: take ~ to stop the row in crime. 2 [C] something done; act. 3 [U] main events in a story, book, etc. 4 [U] fighting in war: He was killed in ~. 5 [C] charge, etc in a law-court: bring an ~ against sb. 6 (idm) into 'action into operation. out of 'action no longer working.

activate /'æktɪveɪt/ v [T] start (sth) working.

active /'æktɪv/ adj 1 doing things; busy or energetic. 2 (grammar) of the verb form used when the subject of a sentence does the action, as in 'She drove the car.'. the active n [sing] active(2) form of a verb. actively adv.

activist /'æktɪvɪst/ n [C] person who takes an active part, in esp politics.

activity /æk'tɪvətɪ/ n (pl -ies) 1 [U] being active; busy action: a lot of ~ in the street. 2 [C, esp pl] something done; action: social activities.

actor /'æktə(r)/ n [C] (fem **actress** /'æktrɪs/) person who acts in plays, films, etc.

actual /'æktʃuəl/ adj existing in fact; real. **actually** /'æktʃuli/ adv 1 really; in fact: what ~ly happened. 2 (used for showing surprise): He ~ly expected me to pay!

acumen /'ækjumen/ n [U] (fml) ability to understand and judge things clearly.

acupuncture /'ækjupʌŋktʃə(r)/ n [U] (medical) treatment of illness by sticking small needles into the body.

acute /ə'kjuːt/ adj (~r, ~st) 1 very great; severe: suffer ~ hardship. 2 very sensitive: an ~ sense of hearing. **acute 'accent** n [C] mark written over a letter, as over the e in café. **acute 'angle** n [C] angle of less than 90°. **acutely** adv. **acuteness** n [U].

AD /ˌeɪ 'diː/ abbr (in the year) since the birth of Jesus Christ.

ad /æd/ n [C] (infml) short for ADVERTISEMENT (ADVERTISE).

adamant /'ædəmənt/ adj (fml) refusing to change one's opinion.

Adam's apple /ˌædəmz 'æpl/ n [C] lump at the front of the throat.

adapt /ə'dæpt/ v [T] make suitable for a new use, situation, etc. **adaptable** adj able to change. **adaptation** /ˌædæp'teɪʃn/ n [C, U] result or process of adapting: an ~ation of the play for television.

adaptor n [C] kind of electrical plug that allows several plugs to be connected to one socket.

add /æd/ v 1 [T] put with sth else: ~ the flour to the milk. 2 [I, T] (up)// put (numbers) together. 3 [T] say (sth more). 4 (phr v) **add up** (infml) seem reasonable; make

sense: It just doesn't ~ up. **add up to sth** result in sth; show.

adder /'ædə(r)/ n [C] small poisonous snake.

addict /'ædɪkt/ n [C] 1 person who cannot stop taking drugs, alcohol, etc. 2 person strongly interested in sth: a TV ~. **addicted** /ə'dɪktɪd/ adj (to)// unable to stop taking or using sth: ~ed to drugs. **addiction** /ə'dɪkʃn/ n [U, C]. **addictive** /ə'dɪktɪv/ adj causing addiction.

addition /ə'dɪʃn/ n 1 [U] adding. 2 [C] something added. 3 (idm) **in addition (to sth/sb)** as an extra thing, person, etc. **additional** /-ʃənl/ adj extra. **additionally** /-ʃənəlɪ/ adv.

additive /'ædɪtɪv/ n [C] substance added to sth, esp food.

address /ə'dres; US 'ædres/ n [C] 1 number, street, town, etc where sb lives. 2 formal speech. **address** v [T] 1 write a name and address on. 2 give a speech to.

adept /'ædept, ə'dept/ adj (at/in)// skilled at (doing sth).

adequate /'ædɪkwət/ adj enough; satisfactory. **adequately** adv.

adhere /əd'hɪə(r)/ v [I] (fml) 1 (to)// (a) stick firmly to sth. 2 to// (fig) (a) act according to a rule, etc. (b) give support to an opinion, etc. **adherent** /əd'hɪərənt/ n supporter of a person, group, etc. **adherence** /-rəns/ n [U].

adhesive /əd'hiːsɪv/ adj able to stick. **adhesion** /əd'hiːʒn/ n [U]. **adhesive** n [C, U] substance, esp glue, that makes things stick together.

ad hoc /ˌæd 'hɒk/ adj, adv (made or arranged) for a particular purpose; not planned.

adjacent /ə'dʒeɪsnt/ adj (to)// next to sth.

adjective /'ædʒɪktɪv/ n [C] (grammar) word that describes a noun, eg green in green grass. **adjectival** /ˌædʒek'taɪvl/ adj.

adjoin /ə'dʒɔɪn/ v [I] (fml) be next to: ~ing rooms.

adjourn /ə'dʒɜːn/ v [T] stop (a meeting) for a time. **adjournment** n [C, U].

adjudicate /ə'dʒuːdɪkeɪt/ v [I, T] (fml) make an official decision or judgement (on). **adjudication** /əˌdʒuːdɪ'keɪʃn/ n [U]. **adjudicator** n [C].

adjunct /'ædʒʌŋkt/ n [C] (to/of)// thing that is attached to sth else but is less important than it.

adjust /ə'dʒʌst/ v 1 [T] change or correct (sth) to make it right. 2 [I, T] (to)// become or make used to new conditions. **adjustable** adj.

adjustment n [C, U].

ad lib /ˌæd 'lɪb/ adj, adv spoken, performed, etc without preparation. **ad lib** v (-bb-) [I] speak, perform, etc without preparation.

administer /əd'mɪnɪstə(r)/ v [T] 1 control or manage: ~ a hospital. 2 (fml) give: ~ punishment/a drug.

administration /əd,mɪnɪ'streɪʃn/ n 1 [U] management of public or business affairs. 2 [U] process of administering. 3 (often **the Administration**) [C] (esp US) the Government: the Bush A~. **administrative** /əd'mɪnɪstrətɪv; US -streɪtɪv/ adj. **administrator** /əd'mɪnɪstreɪtə(r)/ n [C].

admirable /'ædmərəbl/ adj deserving admiration; excellent. **admirably** adv.

admiral /'ædmərəl/ n [C] officer of very high rank in the navy.

admire /əd'maɪə(r)/ v [T] have a good opinion of; look at with pleasure. **admiration** /ˌædmə'reɪʃn/ n [U] feeling of respect, approval or pleasure. **admirer** n [C]. **admiring** adj: admiring glances.

admissible /əd'mɪsəbl/ adj 1 (law) that can be allowed: ~ evidence. 2 (fml) acceptable.

admission /əd'mɪʃn/ n 1 [U] entering or being allowed to enter a building, society, school, etc. 2 [U] money charged for being admitted to a public place. 3 [C] statement that sth is true; confession.

admit /əd'mɪt/ v (-tt-) [T] 1 allow to enter; let in. 2 agree that (sth bad) is true: I ~ that I was wrong. **admittance** n [U] right to enter. **admittedly** adv as must be agreed.

admonish /əd'mɒnɪʃ/ v [T] (fml) tell sb gently that he/she has done sth wrong.

ad nauseam /ˌæd 'nɔːzɪæm/ adv so often as to become annoying: She played the same records ~.

ado /ə'duː/ n [U] trouble; delay: without further ~.

adolescent /ˌædə'lesnt/ adj, n [C] (of a) young person between childhood and adulthood. **adolescence** /-'lesns/ n [U].

adopt /ə'dɒpt/ v [T] 1 take (sb else's child) into one's family, making him/her legally one's son/daughter. 2 take and use (a method, way of life, etc). **adoption** /ə'dɒpʃn/ n [U, C]. **adoptive** adj related by adoption.

adore /ə'dɔː(r)/ v [T] 1 love and respect greatly; worship. 2 (infml) like very much. **adorable** adj lovable: an adorable child/puppy. **adoration** /ˌædə'reɪʃn/ n [U].

adorn /ə'dɔːn/ v [T] add beauty to;

decorate. **adornment** n [C, U].

adrenalin /ə'drenəlɪn/ n [U] substance produced in the body by anger, fear, etc and which makes the heart beat faster.

adrift /ə'drɪft/ adj (of boats) floating freely; not fastened.

adulation /ˌædju'leɪʃn; US ˌædʒʊ'l-/ n [U] (fml) too much praise or admiration.

adult /'ædʌlt, also ə'dʌlt/ n [C], adj (person or animal) grown to full size or strength. **adulthood** n [U] state of being an adult.

adulterate /ə'dʌltəreɪt/ v [T] make lower in quality by adding another substance.

adultery /ə'dʌltərɪ/ n [U] voluntary sexual intercourse between a married person and sb to whom he/she is not married. **adulterer** /-tərə(r)/ n [C] (fem **adulteress** /-tərɪs/) person who commits adultery. **adulterous** /-tərəs/ adj.

advance[1] /əd'vɑːns; US -'væns/ v 1 [I, T] move forward. 2 [I] pay (money) before it is due to be paid; lend. **advanced** adj 1 far on in life or progress: ~d in years; ie old. 2 not basic: ~d studies. **advancement** n [U] act of advancing; progress or promotion.

advance[2] /əd'vɑːns; US -'væns/ n 1 [C, U] forward movement; progress. 2 [C] money paid before it is due; loan. 3 **advances** [pl] attempts to become friendly with sb. 4 (idm) **in advance (of sth)** before sth. **advance** adj done or given before sth: an ~ warning.

advantage /əd'vɑːntɪdʒ; US -'væn-/ n 1 [C] something useful that puts one in a better or more favourable position; benefit. 2 [U] profit or gain. 3 (idm) **take advantage of sb** treat sb unfairly or deceitfully to get what one wants. **take advantage of sth** use sth well, properly, etc. **advantageous** /ˌædvən'teɪdʒəs/ adj.

advent /'ædvənt/ n **the advent** [sing] of/ the coming of an important event.

adventure /əd'ventʃə(r)/ n 1 [C] exciting or dangerous journey or activity. 2 [U] excitement; risk. **adventurer** n [C] person who likes adventures. **adventurous** adj 1 fond of adventures. 2 full of excitement.

adverb /'ædvɜːb/ n [C] (grammar) word that adds information to a verb, adjective, phrase, or another adverb, eg quickly in run quickly. **adverbial** /æd'vɜːbɪəl/ adj, n [C].

adversary /'ædvəsərɪ; US -serɪ/ n [C] (pl -ies) (fml) enemy; opponent.

adverse /ˈædvɜːs/ adj unfavourable: ~ *conditions*. **adversely** adv. **adversity** /ədˈvɜːsəti/ n [C, U] (pl -ies) trouble.

advert /ˈædvɜːt/ n [C] (infml) short for ADVERTISEMENT (ADVERTISE).

advertise /ˈædvətaɪz/ v [T] make (esp sth for sale) known to people by notices in newspapers, etc. **advertisement** /ədˈvɜːtɪsmənt; US ˌædvərˈtaɪzmənt/ n [C] notice in a newspaper, on television, etc of sth for sale. **advertiser** n [C]. **advertising** n [U].

advice /ədˈvaɪs/ n [U] opinion given to sb about what he/she should do.

advise /ədˈvaɪz/ v [T] 1 give advice to. 2 (of/) ((esp commerce) inform (sb) about sth: ~ *sb of a delivery date*. **advisable** adj sensible or wise. **adviser** (also esp US **advisor**) n [C]. **advisory** adj giving advice.

advocate /ˈædvəkət/ n [C] person who speaks in favour of sb (esp in a law-court) or an idea. **advocate** /ˈædvəkeɪt/ v [T] support.

aerial /ˈeərɪəl/ adj in, through or from the air: an ~ *photograph*. **aerial** n [C] wire or rod that receives television or radio signals.

aerobatics /ˌeərəˈbætɪks/ n [pl] acrobatic movements performed by aircraft.

aerobics /eəˈrəʊbɪks/ n [also sing with pl v] physical exercise done to increase the amount of oxygen in the body.

aerodrome /ˈeərədrəʊm/ n [C] (dated esp Brit) small airport.

aerodynamics /ˌeərəʊdaɪˈnæmɪks/ n [U] science which deals with the forces that act on objects moving through the air. **aerodynamic** adj.

aeronautics /ˌeərəˈnɔːtɪks/ n [U] scientific study or practice of flying aircraft.

aeroplane /ˈeərəpleɪn/ n [C] aircraft with wings and one or more engines.

aerosol /ˈeərəsɒl; US -sɔːl/ n [C] small container from which a liquid is forced out as a fine spray.

aerospace /ˈeərəʊspeɪs/ n [U] earth's atmosphere and the space beyond it.

aesthetic /iːsˈθetɪk; US esˈθetɪk/ adj concerned with (the enjoyment of) beauty. **aesthetically** /-klɪ/ adv. **aesthetics** n [U] branch of philosophy dealing with beauty.

afar /əˈfɑː(r)/ adv (idm) **from aˈfar** from a long distance away.

affable /ˈæfəbl/ adj friendly and easy to talk to. **affably** adv.

affair /əˈfeə(r)/ n 1 [C, usu sing] event or series of events. 2 [sing] something to be done; concern. 3 **affairs** [pl] (a) matters of public interest. (b) personal business matters. 4 [C] sexual relationship between people who are not married to each other.

affect /əˈfekt/ v [T] have an influence on: *The cold climate ~ed her health*. **affectation** /ˌæfekˈteɪʃn/ n [C, U] (instance of) unnatural behaviour. **affected** adj not natural; artificial.

affection /əˈfekʃn/ n [U] feeling of fondness; love. **affectionate** /-ʃənət/ adj. **affectionately** adv.

affidavit /ˌæfɪˈdeɪvɪt/ n [C] (law) sworn written statement used as evidence.

affiliate /əˈfɪlɪeɪt/ v [T] (esp of an organization) join a larger organization. **affiliation** /əˌfɪlɪˈeɪʃn/ n [C, U].

affinity /əˈfɪnəti/ n [C, U] (pl -ies) 1 close relationship. 2 strong liking: *She feels a strong ~ for him*.

affirm /əˈfɜːm/ v [T] (fml) state or declare. **affirmation** /ˌæfəˈmeɪʃn/ n [C, U]. **affirmative** adj (of words, answers, etc) showing agreement; meaning 'yes'. **affirmative** n 1 [C] affirmative word, etc. 2 (idm) **in the affirmative** (fml) (of an answer) meaning 'yes'.

affix /əˈfɪks/ v [T] (fml) stick; attach.

affix /ˈæfɪks/ n [C] (grammar) prefix or suffix, eg un- or -ly.

afflict /əˈflɪkt/ v [T] cause pain or trouble to. **affliction** /əˈflɪkʃn/ n [C, U] (fml) (cause of) suffering.

affluent /ˈæfluənt/ adj rich; wealthy. **affluence** /-luəns/ n [U].

afford /əˈfɔːd/ v [T] 1 have enough money, time, space, etc for. 2 be able to do (sth) without risk to oneself: *We can't ~ to lose such experienced workers*.

affront /əˈfrʌnt/ v [T] insult; offend. **affront** n [C] insult.

afield /əˈfiːld/ adv (idm) **far afield** far away, esp from home.

afloat /əˈfləʊt/ adj 1 floating. 2 on board ship. 3 out of debt.

afoot /əˈfʊt/ adj being prepared or planned.

aforementioned /əˌfɔːˈmenʃənd/ (also **aforesaid** /əˈfɔːsed/) adj (fml) mentioned earlier.

afraid /əˈfreɪd/ adj 1 (of/to)) frightened of sb/sth or that sth bad will happen: ~ *of spiders* ○ ~ *to go out in the dark*. 2 (idm) **I'm afraid** I'm sorry: *I'm ~ we'll arrive late*.

afresh /ə'freʃ/ adv (fml) again.

after /'ɑːftə(r)/; US 'æf-/ prep 1 later than: leave ~ lunch. 2 following: C comes ~ B in the alphabet. ○ Year ~ year he would visit her. 3 because of: A~ what he said, I don't ever want to see him again. 4 searching for or chasing: The police are ~ my brother. 5 in spite of: A ~ everything I've done for you, you're leaving me now! 6 in the style of: a painting ~ Rembrandt. 7 (idm) **after all** in spite of what has been said, done or expected.

after adv, conj later in time than): She died three days ~ (I had left). **'after-effect** n [C, usu sing] (esp unpleasant) effect that occurs later. **'afterthought** n [C] idea that comes later.

aftermath /'ɑːftəmæθ (Brit also -mɑːθ)/ n [C] result of a war or other bad event.

afternoon /ˌɑːftə'nuːn; US ˌæf-/ n [U, C] part of the day between noon and evening.

afterwards (US also **afterward**) /'ɑːftəwədz; US 'æf-/ adv at a later time.

again /ə'gen, ə'geɪn/ adv 1 once more; another time: try ~ later. 2 to or in the original place or condition: I was glad to be home ~. 2 in addition: as many/much ~, ie twice as many/much. 4 (idm) **a.gain and a'gain** very often; many times.

against /ə'genst, ə'geɪnst/ prep 1 in contact with: The ladder was leaning ~ the wall. 2 in opposition to: swim ~ the current ○ ~ the law. 3 in contrast to: The trees were black ~ the sky. 4 as a protection from; in preparation for: an injection ~ measles.

age¹ /eɪdʒ/ n 1 [C, U] length of time sb has lived or sth has existed. 2 [U] later part of life; old age: Wisdom comes with ~. 3 [C] period of history: the Elizabethan ~, ie the time of Queen Elizabeth I of England. 4 [C, usu pl] (infml) very long time: waiting for ~ s. 5 (idm) **,be/,come of 'age** be/become an adult in law. **,under 'age** too young. **'age-group** n [C] people in a period of life between two ages. **'age limit** n [C] oldest or youngest age at which a person is allowed to do sth. **,age-'old** adj having existed for a very long time.

age² /eɪdʒ/ v (pres part **ageing** or **aging**, pp **aged** /eɪdʒd/) [I, T] (cause to) become old. **aged** adj /eɪdʒd/ of the age of: a boy ~d ten. 2 /'eɪdʒɪd/ very old. **the aged** /'eɪdʒɪd/ n [pl] very old people.

ageing (also **aging**) n [U] process

of becoming old. **ageing** adj becoming older.

agency /'eɪdʒənsɪ/ n [C] (pl -ies) office or work of an agent(1): a travel ~.

agenda /ə'dʒendə/ n [C] list of things to be discussed at a meeting.

agent /'eɪdʒənt/ n [C] 1 person who arranges business for other people: an estate ~. 2 person or thing that has a particular result: Rain and wind are ~s that wear away rocks.

aggravate /'ægrəveɪt/ v [T] 1 make worse. 2 (infml) annoy: an aggravating delay. **aggravation** /ˌægrə'veɪʃn/ n [C, U].

aggregate /'ægrɪgət/ n [C] total amount.

aggression /ə'greʃn/ n [U] 1 angry feelings. 2 action that may start a quarrel or war. **aggressor** /ə'gresə(r)/ n [C] person or country that starts a quarrel or war.

aggressive /ə'gresɪv/ adj 1 having angry feelings. 2 forceful and eager to succeed: an ~ salesman. **aggressively** adv. **aggressiveness** n [U].

aggrieved /ə'griːvd/ adj (fml) feeling anger and bitterness, esp because of unfair treatment.

aggro /'ægrəʊ/ n [U] (Brit sl) aggressive behaviour likely to cause trouble.

aghast /ə'gɑːst; US ə'gæst/ adj filled with horror or shock.

agile /'ædʒaɪl; US 'ædʒl/ adj able to move quickly and easily. **agility** /ə'dʒɪlətɪ/ n [U].

aging adj ⇔ AGE².

agitate /'ædʒɪteɪt/ v 1 [T] make (sb) anxious; trouble. 2 [I] for/against) argue publicly in favour of/against sth. 3 [T] shake (a liquid) strongly. **agitation** /ˌædʒɪ'teɪʃn/ n [U]. **agitator** n [C] person who agitates for (esp political) change.

aglow /ə'gləʊ/ adj bright with colour or excitement.

AGM /ˌeɪ dʒiː 'em/ abbr (esp Brit) annual general meeting; meeting held once a year by a company, club, etc to elect officials, report on business, etc.

agnostic /æg'nɒstɪk/ n [C], adj (person) believing nothing can be known about God.

ago /ə'gəʊ/ adv before now: The train left five minutes ~.

agog /ə'gɒg/ adj eager and excited.

agonize /'ægənaɪz/ v [I] (over/ about)) be very anxious for a long time about sth. **agonized** adj expressing great pain. **agonizing**

adj causing great pain.

agony /'ægənɪ/ *n* [U, C] (*pl* **-ies**) great pain. **'agony aunt** *n* [C] (*Brit infml* or *joc*) in a newspaper or magazine, woman who gives advice to readers who write for help with their personal problems.

agrarian /ə'greərɪən/ *adj* of land, esp farmland.

agree /ə'griː/ *v* 1 [I] (*with*)// have the same opinion as sb: *I ~ with you that money is the problem.* 2 [I] *to*// be willing to do sth; say yes to sth: *My boss ~d to let me go home early.* 3 [I, T] (*on*)// decide sth. 4 [I, T] (*with*)// approve of sth; accept. 5 [I] be the same; match: *The two descriptions do not ~.* 6 [I] (*with*)// (*grammar*) (of verbs, etc) have the same number, person, etc as another word in the same sentence. 7 [idm] **be agreed** have reached an agreement. 8 (phr v) **agree with sb** (of food) suit sb's health. **agreeable** *adj* 1 pleasant. 2 ready to agree. **agreeably** *adv*. **agreement** *n* 1 [C] arrangement, promise or contract made with sb. 2 [U] state of agreeing: *The two sides failed to reach ~ ment.*

agriculture /'ægrɪkʌltʃə(r)/ *n* [U] science or practice of farming. **agricultural** /ˌægrɪ'kʌltʃərəl/ *adj*.

aground /ə'graʊnd/ *adv, adj* (of ships) touching the bottom in shallow water.

ahead /ə'hed/ *adv* further forward in space or time: *go/plan ~.* **a'head of** *prep* 1 further forward in space or time than. 2 further advanced in space than: *be years ~ of one's rivals.*

aid /eɪd/ *n* 1 [U] help: *with the ~ of a friend.* 2 [C] thing or person that helps: *teaching ~s.* 3 [U] food, money, etc sent to a country in need. 4 (idm) **what is sth in aid of?** (*infml*) what is the purpose of sth? **aid** *v* 1 [T] (*fml*) help. 2 (idm) **aid and a'bet** (esp *law*) help or encourage (sb) to do wrong.

aide /eɪd/ *n* [C] assistant to sb with an important government job: *presidential ~s.*

AIDS (also **Aids**) /eɪdz/ *abbr* Acquired Immune Deficiency Syndrome; very serious disease that destroys a person's natural protection against illness.

ailing /'eɪlɪŋ/ *adj* unwell; ill. **ailment** /'eɪlmənt/ *n* [C] illness, esp a slight one.

aim /eɪm/ *v* 1 [I, T] (*at*)// point (a weapon or object) towards sth. 2 [I] (*at/for*)// direct one's efforts at sth; plan to achieve; intend: *~ at increasing exports.* 3 [T] direct (a

comment, etc): *My remarks were not ~ed at you.* **aim** *n* 1 [C] purpose; intention: *Her ~ is to be famous.* 2 [U] action of aiming. **aimless** *adj* having no purpose. **aimlessly** *adv*.

ain't /eɪnt/ (used in non-standard spoken English) 1 (short for) am/is/are not. 2 (short for) has/have *used to be.* 2 (short for) has/have not; having nothing yet.

air¹ /eə(r)/ *n* 1 [U] mixture of gases that we breathe. 2 (the ~) earth's atmosphere: *travel by ~*, ie in an aircraft. 3 [U] impression or appearance: *an ~ of importance.* 4 (idm) **give oneself/put on 'airs** behave unnaturally to impress others. **in the 'air** (a) (of opinions, etc) passing from one person to another. (b) uncertain. **,on/'off the 'air** broadcasting/not broadcasting. **airborne** /'eəbɔːn/ *adj* 1 transported by air. 2 (of an aircraft) flying. **air-conditioning** *n* [U] system of machines that supply a room or building with cool dry air. **air-conditioned** *adj*. **'aircraft** *n* [C] (*pl* **aircraft**) flying machine, eg an aeroplane or a helicopter. **'aircraft-carrier** *n* [C] warship with a long wide deck for aircraft. **'airfield** *n* [C] area of open ground where aircraft can take off and land. **'air force** *n* [C] part of a country's military forces that is organized for fighting in the air. **'air-hostess** *n* [C] woman whose job is to look after the passengers in an aircraft. **'airlift** *n* [C] transport of people or supplies by air. **'airlift** *v* [T] transport in this way. **'airline** *n* [C] company that carries passengers or goods by aeroplane. **'airliner** *n* [C] large passenger aircraft. **'airmail** *n* [U] system of sending letters, etc by air. **'airplane** /'eəpleɪn/ *n* [C] (*US*) = AEROPLANE. **'airport** *n* [C] place where aircraft land and take off, with buildings for passengers to wait in, etc. **'air raid** *n* [C] attack by aircraft. **'airship** *n* [C] aircraft with no wings which is filled with a gas which is lighter than air, driven by engines. **'airspace** *n* [U] part of the earth's atmosphere above a country, considered to belong to that country. **'airstrip** *n* [C] piece of land cleared for aircraft to take off and land. **'air terminal** *n* [C] building in a town from where passengers travel to an airport. **'airtight** *adj* not allowing air to get in or out. **,air-to-'air** *adj* (fired) from one aircraft to another while flying. **air traffic controller** *n* [C] person whose job is to give radio instructions to pilots about landing, routes, etc. **'air way** n [C] route regularly taken by aircraft. **'airworthy** adj (of an aircraft) safe to fly.

air² /eə(r)/ v 1 [I, T] put (clothes, etc) in a warm place to dry completely. **2** [T] let fresh air into (a room). **3** [T] let people know: ~ *one's opinions*. **airing** n [sing]: *give the blankets a good ~ ing* (fig) *give one's views on ~ ing.* **'airing cupboard** n [C] warm cupboard for drying bedclothes, towels, etc.

airless /'eəlɪs/ adj not having enough fresh air.

airy /'eərɪ/ adj (**-ier, -iest**) **1** having plenty of fresh air moving through it. **2** not serious; casual. **airily** adv.

aisle /aɪl/ n [C] passage between seats in a theatre, etc or between shelves in a supermarket.

ajar /ə'dʒɑː(r)/ adj (of a door) slightly open.

akin /ə'kɪn/ adj to|| (fml) similar to sth.

à la carte /ˌɑː lɑː 'kɑːt/ adj (of a restaurant meal) ordered as separate items from the menu and not as a fixed price for the complete meal.

alacrity /ə'lækrətɪ/ n [U] (fml) prompt or eager action: *He accepted her offer with a ~.*

alarm /ə'lɑːm/ n **1** [U] sudden feeling of fear, caused by danger. **2** [C] (device that gives a) warning sound: *a fire ~* ○ *sound/raise the ~.* **alarm** v [T] cause sudden anxiety to; frighten. **a'larm clock** n [C] clock that can be set to make a noise at a particular time to wake one up. **alarming** adj causing fear.

alas /ə'læs/ interj (dated or rhet) (cry expressing sorrow or regret).

albatross /'ælbətrɒs/ n [C] large white sea-bird.

albeit /ˌɔːl'biːɪt/ conj (dated or fml) although: *a useful, ~ brief, description.*

albino /æl'biːnəʊ; US -'baɪ-/ n [C] (pl ~s) person or animal with white skin and hair and pink eyes.

album /'ælbəm/ n [C] **1** book in which a collection of photographs, stamps, etc can be kept. **2** long-playing record.

alcohol /'ælkəhɒl; US -hɔːl/ n [U] (pure colourless liquid in) drinks such as beer, wine and whisky. **alcoholic** /ˌælkə'hɒlɪk; US -'hɔː-/ adj of or containing alcohol. **alcoholic** n [C] person addicted to alcohol. **alcoholism** n [U] (disease caused by) continual heavy drink-

ing of alcohol.

alcove /'ælkəʊv/ n [C] small area in a room formed by part of the wall being set back.

ale /eɪl/ n [U, C] kind of strong beer.

alert /ə'lɜːt/ adj fully awake and ready to act. **alert** n **1** [C] warning of danger. **2** (idm) **on the a'lert** ready to deal with possible danger. **alert** v [T] warn (sb) of danger.

A level ⇨ A, a¹.

algae /'ældʒiː, also 'ælgaɪ/ n [pl] very simple plants that are mainly found in water.

algebra /'ældʒɪbrə/ n [U] branch of mathematics in which letters represent quantities.

alias /'eɪlɪəs/ n [C] false name, used esp by a criminal. **alias** adv also (falsely) called: *Joe Sykes, alias John Smith.*

alibi /'ælɪbaɪ/ n [C] evidence that proves that sb was somewhere else when a crime was committed.

alien /'eɪlɪən/ n [C] **1** person who has not become a citizen of the country in which he/she lives. **2** creature from another world. **alien** adj **1** foreign. **2** unfamiliar and strange.

alienate /'eɪlɪəneɪt/ v [T] cause (sb) to become unfriendly. **alienation** /ˌeɪlɪə'neɪʃn/ n [U].

alight¹ /ə'laɪt/ adj on fire.

alight² /ə'laɪt/ v [I] (fml) **1** get down from a bus, etc. **2** (of a bird) come down from the air and settle.

align /ə'laɪn/ v [T] **1** place in a straight line. **2** ~ oneself with join sb; come into agreement with: *They ~ ed themselves with the socialists.* **alignment** n [C, U].

alike /ə'laɪk/ adj like one another. **alike** adv in the same way.

alimentary /ˌælɪ'mentərɪ/ adj of food and digestion. **the alimentary ca'nal** n [C] tube-like passage in the body, through which food passes from the mouth to the anus.

alimony /'ælɪmənɪ; US -məʊnɪ/ n [U] money that sb has to pay regularly to a former wife or husband after they have been divorced.

alive /ə'laɪv/ adj **1** living. **2** active; lively. **3** in existence. **4** ~ **to sth** aware of sth. **alive with sth** full of (living things).

alkali /'ælkəlaɪ/ n [C, U] (chemistry) substance that forms a salt when combined with an acid.

all /ɔːl/ adj **1** (used with plural nouns) the whole number of: *A ~ the people have come.* **2** (used with uncountable nouns) the whole

amount of: *We've lost ~ the money.*
3 any: *beyond ~ doubt.*

all² /ɔːl/ *pron* **1** the whole number or amount: *They were ~ broken.* ○ *Take ~ of it.* **2** the only thing; everything: *A ~ I want is some peace.* **3** (idm) **in 'all** when everything is considered. **(not) at all** (not) in any way: *I didn't enjoy it at ~.* **in all** as a total. **not at all** (polite reply when receiving thanks) you are very welcome.

all³ /ɔːl/ *adv* **1** completely: *dressed ~ in black.* **2** (in games) to each side: *The score was four ~.* **3** (idm) **all a'long** (*infml*) all the time. **all 'in** very tired. **all over** everywhere. **all 'right** (also *infml*) **al'right (a)** satisfactory. **(b)** safe and well. **(c)** (used for expressing agreement). **all the better,** harder, etc: *We'll have to work ~ the harder when we get back from our holidays.* ,**all 'there** completely healthy or alert in mind. **all the 'same** ⇨ SAME. **all too** ⇨ TOO. **be all for (doing) sth** believe strongly that sth should be done. **be all the same to sb** not be important to sb: *It's ~ the same to me when you go.* **not all that** very. **the ,all-'clear** *n* [sing] signal that the danger has ended. ,**all-'in** *adj* with everything included: *an ,~-in price.* ,**all out** *adv* using all possible strength: *The team is going ~ out to win.* ○ *an ,~-out effort.* ,**all-'rounder** *n* [C] person with a wide range of abilities.

Allah /ˈælə/ *n* [sing] name of God among Muslims.

allay /əˈleɪ/ *v* [T] (*fml*) make (fears, doubts, etc) less.

allegation /ˌælɪˈgeɪʃn/ *n* [C] statement, esp that sb has done sth wrong, made without proof.

allege /əˈledʒ/ *v* [T] (*fml*) state (sth) as a fact but without proof: *He ~s he was misled about the time.* **alleged** *adj.* **allegedly** *adv.*

allegiance /əˈliːdʒəns/ *n* [U] support or loyalty to a ruler, belief, etc.

allegory /ˈælɪgərɪ; *US* ˈælɪgɔːrɪ/ *n* [C] (*pl* -ies) story in which people are symbols of qualities such as truth or patience. **allegorical** /ˌælɪˈgɒrɪkl/ *adj.*

alleluia /ˌælɪˈluːjə/ *n* [C], *interj* (expression of praise to God).

allergy /ˈælədʒɪ/ *n* [C] (*pl* -ies) medical condition that produces an unfavourable reaction to certain foods, etc. **allergic** /əˈlɜːdʒɪk/ *adj.*

alleviate /əˈliːvɪeɪt/ *v* [T] make (pain or suffering) less. **allevia-**

tion /əˌliːvɪˈeɪʃn/ *n* [U].

alley /ˈælɪ/ *n* [C] **1** narrow passage or street. **2** long narrow track for games such as skittles or ten-pin bowling.

alliance /əˈlaɪəns/ *n* [C] relationship or agreement between countries, groups, etc to work together for the same purpose.

allied ⇨ ALLY².

alligator /ˈælɪgeɪtə(r)/ *n* [C] American reptile like a crocodile.

allocate /ˈæləkeɪt/ *v* [T] give (eg money) as a share or for a purpose. **allocation** /ˌæləˈkeɪʃn/ *n* [C, U].

allot /əˈlɒt/ *v* (*-tt-*) [T] give (sth) as a share. **allotment** /əˈlɒt/ *n* [C] **1** amount or share allotted. **2** (esp *Brit*) small area of land rented for growing vegetables.

allow /əˈlaʊ/ *v* [T] **1** give permission to (sb) to do sth; let (sth be done; permit: *You're not ~ed to smoke in this room.* **2** provide (eg money or time). **3** (phr v) **allow for sth** take sth into consideration: *~ for traffic delays.* **allowable** *adj.* **allowance** *n* **1** [C] money given regularly. **2** (idm) **make allowances for sth** consider sth when making a decision.

alloy /ˈælɔɪ/ *n* [C, U] mixture of metals.

allude /əˈluːd/ *v* [I] *to|| (fml)* mention sth indirectly. **allusion** /əˈluːʒn/ *n* [C, U] indirect reference.

alluring /əˈlʊərɪŋ/ *adj* attractive; charming.

ally¹ /ˈælaɪ/ *n* [C] (*pl* -ies) person or country that has agreed to support another.

ally² /əˈlaɪ/ *v* (*pt*, *pp* -ied) [I, T] ~ oneself with/to join with (sb) by agreement, marriage, etc. **allied** *adj* (*to*)|| connected to sth; similar.

almanac /ˈɔːlmənæk; *US* ˈæl-/ *n* [C] book published yearly with information about the sun, moon, tides, etc.

almighty /ɔːlˈmaɪtɪ/ *adj* (*infml*) very great. **the Almighty** *n* [sing] God.

almond /ˈɑːmənd/ *n* [C] nut of a tree similar to a peach or plum.

almost /ˈɔːlməʊst/ *adv* very nearly: *~ everywhere/impossible.*

alms /ɑːmz/ *n* [pl] (*dated*) money, clothes, etc given to poor people.

aloft /əˈlɒft; *US* əˈlɔːft/ *adv* (*fml*) high up in the air.

alone /əˈləʊn/ *adj, adv* **1** without other people: *living ~.* **2** only: *You ~ can help me.* **3** (idm) **go it a'lone** do sth without help from anyone.

along /əˈlɒŋ; *US* əˈlɔːŋ/ *prep* **1**

from one end to the other end of:
walk ~ the street. 2 close to or on:
a path ~ the river. **along** adv 1 on;
forward: Come ~! 2 with others:
Can I bring some friends ~? 3
(idm) **along with sth** together
with sth. **a'longside** adv, prep
close to the side (of).

aloof /ə'luːf/ adj cool and distant
in character; unfriendly. **aloof-
ness** n [U].

aloud /ə'laʊd/ adv in a voice loud
enough to be heard: read the letter
~.

alphabet /'ælfəbet/ n [C] set of
letters arranged in order, used
when writing a language. **alphabetical** /ˌælfə'betɪkl/ adj in the
order of the alphabet. **alpha-
betically** /-klɪ/ adv.

already /ɔːl'redɪ/ adv 1 before
now: I've ~ told them what happened. 2 earlier than expected:
You're not leaving us ~, are you?

alright = ALL RIGHT (ALL[3]).

Alsatian /æl'seɪʃn/ n [C] large
wolf-like dog.

also /'ɔːlsəʊ/ adv in addition; too.

altar /'ɔːltə(r)/ n [C] table used in
a religious service.

alter /'ɔːltə(r)/ v [I, T] (cause to)
become different; change. **altera-
tion** /ˌɔːltə'reɪʃn/ n [C, U].

alternate[1] /ɔːl'tɜːnət/ adj 1 (of
two things) happening or following
one after the other. 2 every second: on ~
days, eg on Monday, Wednesday
and Friday. **alternately** adv.

alternate[2] /'ɔːltəneɪt/ v [I, T]
(between/with)/ (cause to) occur
one after the other: The weather
will ~ between sunshine and rain.
ˌalternating 'current n [U] electric current that regularly changes direction. **alternation** /ˌɔːlt-
ə'neɪʃn/ n [C, U].

alternative /ɔːl'tɜːnətɪv/ adj 1
that may be used or done instead:
an ~ means of transport. 2 not
based on the usual methods or
standards: A ~ medicine includes
homeopathy and acupuncture. alternative n [C] 1 one of two or
more possibilities. 2 choice between two things. **alternatively**
adv.

although /ɔːl'ðəʊ/ conj though.

altitude /'æltɪtjuːd; US -tuːd/
n [C] height above sea-level.

alto /'æltəʊ/ n [C] (pl ~s) 1 (music for a singer with the) highest
adult male or lowest female voice.
2 musical instrument with the
second highest pitch: an ~ saxophone.

altogether /ˌɔːltə'geðə(r)/ adv 1
completely: It is not ~ surprising

that she failed the exam. 2 including everything.

altruism /'æltruːɪzəm/ n [U] un-
selfishness. **altruist** /-ɪst/ n [C].
altruistic /ˌæltruː'ɪstɪk/ adj.

aluminium /ˌæljʊ'mɪnɪəm/ (US
aluminum /ə'luːmɪnəm/) n [U]
light silvery-white metal.

always /'ɔːlweɪz/ adv 1 at all
times: You should ~ use a seat-belt
in a car. 2 for ever: I'll ~ love her.

am[1] ⇨ BE.

am[2] /ˌeɪ'em/ abbr before noon.

amalgamate /ə'mælgəmeɪt/ v
[I, T] (cause organizations to)
unite; combine. **amalgamation**
/əˌmælgə'meɪʃn/ n [U, C].

amass /ə'mæs/ v [T] gather
together or collect in large quantities.

amateur /'æmətə(r)/ n [C] person
who does sth as a hobby, without
receiving money for it. **amateur-
ish** adj without skill.

amaze /ə'meɪz/ v [T] fill with
great surprise: ~d at the news.
amazement n [U]. **amazing** adj.

ambassador /æm'bæsədə(r)/
n [C] high-ranking official who
represents his/her own country in
a foreign country.

amber /'æmbə(r)/ n [U] (a) hard
yellowish-brown substance used
for making jewels. (b) its colour.

ambidextrous /ˌæmbɪ'dekstrəs/
adj able to use the right hand and
left hand equally well.

ambiguous /æm'bɪgjʊəs/ adj
having more than one meaning.
ambiguity /ˌæmbɪ'gjuːətɪ/ n
[U, C] (pl -ies).

ambition /æm'bɪʃn/ n (a) [U]
strong desire to be successful. (b)
[C] object of such a desire: achieve
one's ~s. **ambitious** /-ʃəs/ adj.

amble /'æmbl/ v [I] walk at a
slow relaxed pace. **amble** n [sing].

ambulance /'æmbjʊləns/ n [C]
vehicle for carrying sick or injured people, esp to hospital.

ambush /'æmbʊʃ/ n [U, C] (waiting in a hidden position to make a)
sudden attack. **ambush** v [T] attack from a place of hiding.

ameba (US) = AMOEBA.

amen /ɑː'men, eɪ'men/ interj
(used at the end of a prayer) may it
be so.

amenable /ə'miːnəbl/ adj willing
to be guided by sth or to do sth.

amend /ə'mend/ v [T] change; improve. **amendment** n [C, U]
change; correction.

amends /ə'mendz/ n [pl] (idm)
make amends (for sth) do sth to
show that one is sorry for some
harm, unkind act, etc.

amenity /ə'miːnətɪ/ n [C] (pl -ies)

something, eg a park or shopping centre, that makes life more convenient or pleasant.

American /ə'merɪkən/ *adj* of North or South America, esp the USA. **American** *n* [C] person from America, esp the USA. **American 'football** *n* [U] American game of football, similar to Rugby.

amethyst /'æmɪθɪst/ *n* [C] purple precious stone.

amiable /'eɪmɪəbl/ *adj* pleasant and friendly. **amiably** *adv*.

amicable /'æmɪkəbl/ *adj* friendly and peaceful: *reach an* ~ *agreement*. **amicably** *adv*.

amid /ə'mɪd/ (also **amidst** /ə'mɪdst/) *prep* (*dated* or *fml*) in the middle of; among.

amiss /ə'mɪs/ *adj, adv* (*dated*) 1 wrong(ly): *Something seems to be* ~. 2 (idm) **take sth a'miss** be offended by sth.

ammonia /ə'məʊnɪə/ *n* [U] gas with a strong smell, used in making explosives, fertilizers, etc.

ammunition /ˌæmjʊ'nɪʃn/ *n* [U] supply of bullets, bombs, etc, fired from weapons.

amnesia /æm'ni:zɪə; *US* -'ni:ʒə/ *n* [U] loss of memory.

amnesty /'æmnəstɪ/ *n* (*pl -ies*) general pardon, esp for political offences.

amoeba /ə'mi:bə/ *n* [C] (*pl* ~s or *-ae* /-bi:/) tiny living creature consisting of only one cell. **amoebic** /-bɪk/ *adj*.

amok /ə'mɒk/ (also **amuck** /ə'mʌk/) *adv* (idm) **run amok** ⇨ RUN[1].

among /ə'mʌŋ/ (also **amongst** /ə'mʌŋst/) *prep* 1 surrounded by: *found it* ~ *a pile of papers*. 2 in the number of; included in: ~ *the best in the world*. 3 (in parts) to each member of: *distribute the books* ~ *the class*.

amorous /'æmərəs/ *adj* showing (esp sexual) love. **amorously** *adv*.

amount /ə'maʊnt/ *n* [C] total or quantity: *a large* ~ *of money*. **amount** *v* [I] *to// be equal to sth.

amp /æmp/ *n* [C] (*infml*) short for AMPERE.

ampere /'æmpeə(r); *US* 'æmpɪər/ *n* [C] unit for measuring electric current.

amphibian /æm'fɪbɪən/ *n* [C] animal, eg a frog, that can live both on land and in water. **amphibious** /-bɪəs/ *adj*.

amphitheatre (*US* **-ter**) /'æmfɪθɪətə(r)/ *n* [C] round unroofed building with rows of seats rising round an open space.

ample /'æmpl/ *adj* (more than) enough. **amply** *adv*.

amplify /'æmplɪfaɪ/ *v* (*pt, pp -ied*) [T] 1 increase in strength: ~ *the sound*, ie make it louder. 2 give more details about. **amplification** /ˌæmplɪfɪ'keɪʃn/ *n* [U]. **amplifier** *n* [C] device that amplifies sounds or signals.

amputate /'æmpjʊteɪt/ *v* [I, T] cut off (an arm or a leg). **amputation** /ˌæmpjʊ'teɪʃn/ *n* [C, U].

amuck ⇨ AMOK.

amulet /'æmjʊlɪt/ *n* [C] object worn to protect one from evil, etc.

amuse /ə'mju:z/ *v* [T] 1 make (sb) laugh or smile. 2 make time pass pleasantly (for sb). **amusement** *n* 1 [C] something that makes time pass pleasantly. 2 [U] state of being amused. **amusing** *adj* causing one to laugh or smile.

an ⇨ A.

anachronism /ə'nækrənɪzəm/ *n* [C] person or thing thought to be out of date.

anaconda /ˌænə'kɒndə/ *n* [C] large South American snake that crushes animals to death.

anaemia /ə'ni:mɪə/ *n* [U] lack of red cells in one's blood, causing a person to look pale. **anaemic** /-mɪk/ *adj*.

anaesthesia /ˌænɪs'θi:zɪə/ *n* [U] state of being unable to feel pain, etc. **anaesthetic** /ˌænɪs'θetɪk/ *n* [C, U] substance that stops one feeling pain. **anaesthetist** /ə'ni:sθətɪst/ *n* [C] doctor who gives anaesthetics to patients before and during surgery. **anaesthetize** /ə'ni:sθətaɪz/ *v* [T] give (sb) an anaesthetic.

anagram /'ænəgræm/ *n* [C] word made by changing the order of the letters of another word: *'Stare' is an* ~ *of 'tears'*.

analogy /ə'nælədʒɪ/ *n* [C] (*pl -ies*) 1 [C] partial likeness: *an* ~ *between the heart and a pump*. 2 [U] explaining one thing by comparing it to sth else. **analogous** /-ləgəs/ *adj* similar.

analyse /'ænəlaɪz/ *v* [T] examine or study, esp by separating sth in to its parts.

analysis /ə'næləsɪs/ *n* (*pl -yses* /-əsi:z/) (a) [U, C] study of sth by examining its parts. (b) [C] statement of the result of this. **analyst** /'ænəlɪst/ *n* [C] 1 person who makes (esp chemical) analyses. 2 psychoanalyst. **analytic** /ˌænə'lɪtɪk/ (also **analytical** /-kl/) *adj*.

analyze (*US*) = ANALYSE.

anarchy /'ænəkɪ/ *n* [U] absence of government; disorder. **anarchist** *n* [C] person who favours anarchy.

anatomy

anatomy /əˈnætəmɪ/ n [U, C] (pl -ies) (study of the) structure of animal bodies. **anatomical** /ˌænəˈtɒmɪkl/ adj.

ancestor /ˈænsestə(r)/ n [C] person who lived a long time ago but to whom one is related. **ancestral** /ænˈsestrəl/ adj of or from one's ancestors. **ancestry** /-trɪ/ n [C] (pl -ies) line of ancestors.

anchor /ˈæŋkə(r)/ n [C] heavy piece of metal lowered from a ship into the water in order to stop the ship from moving. **anchor** v [I, T] lower the anchor (of); prevent from moving. **anchorage** n [C] place where ships may anchor safely.

anchovy /ˈæntʃəvɪ; US ˈæntʃəʊvɪ/ n [C] (pl -ies) small strong-flavoured fish of the herring family.

ancient /ˈeɪnʃənt/ adj 1 belonging to times long ago: ~ Greece. 2 very old.

ancillary /ænˈsɪlərɪ; US ˈænsəlerɪ/ adj giving support; additional.

and /ənd, ən; strong form ænd/ conj 1 also; in addition to: bread ~ butter. 2 then; following this: She came in ~ sat down. 3 as a result of this: Work hard ~ you'll succeed. 4 (showing continuation): for hours ~ hours. 5 (infml) (used instead of to after certain verbs: Try ~ come early.

anecdote /ˈænɪkdəʊt/ n [C] short interesting story about a real person or event.

anemia, anemic (US) = ANAEMIA, ANAEMIC.

anemone /əˈnemənɪ/ n [C] small plant with star-shaped flowers.

anesthesia = ANAESTHESIA.

anew /əˈnjuː; US əˈnuː/ adv (usu rhet) again.

angel /ˈeɪndʒl/ n [C] 1 messenger of God. 2 beautiful or very kind person. **angelic** /ænˈdʒelɪk/ adj.

anger /ˈæŋɡə(r)/ n [U] feeling that makes people want to quarrel or fight. **anger** v [T] make (sb) angry.

angle[1] /ˈæŋɡl/ n [C] 1 space between two lines that meet. 2 corner. 3 (fig) point of view. 4 (idm) at an 'angle not straight. **angle** v [T] 1 move or place in a slanting position. 2 present from a particular point of view.

angle[2] /ˈæŋɡl/ v [I] 1 fish with a line and hook. 2 for|| (infml) try to get (sth) indirectly: ~ for compliments. **angler** n [C]. **angling** n [U].

Anglican /ˈæŋɡlɪkən/ n [C], adj (member) of the Church of England.

Anglicize /ˈæŋɡlɪsaɪz/ v [T] make English.

Anglo- /ˈæŋɡləʊ/ prefix English or British: Anglo-American.

angry /ˈæŋɡrɪ/ adj (-ier, -iest) 1 filled with anger. 2 (of a wound) painful; inflamed. **angrily** adv.

anguish /ˈæŋɡwɪʃ/ n [U] great mental or physical pain. **anguished** adj.

angular /ˈæŋɡjʊlə(r)/ adj 1 having sharp corners. 2 (of a person) thin and bony.

animal /ˈænɪml/ n [C] 1 (a) living creature that can feel and move. (b) any such creature other than a human being. 2 unpleasant wild person. **animal** adj 1 of animals. 2 physical.

animate[1] /ˈænɪmət/ adj living.

animate[2] /ˈænɪmeɪt/ v [T] give life to; make lively. **animated** adj lively. **animated car'toon** n [C] = CARTOON (2.) **animation** /ˌænɪˈmeɪʃn/ n [U] 1 liveliness. 2 process of making animated cartoons.

animosity /ˌænɪˈmɒsətɪ/ n [U, C] (pl -ies) strong hatred.

ankle /ˈæŋkl/ n [C] joint connecting the foot with the leg.

annals /ˈænlz/ n [pl] historical records.

annex /əˈneks/ v [T] take possession of (land, etc). **annexation** /ˌænekˈseɪʃn/ n [U, C].

annexe (also esp US **annex**) /ˈæneks/ n [C] building added to a larger one: the hospital ~.

annihilate /əˈnaɪəleɪt/ v [T] destroy completely. **annihilation** /əˌnaɪəˈleɪʃn/ n [U].

anniversary /ˌænɪˈvɜːsərɪ/ n [C] (pl -ies) day remembered for sth special which happened on that date in a previous year: a wedding ~.

annotate /ˈænəteɪt/ v [T] add notes to (a book, etc). **annotation** /ˌænəˈteɪʃn/ n [C, u].

announce /əˈnaʊns/ v [T] make known publicly. **announcement** n [C] public statement. **announcer** n [C] person who introduces programmes on radio or television.

annoy /əˈnɔɪ/ v [T] make slightly angry; cause trouble to. **annoyance** n [U, C].

annual /ˈænjʊəl/ adj 1 happening once every year. 2 calculated for the year: ~ income. **annual** n [C] 1 book published once a year, having the same title but different contents. 2 plant that lives for one year. **annually** adv.

annuity /əˈnjuːətɪ; US -ˈnuː-/ n [C] (pl -ies) fixed sum of money paid to sb yearly.

annul /əˈnʌl/ v (-ll-) [T] declare (sth) no longer legally valid; cancel. **annulment** n [C, U].

anode /ˈænəʊd/ n [C] positively charged electrode.

anoint /əˈnɔɪnt/ v [T] put oil on, esp as a religious ceremony.

anomaly /əˈnɒməli/ n [C] (pl -ies) (fml) something different from what is normal: *the apparent ~ of the decision.* **anomalous** /-ləs/ adj.

anon[1] /əˈnɒn/ abbr anonymous.

anon[2] /əˈnɒn/ adv (dated) soon.

anonymous /əˈnɒnɪməs/ adj with a name that is not made known; without a name: *The author wishes to remain ~.* **anonymity** /ˌænəˈnɪmətɪ/ n [U].

anorak /ˈænəræk/ n [C] waterproof jacket with a hood.

anorexia /ˌænəˈreksɪə/ n [U] 1 serious illness in which there is a loss of desire to eat food. 2 (also **anorexia nervosa** /nɜːˈvəʊsə/) mental illness that causes fear of gaining weight and eating and leads to dangerous loss of weight. **anorexic** /-ˈreksɪk/ adj.

another /əˈnʌðə(r)/ adj, pron 1 an additional (one): *have ~ cup of tea.* 2 a different (one): *do that ~ time.* 3 a similar (one): *~ Einstein.*

answer /ˈɑːnsə(r); US ˈænsər/ n [C] 1 thing said or written in response to sth/sb; reply. 2 solution: *The ~ to 3 + 7 is 10.* **answer** v [I, T] give an answer to sth/sb: *Think before you ~.* ○ *~ the phone,* ie lift the receiver and speak to the person calling ○ *~ the door,* ie open the door when sb has knocked at it. (phr v) **answer (sb) back** reply rudely (to sb). **answer for sb/sth** (a) be responsible for sth. (b) speak in support of sb/sth. **answerable** adj responsible: *~ for one's actions.*

ant /ænt/ n [C] small crawling insect that lives in organized groups.

antagonism /ænˈtæɡənɪzəm/ n [U] opposition; dislike. **antagonist** /-nɪst/ n [C] opponent. **antagonistic** /ænˌtæɡəˈnɪstɪk/ adj.

antagonize /ænˈtæɡənaɪz/ v [T] cause to become an enemy; anger.

Antarctic /ænˈtɑːktɪk/ adj of the very cold regions around the South Pole. **the Antarctic** n [sing] the very cold regions around the South Pole.

antecedent /ˌæntɪˈsiːdnt/ n 1 [C] (fml) thing or event that comes before another. 2 **antecedents** [pl] ancestors.

antediluvian /ˌæntɪdɪˈluːvɪən/ adj (infml or joc) very out of date; old fashioned.

antelope /ˈæntɪləʊp/ n [C] animal like a deer.

antenatal /ˌæntɪˈneɪtl/ adj (a) existing or occurring before birth. (b) for pregnant women: *an ~ clinic.*

antenna /ænˈtenə/ n [C] 1 (pl ~e /-niː/) insect's feeler. 2 (pl ~s) (US) aerial.

anthem /ˈænθəm/ n [C] piece of music sung in churches or written for a special occasion.

anthology /ænˈθɒlədʒɪ/ n [C] (pl -ies) collection of writings, esp poems.

anthropoid /ˈænθrəpɔɪd/ adj human in form.

anthropology /ˌænθrəˈpɒlədʒɪ/ n [U] study of the human race. **anthropologist** n [C].

anti- /ˈæntɪ/ prefix against: *antiaircraft.*

antibiotic /ˌæntɪbaɪˈɒtɪk/ n [C], adj (powerful substance, eg penicillin) that can destroy bacteria.

antibody /ˈæntɪbɒdɪ/ n [C] (pl -ies) substance formed in the blood which destroys harmful bacteria.

anticipate /ænˈtɪsɪpeɪt/ v [T] 1 expect: *We ~ trouble.* 2 see (what may happen) and take action. **anticipation** /ænˌtɪsɪˈpeɪʃn/ n [U].

anticlimax /ˌæntɪˈklaɪmæks/ n [C] disappointing end to sth exciting.

anticlockwise /ˌæntɪˈklɒkwaɪz/ adv, adj in the direction opposite to the movement of the hands of a clock.

antics /ˈæntɪks/ n [pl] odd or amusing action or behaviour: *the children's ~.*

anticyclone /ˌæntɪˈsaɪkləʊn/ n [C] area of high atmospheric pressure.

antidote /ˈæntɪdəʊt/ n [C] substance that acts against the effects of a poison or disease.

antifreeze /ˈæntɪfriːz/ n [U] substance added to water to stop it freezing, esp in car radiators.

antiquated /ˈæntɪkweɪtɪd/ adj out of date; old fashioned.

antique /ænˈtiːk/ adj, n [C] old and valuable (object): *~ furniture.*

antiquity /ænˈtɪkwətɪ/ n (pl -ies) 1 [U] ancient times. 2 [C, usu pl] ancient building, painting, etc. 3 [U] great age.

antiseptic /ˌæntɪˈseptɪk/ n [C], adj (substance) preventing disease by destroying bacteria.

antisocial /ˌæntɪˈsəʊʃl/ adj 1 not liking to meet other people; unfriendly. 2 harmful to other people.

antithesis /æn'tɪθəsɪs/ n [C] (fml) (pl **-ses** /-siːz/) (fml) direct opposite.

antler /'æntlə(r)/ n [C] horn of a deer.

antonym /'æntənɪm/ n [C] word that is opposite in meaning to another: 'Hot' is the ~ of 'cold'.

anus /'eɪnəs/ n [C] hole through which solid waste matter leaves the body.

anvil /'ænvɪl/ n [C] heavy iron block on which metals are hammered into shape.

anxiety /æŋ'zaɪətɪ/ n (pl **-ies**) 1 [U, C] concern and fear, esp about what might happen. 2 [U] strong desire: ~ to please.

anxious /'æŋkʃəs/ v 1 feeling anxiety. 2 causing anxiety: an ~ time. 3 for; to/ strongly wishing sth: He's very ~ to meet you. **anxiously** adv.

any /'enɪ/ adj, pron 1 some amount (of): Have you got ~ milk? ○ I haven't read ~ books by Tolstoy. 2 no matter which: Take ~ card you like. **any** adv at all: I can't run ~ faster.

anybody /'enɪbɒdɪ/ (also **anyone** /'enɪwʌn/) pron 1 any person: Did ~ see you? 2 one person of many: A ~ will tell you.

anyhow /'enɪhaʊ/ adv 1 (also **anyway** /'enɪweɪ/) in spite of everything: It's too late now, ~. 2 carelessly: do the work ~.

anyone ⇨ ANYBODY.

anyplace /'enɪpleɪs/ (US) = ANYWHERE.

anything /'enɪθɪŋ/ pron 1 any thing (of importance): Has ~ unusual happened? 2 something (whatever it is): I'm so hungry; I'll eat ~! 3 (idm) **anything but** definitely not.

anyway ⇨ ANYHOW 1.

anywhere /'enɪweə(r); US -hweər/ adv 1 in, at or to any place. 2 (idm) **get anywhere** ⇨ GET.

aorta /eɪ'ɔːtə/ n [C] main artery through which blood leaves the heart.

apart /ə'pɑːt/ adv 1 distant: The houses are 500 metres ~. 2 separate(ly): They're living ~. 3 into pieces: It fell ~. **apart from** prep 1 except for. 2 as well as.

apartheid /ə'pɑːthaɪt, -haɪt/ n [U] (in South Africa) former government policy of keeping people of different races separate.

apartment /ə'pɑːtmənt/ n [C] 1 (US) flat. 2 large room.

apathy /'æpəθɪ/ n [U] lack of interest or enthusiasm. **apathetic** /ˌæpə'θetɪk/ adj.

ape /eɪp/ n [C] tailless monkey, eg chimpanzee or gorilla. **ape** v[T] copy (sb's speech or behaviour).

aperitif /ə'perətf; US əˌperə'tiːf/ n [C] alcoholic drink before a meal.

aperture /'æpətʃə(r)/ n [C] (fml) narrow hole or opening, eg in a camera lens.

apex /'eɪpeks/ n [C] (pl **~es** or **apices** /'eɪpɪsiːz/) highest point: the ~ of a triangle.

apiece /ə'piːs/ adv each: costing £1 ~.

aplomb /ə'plɒm/ n [U] confidence and self-control.

apologetic /əˌpɒlə'dʒetɪk/ adj making an apology or feeling regret for (sth). **apologetically** /-klɪ/ adv.

apologize /ə'pɒlədʒaɪz/ v [i] say that one is sorry: I must ~ for being late.

apology /ə'pɒlədʒɪ/ n [C] (pl **-ies**) 1 statement saying that one is sorry for having done wrong, hurt sb's feelings, etc. 2 (idm) **an apology for sth** very poor example of sth.

apostle /ə'pɒsl/ n [C] 1 any of the twelve men sent out by Christ to spread his teaching. 2 leader of a new faith or movement.

apostrophe /ə'pɒstrəfɪ/ n [C] sign (') used for showing the omission of one or more letters as in I'm for I am.

appal (US also **appall**) /ə'pɔːl/ v (-ll-) [T] fill with horror; shock deeply: We were ~led at the news. **appalling** adj.

apparatus /ˌæpə'reɪtəs; US -'rætəs/ n [U, C] set of instruments or equipment used for a purpose.

apparent /ə'pærənt/ adj 1 clearly seen: for no ~ reason. 2 seen but not necessarily real: an ~ lack of knowledge. **apparently** adv.

apparition /ˌæpə'rɪʃn/ n [C] ghost.

appeal /ə'piːl/ v[i] 1 (for)// make a strong request for sth: ~ for help/money. 2 take a matter (to a higher court, etc) for a new decision. 3 to// be attractive to sb: The idea of camping does not ~ to me. **appeal** n 1 [C] strong request. 2 [C] act of appealing(2). 3 [C] attractiveness: 'sex ~. **appealing** adj 1 attractive. 2 causing sb to feel pity.

appear /ə'pɪə(r)/ v[i] 1 come into view; become visible: A ship ~ed on the horizon. 2 arrive. 3 become available; present oneself publicly: Her latest book ~s in the *spring.* **4** be present in a law-court. **5** give the impression of being; seem: *That explanation ~s (to be) reasonable.* **appearance** *n* 1 [C] act of appearing. **2** [C, U] way sb/ sth looks to other people: *an untidy ~ance.* **3** (idm) ˌput in an ap'pearance go to a meeting, party, etc, esp for a short time. to all ap'pearances so far as can be seen.

appease /əˈpiːz/ *v* [T] (*fml*) make (sb) calm or stop (sb) being angry, esp by satisfying demands. **appeasement** *n* [U].

append /əˈpend/ *v* [T] (*fml*) add or attach (sth, esp in writing). **appendage** *n* [C] something added to or joined to sth larger.

appendicitis /əˌpendɪˈsaɪtɪs/ *n* [U] disease of the appendix(2).

appendix /əˈpendɪks/ *n* [C] 1 (*pl -dices* /-dɪsiːz/) something added at the end of a book. **2** (*pl -es*) small organ attached to the intestine.

appetite /ˈæpɪtaɪt/ *n* [C, U] strong desire, esp for food.

appetizer /ˈæpɪtaɪzə(r)/ *n* [C] something eaten or drunk to increase the appetite. **appetizing** *adj* encouraging one's appetite.

applaud /əˈplɔːd/ *v* 1 [I, T] show approval of (sb/sth) by clapping the hands. **2** [T] praise. **applause** /əˈplɔːz/ *n* [U].

apple /ˈæpl/ *n* [C] round fruit with firm flesh.

appliance /əˈplaɪəns/ *n* [C] device; machine.

applicable /əˈplɪkəbl, also ˈæplɪkəbl/ *adj* (*to*)// relevant to sb/sth.

applicant /ˈæplɪkənt/ *n* [C] person who applies for a job, etc.

application /ˌæplɪˈkeɪʃn/ *n* 1 [C, U] request: *an ~ (form) for a job.* **2** [U, C] act of putting sth to practical use: *the practical ~s of the invention.* **3** [U] hard work; great effort.

apply /əˈplaɪ/ *v* (*pt, pp* -ied) 1 [I] (*for*)// ask officially for sth: *~ for a job/visa.* **2** [I] (*to*)// be relevant to sb/sth: *This rule does not ~ to you.* **3** [T] concentrate (one's thoughts and energy): *~ oneself/one's mind to the problem.* **4** [T] put into operation; use: *~ the brakes* ○ *~ modern technology.* **5** [T] put or rub (sth) onto a surface: *~ ointment to the cut.* **applied** *adj* put to practical use: *applied science.*

appoint /əˈpɔɪnt/ *v* [T] 1 choose (sb) for a job. **2** (*fml*) fix or decide: *the ~ed time.* **appointment** *n* 1 (a) [C, U] act of appointing sb for a job. (b) [C] job to which sb is appoin-

ted. **2** [C, U] arrangement to meet sb.

appraise /əˈpreɪz/ *v* [T] (*fml*) consider the value of. **appraisal** *n* [C, U].

appreciable /əˈpriːʃəbl/ *adj* that can be noticed: *an ~ difference.* **appreciably** *adv.*

appreciate /əˈpriːʃɪeɪt/ *v* 1 [T] understand and enjoy (sth): *~ classical music.* **2** [T] be thankful for: *I really ~ all your help.* **3** [T] understand completely: *I ~ your problems, but am not able to help.* **4** [I] (of land, etc) increase in value. **appreciation** /əˌpriːʃɪˈeɪʃn/ *n* [U, C]. **appreciative** /-ʃətɪv/ *adj.*

apprehend /ˌæprɪˈhend/ *v* [T] (*fml*) **1** arrest. **2** understand.

apprehension /ˌæprɪˈhenʃn/ *n* [U, C] worry or fear. **apprehensive** /-ˈhensɪv/ *adj* worried.

apprentice /əˈprentɪs/ *n* [C] person learning a skilled trade. **apprentice** *v* [T] (*to*)// make (sb) work as an apprentice: *He is ~d to a plumber.* **apprenticeship** /əˈprentɪʃɪp/ *n* [C, U] (time of) being an apprentice.

approach /əˈprəʊtʃ/ *v* 1 [I, T] come near(er) to (sb/sth). **2** [T] make a request or offer to: *~ the manager for a pay rise.* **3** [T] begin to deal with: *How shall I ~ this problem?* **approach** *n* [C] 1 [usu sing] act of approaching. **2** road, way, etc. **3** way of dealing with sth. **approachable** *adj* friendly and easy to talk to.

appropriate[1] /əˈprəʊprɪət/ *adj* suitable; correct. **appropriately** *adv.*

appropriate[2] /əˈprəʊprɪeɪt/ *v* [T] **1** take (sth that does not belong to one) for one's own use. **2** set aside for a particular purpose. **appropriation** /əˌprəʊprɪˈeɪʃn/ *n* [C, U].

approval /əˈpruːvl/ *n* [U] 1 feeling or showing that one thinks sb/ sth is good or acceptable: *Your plans have my ~.* **2** (idm) on ap'proval (of goods) to be returned without paying if not satisfactory.

approve /əˈpruːv/ *v* 1 [I] (*of*)// feel or show that sb/sth is good or acceptable. **2** [T] agree to (sth) formally. **approvingly** *adv.*

approximate[1] /əˈprɒksɪmət/ *adj* almost correct or exact, but not completely so. **approximately** *adv*: *~ly 300 students.*

approximate[2] /əˈprɒksɪmeɪt/ *v* [I] *to*// come very near to sth. **approximation** /əˌprɒksɪˈmeɪʃn/ *n* [C].

apricot /ˈeɪprɪkɒt/ *n* (a) [C] small round orange-yellow fruit with a stone. (b) [U] orange-yellow colour.

April /ˈeɪprəl/ n [U, C] the fourth month of the year: on A ~ the first ○ on the first of A ~ ○ (US) on A ~ first ○ She was born in A ~. ○ last/ next A ~.

apron /ˈeɪprən/ n [C] garment worn round the front part of one's body to keep clothes clean.

apt /æpt/ adj 1 suitable: an ~ remark. 2 to/ likely to do sth: ~ to be forgetful. 3 quick to learn. **aptly** adv. **aptness** n [U].

aptitude /ˈæptɪtjuːd; US -tuːd/ n [C, U] natural ability or skill.

Aqualung /ˈækwəlʌŋ/ n [C] (P) breathing unit for underwater swimming.

aquamarine /ˌækwəməˈriːn/ n (a) [C] bluish-green precious stone. (b) [U] bluish-green colour.

aquarium /əˈkweərɪəm/ n [C] (pl ~s or -ria /-rɪə/) building with a) glass tank for keeping live fish.

aquatic /əˈkwætɪk/ adj 1 (of animals or plants) living or growing in water. 2 (of sports) taking place on or in water.

aqueduct /ˈækwɪdʌkt/ n [C] bridge that carries water across a valley.

Arabic /ˈærəbɪk/ adj of the Arabs. **Arabic** n [U] language of the Arabs. **Arabic 'numeral** n [C] sign 1, 2, 3, etc.

arable /ˈærəbl/ adj (of land) used or suitable for growing crops.

arbitrary /ˈɑːbɪtrərɪ; US ˈɑːrbɪtrerɪ/ adj 1 based on chance, not on reason. 2 using an uncontrolled power. **arbitrarily** adv.

arbitrate /ˈɑːbɪtreɪt/ v [I, T] (between)) settle (a dispute, argument, etc) between two groups. **arbitration** /ˌɑːbɪˈtreɪʃn/ n [U] settlement of a dispute by sb chosen as a judge. **arbitrator** n [C].

arc /ɑːk/ n [C] part of the curved line of a circle.

arcade /ɑːˈkeɪd/ n [C] covered passage with shops.

arch /ɑːtʃ/ n [C] curved structure, eg one that is part of the support of a bridge. **arch** v [I, T] form an arch: The cat ~ed its back.

archaeology /ˌɑːkɪˈɒlədʒɪ/ n [U] study of the remains of ancient buildings, tools, etc. **archaeological** /ˌɑːkɪəˈlɒdʒɪkl/ adj. **archaeologist** n [C].

archaic /ɑːˈkeɪɪk/ adj (esp of words) no longer in use; very old.

archangel /ˈɑːkeɪndʒl/ n [C] chief angel(1).

archbishop /ˌɑːtʃˈbɪʃəp/ n [C] chief bishop.

archer /ˈɑːtʃə(r)/ n [C] person who shoots with a bow and arrows. **archery** n [U] skill or sport of shooting with a bow and arrows.

archipelago /ˌɑːkɪˈpeləgəʊ/ n [C] (pl ~s or -es) group of many small islands.

architect /ˈɑːkɪtekt/ n [C] person who designs buildings. **architecture** /-tektʃə(r)/ n [U] art of building; style of building. **architectural** /ˌɑːkɪˈtektʃərəl/ adj.

archives /ˈɑːkaɪvz/ n [pl] (collection of) historical records.

Arctic /ˈɑːktɪk/ adj of the very cold region around the North Pole. **the Arctic** n [sing] the very cold region around the North Pole.

ardent /ˈɑːdnt/ adj very enthusiastic. **ardently** adv.

arduous /ˈɑːdjʊəs; US -dʒʊ-/ adj needing a lot of effort or energy. **arduously** adv.

are ⇨ BE.

area /ˈeərɪə/ n 1 [C, U] extent or measurement of a surface. 2 [C] part of the earth's surface; region: desert ~ s. 3 [C] (fig) range of activity: different ~ s of human experience.

arena /əˈriːnə/ n [C] 1 enclosed area used for sports, etc. 2 (fig) place of competition or activity: in the political ~.

aren't /ɑːnt/ are not. ⇨ BE.

argue /ˈɑːgjuː/ v 1 [I] express disagreement; quarrel. 2 [I, T] for/ against)) give reasons for/against sth. 3 [T] (fml) discuss: The lawyers ~ d the case. **arguable** /ˈɑːgjʊəbl/ adj not certain; questionable. **arguably** adv.

argument /ˈɑːgjʊmənt/ n 1 [C] disagreement. 2 [C, U] discussion; reason for or against. **argumentative** /ˌɑːgjʊˈmentətɪv/ adj fond of arguing(1).

aria /ˈɑːrɪə/ n [C] song for one voice in an opera, etc.

arid /ˈærɪd/ adj 1 (of land) very dry. 2 dull; uninteresting.

arise /əˈraɪz/ v (pt arose /əˈrəʊz/, pp ~n /əˈrɪzn/) [I] come into existence: A difficulty has ~n.

aristocracy /ˌærɪˈstɒkrəsɪ/ n [C] (also sing with pl v) (pl -ies) highest social class, esp people with special titles such as earl and lord. **aristocrat** /ˈærɪstəkræt; US ˈærɪst-/ n [C] member of the aristocracy. **aristocratic** /ˌærɪstəˈkrætɪk; US ˌærɪstə-/ adj.

arithmetic /əˈrɪθmətɪk/ n [U] branch of mathematics that deals with calculations using numbers. **arithmetical** /ˌærɪθˈmetɪkl/ adj.

ark /ɑːk/ n [C] (in the Bible) Noah's ship.

arm¹ /ɑːm/ n [C] 1 (a) upper limb, from the shoulder to the hand. (b) part of a garment that covers this. 2 something shaped like an arm: *the ~ s of a chair.* 3 part or section of a country's military forces. 4 (idm) **with their arms** linked. **'armchair** n [C] chair with supports for the arms. **'armpit** n [C] hollow part under the arm at one's shoulder.

arm² /ɑːm/ v 1 [I, T] supply (sb) with weapons. 2 (idm) **armed to the 'teeth** having very many weapons. **the ,armed 'forces** n [pl] a country's army, navy and air force.

armada /ɑːˈmɑːdə/ n [C] large group of warships.

armadillo /ˌɑːməˈdɪləʊ/ n [C] (pl ~s) small South American animal with large bony scales.

armament /ˈɑːməmənt/ n 1 [C, usu pl] weapons, esp large guns. 2 [U] process of equipping military forces for war.

armistice /ˈɑːmɪstɪs/ n [C] agreement during a war to stop fighting for a time.

armour (US **-or**) /ˈɑːmə(r)/ n [U] 1 protective metal covering for the body in battle. 2 metal covering for tanks, ships, etc. **armoured** (US **-or-**) adj. **armoury** (US **-or-**) n [C] (pl **-ies**) place where weapons are kept.

arms /ɑːmz/ n [pl] 1 weapons. 2 (idm) **take up 'arms** (fml) (prepare to) go to war. **(be) up in 'arms (about/over sth)** protest(ing) strongly about sth. **the 'arms race** n [sing] competition among nations for military strength.

army /ˈɑːmɪ/ n (pl **-ies**) 1 (a) [C] military forces of a country which fight on land. (b) **the army** [sing] profession of being a soldier: *join the ~.* 2 [C] large group: *an ~ of volunteers.*

aroma /əˈrəʊmə/ n [C] pleasant smell. **aromatic** /ˌærəˈmætɪk/ adj.

arose pt of ARISE.

around /əˈraʊnd/ adv, prep 1 with a circular movement (about): *The earth moves ~ the sun.* 2 to or at various points (in): *walk ~ the exhibition.* 3 on all sides (of): *The children gathered ~.* 4 available; present: *Is anyone ~?* 5 near; about: *It's ~ six o'clock.*

arouse /əˈraʊz/ v [T] 1 (fml) wake from sleep. 2 cause to appear or become active: *~ suspicion.*

arr abbr 1 arrives. 2 (of music) arranged (by).

arrange /əˈreɪndʒ/ v 1 [T] organize: *~ a holiday.* 2 [I, T] make plans (to do sth): *We ~ d to meet at one o'clock.* 3 [I, T] come to an agreement about (sth): *~ a loan.* 4 [T] put in order; make attractive: *~ flowers.* 5 [T] adapt (a piece of music) for a particular instrument. **arrangement** n 1 **arrangements** [pl] plans; preparations. 2 [C] agreement; plan. 3 [C] result of arranging(4,5): *a flower ~ment* ○ *an ~ment for piano.* 4 [U] act of arranging.

array /əˈreɪ/ n [C] large impressive series of things.

arrears /əˈrɪəz/ n 1 [pl] money that is owing. 2 (idm) **be in arrears (with sth)** be late in paying money.

arrest /əˈrest/ v [T] 1 seize (sb) by the authority of the law. 2 (fml) stop (a process). 3 attract (attention). **arrest** n 1 [C] act of arresting. 2 (idm) **under arrest** held prisoner by the police.

arrival /əˈraɪvl/ n 1 [U] act of arriving. 2 [C] person or thing that arrives: *The new ~* (ie baby) *is a girl.*

arrive /əˈraɪv/ v [I] 1 reach a place: *~ home.* 2 come: *The great day has ~d!* 3 (infml) become successful. 4 (phr v) **arrive at sth** reach sth: *~ at a decision.*

arrogant /ˈærəgənt/ adj behaving in a proud and rude way. **arrogance** /-gəns/ n [U]. **arrogantly** adv.

arrow /ˈærəʊ/ n [C] 1 pointed stick shot from a bow. 2 sign (➡) used for showing direction.

arse /ɑːs/ n (△ sl) 1 buttocks; bottom(2). 2 person: *You stupid ~!* **arse** v (phr v) **arse about/around** (△ Brit sl) behave in a silly way.

arsenal /ˈɑːsənl/ n [C] place where weapons and ammunition are stored or made.

arsenic /ˈɑːsnɪk/ n [U] very strong poisonous substance.

arson /ˈɑːsn/ n [U] crime of setting fire to property.

art /ɑːt/ n 1 [U] creation or expression of what is beautiful, esp in painting, sculpture, etc: *an '~ gallery.* 2 **arts** [pl] subjects of studying, eg languages or history, that are in contrast to science. 3 [C, U] skill in doing sth.

artefact (also **artifact**) /ˈɑːtɪfækt/ n [C] thing made by a human being.

artery /ˈɑːtərɪ/ n [C] (pl **-ies**) 1 one of the tubes that carry blood from the heart to other parts of the body. 2 main road, railway, etc. **arterial** /ɑːˈtɪərɪəl/ adj.

artful /ˈɑːtfl/ adj clever and deceitful at getting what one wants. **artfully** adv.

arthritis /ɑːˈθraɪtɪs/ n [U] pain and swelling in a joint in the body. **arthritic** /ɑːˈθrɪtɪk/ adj.

artichoke /ˈɑːtɪtʃəʊk/ n [C] 1 (also **globe ˈartichoke**) kind of plant with a head of thick, leaflike scales, used as a vegetable. 2 (also **Jerusalem artichoke** /dʒəˌruːsələm ˈɑːtɪtʃəʊk/) kind of plant with white roots, used as a vegetable.

article /ˈɑːtɪkl/ n [C] 1 separate thing: ~s of clothing. 2 piece of writing in a newspaper, etc. 3 (law) separate part of an agreement. 4 (grammar) word a, an or the.

articulate[1] /ɑːˈtɪkjʊlət/ adj 1 (of a person) able to express his/her opinions clearly in words. 2 (of speech) clearly pronounced. **articulately** adv.

articulate[2] /ɑːˈtɪkjʊleɪt/ v [I, T] 1 speak (sth) clearly. 2 connect by joints. **articulated** adj (of a lorry) having two parts connected by a joint which allows it to turn easily. **articulation** /ɑːˌtɪkjʊˈleɪʃn/ n [U].

artifact ⇨ ARTEFACT.

artificial /ˌɑːtɪˈfɪʃl/ adj 1 not natural; made by human beings. 2 not sincere. **artificially** adv.

artillery /ɑːˈtɪləri/ n [U] (branch of the army that uses) large heavy guns.

artisan /ˌɑːtɪˈzæn; US ˈɑːrtɪzn/ n [C] (fml) person skilled at a craft.

artist /ˈɑːtɪst/ n [C] 1 person who practises one of the arts, esp painting. 2 person who does sth with great skill. 3 = ARTISTE. **artistic** /ɑːˈtɪstɪk/ adj 1 having or showing skill in art. 2 of art and artists. **artistically** /-klɪ/ adv. **artistry** n [U] skill or work of an artist.

artiste /ɑːˈtiːst/ n [C] professional singer, dancer, actor, etc.

arty /ˈɑːti/ adj (infml derog) pretending to be artistic.

as /əz; strong form æz/ prep 1 appearing to be (sb): dressed as a policeman. 2 having the function or character of (sb/sth): a career as a teacher ○ treat as friends. **as** adv **as ... as** (used in comparisons) equally ... as: as tall as his father ○ Run as fast as you can! **as** conj 1 during the time when: I saw her as I was leaving. 2 since; because: As you were out, I left a message. 3 though: Young as I am, I know what I want to be. 4 in the way which: Do as I say. 5 (idm) **as for** sb/sth, **as to** sth with regard to

sb/sth; concerning. **as from**, (esp US) **as of** (showing the time from which sth starts): a new job as from Monday. **as if/though** with the appearance of: as it 'is in reality. ,as it 'were as it might be expressed. **as much** so: I thought as much. **as per** according to: Work as per instructions.

asbestos /æsˈbestɒs/ n [U] soft grey material that does not burn.

ascend /əˈsend/ v [I, T] (fml) go up (sth). 2 (idm) **ascend the throne** (fml) become king or queen. **ascendancy** n [U] (fml) power; influence. **ascendant** n (idm) **in the aˈscendant** having or nearly having controlling power.

ascent /əˈsent/ n [C] act of ascending; way up.

ascertain /ˌæsəˈteɪn/ v [T] (fml) find out; make certain about.

ascribe /əˈskraɪb/ v [T] to// consider to be caused by or belonging to sth/sb: ~ failure to bad luck.

aseptic /ˌeɪˈseptɪk; US əˈsep-/ adj free from bacteria; clean.

asexual /ˌeɪˈsekʃʊəl/ adj 1 without sex or sex organs. 2 having no interest in sexual relations.

ash[1] /æʃ/ n 1 [U] (also **ashes**) [pl] powder left after sth has burnt. 2 [pl] remains of a dead human body after burning. **ˈashtray** n [C] small dish for tobacco ash.

ash[2] /æʃ/ n (a) [C] tree with hard wood. (b) [U] wood of this tree.

ashamed /əˈʃeɪmd/ adj feeling shame.

ashore /əˈʃɔː(r)/ adv on or to the shore.

aside /əˈsaɪd/ adv on or to one side: He laid the book ~. **aside** n [C] remark that others are not supposed to hear.

ask /ɑːsk/ v 1 [I, T] put a question to (sb) in order to get information: I ~ed him where he lived. ○ 'What time is it?' she ~ed. 2 [I, T] say to (sb) that one wants him/her to do sth: I ~ed them to close the window. 3 [T] invite: ~ him to the party. 4 (idm) **'ask for it/trouble** (infml) behave in such a way that trouble is likely. 5 (phr v) **ask after sb** ask about sb's health. **ask for sb/sth** say that one wants to speak to sb or be given sth.

askance /əˈskæns/ adv (idm) **look askance at sb/sth** look at sb/sth with distrust or suspicion.

askew /əˈskjuː/ adj, adv not in a straight or level position.

asleep /əˈsliːp/ adj 1 sleeping. 2 (of an arm or leg) having no feeling.

asp /æsp/ n [C] small poisonous snake of N Africa.

asparagus /ə'spærəgəs/ n [U] plant whose green shoots are eaten as a vegetable.

aspect /'æspekt/ n [C] 1 particular part or side of sth being considered. 2 (fml) direction in which a building faces.

aspersion /ə'spɜːʃn; US -ʒn/ n (idm) cast aspersions on sb/sth ⇨ CAST¹.

asphalt /'æsfælt; US -fɔːlt/ n [U] black substance for making road surfaces. **asphalt** v [T] cover (esp a road) with asphalt.

asphyxiate /əs'fɪksɪeɪt/ v [T] cause (sb) to become very ill or die through lack of air. **asphyxiation** /əs,fɪksɪ'eɪʃn/ n [U].

aspirate /'æspərət/ n [C] (phonetics) sound of 'h'. **aspirate** /'æspəreɪt/ v [T] pronounce with an 'h' sound.

aspire /ə'spaɪə(r)/ v [I] (to) have a strong desire to achieve sth. **aspiration** /,æspə'reɪʃn/ n [C, U] strong desire.

aspirin /'æsprɪn, 'æspərɪn/ n [C, U] (tablet of) medicine that reduces pain and fever.

ass¹ /æs/ n [C] 1 donkey. 2 (infml) stupid person.

ass² /æs/ n [C] (△ US sl) arse(1).

assail /ə'seɪl/ v [T] (fml) attack. **assailant** n [C] attacker.

assassin /ə'sæsɪn; US -sn/ n [C] person who assassinates sb. **assassinate** /ə'sæsɪneɪt; US -sən-/ v [T] murder (sb important). **assassination** /ə,sæsɪ'neɪʃn; US -sə'neɪʃn/ n [C, U].

assault /ə'sɔːlt/ n [C, U] sudden violent attack. **assault** v [T] make an assault on (sb).

assemble /ə'sembl/ v 1 [I, T] gather together. 2 [T] fit together the parts of (sth).

assembly /ə'semblɪ/ n (pl -ies) 1 [C] group of people coming together for a purpose. 2 [U] act of assembling parts. **as'sembly line** n [C] arrangement of machines and workers along which a product moves as it is put together in stages.

assent /ə'sent/ n [U] (fml) agreement. **assent** v [I] (to) (fml) agree to sth.

assert /ə'sɜːt/ v [T] 1 state (sth) firmly. 2 make others recognize (one's authority, etc) by behaving firmly. 3 ~ oneself behave confidently and forcefully. **assertion** /ə'sɜːʃn/ n [U, C]. **assertive** adj confident and forceful.

assess /ə'ses/ v [T] 1 judge the importance, worth, etc of. 2 calculate the value of. **assessment** n [C, U]. **assessor** n [C] person who as-

sesses(2) sth.

asset /'æset/ n [C] 1 valuable person, quality or skill. 2 (usu pl) thing owned, esp property, that can be sold to pay debts.

assign /ə'saɪn/ v [T] 1 give as a share or task. 2 appoint. 3 fix as a time, place, etc; name. **assignment** n [C] 1 piece of work; task. 2 [U] act of assigning.

assimilate /ə'sɪmɪleɪt/ v 1 [T] take in or absorb food, information, ideas, etc. 2 [I, T] (allow sb to) become part of another group or state: immigrants ~d into the country they moved to. **assimilation** /ə,sɪmə'leɪʃn/ n [U].

assist /ə'sɪst/ v [I, T] (fml) help. **assistance** n [U] (fml) help. **assistant** n [C] helper: a 'shop-~.

associate¹ /ə'səʊʃɪeɪt/ v 1 [T] (with)// join together, connect in one's mind: Whisky is often ~d with Scotland. ○ The problems of ~d with homelessness. 2 [I, T] with// act together with (sb/sth); support: ~ with people one doesn't really like.

associate² /ə'səʊʃɪət/ n [C] partner or colleague: business ~ s.

association /ə,səʊsɪ'eɪʃn/ n 1 [C] group of people joined together for a purpose. 2 [U] act of associating. 3 [C] connection in the mind. 4 (idm) in associ'ation with sb together with sb. **As,sociation 'Football** n [U] game in which two teams of eleven players try to kick a round ball into each other's goal.

assorted /ə'sɔːtɪd/ adj of different kinds; mixed. **assortment** /ə'sɔːtmənt/ n [C] assorted collection.

assume /ə'sjuːm; US ə'suːm/ v [T] 1 believe (sth) to be true without proof. 2 begin to use, take or have: ~ control ○ ~ a greater importance. 3 pretend to have (an expression or way of behaving): ~ ignorance. **assumption** /ə'sʌmpʃn/ n 1 [C] something believed to be true without proof. 2 [U] act of assuming.

assurance /ə'ʃɔːrəns; US ə'ʃʊərəns/ n 1 [U] belief in one's own abilities. 2 [C] promise: give an ~. 3 [U] (esp Brit) insurance: life ~.

assure /ə'ʃɔː; US ə'ʃʊə(r)/ v [T] 1 tell (sb) firmly or confidently: I ~ you that the money will be safe with me. 2 cause (sb/oneself) to be sure. 3 insure, esp against death. **assured** adj confident.

asterisk /'æstərɪsk/ n [C] star-shaped symbol (*).

astern /ə'stɜːn/ adv in or at the back end of a ship.

asteroid /'æstərɔɪd/ n [C] very small planet.

asthma /'æsmə; US 'æzmə/ n [U] chest illness that causes difficulty in breathing. **asthmatic** /æs'mætɪk; US æz-/ adj.

astonish /ə'stɒnɪʃ/ v [T] surprise greatly. **astonishing** adj very surprising. **astonishment** n [U].

astound /ə'staʊnd/ v [T] shock or amaze.

astral /'æstrəl/ adj of the stars.

astray /ə'streɪ/ adv away from the right path.

astride /ə'straɪd/ adv, prep with one leg on each side (of).

astrology /ə'strɒlədʒɪ/ n [U] study of the stars in the belief that they influence human affairs. **astrological** /ˌæstrə'lɒdʒɪkl/ adj. **astrologer** /-dʒə(r)/ n [C].

astronaut /'æstrənɔːt/ n [C] person who travels in a spacecraft.

astronomy /ə'strɒnəmɪ/ n [U] scientific study of the stars, planets, etc. **astronomer** /-nəmə(r)/ n. **astronomical** /ˌæstrə'nɒmɪkl/ adj 1 of astronomy. 2 (infml) very large in amount, size, etc.

astute /ə'stjuːt; US ə'stuːt/ adj clever at seeing quickly how to gain an advantage. **astutely** adv. **astuteness** n [U].

asylum /ə'saɪləm/ n [C] (dated) hospital for people with mental illnesses. 2 [U] protection: political ~.

at /ət/ prep 1 (showing a place): at the station ○ study languages at university. 2 towards: look at her ○ guess at the meaning. 3 (showing the distance from sth): hold sth at arm's length. 4 (showing a point in time): at two o'clock. 5 (showing age): He got married at (the age of) 24. 6 (showing a state or continuous activity): at war. 7 by: shocked at the news. 8 (showing a rate, price, speed, etc): driving at 70mph ○ exports valued at £1 million. 9 used after an adj expressing ability: good at music.

ate pt of EAT.

atheism /'eɪθɪɪzəm/ n [U] belief that there is no God. **atheist** /'eɪθɪɪst/ n [C].

athlete /'æθliːt/ n [C] person trained for physical games. **athletic** /æθ'letɪk/ adj 1 of athletes or athletics. 2 physically strong and fit. **athletics** n [U] physical exercises and sports, esp running and jumping.

atlas /'ætləs/ n [C] book of maps.

atmosphere /'ætməsfɪə(r)/ n [sing] 1 the atmosphere gases surrounding the earth. 2 air. 3 general impression of a place: a friendly ~. **atmospheric** /ˌætməs'ferɪk/ adj of the atmosphere.

atoll /'ætɒl/ n [C] ring-shaped coral reef round a lagoon.

atom /'ætəm/ n [C] 1 smallest unit of an element that can take part in chemical change. 2 (fig) very small amount. **atomic** /ə'tɒmɪk/ adj of atoms. **a,tomic 'bomb** (also **'atom bomb**) n [C] bomb whose explosive power comes from splitting atoms.

atrocious /ə'trəʊʃəs/ adj 1 very cruel. 2 (infml) very bad: ~ weather. **atrociously** adv.

atrocity /ə'trɒsətɪ/ n (pl -ies) 1 [C] cruel act. 2 [U] wickedness.

attach /ə'tætʃ/ v 1 [T] fasten or join (sth) to sth. 2 [T] join as a companion or member. 3 [i, T] to// (cause to) connect with sth: ~ importance to her speech. 4 (idm) **be attached to sb/sth** be very fond of sb/sth. **attachment** n 1 [C] thing that can be attached. 2 [U] (to// fondness for sb/sth.

attaché /ə'tæʃeɪ; US ˌætə'ʃeɪ/ n [C] person who works on the staff of an embassy. **at'taché case** n [C] small case for documents.

attack /ə'tæk/ n 1 [C, U] (a) violent attempt to hurt or defeat sb/sth. (b) strong criticism in speech or writing. 2 [C] sudden illness. **attack** v 1 [i, T] begin to deal with (sth) with eagerness and energy. **attacker** n [C].

attain /ə'teɪn/ v [T] (fml) succeed in getting, achieve. **attainable** adj. **attainment** n 1 [U] act of attaining. 2 [C] skill or ability.

attempt /ə'tempt/ v [T] try: ~ to escape. **attempt** n [C] 1 effort to do sth. 2 (idm) **an attempt on sb's life** an attempt to kill sb.

attend /ə'tend/ v 1 [T] be present at: ~ a meeting. 2 [i] to// be concerned with sth; deal with. 3 [i] (to// (fml) give careful thought to sth. **attendance** n 1 [C, U] being present at school, etc. 2 [C] number of people present: a large ~ance. **attendant** n [C] person whose job is to give a service in a public place.

attention /ə'tenʃn/ n [U] 1 careful thought: pay ~. 2 special care or action: My old car needs some ~. 3 position of a soldier standing upright and still.

attentive /ə'tentɪv/ adj giving attention. **attentively** adv.

attest /ə'test/ v [i, T] (to// (fml) show or prove that sth is true.

attic /'ætɪk/ n [C] room in the roof of a house.

attitude /'ætɪtjuːd; US -tuːd/ *n* [C] **1** way of thinking or behaving. **2** (*fml*) position of the body.

attorney /ə'tɜːnɪ/ *n* [C] (*US*) lawyer.

attract /ə'trækt/ *v* [T] **1** pull (sth) towards: *A magnet ~s steel.* **2** get the attention or interest of: *a window display that ~s customers.* **3** find pleasing. **attraction** /ə'trækʃn/ *n* **1** [U] action or power of attracting. **2** [C] something that attracts(2). **attractive** *adj* pleasing or interesting.

attribute /ə'trɪbjuːt/ *v* [T] *to*/ regard (sth) as caused by, produced by or belonging to sb/sth: *~ her success to hard work.* **attribute** /'ætrɪbjuːt/ *n* [C] quality belonging to sb/sth.

attributive /ə'trɪbjʊtɪv/ *adj* (*grammar*) coming in front of a noun.

aubergine /'əʊbəʒiːn/ *n* [C, U] large dark purple fruit, used as a vegetable.

auburn /'ɔːbən/ *adj* (esp of hair) reddish-brown.

auction /'ɔːkʃn/ *n* [C, U] public sale at which goods are sold to the person who offers the most money. **auction** *v* [T] sell by auction. **auctioneer** /ˌɔːkʃə'nɪə(r)/ *n* [C] person in charge of an auction.

audacious /ɔː'deɪʃəs/ *adj* bold and daring (and disrespectful). **audaciously** *adv*. **audacity** /ɔː'dæsətɪ/ *n* [U].

audible /'ɔːdəbl/ *adj* able to be heard. **audibly** *adv*.

audience /'ɔːdɪəns/ *n* [C] **1** group of people gathered together to hear or watch sb/sth. **2** number of people who watch or listen to a broadcast programme. **3** formal meeting with sb important: *an ~ with the Queen.*

audio /'ɔːdɪəʊ/ *adj* of hearing or sound. **ˌaudio-'visual** *adj* using sound and sight.

audit /'ɔːdɪt/ *n* [C] official examination of business accounts. **audit** *v* [T] examine (accounts). **auditor** *n* [C].

audition /ɔː'dɪʃn/ *n* [C] short performance by an actor, singer, etc to test ability. **audition** *v* [I, T] (cause sb to) give an audition.

auditorium /ˌɔːdɪ'tɔːrɪəm/ *n* [C] part of a building in which an audience sits.

augment /ɔːg'ment/ *v* [T] (*fml*) increase.

augur /'ɔːgə(r)/ *v* (*idm*) **augur 'well/'ill for sb/sth** (*fml*) be a good/bad sign for sb/sth in the future.

August /'ɔːgəst/ *n* [U, C] the

eighth month of the year. (See examples of use at *April*).

august /ɔː'gʌst/ *adj* (*fml*) causing respect and awe; grand.

aunt /aːnt; US ænt/ *n* [C] sister of one's father or mother; wife of one's uncle. **auntie** (also **aunty**) *n* [C] (*infml*) aunt.

au pair /ˌəʊ 'peə(r)/ *n* [C] young foreign person who lives with a family in order to learn the language and help with the housework.

aura /'ɔːrə/ *n* [C] quality or feeling that seems to be produced by a person or place.

aural /'ɔːrəl/, also /'aʊrəl/ *adj* of the ear or hearing.

auspices /'ɔːspɪsɪz/ *n* [pl] (*idm*) **under the auspices of sb/sth** (*fml*) helped and supported by sb/sth.

auspicious /ɔː'spɪʃəs/ *adj* (*fml*) showing signs of future success; favourable. **auspiciously** *adv*.

austere /ɒ'stɪə(r)/, also /ɔː'stɪə(r)/ *adj* **1** without decoration; simple and plain. **2** without luxuries or comforts; simple and strict. **austerely** *adv*. **austerity** /ɒ'sterətɪ, also /ɔː'sterətɪ/ *n* [C, U] (*pl* -ies).

authentic /ɔː'θentɪk/ *adj* known to be real or true. **authentically** /-klɪ/ *adv*. **authenticate** *v* [T] prove to be authentic. **authentication** /ɔːˌθentɪ'keɪʃn/ *n* [U]. **authenticity** /ˌɔːθen'tɪsətɪ/ *n* [U] quality of being authentic.

author /'ɔːθə(r)/ *n* [C] **1** writer. **2** person who creates or begins sth. **authoress** /'ɔːθərɪs/ *n* [C] woman author. **authorship** *n* [U] origin of a book.

authoritative /ɔː'θɒrətətɪv; US -teɪtɪv/ *adj* **1** having or showing authority; that can be trusted. **2** given with authority; official. **authoritatively** *adv*.

authority /ɔː'θɒrətɪ/ *n* (*pl* -ies) **1** (a) [U] power to give orders. (b) [C] person or group with this power. **2** [C] expert: *She's an ~ on physics.*

authorize /'ɔːθəraɪz/ *v* [T] give official permission for (sth). **authorization** /ˌɔːθəraɪ'zeɪʃn; US -rɪ'z-/ *n* [U].

autobiography /ˌɔːtəbaɪ'ɒɡrəfɪ/ *n* [C] (*pl* -ies) story of a person's life, written by that person. **autobiographical** /ˌɔːtəbaɪə'ɡræfɪkl/ *adj*.

autocrat /'ɔːtəkræt/ *n* [C] (a) ruler with unlimited power. (b) person who behaves like this. **autocratic** /ˌɔːtə'krætɪk/ *adj*.

autograph /'ɔːtəgrɑːf; US -græf/ *n* [C] signature of sb famous. **autograph** *v* [T] write one's signature on (sth).

automate /ˈɔːtəmeɪt/ v [T] cause to operate by automation.

automatic /ˌɔːtəˈmætɪk/ adj 1 (of a machine) working by itself without human control. 2 (of an action) done without thought. **automatic** n [C] automatic gun, machine, etc. **automatically** /-klɪ/ adv.

automation /ˌɔːtəˈmeɪʃn/ n [U] use of machines to do work previously done by people.

automobile /ˈɔːtəməbiːl/ n [C] (esp US) car.

autonomous /ɔːˈtɒnəməs/ adj self-governing. **autonomy** /-mɪ/ n [U] self-government.

autopsy /ˈɔːtɒpsɪ/ n [C] (pl -ies) medical examination of a body to find the cause of death.

autumn /ˈɔːtəm/ n [U, C] season of the year between summer and winter. **autumnal** /ɔːˈtʌmnəl/ adj.

auxiliary /ɔːɡˈzɪlɪərɪ/ adj giving help or support; additional. **auxiliary** n [C] (pl -ies) person or thing that helps. au,xiliary **verb** n [C] verb used with main verbs to show tense, mood?, etc and to form questions, eg do and has in: Do you know where he has gone?

avail /əˈveɪl/ v (fml) ~ oneself of make use of sth. **avail** n (idm) of **no avail** (fml) not helpful. **to no a'vail**, **without a'vail** with no success.

available /əˈveɪləbl/ adj that can be used or obtained: There are no tickets ~. **availability** /əˌveɪləˈbɪlətɪ/ n [U].

avalanche /ˈævəlɑːnʃ; US -læntʃ/ n [C] 1 mass of snow that falls quickly down the side of a mountain. 2 (fig) large quantity: an ~ of letters.

avarice /ˈævərɪs/ n [U] (fml) greed for money, etc. **avaricious** /ˌævəˈrɪʃəs/ adj.

avenge /əˈvendʒ/ v [T] hurt or punish (sb) for a wrong he/she has done to one: ~ his father's death.

avenue /ˈævənjuː; US -nuː/ n [C] 1 road, esp one with trees on either side. 2 (fig) way of achieving sth: explore several ~s.

average /ˈævərɪdʒ/ n [C] 1 result of adding several amounts together and dividing the total by the number of amounts. 2 [U] usual standard or level. **average** adj: the ~ age. **average** v 1 [I, T] find the average of (sth). 2 [T] be or do as an average: ~ 200 miles a day.

averse /əˈvɜːs/ adj to|| (about) opposed (to sth): not ~ to new ideas.

aversion /əˈvɜːʃn; US əˈvɜːʒn/ n 1 [C, U] strong dislike. 2 [C] thing or person disliked.

avert /əˈvɜːt/ v [T] 1 prevent (sth unpleasant) from happening. 2 (fml) turn away (one's eyes, etc).

aviary /ˈeɪvɪərɪ; US -vɪerɪ/ n [C] (pl -ies) large cage or building in which birds are kept.

aviation /ˌeɪvɪˈeɪʃn/ n [U] science or practice of flying aircraft.

avid /ˈævɪd/ adj very eager; keen. **avidly** adv.

avocado /ˌævəˈkɑːdəʊ/ n [C] (pl ~s) pear-shaped green tropical fruit.

avoid /əˈvɔɪd/ v [T] 1 keep oneself away from. 2 stop (sth) happening; prevent. **avoidable** adj that can be avoided. **avoidance** n [U].

avoirdupois /ˌævədəˈpɔɪz/ n [U] non-metric system of weights, based on the pound.

avow /əˈvaʊ/ v [T] (fml) declare (sth) openly.

await /əˈweɪt/ v [T] (fml) wait for.

awake[1] /əˈweɪk/ adj not asleep.

awake[2] /əˈweɪk/ v (pt awoke /əˈwəʊk/, pp awoken /əˈwəʊkən/) [I, T] wake.

awaken /əˈweɪkən/ v 1 [I, T] wake. 2 [T] cause to become active: ~ sb's interest. 3 (phr v) **awaken sb to sth** make sb aware of sth. **awakening** /-kənɪŋ/ n [sing] act of realizing.

award /əˈwɔːd/ v [T] make an official decision to give (sth) to (sb): ~ her first prize. **award** n [C] something awarded: an ~ for bravery.

aware /əˈweə(r)/ adj ~ of; that|| having knowledge of sth. **awareness** n [U].

away /əˈweɪ/ adv 1 to or at a distance from sth: The sea is two miles ~. 2 continuously: He was working ~. 3 (showing slow disappearance): The water boiled ~. 4 (sport) at the ground of one's opponents: play the next match ~.

awe /ɔː/ n [U] respect and fear. **'awe-inspiring** adj causing awe. **awesome** adj causing awe.

awful /ˈɔːfl/ adj 1 terrible: an ~ accident. 2 (infml) very bad; very great: ~ weather. **awfully** /ˈɔːflɪ/ adv (infml) very (much): ~ly hot.

awhile /əˈwaɪl; US əˈhwaɪl/ adv (fml) for a short time.

awkward /ˈɔːkwəd/ adj 1 lacking skill in movement; clumsy. 2 difficult to use. 3 causing difficulty or inconvenience: arrive at an ~ time. 4 embarrassing: an ~ silence. **awkwardly** adv. **awkwardness** n [U].

awning /ˈɔːnɪŋ/ n [C] roof-like covering of cloth that gives shelter from the rain or sun.

awoke pt of AWAKE[2].

awoken pp of AWAKE².

axe (also esp US **ax**) /æks/ n [C] 1 tool for cutting wood. 2 (idm) ,**have an 'axe to grind** have private reasons for doing sth. **axe** v [T] reduce greatly or end (eg jobs or services).

axiom /ˈæksɪəm/ n [C] statement accepted as true. **axiomatic** /ˌæksɪəˈmætɪk/ adj obviously true.

axis /ˈæksɪs/ n [C] (pl **axes** /ˈæksiːz/) 1 imaginary line through the centre of a turning object: *the earth's ~.* 2 horizontal or vertical line used as a fixed reference on a graph.

axle /ˈæksl/ n [C] rod on which a wheel turns.

aye (also **ay**) /aɪ/ interj (arch) (or used in dialects) yes. **aye** n [C] (person who gives a) vote in favour of sth.

azure /ˈæʒə(r)/, also /ˈæʒjʊə(r)/ adj, n [U] bright blue.

B b

B, b /biː/ n [C] (pl **B's, b's** /biːz/) the second letter of the English alphabet.

b. abbr born.

babble /ˈbæbl/ v [I] talk quickly or foolishly. **babble** n [sing].

babe /beɪb/ n [C] (arch) baby.

baboon /bəˈbuːn; US bæ-/ n [C] kind of large monkey.

baby /ˈbeɪbɪ/ n [C] (pl **-ies**) 1 very young child. 2 (sl esp US) young woman, esp a man's girl-friend. **babyish** adj of or like a baby. **babysit** v (-tt-, pt, pp -sat) [I] look after a child or children while the parents are out. **'babysitter** n [C].

bachelor /ˈbætʃələ(r)/ n [C] 1 unmarried man. 2 **Bachelor** holder of a first university degree: *a ,B~ of 'Arts/'Science.*

back¹ /bæk/ n [C] 1 part of the human body from the neck to the buttocks. 2 part of an object furthest from the front; part that is less used or less important: *sit in the ~ of the car* ○ *the ~ of a cheque.* 3 part of a chair that one leans against. 4 (idm) ,**back to 'front** with the back placed where the front should be. **behind sb's 'back** without sb's knowledge. **get/put sb's 'back up** (infml) make sb angry. **get off sb's 'back** (infml) stop annoying sb. **put one's 'back into sth** work very

hard at sth. **back** adj situated behind or at the back of sth: *the ~ door.* **'backache** n [U, C] pain in the back. **,back-'bencher** n [C] (Brit) member of Parliament who does not hold an official position in the government or opposition. **'backbone** n 1 [C] line of bones down the middle of the back. 2 [sing] (fig) main support. 3 [U] (fig) strength of character. **'back-breaking** adj (of work) extremely hard. **'background** n 1 [sing] (a) part of a scene behind the main things or people. (b) (fig) conditions and events that influence sth. 2 [C] person's social class, education, etc. **'backhand** n [C] stroke in tennis, etc with the back of the hand forward. **,back'handed** adj 1 played as a backhand. 2 indirect and sarcastic: *a ,~handed 'compliment.* **backless** adj. **'backlog** n [C] work still to be done. **,back 'number** n [C] issue of a newspaper, etc of an earlier date. **'backpack** n [C] (esp US) rucksack. **backside** n [C] (infml) buttocks. **,back'stage** adv behind the stage in a theatre. **'backstroke** n [U] swimming stroke done on one's back. **'backwater** n [C] 1 part of a river not reached by its current. 2 (fig) place not affected by progress, new ideas, etc.

back² /bæk/ adv 1 towards or at the back; away from the front or centre: *Stand ~, please.* 2 in(to) an earlier position or condition: *Put the book ~ on the shelf.* 3 (of time) in the past: *a few years ~.* 4 in return: *hit him ~* ○ *I'll phone you ~.* 5 (idm) ,**back and 'forth** backwards and forwards. **'backbiting** n [U] saying of unkind things about sb who is not present. **'backdate** v [T] declare that (sth) is valid from some date in the past. **'backfire** v [I] 1 (of a vehicle) make a loud noise in the engine or exhaust system. 2 (fig) (of a plan, etc) go wrong, esp unpleasantly for those responsible. **'backlash** n [sing] extreme, esp violent, reaction to an event.

back³ /bæk/ v 1 [I, T] move backwards: *~ a car* ○ *[I] onto/[I] face sth at the back: The house ~s onto the park.* 3 [T] give help or support to. 4 [T] bet money on (a horse, etc). 5 [T] cover the back of. 6 (phr v) **back 'down** withdraw a claim, etc made earlier. **back out (of sth)** withdraw from (an agreement, etc). **back sb/sth up** (a) support or encourage sb. (b) give evidence to prove sth. (c) (computing) make a spare copy of (a file, etc). **backer**

n [C] person who gives (esp financial) support. **backing** *n* [U] 1 support or help. 2 material that forms the back of sth. **'backup** *n* 1 [U] extra support. 2 [U, C] (*computing*) (making a) spare copy of a file, etc.

backgammon /'bækgæmən/ *n* [U] game played with draughts and dice.

backward /'bækwəd/ *adj* 1 directed towards the back: *a* ~ *glance*. 2 having made less than normal progress: *a* ~ *child*. **backwards** (also **backward**) *adv* 1 towards the back. 2 with the back or end first: *say the alphabet* ~ s.

bacon /'beɪkən/ *n* [U] salted or smoked meat from the back or sides of a pig.

bacteria /bæk'tɪərɪə/ *n* [pl] (*sing* **-ium** /-ɪəm/) very small living organisms, often the cause of disease. **bacterial** /-rɪəl/ *adj*.

bad /bæd/ *adj* (**worse** /wɜːs/, **worst** /wɜːst/) 1 of a very low standard: *a* ~ *actor*. 2 wicked; immoral. 3 unpleasant: ~ *news*. 4 (of things that are undesirable) serious; severe: *a* ~ *mistake* ⋄ *in a* ~ *mood*. 5 (of health) rotting or rotten: *The fish has gone* ~. 6 unhealthy or diseased: *a* ~ *back*. 7 harmful: *Smoking is* ~ *for you*. 8 (idm) **be in sb's bad 'books** ⇨ BOOK¹. **be bad 'luck** be unfortunate. **,bad 'blood** hate or anger. **go from ,bad to 'worse** (of a bad situation) become even worse. **have a bad night** ⇨ NIGHT. **not (so) 'bad** (*infml*) quite good. **too bad** (*infml*) unfortunate; regrettable: *It's too* ~ *she's ill*. **,bad 'debt** *n* [C] debt that is unlikely to be paid. **baddy** *n* [C] (*pl* **-ies**) (*infml*) bad person in a film, etc. **,bad 'language** *n* [U] rude or offensive words. **badly** *adv* (**worse**, **worst**) 1 in a bad manner. 2 very much; to a great extent: ~ *ly wounded* ⋄ *need some money* ~ *ly*. 3 (idm) **badly 'off** in a poor position, esp financially. **badness** *n* [U]. **,bad-'tempered** *adj* usually cross or angry.

bade *pt* of BID 2.

badge /bædʒ/ *n* [C] something worn to show occupation, membership, rank, etc.

badger¹ /'bædʒə(r)/ *n* [C] small animal with black and white stripes on its head that lives in holes in the ground and is active at night.

badger² /'bædʒə(r)/ *v* [T] annoy (sb) with questions, etc.

badminton /'bædmɪntən/ *n* [U] game similar to tennis, played by hitting a shuttlecock across a high net.

baffle /'bæfl/ *v* [T] be too difficult for (sb) to understand.

bag¹ /bæg/ *n* 1 [C] flexible container with an opening at the top: *a paper* ~. 2 **bags** [pl] *of*// (*infml*) plenty of (sth). 3 (idm) **in the 'bag** (*infml*) certain to be won, achieved, etc.

bag² /bæg/ *v* (**-gg-**) [T] 1 put into a bag. 2 kill (an animal or bird). 3 (*infml*) claim the possession of.

baggage /'bægɪdʒ/ *n* [U] = LUGGAGE.

baggy /'bægɪ/ *adj* (**-ier**, **-iest**) hanging loosely: ~ *trousers*.

bagpipes /'bægpaɪps/ *n* [pl] musical instrument with pipes and a bag to store air.

bail¹ /beɪl/ *n* [U] (a) money paid that allows an accused person to go free until the trial. (b) permission for an accused person to be set free in this way. **bail** *v* (phr *v*) **bail sb out (a)** obtain sb's freedom by payment of bail. (b) (*fig*) help sb out of (esp financial) difficulties.

bail² (also **bale**) /beɪl/ *v* [I, T] throw (water) out of (a boat).

bail³ /beɪl/ *n* [C] (in cricket) small piece of wood over the wicket.

bailiff /'beɪlɪf/ *n* [C] 1 law officer who takes goods, etc from sb who owes money. 2 (*Brit*) landowner's agent.

bait /beɪt/ *n* [U] 1 food put on a hook or in a trap to catch fish or animals. 2 (*fig*) thing used to tempt or attract (sb). **bait** *v* [T] 1 put bait on or in. 2 tease (sb) to make him/her angry.

bake /beɪk/ *v* 1 [I, T] cook in an oven. 2 [I, T] (cause to) become hard by heating. 3 [I] (*infml*) become very hot: *It's baking today!* **baker** *n* [C] person whose job is to bake and sell bread, etc. **bakery** *n* [C] (*pl* **-ies**) place where bread is baked (and sold). **'baking-powder** *n* [U] powder used for making cakes, etc rise and become light.

balance¹ /'bæləns/ *n* 1 [U] condition of being steady: *keep/lose one's* ~. 2 [C] instrument used for weighing. 3 [U, sing] condition when two opposites are equal or in correct proportions: *a* ~ *between work and play*. 4 [C] amount of money in a bank account. 5 [C] amount owed after a part payment. 6 (idm) **in the balance** uncertain or undecided. **on 'balance** having considered everything. **'balance sheet** *n* [C] record of money received and paid out and the difference between these.

balance² /'bæləns/ v 1 (a) [T] keep (sth) steady. (b) [I] be or put oneself steady: *He ~ d on the edge of the table.* 2 [T] compare (two objects, plans, etc); give equal importance to. 3 [T] compare one's debts and what one is owed in (an account).

balcony /'bælkənɪ/ n [C] (*pl* -ies) 1 platform with a wall or railing built onto the outside of a building. 2 upstairs seats in a theatre, etc.

bald /bɔːld/ adj 1 having little or no hair on the head. 2 (*fig*) plain: *a ~ statement.* **balding** adj becoming bald. **baldly** adv. **baldness** n [U].

bale¹ /beɪl/ n [C] large bundle of hay, cloth, etc tied tightly together.

bale² /beɪl/ v 1 = BAIL². 2 (phr v) **bale out (of sth)** jump out of (an aircraft) using a parachute.

balk (also **baulk**) /bɔːk/ v [I] (*at*) be very unwilling to try or do sth.

ball¹ /bɔːl/ n [C] 1 round object used in games. 2 round mass: *a ~ of wool.* 3 round part of the body: *the ~ of one's foot.* 4 [usp pl] (*infml*) testicle. 5 (idm) **keep/start the 'ball rolling** continue/begin an activity. **(be) on the 'ball** (*infml*) be alert and aware of new ideas, etc. **'ball game** n 1 (a) [C] game played with a ball. (b) [U] (*US*) baseball. 2 [C] (*infml*) state of affairs. **'ballpoint** (also **,ball-point 'pen**) n [C] pen that uses a tiny ball at its point to roll ink onto the paper.

ball² /bɔːl/ n [C] 1 large formal social gathering for dancing. 2 (idm) **have a 'ball** (*infml*) have a very good time. **'ballroom** n [C] large room used for dancing.

ballad /'bæləd/ n [C] simple song or poem, esp one that tells a story.

ballast /'bæləst/ n [U] 1 heavy material placed in a ship to keep it steady. 2 sand, etc thrown out of a balloon(2) to make it go higher.

ballerina /,bælə'riːnə/ n [C] woman ballet dancer.

ballet /'bæleɪ/ n 1 (a) [U] style of dancing that tells a story, but without speech. (b) [C] story performed in this way. 2 [C] group of ballet dancers.

ballistics /bə'lɪstɪks/ n [U] study of the movement of objects shot or fired through the air. **bal,listic 'missile** n [C] missile that is at first powered and guided but then falls freely.

balloon /bə'luːn/ n [C] 1 brightly coloured rubber bag filled with air. 2 (also **hot-'air balloon**) large rounded bag filled with air or gas to make it rise in the air, with a basket to carry passengers. **bal,loon** n [I] swell like a balloon. **bal,loonist** n [C] person who flies in a balloon(2).

ballot /'bælət/ n 1 [C, U] (paper used in a) secret vote. 2 [C] number of votes recorded. **ballot** v 1 [I] vote by ballot. 2 [T] find out the opinions of (a group) by organizing a vote. **'ballot-box** n [C] box into which ballot papers are put.

balm /bɑːm/ n [U, C] 1 oil for lessening pain. 2 (*fig*) something that comforts. **balmy** adj (-ier, -iest) 1 (of air) gentle and warm. 2 healing. 3 (esp *US*) = BARMY.

balsa /'bɔːlsə/ n [U, C] (light wood of a) tropical American tree.

balustrade /,bælə'streɪd/ n [C] row of upright posts with a rail along the top, placed on a balcony, etc.

bamboo /,bæm'buː/ n [C, U] tall plant of the grass family with hard hollow stems.

ban /bæn/ v (-nn-) [T] forbid. **ban** n [C] order that forbids sth.

banal /bə'nɑːl; *US* 'beɪnl/ adj ordinary and uninteresting: *~ remarks.*

banana /bə'nɑːnə; *US* bə'nænə/ n [C] long yellow tropical fruit.

band /bænd/ n [C] 1 group of musicians who play popular music. 2 group of people: *a ~ of robbers.* 3 thin flat strip of material for tying things together or putting round an object. 4 range of numbers, amounts, etc within limits: *an income ~.* **band** v [I] (*together*) unite in a group. **'bandstand** n [C] open-air platform for a band(1). **'bandwagon** n (idm) **jump/climb on the 'bandwagon** (*infml*) join others in doing sth fashionable and successful.

bandage /'bændɪdʒ/ n [C] strip of cloth that is wrapped round a wound. **bandage** v [T] wrap a bandage round.

bandit /'bændɪt/ n [C] armed robber.

bandy¹ /'bændɪ/ v (*pt, pp* -ied) 1 (idm) **bandy 'words** (*dated*) quarrel. 2 (phr v) **bandy sth about** pass on (eg information, ideas) in a thoughtless way.

bandy² /'bændɪ/ adj (-ier, -iest) (of the legs) curving outwards at the knees.

bang /bæŋ/ n [C] 1 sudden loud noise; violent blow. 2 (idm) **bang one's head against a brick wall** ⇨ HEAD¹. **bang** v [I, T] make a loud noise; hit violently: *The door ~ed shut.* ○ *She ~ed her knee on the* desk. **bang** *adv* (*infml*) exactly: ~ *in the middle.*

banger /'bæŋə(r)/ *n* [C] (*Brit infml*) 1 sausage. 2 noisy firework. 3 noisy old car.

bangle /'bæŋgl/ *n* [C] ornament worn round the arm or leg.

banish /'bænɪʃ/ *v* [T] 1 send away as a punishment. 2 send (thoughts, etc) out of one's mind. **banishment** *n* [U].

banister /'bænɪstə(r)/ *n* [C, esp pl] upright posts and rail of a staircase.

banjo /'bændʒəʊ/ *n* [C] (*pl* ~s) musical instrument with a round body, played by plucking the strings.

bank¹ /bæŋk/ *n* [C] 1 place where money is kept safely. 2 place for storing things: *a blood* ~. **bank** *v* 1 [T] place or keep (money) in a bank. 2 (phr v) **bank on sb/sth** depend on sb/sth. **banker** *n* [C] owner, director or manager of a bank. **bank 'holiday** *n* [C] official public holiday. **banking** *n* [U] business of running a bank. **'banknote** *n* [C] piece of paper money.

bank² /bæŋk/ *n* [C] 1 land sloping up beside a river, etc. 2 mound of sloping land. 3 mass of snow, clouds, etc. **bank** *v* [I] (of an aircraft) travel with one side higher than the other, while turning.

bank³ /bæŋk/ *n* [C] row or series of similar objects: *a* ~ *of switches.*

bankrupt /'bæŋkrʌpt/ *adj* 1 unable to pay one's debts. 2 (*fig*) completely lacking in sth good. **bankrupt** *n* [C] bankrupt person. **bankruptcy** /-rəpsɪ/ *n* [C, U] (*pl* -**ies**) (instance of) being bankrupt.

banner /'bænə(r)/ *n* [C] long piece of cloth with a message on it, carried by marchers.

banns /bænz/ *n* [pl] public announcement in church of an intended marriage.

banquet /'bæŋkwɪt/ *n* [C] large formal dinner.

bantam /'bæntəm/ *n* [C] small kind of chicken.

banter /'bæntə(r)/ *n* [U] playful joking talk. **banter** *v* [I] speak playfully or jokingly.

baptism /'bæptɪzəm/ *n* 1 [C, U] ceremony of sprinkling water on sb or dipping sb in water, often giving him/her a name as well, as a sign of membership of the Christian Church. 2 (idm) **baptism of 'fire (a)** a soldier's first experience of war. **(b)** introduction to an unpleasant experience. **baptize** /bæp'taɪz/ *v* [T] give baptism to.

bar¹ /bɑː(r)/ *n* 1 [C] long piece of solid material: *a steel* ~ ○ *a* ~ *of chocolate.* 2 [C] length of wood or metal across a door, window, etc: *be behind* ~ *s*, ie be in prison. 3 [C] room or counter where drinks, etc are served. 4 [C] narrow band of colour, light, etc. 5 [C] (*fig*) obstacle: *Poor health is a* ~ *to success.* 6 [C] (*music*) series of notes. 7 [C] barrier in a law-court: *the prisoner at the* ~. **8 the bar** [sing, also sing with pl v] (all those who belong to) the profession of barrister: *be called to the* ~, ie become a barrister. **bar code** *n* [C] group of thick and thin parallel lines printed on goods for sale, containing information for a computer. **'barman** *n* [C] (*fem* **barmaid**) person who serves drinks, etc at a bar(3). **'bartender** *n* [C] (*esp US*) barman.

bar² /bɑː(r)/ *v* (-**rr**-) [T] 1 fasten with a bar. 2 obstruct: ~ *the way.* 3 forbid: *She was* ~ *red from (entering) the competition.*

bar³ /bɑː(r)/ *prep* 1 except. 2 (idm) **bar none** without exception.

barb /bɑːb/ *n* [C] sharp curved point of a hook at the end of a fishing-line, etc. **barbed** *adj* with short sharp points: ~ *ed wire.*

barbarian /bɑː'beərɪən/ *adj*, *n* [C] uncivilized (person). **barbaric** /bɑː'bærɪk/ *adj* 1 of or like barbarians. 2 wild and cruel. **barbarity** /bɑː'bærətɪ/ *n* [U, C] (*pl* -**ies**) great cruelty. **barbarous** /'bɑːbərəs/ *adj* cruel or rough.

barbecue /'bɑːbɪkjuː/ *n* [C] 1 metal frame for cooking food outdoors. 2 party at which food is cooked on a barbecue. **barbecue** *v* [T] cook on a barbecue.

barber /'bɑːbə(r)/ *n* [C] person whose job is to cut men's hair.

barbiturate /bɑː'bɪtjʊrət/ *n* [C] drug that causes sleep.

bard /bɑːd/ *n* [C] (*arch*) poet.

bare /beə(r)/ *adj* (~**r**, ~**st**) 1 without clothing or covering. 2 empty: ~ *cupboards.* 3 just enough; basic. **bare** *v* [T] uncover; reveal. **'bareback** *adj*, *adv* on a horse without a saddle. **'barefaced** *adj* shameless; very rude. **'barefoot** *adj*, *adv* without shoes, socks, etc. **barely** *adv* only just. **bareness** *n* [U].

bargain /'bɑːgɪn/ *n* [C] 1 agreement to do, buy or sell sth. 2 something sold cheaply. 3 (idm) **into the bargain** (*infml*) in addition. **bargain** *v* 1 [I] talk about the price, conditions of sale, etc to reach an agreement. 2 (phr v) **bargain for/on sth** (*infml*) be prepared for sth; expect: *get more* *than you had ~ ed for.*

barge[1] /bɑːdʒ/ *n* [C] flat-bottomed boat.

barge[2] /bɑːdʒ/ *v* (*infml*) **1** [I] rush or bump heavily and awkwardly. **2** (*phr v*) **barge in** interrupt rudely.

baritone /ˈbærɪtəʊn/ *n* [C] (man with a) singing voice between tenor and bass.

bark[1] /bɑːk/ *n* [C] sharp harsh sound made by a dog. **bark** *v* **1** [I] (of dogs) make a bark. **2** [T] say in a fierce voice: *~ out orders.*

bark[2] /bɑːk/ *n* [U] tough outer covering of a tree.

barley /ˈbɑːlɪ/ *n* [U] (grass-like plant producing) grain used for food and making beer and whisky.

barmy /ˈbɑːmɪ/ *adj* (-ier, -iest) (*Brit infml*) foolish; crazy.

barn /bɑːn/ *n* [C] building for storing hay, etc on a farm.

barnacle /ˈbɑːnəkl/ *n* [C] small shellfish that attaches itself to objects under water.

barometer /bəˈrɒmɪtə(r)/ *n* [C] instrument for measuring air pressure and so forecasting the weather: (*fig*) *a ~ of public feeling.*

baron /ˈbærən/ *n* [C] **1** (title of a) British nobleman of the lowest rank of the peerage. **2** powerful and rich industrial leader. **baroness** *n* [C] **1** woman with the same rank as a baron. **2** wife of a baron.

baronet /ˈbærənɪt/ *n* [C] (title of a) man with the lowest hereditary rank in Britain, below a baron but above a knight.

baroque /bəˈrɒk; *US* bəˈrəʊk/ *adj* of the highly decorated style fashionable in Europe in the 17th and 18th centuries.

barrack /ˈbærək/ *v* [I, T] shout loudly at (sb) to interrupt him/her.

barracks /ˈbærəks/ *n* [C, sing or pl *v*] large building(s) for soldiers to live in.

barrage /ˈbærɑːʒ; *US* bəˈrɑːʒ/ *n* [C] **1** heavy continuous gunfire: (*fig*) *a ~ of complaints.* **2** artificial barrier across a river.

barrel /ˈbærəl/ *n* [C] **1** (a) round container for liquids. (b) amount that a barrel contains. **2** tube of a gun through which the bullet is fired. **'barrel-organ** *n* [C] mechanical instrument from which music is produced by turning a handle.

barren /ˈbærən/ *adj* **1** not able to produce crops, fruit or children. **2** (*fig*) without value or interest: *a ~ discussion.*

barricade /ˌbærɪˈkeɪd/ *n* [C] barrier of objects built to block a

street, etc. **barricade** *v* [T] block (a street, etc).

barrier /ˈbærɪə(r)/ *n* [C] **1** something that prevents or controls movement or progress: (*fig*) *~s to world peace.* **2** thing that keeps people apart: *the language ~.*

barring /ˈbɑːrɪŋ/ *prep* except for.

barrister /ˈbærɪstə(r)/ *n* [C] (in English law) lawyer who has the right to speak in higher courts.

barrow /ˈbærəʊ/ *n* [C] **1** = WHEELBARROW (WHEEL). **2** small cart, moved by hand.

barter /ˈbɑːtə(r)/ *v* [I, T] exchange (goods) for other goods. **barter** *n* [U].

base[1] /beɪs/ *n* [C] **1** lowest part of sth, on which it stands. **2** (*fig*) starting-point. **3** main part to which other parts are added: *a drink with a rum ~.* **4** place at which armed forces, etc have their stores. **base** *v* [T] **1** *on// develop (sth) using sth else as a starting-point: *a story ~d on real life.* **2** put (sb) in a place to live and work: *a company ~d in Cairo.* **baseless** *adj* without cause or reason.

base[2] /beɪs/ *adj* (~r, ~st) **1** (*fml*) immoral; dishonourable. **2** (of a metal) low in value.

baseball /ˈbeɪsbɔːl/ *n* [U] American game played with a bat and ball by two teams of nine players.

basement /ˈbeɪsmənt/ *n* [C] lowest floor of a building, below ground level.

bases **1** *pl* of BASIS. **2** *pl* of BASE[1].

bash /bæʃ/ *v* [T] (*infml*) hit heavily. **bash** *n* [C] (*infml*) **1** heavy blow. **2** (*idm*) **have a bash at sth** (*infml*) try to do sth.

bashful /ˈbæʃfl/ *adj* shy. **bashfully** *adv*.

basic /ˈbeɪsɪk/ *adj* simplest or most important; fundamental: *the ~ facts.* **basically** *adv* most importantly. **basics** *n* [pl] basic parts or facts.

basil /ˈbæzl/ *n* [U] sweet-smelling herb.

basin /ˈbeɪsn/ *n* [C] **1** = WASH-BASIN (WASH[1]). **2** round open bowl for liquids or food. **3** hollow place where water collects. **4** area drained by a river.

basis /ˈbeɪsɪs/ *n* [C] (*pl* **bases** /ˈbeɪsiːz/) **1** most important part of sth from which it is developed; foundation: *arguments that have a firm ~.* **2** way in which sth is done: *a service run on a commercial ~.*

bask /bɑːsk; *US* bæsk/ *v* [I] (in//) sit or lie, esp in the sunshine, enjoying its warmth: (*fig*) *~ in sb's approval.*

basket /ˈbɑːskɪt; *US* ˈbæs-/ *n* [C]

container made of woven strips of wood: a 'shopping-~. 'basketball n [U] game in which two teams try to throw a ball into a basket-shaped net above the ground.

bass¹ /beɪs/ n [C] 1 (man with the) lowest singing voice. 2 = DOUBLE-BASS (DOUBLE¹). bass adj low in tone.

bass² /bæs/ n [C] kind of fish of the perch family, eaten as food.

bassoon /bə'su:n/ n [C] wind instrument made of wood, producing very low sounds.

bastard /'ba:stəd; US 'bæs-/ n [C] 1 child of unmarried parents. 2 (derog sl) very unpleasant person. 3 (sl) unfortunate person: The poor ~ has just lost his job.

baste¹ /beɪst/ v [T] pour fat over (meat) while cooking.

baste² /beɪst/ v [T] sew (pieces of material) together with long temporary stitches.

bastion /'bæstiən/ n [C] 1 part of a castle, etc that stands out from the rest. 2 (fig) place where a belief or principle is defended.

bat¹ /bæt/ n [C] 1 shaped piece of wood for hitting the ball in cricket, baseball, etc. 2 (idm) ,off one's own 'bat (infml) without being told to do so. bat v (-tt-) [I] use a bat. 'batsman n [C] player who bats in cricket. batter n [C] (esp in baseball) player who bats.

bat² /bæt/ n [C] small mouse-like animal that flies at night.

bat³ /bæt/ v (-tt-) (idm) not bat an 'eyelid (infml) show no sign of surprise.

batch /bætʃ/ n [C] group of things or people.

bath /ba:θ; US bæθ/ n (pl ~s /ba:ðz; US bæðz/) 1 [C] large container for water in which one sits to wash one's body. 2 [C] act of washing one's body while sitting in the bath. 3 baths [pl] public swimming-pool. bath v 1 [T] give a bath to: ~ a baby. 2 [I] have a bath(2). 'bathrobe n [C] 1 loose towelling garment worn before or after taking a bath. 2 (US) dressing-gown. 'bathroom n [C] 1 room in which there is a bath. 2 (esp US) toilet. 'bath-tub n [C] bath(1).

bathe /beɪð/ v 1 [I] (esp Brit) swim in the sea, etc. 2 [I] (US) have a bath(2). 3 [T] wash with water. bathe n [sing] swim. bather n [C] swimmer.

batman /'bætmən/ n [C] (pl -men /-mən/ (Brit)) army officer's personal servant.

baton /'bætn, 'bætɒn; US 'bætɒn/ n [C] 1 short thin stick used by the

conductor of an orchestra. 2 police officer's short thick stick used as a weapon.

battalion /bə'tæliən/ n [C] army unit that consists of several companies(6).

batten /'bætn/ n [C] long wooden board. batten v [T] down// fasten (sth) with battens.

batter¹ /'bætə(r)/ v [T] hit hard and often. battered adj out of shape because of old age, great use, etc. 'battering-ram n [C] large heavy log formerly used for breaking down walls, etc.

batter² /'bætə(r)/ n [U] mixture of flour, eggs, milk, etc: fish fried in ~.

battery /'bætəri/ n [C] (pl -ies) 1 device for supplying electricity. 2 army unit of big guns. 3 series of cages in which hens are kept. 4 large set of similar things: a ~ of cameras/tests.

battle /'bætl/ n 1 [C, U] fight between armed forces. 2 [C] (fig) any struggle: a ~ of words. battle v [I] fight; struggle: battling against poverty. 'battlefield n [C] place where a battle is fought. 'battleship n [C] large warship with big guns and heavy armour.

battlements /'bætlmənts/ n [pl] (roof surrounded by a) wall on top of a castle, etc, with openings for shooting through.

batty /'bæti/ adj (-ier, -iest) (infml) slightly mad.

bauble /'bɔ:bl/ n [C] cheap showy ornament.

baulk ⇒ BALK.

bawdy /'bɔ:di/ adj (-ier, -iest) rude and amusing about sexual matters.

bawl /bɔ:l/ v [I, T] shout loudly.

bay¹ /beɪ/ n [C] area of the coast where the land curves widely inwards.

bay² /beɪ/ n [C] area or division used for a particular purpose: a 'loading ~. ,bay 'window n [C] window, with glass on three sides, that projects from an outside wall.

bay³ /beɪ/ v [I] (of large dogs) make a deep loud bark, esp when hunting. bay n (idm) hold/keep sb/sth at 'bay prevent (eg an enemy) from coming near.

bay⁴ (also 'bay-tree) /beɪ/ n [C] tree whose dark green leaves are used in cooking.

bayonet /'beɪənɪt/ n [C] long sharp blade fixed to the end of a rifle. bayonet v [T] stab with a bayonet.

bazaar /bə'zɑ:(r)/ n [C] 1 (in eastern countries) group of small shops or stalls. 2 sale of goods to raise money for charity.

bazooka /bə'zu:kə/ n [C] long portable gun that rests on the shoulder and fires rockets esp against tanks.

BBC /ˌbi: bi: 'si:/ abbr British Broadcasting Corporation.

BC /ˌbi: 'si:/ abbr (in the year) before the birth of Jesus Christ.

be¹ /bi/ strong form bi:/ aux v (1st pers sing pres tense am /əm, æm; strong form æm/, 3rd pers sing pres tense is /s, z; strong form ɪz/, 1st pers pl pres tense, 2nd pers sing and pl pres tense, 3rd pers pl pres tense are /ə(r)/; strong form ɑ:(r)/, 1st pers sing pt, 3rd pers sing pt was /wəz/; strong form wɒz/, US /wʌz/, 1st pers pl, 2nd pers pl, 3rd pers pl pt were /wə(r)/; strong form wɜ:(r)/, pres part being /'bi:ɪŋ/, pp been /bi:n (US also)bɪn/) 1 (used with a present participle to form the continuous tense): They are reading. 2 (used with a past participle to form the passive): He was killed. 3 (used with to + infinitive). (a) must: You are to report to the police at 10 o'clock. (b) (showing a future arrangement or intention): The President is to visit London in May.

be² /bi/ strong form bi:/ v (for full present and past tense forms ⇨ BE¹) [I] 1 exist; occur; live: Is there a God? 2 be situated: The lamp is on the table. 3 have a particular name, quality or condition: This is Mrs Khan. ○ The film was very funny. ○ Today is Monday. ○ I'll be 35 next year. 4 (used to show possession): The money's not yours. 5 become: He wants to be a teacher. 6 (used to show equivalence in value, number, etc): That will be £80.95. 7 visit: Have you been to college today? 8 (idm) be out in the open ⇨ OPEN¹.

beach /bi:tʃ/ n [C] sea-shore covered by sand or pebbles. **beach** v [T] move (a boat) onto the shore from the water. **'beach-ball** n [C] large light ball for games on the beach. **'beachhead** n [C] strong position on a shore established by an invading army. **'beachwear** n [U] clothes for sunbathing, swimming, etc.

beacon /'bi:kən/ n [C] light or fire used as a signal or warning.

bead /bi:d/ n 1 (a) [C] small ball of glass, plastic, etc with a small hole through it, for threading on a string. (b) **beads** [pl] necklace of beads. 2 [C] drop of liquid: ~ s of sweat.

beady /'bi:di/ adj (-ier, -iest) (of eyes) small and bright.

beak /bi:k/ n [C] hard horny part of a bird's mouth.

beaker /'bi:kə(r)/ n [C] 1 tall narrow cup for drinking. 2 glass container used in chemistry.

beam /bi:m/ n [C] 1 long piece of wood, metal, etc used for supporting the weight of part of a building. 2 line of light from the sun, a torch, etc. 3 bright happy look or smile. 4 radio signal to direct an aircraft, etc. **beam** v 1 [I] (of the sun, etc) send out light and warmth. 2 [I] (fig) smile happily. 3 [T] send (broadcast signals) in a particular direction.

bean /bi:n/ n [C] 1 (plant with) seed in long pods, used as food: 'soya ~ s ○ 'coffee ~ s. 2 (idm) **full of 'beans** (infml) having a lot of energy; lively.

bear¹ /beə(r)/ n [C] large heavy animal with thick fur.

bear² /beə(r)/ v (pt **bore** /bɔ:(r)/, pp **borne** /bɔ:n/) 1 [T] (fml) carry. 2 [T] support: The ice is too thin to ~ your weight. 3 [T] have; show: The letter bore her signature. 4 [T] accept (sth unpleasant); endure: ~ pain without complaining. 5 [T] produce (flowers, fruit, etc). 6 [T] (fml) give birth to: ~ a child. 7 [T] (fml) have (a particular feeling): I ~ them no sentiment. 8 [I] turn slightly in the stated direction: The road ~ s left. 9 [T] be fit for: The plan will not ~ close examination. 10 (idm) **bear the 'brunt of sth** receive the main force of sth: ~ the brunt of an attack/sb's anger. **bear sth in mind** ⇨ MIND². **bear witness to sth** (fml) be a sign or proof of sth. **bring sth to bear** direct or apply sth: bring pressure to ~ on him to change his mind. **can't bear sb/ sth** dislike sb/sth very much. 11 (phr v) **bear 'down on sb/sth** move quickly and threateningly towards sb/sth. **bear sb/sth 'out** support or confirm sb/sth. **bear 'up** be strong and brave in difficulties. **'bear with sb** be patient with sb; be tolerated. **bearable** adj that can be tolerated.

beard /bɪəd/ n [C] hair growing on the chin and cheeks of a man's face. **bearded** adj.

bearer /'beərə(r)/ n [C] 1 person who brings a letter or message. 2 person who carries a coffin. 3 person who has a cheque for payment.

bearing /'beərɪŋ/ n 1 [sing] (fml) way of standing or behaving. 2 [U] relevance; connection: That has no ~ on the subject. 3 [C] direction shown on a compass. **4 bearings** [pl] knowledge of one's position: *get/lose one's ~ s.*

beast /biːst/ *n* [C] **1** (*dated or fml*) large four-footed animal. **2** cruel or unpleasant person. **beastly** *adj* (*infml*) unpleasant.

beat[1] /biːt/ *v* (*pt* **beat**, *~ en* /'biːtn/) **1** [T] hit repeatedly, esp with a stick. **2** [T] change the shape of (sth), by blows: *~ metal flat.* **3** [I, T] move (up and down) regularly: *His heart was still ~ing.* **4** [T] mix thoroughly: *~ eggs.* **5** [T] defeat: *She ~ me at chess.* **6** (idm) **beat about the 'bush** talk indirectly about sth. **'beat it** (*sl*) go away. **beat a re-'treat** go back hurriedly. **beat 'time** mark the rhythm of music by making regular movements. **off the ,beaten 'track in a quiet** isolated place. **7** (phr v) **beat down** (of the sun) shine with great heat. **beat sb down** persuade (a seller) to reduce a price. **beat sb up** hit and kick sb badly. **beat** *adj* tired out: *I'm dead ~.* **beaten** *adj* shaped by beating. **beater** *n* [C] tool for beating. **beating** *n* [C] **1** punishment by hitting. **2** defeat.

beat[2] /biːt/ *n* [C] **1** (sound of a) repeated stroke: *the ~ of a drum.* **2** rhythm in music or poetry. **3** route along which sb, eg a police officer, goes regularly.

beautician /bjuː'tɪʃn/ *n* [C] person whose job is to give beauty treatments.

beautiful /'bjuːtɪfl/ *adj* giving pleasure to the mind or senses. **beautifully** *adv.* **beautify** /'bjuːtɪfaɪ/ *v* (*pt, pp* **-ied**) [T] make beautiful.

beauty /'bjuːtɪ/ *n* (*pl* **-ies**) **1** [U] quality or state of being beautiful. **2** [C] person or thing that is beautiful. **'beauty salon** (also **'beauty parlour**) *n* [C] place where women receive treatment to become more beautiful. **'beauty spot** *n* [C] place famous for its scenery.

beaver /'biːvə(r)/ *n* [C] fur-coated animal that lives on land and in water and that builds dams across streams. **beaver** (*phr v*) **beaver away** (*infml esp Brit*) work hard.

became *pt* of BECOME.

because /bɪ'kɒz; *US* -kɔːz/ *conj* for the reason that: *I did it ~ they asked me.* **because of** *prep* by reason of: *He couldn't walk fast ~ of his bad leg.*

beckon /'bekən/ *v* [I, T] call (sb) to come nearer by waving one's hand or finger.

become /bɪ'kʌm/ *v* (*pt* **became**

/bɪ'keɪm/, *pp* **become**) (usu used with an *adj*) **1** begin or come to be: *They soon became angry.* ○ *~ a doctor.* **2** [T] (*fml*) be suitable for: *That hat ~ s you.* **3** (idm) **what be-comes of sb** what is happening to sb. **becoming** *adj* (*fml*) attractive.

bed[1] /bed/ *n* [C] **1** piece of furniture that one sleeps on. **2** bottom of the sea or a river. **3** flat base on which sth rests. **4** piece of ground for growing plants. **5** (idm) **go to bed with sb** (*infml*) have sexual intercourse with sb. **'bedclothes** *n* [pl] sheets, blankets, etc on a bed. **'bedpan** *n* [C] container for use as a toilet by sb ill in bed. **'bed-ridden** *adj* too ill or weak to get out of bed. **'bedroom** *n* [C] room for sleeping in. **'bedside** *n* [sing] area beside a bed. **,bed'sitter** (also **'bedsit**) *n* [C] room for both living and sleeping in. **'bedspread** *n* [C] decorative top cover for a bed. **'bedstead** *n* [C] framework supporting the springs and mattress of a bed. **'bedtime** *n* [U] time for going to bed.

bed[2] /bed/ *v* (**-dd-**) [T] **1** place or fix firmly: *The bricks are ~ded in the concrete.* **2** plant. **3** (*infml*) have sexual intercourse with. **4** (phr v) **bed down** settle for the night. **bed sb down** make sb comfortable for the night. **bedding** *n* [U] bed-clothes.

bedevil /bɪ'devl/ *v* (**-ll-**; *US* **-l-**) [T] (*fml*) trouble (sb) greatly.

bedlam /'bedləm/ *n* [U] scene of noisy confusion.

bedraggled /bɪ'dræɡld/ *adj* untidy and wet or dirty.

bee /biː/ *n* [C] **1** stinging insect that makes honey. **2** (idm) **have a 'bee in one's bonnet** think constantly about sth. **make a bee-line for sth/sb** /'biːlaɪn/ go directly towards sth/sb. **'beehive** *n* [C] box for bees to live in.

beech /biːtʃ/ *n* [C] tree with smooth bark, shiny leaves and small nuts.

beef /biːf/ *n* [U] meat of an ox, bull or cow. **beef** *v* [I] (*sl*) complain. **'beefsteak** *n* [U] thick piece of beef. **beefy** *adj* (**-ier, -iest**) (*infml*) strong and muscular.

been *pp* of BE.

beer /bɪə(r)/ *n* [U, C] alcoholic drink made from malt and flavoured with hops. **beery** *adj* smelling of or like beer.

beet /biːt/ *n* [U, C] **1** plant with a fleshy root that is used as a vegetable or for making sugar. **2** (*US*) beetroot. **'beetroot** /'bi:t-/ *n* [C] dark red fleshy root of beet, eaten as a vegetable.

beetle /'biːtl/ n [C] insect with hard wing-covers.

befall /bɪ'fɔːl/ v (pt befell /bɪ'fel/, pp ~en /bɪ'fɔːlən/) [I, T] (arch) happen to (sb).

befit /bɪ'fɪt/ v (-tt-) [T] (fml) be suitable for. **befitting** adj suitable; proper.

before /bɪ'fɔː(r)/ prep 1 earlier than: the day ~ yesterday. 2 in front of; ahead of: B comes ~ C in the alphabet. **before** adv at an earlier time; already: I've seen that film ~. **before** conj earlier in time than: Do it ~ you forget.

beforehand /bɪ'fɔːhænd/ adv in advance; earlier.

befriend /bɪ'frend/ v [T] make a friend of.

beg /beg/ v (-gg-) 1 [I, T] (for) ask for (money, food, etc). 2 [I, T] ask seriously and with feeling: I ~ you to stay. 3 (idm) **I beg to differ** I don't agree. **go 'begging** (of things) be unwanted. **I beg your pardon** (a) please repeat that. (b) I am sorry; please excuse me.

beggar /'begə(r)/ n [C] person who lives by begging.

begin /bɪ'gɪn/ v (-nn-, pt began /bɪ'gæn/, pp begun /bɪ'gʌn/) 1 [I, T] start: ~ to read a new book The film ~s at ten. 2 to feel ill. 3 (idm) **to begin with** at first; firstly. **beginner** n [C] person who is just beginning to learn sth. **beginning** n [C, U] starting-point.

begrudge /bɪ'grʌdʒ/ v [T] feel envy or resentment at: I do not ~ them their success.

behalf /bɪ'hɑːf; US bɪ'hæf/ n (idm) **on behalf of sb** as the representative of sb: I'm speaking on Ann's ~.

behave /bɪ'heɪv/ v 1 [I] act in a particular way: ~ well. 2 ~ oneself show good manners. **behaviour** (US -ior) n [U] way of behaving.

behead /bɪ'hed/ v [T] cut off the head of.

behind¹ /bɪ'haɪnd/ prep 1 at, in or to the back of: Hide ~ the tree. 2 making less progress than: He's ~ the rest of the class. 3 in favour of; supporting. 4 being the reason for; responsible for: What's ~ the smart suit, then? **behind** adv 1 in or to a position at the back of sb/ sth: The children followed ~ their parents. 2 remaining after others have gone: stay ~ after school. 3 (in/with/)// failing to pay money or complete work by the required time: be ~ with the rent.

behind² /bɪ'haɪnd/ n [C] (infml euph) buttocks.

behindhand /bɪ'haɪndhænd/

adv late: be ~ with one's work.

beige /beɪʒ/ adj, n [U] (of a) very light yellowish-brown.

being¹ present participle of BE.

being² /'biːɪŋ/ n 1 [U] existence: The society came into ~ in 1990. 2 [C] living creature: human ~s.

belated /bɪ'leɪtɪd/ adj coming very late or too late. **belatedly** adv.

belch /beltʃ/ v 1 [I] send out gas from the stomach noisily through the mouth. 2 [T] send out (eg smoke) in large amounts. **belch** n [C].

belfry /'belfrɪ/ n [C] (pl -ies) tower for bells.

belief /bɪ'liːf/ n 1 [U] feeling that sth/sb is real and true and can be trusted: ~ in her honesty. 2 [C] something accepted as true: religious ~s.

believe /bɪ'liːv/ v 1 [T] be sure of the truth of. 2 [T] suppose. 3 [I] have religious faith. 4 (phr v) **believe in sb/sth** (a) be sure of the existence of sb/sth. (b) be sure of the value of sth: He ~s in getting plenty of exercise. **believable** adj that can be believed. **believer** n [C].

belittle /bɪ'lɪtl/ v [T] cause to seem unimportant: Don't ~ your achievements.

bell /bel/ n [C] 1 (a) metal object, that makes a ringing sound when struck. (b) instrument, eg a doorbell, that makes a ringing sound. 2 thing shaped like a bell. **'bell-push** n [C] button pushed to ring an electric bell.

belligerent /bɪ'lɪdʒərənt/ adj showing an eagerness to fight or argue.

bellow /'beləʊ/ v [I, T] shout in a deep loud voice.

bellows /'beləʊz/ n [pl] device for blowing air into sth, eg a fire.

belly /'belɪ/ n [C] (pl -ies) 1 (a) part of the body below the chest, containing the stomach and the bowels. (b) stomach. 2 bulging or rounded part of sth. **'bellyache** n [C, U] (infml) stomach pain. **'bellyache** v [I] (infml) complain constantly. **'bellyful** n [C] (infml) enough; too much: I've had a ~ful of your noise.

belong /bɪ'lɒŋ; US -lɔːŋ/ v [I] 1 to// be the property of sb: These books ~ to me. 2 to// be a member of sth: ~ to a club. 3 have as a right place: The plates ~ in this cupboard. **belongings** n [pl] personal articles; possessions.

beloved /bɪ'lʌvd/ adj much loved: He was ~ by all who knew him. 2 /bɪ'lʌvɪd/ much loved: my

~ *husband*. **beloved** /bɪˈlʌvɪd/
n [C] dearly loved person.

below /bɪˈləʊ/ *prep, adv* at or to a
lower place or level (than): *We saw
the sea* ~ *us. The temperature
was* ~ *freezing-point. For details, see* ~.

belt /belt/ *n* [C] **1** strip of material
worn round the waist. **2** circular
piece of material that drives
machinery or carries things
along. **3** area that has a particular
feature; zone: *the copper* ~. **4**
(idm) **below the belt** (*infml*) un-
fair(ly). **belt** *v* **1** [T] fasten with a
belt. **2** [T] (*infml*) hit very hard. **3**
[I] (*infml*) move very fast: ~*ing
along the road.* **4** (phr v) **belt up**
(*sl*) be quiet. **belting** *n* [C] (*infml*)
beating.

bemoan /bɪˈməʊn/ *v* [T] (*fml*)
show sorrow for.

bench /bentʃ/ *n* **1** [C] long seat. **2**
[C] long working-table. **3** **the
bench** [sing] (**a**) judge's seat in a
law-court. (**b**) [also sing with pl v]
judges as a group.

bend /bend/ *v* (*pt, pp* **bent** /bent/)
1 [I, T] move into a curve or away
from being straight or upright: ~
the wire. **2** [I, T] (cause to) bow or
stoop: *B~ down and touch your
toes.* **3** (idm) **be bent on** (**doing**)
sth be determined to do sth. **bend
over backwards** make every
effort. **bend** *n* **1** [C] curve or turn:
a ~ *in the road.* **2 the bends** [pl]
pain suffered by divers coming to
the surface too quickly. **3** (idm)
round the bend (*infml*) crazy or
mad.

beneath /bɪˈniːθ/ *prep, adv* (*fml*)
1 below; under. **2** not worthy of: ~
contempt.

benediction /ˌbenɪˈdɪkʃn/ *n* [C, U]
religious blessing.

benefactor /ˈbenɪfæktə(r)/ *n* [C]
person who gives money, etc. **be-
nefactress** /-fæktrɪs/ *n* [C] woman
benefactor.

beneficial /ˌbenɪˈfɪʃl/ *adj* having
a good effect; useful.

beneficiary /ˌbenɪˈfɪʃərɪ; *US*
-ˈfɪʃɪerɪ/ *n* [C] (*pl* **-ies**) person
who receives sth, esp money, from
a will.

benefit /ˈbenɪfɪt/ *n* **1** (**a**) [sing, U]
advantage; gain: *have the* ~ *of a
good education.* (**b**) [C] something
from which one gains: *the* ~*s of
modern medicine.* **2** [U, C] money
given by the government to people
who are ill, poor, etc: *sickness* ~. **3**
(idm) **for sb's benefit** in order to
help sb. **give sb the benefit of the
doubt** accept that sb is right because there is no clear proof that
he/she is not. **benefit** *v* **1** [T] do

good to. **2** [I] receive benefit or
gain.

benevolent /bɪˈnevələnt/ *adj*
kind and helpful. **benevolence**
/-ləns/ *n* [U].

benign /bɪˈnaɪn/ *adj* **1** (of a person) kind and gentle. **2** (of a disease) not dangerous.

bent *pt* of BEND.

bent[2] /bent/ *n* [C, usu sing] natural skill: *have a* ~ *for languages*.

bent[3] /bent/ *adj* (*sl esp Brit*) **1**
dishonest. **2** homosexual.

bequeath /bɪˈkwiːð/ *v* [T] (*fml*)
give (property, etc) to sb after
death. **bequest** /bɪˈkwest/ *n* [C]
(*fml*) something bequeathed.

berate /bɪˈreɪt/ *v* [T] (*fml*) scold.

bereaved /bɪˈriːvd/ *adj* (*fml*)
having lost a relative or friend by
death. **bereavement** /bɪˈriːv-
mənt/ *n* [U, C].

bereft /bɪˈreft/ *adj* *of*|| (*fml*) com-
pletely without sth: ~ *of all hope.*

beret /ˈbereɪ; *US* bəˈreɪ/ *n* [C]
round flat cap of soft material.

berry /ˈberɪ/ *n* [C] (*pl* **-ies**) small
soft fruit with seeds: *black* ~.

berserk /bəˈzɜːk/ *adj* (idm) **go
berserk** become violently angry.

berth /bɜːθ/ *n* [C] **1** sleeping-place
on a ship, train, etc. **2** place in a
harbour where ships tie up. **berth**
v [I, T] tie up (a ship).

beseech /bɪˈsiːtʃ/ *v* (*pt, pp* **be-
sought** /bɪˈsɔːt/ or ~**ed**) [T] (*fml*)
ask strongly.

beset /bɪˈset/ *v* (-tt-, *pt, pp* **beset**)
[T] (*fml*) (usu passive) trouble constantly: ~ *by problems.*

beside /bɪˈsaɪd/ *prep* **1** at the side
of: *Sit* ~ *me.* **2** (idm) **be'side oneself** having lost one's self-control;
extremely angry, etc.

besides /bɪˈsaɪdz/ *prep* in addition to (sb/sth). **besides** *adv* moreover; also.

besiege /bɪˈsiːdʒ/ *v* [T] surround
(a place) with armed forces: (*fig*)
The Prime Minister was ~*d by reporters.*

bespoke /bɪˈspəʊk/ *adj* (of clothes) made according to the customer's measurements.

best[1] /best/ *adj* **1** superlative of
GOOD[1] of the most excellent kind:
the ~ *dinner I've ever tasted.* **2**
superlative of WELL[2] in the most excellent health, condition, etc: *She
is very ill but always feels* ~ *in the
morning.* **best 'man** *n* [C] man
who supports the bridegroom at a
wedding.

best[2] /best/ *adv* superlative of
WELL[2] in the most excellent manner: *He works* ~ *in the mornings.* **2**
to the greatest degree; most: *I enjoyed her first book* ~. **3** (idm) **as**

,best one 'can as well as one is able to. best 'seller n [C] book, etc that sells in very large numbers.

best³ /best/ n [sing] 1 that which is best: want the ~ for one's children. 2 one's greatest possible effort: do one's ~. 3 (idm) all the 'best (infml) (used when saying goodbye) I hope everything goes well for you. at 'best taking the most favourable view. at its/one's best in the best state or form. the best of both worlds the benefits of two different activities. make the best of sth do as well as one can in (an unsatisfactory situation).

bestial /'bestɪəl; US 'bestʃəl/ adj very cruel. bestiality /ˌbestɪˈæləti; US ˌbestʃiˈælətɪ/ n [U].

bestow /bɪˈstəʊ/ v [T] (fml) give: ~ an honour on her.

bet /bet/ v (-tt-, pt, pp bet or betted) [I, T] 1 risk (money) on a race, doubtful event, etc. 2 (infml) be sure: I ~ they'll come late. bet n [C] (a) arrangement to risk money on a future event. (b) money risked in this way. better n [C] person who bets.

betray /bɪˈtreɪ/ v [T] 1 hand over (sb); show unfaithfulness to. 2 tell (a secret). 3 show unintentionally: His face ~ed his guilt. betrayal /bɪˈtreɪəl/ n [C, U] act of betraying. betrayer n [C].

betrothed /bɪˈtrəʊðd/ adj (fml) engaged to be married.

better¹ /'betə(r)/ adj 1 comparative of GOOD¹ of a more excellent kind: ~ weather than yesterday. 2 comparative of WELL² 1 partly or fully recovered from an illness: She has been much ~ since her operation. 3 (idm) one's better 'half (infml joc) one's wife or husband.

better² /'betə(r)/ adv comparative of WELL² 1 in a more efficient, pleasant, etc way: You play tennis ~ than I do. 2 (idm) be better 'off in a better position, esp financially. had better would be wise to; ought to: You'd ~ go soon. know better (than to do sth) be wise or sensible enough not to do sth.

better³ /'betə(r)/ n [sing] 1 that which is better: I expected ~ from him. 2 (idm) get the better of sb defeat sb.

better⁴ /'betə(r)/ v [T] 1 do better than. 2 improve: ~ oneself, ie improve one's social position or status.

between /bɪˈtwiːn/ prep 1 in the space or time that separates two points: Q comes ~ P and R in the alphabet. ○ Children must go to

school ~ 5 and 16. 2 (showing a connection or relationship): fly ~ London and Paris ○ the link ~ unemployment and crime. 3 shared by: We drank a bottle of wine ~ us. 4 by the actions of: B ~ them, they collected £500. between adv 1 (also in between) in or into the space or time that separates two points. 2 (idm) ˌfew and far be'tween very rare.

bevel /'bevl/ v (-ll-; US -l-) [T] give a sloping edge to.

beverage /'bevərɪdʒ/ n [C] (fml) any kind of drink except water.

bevy /'bevi/ n [C] (pl -ies) large group.

beware /bɪˈweə(r)/ v [I] (of)// be careful about sb/sth dangerous or harmful: B ~ of the dog!

bewilder /bɪˈwɪldə(r)/ v [T] confuse: ~ed by the noise and lights. bewildering adj.

bewitch /bɪˈwɪtʃ/ v [T] 1 put a magic spell on. 2 delight very much; charm. bewitching adj.

beyond /bɪˈjɒnd/ prep 1 on the other side of: The path continues ~ the village. 2 further than the limits of: What happened was ~ my control. 3 (idm) be beyond sb (infml) be too difficult for sb to understand. beyond adv at or to a distance.

bias /'baɪəs/ n [U, C] tendency to be unfair in one's decisions by strongly favouring one's side, person, etc. bias v (-s-, -ss-) [T] (esp passive) give a bias to; influence unfairly: a ~ed jury.

bib /bɪb/ n [C] 1 piece of cloth or plastic tied under a baby's chin. 2 top part of an apron.

bible /'baɪbl/ n 1 (a) the Bible [sing] holy book of the Jewish and Christian religions. (b) [C] copy of this. 2 [C] (fig) authoritative book: the gardeners' ~. biblical /'bɪblɪkl/ adj.

bibliography /ˌbɪblɪˈɒɡrəfɪ/ n [C] (pl -ies) list of books and writings about one subject. bibliographer /-fə(r)/ n [C].

bicentenary /ˌbaɪsenˈtiːnərɪ; US -ˈsentənɪ/ n [C] (pl -ies) (celebration of the) 200th anniversary of an event.

bicentennial /ˌbaɪsenˈtenɪəl/ adj of a bicentenary. bicentennial n [C] = BICENTENARY.

biceps /'baɪseps/ n [C] (pl biceps) large muscle in the upper arm.

bicker /'bɪkə(r)/ v [I] quarrel about unimportant matters.

bicycle /'baɪsɪkl/ n [C] two-wheeled vehicle driven by pedals. bicycle v [I] (dated) ride a bicycle.

bid /bɪd/ v (-dd-, pt, pp bid usu in

sense 2 *pt* **bade** /bæd/, *pp* ~ **den** /'bɪdn/) **1** [I, T] offer (a price) in order to buy sth. **2** [T] (*arch or fml*) (a) order (sb): *She bade me (to) come in.* (b) say as a greeting, etc: ~ *sb farewell.* **bid** *n*[C] **1** attempt to do sth: *a rescue* ~. **2** price offered to buy sth. **bidder** *n*[C]. **bidding** *n*[U].

bide /baɪd/ *v* (idm) **bide one's time** wait for a good opportunity.

biennial /baɪ'enɪəl/ *adj* **1** happening every two years. **2** lasting for two years.

bier /bɪə(r)/ *n*[C] movable stand for a coffin.

bifocal /ˌbaɪ'fəʊkl/ *adj* (of glasses) having lenses that are designed for both distant and near vision. **bifocals** *n*[pl] glasses with bifocal lenses.

big /bɪɡ/ *adj* (~ **ger**, ~**est**) **1** large in size, importance, etc: ~ *feet* ◇ *a* ~ *match.* **2** (*infml*) popular. **3** (idm) **a big noise/shot** (*infml*) an important person. **big 'game** *n*[U] larger animals, hunted for sport. **'big-head** *n*[C] (*infml*) conceited person. **'bigwig** *n*[C] (*infml*) important person.

bigamy /'bɪɡəmɪ/ *n*[U] (crime of) marrying a person when still legally married to sb else. **bigamist** *n*[C] person guilty of bigamy. **bigamous** *adj*.

bigot /'bɪɡət/ *n*[C] person who holds strong unreasonable opinions and will not change them. **bigoted** *adj* intolerant and narrow-minded. **bigotry** *n*[U].

bike /baɪk/ *n*[C] (*infml*) short for BICYCLE.

bikini /bɪ'ki:nɪ/ *n*[C] two-piece swimming costume worn by women.

bilateral /ˌbaɪ'lætərəl/ *adj* between two sides: *a* ~ *agreement.*

bile /baɪl/ *n*[U] liquid produced by the liver.

bilge /bɪldʒ/ *n*[U] (*sl*) foolish talk.

bilingual /ˌbaɪ'lɪŋɡwəl/ *adj* speaking or using two languages.

bilious /'bɪlɪəs/ *adj* feeling sick.

bill[1] /bɪl/ *n*[C] **1** statement of money owed for goods and services. **2** proposed law to be discussed by parliament. **3** (*US*) piece of paper money. **4** printed notice. **5** (idm) **fill/fit the 'bill** be suitable for a purpose. **bill** *v*[T] **1** send a bill(1) to. **2** announce in a programme: *He is* ~*ed to appear as Othello.*

bill[2] /bɪl/ *n*[C] bird's beak.

billet /'bɪlɪt/ *n*[C] private house in which soldiers are put to live with civilians. **billet** *v*[T] put (soldiers) in billets.

billiards /'bɪlɪədz/ *n* (with sing v) game played on a table, using balls and long sticks.

billion /'bɪlɪən/ *pron, adj, n*[C] **1** one thousand million. **2** (*Brit*) one million million.

billow /'bɪləʊ/ *n*[C] swelling mass (eg of smoke) like a wave. **billow** *v*[I] roll like waves. **billowy** *adj*.

billy-goat /'bɪlɪ ɡəʊt/ *n*[C] male goat.

bin /bɪn/ *n*[C] large container for storing things in or for rubbish.

binary /'baɪnərɪ/ *adj* of a system of numbers that uses only the digits 0 and 1.

bind /baɪnd/ (*pt, pp* **bound** /baʊnd/) *v* **1** [T] (a) tie or fasten with a string or rope: ~ *the prisoner's legs to the chair.* **2** (fig) hold together: *bound by friendship.* **2** [T] fasten (a book) to a cover: *a book bound in leather.* **3** [T] make sb obey a duty or promise: ~ *her to secrecy.* **4** [I, T] (cause) to stick together in a solid mass. **bind** *n*[sing] (*infml*) nuisance. **binder** *n*[C] **1** cover that holds sheets of paper together. **2** person or thing that binds books. **binding** *n*[C] book cover.

binge /bɪndʒ/ *n*[C] (*infml*) **1** time of wild eating and drinking. **2** occasion of doing anything far too much: *a shopping* ~.

bingo /'bɪŋɡəʊ/ *n*[U] gambling game using numbers.

binoculars /bɪ'nɒkjələz/ *n*[pl] instrument with a lens for each eye, making distant objects seem nearer.

biochemistry /ˌbaɪəʊ'kemɪstrɪ/ *n*[U] study of the chemistry of living things. **biochemist** *n*[C] student of or expert in biochemistry.

biodegradable /ˌbaɪəʊdɪ'ɡreɪdəbl/ *adj* that can be made to rot by bacteria.

biography /baɪ'ɒɡrəfɪ/ *n*[C] (*pl* **-ies**) story of a person's life, written by sb else. **biographer** /-fə(r)/ *n*[C] person who writes a biography. **biographical** /ˌbaɪə'ɡræfɪkl/ *adj*.

biology /baɪ'ɒlədʒɪ/ *n*[U] scientific study of living things. **biological** /ˌbaɪə'lɒdʒɪkl/ *adj*. **biologist** *n*[C] student of or expert in biology.

birch /bɜ:tʃ/ *n* **1** [U, C] (wood of a) kind of tree with smooth bark and thin branches. **2 the birch** [sing] birch rod, formerly used for punishing.

bird /bɜ:d/ *n*[C] **1** creature with feathers and wings, usu able to fly. **2** (*sl esp Brit*) young woman. **bird**

of '**prey** n [C] bird that kills other animals for food.

biro /'baɪərəʊ/ n [C] (pl ~s) (P) kind of ball-point pen.

birth /bɜːθ/ n 1 [C, U] (process of) being born. 2 [U] family origin: *Russian by* ~. 3 [sing] beginning: *the* ~ *of socialism*. 4 (idm) **give birth (to sb/sth)** produce young. '**birth control** n [U] (method of) preventing pregnancy. '**birthday** n [C] anniversary of the day on which one was born. '**birthmark** n [C] unusual mark on the skin from birth. '**birth rate** n [C] number of births in one year to every thousand people.

biscuit /'bɪskɪt/ n [C] small flat thin crisp cake.

bisect /baɪ'sekt/ v [T] divide into two parts.

bishop /'bɪʃəp/ n [C] 1 Christian clergyman of high rank. 2 chess piece. **bishopric** /-rɪk/ n [C] office or district of a bishop.

bison /'baɪsn/ n [C] (pl **bison**) American buffalo; European wild ox.

bistro /'biːstrəʊ/ n [C] (pl ~s) small restaurant.

bit[1] pt of BITE.

bit[2] /bɪt/ n 1 [C] small piece or amount: *a* ~ *of paper*. 2 (idm) **a bit (a)** slightly; rather: *a* ~ *tired*. **(b)** a short time or distance: *Wait a* ~*!* **bit by bit** gradually. **do one's bit** (*infml*) do one's share of a task. **every bit as good, bad,** etc just as good, etc. **not a bit** not at all.

bit[3] /bɪt/ n [C] 1 part of a bridle that is put inside a horse's mouth. 2 part of a tool for drilling holes.

bit[4] /bɪt/ n [C] (*computing*) unit of information.

bitch /bɪtʃ/ n [C] 1 female dog. 2 (*sl derog*) unpleasant woman.

bite /baɪt/ v (*pt* **bit** /bɪt/, *pp* **bitten** /'bɪtn/) 1 [I, T] cut into (sth) with the teeth. 2 [I, T] (of an insect or snake) sting. 3 [I] (of fish) take the bait. 4 [I] take a strong hold; become effective: *The miners' strike is beginning to* ~. 5 (idm) **bite sb's head off** (*infml*) criticize sb angrily. **bite off ,more than one can 'chew** (*infml*) attempt to do too much. **bite** n 1 [C] (a) act of biting. **(b)** piece cut off by biting. 2 [sing] (*infml*) food: *have a* ~ *to eat*. 3 [C] wound made by a bite or sting. **biting** *adj* sharp; painful: *a biting wind*.

bitter /'bɪtə(r)/ *adj* 1 having a sharp unpleasant taste; not sweet. 2 filled with anger or hatred: ~ *enemies*. 3 causing sorrow: *a* ~ *disappointment*. 4 very cold: *a* ~ *wind*. **bitter** n [U] (*Brit*) bitter beer

strongly flavoured with hops. **bitterly** *adv*: ~ *ly cold/disappointed*. **bitterness** n [U].

bitumen /'bɪtjʊmən; US bə'tuːmən/ n [U] sticky black substance used in making roads.

bivouac /'bɪvʊæk/ n [C] temporary camp without tents. **bivouac** v (*-ck-*) [I] stay in a bivouac.

bizarre /bɪ'zɑː(r)/ *adj* very strange.

blab /blæb/ v (*-bb-*) [I] (*sl*) tell a secret, usu through talking carelessly.

black /blæk/ *adj* 1 of the darkest colour. 2 of a dark-skinned race. 3 very dirty. 4 (of coffee) without milk or cream. 5 without hope: *The future looks* ~. 6 very angry: *a* ~ *look*. 7 (of humour) funny, but about unpleasant events. **black** n 1 [U] black colour. 2 [C] black-skinned person. **black** v [T] 1 make black. 2 refuse to handle (goods, etc): *The strikers* ~*ed the cargo*. 3 (phr v) **black 'out** lose consciousness. **black sth out** switch off (lights) and cover (windows). '**blackberry** n [C] (pl **-ies**) small dark fruit growing wild on bushes. '**blackbird** n [C] common European bird with black or brown feathers. '**blackboard** n [C] board used in schools for writing on. ,**black'currant** n [C] small black fruit of a currant bush. **blacken** v 1 [I, T] become or make black or blacker. 2 [T] say harmful things about. ,**black 'eye** n [C] dark-coloured bruise around the eye. '**blackhead** n [C] spot on the skin, with a black top. ,**black 'ice** n [U] clear thin layer of ice on a road. '**blackleg** n [C] person who works when other workers are on strike. '**blacklist** n [C] list of people considered dangerous or who are to be punished. '**blacklist** v [T] put on a blacklist. **blackly** *adv*. ,**black 'magic** n [U] magic used for evil purposes. '**blackmail** n [U] 1 demanding money from sb by threatening to tell unpleasant information about him/her. 2 use of threats to influence sb. '**blackmail** v [T] force (sb) to do sth by blackmail. '**blackmailer** n [C]. ,**black 'market** n [C, usu sing] illegal buying and selling of goods. **blackness** n [U]. '**blackout** n [C] 1 period in a war when all lights must be switched off and windows must be covered. 2 darkness caused by electrical failure. 3 short loss of consciousness. 4 prevention of the reporting of information: *a news* ~*out*. ,**black 'sheep** n [C] person who brings shame to his/her family. **'black-smith** /-smɪθ/ n [C] person whose job is to make things out of iron.

bladder /'blædə(r)/ n [C] organ in the body in which urine collects.

blade /bleɪd/ n [C] 1 sharp cutting edge of a knife, razor, etc. 2 flat wide part of an oar, propeller, etc. 3 long narrow leaf of grass.

blame /bleɪm/ v 1 [T] consider (sb/sth) to be responsible for sth bad. 2 (idm) **be to blame (for sth)** be responsible for sth bad. **blame** n [U] responsibility for sth bad. **blameless** adj not having done anything wrong. **blameworthy** adj having done sth wrong.

blanch /blɑːntʃ; US blæntʃ/ v [I, T] become or make white.

blancmange /blə'mɒnʒ/ n [C, U] jelly-like pudding made with milk.

bland /blænd/ adj 1 gentle and polite; showing no strong feelings. 2 (of food) having little flavour. 3 uninteresting. **blandly** adv. **blandness** n [U].

blank /blæŋk/ adj 1 (of paper) with nothing written on it. 2 without expression; empty: a ~ look. **blank** n [C] 1 empty space in a document, etc. 2 cartridge without a bullet. **blank 'cheque** n [C] 1 signed cheque with the amount left blank. 2 (fig) complete authority to do what one wants. **blankly** adv. **blank 'verse** n [U] poetry that does not rhyme.

blanket /'blæŋkɪt/ n [C] piece of thick cloth used as a warm covering on a bed. (fig) a ~ of snow. **blanket** v [T] cover. **blanket** adj including all in a group: ~ criticism.

blare /bleə(r)/ v [I, T] make a loud unpleasant noise. **blare** n [U].

blasé /'blɑːzeɪ; US blɑː'zeɪ/ adj showing no excitement or interest in things because one has experienced them before.

blaspheme /blæs'fiːm/ v [I, T] speak in a bad or disrespectful way about God or holy things. **blasphemous** /'blæsfəməs/ adj. **blasphemy** /'blæsfəmɪ/ n [U, C] (pl -ies)

blast /blɑːst; US blæst/ n [C] 1 big (rush of air from an) explosion. 2 sudden rush of wind. 3 sound made by a wind instrument. 4 (idm) **at full 'blast** at the greatest possible power. **blast** v 1 [I, T] break apart or destroy (sth) with explosives. 2 (phr v) **blast 'off** (of spacecraft) leave the ground. **blast** interj (used for showing anger or annoyance). **'blast-furnace** n [C] furnace for melting

iron ore. **'blast-off** n [C] act of a spacecraft leaving the ground.

blatant /'bleɪtənt/ adj very obvious; shameless. **blatantly** adv.

blaze /bleɪz/ n 1 [C] (a) bright flame. (b) large dangerous fire. 2 [sing] bright show: (fig) a ~ of publicity. **blaze** n [i] 1 burn brightly. 2 shine brightly. 3 show strong feeling: blazing with anger. **blazing** adj.

blazer /'bleɪzə(r)/ n [C] loose-fitting jacket, often showing the colours of a school or team.

bleach /bliːtʃ/ v [I, T] become or make white or pale. **bleach** n [U] chemical used to bleach cloth or to clean sth well.

bleak /bliːk/ adj cold and unpleasant: a ~ day ○ (fig) The future looks ~. **bleakly** adv.

bleary /'blɪərɪ/ adj (-ier, -iest) (of eyes) sore and tired. **blearily** adv.

bleat /bliːt/ v [I] n [C] (make the) sound of a sheep or goat.

bleed /bliːd/ v (pt, pp **bled** /bled/) 1 [I] lose blood. 2 [T] draw blood from. 3 [T] draw liquid or air from.

blemish /'blemɪʃ/ n [C] mark that spoils the good appearance of sth. **blemish** v [T] spoil: His reputation has been ~ed.

blend /blend/ v 1 [I, T] mix together. 2 (phr v) **blend** in mix well, so that one cannot notice separate parts. **blend** n [C] mixture. **blender** n [C] (esp US) liquidizer.

bless /bles/ v (pt, pp ~ed /blest/) [T] 1 ask God's favour of. 2 make holy. **blessed** /'blesɪd/ adj 1 holy. 2 giving pleasure. **blessing** n 1 [C] something one is glad of. 2 [U] approval. 3 [C] God's favour.

blew pt of BLOW[1].

blight /blaɪt/ n 1 [U] disease of plants. 2 [C] bad influence. **blight** v [T] be a bad influence on; spoil.

blind[1] /blaɪnd/ adj 1 unable to see. 2 (to)/ unable or unwilling to notice sth: ~ to the dangers involved. 3 without reason: ~ obedience. 4 (idm) **as blind as a 'bat** unable to see well. **blind 'drunk** (infml) very drunk. **the blind** n [pl] blind people. **blind 'alley** n [C] 1 narrow street with no way out. 2 (fig) course of action that has no satisfactory result. **blindly** adv. **blindness** n [U]. **blind spot** n [C] 1 part of a road that a motorist cannot see. 2 (fig) subject that one cannot understand.

blind[2] /blaɪnd/ v [T] 1 make blind. 2 take away reason, judgement, etc from: ~ed by love.

blind[3] /blaɪnd/ n [C] roll of cloth pulled down to cover a window.

blindfold /'blaɪndfəʊld/ v [T] cover the eyes of (sb) with a strip of cloth. **blindfold** n [C] strip of cloth to cover the eyes. **blindfold** adj, adv (as if) with the eyes covered.

blink /blɪŋk/ v 1 [I, T] shut and open (one's eyes) quickly. 2 [I] (of light) shine unsteadily. **blink** n 1 [C] act of blinking. 2 (idm) **on the blink** (infml) (of a machine) not working properly.

blinkers /'blɪŋkəz/ n [pl] leather pieces fixed on a bridle to prevent a horse from seeing sideways.

bliss /blɪs/ n [U] perfect happiness. **blissful** adj. **blissfully** adv.

blister /'blɪstə(r)/ n [C] 1 swelling under the skin, containing watery liquid. 2 swelling on the surface of paint, etc. **blister** v [I, T] (cause to) form blisters.

blithe /blaɪð/ adj happy and carefree.

blitz /blɪts/ n [C] 1 sudden violent attack, esp from the air. 2 (fig) period of great activity or effort (on sth): have a ~ on the garden.

blizzard /'blɪzəd/ n [C] severe snowstorm.

bloated /'bləʊtɪd/ adj swollen.

blob /blɒb/ n [C] drop of liquid; small round mass.

bloc /blɒk/ n [C] group of countries, etc united by a common interest.

block /blɒk/ n [C] 1 large solid piece: a ~ of ice/stone. 2 large building divided into separate parts: a ~ of flats. 3 group of buildings with streets on four sides. 4 large quantity of things considered together: a ~ of theatre seats. 5 obstruction: a ~ in the drain. **block** v [T] 1 make movement on or in difficult or impossible: roads ~ed by snow. 2 prevent from moving. ,block 'letters (also ,block 'capitals) n [pl] capital letters.

blockade /blɒ'keɪd/ n [C] surrounding of a place to prevent goods or people from entering or leaving. **blockade** v [T] make a blockade of.

blockage /'blɒkɪdʒ/ n [C] thing that blocks; obstruction: a ~ in a pipe.

bloke /bləʊk/ n [C] (Brit infml) man.

blond (also of a woman usu **blonde**) /blɒnd/ adj, n (person) having golden or pale-coloured hair.

blood /blʌd/ n [U] 1 red liquid flowing through the body. 2 (fml) family; descent: a woman of noble ~. 3 (idm) **make sb's 'blood boil**

make sb very angry. **make sb's 'blood run cold** fill sb with great fear. **new/fresh 'blood** new member with new ideas. **'blood bath** n [C] violent killing of many people. **'blood-curdling** adj filling one with horror. **'blood donor** n [C] person who gives his/her blood for transfusions. **'blood group** (also **'blood type**) n [C] class of human blood. **'bloodhound** n [C] large dog, used for tracking. **bloodless** adj 1 very pale. 2 without killing. **'blood-poisoning** n [U] infection of the blood with harmful bacteria. **'blood pressure** n [U] measured force of blood in the arteries. **'bloodshed** n [U] killing or wounding of people. **'bloodshot** adj (of eyes) red. **'blood sports** n [pl] sports in which animals or birds are killed. **'bloodstained** adj covered with blood. **'bloodstream** n [C] blood flowing through the body. **'bloodthirsty** adj cruel and eager to kill; showing interest in violence. **'blood-vessel** n [C] tube in the body through which blood flows.

bloody /'blʌdɪ/ adj (-ier, -iest) 1 covered with blood. 2 with a lot of bloodshed. 3 (△ Brit infml) (used for adding emphasis): You ~ idiot! **bloodily** adv. **bloody** adv (△ Brit infml) (used for adding emphasis): too ~ quick. ,bloody-'minded adj (Brit infml) deliberately unhelpful.

bloom /bluːm/ n [C] 1 flower. 2 (idm) **in (full) bloom** producing flowers. **bloom** v [I] 1 produce flowers. 2 (fig) be in a healthy or flourishing condition.

blossom /'blɒsəm/ n 1 [C] flower, esp of a fruit tree. 2 (idm) **in (full) blossom** producing blossom. **blossom** v [I] 1 produce blossom. 2 (fig) develop in a healthy or flourishing way.

blot /blɒt/ n [C] 1 spot of ink, etc. 2 fault: a ~ on his character. **blot** v (-tt-) [T] 1 make a blot on. 2 dry (wet ink) with blotting paper. 3 (phr v) **blot sth out** cover or hide sth: Thick cloud ~ted out the view. **blotter** n [C] large piece of blotting-paper. **'blotting-paper** n [U] absorbent paper for drying wet ink.

blotch /blɒtʃ/ n [C] irregular discoloured mark or spot.

blouse /blaʊz; US blaʊs/ n [C] garment like a shirt, worn by a woman.

blow¹ /bləʊ/ v (pt blew /bluː/, pp ~n /bləʊn/) 1 [I] (of the wind) be moving. 2 [I, T] (of the wind) move:

The wind blew my hat off. **3** [I, T] send out (air) from the mouth. **4** [T] clean (one's nose) by forcing air out of it. **5** [T] make or shape by blowing: ~ *bubbles.* **6** [I, T] produce sound from (a brass instrument, etc). **7** [I, T] (cause to) melt with too strong an electric current: *A fuse has ~n.* **8** [T] (*infml*) spend (a lot of money) wastefully. **9** (idm) **blow sb's 'brains out** (*infml*) kill sb by shooting him/her through the head. **blow sb's 'mind** (*sl*) produce a pleasant or shocking feeling in sb. **blow one's own 'trumpet** (*infml*) praise one's own achievements. **10** (phr v) **blow (sth) out** (cause (sth) to be extinguished by blowing: ~ *out a candle.* **blow over** pass away without serious effect: *The argument will soon* ~ *over.* **blow up** (a) explode. (b) start suddenly and forcefully: *A storm is* ~*ing up.* (c) (*infml*) lose one's temper. **blow sth up** (a) destroy sth by an explosion. (b) fill sth with air or gas. (c) make sth larger. **'blowlamp** (also **'blowtorch**) *n* [C] burner for directing a flame onto a surface, eg to remove old paint. **'blow-out** *n* [C] **1** bursting of a tyre on a motor vehicle. **2** sudden uncontrolled escape of oil or gas from a well. **3** (*sl*) large meal. **'blow-up** *n* [C] enlargement of a photograph.

blow² /bləʊ/ *n* [C] act of blowing: *Give your nose a good* ~.

blow³ /bləʊ/ *n* [C] **1** hard stroke with one's hand or a weapon. **2** unexpected misfortune. **3** (idm) **come to 'blows** start fighting. **,blow-by-'blow** *adj* giving all the details (of an event) as they occur.

blower /'bləʊə(r)/ *n* [C] **1** device that produces a current of air. **2** (*Brit infml*) telephone.

blown *pp* of BLOW¹.

blubber /'blʌbə(r)/ *n* [U] fat of whales.

bludgeon /'blʌdʒən/ *v* [T] **1** (*infml*) hit sb with a heavy object. **2** (*fig*) force (sb) to do sth.

blue /bluː/ *adj* **1** having the colour of a clear sky on a sunny day. **2** (*infml*) sad; depressed. **3** about sex in an indecent way: *a* ~ *film.* **blue** *n* **1** [U] blue colour. **2** **the blues** (a) [also sing with pl v] slow sad music from the southern US. (b) [pl] (*infml*) sadness. **3** (idm) **out of the 'blue** unexpectedly. **'bluebell** *n* [C] plant with blue bell-shaped flowers. **,blue-'blooded** *adj* of noble birth. **'bluebottle** *n* [C] large fly with a blue body. **,blue-'collar** *adj* of

manual workers. **'blueprint** *n* [C] detailed description of a plan. **bluish** *adj* fairly blue.

bluff¹ /blʌf/ *v* [I, T] deceive (sb) by pretending to be cleverer, stronger, etc than one really is. **bluff** *n* [C, U] (act of) bluffing.

bluff² /blʌf/ *adj* (of a person) rough but kind-natured.

blunder /'blʌndə(r)/ *n* [C] stupid or careless mistake. **blunder** *v* [I] **1** make a blunder. **2** move clumsily or uncertainly.

blunt /blʌnt/ *adj* **1** without a sharp edge or point. **2** (of a person) not trying to be polite. **blunt** *v* [T] make blunt or less sharp. **bluntness** *n* [U].

blur /blɜː(r)/ *n* [C] something that cannot be seen clearly. **blur** *v* (-rr-) [I, T] become or make unclear.

blurb /blɜːb/ *n* [C] short description of the contents of a book.

blurt /blɜːt/ *v* (phr v) **blurt sth out** say sth suddenly and thoughtlessly.

blush /blʌʃ/ *v* [I] become red in the face because of embarrassment or shame. **blush** *n* [C].

bluster /'blʌstə(r)/ *v* [I] **1** (of the wind) blow roughly. **2** talk in a noisy angry way. **bluster** *n* [U]. **blustery** *adj* (of the weather) rough and windy.

boa /'bəʊə/ **boa constrictor** *n* [C] large South American snake that crushes animals to death.

boar /bɔː(r)/ *n* [C] **1** male pig. **2** wild pig.

board¹ /bɔːd/ *n* **1** [C] (a) long thin flat piece of wood: *a floor-* ~. (b) flat piece of wood, etc used for a special purpose: *a 'notice-* ~. **2** [C] surface marked with patterns on which certain games are played: *Chess is a '~ game.* **3** [C] group of people controlling a business: *the* ~ *of directors.* **4** [U] food in rented accommodation: *pay for* ~ *and lodging.* **5** (idm) **above 'board** honest and open. **a,cross the 'board** affecting or including all members, groups, etc: *an a,cross-the-~ 'wage increase.* **go by the 'board** fail; be abandoned. **on 'board** on or in a ship, aircraft or train. **take sth on 'board** (*infml*) accept sth.

board² /bɔːd/ *v* **1** cover with boards. **2** [T] (*fml*) get on (a ship, etc). **3** [I, T] get or supply with meals. **boarder** *n* [C] pupil who lives at a boarding-school during the term. **'boarding card** *n* [C] card allowing a person to board a ship or aircraft. **'boarding-house** *n* [C] private house providing meals and accommodation.

'boarding-school n [C] school where pupils live during the term.

boast /bəʊst/ v 1 [I, T] (about/of/) talk (about one's own achievements, possessions, etc) with too much pride: ~ *about one's new car.* 2 [T] possess (sth that one is proud of): *The hotel ~s a fine swimming-pool.* **boast** n [C] boasting statement. **boastful** adj fond of boasting. **boastfully** adv.

boat /bəʊt/ n [C] 1 small open vessel for travelling on water: *a 'rowing-~.* 2 any ship. **boat** v [I] travel in a boat, esp for pleasure: *go ~ing.* **'boat-house** n [C] shed in which boats are stored. **'boat-train** n [C] train that takes people to or from a passenger ship.

boatswain (also **bo'sn, bos'n, bo'sun**) /ˈbəʊsn/ n [C] senior seaman on a ship.

bob¹ /bɒb/ v (-bb-) [I] move up and down: *a cork ~bing on the water.*

bob² /bɒb/ v (-bb-) [T] cut a woman's hair short. **bob** n [C] style of bobbed hair.

bobbin /ˈbɒbɪn/ n [C] small roller for holding thread, etc in a machine.

bobsleigh /ˈbɒbsleɪ/ (also **bobsled** /-sled/) n [C] sledge for racing.

bode /bəʊd/ v (idm) **bode 'well/'ill (for sb/sth)** (fml) be a good/bad sign for (sb/sth) in the future.

bodice /ˈbɒdɪs/ n [C] upper part of a woman's dress.

bodily /ˈbɒdɪlɪ/ adj of the human body; physical. **bodily** adv 1 taking hold of the whole body. 2 as a whole.

body /ˈbɒdɪ/ n [C] (pl **-ies**) 1 (a) whole physical structure of a person or animal. (b) dead body. (c) main part of a human body without the head or limbs. 2 main part of sth: *the ~ of a car.* 3 group of people doing sth together: *a parliamentary ~.* 4 large amount of sth; mass: *a ~ of water.* 5 piece of matter; object: *heavenly bodies,* ie stars and planets. **'bodyguard** n [C] person or group of persons who protect sb important. **'bodywork** n [U] main outside structure of a motor vehicle.

bog /bɒg/ n [C] 1 area of soft wet ground. 2 (Brit sl) toilet. **bog** v (-gg-) (idm) **be/get bogged down** be stuck so that one cannot move: (fig) *get ~ged down in small details.* **boggy** adj.

bogey = BOGY.

boggle /ˈbɒgl/ v [I] (at/) (infml) find sth difficult to imagine or accept: *The mind ~s (at the idea).*

bogus /ˈbəʊgəs/ adj not real.

bogy (also **bogey**) /ˈbəʊgɪ/ n [C] (pl **-ies**) imaginary evil spirit.

boil¹ /bɔɪl/ v 1 [I, T] (of a liquid) (cause to) bubble and change into steam or vapour by being heated: *The kettle* (ie the water in the kettle) *is ~ing.* 2 [T] cook in boiling water: ~ *an egg.* 3 [I] be very angry. 4 (idm) **boil 'dry** (of a liquid) boil until there is none left. 5 (phr v) **boil away** (of a liquid) boil until there is none left. **boil down to** sth have sth as its main point: *It all ~s down to what you really want.* **boil over (a)** (of a liquid) boil and flow over the side of a pan. (b) become uncontrollable; lose one's temper. **boil** n (idm) **bring sth/come to the 'boil** (cause sth to) begin to boil. **boiling 'hot** adj very hot. **'boiling-point** n [C] temperature at which a liquid begins to boil.

boil² /bɔɪl/ n [C] red infected swelling under the skin.

boiler /ˈbɔɪlə(r)/ n [C] device in which water is heated, eg for the central heating in a house. **'boiler suit** n [C] one-piece garment worn for rough work.

boisterous /ˈbɔɪstərəs/ adj (of a person) noisy and cheerful.

bold /bəʊld/ adj 1 not afraid of danger; daring. 2 not shy or modest. 3 clearly seen: ~ *designs.* **boldly** adv. **boldness** n [U].

bollard /ˈbɒləd/ n [C] short thick post on a kerb or traffic island.

bolster /ˈbəʊlstə(r)/ n [C] long pillow. **bolster** v [T] (up/) give support to; strengthen and encourage.

bolt /bəʊlt/ n [C] 1 metal bar that slides into a socket to lock a door, etc. 2 metal screw used with a nut for holding things together. 3 flash of lightning. 4 act of running away quickly: *make a ~ for it.* **bolt** v 1 [T] fasten with a bolt. 2 [I] (esp of a horse) run away quickly. 3 [T] (down/) swallow (food) quickly. **bolt** adv (idm) **bolt 'upright** very straight.

bomb /bɒm/ n 1 [C] container filled with explosive. 2 **the bomb** [sing] the atomic bomb. **bomb** v [T] attack with bombs. **bomber** n [C] 1 aircraft that drops bombs. 2 person who throws or puts bombs in place. **'bombshell** n [C] (infml) great shock.

bombard /bɒmˈbɑːd/ v [T] 1 attack with bombs or shells from big guns. 2 (fig) attack with many questions, etc. **bombardment** n [C, U].

bona fide /ˌbəʊnə ˈfaɪdɪ/ adj, adv

genuine(ly).

bond /bɒnd/ n 1 [C] something that unites people or groups: ~s of friendship. 2 [C] written agreement that has legal force. 3 [C] certificate stating that money has been lent to a government, etc and will be paid back with interest. 4 **bonds** [pl] ropes or chains used for tying up a prisoner. **bond** v [T] join together.

bondage /'bɒndɪdʒ/ n [U] (dated or fml) slavery.

bone /bəʊn/ n 1 [C, U] any of the hard parts that form the skeleton of an animal's body. 2 (idm) **feel certain about sth. have a 'bone to pick with sb** have sth to complain about to sb. **make no bones about (doing) sth** not hesitate to do sth. **bone** v [T] take bones out of. **,bone-'dry** adj completely dry. **,bone 'idle** adj very lazy.

bonfire /'bɒnfaɪə(r)/ n [C] large outdoor fire.

bonnet /'bɒnɪt/ n [C] 1 cover over the engine of a motor vehicle. 2 baby's or woman's hat tied under the chin.

bonny /'bɒnɪ/ adj (-ier, -iest) (approv esp Scot) healthy-looking.

bonus /'bəʊnəs/ n [C] 1 payment in addition to what is usual. 2 anything pleasant in addition to what is expected.

bony /'bəʊnɪ/ adj (-ier, -iest) 1 full of bones: This fish is ~. 2 very thin; having bones that are clearly seen.

boo /buː/ interj, n [C] (pl ~s) sound made to show disapproval. **boo** v [I, T] shout 'boo' (at).

booby prize /'buːbɪ praɪz/ n [C] prize given to someone who comes last in a competition.

booby trap /'buːbɪ træp/ n [C] harmless-looking object that will kill or injure when touched. **booby-trap** v (-pp-) [T] place a booby trap in (sth).

book¹ /bʊk/ n 1 [C] number of printed sheets of paper fastened together in a cover. 2 [C] number of similar items fastened together like a book: a ~ of stamps. 3 **books** [pl] business accounts. 4 [C] main division of a large written work, eg the Bible. 5 (idm) **be in sb's good/bad 'books** (infml) have/not have sb's favour or approval. **'bookcase** n [C] piece of furniture with shelves for books. **book club** n [C] club that sells books cheaply to its members. **'bookkeeping** n [U] keeping of business accounts. **'bookkeeper** n [C]. **'bookmaker** n [C] person who takes

bets on horse races. **'bookmark** n [C] something put in a book to mark the reader's place. **'bookshop** n [C] shop that sells mainly books. **'bookstall** n [C] stall or stand at which books, magazines, etc are sold. **'book token** n [C] card with a voucher that can be exchanged for books. **'bookworm** n [C] person who is very fond of reading.

book² /bʊk/ v 1 [I, T] order (eg tickets) in advance; reserve. 2 [T] write down the name of (sb) when bringing a legal charge: be ~ed for speeding. **bookable** adj that can be reserved. **booking** n [C]. **'booking-office** n [C] office where tickets are sold.

bookie /'bʊkɪ/ n [C] (infml) short for BOOKMAKER (BOOK¹).

booklet /'bʊklɪt/ n [C] small thin book with paper covers.

boom¹ /buːm/ n [C] sudden increase, eg in trade. **boom** v [I] have a boom: Sales are ~ing.

boom² /buːm/ v 1 [I] make a loud deep hollow sound. 2 [I, T] (out)/ say (sth) in a booming voice. **boom** n [C].

boom³ /buːm/ n [C] 1 long pole to keep the bottom of a sail stretched. 2 long movable arm for a microphone.

boomerang /'buːməræŋ/ n [C] curved wooden stick (used by Australian Aboriginals) that returns to the thrower.

boon /buːn/ n [C] something that one is thankful for; benefit.

boor /bʊə(r)/ n [C] rough or rude person. **boorish** adj.

boost /buːst/ v [T] increase the strength or value of. **boost** n [C]. **booster** n [C] 1 something that boosts. 2 additional injection of a drug.

boot /buːt/ n [C] 1 shoe for the foot and ankle, and sometimes also the leg. 2 space for luggage at the back of a motor car. 3 (idm) **give sb/get the 'boot** (infml) dismiss sb/be dismissed from a job. **put the 'boot in** (infml) kick sb brutally. **boot** v 1 [T] kick. 2 (phr v) **boot sb out (of sth)** (infml) force sb to leave a job or place.

booth /buːð; US buːθ/ n [C] 1 small stall where goods are sold. 2 small enclosed area: a telephone ~.

booze /buːz/ n [U] (infml) alcoholic drink. **booze** v [I] (infml) drink alcohol. **boozer** n [C] (infml) 1 person who boozes. 2 (Brit) pub. **'booze-up** n [C] (Brit infml) party, event, etc at which a lot of alcohol is drunk.

bop /bɒp/ n [C, U] (infml) dance or

dancing to pop music. **bop** v (-**pp**-) [I] (*infml*) dance to pop music.

border /'bɔːdə(r)/ n [C] **1** (land near the) dividing line between two countries. **2** edge. **3** strip of land along the edge of a lawn for planting flowers. **border** v **1** [I, T] (*on*)// be next to (another country). **2** (phr v) **border on sth** be almost the same as sth: *a state of excitement ~ ing on madness.* '**borderline** n [C] line that marks a border. '**borderline** adj between two different categories: *a ~ line candidate,* ie one that may or may not pass an examination.

bore[1] /bɔː(r)/ v [T] make (sb) feel tired and uninterested. **bore** n [C] person or thing that bores sb. **boredom** /'bɔːdəm/ n [U] state of being bored. **boring** adj uninteresting; dull.

bore[2] /bɔː(r)/ v [I, T] make (a deep round hole) in sth with a special tool. **bore** n [C] **1** hole made by boring. **2** (diameter of the) hollow part inside a gun barrel.

bore[3] pt of BEAR[2].

born /bɔːn/ v **be born** come into the world by birth: *He was ~ in 1954.* **born** adj having a particular natural ability: *be a ~ leader.* -**born** (forming ns and adjs) having a stated nationality at birth: *Dutch~.* ,**born-a'gain** adj having renewed and very strong faith in sth, esp a religion: *a ~ again Christian.*

borne pp of BEAR[2].

borough /'bʌrə/ US -rəʊ/ n [C] (district in a large) town.

borrow /'bɒrəʊ/ v [I, T] have or use (sth that belongs to sb else), with the promise that it will be returned. **borrower** n [C].

Borstal /'bɔːstl/ n [C, U] prison school for young offenders.

bosom /'bʊzəm/ n **1** [C] (*dated*) person's chest, esp a woman's breasts. **2 the bosom of sth** [sing] (*dated*) loving care and protection of sth: *in the ~ of one's family.* **bosom** '**friend** n [C] very close friend.

boss /bɒs/ n [C] (*infml*) person who controls others or gives orders. **boss** v [T] (*about/around*)// (*infml*) give orders to (sb). **bossy** adj (-**ier**, -**iest**) fond of giving orders.

botany /'bɒtənɪ/ n [U] scientific study of plants. **botanical** /bə'tænɪkl/ adj. **botanist** n [C] student of or expert in botany.

botch /bɒtʃ/ v [T] spoil (sth) by bad or clumsy work. **botch** n [C] piece of badly done work.

both /bəʊθ/ adj, pron the two; the one and the other: *B ~ (the) books are expensive.* ○ *His parents are ~ dead.* **both** adv with equal truth in two cases: *She has houses in ~ London and Paris.*

bother /'bɒðə(r)/ v **1** [T] cause trouble or annoyance to: *Is something ~ ing you?* **2** [I, T] take the time or trouble: *Don't ~ to stand up.* **bother** n [sing] annoying thing; nuisance. **bothersome** adj annoying.

bottle /'bɒtl/ n **1** [C] (a) container with a narrow neck, for liquids. (b) amount contained in this. **2** [C] baby's feeding bottle; milk from this. **3** [U] (*Brit sl*) courage. **bottle** v **1** [T] put in bottles. **2** (phr v) **bottle sth up** not allow (strong feelings) to be shown. '**bottle-neck** n [C] **1** narrow or restricted stretch of road that causes traffic to slow down. **2** anything that slows down movement or progress.

bottom /'bɒtəm/ n **1** [C, usu sing] lowest part or point. **2** [C] part of the body on which one sits. **3** [sing] ground under a sea, lake, etc. **4** [C, usu sing] far end: *at the ~ of the garden.* **5** [sing] lowest position in a class, organization, etc. **6** (idm) **at the 'bottom of sth** the basic cause of sth. **get to the 'bottom of sth** discover the real cause of sth. **bottom** v (phr v) **bottom out** reach its lowest level. **bottomless** adj very deep; unlimited. **the ,bottom 'line** n [sing] (*infml*) most important or deciding point.

bough /baʊ/ n [C] large branch of a tree.

bought pt, pp of BUY.

boulder /'bəʊldə(r)/ n [C] large rock.

bounce /baʊns/ v **1** [I, T] (cause (eg a ball) to) spring back after hitting sth hard. **2** [I, T] move up and down in a lively way. **3** [I, T] move in the direction that is mentioned in a lively way: *She ~ d into the room.* **4** [I] (*infml*) (of a cheque) be returned by a bank because there is not enough money in an account. **bounce** n [C] act of bouncing. **bouncer** n [C] person employed by a club to throw out trouble-makers. **bouncing** adj strong and healthy.

bound[1] pt, pp of BIND.

bound[2] /baʊnd/ adj **1** *to*// (a) certain to do sth: *He is ~ to win.* (b) obliged by law or duty to sth. **2** (idm) **bound 'up in sth** very busy with sth. **bound 'up with sth** closely connected with sth.

bound[3] /baʊnd/ adj (*for*)// going to a place: *a ship ~ for Rotterdam.*

bound⁴ /baʊnd/ v [T] (usu passive) form the boundary of: *an airfield ~ed by woods.*

bound⁵ /baʊnd/ v [I] jump; run with jumping movements. **bound** n [C].

boundary /'baʊndrɪ/ n [C] (pl -ies) line that marks a limit.

boundless /'baʊndlɪs/ adj without limits.

bounds /baʊndz/ n [pl] 1 limits. 2 (idm) **out of 'bounds (to sb)** (of a place) not allowed to be entered (by sb).

bounty /'baʊntɪ/ n (pl -ies) 1 [U] (dated) generosity. 2 [C] (dated) generous gift. 3 [C] money given as a reward. **bountiful** adj generously.

bouquet /bu'keɪ, buː'keɪ/ n 1 [C] bunch of flowers. 2 [sing] smell of wine.

bourgeois /'bɔːʒwɑː, ˌbʊəʒ'wɑː/ n [C], adj 1 (person) of the property-owning middle-class. 2 (derog) (person who is) concerned with material possessions. **bourgeoisie** /ˌbɔːʒwɑː'ziː, ˌbʊəʒwɑː'ziː/ n [sing, also sing with pl v] (derog) middle classes.

bout /baʊt/ n [C] short period of activity or an illness.

boutique /buː'tiːk/ n [C] small shop, esp one that sells fashionable clothes.

bow¹ /baʊ/ v 1 [I, T] bend forward as a sign of respect or as a greeting. 2 (phr v) **bow out (of sth)** stop taking part (in sth). **bow to sb** submit to sth, accept sth: *I ~ to your authority.* **bow** n [C].

bow² /bəʊ/ n [C] 1 piece of wood curved by a tight string, used for shooting arrows. 2 wooden rod with long hairs from a horse stretched from end to end, used for playing the violin, etc. 3 knot made with loops, often in ribbon, for decoration. ˌ**bow-'legged** adj having legs that curve outward at the knees. ˌ**bow-'tie** n [C] man's tie formed as a bow (3). ˌ**bow-'window** n [C] curved window.

bow³ /baʊ/ n [C] front part of a ship.

bowel /'baʊəl/ n [C, usu pl] 1 intestine. 2 deepest part: *in the ~s of the earth.*

bowl¹ /bəʊl/ n [C] 1 (a) deep round container for food or liquid. (b) amount contained in this. 2 hollow rounded part of sth.

bowl² /bəʊl/ v 1 (a) [I, T] send (a ball) to the batsman in cricket. (b) [T] (out)) get (a batsman) out of a game of cricket by hitting the wicket behind him/her with the ball. 2 [I] play a game of bowls or

bowling. 3 (phr v) **bowl sb over** (a) knock sb down. (b) surprise sb greatly. **bowl** n 1 [C] heavy ball used in the game of bowls or ten-pin bowling. 2 **bowls** (with sing v) game in which players try to roll bowls as near as possible to a small ball.

bowler¹ /'bəʊlə(r)/ n [C] person who bowls.

bowler² (also ˌ**bowler 'hat**) /'bəʊlə(r)/ n [C] man's hard round hat.

bowling /'bəʊlɪŋ/ n [U] game in which heavy balls are rolled along a track towards a group of bottle-shaped objects to knock them down.

box¹ /bɒks/ n 1 [C] (a) stiff container, usu with a lid, for holding solids. (b) contents of this. 2 [C] (a) separate enclosed area or compartment: *a ~ in a theatre.* (b) small hut for a particular purpose: *a 'telephone-~.* 3 [C] space on a form, to be filled in. 4 **the box** [sing] (Brit infml) television. **box** v 1 [T] put into a box. 2 (phr v) **box sb/sth in** put sb/sth in a small closed space. ˌ**box number** n [C] number used as an address in a newspaper advertisement, to which replies may be sent. ˌ**box office** n [C] office at a theatre, etc where tickets are sold.

box² /bɒks/ v [I, T] fight (sb) with the fists, esp wearing padded gloves, as a sport. **boxer** n [C] 1 person who boxes. 2 breed of bulldog. **boxing** n [U].

Boxing Day /'bɒksɪŋ deɪ/ n [U, C] the first weekday after Christmas Day.

boy /bɔɪ/ n [C] male child; young man. ˌ**boy-friend** n [C] girl's or woman's special male friend. **boyhood** n [U] the time of being a boy. **boyish** adj of, for or like a boy.

boycott /'bɔɪkɒt/ v [T] refuse to be involved with or take part in (sth). **boycott** n [C].

bra /brɑː/ n [C] woman's undergarment worn to support the breasts.

brace /breɪs/ v 1 ~ **oneself (for/to)** prepare oneself for sth difficult or unpleasant. 2 [T] place (one's hand or foot) to steady one's body. 3 [T] make stronger or firmer; support. **brace** n 1 [C] wire device worn esp by children to straighten the teeth. 2 [C] device that straightens or supports. 3 **braces** [pl] (Brit) straps that pass over the shoulders to hold trousers up. **bracing** adj giving energy: *the bracing sea air.*

bracelet /'breɪslɪt/ n [C] decorative band worn around one's wrist.

bracken /'brækən/ n [U] large fern.

bracket /'brækɪt/ n [C] 1 [usu pl] either of certain pairs of written marks, eg (), used for enclosing words. 2 wood or metal support for a shelf. 3 group within particular limits: *the 20-30 age ~*. **bracket** v [T] 1 put in brackets. 2 put together.

brackish /'brækɪʃ/ adj (of water) slightly salty.

brag /bræg/ v (-gg-) [I, T] talk with too much pride (about sth).

braid /breɪd/ n 1 [U] threads of silk, etc woven together to make a decorative band for clothes or material. 2 [C] (*US*) plait. **braid** v [T] (*US*) plait.

Braille /breɪl/ n [U] system of writing for blind people, using raised dots.

brain /breɪn/ n [C] 1 organ in the body that controls thought, feeling, etc. 2 mind; intelligence: *have a good ~*. 3 (*infml*) clever person. 4 (idm) **have sth on the brain** (*infml*) think about sth constantly. **brain** v [T] kill with a heavy blow on the head. '**brain-child** n [sing] person's **o**riginal idea. '**brain drain** n [C] movement of skilled clever people to other countries. **brainless** adj stupid. '**brainstorm** n [C] (*Brit*) sudden mental disturbance. '**brainwash** v [T] force (sb) to accept new beliefs by use of extreme mental pressure. '**brainwave** n [C] (*infml*) sudden clever idea. **brainy** adj (-ier, -iest) (*infml*) clever.

braise /breɪz/ v [T] cook (meat or vegetables) slowly in a covered container.

brake /breɪk/ n [C] device for reducing the speed of or stopping a vehicle. **brake** v [I, T] slow down or stop using a brake.

bramble /'bræmbl/ n [C] wild prickly shrub; blackberry bush.

bran /bræn/ n [U] outer covering of grain.

branch /brɑ:ntʃ; *US* bræntʃ/ n [C] 1 part of a tree growing out from a trunk. 2 division of a railway, road, etc. 3 division of a family, organization, etc: *a ~ office*. **branch** v 1 [I] divide into branches. 2 (phr v) **branch 'off** turn from one road into a smaller one. **branch 'out** extend or expand one's range of activities.

brand /brænd/ n [C] 1 particular make of goods: *the cheapest ~ of margarine.* 2 particular kind: *a strange ~ of humour.* 3 mark

burnt onto the skin of an animal to show ownership. **brand** v [T] 1 mark with a brand(3). 2 give a bad name to: *He was ~ed (as) a thief.* ,**brand-'new** adj completely new.

brandish /'brændɪʃ/ v [T] wave (esp a weapon) threateningly in the air.

brandy /'brændɪ/ n [U, C] (*pl* -ies) strong alcoholic drink made from wine.

brash /bræʃ/ adj confident in a rude or aggressive way.

brass /brɑ:s; *US* bræs/ n 1 [U] bright yellow metal. 2 [U, C, usu pl] thing(s) made from brass. 3 **the brass** (sing, also sing with pl v) (people who play) wind instruments made from brass. 4 [U] (*Brit sl*) money. ,**brass 'band** n [C] band which plays brass and percussion instruments only.

brassière /'bræsɪə(r); *US* brə'zɪər/ n [C] (*fml*) = BRA.

brat /bræt/ n [C] (*derog*) (badly-behaved) child.

bravado /brə'vɑ:dəʊ/ n [U] unnecessary or false show of boldness.

brave /breɪv/ adj (~r, ~st) 1 ready to meet danger or suffering; showing no fear. 2 showing courage. **brave** v [T] meet (eg a danger) without showing fear. **bravely** adv. **bravery** /'breɪvərɪ/ n [U].

bravo /,brɑ:'vəʊ/ interj, n [C] (*pl* ~s) shout meaning 'Well done!'.

brawl /brɔ:l/ n [C] noisy quarrel. **brawl** v [I] quarrel noisily.

brawny /'brɔ:nɪ/ adj strong and muscular.

bray /breɪ/ n [C] cry of a donkey. **bray** v [I] make this cry or a sound like it.

brazen /'breɪzn/ adj very bold; shameless.

brazier /'breɪzɪə(r)/ n [C] metal container for holding a charcoal or coal fire.

breach /bri:tʃ/ n 1 [C, U] breaking or neglect of a law, agreement, etc. 2 [C] break in a friendly relationship. 3 [C] (*fml*) opening, eg in a wall. **breach** v [T] 1 break (a law, etc). 2 (*fml*) make an opening in. ,**breach of the 'peace** n [C, usu sing] (*law*) fighting in a public place.

bread /bred/ n [U] 1 food made of flour, water and usu yeast, baked in an oven. 2 (*sl*) money. 3 (idm) **on the 'breadline** very poor. '**breadcrumb** n [C, usu pl] tiny piece of bread. '**breadwinner** n [C] person whose earnings support his/her family.

breadth /bredθ, bretθ/ n [U] 1 distance from side to side; width. 2

break

wide extent; range.

break¹ /breɪk/ v (pt **broke** /brəʊk/, pp **broken** /ˈbrəʊkən/) **1** [I, T] (cause to) separate into pieces: Glass ~s easily. ○ ~ a plate. **2** [I, T] become or make by breaking: ~ open the boxes. **3** [I, T] become or make useless by being damaged: My watch has broken. **4** [T] disobey (a law, promise, etc.). **5** [I] (off)// stop doing sth. **6** [T] interrupt: ~ one's journey ○ ~ the silence. **7** [I] become lighter; begin: Day was ~ing. **8** [I, T] (cause (sb/sth) to) be weakened or destroyed: ~ the power of the unions ○ His wife's death broke him. **9** [T] weaken the effect of (a fall). **10** [T] (of)// succeed in getting (sb) to end (a habit). **11** [I] (of the weather) change suddenly after a settled period. **12** [I, T] become or make known: ~ the news. **13** [I] (of a boy's voice) become deeper. **14** [T] do better than (a previous record). **15** [T] solve (a code). **16** (idm) **break the 'back of sth** finish the largest or most difficult part of sth. **break 'even** make neither a loss nor a profit. **break fresh/new 'ground** introduce or discover a new method, activity, etc. **break the 'ice** make people feel friendly towards one another, eg at the beginning of a party. **break 'wind** (euph) let out air from the bowels. **make or break sb/sth** cause sb/ sth to either succeed or fail. **17** (phr v) **break away (from sb/sth)** go away from sb/sth; leave (eg a political party). **break down** (a) (of machinery) stop working. (b) fail; collapse: Talks between the two sides have broken down. (c) lose control of one's feelings. **break sth down** (a) destroy sth: ~ down resistance. (b) analyse sth; classify: ~ down expenses. **break in** (a) enter a building by force. (b) (on)// interrupt sb's conversation. **break sb/sth in** train and discipline sb/sth. **break into sth** (a) enter (a building) by force. (b) suddenly begin sth: ~ into laughter/a run. (c) start to spend (money saved). **break off** stop speaking. **break (sth) off** (cause to) separate by force. **break sth off** end sth suddenly: They've broken off their engagement. **break out** (a) start suddenly (of sth bad): Fire broke out. (b) (of)// escape from a prison. (c) (in)// suddenly become covered in sth: ~ out in spots. **break through (sth)** (a) force a way through sth. (b) (of the sun) appear from behind (clouds). **break up** (a) (of a group of people) go

away in different directions. (b) (Brit) (of a school or its pupils) begin the holidays. (c) (with)// end a relationship with sb. **break (sth) up** (cause sth to) separate into smaller pieces. (b) (cause sth to) come to an end: Their marriage is ~ing up. **breakable** adj easily broken. **'breakaway** adj of a group of people who have left eg a political party. **'break-in** n [C] entering a building by force. **'breakout** n [C] escape from a prison. **'breakthrough** n [C] important development or discovery. **'breakup** n [C] end (esp of a relationship).

break² /breɪk/ n [C] **1** place where sth is broken: a ~ in a pipe. **2** space or gap. **3** rest; pause: a 'lunch-~. **4** interruption of sth continuous: a ~ with tradition. **5** (infml) piece of luck that leads to success. **6** (idm) **break of day** dawn. **make a break for it** (try to) escape.

breakage /ˈbreɪkɪdʒ/ n **1** [C] something that has been broken. **2** [C, U] act of breaking.

breakdown /ˈbreɪkdaʊn/ n [C] **1** failure in machinery. **2** collapse or failure. **3** weakness or collapse of sb's (esp mental) health: a ˌnervous '~. **4** analysis of statistics: a ~ of expenses.

breaker /ˈbreɪkə(r)/ n [C] **1** large wave that breaks into foam. **2** person or thing that breaks sth: a 'law-~.

breakfast /ˈbrekfəst/ n [C, U] first meal of the day. **breakfast** v [I] eat breakfast.

breakneck /ˈbreknek/ adj dangerously fast: at ~ speed.

breakwater /ˈbreɪkwɔːtə(r)/ n [C] wall built out into the sea to protect a harbour.

breast /brest/ n [C] **1** either of the two parts of a woman's body that produce milk. **2** (rhet) upper front part of the body. **'breastbone** n [C] thin flat vertical bone in the chest between the ribs. **'breast-stroke** n [U] kind of swimming stroke.

breath /breθ/ n **1** [U] air taken into and sent out of the lungs. **2** [C] single act of taking air into the lungs. **3** [sing] slight movement of air. **4** (idm) **get one's 'breath back** return to one's usual rate of breathing. **out of 'breath** breathing very quickly, eg after running fast. **take sb's 'breath away** surprise sb greatly. **under one's 'breath** in a whisper. **breathless** adj **1** out of breath. **2** almost stopping breathing, eg because of fear. **breathlessly** adv. **'breathtaking**

adj amazing.

breathalyser (*US* **-lyz-**) /ˈbreθə-laɪzə(r)/ *n* [C] device used by the police for measuring the amount of alcohol in a driver's breath.

breathe /briːð/ *v* 1 [I, T] take (air) into the lungs and send it out again. 2 [T] say very quietly; whisper. 3 [T] give out (a feeling, quality, etc). 4 (idm) **breathe again** feel calm or relaxed after a difficult or anxious time. **breathe down sb's 'neck** (*infml*) watch sb too closely. **breather** *n* [C] (*infml*) short rest.

breeches /ˈbrɪtʃɪz/ *n* [pl] short trousers fastened just below the knee.

breed /briːd/ *v* (*pt, pp* **bred** /bred/) 1 [T] keep (animals) for the purpose of producing young: ~ *horses/cattle.* 2 [I] (of animals) produce young. 3 [T] bring up; train: *a well-bred child.* 4 [T] lead to; cause: *Dirt ~s disease.* **breed** *n* [C] 1 kind of animal. 2 particular kind of person: *a new ~ of manager.* **breeder** *n* [C] person who breeds animals. **breeding** *n* [U] 1 producing of animal young. 2 good manners; education: *a man of good ~ing.*

breeze /briːz/ *n* [C, U] gentle wind. **breeze** (*phr v*) **breeze in, out, etc** (*infml*) move casually and cheerfully in the direction that is mentioned. **breezy** *adj* 1 slightly windy. 2 cheerful and confident. **breezily** *adv*.

brethren /ˈbreðrən/ *n* [pl] (*arch*) brothers.

brevity /ˈbrevətɪ/ *n* [U] (*fml*) shortness: *the ~ of life.*

brew /bruː/ *v* 1 [I, T] prepare (tea, coffee or beer). 2 [I] (of sth unpleasant) develop. **brew** *n* [C] result of brewing. **brewer** *n* [C]. **brewery** /ˈbruːərɪ/ *n* [C] (*pl* **-ies**) place where beer is brewed.

bribe /braɪb/ *n* [C] something given to sb to persuade him/her to do sth. **bribe** *v* [T] give a bribe to. **bribery** /ˈbraɪbərɪ/ *n* [U] giving or taking bribes.

bric-à-brac /ˈbrɪkəbræk/ *n* [U] small ornaments of little value.

brick /brɪk/ *n* [C, U] (block of) baked clay used for building. **brick** *v* (*phr v*) **brick sth in/up** fall or block (an opening) with bricks. **'bricklayer** *n* [C] person whose job is to build with bricks. **'brickwork** *n* [U] structure built of bricks.

bridal /ˈbraɪdl/ *adj* of a bride or wedding.

bride /braɪd/ *n* [C] woman on her wedding day; newly married woman. **'bridegroom** *n* [C] man on his wedding day; newly married man. **'bridesmaid** *n* [C] girl attending the bride at her wedding.

bridge[1] /brɪdʒ/ *n* [C] 1 structure providing a way across a river, etc. 2 (*fig*) thing which links two or more different things. 3 raised part of a ship from which it is controlled. 4 upper part of the nose. 5 part on a violin, etc over which the strings are stretched. **bridge** *v* [T] build a bridge across. **'bridgehead** *n* [C] strong position captured in enemy territory.

bridge[2] /brɪdʒ/ *n* [U] card-game for four players.

bridle /ˈbraɪdl/ *n* [C] part of a horse's harness that goes on its head. **bridle** *v* 1 [T] put a bridle on (a horse). 2 [T] (*fig*) control: ~ *one's emotions.* 3 [I] show anger by moving one's head up or back.

brief[1] /briːf/ *adj* 1 lasting only a short time. 2 using few words. 3 (of clothes) short. 4 (idm) **in brief** in a few words. **briefly** *adv*.

brief[2] /briːf/ *n* [C] instructions and information for a particular task. **brief** *v* [T] give a brief to. **'briefcase** *n* [C] flat leather case for papers, etc.

briefs /briːfs/ *n* [pl] short close-fitting pants or knickers.

brigade /brɪˈgeɪd/ *n* [C] 1 army unit usu of three battalions. 2 organization for a particular purpose: *the fire ~.* **brigadier** /ˌbrɪgəˈdɪə(r)/ *n* [C] officer commanding a brigade(1).

bright /braɪt/ *adj* 1 giving out or reflecting a lot of light; shining. 2 (of colour) strong. 3 cheerful; happy. 4 clever. 5 likely to be successful: *The future looks ~.* **brighten** *v* [I, T] become or make brighter. **brightly** *adv*. **brightness** *n* [U].

brilliant /ˈbrɪlɪənt/ *adj* 1 very bright. 2 very clever. 3 (*infml*) very good. **brilliance** /-lɪəns/ *n* [U]. **brilliantly** *adv*.

brim /brɪm/ *n* [C] 1 edge of a cup, etc. 2 bottom edge of a hat. **brim** *v* (**-mm-**) 1 [I] (*with*)// be full with sth. 2 (*phr v*) **brim over** overflow.

brine /braɪn/ *n* [U] salt water, esp for preserving food.

bring /brɪŋ/ *v* (*pt, pp* **brought** /brɔːt/) [T] 1 carry or lead towards the speaker or to the place to which he/she is referring: *B~ me my coat.* ○ *He brought his dog with him.* 2 cause; produce: *Spring ~s warm weather.* ○ *The story brought tears to her eyes.* 3 cause to reach a certain state or condition:

~ *water to the boil*, ie boil it. 4 force or persuade sb/oneself to do sth: *I can't ~ myself to tell him*. 5 (*against*)|| (*law*) start a case, etc): ~ *a charge against sb*. 6 (idm) **bring sth to a 'head** ⇨ HEAD¹. **bring sth to mind** ⇨ MIND¹. **bring sth into the open** ⇨ OPEN¹. 7 (phr v) **bring sth about** cause sth to happen. **bring sb/sth back** (a) return sb/sth: ~ *back a book* ◇ *I brought the children back*, ie home. (b) cause sth to be remembered. (c) introduce sth again: ~ *back hanging*. **bring sth/sb down** (a) cause sth to fall: ~ *down the government* ◇ *brought him down with a rugby tackle*. (b) reduce: ~ *prices down*. (c) cause (an aircraft) to fall out of the sky or to land. **bring sth forward** (a) cause to be earlier: ~ *the meeting forward*. (b) propose for discussion; raise. **bring sth/sb in** (a) introduce sth: ~ *in a new fashion/legislation*. (b) produce sth as profit. (c) use sb's services as an adviser, etc: ~ *in a scientist to check pollution*. **bring sth off** (*infml*) manage to do sth successfully. **bring sth on** result in sth; cause sth: *The rain brought on his cold*. **bring sb out** (a) cause sb to strike: *Union leaders brought out the workers*. (b) cause sb to become less shy: *His first year at college brought him out a little*. **bring sth out** (a) cause sth to be seen; reveal sth: ~ *out the meaning* ◇ *brought out her kindness*. (b) produce or publish sth: ~ *out a new type of computer*. **bring sb round** (a) cause sb to regain consciousness. (b) convert sb to one's own views. **bring sb up** look after and train (children): *brought up to be polite*. **bring sb/sth up** (a) call attention to sb/sth; mention sb/sth: ~ *up the subject of salaries*. (b) vomit sth.

brink /brɪŋk/ *n* [C] edge of a steep or dangerous place: (*fig*) *on the ~ of war*.

brisk /brɪsk/ *adj* moving quickly; lively: *walk at a ~ pace*. **briskly** *adv*.

bristle /'brɪsl/ *n* [C, U] short stiff hair, esp on a brush. **bristle** *v* [I] 1 (of hair) stand up stiffly. 2 (*fig*) show anger. 3 (phr v) **bristle with sth** have a large number of sth.

brittle /'brɪtl/ *adj* hard but easily broken: ~ *glass*.

broach /brəʊtʃ/ *v* [T] begin a discussion (of a subject).

broad /brɔːd/ *adj* 1 measuring a large amount from one side to the other; wide. 2 covering a wide area; extensive: (*fig*) *a ~ range of*

subjects. 3 clear; obvious: *a ~ grin*. 4 not detailed; general: *a ~ outline of a speech*. 5 (of speech) with a strong accent. 6 (idm) **in broad 'daylight** in the full light of day. **broaden** *v* [I, T] become or make broader. **broadly** *adv* generally: ~ *ly speaking*. **broad-'minded** *adj* liberal and tolerant.

broadcast /'brɔːdkɑːst; *US* -kæst/ *n* [C] radio or television programme. **broadcast** *v* (*pt, pp* **broadcast**) [I, T] send out (radio or television programmes). **broadcaster** *n* [C]. **broadcasting** *n* [U].

broadside /'brɔːdsaɪd/ *n* [C] 1 firing of all the guns on a ship's side. 2 (*fig*) fierce attack in words.

broccoli /'brɒkəlɪ/ *n* [U] kind of cauliflower with greenish flower-heads.

brochure /'brəʊʃə(r); *US* brəʊ'ʃʊər/ *n* [C] booklet containing information or advertisements.

broil /brɔɪl/ *v* [T] (esp *US*) grill (food).

broke /brəʊk/ *pt* of BREAK¹.

broke² /brəʊk/ *adj* (*infml*) 1 having no money. 2 (idm) **flat broke** completely broke.

broken¹ /'brəʊkən/ *pp* of BREAK¹.

broken² /'brəʊkən/ *adj* 1 not continuous; interrupted: ~ *sleep*. 2 (of a foreign language) spoken imperfectly. 3 (of a person) weakened by illness or misfortune. **broken 'home** *n* [C] family in which the parents have divorced or separated.

broker /'brəʊkə(r)/ *n* [C] person who buys and sells eg business shares for others.

brolly /'brɒlɪ/ *n* [C] (*pl* **-ies**) (*infml* esp *Brit*) umbrella.

bronchial /'brɒŋkɪəl/ *adj* of the tubes of the windpipe.

bronchitis /brɒŋ'kaɪtɪs/ *n* [U] inflammation of the tubes of the windpipe.

bronze /brɒnz/ *n* 1 [U] metal that is a mixture of copper and tin. 2 [U] reddish-brown colour. 3 [C] something made of bronze; bronze medal. **bronze** *v* [T] make bronze in colour. **bronze 'medal** *n* [C] medal awarded as third prize in a competition, esp a sports contest.

brooch /brəʊtʃ/ *n* [C] ornament pinned to a dress.

brood /bruːd/ *n* [C] 1 young birds produced at one hatching or birth. 2 (*joc*) family of children. **brood** *v* [I] 1 sit on eggs to hatch them. 2 think for a long time in a troubled way: ~ *ing over her problems*.

broody *adj* 1 (of a hen) wanting to

brood. **2** sad and very quiet.

brook /bruk/ n [C] small stream.

broom /bru:m/ n [C] brush with a long handle for sweeping floors.

broth /brɒθ; US brɔ:θ/ n [U] kind of soup.

brothel /'brɒθl/ n [C] house of prostitutes.

brother /'brʌðə(r)/ n [C] **1** son of the same parents as oneself or another person mentioned. **2** man who is a member of the same society, profession, etc. **3** (pl **brethren** /'breðrən/) **(a)** male member of a religious society. **(b)** member of certain Christian churches. **brotherhood** n **1** [U] (feeling of) friendship between brothers. **2** [C] (members of) a society or organization. **brother-in-law** n [C] (pl ~s-in-law) brother of one's husband or wife; husband of one's sister. **brotherly** adj.

brought pt, pp of BRING.

brow /braʊ/ n [C] **1** forehead. **2** eyebrow. **3** slope leading to the top of a hill.

browbeat /'braʊbi:t/ v (pt browbeat, pp ~en /-bi:tn/) [T] frighten (sb) into doing sth.

brown /braʊn/ adj, n [C, U] (having the) colour of toasted bread or coffee with milk. **brown** v [I] become or make brown.

browse /braʊz/ v [I] **1** read books in a casual leisurely way. **2** feed on grass, leaves, etc. **browse** n [C, usu sing].

bruise /bru:z/ n [C] injury caused by a blow to the body so that the skin is discoloured. **bruise** v **1** [T] cause a bruise to. **2** [I] show the effects of a bruise.

brunette /bru:'net/ n [C] white woman with dark brown hair.

brunt /brʌnt/ n (idm) bear the 'brunt of sth ⇨ BEAR².

brush¹ /brʌʃ/ n **1** [C] tool with bristles for cleaning, painting, etc: a 'tooth-~. **2** [sing] act of brushing. **3** [C] argument or fight: a nasty ~ with his boss. **4** [U] (land covered by) small trees and shrubs.

brush² /brʌʃ/ v [T] **1** clean with a brush. **2** touch lightly when passing. **3** (phr v) brush sth aside pay little or no attention to sth. brush sth up, brush up on sth study or practise (sth forgotten): ~ up (on) your French.

brusque /bru:sk; US brʌsk/ adj rough and impolite. **brusquely** adv. **brusqueness** n [U].

Brussels sprout /ˌbrʌslz 'spraʊt/ n [C] kind of vegetable that looks like a very small cabbage.

brutal /'bru:tl/ adj cruel; savage. **brutality** /bru:'tælətɪ/ n [U, C] (pl -ies). **brutally** adv.

brute /bru:t/ n [C] **1** (esp large or fierce) animal. **2** cruel insensitive person. **brute** adj unthinking and physical: ~ force. **brutish** adj or like a brute.

bubble /'bʌbl/ n [C] **1** (in the air) floating ball of liquid containing air or gas. **2** (in a liquid) ball of air or gas. **bubble** v [I] **1** send up, rise in or make the sound of bubbles. **2** (fig) be full of happy feelings. '**bubble gum** n [U] chewing-gum that can be blown into bubbles. **bubbly** adj (-ier, -iest) **1** full of bubbles. **2** happy and lively.

buck¹ /bʌk/ n [C] male deer, hare or rabbit.

buck² /bʌk/ v **1** [I] (of a horse) jump up with all four feet together. **2** (phr v) buck 'up hurry. buck (sb) up (cause sb to) become more cheerful.

buck³ /bʌk/ n [C] (US infml) US dollar.

buck⁴ /bʌk/ n the buck [sing] (infml) responsibility: to pass the ~.

bucket /'bʌkɪt/ n [C] **1** round open container with a handle, for carrying liquids. **2** (also '**bucketful**) amount a bucket contains. **bucket** v [I] (down)// (infml) (of rain) pour down heavily.

buckle /'bʌkl/ n [C] metal or plastic fastener for a belt, etc. **buckle** v [I, T] **1** fasten with a buckle. **2** bend, esp because of force or heat. **3** (phr v) buckle down (to sth) (infml) start sth in a determined way.

bud /bʌd/ n [C] flower or leaf before it opens. **bud** v (-dd-) [I] produce buds. **budding** adj beginning to develop well.

Buddhism /'budɪzəm/ n [U] Asian religion based on the teachings of the N Indian philosopher Gautama Siddartha or Buddha. **Buddhist** /'budɪst/ n [C], adj.

buddy /'bʌdɪ/ n [C] (pl -ies) (infml esp US) friend.

budge /bʌdʒ/ v [I, T] move slightly: The stone won't ~.

budgerigar /'bʌdʒərɪgɑ:(r)/ n [C] small brightly-coloured Australian bird, often kept as a pet.

budget /'bʌdʒɪt/ n [C] plan of how much money will be spent over a period of time. **budget** v [I] (for)// plan the amount of money to be spent on sth. **budget** adj cheap: ~ holidays.

buff¹ /bʌf/ n [U] dull-yellow colour. **buff** v [T] polish with a soft material.

buff² /bʌf/ n [C] person who knows a lot about the subject that is mentioned: *a computer* ~.

buffalo /'bʌfələʊ/ n [C] (*pl* **buffalo** or ~ **es**) kind of large wild ox.

buffer /'bʌfə(r)/ n [C] device on a railway engine, etc to reduce the effect of a collision.

buffet¹ /'bʊfeɪ; *US* bə'feɪ/ n [C] 1 counter where food and drink may be bought and consumed, eg at a railway station. 2 meal at which guests serve themselves from a number of dishes.

buffet² /'bʌfɪt/ v [T] push or knock roughly from side to side: ~ *ed by the wind.*

buffoon /bə'fuːn/ n [C] clown.

bug /bʌɡ/ n [C] 1 small insect. 2 (*infml*) (illness caused by a) germ. 3 (*infml*) great interest in sth mentioned: *He's got the cooking* ~! 4 (*infml*) fault in a machine, esp a computer. 5 (*infml*) small hidden microphone. **bug** v (**-gg-**) [T] 1 fit with a bug(5). 2 (*infml*) annoy constantly.

bugbear /'bʌɡbeə(r)/ n [C] thing that is disliked or causes annoyance.

bugger /'bʌɡə(r)/ n [C] (△ *infml esp Brit*) 1 annoying person or thing. 2 person: *Poor* ~ ! *His wife left him last week.* **bugger** *interj* (△ *infml esp Brit*) (used for expressing anger or annoyance).

bugle /'bjuːɡl/ n [C] musical instrument like a small trumpet. **bugler** n [C].

build¹ /bɪld/ v (*pt, pp* **built** /bɪlt/) [T] 1 make by putting parts, etc together. 2 develop, establish: ~ *a better future.* 3 (*phr v*) **build on** sth use sth as a foundation for further progress. **build sth on** sth base sth on sth. **build (sth) up** (cause to) become greater; increase: *Traffic is* ~ *ing up.* ○ ~ *up a business.* **build sb/sth up** speak with great praise about sb/sth. **builder** n [C]. **build-up** n [C] 1 gradual increase. 2 favourable description. **built-'in** *adj* included to form part of a structure. **built-'up** *adj* covered with buildings.

build² /bɪld/ n [U, C] shape and size of the human body.

building /'bɪldɪŋ/ n 1 [C] structure with a roof and walls. 2 [U] (business of) constructing houses, etc. **'building society** n [C] (*Brit*) organization that accepts money to be invested and lends money to people who want to buy houses.

bulb /bʌlb/ n [C] 1 pear-shaped glass part of an electric lamp. 2 thick rounded underground stem

of certain plants. **bulbous** *adj* round and fat.

bulge /bʌldʒ/ v [I] swell outwards. **bulge** n [C] rounded swelling.

bulk /bʌlk/ n 1 [U] (esp great) size or quantity. 2 [C] large shape or mass. 3 the **bulk of** sth [sing] the main part of sth. 4 (*idm*) **in 'bulk** in large quantities. **bulky** *adj* (**-ier, -iest**) large; difficult to move.

bull /bʊl/ n [C] 1 male of the ox family which has not been castrated. 2 male of the elephant, whale and other large animals. 3 (*idm*) **a bull in a 'china shop** person who is clumsy where skill or care is needed. **take the bull by the 'horns** face a difficulty boldly. **'bulldog** n [C] strong dog with a large head and a short thick neck. **'bull's-eye** n [C] centre of a target. **'bullshit** n [U], *interj* (△ *sl*) nonsense, rubbish.

bulldoze /'bʊldəʊz/ v [T] 1 remove or flatten with a bulldozer. 2 (*fig*) force (sb) to do sth. **bulldozer** n [C] powerful tractor for moving large quantities of earth.

bullet /'bʊlɪt/ n [C] round or pointed piece of metal shot from a gun. **'bullet-proof** *adj* that can stop bullets passing through it: ~ *-proof glass.*

bulletin /'bʊlətɪn/ n [C] short official news report.

bullion /'bʊliən/ n [U] gold or silver in bulk or bars.

bullock /'bʊlək/ n [C] castrated bull.

bully /'bʊlɪ/ n [C] (*pl* **-ies**) person who uses his/her strength to frighten or hurt weaker people. **bully** v (*pt, pp* **-ied**) [T] use strength in this way.

bulrush /'bʊlrʌʃ/ n [C] tall strong weed that grows on marshy land.

bulwark /'bʊlwək/ n [C] 1 wall built as a defence. 2 (*fig*) something that defends or protects.

bum¹ /bʌm/ n [C] (*infml esp Brit*) buttocks.

bum² /bʌm/ n [C] (*infml esp US*) 1 tramp. 2 lazy person. **bum** v (*phr v*) **bum a'round** (*infml*) pass one's time doing nothing in particular.

bumble-bee /'bʌmblbiː/ n [C] large hairy bee with a loud hum.

bump /bʌmp/ v 1 [I, T] hit or strike (sth): *I* ~ *ed into the chair in the dark.* 2 [I] move with a rough action: *The old bus* ~ *ed along the mountain road.* 3 (*phr v*) **bump into to sb** (*infml*) meet sb by chance. **bump sb off** (*infml*) kill sb. **bump sth up** (*infml*) increase sth. **bump** n [C] 1 (dull sound of a) blow or knock. 2 uneven area on a road

surface. **3** swelling on the body.
bumpy /'bʌmpɪ/ adj (**-ier, -iest**) uneven.

bumper¹ /'bʌmpə(r)/ n [C] bar on the front and back of a motor vehicle to protect it from damage.

bumper² /'bʌmpə(r)/ adj unusually large: a ~ harvest.

bumpkin /'bʌmpkɪn/ n [C] (usu derog) awkward or simple person from the country.

bun /bʌn/ n [C] **1** small round sweet cake. **2** (esp woman's) hair twisted round into a tight knot at the back of the head.

bunch /bʌntʃ/ n [C] **1** number of small similar things fastened or growing together: a ~ of flowers/grapes. **2** (infml) group: They're an interesting ~ of people. **bunch** v [I, T] (together/up)) form into a bunch.

bundle /'bʌndl/ n **1** [C] number of things fastened or wrapped together: old clothes tied into a ~. **2 a bundle of sth** [sing] a mass of sth: He's a ~ of nerves, ie He is very nervous. **bundle** v **1** [T] (up)) make or tie into a bundle. **2** [I, T] go or send hurriedly or roughly: They ~d him into a taxi.

bung /bʌŋ/ n [C] stopper for closing the hole in a barrel or jar. **bung** v [T] **1** (Brit infml) throw or put roughly or carelessly. **2** up)) block or close (a hole).

bungalow /'bʌŋgələʊ/ n [C] house with only one storey.

bungle /'bʌŋgl/ v [I, T] do (sth) badly or clumsily.

bunion /'bʌnjən/ n [C] painful swelling, esp on sb's big toe.

bunk¹ /bʌŋk/ n [C] **1** narrow bed fixed to a wall, eg on a ship. **2** one of a pair of single beds fixed one above the other.

bunk² /bʌŋk/ n (idm) **do a 'bunk** (Brit infml) run away.

bunker /'bʌŋkə(r)/ n [C] **1** container for storing coal. **2** strongly built underground shelter for soldiers. **3** sandy hollow on a golf-course.

bunny /'bʌnɪ/ n [C] (pl **-ies**) (used by children) rabbit.

buoy /bɔɪ/ n [C] floating object attached to the sea bottom to show danger, rocks, etc. **buoy** v (phr v) **buoy sb/sth up** (a) keep sb afloat. (b) (fig) encourage sb.

buoyant /'bɔɪənt/ adj **1** able to float. **2** (fig) cheerful. **3** (fig) (of the stock market, etc) having a lot of trade and so keeping prices high. **buoyancy** /-ənsɪ/ n [U]. **buoyantly** adv.

burden /'bɜːdn/ n [C] **1** (fml) heavy load. **2** (fig) responsibility or duty that causes worry or is

hard to bear: the ~ of ta...
burden v [T] put a burden...
burdensome /-səm/ adj hard...
bear, causing worry.

bureau /'bjʊərəʊ/ n [C] (pl **-x** or **-s** /-rəʊz/) **1** (Brit) writing-desk with drawers. **2** (US) chest of drawers. **3** (esp US) government department. **4** office.

bureaucracy /bjʊə'rɒkrəsɪ/ n (pl **-ies**) **1** (a) [C] group of government officials who are appointed, not elected. (b) [U] system of government by such officials. **2** [U] (derog) unnecessary and complicated official rules. **bureaucrat** /'bjʊərəkræt/ n [C] (often derog) official who works in a government department. **bureaucratic** /ˌbjʊərə'krætɪk/ adj.

burglar /'bɜːglə(r)/ n [C] person who breaks into a building to steal things. **'burglar-proof** adj made so that burglars cannot break into it. **burglary** n [C, U] (pl **-ies**) (instance of the) crime of entering a building in order to steal. **burgle** (US **burglarize**) /'bɜːgl/ v break into (a building) to steal things.

burial /'berɪəl/ n [C, U] (ceremony of) burying a dead body.

burly /'bɜːlɪ/ adj (**-ier, -iest**) having a strong heavy body.

burn /bɜːn/ v (pt, pp ~**t** /bɜːnt/ or esp US ~**ed** /bɜːnd/) **1** [I] be on fire. **2** [T] destroy or injure by fire or acid: ~ old papers. **3** [T] use for heating or lighting: ~ coal in a fire. **4** [I, T] spoil (sth being cooked) with too much heat: Sorry, I've ~t the toast. **5** [I] (of sb's face) be red because of embarrassment. **6** [I] with)) be filled with anger, etc. **7** (phr v) **burn (sth) down** (cause sth to) be completely destroyed by fire. **burn (itself) out** (of a fire) stop burning because there is no more fuel. **burn oneself out** exhaust oneself or ruin one's health by working too hard. **burn sth out** destroy sth completely by burning: the ~t-out wreck of a car. **burn** n [C] injury or mark caused by burning. **burner** n [C] part of a cooker, heater, etc from which the flame comes. **burning** adj **1** intense: a ~ing thirst/desire. **2** very important; urgent: the ~ing question.

burnish /'bɜːnɪʃ/ v [T] polish by rubbing.

burp /bɜːp/ n [C], v [I] (infml) belch.

burrow /'bʌrəʊ/ n [C] hole made in the ground by rabbits, etc. **burrow** v [I, T] dig (a hole).

bursar /'bɜːsə(r)/ n [C] person

who manages the money in a school or college. **bursary** n [C] (pl **-ies**) grant given to a student.

burst /bɜːst/ v (pt, pp **burst**) 1 [I, T] break open or apart, esp because of pressure from inside: *The tyre ~ suddenly.* ○ *The river ~ its banks.* 2 [I] (*with*)// be full of sth to the point of breaking open: *She was ~ing with anger.* 3 (idm) **be bursting to do sth** be very eager to do sth. **burst (sth) 'open** open (sth) suddenly or violently. 4 (phr v **burst in on sb/sth** interrupt sb/ sth suddenly. **burst into sth** suddenly produce sth: *~ into tears/ laughter.* **burst into, out of, etc sth** move suddenly and forcefully in the direction that is mentioned. **burst out (a)** say suddenly and with feeling. **(b)** begin suddenly (doing sth): *~ out crying.* **burst** n [C] 1 bursting; explosion or split. 2 brief violent effort: *a ~ of energy.* 3 outbreak: *a ~ of gunfire.*

bury /'beri/ v (pt, pp **-ied**) [T] 1 put (a dead body) in a grave. 2 put underground; hide from view: *buried treasure* ○ *She buried her face in her hands.* 3 ~ **oneself** in concentrate deeply on sth. 4 (idm) **bury the 'hatchet** stop quarrelling.

bus /bʌs/ n [C] large motor vehicle that carries passengers. **bus** v (*-s-* also **-ss-**) [I, T] go or take by bus. **'bus-stop** n [C] regular stopping place for a bus.

bush /bʊʃ/ n 1 [C] low thickly-growing woody plant. 2 **the bush** [U] wild uncultivated land, eg in Australia or Africa. **bushy** adj (**-ier, -iest**) growing thickly: *~y eyebrows.*

business /'bɪznɪs/ n 1 [U] activity of buying and selling; commerce or trade. 2 [C] organization that sells goods or provides a service. 3 [C, U] one's usual occupation. 4 [U] duty; task. 5 [U] things that need to be dealt with. 6 [sing] matter; affair: *Let's forget the whole ~.* 7. (idm) **get down to 'business** start the work that must be done. **go out of 'business** become bankrupt. **have no 'business to do sth** have no right to do sth. **'business-like** adj well-organized; efficient. **'businessman, 'businesswoman** n [C] person who works in business.

busker /'bʌskə(r)/ n [C] (infml) person who plays music in the street, etc to try to earn money.

bust¹ /bʌst/ v (pt, pp **bust** or **~ed**) [T] (infml) break (sth); smash (sth). **bust** adj (infml) 1 broken. 2 (idm) **go bust** (of a business) become bankrupt.

bust² /bʌst/ n [C] 1 sculpture of a person's head and shoulders. 2 woman's breasts.

bustle /'bʌsl/ v [I] move busily and energetically. **bustle** n [U].

busy /'bɪzɪ/ adj (**-ier, -iest**) 1 having a lot to do; already working on sth: *I'm ~ all day so I won't be able to help you.* 2 full of activity: *a ~ day.* 3 (of a telephone line) in use. **busily** adv. **busy** v (pt, pp **-ied**) [T] ~ **oneself** keep oneself busy.

but¹ /bət; strong form bʌt/ conj (used for showing a contrast): *Tom went to the party, ~ his brother didn't.*

but² /bət; strong form bʌt/ prep 1 except: *nothing to eat ~ bread and cheese.* 2 (idm) **'but for sb/sth** except for sb/sth: *B~ for your help we should not have finished on time.*

but³ /bʌt, also bət/ adv (fml or dated) only: *We can ~ try.*

butcher /'bʊtʃə(r)/ n [C] 1 person whose job is killing animals for food or selling meat. 2 cruel murderer. **butcher** v [T] 1 kill and prepare (animals) for meat. 2 kill cruelly. **butchery** n [U] unnecessary cruel killing.

butler /'bʌtlə(r)/ n [C] chief male servant in a house.

butt¹ /bʌt/ n [C] 1 thicker end of a weapon, eg a rifle. 2 unburned end of a cigarette, etc.

butt² /bʌt/ n [C] large barrel.

butt³ /bʌt/ n [C] person who is often mocked or teased.

butt⁴ /bʌt/ v 1 [T] hit or push with the head. 2 (phr v) **butt in (on sb/ sth)** interrupt sb's conversation.

butter /'bʌtə(r)/ n [U] yellow fatty food made from cream, spread on bread, etc. **butter** v [T] 1 spread butter on. 2 (phr v) **butter sb up** (infml) flatter sb. **'buttercup** n [C] wild plant with small yellow flowers. **'butterscotch** n [U] hard sweet substance made by boiling sugar and butter together.

butterfly /'bʌtəflaɪ/ n [C] (pl **-ies**) insect with a long thin body and large colourful wings.

buttock /'bʌtək/ n [C, esp pl] either of the two fleshy rounded parts of the body on which a person sits.

button /'bʌtn/ n [C] 1 small round disc sewn onto a garment as a fastener. 2 small knob that is pressed to operate a machine, bell, etc. **button** v [I, T] fasten with buttons. **'buttonhole** n [C] 1 hole through which a button is passed. 2 flower worn on a coat or jacket.

'buttonhole v [T] stop (sb) and make him/her listen to one.

buttress /'bʌtrɪs/ n [C] support built against a wall. **buttress** v [T] support or strengthen.

buxom /'bʌksəm/ adj (of a woman) large and healthy-looking.

buy /baɪ/ v (pt, pp **bought** /bɔːt/) [T] 1 get (sth) by paying money. 2 (infml) accept or believe. 3 (phr v) **buy sb out** pay sb to give up a share in a business so that one can gain control. **buy** n [C] thing bought: a good ~. **buyer** n [C] person who buys, esp one who chooses goods to be sold in a large shop.

buzz /bʌz/ v 1 [I] make a humming sound. 2 [I] (with/) be full of excited talk. 3 [I] move quickly and busily. 4 [T] call (sb) with a buzzer. 5 (phr v) **buzz 'off** (infml) go away. **buzz** n 1 [C] buzzing sound. 2 [sing] (infml esp US) feeling of pleasure or excitement. 3 (idm) **give sb a 'buzz** (infml) telephone sb. **buzzer** n [C] electrical device that produces a buzzing sound.

buzzard /'bʌzəd/ n [C] kind of large hawk.

by¹ /baɪ/ prep 1 at the side of; near: Sit by me. 2 through, along: come in by the back door. 3 past: She walked by me. 4 not later than: finish the work by tomorrow. 5 during: The enemy attacked by night. 6 through the action, power or means of: The soldiers were shot by terrorists. ○ a play by Shaw ○ pay by cheque ○ travel by train. 7 as a result of; because of: meet by chance. 8 (showing a part of the body, etc touched): take sb by the hand. 9 using (sth) as a standard or unit: get paid by the hour ○ sell material by the metre. 10 in units: The children came in two by two. 11 (showing the dimensions of a rectangle, etc): a room 18 feet by 20 feet. 12 to the extent of: The bullet missed him by ten millimetres. 13 according to: By law, his parents should be informed.

by² /baɪ/ adv 1 past: drive by. 2 near.

bye /baɪ/ (also **bye-bye** /ˌbaɪˈbaɪ/) interj (infml) goodbye.

by-election /'baɪɪlekʃn/ n [C] election of a new Member of Parliament in a place when the member has died or resigned.

bygone /'baɪɡɒn/ adj past: in ~ days. **bygones** n (idm) **let ˌbygones be 'bygones** forgive and forget past quarrels.

by-law (also **bye-law**) /'baɪlɔː/ n [C] law made by a local authority.

bypass /'baɪpɑːs; US -pæs/ n [C] main road that goes round a town instead of through it. **bypass** v [T] 1 provide with a bypass. 2 avoid (sth), using a bypass: (fig) ~ the problem.

by-product /'baɪprɒdʌkt/ n [C] something made during the manufacture of some other product.

bystander /'baɪstændə(r)/ n [C] person standing near, but not taking part, when sth happens.

byte /baɪt/ n [C] (computing) fixed number of binary digits, often representing a single character, used to measure a computer's memory.

byword /'baɪwɜːd/ n [C] 1 for// person or thing that is well-known for a particular quality. 2 common word or expression.

C c

C, c /siː/ n [C] (pl **C's, c's**) /siːz/) the third letter of the English alphabet.

C abbr 1 Celsius. 2 Roman numeral for 100.

c abbr 1 cent(s). 2 century. 3 (also **ca**) (esp before dates) about.

cab /kæb/ n [C] 1 taxi. 2 part of a railway engine, lorry, etc where the driver sits.

cabaret /'kæbəreɪ; US ˌkæbəˈreɪ/ n [U, C] singing and dancing provided in a restaurant or nightclub.

cabbage /'kæbɪdʒ/ n [C, U] vegetable with a round head of thick green leaves.

cabin /'kæbɪn/ n [C] 1 small room or compartment in a ship or aircraft. 2 small wooden hut. **'cabin cruiser** n [C] = CRUISER 2 (CRUISE).

cabinet /'kæbɪnɪt/ n [C] 1 piece of furniture with drawers or shelves for storing things. 2 **the Cabinet** [also sing with pl v] group of chief ministers of a government.

cable /'keɪbl/ n 1 [C, U] thick strong rope. 2 [C] bundle of wires for carrying electricity. 3 [C] telegram. **cable** v [T] send (a message, etc) to (sb) by telegram. **'cable-car** n [C] car supported and pulled by a moving cable, for taking people up a mountain, etc. **cable 'television** n [U] system of broadcasting television programmes by wires to subscribers.

cache /kæʃ/ n [C] hidden store: a drugs ~.

cackle /'kækl/ n 1 [U] loud cluck-ing noise that a hen makes. 2 [C] loud laugh. **cackle** v [I] 1 (of a hen) make a cackle. 2 (of a person) laugh noisily.

cactus /'kæktəs/ n [C] (pl -es or -ti /-taɪ/) plant with a thick fleshy stem and usu prickles.

cadet /kə'det/ n [C] young person training in the police or armed for-ces.

cadge /kædʒ/ v [I, T] (infml) (try to) get by asking, often unreason-ably.

café /'kæfeɪ; US kæ'feɪ/ n [C] small restaurant where light meals and drinks are served.

cafeteria /ˌkæfə'tɪərɪə/ n [C] res-taurant in which customers col-lect their own food from a counter.

caffeine /'kæfi:n/ n [U] stimulat-ing drug found in tea-leaves and coffee beans.

cage /keɪdʒ/ n [C] structure of bars or wires in which birds or animals are kept. **cage** v [T] put in a cage.

cagey /'keɪdʒɪ/ adj secretive.

cagoule /kə'gu:l/ n [C] light long waterproof jacket with a hood.

cairn /keən/ n [C] pile of stones as a landmark(1) or memorial.

cajole /kə'dʒəʊl/ v [T] persuade (sb) by flattery or deceit.

cake /keɪk/ n 1 [C, U] sweet food made from a mixture of flour, eggs, butter, etc baked in an oven. 2 [C] other food mixture cooked in a round flat shape: *fish ~s*. 3 [C] shaped piece of a substance: *a ~ of soap*. **cake** v [T] cover thickly (with mud, etc).

calamity /kə'læmətɪ/ n [C] (pl -ies) great disaster.

calcium /'kælsɪəm/ n [U] soft white metallic element.

calculable /'kælkjʊləbl/ adj that can be calculated.

calculate /'kælkjʊleɪt/ v 1 [I, T] find out by working with num-bers: *~ the cost*. 2 (idm) **be cal-culated to do sth** be intended to do sth: *~d to attract attention*. **cal-culating** adj (derog) using deceit or trickery to get what one wants. **calculation** /ˌkælkjʊ'leɪʃn/ n [C, U]. **calculator** n [C] small elec-tronic device for making calcula-tions.

calendar /'kælɪndə(r)/ n [C] 1 chart showing the days, weeks and months of a particular year. 2 system by which time is divided: *the Muslim ~*.

calf¹ /kɑ:f; US kæf/ n (pl calves /kɑ:vz; US kævz/) 1 [C] (a) young of cattle. (b) young of the seal, whale and certain other animals.

2 (also **'calfskin**) leather from the skin of a calf.

calf² /kɑ:f; US kæf/ n [C] (pl calves /kɑ:vz; US kævz/) back of the human leg, between the knee and the ankle.

calibre (US -ber) /'kælɪbə(r)/ n 1 [U] quality; ability: *Her work is of the highest ~*. 2 [C] diameter of the inside of a tube or gun-barrel.

calipers = CALIPERS.

call¹ /kɔ:l/ v 1 [I, T] say (sth) loud-ly; shout. 2 [T] order or ask (sb) to come by telephoning, shouting, etc: *~ the police*. 3 [I] make a short visit. 4 [I, T] telephone (sb). 5 [T] order (sth) to take place; an-nounce: *~ a meeting/election/strike*. 6 [T] name: *Her husband is ~ed Dick*. 7 [T] consider to be: *I ~ his behaviour very selfish*. 8 [T] wake: *Please ~ me at 7 o'clock*. 9 (idm) **call sb's bluff** invite sb to do what he/she is threatening to do. **call it a day** (infml) decide to stop doing sth. **call sth to mind** ⇨ MIND¹. **call sb 'names** insult sb. **call the 'tune** (infml) be in a posi-tion to control a situation. 10 (phr v) **call by** visit for a short time when passing. **call for sb/sth (a)** visit a house, etc to collect sb/sth. (b) demand or need sth: *the prob-lem ~s for immediate action*. **call sb in** ask sb to come and help one. **call sb/sth off** order (eg dogs or soldiers) to stop attacking or searching. **call sth off** cancel (a planned event): *The trip was ~ed off*. **call on sb** visit sb for a short time. **call on/upon sb** formally ask or invite sb (to do sth). **call sb out (a)** ask sb to help in an emer-gency: *~ out the fire brigade*. (b) order sb to go on strike. **call sb up (a)** (esp US) telephone sb. (b) order sb to join the armed forces. **caller** n [C] person who makes a short visit or a telephone call. **'call-up** n [U, C] order to join the armed forces.

call² /kɔ:l/ n 1 [C] shout; cry. 2 [C] telephone conversation. 3 [C] characteristic cry of a bird. 4 [C] short visit. 5 [C] order or invita-tion to come. 6 [U] need or demand for sth. 7 (idm) **(be) on 'call** (eg of doctor) available for work if needed. **'call-box** n [C] = TELE-PHONE-BOX (TELEPHONE). **'call-girl** n [C] prostitute who makes ap-pointments by telephone.

calligraphy /kə'lɪɡrəfɪ/ n [U] (art of) beautiful handwriting.

calling /'kɔ:lɪŋ/ n [C] profession or trade.

calipers (also **callipers**) /'kælɪpəz/ n [pl] 1 instrument for measuring the diameter of round objects. **2** metal supports for weak or injured legs.

callous /'kæləs/ *adj* cruelly unkind and insensitive.

callow /'kæləʊ/ *adj* (*derog*) young and inexperienced.

callus /'kæləs/ *n* [C] area of thick hardened skin.

calm /kɑːm *also*; *US* kɑːlm/ *adj* **1** not excited; quiet; untroubled. **2 (a)** (of the sea) without large waves. **(b)** (of the weather) not windy. **calm** *n* [U, C] calm state or period. **calm** *v* [I, T] (*down*)// become or make calm. **calmly** *adj*.

calmness *n* [U].

calorie /'kælərɪ/ *n* [C] **1** unit of heat. **2** unit of the energy value of food.

calve /kɑːv; *US* kæv/ *v* [I] give birth to a calf.

calves *pl* of CALF[1,2].

calypso /kə'lɪpsəʊ/ *n* [C] (*pl* ~s) kind of West Indian song.

camber /'kæmbə(r)/ *n* [C] slight rise in the middle of a road surface.

camcorder /'kæmkɔːdə(r)/ *n* [C] portable video camera with a built-in video recorder.

came *pt* of COME.

camel /'kæml/ *n* [C] animal with a long neck and one or two humps on its back.

cameo /'kæmɪəʊ/ *n* [C] (*pl* ~s) **1** hard stone with a raised design, used as an ornament. **2** short piece of fine descriptive acting or writing.

camera /'kæmərə/ *n* [C] apparatus for taking photographs or moving pictures.

camouflage /'kæməflɑːʒ/ *n* [C, U] (use of) colour, nets, branches, etc that help to hide sb/sth. **camouflage** *v* [T] hide (sb/sth) by camouflage.

camp /kæmp/ *n* [C] **1** place where people live in tents or huts for a short time. **2** group of people with the same esp political ideas. **camp** *v* [I] put up a tent; spend a holiday in a tent: *We go ~ing every summer.* **camper** *n* [C] person who camps.

campaign /kæm'peɪn/ *n* [C] **1** series of planned activities with a particular aim: *an advertising ~.* **2** series of military operations in a war. **campaign** *v* [I] take part in a campaign. **campaigner** *n* [C].

campus /'kæmpəs/ *n* [C] grounds of a university, college or school.

can[1] /kən; strong form kæn/ *modal v* (*neg* **cannot** /'kænɒt/, contracted form **can't** /kɑːnt; *US* kænt/, *pt* **could** /kəd; strong

form kʊd/, *neg* **could not**, contracted form **couldn't** /'kʊdnt/) **1** be able to or know how to: *C ~ you ski?* **2** (used of verbs of perception): *C ~ you hear that cuckoo?* **3** be allowed to: *You ~ borrow my car if you want to.* **4** (indicating requests): *C ~ you help me?* **5** (showing possibility in the present): *That ~'t be true!*

can[2] /kæn/ *n* [C] **(a)** metal container for food or liquids: *a ~ of beans.* **(b)** contents of such a container. **can** *v* (-nn-) [T] put (food, etc) in a can. **cannery** *n* [C] (*pl* -ies) place where food is canned.

canal /kə'næl/ *n* [C] man-made waterway for boats to travel along or for irrigation.

canary /kə'neərɪ/ *n* [C] (*pl* -ies) small yellow bird, often kept in a cage as a pet.

cancel /'kænsl/ *v* (-ll-; *US* -l-) [T] **1** say that (sth already arranged) will not be done or happen: *The meeting was ~led.* **2** cross out (sth written); make a mark on (eg a postage stamp). **3** (*phr v*) **cancel (sth) out** be equal (to sth) in effect; balance. **cancellation** /,kænsə'leɪʃn/ *n* [C, U].

cancer /'kænsə(r)/ *n* **1** [C, U] diseased growth in the body. **2 Cancer** ⇨ TROPIC. **cancerous** *adj* of or like cancer.

candid /'kændɪd/ *adj* not hiding one's thoughts; frank: *a ~ discussion.* **candidly** *adj*.

candidate /'kændɪdət; *US* -deɪt/ *n* [C] **1** person being considered for a job or in an election. **2** person taking an examination.

candied /'kændɪd/ *adj* having a covering of sugar.

candle /'kændl/ *n* [C] stick of wax with a string (= WICK) through it, which gives out light when it burns. **'candlestick** *n* [C] holder for a candle.

candour (*US* **-dor**) /'kændə(r)/ *n* [U] quality of being candid.

candy /'kændɪ/ *n* (*pl* -ies esp *US*) **1** [U] sweets or chocolate. **2** [C] sweet or chocolate.

cane /keɪn/ *n* **1 (a)** [C] hollow stem of certain plants, eg bamboo or sugar-cane. **(b)** [U] such stems used as a material for making furniture. **2** [C] length of cane, etc, used as a support, for a plant or as a walking-stick. **3 the cane** [sing] punishment of children by being hit with a cane. **cane** *v* [T] hit with a cane.

canine /'keɪnaɪn/ *adj* of or like a dog.

canister /'kænɪstə(r)/ *n* [C] **1** small (usu metal) box with a lid. **2**

cylinder fired from a gun.

canker /'kæŋkə(r)/ n [U] **1** disease of trees. **2** disease that causes ulcers. **3** (fig) bad influence that spreads.

cannabis /'kænəbɪs/ n [U] drug made from the hemp plant, smoked for its intoxicating effect.

cannery ⇨ CAN².

cannibal /'kænɪbl/ n [C] **(a)** person who eats human flesh. **(b)** animal that eats its own kind. **cannibalism** /-bəlɪzəm/ n [U]. **cannibalize** /-bəlaɪz/ v [T] use (a machine, vehicle, etc) to provide spare parts for another.

cannon /'kænən/ n [C] (pl **cannon**) **1** old kind of large heavy gun firing solid metal balls. **2** automatic gun firing shells(3) from an aircraft.

cannot ⇨ CAN¹.

canoe /kə'nuː/ n [C] light narrow boat moved by a paddle. **canoe** v [I] travel by canoe. **canoeist** n [C] person who paddles a canoe.

canon /'kænən/ n [C] **1** priest with special duties in a cathedral. **2** (fml) general standard or principle: offend the ~s of good taste. **canonical** /kə'nɒnɪkl/ adj according to canon law. **canonize** /'kænənaɪz/ v [T] officially declare (sb) to be a saint. ˌcanon 'law n [U] church law.

canopy /'kænəpɪ/ n [C] (pl **-ies**) **1** (usu cloth) covering over a bed, throne, etc. **2** cover for the cockpit of an aircraft.

cant /kænt/ n [U] insincere talk.

can't cannot. ⇨ CAN¹.

cantankerous /kæn'tæŋkərəs/ adj bad-tempered; quarrelsome.

canteen /kæn'tiːn/ n [C] **1** place, eg in a factory, office or school where food is served. **2** (Brit) box containing a set of knives, forks and spoons.

canter /'kæntə(r)/ n [C, usu sing] horse's movement that is faster than a trot but slower than a gallop. **canter** v [I, T] move at a canter.

cantilever /'kæntɪliːvə(r)/ n [C] beam or bracket extending from a wall or base eg to support a bridge.

canvas /'kænvəs/ n **(a)** [U] strong course cloth used for tents, sails, oil-painting, etc. **(b)** [C] (piece of this for an) oil-painting.

canvass /'kænvəs/ v [I, T] go round an area asking (people) for (political support or opinions). **canvasser** n [C].

canyon /'kænjən/ n [C] deep valley.

cap /kæp/ n [C] **1** soft flat hat without a brim. **2** top covering eg

on a bottle or tube of toothpaste.

cap v (-pp-) [T] **1** put a cap on; cover the top of. **2** do or say sth better than sth previously said or done. **3** choose (a player) for a national team.

capability /ˌkeɪpə'bɪlətɪ/ n (pl **-ies**) **1** [U, C] quality of being able to do sth; ability: a country's nuclear ~, ie power to fight with nuclear weapons. **2** [usu pl] undeveloped ability.

capable /'keɪpəbl/ adj **1** of// having the ability necessary for sth;: You are ~ of producing better work than this. **2** having ability; clever: a ~ person. **capably** adv.

capacity /kə'pæsətɪ/ n (pl **-ies**) **1** [U] amount that sth can hold or produce: a hall with a seating ~ of 750. **2** [C, U] power or ability. **3** [C] position: in my ~ as manager.

cape¹ /keɪp/ n [C] loose sleeveless garment like a short cloak.

cape² /keɪp/ n [C] piece of land that projects into the sea.

capillary /kə'pɪlərɪ; US 'kæplərɪ/ n [C] (pl **-ies**) small narrow tube, esp a very small blood-vessel.

capital /'kæpɪtl/ n **1** [C] town or city that is the centre of government of a country, etc. **2** [U] wealth used to produce more wealth; money with which a business is started. **3** [C] (also **capital letter**) large letter, eg A. **4** (idm) **make capital (out) of sth** use (a situation) to one's advantage. **capital** adj involving punishment by death.

capitalism /'kæpɪtəlɪzəm/ n [U] economic system in which a country's trade and industry are controlled by private owners and not the state. **capitalist** /-lɪst/ n [C] **1** person who supports capitalism. **2** person who owns capital(2). **capitalist** adj.

capitalize /'kæpɪtəlaɪz/ v **1** [T] write with capital letters. **2** [T] convert into capital(2). **3** (phr v) **capitalize on sth** use sth to one's own advantage.

capitulate /kə'pɪtʃʊleɪt/ v [I] (to)// surrender to sb. **capitulation** /kəˌpɪtʃʊ'leɪʃn/ n [U].

Capricorn ⇨ TROPIC.

capsize /kæp'saɪz; US 'kæpsaɪz/ adj [I, T] (of a boat) (cause to) turn over.

capstan /'kæpstən/ n [C] upright post turned to raise a ship's anchor.

capsule /'kæpsjuːl; US 'kæpsl/ n [C] **1** very small container of medicine that is swallowed. **2** compartment for people or instruments in a spacecraft.

captain /'kæptɪn/ n [C] **1** leader of a sports team. **2** person in charge of a ship or aircraft. **3** middle-ranking officer in the army. **captain** v [T] be captain of.

caption /'kæpʃn/ n [C] words painted with a picture or cartoon in order to explain it.

captivate /'kæptɪveɪt/ v [T] fascinate: ~d by her beauty.

captive /'kæptɪv/ n [C], adj (person or animal) taken prisoner. **captivity** /kæp'tɪvətɪ/ n [U] state of being captive.

captor /'kæptə(r)/ n [C] person who captures a person or animal.

capture /'kæptʃə(r)/ v [T] **1** take as a prisoner. **2** take or win by force. **3** succeed in representing in a picture, film, etc. **capture** n [U] act of capturing. **2** [C] person or thing captured.

car /kɑː(r)/ n [C] **1** motor vehicle for carrying passengers. **2** railway carriage: a dining-~. **'car-boot sale** n [C] outdoor sale at which people sell unwanted goods from the boots of their cars. **'car park** n [C] area where cars may be parked.

carafe /kə'ræf/ n [C] glass container in which water or wine is served.

caramel /'kærəmel/ n **1** [U] burnt sugar used for colouring and flavouring food. **2** [C] chewy sweet of boiled sugar.

carat /'kærət/ n [C] **1** unit of weight for precious stones. **2** measure of the purity of gold.

caravan /'kærəvæn/ n [C] **1** small home on wheels, pulled by a car. **2** covered cart for living in. **3** group of people and animals travelling across a desert.

carbohydrate /ˌkɑːbə'haɪdreɪt/ n [C, U] substance found in food, eg sugar and potatoes, that provides energy.

carbon /'kɑːbən/ n **1** [U] non-metallic element found in diamonds, coal and all living matter. **2** [C] = CARBON COPY. **3** [C, U] = CARBON PAPER. **,carbon 'copy** n [C] copy made with carbon paper. **'carbon paper** n [C, U] (sheet of) thin paper coated with a coloured substance, used for making copies.

carbuncle /'kɑːbʌŋkl/ n [C] large painful swelling under the skin.

carburettor /ˌkɑːbə'retə(r)/ (US -t- /US 'kɑːrbəreɪtər/) n [C] part of a car engine in which petrol and air are mixed.

carcass /'kɑːkəs/ n [C] dead body of an animal.

card /kɑːd/ n **1** [C, U] piece of stiff paper with various purposes: a 'Christmas ~ ○ a membership ~ ○ a 'post~. **2** [C] = PLAYING-CARD (PLAY²). **3** (idm) lay/put one's **'cards on the table** be honest about one's intentions. on the cards (infml) likely.

cardboard /'kɑːdbɔːd/ n [U] thick stiff kind of paper.

cardiac /'kɑːdiæk/ adj of the heart.

cardigan /'kɑːdɪgən/ n [C] knitted woollen jacket with buttons or a zip at the front.

cardinal¹ /'kɑːdɪnl/ adj (fml) most important. **cardinal** (also **,cardinal 'number**) n [C] whole number representing a quantity, eg 1, 2, or 5.

cardinal² /'kɑːdɪnl/ n [C] senior Roman Catholic priest.

care¹ /keə(r)/ n **1** [U] serious attention or thought: arrange the flowers with ~ ○ Take ~ when crossing the road. **2** [U] protection: The child was left in his sister's ~. **3** [C, U] worry or anxiety: without a ~ in the world. **4** (idm) take care of oneself/sb/sth (a) make sure that one/sb is safe and well. (b) be responsible for sb/sth. **take sb into care** put (esp a child) in a home owned by a local authority for proper treatment. **'carefree** adj without worries. **careful** adj **1** (of a person) cautious; thinking of what one does. **2** done with care: a ~ful piece of work. **carefulness** n [U]. **careless** adj **1** not taking care; thoughtless. **2** resulting from lack of care. **3** unconcerned; casual. **carelessly** adv. **carelessness** n [U].

care² /keə(r)/ v [I] **1** (about)// be worried, concerned or interested (about sth): I ~ about this country's future. **2** for; to// (fml) wish or like (to do) sth: Would you ~ to go for a walk? **3** (phr v) **care for sb** (a) take care of sb; look after. (b) love or love sb.

career /kə'rɪə(r)/ n [C] **1** profession or occupation. **2** progress through life. **career** v [I] rush wildly: ~ down the hill.

caress /kə'res/ n [C] loving touch. **caress** v [T] give a caress to.

caretaker /'keəteɪkə(r)/ n [C] person whose job is to look after a building.

cargo /'kɑːgəʊ/ n [C, U] (pl ~es; US ~s) goods carried in a ship or aircraft.

caricature /'kærɪkətjʊə(r)/ n [C] picture or description of a person that emphasizes certain features to cause amusement or ridicule.

caricature v [T] make a caricature of (sb).

carnage /'kɑːnɪdʒ/ n [U] killing of a lot of people.

carnal /'kɑːnl/ adj (fml) of the body; sexual or sensual.

carnation /kɑː'neɪʃn/ n [C] plant with sweet-smelling white, pink or red flowers.

carnival /'kɑːnɪvl/ n [C] public festival.

carnivore /'kɑːnɪvɔː(r)/ n [C] flesh-eating animal. **carnivorous** (/kɑː'nɪvərəs/) adj.

carol /'kærəl/ n [C] joyful song, esp a Christmas hymn.

carp[1] /kɑːp/ n [C] (pl carp) large freshwater fish.

carp[2] /kɑːp/ v [I] (at/about)(I) complain continually about unimportant matters.

carpenter /'kɑːpəntə(r)/ n [C] person whose job is to make and repair wooden objects. **carpentry** (/-trɪ/) n [U] work of a carpenter.

carpet /'kɑːpɪt/ n [C] thick piece of cloth for covering floors. **carpet** v [T] cover with or as if with a carpet.

carriage /'kærɪdʒ/ n 1 [C] railway coach for carrying passengers. 2 [C] vehicle pulled by a horse. 3 [U] (cost of) transporting goods. 4 [C] moving part of a machine: *a typewriter ~.* '**carriageway** n [C] part of a motorway, etc on which vehicles travel.

carrier /'kærɪə(r)/ n [C] 1 person or company that carries goods. 2 person or animal that can pass a disease to others without suffering from it. '**carrier bag** n [C] paper or plastic bag for carrying shopping.

carrot /'kærət/ n [C] long orange-coloured root vegetable.

carry /'kærɪ/ v (pt, pp -ied) 1 (a) support the weight of and take from place to place: *~ the boxes upstairs.* (b) support the weight of: *The pillars ~ the whole roof.* 2 [T] have with one: *I never ~ much money.* 3 [T] (of pipes, wires, etc) contain and direct (water, oil, electricity, etc). 4 [T] have as a result: *Power carries great responsibility.* 5 [T] (of a newspaper) include or contain (eg a story). 6 [T] (usu passive) approve in a vote: *The proposal was carried.* 7 [I] (of a sound) be able to be heard at a distance: *His voice doesn't ~ very far.* 8. (idm) **be/get carried away** become so excited that one loses self-control. 9 (phr v) **carry sth off** win sth. **carry on (with/doing sth)** continue doing sth: *~ on reading.* **carry on (with sb)**

(infml) have an affair(4) with sb. **carry sth on** take part in sth; conduct. **carry sth out** do sth; fulfil or complete: *~ out a plan.* **carry sth through** complete sth successfully. **carry sb through sth** help sb to survive (a difficult period).

cart /kɑːt/ n [C] 1 vehicle for carrying loads, usu pulled by a horse. 2 (idm) **put the cart before the horse** do things in the wrong order. **cart** /kɑːt/ v 1 carry in a cart. 2 (infml) carry: *~ing parcels around.* '**cart-horse** n [C] large strong horse used for heavy work. '**cart-wheel** n [C] sideways somersault with arms and legs stretched out.

carte blanche /ˌkɑːt 'blɒnʃ/ n [C] complete freedom.

cartilage /'kɑːtɪlɪdʒ/ n [U] strong white flexible tissue attached to the bones of animals.

carton /'kɑːtn/ n [C] cardboard or plastic box.

cartoon /kɑː'tuːn/ n [C] 1 amusing drawing or series of drawings in a newspaper, etc. 2 film made by photographing a series of drawings. **cartoonist** n [C] person who draws cartoons.

cartridge /'kɑːtrɪdʒ/ n [C] 1 tube or case containing explosive with a bullet, for firing from a gun. 2 part of a record-player that holds the stylus. 3 small sealed container: *an ink ~.*

carve /kɑːv/ v [I, T] 1 form (sth) by cutting away material from stone or wood: *~ one's initials on a tree.* 2 cut (cooked meat) into slices. 3 (phr v) **carve sth out** build (eg one's career) by hard work. **carver** n [C] person who carves. **carving** n [C] something carved in stone, etc. '**carving knife** n [C] large sharp knife used for carving meat.

cascade /kæ'skeɪd/ n [C] waterfall. **cascade** v [I] fall like a cascade.

case[1] /keɪs/ n 1 [C] example of the occurrence of sth: *a clear ~ of blackmail* ○ *In most ~s, no extra charge is made.* 2 the **case** [sing] actual state of affairs: *If that is the ~, you will have to work harder.* 3 [C] instance of a disease or injury. 4 [C] matter being investigated by the police. 5 [C] (a) matter to be decided in a law-court. (b) [usu sing] set of facts, etc to support or oppose one side in a discussion, etc. 6 [U, C] form of a word that shows its relationship to another word. 7 (idm) **a case in point** example that is relevant to the matter being discussed. **in any case**

whatever happens. **in case of sth** if sth happens: *In ~ of emergency, phone the police.* **in 'that case** if that is the state of affairs. **(just) in case** because of the possibility of sth happening: *Take an umbrella in ~ it rains.* **,case** 'history *n* [C] record of a person's background, health, etc.

case² /keɪs/ *n* [C] **1** box or other container. **2** suitcase. **case** *v* [T] enclose in a case.

casement /'keɪsmənt/ *n* [C] window that opens like a door.

cash /kæʃ/ *n* [U] **1** money in coins or notes. **2** (*infml*) money in any form. **cash o 1** [T] exchange (eg a cheque) for cash. **2** (phr v) **cash in on sth** take advantage of sth; profit from sth. **'cash crop** *n* [C] crop grown for selling. **'cash dispenser** *n* [C] machine outside a bank from which cash can be obtained when a personal card is inserted and a code-number keyed. **'cash register** *n* [C] machine in a shop for recording and storing cash received.

cashew /'kæʃuː/ *n* [C] (tropical American tree with a) small kidney-shaped nut.

cashier /kæ'ʃɪə(r)/ *n* [C] person whose job is to receive and pay out money in a bank, shop, etc.

cashmere /'kæʃmɪə(r)/ *n* [U] fine soft wool.

casing /'keɪsɪŋ/ *n* [C] (esp protective) covering.

casino /kə'siːnəʊ/ *n* [C] (*pl* ~s) building or room for gambling and other entertainments.

cask /kɑːsk; *US* kæsk/ *n* [C] barrel for liquids.

casket /'kɑːskɪt; *US* 'kæs-/ *n* [C] **1** small box to hold jewels, letters, etc. **2** (*US*) coffin.

cassava /kə'sɑːvə/ *n* [C, U] (tropical plant with) starchy roots eaten as food.

casserole /'kæsərəʊl/ *n* (a) [C] covered dish in which food is cooked. (b) [C, U] food so cooked.

cassette /kə'set/ *n* [C] small sealed case containing magnetic tape or film.

cassock /'kæsək/ *n* [C] long outer garment worn by certain clergymen.

cast¹ /kɑːst; *US* kæst/ *v* (*pt, pp* **cast**) [T] **1** throw; allow to fall: *~ a net* ○ *Snakes ~ their skins.* ○ (*fig*) *The tree ~ a long shadow.* ○ *~ a glance at sb* ○ *~ doubt on his claims.* **2** make (an object) by pouring metal into a mould: *~ a statue.* **3** give (an actor) a part in a play. **4** (idm) **cast aspersions on sb/sth** (*fml*) make unkind or damaging

remarks about sb/sth. **cast an eye/one's eyes over sth** look at or examine sth quickly. **cast light on sth** ⇨ LIGHT¹. **cast lots** ⇨ LOT³. **5** (phr v) **cast sb/sth aside** get rid of sb/sth. **cast (sth) off** untie the ropes (of a boat). **cast sth off** get rid of sth. **casting** *n* [C] object made by pouring metal into a mould. **,casting 'vote** *n* [C] vote given to decide a matter when votes on each side are equal. **cast 'iron** *n* [U] hard alloy of iron made by casting in a mould. **cast-iron** *adj* **1** made of cast iron. **2** (*fig*) very strong: *a ~-iron excuse.* **'cast-off** *n* [C, usu *pl*], *adj* (garment) no longer wanted by original owner.

cast² /kɑːst; *US* kæst/ *n* [C] **1** all the actors in a play, etc. **2** act of throwing sth. **3** (a) object made by pouring or pressing soft material into a mould. (b) mould used for this.

castanets /,kæstə'nets/ *n* [pl] pair of shell-shaped pieces of wood, etc clicked together with the fingers.

castaway /'kɑːstəweɪ/ *n* [C] shipwrecked person.

caste /kɑːst/ *n* [C] one of the Hindu social classes.

castigate /'kæstɪgeɪt/ *v* [T] (*fml*) criticize severely.

castle /'kɑːsl; *US* 'kæsl/ *n* [C] **1** old large building with thick walls, used for protection from enemies. **2** chess piece.

castor (also **caster**) /'kɑːstə(r); *US* 'kæs-/ *n* [C] **1** small wheel fixed to a chair, etc. **2** small container for sugar, with holes at the top. **,castor 'sugar** *n* [U] very fine white sugar.

castor oil /,kɑːstər 'ɔɪl; *US* 'kæstər ɔɪl/ *n* [U] thick yellowish oil used as a medicine.

castrate /kæ'streɪt; *US* 'kæstreɪt/ *v* [T] remove the testicles of (a male animal). **castration** /kæ'streɪʃn/ *n* [U].

casual /'kæʒʊəl/ *adj* **1** informal; not serious: *~ clothes.* **2** happening by chance: *a ~ meeting.* **3** not permanent: *~ work.* **casually** *adv*.

casualty /'kæʒʊəltɪ/ *n* [C] (*pl* -ies) person injured or killed in war or an accident.

cat /kæt/ *n* [C] (a) small furry animal often kept as a pet. (b) wild animal, eg lion or tiger, related to this. **'cat burglar** *n* [C] burglar who enters buildings by climbing up walls, etc. **'catcall** *n* [C] loud shrill whistle expressing disapproval. **'catnap** *n* [C] short sleep.

catacombs /'kætəkuːmz; *US* -kəʊmz/ *n* [pl] series of underground tunnels for burying dead bodies.

catalogue (US also **-log**) /'kætəlɒg; US -lɔːg/ n [C] list of items, eg goods for sale. **catalogue** v [T] list in a catalogue.

catalyst /'kætəlɪst/ n [C] something that speeds up or causes a change without itself changing.

catapult /'kætəpʌlt/ n [C] Y-shaped stick with a piece of elastic, for shooting stones, etc. **catapult** v [T] shoot (as if) from a catapult.

cataract /'kætərækt/ n [C] 1 large steep waterfall. 2 disease of the eye, causing blindness.

catarrh /kə'tɑː(r)/ n [C] inflammation in the nose and throat, causing a flow of liquid.

catastrophe /kə'tæstrəfi/ n [C] sudden great disaster or misfortune. **catastrophic** /ˌkætə'strɒfɪk/ adj.

catch¹ /kætʃ/ v (pt, pp **caught** /kɔːt/) 1 [T] stop and hold (sth moving) esp in the hands: ~ a ball. 2 [T] capture; seize: ~ a thief. 3 [T] find or discover (sb doing sth): ~ sb stealing. 4 [T] be in time for and get on (a train, etc). 5 [I, T] (cause to) become trapped: I caught my fingers in the door. 6 [T] become ill with: ~ a cold. 7 [T] hear (sth); understand: I didn't quite ~ your name. 8 [T] hit. 9 (idm) be **caught 'up in** sth be involved in sth. **catch sb's at'tention/'eye** attract sb's attention. **catch sb's fancy** ⇒ FANCY¹. **catch 'fire** begin to burn. **catch sb 'napping** (infml) find sb not paying attention. **catch sb red-'handed** discover sb in the act of doing wrong. **catch sight of sb/sth** see sb/sth for a moment. 10 (phr v) **,catch 'on** (infml) become popular. **,catch 'on (to sth)** (infml) understand sth. **,catch sb 'out** show that sb is ignorant or doing wrong. **,catch 'up (with sb)**, **catch sb 'up** reach the same level as sb. **,catch 'up on** sth spend extra time doing sth. **catching** adj (of a disease) infectious. **'catchment ,area** /'kætʃmənt/ n [C] area from which people are sent to a particular school, hospital, etc. **'catch-phrase** n [C] phrase used often and by many people (often for a short period). **catchy** adj (-ier, -iest) (of a tune) easy to remember.

catch² /kætʃ/ n [C] 1 act of catching sth, esp a ball. 2 (amount of) sth caught. 3 device for fastening sth. 4 hidden difficulty: There must be a ~ in this somewhere.

categorical /ˌkætə'gɒrɪkl; US -'gɔːr-/ adj (of a statement) unconditional; absolute. **categorically** /-klɪ/ adv.

category /'kætəgərɪ; US -gɔːrɪ/ n [C] (pl **-ies**) group in a complete system; class. **categorize** /-gəraɪz/ v [T] put in a category.

cater /'keɪtə(r)/ v [I] (for)// 1 provide food and services for sb, esp at social functions. 2 provide what is needed or desired by sb: television programmes ~ing for all tastes. **caterer** n [C].

caterpillar /'kætəpɪlə(r)/ n [C] 1 larva of a butterfly or moth. 2 (also **Caterpillar track**) (P) endless belt passing round the wheels of a tractor or tank(2).

catgut /'kætgʌt/ n [U] thin strong cord used for the strings of violins, tennis rackets, etc.

cathedral /kə'θiːdrəl/ n [C] main church in a diocese.

cathode /'kæθəʊd/ n [C] negative electrode in a battery, etc.

catholic /'kæθəlɪk/ adj 1 **Catholic** = ROMAN CATHOLIC (ROMAN). 2 (fml) including many things; general: have ~ tastes. **Catholic** n [C] = ROMAN CATHOLIC (ROMAN). **Catholicism** /kə'θɒləsɪzəm/ n [U] teaching, beliefs, etc of the Roman Catholic Church.

cattle /'kætl/ n [pl] cows and bulls, etc.

catty /'kætɪ/ adj (-ier, -iest) very unkind and spiteful.

caught pt, pp of CATCH¹.

cauldron /'kɔːldrən/ n [C] large deep pot for boiling things in.

cauliflower /'kɒlɪflaʊə(r); US 'kɔːlɪ-/ n [C, U] vegetable with a large white flower-head.

cause /kɔːz/ n 1 [C, U] something that produces an effect; thing, etc that makes sth happen: the ~ of the fire. 2 [U] (for)// reason: have ~ for complaint. 3 [C] aim or movement that is strongly supported: the ~ of world peace. **cause** v [T] be the cause of: What ~d his death?

causeway /'kɔːzweɪ/ n [C] raised road or path across wet ground.

caustic /'kɔːstɪk/ adj 1 able to burn by chemical action: ~ soda. 2 (fig) (of remarks) very bitter or critical. **caustically** /-klɪ/ adv.

caution /'kɔːʃn/ n 1 [U] great care. 2 warning words. **caution** v [T] warn. **cautionary** /'kɔːʃənərɪ; US -nerɪ/ adj giving a warning.

cautious /'kɔːʃəs/ adj having or showing caution(1); very careful. **cautiously** adv.

cavalcade /ˌkævl'keɪd/ n [C] procession of people on horseback, in cars, etc.

cavalry /'kævlrɪ/ n [C, also sing with pl v] (pl -ies) soldiers fighting on horseback (esp formerly), or in armoured vehicles.

cave /keɪv/ n [C] hollow place in the side of a cliff or hill, or underground. **cave** v (phr v) **cave in** fall inwards; collapse.

cavern /'kævən/ n [C] large cave. **cavernous** adj like a cavern; large and deep.

caviare (also **caviar**) /'kævɪɑː(r)/ n [U] salted eggs of certain types of large fish, eaten as food.

cavity /'kævətɪ/ n [C] (pl -ies) (fml) small hole in sth solid, eg a tooth.

cayenne /keɪ'en/ ,**cayenne 'pepper** /keɪ'en/ n [U] kind of hot red powdered pepper.

CB /,si: 'bi:/ abbr citizens' band.

cc /,si:'si:/ abbr cubic centimetre, as a measure of the power of an engine.

CD /,si: 'di:/ abbr compact disc.

cease /si:s/ v [I, T] (fml) stop. ,**cease-'fire** n [C] agreement to stop fighting. **ceaseless** adj not stopping. **ceaselessly** adv.

cedar /'si:də(r)/ n (a) [C] tall evergreen tree with a hard sweet-smelling wood. (b) [U] wood of this tree.

ceiling /'si:lɪŋ/ n [C] 1 upper surface of a room. 2 official upper limit: a price/wage ~.

celebrate /'selɪbreɪt/ v 1 [I, T] mark (a special occasion) by enjoying oneself. 2 [T] (fml) praise; honour. **celebrated** adj famous. **celebration** /,selɪ'breɪʃn/ n [C, U].

celebrity /sɪ'lebrətɪ/ n (pl -ies) 1 [C] famous person. 2 [U] fame.

celery /'selərɪ/ n [U] plant whose white stems are eaten raw.

celestial /sɪ'lestɪəl/ US -tʃl/ adj (in/ml) of the sky; of heaven.

celibate /'selɪbət/ adj remaining unmarried or not sexually active, esp for religious reasons. **celibacy** /-bəsɪ/ n [U]. **celibate** n [C] celibate person.

cell /sel/ n [C] 1 small room: a prison ~. 2 device for producing electric current by chemical action. 3 tiny unit of living matter. 4 small group of people, eg in a secret organization.

cellar /'selə(r)/ n [C] underground room for storing things: a wine ~.

cello /'tʃeləʊ/ n [C] (pl ~s) kind of large violin, held between the knees. **cellist** /'tʃelɪst/ n [C] person who plays a cello.

Cellophane /'seləfeɪn/ n [U] (P)

thin transparent material used for wrapping things in.

cellular /'seljʊlə(r)/ adj 1 consisting of cells(3). 2 (of blankets, etc) loosely woven.

Celsius /'selsɪəs/ adj, n [U] (in the) temperature scale with the freezing-point of water 0°and the boiling-point at 100°.

cement /sɪ'ment/ n [U] 1 grey powder that when mixed with water becomes hard like stone, used in building. 2 kind of glue. **cement** v [T] join (as if) with cement.

cemetery /'semətrɪ; US -terɪ/ n [C] (pl -ies) place where dead people are buried.

cenotaph /'senətɑːf; US -tæf/ n [C] monument built in memory of people killed in a war.

censor /'sensə(r)/ n [C] official with authority to examine books, films, etc and to remove parts considered indecent, offensive, etc. **censor** v [T] examine or remove parts of (a book, etc). **censorship** n [U] act or policy of censoring.

censure /'senʃə(r)/ v (fml) criticize strongly; condemn. **censure** n [U].

census /'sensəs/ n [C] official counting, esp of the population of a country.

cent /sent/ n [C] one 100th part of a main unit of money eg a dollar.

centaur /'sentɔː(r)/ n [C] (in Greek mythology) creature that is half man and half horse.

centenarian /,sentɪ'neərɪən/ n [C], adj (person who is) 100 years old or more.

centenary /sen'ti:nərɪ; US 'sentənerɪ/ n [C] (pl -ies) 100th anniversary.

centennial /sen'tenɪəl/ n [C] (US) centenary.

center (US) = CENTRE.

centigrade /'sentɪgreɪd/ adj, n [U] = CELSIUS.

centimetre (US -meter) [C] metric unit of length; 100th part of a metre.

centipede /'sentɪpiːd/ n [C] small crawling creature with many legs.

central /'sentrəl/ adj 1 at or of the centre. 2 most important; main. ,**central 'heating** n [U] system of heating a building from one main source through pipes and radiators. **centrally** adv.

centralize /'sentrəlaɪz/ v [I, T] (cause to) come under the control of one central authority. **centralization** /,sentrəlaɪ'zeɪʃn; US -lɪ'z-/ n [U].

centre /'sentə(r)/ n 1 [C] middle point or part. 2 [C] place for a particular activity: *a 'shopping ~*. **3** point towards which people's interest is directed: *the ~ of attention*. **4** (esp **the centre**) [sing] moderate political position, between the extremes of left and right. **centre** *v* (phr v) **centre (sth) on/around sb/sth** (cause sth to) have sb/sth as its main concern.

centrifugal /ˌsentrɪ'fjuːgl, also sen'trɪfjʊgl/ *adj* moving away from the centre: *~ force*.

century /'sentʃərɪ/ *n* [C] (*pl* **-ies**) **1** period of 100 years. **2** (in cricket) 100 runs by one player.

ceramic /sɪ'ræmɪk/ *adj* of or relating to pottery. **ceramics** *n* **1** [U] art of making and decorating pottery. **2** [pl] objects made of clay, porcelain, etc.

cereal /'sɪərɪəl/ *n* [U, C] **1** (edible grain produced by a) kind of grass, eg wheat or barley. **2** food made from cereal grain: *'breakfast ~ s*.

ceremonial /ˌserɪ'məʊnɪəl/ *adj* of or used for a ceremony: *a ~ occasion*. **ceremonial** *n* [C, U] system of rules, etc for ceremonies. **ceremonially** /-nɪəlɪ/ *adj*.

ceremonious /ˌserɪ'məʊnɪəs/ *adj* very formal and polite. **ceremoniously** *adj*.

ceremony /'serɪmənɪ/ *n* (*pl* **-ies**) **1** [C] formal act(s), religious service, etc on a special occasion. **2** formal behaviour.

certain /'sɜːtn/ *adj* **1** having no doubts; sure. **2** (*to*)|| sure to happen: *They're ~ to win the game.* **3** particular, but not named: *on ~ conditions*. **4** slight; some: *a ~ coldness in his attitude*. **5** (idm) **make certain** do sth to be sure: *Make ~ that no bones are broken.* **certainly** *adj* **1** without doubt. **2** (in answer to questions) of course; yes. **certainty** *n* (*pl* **-ies**) **1** [U] state of being sure. **2** [C] thing that is certain.

certificate /sə'tɪfɪkət/ *n* [C] official paper that states certain facts: *a 'birth ~*.

certify /'sɜːtɪfaɪ/ *v* (*pt, pp* **-ied**) [T] declare formally (that sth is true): *~ him dead/insane*.

cessation /se'seɪʃn/ *n* [U, C] (*fml*) action of stopping.

cesspit /'sespɪt/ *n* [C] (also **cesspool** /sespuːl/) *n* [C] underground hole or tank into which drains empty.

CFC /ˌsiː ef 'siː/ *abbr* chlorofluorocarbon, any of several gasses, used in refrigerators and aerosols, etc and thought to harm the atmosphere around the earth.

chafe /tʃeɪf/ *v* **1** [I] [T] (cause to)

become sore by rubbing. **2** [I] (*at/ under*)|| become impatient because of sth: *~ at the delay*.

chaff /tʃɑːf; *US* tʃæf/ *n* [U] outer covering of grain, removed before the grain is used as food.

chagrin /'ʃægrɪn; *US* ʃə'grɪːn/ *n* [U] (*fml*) disappointment or annoyance.

chain /tʃeɪn/ *n* **1** [C, U] length of metal rings joined together. **2** [C] series of connected things: *a ~ of mountains/shops/events*. **chain** *v* [T] fasten (as if) with a chain. **chain re'action** [C] series of events each of which causes the next. **'chain-smoke** *v* [I, T] smoke (cigarettes) continuously. **'chain-smoker** *n* [C]. **'chain-store** *n* [C] one of several similar shops owned by the same company.

chair /tʃeə(r)/ *n* **1** [C] moveable seat with a back, for one person. **2** **the chair** [sing] (position of the) person in charge of a meeting. **3** [C] position of a professor at a university. **chair** *v* [T] be in charge of (a meeting). **'chairman, 'chairperson, 'chairwoman** *n* [C] person in charge of a meeting.

chalet /'ʃæleɪ/ *n* [C] **1** Swiss mountain hut built of wood. **2** small house in a holiday camp.

chalk /tʃɔːk/ *n* **(a)** [U] kind of soft white rock. **(b)** [C, U] this material made into sticks for writing or drawing. **chalk** *v* **1** [I, T] write or draw (sth) with chalk. **2** (phr v) **chalk sth up** achieve (a success). **chalky** *adj* (**-ier, -iest**) of or like chalk.

challenge /'tʃælɪndʒ/ *n* [C] **1** difficult or demanding task. **2** invitation to take part in a game, fight, etc. **challenge** *v* [T] **1** invite (sb) to take part in a game, fight, etc. **2** question the truth, rightness, etc of (sth). **challenger** *n* [C]. **challenging** *adj* difficult and demanding.

chamber /'tʃeɪmbə(r)/ *n* **1** [C] (formerly) room. **2** [C] (room used by a) law-making group. **3** **chambers** [pl] set of rooms used by judges and barristers. **4** [C] enclosed space: *the ~s of the heart*. **'chambermaid** *n* [C] woman who cleans and tidies bedrooms in a hotel. **'chamber music** *n* [U] classical music for a small group of players. **ˌchamber of 'commerce** *n* [C] group of business people or organized to improve local trade interests.

chameleon /kə'miːlɪən/ *n* [C] small lizard whose skin colour changes to match its surroundings.

chamois /ˈʃæmwɑː; US ˈʃæmɪ/ n [C] (pl chamois) small goat-like antelope. **'chamois leather** /ˈʃæmɪ/ n [C, U] (piece of) soft leather cloth from the skin of goats, etc.

champ¹ /tʃæmp/ v [I] 1 (esp of horses) bite noisily. 2 be impatient.

champ² /tʃæmp/ n [C] (infml = CHAMPION¹.

champagne /ʃæmˈpeɪn/ n [U, C] sparkling white French wine.

champion /ˈtʃæmpɪən/ n [C] 1 person, team, etc that wins a competition. 2 person who supports or defends sb or a principle: a ~ of women's rights. **champion** v [T] support; defend. **championship** n 1 [C] competition to find the champion(1). 2 position of being a champion. 3 [U] act of championing.

chance /tʃɑːns; US tʃæns/ n 1 [U] way in which things happen without any cause that can be seen; luck. 2 [C, U] possibility; likelihood: no ~ of winning. 3 [C] opportunity: have a ~ to make an apology. 4 (idm) by **'chance** by accident. **on the (off) chance** in the hope of. **take a 'chance (on sth)** try to do sth risky. **chance** v [I] (fml) happen by chance: I ~d to be there. 2 [T] take a risk. **chancy** adj (-ier, -iest) (infml) risky.

chancel /ˈtʃɑːnsl; US ˈtʃænsl/ n [C] eastern part of a church, containing the altar.

chancellor /ˈtʃɑːnsələ(r); US ˈtʃæns-/ n [C] 1 head of government in some countries. 2 (Brit) honorary head of some universities. ˌChancellor of the Ex'chequer n [C] (Brit) government minister responsible for finance.

chandelier /ˌʃændəˈlɪə(r)/ n [C] decorative hanging light with branches for several bulbs or candles.

change¹ /tʃeɪndʒ/ v 1 [I, T] become or make different: Our plans have ~d. ○ Water ~s into steam. ○ ~ one's attitude. 2 [T] replace (sth) with another: ~ a light bulb. 3 [I, T] take off (one's clothes) and put others on. 4 [I, T] go from one (train, bus, etc) to another. 5 [T] give and receive (money) in exchange for money of smaller value or in a foreign currency. 6 (idm) **change 'hands** pass to another owner. **change one's mind** change one's decision or opinion. ˌchange one's 'tune change one's attitude, behaviour, etc. 7 (phr v) ˌchange 'over (from sth) (to sth) change from one system to another. **changeable** adj often changing. **'change-over** n [C] change from one system to another.

change² /tʃeɪndʒ/ n 1 [C, U] act of changing. 2 [C] something used in place of another: ~ of name/clothes. 3 [U] (a) money returned when the price of sth is less than the amount given. (b) coins of low value. 4 (idm) **for a change** to be different from what usually happens, for the sake of variety.

channel /ˈtʃænl/ n [C] 1 passage along which a liquid flows. 2 narrow stretch of water: the English C~. 3 way by which news, information, may travel: your complaint must be made through the proper ~s. 4 television station. **channel** v (-ll-; US also -l-) [T] 1 form a channel in. 2 cause to go through channels; direct: (fig) ~ all our resources into the new scheme.

chant /tʃɑːnt/ v [I, T] 1 sing (sth) on one note. 2 sing or shout (sth) rhythmically and repeatedly. **chant** n [C].

chaos /ˈkeɪɒs/ n [U] complete disorder or confusion. **chaotic** /keɪˈɒtɪk/ adj.

chap¹ /tʃæp/ n [C] (infml esp Brit) man or boy.

chap² /tʃæp/ v (-pp-) [I, T] (of the skin) (cause) to become cracked, rough and sore: ~ped lips.

chapel /ˈtʃæpl/ n [C] 1 place used for Christian worship, eg in a school or hospital. 2 small place within a church, with an altar.

chaplain /ˈtʃæplɪn/ n [C] clergyman in the armed forces, a hospital, prison, etc.

chapter /ˈtʃæptə(r)/ n [C] 1 (usu numbered) main division of a book. 2 period of time.

char¹ /tʃɑː(r)/ n (-rr-) [I, T] (cause to) become black by burning.

char² /tʃɑː(r)/ n **'charwoman** n [C] (Brit) woman who is employed to clean a house or office.

character /ˈkærəktə(r)/ n 1 [C] qualities that make sb, a country, etc different from others: The ~ of the town has changed over the years. 2 [U] particular quality of sth: discussions that were confidential in ~. 3 [U] (a) striking individuality: house with no ~. (b) moral strength: a woman of ~. 4 [C] person in a play, novel, etc. 5 [C] (infml) person, esp an odd one. 6 [C] letter or sign used in writing or printing: Chinese ~s. 7 (idm) **in/out of character** typical/not typical of sb's character. **characterless** adj uninteresting; ordinary.

characteristic /ˌkærəktəˈrɪstɪk/ *adj* typical. **characteristic** *n* [C] typical quality or feature. **characteristically** /-klɪ/ *adv*.

characterize /ˈkærəktəraɪz/ *v* [T] 1 describe the character of. 2 be typical of.

charade /ʃəˈrɑːd; US ʃəˈreɪd/ *n* 1 **charades** (with sing *v*) party game in which one team acts a word that has to be guessed by the other team. 2 [C] (*fig*) absurd and obvious pretence.

charcoal /ˈtʃɑːkəʊl/ *n* [U] black substance of burnt wood, used as a fuel, for drawing, etc.

charge¹ /tʃɑːdʒ/ *v* 1 [I, T] ask in payment: *They ~d me £50 for the repair.* 2 [T] *to// record* (sth) as a debt to be paid by sb/sth: *C~ it to his account.* 3 [T] (*with//*) accuse (sb) of sth, esp in a law-court: *He was ~d with murder.* 4 [I, T] rush forward and attack (sb/sth). 5 [T] put electricity into (a battery). 6 [T] *with//* (esp passive) fill with an emotion: *a voice ~d with tension.* 7 [T] *with//* (*fml*) give (sb) a duty or responsibility.

charge² /tʃɑːdʒ/ *n* 1 [C] price asked for goods or services. 2 [C] formal claim that sb has done wrong: *a ~ of murder.* 3 [U] responsibility and control: *take ~ of the department.* 4 [C, U] rushing attack. 5 [C] electricity put into a battery. 6 (idm) **in charge (of sb/sth)** having responsibility for and control of sb/sth.

chargé d'affaires /ˌʃɑːʒeɪ dæˈfeə(r)/ *n* [C] (*pl* **chargés d'affaires**) deputy ambassador.

chariot /ˈtʃærɪət/ *n* [C] horse-drawn open vehicle with two wheels used in ancient times in fighting. **charioteer** /ˌtʃærɪəˈtɪə(r)/ *n* [C] driver of a chariot.

charisma /kəˈrɪzmə/ *n* [U] power to inspire devotion and enthusiasm. **charismatic** /ˌkærəzˈmætɪk/ *adj*: *a ~tic politician.*

charitable /ˈtʃærətəbl/ *adj* 1 kind in one's attitude to others. 2 of or connected with a charity(1). **charitably** *adv*.

charity /ˈtʃærətɪ/ *n* (*pl* -**ies**) 1 [C] organization that helps the needy. 2 [U] kindness towards others. 3 [U] money, food, etc given to very poor people.

charlatan /ˈʃɑːlətən/ *n* [C] person who falsely claims to have special skill or knowledge.

charm /tʃɑːm/ *n* 1 (a) [U] power of pleasing people; attractiveness. (b) [C] pleasing quality. 2 [C] object worn for good luck. 3 [C] magic spell. **charm** *v* [T] 1 please or

attract. 2 influence by magic. **charming** *adj* delightful.

chart /tʃɑːt/ *n* 1 [C] diagram, graph, etc giving information. 2 [C] map of the sea. 3 **the charts** [pl] weekly list of the best-selling pop music records. **chart** *v* [T] make a chart of.

charter /ˈtʃɑːtə(r)/ *n* [C] 1 official written statement giving certain rights, privileges, principles, etc. 2 hiring of an aircraft or ship: *a ~ flight.* **charter** *v* [T] hire (an aircraft, etc) for a particular purpose. **chartered** *adj* qualified according to the rules of a certain profession: *a ~ed accountant.*

charwoman ⇨ CHAR².

chase /tʃeɪs/ *v* [I, T] (*after*)// run after (sb) in order to catch or drive away. **chase** *n* [C] act of chasing.

chasm /ˈkæzəm/ *n* [C] 1 deep opening in the ground. 2 (*fig*) very wide difference of interest, etc.

chassis /ˈʃæsɪ/ *n* [C] (*pl* **chassis** /ˈʃæsɪz/) framework on which the body of a vehicle is built.

chaste /tʃeɪst/ *adj* 1 pure; virtuous. 2 avoiding wrong sexual activity. 3 of style or taste) simple.

chasten /ˈtʃeɪsn/ *v* [T] (*fml*) correct by punishment or suffering; humble and improve.

chastise /tʃæˈstaɪz/ *v* [T] (*fml*) punish severely. **chastisement** *n* [C].

chastity /ˈtʃæstətɪ/ *n* [U] state of being chaste(1, 2).

chat /tʃæt/ *n* [C] friendly informal talk. **chat** *v* (-tt-) 1 [I] talk in an informal way. 2 (phr *v*) **chat sb up** (*Brit infml*) talk to (sb, esp of the opposite sex) in a friendly way, esp in order to begin a relationship. **chatty** *adj* (-**ier**, -**iest**) fond of chatting.

château /ˈʃætəʊ; US ʃæˈtəʊ/ *n* [C] (*pl* ~**x** /-təʊz/) castle or large country house in France.

chatter /ˈtʃætə(r)/ *v* [I] 1 talk quickly and continuously about unimportant things. 2 (of birds or monkeys) make short repeated high-pitched noises. 3 (of the teeth) strike together from cold or fear. **chatter** *n* [C] 1 continuous quick talk. 2 chattering sound. **chatterbox** *n* [C] person who chatters(1).

chauffeur /ˈʃəʊfə(r); US ʃəˈfɜːr/ *n* [C] person paid to drive a private car. **chauffeur** *v* [T] drive (sb) as a chauffeur.

chauvinism /ˈʃəʊvɪnɪzəm/ *n* [U] excessive and unreasonable belief that one's own country, or sex, is the best. **chauvinist** /-ɪst/ *n* [C]. **chauvinistic** /ˌʃəʊvɪˈnɪstɪk/ *adj*.

cheap /tʃiːp/ *adj* **1** costing little money. **2** of poor quality: ~ *and nasty*. **3** mean and unfair: *a* ~ *joke*. **cheapen** *v* [I, T] become or make cheap. **cheaply** *adv*. **cheapness** *n* [U].

cheat /tʃiːt/ *v* **1** [I] act dishonestly: ~ *in an examination*. **2** (phr v) **cheat sb (out) of sth** get sth from sb by dishonest behaviour. **cheat** *n* [C] person who cheats.

check¹ /tʃek/ *v* **1** (a) [I, T] make sure (of sth) by examining or investigating. (b) [T] examine (sth) to make sure it is correct, safe, satisfactory, etc. **2** [T] cause to stop; control: ~ *the enemy's progress*. **3** (phr v) **check in** register one's arrival at an airport, hotel, etc. **check-out** pay one's bill and leave a hotel. **check up on sth** (or *esp US*) **check sth out** examine sth to discover if it is true, safe, correct, etc. **'check-in** *n* [C] place where one checks in at an airport, etc. **'check-out** *n* [C] place where customers pay for goods in a supermarket. **'checkpoint** *n* [C] place, eg on a frontier, where travellers and vehicles are inspected. **'check-up** *n* [C] medical examination.

check² /tʃek/ *n* **1** [C] examination to make sure that sth is correct, safe, satisfactory, etc. **2** [U] control: *hold/keep one's emotions in* ~. **3** [sing] (in chess) position of directly threatening one's opponent's king. **4** [C] (*US*) bill in a restaurant. **5** [C] (*US*) = CHEQUE.

check³ /tʃek/ *n* [U, C] pattern of crossed lines forming squares. **checkered** (*US*) = CHEQUERED.

checkmate /ˈtʃekmeɪt/ *n* **1** (in chess) situation in which one player cannot prevent the capture of his/her king meaning the other player is the winner. **2** (*fig*) total defeat.

cheek /tʃiːk/ *n* **1** [C] either side of the face below the eye. **2** [U] rude and disrespectful behaviour or talk. **cheek** *v* [T] speak cheekily to. **cheeky** *adj* (-ier, -iest) rude and disrespectful. **cheekily** *adv*.

cheer¹ /tʃɪə(r)/ *v* **1** [I, T] give shouts of praise, support, etc to (sb). **2** [T] give comfort or encouragement to: ~ *ing news*. **3** (phr v) **cheer (sb) up** (cause sb to) become happier or more cheerful.

cheer² /tʃɪə(r)/ *n* **1** [C] shout of praise, support, etc. **2** [U] (*arch*) happiness. **3 cheers** [pl] (said just before people drink an alcoholic drink) good health. **cheerful** /ˈtʃɪəfl/ *adj* happy. **cheerfully** *adv*. **cheerless** *adj* sad; gloomy.

cheerio /ˌtʃɪəriˈəʊ/ *interj* (*Brit infml*) goodbye.

cheery /ˈtʃɪərɪ/ *adj* (-ier, -iest) lively and happy. **cheerily** *adv*.

cheese /tʃiːz/ *n* [U, C] solid food made from milk. **'cheesecake** *n* [C, U] kind of tart made with cream cheese on a base of crushed biscuits. **'cheesecloth** *n* [U] loosely woven cotton cloth. **'cheesed 'off** *adj* (*Brit infml*) annoyed, bored or frustrated.

cheetah /ˈtʃiːtə/ *n* [C] spotted African wild animal of the cat family, able to run very fast.

chef /ʃef/ *n* [C] chief cook in a restaurant, hotel, etc.

chemical /ˈkemɪkl/ *adj* of or relating to chemistry. **chemical** *n* [C] substance used in chemistry. **chemically** *-klɪ/ adv*.

chemist /ˈkemɪst/ *n* **1** person who prepares and sells medicines, and usu cosmetics and toiletries. **2** student of or expert in chemistry. **chemistry** /ˈkemɪstrɪ/ *n* [U] scientific study of the structure of substances and how they combine together.

cheque /tʃek/ *n* [C] written order to a bank to pay money. **'chequebook** *n* [C] book of printed cheques. **'cheque card** *n* [C] card issued by a bank to sb who has an account with it, guaranteeing payment of his/her cheques up to a stated amount.

chequered /ˈtʃekəd/ *adj* having good and bad parts: *a* ~ *history*.

cherish /ˈtʃerɪʃ/ *v* [T] (*fml*) **1** protect lovingly; care for. **2** keep (hope, etc) in one's mind: ~ *ed memories*.

cherry /ˈtʃerɪ/ *n* [C] (*pl* -ies) small round red or black fruit with a stone.

cherub /ˈtʃerəb/ *n* [C] **1** (*pl* ~im /-ɪm/) kind of angel. **2** (*pl* ~s) beautiful young child.

chess /tʃes/ *n* [U] board game for two players.

chest /tʃest/ *n* **1** [C] upper front part of the body. **2** [C] large strong box. **3** (idm) **get sth off one's 'chest** (*infml*) say sth that one has wanted to say for a long time. **,chest of 'drawers** *n* [C] piece of furniture with drawers.

chestnut /ˈtʃesnʌt/ *n* [C] (tree producing a) smooth reddish-brown nut. **chestnut** *adj* reddish-brown.

chew /tʃuː/ *v* **1** [I, T] crush (food) with the teeth. **2** (phr v) **chew sth over** (*infml*) think about sth slowly and carefully. **chew** *n* act of chewing. **'chewing-gum** *n* [C] sweet sticky substance to be chewed for a long time but not swallowed. **chewy** adj (-ier, -iest).

chic /ʃiːk/ adj fashionable; stylish.

chick /tʃɪk/ n [C] young bird, esp a young chicken.

chicken /'tʃɪkɪn/ n (a) [C] young bird, esp a hen. (b) [U] its meat. **chicken** adj (sl) cowardly. **chicken** v (phr v) **chicken out (of sth)** (infml) decide not to do sth because one is afraid. **'chickenpox** /-pɒks/ n [U] disease, esp of children, causing red spots on the skin.

chicory /'tʃɪkərɪ/ n [U] (a) plant, the leaves of which are eaten raw in salads. (b) root of this plant, roasted and made into a powder and used with coffee.

chief /tʃiːf/ n [C] leader or ruler; highest official. **chief** adj 1 most important; main. 2 having the highest rank. **Chief 'Constable** n [C] (Brit) head of the police force in a particular area. **chiefly** adv mainly. **-in-'chief** (in compound nouns) highest in rank: the Commander-in-∼.

chieftain /'tʃiːftən/ n [C] leader of a tribe.

child /tʃaɪld/ n [C] (pl **children** /'tʃɪldrən/) 1 young human being. 2 son or daughter. **'childbirth** n [U] act of giving birth to a child. **childhood** n [U] state or time of being a child. **childish** adj (of an adult) behaving like a child. **childless** adj having no children. **'childlike** adj simple; innocent. **'child-minder** n [C] person whose job is to look after other people's children, esp those of parents who are at work.

chill /tʃɪl/ v 1 [I, T] become or make cold. 2 [T] make (sb) feel very afraid. **chill** n 1 [sing] unpleasant coldness. 2 [C] illness caused by cold and damp. **chilly** adj (-ier, -iest) 1 rather cold. 2 (fig) unfriendly.

chilli (US **chili**) /'tʃɪlɪ/ n [C, U] (pl ∼es) dried pod of a red or green pepper, tasting very hot. **,chilli con 'carne** n [C, U] stew made with meat, tomatoes and beans and flavoured with chillies.

chime /tʃaɪm/ n [C] (sound of a) set of tuned bells. **chime** v [I, T] (of bells) ring.

chimney /'tʃɪmnɪ/ n [C] passage through which smoke is carried away from a fire. **'chimney-pot** n [C] short pipe fitted to the top of a chimney. **'chimney-stack** n [C] group of chimneys on a roof. **'chimney-sweep** n [C] person whose job is to remove soot from inside chimneys.

chimp /tʃɪmp/ n [C] (infml) chimpanzee.

chimpanzee /,tʃɪmpən'ziː, -pæn-/ n [C] kind of small African ape.

chin /tʃɪn/ n [C] part of the face below the mouth.

china /'tʃaɪnə/ n [U] (a) fine baked and glazed white clay. (b) objects, eg cups and plates, made from this.

chink¹ /tʃɪŋk/ n [C] narrow crack.

chink² /tʃɪŋk/ v [I] n [C] (make the) sound of glasses, coins, etc striking together.

chip /tʃɪp/ n [C] 1 [usu pl] thin strip of potato fried in deep fat: fish and '∼s. 2 (a) thin piece (of sth) which has broken off. (b) place from which such a piece has been broken. 3 flat plastic counter used in gambling to represent money. 4 short for MICROCHIP. 5 (idm) **have a 'chip on one's shoulder** (infml) be bitter, angry, etc because one considers that one has been unfairly treated. **chip** v (-pp-) 1 [I, T] (cause to) break a small piece off the edge. 2 (phr v) **chip 'in (with sth)** (infml) (a) interrupt a conversation: She ∼ped in with a couple of useful comments. (b) give (money).

chiropodist /kɪ'rɒpədɪst/ n [C] person whose job is to treat minor problems people have with their feet. **chiropody** /-dɪ/ n [U].

chirp /tʃɜːp/ v [I] n [C] (make the) short sharp sound of small birds. **chirpy** adj (-ier, -iest (Brit)) (infml) lively and happy.

chisel /'tʃɪzl/ n [C] tool with a sharp end for cutting wood or stone. **chisel** v (-ll-, US also -l-) [T] cut or shape with a chisel.

chit /tʃɪt/ n [C] note showing an amount of money owed, eg for drinks.

chivalry /'ʃɪvəlrɪ/ n [U] 1 rules and customs of knights in the Middle Ages. 2 good manners, esp honour and politeness, esp as shown by men towards women. **chivalrous** /'ʃɪvlrəs/ adj.

chlorine /'klɔːriːn/ n [U] strong-smelling chemical substance used as a disinfectant.

chloro-fluorocarbon /klɔːrə,flʊərəʊ'kɑːbən/ n [C] = CFC.

chlorophyll /'klɒrəfɪl; US 'klɔːr-/ n [U] green substance in plants that absorbs energy from sunlight to help them grow.

chocolate /'tʃɒklət/ n (a) [U] brown substance made from cocoa and eaten as a sweet. (b) [C] sweet covered with this. (c) [U] hot drink made from this. **chocolate**

adj dark brown.

choice /tʃɔɪs/ n 1 [C] act of choosing. 2 [U] right or possibility of choosing: I had no ~ but to leave. 3 [C] variety from which to choose: a large ~ of restaurants. 4 [C] person or thing chosen: I don't like his ~ of friends. **choice** adj unusually good: ~ fruit.

choir /ˈkwaɪə(r)/ n [C] (a) group of singers. (b) part of a church in which these singers sit.

choke /tʃəʊk/ v 1 [I, T] (cause to) be unable to breathe because one's windpipe is blocked. 2 [T] block or fill (a passage): the drains are ~d with dead leaves. 3 (phr v) **choke sth back** suppress (a strong emotion). **choke** n [C] (knob that operates) the valve controlling the flow of air into a petrol engine.

cholera /ˈkɒlərə/ n [U] kind of infectious and often fatal disease, common in hot countries.

cholesterol /kəˈlestərɒl/ n [U] fatty substance found in animal fluids and tissue.

choose /tʃuːz/ v (pt **chose** /tʃəʊz/, pp **chosen** /ˈtʃəʊzn/) 1 [I, T] decide to have (sb/sth) from many available: You can't have all of the sweets, you must ~ one. 2 [T] decide: She chose to become a doctor.

chop /tʃɒp/ v (-pp-) [T] cut into pieces with an axe, knife, etc. **chop** n [C] 1 chopping blow. 2 thick slice of pork or lamb with a bone in it.

chopper /ˈtʃɒpə(r)/ n [C] 1 heavy tool for chopping. 2 (infml) helicopter.

choppy /ˈtʃɒpɪ/ adj (-ier, -iest) (of the sea) moving in short broken waves.

chopsticks /ˈtʃɒpstɪks/ n [pl] pair of thin sticks used in China, Japan, etc for lifting food to the mouth.

choral /ˈkɔːrəl/ adj of or for a choir.

chord /kɔːd/ n [C] 1 musical notes sounded together. 2 (mathematics) straight line that joins two points on the circumference of a circle.

chore /tʃɔː(r)/ n [C] ordinary or boring task.

choreography /ˌkɒrɪˈɒɡrəfɪ; US ˌkɔːrɪ-/ n [U] art of designing and arranging steps for dances on stage. **choreographer** /-fə(r)/ n [C].

chorister /ˈkɒrɪstə(r)/ n [C] person who sings in a choir.

chorus /ˈkɔːrəs/ n [C] 1 (music for a) large group of singers. 2 part of a song that is sung after each verse. 3 something said by many people together: a ~ of approval. **chorus** v [T] sing or say together.

chose pt of CHOOSE.

chosen pp of CHOOSE.

Christ /kraɪst/ (also ˌJesus ˈChrist /ˈdʒiːzəs/) n [sing] founder of the Christian religion.

christen /ˈkrɪsn/ v [T] 1 receive (esp a baby) into the Christian Church by baptism; give a name to (sb) at baptism. 2 (fig) use (sth) for the first time. **christening** n [C].

Christendom /ˈkrɪsndəm/ n [sing] (fml) all Christian people throughout the world.

Christian /ˈkrɪstʃən/ n [C] person who believes in the Christian religion. **Christian** adj 1 of Christianity. 2 showing the qualities of a Christian; kind. **Christianity** /ˌkrɪstɪˈænətɪ/ n [U] religion based on the belief that Christ was the son of God, and on his teachings. **ˈChristian name** n [C] first name.

Christmas /ˈkrɪsməs/ (also ˌChristmas ˈDay) n [U, C] yearly celebration of the birth of Christ; 25 December.

chrome /krəʊm/ n [U] chromium, esp as a protective covering on other metals.

chromium /ˈkrəʊmɪəm/ n [U] metallic element used eg as a shiny protective covering on other metals.

chromosome /ˈkrəʊməsəʊm/ n [C] one of the fine threads in animal and plant cells, carrying genes.

chronic /ˈkrɒnɪk/ adj 1 (of an illness) lasting for a long time. 2 (Brit infml) very bad. **chronically** /-klɪ/ adv.

chronicle /ˈkrɒnɪkl/ n [C] record of historical events. **chronicle** v [T] make a chronicle of.

chronology /krəˈnɒlədʒɪ/ n (pl -ies) 1 [U] science of fixing dates. 2 [C] series of events in order. **chronological** /ˌkrɒnəˈlɒdʒɪkl/ adj arranged in order of time. **chronologically** -klɪ/ adv.

chronometer /krəˈnɒmɪtə(r)/ n [C] very accurate clock.

chrysalis /ˈkrɪsəlɪs/ n [C] shell-like form of an insect just before it becomes a butterfly or moth.

chrysanthemum /krɪˈsænθəməm/ n [C] garden plant with brightly coloured flowers.

chubby /ˈtʃʌbɪ/ adj (-ier, -iest) slightly fat.

chuck[1] /tʃʌk/ v [T] (infml) 1 throw. 2 give up; abandon: She's just ~ed her boy-friend, ie She ended her relationship with him.

chuck² /tʃʌk/ n [C] **1** part of a lathe that grips the object to be worked on. **2** part of a drill that grips the bit²(2).

chuckle /'tʃʌkl/ v [I] laugh quietly. **chuckle** n [C].

chum /tʃʌm/ n [C] (dated infml) friend. **chummy** adj (-ier, -iest) friendly.

chump /tʃʌmp/ n [C] **1** (infml) foolish person. **2** thick piece of meat.

chunk /tʃʌŋk/ n [C] **1** thick piece or lump. **2** (infml) fairly large amount. **chunky** adj (-ier, -iest) short and thick.

church /tʃɜːtʃ/ n **1** [C] building for public Christian worship. **2 Church** [C] particular group of Christians: the Anglican C~. **3 the Church** [sing] profession of being a Christian minister: go in-to/enter the C~. **'churchyard** n [C] burial-ground round a church.

churn /tʃɜːn/ n [C] **1** container in which cream is shaken to make butter. **2** large (usu metal) container in which milk is carried. **churn** v **1** [T] beat (milk or cream) to make butter. **2** [I, T] move about violently. **3** (phr v) **churn sth out** (infml) produce sth in large amounts.

chute /ʃuːt/ n [C] sloping passage down which things can slide.

chutney /'tʃʌtnɪ/ n [U] hot-tasting mixture of fruit, spices, etc.

cider /'saɪdə(r)/ n [U] alcoholic drink made from apples.

cigar /sɪ'gɑː(r)/ n [C] tight roll of tobacco leaves for smoking.

cigarette /ˌsɪgə'ret/; US /'sɪgəret/ n [C] roll of finely cut tobacco in thin paper for smoking.

cinder /'sɪndə(r)/ n [C, usu pl] small piece of partly burnt coal, etc.

cinema /'sɪnəmə, 'sɪnəmɑː/ n **1** [C] place where films are shown. **2** [sing] films as an art or industry.

cinnamon /'sɪnəmən/ n [U] yellowish-brown spice used in cooking.

cipher (also **cypher**) /'saɪfə(r)/ n **1** [C, U] secret system of writing in which symbols or letters represent other letters. **2** (fig derog) person or thing of no importance.

circa /'sɜːkə/ prep (used with dates) about: born ~ 150 BC.

circle /'sɜːkl/ n [C] **1** (space enclosed by a) curved line, every point on which is the same distance from the centre. **2** ring. **3** group of people: our ~ of friends. **4** upstairs seats in a theatre, etc. **cir-**

cle v [I, T] move in a circle, go round.

circuit /'sɜːkɪt/ n [C] **1** line or journey round a place: a racing ~. **2** complete path along which an electric current flows. **3** series of places or events: a lecture ~. **circuitous** /sə'kjuːɪtəs/ adj (fml) long and indirect: a ~ous route.

circular /'sɜːkjʊlə(r)/ adj **1** shaped like a circle; round. **2** moving round: a ~ route. **circular** n [C] printed letter, advertisement, etc sent to a large number of people.

circulate /'sɜːkjʊleɪt/ v [I, T] **1** (cause to) go round continuously; move about freely. **2** pass from one person to another. **circulation** /ˌsɜːkjʊ'leɪʃn/ n **1** [C, U] movement of blood round the body. **2** [U] (a) passing of sth from one person to another: the ~ of news. (b) state of being circulated: There are only a few of the new coins in ~, ie being used. **3** [C] number of copies of a newspaper, etc sold.

circumcise /'sɜːkəmsaɪz/ v [T] cut off the skin at the end of the penis of (a man or boy). **circumcision** /ˌsɜːkəm'sɪʒn/ n [C, U].

circumference /sə'kʌmfərəns/ n [C] (a) line that is the boundary of a circle. (b) distance round this: the earth's ~.

circumflex /'sɜːkəmfleks/ n [C] mark placed over a vowel, as in French: rôle.

circumnavigate /ˌsɜːkəm-'nævɪget/ v [T] (fml) sail round (esp the world). **circumnavigation** /ˌsɜːkəmˌnævɪ'geɪʃn/ n [C, U].

circumspect /'sɜːkəmspekt/ adj (fml) cautious.

circumstance /'sɜːkəmstəns/ n **1** [C, usu pl] condition connected with an event or action: the ~s of his death. **2 circumstances** [pl] financial position. **3** (idm) **in/under the 'circumstances** this being the case. **in/under no circumstances** never.

circumstantial /ˌsɜːkəm-'stænʃl/ adj **1** (of evidence) having details that strongly suggest sth but do not prove it. **2** (of a description) very detailed.

circus /'sɜːkəs/ n [C] **1** show of performing animals, acrobats, etc, usu in a large tent. **2** (Brit) (in place-names) open space in a town where several streets meet: Piccadilly C~.

cistern /'sɪstən/ n [C] water tank, eg above a toilet.

cite /saɪt/ v [T] (fml) **1** mention as

an example or to support an argument. **2** (*law*) order to appear in court. **citation** /saɪˈteɪʃn/ *n* (a) [U] act of citing sb/sth. (b) [C] quotation.

citizen /ˈsɪtɪzn/ *n* [C] **1** person who has full rights as a member of a country. **2** person who lives in a town or city. **citizens' 'band** *n* [sing] range of radio frequencies used by members of the public for local communication. **citizenship** *n* [U] rights, duties and state of being a citizen.

citric acid /ˌsɪtrɪk ˈæsɪd/ *n* [U] kind of weak acid from such fruits as oranges and lemons.

citrus /ˈsɪtrəs/ *n* [C] any of a group of related trees including the lemon, lime and orange: ~ *fruit*.

city /ˈsɪtɪ/ *n* (*pl* -ies) **1** [C] (a) large important town. (b) [also sing with pl v] all the people living in a city. **2 the City** [sing] financial centre of London.

civic /ˈsɪvɪk/ *adj* of a town or city or its citizens.

civil /ˈsɪvl/ *adj* **1** of the citizens of a country. **2** not concerning the armed forces. **3** polite. **,civil engi'neering** *n* [U] design and building of roads, bridges, etc. **civility** /sɪˈvɪlətɪ/ *n* (*pl* -ies) (*fml*) **1** [U] politeness. **2** [C, usu pl] polite acts. **civilly** /ˈsɪvəlɪ/ *adv*. **civil 'rights** *n* [pl] rights of each citizen to freedom and equality. **,civil 'servant** *n* [C] person who works in the Civil Service. **the ,Civil 'Service** *n* [sing] (a) all government departments. (b) [with sing or pl v] all the people who work in these. **,civil 'war** *n* [C, U] war between groups of people from the same country.

civilian /sɪˈvɪlɪən/ *n* [C], *adj* (person) not of the armed forces.

civilization /ˌsɪvəlaɪˈzeɪʃn; *US* -əlɪˈz-/ *n* **1** [U] (esp advanced) state of human social development and organization. **2** [C, U] culture and way of life of a society at a particular time and place: *the history of western* ~.

civilize /ˈsɪvəlaɪz/ *v* **1** bring to civilization: *a* ~*d society*. **2** improve the behaviour and manners of.

clad /klæd/ *adj* (*dated* or *fml*) clothed; dressed.

claim /kleɪm/ *v* [T] **1** say as a fact (without being able to prove it): *He* ~*s to be a British citizen*. **2** ask for or demand as one's right. **3** (*fml*) (of a disaster, etc) cause the death of: *The earthquake* ~*ed thousands of lives*. **claim** *n* **1** [C] statement of sth as a fact. **2** [C] demand for sth

as one's right: *an insurance* ~. **3** [C, U] right to sth. **claimant** *n* [C] person who claims(2) sth.

clairvoyance /kleəˈvɔɪəns/ *n* [U] supposed power of seeing in the mind future events. **clairvoyant** /-ənt/ *n* [C], *adj* (person) having such power.

clam /klæm/ *n* [C] shellfish. **clam** *v* (-mm-) (phr v) **clam up** (*infml*) become silent.

clamber /ˈklæmbə(r)/ *v* [I] climb with difficulty.

clammy /ˈklæmɪ/ *adj* (-ier, -iest) unpleasantly hot and damp.

clamour (*US* -or) /ˈklæmə(r)/ *n* [C, U] loud confused noise. **clamour** [I] (*for*)/ demand (sth) noisily.

clamp /klæmp/ *n* [C] device for holding things together tightly, usu with a screw. **clamp** *v* **1** [T] fasten with a clamp. **2** (phr v) **clamp down on sb/sth** control sb/sth officially. **'clamp-down** *n* [C].

clan /klæn/ *n* [C] large family group, esp in Scotland.

clandestine /klænˈdestɪn/ *adj* (*fml*) secret: *a* ~ *organization*.

clang /klæŋ/ *n* [C] loud ringing sound. **clang** *v* [I, T] (cause sth to) make this sound.

clank /klæŋk/ *n* [C] dull sound of metal chains striking together. **clank** *v* [I, T] (cause sth to) make this sound.

clap /klæp/ *v* (-pp-) **1** [I, T] strike (one's hands) together, esp to show approval. **2** [T] strike lightly with an open hand: ~ *sb on the back*. **3** [T] (*infml*) put quickly (esp in prison). **clap** *n* [C] **1** act or sound of clapping. **2** sudden loud noise, esp of thunder. **clapped 'out** *adj* (*Brit infml*) completely worn out: *a* ~ *ped out old car*.

claret /ˈklærət/ *n* [U, C] kind of red French wine. **claret** *adj* dark red.

clarify /ˈklærɪfaɪ/ *v* (*pt, pp* -ied) [T] make clearer and easier to understand. **clarification** /ˌklærɪfɪˈkeɪʃn/ *n* [U].

clarinet /ˌklærəˈnet/ *n* [C] kind of woodwind musical instrument. **clarinettist** *n* [C] person who plays the clarinet.

clarity /ˈklærətɪ/ *n* [U] clearness.

clash /klæʃ/ *v* **1** [I] fight or argue. **2** [I] (of ideas, designs, etc) be opposed to one another; not match. **3** [I] (of events) happen inconveniently at the same time. **4** [I, T] strike together with a loud harsh noise. **clash** *n* [C] **1** disagreement. **2** clashing noise.

clasp /klɑːsp; *US* klæsp/ *n* [C] **1**

device for fastening things together. **2** firm hold. **clasp** *v* [T] **1** hold tightly. **2** fasten with a clasp(1).

class /klɑːs; *US* klæs/ *n* **1** (a) [C] social group at a particular level: *the middle ~es.* (b) [U] system that divides people into such groups. **2** [C] (a) group of students taught together. (b) period of time when such a group meets. **3** [C] group of things with similar qualities. **4** [U] (*infml*) elegance. **class** *v* [T] put in a class(3); classify. 'class'room *n* [C] room in a school in which a class of students is taught. **classy** *adj* (-ier, -iest) (*infml*) fashionable; stylish.

classic /ˈklæsɪk/ *adj* **1** typical: *a ~ example.* **2** of very high quality: *a ~ film.* **classic** *n* **1** [C] writer, work of art, book, etc of high quality and lasting value. **2 classics** (with sing *v*) (study of the) literature of ancient Greece and Rome.

classical /ˈklæsɪkl/ *adj* **1** of the style of ancient Greece and Rome. **2** traditional. **3** (of music) serious, esp of the period 1750-1800. **classically** /-klɪ/ *adv.*

classify /ˈklæsɪfaɪ/ *v* (*pt, pp* -ied) [T] arrange into classes(3). **classification** /ˌklæsɪfɪˈkeɪʃn/ *n* [C, U]. **classified** *adj* officially secret.

clatter /ˈklætə(r)/ *n* [sing] continuous noise of hard things hitting each other. **clatter** *v* [I] make a clatter.

clause /klɔːz/ *n* [C] **1** (*grammar*) group of words that contains a subject and a verb. **2** (*law*) section of a legal document.

claustrophobia /ˌklɔːstrəˈfəʊbɪə/ *n* [U] abnormal fear of being in an enclosed space.

claw /klɔː/ *n* [C] **1** hard curved nail at the end of the foot of an animal or bird. **2** pointed part at the end of the leg of a shellfish. **3** device like a claw for gripping and lifting things. **claw** *v* [I, T] (*at*)// tear or scratch with claws.

clay /kleɪ/ *n* [U] stiff sticky earth that becomes hard when baked, used for making bricks, pots, etc.

clean¹ /kliːn/ **1** free from dirt. **2** not yet used: *a ~ piece of paper.* **3** not indecent: *a ~ joke.* **4** smooth; regular: *a ~ cut.* **5** (idm) **make a clean 'breast of** sth make a full confession of sth. **clean** *adv* **1** completely: *I ~ forgot about it.* **2** (idm) **come clean** make a full and honest confession. ˌclean-'cut *adj* **1** clearly outlined. **2** neat and tidy. ˌclean-'shaven *adj* not having a beard or moustache.

clean² /kliːn/ *v* **1** [T] make (sth) clean. **2** (phr v) **clean sb out**

(*infml*) take all sb's money. **clean sth out** clean the inside of (a cupboard, room, etc). **clean (sth) up** (a) remove (dirt, rubbish, etc) from (a place). (b) (*infml*) make or win (a lot of money). **clean sth up** remove criminals, bad influence, etc from (a place). **clean** *n* [sing] act of cleaning. **cleaner** *n* [C] **1** person or thing that cleans: *a vacuum ~.* **2** shop where clothes, etc are cleaned with chemicals, not water.

cleanliness /ˈklenlɪnəs/ *n* [U] state of being clean.

cleanly /ˈkliːnlɪ/ *adv* easily; smoothly.

cleanse /klenz/ *v* [T] make pure or thoroughly clean. **cleanser** *n* [C] substance that cleanses.

clear¹ /klɪə(r)/ *adj* **1** easy to see through: *~ glass.* **2** easy to understand, see or hear: *a ~ explanation of the problems.* **3** obvious; definite: *a ~ case of cheating.* **4** without doubt or confusion; certain: *I'm not ~ about what I should do.* **5** free from obstructions. **6** (*of*)// not touching sth. **7** without cloud or mist: *a ~ sky.* **8** without spots: *~ skin.* **9** free from guilt: *a ~ conscience.* **10** (of a sum of money) with nothing to be taken away: *~ profit.* **11** (idm) **make sth/oneself 'clear** express sth/oneself clearly so that one's wishes, etc are fully understood. **clear** *n* (idm) **in the 'clear** (*infml*) no longer in danger or suspected of sth. **clear** *adv* **1** clearly: *I can hear you loud and ~.* **2** completely: *The prisoner got ~ away.* **3** out of the way: *Stand ~ of the doors.* **4** (idm) **keep/stay/steer clear of** sb/sth avoid meeting sb or going near sb/sth. ˌclear-'cut *adj* easy to understand; not vague. ˌclear-'headed *n* able to think clearly. **clearly** *adv* in a clear manner; obviously. ˌclear-'sighted *adj* understanding or thinking clearly.

clear² /klɪə(r)/ *v* **1** [T] remove (sth unwanted) from (a place). **2** [T] get past or over without touching: *The horse ~ed the fence.* **3** [I] (of fog or mist) disappear gradually. **4** [T] approve (sth) officially. **5** [T] (*of*)// declare (sb) to be not guilty of a crime. **6** (idm) **clear the 'air** lessen or remove fears, suspicions, etc by talking about them openly. **7** (phr v) **clear (sth) away** remove (objects) in order to leave a place tidy. **clear off** (*infml*) go away. **clear out** (*of*) (*infml*) leave (a place). **clear sth out** make sth empty or tidy by removing unwanted things: *~ out the cup-*

boards. **clear up** (of the weather) become bright or fine. **clear (sth) up** make (sth) tidy. **clear sth up** remove doubt about sth; solve: ~ *up a mystery.*

clearance /'klɪərəns/ n 1 [C, U] act of removing unwanted things. 2 [C, U] clear space between two things. 3 [U] official approval or permission.

clearing /'klɪərɪŋ/ n [C] open space from which trees have been cleared in a forest.

cleavage /'kliːvɪdʒ/ n [C] 1 space between a woman's breasts. 2 (*fml*) division or split.

clef /klef/ n [C] musical symbol showing the pitch of the notes.

clemency /'klemənsɪ/ n [U] (*fml*) mercy.

clench /klentʃ/ v [T] close tightly; press firmly together: ~ *one's fists.*

clergy /'klɜːdʒɪ/ n [pl] people appointed as priests. **'clergyman** /'klɜːdʒɪmən/ n [C] Christian priest or minister.

clerical /'klerɪkl/ *adj* 1 of or for a clerk. 2 of or for the clergy.

clerk /klɑːk; US klɜːrk/ n [C] person who works in an office, shop, etc and whose job is to keep records, accounts, etc.

clever /'klevə(r)/ *adj* 1 quick at learning and understanding. 2 showing skill; effective: a ~ *scheme.* **cleverly** *adv.* **cleverness** n [U].

cliché /'kliːʃeɪ; US kliːˈʃeɪ/ n [C] idea or expression that is used so often that it no longer has any meaning.

click /klɪk/ n [C] short sharp sound (like that of a key turning in a lock). **click** v [I, T] make a click. 2 [I] (*infml*) suddenly become understood.

client /'klaɪənt/ n 1 person who receives help or advice from a professional person. 2 customer in a shop.

clientele /ˌkliːɒnˈtel; US ˌklaɪən-/ n [sing] (with sing or pl v) customers or clients as a group.

cliff /klɪf/ n [C] steep rock face, esp by the sea.

climactic /klaɪˈmæktɪk/ *adj* (*fml*) forming a climax.

climate /'klaɪmɪt/ n 1 [C, U] general weather conditions of a place. 2 [C] general attitude or feeling. **climatic** /klaɪˈmætɪk/ *adj.*

climax /'klaɪmæks/ n [C] most exciting or interesting moment in a story, etc, usu near the end. **climax** v [I, T] bring (sth) or come to a climax.

climb /klaɪm/ v 1 [I, T] go up (sth), esp using one's hands and feet. 2 [I] move in the direction mentioned, with difficulty: ~ *out of the lorry.* 3 [I] (of aircraft) go higher in the sky. 4 [I] (of plants) grow upwards. 5 (*idm*) **climb on the bandwagon** ⇨ BAND. 6 (*phr v*) **climb down** (*infml*) admit that one has made a mistake. **climb** n [C] 1 act of climbing. 2 place to climb. **'climb-down** [C] act of admitting one was mistaken. **climber** n [C] 1 person who climbs. 2 climbing plant.

clinch /klɪntʃ/ v [T] 1 (*infml*) settle (an argument or agreement) firmly. 2 hold with the arms; embrace. **clinch** n [C] embrace.

cling /klɪŋ/ v (*pt, pp* **clung** /klʌŋ/) [I] hold tightly. **'cling film** n [U] clear thin plastic film used for wrapping food.

clinic /'klɪnɪk/ n [C] (part of a) hospital or building where people go for specialized medical treatment or advice: a *children's* ~. **clinical** *adj* 1 of clinics or medical treatment. 2 cold and unfeeling. 3 (of a room or building) very plain and undecorated.

clink /klɪŋk/ n [C] sound of small pieces of glass, etc knocking together. **clink** v [I, T] (cause sth to) make this sound.

clip¹ /klɪp/ n [C] small wire, etc device for holding things together: a *paper-* ~. **clip** v (*-pp-*) [T] fasten with a clip. **'clipboard** n [C] portable board with a clip at the top for holding papers.

clip² /klɪp/ v (*-pp-*) [T] 1 cut with scissors, etc. 2 (*infml*) hit sharply. **clip** n [C] 1 act of clipping. 2 (*infml*) sharp blow. **clippers** n [pl] instrument for clipping. **clipping** n [C] 1 piece cut off. 2 (esp US) cutting²(1).

clique /kliːk/ n [C] (often *derog*) closely united group of people.

cloak /kləʊk/ n 1 [C] loose outer garment without sleeves. 2 [sing] (*fig*) thing that hides or covers: a ~ *of secrecy.* **cloak** v [T] cover or hide. **'cloakroom** n [C] 1 place where coats, etc may be left. 2 (*Brit euph*) toilet.

clock /klɒk/ n 1 [C] instrument for measuring and showing the time. 2 (*idm*) **put/turn the 'clock back** return to old-fashioned ideas, etc. **round the 'clock** all day and all night. **clock** v 1 [T] measure the time of. (*phr v*) **clock in/out** record the time that one arrives at/leaves work. **clock sth up** reach (a time, speed, etc). **'clockwise** *adv, adj* in the direction of the movement of the hands of a clock. **'clockwork** n [U] 1 machinery wound up with a key. 2 (idm) **like 'clockwork** with no problems; smoothly.

clod /klɒd/ n [C] lump of earth or clay.

clog¹ /klɒg/ n [C] wooden shoe.

clog² /klɒg/ v (-gg-) [I, T] (up)/ (cause to) become blocked.

cloister /'klɔɪstə(r)/ n [C] covered passage round a square in a convent, college, cathedral, etc. **cloistered** adj sheltered from the busy world.

close¹ /kləʊz/ v 1 [I, T] shut: ~ the door ○ The shop ~s at 5pm. 2 [I, T] (cause to) come to an end: ~ a meeting. 3 (idm) **close one's eyes to sth** ignore sth. 4 (phr v) **close 'down** (of a radio or television station) stop broadcasting. **close (sth) down** (of a factory, business, etc) shut completely. **close in (on sb/sth)** come nearer to sb/sth; gradually surround. **close** n [sing] (fml) end of a period of time or activity: at the ~ of the day. **,closed-circuit 'television** n [U] system in which television signals are sent by wires to a limited number of receivers. **'close-down** n [C] act of closing sth down. **closed 'shop** n [C] place of work where the employees must be members of a particular trade union.

close² /kləʊs/ adj (~r, ~st) 1 near. 2 (a) near in relationship: ~ relatives. (b) intimate: a ~ friend. 3 thorough: ~ inspection. 4 won by a small difference: a ~ race. 5 uncomfortably hot and without fresh air. 6 (idm) a ,close 'call/ 'shave situation in which a disaster or failure is only just avoided. **close** adv in a close position: follow ~ behind. **,close-'fitting** adj (of clothes) fitting tightly to the body. **,close-'knit** adj (of a group of people) joined together closely by shared beliefs, activities, etc. **closely** adv. **closeness** n [U]. **,close-'set** adj situated very close together: ~ ,set 'eyes. **'close-up** n [C] photograph taken very near.

close³ /kləʊs/ n [C] 1 street closed at one end. 2 grounds of a cathedral.

closet /'klɒzɪt/ n [C] (esp US) cupboard. **closet** adj secret. **closet** v [T] shut away in a private room.

closure /'kləʊʒə(r)/ n [C, U] closing: the ~ of the factory.

clot /klɒt/ n [C] 1 lump formed from a liquid, esp blood. 2 (Brit infml) fool. **clot** v (-tt-) [I, T] form

into clots(1).

cloth /klɒθ; US klɔ:θ/ n (a) [U] material made by weaving cotton, wool, etc. (b) [C] piece of cloth used for a special purpose: a 'table ~.

clothe /kləʊð/ v [T] provide clothes for.

clothes /kləʊðz; US kləʊz/ n [pl] covering for a person's body. **'clothes-horse** n [C] frame on which clothes are hung to dry, esp indoors. **'clothes-line** n [C] rope stretched between posts on which washed clothes are hung to dry. **'clothes-peg** n [C] wooden or plastic clip for fastening clothes to a clothes-line.

clothing /'kləʊðɪŋ/ n [U] clothes.

cloud /klaʊd/ n 1 [C, U] (mass of) visible water vapour floating in the sky. 2 [C] mass of eg dust or smoke in the air. 3 [C] (fig) thing causing unhappiness, uncertainty, etc. 4 (idm) **under a 'cloud** in disgrace; under suspicion. **cloud** v 1 [I, T] become or make unclear: The sky ~ed over. 2 [T] confuse. **cloudy** adj (-ier, -iest) 1 cover with clouds. 2 not clear.

clout /klaʊt/ n [T] (infml) hit, esp with the hand. **clout** n (infml) 1 [C] heavy blow, esp with the hand. 2 [U] power or influence.

clove¹ /kləʊv/ n [C] dried flower-bud of a tropical tree, used as a spice.

clove² /kləʊv/ n [C] one of the small separate sections of a bulb(2): a ~ of garlic.

clover /'kləʊvə(r)/ n [U, C] small plant with (usu) three leaves on each stalk.

clown /klaʊn/ n [C] (a) performer in a circus who does silly things to make people laugh. (b) person behaving foolishly. **clown** v [I] behave foolishly.

club /klʌb/ n [C] 1 (a) group of people who meet for sport, social entertainment, etc. (b) building where such a group meets. 2 thick heavy stick used as a weapon. 3 stick for hitting the ball in golf. 4 playing-card with black three-leaved shapes. **club** v (-bb-) 1 [T] hit with a club(2). 2 (phr v) **club together** join together to give money for sth.

cluck /klʌk/ v [I] n [C] (make the) noise of a hen.

clue /klu:/ n [C] 1 something that gives help in finding an answer to a problem. 2 (idm) **not have a 'clue** (infml) not know anything. **clueless** adj (infml derog) stupid.

clump¹ /klʌmp/ n [C] group (esp of trees or plants).

73 cockroach

clump² /klʌmp/ v [I] walk heavily and awkwardly.

clumsy /'klʌmzɪ/ adj (-ier, -iest) 1 lacking in skill and ungraceful in movement. 2 difficult to use. 3 tactless. **clumsily** adv. **clumsiness** n [U].

clung pt, pp of CLING.

cluster /'klʌstə(r)/ n [C] group of things close together. **cluster** v [I] form a close group.

clutch¹ /klʌtʃ/ v [I, T] (try to) hold tightly, esp with the hands. **clutch** n [C] 1 act of clutching. 2 **clutches** [pl] (infml) power of control: be in sb's ~es. 3 [C] device that connects and disconnects the engine and gears in a motor vehicle.

clutch² /klʌtʃ/ n [C] group of bird's eggs that hatch together.

clutter /'klʌtə(r)/ n [U] (esp unnecessary or unwanted) things lying about untidily. **clutter** v [T] make (a room, desk, etc) untidy.

cm abbr (pl **cm** or ~s) centimetre(s).

CND /ˌsiː en 'diː/ abbr Campaign for Nuclear Disarmament.

Co abbr company(1).

c/o /ˌsiː 'əʊ/ abbr (on letters, etc addressed to sb staying at sb else's house) care of.

coach¹ /kəʊtʃ/ n [C] 1 bus for carrying passengers on long journeys. 2 railway carriages. 3 carriage pulled by horses.

coach² /kəʊtʃ/ v [T] teach (sb), esp for an examination or in a game. **coach** n [C] person who coaches sb or a team.

coagulate /kəʊˈægjʊleɪt/ v [I, T] change from a liquid to a thick semi-solid state.

coal /kəʊl/ n [C, U] (piece of) black mineral that is burnt as a fuel. 'coal-face n [C] surface in a coal-mine from which coal is cut. 'coalfield n [C] district in which coal is mined. 'coal-mine n [C] place underground where coal is dug. 'coal-miner n [C] person whose job is digging coal in a coal-mine.

coalesce /ˌkəʊəˈles/ v [I] (fml) come together and unite.

coalition /ˌkəʊəˈlɪʃn/ n [C] union of political parties for a special purpose.

coarse /kɔːs/ adj (~r, ~st) 1 rough; not fine. 2 rude and offensive. **coarsely** adv. **coarsen** /'kɔːsn/ v [I, T] become or make coarse. **coarseness** n [U].

coast /kəʊst/ n [C] 1 land next to the sea. 2 (idm) the coast is 'clear (infml) there is no danger of being seen or caught. **coast** v [I] move, esp downhill, without using power. **coastal** adj. 'coastguard n [C,

also sing with pl v] (one of a) group of people on police duty on the coast. 'coastline n [C] shape or outline of a coast.

coat /kəʊt/ n [C] 1 outer garment with sleeves, usu fastened at the front with buttons. 2 fur or hair on an animal. 3 layer on a surface: a ~ of paint. **coat** v [T] cover (sth) with a layer of sth. 'coat-hanger n [C] curved piece of wood, metal, etc used for hanging a garment on. **coating** n [C] thin layer. coat of 'arms n [C] design on a shield used as a sign by a noble family, town, etc.

coax /kəʊks/ v [T] 1 persuade gently or gradually. 2 (phr v) **coax sth out of/from sb** obtain sth from sb by persuading them gently.

cob /kɒb/ n [C] 1 strong short-legged horse. 2 male swan. 3 = CORN-COB (CORN¹).

cobble¹ /'kɒbl/ (also 'cobble-stone) n rounded stone used for covering the surface of a road. **cobbled** adj.

cobble² /'kɒbl/ v (phr v) **cobble sth together** put sth together quickly or roughly.

cobbler /'kɒblə(r)/ n [C] person who repairs shoes.

cobra /'kəʊbrə/ n [C] poisonous snake of India and Africa.

cobweb /'kɒbweb/ n [C] spider's web.

cocaine /kəʊˈkeɪn/ n [U] drug taken for pleasure by addicts.

cock¹ /kɒk/ n [C] male bird, esp an adult male chicken.

cock² /kɒk/ n [C] 1 tap or valve for controlling the flow of a liquid in a pipe. 2 hammer of a gun.

cock³ /kɒk/ v [T] 1 raise or turn (sth) upwards: The horse ~ed its ears. 2 raise the hammer of (a gun) ready for firing. 3 (phr v) **cock sth up** (Brit infml) spoil or ruin sth. 'cock-up n [C] (Brit infml) act of making a bad mistake.

cockatoo /ˌkɒkəˈtuː/ n [C] (pl ~s) kind of parrot with a large crest.

cockerel /'kɒkərəl/ n [C] young cock¹.

cock-eyed /'kɒk aɪd/ adj (infml) 1 not straight or level; crooked. 2 stupid: a ~ plan.

cockle /'kɒkl/ n [C] small edible shellfish.

cockney /'kɒknɪ/ n (a) [C] native of London, esp sb from the east of the city. (b) [U] dialect spoken by cockneys.

cockpit /'kɒkpɪt/ n [C] part of a small aircraft in which the pilot sits.

cockroach /'kɒkrəʊtʃ/ n [C]

large dark-brown insect that lives esp in damp rooms.

cocksure /ˈkɒkˈʃɔː(r); US ·ˈʃʊər/ adj (infml) too confident.

cocktail /ˈkɒkteɪl/ n [C] 1 mixed alcoholic drink. 2 mixture of fruit or shellfish: a ,prawn '~.

cocky /ˈkɒkɪ/ adj (-ier, -iest) (infml) too self-confident.

cocoa /ˈkəʊkəʊ/ n (a) [U] brown powder tasting like bitter chocolate. (b) [U, C] hot drink made from this.

coconut /ˈkəʊkənʌt/ n [C] large nut having a hard hairy shell and an edible white lining and filled with milky juice.

cocoon /kəˈkuːn/ n [C] silky covering made by an insect larva to protect itself while it is a chrysalis.

cod /kɒd/ n (a) [C] (pl cod) large sea-fish. (b) [U] its flesh eaten as food.

coddle /ˈkɒdl/ v [T] treat (sb) too kindly.

code /kəʊd/ n 1 [C] system of rules and principles: a ~ of behaviour. 2 [C, U] system of secret writing in which letters, words, etc represent others: break the ~ the enemy use to send messages. 3 [C] system of signs or symbols used to send messages by machine. **code** v [T] put into a code.

coed /ˌkəʊˈed/ n [C] (esp US infml) female student at a coeducational college, etc. **coed** adj (infml) coeducational.

coeducation /ˌkəʊedʒʊˈkeɪʃn/ n [U] education of boys and girls together. **coeducational** adj.

coerce /kəʊˈɜːs/ v [T] (fml) force (sb) to do sth. **coercion** /-ˈɜːʃn; US -ˈɜːʒn/ n [U]. **coercive** adj.

coexist /ˌkəʊɪgˈzɪst/ v [I] exist at the same time or in the same place. **coexistence** n [U] (of countries) existing together: peaceful ~ ence.

coffee /ˈkɒfɪ; US ˈkɔːfɪ/ n (a) [U] (powder obtained by grinding the roasted) seeds of the coffee tree. (b) [U, C] drink made by adding hot water to powdered coffee.

coffer /ˈkɒfə(r)/ n 1 [C] large strong box for holding money, etc. 2 **coffers** [pl] (fml) store of money.

coffin /ˈkɒfɪn/ n [C] box in which a dead body is buried or cremated.

cog /kɒg/ n [C] 1 one of the teeth on a wheel that moves the teeth of a similar wheel. 2 (idm) **a cog in a ma'chine** unimportant but necessary person in a large organization. **'cog-wheel** n [C] wheel with teeth round the edge.

cogent /ˈkəʊdʒənt/ adj (fml) (of an argument, reason, etc) strong; convincing.

cognac /ˈkɒnjæk/ n [U] kind of brandy.

cohabit /kəʊˈhæbɪt/ v [I] (fml) (of an unmarried couple) live together as husband and wife. **cohabitation** /ˌkəʊhæbɪˈteɪʃn/ n [U].

cohere /kəʊˈhɪə(r)/ v [I] 1 stick together in a mass. 2 (of ideas, etc) be connected logically. **coherent** /-ˈhɪərənt/ adj (of ideas, speech, etc) connected logically; clear and easy to understand. **coherence** /-rəns/ n [U]. **coherently** adv.

cohesion /kəʊˈhiːʒn/ n [U] tendency to stick together; unity. **cohesive** /-ˈhiːsɪv/ adj.

coil /kɔɪl/ v [I, T] twist into a continuous circular shape. **coil** n [C] 1 length of rope, etc wound into a series of loops. 2 single ring or loop of rope, etc. 3 device put inside a woman's womb to stop her from becoming pregnant.

coin /kɔɪn/ n [C] piece of metal used as money. **coin** v [T] 1 make (coins). 2 invent (a new word or phrase). **coinage** /ˈkɔɪnɪdʒ/ n [U] coins in use in a country.

coincide /ˌkəʊɪnˈsaɪd/ v [I] 1 (of events) happen at the same time. 2 (of opinions or ideas) agree. 3 (of objects) occupy the same amount of space.

coincidence /kəʊˈɪnsɪdəns/ n [C, U] (instance of the) happening of two or more things at the same time by chance: It was pure ~ that we were both travelling on the same plane. **coincidental** /kəʊˌɪnsɪˈdentl/ adj happening by chance.

coke /kəʊk/ n [U] substance that remains when gas has been taken out of coal, used as a fuel.

colander (also **cullender**) /ˈkʌləndə(r)/ n [C] bowl with many small holes in it, used to drain water from food.

cold[1] /kəʊld/ adj 1 of low temperature. 2 (of food) not heated; having cooled after being heated. 3 unfriendly; unfeeling: a ~ stare/ welcome. 4 unconscious: knock sb out ~. 5 (idm) **get/have cold 'feet** (infml) become/be afraid to do sth. **give sb/get the cold 'shoulder** treat sb/be treated in an unfriendly way. **in cold 'blood** deliberately cruel and without feeling: kill sb in ~ blood. **pour/throw cold 'water on sth** be discouraging or not enthusiastic about sth. **cold-'blooded** adj 1 (of animals) having a blood temperature that varies with the surroundings. 2 without pity; cruel. **cold-'hearted** adj unkind. **coldly** adj. **coldness** n [U].

,cold 'war n [sing] extreme political struggle between nations without actually fighting.

cold² /kəʊld/ n **1** [U] low temperature. **2** [C, U] illness of the nose or throat. **3** (idm) (**be left**) **out in the 'cold** (be) ignored.

coleslaw /'kəʊlslɔː/ n [U] finely shredded raw cabbage, carrots, etc mixed with mayonnaise.

colic /'kɒlɪk/ n [U] severe pain in the stomach and bowels.

collaborate /kə'læbəreɪt/ v [I] **1** work together. **2** (with)// help the enemy. **collaboration** /kə,læbə'reɪʃn/ n [U]. **collaborator** n [C].

collage /'kɒlɑːʒ; US kə'lɑːʒ/ n [C] picture made by sticking pieces of paper, cloth, etc onto a surface.

collapse /kə'læps/ v **1** [I] fall down suddenly: *The building ~d in the earthquake.* **2** [I] fall down (and become unconscious) because of illness or tiredness. **3** [I] fail suddenly and completely. **4** [I, T] fold into a flat compact shape: *The table ~s to fit into the cupboard.* **collapse** n [sing]: *the ~ of the company.* **collapsible** adj that can be collapsed(4) for packing, etc.

collar /'kɒlə(r)/ n [C] **1** part of a garment that fits round the neck. **2** band of leather, etc put round the neck of a dog or other animal. **collar** v [T] seize or catch. **'collarbone** n [C] bone joining the breastbone and the shoulder-blade.

collate /kə'leɪt/ v [T] gather (information) to examine and compare it.

collateral /kə'lætərəl/ n [U] property or money used as a security(3) for a loan.

colleague /'kɒliːɡ/ n [C] person with whom one works.

collect /kə'lekt/ v **1** [I, T] come or bring together: *~ the empty glasses* ○ *A crowd ~ed at the scene of the accident.* **2** [I] save (stamps, etc) as a hobby. **3** [I, T] (for)// obtain money from a number of people for sb/sth: *~ money for charity.* **4** [T] fetch: *~ a child from school.* **5** [T] regain control of (oneself or one's thoughts). **collect** adj, adv (US) (of a telephone call) to be paid for by the receiver. **collected** adj calm and self-controlled. **collection** /kə'lekʃn/ n **1** [U] collecting. **2** [C] group of things collected. **3** [C] sum of money collected. **collective** adj of a group or society as a whole; shared. **collectively** adv. **collector** n [C] person who coll-

ects sth: *a 'ticket-~ or.*

college /'kɒlɪdʒ/ n [C] **1** institution for higher education; part of a university. **2** organized group of professional people: *the Royal C~ of Surgeons.*

collide /kə'laɪd/ v [I] **1** (of moving objects or people) hit each other or against sb/sth. **2** be opposed.

collier /'kɒlɪə(r)/ n [C] coalminer. **colliery** /'kɒlɪərɪ/ n [C] (pl -ies) coalmine.

collision /kə'lɪʒn/ n [C, U] (instance of) colliding.

colloquial /kə'ləʊkwɪəl/ adj (of words, style, etc) suitable for normal conversation; not formal or literary. **colloquialism** n [C] colloquial word or phrase. **colloquially** adv.

collude /kə'luːd/ v [I] (with)// (fml) work together with sb secretly and dishonestly. **collusion** /kə'luːʒn/ n [U].

colon¹ /'kəʊlən/ n [C] punctuation mark (:).

colon² /'kəʊlən/ n [C] lower part of the large intestine.

colonel /'kɜːnl/ n [C] middle-ranking officer in the army or US air force.

colonial /kə'ləʊnɪəl/ adj of a colony(1) or colonies. **colonial** n [C] person living in a colony(1). **colonialism** n [U] policy of having colonies/1. **colonialist** n [C], adj.

colonist /'kɒlənɪst/ n [C] person who settles in an area and colonizes it.

colonize /'kɒlənaɪz/ v [T] establish (an area) as a colony(1). **colonization** /,kɒlənaɪ'zeɪʃn; US -nɪ'z-/ n [U].

colonnade /,kɒlə'neɪd/ n [C] row of columns(1).

colony /'kɒlənɪ/ n [C] (pl -ies) **1** country lived in and controlled by people from another country. **2** group of people with the same interest, etc living in the same place.

color (US) = COLOUR¹·².

colossal /kə'lɒsl/ adj very large.

colossus /kə'lɒsəs/ n [C] (pl -lossi /-lɒsaɪ/ or ~es) **1** very large statue. **2** person of very great size, importance, etc.

colour¹ /'kʌlə(r)/ n **1** (a) [U] appearance of sth as a result of rays of light of different wavelengths being reflected. (b) [C] particular kind of this; red, green, etc. **2** [U] appearance of the skin. **3** colours [pl] (a) badge, etc worn to show that one is a member of a particular team, school, etc. (b) flag. **4** [C] lively detail of sth; interest. **5** (idm) **off colour** (infml) unwell;

ill. **with ,flying 'colours** with great success. **'colour bar** *n* [C] discrimination against people of certain races, esp towards black people. **,colour-'blind** *adj* unable to distinguish between colours(1). **colourful** *adj* 1 brightly coloured. 2 interesting or exciting. **colourless** *adj* 1 without colour(1). 2 dull and uninteresting. **'colour supplement** *n* [C] (*Brit*) magazine with coloured pictures, given free with a Sunday newspaper.

colour² /'kʌlə(r)/ *v* 1 [T] give colour to. 2 [I] blush. 3 [T] affect or influence. 4 (phr v) **colour sth in** fill (a picture, etc) with colour. **coloured** *adj* 1 having the colour that is mentioned; not just black or white. 2 of a race that does not have a white skin. **colouring** *n* 1 [U] (a) colours of sth. (b) colours of sb's skin. 2 [C, U] substance that gives colour to food.

colt /kəʊlt/ *n* [C] young male horse.

column /'kɒləm/ *n* [C] 1 (a) tall pillar supporting part of a building or standing alone. (b) something shaped like this: *a ~ of smoke.* 2 group of people, etc moving in a long line. 3 (a) newspaper article. (b) vertical division of a printed page. **columnist** /-nɪst/ *n* [C] person who writes a newspaper column.

coma /'kəʊmə/ *n* [C] state of deep unconsciousness.

comb /kəʊm/ *n* [C] 1 piece of plastic or metal with teeth, used for making the hair tidy. 2 [usu sing] act of combing: *give one's hair a ~.* 3 *n* [C, U] = HONEYCOMB (HONEY). **comb** *v* [T] 1 tidy (one's hair) with a comb. 2 search thoroughly.

combat /'kɒmbæt/ *n* [C, U], *v* [I, T] fight; struggle. **combatant** /-bətənt/ *n* [C] person who fights. **combatant** *adj* fighting.

combination /ˌkɒmbɪ'neɪʃn/ *n* 1 [C] number of things or people joined or mixed together: *a ~ of traditional and modern architecture.* 2 [U] act of combining. 3 [C] series of numbers or letters needed to open the lock of a safe, etc.

combine¹ /kəm'baɪn/ *v* [I, T] join or mix together.

combine² /'kɒmbaɪn/ *n* [C] group of people or business firms working together. **,combine 'harvester** *n* [C] machine that both cuts and threshes grain.

combustible /kəm'bʌstəbl/ *adj* that can catch fire and burn easily.

combustion /kəm'bʌstʃən/ *n* [U]

process of burning.

come /kʌm/ *v* (*pt* **came** /keɪm/, *pp* **come**) [I] 1 (a) move towards the speaker or the place to which he/she is referring: *~ and talk to me.* (b) arrive. 2 travel a specified distance: *We've ~ thirty miles since lunch.* 3 reach; extend: *The path ~s right up to the gate.* 4 occur; take place: *Christmas ~s once a year.* 5 exist; be available: *This dress ~s in several different colours.* 6 become: *~ loose.* 7 *to/* **begin:** *~ to realize the truth.* 8 *to/ into/* reach a certain state or condition: *~ to an end.* 9 (idm) **come to grips with sth** ⇒ GRIP. **come to a 'head** ⇒ HEAD¹. **come loose** ⇒ LOOSE. **come to nothing** be unsuccessful. **come out into the open** ⇒ OPEN¹. **come what may** whatever may happen. **how come** (*...*)? (*infml*) how does/did it happen (that *...*)? **to come** in the future: *for several years to ~.* 10 (phr v) **come a'bout** happen. **come across sb/sth** find or meet by chance. **come a'long (a)** arrive: *When the right job ~s along, she'll take it.* (b) progress, develop or improve: *Her work is coming along nicely.* (c) = COME ON C. **come a'part** fall to pieces. **come at sb** (with sth) attack: *He came at me with a knife.* **come 'back** return. **come 'back (to sb)** be remembered. **come before sb/sth** be dealt with by sb/sth. **come between A and B** interfere. **'come by sth** obtain or receive: *Good jobs are hard to ~ by these days.* **come 'down (a)** collapse. (b) (of rain, prices, etc) fall. (c) reach a decision (against, for, or in favour of sth). **come down to sb** (of traditions, stories, etc) be passed on to younger members of the family, etc. **come down to sth (a)** reach as far down as (a stated point): *Her hair ~s down to her waist.* (b) be able to be expressed in a certain way: *What it ~s down to is that if your work doesn't improve you'll have to leave.* **come in (a)** (of the tide) move towards the land. (b) become fashionable. (c) be received as income, etc. (d) have a part to play: *Where do I ~ in?* **come in for sth** be the object of (punishment, criticism, etc). **come into sth** inherit sth. **'come off sth (a)** be able to be removed: *Will these dirty marks ~ off?* (b) take place: *Did your holiday ~ off?* (c) (of plans, etc) succeed: *The experiment did not ~ off.* **come off (sth) (a)** be separated from sth: *The but-*

ton has ~ off my coat. (b) fall off eg a horse, bicycle, etc. **come on** (a) (of an actor) walk onto the stage. (b) = COME ALONG b. (c) (said to encourage or challenge sb): *C~ on, if we don't hurry we'll be late.* (d) (of rain, night, illness, etc) begin: *I think he has a cold coming on.* **come 'out** (a) become visible; appear: *The rain stopped and the sun came out.* (b) become known; be published: *The truth came out eventually.* (c) (of workers) strike. (d) be clearly revealed, eg in a photograph. **come 'out (of sth)** be removed from sth: *Will the stains ~ out?* **come out in sth** become (partly) covered in spots, etc: ~ *out in a rash.* **come out with sth** say sth: ~ *out with the strangest remarks.* **come over** (a) move from one place to another, esp for a visit: ~ *over to Scotland for a holiday.* (b) be communicated: *Your position didn't really ~ over in your speech.* **come over sb** (of feelings, etc) affect sb: *A feeling of dizziness came over him.* **come 'round** (a) come by an indirect route. (b) visit: *C~ round to my place for the evening.* (c) occur again: *Christmas seems to ~ round quicker every year.* (d) become conscious again. (e) be converted to sb else's opinions, views, etc. **come 'through** (of a message, signal, etc) arrive. **come through (sth)** recover from a serious illness or escape injury. **come 'to** = COME ROUND d. **,come to 'sth** amount to sth; be equal to sth: *The bill came to £20.* **come to sb** occur to sb: *The idea came to me in a dream.* **come under sth** (a) be in (a certain category, etc). (b) be subjected to sth: ~ *under her influence.* **come 'up** (a) (of plants, etc) become visible above the ground. (b) be mentioned: *The question hasn't ~ up yet.* (c) occur: *A couple of problems have ~ up so I'll be late home from work.* **come up against sb/sth** meet (difficulties, etc). **come up (to sth)** reach (sth): *The water came up to my waist.* **come up with sth** produce or find: ~ *up with a solution.* **come upon sb/sth** find unexpectedly: ~ *upon a group of children playing.* **come-back** *n* [C, usu sing] return to a previous (successful) position. **come-down** *n* [C, usu sing] loss of power, status, dignity, etc. **coming** *adj* future: *in the coming months.* **coming** 1 [sing] arrival: *the coming of spring.* 2 (idm) **,comings and 'goings** arrivals and departures.

comedian /kə'mi:dɪən/ *n* [C] 1 (*fem* **comedienne** /kə,mi:dɪ'en/) performer who makes people laugh. 2 person who behaves in a comic way.

comedy /'kɒmədɪ/ *n* (*pl* -**ies**) 1 [C] amusing play, film, etc. 2 [U] amusing aspect of sth.

comet /'kɒmɪt/ *n* [C] bright object, like a star with a long tail, that moves round the sun.

comfort /'kʌmfət/ *n* 1 [U] state of being relaxed and free from pain or worry. 2 [U] kindness to sb who is suffering: *words of* ~. 3 [sing] person or thing that brings help or relief. 4 [C, usu pl] thing that gives physical ease and makes life more pleasant. **comfort** *v* [T] make (sb) less unhappy or worried. **comfortable** /'kʌmftəbl; US -fət-/ *adj* 1 giving comfort to the body: *a ~able chair.* 2 giving freedom from worry: *a ~able job.* 3 (*infml*) fairly rich. 4 more than adequate. **comfortably** *adv.*

comic /'kɒmɪk/ *adj* 1 causing people to laugh. 2 of comedy. **comic** *n* [C] 1 comedian. 2 children's magazine with stories told in pictures. **comical** *adj* causing people to laugh. **comic 'strip** *n* [C] series of drawings telling an amusing story.

comma /'kɒmə/ *n* [C] punctuation mark (,).

command /kə'mɑːnd; US -'mænd/ *v* 1 [I, T] order. 2 deserve and obtain: ~ *respect.* 3 [T] be in charge of: ~ *a regiment.* 4 [T] have a clear view of (a place): *a ~ ing position over the valley.* **command** *n* 1 [C] order. 2 [U] control; authority: *in ~ of a ship.* 3 **Command** [C] part of an army, air force, etc. 4 [U, sing] ability to use sth: *a good ~ of French.*

commandant /,kɒmən'dænt/ *n* [C] officer in command of a military establishment.

commandeer /,kɒmən'dɪə(r)/ *v* [T] take possession or control of (sth) for official, esp military, purposes.

commander /kə'mɑːndə(r); US -'mæn-/ *n* [C] 1 person who commands. 2 middle-ranking officer in the navy.

commandment /kə'mɑːndmənt; US -'mænd-/ *n* [C] law given by God.

commando /kə'mɑːndəʊ; US -'mæn-/ *n* [C] (*pl* ~**s** or ~**es**) (member of a) group of soldiers trained to make quick raids.

commemorate /kə'meməreɪt/ *v* [T] honour the memory of (sb, an event, etc). **commemoration**

/kə,meməˈreɪʃn/ n [C, U].
commemorative /-rətɪv/ adj.

commence /kəˈmens/ v [I, T] (fml) begin; start. **commencement** n [C, U].

commend /kəˈmend/ v [T] (fml) 1 praise; recommend. 2 ~ **oneself** to be approved by sb. **commendable** adj deserving praise. **commendation** /ˌkɒmenˈdeɪʃn/ n [U, C].

commensurate /kəˈmenʃərət/ adj with|| (fml) in the right proportion to sth: pay ~ with the importance of the job.

comment /ˈkɒment/ n [C, U] written or spoken statement of opinion. **comment** v [I] (on)|| give one's opinion on sth.

commentary /ˈkɒməntri; US -teri/ n (pl -ies) 1 [C] broadcast description of an event as it happens: a ~ on a football match. 2 [C] set of explanations on a book, etc.

commentate /ˈkɒmənteɪt/ v [I] give a commentary(1). **commentator** n [C].

commerce /ˈkɒmɑːs/ n [U] buying and selling of goods; trade.

commercial /kəˈmɑːʃl/ adj 1 of or relating to commerce. 2 making a profit. 3 (of television or radio) paid for by advertisements. **commercial** n [C] advertisement on television or radio. **commercialized** adj concerned mainly with making a profit. **commercially** /-ʃəli/ adv. com,**mercial ˈtraveller** n [C] person whose job is to go to different shops, etc to sell a company's products and get orders for them.

commiserate /kəˈmɪzəreɪt/ v [I] (with)|| (fml) show sympathy to sb: I ~ d with her on the loss of her job. **commiseration** /kəˌmɪzəˈreɪʃn/ n [C, U].

commission /kəˈmɪʃn/ n 1 [C] task or piece of work given to sb to do. 2 [C, U] money paid to sb who sells goods for making a sale. 3 [C] group of people officially appointed to find out sth and to report on it. 4 [C] official paper appointing an officer in the armed forces. **commission** v [T] 1 formally ask (sb) to do a piece of work. 2 appoint (sb) officially by means of a commission(4).

commissionaire /kəˌmɪʃəˈneə(r)/ n [C] (esp Brit) uniformed attendant at the entrance to a cinema, theatre, hotel, etc.

commissioner /kəˈmɪʃənə(r)/ n [C] 1 member of a commission(3). 2 government representative.

commit /kəˈmɪt/ v (-tt-) [T] 1 do (sth wrong or foolish). 2 (to)|| promise that sb/one will do sth: The government has ~ ted itself to fighting inflation. 3 ~ **oneself** give one's opinion firmly. 4 send (sb) to a prison or hospital. **commitment** n 1 [C] something that one has promised to do. 2 [U] loyalty.

committee /kəˈmɪti/ n [C, also sing with pl v] group of people appointed to deal with a particular matter.

commodity /kəˈmɒdəti/ n [C] (pl -ies) useful thing, esp an article of trade; product.

common¹ /ˈkɒmən/ adj 1 happening or found often and in many places; usual. 2 shared or used by two or more people: a ~ interest ○ ~ knowledge. 3 (derog) (of people) having bad manners; vulgar. ,common 'ground n [U] shared opinions or aims. ,common 'law n [U] (esp in England) unwritten law based on customs and earlier legal decisions. 'common-law adj. commonly adv. the ,Common 'Market n [sing] the European Economic Community; economic association of certain European countries which helps to promote trade between the members. 'commonplace adj ordinary. ,common 'sense n [U] practical good sense gained from experience of life.

common² /ˈkɒmən/ n 1 [C] area of unfenced land which everyone may use. 2 (idm) have sth in common share interests, characteristics, etc. in common with sb/sth together with sb/sth.

commoner /ˈkɒmənə(r)/ n [C] person who is not a member of the nobility.

Commons /ˈkɒmənz/ n the Commons [sing, also sing with pl v] (members of) the House of Commons, that part of the British government which is elected.

commonwealth /ˈkɒmənwelθ/ n 1 [C] group of States that have chosen to be politically linked: the C~ of Australia. 2 the Commonwealth [sing] association of independent States that were formerly colonies and dominions of Britain.

commotion /kəˈməʊʃn/ n [sing, U] noisy confusion.

communal /ˈkɒmjʊnl, kəˈmjuːnl/ adj shared by a group of people.

commune¹ /ˈkɒmjuːn/ n [C] 1 group of people who live together and share property and responsibilities. 2 (in France, etc) smallest unit of local government.

commune² /kəˈmjuːn/ v [I] *with/* feel close to sth; talk to sb: ~ *with nature.*

communicate /kəˈmjuːnɪkeɪt/ v 1 [I, T] make (sth) known. 2 [T] pass on (a disease). 3 [I] (of rooms) be connected: *a communicating door.* **communication** /kə,mjuːnɪˈkeɪʃn/ n 1 [U] communicating. 2 [C] (*fml*) letter, telephone call, etc. 3 **communications** [pl] ways of sending information, esp electronically; ways of travelling. **communicative** /-kətɪv; US -keɪtɪv/ adj willing to give information or talk.

communion /kəˈmjuːnɪən/ n [U] 1 (*fml*) sharing thoughts, feelings, etc. 2 **Communion** Christian service of sharing bread and wine.

communiqué /kəˈmjuːnɪkeɪ; US kə,mjuːnəˈkeɪ/ n [C] official announcement.

communism /ˈkɒmjunɪzəm/ n [U] (a) social and economic system in which there is no private ownership and the means of production belongs to all members of society. (b) **Communism** political doctrine or movement that aims to establish such a society; such a system established eg in the USSR. **communist** /-nɪst/ n [C], adj.

community /kəˈmjuːnətɪ/ n (pl -ies) 1 **the community** [sing] all the people living in one place. 2 [C, also sing with pl v] group of people with the same interests, etc. 3 [U] condition of sharing or having things in common. **community charge** [sing] (in the UK) form of local tax paid by every adult.

commute /kəˈmjuːt/ v 1 [I] travel regularly between one's home and work. 2 [T] replace (a punishment) by one that is less severe. **commuter** n [C] person who commutes(1).

compact¹ /kəmˈpækt/ adj closely packed together; neatly fitted in a small space. **,compact 'disc** n [C] small disc on which information or sound is recorded and reproduced by laser action. **compactly** adv. **compactness** n [U].

compact² /ˈkɒmpækt/ n [C] small flat container for face-powder.

companion /kəmˈpænɪən/ n [C] person who spends time or travels with another. **companionship** n [U] relationship between friends or companions.

company /ˈkʌmpənɪ/ n (pl -ies) 1 [C] business organization. 2 [U] group of people working together: *an opera* ~. 3 [U] being together with others: *He is good/bad* ~, ie

he is pleasant/unpleasant to be with. 4 [U] group of people; visitors. 5 [U] people with whom one spends one's time: *That girl keeps very bad* ~. 6 [C] group of soldiers that forms part of a battalion.

comparable /ˈkɒmpərəbl/ adj that can be compared; similar.

comparative /kəmˈpærətɪv/ adj 1 of a comparison or comparing. 2 measured by comparing; relative: *living in* ~ *comfort.* 3 (*grammar*) (of adjectives and adverbs expressing a greater degree or 'more', eg *better, worse*: *'Better' is the* ~ *form of 'good'.* **comparative** n [C] (*grammar*) comparative form of an adjective or adverb. **comparatively** adv.

compare /kəmˈpeə(r)/ v 1 [T] (*with/to*)] examine things to see how they are alike and how they are different: ~ *the results of one test with the results of another.* 2 [T] *A to B*/] show the likeness between sb/sth and sb/sth else. 3 [I] *with/*] be worthy of being compared with sth. 4 (idm) **compare 'notes** exchange opinions.

comparison /kəmˈpærɪsn/ n 1 [C, U] 2 [U] likeness: *There is no* ~ *between them.* 3 (idm) **by/in comparison (with sb/sth)** when compared with sb/sth.

compartment /kəmˈpɑːtmənt/ n [C] section of a railway carriage; separate part of sth.

compass /ˈkʌmpəs/ n 1 [C] device for finding direction, with a needle that points north. 2 **compasses** [pl] V-shaped instrument for drawing circles. 3 [C] (*fml*) range; scope: *beyond the* ~ *of the human mind.*

compassion /kəmˈpæʃn/ n [U] feeling of pity for the suffering of others. **compassionate** /-ʃənət/ adj showing or feeling compassion. **compassionately** adv.

compatible /kəmˈpætəbl/ adj (eg of people, ideas or principles) able to exist together. **compatibility** /kəm,pætəˈbɪlətɪ/ n [U].

compatriot /kəmˈpætrɪət; US -ˈpeɪt-/ n [C] person from the same country as another.

compel /kəmˈpel/ v (-ll-) [T] (*fml*) force (sb) to do sth. **compelling** adj convincing.

compensate /ˈkɒmpenseɪt/ v [I, T] (*for*)/] pay or give (sb) sth to balance or lessen the bad effect of damage, loss, etc. **compensation** /,kɒmpenˈseɪʃn/ n 1 [U] compensating. 2 [U, C] something given to compensate.

compère /ˈkɒmpeə(r)/ n [C] person who introduces the performers or guests in a radio or television show. **compère** *v* [T] act as a compère for.

compete /kəm'pri:t/ *v* [I] take part in a race, contest, etc; try to win by defeating others: ~ *against/with others*.

competence /'kɒmpɪtəns/ *n* [U] 1 being competent; ability. 2 (*fml*) legal authority. **competent** /-tənt/ *adj* having the ability, skill, knowledge, etc to do sth. **competently** *adv*.

competition /ˌkɒmpə'tɪʃn/ *n* 1 [C] event in which people compete: *a photography* ~. 2 [U] trying to win; competing. **competitive** /kəm'petətɪv/ *adj* 1 of or involving competition. 2 eager to compete.

competitor /kəm'petɪtə(r)/ *n* [C] person who competes.

compile /kəm'paɪl/ *v* [T] produce (a book, report, etc) by collecting information. **compilation** /ˌkɒmpɪ'leɪʃn/ *n* 1 [U] compiling. 2 [C] something that is compiled. **compiler** *n* [C].

complacent /kəm'pleɪsnt/ *adj* (*usu derog*) calmly satisfied. **complacency** /-snsɪ/ *n* [U]. **complacently** *adv*.

complain /kəm'pleɪn/ *v* [I] say that one is dissatisfied or unhappy: ~ *about the food*.

complaint /kəm'pleɪnt/ *n* 1 [C, U] (statement of) complaining. 2 [C] illness; disease.

complement /'kɒmplɪmənt/ *n* [C] 1 something that goes well with sth else; making it complete: *Wine is the perfect* ~ *to a meal*. 2 total number needed. 3 (*grammar*) word(s), esp adjectives and nouns, used after a verb such as *be* or *become* describing the subject of the verb: *In 'I'm unhappy', 'unhappy'is the* ~. **complement** /-ment/ *v* [T] go well with (sth) to form a whole. **complementary** /ˌkɒmplɪ'mentrɪ/ *adj* going well with each other to form a whole.

complete /kəm'pli:t/ *adj* 1 having all its parts; whole. 2 finished; ended. 3 in every way; total: *a* ~ *surprise*. **complete** *v* [T] finish; make whole. 2 fill in (a form). **completely** *adv* in every way. **completeness** *n* [U]. **completion** /kəm'pli:ʃn/ *n* [U].

complex[1] /'kɒmpleks; *US* kəm'pleks/ *adj* made up of many different parts; difficult to understand or explain. **complexity** /kəm'pleksətɪ/ *n* [C, U] (*pl* -ies).

complex[2] /'kɒmpleks/ *n* [C] 1 group of connected or similar things: *a sports* ~. 2 abnormal

mental state resulting from a past experience.

complexion /kəm'plekʃn/ *n* [C] 1 natural appearance or quality of the skin: *a dark/fair* ~. 2 (*usu sing*) general character of sth.

compliance /kəm'plaɪəns/ *n* [U] (*fml*) action of complying. **compliant** /-ənt/ *adj* obedient.

complicate /'kɒmplɪkeɪt/ *v* [T] make (sth) difficult to do, understand or deal with. **complicated** *adj* difficult to understand or explain because there are many different parts. **complication** /ˌkɒmplɪ'keɪʃn/ *n* [C] something that makes a situation more difficult.

complicity /kəm'plɪsətɪ/ *n* [U] (*fml*) taking part with another person in a crime.

compliment /'kɒmplɪmənt/ *n* 1 [C] expression of praise, admiration, etc. 2 **compliments** [pl] (*fml*) greetings or good wishes. **compliment** /-ment/ *v* [T] express praise or admiration of. **complimentary** /ˌkɒmplɪ'mentrɪ/ *adj* 1 expressing admiration. 2 given free of charge: ~ *ary tickets*.

comply /kəm'plaɪ/ *v* (*pt, pp* -**ied**) [I] (*with*)// (*fml*) agree to do sth; obey.

component /kəm'pəʊnənt/ *n* [C] any of the parts of which sth is made. **component** *adj*.

compose /kəm'pəʊz/ *v* 1 [I, T] write (music, a poem, a letter, etc). 2 ~ *oneself* bring oneself under control. 3 (idm) **be composed of** *sb/sth* have sb/sth as its parts or members. **composed** *adj* calm. **composer** *n* [C] person who composes music.

composite /'kɒmpəzɪt/ *n* [C], *adj* (thing) made up of different parts.

composition /ˌkɒmpə'zɪʃn/ *n* 1 [C] sth, eg a piece of music, that is composed. 2 [U] action of composing sth. 3 [C] short piece of written work done at school. 4 [U] parts of which sth is made: *the chemical* ~ *of the soil*.

compost /'kɒmpɒst/ *n* [U] mixture of decayed plants, manure, etc, added to the soil to help plants grow.

composure /kəm'pəʊʒə(r)/ *n* [U] (*fml*) calmness.

compound[1] /'kɒmpaʊnd/ *n* [C] 1 thing made up of two or more parts. 2 (*grammar*) word made up of two or more words, eg *policeman*. **compound** *adj*. ˌ**compound** '**interest** *n* [U] interest paid on both the original amount of money and on the interest(5) added to it.

compound² /kəmˈpaʊnd/ v [T] (fml) 1 mix together: ~ *several chemicals*. 2 make (sth bad) worse.

compound³ /ˈkɒmpaʊnd/ n [C] enclosed area with buildings, etc.

comprehend /ˌkɒmprɪˈhend/ v [T] (fml) 1 understand fully. 2 (fml) include.

comprehension /ˌkɒmprɪˈhenʃn/ n 1 [U] power to understand sth. 2 [C] exercise to improve one's understanding. **comprehensible** /-ˈhensəbl/ adj that can be understood fully.

comprehensive /ˌkɒmprɪˈhensɪv/ adj 1 including (nearly) everything: *a ~ description*. 2 (Brit) (of education) for pupils of all abilities in the same school. **comprehensive school** n [C] (Brit) large secondary school which teaches pupils of all abilities.

compress /kəmˈpres/ v [T] 1 force into a small(er) space; press together. 2 put (ideas, etc) into fewer words. **compression** /-ˈpreʃn/ n [U].

comprise /kəmˈpraɪz/ v [T] have as parts; be composed of.

compromise /ˈkɒmprəmaɪz/ n [C, U] settling of an argument by which each side gives up sth it had asked for. **compromise** v [I] 1 make a compromise. 2 [T] put into a dangerous or embarrassing position.

compulsion /kəmˈpʌlʃn/ n 1 [U] act of compelling. 2 [C] strong desire; urge.

compulsive /kəmˈpʌlsɪv/ adj 1 caused by a strong desire or obsession: *a ~ liar*. 2 (of a book, film, etc) very interesting.

compulsory /kəmˈpʌlsəri/ adj that must be done; required by the law, etc.

compunction /kəmˈpʌŋkʃn/ n [U] (fml) feeling of guilt.

compute /kəmˈpjuːt/ v [T] (fml) calculate. **computation** /ˌkɒmpjuːˈteɪʃn/ n [U, C] calculation.

computer /kəmˈpjuːtə(r)/ n [C] electronic device for storing, analysing and producing information, for making calculations, or controlling machines. **computerize** v [T] provide a computer to do the work of. **computerization** /kəmˌpjuːtəraɪˈzeɪʃn; US -rɪˈz-/ n [U].

comrade /ˈkɒmreɪd; US -ræd/ n [C] 1 fellow member of a trade union or political party. 2 (dated) friend or companion. **comradeship** n [U].

Con /kɒn/ abbr (Brit politics)

Conservative (party).

con /kɒn/ v (-nn-) [T] (infml) trick; deceive. **con** n [C] (infml) trick. '**con man** n [C] man who persuades others to give him their money, etc.

concave /ˈkɒŋkeɪv/ adj curved inwards.

conceal /kənˈsiːl/ v [T] hide; keep secret. **concealment** n [U].

concede /kənˈsiːd/ v [I, T] 1 admit that (sth) is true. 2 [I, T] admit that one has lost (a game, etc). 3 [T] give (sth) as a right.

conceit /kənˈsiːt/ n [U] too high an opinion of oneself. **conceited** adj.

conceive /kənˈsiːv/ v [I, T] 1 (of)// form (an idea, etc) in the mind; imagine. 2 become pregnant with (a child). **conceivable** adj that can be believed; imaginable. **conceivably** adv.

concentrate /ˈkɒnsntreɪt/ v 1 [I] (on)// give one's full attention to sth: *~ on one's work*. 2 [I, T] come or bring together at one place. 3 [T] increase the strength of (a liquid, etc). **concentrate** n [C, U] substance or liquid made by concentrating(3).

concentration /ˌkɒnsnˈtreɪʃn/ n 1 [U] giving one's full attention to sth. 2 [C] grouping of people or things. **concen'tration camp** n [C] prison for political prisoners.

concentric /kənˈsentrɪk/ adj (of circles) having the same centre.

concept /ˈkɒnsept/ n [C] general idea.

conception /kənˈsepʃn/ n 1 (a) [U] forming of an idea in the mind. (b) [C] idea formed in the mind. 2 [U] act of conceiving(2).

concern¹ /kənˈsɜːn/ v 1 [T] worry (sb): *I'm ~ed about her safety*. 2 ~ oneself with be busy with (sth). 3 [T] be important to (sb); affect. 4 [T] be about (sth). 5 (idm) as far as sb/sth is concerned in the way or to the degree that sb/sth is involved or affected: *As far as I'm ~ed, it doesn't matter what you do*. **concerning** prep about.

concern² /kənˈsɜːn/ n 1 [U] worry. 2 [C] something that is important to sb. 3 [C] business; company: *a profitable ~*.

concert /ˈkɒnsət/ n 1 [C] musical performance. 2 (idm) **in 'concert** (a) giving a concert. (b) (fml) working together.

concerted /kənˈsɜːtɪd/ adj arranged or done by people working together: *make a ~ effort*.

concertina /ˌkɒnsəˈtiːnə/ n [C] musical instrument like a small accordion. **concertina** v [I] fold up (as if) by being pressed together from each end.

concerto /kənˈtʃeətəʊ, -ˈtʃɜːt-/ n [C] (pl ~s) musical composition for one instrument supported by an orchestra.

concession /kənˈseʃn/ n 1 (a) [U] conceding. (b) [C] something conceded, eg after an argument. 2 [C] special right given to sb to do sth: a ~ to drill for oil.

conciliate /kənˈsɪlɪeɪt/ v [T] (fml) make (sb) less angry. **conciliation** /kənˌsɪlɪˈeɪʃn/ n [U]. **conciliatory** /-ɪətərɪ; US -ɪetɔːrɪ/ adj wishing or likely to conciliate.

concise /kənˈsaɪs/ adj giving a lot of information in a few words: a ~ report. **concisely** adv. **conciseness** n [U].

conclude /kənˈkluːd/ v 1 [I, T] usu (fml) come or bring to an end. 2 [T] come to believe (sth) as a result of reasoning: The jury ~d that he was guilty. 3 [T] arrange and settle: ~ an agreement. **conclusion** /-ˈkluːʒn/ n [C] 1 end. 2 decision; settlement. **conclusive** /-ˈkluːsɪv/ (of evidence, etc) ending doubt; convincing. **conclusively** adv.

concoct /kənˈkɒkt/ v [T] 1 make by mixing several things together. 2 invent (a story, excuse, etc). **concoction** /-ˈkɒkʃn/ n 1 [C] mixture. 2 [U] mixing.

concord /ˈkɒŋkɔːd/ n [U] (fml) agreement or harmony.

concourse /ˈkɒŋkɔːs/ n [C] place where a large number of people come together.

concrete /ˈkɒŋkriːt/ n [U] building material made by mixing cement with sand, gravel, etc. **concrete** v [T] cover with concrete. **concrete** adj 1 existing in material form; that can be touched, etc. 2 definite; not vague: a ~ suggestion.

concur /kənˈkɜː(r)/ v (-rr-) [I] (fml) 1 agree. 2 (of events, etc) happen together. **concurrence** /-ˈkʌrəns/ n [U]. **concurrent** /-ˈkʌrənt/ adj at the same time. **concurrently** adv.

concuss /kənˈkʌs/ v [T] injure (sb's brain) by a blow or violent shaking. **concussion** /-ˈkʌʃn/ n [U].

condemn /kənˈdem/ v [T] 1 say that one disapproves of (sb/sth). 2 to// (a) (law) declare the punishment for (sb): He was ~ed to death. (b) make (sb) accept sth unpleasant: ~ed to a job she hates. 3 declare officially that (a building, etc) is unfit for use. **condemnation** /ˌkɒndemˈneɪʃn/ n [U, C].

condense /kənˈdens/ v 1 [I, T] (a) (of a liquid) become or make thicker. (b) (of a gas or vapour) change into a liquid. 2 [T] put into fewer words: ~ a speech. **condensation** /ˌkɒndenˈseɪʃn/ n [U] 1 act of condensing. 2 drops of liquid formed on a surface when vapour condenses. **condenser** n [C].

condescend /ˌkɒndrˈsend/ v [T] (to)// (derog) do sth, thinking that one is superior to others: The manager ~ed to talk to the workers. **condescending** adj. **condescension** /-ˈsenʃn/ n [U].

condiment /ˈkɒndɪmənt/ n [C] seasoning, eg salt or pepper.

condition¹ /kənˈdɪʃn/ n 1 [sing] what sth is like; state: a car in good ~. 2 **conditions** [pl] circumstances. 3 [C] (a) something needed to make sth else happen: One of the ~s of the job is that you can drive. (b) thing required as part of an agreement or contract. 4 [U] physical fitness: be out of ~. 5 [C] illness. 6 (idm) **on condition that** only if.

condition² /kənˈdɪʃn/ v [T] 1 have an important effect on; determine. 2 train to act or think in a certain way. **conditioner** n [C] liquid put on hair to make it healthy and shiny. **conditioning** n [U].

conditional /kənˈdɪʃənl/ adj (on)// depending on sth: Payment is ~ on satisfactory completion of the work. 2 (grammar) (of a clause) beginning with if or unless. **conditionally** /-ʃənəlɪ/ adv.

condolence /kənˈdəʊləns/ n [U, C, esp pl] expression of sympathy.

condom /ˈkɒndəm/ n [C] rubber covering worn by a man on his penis during sexual intercourse, as a contraceptive.

condone /kənˈdəʊn/ v [T] regard (wrong behaviour) as if it were not serious; forgive.

conducive /kənˈdjuːsɪv; US -ˈduːs-/ adj to// allowing or helping sth to happen: ~ to health.

conduct¹ /kənˈdʌkt/ v 1 [T] organize and direct: ~ a survey. 2 ~ **oneself** (fml) behave in a certain way. 3 [I, T] direct the performance of (an orchestra, etc). 4 [T] allow (heat, electricity, etc) to pass along or through. **conduction** /-ˈdʌkʃn/ n [U] conducting of heat or electricity. **conductor** n [C] 1 person who conducts an orchestra, etc. 2 (fem **conductress** /-ˈdʌktrɪs/) (Brit) person who sells tickets on a bus. 3 substance that conducts heat or electricity.

conduct² /ˈkɒndʌkt/ n [U] 1 behaviour. **2** manner of directing or managing sth.

cone /kəʊn/ n [C] **1** (**a**) solid body that narrows to a point from a circular flat base. (**b**) something with this shape: *an ice-cream ~*. **2** fruit of certain evergreen trees, eg fir or pine.

confection /kən'fekʃn/ n [C] (*fml*) food made with sweet ingredients. **confectioner** /-ʃənə(r)/ n [C] person who (makes and sells) sweets and cakes. **confectionery** n [U] sweets, cakes, etc.

confederacy /kən'fedərəsɪ/ n [C] (*pl* -ies) union of states, people, etc.

confederate /kən'fedərət/ n [C] person who works with sb (esp in sth illegal or secret).

confederation /kən,fedə'reɪʃn/ n [C] organization of smaller groups or states.

confer /kən'fɜː(r)/ v (-rr-) (*fml*) **1** [I] (*with*)// have discussions with sb. **2** [T] (*on*)// give (eg an advantage or honour) to (sb): *~ authority on sb.*

conference /'kɒnfərəns/ n [C] **1** meeting for discussion or exchange of opinions. **2** (idm) **in conference** in a formal meeting.

confess /kən'fes/ v [I, T] **1** admit (that one has done wrong). **2** (esp in the Roman Catholic Church) tell (one's sins) formally to a priest. **confession** /-'feʃn/ n [C, U] **1** statement admitting that one has done wrong. **2** telling of one's sins. **confessional** /-'feʃənl/ n [C] private place in a church where a priest hears confessions.

confetti /kən'fetɪ/ n (with sing v) small pieces of coloured paper thrown at weddings.

confidant (*fem* -**dante**) /,kɒnfɪ'dænt/ n [C] trusted person to whom one speaks about one's secrets.

confide /kən'faɪd/ v **1** [T] tell (a secret) to sb. **2** (phr v) **confide in sb** tell (a secret, etc) to sb one trusts a lot.

confidence /'kɒnfɪdəns/ n **1** [U] firm trust. **2** [U] feeling sure about one's ability. **3** [C] secret that is told to sb. **4** (idm) **in (strict) confidence** as a secret. **take sb into one's confidence** tell sb a secret. **confident** /-dənt/ adj very sure. **confidently** adv.

confidential /,kɒnfɪ'denʃl/ adj **1** to be kept secret. **2** trusted with secrets. **confidentiality** /-,denʃɪ'ælətɪ/ n [U]. **confidentially** /-ʃəlɪ/ adv.

configuration /kən,fɪgə'reɪʃn;

US -,fɪgjʊ'reɪʃn/ n (*fml*) arrangement of the parts of sth.

confine /kən'faɪn/ v [T] **1** (*to*)// keep within certain limits: *The illness was ~d to the village.* **2** keep (sb) shut in: *~d to bed with a fever.* **confined** adj (of space) limited; restricted. **confinement** n **1** [U] being shut in. **2** [C, U] giving birth to a child. **confines** /'kɒnfaɪnz/ n [pl] (*fml*) limits; borders.

confirm /kən'fɜːm/ v [T] **1** show or say that (sth) is true: *The announcement ~ed my suspicions.* **2** say or write that (sth) is definite: *Please write to ~ the details.* **3** (usu passive) admit (sb) to membership of the Christian Church. **confirmation** /,kɒnfə'meɪʃn/ n [C, U]. **confirmed** adj unlikely to change: *a ~ed bachelor.*

confiscate /'kɒnfɪskeɪt/ v [T] take possession of (sb's property) officially, without payment and esp as a punishment. **confiscation** /,kɒnfɪ'skeɪʃn/ n [C, U].

conflagration /,kɒnflə'greɪʃn/ n [C] (*fml*) large and destructive fire.

conflict /'kɒnflɪkt/ n [C, U] **1** struggle, fight or serious disagreement. **2** (of opinions, etc) opposition; difference. **conflict** /kən'flɪkt/ v [I] be in opposition.

conform /kən'fɔːm/ v [I] **1** (*to*)// keep to generally accepted rules, standards, etc. **2** *with/to*// agree with sth. **conformist** n [C] person who conforms. **conformity** n [U].

confound /kən'faʊnd/ v [T] (*dated fml*) puzzle and surprise (sb).

confront /kən'frʌnt/ v [T] (*with*)// make (sb) face sth unpleasant or difficult. **2** make (sb) face sth unpleasant or difficult. **3** meet face to face; oppose. **confrontation** /,kɒnfrʌn'teɪʃn/ n [C, U] (instance of) angry opposition.

confuse /kən'fjuːz/ v [T] **1** mistake sb/sth for another: *You have ~d him and/with his brother.* **2** make (sb) unable to think clearly: *I'm ~d.* **3** make sth unclear. **confusion** /-'fjuːʒn/ n [U].

congeal /kən'dʒiːl/ v [I, T] (of a liquid) (cause to) become thick and solid.

congenial /kən'dʒiːnɪəl/ adj **1** pleasant: *a ~ atmosphere.* **2** having similar interests. **congenially** adv.

congenital /kən'dʒenɪtl/ adj (of diseases, etc) present from or before birth.

congested /kən'dʒestɪd/ adj too full; overcrowded: *streets ~ with* *traffic.* **congestion** /-'dʒestʃən/ *n* [U].

conglomerate /kən'glɒmərət/ *n* [C] large business organization consisting of several different firms. **conglomeration** /kən-ˌglɒmə'reiʃn/ *n* [C] group of things put together.

congratulate /kən'grætʃuleit/ *v* [T] express pleasure at the success, good fortunes, etc of (sb): ~ *sb on good exam results.* **congratulations** /kənˌgrætʃu'leiʃnz/ *interj* (used for congratulating sb).

congregate /'kɒŋgrigeit/ *v* [I] gather together. **congregation** /ˌkɒŋgri'geiʃn/ *n* [C] group of people who regularly attend a church. **congregational** *adj*.

congress /'kɒŋgres; *US* -grəs/ *n* [C, also sing with pl v] 1 formal meeting for discussion. 2 **Congress** law-making body, eg of the USA. **congressional** /kən-'greʃənl/ *adj*. **'Congressman**. **'Congresswoman** *n* [C] member of the US Congress.

congruent /'kɒŋgruənt/ *adj* (of triangles) having the same size and shape.

congruous /'kɒŋgruəs/ *adj* (*fml*) suitable; fitting.

conical /'kɒnikl/ *adj* cone-shaped.

conifer /'kɒnifə(r), also 'kəun-/ *n* [C] tree, eg pine or fir, that produces cones. **coniferous** /kə'nifərəs; *US* kəʊ'n-/ *adj*.

conjecture /kən'dʒektʃə(r)/ *v* [I, T] (*fml*) guess. **conjecture** *n* [I, C] (*fml*) guessing; guess. **conjectural** *adj*.

conjugal /'kɒndʒʊgl/ *adj* (*fml*) of the relationship between a husband and wife.

conjunction /kən'dʒʌŋkʃn/ *n* 1 [C] (*grammar*) word, eg *and, but* or *or* that joins words, phrases or sentences. 2 [C, U] (*fml*) (instance of) being joined. 3 (idm) **in conjunction with sb/sth** together with sb/sth.

conjure /'kʌndʒə(r)/ *v* 1 [I] do clever tricks that appear magical. 2 (phr v) **conjure sth up** cause sth to appear as a picture in the mind. **conjurer** (also **-or**) *n* [C] person who performs conjuring tricks.

conk /kɒŋk/ (phr v) **conk out** (*infml*) (a) (of a machine) stop working: *His old car has ~ed out.* (b) (of a person) become exhausted, fall asleep or die.

connect /kə'nekt/ *v* 1 [I, T] come or bring together; join: ~ *two wires.* 2 [T] think of as being related.

connection (*Brit* also **con-**

nexion) /kə'nekʃn/ *n* 1 (a) [U] connecting or being connected. (b) [C] point where two things are connected; relationship. 2 [C] train, aircraft, etc that takes passengers on the next stage of their journey. 3 [C, usu pl] person one knows in business. 4 (idm) **in connection with sb/sth** about sb/sth; concerning.

connive /kə'naiv/ *v* [I] *at//* take no notice of or seem to allow sth wrong. **connivance** *n* [U].

connoisseur /ˌkɒnə'sɜː(r)/ *n* [C] expert, eg on food or art.

connotation /ˌkɒnə'teiʃn/ *n* [C, esp pl] idea or quality suggested by a word in addition to its main meaning: *Be careful not to use slang words that have obscene ~s.*

conquer /'kɒŋkə(r)/ *v* [T] 1 take possession of (sth) by force. 2 defeat or overcome: (*fig*) *You must ~ your fear of driving.* **conqueror** *n* [C].

conquest /'kɒŋkwest/ *n* 1 [U] conquering, eg of a country or people. 2 [C] something gained by conquering.

conscience /'kɒnʃəns/ *n* 1 [C, U] sense of right and wrong: *have a clear/guilty ~* (ie feel that one has done right/wrong). 2 (idm) **(have sth) on one's conscience** (feel) troubled about sth one has done.

conscientious /ˌkɒnʃi'enʃəs/ *adj* (of a person or his/her actions) very careful. **conscientiously** *adv*. **conscientiousness** *n* [U].

conscious /'kɒnʃəs/ *adj* 1 awake. 2 (*of*)// aware of sth. 3 intentional: *make an ~ effort.* **consciously** *adv*. **consciousness** *n* [U]: *regain ~ness after an accident.*

conscript /kən'skript/ *v* [T] force (sb) by law to serve in the armed forces. **conscript** /'kɒnskript/ *n* [C] person who has been conscripted. **conscription** /-'skripʃn/ *n* [U].

consecrate /'kɒnsikreit/ *v* [T] 1 declare officially to be holy: ~ *a church.* 2 reserve for a special (esp religious) purpose. **consecration** /ˌkɒnsi'kreiʃn/ *n* [U].

consecutive /kən'sekjutiv/ *adj* coming one after the other without interruption. **consecutively** *adv*.

consensus /kən'sensəs/ *n* [C, U] general agreement.

consent /kən'sent/ *v* [I] (*to*)// give agreement to or permission for sth. **consent** *n* [U] agreement; permission.

consequence /'kɒnsikwəns; *US* -kwens/ *n* 1 [C] result or effect: *the political ~s of the decision.* 2

[U] (*fml*) importance: *It is of no ~.*

consequent /'kɒnsɪkwənt/ *adj* (*fml*) following as a result. **consequently** *adv* therefore.

consequential /ˌkɒnsɪ'kwenʃl/ *adj* (*fml*) 1 consequent. 2 important.

conservation /ˌkɒnsə'veɪʃn/ *n* [U] 1 prevention of loss, waste, etc. 2 preservation of the natural environment. **conservationist** *n* [C] person interested in conservation(2).

conservative /kən'sɜːvətɪv/ *adj* 1 opposed to great or sudden change. 2 **Conservative** of the Conservative Party. 3 cautious; moderate: *a ~ estimate.* **conservative** *n* [C] 1 conservative person. 2 **Conservative** member of the Conservative Party. **conservatively** *adv*. the **Con'servative Party** *n* [sing] (*Brit politics*) major political party which supports capitalism and opposes socialism. **conservatism** /-tɪzəm/ *n* [U].

conservatory /kən'sɜːvətrɪ; *US* -tɔːrɪ/ *n* [C] (*pl* -ies) 1 room with glass walls and roof in which plants are grown. 2 school of music, drama, etc.

conserve /kən'sɜːv/ *v* [T] prevent (sth) from being changed, lost or destroyed. **conserve** /'kɒnsɜːv/ *n* [C, U] (*fml*) jam, with quite large pieces of fruit.

consider /kən'sɪdə(r)/ *v* [T] 1 think about. 2 believe to be; regard as: *We ~ this (to be) very important.* 3 take into account: *~ the feelings of others.* **considered** *adj* as a result of careful thought: *a ~ed opinion.*

considerable /kən'sɪdərəbl/ *adj* great in amount or size. **considerably** /-əblɪ/ *adv* much: *It's considerably colder today.*

considerate /kən'sɪdərət/ *adj* kind and thinking of the needs of others. **considerately** *adv*.

consideration /kənˌsɪdə'reɪʃn/ *n* 1 [U] careful thought. 2 [U] being thoughtful towards others. 3 [C] something that must be thought about, esp when deciding sth: *Cost is just one of the ~ s.* 4 [C] (*fml*) reward; payment. 5 (*idm*) **take sth into consideration** think about sth when making a judgement or decision.

considering /kən'sɪdərɪŋ/ *prep*, *conj* if one takes into consideration: *She's very active, ~ her age.*

consign /kən'saɪn/ *v* [T] 1 send (goods, etc) for delivery. 2 (*fml*) hand (sb/sth) over; give up: *~ the boy to his brother's care.* **consignment** *n* 1 [U] consigning. 2 [C]

goods consigned.

consist /kən'sɪst/ *v* [I] (phr *v*) **consist of** be made up of: *a meal ~ing of soup and bread.* **consist in** have as the main element.

consistency /kən'sɪstənsɪ/ *n* 1 [U] quality of being consistent(1). 2 [C, U] (*pl* -ies) degree of thickness, esp of a liquid.

consistent /kən'sɪstənt/ *adj* 1 (*approv*) (of a person's behaviour, etc) not changing. 2 (*with*)|| in agreement: *injuries ~ with the accident.* **consistently** *adv*.

consolation /ˌkɒnsə'leɪʃn/ *n* 1 [U] consoling: *a few words of ~.* 2 [C] person or thing that consoles. **console**[1] /kən'səʊl/ *v* [T] give comfort or sympathy to.

console[2] /'kɒnsəʊl/ *n* [C] panel for the controls of electronic equipment.

consolidate /kən'sɒlɪdeɪt/ *v* [I, T] 1 become or make stronger, more secure, etc. 2 (*commerce*) unite or combine (into one): *~ all his debts.* **consolidation** /kənˌsɒlɪ'deɪʃn/ *n* [C, U].

consommé /kən'sɒmeɪ; *US* ˌkɒnsə'meɪ/ *n* [U] clear meat soup.

consonant /'kɒnsənənt/ *n* [C] (a) speech sound made by (partly) stopping the breath with the tongue, lips, etc. (b) letter used for representing these, eg *b*, *c* and *d*.

consort[1] /'kɒnsɔːt/ *n* [C] husband or wife, esp of a ruler.

consort[2] /kən'sɔːt/ *v* [I] (*with*)|| (*usu derog*) spend time with: *~ing with criminals.*

consortium /kən'sɔːtɪəm; *US* 'sɔːrʃɪəm/ *n* (*pl* -tia -tɪə; *US* -ʃɪə/) [C] (with sing *or* pl *v*) group of businesses, banks, etc with a common purpose.

conspicuous /kən'spɪkjʊəs/ *adj* easily seen; noticeable. **conspicuously** *adv*.

conspiracy /kən'spɪrəsɪ/ *n* (*pl* -ies) 1 [U] act of conspiring. 2 [C] plan made by conspiring.

conspire /kən'spaɪə(r)/ *v* [I] 1 (*with*; *against*)|| make secret plans with other people: *~ to kill the king* ◦ *He ~d with others against the government.* 2 (*against*)|| act together; combine: *Circumstances ~d against them.* **conspirator** /kən'spɪrətə(r)/ *n* [C] person who conspires.

constable /'kʌnstəbl; *US* 'kɒn-/ *n* [C] (*Brit dated*) policeman or policewoman of the lowest rank. **constabulary** /kən'stæbjʊlərɪ; *US* -lerɪ/ *n* [C], (also sing with pl *v*) (*pl* -ies) police force of a particular area.

constant /'kɒnstənt/ adj 1 continuing all the time: ~ noise. 2 not changing: a ~ temperature. **constancy** n [U] state of being constant(2).

constellation /ˌkɒnstə'leɪʃn/ n [C] group of stars with a name.

consternation /ˌkɒnstə'neɪʃn/ n [U] feeling of surprise, fear and worry.

constipated /'kɒnstɪpeɪtɪd/ adj not able to empty waste matter from the bowels easily. **constipation** /ˌkɒnstɪ'peɪʃn/ n [U] state of being constipated.

constituency /kən'stɪtjʊənsɪ/ n [C] (with sing or pl v) (pl -ies) (voters living in) area that sends a representative to parliament.

constituent /kən'stɪtjʊənt/ adj 1 being part of a whole. 2 (of an assembly, etc) having the power or right to alter a political constitution. **constituent** n [C] 1 member of a constituency. 2 part of a whole.

constitute /'kɒnstɪtjuːt/ v [T] make up or form (a whole): Twelve months ~ a year. 2 be: The decision to build the road ~ s a real threat to the countryside.

constitution /ˌkɒnstɪ'tjuːʃn; US ·'tuːʃn/ n 1 [C] set of laws and principles according to which a country is governed. 2 [C] person's physical structure and condition: a strong ~. 3 [C] general structure of sth. **constitutional** adj conforming to the laws, etc by which a country is governed. **constitutionally** /-əlɪ/ adv.

constrain /kən'streɪn/ v [T] (fml) make (sb) do sth by force or strong persuasion: I felt ~ ed to obey.

constraint /kən'streɪnt/ n 1 [C] thing that limits or restricts (sb's actions, etc): One of the ~ s on the project will be the money available. 2 [U] constraining or being constrained.

constrict /kən'strɪkt/ v [T] make tighter, smaller or narrower: a tight collar ~ ing the neck. **constriction** /kən'strɪkʃn/ n 1 [U] constricting. 2 [C] something that constricts: (fig) the ~ s of prison life.

construct /kən'strʌkt/ v [T] build or put together.

construction /kən'strʌkʃn/ n 1 [U] way or act of constructing: The new bridge is still under ~. 2 [C] structure; building. 3 [C] (fml) way in which sth is understood; meaning: I would put a different ~ on her behaviour.

constructive /kən'strʌktɪv/ adj helpful; useful: ~ suggestions. **constructively** adv.

consul /'kɒnsl/ n [C] official sent by his/her government to live in a foreign country and help people from his/her own country who are living there. **consular** /'kɒnsjʊlə(r); US -sel-/ adj of a consul or his/her work. **consulate** /'kɒnsjʊlət; US -səl-/ n [C] consul's office.

consult /kən'sʌlt/ v 1 [T] go to (a person, book, etc) for information, advice or help: ~ the doctor about a sore throat. 2 [I] with// discuss matters with sb: ~ with one's friends.

consultant /kən'sʌltənt/ n [C] 1 person who is paid to give expert advice. 2 (Brit) senior hospital doctor who specializes in a particular branch of medicine: a ~ surgeon.

consultation /ˌkɒnsl'teɪʃn/ n 1 [U] act of consulting or being consulted. 2 [C] meeting for discussion, eg about a sick person.

consume /kən'sjuːm; US ·'suːm/ v [T] 1 use: Some types of car ~ less petrol than others. 2 (of fire, etc) destroy. 3 (fml) eat or drink. **consuming** adj very strong: a ~ passion.

consumer /kən'sjuːmə(r); US -suː-/ n [C] person who buys goods. **consumer durables** = DURABLES (DURABLE). **consumer goods** n [pl] goods bought by individual customers, such as food, clothes, etc.

consummate /'kɒnsəmeɪt/ v [T] (fml) 1 make perfect. 2 make (a marriage) legally complete by having sexual intercourse. **consummation** /ˌkɒnsə'meɪʃn/ n [C, U].

consumption /kən'sʌmpʃn/ n [U] (a) using of food, resources, etc: This food is not fit for human ~. (b) amount used: measure a car's fuel ~.

contact /'kɒntækt/ n 1 [U] state of touching: Her hand came into ~ with a hot surface. 2 [U] communication: Stay in ~ with your parents. 3 [C] instance of meeting or communicating: a job involving contacts with other companies. 4 [C] person one has met or will meet, esp one who is or can be helpful: He has several ~ s in the building trade. 5 [C] electrical connection. **contact** /'kɒntækt, kən'tækt/ v [T] reach (sb) by telephone, letter, etc: Where can I ~ you next week? **'contact lens** n [C] thin lens placed on the surface of the eye to improve a person's eyesight.

contagion /kən'teɪdʒn/ n 1 [U] spreading of disease by being close to or touching other people. 2 [C] disease spread by contact.
contagious /-'teɪdʒəs/ adj 1 (a) (of a disease) spreading by contact. (b) (of a person) having a disease that can be spread to others by contact. 2 easily spread from person to person: *contagious laughter.*

contain /kən'teɪn/ v [T] 1 have or hold within itself: *a bottle ~ing two litres of milk.* 2 control (feelings, enemy forces, etc): *trying to ~ her anger.*
container /kən'teɪnə(r)/ n [C] 1 bottle, box, etc for holding sth: *a ~ for sugar.* 2 large metal box, etc for transporting goods.

contaminate /kən'tæmɪneɪt/ v [T] make dirty or impure: *~d food.* **contamination** /kən,tæmɪ'neɪʃn/ n [U].

contemplate /'kɒntəmpleɪt/ v [T] 1 think about; consider doing: *~ visiting London.* 2 (*fml*) look at thoughtfully: *~ a picture.* **contemplation** /,kɒntəm'pleɪʃn/ n [U] act of contemplating; deep thought. **contemplative** /kən'templətɪv/ adj thoughtful.

contemporary /kən'temprərɪ; US -pərerɪ/ adj 1 of the present time; modern. 2 belonging to the same time: *a play by Shakespeare accompanied by ~ music.* **contemporary** n [C] (*pl* -ies) person who lived or lives at the same time as another person: *Shakespeare and his contemporaries.*

contempt /kən'tempt/ n [U] (*for*)|| 1 feeling that sb/sth is of no value and cannot be respected: *feel ~ for people who are cruel to animals.* 2 lack of respect for (rules, danger, etc): *her ~ for the risks.* **contemptible** /-əbl/ adj deserving contempt(1). **con,tempt of 'court** n [U] not obeying a court or judge. **contemptuous** /-t'tʃuəs/ adj feeling or showing contempt.

contend /kən'tend/ v 1 [I] *with/against*|| compete or struggle with sb/sth. 2 [T] argue; put forward as one's opinion: *~ that the theory was wrong.* **contender** n [C] person who tries to win sth in competition with others.

content[1] /kən'tent/ adj satisfied; happy: *~ to stay at home.* **content** n [U] state of being content. **content** v [T] make (sb) content. **contented** adj satisfied. **contentedly** adv. **contentment** n [U] state of being content.

content[2] /'kɒntent/ n 1 **contents**

[pl] what is contained in sth: *the ~s of her bag.* 2 **contents** [pl] list of chapters in a book. 3 [sing] the subject written or spoken about in a book, programme, etc. 4 [sing] amount of sth contained in a substance, etc: *the silver ~ of a coin.*

contention /kən'tenʃn/ n 1 [U] quarrelling or arguing; contending(2). 2 [C] claim made in an argument, etc. **contentious** /-ʃəs/ adj liking or causing argument.

contest[1] /'kɒntest/ n [C] fight; competition.

contest[2] /kən'test/ v [T] 1 claim that (sth) is wrong. 2 take part in and try to win (a competition, etc): *~ an election.* **contestant** n [C] person who takes part in a competition.

context /'kɒntekst/ n [C, U] 1 sentence, phrase, etc in which a word appears. 2 circumstances in which an event happens.

continent /'kɒntɪnənt/ n 1 [C] one of the main land masses (Europe, Asia, Africa, etc). 2 **the Continent** [sing] the mainland of Europe. **continental** /,kɒntɪ'nentl/ adj 1 of or typical of a continent. 2 (also **Continental**) of the mainland of Europe: *a ~al holiday.*

contingency /kən'tɪndʒənsɪ/ n [C] (*pl* -ies) event that may or may not occur: *prepared for every ~.*

contingent[1] /kən'tɪndʒənt/ n [C] 1 part of a larger force of troops, ships, etc. 2 part of a larger group of people.

contingent[2] /kən'tɪndʒənt/ adj depending on chance.

continual /kən'tɪnjʊəl/ adj happening all the time or very frequently: *~ rain* ○ *~ interruptions.* **continually** adv again and again; without stopping.

continuation /kən,tɪnjʊ'eɪʃn/ n 1 [U, sing] act of continuing. 2 [C] thing which continues beyond or extends sth else: *This road is a ~ of the motorway.*

continue /kən'tɪnjuː/ v [I, T] 1 (cause to) go or move further: *~ up the hill.* 2 (cause to) go on being or happening: *~ running* ○ *~d her visits to the hospital.* 3 start again after stopping.

continuity /,kɒntɪ'njuːətɪ/ n [U] 1 state of being continuous. 2 logical connection between parts of a whole: *The story lacks ~.*

continuous /kən'tɪnjʊəs/ adj going on without stopping: *a ~ line/ noise/flow.* **continuously** adv. **con'tinuous tense** n [C] (*grammar*) phrase formed from part of the verb *be* and a verb ending in

-ing, used to show action that continues over a period of time, as in: *I am singing.*

contort /kən'tɔ:t/ *v* [T] force or twist out of the usual shape: *a face ~ed with pain.* **contortion** /kən'tɔ:ʃn/ *n* [C, U].

contour /'kɒntʊə(r)/ *n* [C] outline of a coast, a human figure, etc. **'contour line** *n* [C] line on a map joining points at the same height above sea level.

contraband /'kɒntrəbænd/ *n* [U] goods brought illegally into or out of a country.

contraception /ˌkɒntrə'sepʃn/ *n* [U] preventing of pregnancy. **contraceptive** /-'septɪv/ *n*[C], *adj* (device, drug, etc for) preventing pregnancy.

contract[1] /'kɒntrækt/ *n* [C, U] formal agreement between two people, groups, states, etc: *a ~ between a person and his/her employer* ○ *The builder is under ~ to finish the house by the end of June.* **contractual** /kən'træktʃuəl/ *adj* of or in a contract.

contract[2] /kən'trækt/ *v* 1 [I, T] make a legal agreement: *~ with the firm to supply goods.* 2 [T] catch (a disease). 3 [T] *(fml)* acquire (debts, etc). 4 (phr v) **contract out (of sth)** not take part (in sth).

contract[3] /kən'trækt/ *v*[I, T] (cause to) become smaller: *metal ~s as it cools.* **contraction** /kən'trækʃn/ *n* 1 [U] contracting. 2 [C] short form of a word: *'Can't' is a ~ion of 'cannot'.* 3 [C] tightening of the womb before birth.

contradict /ˌkɒntrə'dɪkt/ *v* [T] 1 say that a person, statement, etc is wrong: *Don't ~ your mother.* 2 (of facts, statements, etc) be contrary to: *Her account ~s what you said.* **contradiction** *n* [C, U]. **contradictory** *adj* not agreeing: *~ory accounts of the accident.*

contraflow /'kɒntrəfləʊ/ *n* [C, U] transferring of traffic from its usual half of the road to the other half, so that it shares the lane with traffic coming in the other direction.

contralto /kən'træltəʊ/ *n* [C, U] = ALTO 1.

contraption /kən'træpʃn/ *n* [C] *(infml)* strange or complicated device.

contrary[1] /'kɒntrəri/ *adj* (*to*)// opposite; quite different: *~ to what you believe.*

contrary[2] /'kɒntrəri/ *US* -treri/ *n* 1 **the contrary** [sing] the opposite: *The ~ is true.* 2 (idm) **on the 'contrary** the opposite is true: *I've never said I don't like music;*

on the ~, I like it a lot. **to the 'contrary** showing the opposite: *I shall continue to believe this until I get proof to the ~.*

contrary[3] /kən'treəri/ *adj (infml)* not willing to help, obey, etc: *Don't be so ~!* **contrariness** *n* [U].

contrast /kən'trɑ:st/ *v* 1 [T] compare so that differences are made clear. 2 [I] show a difference: *the ~ing cultures of Africa and Europe.* **contrast** /'kɒntrɑ:st/ *n* [C, U] difference which is clearly seen.

contravene /ˌkɒntrə'vi:n/ *v* [T] break (a law, rule, etc). **contravention** /ˌkɒntrə'venʃn/ *n* [C, U].

contretemps /'kɒntrətɒm/ *n* [C] unlucky event; set-back.

contribute /kən'trɪbju:t/ *v* 1 [I, T] (*to/towards*)// join with others in giving (help, money, ideas, etc). 2 [I] *to*// help to cause: *~ to her success.* 3 [I, T] write (articles, etc) for newspapers, etc. **contribution** /ˌkɒntrɪ'bju:ʃn/ *n* [C, U]. **contributor** *n* [C] person who contributes(1, 3). **contributory** /kən'trɪbjʊtəri/ *adj.*

contrite /'kɒntraɪt/ *adj* sorry that one has done sth wrong. **contritely** *adv.* **contrition** /kən'trɪʃn/ *n* [U].

contrive /kən'traɪv/ *v* [T] 1 find a way of doing (sth): *~ to live on a small income.* 2 invent, plan or design: *~ a way of avoiding paying tax.* **contrivance** *n* 1 [U] contriving. 2 [C] something invented.

control /kən'trəʊl/ *n* 1 [U] power to direct, order or limit: *She lost ~ of the car on the ice.* 2 [C] means of keeping control: *~s on pollution.* 3 [C] standard of comparison for the results of an experiment. 4 [usu pl] means by which a machine, etc is operated or regulated. 5 (idm) **be in control (of sth)** manage, direct or rule (sth). **out of con'trol** no longer able to be properly directed, ordered, etc: *The car went out of ~.* **under control** successfully managed, ruled or directed: *The fire was brought under ~.* **control** *v* (-ll-) [T] 1 have power or authority over: *~ one's temper.* 2 regulate (traffic, prices, etc). 3 check; inspections to *~ quality.* **controller** *n* [C] person who controls sth, esp a department of a large organization.

controversy /'kɒntrəvɜ:si, kən'trɒvəsi/ *n* (*pl* **-ies**) [C, U] public argument or debate about sth many people do not agree with: *~ over the building of a new motorway.* **controversial** /ˌkɒntrə-'vɜ:ʃl/ *adj* causing controversy.

controversially adv.

conundrum /kə'nʌndrəm/ n [C, usu sing] 1 question, usu with a pun or joke in its answer, asked for fun. 2 puzzling problem.

conurbation /ˌkɒnɜː'beɪʃn/ n [C, large urban area formed by several towns which have spread towards each other.

convalesce /ˌkɒnvə'les/ v [I] become healthy and strong again after an illness. **convalescence** n [sing, U] (period of) recovery from an illness. **convalescent** n [C], adj (person who is) recovering from an illness.

convene /kən'viːn/ v [I, T] (cause to) come together (for a meeting, etc). **convener** (also **-venor**) n [C] person who arranges meetings.

convenience /kən'viːnɪəns/ n 1 [U] quality of being convenient or suitable. 2 [C] device, tool, etc that is useful, suitable, etc: *Central heating is one of the ~s of modern houses.*

convenient /kən'viːnɪənt/ adj fitting in well with sb's needs; suitable: *a ~ place to stay.* **conveniently** adv.

convent /'kɒnvənt/ *US* -vent/ n [C] building where a community of nuns lives.

convention /kən'venʃn/ n 1 [C] meeting of the members of a society, political party, etc: *a scientists' ~.* 2 (a) [U] general, usu unspoken, agreement on how people should behave. (b) [C] custom: *the ~s of international trade.* 3 [C] agreement between states, rulers, etc. **conventional** adj based on or following convention(2). **conventionally** adv.

converge /kən'vɜːdʒ/ v [I] (of lines, moving objects) come towards each other and meet at a point: *a village where two roads ~.* **convergence** n [U]. **convergent** adj.

conversant /kən'vɜːsnt/ adj with// having knowledge or experience of sth: *~ with modern teaching methods.*

conversation /ˌkɒnvə'seɪʃn/ n 1 [U] informal talking: *the art of ~.* 2 [C] informal talk: *hold a ~.* **conversational** adj (of words, etc) used in conversation: *a ~ tone/style.*

converse¹ /kən'vɜːs/ v [I] (with)// (fml) talk.

converse² /'kɒnvɜːs/ the converse n [sing] the opposite: *The ~ is true.* **converse** adj opposite. **conversely** adv.

conversion /kən'vɜːʃn; *US* kən'vɜːrʒn/ n [C, U] (instance of)

converting: *the ~ of the barn into a house.*

convert¹ /kən'vɜːt/ v [I, T] 1 change (sth) from one form, use, etc to another: *~ a house into flats.* 2 (cause sb) to change one's/his/her beliefs, etc: *~ him to Christianity.* **convertible** /-əbl/ adj able to be converted. **convertible** n [C] car with a roof that can be folded down or removed.

convert² /'kɒnvɜːt/ n [C] person who has converted, esp to a different religion.

convex /'kɒnveks/ adj curved outwards: *~ mirror.*

convey /kən'veɪ/ v [T] 1 take; carry: *goods ~ed by rail.* 2 (to)// make (feelings, ideas, etc) known to another person: *She ~ed her fears to her friends.* **conveyance** n [C, U] (vehicle for) transporting. **conveyancing** n [U] legal transfer of property from one person to another. **conveyor** (also **-veyer**) n [C] person or thing that conveys. **con'veyor belt** n [C] (eg in a factory) band moving over wheels for carrying packages, etc.

convict /kən'vɪkt/ v [T] (of a judge, court, etc) declare that sb is guilty of a crime): *She was ~ed of theft.* **convict** /'kɒnvɪkt/ n [C] person who has been convicted and sent to prison.

conviction /kən'vɪkʃn/ n [C, U] 1 (instance of the) convicting of a person for a crime. 2 firm belief: *a ~ that what she said was true.*

convince /kən'vɪns/ v [T] (of)// make (sb) feel certain; cause (sb) to realize: *I ~ed her that I was right.* ○ *~ sb of the truth.* **convincing** adj that convinces: *a convincing argument.* **convincingly** adv.

convivial /kən'vɪvɪəl/ adj cheerful and merry: *a ~ person/evening.* **conviviality** /kənˌvɪvɪ'ælətɪ/ n [U].

convoluted /'kɒnvəluːtɪd/ adj 1 twisted; coiled. 2 (fig) (of an argument, etc) not easy to follow; complicated.

convolution /ˌkɒnvə'luːʃn/ n [C, usu pl] twist; coil: (fig) *the ~s of the plot.*

convoy /'kɒnvɔɪ/ n [C] (a) group of vehicles or ships travelling together. (b) group of ships escorted and protected by warships, etc. **convoy** v [T] (of a warship, etc) travel with (other ships) to protect them.

convulse /kən'vʌls/ v [T] cause violent and uncontrollable movements: *a city ~d by riots.* **convulsion** /-'vʌlʃn/ n [C] 1 [usu pl] sudden uncontrollable and violent body movement. **2** violent disturbance. **convulsive** *adj.*

coo /kuː/ *v* **1** [I] make a soft murmuring sound like that of a dove. **2** [T] say (sth) in a soft murmuring voice. **coo** *n* [C].

cook /kʊk/ *v* **1** (a) [I, T] prepare (food) by heating it: ~ *breakfast/dinner.* (b) [I] be prepared in this way. **2** [T] (*infml derog*) change (accounts, etc) in order to deceive: ~ *the figures.* **cook** *n* [C] person who cooks food. **cook** *n* [C] device for cooking food by heating. **cookery** *n* [U] art and practice of cookery. **cooking** *n* [U] process of preparing food by heating.

cookie /'kʊkɪ/ *n* [C] (*US*) **1** biscuit. **2** (*infml*) person: *a tough* ~.

cool¹ /kuːl/ *adj* **1** not hot or cold; fairly cold: *It feels* ~ *in the shade.* **2** calm; not excited: *stay* ~ *in spite of danger.* **3** showing no interest, enthusiasm, etc: *He was* ~ *about the suggestion.* **4** (*infml*) (used for suggesting an amount, etc is very large): *a* ~ *five million pounds!* **5** (*infml*) very good; fine: *real* ~ *music.* **cool** *n* **1** **the cool** [sing] cool air or place; coolness: *sitting in the* ~. **2** (idm) **keep/lose one's cool** (*infml*) remain/not remain calm. ,**cool-'headed** *adj* not easily excited or worried; calm. **coolly** *adv.* **coolness** *n* [U].

cool² /kuːl/ *v* [I, T] **1** (*down/off*) make or become cooler: *Have a drink to* ~ *down.* **2** (phr v) **cool down/off** become calm or less excited.

coop /kuːp/ *n* [C] cage, esp for hens. **coop** *v* (phr v) **coop up** confine in a small space: *prisoners* ~*ed up in cells.*

co-operate /kəʊˈɒpəreɪt/ *v* [I] work or act together to achieve (sth): *They* ~*d on the project.* **co-operation** /kəʊˌɒpəˈreɪʃn/ *n* [U] **1** acting or working together with a common purpose. **2** willingness to be helpful. **co-operative** /-ətɪv/ *adj* **1** joint. **2** willing to co-operate. **co-operative** *n* [C] business, farm, etc owned by the people who work there.

co-opt /kəʊˈɒpt/ *v* [T] (of members of a committee) make (sb) a member by voting for him/her.

co-ordinate¹ /ˌkəʊˈɔːdɪneɪt/ *v* [T] (*with*/) make (actions, limbs, etc) work together: ~ *efforts to get the project finished.* **co-ordination** /ˌkəʊˌɔːdɪˈneɪʃn/ *n* [U]. **co-ordinator** *n* [C].

co-ordinate² /ˌkəʊˈɔːdɪnət/ *n* **1** [C] either of the two numbers or letters used to fix the position of a point on a map, etc. **2** **co-ordina-**tes [pl] separate garments in matching colours for wearing together.

cop¹ /kɒp/ *n* [C] (*sl*) policeman.

cop² /kɒp/ *v* (-pp-) [T] (*sl*) **1** receive; get: ~ *a bang on the head.* **2** (phr v) **cop out** (*derog*) avoid doing sth. '**cop-out** *n* [C] (*sl derog*) act of or excuse for not doing sth.

cope /kəʊp/ *v* [I] (*with*/) deal with successfully: *She couldn't* ~ *with all her work.*

copier ⇨ COPY².

copious /'kəʊpɪəs/ *adj* (*fml*) plentiful: *a* ~ *supply.* **copiously** *adv.*

copper¹ /'kɒpə(r)/ *n* **1** [U]: common reddish-brown metal: ~ *wire.* **2** [U] reddish-brown colour. **3** [C] coin made of copper, of very low value.

copper² /'kɒpə(r)/ *n* [C] (*sl*) policeman.

copse /kɒps/ *n* [C] small area of shrubs and trees.

copulate /'kɒpjʊleɪt/ *v* [I] (*with*/) (*fml*) (esp of animals) have sexual intercourse. **copulation** /ˌkɒpjʊˈleɪʃn/ *n* [U].

copy¹ /'kɒpɪ/ *n* [C] (*pl* **-ies**) **1** thing made to be like another, esp a reproduction of a letter, pictures, etc: *Put a* ~ *of the letter in the file.* **2** one example of a book, newspaper, etc of which many have been made: *The library has two copies of this book.* '**copycat** *n* [C] (*infml derog*) person who imitates another's behaviour, clothes, etc.

copy² /'kɒpɪ/ *v* (*pt, pp* **-ied**) [T] **(a)** make a written copy: *He wrote the sentence on the blackboard and told the children to* ~ *it into their books.* **(b)** make a copy: ~ *a document on the photocopier.* **2** [T] (try to) do the same as: *The teacher told the class to* ~ *his movements.* **3** [I] cheat in an exam, etc by copying what sb else has done, written, etc. **copier** *n* [C] machine that copies documents.

copyright /'kɒpɪraɪt/ *n* [U, C] author's legal right to print, publish and sell his/her work. **copyright** *v* [T] protect (a book, etc) in this way.

coral /'kɒrəl; *US* 'kɔːrəl/ *n* [U] hard red, pink or white substance formed on the sea bed by small creatures. **coral** *adj* made of coral.

cord /kɔːd/ *n* **1** [C, U] (length of) long thin material made of twisted strands, thicker than string. **2** [C] part of the body like a cord: *the vocal* ~*s.*

cordial¹ /'kɔːdɪəl; *US* 'kɔːrdʒəl/ *adj* warm and friendly: *a* ~ *wel-*

come/smile. **cordially** adv.

cordial² /'kɔːdɪəl/ n [U] (Brit) non-alcoholic sweet drink: lime ~.

cordon /'kɔːdn/ n [C] ring or line of people acting as guards, barriers, etc to stop people entering or leaving an area: a police ~. **cordon** v (phr v) **cordon off** place a cordon around: The army ~ed off the area.

corduroy /'kɔːdərɔɪ/ n [U] thick cotton cloth with raised ridges: ~ trousers.

core /kɔː(r)/ n [C] 1 usu hard centre of such fruits as the apple or pear. 2 central or most important part of anything: the ~ of the problem. 3 (idm) **to the 'core** completely; thoroughly: shocked to the ~. **core** v [T] take the core out of (eg an apple).

cork /kɔːk/ n 1 [U] light springy bark from a type of oak tree: ~ table mats. 2 [C] round piece of this used to seal a bottle. **cork** v [T] seal (a bottle, etc) with a cork. **'corkscrew** n [C] tool for pulling corks from bottles.

corn¹ /kɔːn/ n 1 [U] 1 (seed of) various grain plants. 2 (esp US) maize. **corn-cob** n [C] hard part at the top of a maize stalk on which the grains grow. **'cornflour** n [U] flour made from maize. **corn on the 'cob** n [C] maize cooked with all the grains still attached to the stalk.

corn² /kɔːn/ n [C] small area of hardened skin on the foot.

cornea /'kɔːnɪə/ n [C] tough transparent covering of the eyeball.

corned beef /ˌkɔːnd 'biːf/ n [U] beef preserved in salt.

corner /'kɔːnə(r)/ n [C] 1 place where two lines or surfaces meet. 2 hidden or secret place. 3 region: from all ~s of the earth. 4 (infml) difficult or awkward situation: in a (tight) ~. 5 (idm) **turn the 'corner** pass the most difficult, dangerous, etc stage of sth. **corner** v 1 [T] put in a difficult position; trap: ~ed by the police. 2 [I] turn a corner on a road, etc: a car designed for fast ~ing.

cornet /'kɔːnɪt/ n [C] 1 small musical instrument like a trumpet. 2 cone-shaped container of thin biscuit for ice-cream, etc.

cornice /'kɔːnɪs/ n [C] ornamental border around a ceiling or at the top of a column.

corny /'kɔːnɪ/ adj (-ier, -iest) too familiar or sentimental.

coronary /'kɒrənrɪ; US 'kɔːrənærɪ/ adj of the arteries carrying blood to the heart. **coronary** n [C] (pl -ies) (also **coronary thrombosis**) blocking of an artery in the heart by a clot of blood, often damaging the heart or causing death.

coronation /ˌkɒrə'neɪʃn; US ˌkɔːr-/ n [C] ceremony of crowning a king or queen.

coroner /'kɒrənə(r); US 'kɔːr-/ n [C] (Brit) official who tries to find the cause of any accidental or suspicious death.

coronet /'kɒrənɛt; US 'kɔːr-/ n [C] small crown worn by a peer² or peeress.

corporal¹ /'kɔːpərəl/ adj involving physical punishment: ~ punishment.

corporal² /'kɔːpərəl/ n [C] non-commissioned officer below the rank of sergeant in the army.

corporate /'kɔːpərət/ adj 1 of or belonging to a corporation(2). 2 of or shared by all the members of a group: ~ responsibility.

corporation /ˌkɔːpə'reɪʃn/ n [C, also sing with pl v] 1 (esp Brit) group of people elected to govern a town. 2 large business or company.

corps /kɔː(r)/ n [C] (pl corps /kɔːz/) 1 military force formed from part of the full army, etc. 2 one of the technical branches of an army: the Medical C~. 3 group of people involved in a particular activity: the diplomatic ~.

corpse /kɔːps/ n [C] dead body, esp of a human being.

corpulent /'kɔːpjʊlənt/ adj (fml) fat.

corpuscle /'kɔːpʌsl/ n [C] one of the red or white cells in the blood.

corral /kə'rɑːl/ n [C] enclosure for horses, cattle, etc. **corral** v (-ll-; US -l-) [T] drive (cattle, etc) into or enclose in a corral.

correct¹ /kə'rekt/ adj 1 true; right; accurate: the ~ answer ○ the ~ way to do it. 2 (of manners, dress, etc) proper; decent. **correctly** adv. **correctness** n [U].

correct² /kə'rekt/ v [T] 1 make correct; remove the mistakes from: ~ sb's spelling. 2 change sth so that it is accurate: glasses to ~ your eyesight. **correction** /kə'rekʃn/ n 1 [C] change that corrects sth: corrections written in red ink. 2 [U] correcting. 3 [U] punishment. **corrective** n [C], adj (something that) corrects.

correlate /'kɒrəleɪt; US 'kɔːr-/ v [I, T] (with/to) (of two things) be closely related or connected; show such a relation between (two things): The results of the two tests do not ~. **correlation**

/ˌkɒrɪˈleɪʃn/ n [sing, U] close relationship or connection.

correspond /ˌkɒrɪˈspɒnd; US ˌkɔːr-/ v [I] 1 (with/to)) be the same or similar; be in agreement: Your account doesn't ~ with hers. 2 (with)) exchange letters. **corresponding** adj that agrees. **correspondingly** adv.

correspondence /ˌkɒrɪˈspɒndəns; US ˌkɔːr-/ n 1 [C, U] agreement; similarity: a close ~ between the two texts. 2 [U] letter-writing; letters. **correspondent** n [C] 1 person with whom one exchanges letters. 2 person who reports for a newspaper, radio or TV station, usu from abroad.

corridor /ˈkɒrɪdɔː(r); US ˈkɔːr-/ n [C] long narrow passage from which doors open into rooms.

corroborate /kəˈrɒbəreɪt/ v [T] confirm the correctness of (a belief, statement, etc): I can ~ what she said. **corroboration** /kəˌrɒbəˈreɪʃn/ n [U].

corrode /kəˈrəʊd/ v [I, T] be destroyed or destroy, esp by chemical action. **corrosion** /kəˈrəʊʒn/ n [U] (a) corroding. (b) corroded area or part. **corrosive** /kəˈrəʊsɪv/ n [C], adj (substance) that corrodes.

corrugated /ˈkɒrəgeɪtɪd; US ˈkɔːr-/ adj having rounded parallel folds: ~ iron/cardboard.

corrupt /kəˈrʌpt/ adj 1 immoral: a ~ society/mind. 2 dishonest, esp because of taking bribes: a ~ business deal. **corrupt** v [I, T] become or make corrupt: ~ing young people. **corruption** /kəˈrʌpʃn/ n [U]. **corruptly** adv.

corset /ˈkɔːsɪt/ n [C] garment worn under the clothes to shape the waist and hips.

cortege /kɔːˈteɪʒ/ n [C] procession, esp at a funeral.

cosh /kɒʃ/ n [C] (Brit) length of pipe, rubber tubing filled with metal, etc for hitting people.

cosmetic /kɒzˈmetɪk/ n [C] substance put on the body, esp the face, to make it beautiful. **cosmetic** adj 1 used as a cosmetic. 2 (often derog) used to make (sth) look better: These are just ~ improvements to the system, they do not really change anything.

cosmic /ˈkɒzmɪk/ adj of the whole universe or cosmos.

cosmonaut /ˈkɒzmənɔːt/ n [C] a Soviet astronaut.

cosmopolitan /ˌkɒzməˈpɒlɪtən/ adj 1 of or from all parts of the world: a ~ gathering. 2 (approv) (open-minded and tolerant through) having wide experience of the world.

cosmos /ˈkɒzmɒs/ **the cosmos** n [sing] the universe.

cost[1] /kɒst; US kɔːst/ n 1 [C, U] price paid for a thing: the high ~ of repairs. 2 [sing, U] what is needed to gain sth: the ~ of victory. 3 **costs** [pl] expenses of a case in a lawcourt. 4 (idm) **at all costs** be the most important thing. **to one's 'cost** to one's loss or disadvantage. **costly** adj (-ier, -iest) 1 costing a lot; of great value. 2 causing much loss, effort, etc: a ~ly mistake.

cost[2] /kɒst; US kɔːst/ v (pt, pp **cost** in sense 3 ~ed) 1 [I] have as a price; be obtainable at the price of: shoes ~ ing £20. 2 [I] result in the loss of; need: a mistake that ~ him his life ◇ ~ a great deal of effort. 3 [T] (commerce) estimate the cost of. **costing** n [C, U] (commerce) estimation or fixing of prices or costs.

co-star /ˈkəʊstɑː(r)/ n [C] well-known actor who appears in a film, etc with other actors of the same status. **co-star** v (-rr-) [I] be a co-star.

costume /ˈkɒstjuːm; US -tuːm/ n 1 [C, U] garment or style of dress, esp that of a particular period. 2 [C] clothes worn by actors on stage.

cosy /ˈkəʊzɪ/ adj (-ier, -iest) warm and comfortable: a ~ room/feeling ◇ (fig) a ~ little talk. **cosily** adv. **cosiness** n [U]. **cosy** n [C] (pl -ies) cover to keep a teapot warm.

cot /kɒt/ n [C] 1 (Brit) small bed for a young child. 2 (US) simple narrow bed, eg on a ship.

cottage /ˈkɒtɪdʒ/ n [C] small house, esp in the country.

cotton[1] /ˈkɒtn/ n [U] 1 soft, white substance used for making thread, cloth, etc. 2 thread or cloth made from this: a ~ dress. ˌcotton 'wool n [U] soft absorbent material used for padding, bandages, etc.

cotton[2] /ˈkɒtn/ v (phr v) **cotton on (to sth)** (infml) come to understand or realize (sth).

couch[1] /kaʊtʃ/ n [C] long seat like a bed.

couch[2] /kaʊtʃ/ v [T] (in)) (fml) express: a reply ~ed in friendly terms.

couchette /kuːˈʃet/ n [C] folding bed in a railway carriage.

cougar /ˈkuːgə(r)/ n [C] (esp US) = PUMA.

cough /kɒf/ v 1 [I] push air out from the lungs violently and noisily: The smoke made me ~. 2 [T] (up)) produce by coughing. **cough** n 1 [C] act or sound of coughing. 2 [sing] illness that makes one cough.

could[1] /kəd; strong form kʊd/ *modal v* (*neg* **could not**, *contracted form* **couldn't** /'kʊdnt/) 1 (used in requests): C~ I use your phone? 2 (indicating a result): We were so tired, we ~ have slept for days! 3 (indicating a possibility): You ~ be right. 4 (used in suggestions): You ~ ask her to go with you.

could[2] *pt of* CAN[1].

couldn't could not. ⇨ COULD[1].

council /'kaʊnsl/ *n* [C, also sing with pl v] group of people elected to manage the affairs of a city, town, etc, give advice, make rules, etc: a ~ meeting. **'council house** *n* [C] house owned by a local council and rented out to people. **councillor** (*US* **councilor**) /'kaʊnsələ(r)/ *n* [C] member of a council.

counsel /'kaʊnsl/ *n* 1 [U] advice; suggestions. 2 [C] (*pl* **counsel**) barrister acting in a law case. **counsel** *v* (-**ll**-; *US* -**l**-) [T] (*fml*) advise: He ~ed her to leave. **counsellor** (*US* **counselor**) /'kaʊnsələ(r)/ *n* [C] 1 adviser. 2 (*US*) lawyer.

count[1] /kaʊnt/ *v* 1 [I] say or name numbers in order: C~ from 1 to 10. 2 [T] (*up*)) find the total of: ~ the people in the room. 3 [T] (indicate: ten people, ~ing Ann. 4 [T] consider to be: ~ oneself lucky. 5 [I] (a) be important or of value: every minute ~ s. (b) be accepted as valid: That didn't ~ because the game was over. 6 (phr v) **count (sth) against sb** be to the disadvantage of sb: Will my past mistakes ~ against me? **count on sb** rely or depend on sb: I'm ~ing on you to help. **count sb/sth out** (a) count (eg coins) slowly, one by one. (b) not include: C~ me out, I'm not going. **countable** *adj* that can be counted: 'House' is a ~able noun. **'countdown** *n* [C] act of counting backwards to zero, eg before firing a rocket.

count[2] /kaʊnt/ *n* [C] 1 act of counting; number reached by counting: There were 50 at the last ~. 2 (*law*) crime that sb is accused of: a ~ of robbery. 3 (idm) **keep/ lose 'count of sth** know/not know how many there are of sth.

count[3] /kaʊnt/ *n* [C] nobleman in France, Italy, etc.

countenance /'kaʊntənəns/ *n* 1 [C] (*fml*) (expression of a) face. 2 [U] support; approval: give/lend ~ to a plan. **countenance** *v* [T] (*fml*) support; approve: I cannot ~ violence.

counter[1] /'kaʊntə(r)/ *n* [C] flat surface where goods are shown, items sold, etc in a shop, bank, etc.

counter[2] /'kaʊntə(r)/ *n* [C] 1 small disc used for counting games, etc. 2 thing that can be exchanged for sth else: a bargaining ~.

counter[3] /'kaʊntə(r)/ *adv to*|| in the opposite direction; against: Her theories ran ~ to the evidence.

counter[4] /'kaʊntə(r)/ *v* [I, T] (*with*)|| respond to an attack, etc with an opposing view, etc: ~ his arguments with her own opinion.

counter- /'kaʊntə(r)-/ (in compounds) 1 opposite in direction or effect: ~-pro'ductive. 2 made as a response to: '~-attack. 3 corresponding: '~-part.

counteract /ˌkaʊntər'rækt/ *v* [T] reduce the effect of (an action, force, poison, etc): try to ~ the bad influence of TV.

counter-attack /'kaʊntər ətæk/ *n* [C], *v* [I] (make) an attack in response to an enemy's attack.

counterbalance /'kaʊntə-'bæləns/ *n* [C] weight or force that is equal to another and balances it. **counterbalance** /ˌkaʊntə'bæləns/ *v* [T] act as a counterbalance to.

counter-espionage /ˌkaʊntər 'espɪənɑːʒ/ *n* [U] action taken against an enemy's spying.

counterfeit /'kaʊntəfɪt/ *n* [C], *adj* (something) made to look exactly like sth else in order to deceive: ~ banknotes. **counterfeit** *v* [T] copy (coins, handwriting, etc) in order to deceive. **counterfeiter** *n* [C] person who counterfeits money.

counterfoil /'kaʊntəfɔɪl/ *n* [C] detachable part of a cheque, etc that can be kept as a record.

countermand /ˌkaʊntə'mɑːnd; *US* -'mænd/ *v* [T] cancel or change (a command already given).

counterpart /'kaʊntəpɑːt/ *n* [C] person or thing similar or corresponding to another.

counter-productive /ˌkaʊntə prə'dʌktɪv/ *adj* producing the opposite effect to what is intended: Her anger was ~: it just made him refuse to help at all.

countersign /'kaʊntəsaɪn/ *v* [T] sign (a document, etc that has already been signed) to make it valid.

countess /'kaʊntɪs/ *n* [C] 1 wife of a count or earl. 2 woman with the rank of a count or earl.

countless /'kaʊntlɪs/ *adj* numerous: I've been there ~ times.

country /'kʌntrɪ/ *n* (*pl* -**ies**) 1 [C]

area of land that forms a politically independent unit; nation. **2 the country** [sing] the people of a country: *a politician loved by the whole ~.* **3 the country** [sing] land outside towns; fields, woods, etc used for farming, etc: *~ life/ people.* **4** (idm) **go to the country** (of a government) call a general election.

countryman /ˈkʌntrɪmən/ (*fem* **countrywoman** /ˈkʌntrɪwʊmən/) *n* [C] **1** person living in the country(3). **2** person from or living in the same country(1) as sb else.

countryside /ˈkʌntrɪsaɪd/ **the countryside** *n* [sing] the country(3).

county /ˈkaʊntɪ/ *n* [C] (*pl* -ies) division of a country or state for the purpose of local government.

coup /kuː/ *n* [C] (*pl* ~s /kuːz/) **1** sudden successful action: *This deal was a ~ for her.* **2** (also **coup d'état** /kuː deɪˈtɑː/) illegal seizing of power in a state, often by violence.

couple¹ /ˈkʌpl/ *n* [C] **1** two people or things, seen together or associated: *a married ~.* **2** (idm) **a couple of** (*infml*) a few: *a ~ of drinks/days.*

couple² /ˈkʌpl/ *v* (*with*)// **1** [T] fasten or join (two things) together. **2** [T] link or associate (two ideas, facts, etc): *His illness, ~d with his lack of money, prevented him leaving.* **3** [I] (*arch* or *rhet*) have sexual intercourse.

coupon /ˈkuːpɒn/ *n* [C] **1** ticket which gives the holder the right to receive or do sth. **2** printed form, often cut out from a newspaper, used to enter a competition, order goods, etc.

courage /ˈkʌrɪdʒ/ *n* [U] ability to control one's fear when facing danger, pain, etc: *show ~ in a battle.* **courageous** /kəˈreɪdʒəs/ *adj.* **courageously** *adv.*

courgette /kɔːˈʒet/ *n* [C] small green marrow¹, eaten as a vegetable.

courier /ˈkʊrɪə(r)/ *n* [C] **1** person who arranges travel, accompanies groups of travellers, etc. **2** messenger carrying news, important papers, etc.

course¹ /kɔːs/ *n* **1** [C] path or direction followed by sth: *the ~ of a river/aircraft.* **2** [C] (often in compounds) area where sports events, esp races, are held: *a golf ~ ○ a race~.* **3** [sing] forward movement in time: *the ~ of history.* **4** [C] series of lessons, lectures, etc: *a French ~.* **5** [C] (*medicine*) series of treatments: *a ~ of injec-*

tions. **6** [C] one of several parts of a meal: *the fish ~.* **7** (idm) **(as) a matter of course** (as) sth that is quite normal and expected. **in the course of during. in due 'course** at the proper time. **of course** naturally; certainly. **run/take its 'course** continue to end in the usual way.

course² /kɔːs/ *v* [I] (*fml*) (of liquids) move quickly: *The blood ~ed round its veins.*

court¹ /kɔːt/ *n* **1** [C, U] place where legal cases are heard. **2 the court** [sing] those present in a court, esp the judges, etc. **3** [C, U] (residence of a) great ruler, his family and officials, etc. **4** [C] (often in compounds) space marked out for certain ball games: *a tennis ~.* **5** [C] (also **'courtyard**) space surrounded by walls but with no roof.

court² /kɔːt/ *v* **1** (*dated*) (a) [T] try to win the affection of (sb), esp when hoping to marry him/her. (b) [I] (of a couple) spend time together, esp when intending to marry. **2** [T] (often *derog*) try to gain the favour or support of: *~ sb's favour.* **3** [T] risk (trouble, etc): *~ disaster.*

courteous /ˈkɜːtɪəs/ *adj* having good manners; polite: *a ~ person/ request.* **courteously** *adv.*

courtesy /ˈkɜːtəsɪ/ *n* (*pl* -ies) **1** [U] courteous behaviour. **2** [C] courteous remark, action, etc. **3** (idm) **by courtesy of** with the favour or permission of.

courtier /ˈkɔːtɪə(r)/ *n* [C] member of a king or queen's court¹(3).

court martial /ˌkɔːt ˈmɑːʃl/ *n* [C] (*pl* **courts martial**) court for trying crimes against military law; trial in such a court. **court martial** *v* (-ll-; *US* -l-) [T] (*for*)// try (sb) in a court martial.

courtship /ˈkɔːtʃɪp/ *n* [C, U] (period of) courting²(1).

courtyard /ˈkɔːtjɑːd/ = COURT¹(5).

cousin /ˈkʌzn/ *n* [C] child of one's uncle or aunt.

cove /kəʊv/ *n* [C] small bay¹.

cover¹ /ˈkʌvə(r)/ *v* **1** [T] (*up/ over*)// place (one thing) over or in front of (another); hide or protect (sth) in this way: *~ a table with a cloth ○ ~ one's face ○ ~ (up) the body.* **2** [T] (*in/with*)// (esp passive) spread, or lay a layer of (sth) on the surface of (sth): *hills ~ed with snow ○ boots ~ed in mud.* **3** [T] travel (a certain distance): *~ 100 miles in a day.* **4** [T] (of money) be enough for: *Will £20 ~ your expenses?* **5** [T] include: *Her researches*

~ed a wide field. 6 [T] (of a journalist) report (an event): *I've been asked to ~ the election.* 7 [I] (*for*)// do sb's work, etc during his/her absence. 7 [T] keep (a gun) aimed at sb: *We've got him ~ed.* 9 (idm) **cover one's tracks** leave no evidence of where one has been or what one has been doing. 10 (phr v) **cover up** (*derog*) keep (a scandal, an embarrassment, etc) secret. **cover up for sb** keep sb's mistakes, crimes, etc secret to protect him/her. **coverage** *n* [U] covering of events, etc by a reporter. **covered** *adj* (*in/with*)// having a great number or amount of sth: *trees ~ed in blossom.* '**cover-up** *n* [C] (*derog*) act of hiding a mistake, crime, etc.

cover² /'kʌvə(r)/ *n* 1 [C] (**a**) thing that covers: *a chair ~.* (**b**) top; lid. 2 [C] thick outside papers of a book, magazine, etc. 3 [U] place or area giving shelter: *seek ~ under some trees.* 4 **the covers** [pl] bedclothes. 5 [usu sing] (*for*)// means of keeping sth secret: *a business that is a ~ for drug dealing.* 6 [U] protection from attack: *Aircraft gave the infantry ~.* 7 [U] insurance against loss, damage, etc. 8 [C] wrapper or envelope. 9 (idm) **under cover of** hidden by: *under ~ of darkness.*

covert /'kʌvət; *US* 'kəʊvɜːrt/ *adj* half-hidden; not open; secret: *a ~ glance/threat.* **covertly** *adv.*

cow¹ /kaʊ/ *n* [C] 1 fully grown female of any animal of the ox family. 2 female of some mammals, eg elephant, rhinoceros and whale. 3 (*derog sl*) woman: *You silly ~!* '**cowboy** *n* [C] 1 man who looks after cattle in the western parts of the US. 2 (*Brit infml*) builder, plumber, etc who does work poorly or dishonestly.

cow² /kaʊ/ *v* [T] frighten (sb) into doing what one wants: *He was ~ed into giving them all his money.*

coward /'kaʊəd/ *n* [C] (*derog*) person who cannot control his/her fear; person who avoids danger, responsibility, etc. **cowardly** *adj* (*derog*) of or like a coward; not brave: *a ~ attack.* **cowardice** /-dɪs/ *n* [U] (*derog*) feelings or behaviour of a coward.

cower /'kaʊə(r)/ *v* [I] lower the body or move back from fear, cold, etc.

cowl /kaʊl/ *n* [C] 1 large hood on a monk's gown. 2 metal cap for a chimney, etc.

cox /kɒks/ *n* [C] (also (*fml*) **coxswain** /'kɒksn/) *n* [C] person who steers a rowing-boat, esp in races. **cox**

v [I, T] act as a cox (of).

coy /kɔɪ/ *adj* 1 (pretending to be) shy, modest, etc: *a ~ smile.* 2 not willing to give information, answer questions, etc: *She was a little ~ about her past.* **coyly** *adv.* **coyness** *n* [U].

coyote /kɔɪˈəʊtɪ; *US* 'kaɪəʊt/ *n* [C] small wolf of western N America.

crab /kræb/ *n* (**a**) [C] ten-legged shellfish. (**b**) [U] its flesh eaten as food.

crabby /'kræbɪ/ *adj* (**-ier, -iest**) (*infml*) bad-tempered; irritable: *in a ~ mood.*

crack¹ /kræk/ *n* [C] 1 line where sth has broken, but not into separate parts: *a ~ in a cup/the ice.* 2 sudden sharp noise: *the ~ of a whip/rifle.* 3 sharp blow: *a ~ on the head.* 4 (*infml*) clever or amusing remark; joke: *She made a ~ about my baldness.* 5 (idm) **the crack of dawn** (*infml*) very early in the morning. **crack** *adj* excellent; very skilful: *She's a ~ shot.*

crack² /kræk/ *v* 1 [I, T] (cause) to form a crack¹(1) or cracks in: *~ a plate* ○ *The ice ~ed.* 2 [I, T] make a crack or cracks¹(2): *~ a whip.* 3 [T] break (sth) open or into pieces: *~ a safe* ○ *~ nuts.* 4 [T] hit (sth) sharply: *~ one's head on the door.* 5 [I, T] (cause to) stop resisting or fail: *She finally ~ed and told the truth.* 6 [T] (*infml*) solve (a problem, etc): *~ a code.* 7 [I] (of the voice) suddenly become harsh; (of a boy's voice) become deeper. 8 [T] (*infml*) tell (a joke). 9 (idm) **get 'cracking** (*infml*) start to be very busy. 10 (phr v) **crack down (on sb/sth)** become more strict or severe: *~ down on crime.* **crack up** (*infml*) lose physical or mental health. '**crack-down** *n* [C] sudden strict or severe measures: *a police ~ down on vandalism.* **cracked** (*adj*) (*infml*) slightly mad: *You must be ~ed to drive so fast!*

crack³ /kræk/ *n* [U] (*sl*) very strong pure form of cocaine.

cracker /'krækə(r)/ *n* [C] 1 thin dry biscuit, often eaten with cheese. 2 firework that makes cracking noises. 3 toy consisting of a cardboard tube wrapped in paper that makes a cracking noise when pulled apart.

crackers /'krækəz/ *adj* (*Brit infml*) mad; crazy.

crackle /'krækl/ *v* [I] make a number of small cracking sounds, as when dry sticks burn: *Dry leaves ~d under our feet.* **crackle** *n* [sing, U] crackling sound.

crackpot /'krækpɒt/ *n* [C] (*infml*)

eccentric or mad person: *a ~ idea/ person.*

cradle /'kreɪdl/ *n* [C] **1** small bed for a baby. **2** (*fig*) place where sth begins: *the ~ of Western culture.* **3** any framework like a cradle. **cradle** *v* [T] place or hold (sb/sth) (as if) in a cradle.

craft /krɑːft; US kræft/ *n* **1** [C] (occupation needing) skill with the hands: *the potter's ~.* **2** [C] (*pl* craft) ship, boat, aircraft or spacecraft. **3** [U] (*fml derog*) skill in deceiving; cunning. **-craft** (in compounds): *handi~/needle~.* **'craftsman** *n* [C] (*pl* **-men**) skilled worker who practises a craft. **'craftsmanship** *n* [U] skill as a craftsman.

crafty /'krɑːftɪ; US 'kræftɪ/ *adj* (**-ier, -iest**) showing great skill in deceiving; cunning. **craftily** *adv.* **craftiness** *n* [U].

crag /kræg/ *n* [C] steep mass of rock. **craggy** *adj* (**-ier, -iest**) **1** having many crags. **2** (of sb's face) having strong features and deep lines.

cram /kræm/ *v* (**-mm-**) **1** [T] (*in/ into/with*))/ push too much of (sth) into (sth): *~ the clothes into the suitcase* ○ *~ the file with papers.* **2** [I] (*for*)/ study very hard for an exam, etc.

cramp¹ /kræmp/ *n* [C, usu pl, U] sudden and painful tightening of the muscles.

cramp² /kræmp/ *v* **1** [T] (usu passive) give too little space to; prevent the movement or development of: *feel ~ed by the rules.* **2** (idm) **cramp sb's 'style** (*infml*) stop sb doing things in the way he/ she wants to. **cramped** *adj* having too little space: *~ conditions.*

crampon /'kræmpɒn/ *n* [C] iron plate with spikes, worn over shoes for climbing on ice.

cranberry /'krænbərɪ; US -berɪ/ *n* [C] small red slightly sour berry, used for making jelly and sauce.

crane¹ /kreɪn/ *n* [C] **1** large wading bird with long legs and neck. **2** machine with a long arm, used for lifting heavy weights.

crane² /kreɪn/ *v* [I, T] stretch (one's neck), eg to see better: *Children ~d to see the animals.*

cranium /'kreɪnɪəm/ *n* [C] (*pl* **-s** or **crania** /'kreɪnɪə/) (*anatomy*) skull. **cranial** *adj.*

crank¹ /kræŋk/ *n* [C] L-shaped handle for turning things. **crank** *v* [T] (*up*)/ move by turning a crank: *~ the engine* (ie start it with a crank). **'crankshaft** *n* [C] shaft that turns or is turned by a crank.

crank² /kræŋk/ *n* [C] (*derog*) person with fixed strange ideas. **cranky** *adj* (**-ier, -iest**) (*infml derog*) **1** (of people) odd; eccentric. **2** (*US*) bad-tempered.

cranny /'krænɪ/ *n* [C] **1** small opening in a wall, etc. **2** (idm) **every nook and cranny** ⇨ NOOK.

crap /kræp/ *n* (*sl* △) **1** [U] empty waste matter from the bowels. **crap** *n* (△) **1** [U] excrement. **2** [sing] act of emptying the bowels. **3** [U] nonsense; rubbish. **crappy** *adj* (**-ier, -iest**) (*sl*) useless; worthless.

crash¹ /kræʃ/ *n* [C] **1** [usu sing] (noise made by a) violent fall, blow, etc: *The dishes fell with a ~ to the floor.* **2** accident involving a vehicle in collision with (sth): *a car ~.* **3** complete ruin or collapse, eg of a business. **crash** *adj* done to achieve quick results: *a ~ course in French.* **crash** *adv* with a crash. **'crash-helmet** *n* [C] helmet worn, eg by a motor-cyclist, to protect the head. **,crash-'land** *v* [I, T] land (an aircraft) in an emergency. **,crash-'landing** *n* [C] landing made in this way.

crash² /kræʃ/ *v* **1** [I, T] fall or strike (sth) violently or noisily: *The tree ~ed through the window.* **2** [I, T] (cause) to collide with (sth): *~ the car (into a wall).* **3** [I] make a loud noise: *The thunder ~ed.* **4** [I, T] (cause) to move suddenly or violently: *an elephant ~ing through the trees.* **5** [I] (of a business, etc) fail suddenly.

crass /kræs/ *adj* (*fml derog*) **1** very stupid, ignorant, etc: *a ~ idiot.* **2** very great or complete: *~ stupidity.*

crate /kreɪt/ *n* [C] large wooden container for goods. **crate** *v* [T] put in a crate.

crater /'kreɪtə(r)/ *n* [C] **1** opening at the top of a volcano. **2** hole made by a bomb.

cravat /krə'væt/ *n* [C] piece of cloth worn by men round the neck.

crave /kreɪv/ *v* [T] (*for*)/ desire strongly: *~ for a cigarette.* **craving** *n* [C].

crawl /krɔːl/ *v* [I] **1** move slowly along the ground or on the hands and knees: *The baby ~ed along the floor.* **2** move very slowly: *traffic ~ing into London.* **3** (*with*)/ (esp in the continuous tense) be covered with or full of things that crawl, etc: *a floor ~ing with ants.* **4** (*to*)/ (*infml*) try to gain sb's favour by doing as he/she wants, flattering him/her, etc. **5** (idm) **make one's flesh crawl** ⇨ FLESH. **crawl** *n* **1** [C] crawling movement. **2** the

crawl [sing] fast swimming stroke. **crawler** n (*infml derog*) person who crawls(4).

crayon /'kreɪən/ n [C] pencil of soft coloured chalk or wax. **crayon** v [T] draw with crayons.

craze /kreɪz/ n [C] (a) enthusiastic, usu brief, popular interest in sth. (b) object of such an interest.

crazed /kreɪzd/ adj (*with*) very excited; mad.

crazy /'kreɪzɪ/ adj (-ier, -iest) 1 wildly excited or enthusiastic: ~ *about football*. 2 (*infml*) insane; mad. 3 (*infml*) foolish; not sensible: a ~ *idea*. **crazily** adv. **craziness** n [U].

creak /kriːk/ v [I] n [C] (make a) harsh sound like a badly-oiled hinge: *The branches ~ed in the wind*. **creaky** adj (-ier, -iest) making creaking sounds.

cream /kriːm/ n 1 [U] thick yellowish liquid that is the fatty part of milk. 2 [U] any substance like cream: *furniture* ~. 3 **the cream** [sing] the best part: *the* ~ *of society*. 4 [U] yellowish-white colour. **cream** adj yellowish-white. **cream** v [T] 1 take cream out of (milk). 2 make (potatoes, etc) into soft paste. 3 (phr v) **cream off** take the best part. **creamy** adj (-ier, -iest) like cream; containing cream.

crease /kriːs/ n [C] 1 line made in cloth, paper, etc by crushing, folding or pressing. 2 wrinkle on the skin. 3 white line near the wicket on a cricket pitch. **crease** v [I, T] (cause to) develop a crease.

create /kriːˈeɪt/ v [T] 1 cause (sth) to exist; make (sth new or original). 2 result in; produce: ~ *problems*.

creation /kriːˈeɪʃn/ n 1 [U] creating: *the* ~ *of the world*. 2 (also **Creation**) [U] all created things. 3 [C] something created or made.

creative /kriːˈeɪtɪv/ adj able to create: a ~ *person who writes and paints*. 2 of creation: *the* ~ *act*. **creatively** adv. **creativity** /ˌkriːeɪˈtɪvətɪ/ n [U].

creator /kriːˈeɪtə(r)/ n 1 [C] person who creates: *the* ~ *of this novel*. 2 **the Creator** [sing] God.

creature /'kriːtʃə(r)/ n [C] living animal or person: *all God's* ~*s*.

crèche /kreɪʃ/ n [C] place where babies are cared for while their parents are at work.

credentials /krɪˈdenʃls/ n [pl] 1 documents showing a person is who he/she claims to be. 2 qualities, etc that make one suitable: *Does she have the* ~ *for this demanding work?*

credible /'kredəbl/ adj that can be believed: a ~ *story/explanation*. **credibility** /ˌkredəˈbɪlɪtɪ/ n [U] quality of being credible. **credibly** /-əblɪ/ adv in a credible way.

credit[1] /'kredɪt/ n 1 [U] agreement to buy sth and pay later: *buy a car on* ~. 2 [U] belief of others that a person, company, etc can pay debts: *have good/poor* ~. 3 [U] sum of money in a bank account. 4 [C] sum of money lent by a bank, etc. 5 [C] entry in an account of money received. 6 [U] belief; trust: *give* ~ *to her story*. 7 [U] praise; approval: *get/be given all the* ~ *for sth*. 8 [sing] to/l person or thing that makes a reputation better: *She's a* ~ *to her family*. 9 [C] (*US*) course completed by a student. 10 (idm) **be to sb's credit** make sb worthy of praise. **'credit card** n [C] card allowing the holder to buy goods on credit(1). **'credit-worthy** adj accepted as safe for receiving credit. **'credit-worthiness** n [U].

credit[2] /'kredɪt/ v [T] 1 (*with*)/l think that sb has sth: *I* ~*ed you with more sense*. 2 put a sum of money into (an account). 3 believe: *Would you* ~ *it?*

creditable /'kredɪtəbl/ adj deserving praise (although not perfect): a ~ *piece of work*. **creditably** adv.

creditor /'kredɪtə(r)/ n [C] person to whom sb owes money.

credulous /'kredjʊləs; *US* -dʒə-/ adj too willing to believe things. **credulity** /krɪˈdjuːlətɪ/ n [U].

creed /kriːd/ n [C] set of beliefs, esp religious ones.

creek /kriːk; *US* krɪk/ n [C] 1 (*Brit*) narrow stretch of river cutting into a coast or river-bank. 2 (*US*) small river.

creep /kriːp/ v [I] (*pt, pp* **crept** /krept/) 1 move along slowly or quietly, esp crouching low: *The thief crept along the corridor.* ○ (*fig*) *Old age is* ~*ing up on me*. 2 (of plants, etc) grow over the surface of a wall, etc. 3 (idm) **make one's flesh creep** ⇨ FLESH. **creep** n 1 [C] (*infml derog*) unpleasant person, esp one who tries to gain sb's favour by doing what he/she wants, etc. 2 (idm) **give sb the creeps** (*infml*) make sb feel fear or dislike. **creeper** n [C] plant that creeps(2).

creepy /'kriːpɪ/ adj (-ier, -iest) (*infml*) causing or feeling fear: a ~ *house/atmosphere*.

creepy-crawly /ˌkriːpɪˈkrɔːlɪ/ n [C] (*infml esp joc*) insect, spider, etc.

cremate /krɪˈmeɪt/ v [T] burn (the body of a dead person) to ashes. **cremation** /-ˈmeɪʃn/ n [C, U] (act of) cremating. **crematorium** /ˌkremaˈtɔːrɪəm/ n [C] (pl ~s or -**oria** /-ˈɔːrɪə/) place where bodies are cremated.

creosote /ˈkrɪəsəʊt/ n [U] brown oily liquid used for preserving wood.

crepe (also **crêpe**) /kreɪp/ n [U] 1 any of various types of wrinkled cloth or paper: a ~ blouse. 2 rubber with wrinkled surface. 3 thin pancake.

crept pt, pp of CREEP.

crescendo /krɪˈʃendəʊ/ n [C] (pl ~ s) 1 (music) gradual increase in loudness. 2 (fig) (gradual increase in intensity, noise, etc to a) climax. **crescendo** adj, adv of or with increasing loudness: a ~ passage.

crescent /ˈkreznt, ˈkresnt/ n [C] 1 (something shaped like the) curve of the new moon. 2 row of houses built in a curve.

cress /kres/ n [U] plant with hot-tasting leaves, used for salad.

crest /krest/ n [C] 1 tuft of feathers on a bird's head. 2 (a) top of a hill. (b) white top of a large wave. 3 design over the shield of a coat of arms, often representing on notepaper, etc. 4 decoration on top of a soldier's helmet. **crest** v [T] reach the top of (a hill, etc).

crestfallen /ˈkrestfɔːlən/ adj very sad or disappointed.

cretin /ˈkretɪn/ n [C] 1 (offensive △) stupid person. 2 (medical) person who is deformed and of very low intelligence.

crevasse /krɪˈvæs/ n [C] deep open crack in thin ice.

crevice /ˈkrevɪs/ n [C] narrow opening or crack in a rock, wall, etc.

crew /kruː/ n [C] 1 people working on a ship or aircraft; these people, except the officers. 2 group of people working together: a camera ~. **crew** v [I, T] act as the crew (of).

crib[1] /krɪb/ n [C] 1 small bed for a baby. 2 wooden framework for holding an animal's food.

crib[2] /krɪb/ n [C] 1 something copied dishonestly from the work of another person: The teacher said my exam answer was a ~. 2 something used as an aid to understanding, eg a translation of a foreign text one is studying. **crib** v (-**bb**-) [I, T] copy (sb's work) dishonestly.

crick /krɪk/ n [sing] painful stiffness, esp in the neck.

cricket[1] /ˈkrɪkɪt/ n [U] ball game

played on grass by two teams of eleven players, in which a ball is bowled at a wicket and a batsman tries to hit it: a ~ match. **cricketer** n [C] cricket player.

cricket[2] /ˈkrɪkɪt/ n [C] small brown jumping insect that makes a shrill noise.

cried pt, pp of CRY[2].

cries 1 3rd pers sing pres t of ⇨ CRY[2]. 2 pl of CRY[1].

crime /kraɪm/ n 1 [C] offence for which there is a punishment by law: commit a ~. 2 [U] such offences. 3 a crime [sing] a foolish or shameful act: It's a ~ to waste money like that. **criminal** /ˈkrɪmɪnl/ adj 1 of or concerning crime: a ~ offence ○ ~ law. 2 foolish or shameful: It's ~ not to use your talents fully. **criminal** n [C] person who commits a crime or crimes. **criminally** /-nəlɪ/ adv.

crimson /ˈkrɪmzn/ adj, n [U] (of a) deep red.

cringe /krɪndʒ/ v [I] 1 move back or lower (the body) in fear. 2 (to/ before)// behave too humbly towards sb who is more powerful: Don't always ~ to the boss.

crinkle /ˈkrɪŋkl/ n [C] small narrow wrinkle in paper, skin, etc. **crinkle** v [I, T] (cause to) form crinkles: ~d paper.

cripple /ˈkrɪpl/ n [C] person unable to move properly because of injury or disease, esp to the spine or legs. **cripple** v [T] (usu passive) 1 make(sb) a cripple: ~d by a back injury. 2 (fig) seriously damage or weaken: ~d by debt.

crisis /ˈkraɪsɪs/ n [C, U] (pl **crises** /-siːz/) time of difficulty, danger, etc; decisive moment: an economic ~ ○ a country in ~.

crisp /krɪsp/ adj 1 (a) (esp of food) hard, dry and easily broken: a ~ biscuit ○ ~ snow. (b) (esp of fruit or vegetables) fresh and firm: a ~ lettuce. (c) (esp of paper) slightly stiff: ~ banknotes. 2 (of the weather) frosty, cold: a ~ winter morning. 3 (of sb's way of speaking, behaving, etc) precise and brisk: a ~ reply. **crisp** n [C, usu pl] thin slice of potato, fried and dried and sold in packets. **crisp** v [I, T] make or become crisp. **crisply** adv. **crispness** n [U]. **crispy** adj (-ier, -iest) (infml) crisp(1a, b).

criss-cross /ˈkrɪskrɒs/ adj with crossed lines: a ~ pattern. **criss-cross** v [I, T] form or make a criss-cross pattern (on): roads ~ ing the country.

criterion /kraɪˈtɪərɪən/ n [C] (pl **-ria** /-rɪə/) standard by which sb/

sth is judged.

critic /ˈkrɪtɪk/ n [C] 1 person who forms and gives opinions about literature, art, music, etc: *The ~s liked the play.* 2 person who points out faults, disapproves, etc.

critical /ˈkrɪtɪkl/ adj 1 pointing out faults; disapproving: *a ~ remark.* 2 forming or giving judgment, esp about art, literature, etc: *a ~ review.* 3 of or at a crisis: *a ~ decision.* **critically** /-ɪklɪ/ adv in a critical way: *~ly ill.*

criticism /ˈkrɪtɪsɪzəm/ n 1 (a) [U] art of judging literature, books, etc: *literary ~.* (b) [C] such a judgement. 2 (a) [U] pointing out faults; disapproval: *I can't stand her constant ~.* (b) [C] remark that points out a fault.

criticize /ˈkrɪtɪsaɪz/ v 1 [I, T] point out the faults of: *Don't ~ my work.* 2 [T] form and give opinions about (esp art, literature, etc).

critique /krɪˈtiːk/ n [C] critical judgement: *The book contains a ~ of her ideas.*

croak /krəʊk/ n [C] deep, hoarse sound as made by a frog. **croak** v 1 [I] make this kind of sound. 2 [I, T] say (sth) in a croaking voice.

crockery /ˈkrɒkərɪ/ n [U] plates, cups, etc made of baked clay.

crocodile /ˈkrɒkədaɪl/ n [C] 1 large river reptile with a long body and tail, found in hot countries. 2 (*infml*) long line of people, esp schoolchildren, walking in pairs. 3 (*idm*) **crocodile tears** insincere sorrow.

crocus /ˈkrəʊkəs/ n [C] small plant with white, yellow or purple flowers appearing early in spring.

croissant /ˈkrwæsɒ̃/; US krʌˈsɒ̃/ n [C] crescent-shaped bun of light flaky pastry.

crony /ˈkrəʊnɪ/ n [C] (*infml*, derog) friend or companion.

crook /krʊk/ n [C] 1 (*infml*) criminal. 2 bend or curve. 3 stick with a rounded hook at one end, esp as used by a shepherd. **crook** v [T] bend (esp one's finger or arm).

crooked /ˈkrʊkɪd/ adj 1 not straight: *a ~ line.* 2 (*infml*) dishonest: *a ~ politician.* **crookedly** adv.

crop¹ /krɒp/ n 1 [C] amount of grain, grass, fruit, etc produced in a year or season: *a good ~ of wheat.* 2 **crops** [pl] agricultural plants in the fields. 3 [sing] of// group of people or things: *a new ~ of problems.*

crop² /krɒp/ v (-pp-) [T] 1 cut short (sb's hair, a horse's tail). 2 (of animals) bite off the tops of (grass, plants, etc); graze. 3 (phr v)

crop up appear or occur, esp unexpectedly: *A new problem has ~ped up.*

croquet /ˈkrəʊkeɪ; US krəʊˈkeɪ/ n [U] game played on grass with balls that are knocked through hoops.

cross¹ /krɒs; US krɔːs/ n [C] 1 mark made by drawing one line across another, eg x. 2 (a) **the Cross** [sing] the frame made of an upright post with another across it near the top, on which Christ was crucified. (b) [C] thing representing this, worn as an emblem. (c) [C] sign of the cross made by a member of the clergy. 3 (*fml*) source of suffering or sorrow: *We all have our ~ to bear.* 4 (a) animal or plant that is the offspring of two different breeds or varieties. (b) mixture of two things.

cross² /krɒs; US krɔːs/ v 1 [I, T] go across; extend from one side to the other of sth: *a bridge ~ing the road.* 2 [T] put or place (one thing) over another of the same kind: *~ one's arms.* 3 [T] draw a line or lines: *~ a cheque,* ie draw two lines on it to show that it must be paid into a bank account. 4 [I] meet and pass each other: *The letters ~ed in the post.* 5 [T] prevent (sb) doing sth; oppose (sb's plans, etc): *You shouldn't ~ her in business.* 6 [T] (*with*)// cause (two different types of animal or plant) to produce offspring: *~ different varieties of rose.* 7 ~ **oneself** make the sign of a cross. 8 (*idm*) **cross one's mind** (of ideas, etc) come into one's mind. 9 (phr v) **cross sth off/out/through** remove sth by drawing a line through it: *~ her name off the list* ○ *~ his name out.*

cross³ /krɒs; US krɔːs/ adj 1 angry: *I was ~ with him for being late.* ○ *She's ~ about this.* 2 (of winds) blowing from one side: *a ~ breeze.* **crossly** adv. **crossness** n [U].

crossbow /ˈkrɒsbəʊ; US krɔːs-/ n [C] powerful bow²(1) with a grooved support, using a trigger to release the arrow.

crossbred /ˈkrɒsbred; US ˈkrɔːs-/ adj produced by crossing breeds: *a ~ horse.*

crossbreed /ˈkrɒsbriːd; US krɔːs-/ n [C] animal, plant, etc produced by crossing breeds.

cross-check /ˌkrɒs ˈtʃek; US ˌkrɔːs-/ v [I, T] test (eg a method, calculation, etc) by using a different method, source of information, etc. **cross-check** /ˈkrɒstʃek/ n [C] test of this kind.

cross-country /ˌkrɒs ˈkʌntrɪ; US krɔːs-/ adj, adv across the country or fields, not on roads: *a ~ race.*

cross-examine /ˌkrɒs ɪɡˈzæmɪn; *US* ˌkrɔːs-/ *v* [T] question closely, esp to test answers already given, as in a law-court. **cross-examination** *n* [C, U] (act of) cross-examining.

cross-eyed /ˈkrɒsaɪd; *US* ˈkrɔːs-/ *adj* with one or both eyes turned towards the nose.

crossfire /ˈkrɒsfaɪə(r); *US* ˈkrɔːs-/ *n* [U] firing of guns from two or more points, so that the bullets cross.

crossing /ˈkrɒsɪŋ; *US* ˈkrɔːs-/ *n* [C] 1 place where two roads, railways, etc meet. 2 short for LEVEL CROSSING (LEVEL¹). 3 journey across the sea, a wide river, etc: *a stormy ~ of the Atlantic.*

cross-legged /ˌkrɒs ˈleɡd; *US* ˌkrɔːs-/ *adv* with one leg over the other: *sitting ~.*

cross-piece /ˈkrɒspiːs; *US* ˈkrɔːs-/ *n* [C] piece (of a structure, tool, etc) lying or fixed across another piece.

cross purposes /ˌkrɒs ˈpɜːpəsɪz; *US* ˌkrɔːs-/ *n* (idm) **at cross 'purposes** (of two people or groups) misunderstanding what the other is talking about.

cross-reference /ˌkrɒs ˈrefrəns; *US* ˌkrɔːs-/ *n* [C] note directing the reader to another part of the book, file, etc.

crossroads /ˈkrɒsrəʊdz; *US* ˈkrɔːs-/ *n* [C] (*pl* **crossroads**) 1 place where two or more roads meet. 2 (idm) **at a/the 'crossroads** at a point where an important decision is to be taken.

cross-section /ˌkrɒs ˈsekʃn; *US* ˌkrɔːs-/ *n* [C] 1 (drawing of a) surface formed by cutting or slicing through sth. 2 (*fig*) representative sample of a group: *a ~ of society.*

crossword /ˈkrɒswɜːd; *US* ˈkrɔːs-/ *n* [C] puzzle in which words have to be guessed from clues and written in spaces in a grid.

crotch /krɒtʃ/ *n* [C] place where a person's legs, or trouser legs, join.

crouch /kraʊtʃ/ *v* [I] lower the body by bending the knees: *~ down on the floor.* **crouch** *n* [sing] crouching position.

croupier /ˈkruːpɪə; *US* -pɪər/ *n* [C] person in charge of a table where people gamble money on cards, etc.

crow¹ /krəʊ/ *n* 1 [C] any of various types of large black bird with a harsh cry. 2 (idm) **as the 'crow flies** in a straight line: *It's ten miles away, as the ~ flies.*

'crow's-feet *n* [pl] lines on the skin near the corner of the eye.

'crow's-nest *n* [C] look-out platform on the mast of a ship.

crow² /krəʊ/ *v* [I] 1 (of a cock) make a loud shrill cry. 2 (*over*)// express glee about a success, etc: *~ ing over her profits.* **crow** *n* [usu sing] crowing sound.

crowbar /ˈkrəʊbɑː(r)/ *n* [C] straight iron bar used as a lever for opening crates, moving heavy objects, etc.

crowd /kraʊd/ *n* [C, also sing with pl v] 1 large number of people together: *a ~ of tourists.* 2 (*infml*) group of people associated in some way: *the golfing ~.* **crowd** *v* 1 [I] come together in a crowd: *~ around the stage.* 2 [T] fill (a space, room, etc): *Tourists ~ed the beach.* 3 [T] (*infml*) put pressure on sb. **crowded** *adj* (too) full of people: *a ~ room.*

crown¹ /kraʊn/ *n* 1 [C] ornamental head-dress of a king or queen. 2 **the Crown** [sing] royal power. 3 [C] top of a hill, head, hat, etc.

crown² /kraʊn/ *v* [T] 1 put a crown on (a king or queen). 2 (*with*)// (usu passive) (a) (*fml*) form the top of: *a hill ~ed with a wood.* (b) complete in a suitable or perfect way: *a project ~ed with success.* 3 (idm) **to crown it 'all** to be the last in a series of bad events. **crowning** *adj* making perfect or complete: *a ~ing achievement.*

crucial /ˈkruːʃl/ *adj* of decisive importance: *a ~ decision.* **crucially** /-ʃəlɪ/ *adv.*

crucifix /ˈkruːsɪfɪks/ *n* [C] model of the Cross with a figure of Christ on it.

crucifixion /ˌkruːsɪˈfɪkʃn/ *n* [C, U] (act of) crucifying.

crucify /ˈkruːsɪfaɪ/ *v* (*pt, pp* -**ied**) [T] 1 kill sb by nailing him/her to a cross. 2 (*infml*) criticize, punish, etc very severely.

crude /kruːd/ *adj* 1 (of materials) in a natural state and not refined: *~ oil.* 2 (a) not well made or prepared; rough: *~ tools.* (b) rude and vulgar: *~ jokes.* **crudely** *adv.*

cruel /ˈkruːəl/ *adj* 1 (of people) enjoying the suffering of others. 2 causing suffering: *~ treatment.* **cruelly** *adv.* **cruelty** *n* 1 [U] cruel actions. 2 [C, usu pl] (*pl* -**ies**) cruel act.

cruet /ˈkruːɪt/ *n* [C] small stand for salt and pepper, oil and vinegar, etc on a table.

cruise /kruːz/ *v* [I] 1 sail about for pleasure, or look for enemy ships in wartime. 2 (of cars, aircraft, etc) travel at the speed which uses least fuel: ~ *along at 50 miles per hour.* **cruise** *n* [C] pleasure voyage. **cruiser** *n* [C] 1 fast warship. 2 motor boat with sleeping accommodation. '**cruise missile** *n* [C] missile that flies low and can guide itself.

crumb /krʌm/ *n* [C] 1 very small piece of dry food, esp bread. 2 very small amount.

crumble /'krʌmbl/ *v* 1 [I, T] break, rub or fall into very small pieces. 2 [I] (*fig*) come to an end: *Their marriage ~d.* **crumbly** *adj* (-**ier, -iest**) easily crumbled.

crumple /'krʌmpl/ *v* (*up*)‖ 1 [I, T] (cause) to be pressed or crushed into creases: *material that ~s easily.* 2 [I] (*fig*) come to an end; collapse: *Her resistance ~d.*

crunch /krʌntʃ/ *v* 1 [I, T] (*up*)‖ crush noisily with the teeth when eating. 2 [I, T] crush or be crushed noisily: *The snow ~ed under our feet.* **crunch** *n* [sing] 1 act or sound of crunching. 2 **the crunch** (*infml*) crisis: *when the ~ comes.*

crusade /kru:'seɪd/ *n* [C] (*for/ against*)‖ any struggle for sth good or against sth bad. **crusade** *v* [I] take part in a crusade. **crusader** *n* [C].

crush¹ /krʌʃ/ *v* 1 [T] press so hard there is breakage or injury: *Her hand was ~ed by the heavy door.* 2 [T] break (sth hard) into small pieces or powder. 3 [I, T] (cause) to become full of creases: *clothes ~ed in a suitcase.* 4 [T] defeat completely. 5 [I] move through or into a narrow space by pushing: *Crowds ~ed into the theatre.* **crushing** *adj* 1 overwhelming: *a ~ing defeat.* 2 humiliating: *a ~ing remark.*

crush² /krʌʃ/ *n* 1 [sing] crowd of people pressed together. 2 [C] (*on*)‖ strong but often brief liking.

crust /krʌst/ *n* [C, U] 1 hard surface of a loaf, pie, tart, etc. 2 hard surface: *the earth's ~.* **crusty** *adj* (-**ier, -iest**) 1 having a crust; like a crust: *~y bread.* 2 (*infml*) badtempered.

crustacean /krʌ'steɪʃn/ *n* [C] shellfish.

crutch /krʌtʃ/ *n* [C] 1 stick used as a support under the arm to help a lame person walk. 2 (*fig*) person or thing that helps or supports. 3 = CROTCH.

crux /krʌks/ *n* [C] most important or difficult part of a problem.

cry¹ /kraɪ/ *n* (*pl* -**ies**) 1 [C] loud sound expressing pain, grief, etc: *a ~ for help.* 2 [sing] act or period of weeping: *have a good ~.* 3 [C] sound made by a bird or animal:

the ~ of the thrush. 4 (*idm*) **a far cry from** very different from.

cry² /kraɪ/ *v* (*pt, pp* -**ied**) 1 [I] (*for; over; with*)‖ produce tears from the eyes; weep: *~ with pain ○ He was ~ing for his mother.* 2 [I] (of people or animals) make sounds expressing pain, fear, etc: *~ out in surprise.* 3 [I, T] call loudly: *'Get out!' he cried.* 4 (*phr v*) **cry off** cancel an appointment, etc. **cry out for** need urgently. '**cry-baby** *n* [C] person who cries too easily or for no good reason.

crypt /krɪpt/ *n* [C] room under a church.

cryptic /'krɪptɪk/ *adj* having a hidden meaning.

crystal /'krɪstl/ *n* 1 (**a**) [U] transparent colourless mineral, eg quartz. (**b**) [C] piece of this, esp as an ornament. 2 [U] high quality glass. 3 [C] regular shape taken naturally by certain substances: *salt ~s.* 4 [C] (*US*) glass or plastic cover on the face of a watch. **crystalline** *adj* 1 made of crystal(s); like crystal. 2 (*fml*) very clear: *~ water.* **crystallize** *v* 1 [I, T] (cause to) form into crystals. 2 [I, T] (*fig*) (cause ideas, plans, etc to become) clear and definite. 3 [T] preserve (fruit) in sugar.

cub /kʌb/ *n* [C] young lion, bear, fox, etc.

cubby-hole /'kʌbɪ həʊl/ *n* [C] small enclosed space or room.

cube /kju:b/ *n* [C] 1 solid body having six equal square sides. 2 (*mathematics*) result of multiplying a number by itself twice. **cube** *v* [T] (*esp passive*) multiply a number by itself twice: *3 ~d is 27.* **cubic** /'kju:bɪk/ *adj* 1 having the shape of a cube; of a cube. 2 produced by multiplying length, width and height: *a ~ metre.*

cubicle /'kju:bɪkl/ *n* [C] small space formed by dividing a larger room.

cuckoo /'kʊku:/ *n* [C] bird whose call is like its name, and which lays its eggs in the nests of other birds.

cucumber /'kju:kʌmbə(r)/ *n* [C, U] (creeping plant producing a) long green fleshy vegetable, eaten raw.

cud /kʌd/ *n* [U] food which cattle, etc bring back from the stomach and chew again.

cuddle /'kʌdl/ *v* 1 [T] hold close and lovingly in one's arms: *~ a child.* 2 (*phr v*) **cuddle up** lie close and comfortably: *She ~d up to her father.* **cuddle** *n* [C] act of cuddling; hug. **cuddly** *adj* (-**ier, -iest**) (*infml*) pleasant to cuddle.

cudgel /'kʌdʒl/ n [C] 1 short thick stick. 2 (idm) **take up the 'cudgels** strongly defend or support sb/sth. **cudgel** v (-ll-; US -l-) [T] hit with a cudgel.

cue¹ /kju:/ n [C] 1 word, gesture, etc showing that it is sb's turn to do or say sth, esp in a play: *The actor came in on ~.* 2 hint about how to behave, what to do, etc.

cue² /kju:/ n [C] long thin stick used for striking the ball in snooker, billiards, etc.

cuff¹ /kʌf/ n [C] 1 end of a sleeve at the wrist. 2 (idm) **off the 'cuff** (of a remark, etc) said without thinking beforehand. **'cuff-link** n [C] fastener for a shirt cuff.

cuff² /kʌf/ v[T] give (sb) a light blow with an open hand. **cuff** n [C].

cuisine /kwɪ'zi:n/ n [U] (style of) cooking.

cul-de-sac /'kʌl də sæk/ n [C] street open at one end only.

culinary /'kʌlɪnərɪ; US -neri/ adj of or for cooking.

cullender = COLANDER.

culminate /'kʌlmɪneɪt/ v [I] in// have as a final result or highest point: ~ *in success.* **culmination** /ˌkʌlmɪ'neɪʃn/ n [sing] final result or highest point.

culpable /'kʌlpəbl/ adj deserving blame. **culpability** n [U]. **culpably** adv.

culprit /'kʌlprɪt/ n [C] person who has done sth wrong.

cult /kʌlt/ n [C] 1 system of religious worship. 2 devotion to a person, thing, practice, etc. 3 popular fashion: *a ~ film.*

cultivate /'kʌltɪveɪt/ v [T] 1 prepare and use (land) for crops by ploughing. 2 help (crops) to grow. 3 give care, time, etc to develop (sth): *~ her interest in literature.* 4 give time, attention, etc to seeking the friendship of (sb). **cultivated** adj showing good taste and refinement. **cultivation** /ˌkʌltɪ'veɪʃn/ n [U].

culture /'kʌltʃə(r)/ n 1 [U] (capacity to appreciate or understand) art, literature, etc. 2 [U, C] particular expression of art, thought, etc: *Greek ~.* 3 [U] cultivating of crops, etc. 4 [C] (biology) group of cells grown for study. **cultural** adj concerning culture. **cultured** adj (of people) able to appreciate art, literature, etc. **'culture shock** n [U] feeling of confusion, worry, etc sometimes felt by people when they first come into contact with people from another country.

cumbersome /'kʌmbəsʌm/ adj 1

heavy and awkward to carry. 2 slow and inefficient.

cumulative /'kju:mjʊlətɪv; US -leɪtɪv/ adj increasing in amount, force, etc by one addition after another.

cunning /'kʌnɪŋ/ adj having or showing skill in deceiving: *a ~ trick.* **cunning** n [U] quality of being cunning. **cunningly** adv.

cunt /kʌnt/ n [C] (offensive △ sl) 1 female sexual organs. 2 (derog) unpleasant person.

cup¹ /kʌp/ n [C] 1 small bowl with a handle for drinking tea, coffee, etc. 2 contents of a cup. 3 gold or silver vessel given as a prize in a competition. 4 something shaped like a cup. 5 (idm) **not sb's cup of 'tea** (infml) not what sb likes. **cupful** n [C] amount that a cup will hold.

cup² /kʌp/ v (-pp-) [T] 1 put (one's hands) in the shape of a cup; hold as if in a cup: *~ one's chin in one's hands.*

cupboard /'kʌbəd/ n [C] set of shelves with doors in the front.

curable /'kjʊərəbl/ adj able to be cured.

curate /'kjʊərət/ n [C] clergyman who helps a parish priest.

curative /'kjʊərətɪv/ adj helping to cure.

curator /kjʊə'reɪtə(r)/ also; US 'kjʊərətər/ n [C] person in charge of a museum, art gallery, etc.

curb /kɜ:b/ n [C] 1 (on//) something that restrains or controls. 2 strap passing under a horse's jaw, used to control it. 3 (esp US) = KERB. **curb** v [T] 1 restrain; control: *~ one's joy.* 2 control (a horse) with a curb.

curd /kɜ:d/ n [C, usu pl] thick soft substance formed when milk turns sour. 2 [U] (used in compounds) substance resembling curd: *lemon-~s.*

curdle /'kɜ:dl/ v [I, T] form into curds.

cure /kjʊə(r)/ v [T] 1 (of//) bring (sb) back to health: *~ d of a serious illness.* 2 put an end to (sth): *a policy to ~ inflation.* 3 stop (sb) doing sth unpleasant foolish, etc: *~ sb of an obsession.* 4 treat (meat, fish, etc) in order to preserve it. **cure** n 1 [C, usu sing] return to health. 2 [C] something that cures: *a ~ for arthritis.*

curfew /'kɜ:fju:/ n [C] time or signal for people to stay indoors.

curio /'kjʊərɪəʊ/ n [C] (pl ~s) rare or unusual small object.

curiosity /ˌkjʊərɪ'ɒsɪtɪ/ n (pl -ies) 1 [U] being interested in or eager to learn about, etc (sth). 2 [C] strange or rare object.

curious /ˈkjʊərɪəs/ *adj* **1** eager to learn, know, etc: ~ *about how a machine works*. **2** *often|| (derog)* having or showing too much interest in the affairs of others. **3** strange; unusual. **curiously** *adv*.

curl /kɜːl/ *n* [C] something with a spiral shape, esp a lock of hair. **curl** *v* **1** [I, T] form into a curl or curls. **2** [I] grow into curls; coil: *a plant ~ing round a post*. **3** (phr v) **curl up** lie or sit with a curved back and legs close to the body. **curly** *adj* (**-ier, -iest**) having curls.

currant /ˈkʌrənt/ *n* [C] **1** small dried grape used in cakes, etc. **2** (used in compounds) (bush with) small black, red or white fruit: *black ~s*.

currency /ˈkʌrənsɪ/ *n* (*pl* **-ies**) **1** [U, C] money in use in a country. **2** [U] state of being generally used or believed.

current /ˈkʌrənt/ *adj* **1** of the present time; happening now: ~ *affairs*. **2** in general use; generally accepted. ,**current ac'count** *n* [C] bank account from which money can be drawn without notice. **currently** *adv* at the present time; now.

current [2] /ˈkʌrənt/ *n* **1** [C] stream of water, air, gas, etc. **2** [U, sing] flow of electricity. **3** [C] course or movement of events, opinions, etc.

curriculum /kəˈrɪkjʊləm/ *n* [C] (*pl* ~s or **-la** /-lə/) course of study in a school, college, etc. **curriculum vitae** /ˈviːtaɪ/ *n* [C] brief written account of one's past education, career, etc used in applying for jobs.

curry [1] /ˈkʌrɪ/ *n* [C, U] (*pl* **-ies**) (dish of) meat, fish, eggs, etc cooked with hot-tasting spices. **curried** *adj* (of meat, etc) cooked with hot-tasting spices.

curry [2] /ˈkʌrɪ/ *v* (*pt, pp* **-ied**) (idm) **curry favour (with sb)** try to win favour or approval (from sb) by using flattery, etc.

curse [1] /kɜːs/ *n* **1** [C] offensive word or words intended to express anger, etc. **2** [sing] word or words spoken with the aim of punishing, destroying, etc: *The witch put a ~ on him*. **3** [C] cause of suffering unhappiness, etc.

curse [2] /kɜːs/ *v* **1** [I, T] speak a curse or curses[1] against sb/sth: *cursing her bad luck*. **2** [T] use a curse[1](2) against. **3** [T] *with|| (usu passive)* suffer unhappiness, etc because of: *a man ~ with arthritis*. **cursed** /ˈkɜːsɪd/ *adj* very

bad: *a ~d nuisance*.

cursor /ˈkɜːsə(r)/ *n* [C] (*computing*) movable dot on a computer screen that indicates where one may enter data, etc.

cursory /ˈkɜːsərɪ/ *adj* (*often derog*) done quickly; (too) hurried or brief. **cursorily** *adv*.

curt /kɜːt/ *adj* (of a speaker or sth spoken) abrupt; brief: *a ~ refusal*. **curtly** *adv*. **curtness** *n* [U].

curtail /kɜːˈteɪl/ *v* [T] make short; limit: ~ *sb's activities*. **curtailment** *n* [C, U] (act of) curtailing.

curtain /ˈkɜːtn/ *n* **1** [C] piece of cloth, etc hung up to cover a window, divide a room, etc: *draw the ~s*. **2** [C] sheet of heavy material across the front of a stage in a theatre. **3** [C] anything that screens, covers, protects, etc: *a ~ of mist*. **4** **curtains** [pl] (*for*)|| (*infml*) death or the end: *It's ~s for us if they find out what you've done!* **curtain** *v* [T] provide with curtains.

curtsey (also **curtsy**) /ˈkɜːtsɪ/ *n* [C] (*pl* ~s, **-ies**) act of bending the knees (by a woman) to show respect. **curtsey** (also **curtsy**) *v* (*pt, pp* **-ed** or **-ied**) [I] make a curtsey.

curve /kɜːv/ *n* [C] line of which no part is straight and which has no angles. **curve** *v* **1** [I, T] form a curve. **2** [I] move in a curve.

cushion /ˈkʊʃn/ *n* [C] **1** small bag filled with soft material, to make a seat more comfortable, to kneel on, etc. **2** something like a cushion: *a ~ of air*. **cushion** *v* [T] **1** reduce the force of (a blow, etc). **2** (*from*)|| protect (sb) from sth unpleasant.

cushy /ˈkʊʃɪ/ *adj* (**-ier, -iest**) *usu derog* (of a job, etc) not needing much effort; easy.

custard /ˈkʌstəd/ *n* [U] mixture of eggs and milk, sweetened and flavoured.

custodian /kʌˈstəʊdɪən/ *n* [C] person who is in charge of sb or sth, esp a public building.

custody /ˈkʌstədɪ/ *n* [U] **1** (right or duty of) caring for or guarding: ~ *of her child*. **2** imprisonment while awaiting trial: *be in ~*.

custom /ˈkʌstəm/ *n* **1** [U] generally accepted behaviour among members of a social group. **2** [C] way of behaving or doing things: *ancient ~s*. **3** [U] regular use of a shop, etc. **customary** /-mərɪ; *US* -merɪ/ *adj* according to custom, usual. ,**custom-'built**, ,**custom-'made** *adj* made in the way that the customer wants.

customer /ˈkʌstəmə(r)/ *n* [C] person who buys sth in a shop, etc, uses a service, etc.

customs /ˈkʌstəmz/ n [pl] 1 taxes payable on imported goods. 2 **Customs** place where customs are collected, eg at an airport.

cut[1] /kʌt/ v (-tt-, *pt, pp* **cut**) 1 [I, T] make an opening, wound, etc with sth sharp: *I ~ my hand with a knife.* 2 [T] (a) *(off)//* remove sth from (sth larger) with a knife, etc: ~ *(off) a piece of cake.* (b) divide into smaller pieces with a knife, etc: ~ *the cake.* 3 [T] shorten sth by cutting: ~ *sb's hair.* 4 [I] (a) (of a knife, etc) be capable of cutting. (b) (of material, etc) be able to cut. 5 [T] cause physical or mental pain to: *His remarks ~ me deeply.* 6 [T] (of a line) cross (another line). 7 [T] reduce: ~ *taxes.* 8 [T] remove (a part or parts) from (a film, tape, etc); edit: ~ *some scenes from a film.* (b) [I] stop filming or recording. 9 [T] *(infml)* stay away from (a class, etc). 10 (idm) **cut and dried** completely settled and decided and unlikely to be changed. **cut both/two 'ways** having an effect both for and against sb/sth. **cut 'corners** do things in the easiest and quickest way, often by being careless. **cut sb dead** pretend not to see sb, etc in order to show one's anger, etc. **cut it 'fine** allow only just enough time, money, space or material needed for a purpose. **cut 'loose** *(infml)* act, speak, etc freely and without restraint. **cut one's 'losses** stop an unprofitable business, activity, etc before one suffers any further loss, harm, etc. **cut no 'ice (with sb)** not impress or influence (sb). **cut sb to the 'quick** hurt sb's feelings. **cut sb/sth 'short** stop sb speaking; interrupt a conversation, remark, etc. 11 (phr v) **cut across sth** (a) go across (a field, etc) to shorten one's route. (b) not correspond to (divisions between groups): ~ *across social barriers.* **cut sth back, cut back (on sth)** (a) cut (shrubs, etc) close to the stem. (b) reduce: ~ *back (on) the number of workers.* **cut down** cause to fall by cutting: ~ *down a tree.* **cut sth down, cut down on (sth)** reduce: ~ *down on one's smoking.* **cut 'in (on)** (a) interrupt a conversation, etc. (b) move in front of another vehicle, leaving too little space. **cut sth 'off** (a) remove (sth) by cutting. (b) block or obstruct: ~ *off*

their retreat. (c) isolate: *a town ~ off by floods.* **cut sth open** make an opening or split in sth by cutting. **cut out** (of an engine, etc) stop functioning. **cut sth out** (a) remove sth by cutting. (b) make or shape sth by cutting: ~ *out a dress.* (c) *(infml)* omit sth. (d) *(infml)* stop doing or using sth: ~ *out cigarettes.* **(not) be cut out for/to be sth** (not) have the abilities needed for sth: *I'm not ~ out to be a teacher.* **cut up** (a) cut (sth) into pieces. (b) *(infml)* make (sb) unhappy. **'cut-back** n [C] reduction. **'cut-out** n [C] 1 shape cut out of paper, etc. 2 device that stops a machine, etc working. **,cut-'price** reduced in price; cheap.

cut[2] /kʌt/ n [C] 1 opening made with a knife, etc. 2 blow with a knife, etc. 3 act of cutting: *Your hair needs a ~.* 4 (*in*) *(infml)* reduction: *a ~ in taxes.* 5 act of removing part of sth: *make some ~s in the film.* 6 part that is cut from sth larger: *a ~ of beef.* 7 style in which clothes, hair, etc is cut: *a suit with a loose ~.* 8 *(infml)* share: *a ~ of the profits.* 9 (idm) **a cut above sb/sth** better than sb/sth.

cute /kjuːt/ *adj* 1 attractive, pretty or charming. 2 *(infml* esp *US)* (too) clever; sharp-witted. **cutely** *adv.* **cuteness** n [U].

cuticle /ˈkjuːtɪkl/ n [C] layer of skin at the base of a finger-nail or toe-nail.

cutlery /ˈkʌtləri/ n [U] knives, forks, etc used for eating.

cutlet /ˈkʌtlɪt/ n [C] slice of meat or fish.

cutter /ˈkʌtə(r)/ n 1 [C] person or thing that cuts. 2 **cutters** [pl] (used esp in compounds) tool for cutting. 3 [C] type of small sailing-boat.

cutthroat /ˈkʌtθrəʊt/ *adj* ruthless.

cutting[1] /ˈkʌtɪŋ/ *adj* (of remarks, etc) sarcastic; hurtful.

cutting[2] /ˈkʌtɪŋ/ n [C] 1 article, etc cut from a newspaper, etc. 2 uncovered passage cut through the ground for a road, railway, etc. 3 short piece of the stem of a plant, used for growing a new plant.

cv /ˌsiː ˈviː/ *abbr* curriculum vitae.

cyanide /ˈsaɪənaɪd/ n [U] strong poison.

cycle /ˈsaɪkl/ n [C] 1 series of events in a regularly repeated order: *the ~ of the seasons.* 2 *(infml)* bicycle or motor cycle. — *v* [I] ride a bicycle. **cyclical** /ˈsɪklɪkl/ *adj* happening in cycles(1). **cyclist** n [C] person who cycles.

cyclone /'saɪkləʊn/ n [C] wind rotating very fast round a calm centre. **cyclonic** /saɪ'klɒnɪk/ adj.

cygnet /'sɪgnɪt/ n [C] young swan.

cylinder /'sɪlɪndə(r)/ n [C] 1 long solid or hollow body with circular ends and straight sides. 2 space inside an engine in which gas or steam moves a piston. **cylindrical** /sɪ'lɪndrɪkl/ adj cylinder-shaped.

cymbal /'sɪmbl/ n [C] one of a pair of round brass plates struck together to make clanging sounds.

cynic /'sɪnɪk/ n [C] person who does not believe that anyone has good or sincere reasons for what he/she does. **cynical** adj of or like a cynic: a ~ al remark. **cynically** /-klɪ/ adv. **cynicism** /'sɪnɪsɪzəm/ n [U] cynic's opinions or attitudes.

cypher = CIPHER.

cypress /'saɪprəs/ n [C] any of various types of evergreen tree with dark leaves and hard wood.

cyst /sɪst/ n [C] hollow organ in the body containing liquid.

cystitis /sɪ'staɪtɪs/ n [U] inflammation of the bladder.

czar, czarina = TSAR, TSARINA.

D d

D, d /diː/ n [C] (pl **D's, d's** /diːz/) 1 the fourth letter of the English alphabet. 2 Roman numeral for 500.

d. abbr died: d. 1924.

'd short for HAD or WOULD: I'd ◇ she'd.

dab /dæb/ v (-bb-) [T] touch (sth) lightly or gently: ~ one's face dry. **dab** n [C] small quantity of paint, etc put on a surface.

dabble /'dæbl/ v 1 [I] (in)// be interested in a subject in a way that is not serious. 2 [T] move (one's hands, feet, etc) gently about in water.

dachshund /'dækshʊnd/ n [C] small dog with very short legs.

dad /dæd/ n [C] (infml) father.

daddy /'dædɪ/ n [C] (pl -ies) (used by children) father.

daffodil /'dæfədɪl/ n [C] yellow trumpet-shaped flower that grows in spring.

daft /dɑːft/ adj (infml) silly.

dagger /'dægə(r)/ n [C] short sharp knife used as a weapon.

daily /'deɪlɪ/ adj, adv happening or appearing every day or every weekday. **daily** n [C] (pl -ies) daily newspaper.

dainty /'deɪntɪ/ adj (-ier, -iest) pretty and delicate. **daintily** adv.

dairy /'deərɪ/ n [C] (pl -ies) 1 building where butter, cheese, etc are made. 2 shop where milk, butter, eggs, etc are sold. '**dairy cattle** n [U] cows kept to produce milk.

daisy /'deɪzɪ/ n [C] (pl -ies) small flower with a yellow centre and white petals.

dale /deɪl/ n [C] (poet) valley.

dam /dæm/ n [C] wall built to keep back water. **dam** v (-mm-) [T] 1 make a dam across. 2 (fig) hold back or control (feelings).

damage /'dæmɪdʒ/ n 1 [U] harm; loss: The fire caused great ~. 2 **damages** [pl] (law) money claimed from a person who has caused loss or injury. **damage** v [T] cause damage to.

dame /deɪm/ n [C] 1 (title of a) woman awarded an honour equal to a knight: D~ Janet Baker. 2 (US sl) woman.

damn /dæm/ interj (infml) (used for showing anger or annoyance). **damn** v [T] 1 (of God) condemn to everlasting punishment. 2 say that (sth) is bad or worthless. **damn** n (idm) **not care/give a damn** (infml) not care at all. **damnation** /-'neɪʃn/ n [U] state of suffering in hell.

damned /dæmd/ adj (infml) (used for showing annoyance): You ~ fool! **damned** adv (infml) very: ~ lucky.

damp¹ /dæmp/ adj slightly wet: a ~ cloth. **damp** n [U] state of being damp. **dampness** n [U].

damp² /dæmp/ v [T] 1 make damp. 2 (also **dampen** /'dæmpən/) make sad or less strong: ~ his enthusiasm. 3 (phr v) **damp sth down** make (a fire) burn more slowly.

damper /'dæmpə(r)/ n [C] 1 person or thing that discourages: put a ~ on the party. 2 small flat piece of metal that controls the flow of air into a fire.

damson /'dæmzn/ n [C] (tree producing a) small dark-purple plum.

dance /dɑːns/ n [C] 1 movements and steps in time to music. 2 social meeting for dancing. **dance** v 1 [I] move with steps in time to music. 2 [T] perform a (named dance). **dancer** n [C]. **dancing** n [U]: a dancing teacher.

dandelion /'dændɪlaɪən/ n [C] small wild plant with bright yellow flowers.

dandruff /'dændrʌf/ n [U] small pieces of dead skin in the hair on

one's head.
danger /'deɪndʒə(r)/ n 1 [U] possibility of being hurt or killed. 2 [C] thing or person that may cause danger. 3 (idm) **in danger** likely to be hurt or killed. **out of danger** no longer seriously ill. **dangerous** adj likely to cause danger. **dangerously** adv.

dangle /'dæŋgl/ v [I, T] hang or swing loosely.

dank /dæŋk/ adj unpleasantly damp and cold: a ~ cellar/cave.

dare¹ /deə(r)/ modal v (pres tense, all persons **dare**, neg **dare not** or **daren't** /deənt/) have the courage to (do sth): I ~ n't ask him. ○ D~ we try again?

dare² /deə(r)/ v 1 [T] to// challenge (sb) to do sth dangerous or difficult: I ~ you to jump off the tree. 2 [I] (to)// be brave enough to do sth: No one ~d (to) speak. **dare** n (idm) **do sth for a dare** do sth because one is dared(1). **'daredevil** n [C] person who is very daring.

daring /'deərɪŋ/ adj bold and adventurous. **daringly** adv.

dark¹ /dɑːk/ adj 1 with no or very little light: a ~ night/room. 2 (of colour) nearer black than white: ~ blue. 3 (of the skin) not fair. 4 hopeless; sad: look on the ~ side of things. 5 (idm) a **dark 'horse** person who hides special abilities. **darken** v [I, T] make or become dark. **darkly** adv. **darkness** n [U].

dark² /dɑːk/ n [U] 1 absence of light: sit in the ~. 2 (idm) **after/before dark** after/before the sun sets. **be/keep sb in the dark** keep sb ignorant.

darling /'dɑːlɪŋ/ n [C] person who is loved very much.

darn /dɑːn/ v [I, T] mend (sth) by sewing: ~ sb's socks. **darn** n [C] hole mended by darning.

dart¹ /dɑːt/ n 1 [C] small sharp-pointed object used in the game of darts. 2 **darts** (with sing v) game in which darts are thrown at a target.

dart² /dɑːt/ v [I] move suddenly and quickly.

dash¹ /dæʃ/ n 1 sudden quick movement: make a ~ for the bus. 2 small amount of sth added: a ~ of pepper. 3 punctuation mark (—). **'dashboard** n [C] board below the windscreen in a car, with a speedometer, etc.

dash² /dæʃ/ v 1 [I] run quickly: ~ across the road. 2 [T] throw violently. 3 [T] destroy (sb's hopes). **dashing** adj having a lot of style and self-confidence.

data /'deɪtə/ n [U] information or

facts, eg to be analysed by a computer. **'database** n [C] organized store of computer data. **data-'processing** n [U] operations performed on computer data.

date¹ /deɪt/ n [C] 1 the day, month and year of an event: His ~ of birth is 18 May 1930. 2 (infml) (a) social meeting between a boy-friend and girl-friend. (b) (esp US) boy-friend or girl-friend with whom one has a date. 3 (idm) (**be/go) out of date** (be) no longer valid or fashionable. **to date** so far; until now. **(be/bring) up to date** (be/make) modern.

date² /deɪt/ v 1 [T] write a date on: The letter was ~d 23 July. 2 [I] from//back to// have existed since: The church ~s from the twelfth century. 3 [I] become out of date. 4 [T] (infml esp US) have one or many dates¹(2a) with (sb). **dated** /'deɪtɪd/ adj out of fashion.

date³ /deɪt/ n [C] small brown sticky fruit.

daub /dɔːb/ v [T] put (paint, plaster, etc) roughly on a surface.

daughter /'dɔːtə(r)/ n [C] person's female child. **'daughter-in-law** /ɪn lɔː/ n [C] (pl ~s-in-law) wife of one's son.

daunting /'dɔːntɪŋ/ adj discouraging because difficult.

dawdle /'dɔːdl/ v [I] move slowly and lazily.

dawn /dɔːn/ n 1 [C, U] first light of day. 2 [sing] (fig) beginning: the ~ of civilization. **dawn** v [I] 1 begin to become light. 2 (on)// become clear to sb: The truth began to ~ on him.

day /deɪ/ n 1 [C] period of 24 hours. 2 [C, U] time between sunrise and sunset. 3 [C] hours of the day spent working. 4 [C, U] period of time: in the ~s of the Roman Empire. 5 (idm) **any day (now)** very soon. **day and night** ⇨ NIGHT. **in, day out, day after day** for many days together. **sb/sth's days are numbered** sb/sth will soon die, fail, etc. **make sb's day** (infml) make sb very happy. **one day** on a day (past or future). **'daybreak** n [U] dawn. **'day-dream** n [U] (enjoy) imaginary pleasant thoughts. **'daylight** n [U] 1 light of day. 2 dawn. **'day-time** n [U] time between sunrise and sunset.

daze /deɪz/ v [T] make (sb) unable to think clearly. **daze** n (idm) **in a daze** unable to think clearly.

dazzle /'dæzl/ v [T] 1 make (sb) unable to see clearly because of too much strong light. 2 amaze by a splendid display.

decant

dB *abbr* decibel(s).

DDT /ˌdiː diː ˈtiː/ n [U] powerful dangerous insecticide.

dead /ded/ *adj* 1 (of people, animals or plants) no longer living. 2 (of languages, customs, etc) no longer used. 3 (of part of one's body) no longer able to feel anything, eg because of cold. 4 complete; absolute: *a ~ stop.* 5 no longer water: *The telephone went ~.* 6 without activity: *The town is ~ after 10 o'clock.* 7 (*fig*) (of colour, sound, etc) dull. 8 (idm) **a dead 'loss** (*sl*) person or thing that is useless or worthless. **dead** *adv* completely; absolutely: *~ certain/ accurate.* **the dead** n [pl] dead people. ˌ**dead 'end** n [C] place or situation where more progress is impossible. **'deadline** n [C] fixed date for completing a task: *meet/ miss a ~ line.*

deaden /dedn/ v [T] make less strong, bright, etc.

deadlock /ˈdedlɒk/ n [C, U] total failure to reach agreement.

deadly /ˈdedlɪ/ *adj* (-ier, -iest) 1 likely to cause death: *a ~ poison.* 2 (*infml*) boring; dull. **deadly** *adv* (*infml*) extremely: *~ serious.*

deaf /def/ *adj* 1 unable to hear. 2 *to*// unwilling to listen. **the deaf** n [pl] deaf people. ˌ**deaf-and- 'dumb** *adj* unable to hear or speak. ˌ**deaf'mute** n [C] somebody who is deaf and dumb. **deafness** n [U].

deafen /ˈdefn/ v [T] make it difficult for (sb) to hear sth: *~ed by the noise.*

deal¹ /diːl/ n (idm) **a good/great deal** a large quantity: *a good ~ of money* ○ *I see him a great ~, ie very often.*

deal² /diːl/ n [C] 1 (business) agreement. 2 giving out of playing-cards in a card game.

deal³ /diːl/ v (pt, pp ~t /delt/) 1 [I, T] give out (cards) to a number of players. 2 [T] deliver or inflict (a blow). 3 (phr v) **deal in sth** buy and sell (goods); trade in sth: *~ in second-hand cars.* **deal with sb** do business with sb. **deal with sth** (a) attend to sth; handle. (b) be about sth; discuss: *a book ~ing with Africa.* **dealer** n [C] 1 person who deals out playing-cards. 2 trader. **dealings** n [pl] business or personal relations: *have ~ings with sb.*

dean /diːn/ n [C] 1 clergyman responsible for several parishes or a church. 2 head of a university department.

dear /dɪə(r)/ *adj* 1 loved; lovable. 2 (used at the beginning of letters): *D~ Madam/Sir.* 3 (*Brit*) expensive. 4 (*to*)// precious to sb. **dear** *adv* at a high cost. **dear** n [C] 1 lovable person. 2 (used for speaking kindly to sb): *Yes, ~.* **dear** *interj* (used for expressing surprise, impatience, etc): *Oh ~! ○ D~ me!* **dearly** *adv* 1 very much. 2 (*fig*) with great loss, damage, etc.

dearth /dɜːθ/ n [sing] (*of*)// (*fml*) shortage of sth.

death /deθ/ n 1 [C] dying; being killed. 2 [U] end of life; state of being dead. 3 [sing] (*fig*) destruction: *the ~ of one's hopes.* 4 (idm) **bored/sick, etc to death of sth** very tired of/bored with sth. **put sb to death** execute sb; kill sb. **deathly** *adj, adv* like death. **'death penalty** n [sing] punishment of being executed for a crime. **'death-trap** n [C] very dangerous place or vehicle. **'death-warrant** n [C] official order for sb's execution.

débâcle /derˈbɑːkl/ n [C] sudden and complete failure.

debase /dɪˈbeɪs/ v [T] lower the value or quality of (sth). **debasement** n [U].

debate /dɪˈbeɪt/ n [C, U] formal discussion at a public meeting or in Parliament. **debate** v [I, T] discuss formally; think about. **debatable** *adj* not certain; open to question.

debauched /dɪˈbɔːtʃt/ *adj* (*fml*) immoral. **debauchery** /-tʃərɪ/ n [U] wild immoral behaviour.

debilitating /dɪˈbɪlɪteɪtɪŋ/ *adj* making sb weak: *a ~ illness.*

debit /ˈdebɪt/ n [C] written note in an account of money paid or owing. **debit** v [T] take money from (an account) to pay for sth.

debris /ˈdeɪbriː; US dəˈbriː/ n [U] scattered broken pieces.

debt /det/ n 1 [C] sum of money owed to sb. 2 [U] state of owing money: *be in/out of ~.* 3 [C, U] condition of needing to do sth in return for sb's help or kindness. **debtor** n [C] person who owes money to sb.

début /ˈdeɪbjuː; US deɪˈbjuː/ n [C] first public appearance of an actor, musician, etc: *make one's ~.*

decade /ˈdekeɪd; also esp US dɪˈkeɪd/ n [C] period of ten years.

decadent /ˈdekədənt/ *adj* showing a falling to a lower level of morals: *~ behaviour/society.* **decadence** /-dəns/ n [U].

decaffeinated /ˌdiːˈkæfɪneɪtɪd/ *adj* (of coffee) with the caffeine removed.

decant /dɪˈkænt/ v [T] pour (wine, etc) from a bottle into another container. **decanter** n [C] glass bottle with a stopper, for wine.

decapitate /dɪˈkæpɪteɪt/ v [T] (fml) kill (sb) by cutting off his/her head.

decay /dɪˈkeɪ/ v 1 [I] become or make bad. 2 [I] lose health, strength, etc. **decay** n [U] decaying: tooth ~.

deceased /dɪˈsiːst/ adj. **the deceased** n [C] (pl the deceased) (fml) person who has recently died.

deceit /dɪˈsiːt/ n [U, C] behaviour that causes sb to believe sth that is false. **deceitful** adj 1 often deceiving. 2 intended to deceive: ~ful words. **deceitfully** adv. **deceitfulness** n [U].

deceive /dɪˈsiːv/ v [T] make (sb) believe sth that is false. **deceiver** n [C].

December /dɪˈsembə(r)/ n [U, C] twelfth month of the year. (See examples of use at April).

decent /ˈdiːsnt/ adj 1 right and suitable; acceptable: wear ~ clothes to the party. 2 not likely to shock or embarrass people: ~ behaviour. **decency** /ˈdiːsnsɪ/ n [U]. **decently** adv.

deception /dɪˈsepʃn/ n 1 [U] deceiving: obtain sth by ~. 2 [C] action intended to deceive.

deceptive /dɪˈseptɪv/ adj misleading: a ~ appearance. **deceptively** adv.

decibel /ˈdesɪbel/ n [C] unit for measuring the loudness of sounds.

decide /dɪˈsaɪd/ v 1 [I] think about sth and come to a conclusion: I ~d to leave. 2 [T] cause (sb) to decide(1). 3 [T] settle (a question or a doubt); give a judgement about. **decided** adj 1 clear; definite. 2 (of people) determined. **decidedly** adv definitely.

deciduous /dɪˈsɪdjʊəs/ adj (of trees) losing their leaves every autumn.

decimal /ˈdesɪml/ adj of tens or tenths: ~ currency. **decimal** n [C] fraction expressed in tenths, hundredths, etc, eg 0·25. **decimalize** /-məlaɪz/ v [I, T] change to a decimal system. **decimalization** /ˌdesɪməlaɪˈzeɪʃn; US -lɪˈzæ-/ n [U]. **decimal 'point** n [C] dot placed after the unit figure in decimals: 10·25.

decimate /ˈdesɪmeɪt/ v [T] 1 kill or destroy a large number of. 2 (fig) reduce.

decipher /dɪˈsaɪfə(r)/ v [T] find the meaning of (sth written in code, bad handwriting, etc).

decision /dɪˈsɪʒn/ n 1 [C, U] (result of) deciding: come to/reach/

make a ~. 2 [U] ability to decide and act quickly. **decisive** /dɪˈsaɪsɪv/ adj 1 having a clear result. 2 having or showing the ability to decide quickly. **decisively** adv. **decisiveness** n [U].

deck¹ /dek/ n [C] 1 floor in a ship, bus, etc. 2 part of a stereo system that plays records or tapes. 3 pack of playing-cards. '**deck-chair** n [C] folding canvas chair, used outside.

deck² /dek/ v [T] (out) decorate (sb/sth): streets ~ed out with flags.

declare /dɪˈkleə(r)/ v [I, T] 1 make (sth) known formally; announce. 2 say firmly and solemnly. 3 tell a customs officer about (imported goods): Have you anything to ~? **declaration** /ˌdekləˈreɪʃn/ n [C].

decline¹ /dɪˈklaɪn/ n [C, U] gradual and continuous loss of quality, importance, power, etc: a ~ in population.

decline² /dɪˈklaɪn/ v 1 [I] become weaker, lower, etc. 2 [I, T] say 'no' to (sth); refuse.

decode /ˌdiːˈkəʊd/ v [T] find the meaning of (a message in code).

decompose /ˌdiːkəmˈpəʊz/ v [I, T] become or make rotten. **decomposition** /ˌdiːkɒmpəˈzɪʃn/ n [U].

décor /ˈdeɪkɔː(r); US ˈdeɪkɔːr/ n [U, sing] style of decorations and furnishings of a room.

decorate /ˈdekəreɪt/ v 1 [T] make (more) beautiful by placing ornaments on or in (sth). 2 [I, T] put paint or wallpaper on the walls of (a room or building). 3 [T] give a medal to (sb): ~d for bravery. **decoration** /ˌdekəˈreɪʃn/ n 1 [U] decorating. 2 [C] something used for decorating: Christmas ~s. 3 [C] medal, etc given as an honour. **decorative** /ˈdekərətɪv; US -reɪt-/ adj suitable for decorating(1). **decorator** n [C] person who decorates(2).

decoy /ˈdiːkɔɪ/ n [C] 1 (real or imitation) bird used to attract others so that they can be caught or shot. 2 (fig) person or thing that is used to tempt sb into a trap.

decrease /dɪˈkriːs/ v [I, T] become or make shorter, smaller or less: Sales are decreasing. **decrease** /ˈdiːkriːs/ n [C, U] (result or amount of) decreasing: a small ~ in exports.

decree /dɪˈkriː/ n [C] 1 order that has the force of the law: by royal ~. 2 judgement of certain lawcourts. **decree** v [T] order by a decree.

decrepit /dɪˈkrepɪt/ adj made weak by old age.

dedicate /'dedɪkeɪt/ v[T] *to*|| give (oneself or one's time, energy, etc) to a special purpose. 2 (of an author) write sb's name at the beginning of (a book) as a sign of friendship or respect. **dedicated** *adj* committed. **dedication** /ˌdedɪ'keɪʃn/ n[C, U].

deduce /dɪ'djuːs/ v[T] reach (a conclusion, theory, etc) by reasoning.

deduct /dɪ'dʌkt/ v[T] take away (an amount or part): ~ £50 *from her salary*.

deduction /dɪ'dʌkʃn/ n[C, U] 1 (amount or result of) deducting: *tax* ~s. 2 (conclusion reached by) reasoning.

deed /diːd/ n[C] 1 (*fml*) something done; act. 2 (*law*) signed agreement, esp about ownership.

deem /diːm/ v[T] consider.

deep[1] /diːp/ *adj* 1 going a long way down from the top or surface: *a* ~ *river* ○ *a hole one metre* ~. 2 (*fig*) serious: *a* ~ *book*. 3 (of sounds) low. 4 (of colours or feelings) strong; intense: ~ *hatred*. 5 (of sleep) from which one is not easily wakened. 6 *in*|| absorbed in (sth): ~ *in thought*|*a book*. 7 (idm) **go off the 'deep end** become very angry. **in deep 'water** in trouble. **deeply** *adv* intensely: ~ *ly hurt by your remarks*.

deep[2] /diːp/ *adv* far down or in. ˌdeep-'freeze /|| n[C] freezer. ˌdeep-'rooted *adj* not easily removed: ~ *rooted suspicions*. ˌdeep-'seated *adj* firmly established: ~ *seated fears*.

deepen /'diːpən/ v[I, T] become or make deep, deeper or more intense.

deer /dɪə(r)/ n[C] (*pl* deer) fast graceful animal, the male of which has branching horns (= ANTLERS).

deface /dɪ'feɪs/ v[T] spoil the appearance or surface of.

defame /dɪ'feɪm/ v[T] (*fml*) attack the good reputation of (sb). **defamation** /ˌdefə'meɪʃn/ n[U].

default /dɪ'fɔːlt/ v[I] fail to pay a debt, perform a duty or appear (eg in a lawcourt) when required. **default** n[U] failure to do sth, appear, etc: *win a game by* ~. **defaulter** n[C] person who defaults.

defeat /dɪ'fiːt/ v[T] 1 win a victory over (sb). 2 cause to fail: *Our hopes were* ~*ed*. **defeat** n[C, U] (instance of) defeating or being defeated.

defect[1] /'diːfekt/ n[C] fault; imperfection. **defective** /dɪ'fektɪv/ *adj*.

defect[2] /dɪ'fekt/ v[I] leave one's country, political party, etc and join an opposing one. **defection** /dɪ'fekʃn/ n[C, U]. **defector** n[C] person who defects.

defence (*US* **-fense**) /dɪ'fens/ n 1 [U] defending from attack. 2 [C] something used for defending or protecting: *the country's* ~*s*. 3 [C, U] (*law*) (a) argument used to answer an accusation. (b) **the defence** (with sing or pl v) the lawyer(s) acting for an accused person. **defenceless** *adj* unable to defend oneself.

defend /dɪ'fend/ v[T] 1 (*from*| *against*)|| protect or guard; make safe. 2 speak or write in support of: ~ *a decision*. **defendant** n[C] person against whom a case is brought in a lawcourt. **defender** n[C] 1 person who defends. 2 (in sport) player who guards the goal area. **defensible** /dɪ'fensəbl/ *adj* able to be defended.

defensive /dɪ'fensɪv/ *adj* used for defending. **defensive** n (idm) **on the defensive** ready to protect oneself against criticism. **defensively** *adv*.

defer /dɪ'fɜː(r)/ v (-rr-) 1 [I] *to*|| agree with sb, an opinion, etc, esp to show respect: *I* ~ *to her experience*. 2 [T] delay: ~ *payment*. **deference** /'defərəns/ n[U] giving way to the wishes of others as a sign of respect.

defiance /dɪ'faɪəns/ n[U] obvious disobedience or resistance; defying: *in* ~ *of my orders*. **defiant** /-ənt/ *adj* obviously and aggressively disobedient. **defiantly** *adv*.

deficiency /dɪ'fɪʃnsɪ/ n[C, U] (*pl* -ies) (instance of) being short of or less than what is needed. **deficient** /-ʃnt/ *adj* not having enough of sth; inadequate: ~ *in vitamins*.

deficit /'defɪsɪt/ n[C] amount by which sth, esp a sum of money, is too small.

defile /dɪ'faɪl/ v[T] (*fml*) make dirty or impure.

define /dɪ'faɪn/ v[T] 1 state precisely the meaning of (eg words). 2 state or show clearly: ~ *a judge's powers*. **definable** *adj* that can be defined.

definite /'defɪnət/ *adj* clear; not doubtful. ˌ**definite 'article** n[C] the word *the*. **definitely** *adv* 1 without doubt: ~*ly not true*. 2 (*infml*) (used in answer to a question) yes; certainly.

definition /ˌdefɪ'nɪʃn/ n 1 [C] statement that defines a word. 2 [U] clearness of outline: *The photograph lacks* ~.

definitive /dɪ'fɪnətɪv/ *adj* fixed;

decisive; without the need for change or addition.

deflate /dɪˈfleɪt/ v [T] 1 make (a tyre, etc) smaller by letting out air or gas. 2 (*fig*) cause to seem less important. 3 /ˌdiːˈfleɪt/ reduce the amount of money in circulation in (an economy). **deflation** /dɪˈfleɪʃn/ n [U].

deflect /dɪˈflekt/ v [I, T] (cause to) turn from the intended course or aim: ~ *a bullet/criticism.* **deflection** /dɪˈflekʃn/ n [C, U].

deform /dɪˈfɔːm/ v [T] spoil the shape or appearance of: *a ~ed foot.* **deformity** n [C, U] (*pl* -ies).

defraud /dɪˈfrɔːd/ v [T] trick or cheat (sb): ~ *him of £100.*

defrost /ˌdiːˈfrɒst; *US* -frɔːst/ v [T] remove ice from (a refrigerator, food, etc).

deft /deft/ adj (at)// quick and skilful (esp with one's hands). **deftly** adv. **deftness** n [U].

defunct /dɪˈfʌŋkt/ adj (*fml*) no longer used or effective.

defuse /ˌdiːˈfjuːz/ v [T] 1 remove the fuse from (a bomb). 2 (*fig*) reduce the dangerous tension in (a difficult situation).

defy /dɪˈfaɪ/ v (*pt, pp* -ied) [T] 1 resist openly; refuse to obey. 2 challenge (sb) to do sth. 3 be so difficult as to make (sth) impossible: ~ *description.*

degenerate /dɪˈdʒenəreɪt/ v [I] become worse in quality, actions, etc. **degenerate** /-nərət/ adj having lost good moral or mental qualities.

degrade /dɪˈɡreɪd/ v [T] make (sb) less deserving of respect: ~ *oneself by cheating.* **degradation** /ˌdeɡrəˈdeɪʃn/ n [U].

degree /dɪˈɡriː/ n [C] 1 a degree shows how much of sth exists: *a high ~ of accuracy* ○ *not in the slightest ~ interested.* 2 unit of measurement for temperature: *ten ~s Celsius (10°C).* 3 unit of measurement of angles (in a circle): *an angle of 30 ~s (30°).* 4 qualification given by a university or college to sb who has completed a course. 5 (*idm*) **by degrees** gradually.

dehydrate /ˌdiːˈhaɪdreɪt/ v [T] remove water from (esp food, to preserve it).

de-ice /ˌdiːˈaɪs/ v [T] remove ice from.

deign /deɪn/ v [T] be kind or gracious enough (to do sth): *She didn't ~ to speak to me.*

deity /ˈdeɪəti/ n (*pl* -ies) god or goddess.

dejected /dɪˈdʒektɪd/ adj sad or gloomy. **dejection** /-kʃn/ n [U].

delay /dɪˈleɪ/ v [I, T] be or make slow or late: *I was ~ed by the traffic.* 2 [T] postpone. **delay** n [C, U] (instance of) delaying or being delayed.

delectable /dɪˈlektəbl/ adj (*fml*) (esp of food) delightful.

delegate[1] /ˈdelɪɡət/ n [C] person chosen by others to express their views at a meeting.

delegate[2] /ˈdelɪɡeɪt/ v [T] appoint (sb) as a representative; give (duties, rights, etc) to sb. **delegation** /ˌdelɪˈɡeɪʃn/ n 1 [U] delegating. 2 [C] group of delegates.

delete /dɪˈliːt/ v [T] remove or cross out (sth written or printed). **deletion** /dɪˈliːʃn/ n [C, U].

deliberate[1] /dɪˈlɪbərət/ adj 1 intentional: *a ~ insult.* 2 slow and cautious (in action, speech, etc). **deliberately** adv.

deliberate[2] /dɪˈlɪbəreɪt/ v [I, T] (about/on)// (*fml*) think or talk about sth very carefully. **deliberation** /dɪˌlɪbəˈreɪʃn/ n 1 [C, U] careful thought. 2 [U] slowness of action or speech.

delicacy /ˈdelɪkəsi/ n (*pl* -ies) 1 [U] quality of being delicate. 2 [C] tasty food: *a local ~.*

delicate /ˈdelɪkət/ adj 1 small and pretty; fine. 2 (of colours) soft; not strong. 3 needing careful handling or treatment: *a ~ vase/ situation.* 4 becoming ill easily: *in ~ health.* 5 able to show very small changes or differences: *a ~ instrument.* **delicately** adv.

delicatessen /ˌdelɪkəˈtesn/ n [C] shop selling prepared, esp unusual or imported food.

delicious /dɪˈlɪʃəs/ adj having a very pleasant taste or smell.

delight[1] /dɪˈlaɪt/ n 1 [U] great pleasure: *take ~ in being a parent.* 2 [C] cause or source of great pleasure. **delightful** adj. **delightfully** adv.

delight[2] /dɪˈlaɪt/ v 1 [T] give great pleasure to (sb). 2 [I] find great pleasure: *She ~s in working hard.* 3 (*idm*) **be delighted** be greatly pleased.

delineate /dɪˈlɪnieɪt/ v [T] (*fml*) show (sth) by drawing or describing.

delinquent /dɪˈlɪŋkwənt/ n [C], adj (person) behaving badly or doing wrong. **delinquency** /-kwənsi/ n [C, U] (*pl* -ies) bad behaviour or wrongdoing.

delirious /dɪˈlɪriəs/ adj 1 suffering from delirium. 2 (*fig*) very excited and happy. **deliriously** adv.

delirium /dɪˈlɪriəm/ n [U] 1 mental disturbance, esp during illness. 2 (*fig*) wild excitement.

deliver /dɪ'lɪvə(r)/ *v* 1 [I, T] take (letters, goods, etc) to houses or buyers: ~ *milk/newspapers*. 2 [T] give (a speech) in public: ~ *a lecture*. 3 [T] help a woman in the birth of (a baby). 4 (idm) **deliver the goods** ⇨ GOODS.

delivery /dɪ'lɪvərɪ/ *n* (*pl* -ies) 1 [U, C] delivering (of letters, goods, etc). 2 [C] birth of a child: *The mother had an easy ~*. 3 [C, sing, U] manner of speaking in lectures, etc. 4 (idm) **take delivery (of sth)** receive sth.

delta /'deltə/ *n* [C] land in the shape of a triangle where a river separates into branches.

delude /dɪ'luːd/ *v* [T] deceive or mislead.

deluge /'deljuːdʒ/ *n* [C] 1 heavy fall of rain. 2 (*fig*) great quantity of sth: *a ~ of letters.* **deluge** *v* [T] present (sb) with a great quantity of things: *~d with questions.*

delusion /dɪ'luːʒn/ *n* [C, U] mistaken belief: *under the ~ that he is Napoleon.*

deluxe /dɪ'lʌks/ *adj* of very high quality: *a ~ hotel.*

delve /delv/ *v* [I] *in/into/* investigate sth: ~ *into the past.*

Dem *abbr* Democrat(ic).

demand[1] /dɪ'mɑːnd; *US* dɪ'mænd/ *n* 1 [C] act of demanding(1); sth that is demanded(1): *the workers' ~s for higher pay.* 2 [U] people's desire for sth/sb that they want to buy/employ: *no ~ for history graduates ○ Our goods are in great ~*, ie many people want them. (idm) **on demand** when asked for.

demand[2] /dɪ'mɑːnd; *US* dɪ'mænd/ *v* [T] 1 ask for (sth) as if ordering. 2 (*fml*) need: *work ~ing great care.* **demanding** *adj* (a) needing much skill, effort, etc: *a ~ing job.* (b) making others work hard: *a ~ing boss.*

demarcate /'diːmɑːkeɪt/ *v* [T] fix the limits of. **demarcation** /,diːmɑː'keɪʃn/ *n* [U, C].

demean /dɪ'miːn/ *v* [T] (*fml*) ~ **oneself** behave in a way that causes oneself to be less respected by other people.

demeanour (*US* -or) /dɪ'miːnə(r)/ *n* [C, usu sing] (*fml*) way of behaving.

demented /dɪ'mentɪd/ *adj* mad.

demerara (also **demerara sugar**) /,demə'reərə/ *n* [U] light-brown sugar.

demilitarize /,diː'mɪlɪtəraɪz/ *v* [T] remove military forces from a place.

demise /dɪ'maɪz/ *n* [sing] 1 (*fml*) death. 2 (*fig*) end or failure.

demist /,diː'mɪst/ *v* [T] remove the mist from (a car windscreen).

democracy /dɪ'mɒkrəsɪ/ *n* (*pl* -ies) 1 [C, U] (country with a) government in which all citizens share through their elected representatives. 2 [U] control of an organization by its members, who take part in the making of decisions: *industrial ~.*

democrat /'deməkræt/ *n* [C] 1 person who favours or supports democracy. 2 **Democrat** (*US*) member of the Democratic Party. **democratic** /,demə'krætɪk/ *adj* of or supporting democracy. **democratically** *adv.*

demolish /dɪ'mɒlɪʃ/ *v* [T] 1 pull down (old buildings). 2 (*fig*) destroy (an argument, theory, etc). **demolition** /,demə'lɪʃn/ *n* [C, U].

demon /'diːmən/ *n* 1 evil spirit. 2 (*fml*) person with great skill or energy. **demonic** /diː'mɒnɪk/ *adj.*

demonstrable /'demənstrəbl; *US* dɪ'mɒnstrəbl/ *adj* that can be proved. **demonstrably** *adv.*

demonstrate /'demənstreɪt/ *v* 1 [T] show clearly or prove by giving facts or examples. 2 [I] take part in a demonstration(2). **demonstrator** *n* [C] 1 person who takes part in a demonstration(2). 2 person who explains by demonstrating(1).

demonstration /,demən'streɪʃn/ *n* 1 [C, U] act of showing clearly the facts, how sth works, etc. 2 [C] public display of opinion or feeling by a group, eg of workers or students. **demonstrative** /dɪ'mɒnstrətɪv/ *adj* 1 showing feelings. 2 (*grammar*) (of a pronoun) used for showing or explaining who or which, eg *this, those.*

demoralize /dɪ'mɒrəleɪz/ *US* -'mɔːr-/ *v* [T] destroy the courage, confidence, etc of (sb): *~d unemployed school-leavers.*

demote /,diː'məʊt/ *v* [T] reduce to a lower rank.

demure /dɪ'mjʊə(r)/ *adj* quiet, serious and shy: *a ~ young woman.* **demurely** *adv.*

den /den/ *n* [C] 1 a wild animal's hidden home. 2 (*infml*) small quiet room in a home where sb can work, eg at his/her hobbies.

denationalize /,diː'næʃənəlaɪz/ *v* [T] transfer (a nationalized industry) to private ownership again; privatize. **denationalization** /,diː,næʃənəlaɪ'zeɪʃn; *US* -lɪ'z-/ *n* [U].

denial /dɪ'naɪəl/ *n* 1 statement that sth is not true. 2 [C, U] denying; refusing a request.

denigrate /'denɪgreɪt/ v [T] claim (unfairly) that (sb/sth) is inferior, worthless, etc.

denim /'denɪm/ n 1 [U] strong cotton cloth. 2 **denims** [pl] (esp blue) jeans made from denim.

denomination /dɪˌnɒmɪ'neɪʃn/ n [C] 1 religious group. 2 unit of money or measurement. **denominational** adj of religious groups.

denominator /dɪ'nɒmɪneɪtə(r)/ n [C] number below the line in a fraction, eg 4 in ¾.

denote /dɪ'nəʊt/ v [T] 1 be the symbol or name of; represent. 2 indicate: His silence ~d criticism.

denounce /dɪ'naʊns/ v [T] speak publicly against: ~ sb as a spy.

dense /dens/ adj (~r, ~st) 1 (of people and things) crowded together: ~ through: ~ fog. 3 (infml) stupid. **densely** adv.

density /'densətɪ/ n (pl -ies) 1 [U] the quality of being dense(1, 2). 2 [C, U] (physics) relation of mass to volume.

dent /dent/ n hollow place in a hard surface made by a blow. **dent** v [T] make a dent in.

dental /'dentl/ adj of or for the teeth.

dentist /'dentɪst/ n [C] person whose job is to care for teeth. **dentistry** n [U] work of a dentist.

denunciation /dɪˌnʌnsɪ'eɪʃn/ n [C, U] (act of) denouncing

deny /dɪ'naɪ/ v (pt, pp -ied) 1 say that (sth) is not true. 2 refuse to give (sth) asked for or needed by sb.

deodorant /diː'əʊdərənt/ n [C, U] substance that hides or removes body odours.

dep abbr departs.

depart /dɪ'pɑːt/ v [I] (fml) go away; leave: The train ~s from platform 3. ○ ~ from the truth.

department /dɪ'pɑːtmənt/ n [C] one of several divisions of a government, business, shop, university, etc. **de'partment store** n [C] large shop where many kinds of goods are sold in different departments.

departure /dɪ'pɑːtʃə(r)/ n [C, U] (act of) going away.

depend /dɪ'pend/ v [I] 1 on// (a) need the support of sb/sth in order to survive: Children ~ on their parents. (b) trust; be certain about sth: You can ~ on John not to be late. 2 on// follow directly or logically from sth: Our success ~s on how hard we work. **dependable** adj that may be depended on:

a ~able friend.

dependant (also esp US **-ent**) /dɪ'pendənt/ n [C] person who depends on another for a home, food, etc.

dependence /dɪ'pendəns/ n [U] 1 constant need for sth in order to survive: ~ on drugs/foreign imports. 2 confident trust.

dependent /dɪ'pendənt/ adj 1 needing sth for support: ~ on her parents. 2 decided (by facts, a decision, etc): ~ on your passing the exam. **dependent** n [C] (esp US) dependant.

depict /dɪ'pɪkt/ v [T] show in a picture; describe in words. **depiction** /-kʃn/ n [U, C].

deplete /dɪ'pliːt/ v [T] reduce greatly in amount: Our food supplies are badly ~d. **depletion** /-i:ʃn/ n [U].

deplore /dɪ'plɔː(r)/ v [T] express strong disapproval of. **deplorable** adj very bad; deserving strong disapproval.

deploy /dɪ'plɔɪ/ v [I, T] (of troops) move into position for battle.

deport /dɪ'pɔːt/ v [T] force (sb unwanted) to leave a country. **deportation** /ˌdiːpɔː'teɪʃn/ n [C, U].

depose /dɪ'pəʊz/ v [T] remove (a ruler) from power.

deposit[1] /dɪ'pɒzɪt/ n 1 [C] amount of money in an (esp savings) account. 2 [C] payment of part of a larger sum, the rest of which is to be paid later. 3 [C] amount of money that sb pays when beginning to rent sth. 4 [C, U] layer of matter left by a river, etc. **de'posit account** n [C] account at a bank, etc in which the money earns interest.

deposit /dɪ'pɒzɪt/ v [T] 1 (fml) lay or put down. 2 (eg of a river) leave (mud, etc) on sth. 3 put (money) into a bank, esp to earn interest; put (sth valuable) in a safe place.

depot /'depəʊ; US 'diːpəʊ/ n 1 (a) storehouse; warehouse. (b) place where buses, etc are kept. 2 (US) railway or bus station.

depraved /dɪ'preɪvd/ adj morally bad. **depravity** /dɪ'prævətɪ/ n [U, C].

deprecate /'deprəkeɪt/ v [T] (fml) show disapproval of.

depreciate /dɪ'priːʃɪeɪt/ v [I] become less valuable. **depreciation** /dɪˌpriːʃɪ'eɪʃn/ n [U, C].

depress /dɪ'pres/ v [T] 1 make (sb) sad: feel very ~d. 2 make lower in value: ~ prices. 3 (fml) press down. **depressing** adj making one feel sad: a ~ing film.

depression /dɪ'preʃn/ n 1 [U] state of being depressed(1). 2 [U] period of little economic activity and poverty and unemployment. **3** [C] hollow sunken place. **4** [C] area of low atmospheric pressure.

deprive /dɪˈpraɪv/ v[T] *off*/ take sth away from (sb): ~ *people of freedom.* **deprivation** /ˌdeprɪˈveɪʃn/ n[C, U]. **deprived** *adj* without adequate food, housing, health care, etc.

Dept *abbr* Department.

depth /depθ/ n **1** [C, U] distance from the top to the bottom or from the front to the back. **2** [U] deep thought, feeling, etc: *a writer of great* ~. **3** (idm) **in 'depth** in detail; thoroughly. **out of one's depth (a)** in water that is deeper than one's height. **(b)** (fig) in a situation that is beyond one's understanding or ability.

deputation /ˌdepjuˈteɪʃn/ n[C] (with sing or pl v) group of people with the right to act or speak for others.

deputize /ˈdepjutaɪz/ v[I] act as deputy: ~ *for the manager.*

deputy /ˈdepjuti/ n[C] (pl -ies) **1** person immediately below the head of a school or organization. **2** person to whom authority is given (eg when sb is absent).

derail /dɪˈreɪl/ v[T] cause (a train) to leave the rails. **derailment** n[C, U].

deranged /dɪˈreɪndʒd/ *adj* unable to act and think normally, esp because of mental illness.

derelict /ˈderəlɪkt/ *adj* left to fall into ruin: *a ~ house.* **dereliction** /ˌderəˈlɪkʃn/ n[U].

derision /dɪˈrɪʒn/ n[U] ridicule. **derisory** /dɪˈraɪsərɪ/ *adj* not to be considered seriously.

derivation /ˌderɪˈveɪʃn/ n[C, U] origin or development of a word. **derivative** /dɪˈrɪvətɪv/ *adj*, n[C] (something, esp a word) derived from another.

derive /dɪˈraɪv/ v **1** [T] get; gain: ~ *pleasure from sth.* **2** [I] *from*/ come from: *words ~d from Latin.*

derogatory /dɪˈrɒgətrɪ; *US* -tɔːrɪ/ *adj* showing a lack of respect for sb/sth.

derrick /ˈderɪk/ n[C] **1** large crane for moving cargo on a ship. **2** framework over an oil well to hold the drilling machinery, etc.

descend /dɪˈsend/ v **1** [I, T] (*fml*) come or go down (sth). **2** (idm) **be descended from sb/sth** have sb/sth as ancestors. **3** (phr v) **descend on sb/sth** visit or attack sb/sth suddenly. **descendant** n person or animal that is descended from another: *the ~ants of Queen Victoria.*

descent /dɪˈsent/ n **1** [C, usu sing] coming or going down. **2** [C] downward slope. **3** [U] family; origin: *of French* ~.

describe /dɪˈskraɪb/ v[T] **1** say what (sb/sth) is like. **2** (*fml*) draw: ~ *a circle.*

description /dɪˈskrɪpʃn/ n **1** [C, U] statement of what sb/sth is like. **2** [C] kind or type: *boats of every* ~. **descriptive** /dɪˈskrɪptɪv/ *adj* intending to describe sb/sth.

desecrate /ˈdesɪkreɪt/ v[T] spoil or damage (a sacred thing or place). **desecration** /ˌdesɪˈkreɪʃn/ n[U].

desegregate /ˌdiːˈsegrɪgeɪt/ v[T] end (esp racial) segregation in: ~ *schools.* **desegregation** /ˌdiːˌsegrɪˈgeɪʃn/ n[U].

desert¹ /dɪˈzɜːt/ v **1** [T] go away from. **2** [T] leave (sb) without help or support: ~ *one's family.* **3** [I, T] leave (esp the armed forces) without permission. **deserter** n person who deserts(3). **desertion** /dɪˈzɜːʃn/ n[C, U].

desert² /ˈdezət/ n[C, U] large area of land, without water and trees, often covered with sand. **,desert 'island** n[C] tropical island without people.

deserts /dɪˈzɜːts/ n[pl] what sb deserves: *get one's just* ~s.

deserve /dɪˈzɜːv/ v[T] be sth or have done sth for which one should receive (a reward, punishment, etc): *She* ~d *to win.*

design /dɪˈzaɪn/ n **1 (a)** [C] drawing from which sth may be made. **(b)** [U] art of making such drawings, etc. **2** [C] decorative pattern of lines, shapes, etc. **3** [U] general planning of a machine, building, etc. **4** [C, U] plan; intention. **design** v[T] **1** prepare a plan or sketch of (sth to be made). **2** intend or plan: *a room* ~*ed for the children.* **designer** n[C].

designate /ˈdezɪgneɪt/ v[T] **1** choose (sb) for a particular job or purpose. **2** mark out clearly.

desirable /dɪˈzaɪərəbl/ *adj* worth having or doing. **desirability** /dɪˌzaɪərəˈbɪlətɪ/ n[U].

desire /dɪˈzaɪə(r)/ n **1** [C, U] strong wish: *no* ~ *to be rich/for wealth.* **2** [C] something that is wished for. **desire** v[T] (*fml*) want very much.

desist /dɪˈzɪst/ v[I] (*from*)// (*fml*) stop doing sth.

desk /desk/ n[C] table with a flat or sloping top at which to read, write or work. **,desk-top 'publishing** n[U] preparing and printing books, etc using a computer and laser printer.

desolate /'desələt/ *adj* **1** (of a place) neglected and without people. **2** lonely and sad. **desolation** /,desə'leɪʃn/ *n* [U].

despair /dɪ'speə(r)/ *n* [U] loss of all hope. **despair** *v* [I] (*of*)// be in despair: ~ *of ever getting better.*

despatch = DISPATCH.

desperate /'despərət/ *adj* **1** ready to do anything to change one's hopeless situation. **2** done when everything else has failed: a ~ *attempt to save her.* **3** in great need: ~ *for money.* **4** extremely serious: *a ~ situation.* **desperately** *adv.* **desperation** /,despə'reɪʃn/ *n* [U].

despicable /dɪ'spɪkəbl/ *adj* deserving to be despised.

despise /dɪ'spaɪz/ *v* [T] strongly dislike because one considers as not important or of no value.

despite /dɪ'spaɪt/ *prep* (used to introduce a contrast): *still a clear thinker, ~ his old age.*

despondent /dɪ'spɒndənt/ *adj* having or showing loss of hope. **despondency** /-dənsɪ/ *n* [U]. **despondently** *adv.*

despot /'despɒt/ *n* [C] ruler with unlimited powers, esp one who rules unfairly. **despotic** /dɪ'spɒtɪk/ *adj* who rules unfairly.

dessert /dɪ'zɜːt/ *n* [C, U] sweet food eaten at the end of a meal. **des'sert-spoon** *n* [C] medium-sized spoon.

destination /,destɪ'neɪʃn/ *n* [C] place to which sb/sth is going.

destined /'destɪnd/ *adj* **1** intended or certain: ~ *to become famous.* **2** *for*// on the way to: bound for a place.

destiny /'destɪnɪ/ *n* (*pl* **-ies**) **1** [C] the future as controlled by fate. **2** [U] fate.

destitute /'destɪtjuːt; US -tuːt/ *adj* without food, money, shelter, etc. **destitution** /,destɪ'tjuːʃn; US -'tuː-/ *n* [U].

destroy /dɪ'strɔɪ/ *v* [T] **1** break to pieces; put an end to. **2** kill (an animal), usu because it is sick. **destroyer** *n* [C] (**a**) person or thing that destroys. (**b**) small fast warship.

destruction /dɪ'strʌkʃn/ *n* [U] destroying or being destroyed. **destructive** /-ktɪv/ *adj* causing destruction; fond of destroying.

detach /dɪ'tætʃ/ *v* [T] unfasten and separate. **detached** *adj* (**a**) (of a house) not joined to another. (**b**) not involved; unemotional. **detachment** *n* (**a**) [U] state of being detached. (**b**) [C] group of soldiers

sent away from the main group.

detail[1] /'diːteɪl; US dɪ'teɪl/ *n* [C, U] small particular fact or item: *describe sth in ~.*

detail[2] /'diːteɪl; US dɪ'teɪl/ *v* [T] **1** list and describe fully. **2** appoint for special duty.

detain /dɪ'teɪn/ *v* [T] prevent from leaving; delay. **detainee** /,diːteɪ'niː/ *n* [C] person who is detained by the authorities, esp for political reasons.

detect /dɪ'tekt/ *v* [T] discover the existence or presence of. **detection** *n* [U]. **detective** *n* [C] person, esp a police officer, whose job is to investigate crimes. **detector** *n* [C] device for detecting sth.

detention /dɪ'tenʃn/ *n* **1** [U] act of detaining sb, esp for political reasons. **2** [C, U] punishment of keeping badly behaved school-children at school after school hours.

deter /dɪ'tɜː(r)/ *v* (**-rr-**) [T] (*from*)// prevent or discourage (sb) from doing sth.

detergent /dɪ'tɜːdʒənt/ *n* [C, U] liquid or powder used for washing clothes or plates, etc.

deteriorate /dɪ'tɪərɪəreɪt/ *v* [I] become worse: *His health ~d.* **deterioration** /dɪ,tɪərɪə'reɪʃn/ *n* [U].

determination /dɪ,tɜːmɪ'neɪʃn/ *n* [U, C] **1** seriousness in wanting to do sth successfully: *a ~ to improve one's English.* **2** act of deciding.

determine /dɪ'tɜːmɪn/ *v* **1** [T] control or cause: *Our living standards are ~d by our income.* **2** [T] find out (sth) precisely: ~ *what happened.* **3** [T] settle or decide: ~ *party policy.* **4** [T] (*fml*) decide firmly to do sth. **determined** *adj* showing a serious wish to do sth successfully: ~ *d to win.*

deterrent /dɪ'terənt; US -'tɜː-/ *n* [C] something that deters sb from doing sth: *the nuclear ~,* ie nuclear weapons that discourage countries from starting a war.

detest /dɪ'test/ *v* [T] hate strongly. **detestable** *adj* that one hates.

dethrone /diː'θrəʊn/ *v* [T] remove (a ruler) from the throne.

detonate /'detəneɪt/ *v* [I, T] (cause to) explode. **detonation** /,detə'neɪʃn/ *n* [C, U]. **detonator** *n* [C] part of a bomb that causes it to explode.

detour /'diːtʊə(r); US dɪ'tʊər/ *n* [C] way round; diversion: *make a ~ round the floods.*

detract /dɪ'trækt/ *v* [I, *from*// lessen the effect or value of sth.

detriment /'detrɪmənt/ *n* [U] damage; harm: *to the ~ of her*

health ○ *without ~ to her health.*
detrimental /ˌdetrɪ'mentl/ *adj* (*to*)|| harmful.
deuce /djuːs; *US* duːs/ *n* [C] (in tennis) score of 40 points to each player.
devalue /ˌdiːˈvæljuː/ *v* [T] make the value of (a currency) less. **devaluation** /ˌdiːˌvæljuˈeɪʃn/ *n* [C, U].
devastate /'devəsteɪt/ *v* [T] completely destroy; ruin. (*fig*) *~d by his death.* **devastation** /ˌdevəˈsteɪʃn/ *n* [U].
develop /dɪˈveləp/ *v* 1 [I, T] become or make larger, fuller or more mature: *The argument ~ed into a fight.* 2 [I, T] come or bring gradually into existence: *a ~ cough.* 3 [T] treat (an exposed film) so that the photograph can be seen. 4 [T] use (an area of land) for buildings and so increase its value. **developer** *n* [C] person or company that develops land. **development** *n* [U] (a) developing. (b) new event or situation. (c) area of land with new buildings on it.
deviate /'diːvɪeɪt/ *v* [I] *from*|| turn away from what is usual, accepted, etc. **deviation** /ˌdiːvɪˈeɪʃn/ *n* [C, U].
device /dɪˈvaɪs/ *n* [C] 1 object made for a particular purpose. 2 careful scheme; trick.
devil /'devl/ *n* [C] 1 **the Devil** the supreme spirit of evil; Satan. 2 evil spirit. 3 (*infml*) mischievous person. 4 (idm) **devil's 'advocate** person who speaks against sb/sth to encourage discussion.
devious /'diːvɪəs/ *adj* cunning; deceitful.
devise /dɪˈvaɪz/ *v* [T] think out (a plan, system, etc).
devoid /dɪˈvɔɪd/ *adj of*|| without sth: *~ of any ability.*
devolution /ˌdiːvəˈluːʃn; *US* ˌdev-/ *n* [U] transfer of power from central to regional government.
devote /dɪˈvəʊt/ *v* [T] *to*|| give (oneself or one's time, energy, etc) to sth. **devoted** *adj* (*to*)|| very loving or loyal. **devotee** /ˌdevəˈtiː/ *n* [C] person who is devoted to sth. **devotion** /dɪˈvəʊʃn/ *n* [U] (a) deep strong love. (b) [C, usu pl] prayer.
devour /dɪˈvaʊə(r)/ *v* [T] 1 eat hungrily or greedily. 2 (*fig*) absorb, use up or destroy: *forests ~ed by fire.*
devout /dɪˈvaʊt/ *adj* 1 very religious. 2 (of prayers, wishes, etc) serious; sincere.
dew /djuː; *US* duː/ *n* [U] tiny drops of water that form on cool surfaces in the night. **dewy** *adj.*

'dewdrop *n* [C] drop of dew.
dexterity /ˌdekˈsterətɪ/ *n* [U] great skill, esp with one's hands. **dexterous, dextrous** /'dekstrəs/ *adj.*
diabetes /ˌdaɪəˈbiːtiːz/ *n* [U] disease in which there is too much sugar in the blood. **diabetic** /ˌ-'betɪk/ *adj, n* [C] (of or for a) person with diabetes.
diabolical /ˌdaɪəˈbɒlɪkl/ *adj* 1 very cruel or wicked. 2 (*infml*) very bad: *~ weather.*
diagnose /ˌdaɪəgˈnəʊz/ *v* [T] identify precisely (an illness or error) by careful examination. **diagnosis** /ˌdaɪəgˈnəʊsɪs/ *n* [C, U] (*pl* **-noses** /-siːz/) act or result of diagnosing. **diagnostic** /ˌdaɪəgˈnɒstɪk/ *adj.*
diagonal /daɪˈægənl/ *n* [C], *adj* (straight line) going across a square or oblong. **diagonally** *adv.*
diagram /'daɪəgræm/ *n* [C] drawing, design or plan used for explaining or illustrating sth. **diagrammatic** /ˌdaɪəgrəˈmætɪk/ *adj.*
dial /'daɪəl/ *n* [C] 1 marked face of a clock, watch or measuring instrument. 2 movable disc on a telephone, with numbered holes, used for making a connection. **dial** *v* (-ll-; *US* -l-) [I, T] use a telephone dial to call (a number). **'dialling tone** *n* [C] sound heard on the telephone before one dials the number.
dialect /'daɪəlekt/ *n* [C, U] form of a language used in part of a country: *the Yorkshire ~.*
dialogue (*US* **-log**) /'daɪəlɒg; *US* -lɔːg/ *n* 1 [U] communication between representatives of two groups: *~ between the superpowers.* 2 [U] conversation or talk, eg in a play or in real life.
diameter /daɪˈæmɪtə(r)/ *n* [C] length of a straight line drawn from side to side through the centre of a circle.
diametrically /ˌdaɪəˈmetrɪklɪ/ *adv* completely: *~ opposed.*
diamond /'daɪəmənd/ *n* 1 [C, U] very hard brilliant precious stone. 2 [C] figure with four equal sides whose angles are not right angles. 3 [C] playing-card with red shapes like diamonds(2). **diamond 'jubilee** *n* [C] 60th anniversary of an important event.
diaper /'daɪəpə(r); *US* also 'daɪpər/ *n* [C] (*US*) nappy.
diaphragm /'daɪəfræm/ *n* [C] 1 muscle between the chest and the abdomen. 2 thin vibrating disc or plate in an instrument.
diarrhoea (*US* **-rrhea**) /ˌdaɪəˈrɪə/

n [U] too frequent and too watery emptying of one's bowels.

diary /ˈdaɪərɪ/ *n* [C] (*-ies*) (book used for a) daily record of events, appointments, etc: *keep* (ie write regularly in) *a* ~.

dice /daɪs/ *n* [C] (*pl* **dice**) small cube marked with spots to indicate numbers, used in games. **dice** *v* [T] **1** cut (food) into small cubes. **2** (idm) **dice with 'death** risk one's life.

dictate /dɪkˈteɪt; *US* ˈdɪkteɪt/ *v* [I, T] **1** read (a letter, etc) aloud for sb else to write down. **2** order or state with authority. **dictation** /-ˈteɪʃn/ *n* **1** [U] act of dictation. **2** [C] piece of writing that is dictated.

dictator /dɪkˈteɪtə(r); *US* ˈdɪkteɪtər/ *n* (*derog*) ruler who has complete power in a country. **dictatorial** /ˌdɪktəˈtɔːrɪəl/ *adj*. **dictatorship** *n* [C, U] (country with) government by a dictator.

diction /ˈdɪkʃn/ *n* [U] clearness with which sb speaks.

dictionary /ˈdɪkʃənrɪ; *US* -nerɪ/ *n* [C] (*pl* **-ies**) book containing the words of a language, with their meanings, arranged in alphabetical order.

did *pt* of DO.

didn't did not. ⇨ DO.

die[1] /daɪ/ *n* [C] metal block used to stamp designs on coins, medals, etc.

die[2] /daɪ/ *v* (*pres part* **dying** /ˈdaɪɪŋ/) [I] **1** stop living; reach the end of one's life. **2** (*fig*) cease to exist: *love that will never* ~. **3** *for; to*// have a strong wish for sth: *dying for a drink* ◇ *dying to tell her*. **4** (idm) **die laughing** (*infml*) laugh a lot. **5** (phr v) **die away** become weaker and disappear. **die down** become less strong. **die out** disappear completely.

diesel /ˈdiːzl/ *n* **1** [C] vehicle, esp a train, with a diesel engine. **2** [U] (also **'diesel oil**) heavy fuel used in a diesel engine. **'diesel engine** *n* [C] internal-combustion engine used in buses, trains, lorries, etc.

diet /ˈdaɪət/ *n* **1** [C, U] food that is usually eaten. **2** [C] food eaten by sb in order to lose weight: *be/go on a* ~. **diet** *v* [I] eat special food in order to lose weight.

differ /ˈdɪfə(r)/ *v* [I] **1** (*from*)// be unlike. **2** disagree: *I'm sorry to* ~ *with you on that.* **difference** /ˈdɪfrəns/ *n* **1** [C, U] example of being unlike: *the* ~ *in their ages.* **2** [sing] amount by which two things are unlike: *The* ~ *between 7 and 18 is 11.* **3** [C] disagreement. **4** (idm) **not make any/the slight-**

est difference not be important.

different /ˈdɪfrənt/ *adj* **1** (*from; in/from; to; US than*)// not the same as sb/sth. **2** separate; distinct: *several* ~ *people.*

differentiate /ˌdɪfəˈrenʃɪeɪt/ *v* [I, T] (*between A and B; A from B*)// show the difference between two or more things; distinguish one thing from others.

difficult /ˈdɪfɪkəlt/ *adj* **1** not easy; requiring effort, skill, etc: *find sth* ~ *to understand.* **2** (of people) not easily pleased; easily offended. **difficulty** *n* (*pl* **-ies**) **1** [C] something that is hard to understand. **2** [U] fact or quality of being difficult.

diffident /ˈdɪfɪdənt/ *adj* lacking confidence; shy. **diffidence** /-dəns/ *n* [U].

diffuse /dɪˈfjuːz/ *v* [I, T] (of light) cause to spread out in every direction. **diffuse** /dɪˈfjuːs/ *adj* **1** scattered: ~ *light.* **2** using too many words; not precise. **diffusion** /-ˈuːʒn/ *n* [U].

dig[1] /dɪg/ *n* [C] **1** small push or thrust: *a* ~ *in the ribs.* **2** critical remark: *That was a* ~ *at Ray.* **3** archaeological excavation. **4** **digs** [pl] (*Brit*) lodgings.

dig[2] /dɪg/ *v* (*-gg-*, *pt, pp* **dug** /dʌg/) **1** [I, T] break up and move (earth) with a spade, etc; make (a way) through, into, etc by doing this; make (a hole, etc) by doing this. **2** [T] obtain by digging: ~ *potatoes.* **3** (phr v) **dig sb/sth out** (of sth) (a) get sb/sth out by digging. (b) (*infml*) find sth by searching. **dig sth up** remove or find sth by digging or careful searching.

digest[1] /dɪˈdʒest, daɪ-/ *v* **1** (a) [T] change (food) in the stomach so that it can be used by the body. (b) [I] of food be changed in this way. **2** [T] understand fully.

digest[2] /ˈdaɪdʒest/ *n* [C] short concise account; summary.

digit /ˈdɪdʒɪt/ *n* [C] **1** one of the ten numbers from 0 to 9. **2** (*fml*) finger or toe. **digital** *adj* showing amounts by numbers: *a* ~ *al watch.*

dignified /ˈdɪgnɪfaɪd/ *adj* having or showing dignity.

dignitary /ˈdɪgnɪtərɪ; *US* -terɪ/ *n* [C] (*pl* **-ies**) (*fml*) person with a high rank.

dignity /ˈdɪgnətɪ/ *n* **1** [U] calm and serious manner. **2** [U] quality that deserves respect; true worth. **3** (idm) **beneath one's dignity** not important enough for one to do.

digress /daɪˈgres/ *v* [I] (*from*)// turn from the main subject in

speaking or writing. **digression**
/-'greʃn/ n [U, C].

digs ⇨ DIG⁴.

dike (also **dyke**) /daɪk/ n [C] **1**
long wall of earth, for holding
back water. **2** ditch.

dilapidated /dɪ'læpɪdeɪtɪd/ adj
(of buildings) old and falling to
pieces.

dilate /daɪ'leɪt/ v [I, T] (esp of
eyes) become or make wider or
larger.

dilemma /dɪ'lemə/ n [C] difficult
situation in which one has to
choose between two things.

diligent /'dɪlɪdʒənt/ adj hard-
working; showing care and effort:
a ~ worker. **diligence** /-dʒəns/
n [U]. **diligently** adv.

dilute /daɪ'luːt/ v [T] (with))//
make (a liquid) weaker by adding
water or another liquid. **dilution**
/-'luːʃn/ n [U, C].

dim /dɪm/ adj (-mer, -mest) **1** not
bright: in a ~ light. **2** not easy to
see. **3** (fig) unclear; vague: ~
memories. **4** (infml) not intelligent.
5 (idm) **take a dim view of sth**
think that sth is bad or wrong.
dim v (-mm-) [I, T] become or
make dim. **dimly** adv. **dimness**
n [U].

dime /daɪm/ n [C] coin of USA
and Canada worth ten cents.

dimension /dɪ'menʃn/ n **1** [C]
measurement of length, width or
height. **2** dimensions [pl] scope
or extent: the ~s of the problem. **3**
[C] (fig) aspect. **dimensional**
/-ʃənəl/ (in compound adjectives)
having the number of dimensions
that is mentioned: two-~al.

diminish /dɪ'mɪnɪʃ/ v [I, T] become or make smaller: Our chances of success are ~ing.

diminutive /dɪ'mɪnjʊtɪv/ adj
very small.

dimple /'dɪmpl/ n [C] small natural hollow in sb's cheek or chin.

din /dɪn/ n [C, sing] loud unpleasant noise. **din** v (-nn-) (phr v)
din sth into sb tell sth to sb again
and again.

dine /daɪn/ v **1** [I] (fml) eat dinner. **2** (phr v) **dine out** eat dinner
in a restaurant, hotel, etc. **'dining-
car** n [C] railway carriage where
meals are served. **'dining-room**
n [C] room in which meals are
eaten.

dinghy /'dɪŋgɪ/ n [C] (pl -ies)
small open boat.

dingy /'dɪndʒɪ/ adj (-ier, -iest)
dirty-looking; not bright or pleasant. **dinginess** n [U].

dining ⇨ DINE.

dinner /'dɪnə(r)/ n [C, U] main
meal of the day, eaten at midday

or in the evening. **'dinner-jacket**
n [C] man's black jacket worn at
formal evening events.

dinosaur /'daɪnəsɔː(r)/ n [C]
large prehistoric reptile that no
longer exists.

diocese /'daɪəsɪs/ n [C] area for
which a bishop is responsible.

dip /dɪp/ v (-pp-) **1** [T] put into a
liquid for a short time. **2** [I] go
down; drop: The sun ~ped below
the horizon. **3** [T] lower (a beam of
light): ~ the headlights of a car. **4**
(phr v) **dip into sth (a)** use money
from (eg one's savings). **(b)** read (a
book) for a short time. **dip** n **1** [C]
act of dipping. **2** [C] quick swim. **3**
[C, U] creamy sauce into which
food is dipped. **4** [C] downward
slope.

diphtheria /dɪf'θɪərɪə/ n [U]
serious disease of the throat.

diphthong /'dɪfθɒŋ; US -θɔːŋ/
n [C] union of two vowels, eg /aɪ/
in pipe /paɪp/.

diploma /dɪ'pləʊmə/ n [C] official
paper showing that a student has
passed an examination, etc.

diplomacy /dɪ'pləʊməsɪ/ n [U] **1**
management of relations between
countries. **2** skill in dealing with
people; tact.

diplomat /'dɪpləmæt/ n [C] person whose job is diplomacy(1). **diplomatic** /ˌdɪplə'mætɪk/ adj **1** of
diplomacy(1): work in the ~ ic service. **2** having or showing diplo-
macy(2); tactful. **diplomatically**
adv.

dire /'daɪə(r)/ adj terrible.

direct¹ /dɪ'rekt, daɪ-/ adj **1** going
straight: a ~ route. **2** with nothing
or nobody in between: a ~ result.
3 frank and honest; straightforward. **4** exact: the ~ opposite. **direct** adv without interrupting a
journey: travel ~ to Rome. **direct**
'current n [U] electric current
that flows in one direction only.
direct 'debit n [C] order to a bank
that allows sb else to take money
from one's account. **directness**
n [U]. **direct 'object** n [C] (grammar) noun, noun phrase or noun
clause that is affected by the action of the verb, eg the money in He
took the money. **direct 'speech**
n [U] speaker's actual words.

direct² /dɪ'rekt, daɪ-/ v [T] **1** tell
(sb) how to get somewhere: Can
you ~ me to the station, please? **2**
organize or control; manage: ~ a
project/film. **3** aim or turn: ~ one's
attention to a more important matter. **4** (fml) order or instruct.

direction /dɪ'rekʃn, daɪ-/ n **1** [C]
point towards which a person or
thing moves or looks: run off in the

opposite ~. **2 directions** [pl] instructions. **3** [U] organization or management: *under my ~.*

directive /dɪˈrektɪv, daɪ-/ *n* [C] (*fml*) official order.

directly /dɪˈrektlɪ, daɪ-/ *adv* **1** in a direct manner; exactly. **2** immediately. **directly** *conj* as soon as: *I came ~ I knew.*

director /dɪˈrektə(r), daɪ-/ *n* [C] **1** person who manages sth, esp a business company. **2** person who directs a play or a film. **directorship** *n* [C] position of a company director.

directory /dɪˈrektərɪ, daɪ-/ *n* [C] (*pl* **-ies**) book with a list of names, addresses and telephone numbers.

dirt /dɜːt/ *n* [U] **1** unclean matter, eg dust or mud. **2** (*infml*) nasty talk; scandal. **3** (*infml*) excrement: *dog ~ on my shoe.* **dirt cheap** *adj* (*infml*) very cheap.

dirty /ˈdɜːtɪ/ *adj* (**-ier, -iest**) **1** not clean: *~ water.* **2** cruel; unfair: *a ~ trick.* **3** unpleasantly concerned with sex: *a ~ joke.* **4** disapproving: *give sb a ~ look.* **dirty** *v* (*pt, pp* **-ied**) [T] make dirty.

disable /dɪsˈeɪbl/ *v* [T] make (sb) unable to use his/her body properly, esp to move about. **disability** /ˌdɪsəˈbɪlətɪ/ *n* (*pl* **-ies**) **1** [C] something that disables sb. **2** [U] (*fml*) state of being disabled. **disabled** *adj.* **disablement** *n* [U].

disabuse /ˌdɪsəˈbjuːz/ *v* [T] (*of*) free (sb) of wrong ideas.

disadvantage /ˌdɪsədˈvɑːntɪdʒ; *US* -ˈvæn-/ *n* [C] **1** unfavourable condition. **2** (idm) to **sb's disadvantage** (*fml*) damaging sth. **disadvantaged** *adj* suffering from social or economic disadvantages. **disadvantageous** /ˌdɪsædvɑːnˈteɪdʒəs; *US* -væn-/ *adj.*

disagree /ˌdɪsəˈgriː/ *v* [I] **1** have different opinions: *I ~ with you/ with what you say.* **2** be different. **3** (phr v) **disagree with sb** (of food) make sb feel ill. **disagreeable** *adj* unpleasant. **disagreeably** *adv.* **disagreement** *n* [C, U] difference of opinion.

disappear /ˌdɪsəˈpɪə(r)/ *v* [I] **1** go out of sight. **2** stop existing. **disappearance** *n* [C, U].

disappoint /ˌdɪsəˈpɔɪnt/ *v* [T] fail to do or be what is hoped for by (sb). **disappointed** *adj* sad at not getting what was hoped for. **disappointing** *adj.* **disappointingly** *adv.* **disappointment** *n* **1** [U] state of being disappointed. **2** [C] person or thing that is disappointing.

disapprove /ˌdɪsəˈpruːv/ *v* [I]

(*of*)|| say or think that sb/sth is bad. **disapproval** *n* [U].

disarm /dɪsˈɑːm/ *v* **1** [T] take away all weapons from. **2** [I] (of a country) stop using (esp nuclear) weapons. **3** [T] make (sb) less angry, hostile, etc. **disarmament** *n* [U] act of disarming(2).

disarray /ˌdɪsəˈreɪ/ *n* [U] (*fml*) state of bad organization: *in ~.*

disassociate ⇒ DISSOCIATE.

disaster /dɪˈzɑːstə(r); *US* -ˈzæs-/ *n* [C] serious sudden misfortune; terrible accident. **disastrous** /dɪˈzɑːstrəs; *US* -ˈzæs-/ *adj.* **disastrously** *adv.*

disband /dɪsˈbænd/ *v* [I, T] break up (a group of people or an organization).

disbelieve /ˌdɪsbɪˈliːv/ *v* [T] refuse to believe. **disbelief** /-bɪˈliːf/ *n* [U] lack of belief.

disc (also esp *US* **disk**) /dɪsk/ *n* [C] **1** something that is flat, thin and round, eg a record. **2** flat piece of cartilage in one's spine: *a slipped ~.* **'disc jockey** *n* person who plays and introduces records of popular music on the radio or at a disco.

discard /dɪˈskɑːd/ *v* [T] get rid of; throw away.

discern /dɪˈsɜːn/ *v* [T] (*fml*) understand; see with one's eyes. **discernible** *adj.* **discerning** *adj* (*approv*) showing careful judgement. **discernment** *n* [U] ability to judge well.

discharge /dɪsˈtʃɑːdʒ/ *v* **1** [T] allow (sb) to leave; send (sb) away. **2** [T] (*fml*) perform (a duty). **3** [I, T] send out (liquid, gas, etc). **4** [T] take (cargo) off a ship. **5** [T] (*fml*) pay (a debt). **discharge** /ˈdɪstʃɑːdʒ/ *n* **1** [U] discharging or being discharged. **2** [U, C] something that is discharged.

disciple /dɪˈsaɪpl/ *n* [C] follower of a religious, political, etc leader.

discipline /ˈdɪsɪplɪn/ *n* **1** (a) [U] training to produce obedience, self-control, etc. (b) [U] result of such training, eg of soldiers. **2** [U] punishment. **3** [C] (*fml*) area of knowledge. **discipline** *v* [T] **1** train to be obedient. **2** punish.

disclaim /dɪsˈkleɪm/ *v* [T] (*fml*) say that one does not have (responsibility for sth).

disclose /dɪsˈkləʊz/ *v* [T] (a) make (sth) known. (b) allow (sth) to be seen. **disclosure** /-ˈkləʊʒə(r)/ *n* [U, C].

disco /ˈdɪskəʊ/ (also **discotheque** /ˈdɪskətek/) *n* [C] (*pl* **~s**) club, party, etc where people dance to pop records.

discolour (*US* **-or**) /dɪsˈkʌlə(r)/

v [I, T] (cause to) change colour in an unpleasant way. **discoloration** /ˌdɪskʌləˈreɪʃn/ *n* [U, C].

discomfort /dɪsˈkʌmfət/ *n* (a) [U] lack of comfort; slight pain. (b) [C] something that causes this.

disconcert /ˌdɪskənˈsɜːt/ *v* [T] embarrass, upset or worry.

disconnect /ˌdɪskəˈnekt/ *v* [T] A *(from B)*|| detach sth (from sth); undo a connection. **disconnected** *adj* (of ideas in a speech or writing) badly ordered.

disconsolate /dɪsˈkɒnsələt/ *adj* *(fml)* very unhappy and without hope. **disconsolately** *adv*.

discontent /ˌdɪskənˈtent/ *n* [U] *(with)*|| lack of satisfaction. **discontented** *adj* not satisfied.

discontinue /ˌdɪskənˈtɪnjuː/ *v* [T] *(fml)* put an end to; stop.

discord /ˈdɪskɔːd/ *n* 1 [U] *(fml)* disagreement; quarrelling. 2 (a) [U] lack of harmony between musical sounds. (b) [C] unpleasant instance of this. **discordant** /dɪsˈkɔːdənt/ *adj*.

discotheque = DISCO.

discount¹ /ˈdɪskaʊnt/ *n* [C] reduction in price.

discount² /dɪsˈkaʊnt; US ˈdɪskaʊnt/ *v* [T] consider (sth) to be unimportant or untrue.

discourage /dɪsˈkʌrɪdʒ/ *v* [T] 1 take away the hope or enthusiasm from: *~ sb by failure*. 2 persuade (sb) not to do sth: *~ children from smoking*. **discouragement** *n* [U, C].

discourse /ˈdɪskɔːs/ *n* [C, U] *(fml)* serious speech or conversation.

discourteous /dɪsˈkɜːtɪəs/ *adj* *(fml)* impolite; rude. **discourteously** *adv*. **discourtesy** /-ˈkɜːtəsɪ/ *n*.

discover /dɪsˈkʌvə(r)/ *v* [T] 1 find or learn about for the first time. 2 come to know or realize; find out. **discoverer** /dɪsˈkʌvərə(r)/ *n* (*pl* -ies) 1 [U] discovering. 2 [C] something that is discovered.

discredit /dɪsˈkredɪt/ *v* [T] 1 cause people to think badly of. 2 cause to appear untrue or doubtful. **discredit** *n* [U] loss of respect or reputation.

discreet /dɪsˈkriːt/ *adj* showing careful judgement in what one says or does. **discreetly** *adv*.

discrepancy /dɪsˈkrepənsɪ/ *n* [C] (*pl* -ies) difference between two things.

discretion /dɪsˈkreʃn/ *n* [U] 1 good judgement. 2 freedom to decide what to do: *use your own ~*.

discriminate /dɪsˈkrɪmɪneɪt/ *v* [I] 1 *(between)*|| see or make a difference. 2 *against/in favour of*|| treat (sb) worse/better than others. **discriminating** *adj*. **discrimination** /dɪˌskrɪmɪˈneɪʃn/ *n* [U].

discus /ˈdɪskəs/ *n* [C] heavy round disc thrown as a sport.

discuss /dɪsˈkʌs/ *v* [T] talk or write about (sth). **discussion** *n* [C, U].

disdain /dɪsˈdeɪn/ *n* [U] feeling that sb/sth is not good enough to deserve respect. **disdain** *v* [T] 1 treat with disdain. 2 refuse (to do sth) because of one's disdain. **disdainful** *adj*.

disease /dɪˈziːz/ *n* [C, U] illness. **diseased** *adj* having a disease.

disembark /ˌdɪsɪmˈbɑːk/ *v* [I] *(from)*|| leave a ship, aircraft or bus. **disembarkation** /ˌdɪsembɑːˈkeɪʃn/ *n* [U].

disenchanted /ˌdɪsɪnˈtʃɑːntɪd; US -ˈtʃænt-/ *adj* *(with)*|| having lost one's good opinion of sth.

disengage /ˌdɪsɪnˈgeɪdʒ/ *v* 1 [T] *(from)*|| free or separate. 2 [I] stop fighting.

disentangle /ˌdɪsɪnˈtæŋgl/ *v* [T] 1 make (string, etc) free of knots. 2 *(from)*|| free (sb/sth) from sth complicated or confused.

disfigure /dɪsˈfɪgə(r); US -gjər/ *v* [T] spoil the appearance of. **disfigurement** *n* [C, U].

disgorge /dɪsˈgɔːdʒ/ *v* [I, T] (cause) to flow or pour out.

disgrace /dɪsˈgreɪs/ *n* 1 [U] shame or loss of respect because of one's bad behaviour. 2 [sing] person or thing that is so bad that it causes shame. **disgrace** *v* [T] bring disgrace on. **disgraceful** *adj* very bad; causing disgrace.

disgruntled /dɪsˈgrʌntld/ *adj* annoyed and dissatisfied.

disguise /dɪsˈgaɪz/ *v* [T] 1 change the appearance of (oneself/sth) in order not to be recognized. 2 hide: *~ one's anger*. **disguise** *n* 1 [C] something worn in order to disguise oneself. 2 [U] disguising.

disgust /dɪsˈgʌst/ *n* [U] strong dislike. **disgust** *v* [T] cause disgust in. **disgusted** *adj* feeling disgust. **disgusting** *adj* causing disgust.

dish /dɪʃ/ *n* [C] 1 shallow container for serving food. 2 [C] particular kind of food in a meal. 3 **the dishes** [pl] plates, bowls, cups, etc used for a meal. **dish** *v* (phr *v*) **dish sth out** give away a lot of sth: *~ out leaflets/compliments*. **dish sth up** put (food) onto plates. **dishcloth** *n* [C] cloth for washing plates, pans, etc. **dishwasher** *n* [C] machine that washes plates, bowls, etc.

dishearten /dɪsˈhɑːtn/ v [T]
cause (sb) to lose hope or confidence.

dishevelled (US **-l-**) /dɪˈʃevld/
adj (of clothes or hair) very untidy.

dishonest /dɪsˈɒnɪst/ adj not
honest. **dishonestly** adv. **dishonesty** n [U].

dishonour (US **-or**) /dɪsˈɒnə(r)/
n [U, sing] (fml) feeling of shame or
disgrace. **dishonour** v [T] (fml) 1
bring dishonour to. 2 (of a bank)
refuse to pay (a cheque). **dishonourable** adj not honourable.

disillusion /ˌdɪsɪˈluːʒn/ v [T] destroy the pleasant beliefs of (sb) by
telling him/her the truth. **disillusioned** adj. **disillusionment**
n [U].

disinclined /ˌdɪsɪnˈklaɪnd/ adj
(for; to)// not willing: ~ for study ○
~ to leave.

disinfect /ˌdɪsɪnˈfekt/ v [T] clean
(sth) with a substance that destroys germs: ~ a wound. **disinfectant** n [U, C] substance used for
disinfecting things.

disinformation /ˌdɪsˌɪnfəˈmeɪʃn/
n [U] false information, esp from a
government.

disinherit /ˌdɪsɪnˈherɪt/ v [T]
stop (sb) inheriting one's
property.

disintegrate /dɪsˈɪntɪɡreɪt/ v [I]
break into small pieces. **disintegration** /dɪsˌɪntɪˈɡreɪʃn/ n [U].

disinterested /dɪsˈɪntrəstɪd/ adj
not influenced by personal interests.

disjointed /dɪsˈdʒɔɪntɪd/ adj (of
words, thoughts, etc) not having a
clear order.

disk /dɪsk/ n [C] 1 (esp US) =
DISC. 2 flat round magnetic plate
used for storing computer information. **'disk drive** n [C] device in a computer that transfers
information to and from a disk(2).

dislike /dɪsˈlaɪk/ v [T] not like.
dislike n [U] feeling of not liking
sb/sth. 2 [C] something that one
dislikes.

dislocate /ˈdɪsləkeɪt; US -ləʊ-/
v [T] 1 put (a bone) out of its usual
position. 2 put (traffic, a system,
etc) out of order. **dislocation**
/ˌdɪsləˈkeɪʃn; US -ləʊ-/ n [U, C].

dislodge /dɪsˈlɒdʒ/ v [T] move or
force from a fixed position.

disloyal /dɪsˈlɔɪəl/ adj not loyal.
disloyally adv. **disloyalty** n [U].

dismal /ˈdɪzməl/ adj sad; miserable. **dismally** adv.

dismantle /dɪsˈmæntl/ v [T] take
to pieces: ~ a machine/engine.

dismay /dɪsˈmeɪ/ n [U] feeling of
fear and discouragement. **dismay**

v [T] fill (sb) with dismay.

dismember /dɪsˈmembə(r)/ v [T]
1 cut or tear off the arms and legs
of. 2 divide (a country, etc) into
smaller parts.

dismiss /dɪsˈmɪs/ v [T] 1 remove
(a worker) from a job. 2 allow to
leave; send away. 3 put (thoughts,
etc) out of one's mind. 4 (law) end
(a court case). **dismissal** n [U, C].

disobedient /ˌdɪsəˈbiːdiənt/ adj
not obedient. **disobedience**
/-əns/ n [U]. **disobediently** adv.

disobey /ˌdɪsəˈbeɪ/ v [I, T] not
obey (a person, law, etc).

disorder /dɪsˈɔːdə(r)/ n 1 [U] lack
of order; confusion. 2 [C, U] public
rioting. 3 [C, U] illness of the mind
or body. **disorder** v [T] put into
disorder. **disorderly** adj.

disorganize /dɪsˈɔːɡənaɪz/ v [T]
cause (sth organized) to be confused.

disorientate /dɪsˈɔːriənteɪt/ (also
esp US **disorient** /dɪsˈɔːriənt/)
v [T] cause (sb) to lose all sense of
direction; confuse. **disorientation** /dɪsˌɔːriənˈteɪʃn/ n [U].

disown /dɪsˈəʊn/ v [T] say that
one no longer wants to be connected with (sb/sth).

disparaging /dɪˈspærɪdʒɪŋ/ adj
suggesting that sb/sth is not important; scornful.

disparate /ˈdɪspərət/ adj (fml) so
different that they cannot be compared. **disparity** /dɪˈspærətɪ/
n [C, U] (pl **-ies**) difference.

dispassionate /dɪˈspæʃənət/ adj
not influenced by emotion; fair.
dispassionately adv.

dispatch (also **despatch**)
/dɪˈspætʃ/ v [T] (fml) 1 send. 2 finish quickly. **dispatch** (also **despatch**) n 1 [U] (fml) dispatching. 2
[C] message or report that is sent.
3 [U] (fml) speed.

dispel /dɪˈspel/ v (**-ll-**) [T] cause to
vanish: ~ doubts.

dispense /dɪˈspens/ v [T] 1 (fml)
give (sth) out; distribute. 2
prepare and give out (medicine). 3
(phr v) **dispense with sth** do
without sth; get rid of. **dispensary**
/dɪˈspensərɪ/ n [C] (pl **-ies**) place
where medicines are dispensed.
dispensation /ˌdɪspenˈseɪʃn/ n
(fml) 1 [U] act of dispensing sth. 2
[U, C] permission to do sth usually
forbidden.

disperse /dɪˈspɜːs/ v [I, T] go or
send in different directions. **dispersal** n [U].

dispirited /dɪˈspɪrɪtɪd/ adj without enthusiasm; discouraged.

displace /dɪsˈpleɪs/ v [T] 1 move
(sth) from its usual place. 2 take
the place of. **displacement** n [U].

display /dɪˈspleɪ/ v [T] show; exhibit. **display** n [C] act of being displayed; something displayed.

displease /dɪsˈpliːz/ v [T] annoy. **displeasure** /dɪsˈpleʒə(r)/ n [U] annoyance.

dispose /dɪˈspəʊz/ v (phr v) **dispose of sth** get rid of sth unwanted. **disposable** /dɪˈspəʊzəbl/ adj 1 that can be thrown away after use: ~ nappies. 2 that can be used: ~ income. **disposal** n 1 [U] action of getting rid of sth. 2 (idm) **at one's disposal** available for use as one wants. **disposed** adj 1 (to) willing to do sth. 2 (idm) **well/favourably disposed towards sb/sth** thinking that sb/sth is good. **disposition** /ˌdɪspəˈzɪʃn/ n [U] (fml) person's natural character.

dispossess /ˌdɪspəˈzes/ v [T] (of) take away property, etc from (sb).

disproportionate /ˌdɪsprəˈpɔːʃənət/ adj too large or too small. **disproportionately** adv.

disprove /ˌdɪsˈpruːv/ v [T] show (sth) to be wrong or false.

dispute /dɪˈspjuːt/ n [C, U] disagreement or argument. **dispute** v 1 [T] argue about; question. 2 [I] (with/i) argue; debate.

disqualify /dɪsˈkwɒlɪfaɪ/ v (pt, pp -ied) [T] (from/i) prevent (sb) officially from doing sth. **disqualification** /dɪsˌkwɒlɪfɪˈkeɪʃn/ n [U, C].

disquiet /dɪsˈkwaɪət/ n [U] (fml) worry or anxiety. **disquiet** v [T] (fml) make anxious.

disregard /ˌdɪsrɪˈgɑːd/ v [T] pay no attention to; ignore. **disregard** n [U] lack of attention or care.

disrepair /ˌdɪsrɪˈpeə(r)/ n [U] state of needing repair.

disrepute /ˌdɪsrɪˈpjuːt/ n [U] state of having lost the good opinion of people: bring the sport into ~. **disreputable** /dɪsˈrepjʊtəbl/ adj not respectable: a disreputable nightclub.

disrespect /ˌdɪsrɪˈspekt/ n [U] lack of respect; rudeness. **disrespectful** adj.

disrupt /dɪsˈrʌpt/ v [T] cause disorder in (sth): ~ a public meeting. **disruption** /-ˈrʌpʃn/ n [C, U]. **disruptive** adj causing disruption: a ~ive influence.

dissatisfy /dɪˈsætɪsfaɪ/ v (pt, pp -ied) [T] fail to satisfy; make unhappy. **dissatisfaction** /ˌdɪˌsætɪsˈfækʃn/ n [U]. **dissatisfied** adj.

dissect /dɪˈsekt/ v [T] cut up (a dead body) to examine it. **dissection** /dɪˈsekʃn/ n [C, U].

disseminate /dɪˈsemɪneɪt/ v [T] (fml) spread (information) widely.

dissemination /dɪˌsemɪˈneɪʃn/ n [U].

dissension /dɪˈsenʃn/ n [U, C] disagreement or quarrel.

dissent /dɪˈsent/ n [U] disagreement. **dissent** v [I] (from/i) (fml) disagree with an opinion. **dissenter** n [C] person who dissents.

dissertation /ˌdɪsəˈteɪʃn/ n [C] (on/i) long written account.

disservice /dɪsˈsɜːvɪs/ n [C, usu sing] harmful action: do sb a ~.

dissident /ˈdɪsɪdənt/ n [C] person who disagrees with official government views.

dissimilar /dɪˈsɪmɪlə(r)/ adj not similar. **dissimilarity** /ˌdɪsɪmɪˈlærəti/ n [U, C] (pl -ies).

dissipated /ˈdɪsɪpeɪtɪd/ adj wasting one's life on foolish harmful pleasures.

dissociate /dɪˈsəʊʃɪeɪt/ (also **disassociate** /ˌdɪsəˈsəʊʃɪeɪt/) v [T] 1 ~ **oneself from** say that one does not support sb/sth. 2 A from B/i separate two things in one's mind. **dissociation** /dɪˌsəʊsɪˈeɪʃn/ n [U].

dissolve /dɪˈzɒlv/ v 1 [I] (of a solid) become liquid: Salt ~s in water. 2 [T] make (a solid) become liquid: D~ the salt in water. 3 [T] bring to an end: ~ parliament. 4 (idm) **dissolve into tears/laughter** begin to cry/laugh without being able to control one's feelings.

dissolution /ˌdɪsəˈluːʃn/ n [U] breaking up of a marriage, formal meeting, etc.

dissuade /dɪˈsweɪd/ v [T] (from/i) advise sb not to do sth: ~ sb from leaving.

distance /ˈdɪstəns/ n 1 [C, U] amount of space between two points or places or time. 2 [U] being far away in space or time. 3 [C, U] distant place or point: listen from a ~. 4 (idm) **go the distance** continue to run, fight, etc until the end of the contest. **distance** v [T] (from/i) separate (oneself) from sb/sth in one's mind or feelings.

distant /ˈdɪstənt/ adj 1 far away. 2 (of people) not closely related: a ~ cousin. 3 unfriendly. **distantly** adv.

distaste /dɪsˈteɪst/ n [U, sing] dislike. **distasteful** adj unpleasant.

distil (US distill) /dɪˈstɪl/ v (-ll-) [T] 1 (from/i) (a) change a (liquid) to gas by heating, and then cool the gas and collect drops of liquid. (b) make (whisky, etc) in this way. 2 (from/i) derive (sth) from sth: advice ~ led from years of experience. **distillation** /ˌdɪstɪˈleɪʃn/ n [U]. **distillery** n [C] place where whisky, etc is distilled.

distinct /dɪ'stɪŋkt/ adj 1 clearly different; separate. 2 easily heard or seen. **distinctly** adv.

distinction /dɪ'stɪŋkʃn/ n 1 [C, U] (between A and B) difference between two things. 2 [U] excellence. 3 [C] mark of honour or high achievement.

distinctive /dɪ'stɪŋktɪv/ adj marking sth as clearly different. **distinctively** adv.

distinguish /dɪ'stɪŋgwɪʃ/ v 1 [I, T] (between) A and B; A (from B)| see or understand the difference between two things. 2 [T] A (from B)| (a) show the difference between two things. (b) be a particular mark that makes sth/sb different. 3 [T] be able to see or hear (sth). 4 ~ oneself do sth very well. **distinguishable** adj. **distinguished** adj successful and famous.

distort /dɪ'stɔːt/ v [T] 1 pull or twist (sth) out of its usual shape. 2 give a false account of: ~ the facts. **distortion** /dɪ'stɔːʃn/ n [C, U].

distract /dɪ'strækt/ v [T] take (one's attention) away from sth. **distracted** adj unable to think properly because one is worried. **distraction** /dɪ'strækʃn/ n 1 [C, U] something, eg noise, that distracts sb's attention. 2 [C] something that amuses or entertains.

distraught /dɪ'strɔːt/ adj very upset and worried.

distress /dɪ'stres/ n [U] 1 great pain or sorrow. 2 state of danger: a ship in ~. **distress** v [T] cause distress(1) to. **distressing** adj causing distress(1): ~ ing news.

distribute /dɪ'strɪbjuːt/ v [T] 1 give out. 2 spread or scatter. **distribution** /ˌdɪstrɪ'bjuːʃn/ n [C, U]. **distributor** /dɪ'strɪbjʊtə(r)/ n [C] 1 person that supplies goods to shops, etc. 2 device that sends electric current to the sparking-plugs in an engine.

district /'dɪstrɪkt/ n [C] part of a town or country.

distrust /dɪs'trʌst/ v [T] have no trust in (sb). **distrust** n [U, sing] lack of trust; suspicion. **distrustful** adj.

disturb /dɪs'tɜːb/ v [T] 1 break the peace or order of; interrupt. 2 worry. **disturbance** n 1 [C, U] act of disturbing sb/sth. 2 [C] violent public disorder. **disturbed** adj emotionally or mentally ill.

disunity /dɪs'juːnəti/ n [U] (fml) lack of unity; disagreement.

disuse /dɪs'juːs/ n [U] state of not being used: fall into ~. **disused** /-'juːzd/ adj.

ditch /dɪtʃ/ n [C] narrow channel

dug to hold or carry off water. **ditch** v [T] (infml) end a relationship with (sb): She ~ed her boyfriend.

dither /'dɪðə(r)/ v [I] be unable to decide what to do.

ditto /'dɪtəʊ/ n [C] (pl ~s) (used in lists to avoid repeating a word, etc) the same thing again.

ditty /'dɪti/ n [C] (pl -ies) short simple song.

divan /dɪ'væn; US 'daɪvæn/ n [C] long low seat without a back.

dive /daɪv/ v (pt, pp dived; US also pt dove /dəʊv/) [I] 1 go head first into water. 2 go under water. 3 (of an aircraft) go steeply downwards. 4 move quickly in the direction that is mentioned: ~ under the bed. 5 (phr v) dive in start to do sth with great enthusiasm. **dive** n [C] 1 act of diving into water. 2 bar or club that is not thought respectable. **diver** n [C] person who dives, esp one who works under water. **'diving-board** n [C] board from which people dive into a swimming-pool.

diverge /daɪ'vɜːdʒ/ v [I] become further apart; differ. **divergence** /-dʒəns/ n [C, U]. **divergent** /-dʒənt/ adj.

diverse /daɪ'vɜːs/ adj of different kinds: ~ interests. **diversity** n [U, sing] difference; variety.

diversify /daɪ'vɜːsɪfaɪ/ v (pt, pp -ied) [I, T] widen the range of (goods, interests, etc). **diversification** /daɪˌvɜːsɪfɪ'keɪʃn/ n [U].

diversion /daɪ'vɜːʃn; US -'vɜːrʒn/ n 1 [C] something that draws attention away from sth that one does not want to be noticed: create a ~. 2 [C] different route for traffic. 3 [U, C] change of direction: the ~ of a river. **diversionary** adj: ~ary tactics.

divert /daɪ'vɜːt/ v [T] (from, to)| 1 turn sth from one course, use, etc to another: ~ traffic ○ ~ money to education. 2 entertain.

divide /dɪ'vaɪd/ v 1 [I, T] break into parts; separate. 2 [T] cause (people) to disagree. 3 [T] by| find out how many times one number is contained in another: 30 ~d by 6 is 5. **divide** n [C] something that divides. **dividers** n [pl] instrument for measuring lines, angles, etc.

dividend /'dɪvɪdend/ n [C] part of the profits paid to people who have shares in a company.

divine[1] /dɪ'vaɪn/ adj 1 of or like God or a god. 2 (infml) wonderful. **divinely** adv. **divinity** /dɪ'vɪnəti/ n 1 [U] study of religion. 2 [U] quality of being divine(1). 3 [C] god or goddess.

divine² /dɪ'vaɪn/ v [T] (fml) discover by guessing.

divisible /dɪ'vɪzəbl/ adj that can be divided: 4 is ~ by 2.

division /dɪ'vɪʒn/ n 1 [U] dividing or being divided. 2 [C] one of the parts into which sth is divided. 3 [C] big part of an organization: the 'sales division. 4 [C, U] disagreement. 5 [U] process of dividing numbers. 6 [C] (esp Brit) (in Parliament) vote. 7 [C] group of sports teams. **divisional** /-ʒənl/ adj.

divisive /dɪ'vaɪsɪv/ adj causing disagreement.

divorce /dɪ'vɔːs/ n 1 [C, U] legal ending of a marriage. 2 [C] ending of a connection; separation. **divorce** v 1 [T] end a marriage by law: ~ sb ○ get ~d. 2 [T] /from// separate sth from sth else. **divorcee** /dɪˌvɔː'siː/ n [C] divorced person.

divulge /daɪ'vʌldʒ/ v [T] make known (a secret).

D I Y /ˌdiː aɪ 'waɪ/ n [U] do it yourself; doing house repairs, decorating rooms, etc oneself.

dizzy /'dɪzi/ adj (-ier, -iest) 1 (of a person) feeling as if everything is turning round and round; unable to balance. 2 of or causing this feeling: ~ heights. **dizzily** adv. **dizziness** n [U].

DJ /ˌdiː 'dʒeɪ/ abbr (infml) 1 dinner-jacket. 2 disc jockey.

do¹ /duː/ aux v (neg do not, contracted form don't /dəʊnt/; 3rd pers sing pres tense does /dʌz/; strong form dʌz/, neg does not, contracted form doesn't /'dʌznt/; pt did /dɪd/, neg did not, contracted form didn't /'dɪdnt/; pp done /dʌn/) 1 (a) (used in front of a verb to form negative sentences and questions): I don't like fish. ○ Do you believe him? (b) (used at the end of a sentence to form a question): You live in Hastings, don't you? 2 (used for emphasizing that a verb is positive): He does look tired. ○ 'Do shut up! 3 (used to avoid repeating a verb): She runs faster than I do.

do² /duː/ v (3rd pers sing pres tense does /dʌz/, pt did /dɪd/, pp done /dʌn/) 1 [T] perform (an action): What are you doing now? 2 [T] produce or make; work at: do a drawing ○ do science (ie study) at school. 3 [T] find the answer to; solve: do a puzzle. 4 [T] arrange, tidy, clean, etc (sth): do one's hair ○ do the cooking. 5 [I, T] behave; perform: do as you please ○ do one's best. 6 [T] travel (a distance): How many miles did you do? 7 [I, T]

(for)// be (good) enough for (sb): 'Can you lend me some money?' 'Yes—will £10 do (you)?' 8 [I] progress: She's doing well at school. 9 [T] cheat or swindle (sb): You've been done! 10 (idm) be/have to do with sb/sth be connected with sb/sth: The letter is to do with the trip to France. ˌhow do you 'do? (used when being introduced to sb). what do you do (for a living)? what is your job? 11 (phr v) do away with oneself/sb kill oneself/sb. do away with sth get rid of sth; abolish. do sb/sth down (infml) make sb/sth seem unimportant. do for sb do housework for sb. do for sb/sth (infml) (usu passive) ruin or kill sb/sth: If we can't borrow the money, we're done for. do for sb (infml) manage to get sth: What will you do for lunch? do sb 'in (infml) (a) kill sb. (b) tire sb completely: You look done in! do sth out (infml) make (a room, cupboard, etc) clean and tidy. do sb out of sth (infml) stop sb having sth, esp by cheating. do sb 'over (infml) hit and hurt sb very badly. do (sth) up fasten or be fastened. do sth up decorate or modernize a room, building, etc. do with sth need sth: I could do with a cold drink! do sth with oneself use one's time doing sth: What does Simon do with himself at weekends? do sth with sth put, hide, use, etc sth: What have you done with (ie Where have you put) my keys? do without (sb/sth) manage, work, exist, etc without sth. sth. do'gooder n [C] (often derog) person who tries too hard to do good things for others.

do³ /duː/ n [C] (pl dos or do's /duːz/) 1 (Brit infml) party. 2 (idm) **do's and don'ts** /ˌduːzən'dəʊnts/ rules.

docile /'dəʊsaɪl; US 'dɒsl/ adj quiet and easily controlled.

dock¹ /dɒk/ n [C] place where ships are loaded and unloaded, or repaired. **dock** v 1 [I, T] (of a ship) come or bring into a dock. 2 [I] (of two spacecraft) join together in space. **docker** n [C] person who loads and unloads ships. **'dockland** n [U, C] district near a dock-yard. **'dockyard** [n [C] place where ships are built or repaired.

dock² /dɒk/ n [C] part of a law-court where the prisoner stands.

dock³ /dɒk/ v [T] 1 cut short (an animal's tail). 2 take away (part of sb's wages).

doctor /'dɒktə(r)/ n [C] 1 person who has been trained in medicine.

2 person who has received the highest university degree. **doctor** *v* [T] **1** change (sth) in order to deceive people: ~ *the figures.* **2** make (a cat or dog) unable to breed. **doctorate** /-tərət/ *n* [C] degree of a doctor(2).

doctrinaire /ˌdɒktrɪ'neə(r)/ *adj* (*fml derog*) strictly applying a theory without thinking about practical problems: ~ *attitudes.*

doctrine /'dɒktrɪn/ *n* [C, U] set of teachings; belief. **doctrinal** /dɒk'traɪnl; *US* 'dɒktrɪnl/ *adj.*

document /'dɒkjʊmənt/ *n* [C] paper giving information, evidence, etc. **document** /-ment/ *v* [T] prove or support with documents; record. **documentation** /ˌdɒkjʊmen'teɪʃn/ *n* [U] documents used as evidence or proof.

documentary /ˌdɒkjʊ'mentri/ *n* [C] (*pl* -ies) film, radio or television programme that gives information and facts. **documentary** *adj* of documents: ~ *evidence.*

dodge /dɒdʒ/ *v* [I, T] move suddenly to one side in order to avoid (sb/sth). **2** [T] avoid (sth) by dishonesty. **dodge** *n* [C] **1** sudden movement to avoid sb/sth. **2** clever trick. **dodger** *n* [C] person who dodges(2). **dodgy** /'dɒdʒɪ/ *adj* (*infml*) dishonest; risky.

doe /dəʊ/ *n* [C] adult female deer, reindeer, rabbit or hare.

does ⇨ DO[1,2].

doesn't does not. ⇨ DO[1].

dog[1] /dɒg; *US* dɔːg/ *n* [C] **1** (a) common animal kept by people for hunting, guarding, etc or as a pet. (b) male of this animal. **2** the dogs [pl] (betting on the races) of greyhound racing. **3** (idm) **a ˌdog in the ˈmanger** person who stops others enjoying sth even though he/she does not need or want it. **a dog's life** a very unhappy life. **go to the ˈdogs** (of a country or organization) lose its good qualities. **ˈdog-collar** *n* [C] **1** collar for a dog. **2** (*infml*) stiff white collar worn by a clergyman. **ˈdog-eared** *adj* (of a book) having the corners of many pages turned down with use. **ˈdoghouse** *n* [C] **1** (*US*) kennel. **2** (idm) **in the doghouse** (*infml*) in disgrace. **dog-tired** *adj* (*infml*) very tired.

dog[2] /dɒg; *US* dɔːg/ *v* (-gg-) [T] follow (sb/sth) closely: (*fig*) ~ *ged by illness.*

dogged /'dɒgɪd/ *adj* not giving up easily; determined. **doggedly** *adv.*

dogma /'dɒgmə; *US* 'dɔːgmə/ *n* [C, U] (esp religious) belief(s) to be accepted without questioning.

dogmatic /dɒg'mætɪk; *US* dɔːg-/ *adj* giving opinions forcefully, without thinking that different opinions might be right. **dogmatically** /-klɪ/ *adv.*

do-gooder ⇨ DO[2].

dogsbody /'dɒgzbɒdɪ; *US* 'dɔːg-/ *n* [C] (*pl* -ies) (*Brit infml*) person who does boring and unpleasant jobs for others.

doldrums /'dɒldrəmz/ *n* (idm) **in the ˈdoldrums 1** sad; depressed. **2** not making progress.

dole /dəʊl/ *n* the dole [sing] (*Brit infml*) money paid regularly by the government to people without jobs: *be/go on the ~,* ie receive such money. **dole** *v* (phr v) **dole sth out** distribute (food, money, etc) in small amounts.

doleful /'dəʊlfl/ *adj* sad; unhappy. **dolefully** *adv.*

doll /dɒl; *US* dɔːl/ *n* [C] model of a baby or a person, used as a child's toy. **doll** *v* (phr v) **doll oneself up** (*infml*) dress smartly.

dollar /'dɒlə(r)/ *n* [C] **1** unit of money in the USA, Canada, Australia, etc. **2** banknote or coin worth one dollar.

dollop /'dɒləp/ *n* [C] (*infml*) soft shapeless mass of sth, esp food.

dolphin /'dɒlfɪn/ *n* [C] intelligent animal that looks like a large fish and lives in the sea.

domain /də'meɪn/ *n* [C] (*fml*) **1** area of activity or knowledge. **2** area under sb's control.

dome /dəʊm/ *n* [C] round roof with a circular base. **domed** *adj* shaped like a dome.

domestic /də'mestɪk/ *adj* **1** of the home, house or family: ~ *duties.* **2** within a particular country; not foreign: ~ *policies.* **3** (of animals) not wild; kept in a house or on a farm. **domestic** (also **domestic ˈhelp**) *n* [C] person who is paid to do housework. **domesticated** *adj* **1** (of animals) tame. **2** (of people) enjoying housework and home life. **domestic ˈscience** *n* [U] = HOME ECONOMICS (HOME[1]).

dominant /'dɒmɪnənt/ *adj* most important or powerful: *a ~ position.* **dominance** /-nəns/ *n* [U].

dominate /'dɒmɪneɪt/ *v* **1** [I, T] have control or power over (people, events, etc). **2** [T] be the most important thing in. **3** [T] be most noticeable in (an area): *The castle ~s the whole city.* **domination** /ˌdɒmɪ'neɪʃn/ *n* [U].

domineering /ˌdɒmɪ'nɪərɪŋ/ *adj* trying to control other people in an unpleasant way.

dominion /də'mɪnɪən/ *n* **1** [U] (*fml*) authority to rule. **2** [C] land controlled by a ruler.

domino /'dɒmɪnəʊ/ n (pl ~es) 1 [C] small flat piece of wood marked with spots. 2 dominoes (with sing v) game played with dominoes.

don /dɒn/ n [C] (Brit) teacher at a university.

donate /dəʊ'neɪt; US 'dəʊneɪt/ v [T] (to)// give (money, goods, etc) to an organization. **donation** /dəʊ'neɪʃn/ n [C, U].

done[1] pt of DO[1,2].

done[2] /dʌn/ adj 1 finished. 2 (of food) cooked enough. 3 socially correct.

donkey /'dɒŋkɪ/ n [C] 1 animal like a small horse, but with longer ears. 2 (idm) **donkey's years** (infml) a very long time.

donor /'dəʊnə(r)/ n [C] person who gives sth: a blood ~.

don't do not. ⇨ DO[1].

doodle /'du:dl/ v [I] do small drawings while one is thinking about sth else. **doodle** n [C].

doom /du:m/ n [U] unavoidable evil. **doomed** adj (of sth bad) that will certainly happen: be ~ed to die/to failure. **doomsday** /'du:mzdeɪ/ n [sing] end of the world.

door /dɔ:(r)/ n [C] 1 piece of wood, etc used for closing the entrance to a building, room, etc. 2 = DOORWAY. 3 (idm) **door-to-'door** going from one house, then the next house, etc along a street trying to sell goods: a ~-to- 'salesman. **next 'door (to sb/sth)** to/in the next building, room, etc: go next ~ to borrow some milk. **(be) on the 'door** (at a public meeting) (stand) at the door to collect tickets, etc. **out of 'doors** not inside a building; outside. **'doorbell** n [C] bell that is rung by visitors to a house. **'doorstep** n [C] step in front of a door. **'doorway** n [C] opening for a door.

dope /dəʊp/ n (infml) 1 [U] harmful drug. 2 [C] stupid person. **dope** v [T] give dope to. **dopey** (also **dopy**) adj (infml) 1 sleepy, as if drugged. 2 stupid.

dormant /'dɔ:mənt/ adj not active: a ~ volcano.

dormitory /'dɔ:mɪtrɪ; US -'tɔ:rɪ/ n [C] (pl -ies) large bedroom where several people sleep.

dormouse /'dɔ:maʊs/ n [C] (pl **dormice** /'dɔ:maɪs/) small animal like a mouse.

dosage /'dəʊsɪdʒ/ n [C, usu sing] amount of medicine.

dose /dəʊs/ n [C] 1 amount of medicine to be taken at one time. 2 experience of sth unpleasant: a ~ of flu. **dose** v [T] (with)// give (sb/

oneself) a dose of sth.

doss /dɒs/ v (phr v) **doss down** (Brit sl) lie down to sleep, esp not in a proper bed. **'doss-house** n [C] (Brit sl) very cheap lodging-house.

dossier /'dɒsɪeɪ; US also 'dɔ:sɪər/ n [C] set of papers containing information about a person or event.

dot /dɒt/ n [C] 1 small round mark. 2 (idm) **on the dot** at exactly the right moment. **dot** v (-tt-) [T] 1 mark with a dot. 2 (usu passive) put all over (an area); scatter: The sky was ~ted with stars.

dotage /'dəʊtɪdʒ/ n (idm) **in one's dotage** weak in one's mind because of old age.

dote /dəʊt/ v [I] on// show too much fondness for sb/sth: ~ on a child.

dotty /'dɒtɪ/ adj (-ier, -iest) (Brit infml) slightly mad.

double[1] /'dʌbl/ adj 1 twice as much, big, good, etc: Her income is ~ what it was a year ago. 2 having two parts or uses: ~ doors ○ 'Otter' is spelt with a ~ t. 3 made for two people: a ~ bed. **double-'bass** n [C] largest instrument of the violin family. **double 'chin** n [C] fold of fat below the chin. **double-'dealing** n [U] deceitful behaviour. **double-'decker** n [C] bus with two floors. **double 'Dutch** n [U] (Brit infml) talk or writing that one cannot understand.

double[2] /'dʌbl/ adv twice; in two parts: fold a blanket ~. **double-'barrelled** adj (of a gun) having two barrels. **double-'book** v [I, T] reserve (a ticket, hotel room, etc) for more than one person at a time. **double-'breasted** adj (of a coat) made to cross over at the front with two rows of buttons. **double-'check** v [I, T] check (sth) twice. **double-'cross** v [T] (infml) cheat or betray (sb) after winning his/her trust. **double-'edged** adj (fig) (of a comment) having a good meaning and a bad meaning. **double-'glazing** n [U] two layers of glass in a window, to reduce the loss of heat. **double-'jointed** adj (of fingers, arms, etc) having joints that can bend backwards as well as forwards. **double-'quick** adj, adv (infml) very quick(ly).

double[3] /'dʌbl/ n 1 [U] twice the quantity: He's paid ~ for the same job. 2 [C] person who looks exactly like another. 3 **doubles** [pl] game with two players on each side. 4 (idm) **at the double** (infml) quickly.

double[4] /'dʌbl/ v 1 [I, T] become or make twice as much or as many: *the price has* ~*d.* **2** [T] fold to make two layers. **3** (phr v) **double as sb/sth** have ~ as a second job or use. **double back** turn back in the opposite direction. **double (sb) up** (cause sb to) bend the body: *be* ~*d up with laughter.*

doubly /'dʌblɪ/ *adv* (used before an adj) twice as: *make* ~ *sure.*

doubt /daʊt/ *n* **1** [C, U] feeling of uncertainty. **2** (idm) **in doubt** uncertain. **no doubt** very probably. **without doubt** certainly. **doubt** *v* [I, T] feel uncertain about (sth); think that (sth) is not true. **doubtful** *adj* **1** uncertain. **2** unlikely. **doubtless** *adv* almost certainly, probably.

dough /dəʊ/ *n* [U] **1** mixture of flour, water, etc for making bread. **2** (*sl*) money. **'doughnut** *n* [C] small cake, usu ring-shaped, made from sweet dough cooked in fat.

douse (also **dowse**) /daʊs/ *v* **1** throw water over. **2** put out (a light).

dove¹ /dʌv/ *n* [C] **1** kind of pigeon. **2** (*fig*) person in favour of peace. **dovecote** /'dʌvkɒt/, also **'dʌvkaʊt/** *n* [C] small shelter for pigeons and doves.

dove² (*US*) *pt* of DIVE.

dovetail /'dʌvteɪl/ *n* [C] joint for fitting two pieces of wood together. **dovetail** *v* [T] **1** join (two pieces of wood) with a dovetail. **2** [I] (*fig*) fit neatly together.

dowdy /'daʊdɪ/ *adj* (-**ier**, -**iest**) (of people) wearing dull unfashionable clothes.

down¹ /daʊn/ *adv* **1** to or at a lower level: *jump* ~ . **2** to a horizontal position: *knock sb* ~ . **3** (a) away from an important place: *move* ~ *from London.* (b) to the south. **4** (showing a reduction): *calm/settle* ~ ○ *Prices are* ~ . **5** (written) on paper: *Copy/Take this* ~ . **6** (idm) **be/go down with sth** have or catch an illness. **down 'under** (*infml*) in Australia. **down with sb/sth** used for expressing a wish to get rid of sb/sth: *D~ with fascism!* **'down-and-out** *n* [C] very poor person with no job or home. **down-to-'earth** *adj* practical, sensible.

down² /daʊn/ *prep* **1** at or to a lower level on: *roll ~ the hill.* **2** (of flat places) along: *live* ~ *the street.*

down³ /daʊn/ *adj* **1** going downwards: *the* ~ *escalator.* **2** sad: *feel* ~ . **3** not operating: *The computer is* ~ *again.* **down 'payment** *n* [C] part of the total cost of sth paid at the time of buying, with the rest paid later.

down⁴ /daʊn/ *v* [T] **1** swallow

quickly. **2** knock (sb) to the ground.

down⁵ /daʊn/ *n* [U] fine soft feathers or hair: *duck* ~ .

downcast /'daʊnkɑːst; *US* -kæst/ *adj* **1** sad; depressed. **2** (of eyes) looking down.

downfall /'daʊnfɔːl/ *n* [sing] fall from power or success; cause of such a fall.

downgrade /ˌdaʊnˈgreɪd/ *v* [T] make (sth) less important.

down-hearted /ˌdaʊnˈhɑːtɪd/ *adj* sad; depressed.

downhill /ˌdaʊnˈhɪl/ *adv* **1** down a slope. **2** (idm) **go downhill** become worse. **downhill** *adj* going down a slope.

Downing Street /'daʊnɪŋ striːt/ *n* [sing] (a) street in London where the Prime Minister lives. (b) (*fig*) the British Prime Minister or the British Government.

downpour /'daʊnpɔː(r)/ *n* [C] heavy fall of rain.

downright /'daʊnraɪt/ *adj* (of sth bad) complete: *a* ~ *lie.* **downright** *adv* thoroughly: ~ *rude.*

downs /daʊnz/ *n* **the downs** [pl] area of low hills.

downstairs /ˌdaʊnˈsteəz/ *adv*, *adj* to or on a lower floor.

downstream /ˌdaʊnˈstriːm/ *adv* in the direction in which a river flows.

downtown /ˌdaʊnˈtaʊn/ *adv*, *adj* (*esp US*) to or in the centre of a town or city.

downtrodden /'daʊntrɒdn/ *adj* treated badly: ~ *workers.*

downward /'daʊnwəd/ *adj* going down. **downwards** (also **downward**) *adv* going down.

dowry /'daʊərɪ/ *n* [C] (-**ies**) property or money that a bride's father gives to her husband.

dowse = DOUSE.

doz *abbr* dozen.

doze /dəʊz/ *v* [I] sleep lightly. **doze** *n* [C, usu sing] light sleep. **dozy** *adj* (-**ier**, -**iest**) **1** sleepy. **2** (*infml*) stupid.

dozen /'dʌzn/ *n* (*pl* ~ **s** or **dozen** when counting sth) **1** set of twelve. **2** (idm) **talk, etc nineteen to the dozen** talk, etc quickly and continually.

Dr *abbr* **1** Doctor. **2** (in street names) Drive.

drab /dræb/ *adj* (~**ber**, ~**best**) dull; not interesting. **drabness** *n* [U].

draft /drɑːft; *US* dræft/ *n* **1** [C] rough written plan of sth. **2** [C] written order for payment of money by a bank. **3** **the draft** [sing] (*US*) = CALL-UP (CALL¹). **4** [C] (*US*) ⇨ DRAUGHT. **draft** *v* [T] **1** make a draft(1) of. **2** send (people) somewhere for a special task. **3** (*US*) conscript. **draftsman** *n* [C] (*pl* -men) **1** person who drafts new laws. **2** (*US*) = DRAUGHTSMAN (DRAUGHT).

drafty /'dræftɪ/ *adj* = DRAUGHTY (DRAUGHT).

drag /dræg/ *v* (-**gg**-) **1** [T] pull (sth big or heavy) along with effort and difficulty. **2** [I] move slowly and with effort. **3** [T] force sb to go somewhere: *She ~ged herself out of bed.* **4** [I] (of time) pass slowly. **5** [T] search the bottom of (a river, lake, etc) with nets, etc. **6** (idm) **drag one's feet/heels** deliberately do sth slowly. **7** (*phr v*) **drag on** last for what seems a long time. **drag sth out** cause a meeting, etc to last longer than necessary. **drag sth out of sb** force sb to give information. **drag sth up** talk about an unpleasant or embarrassing event. **drag** *n* **1** [sing] (*sl*) boring thing or person. **2** [U] (*sl*) women's clothes worn by a man: *in ~.* **3** [C] (*sl*) act of breathing in smoke from a cigarette, etc. **4** [sing] *on*|| (*infml*) person or thing that makes progress difficult.

dragon /'drægən/ *n* [C] **1** imaginary animal with wings and claws, able to breathe out fire. **2** fierce unpleasant old woman.

drain /dreɪn/ *n* **1** [C] pipe or channel for carrying away water or sewage. **2** (idm) **a drain on sth** something that uses a lot of money, strength, etc: *a ~ on one's resources.* **(go) down the drain** be wasted. **drain** *v* **1** [I, T] (*away/off; from*)|| (cause liquid to) flow away: *The water ~ed away.* ○ *She ~ed the oil from the engine.* **2** [T] empty (a glass). **3** [I, T] become or make dry as liquid flows away: *Leave the dishes to ~.* **4** [T] make weaker or poorer. **drainage** *n* [U] **1** system of drains. **2** act of draining. **'draining-board** (*US* **'drainboard**) *n* [C] surface next to a sink, on which dishes, etc drain. **'drainpipe** *n* [C] pipe for carrying water from the roof of a building to the ground.

drake /dreɪk/ *n* [C] male duck.

drama /'drɑːmə/ *n* **1** [C] play for the theatre, radio or television. **2** [U] plays in general: *Elizabethan ~.* **3** [C, U] series of exciting events. **dramatic** /drə'mætɪk/ *adj* **1** exciting or impressive: *a ~tic development.* **2** of the theatre. **dramatically** /-klɪ/ *adv.* **dramatics** /drə'mætɪks/ *n* [U] **1** (with sing *v*) producing plays or acting. **2** [pl] (*derog*) behaviour that is too

excited. **dramatist** /'dræmətɪst/ *n* [C] writer of plays. **dramatize** /'dræmətaɪz/ *v* [T] **1** make (a story) into a play. **2** make (an event) seem more exciting. **dramatization** /ˌdræmətaɪ'zeɪʃn/ *n* [C, U] = *a ~tization of the novel.*

drank *pt* of DRINK.

drape /dreɪp/ *v* [T] **1** hang (cloth, etc) loosely on sth. **2** (*in/with*)|| cover or decorate (sth) with cloth, etc. **3** *round/over*|| allow (part of one's body) to rest loosely on sth. **drape** *n* [C, usu *pl*] (*US*) curtain. **draper** *n* [C] (*Brit*) shopkeeper who sells cloth. **drapery** *n* (*pl*-ies) **1** [C, U] cloth, etc hanging in loose folds. **2** [U] (*Brit*) draper's trade or goods.

drastic /'dræstɪk/ *adj* severe; very significant: *a ~ shortage of food.* **drastically** /-klɪ/ *adv.*

draught /drɑːft/ (*US* **draft** /dræft/) *n* **1** [C] current of air. **2** [C] amount of liquid swallowed at one time. **3** (idm) **on draught** (of beer, etc) taken from a barrel. **draught** *adj* **1** (of beer, etc) served on draught. **2** (of animals) used for pulling loads. **draughtsman** (*US* **draftsman**) *n* [C] (*pl*-men) **1** person who draws plans of machines, buildings, etc. **2** person who is skilled at drawing. **draughty** *adj* (-ier, -lest) with currents of cold air blowing through.

draughts /drɑːfts/ *n* (with sing *v*) table game for two players using 24 pieces on a board.

draw¹ /drɔː/ *v* (*pt* **drew** /druː/, *pp* ~**n** /drɔːn/) **1** [I, T] make a (picture) with a pen, pencil, etc. **2** [I] move in the direction that is mentioned: *The train drew into the station.* **3** [T] move by pulling: *The horses drew the coach along.* ○ *the curtains,* ie pull them across a window to cover or uncover it. **4** [T] *from/out of*|| take or pull (sth) out of sth: *~ a gun from one's pocket.* **5** [T] attract: *~ a crowd.* **6** [T] obtain from a source: *~ water from a well* ○ *~ one's salary.* **7** [T] make or obtain by study, reasoning, etc: *~ a conclusion/comparison.* **8** [I, T] finish (a game) with neither side winning: *The match was ~n.* **9** [I, T] take in (breath). **10** [I, T] (*from*)|| get or take sth by chance: *~ the winning ticket.* **11** (idm) **draw a 'blank** fail to find sth. **draw lots** ⇨ LOT³. **draw the line at sth** refuse to do sth. **12** (*phr v*) **draw back (from sth/doing sth)** not take action, esp because one is uncertain. **draw in** (of the day) become shorter. **draw sb in, draw sb into sth**

make sb take part in sth, esp when he/she does not want to. **draw on** (of a time) come near. **draw on sth** use sth: ~ *on sb's experience.* **draw out** (of the day) become longer. **draw sb out** encourage sb to talk. **draw sth out** make (eg a discussion) longer than usual. **draw up** (of a vehicle) stop. **draw oneself up** stand up straight. **draw sth up** write out (a list, etc).

draw² /drɔː/ n [C] 1 result of a game in which neither side wins. 2 [usu sing] choosing tickets, etc by chance; lottery or raffle. 3 [usu sing] person or thing that attracts many people.

drawback /'drɔːbæk/ n [C] disadvantage; problem.

drawer /drɔː(r)/ n [C] box-like container that slides in and out of a desk, chest, etc.

drawing /'drɔːɪŋ/ n 1 [C] picture. 2 [U] skill of representing objects, scenes, etc by lines. **'drawing-pin** n [C] short pin with a flat top. **'drawing-room** n [C] (*dated*) room in which guests are received.

drawl /drɔːl/ v [I, T] speak or say (sth) slowly, making the vowels longer. **drawl** n [sing].

drawn pp of DRAW¹.

drawn² /drɔːn/ adj (of a person or his/her face) looking very tired or worried.

dread /dred/ v [T] fear greatly. **dread** n [U] great fear and anxiety. **dreaded** adj greatly feared; terrible. **dreadful** adj very bad; terrible. **dreadfully** adv terribly; very.

dream /driːm/ n 1 [C] thoughts or images experienced in a person's mind during sleep. 2 [C] something that one thinks about a lot but is unlikely to happen: his ~ *of becoming president.* 3 [sing] (*infml*) wonderful person or thing. **dream** v (pt, pp ~t /dremt/ or esp US ~ed) 1 [I, T] have a dream; experience (sth) in a dream. 2 [I, T] imagine (sth). 3 (idm) **not dream of sth/doing sth** not consider doing sth; never do sth: *I wouldn't ~ of allowing you to pay.* 4 (phr v) **dream sth up** think of sth foolish. **dream** adj (*infml*) wonderful: *a ~ house.* **dreamer** n [C] 1 person who dreams. 2 (*derog*) person with impractical ideas. **dreamless** adj (of sleep) without dreams. **dreamlike** adj like a dream; strange and unreal. **dreamy** adj (-ier, -iest) 1 (of a person) with thoughts far away from his/her work, etc. 2 vague; unreal. 3 pleasant and peaceful. **dreamily** adv.

dreary /'drɪərɪ/ adj (-ier, -iest) dull or boring; making one feel depressed. **drearily** /-rəlɪ/ adv. **dreariness** n [U].

dredge /dredʒ/ v 1 [T] clear (a river, etc) using a dredger. 2 (phr v) **dredge sth up** mention sth unpleasant that has been forgotten. **dredger** n [C] boat that can clear mud, etc from the bottom of rivers, canals, etc.

dregs /dregz/ n [pl] 1 little bits of solid matter that sink to the bottom of liquid. 2 (*derog*) worst and most useless part: *the ~ of society.*

drench /drentʃ/ v [T] make completely wet: *We were ~ed in the rain.*

dress¹ /dres/ n 1 [C] one-piece outer garment worn by a woman or girl. 2 [U] clothing: *formal ~.* **'dressmaker** n [C] person, esp a woman, who makes clothes. **'dress rehearsal** n [C] final rehearsal of a play, with costumes, lighting, etc.

dress² /dres/ v 1 [I, T] put clothes on (sb/oneself). 2 [I] put on formal clothes for a special occasion: ~ *for dinner.* 3 [T] decorate: ~ *a shop window.* 4 [T] clean and bandage (a wound). 5 [T] prepare (food) for cooking or eating. 6 (idm) **dressed to 'kill** (*infml*) dressed so as to attract attention, esp from the opposite sex. 7 (phr v) **dress sb down** criticize sb angrily. **dress up** (a) put on one's best clothes. (b) (esp of children) put on unusual clothes for fun.

dresser /'dresə(r)/ n [C] (esp *Brit*) piece of kitchen furniture with shelves for dishes, and cupboards below.

dressing /'dresɪŋ/ n 1 [C, U] bandage for treating a wound. 2 [C, U] sauce for salads. **'dressing-gown** n [C] loose coat worn over pyjamas, etc. **'dressing-table** n [C] table with drawers and a mirror, in a bedroom.

drew pt of DRAW¹.

dribble /'drɪbl/ v 1 [I] allow a liquid to flow slowly from the mouth. 2 [I, T] (cause a liquid) to fall in small drops. 3 [I, T] move a (ball) forward with many short kicks. **dribble** n [C, usu sing].

dried pt, pp of DRY.

drier ⇨ DRY.

drift /drɪft/ v [I] 1 move along in a current of air or water. 2 (of people) live or move aimlessly. **drift** n 1 [U] drifting movement. 2 [C] mass of snow piled up by the wind. 3 [C, U] (*fig*) gradual movement or change. 4 [sing] general meaning: *the ~ of her argument.*

drifter n [C] person who drifts(2).

drill¹ /drɪl/ n [C] tool for making holes. **drill** v [I, T] make (a hole), using a drill.

drill² /drɪl/ n 1 [C] exercise for teaching sth, using repetition: *pronunci'ation* ~ s. 2 [U] method of training soldiers. 3 [C] right way to act in an emergency: *a fire* ~. **drill** v [I, T] train with drills.

drily ⇨ DRY.

drink /drɪŋk/ v (pt **drank** /dræŋk/, pp **drunk** /drʌŋk/) 1 [I, T] take (liquid) into the mouth and swallow it. 2 [I] drink alcohol. 3 (idm) **drink sb's health** (fml) show one's respect for sb, by drinking a toast. **drink like a fish** (infml) drink a lot of alcohol. 4 (phr v) **drink sth in** watch or listen to sth with great interest. **drink to sb/sth** wish sb/sth happiness. **drink** n [C, U] 1 liquid for drinking. 2 alcoholic liquid. **drinkable** adj. **drinker** n [C] person who drinks (usu too much) alcohol.

drip /drɪp/ v (-pp-) [I, T] 1 (allow liquid to) fall in small drops. 2 (idm) **dripping 'wet** very wet. **drip** n [C] 1 series of drops of falling liquid. 2 (medical) device that puts liquid food, etc directly into a patient's veins. 3 (sl) dull weak person. **drip-'dry** adj (of clothes) able to dry easily when hung up to drip. **dripping** n [U] fat from roasted meat.

drive¹ /draɪv/ n (pt **drove** /drəʊv/, pp ~ **n** /'drɪvn/) 1 [I, T] operate and control (a vehicle). 2 [T] take (sb) somewhere in a car, etc. 3 [T] force (animals or people) to move. 4 [T] be the power for (a machine). 5 [T] hit (a ball) with force. 6 [T] force (sth) to go into sth mentioned: ~ *a nail into wood*. 7 [T] force (sb) to be in a certain state: *You're driving me mad!* 8 (idm) **be driving at mean**: *What are you driving at?* **drive a hard 'bargain** not give way easily to another person in a business deal. **'drive-in** n, adj (place) where people can be entertained, served, etc while staying in their cars. **driver** n [C] person who drives a vehicle. **'driving-licence** (US **driver's license**) n [C] official proof that one is allowed to drive(1).

drive² /draɪv/ n 1 [C] journey in a car, van, etc. 2 [C] (US usu **'driveway**) private road leading to a house. 3 [C] hard stroke in golf, tennis, etc. 4 [U] energy. 5 [C] strong need. 6 [C] organized effort; campaign: *an 'export* ~.

drivel /'drɪvl/ n [U] silly nonsense.

drizzle /'drɪzl/ n [U] fine light rain. **drizzle** v [I] (used with *it*) rain in fine drops.

drone /drəʊn/ v 1 [I] make a low humming sound. 2 (phr v) **drone on** speak for a long time in a boring manner. **drone** n 1 [sing] low humming sound. 2 [C] male bee.

drool /druːl/ v [I] 1 let saliva flow from the mouth. 2 (over)|| (infml) foolishly show how much one likes sb/sth.

droop /druːp/ v (-pp-) [I, T] hang or bend downwards because of weakness.

drop¹ /drɒp/ v (-pp-) 1 [I, T] fall or allow (sth) to fall. 2 [I] become less. 3 [T] (off)|| allow (sb) to get out of a car, etc. 4 [T] (from)|| omit (sb) from sth: *He's been* ~ *ped from the team.* 5 [T] (infml) send a (letter) to sb; say casually. 6 [T] stop doing or discussing (sth). 7 (idm) **drop sb a line** write a short letter to sb. 8 (phr v) **drop back** move slowly and so get behind other people. **drop by/in/round, drop in on sb** visit sb informally. **drop off** (a) fall asleep. (b) become less. **drop out (of sth)** (a) leave college, etc without finishing one's course. (b) withdraw from an activity. **'drop-out** n [C] person who drops out (a).

droppings n [pl] solid waste matter from animals and birds.

drop² /drɒp/ n 1 [C] small round mass of liquid. 2 **drops** [pl] liquid medicine taken in drops. 3 [C] small round sweet. 4 [sing] steep or vertical distance: *a* ~ *of 500 metres.* 5 [sing] (fig) decrease: *a* ~ *in prices.* 6 (idm) **at the ,drop of a 'hat** without hesitation.

drought /draʊt/ n [C, U] long period of very dry weather.

drove¹ pt of DRIVE¹.

drove² /drəʊv/ n [C] very large group: ~ *s of visitors.*

drown /draʊn/ v 1 [I, T] (cause to) die in water because one is unable to breathe. 2 [T] (out)|| (of a sound) be louder than another sound and prevent it being heard. 3 (idm) **drown one's 'sorrows** drink alcohol in order to forget one's problems.

drowsy /'draʊzɪ/ adj (-ier, -iest) feeling sleepy. **drowsily** adv. **drowsiness** n [U].

drudge /drʌdʒ/ n [C] person who does hard boring work. **drudgery** /-ərɪ/ n [U] hard boring work.

drug /drʌg/ n [C] 1 substance used as a medicine. 2 substance, eg cocaine or heroin, used for pleasure: *He's on ~s.* **drug** *v* (**-gg-**) [T] **1** add harmful drugs to (food, etc). **2** give drugs to (sb), to make him/her unconscious. **'drug addict** *n* [C] person who cannot stop taking drugs(2). **'drugstore** *n* [C] (*US*) chemist's shop that sells a range of goods and also simple meals.

drum /drʌm/ *n* [C] **1** musical instrument made of skin stretched tightly across a hollow round frame. **2** large round metal container: *an oil ~.* **drum** *v* (**-mm-**) **1** [I] play a drum. **2** [I, T] tap (one's fingers) continuously on a surface. **3** (phr *v*) **drum sth into sb** make sb remember sth by repeating it often. **drum sth up** try hard to get support, customers, etc. **drummer** *n* [C] person who plays a drum. **'drumstick** *n* [C] stick used for beating a drum.

drunk¹ *pp* of DRINK.

drunk² /drʌŋk/ *adj* excited or confused by alcoholic drink. **drunk** (also **drunkard** /-əd/) *n* [C] person who often gets drunk. **drunken** *adj* **1** showing the effects of drink. **2** often drunk. **drunkenly** *adv.* **drunkenness** *n* [U].

dry /draɪ/ *adj* (**drier, driest**) **1** not wet: *a ~ cloth ○ ~ paint ○ ~ weather.* **2** (of wine) not sweet. **3** (of humour) pretending to be serious; ironic. **4** boring; dull: *a ~ speech.* **drier** (also **dryer**) /'draɪə(r)/ *n* [C] machine that dries: *a clothes drier.* **dry** *v* (*pt, pp* **dried**) **1** [I, T] become or make dry. **2** (phr *v*) **dry (sth) out** (cause sth to) become completely dry. **dry up** (a) (of a supply) come to an end. (b) be unable to continue talking because one has forgotten one's words. **dry (sth) up** dry dishes, etc with a cloth after washing them. **dryly** (also **drily**) /'draɪlɪ/ *adv.* **dryness** *n* [U]. **dry 'rot** *n* [U] disease that turns wood to powder.

dual /'djuːəl; *US* 'duːəl/ *adj* having two parts; double. **dual 'carriageway** *n* [C] road divided down the centre by a barrier or grass.

dub /dʌb/ *v* (**-bb-**) [T] **1** give (sb) a particular name. **2** translate the words in (a film) into a different language.

dubious /'djuːbɪəs; *US* 'duː-/ *adj* causing or feeling doubt. **dubiously** *adv.*

duchess /'dʌtʃɪs/ *n* [C] **1** wife or widow of a duke. **2** woman with the same rank as a duke.

duchy /'dʌtʃɪ/ *n* [C] (*pl* **-ies**) land of a duke or duchess.

duck¹ /dʌk/ *n* (*pl* **duck** or **~s**) **1** (a) [C] common water-bird. (b) [C] female of this. (c) [U] its meat. **2** [C] (in cricket) batsman's score of 0.

duck² /dʌk/ *v* **1** [I, T] move (one's head) down quickly. **2** [T] push (sb) under water for a short time. **3** [I, T] (*out of*)) try to avoid a responsibility.

duckling /'dʌklɪŋ/ *n* [C] young duck.

duct /dʌkt/ *n* [C] tube or channel carrying liquids or air.

dud /dʌd/ *n* [C], *adj* (*infml*) (something) that is useless or worthless: *a ~ cheque.*

due /djuː;; *US* duː/ *adj* **1** needing to be paid; owed. **2** arranged or expected: *The train is ~ to arrive)* at 1.30. **3** proper; right. **4** *to*|| because of: *Her success is ~ to hard work.* **due** *adv* (of points of the compass) exactly: *~ east.* **due** *n* **1** [sing] something that should be given to sb by right. **2 dues** [pl] money to be paid, eg for membership of a club.

duel /'djuːəl; *US* 'duːəl/ *n* [C] **1** (formerly) formal fight with guns or swords between two people **2** contest between two people or groups. **duel** *v* (**-ll-**; *US* **-l-**) [I] fight a duel.

duet /dju:'et; *US* du:'et/ *n* [C] piece of music for two players or singers.

duffle-coat (also **duffel-coat**) /'dʌflkəut/ *n* [C] coat made of a heavy cloth, usu with a hood.

dug *pt, pp* of DIG².

dug-out /'dʌgaut/ *n* [C] **1** canoe made by hollowing out a tree trunk. **2** covered shelter made by digging in the ground.

duke /djuːk; *US* duːk/ *n* [C] (title of a) nobleman of the highest rank. **dukedom** /-dəm/ *n* [C] **1** position or rank of a duke. **2** land ruled by a duke.

dull /dʌl/ *adj* **1** not bright or clear. **2** slow in understanding. **3** not exciting; boring. **4** not sharp: *a ~ knife/ache.* **dull** *v* [I, T] become or make dull. **dullness** *n* [U]. **dully** /'dʌl-lɪ/ *adv.*

duly /'djuːlɪ; *US* 'duːlɪ/ *adv* in a correct manner; at the proper time.

dumb /dʌm/ *adj* **1** unable to speak. **2** not willing to say anything. **3** (*infml derog*) stupid. **dumbly** *adv.* **dumbness** *n* [U].

dumbfounded /dʌmˈfaundɪd/

adj so surprised that one cannot say anything.

dummy /'dʌmɪ/ *n* [C] (*pl* **-ies**) **1** object made to look like a real person, used eg for showing clothes in a shop. **2** (*Brit*) rubber object, shaped like a nipple, for a baby to suck. **dummy 'run** *n* [C] practice attempt before the real performance.

dump /dʌmp/ *v* [T] **1** put (sth unwanted) in a place: ~ *rubbish in the river*. **2** put (sth) down carelessly. **3** (*derog*) sell (goods) abroad at a very low price. **dump** *n* [C] **1** place where rubbish may be left. **2** store of military supplies. **3** (*infml derog*) dirty unattractive place. **4** (*idm*) **down in the dumps** unhappy. **'dumper truck** *n* [C] vehicle for carrying earth, etc.

dumpling /'dʌmplɪŋ/ *n* [C] ball of cooked dough, eaten with meat or fruit.

dumpy /'dʌmpɪ/ *adj* (**-ier, -iest**) short and fat.

dunce /dʌns/ *n* [C] (*derog*) person, esp at school, who is slow to learn.

dune /dju:n; *US* du:n/ (*also* **'sand-dune**) *n* [C] long low hill of sand formed by the wind.

dung /dʌŋ/ *n* [U] solid waste matter from animals.

dungarees /,dʌŋgə'ri:z/ *n* [pl] overalls *or* trousers made of cotton cloth.

dungeon /'dʌndʒən/ *n* [C] dark underground prison.

dunk /dʌŋk/ *v* [T] dip (food) into liquid before eating it.

duo /'dju:əʊ; *US* 'du:əʊ/ *n* [C] (*pl* ~**s**) pair of performers.

dupe /dju:p; *US* du:p/ *v* [T] trick or deceive. **dupe** *n* [C] person who is duped.

duplex /'dju:pleks; *US* 'du:-/ *n* [C] (*US*) **1** semi-detached house. **2** flat on two floors.

duplicate¹ /'dju:plɪkət; *US* 'du:pləkeɪt/ *v* [T] make an exact copy of. **duplication** /,dju:plɪ'keɪʃn; *US* ,du:plə'keɪʃn/ *n* [U]. **duplicator** *n* [C] machine that copies documents.

duplicate² /'dju:plɪkət; *US* 'du:pləkət/ *adj* exactly like sth else; identical. **duplicate** *n* [C] **1** something that is exactly like sth else. **2** (*idm*) **in duplicate** as two copies that are exactly the same.

durable /'djʊərəbl; *US* 'dʊ-/ *adj* lasting for a long time. **durables** *n* [pl] goods expected to last for years, eg washing-machines.

duration /dju'reɪʃn; *US* dʊ-/ *n* [U] time during which sth lasts.

duress /dju'res; *US* dʊ-/ *n* [U] threats or force: *under* ~ .

during /'djʊərɪŋ; *US* 'dʊ-/ *prep* **1** through all (a period of time). **2** at a point of time in: *He died* ~ *the night.*

dusk /dʌsk/ *n* [U] time just before night. **dusky** *adj* (**-ier, -iest**) dim; dark-coloured.

dust /dʌst/ *n* [U] fine dry powder of earth or other matter. **dust** *v* [T] **1** remove the dust from (sth) by wiping, etc. **2** sprinkle with powder. **'dustbin** *n* [C] container for household rubbish. **'dust bowl** *n* [C] area that has no vegetation because of drought, etc. **'dust-cart** *n* [C] lorry for collecting rubbish from dustbins. **duster** *n* [C] cloth for removing dust from furniture. **'dust-jacket** *n* [C] loose paper cover for a book. **'dustman** /-mən/ *n* [C] (*pl* **-men**) man who empties dustbins. **dustpan** *n* [C] small flat container into which dust is swept. **dust-sheet** *n* [C] large sheet for covering furniture, to protect it from dust. **dusty** *adj* (**-ier, -iest**) covered with dust.

Dutch /dʌtʃ/ *adj* **1** of the Netherlands (=HOLLAND), its people or their language. **2** (*idm*) **go Dutch (with sb)** share expenses.

duty /'dju:tɪ; *US* 'du:tɪ/ *n* [C, U] (*pl* **-ies**) **1** something that one must do. **2** tax: *customs duties.* **3** (*idm*) **on/off duty** doing/not doing one's regular work. **dutiful** *adj* showing respect and obedience. **dutifully** *adv*. **duty-'free** *adj, adv* (of goods) able to be taken into a country without payment of customs duties.

duvet /'du:veɪ/ *n* [C] large bag filled with soft feathers used as a bed covering.

dwarf /dwɔ:f/ *n* [C] (*pl* ~**s**) person, animal or plant that is much smaller than usual. **dwarf** *v* [T] make (sb/sth) seem small.

dwell /dwel/ *v* (*pt, pp* **dwelt** /dwelt/) **1** [I] (*arch or rhet*) live (in a place). **2** (*phr v*) **dwell on sth** think, speak or write a lot about sth. **dweller** *n* [C] (in compound nouns) person who lives in the place mentioned: *city-* ~*ers.*

dwelling *n* [C] (*fml*) home.

dwindle /'dwɪndl/ *v* [I] become gradually less, fewer or smaller.

dye /daɪ/ *v* (*pres part* ~**ing**) [T] colour (sth) by dipping it in a liquid. **dye** *n* [C, U] substance used to dye cloth, etc. **dyed-in-the-'wool** *adj* totally fixed in one's opinions.

dying ⇨ DIE².

dyke /daɪk/ = DIKE.

dynamic /daɪ'næmɪk/ *adj* **1** of a force that produces power or movement. **2** energetic and forceful. **dynamically** /-klɪ/ adv. **dynamics** n [U] (with sing v) branch of physics dealing with movement and force. **dynamism** /'daɪnəmɪzəm/ n [U] quality of being dynamic(2).

dynamite /'daɪnəmaɪt/ n [U] 1 powerful explosive. 2 (fig) person or thing that is likely to shock or excite. **dynamite** v [T] blow (sth) up with dynamite.

dynamo /'daɪnəməʊ/ n [C] (pl ~s) machine that uses the movement of sth, eg water, to produce electricity.

dynasty /'dɪnəstɪ; US 'daɪ-/ n [C] (pl -ies) series of rulers belonging to the same family.

dysentery /'dɪsəntrɪ; US -terɪ/ n [U] painful disease of the bowels.

dyslexia /dɪs'leksɪə; US -'lek-/ n [U] abnormal difficulty in reading and spelling. **dyslexic** /-'leksɪk/ n [C], adj (person) with dyslexia.

E e

E, e /iː/ n [C] (pl E's, e's /iːz/) the fifth letter of the English alphabet. '**E number** n [C] code number used for showing a substance added to food.

E abbr 1 (esp on electric plugs) earth. 2 east(ern): E Sussex.

each /iːtʃ/ adj (of two or more) every one considered individually: a ring on ~ finger. each pron every individual member (of a group): ~ of the girls. each adv for every one: They cost £10 each. **each 'other** (used only as the object of a v or as a prep) the other one: Paul and Sue helped ~ other, ie Paul helped Sue and Sue helped Paul.

eager /'iːgə(r)/ adj (for; to)) wanting to have sth or to do sth very much: ~ for success. **eagerly** adv. **eagerness** n [U].

eagle /'iːgl/ n [C] large strong bird that eats small animals. '**eagle-eyed** adj good at noticing small details.

ear¹ /ɪə(r)/ n 1 [C] part of the head on each side of the head used for hearing. 2 [sing] sense of hearing: She has a good ~ for music. 3 (idm) (be) all 'ears (be) listening with great interest. (be) up to one's 'ears in sth (be) very busy with sth. '**earache** n [U, sing] pain inside the ear. '**ear-drum** n [C] tightly stretched skin inside the ear

which vibrates when sounds reach it. '**ear-ring** n [C] piece of jewellery worn at the bottom of the ear. '**earshot** n [U] (idm) out of/within earshot not close/close enough to hear what sb is saying.

ear² /ɪə(r)/ n [C] top part of wheat, barley, etc that contains the seeds.

earl /ɜːl/ n [C] (fem **countess**) (title of a) British nobleman with the rank between a marquis and a viscount. **earldom** n [C] rank or lands of an earl.

early /'ɜːlɪ/ adj, adv (-ier, -iest) 1 near to the beginning: in the ~ morning. 2 before the usual or expected time: The bus arrived ~. 3 (idm) **at the earliest** not before the time mentioned. an '**early bird** (joc) person who gets up or arrives early. early '**closing day** n [C] (Brit) particular day every week on which shops are shut in the afternoons. early '**warning system** n [C] radar stations that give warning when enemy aircraft or missiles are coming.

earmark /'ɪəmɑːk/ v [T] keep for a special purpose: money ~ed for research.

earn /ɜːn/ v 1 [I, T] get (money) by working. 2 [T] gain (sth deserved) because of one's achievements. **earner** n [C]. **earnings** n [pl] money earned.

earnest /'ɜːnɪst/ adj serious; determined. **earnest** n (idm) **in earnest** in a determined way; seriously. **earnestly** adv. **earnestness** n [U].

earth /ɜːθ/ n 1 (usu the **earth**) [sing] this world. 2 [sing] the surface of the world; land. 3 [U] soil. 4 [C] a wild animal's hole. 5 [C, usu sing] (esp Brit) wire for electrical contact with the ground. 6 (idm) **charge, cost, etc the earth** (infml) charge, etc a lot of money. **how, why, etc on 'earth** (infml) (used for emphasis): What on ~ are you doing? **earth** v [T] (Brit) (usu passive) connect (an electrical appliance) with an earth(5). **earthly** adj 1 of this world; not spiritual. 2 (infml) possible: no ~ly use. **earthquake** /'ɜːθkweɪk/ n [C] sudden violent movement of the earth's surface. '**earthworm** n [C] worm that lives in the soil. **earthy** adj 1 of or like soil. 2 not sensitive or refined: an ~y sense of humour.

earthenware /'ɜːθənweə(r)/ n [U] bowls, etc made of baked clay.

ease /iːz/ n [U] 1 lack of difficulty: do sth with ~. 2 comfort. 3 (idm) at (one's) 'ease comfortable and relaxed. **ease** v 1 [I, T] become or make less difficult or painful. 2 [I, T] become or make less intense or severe. 3 [T] move (sb/sth) slowly and carefully: ~ *the injured man out of the car.* 4 (phr v) ,**ease 'off**/ '**up** become less intense or severe.

easel /'i:zl/ *n* [C] wooden frame for supporting a blackboard or a picture.

east /i:st/ *n* [sing] 1 **the east** point on the horizon where the sun rises. 2 **the East** (a) countries of Asia, esp China and Japan. (b) any part of the world to the east of Europe: *the Middle E~.* (c) part of a particular country towards the east. 2 (of winds) from the east. **east** *adj* 1 in or towards the east. 2 (of winds) from the east. **east** *adv* towards the east. **eastbound** /'i:stbaund/ *adj* travelling towards the east. **easterly** /'i:stəli/ *adj, adv* 1 in or towards the east. 2 (of winds) from the east. **eastern** /'i:stən/ (*also* **Eastern**) *adj* of the east part of the world or a particular country. **eastward** /'i:stwəd/ *adj* towards the east. **eastward(s)** *adv.*

Easter /'i:stə(r)/ *n* [U] day when Christians celebrate the resurrection of Christ.

easy /'i:zɪ/ *adj* (**-ier, -iest**) 1 not difficult. 2 free from anxiety, pain or trouble. **easily** /'i:zəlɪ/ *adv* 1 without difficulty. 2 without doubt: *easily the best.* **easy** *adv* (**idm**) **go easy on sb** be less severe with sb. **go easy on sth** not use too much of sth: *Go ~ on the milk.* **take it/things easy** not work too hard. ,**easy 'chair** *n* [C] large comfortable armchair. **easy'going** *adj* not easily annoyed or worried.

eat /i:t/ *v* (*pt* **ate** /et; *US* eɪt/, *pp* ~**en** /'i:tn/) 1 [I, T] put (food) into one's mouth and swallow it. 2 (**idm**) **eat one's heart out** be very sad or troubled. ,**eat one's 'words** admit that one was wrong. 3 (phr v) **eat sth away** destroy sth gradually. **eat into sth** (**a**) destroy or corrode sth. (**b**) use up time, supplies, savings, etc. **eatable** *adj* that can be eaten. **eater** *n* [C] person who eats in a particular way: *a big eater,* ie a person who eats a lot.

eaves /i:vz/ *n* [pl] overhanging edges of a roof.

eavesdrop /'i:vzdrɒp/ *v* (**-pp-**) [I] (*on*)|| listen secretly to a private conversation. **eavesdropper** *n* [C].

ebb /eb/ *v* [I] 1 (of the tide) flow back from the land to the sea. 2 (*fig*) become less or weaker. **ebb** *n* (*usu* **the ebb**) [sing] flowing out of the tide.

ebony /'ebənɪ/ *n* [U] hard black wood. **ebony** *adj* black.

eccentric /ɪk'sentrɪk/ *adj* 1 (of a person or his/her behaviour) unusual; peculiar. 2 (of circles) not having the same centre. **eccentric** *n* [C] eccentric person. **eccentricity** /ˌeksen'trɪsətɪ/ *n* [C, U] (*pl* **-ies**) (example of) eccentric behaviour.

ecclesiastical /ɪˌkli:zɪ'æstɪkl/ *adj* of the Christian Church or its clergymen.

echo /'ekəʊ/ *n* [C] (*pl* ~**es**) sound reflected from a surface. **echo** *v* 1 [I] be sent back as an echo. 2 [T] repeat or agree with (sb's words).

éclair /eɪ'kleə(r), er'kleə(r)/ *n* [C] pastry filled with cream and with chocolate on top.

eclipse /ɪ'klɪps/ *n* [C] 1 (of the sun) blocking of the sun's light by the moon. 2 (of the moon) blocking of the moon's light when the earth's shadow falls on the moon. **eclipse** *v* [T] (*fig*) make (sb/sth) seem less important by comparison.

ecology /ɪ'kɒlədʒɪ/ *n* [U] (study of the) relations of living things to their surroundings. **ecological** /ˌi:kə'lɒdʒɪkl/ *adj.* **ecologist** /ɪ'kɒlədʒɪst/ *n* [C] student of or expert in ecology.

economic /ˌi:kə'nɒmɪk, ˌekə-/ *adj* 1 connected with trade and industry; of economics. 2 profitable. **economical** *adj* careful in using money, time, etc. **economically** /-klɪ/ *adv.*

economics /ˌi:kə'nɒmɪks, ˌekə-/ *n* (with *sing v*) study of the production, distribution and use of goods and wealth. **economist** /ɪ'kɒnəmɪst/ *n* [C] student of or expert in economics.

economize /ɪ'kɒnəmaɪz/ *v* [I] save money; spend less than before.

economy /ɪ'kɒnəmɪ/ *n* (*pl* **-ies**) 1 (*often* **the economy**) [C] economic system of a country. 2 [C, U] (example of) avoidance of waste of money, time, etc. **economy** *adj* cheap: ~ *class air travel.*

ecstasy /'ekstəsɪ/ *n* [U, C] (*pl* **-ies**) feeling of great happiness. **ecstatic** /ɪk'stætɪk/ *adj.* **ecstatically** /-klɪ/ *adv.*

eddy /'edɪ/ *n* [C] (*pl* **-ies**) circular movement of water or air. **eddy** *v* (*pt, pp* **-ied**) [I] move in eddies.

edge /edʒ/ *n* [C] 1 outer limit of an object or surface: *the ~ of the bed.* 2 sharp cutting part of a knife, etc. 3 (**idm**) **have the edge on/over sb/sth** (*infml*) be slightly better than sb/sth. **on 'edge** nervous or tense. **take the edge off sth** make sth weaker. **edge** v 1 [T] supply with a border. 2 [I, T] move slowly in the direction that is mentioned: *She ~ d (her way) along the cliff.* **edging** n [C, U] narrow border. **edgy** adj (infml) nervous.

edible /'edɪbl/ adj that can be eaten.

edit /'edɪt/ v [T] 1 prepare (sb else's writing) for publication. 2 direct the publishing of (a newspaper, magazine, etc). 3 prepare (a film, television programme, etc) by choosing and putting together different parts. **editor** n [C] person who edits a newspaper, book, etc.

edition /ɪ'dɪʃn/ n [C] 1 form in which a book is printed: *a paperback ~.* 2 total number of copies of a book, etc issued at one time.

editorial /ˌedɪ'tɔːrɪəl/ adj of an editor. **editorial** n [C] article in a newspaper giving the editor's opinion.

educate /'edʒukeɪt/ v [T] train the mind and character of (sb); teach. **education** /ˌedʒu'keɪʃn/ n [U] 1 training and instruction. 2 knowledge and character resulting from such training. **educational** /ˌedʒu'keɪʃənl/ adj.

EEC /ˌiː iː 'siː/ abbr European Economic Community (the Common Market).

eel /iːl/ n [C] long fish like a snake.

eerie /'ɪərɪ/ adj (~ r, ~ st) strange and frightening. **eerily** /'ɪərəlɪ/ adv.

effect /ɪ'fekt/ n 1 [C, U] change caused by sb/sth; result. 2 [C] impression produced on a reader, hearer, etc. **effects** [pl] (fml) personal possessions. 4 (idm) **bring/put sth into effect** put sth into use or operation. **in effect** (a) in fact; really. (b) in operation. **take effect** come into operation. **effect** v [T] (fml) make (sth) happen.

effective /ɪ'fektɪv/ adj 1 producing the results that one wants: *the most ~ method.* 2 actual or existing: *the club's ~ membership.* **effectively** adv. **effectiveness** n [U].

effectual /ɪ'fektʃuəl/ adj (fml) producing the results that one wants: *an ~ remedy.*

effeminate /ɪ'femɪnət/ adj (derog) (of a man) like a woman.

effervesce /ˌefə'ves/ v [I] release bubbles of gas. **effervescence** /-'vesns/ n [U] 1 effervescing. 2 lively excited behaviour. **effervescent** /-'vesnt/ adj.

efficient /ɪ'fɪʃnt/ adj 1 able to work well: *an ~ manager.* 2 (of a

machine, etc) producing good results. **efficiency** /-'fɪʃnsɪ/ n [U]. **efficiently** adv.

effigy /'efɪdʒɪ/ n [C] (pl -ies) figure or model of a person.

effort /'efət/ n 1 [U] use of strength: *a waste of time and ~.* 2 [C] attempt: *make an ~ to escape.* **effortless** adj done easily, without effort. **effortlessly** adv.

effrontery /ɪ'frʌntərɪ/ n [U] boldness or rudeness without shame.

effusive /ɪ'fjuːsɪv/ adj showing too much feeling. **effusively** adv.

EFL /ˌiː ef 'el/ abbr English as a Foreign Language.

eg /ˌiː 'dʒiː/ abbr for example.

egg[1] /eg/ n 1 [C] round object with a hard shell, containing a baby bird. 2 [C, U] hen's egg used as food. 3 [C] female reproductive cell. 4 (idm) **put all one's eggs in one 'basket** risk all one's money, time, etc on one single opportunity. **'egg-cup** n [C] small container for a boiled egg. **'egghead** n [C] (infml derog) very intellectual person. **'egg-plant** n [C, U] (esp US) aubergine.

egg[2] /eg/ v (phr v) **egg sb on** encourage sb to do sth.

ego /'egəʊ, 'iːgəʊ/ n [C] (pl ~ s) (often high) opinion of oneself.

egocentric /ˌegəʊ'sentrɪk; US ˌiːg-/ adj thinking only about oneself.

egoism /'egəʊɪzəm; US 'iːg-/ n [U] self-centredness; selfishness. **egoist** /-ɪst/ n [C] self-centred person.

egotism /'egəʊtɪzəm; US 'iːg-/ n [U] practice of talking too much about oneself; selfishness. **egotist** /-tɪst/ n [C] selfish person. **egotistic** /ˌegə'tɪstɪk; US ˌiːg-/ (also **egotistical**) adj.

eiderdown /'aɪdədaʊn/ n [C] thick, warm bed covering.

eight /eɪt/ pron, adj, n [C] 8. **eighth** /eɪtθ/ pron, adj 8th. **eighth** pron, n [C] ⅛.

eighteen /ˌeɪ'tiːn/ pron, adj, n [C] 18. **eighteenth** /ˌeɪ'tiːnθ/ pron, adj 18th. **eighteenth** pron, n [C] ¹⁄₁₈.

eighty /'eɪtɪ/ pron, adj, n [C] (pl -ies) 80. **eightieth** pron, adj 80th. **eightieth** pron, n [C] ¹⁄₈₀.

either /'aɪðə(r), 'iːðər/ adj, pron one or the other of two: *park on ~ side of the road.* **either** adv, conj 1 (used after two negative verbs): *I don't like the red tie and I don't like the blue one ~,* ie I dislike both. 2 **either...or...** (used for showing alternatives): *You can ~ write or phone for the book.*

eject /ɪ'dʒekt/ v [T] (from)) send or throw out. **ejection** /ɪ'dʒekʃn/ n [U]. **ejector seat** n [C] seat that throws the pilot out of an aircraft in an emergency.

eke /iːk/ v (phr v) **eke sth out** make a small supply of sth last as long as possible.

elaborate /ɪˈlæbərət/ adj complicated; very detailed. **elaborate** /ɪˈlæbəreɪt/ v [I, T] (on)// work out or describe (sth) in detail. **elaborately** adv. **elaboration** /ɪˌlæbəˈreɪʃn/ n [U, C].

elapse /ɪˈlæps/ v [I] (fml) (of time) pass.

elastic /ɪˈlæstɪk/ adj **1** able to go back into its original shape after being pulled or pressed. **2** (fig) not fixed: *Our plans are fairly ~.* **elastic** n [U] elastic material. **e,lastic 'band** n [C] thin circular strip of rubber, used to keep papers, etc together. **elasticity** /ˌelæˈstɪsəti, ˌiːl-/ n [U].

elated /ɪˈleɪtɪd/ adj (at/by)// very happy, pleased, etc. **elation** /ɪˈleɪʃn/ n [U].

elbow /ˈelbəʊ/ n [C] (a) joint where the arm bends. (b) part of the sleeve of a coat that covers this. **elbow** v [I] (phr v) **elbow sb aside** push sb to one side with one's elbows. **elbow one's way** force one's way using one's elbows. **'elbow-grease** n [U] (infml) hard work with the hands. **'elbow-room** n [U] (infml) space to move or work freely.

elder[1] /ˈeldə(r)/ adj (of two members of a family) older: *my ~ brother.* **elder** n **1** my, etc elder [sing] person older than me, etc. **2** [C] person of greater age and authority. **3** [C] officer in some Christian churches. **elderly** adj rather old. **,elder 'statesman** n [C] old and respected politician.

elder[2] /ˈeldə(r)/ n [C] small tree with white flowers and red or black berries.

eldest /ˈeldɪst/ adj, n [C] (of three or more people) oldest (person).

elect /ɪˈlekt/ v [T] **1** choose (sb) by voting. **2** (fml) decide: *They ~ed to stay.* **elect** adj (fml) chosen but not yet doing the job: *the president ~.* **elector** n [C] person with the right to vote. **electoral** /ɪˈlektərəl/ adj of elections. **electorate** /ɪˈlektərət/ n [C, also sing with pl v] all the electors.

election /ɪˈlekʃn/ n [C, U] choosing representatives by voting.

electric /ɪˈlektrɪk/ adj **1** worked by or producing electricity: *an ~ fire.* **2** (fig) exciting. **electrical** adj worked by or concerned with electricity. **electrically** /-klɪ/ adv. **the e,lectric 'chair** n [sing] (esp in the US) chair in which sb is elec-

trocuted. **e,lectric 'shock** n [C] sudden pain caused by electricity passing through one's body.

electrician /ɪˌlekˈtrɪʃn/ n [C] person whose job is to fit and repair electrical equipment.

electricity /ɪˌlekˈtrɪsəti/ n [U] **1** form of energy used for heating, lighting, driving machines, etc. **2** supply of such energy: *Don't waste ~.*

electrify /ɪˈlektrɪfaɪ/ v (pt, pp -ied) [T] **1** provide with electricity. **2** (fig) excite suddenly.

electrocute /ɪˈlektrəkjuːt/ v [T] kill (sb) using an electric current. **electrocution** /ɪˌlektrəˈkjuːʃn/ n [C].

electrode /ɪˈlektrəʊd/ n [C] point by which an electric current enters or leaves a battery, etc.

electron /ɪˈlektrɒn/ n [C] tiny particle of matter inside an atom, with a negative electric charge. **electronic** /ˌɪlekˈtrɒnɪk/ adj **1** produced or operated by a flow of electrons: *an ~ calculator.* **2** concerned with electronic equipment, eg computers. **electronically** /-klɪ/ adv. **electronics** /ˌɪlekˈtrɒnɪks/ n (with sing v) science and development of electronic devices.

elegant /ˈelɪgənt/ adj showing good taste; graceful. **elegance** /-gəns/ n [U]. **elegantly** adv.

element /ˈelɪmənt/ n **1** [C] (in/ of)// part of a whole: *Justice is only one ~ in good government.* **2** [C, usu sing] small amount: *an ~ of truth in their story.* **3** [C] chemical substance that cannot be divided into simpler substances. **4 the elements** [pl] forces of nature; bad weather. **5 elements** [pl] basic principles of a subject. **6** [C] part of an electric kettle, etc that gives out heat. **7** (idm) **in/out of one's 'element** doing/not doing what one is good at and enjoys.

elementary /ˌelɪˈmentrɪ/ adj **1** of the basic and first stages of sth: *~ maths.* **2** simple; not advanced: *an ~ question.* **ele'mentary ,school** n [C] (US) school for children aged about 5 to12.

elephant /ˈelɪfənt/ n [C] very large animal with four feet, tusks and a trunk.

elevate /ˈelɪveɪt/ v [T] (fml) **1** lift up; raise. **2** improve (the mind or morals).

elevation /ˌelɪˈveɪʃn/ n **1** [sing] act of elevating. **2** [C] height above sea-level. **3** [C] drawing of one side of a building.

elevator /ˈelɪveɪtə(r)/ n [C] **1** (US) lift. **2** machine for moving grain, goods, etc from one floor of a building to another.

eleven /ɪ'levn/ *pron, adj, n* [C] 11. **elevenses** /-zɪz/ *n* [U] (with sing v) (*Brit infml*) a mid-morning snack, often coffee and biscuits. **eleventh** /ɪ'levnθ/ *pron, adj* 11th. **eleventh** *pron, n* [C] ⚹.

elf /elf/ *n* [C] (*pl* **elves** /elvz/) small mischievous fairy.

elicit /ɪ'lɪsɪt/ *v* [T] (*from*)// (*fml*) get (information, etc) from sb.

eligible /'elɪdʒəbl/ *adj* (*for; to*)// suitable; having the right qualifications: ~ *for a job.* **eligibility** /,elɪdʒə'bɪlɪtɪ/ *n* [U].

eliminate /ɪ'lɪmɪneɪt/ *v* [T] remove completely. **elimination** /ɪ,lɪmɪ'neɪʃn/ *n* [U].

élite /eɪ'liːt/ *n* [C] group of powerful important people in society. **élitism** /-ɪzəm/ *n* [U] (often *derog*) (belief in a) system that aims to develop an élite. **élitist** /-tɪst/ *n* [C], *adj.*

elk /elk/ *n* [C] very large deer.

ellipse /ɪ'lɪps/ *n* [C] regular oval. **elliptical** /ɪ'lɪptɪkl/ *adj.*

elm /elm/ *n* (**a**) [C] (also **elm tree**) tall tree with broad leaves. (**b**) [U] its hard heavy wood.

elocution /,elə'kjuːʃn/ *n* [U] art of speaking clearly.

elongate /'iːlɒŋgeɪt; *US* ɪ'lɔːŋ-/ *v* [T] make longer.

elope /ɪ'ləʊp/ *v* [I] run away secretly to get married. **elopement** *n* [C, U].

eloquence /'eləkwəns/ *n* [U] skilful use of language to express oneself or to persuade others. **eloquent** /-ənt/ *adj.* **eloquently** *adv.*

else /els/ *adv* 1 in addition; apart from (that already mentioned): *Have you anything ~ to do?* ○ *We went to the cinema and nowhere ~,* ie to no other place. 2 (idm) **or else** otherwise; if not: *Run or ~ you'll be late.* **elsewhere** /,els'weə(r); *US* -'hweər/ *adv* in, at or to some other place.

ELT /,iː el 'tiː/ *abbr* English Language Teaching.

elucidate /ɪ'luːsɪdeɪt/ *v* [T] (*fml*) make (sth) clear; explain. **elucidation** /ɪ,luːsɪ'deɪʃn/ *n* [U].

elude /ɪ'luːd/ *v* [T] 1 escape from (sb/sth); avoid. 2 (of a fact, name, etc) be difficult for (sb) to remember. **elusive** /ɪ'luːsɪv/ *adj* hard to find, describe or remember.

elves *pl* of **elf**.

emaciated /ɪ'meɪsɪeɪtɪd/ *adj* very thin and weak. **emaciation** /ɪ,meɪsɪ'eɪʃn/ *n* [U].

emanate /'emaneɪt/ *v* [I] *from*// (*fml*) come or flow from sb/sth.

emancipate /ɪ'mænsɪpeɪt/ *v* [T] set (sb) free, esp politically or socially. **emancipation** /ɪ,mænsɪ'peɪʃn/ *n* [U].

embalm /ɪm'bɑːm; *US* also -'bɑːlm/ *v* [T] preserve (a dead body) with chemicals, etc.

embankment /ɪm'bæŋkmənt/ *n* [C] wall of earth, etc that holds back water or supports a railway or road.

embargo /ɪm'bɑːgəʊ/ *n* [C] (*pl* ~ es /-gəʊz/) (*on*)// official order stopping trade. **embargo** *v* (*pt, pp* ~ ed /-gəʊd/) [T] put an embargo on.

embark /ɪm'bɑːk/ *v* 1 [I] go on board a ship. 2 (phr v) **embark on/upon sth** start sth new or difficult. **embarkation** /,embɑː'keɪʃn/ *n* [U, C].

embarrass /ɪm'bærəs/ *v* [T] make (sb) feel self-conscious, ashamed or awkward: *His smile ~ed her.* **embarrassing** *adj*: an *~ ing mistake.* **embarrassingly** *adv.* **embarrassment** *n* [U, C].

embassy /'embəsɪ/ *n* [C] (*pl* -ies) office of an ambassador and his/ her staff.

embed /ɪm'bed/ *v* (-dd-) [T] (*in*)// (usu passive) fix (sth) firmly in a surrounding mass.

embellish /ɪm'belɪʃ/ *v* [T] 1 (*with*)// (usu passive) make (sth) attractive by adding decorations. 1 add details to (a story) to make it more interesting. **embellishment** *n* [C, U].

ember /'embə(r)/ *n* [C, usu pl] piece of hot coal, etc in a dying fire.

embezzle /ɪm'bezl/ *v* [I, T] use (money placed in one's care) illegally to benefit oneself.

embitter /ɪm'bɪtə(r)/ *v* [T] (usu passive) make (sb) feel hate, envy and anger.

emblem /'embləm/ *n* [C] design or symbol that represents sth: *The dove is an ~ of peace.*

embody /ɪm'bɒdɪ/ *v* (*pt, pp* -ied) [T] (*in*)// (*fml*) express (an idea or feature); include. **embodiment** *n* [sing]: *She is the embodiment of honesty.*

emboss /ɪm'bɒs; *US* -'bɔːs/ *adj* 1 (of a surface) with a raised design. 2 (of a design) raised from a surface.

embrace /ɪm'breɪs/ *v* [I, T] take (sb) into one's arms as a sign of affection. 2 [T] (*fml*) accept (an idea, religion) willingly. 3 [T] (*fml*) include. **embrace** *n* [C] act of embracing(1): *a loving ~.*

embroider /ɪm'brɔɪdə(r)/ *v* [I, T] decorate (cloth) with needlework. 2 [T] add untrue details to (a

story) to make it more interesting.
embroidery n [C, U].

embryo /'embriəʊ/ n [C] (pl ~s /-əʊz/) 1 young animal before birth. 2 (idm) **in 'embryo** existing but not developed. **embryonic** /,embri'ɒnɪk/ adj.

emerald /'emərəld/ n [C] bright green precious stone. **emerald** adj bright green in colour.

emerge /ɪ'mɜːdʒ/ v [I] 1 come out; come into view. 2 (of facts) become known. **emergence** /-dʒəns/ n [U]. **emergent** /-dʒənt/ adj beginning to develop; new.

emergency /ɪ'mɜːdʒənsɪ/ n [C, U] (pl -ies) serious situation needing quick action.

emigrate /'emɪɡreɪt/ v [I] leave one's own country to go and live in another. **emigrant** /'emɪɡrənt/ n [C] person who emigrates. **emigration** /,emɪ'ɡreɪʃn/ n [U].

eminent /'emɪnənt/ adj (of a person) famous and respected. **eminence** /-əns/ n [U]. **eminently** adv (fml) very; obviously: ~ly qualified.

emir /e'mɪə(r)/ n [C] Muslim ruler. **emirate** /'emɪəreɪt/ n [C] lands, etc ruled by an emir.

emit /ɪ'mɪt/ v (-tt-) [T] (fml) give or send out: ~ heat. **emission** /ɪ'mɪʃn/ n [U, C].

emotion /ɪ'məʊʃn/ n [C, U] strong feeling, eg love, joy, fear or hate. **emotional** /-ʃənl/ adj 1 of the emotions. 2 causing emotion: an ~al speech. 3 showing (too much) emotion. **emotionally** adv.

emotive /ɪ'məʊtɪv/ adj causing strong feelings.

emperor /'empərə(r)/ n [C] ruler of an empire.

emphasis /'emfəsɪs/ n [C, U] (pl -ases /-əsiːz/) 1 special importance given to sth. 2 extra force given to a word or words. **emphasize** /-saɪz/ v [T] put emphasis on (sth). **emphatic** /ɪm'fætɪk/ adj having or using emphasis. **emphatically** /-klɪ/ adv.

empire /'empaɪə(r)/ n [C] group of countries controlled by one ruler or government.

empirical /ɪm'pɪrɪkl/ adj (of knowledge) based on observation and experiment, not on theory.

employ /ɪm'plɔɪ/ v [T] 1 give work to (sb) for payment. 2 (fml) use. **employable** adj capable of being employed. **employee** /,emplɔɪ'iː; also ɪm'plɔɪ-/ n [C] person who is employed. **employer** n [C] person who employs others. **employment** n [U] 1 regular paid work. 2 act of employing people.

embroidery *(second column)*

empower /ɪm'paʊə(r)/ v [T] (fml) (usu passive) give legal power to (sb).

empress /'empris/ n [C] female ruler of an empire; wife of an emperor.

empty /'emptɪ/ adj (-ier, -iest) 1 containing nothing. 2 having no value or meaning: ~ promises. **empties** n [pl] empty bottles, boxes, etc. **emptiness** /-tɪnɪs/ n [U]. **empty** v (pt, pp -ied) [I, T] become or make empty. **,empty-'handed** adj bringing or taking nothing. **,empty-'headed** adj foolish; silly.

emu /'iːmjuː/ n [C] large Australian bird that cannot fly.

emulate /'emjʊleɪt/ v [T] (fml) try to do as well as or better than (sb). **emulation** /,emjʊ'leɪʃn/ n [U].

emulsion /ɪ'mʌlʃn/ n [U, C] creamy medicine or paint containing oil or fat.

enable /ɪ'neɪbl/ v [T] to// make (sb) able to do sth.

enamel /ɪ'næml/ n [U] 1 glass-like covering for metal, pottery, etc. 2 hard covering of the teeth. **enamel** v (-ll-; US also -l-) [T] cover with enamel.

enamoured (US -ored) /ɪ'næməd/ adj of// very fond of sth.

enchant /ɪn'tʃɑːnt/ v [T] delight. **enchanted** /-ɪd/ adj placed under a magic spell. **enchanting** adj delightful. **enchantment** n [U, C].

encircle /ɪn'sɜːkl/ v [T] surround.

enclave /'enkleɪv/ n [C] part of a country surrounded by another.

enclose /ɪn'kləʊz/ v [T] 1 put a wall, etc round. 2 put in an envelope. **enclosure** /ɪn'kləʊʒə(r)/ n [C] 1 area of land that is enclosed. 2 something put in the same envelope as a letter.

encore /'ɒŋkɔː(r)/ interj, n [C] (used by an audience to ask for a) repeated performance.

encounter /ɪn'kaʊntə(r)/ v [T] (fml) meet (sth/sb difficult or unexpected). **encounter** n [C] unexpected (esp unpleasant) meeting.

encourage /ɪn'kʌrɪdʒ/ v [T] give support, confidence or hope to: They ~d him to come. **encouragement** n [U, C]. **encouraging** adj: encouraging news.

encroach /ɪn'krəʊtʃ/ v [I] (on)// (fml) go beyond what is right or natural: ~ on sb's rights.

encyclopedia (also **-paedia**) /ɪn,saɪklə'piːdɪə/ n [C] book(s) giving information on all subjects or on one subject, usu in alphabetical order. **encyclopedic** (also **-paedic**) /-'piːdɪk/ adj complete and thorough.

end /end/ *n* [C] **1** point where sth stops; last part of sth: *at the ~ of the street/war.* **2** small piece that remains: *cigarette ~s.* **3** aim or purpose: *with this ~ in view.* **4** (idm) **in the 'end** at last; finally. **make ends meet** earn just enough money to live. **no 'end of sth** (*infml*) very many or much. **on 'end** (a) upright. (b) continuously: *rain for days on ~.* **put an end to sth** stop sth. *end v* **1** [I, T] come or bring to an end. **2** (phr v) **end up** reach a certain place or state finally. **ending** *n* [C] last part of a word, story, etc. **endless** /-lɪs/ *adj* having no end. **endlessly** *adv.*

endanger /ɪn'deɪndʒə(r)/ *v* [T] cause danger to.

endear /ɪn'dɪə(r)/ *v* [T] *to/ι* (*fml*) make (sb/oneself) liked or loved by sb. **endearment** *n* [C, U] expression of affection.

endeavour (*US -or*) /ɪn'devə(r)/ *v* [I] *to/ι* try to do sth. **endeavour** *n* (*fml*) **1** [C] attempt. **2** [U] hard work; effort.

endemic /en'demɪk/ *adj* (*fml*) (esp of a disease) often found in a particular place.

endorse /ɪn'dɔːs/ *v* [T] **1** approve of or support (sb/sth) publicly. **2** write one's name on the back of (a cheque). **3** (usu passive) record a driving offence on (a driving licence). **endorsement** *n* [C, U].

endow /ɪn'daʊ/ *v* [T] **1** give money that provides a regular income for (a school, etc). **2** (idm) **be endowed with sth** be born with a good quality or ability. **endowment** *n* [C, U].

endure /ɪn'djʊə(r); *US* -'dʊər/ *v* **1** [T] suffer (pain, etc) patiently. **2** [I] continue to exist. **endurance** *n* [U] ability to endure sth. **enduring** *adj* lasting.

enemy /'enəmɪ/ *n* (*pl* -**ies**) **1** [C] person who hates or wants to harm sb. **2 the enemy** [sing] (with sing or pl v) (armed forces of a) country that one is fighting against.

energy /'enədʒɪ/ *n* **1** [U] ability to act or work with strength or enthusiasm. **2 energies** [pl] person's powers available for working. **3** [U] power used for operating machinery, etc: *atomic ~.* **energetic** /ˌenə'dʒetɪk/ *adj* full of or done with energy(1). **energetically** /-klɪ/ *adv.*

enfold /ɪn'fəʊld/ *v* [T] (*fml*) take (sb) into one's arms.

enforce /ɪn'fɔːs/ *v* [T] force people to obey (a law, etc). **enforceable** *adj.* **enforcement** *n* [U].

engage /ɪn'geɪdʒ/ *v* **1** [T] (*fml*) arrange to employ (sb). **2** [T] (*fml*) keep (one's attention, etc). **3** [I, T] (of parts of a machine) lock together. **4** (phr v) **engage (sb) in sth** (make sb) take part or be busy in sth. **engaged** *adj* **1** having agreed to marry. **2** arrangement to meet sb. **3** (*fml*) battle. **engaging** *adj* pleasant; charming.

engine /'endʒɪn/ *n* [C] **1** machine that changes energy into movement. **2** vehicle that pulls a train. **'engine-driver** *n* [C] person who drives a railway engine.

engineer /ˌendʒɪ'nɪə(r)/ *n* [C] **1** person who designs machines, bridges, railways, etc. **2** person who controls an engine. **engineer** *v* [T] arrange (sth), esp secretly or indirectly. **engineering** *n* [U] work or profession of an engineer(1).

English /'ɪŋglɪʃ/ *n* [U] the English language. **2 the English** [pl] English people. **English** *adj* of England, its people or their language. **Englishman** /-mən/ (*pl* -**men**) **Englishwoman** /-**women**) *n* [C] person born in England.

engrave /ɪn'greɪv/ *v* [T] **1** *A on B/ B (with A)/* cut words or a design on a hard surface. **2** (idm) **be engraved on sb's mind, memory**, etc be impressed deeply on sb's mind, etc. **engraver** *n* [C]. **engraving** *n* **1** [C] picture printed from an engraved metal plate. **2** [U] work of an engraver.

engross /ɪn'grəʊs/ *v* [T] (usu passive) take all the attention of (sb): ~ *ed in her work.*

engulf /ɪn'gʌlf/ *v* [T] surround or cause to disappear: *The hotel was ~ed in flames.*

enhance /ɪn'hɑːns; *US* -'hæns/ *v* [T] improve the good qualities of sth). **enhancement** *n* [C, U].

enigma /ɪ'nɪgmə/ *n* [C] mystery. **enigmatic** /ˌenɪg'mætɪk/ *adj.* **enigmatically** /-klɪ/ *adv.*

enjoy /ɪn'dʒɔɪ/ *v* [T] **1** get pleasure from. **2** be fortunate to have (sth): ~ *good health.* **3** ~ **oneself** be happy. **enjoyable** *adj* pleasant. **enjoyably** *adv.* **enjoyment** *n* [C, U].

enlarge /ɪn'lɑːdʒ/ *v* **1** [I, T] become or make larger. **2** (phr v) **enlarge on sth** (*fml*) say or write more about sth. **enlargement** *n* [C, U].

enlighten /ɪn'laɪtn/ *v* [T] give more knowledge or understanding to (sb). **enlightenment** *n* [U].

enlist /ɪn'lɪst/ v 1 [I, T] (make sb) join the armed forces. 2 [T] obtain (sb's help or support). **enlistment** n [C, U].

enormity /ɪ'nɔːmətɪ/ n (pl -ies) 1 [C, U] (fml) great wickedness. 2 [U] very large size.

enormous /ɪ'nɔːməs/ adj very large. **enormously** adv greatly; very.

enough /ɪ'nʌf/ adj, pron as many or as much (of sth) as necessary: Is £100 ~? **enough** adv 1 sufficiently: not old ~. 2 (idm) oddly, strangely, etc enough it is very strange, but....

enquire, enquiry ⇨ INQUIRE, INQUIRY.

enraged /ɪn'reɪdʒd/ adj very angry.

enrich /ɪn'rɪtʃ/ v [T] 1 (with)) improve (sth) by adding sth: soil ~ed with fertilizer. 2 make richer. **enrichment** n [U].

enrol (also esp US -ll) /ɪn'rəʊl/ v (-ll-) [I, T] become or make (sb) a member of a college or course. **enrolment** n [C, U].

en route /ˌɒn 'ruːt/ adv (French) on the way.

ensemble /ɒn'sɒmbl/ n [C] 1 group of things considered as a whole. 2 small group of musicians who often play together.

ensign /'ensən, also 'ensaɪn/ n [C] 1 ship's flag. 2 junior officer in the US navy.

ensue /ɪn'sjuː; US -'suː/ v [I] happen later or as a result; follow.

ensure (US **insure**) /ɪn'ʃɔː(r); US m'ʃʊər/ v [T] make certain that (sth) happens.

entail /ɪn'teɪl/ v [T] make necessary: Your plan ~s a lot of work.

entangle /ɪn'tæŋgld/ adj (in)) twisted or caught in sth. **entanglement** n [C, U].

enter /'entə(r)/ v 1 [I, T] come or go into (sth). 2 [T] become a member of; join: ~ university. 3 [T] write details of (sb/sth) in a book or list. 4 [I, T] take part in (a competition, examination, etc). 5 (phr v) **enter into sth** (a) begin to deal with sth. (b) form part of sth. **enter on/upon sth** (fml) begin sth.

enterprise /'entəpraɪz/ n 1 [C] new or difficult plan. 2 [U] courage and enthusiasm. 3 [C] business company; firm. 4 [U] business activity: private ~. **enterprising** adj having enterprise(2).

entertain /ˌentə'teɪn/ v 1 [I, T] amuse and interest (sb). 2 [T] give food and drink to (sb) in one's home. 3 [T] be willing to think about: ~ an idea. **entertainer** n [C] person whose job is to enter-

tain(1) people. **entertaining** adj amusing. **entertainment** n 1 [U] entertaining or being entertained. 2 [C] public performance.

enthral (also esp US -ll) /ɪn'θrɔːl/ v (-ll-) [T] capture the complete attention of.

enthuse /ɪn'θjuːz; US -θuːz/ v [I] (about/over)) talk about sth with great enthusiasm.

enthusiasm /ɪn'θjuːzɪæzəm; US -'θuː-/ n [U] great interest or admiration; eagerness. **enthusiast** /-æst/ n [C] person with a strong interest in sth. **enthusiastic** /ɪnˌθjuːzɪ'æstɪk; US -θuː-/ adj full of enthusiasm. **enthusiastically** /-klɪ/ adv.

entice /ɪn'taɪs/ v [T] tempt or persuade (sb), by offering sth attractive. **enticement** n [C, U].

entire /ɪn'taɪə(r)/ adj complete. **entirely** adv. **entirety** /ɪn'taɪərətɪ/ n [U].

entitle /ɪn'taɪtl/ v [T] 1 give a title to (a book, etc). 2 to)) give (sb) a right to have or do sth. **entitlement** n [C, U].

entity /'entətɪ/ n [C] (pl -ies) (fml) something that has a separate existence.

entourage /ˌɒntʊ'rɑːʒ/ n [C, also sing with pl v] people who accompany an important person.

entrance¹ /'entrəns/ n 1 [C] door, gate, etc by which one enters. 2 [U, C] act of entering. 3 [U] right to enter.

entrance² /ɪn'trɑːns; US -'træns/ v [T] fill with wonder and delight: ~d by the music.

entrant /'entrənt/ n [C] person who enters a competition, profession, etc.

entreat /ɪn'triːt/ v [T] (fml) ask (sb) earnestly. **entreaty** n [C, U] (pl -ies) act of entreating.

entrenched /ɪn'trentʃt/ adj (of ideas, etc) firmly fixed.

entrepreneur /ˌɒntrəprə'nɜː(r)/ n [C] person who starts a business.

entrust /ɪn'trʌst/ v [T] with; to)) give sth to sb to look after: ~ the job to him ○ ~ him with the job.

entry /'entrɪ/ n (pl -ies) 1 [C] act of coming or going in. 2 [U] right of entering. 3 [C] (place of) entrance. 4 [C] something written in a list: dictionary entries.

enumerate /ɪ'njuːməreɪt; US ɪ'nuː-/ v [T] name (things on a list) one by one. **enumeration** /ɪˌnjuːmə'reɪʃn; US ɪˌnuː-/ n [U].

enunciate /ɪ'nʌnsɪeɪt/ v [T] speak (words) clearly. **enunciation** /ɪˌnʌnsɪ'eɪʃn/ n [U].

envelop /ɪn'veləp/ v [T] cover or surround completely: ~ed in fog.

envelopment n [U].
envelope /'envələʊp, also 'ɒn-/ n [C] paper covering for a letter.
enviable /'envɪəbl/ adj very desirable; causing envy.
envious /'envɪəs/ adj feeling or showing envy. **enviously** adv.
environment /ɪn'vaɪərənmənt/ n [C, U] surroundings and conditions in which people live. **environmental** /ɪn,vaɪərən'mentl/ adj. **environmentalist** /ɪn,vaɪərən'mentəlɪst/ n [C] person who wants to protect our natural environment.
envisage /ɪn'vɪsɪdʒ/ v [T] have an idea of (sth) as a future possibility.
envoy /'envɔɪ/ n [C] 1 messenger or representative. 2 diplomatic agent.
envy /'envɪ/ n 1 [U] feeling of discontent when one wants that sb else has. 2 (idm) **the envy of sb** thing that sb wants to have or be. **envy** v (pt, pp **-ied**) [T] feel envy towards (sb) or at (sth).
enzyme /'enzaɪm/ n [C] chemical substance formed in living cells that causes chemical change.
epaulette (also esp US **-let**) /'epəlet/ n [C] decoration on the shoulder of a uniform.
ephemeral /ɪ'femərəl/ adj lasting for a very short time.
epic /'epɪk/ n [C] long poem, film, etc about the actions of great heroes. **epic** adj impressive; grand.
epidemic /,epɪ'demɪk/ n [C] disease that spreads quickly among many people.
epilepsy /'epɪlepsɪ/ n [U] disease that causes sb to become unconscious and to have violent fits. **epileptic** /,epɪ'leptɪk/ adj, n [C].
epilogue /'epɪlɒg/ (US **-log** /-lɔːg/) n [C] last part of a book or play.
episode /'epɪsəʊd/ n [C] 1 one important event or period of time. 2 one of several parts of a story on television, etc.
epitaph /'epɪtɑːf; US -tæf/ n [C] words on a tombstone.
epithet /'epɪθet/ n [C] adjective used to describe sb.
epitome /ɪ'pɪtəmɪ/ n [C] person or thing that is the perfect example of a quality or type: She is the ~ of kindness. **epitomize** /ɪ'pɪtəmaɪz/ v [T] be an epitome of.
epoch /'iːpɒk; US 'epək/ n [C] period of time marked by important events or characteristics.
equable /'ekwəbl/ adj moderate; not changing much: an ~ climate/temper.
equal /'iːkwəl/ adj 1 the same in size, number, value, etc. 2 to//

having the ability or strength for sth: ~ to the task. **equal** n [C] person or thing equal to another. **equal** v (-ll-; US -l-) [T] be equal to (sb/sth). **equality** /ɪ'kwɒlətɪ/ n [U] state of being equal. **equalize** v [I, T] become or make equal. **equally** adv 1 in an equal manner. 2 similarly.
equate /ɪ'kweɪt/ v [T] consider as equal: You cannot ~ these two systems of government.
equation /ɪ'kweɪʒn/ n [C] statement that two amounts are equal: $2x + 5 = 11$ is an equation.
equator /ɪ'kweɪtə(r)/ n the **equator** [sing] imaginary line round the earth, half-way between the North and South Poles. **equatorial** /,ekwə'tɔːrɪəl/ adj.
equestrian /ɪ'kwestrɪən/ adj of horse-riding.
equilibrium /,iːkwɪ'lɪbrɪəm, also ,ek-/ n [U] (fml) state of being balanced.
equinox /'iːkwɪnɒks, also 'ek-/ n [C] time of the year when day and night are of equal length.
equip /ɪ'kwɪp/ v (-pp-) [T] (with//) supply sb with sth needed for a particular purpose. **equipment** n [U] things needed for a particular purpose: office ~ment.
equitable /'ekwɪtəbl/ adj fair and just: an ~ tax system. **equitably** adv.
equity /'ekwətɪ/ n 1 [U] (fml) fairness. 2 **equities** [pl] stocks and shares on which fixed interest is not paid.
equivalent /ɪ'kwɪvələnt/ adj, n [C] (something) that has the same function, importance, etc.
equivocal /ɪ'kwɪvəkl/ adj (fml) having a doubtful or double meaning: an ~ answer. **equivocate** /ɪ'kwɪvəkeɪt/ v [I] (fml) speak in an equivocal way.
era /'ɪərə/ n [C] period in history marked by an important event or development.
eradicate /ɪ'rædɪkeɪt/ v [T] put an end to (sth bad). **eradication** /ɪ,rædɪ'keɪʃn/ n [U].
erase /ɪ'reɪz; US -s/ v [T] remove (marks, etc): (fig) ~ the event from his memory. **eraser** n [C] (esp US) rubber(2).
erect /ɪ'rekt/ v [T] 1 (fml) build; establish. 2 fix or set upright: ~ a tent. **erect** adj upright: stand ~. **erection** /ɪ'rekʃn/ n 1 [U] act of erecting sth. 2 [C] (fml) building. 3 [C] swelling and hardening of a man's penis. **erectness** n [U].
erode /ɪ'rəʊd/ v [T] (usu passive) (of the sea, wind, etc) destroy (rock, etc) gradually. **erosion**

/ɪˈrəʊʒn/ n [U].

erotic /ɪˈrɒtɪk/ adj arousing sexual desire.

err /ɜː(r); US eə/ v [I] (fml) make a mistake.

errand /ˈerənd/ n [C] short journey, eg to buy goods from a shop.

erratic /ɪˈrætɪk/ adj not regular or reliable. **erratically** /-klɪ/ adv.

erroneous /ɪˈrəʊniəs/ adj (fml) (of beliefs, etc) incorrect.

error /ˈerə(r)/ n 1 [C] mistake. 2 [U] being wrong: do it in ~.

erudite /ˈeruːdaɪt/ adj (fml) having or showing great knowledge.

erupt /ɪˈrʌpt/ v [I] 1 (of a volcano) throw out lava. 2 break out violently: Fighting ~ed on the streets. **eruption** /ɪˈrʌpʃn/ n [C, U].

escalate /ˈeskəleɪt/ v [I, T] become or make bigger or more serious. **escalation** /ˌeskəˈleɪʃn/ n [U, C].

escalator /ˈeskəleɪtə(r)/ n [C] moving stairs for carrying people up or down.

escapade /ˈeskəpeɪd/ n [C] daring or adventurous act.

escape /ɪˈskeɪp/ v 1 [I] (from)// get free from prison or sb's control. 2 [I] (from)// (of gases, liquids, etc) find a way out. 3 [I, T] avoid (sth unpleasant). 4 [T] be forgotten by: Her name ~s me, ie I can't remember it. **escape** n 1 [C, U] (act of) escaping. 2 [C] leak of gas or a liquid. **escapism** n [U] activity that helps one forget one's problems, etc. **escapist** adj, n [C].

escort /ˈeskɔːt/ n [C] person or group of people or vehicles that go with sb to protect him/her. **escort** /ɪˈskɔːt/ v [T] go with (sb) as an escort.

esophagus (US) = OESOPHAGUS.

esoteric /ˌesəʊˈterɪk, ˌiːsəʊ-/ adj (fml) understood by only a small group of people.

especially /ɪˈspeʃəlɪ/ adj 1 in particular: I love the country, ~ in spring. 2 to a very great degree: This is ~ true of old people.

espionage /ˈespɪənɑːʒ/ n [U] activity of spying.

essay /ˈeseɪ/ n [C] short piece of writing on one subject. **essayist** n [C] writer of essays.

essence /ˈesns/ n 1 [U] most important quality of sth. 2 [C, U] flavouring in concentrated liquid form. 3 (idm) in 'essence really.

essential /ɪˈsenʃl/ adj 1 most important; necessary. 2 fundamental: an ~ part of the English character. **essential** n [C, usu pl] most important or necessary thing. **ess-**

entially /-ʃəlɪ/ adv basically or really.

establish /ɪˈstæblɪʃ/ v [T] 1 start and organize (a business, system, etc); create. 2 settle (oneself) firmly in a position or activity. 3 show (a fact, etc) to be true; prove. **establishment** n 1 [U] act of establishing sth. 2 [C] (fml) business or large institution. 3 **the Establishment** [sing] (esp Brit often derog) people in positions of power.

estate /ɪˈsteɪt/ n 1 [C] land in the country, with one owner. 2 [C] (esp Brit) large area of land with factories or houses on it: a housing ~. 3 [U, C] (law) all of a person's money and property. **estate agent** n [C] person who buys and sells houses for others. **estate car** n [C] car with an area for luggage behind the back seats and a door at the back.

esteem /ɪˈstiːm/ n [U] (fml) good opinion; respect. **esteem** v [T] (fml) respect greatly.

esthetic (US) = AESTHETIC.

estimate /ˈestɪmeɪt/ v [T] 1 calculate (a quantity or cost) approximately. 2 form an opinion about (sth). **estimate** /ˈestɪmət/ n [C] approximate calculation of cost, quantity, etc. **estimation** /ˌestɪˈmeɪʃn/ n [U] judgement; opinion.

estuary /ˈestjʊərɪ; US -ʊerɪ/ n (pl -ies) mouth of a river into which the tide flows.

etc /ɪt ˈsetərə, et-/ abbr and other similar things; and the rest.

etch /etʃ/ v [I, T] use a needle and acid to draw (a picture, etc) on a metal plate. **etching** n 1 [U] art of making etched prints. 2 [C] picture printed from an etched metal plate.

eternal /ɪˈtɜːnl/ adj 1 lasting for ever. 2 (infml) seeming never to stop: ~ fighting. **eternally** /-nəlɪ/ adv.

eternity /ɪˈtɜːnətɪ/ n 1 [U] (fml) time without end, esp after death. 2 [usu sing] (infml) a very long time.

ether /ˈiːθə(r)/ n [U] colourless liquid made from alcohol. **ethereal** /ɪˈθɪərɪəl/ adj very delicate and light.

ethic /ˈeθɪk/ n 1 [sing] system of moral principles: the Christian ~. 2 **ethics** (a) [pl] moral principles. (b) (with sing v) study of morals. **ethical** adj 1 of morals. 2 morally right. **ethically** adv.

ethnic /ˈeθnɪk/ adj of a national, racial or tribal group. **ethnically** /-klɪ/ adv.

etiquette /ˈetɪket/ n [U] rules for

correct and polite behaviour.

etymology /ˌetɪˈmɒlədʒɪ/ n [U] study of the history of words.

eucalyptus /ˌjuːkəˈlɪptəs/ n [C] tall evergreen tree from which an oil, used as medicine, is obtained.

euphemism /ˈjuːfəmɪzəm/ n [C, U] use of a pleasant mild word for sth unpleasant: *'Pass away' is a euphemism for 'die'.* **euphemistic** /ˌjuːfəˈmɪstɪk/ adj.

euphoria /juːˈfɔːrɪə/ n [U] feeling of great happiness and excitement. **euphoric** /juːˈfɒrɪk; US -ˈfɔːr-/ adj.

euthanasia /ˌjuːθəˈneɪzɪə; US -ˈneɪʒə/ n [U] painless killing of people who have a painful incurable disease.

evacuate /ɪˈvækjʊeɪt/ v [T] take people away from a dangerous place to a safer place: ~ *(children from) the city.* **evacuation** /ɪˌvækjʊˈeɪʃn/ n [C, U].

evade /ɪˈveɪd/ v [T] 1 find a way of not doing or dealing with (sth): ~ *(answering) a question.* 2 keep out of the way of (sb/sth).

evaluate /ɪˈvæljʊeɪt/ v [T] decide the value or quality of. **evaluation** /ɪˌvæljʊˈeɪʃn/ n [C, U].

evangelical /ˌiːvænˈdʒelɪkl/ adj of a Christian group that emphasizes salvation by personal belief in Christ.

evangelist /ɪˈvændʒəlɪst/ n [C] 1 one of the writers of the Gospels. 2 person who travels around holding Christian meetings. **evangelistic** /ɪˌvændʒəˈlɪstɪk/ adj.

evaporate /ɪˈvæpəreɪt/ v 1 [I, T] (cause to) change into vapour and disappear. 2 [I] disappear. **evaporation** /ɪˌvæpəˈreɪʃn/ n [U].

evasion /ɪˈveɪʒn/ n [C, U] act of evading sth. **evasive** /ɪˈveɪsɪv/ adj trying to avoid sth. **evasively** adv.

eve /iːv/ n [C, usu sing] 1 day before a religious festival. 2 time just before sth: *on the ~ of the election.*

even[1] /ˈiːvn/ adv 1 (used for emphasizing sth unexpected or surprising): *Anyone can understand this. E~ a child.* 2 (used for emphasizing a comparative): still: *You know ~ less than I do.* 3 (idm) **even if/though** in spite of the fact that: *I'll get there ~ if I have to walk.* **even 'now/'so/'then** in spite of these circumstances, etc: *I told him, but ~ then he didn't believe me.*

even[2] /ˈiːvn/ adj 1 level and smooth: *an ~ surface.* 2 regular; steady: *an ~ temperature.* 3 (of amounts or distances) equal. 4 (of numbers) that can be divided by

two. 5 equally balanced: *The two teams are very ~.* 6 (idm) **get even with sb** get revenge on sb. **on an even keel** steady. **even** v (phr v) **even (sth) out/up** become or make level, equal or balanced. **even-'handed** adj fair. **evenly** adv. **evenness** n [U]. **even-'tempered** adj not easily made angry.

evening /ˈiːvnɪŋ/ n [C, U] part of the day between the afternoon and bedtime. **'evening dress** n 1 [U] clothes worn for formal occasions in the evening. 2 [C] woman's formal dress.

event /ɪˈvent/ n [C] 1 something that happens, esp sth important. 2 one race, competition, etc in a sports programme. 3 (idm) **at all events** whatever happens. **in the event of sth** (*fml*) if sth happens. **eventful** /-fl/ adj full of interesting or important events.

eventual /ɪˈventʃʊəl/ adj happening at last as a result. **eventuality** /ɪˌventʃʊˈælətɪ/ n [C] (pl -ies) (*fml*) possible event or result. **eventually** adv in the end: *They ~ly agreed to pay the bill.*

ever /ˈevə(r)/ adv 1 at any time: *Nothing ~ happens here.* ○ *Do you ~ wish you were rich?* ○ *the best work you've ~ done.* 2 **ever-** (in compounds) always; continuously: *the ~-increasing number of students.* 3 (used for showing surprise in questions): *What ~ do you mean?* 4 (idm) **for ever** ⇨ FOREVER 1. **ever since** from (a certain time) until now: *She's liked reading ~ she was a child.* **ever so/such** (*infml*) very: ~ *so rich.*

evergreen /ˈevəgriːn/ n [C], adj (tree or bush) that has green leaves throughout the year.

everlasting /ˌevəˈlɑːstɪŋ; US -ˈlæst-/ adj lasting for ever.

every /ˈevrɪ/ adj 1 each (one): *E~ child passed the exam.* 2 all possible: *You have ~ reason to be satisfied.* 3 (used for showing that sth happens regularly): *She phones ~ week.* 4 (idm) **every other** each alternate: ~ *other day* (eg Monday, Wednesday and Friday). **'everybody** (also **'everyone**) pron every person. **'everyday** adj ordinary; daily. **'everything** pron all things: *E~thing was destroyed.* **'everywhere** adv in or to every place.

evict /ɪˈvɪkt/ v [T] force (sb) to leave a house by official authority of the law. **eviction** /-kʃn/ n [C, U].

evidence /ˈevɪdəns/ n [U] 1 (esp *law*) anything that gives a reason for believing sth or proves sth. 2

(idm) **in evidence** present and clearly seen.

evident /'evidənt/ *adj* plain and clear; obvious. **evidently** *adv*.

evil /'i:vl/ *adj* wickedness; harmful. **evil** *n* 1 [U] wickedness. 2 [C] very bad thing. **evilly** /-vəli/ *adv*.

evocative /ɪ'vɒkətɪv/ *adj* that brings memories, feelings, etc of sth: *an ~ picture.*

evoke /ɪ'vəʊk/ *v* [T] produce (a memory, feeling, etc).

evolution /ˌi:və'lu:ʃn; US ˌev-/ *n* [U] (theory of) gradual development, esp of animals and plants from earlier simpler forms.

evolve /ɪ'vɒlv/ *v* [I, T] (cause to) develop gradually.

ewe /ju:/ *n* [C] female sheep.

exacerbate /ɪg'zæsəbeɪt/ *v* [T] (*fml*) make (sth bad) much worse.

exact[1] /ɪg'zækt/ *adj* correct in every detail; precise: *the ~ time.* **exactitude** /-ɪtju:d; US -tu:d/ *n* [U] correctness. **exactly** *adv* 1 correctly; precisely. 2 (as an answer) you are right. **exactness** *n* [U].

exact[2] /ɪg'zækt/ *v* [T] (*fml*) demand and obtain (sth): *~ obedience.* **exacting** *adj* requiring hard work and care.

exaggerate /ɪg'zædʒəreɪt/ *v* [I, T] make (sth) seem better, larger, etc than it really is. **exaggeration** /ɪgˌzædʒə'reɪʃn/ *n* [C, U].

exam /ɪg'zæm/ *n* [C] (*infml*) short for EXAMINATION 1.

examination /ɪgˌzæmɪ'neɪʃn/ *n* 1 [C] test of knowledge or ability. 2 [U, C] action of examining.

examine /ɪg'zæmɪn/ *v* [T] 1 look at carefully. 2 question (sb) in order to test knowledge or ability. **examiner** *n* [C] person who tests knowledge or ability.

example /ɪg'zɑ:mpl; US -'zæm-/ *n* [C] 1 fact, thing, etc that shows a general rule or represents a group: *a fine ~ of Norman architecture.* 2 person or quality to be copied: *His bravery is an ~ to us all.* 3 (idm) **for example** as an example(1): *Many women, Alison for ~, have a job and a family.* **make an example of sb** punish sb as a warning to others.

exasperate /ɪg'zæspəreɪt/ *v* [T] annoy (sb) very much. **exasperation** /ɪgˌzæspə'reɪʃn/ *n* [U].

excavate /'ekskəveɪt/ *v* [T] make or uncover (sth) by digging: *~ a hole/buried city.* **excavation** /ˌekskə'veɪʃn/ *n* [C, U]. **excavator** *n* [C] person or machine that excavates sth.

exceed /ɪk'si:d/ *v* [T] 1 be greater than. 2 go beyond (a limit or rule): *~ the speed limit,* ie drive faster

than is allowed. **exceedingly** *adv* (*fml*) extremely.

excel /ɪk'sel/ *v* (-ll-) [I] *at/in//* be very good at sth.

Excellency /'eksələnsi/ *n* [C] (*pl* -ies) title of some officials, eg ambassadors or governors.

excellent /'eksələnt/ *adj* very good. **excellence** /-ləns/ *n* [U]. **excellently** *adv*.

except /ɪk'sept/ *prep* not including; but not: *The shop is open every day ~ Sunday.* **except** *v* [T] (*fml*) (usu passive) exclude; leave out.

exception /ɪk'sepʃn/ *n* 1 [C] person, thing, etc that is not included: *All the students did well, with the ~ of Jo, who failed.* 2 (idm) **make an exception (of sb/sth)** treat sb/ sth as a special case. **take exception to sth** be annoyed by sth. **exceptional** /-ʃənl/ *adj* unusual; very good. **exceptionally** /-ʃənəli/ *adv*.

excerpt /'eksɜ:pt/ *n* [C] piece taken from a book, film, etc.

excess /ɪk'ses/ *n* 1 [sing] *of// * larger amount of sth than is needed or usual. 2 **excesses** [pl] (*fml*) bad or cruel behaviour. 3 (idm) **in excess of sth** more than sth. **to excess** too much: *drink to ~.* **excess** /'ekses/ *adj* extra: *~ baggage.* **excessive** *adj* too much. **excessively** *adv*.

exchange /ɪks'tʃeɪndʒ/ *v* [T] give and receive (sth) in return: *~ pounds for dollars.* **exchange** *n* 1 [C, U] act of exchanging. 2 [C] (angry) conversation. 3 [C] place where people meet for business: *the Stock E~.* 4 = TELEPHONE EXCHANGE (TELEPHONE). **exchange rate** *n* [C] value of the money of one country against the money of another country.

exchequer /ɪks'tʃekə(r)/ *n* **the Exchequer** [sing] (*Brit*) government department in charge of public money: *the Chancellor of the E~,* ie the minister at the head of this department.

excise /'eksaɪz/ *n* [U] tax on certain goods produced inside a country.

excite /ɪk'saɪt/ *v* [T] 1 cause strong, esp pleasant feelings in (sb). 2 cause (a feeling or response) in (sb). **excitable** *adj* easily excited. **excited** *adj* full of strong happy feelings. **excitedly** *adv*. **excitement** *n* [U, C]. **exciting** *adj* causing great interest and excitement.

exclaim /ɪk'skleɪm/ *v* [I, T] speak or say suddenly or loudly. **exclamation** /ˌeksklə'meɪʃn/ *n* [C] sound(s) or word(s) exclaimed. **ex-**

clamation mark (US exclamation point) n [C] mark (!) written after an exclamation.

exclude /ɪkˈskluːd/ v [T] 1 keep (sb/sth) out; not include. 2 put (sth) out of one's mind: ~ *the idea of failure*. **exclusion** /-luːʒn/ n [U].

exclusive /ɪkˈskluːsɪv/ *adj* 1 (of a group) admitting only carefully chosen people. 2 limited to a particular group of people, esp rich people. **exclusive** n [C] report published by only one newspaper. **exclusively** *adv* only.

excommunicate /ˌekskəˈmjuːnɪkeɪt/ v [T] exclude (sb) from the Christian church. **excommunication** /ˌekskəˌmjuːnɪˈkeɪʃn/ n [U, C].

excrement /ˈekskrɪmənt/ n [U] (*fml*) solid waste matter from the body.

excrete /ɪkˈskriːt/ v [T] pass out (waste matter) from the body.

excruciating /ɪkˈskruːʃɪeɪtɪŋ/ *adj* (of pain) very bad. **excruciatingly** *adv*.

excursion /ɪkˈskɜːʃn; US -ɜːrʒn/ n [C] short journey, esp for pleasure.

excuse /ɪkˈskjuːs/ n [C] reason given to explain or defend one's behaviour. **excusable** /ɪkˈskjuːzəbl/ *adj* forgivable. **excuse** /ɪkˈskjuːz/ v [T] 1 forgive or pardon. 2 (*from*) set (sb) free from a duty. 3 justify: *Nothing can ~ such rudeness*. 4 (*idm*) **excuse me** (a) (used as an apology when one interrupts, disagrees, etc). (b) (US) please repeat what you said.

execute /ˈeksɪkjuːt/ v [T] 1 (*fml*) perform (what one is asked to do); carry out: ~ *a plan*. 2 kill (sb) as a legal punishment. **execution** /ˌeksɪˈkjuːʃn/ n 1 [U] (*fml*) carrying out of a plan, piece of work, etc. 2 [C, U] killing sb as a legal punishment. **executioner** /ˌeksɪˈkjuːʃənə(r)/ n [C] official who executes criminals.

executive /ɪgˈzekjʊtɪv/ *adj* concerned with managing and, carrying out decisions. **executive** n 1 [C] person in an executive position in a business organization. 2 **the executive** [sing] branch of government concerned with carrying out decisions, laws, etc.

executor /ɪgˈzekjʊtə(r)/ n [C] person who is appointed to carry out the terms of a will.

exemplify /ɪgˈzemplɪfaɪ/ v (*pt, pp* -**ied**) [T] be or give an example of (sth). **exemplification** /ɪgˌzemplɪfɪˈkeɪʃn/ n [U, C].

exempt /ɪgˈzempt/ *adj* (*from*)|| free from a duty or obligation. **exempt** v [T] (*from*)|| make (sb/sth)exempt from sth. **exemption** /ɪgˈzempʃn/ n [U, C].

exercise /ˈeksəsaɪz/ n 1 [U] use of one's body to make oneself healthier: *Jogging is good ~.* 2 [C] activity intended for training: *maths ~s.* 3 [U] careful use or practice: *the ~ of authority.* **exercise** v 1 [I, T] train (one's body) by means of exercises. 2 [T] use (authority or a right) carefully. **'exercise book** n [C] book for writing in, esp at school.

exert /ɪgˈzɜːt/ v [T] 1 use (sth powerful) to produce an effect: ~ *pressure on sb to do sth.* 2 ~ **oneself** make an effort. **exertion** /ɪgˈzɜːʃn; US -ɜːrʒn/ n [C, U].

exhale /eksˈheɪl/ v [I, T] breathe out. **exhalation** /ˌekshəˈleɪʃn/ n [C, U].

exhaust /ɪgˈzɔːst/ v [T] 1 make (sb) very tired. 2 use (sth) completely. **exhaust** n (a) [C] pipe through which gas, fumes, etc escape from an engine. (b) [U] this gas. **exhausted** *adj* very tired. **exhaustion** /ɪgˈzɔːstʃən/ n [U]. **exhaustive** *adj* thorough.

exhibit /ɪgˈzɪbɪt/ v [T] 1 (*fml*) show clearly that one has (a quality). 2 show publicly for sale, etc. **exhibit** n [C] 1 something shown in a museum, etc. 2 something shown as evidence in a lawcourt. **exhibitor** n [C] person who exhibits(2) pictures, etc.

exhibition /ˌeksɪˈbɪʃn/ n 1 [C] public show of pictures, etc. 2 [C] (usu sing) act of showing: *an ~ of bad manners.* **exhibitionism** /-ɪzəm/ n [U] behaviour intended to attract attention to oneself. **exhibitionist** n [C].

exhilarate /ɪgˈzɪləreɪt/ v [T] (usu passive) make (sb) feel very happy and excited. **exhilaration** /ɪgˌzɪləˈreɪʃn/ n [U].

exhort /ɪgˈzɔːt/ v [T] (*fml*) urge strongly: ~ *them to try harder.* **exhortation** /ˌegzɔːˈteɪʃn/ n [C, U].

exile /ˈeksaɪl/ n 1 [U] being sent away from one's own country: *live in ~.* 2 [C] person who is sent away from his/her own country. **exile** v [T] send into exile.

exist /ɪgˈzɪst/ v [I] 1 be real; continue living. **existence** n 1 [U] state of existing: *believe in the ~ence of God.* 2 [sing] way of life: *a miserable ~ence.* **existent** *adj* (*fml*) existing; actual.

exit /ˈeksɪt/ n [C] 1 way out of a public building. 2 act of leaving a place. **exit** v [I] go out; (esp of an actor) leave the stage.

exonerate /ɪgˈzɒnəreɪt/ v [T] (fml) free (sb) from blame. **exoneration** /ɪg.zɒnəˈreɪʃn/ n [U].

exorbitant /ɪgˈzɔːbɪtənt/ adj (of a price) much too high. **exorbitantly** adv.

exorcize /ˈeksɔːsaɪz/ v [T] drive out an evil spirit by prayer. **exorcism** /-sɪzəm/ n [U, C]. **exorcist** n [C].

exotic /ɪgˈzɒtɪk/ adj 1 from another country; not native: ~ fruits. 2 attractive or pleasing because unusual.

expand /ɪkˈspænd/ v 1 [I, T] become or make larger: Metals ~ when heated. ○ ~ a business. 2 (phr v) **expand on sth** give more information about sth.

expanse /ɪkˈspæns/ n [C] wide open area (of land, sea, etc).

expansion /ɪkˈspænʃn/ n [U] action of expanding. **expansionism** /-ʃənɪzəm/ n [U] (esp derog) policy of expanding one's land or business. **expansionist** adj.

expansive /ɪkˈspænsɪv/ adj (of people) willing to talk a lot.

expatriate /ˌeksˈpætrɪət; US -ˈpeɪt-/ n [C] (person) living outside his/her own country.

expect /ɪkˈspekt/ v 1 [T] think or believe that (sth) will happen. 2 (idm) **be expecting** be pregnant. **expectancy** n [U] (fml) state of expecting (sth to happen). **expectant** adj 1 expecting (esp sth good). 2 pregnant. **expectation** /ˌekspekˈteɪʃn/ n [C, U] strong hope or belief that sth will happen.

expedient /ɪkˈspiːdɪənt/ adj, n [C] (fml) (plan or action that is) useful for a particular purpose, but perhaps not fair or moral. **expediency** /-ənsɪ/ n [U].

expedition /ˌekspɪˈdɪʃn/ n [C] (a) organized journey for a purpose, eg exploration. (b) people making such a journey. **expeditionary** /-ʃənərɪ; US -nerɪ/ adj (of an army) sent abroad to fight.

expel /ɪkˈspel/ v (-ll-) [T] 1 to force (sb) to leave a school, club, etc. 2 force (sth) out: ~ air from the lungs.

expend /ɪkˈspend/ v [T] (fml) spend or use (money, time or energy). **expendable** adj (of sth) that may be used, destroyed, etc for a purpose.

expenditure /ɪkˈspendɪtʃə(r)/ n [U, C] 1 amount of money spent on sth. 2 spending or using money, energy, etc.

expense /ɪkˈspens/ n 1 [U, C] spending of money; cost. 2 **expenses** [pl] money used for a particular purpose: travelling ~s. 3

(idm) **at sb's expense** (a) with sb paying. (b) (of a joke) to make sb look foolish.

expensive /ɪkˈspensɪv/ adj costing a lot of money. **expensively** adv.

experience /ɪkˈspɪərɪəns/ n 1 [U] knowledge or skill gained by doing or seeing things: learn by ~. 2 [C] event or activity that affects one: a happy ~. **experience** v [T] have an experience of (sth); feel: ~ difficulty/pain. **experienced** adj having a lot of experience(1).

experiment /ɪkˈsperɪmənt/ n [C, U] (esp in science) test done carefully to study sth. **experiment** v [I] do an experiment. **experimental** /ɪkˌsperɪˈmentl/ adj of or using experiments. **experimentation** /ɪkˌsperɪmenˈteɪʃn/ n [U].

expert /ˈekspɜːt/ n [C] person with special knowledge or skill. **expert** adj having or involving great knowledge or skill. **expertly** adv.

expertise /ˌekspɜːˈtiːz/ n [U] great knowledge or skill.

expire /ɪkˈspaɪə(r)/ v [I] 1 (of sth that lasts for a time) become no longer available for use: My passport has ~ d. 2 (dated fml) die. **expiry** /ɪkˈspaɪərɪ/ n [U] ending of the period when a contract, etc is valid.

explain /ɪkˈspleɪn/ v 1 [I, T] make (sth) clear, give the meaning of. 2 [T] give reasons for: ~ one's behaviour. 3 (phr v) **explain sth away** give reasons why one should not be blamed for sth. **explanation** /ˌekspləˈneɪʃn/ n 1 [C] statement that explains sth. 2 [U] act of explaining sth. **explanatory** /ɪkˈsplænətrɪ; US -tɔːrɪ/ adj (of statements) intended to explain.

explicit /ɪkˈsplɪsɪt/ adj 1 (of statements) clearly and fully expressed. 2 (of people) saying sth clearly and openly. **explicitly** adv. **explicitness** n [U].

explode /ɪkˈspləʊd/ v 1 [I, T] (cause to) burst with a loud noise, usu causing damage. 2 [I] (of people) show strong feelings suddenly.

exploit¹ /ɪkˈsplɔɪt/ v [T] 1 treat (sb) selfishly and unfairly, for profit. 2 use or develop (sth), esp for profit: ~ oil reserves. **exploitation** /ˌeksplɔɪˈteɪʃn/ n [U].

exploit² /ˈeksplɔɪt/ n [C] brave or adventurous act.

explore /ɪkˈsplɔː(r)/ v [T] 1 travel through (a country) to learn about it. 2 examine (sth) carefully: ~ different possibilities. **exploration**

/ˌekspləˈreɪʃn/ n [U, C]. **exploratory** /ɪkˈsplɒrətrɪ; US -tɔːrɪ/ adj done in order to find out sth. **explorer** n [C] person who explores(1).

explosion /ɪkˈspləʊʒn/ n [C] 1 (loud noise caused by) exploding. 2 sudden burst of anger. 3 great and sudden increase: *the population* ~.

explosive /ɪkˈspləʊsɪv/ n, adj (substance) that can explode. **explosively** adv.

exponent /ɪkˈspəʊnənt/ n [C] person who supports and explains a belief, etc.

export /ɪkˈspɔːt/ v [I, T] send (goods) to another country for sale. **export** /ˈekspɔːt/ n 1 [U] (business of) exporting. 2 [C] something exported. **exporter** n [C] person, company or country that exports goods.

expose /ɪkˈspəʊz/ v [T] 1 uncover; make visible; leave unprotected. 2 reveal; make known (sth secret or dishonest). 3 (in photography) allow light to reach (film). **exposure** /ɪkˈspəʊʒə(r)/ n [U, C].

expound /ɪkˈspaʊnd/ v [T] (fml) explain or make (sth) clear by giving details: ~ *a theory*.

express¹ /ɪkˈspres/ v [T] 1 make known by words or looks: ~ *an opinion*. 2 ~ *oneself* speak or write clearly one's thoughts or feelings.

express² /ɪkˈspres/ adj 1 going quickly: *an* ~ *letter*. 2 (fml) clearly stated: *his* ~ *wish*. **express** adv by express post. **express** (also **express train**) n [C] fast train. **expressly** adv definitely; clearly. **expressway** n [C] (US) motorway.

expression /ɪkˈspreʃn/ n 1 [C, U] (an example of) act or process of expressing. 2 [C] word or phrase: *a polite* ~. 3 [C] look on sb's face that shows a feeling: *an angry* ~. 4 [U] feeling shown when acting, singing, etc. **expressionless** adj not showing one's feelings.

expressive /ɪkˈspresɪv/ adj showing one's feelings or thoughts. **expressively** adv. **expressiveness** n [U].

expropriate /eksˈprəʊprɪeɪt/ v [T] (fml) take away for public use.

expulsion /ɪkˈspʌlʃn/ n [C, U] (act of) expelling.

exquisite /ˈekskwɪzɪt, also ɪkˈskwɪzɪt/ adj very beautiful; skilfully made. **exquisitely** adv.

extend /ɪkˈstend/ v 1 [I] (of space or land) reach or stretch: *The park* ~ *s to the river*. 2 [T] make longer or larger: ~ *the house*. 3 [T] stretch out (part of one's body) fully. 4 [T] (fml) offer: ~ *an invitation*.

extension /ɪkˈstenʃn/ n 1 [U] act of extending. 2 [C] added part: *a new* ~ *to the hospital*. 3 [C] telephone line inside an organization.

extensive /ɪkˈstensɪv/ adj large in area or amount. **extensively** adv.

extent /ɪkˈstent/ n 1 [U] length; range: *the* ~ *of the damage*. 2 [sing] degree: *to some* ~.

extenuating /ɪkˈstenjʊeɪtɪŋ/ adj (fml) making bad behaviour less serious by giving reasons for it: ~ *circumstances*.

exterior /ɪkˈstɪərɪə(r)/ n [C] outside surface or appearance. **exterior** adj on or coming from the outside.

exterminate /ɪkˈstɜːmɪneɪt/ v [T] destroy (people or animals) completely. **extermination** /ɪkˌstɜːmɪˈneɪʃn/ n [U].

external /ɪkˈstɜːnl/ adj outside: ~ *injuries*, ie not inside the body. **externally** /-nəlɪ/ adv.

extinct /ɪkˈstɪŋkt/ adj 1 (of a kind of animal) no longer existing. 2 (of a volcano) no longer active. **extinction** /ɪkˈstɪŋkʃn/ n [U] being or becoming extinct.

extinguish /ɪkˈstɪŋgwɪʃ/ v [T] (fml) 1 cause (a fire, etc) to stop burning. 2 destroy (hope, love, etc). **extinguisher** = FIRE EXTINGUISHER (FIRE¹).

extol /ɪkˈstəʊl/ v (-ll-) [T] (fml) praise greatly.

extort /ɪkˈstɔːt/ v [T] obtain by violence, threats, etc. **extortion** /ɪkˈstɔːʃn/ n [U, C]. **extortionate** /-ʃənət/ adj (derog) (of demands or prices) much too high.

extra /ˈekstrə/ adj more than usual or necessary; additional: ~ *pay*, **extra** adv 1 more than usually: *an* ~ *strong box*. 2 in addition: *price £1.75, postage* ~. **extra** n [C] 1 additional things. 2 person employed for a small part in a film, eg in a crowd scene. 3 special edition of a newspaper.

extract /ɪkˈstrækt/ v [T] 1 pull (sth out, esp with effort). 2 obtain by force: ~ *money from sb*. 3 obtain (juices, etc) by crushing. **extract** /ˈekstrækt/ n [C] 1 short part of a book, film, etc. 2 substance obtained by extracting: *beef* ~. **extraction** /ɪkˈstrækʃn/ n [C, U]: *the* ~ *ion of information/a tooth*. 2 [U] origin (of a family): *of French* ~ *ion*.

extra-curricular /ˌekstrəkəˈrɪkjələ(r)/ adj outside the regular course of work at a school or college.

extradite /'ekstrədaɪt/ *v* [T] send (sb accused of a crime) to the country where the crime was said to have been committed. **extradition** /ˌekstrə'dɪʃn/ *n* [U, C].

extra-marital /ˌekstrə'mærɪtl/ *adj* (of sexual relationships) outside marriage.

extraneous /ɪk'streɪnɪəs/ *adj* (*fml*) not connected with what is being dealt with.

extraordinary /ɪk'strɔːdnrɪ; US -dəneri/ *adj* 1 beyond what is usual or ordinary; remarkable: ~ *beauty*. 2 very strange. **extraordinarily** *adv*.

extrapolate /ɪk'stræpəleɪt/ *v* [I, T] (*fml*) estimate (sth unknown) from facts that are already known. **extrapolation** /ɪkˌstræpə'leɪʃn/ *n* [U].

extraterrestrial /ˌekstrətə-'restrɪəl/ *adj* of or from outside the earth.

extravagant /ɪk'strævəgənt/ *adj* 1 wasting money, etc. 2 (of ideas or behaviour) unreasonable; unnecessary. **extravagance** /-gəns/ *n* [U, C]. **extravagantly** *adv*.

extravaganza /ɪkˌstrævə-'gænzə/ *n* [C] elaborate, colourful and expensive activity or entertainment.

extreme /ɪk'striːm/ *adj* 1 greatest or most intense: *in* ~ *pain*. 2 furthest possible: *the* ~ *north of the country*. 3 (often *derog*) beyond the normal limits; not moderate: ~ *opinions*. **extreme** *n* [C] 1 opposite feeling or condition: *Love and hate are* ~*s*. 2 greatest degree: *the* ~*s of heat in the desert*. **extremely** *adv* very.

extremist /ɪk'striːmɪst/ *n* [C], *adj* (usu *derog*) (a person) holding extreme(3) political opinions.

extremity /ɪk'stremətɪ/ *n* (*pl* -ies) 1 [sing] (*fml*) highest degree. 2 (a) [C] (*fml*) furthest point. (b) **extremities** [pl] human hands and feet.

extricate /'ekstrɪkeɪt/ *v* [T] set free from a difficult situation, trap, etc.

extrovert /'ekstrəvɜːt/ *n* [C] lively cheerful person.

exuberant /ɪg'zjuːbərənt; US -'zuː-/ *adj* full of energy and excitement; lively. **exuberance** /-əns/ *n* [U].

exude /ɪg'zjuːd; US -'zuːd/ *v* [I, T] 1 (of drops of liquid, etc) (cause to) come out slowly. 2 [T] express (a feeling) strongly: ~ *happiness*.

exult /ɪg'zʌlt/ *v* [I] (*fml*) show great happiness; rejoice. **exultant** *adj*. **exultation** /ˌegzʌl'teɪʃn/

n [U].

eye /aɪ/ *n* 1 [C] one of the two organs of sight. 2 [sing] observation; judgement: *have a good* ~ *for detail*. 3 [C] hole in a needle. 4 [C] calm area in the centre of a storm. 5 (idm) **(be) all 'eyes** (be) looking with great attention. **in the eyes of sb/sth** in the opinion of sb/sth. **make 'eyes at sb** (*infml*) look at sb in a way that shows one is attracted to him/her. **with one's 'eyes open** fully aware of what one is doing. **eye** *v* [T] look at (sb/sth) carefully. **'eyeball** *n* [C] round ball-shaped part of the eye. **'eyebrow** *n* [C] line of hairs above each eye. **'eyelash** *n* [C] hair on the edge of the eyelid. **'eyelid** *n* [C] one of two folds of skin that cover the eyes when they close. **'eye-opener** *n* [C, usu sing] something surprising or revealing. **'eyesight** *n* [U] ability to see. **'eyesore** *n* [C] something that is ugly, eg a building. **'eyewitness** *n* = WITNESS 1.

F f

F, f /ef/ *n* [C] (*pl* **F's**, **f's** /efs/) the sixth letter of the English alphabet.

F *abbr* Fahrenheit.

fable /'feɪbl/ *n* 1 [C] short story, esp with animals as characters, that teaches a lesson. 2 [C, U] legend. **fabled** *adj* well-known in history; legendary.

fabric /'fæbrɪk/ *n* 1 [C, U] woven cloth. 2 **the fabric** (of sth) [sing] the structure of sth: *the* ~ *of society a building*.

fabricate /'fæbrɪkeɪt/ *v* [T] 1 invent (a false story). 2 make or manufacture. **fabrication** /ˌfæbrɪ'keɪʃn/ *n* [C, U].

fabulous /'fæbjʊləs/ *adj* 1 (*infml*) wonderful. 2 very great: ~ *wealth*. 3 existing in stories and legends: ~ *monsters*. **fabulously** *adv* extremely: ~*ly rich*.

façade /fə'sɑːd/ *n* [C] 1 front of a building. 2 (*fig*) false appearance: *behind a* ~ *of respectability*.

face /feɪs/ *n* 1 [C] front part of the head. 2 expression shown on a face. 3 surface or (front) side of sth: *the north* ~ *of the mountain*. 4 (idm) **face to face (with sb/sth)** close to and looking at sb/sth. **make/pull 'faces/a 'face** make an amusing, rude, etc expression with one's face. **to sb's 'face** open-

ly and directly in sb's presence.
face *v* 1 [I, T] have or turn the face towards. 2 [T] meet confidently: ~ *danger*. 3 [T] need the attention of: *the problems that ~ the government*. 4 [T] cover (a surface) with a layer of material. 5 (idm) **face the 'music** (*infml*) accept criticism of one's own decision or action. 6 (phr v) **face up to sth** accept and deal with sth bravely. **'face-cloth** *n* [C] small cloth used for washing one's face. **faceless** *adj* with no clear character or identity. **'face-lift** *n* [C] 1 medical operation performed to make the face look younger. 2 (*fig*) improvement in the appearance of a building, etc. **,face 'value** *n* 1 [C, U] value shown on money or postage stamps. 2 (idm) **take sth at 'face value** accept sth as it seems to be from its appearance.

facet /'fæsɪt/ *n* [C] 1 any of the many sides of a cut jewel. 2 aspect, eg of a situation or problem.

facetious /fə'si:ʃəs/ *adj* trying to be amusing, esp cleverly or at the wrong time. **facetiously** *adv*.

facial /'feɪʃl/ *adj* of or for the face.

facile /'fæsaɪl; *US* 'fæsl/ *adj* (usu *derog*) produced easily but without careful thought: ~ *comments*.

facilitate /fə'sɪlɪteɪt/ *v* [T] (*fml*) make (sth) easy.

facility /fə'sɪlətɪ/ *n* (*pl* -ies) 1 [C, usu *pl*] equipment, service, etc that is provided for a particular purpose: *'sports facilities*. 2 [sing, U] ability to learn or do things easily: *a ~ for learning languages*.

facsimile /fæk'sɪmɪlɪ/ *n* [C] exact copy of writing, a picture, etc.

fact /fækt/ *n* 1 [C] something that is known to have happened or to be true. 2 [U] truth; reality. 3 (idm) **the ,facts of 'life** details of sex and how babies are born. **in 'fact** really.

faction /'fækʃn/ *n* [C] small group in a larger group, esp in politics.

factor /'fæktə(r)/ *n* [C] fact, circumstance, etc that helps to produce a result: *a major ~ in making a decision*.

factory /'fæktərɪ/ *n* [C] (*pl* -ies) building(s) where goods are made, esp by machinery.

factual /'fæktʃʊəl/ *adj* concerned with or based on facts. **factually** *adv*.

faculty /'fækltɪ/ *n* [C] (*pl* -ies) 1 natural ability of the body or mind: *her mental faculties*. 2 (a) university department. (b) [also sing with *pl* v] teachers, etc in one

of these.

fade /feɪd/ *v* 1 [I, T] (cause sth to) lose colour or freshness. 2 [I] (*away*) disappear gradually from sight or hearing. 3 (phr v) **fade away** (of people) become weaker; die.

faeces /'fi:si:z/ *n* [*pl*] (*fml*) solid waste matter passed from the bowels.

fag /fæg/ *n* 1 [C] (*Brit infml*) cigarette. 2 [C] (*infml derog* esp *US*) male homosexual. **fagged out** /fægd/ *adj* (*infml*) very tired.

faggot (*US* **fagot**) /'fægət/ *n* 1 ball of chopped meat. 2 bundle of sticks for burning. 3 (*infml derog*) male homosexual.

Fahrenheit /'færənhaɪt/ *n* [U] temperature scale with the freezing-point of water at 32° and the boiling-point at 212°.

fail /feɪl/ *v* 1 [I, T] be unsuccessful. 2 [T] (of an examiner) decide that (a candidate) has been unsuccessful. 3 [I, T] not be enough for (sb/sth); disappoint: *The crops ~ed because of drought.* ○ *All his friends ~ed him.* 4 [I] (of health, eyesight, etc) become weak. 5 [I] forget or neglect (to do sth): ~ *to keep an appointment.* 6 [I] become bankrupt: *The company ~ed.* **fail** *n* 1 [C] failure in an examination. 2 (idm) **without 'fail** definitely.

failing /'feɪlɪŋ/ *n* [C] fault or weakness. **failing** *prep* [I] (of sth) does not happen or is not possible.

failure /'feɪljə(r)/ *n* 1 [U] lack of success. 2 [C] person or thing that fails. 3 [C, U] (instance of) not doing sth: *His ~ to help us was disappointing.* 4 [C, U] (instance of) not operating normally: *engine/heart ~*.

faint /feɪnt/ *adj* 1 (of things known by one's senses) weak; not clear: ~ *sounds*. 2 (of ideas, etc) weak; vague: *a ~ hope*. 3 (of people) about to lose consciousness. **faint** *v* [I] lose consciousness. **faint** *n* [C] act of fainting. **,faint-'hearted** *adj* not brave or confident. **faintly** *adv*. **faintness** *n* [U].

fair¹ /feə(r)/ *adj* 1 just; honest: *a ~ decision*. 2 quite good: *a ~ chance of success*. 3 (of the weather) dry and fine. 4 (of the skin or hair) light in colour: *a ,~ 'haired boy*. 5 neat; clean: *a ~ copy*. 6 (idm) **fair 'play** equal treatment for everyone. **fair** *adv* 1 in a fair(1) manner. 2 (idm) **fair enough** all right; true. **fairly** *adv* 1 moderately: ~ *ly easy*. 2 honestly. **fairness** *n* [U].

fair² /feə(r)/ *n* [C] 1 fun-fair. 2

market for farm animals and farm products. **3** large exhibition of goods: *a book ~.* **'fairground** *n* [C] open area where fun-fairs are held.

fairy /'feərɪ/ *n* [C] (*pl* -ies) small imaginary creature with magical powers. **'fairy story, 'fairy-tale** *n* [C] **1** story about fairies, magic, etc usu for children. **2** untrue story.

fait accompli /ˌfeɪt ə'kɒmplɪ:; *US* əkɒm'pli:/ *n* [C] (*French*) something that has already happened and cannot be changed.

faith /feɪθ/ *n* **1** [U] strong trust and confidence. **2** [U, sing] strong religious belief. **3** [C] religion: *the Jewish ~.* **4** (idm) **in good faith** with honest intentions.

faithful /'feɪθfl/ *adj* **1** (*to*) loyal. **2** accurate: *a ~ description.* **the faithful** *n* [pl] true believers in a religion. **faithfully** /-fəlɪ/ *adv.* **faithfulness** *n* [U].

faithless /'feɪθlɪs/ *adj* not loyal; false.

fake /feɪk/ *n* [C] **1** something that looks genuine but is not. **2** person who tries to deceive others by pretending to be or have sth. **fake** *v* [T] **1** make (eg a work of art) so that it seems genuine. **2** pretend (a feeling).

falcon /'fɔ:lkən; *US* 'fælkən/ *n* [C] small bird that can be trained to hunt and kill other birds and animals.

fall¹ /fɔ:l/ *v* (*pt* **fell** /fel/, *pp* **-en** /'fɔ:lən/) [I] **1** come or go down freely: *Leaves ~ in autumn.* ○ *~ off a ladder.* **2** stop standing; collapse: *The tree fell (down) in the storm.* **3** hang down: *Her hair ~s over her shoulders.* **4** become less in amount, number or intensity: *The temperature fell sharply.* **5** (of land) slope downwards. **6** lose power: *The government fell after the revolution.* **7** die in battle; (of a city) be captured. **8** pass into the state that is mentioned: become: *~ asleep* ○ *~ into disuse.* **9** happen or occur as a date: *Christmas ~s on a Friday this year.* **10** (idm) **fall flat** (of a joke or act) fail to produce the effect that was wanted. **fall foul of sb/sth** get into trouble with sb/sth. **fall in love with sb** feel a sudden strong attraction for sb. **fall on one's feet** ⇨ FOOT. **fall short of sth** fail to reach a necessary standard. **11** (phr v) **fall apart** break into pieces. **fall back** retreat. **fall back on sth** use sth, when other things have been tried without success. **fall behind (sb/sth)** fail

to keep level (with sb/sth). **fall behind with sth** fail to pay sth, eg rent. **fall for sb** (*infml*) be very attracted to sb. **fall for sth** (*infml*) be tricked into believing sth. **fall in** collapse: *The roof fell in.* **fall off** become less: *Attendance has ~en off.* **fall on sb/sth** (a) be the duty of sb. (b) (of the eyes) be directed towards sb/sth. **fall out (with sb)** quarrel (with sb). **fall through** fail to be completed: *The business deal fell through.*

fall² /fɔ:l/ *n* [C] **1** act of falling. **2** amount of sth that has fallen: *a heavy ~ of snow.* **3** distance through which sth falls. **4** (also **falls** [pl]) waterfall. **5** (*US*) autumn.

fallacy /'fæləsɪ/ *n* [C, U] (*pl* -ies) false belief or argument. **fallacious** /fə'leɪʃəs/ *adj* (*fml*) based on a fallacy.

fallen *pp* of FALL¹.

fallible /'fæləbl/ *adj* liable to make mistakes. **fallibility** /ˌfælə'bɪlətɪ/ *n* [U].

fall-out /'fɔ:laʊt/ *n* [U] radioactive dust in the air after a nuclear explosion.

fallow /'fæləʊ/ *adj* (of land) ploughed but not sown or planted.

false /fɔ:ls/ *adj* **1** wrong; incorrect. **2** not real; artificial: *~ teeth.* **3** deceitful; disloyal: *a ~ friend.* **4** (idm) **a false 'alarm** warning of sth dangerous that does not happen. **a false 'start** (a) (in a race) start before the signal has been given. (b) unsuccessful beginning to sth. **on/under false pretences** pretending to be sb else in order to deceive. **falsehood** /'fɔ:lshʊd/ *n* [C, U] untrue statement; lie; lying. **falsely** *adv.* **falseness** *n* [U].

falsify /'fɔ:lsɪfaɪ/ *v* (*pt, pp* -**ied**) [T] alter (a document, etc) so it is false. **falsification** /ˌfɔ:lsɪfɪ'keɪʃn/ *n* [C, U].

falsity /'fɔ:lsətɪ/ *n* (*pl* -ies) [U] falsehood; error.

falter /'fɔ:ltə(r)/ *v* [I] **1** move or act in an uncertain or hesitating way. **2** speak hesitantly. **falteringly** *adv.*

fame /feɪm/ *n* [U] state of being well known. **famed** *adj* famous.

familiar /fə'mɪlɪə(r)/ *adj* **1** (*to*) well known to sb; often seen or heard. **2** *with/* having a good knowledge of sth. **3** close and friendly. **familiarity** /fəˌmɪlɪ'ærətɪ/ *n* [C, U] (*pl* -ies). **familiarly** *adv.*

familiarize /fə'mɪlɪəraɪz/ *v* [T] *with/* make (oneself/sb) well informed about sth.

family /'fæməlɪ/ *n* (*pl* -ies) **1** [C,

also sing with pl v] (a) group of parents and children. (b) group of parents, children and close relatives, eg uncles, cousins and grandparents. 2 [C, U, also sing with pl v] person's children. 3 [C, also sing with pl v] all the people descended from the same ancestor. 4 [C] group of living creatures or languages: *the cat ~.* **'family 'planning** *n* [U] controlling the number of children in a family by using contraception. **family 'tree** *n* [C] chart showing the relationship of family members.

famine /'fæmɪn/ *n* [C, U] serious shortage of food.

famished /'fæmɪʃt/ *adj* (*infml*) very hungry.

famous /'feɪməs/ *adj* known to very many people. **famously** *adv* very well: *They get on ~ly.*

fan¹ /fæn/ *n* [C] object for making a current of air, eg to cool a room. **fan** *v* (**-nn-**) **1** [T] send a current of air onto. **2** (phr v) **fan out** spread out from a central point: *The troops ~ned out across the field.* **'fan belt** *n* [C] rubber belt used to turn the fan that cools a car engine.

fan² /fæn/ *n* [C] very keen supporter: *football ~ s.* **'fan mail** *n* [U] letters from fans to a famous person.

fanatic /fə'nætɪk/ *n* [C] person who is too enthusiastic about sth: *a religious ~.* **fanatical** *adj* too enthusiastic. **fanatically** /-klɪ/ *adv.* **fanaticism** /-tɪsɪzəm/ *n* [U].

fanciful /'fænsɪfl/ *adj* **1** (*of people*) guided by imagination, not reason. **2** unreal: *~ ideas.* **fancifully** *adv.*

fancy¹ /'fænsɪ/ *n* (*pl* **-ies**) **1** [C] (*for*)|| liking or desire: *a ~ for some cake.* **2** [U] ability to create images in the mind. **3** [C] vague opinion or idea. **4** (idm) **catch/ take sb's fancy** please or attract sb. **take a fancy to sb/sth** become fond of sb/sth. **fancy** *v* (*pt, pp* **-ied**) [T] **1** (*infml*) want: *I ~ a cup of tea.* **2** (*infml*) find (sb) attractive: *I think she fancies you.* **3** think or believe (sth). **4** (used for showing surprise, shock, etc): *F~ that!*

fancy² /'fænsɪ/ *adj* **1** decorated and unusual; not plain: *~ cakes.* **2** extravagant or exaggerated: *~ ideas.* **fancy 'dress** *n* [U] unusual clothing worn for a party.

fanfare /'fænfeə(r)/ *n* [C] short piece of music played on trumpets.

fang /fæŋ/ *n* [C] long sharp tooth.

fanny /'fænɪ/ *n* [C] (*pl* **-ies**) **1** (*Brit* △ *sl*) female sex organs. **2** (*sl esp US*) buttocks.

fantasize /'fæntəsaɪz/ *v* [I, T] (*about*)|| imagine fantasies about sth.

fantastic /fæn'tæstɪk/ *adj* **1** (*infml*) wonderful: *a ~ party.* **2** (*infml*) very large. **3** wild and strange. **4** (of ideas) not practical. **fantastically** /-klɪ/ *adv.*

fantasy /'fæntəsɪ/ *n* [C, U] (*pl* **-ies**) (pleasant idea or dream of the) imagination: *childhood ~ies.*

far¹ /fɑ:(r)/ *adv* (~**ther** /'fɑ:ðə(r)/ or **further** /'fɜ:ðə(r)/, ~**thest** /'fɑ:ðɪst/ or **furthest** /'fɜ:ðɪst/) **1** at or to a great distance: *How ~ is it to London?* **2** to a great extent: *fallen ~ behind with his work.* **3** very much: ~ *easier.* **4** (idm) **as/so far as, in so far as** to the extent that: *As ~ as I know, they're still coming.* **far from doing sth** instead of doing sth: *F~ from hating the music, I love it!* **far from sth** not at all sth: *The work is ~ from easy,* ie it is very difficult. **go 'far** (of money) buy many things. **go 'far, go a long 'way** (of people) be very successful. **go too 'far** behave in a way that is beyond reasonable limits. **'so far** until now. **'far-away** *adj* **1** distant. **2** (of a look in sb's eyes) dreamy. **,far-'fetched** *adj* difficult to believe. **,far-'off** *adj* distant. **,far-'reaching** *adj* having a wide influence: *a ~ reaching decision.* **,far-'sighted** *adj* seeing what may happen in the future and so making wise plans.

far² /fɑ:(r)/ *adj* (~**ther** /'fɑ:ðə(r)/ or **further** /'fɜ:ðə(r)/, ~**thest** /'fɑ:ðɪst/ or **furthest** /'fɜ:ðɪst/) **1** more distant: *the ~ end of the street ○ on the ~ right,* ie with extreme right-wing views. **2** (*dated* or *fml*) distant: *a ~ country.* **the Far 'East** *n* [sing] China, Japan and other countries of E and SE Asia.

farce /fɑ:s/ *n* **1** (a) [C] funny play, with unlikely ridiculous situations. (b) [U] this kind of play. **2** [C] series of actual ridiculous events. **farcical** *adj.*

fare /feə(r)/ *n* [C] money charged for a journey: *bus ~ s.* **fare** *v* [I] (*fml*) progress; get on: *~ well/ badly.*

farewell /,feə'wel/ *interj*, *n* [C] (*dated* or *fml*) goodbye.

farm /fɑ:m/ *n* [C] area of land and buildings for growing crops and raising animals. **farm** *v* [I, T] use (land) for growing crops and raising animals. **farmer** *n* [C] person who owns or manages a farm. **'farm-hand** *n* [C] person who works for a farmer. **'farmyard** *n* [C] space enclosed by or next to farm buildings.

fart /fɑːt/ v [I] (△) send air from the bowels out through the anus.

fart n [C] (△) 1 sending of air out through the anus. 2 (sl derog) person who is disliked.

farther, farthest adv, adj ⇨ FAR.

fascinate /'fæsɪneɪt/ v [T] attract or interest (sb) greatly. **fascinating** adj. **fascination** /ˌfæsɪ'neɪʃn/ n [U, C].

fascism (also **Fascism**) /'fæʃɪzəm/ n [U] right-wing dictatorial political system. **fascist** (also **Fascist**) adj, n [C].

fashion /'fæʃn/ n 1 [sing] way of doing sth: walk in a strange ~. 2 [C, U] popular style of clothes at a particular time: wearing the latest ~. 3 (idm) after a 'fashion not particularly well. in/out of fashion fashionable/no longer fashionable. **fashion** v [T] give form or shape to.

fashionable /'fæʃnəbl/ adj 1 following a style that is popular at a particular time. 2 used by many (esp rich) people: a ~ restaurant. **fashionably** adv.

fast[1] /fɑːst; US fæst/ adj 1 quick: ~ cars. 2 (of a watch or clock) showing a time later than the true time. **fast** adv quickly. **fast 'food** n [U] food, eg hamburgers and chips, that can be cooked easily.

fast[2] /fɑːst; US fæst/ adj 1 firmly fixed. 2 (of colours) not likely to fade or spread when washed. 3 (idm) **stand fast** ⇨ STAND[2] 11. **fast** adv 1 firmly; tightly. 2 (idm) **fast asleep** sleeping deeply.

fast[3] /fɑːst; US fæst/ v [I] go without food, esp for religious reasons. **fast** n [C] period of fasting.

fasten /'fɑːsn; US 'fæsn/ v 1 [I, T] become or make firmly fixed: ~ your seat-belt. 2 (phr v) **fasten on sth** take and use sth with enthusiasm. **fasten sth on sth** direct (one's attention, thoughts, etc) on sth. **fastener, fastening** n [C] something that fastens things together: a zip-~er.

fastidious /fə'stɪdɪəs, fæ-/ adj difficult to please; not liking things to be dirty or untidy. **fastidiously** adv.

fat[1] /fæt/ adj (~ter, ~test) 1 (of sb's body) large in size; having too much fat. 2 thick or wide: a ~ book. 3 (infml) large in quantity: ~ profits. **fatness** n [U].

fat[2] /fæt/ n 1 [U] substance under animals' skins, used for keeping them warm. 2 [C, U] substance from animals or plants used in cooking.

fatal /'feɪtl/ adj 1 causing or ending in death: a ~ accident. 2 causing disaster: a ~ mistake. **fatally** adv.

fatalism /'feɪtəlɪzəm/ n [U] belief that events are controlled by fate(1). **fatalist** n [C].

fatality /fə'tæləti/ n (pl -ies) 1 [C] death caused by accident or violence. 2 [U] sense of being controlled by fate(1).

fate /feɪt/ n 1 [U] power believed to control all events. 2 [C] person's future, esp death. **fateful** adj important: that ~ day. **fatefully** adv.

father /'fɑːðə(r)/ n 1 [C] male parent. 2 [C] (usu pl) ancestor. 3 [C] first leader: city ~ s. 4 [C] clergyman. 5 **Father** [sing] God. father v [T] be the father of. **Father 'Christmas** n [C] old man who is believed by children to bring presents at Christmas. **'father-in-law** n [C] (pl ~s-in-law) father of one's wife or husband. **'fatherland** n [C] country in which one was born. **fatherly** adj of or like a father.

fathom /'fæðəm/ n [C] measurement of the depth of water (1.8 metres or 6 feet). **fathom** v [T] understand fully. **fathomless** adj too deep to measure or understand.

fatigue /fə'tiːg/ n 1 [U] great tiredness. 2 [U] weakness in metals, etc caused by constant stress. 3 **fatigues** [pl] clothes worn by soldiers when cleaning, cooking, etc. **fatigue** v [T] (fml) make (sb) very tired.

fatten /'fætn/ v [I, T] become or make fat.

fatty /'fæti/ adj (-ier, -iest) containing (too much) fat. **fatty** n [C] (pl -ies) (infml derog) fat person.

fatuous /'fætjʊəs/ adj foolish: ~ remarks. **fatuously** adv.

faucet /'fɔːsɪt/ n [C] (US) tap.

fault /fɔːlt/ n 1 [sing] responsibility for being wrong: It was Pat's ~. 2 [C] mistake or imperfection: an electrical ~. 3 [C] crack in the surface of the earth. 4 (idm) **at fault** in the wrong. **fault** v [T] find a fault in: I cannot ~ her performance. **faultless** adj perfect. **faultlessly** adv. **faulty** adj (esp of a machine) not working properly.

fauna /'fɔːnə/ n [U] all the animals of an area or period of time.

faux pas /ˌfəʊ 'pɑː/ n [C] (pl faux pas /-'pɑːz/) (French) embarrassing mistake.

favour (US **-or**) /'feɪvə(r)/ n 1 [U] liking or approval: look with ~ on the idea. 2 [U] treatment of sb more generously than others: show ~ to sb. 3 [C] act of kindness: Do me a ~

and lend me your pen. 4 (idm) **be out of 'favour with sb** not have sb's approval. **in favour of sb/sth** supporting sb/sth. **in sb's favour** to the advantage of sb. **favour** *v* [T] 1 support. 2 treat (sb) more generously than others. **favourable** *adj* 1 showing approval. 2 helpful; suitable. **favourably** *adv*.

favourite (*US* favor-) /ˈfeɪvərɪt/ *n* 1 [C] person or thing liked more than others. 2 **the favourite** [sing] horse, etc expected to win a race. **favourite** *adj* liked more than any other. **favouritism** /-ɪzəm/ *n* [U] practice of being unfairly generous to one person or group.

fawn¹ /fɔːn/ *n* [C] young deer. **fawn** *adj* light yellowish brown in colour.

fawn² /fɔːn/ *v* (phr v) **fawn on sb** try to gain sb's favour by pretending to like him/her.

fax /fæks/ *n* [C] copy of written or printed material sent electronically by a telephone line. **fax** *v* [T] send (such a copy).

FBI /ˌef biː/ *abbr* **the FBI** (*US*) Federal Bureau of Investigation.

fear /fɪə(r)/ *n* 1 [C, U] feeling caused by the possibility of danger, pain, etc. 2 [U] possibility: *There's no ~ of me going.* 3 (idm) **in fear of one's 'life** worried about one's own safety. **no fear** (*infml*) certainly not. **fear** *v* 1 [T] be afraid of. 2 [I] *for// be* anxious or worried about sth: *~ for one's life.* **fearful** *adj* 1 afraid. 2 very unpleasant. 3 (*infml*) great: *a ~ful mess.* **fearless** *adj* not afraid. **fearlessly** *adv*.

feasible /ˈfiːzəbl/ *adj* that can be done. **feasibility** /ˌfiːzəˈbɪlətɪ/ *n* [U].

feast /fiːst/ *n* [C] 1 large splendid meal. 2 religious festival, eg Christmas. **feast** *v* 1 [I] take part in a feast. 2 [T] provide (sb) with a feast. 3 (idm) **feast one's eyes on sth** look at sth with pleasure.

feat /fiːt/ *n* [C] difficult act that is well done.

feather /ˈfeðə(r)/ *n* [C] 1 one of the many light coverings that grow from a bird's skin. 2 (idm) **a 'feather in one's cap** something that one can be proud of. **feather** *v* [T] cover or fit with feathers. 2 (idm) **feather one's 'nest** make oneself richer or more comfortable. **feather 'bed** *n* [C] mattress filled with feathers. **feathery** *adj* light and soft.

feature /ˈfiːtʃə(r)/ *n* [C] 1 noticeable part: *an important ~ of city life.* 2 **features** parts of sb's face,

eg the eyes and mouth. 3 special article in a newspaper. 4 full-length film shown at a cinema. **feature** *v* 1 [T] give an important part to (sb/sth). 2 [I] *in// have an important part in sth. **featureless** *adj* uninteresting.

February /ˈfebruərɪ; *US* -ʊerɪ/ *n* [U, C] second month of the year. (See examples of use at *April*).

feces (*US*) = FAECES.

fed *pt, pp* of FEED.

federal /ˈfedərəl/ *adj* 1 of a system of government in which several states unite, eg for defence. 2 of the central government, not the government of states.

federation /ˌfedəˈreɪʃn/ *n* [C] 1 union of states with a central federal government. 2 similar union of societies, etc.

fed up /ˌfed ˈʌp/ *adj* (*infml*) tired and unhappy.

fee /fiː/ *n* [C] 1 money paid to take an examination, join a club, etc: *entrance ~.* 2 [usu pl] money paid for professional services.

feeble /ˈfiːbl/ *adj* (~r, ~st) weak. **feeble-'minded** *adj* having less than usual intelligence. **feebly** /-blɪ/ *adv*.

feed /fiːd/ *v* (*pt, pp* fed /fed/) 1 [T] give food to. 2 [I] (on)// (esp of animals) eat. 3 [T] *A (with B; B to A)// supply (sth) with material; supply (material) to sth. **feed** *n* 1 [C] meal for an animal or baby. 2 [U] food for animals. 3 [C] pipe, channel, etc that carries material to a machine. **'feedback** *n* [U] information about a product, etc sent back to the person in charge. **'feeding-bottle** *n* [C] bottle from which a baby is given milk.

feel /fiːl/ *v* (*pt, pp* felt /felt/) 1 [T] learn about (sth) by touching or holding in one's hands. 2 [T] be aware of; experience: *~ the pain ○ ~ concern.* 3 (usu used with an adj) (a) be in the state that is mentioned: *~ happy/tired.* (b) have the quality mentioned: *These shoes ~ tight.* 4 [T] suffer because of: *~ the cold.* 5 [T] have as an opinion; believe: *He felt he would succeed.* 6 (idm) **feel like (doing) sth** want (to do) sth: *~ like (having) a drink.* 7 (phr v) **feel for sb** have sympathy for sb. **feel** *n* [sing] 1 act of feeling. 2 sensation caused by touching sth. 3 general impression of a place, etc.

feeler /ˈfiːlə(r)/ *n* [C] 1 long thin part of an insect's head, used for touching things. 2 (idm) **put out feelers** ask questions, etc to test the opinions of others.

feeling /'fiːlɪŋ/ n 1 [C] something felt through the mind or the senses. 2 [U] ability to feel. 3 [C, usu sing] belief; vague idea: *a ~ that something awful is going to happen.* 4 [sing] opinion. 5 [U] sympathy or sensitivity. 6 **feelings** [pl] sb's emotions rather than thoughts. 7 (idm) **bad/ill 'feeling** anger or dissatisfaction.

feet pl of FOOT.

feign /feɪn/ v [T] (*fml*) pretend (sth).

feint /feɪnt/ n [C, U] pretended action or attack. **feint** v [I] make a feint.

felicity /fə'lɪsətɪ/ n [U] (*fml*) great happiness.

feline /'fiːlaɪn/ adj of or like a cat.

fell¹ pt of FALL¹.

fell² /fel/ n [C] area of rocky moorland in N England.

fell³ /fel/ v [T] 1 cut down (a tree). 2 knock (sb) down.

fellow /'feləʊ/ n [C] 1 (*dated infml*) man; chap. 2 [usu pl] companion: *'school ~s.* **fellow** adj of the same group or kind: *one's ~ men.* **fellowship** n 1 [U] feeling of friendship. 2 [C] group or society. 3 [C] position of a college fellow.

felony /'felənɪ/ n [C, U] (pl **-ies**) (*law*) serious crime, eg murder. **felon** /'felən/ n [C] person guilty of a felony.

felt¹ pt, pp of FEEL.

felt² /felt/ n [U] thick cloth made from pressed wool, hair or fur. **felt-tip 'pen** (also **felt-'tip**) n [C] pen with a pointed top made of felt.

female /'fiːmeɪl/ adj 1 of the sex that produces young. 2 (of a plant) producing fruit. 3 (of part of a device) having a hollow part into which another part fits. **female** n [C] female person or animal.

feminine /'femənɪn/ adj 1 of or like women. 2 (*grammar*) of a particular class of nouns, pronouns, etc. **femininity** /,femə'nɪnətɪ/ n [U] quality of being feminine.

feminism /'femɪnɪzəm/ n [U] belief in the principle that women should have the same rights as men. **feminist** n [C], adj.

fen /fen/ n [C] area of low flat wet land.

fence¹ /fens/ n [C] wall made of wood or wire. **fence** v [T] (in/off|) surround or divide (sth) with a fence. **fencing** n [U] material for making fences.

fence² /fens/ v [I] 1 fight with a long thin sword as a sport. 2 avoid giving a direct answer to a question. **fencing** n [U] sport of fight-

ing with long thin swords.

fend /fend/ v (phr v) **fend for one'self** look after oneself. **fend sb/sth off** defend oneself from sb/sth.

ferment¹ /fə'ment/ v [I, T] 1 (make sth) change chemically so that glucose becomes alcohol, eg in beer and wine. 2 become or make excited. **fermentation** /,fɜːmen'teɪʃn/ n [U].

ferment² /'fɜːment/ n [U] excitement and trouble.

fern /fɜːn/ n [C, U] flowerless plant with feathery green leaves.

ferocious /fə'rəʊʃəs/ adj fierce or violent. **ferociously** adv.

ferocity /fə'rɒsətɪ/ n [U] quality of being ferocious.

ferret /'ferɪt/ n [C] small animal of the weasel family that hunts rabbits and rats. **ferret** v 1 (*about*)| (*infml*) search. 2 (phr v) **ferret sth out** (*infml*) find sth by searching thoroughly.

ferry (also **'ferry-boat**) /'ferɪ/ n [C] (pl **-ies**) boat that carries people and goods across a river or short stretch of sea. **ferry** v (pt, pp **-ied**) [T] transport (people or goods), esp regularly.

fertile /'fɜːtaɪl; US 'fɜːrtl/ adj 1 (of land or soil) able to produce strong plants. 2 (of a person's mind) full of new ideas. 3 (of plants or animals) able to produce fruit or young. **fertility** /fə'tɪlətɪ/ n [U].

fertilize /'fɜːtəlaɪz/ v [T] make fertile. **fertilization** /,fɜːtəlaɪ'zeɪʃn; US -lɪ'z-/ n [U]. **fertilizer** n [U, C] substance added to soil to make it more fertile.

fervent /'fɜːvənt/ adj showing strong feeling: *~ belief/supporter.* **fervently** adv.

fervour (*US* **-or**) /'fɜːvə(r)/ n [U] very strong feeling; enthusiasm.

fester /'festə(r)/ v [I] 1 (of a wound) become infected. 2 (*fig*) (of feelings or thoughts) become more bitter and angry.

festival /'festəvl/ n [C] 1 organized series of performances of music, drama, etc. 2 (day or time for a) public, esp religious, celebration.

festive /'festɪv/ adj joyous.

festivity /fe'stɪvətɪ/ n [U, C] (pl **-ies**) happy celebration.

fetch /fetʃ/ v [T] 1 collect (from a place): *~ the children (from school).* 2 (of goods) be sold for (a price): *The vase ~ed £1000.*

fête /feɪt/ n [C] outdoor entertainment, usu to collect money for a particular purpose. **fête** v [T] (usu passive) honour in a special way.

fetish /'fetɪʃ/ n [C] something to which too much attention is given.

fetter /'fetə(r)/ n [C] 1 chain for a prisoner's foot. 2 (fig) (usu pl) something that hinders progress: *the ~s of government controls.* **fetter** v [T] 1 put in chains. 2 prevent, hinder.

fetus (US) = FOETUS.

feud /fju:d/ n [C] long bitter quarrel. **feud** v [I] carry on a feud.

feudal /'fju:dl/ adj of the system of receiving land from a landowner, and working and fighting for him in return, during the Middle Ages in Europe. **feudalism** /-dəlɪzəm/ n [U].

fever /'fi:və(r)/ n 1 [C, U] very high temperature of the body. 2 [U] disease causing a high fever. 3 [sing] state of excitement: *in a ~ of impatience.* **feverish** adj 1 having a fever. 2 excited; very fast. **feverishly** adv.

few /fju:/ adj 1 a few a small number (of). 2 (used without a) not many: *F~ people live to be 100.*

fiancé /fɪ'ɒnseɪ; US ˌfiːɑːn'seɪ/ n [C] (fem **fiancée**) person to whom one is engaged to be married.

fiasco /fɪ'æskəʊ/ n [C] (pl ~s; US also ~es) complete failure.

fib /fɪb/ n [C] (infml) small lie, esp about sth unimportant. **fib** v (-bb-) [I] tell a fib. **fibber** n [C].

fibre (US **fiber**) /'faɪbə(r)/ n [C] 1 thin thread in an animal or vegetable growth: *muscle ~s.* 2 [U] material formed from a mass of fibres. 3 [U] person's character: *strong moral ~.* **fibreglass** (US '**fiber-**) n [U] material made from glass fibres, used for keeping heat in. **fibrous** /-brəs/ adj made of, or like, fibres.

fickle /'fɪkl/ adj often changing.

fiction /'fɪkʃn/ n 1 [U] writing that describes invented people and events, not real ones. 2 [C, U] story or statement that is not true. **fictional** /-ʃənl/ adj.

fictitious /fɪk'tɪʃəs/ adj untrue; invented.

fiddle /'fɪdl/ n [C] 1 (sl) dishonest action. 2 (infml) violin. **fiddle** v 1 [I] *with// play aimlessly with sth in one's hands. 2 [T] (infml) change (accounts) dishonestly; get (sth) by cheating. 3 [I] play the violin. **fiddler** n [C] 1 person who plays a violin. 2 (infml) person who cheats. **fiddling** adj small and unimportant. **fiddly** adv awkward to do or use.

fidelity /fɪ'delətɪ; US faɪ-/ n [U] 1 faithfulness. 2 accuracy of a translation, report, etc.

fidget /'fɪdʒɪt/ v [I] move one's body about restlessly. **fidget** n [C] person who fidgets. **fidgety** adj.

field /fi:ld/ n 1 [C] area of land on which crops are grown or cattle are kept. 2 [C] open area: *a football ~/bil ~/battle ~.* 3 [C] area of study or activity. 4 [C] area in which a force can be felt: *a magnetic ~.* '**field-day** n (idm) **have a field-day** have great fun, success, etc. '**field 'marshal** n [C] officer of the highest rank in the British army.

field /fi:ld/ v 1 [I, T] (in cricket, etc) (stand ready to) catch or stop (the ball). 2 [T] put (a team) into the field. 3 [T] deal with (a question) skilfully. **fielder** n [C] (in cricket, etc) person who fields.

fiend /fi:nd/ n [C] 1 very wicked person. 2 person who is very keen on sth mentioned: *a health ~.* **fiendish** adj. **fiendishly** adv very.

fierce /fɪəs/ adj (~r, ~st) 1 angry and violent. 2 intense; strong: *~ heat/opposition.* **fiercely** adv. **fierceness** n [U].

fiery /'faɪərɪ/ adj (-ier, -iest) 1 of or like fire; flaming. 2 (of a person) quickly made angry. **fierily** /-rəlɪ/ adv.

fifteen /ˌfɪf'ti:n/ pron, adj, n [C] 15. **fifteenth** /ˌfɪf'ti:nθ/ pron, adj, n [C] 15th. **fifteenth** n [C] $\frac{1}{15}$.

fifth /fɪfθ/ pron, adj, n [C] 5th. **fifth** pron, n [C] $\frac{1}{5}$.

fifty /'fɪftɪ/ pron, adj, n [C] (pl -ies) 50. **fiftieth** pron, adj, n [C] 50th. **fiftieth** pron, n [C] $\frac{1}{50}$. ,**fifty-'fifty** adj, adv shared equally between two.

fig /fɪg/ n [C] 1 (tree with a) soft sweet fruit full of small seeds. 2 (idm) **not care/give a 'fig** (about sth) not care about sth at all.

fig abbr 1 figure; illustration: *See fig 3.* 2 figurative.

fight /faɪt/ v (pt, pp fought /fɔːt/) 1 [I, T] use force with the hands or weapons against sb: *(fig) ~ against poverty.* 2 [T] carry on (a battle or war). 3 [I] quarrel or argue. 4 (phr v) **fight back** (a) show resistance. (b) try hard to return to a previous good position. **fight sb/sth off** resist or repel sb/sth: *~ off an attacker/a cold.* **fight sth out** decide a quarrel by fighting. **fight** n 1 [C] act of fighting. 2 [U] desire or ability to fight. **fighter** n [C] 1 person who fights in war or in sport. 2 fast military aircraft.

figment /'fɪgmənt/ n [C] something not real: *a ~ of her imagination.*

figurative /'fɪgərətɪv/ adj (of words) used not in the ordinary literal sense but in an imaginative way. **figuratively** adv.

figure /'fɪgə(r); US 'fɪgjər/ n 1 [C] symbol for a number. 2 [C] price. 3 [C] human form or shape: ~ approaching in the darkness ○ a good ~, ie slim or shapely. 4 [C] person: important ~ s in history. 5 [C] form of a person that is drawn, carved, etc. 6 [C] diagram. 7 **figures** [pl] arithmetic. **figure** v 1 [I] (in)// appear in sth. 2 [T] (esp US) think. 3 [I] (infml) (used with it or that) be likely: That ~ s. 4 (phr v) **figure on sth** (US) include sth in one's plans. **figure sth out** discover sth by thinking; calculate. **'figure-head** n [C] person in a high position but with no real authority. **,figure of 'speech** n [C] figurative expression.

filament /'fɪləmənt/ n [C] thin wire inside a light bulb; thin thread.

file[1] /faɪl/ n [C] metal tool with a rough surface for cutting or shaping hard substances. **file** v [T] cut or shape with a file: ~ one's fingernails. **filings** /'faɪlɪŋz/ n [pl] small bits removed by a file.

file[2] /faɪl/ n [C] 1 holder, box, cover, etc for keeping papers. 2 papers in a file. 3 organized computer data. 4 (idm) **on file** kept in a file. **file** v 1 [T] put (sth) in a file. 2 [I, T] (for)// make (a formal request, etc) officially: ~ for divorce. **'filing cabinet** n [C] cabinet for holding files.

file[3] /faɪl/ n [C] line of people one behind the other. **file** v [I] walk in a file: ~ out of the room.

fill /fɪl/ v 1 [I, T] become or make full. 2 hold (a job); put sb into (a job): ~ a vacancy. 3 [T] perform (a function); fulfil. 4 (phr v) **fill in** (**for sb**) take sb's place. **fill sth in**, (US also) **fill sth out** add what is necessary to make complete: ~ in a form. **fill 'out** become larger or fatter. **fill** (**sth**) **up** become or make full. **fill in** (idm) **one's fill of sth** (a) as much as one can eat or drink. (b) as much as one can bear: I've had my ~ of your rudeness! **filler** n [C] material used to fill a hole in sth. **filling** n [C] material used to fill a hole in a tooth. **'filling station** n [C] petrol station.

fillet /'fɪlɪt/ n [C] piece of meat or fish without bones. **fillet** v [T] cut into fillets.

film /fɪlm/ n 1 [C] cinema picture; movie. 2 [C, U] roll of thin flexible material used in photography. 3 [C, usu sing] thin covering: a ~ of oil. **film** v [I, T] make a film(1) of

(sb/sth). **'film star** n [C] popular cinema actor or actress.

filter /'fɪltə(r)/ n [C] 1 device used for holding back solid material in a liquid passed through it. 2 coloured glass that allows light only of certain wavelengths to pass through. **filter** v 1 [I, T] (cause to) flow through a filter. 2 [I] pass or flow slowly; become known gradually.

filth /fɪlθ/ n [U] 1 disgusting dirt. 2 very rude and offensive words, pictures, etc. **filthy** adj (-ier, -iest).

fin /fɪn/ n [C] 1 wide thin winglike part of a fish. 2 thing shaped like this, eg on the back of an aircraft.

final /'faɪml/ adj 1 coming at the end; last. 2 (of a decision) that cannot be changed. 3 (idm) **final straw** ⇨ STRAW. **final** n [C] 1 last of a series of competitions: the tennis ~ s. 2 **finals** [pl] last set of university examinations. **finalist** /-nəlɪst/ n [C] player in a final competition. **finalize** /-nəlaɪz/ v [T] put into final form. **finally** /-nəli/ adv 1 eventually. 2 conclusively: settle the matter ~ ly.

finale /fɪ'nɑːlɪ; US -'næli/ n [C] last part of a piece of music or drama.

finance /'faɪnæns, fɪ'næns/ n 1 [U] management of (esp public) money. 2 [U] money needed to pay for a project: obtain ~ from the bank. 3 **finances** [pl] money available to a person, company, etc. **finance** v [T] provide money for (a project, etc). **financial** /faɪ'nænʃl, fɪ'næn-/ adj. **financially** adv. **financier** /faɪ'nænsɪə(r); US fɪnən'sɪər/ n [C] person who finances businesses.

finch /fɪntʃ/ n [C] small songbird.

find /faɪnd/ v (pt, pp **found** /faʊnd/) [T] 1 discover (sth/sb) by searching. 2 discover (sth/sb) unexpectedly. 3 get back (sth/sb that was lost). 4 succeed in obtaining (sth): ~ time to study. 5 become aware of (sth) by experience; consider to be: I ~ it difficult to understand him. 6 arrive at naturally: Water always ~ s its own level. 7 exist in a particular place: Tigers are found in India. 8 (law) declare a judgement on (a person): ~ her innocent. 9 (idm) **find fault with sth/sb** look for mistakes in sth/sb; complain about. 10 (phr v) **find sth out** learn sth by study or inquiry: ~ out when the next train leaves. **find** n [C] something interesting or valuable that is found.

finder *n* [C]. **finding** *n* [C, usu pl] 1 what is learnt by study or inquiry. 2 (*law*) decision reached by a court.

fine¹ /faɪn/ *adj* (~**r**, ~**st**) 1 enjoyable or pleasing: *a ~ view*. 2 in good health. 3 (of weather) bright; clear. 4 made of very small particles: ~ *powder*. 5 delicate; carefully made. 6 (able to be) seen or noticed only with difficulty or effort: *a ~ distinction*. **fine** *adv* very well. **fine 'art** *n* [U] (also **the fine 'arts** [pl]) paintings, sculptures, etc. **finely** *adv* 1 very well. 2 into small pieces: ~ *ly cut meat*. **fineness** *n* [U].

fine² /faɪn/ *n* [C] money paid as a punishment for breaking the law. **fine** *v* [T] punish (sb) by ordering him/her to pay a fine.

finery /'faɪnrɪ/ *n* [U] beautiful clothing.

finesse /fɪ'nes/ *n* [U] skilful way of dealing with a situation.

finger /'fɪŋgə(r)/ *n* [C] 1 any of the five parts at the end of each hand. 2 part of a glove that fits over a finger. 3 (idm) **get, pull, etc one's 'finger out** (*infml*) stop being lazy; start to work hard. **put one's finger on sth** find precisely (an error, etc). **finger** *v* [T] touch or feel with one's fingers. **'fingernail** *n* [C] hard layer that covers the end of each finger. **'fingerprint** *n* [C] mark made by a finger when pressed on a surface. **'fingertip** *n* [C] 1 end of a finger. 2 (idm) **have sth at one's fingertips** know sth very well.

finish /'fɪnɪʃ/ *v* 1 [I, T] come or bring to an end; reach the end of (a task). 2 [T] eat, drink or use what is left of (sth). 3 [T] make (sth) complete. 4 (phr v) **finish sb/sth off** destroy sb/sth. **finish with sb/sth** no longer be dealing with sb/sth; end a relationship with sb. **finish** *n* 1 [C] last part. 2 [C, U] appearance after being polished, painted, etc: *a highly-polished ~*.

finite /'faɪnaɪt/ *adj* 1 limited. 2 (*grammar*) (of a verb form) agreeing with its subject in person and number: '*Is' and 'was' are ~ forms of 'be'*.

fir (also **'fir-tree**) /fɜː(r)/ *n* [C] evergreen tree with leaves like needles. **'fir-cone** *n* [C] fruit of the fir-tree.

fire¹ /'faɪə(r)/ *n* 1 [U] burning that produces light and heat. 2 **(a)** [C] burning that causes destruction: *forest ~s*. **(b)** [U] destruction by fire. 3 [C] fuel burning for heating, cooking, etc: *light a ~*. 4 [C] apparatus for heating a room: *a gas*

~. 5 [U] shooting from guns. 6 (idm) **on 'fire** burning. **under 'fire** being shot at. **'fire-alarm** *n* [C] bell that warns people of a fire. **'firearm** *n* [C, usu pl] gun. **the 'fire brigade** *n* [sing] team of people who put out fires. **'fire-drill** *n* [C, U] practice of leaving a burning building, etc safely. **'fire-engine** *n* [C] vehicle that carries firemen and equipment to put out fires. **'fire-escape** *n* [C] outside staircase for leaving a burning building. **'fire extinguisher** *n* [C] metal cylinder containing water or chemicals for putting out a small fire. **'fire-fighter** *n* [C] person who helps put out large fires. **'fireguard** *n* [C] protective metal framework round a fire in a room. **'fireman** /-mən/ *n* [C] (*pl* -**men**) person whose job is to put out fires. **'fireplace** *n* [C] open space in a wall for a fire in a room. **'fireproof** *v* [T] *adj* (make sth) unable to be damaged by fire. **'fireside** *n* [C, usu sing] part of a room near the fireplace. **'fire station** *n* [C] building for a fire brigade. **'firewood** *n* [U] wood used for lighting fires or as fuel. **'firework** *n* [C] device containing chemicals that burn or explode with coloured flames.

fire² /'faɪə(r)/ *v* 1 [I, T] shoot with a gun; shoot (a bullet). 2 [T] (*infml*) dismiss (an employee) from a job. 3 [T] excite: ~ *sb's imagination*. 4 [T] heat (a clay object) in a special oven. **'firing-line** *n* [sing] front line of battle, nearest the enemy. **'firing-squad** *n* [C, U] group of soldiers ordered to shoot a condemned person.

firm¹ /fɜːm/ *adj* 1 fairly hard. 2 strongly fixed in place. 3 not likely to change. 4 (of a person's movements) steady; stable. 5 (idm) **stand firm** ⇨ STAND² 11. **firm** *v* [I, T] become or make firm. **firm** *adv* firmly. **firmly** *adv* in a firm way. **firmness** *n* [U].

firm² /fɜːm/ *n* [C] business company.

first¹ /fɜːst/ *adj* 1 coming before all others. 2 (idm) **at first 'sight** when seen for the first time. **first 'thing** as soon as possible, esp on a particular day. **first 'aid** *n* [U] treatment given immediately to an injured person before a doctor comes. **first 'class** *n* [U] most comfortable conditions on a train, ship, etc. **'first-class** *adj, adv* of by the best class. **'first 'floor** *n* [C] 1 (*Brit*) floor immediately above the ground floor. ⇨ 2 (*US*) ground floor. **first 'hand** *adj, adv* (of information) (obtained) directly from the origin. **firstly** adv (in giving a list) to begin with. **'first name** n [C] name that goes before one's family name. **'first 'person** n [sing] (grammar) set of pronouns, eg I, we, me, and the verb forms, eg am, used with them. **first-rate** adj excellent.

first¹ /fɜːst/ adv 1 before anyone or anything else: She spoke first. 2 for the first time: when I ~ came to London. 3 in preference to sth else.

first² /fɜːst/ n, pron 1 the **first** [sing] first person or thing: the ~ to leave. 2 [C] (infml) important new achievement. 3 [C] university examination result of the highest class. 4 (idm) **at 'first** at the beginning.

fish /fɪʃ/ n (pl **fish** or ~es) 1 [C] cold blooded animal that lives in water. 2 [U] flesh of a fish eaten as food: ~ and chips. **fish** v 1 [I] try to catch fish. 2 (phr v) **fish for sth** try to obtain (compliments, etc) indirectly. **fish sth out (of sth)** take sth out (of sth): He ~ed a coin out of his pocket. **fisherman** /'fɪʃəmən/ n [C] (pl **-men**) person who catches fish, esp as a job. **fishery** n [C, usu pl] (pl **-ies**) part of the sea where fishing is carried on. **fishing** n [U] sport or job of catching fish: go ~ing ○ '~-ing-rod. **fishmonger** /'fɪʃmʌŋgə(r)/ n [C] person who sells fish in a shop. **fishy** adj (-ier, -iest) 1 like fish. 2 (infml) causing doubt: a ~y story.

fission /'fɪʃn/ n [U] splitting, esp of an atom: nuclear ~.

fissure /'fɪʃə(r)/ n [C] deep crack in rock.

fist /fɪst/ n [C] hand when tightly closed. **fistful** n [C] number or quantity that can be held in a fist.

fit¹ /fɪt/ v (-tt-) 1 [I, T] be the right size and shape for (sb): These shoes don't ~ (me). 2 [T] put on (clothing) to see that it is the right size, shape, etc: have a new coat ~ted. 3 [T] put into place: ~ a new window. 4 [T] make suitable for: make the punishment ~ the crime. 5 (phr v) **fit sb/sth in** find time or room for sb/sth. **fit in (with sb/sth)** be in harmony (with sb/sth). **fit sb/sth out** equip sb/sth. **fit** n [C] way in which sth, esp a garment, fits: a tight ~. **fitted** adj fixed in place: ~ted carpets/cupboards. **fitter** n [C] 1 person whose job is to put together and fit machinery. 2 person who cuts out and fits clothes.

fit² /fɪt/ adj (~ter, ~test) 1 for; to// suitable or suited, good enough; right: not ~ to eat ○ Do as you think ~. 2 in good health. 3 to//

ready to do sth: laughing ~ to burst. **fitness** n [U] 1 state of being physically fit. 2 for; suitability for sth.

fit³ /fɪt/ n [C] 1 sudden short attack of illness; sudden attack with loss of consciousness and violent movements. 2 sudden short period of intense feeling or activity: a ~ of anger/enthusiasm. 3 (idm) **by/in 'fits and 'starts** not regularly over a period of time. **have/throw a 'fit** (a) suffer a fit(1). (b) (infml) be very shocked or angry. **fitful** /-fl/ adj occurring irregularly. **fitfully** /-fəli/ adv.

fitting /'fɪtɪŋ/ adj right; suitable. **fitting** n [C] 1 [usu pl] small part of equipment: electrical ~ s. 2 [usu pl] something, eg a cooker, that is fixed in a building but can be removed.

five /faɪv/ pron, adj, n [C] 5. **fiver** /-ə(r)/ n [C] (Brit infml) £5 (note).

fix¹ /fɪks/ v [T] 1 fasten (sth) firmly to sth. 2 direct (one's eyes, thoughts, etc) onto sth. 3 arrange: ~ a date for a meeting. 4 repair. 5 put in order: He ~ed his hair. 6 (esp US) prepare (food or drink). 7 unfairly influence the result of (sth). 8 (phr v) **fix on sb/sth** choose sb/sth. **fix sb up (with sth)** provide sb with sth. **fixation** /fɪk'seɪʃn/ n [C] unhealthy emotional attachment; obsession.

fix² /fɪks/ n [C] 1 [usu sing] awkward situation. 2 position found by taking measurements, etc, eg when sailing. 3 (sl) injection of a narcotic drug.

fixture /'fɪkstʃə(r)/ n [C] 1 [usu pl] something, eg a bath, that is fixed in a building and is not removed when the owner moves house. 2 sporting event on an agreed date.

fizz /fɪz/ v [I] make a hissing sound of bubbles of gas in a liquid. **fizz** n [U] quality of having a lot of bubbles of gas in a liquid. **fizzy** adj (-ier, -iest).

fizzle /'fɪzl/ v [I] make a weak fizzing sound. 2 (phr v) **fizzle out** come to a weak disappointing end.

flab /flæb/ n [U] (infml) soft loose fatty flesh. **flabby** adj (-ier, -iest) 1 (of the muscles) not strong. 2 (fig) feeble and weak. **flabbiness** n [U].

flabbergasted /'flæbəgɑːstɪd; US -gæst-/ adj very shocked and surprised.

flag¹ /flæg/ n [C] piece of cloth used as a symbol of a country, or as a signal. **flag** v (-gg-) (phr v) **flag sth down** signal to (a vehicle) to stop. **'flagship** *n* [C] 1 ship that has the commander of a fleet on board. 2 (*fig*) most important of a group of products or services.

flag² /flæg/ *v* (**-gg-**) [I] become weak: *Interest/Enthusiasm is* ~*ging*.

flagon /'flægən/ *n* [C] large round bottle for wine, cider, etc.

flagrant /'fleɪgrənt/ *adj* openly bad: ~ *disobedience*. **flagrantly** *adv*.

flagstone /'flægstəʊn/ *n* [C] large flat stone for a floor, path or pavement.

flair /fleə(r)/ *n* [U, sing] natural ability to do sth well: *She has a* ~ *for languages*, ie is quick at learning them.

flake /fleɪk/ *n* [C] small thin layer; small loose bit: *'snow* ~*s*. **flake** *v* [I] 1 fall off in flakes. 2 (*phr v*) **flake out** (*infml*) collapse with exhaustion. **flaky** *adj* (**-ier, -iest**) made of flakes; tending to flake.

flamboyant /flæm'bɔɪənt/ *adj* 1 (of a person) very showy and lively. 2 brightly coloured. **flamboyance** /-əns/ *n* [U]. **flamboyantly** *adv*.

flame /fleɪm/ *n* [C, U] hot glowing burning gas coming from sth on fire: *The house was in* ~*s*, ie was burning. **flame** *v* [I] 1 burn with a bright flame. 2 have the colour of flames; blaze. **flaming** *adj* violent: *a flaming argument*.

flamingo /flə'mɪŋgəʊ/ *n* [C] (*pl* ~*s*) wading-bird with long legs, a long neck and pink feathers.

flammable /'flæməbl/ *adj* that can burn easily.

flan /flæn/ *n* [C] open pastry case with fruit, jam, etc in it.

flank /flæŋk/ *n* [C] 1 side of an animal or person between the ribs and the hip. 2 left or right side of an army. **flank** *v* [T] place on each side of or at the side of (sb/sth).

flannel /'flænl/ *n* 1 [U] soft loosely woven woollen cloth. 2 **flannels** [pl] men's trousers made of flannel. 3 ⇨ FACE-CLOTH (FACE).

flap /flæp/ *n* [C] 1 flat piece of material that covers an opening. 2 action or sound of flapping. 3 part of the wing of an aircraft that can be lifted. 4 (idm) **be/get into a flap** (*infml*) become excited or confused. **flap** *v* (**-pp-**) 1 [I, T] move up and down or from side to side: *sails* ~*ping in the wind*. 2 [I, T] give a light blow at (sth): ~ *the flies away* ○ *The bird* ~*ped its wings*. 3 [I] (*infml*) become excited and anxious.

flare¹ /fleə(r)/ *v* 1 [I] burn with a bright unsteady flame. 2 (*phr v*)

flare up (**a**) burst into a bright flame. (**b**) (*fig*) become more violent. **flare** *n* [C] 1 [usu sing] flaring light or flame. 2 (device that produces a) flaring light used as a signal. **'flare-up** *n* [C] 1 sudden burst of light or flame. 2 (*fig*) sudden outburst of violent activity.

flare² /fleə(r)/ *v* [I, T] become or make wider at the bottom: *a* ~*d skirt*. **flare** *n* [C] gradual widening.

flash /flæʃ/ *n* 1 [C] sudden bright burst of light: *a* ~ *of lightning* ○ (*fig*) *a* ~ *of inspiration*. 2 [C, U] (device that produces a) brief bright light for taking photographs indoors. 3 (idm) **in a flash** immediately. **flash** *adj* (*infml*) expensive-looking; showy. **flash** *v* 1 [I, T] (cause sth to) shine with a sudden bright light. 2 [I] come suddenly into view or into the mind. 3 [T] send (news, information, etc) by television, satellite, etc. 4 [I] move quickly: *The train* ~*ed past us*. **'flashback** *n* [C] part of a film, etc that shows a scene in the past. **'flashbulb** *n* [C] electric bulb in a flash(3). **'flashlight** *n* [C] 1 = FLASH 2. 2 (*esp US*) small electric torch. **flashy** *adj* (**-ier, -iest**) attractive, but not in good taste: ~*y clothes*. **flashily** *adv*.

flask /flɑːsk; *US* flæsk/ *n* [C] 1 bottle with a narrow neck. 2 vacuum flask. 3 = HIP-FLASK (HIP).

flat¹ /flæt/ *n* [C] (*esp Brit*) (also *esp US* **apartment**) set of rooms on one floor of a building, used as a home.

flat² /flæt/ *adj* (~**ter**, ~**test**) 1 smooth and level. 2 at full length; spread out fully: *lying* ~ *on her back*. 3 having a broad level surface but not deep: *a* ~ *dish*. 4 dull; boring. 5 (of a battery) no longer producing electricity. 6 (of a tyre) no longer having air inside. 7 (of drinks) no longer fizzy. 8 absolute: *a* ~ *refusal*. 9 at a fixed price: *a* ~ *rate*. 10 (*music*) lower than the true or acceptable note. **flat** *adv* 1 in or into a flat position. 2 exactly: *in 10 seconds* ~. 3 (*music*) lower than the true or acceptable note. 4 (idm) **flat 'out** (*infml*) using all one's energy and strength and not stopping. **flat-'footed** *adj* having feet with flat soles.

flat³ /flæt/ *n* 1 [sing] flat level part of sth. 2 [C, usu *pl*] stretch of low level land, esp near water: *'mud* ~*s*. 3 [C] (*music*) flat²(10) note. 4 [C] (*esp US*) flat tyre.

flatten /'flætn/ *v* [I, T] become or make (sth) flat.

flatter /'flætə(r)/ v [T] 1 praise too much or insincerely. 2 (usu passive) give a feeling of pleasure to. 3 (of a picture) show (sb) as better-looking than he/she is. **flatterer** n [C]. **flattery** n [U] flattering remarks.

flaunt /flɔ:nt/ v [T] (usu derog) show (sth valuable) in order to gain admiration: ~ one's wealth.

flautist /'flɔ:tɪst/ n [C] flute-player.

flavour (US -or) /'fleɪvə(r)/ n 1 [U] taste and smell of food: add salt to improve the ~. 2 [C] particular taste: six ~s of ice-cream. 3 [C, U] special quality. **flavour** v [T] give flavour to. **flavouring** n [C, U] something added to food to give flavour. **flavourless** adj.

flaw /flɔ:/ n [C] fault or mistake; imperfection. **flaw** v [T] cause (sth) to have a flaw. **flawless** adj perfect. **flawlessly** adv.

flax /flæks/ n [U] plant grown for its fibres, used for making linen. **flaxen** /'flæksn/ adj (of hair) pale yellow.

flea /fli:/ n [C] small jumping insect that feeds on blood.

fleck /flek/ n [C] very small patch, spot or grain. **fleck** v [T] mark with flecks.

flee /fli:/ v (pt, pp **fled** /fled/) [I, T] (fml)// run or hurry away from (sb/sth); escape.

fleece /fli:s/ n [C] woolly covering of a sheep. **fleece** v [T] (infml) rob (sb) by trickery, esp by charging too much money. **fleecy** adj like fleece; woolly.

fleet /fli:t/ n [C] 1 group of ships under one commander. 2 group of buses, cars, etc owned by one organization.

fleeting /'fli:tɪŋ/ adj lasting only a short time: a ~ glimpse.

flesh /fleʃ/ n 1 [U] soft part between the skin and bones of animal bodies. 2 [U] soft juicy part of a fruit. 3 **the flesh** [sing] the body, contrasted with the mind or the soul. 4 (idm) **in the 'flesh** in person; in real life. **make one's flesh crawl/creep** make one feel nervous or frightened. **one's 'own flesh and 'blood** close relatives in one's family. **fleshy** adj fat.

flew pt of FLY¹.

flex¹ /fleks/ n [C, U] wire for electric current, in a covering of plastic, etc.

flex² /fleks/ v [T] bend or move (one's legs, muscles, etc).

flexible /'fleksəbl/ adj 1 that can bend easily without breaking. 2 easily changed: ~ plans. **flexibility** /ˌfleksə'brlətɪ/ n [U].

flick /flɪk/ n [C] 1 quick light blow. 2 quick sharp movement: with a ~ of his wrist. **flick** v 1 [T] touch lightly; hit with a flick. 2 (phr v) **flick through sth** turn over the pages of (a book, etc) quickly.

flicker /'flɪkə(r)/ v [I] 1 (of a light or flame) burn or shine unsteadily. 2 (of hopes, etc) appear briefly. 3 move backwards and forwards lightly. **flicker** n [C, usu sing] 1 flickering movement. 2 (fig) weak short-lived feeling: a ~ of hope.

flier (also **flyer**) /'flaɪə(r)/ n [C] pilot of an aircraft.

flight¹ /flaɪt/ n 1 [U] flying through the air: the development of ~. 2 [C] (a) journey made by air. (b) aircraft making a journey: ~ number BA 4793 from London. 3 [C] group of aircraft or birds flying together. 4 [C] set of stairs between two floors. 5 (idm) **a flight of 'fancy** unrealistic imaginative idea. '**flight path** n [C] course of an aircraft through the air.

flight² /flaɪt/ n [C, U] fleeing or running away.

flimsy /'flɪmzɪ/ adj (-ier, -iest) 1 light and thin; easily destroyed. 2 (fig) weak: a ~ excuse. **flimsily** adv.

flinch /flɪntʃ/ v [I] move back because of shock, fear or pain.

fling /flɪŋ/ v (pt, pp **flung** /flʌŋ/) [T] 1 throw or move (sth) violently. 2 (phr v) **fling oneself into sth** do sth with a lot of energy and enthusiasm. **fling** n [C] 1 act or movement of flinging. 2 short period of enjoyment and fun: have a ~ after the exams. 3 lively Scottish dance.

flint /flɪnt/ n 1 [C, U] hard stone, used for making sparks. 2 [C] piece of hard metal in a cigarette lighter that is used for making sparks.

flip /flɪp/ v (-pp-) 1 [T] make (sth) move, esp through the air, by hitting it lightly: ~ a coin. 2 [I] (infml) become very angry. **flip** n [C] quick light blow.

flippant /'flɪpənt/ adj not showing enough respect. **flippancy** /-ənsɪ/ n [U]. **flippantly** adv.

flipper /'flɪpə(r)/ n [C] 1 broad flat limb of a seal, turtle, etc. 2 large flat rubber shoe used when swimming underwater.

flirt /flɜ:t/ v [I] 1 (with)// behave towards sb in a romantic but not serious way. 2 with// think about sth, but not seriously. **flirt** n [C] person who flirts(1). **flirtation** /flɜ:'teɪʃn/ n [C, U]. **flirtatious**

flit /flɜː'teɪʃəs/ *adj* fond of flirting.

flit /flɪt/ *v* (-tt-) [I] fly or move lightly and quickly.

float /fləʊt/ *v* 1 [I, T] (cause sth to) stay on the surface of a liquid or up in air. 2 [T] suggest (an idea or plan). 3 [T] start (a business company) by selling shares. 4 [I, T] (of a currency) (allow) to change in value with foreign currencies. **float** *n* [C] 1 light object that floats (often used to support a heavier object in water). 2 low vehicle, esp one used for showing things in a procession. 3 amount of money used, esp by a shopkeeper to provide change. **floating** *adj* not fixed.

flock /flɒk/ *n* [C] 1 group of sheep, birds or goats. 2 large crowd of people. 3 Christian congregation. **flock** *v* [I] move in great numbers: *Crowds ~ed to the football match.*

flog /flɒg/ *v* (-gg-) [T] 1 beat severely. 2 (*sl*) sell. 3 (idm) **flog a dead 'horse** (*infml*) waste one's efforts doing sth that cannot succeed. **flog sth to 'death** (*infml*) repeat (a story, joke, etc) too often. **flogging** *n* [C, U] severe beating.

flood /flʌd/ *n* [C] 1 (coming of a) great quantity of water, esp over a place that is usually dry. 2 (*fig*) large quantity: *a ~ of tears/letters.* **flood** *v* [I, T] 1 fill or cover with water. 2 cover or fill (sth) completely: (*fig*) *A sense of relief ~ed over her.* 3 (phr v) **flood in** arrive in great numbers. **'flood-tide** *n* [C, U] rising tide.

floodlight /'flʌdlaɪt/ *n* [C, usu pl] large powerful light that produces a wide beam. **floodlight** *v* (*pt, pp* **floodlit** /-lɪt/) [T] light (sth) with floodlights.

floor /flɔː(r)/ *n* 1 [C] surface of a room on which one stands and walks. 2 [C] bottom of the sea; ground surface of a cave, forest, etc. 3 [C] number of rooms on the same level in a building: *I live on the fourth ~.* 4 [C, usu sing] area where an activity that is mentioned takes place: *the dance ~ the factory/shop ~*, ie where the ordinary workers, not the managers work. 5 (idm) **take the 'floor** stand up to speak in a debate. **floor** *v* [T] 1 provide with a floor. 2 knock (sb) down. 3 (of a question, problem, etc) defeat or confuse (sb). **'floor-board** *n* [C] wooden plank for a floor. **'floor show** *n* [C] cabaret entertainment.

flop /flɒp/ *v* (-pp-) [I] 1 move or fall clumsily or helplessly: *~ exhausted into a chair.* 2 (*infml*) (of a

book, film, etc) fail. **flop** *n* [C] 1 [usu sing] flopping movement or sound. 2 (*infml*) failure of a book, film, etc. **floppy** *adj* (-ier, -iest) hanging down loosely; soft and flexible: *a ~py hat.* **floppy 'disk** *n* [C] (*computing*) flexible disk used for storing information.

flora /'flɔːrə/ *n* [pl, U] all the plants of an area or period of time. **floral** /'flɔːrəl/ *adj* of flowers.

florid /'florɪd; US 'flɔːrɪd/ *adj* 1 (usu *derog*) decorated too much. 2 (of a person's face) red.

florist /'florɪst; US 'flɔːr-/ *n* [C] person who has a shop that sells flowers.

flotation /fləʊ'teɪʃn/ *n* [C, U] act of floating(3) a business company.

flotilla /flə'tɪlə/ *n* [C] group of small, esp military, ships.

flounce /flaʊns/ *v* [I] move in a quick angry manner: *She ~d out of the room.*

flounder /'flaʊndə(r)/ *v* [I] 1 make wild and usu useless efforts, as in trying to move through water. 2 (*fig*) hesitate or make mistakes when speaking, etc.

flour /'flaʊə(r)/ *n* [U] fine powder made from grain, used for making bread, etc.

flourish /'flʌrɪʃ/ *v* [I] 1 be successful: *Her business is ~ing.* 2 [I] grow healthily. 3 [T] wave (sth) about: *~ a pen.* **flourish** *n* [C, usu sing] 1 bold sweeping movement made to attract attention. 2 short loud piece of music.

flout /flaʊt/ *v* [T] disobey (rules, etc) openly and without respect.

flow /fləʊ/ *v* [I] 1 (of a liquid) move freely and smoothly: (*fig*) *Keep the traffic ~ing.* 2 (of the tide) come in from the sea to the land. 3 (of hair) hang down loosely. 4 (phr v) **flow from sth** come or result from sth. **flow** *n* 1 [C, usu sing] flowing movement; constant stream or supply. 2 (usu **the flow**) [sing] coming in of the tide.

flower /'flaʊə(r)/ *n* 1 [C] part of a plant that produces seeds, often brightly coloured. 2 [sing] (*rhet*) finest part: *the ~ of the nation's youth.* **flower** *v* [I] produce flowers. **'flower-bed** *n* [C] piece of ground where flowers are grown. **'flowerpot** *n* [C] pot in which a plant is grown. **flowery** *adj* 1 having many flowers. 2 (of language) too elaborate: *a ~y speech.*

flown *pp* of FLY[1].

flu /fluː/ *n* [U] (*infml*) influenza.

fluctuate /'flʌktʃʊeɪt/ *v* [I] 1 (of a level) move up and down. 2 (of an attitude) change continually. **fluctuation** /ˌflʌktʃʊ'eɪʃn/

n [C, U].

fluent /'fluːənt/ *adj* 1 (of a person) able to speak a language smoothly and easily: He's ~ in Spanish. 2 (of speech, a language or action) expressed in a smooth easy way: speak ~ English. **fluency** /-ənsɪ/ *n* [U]. **fluently** *adv*.

fluff /flʌf/ *n* [U] 1 soft light pieces that come from woolly material. 2 soft fur or hair on a young animal. **fluff** *v* [T] 1 shake into a soft full mass; spread out lightly: ~ *up* a pillow. 2 (*infml*) do (sth) badly or unsuccessfully: He ~ed his exams. **fluffy** *adj* (-ier, -iest) soft and light; covered with fluff: a ~ y cat.

fluid /'fluːɪd/ *adj* 1 able to flow. 2 (of ideas, etc) not fixed. **fluid** *n* [C, U] liquid.

fluke /fluːk/ *n* [C, usu sing] accidental good luck.

flung *pt*, *pp* of FLING.

fluorescent /flɔːˈresnt; *US* flʊəˈr-/ *adj* giving out a bright glowing light when exposed to another light.

fluoride /'flɔːraɪd; *US* 'flʊər-/ *n* [U] chemical compound thought to prevent teeth from decaying.

flurry /'flʌrɪ/ *n* [C] (*pl* -ies) 1 sudden rush of wind, snow, etc. 2 (*fig*) burst of activity: a ~ *of activity/ excitement*. **flurry** *v* (*pt, pp* -ied) [T] make (sb) confused, rushed, etc: Don't get flurried!

flush[1] /flʌʃ/ *n* 1 [sing] rush of water, esp for cleaning a toilet. 2 [C, usu sing] redness of the face. 3 [C, usu sing] sudden rush of excitement. **flush** *v* 1 [I, T] (of the face) become or make red. 2 [T] clean with a rush of water: ~ *the toilet*. **flushed** *adj* very excited and pleased.

flush[2] /flʌʃ/ *adj* 1 level. 2 (*infml*) having plenty of money.

fluster /'flʌstə(r)/ *v* [T] make (sb) nervous and confused. **fluster** *n* [sing] nervous confused state.

flute /fluːt/ *n* [C] metal or wooden musical instrument, played by blowing across a mouth-hole at the side.

flutter /'flʌtə(r)/ *v* 1 [I, T] (of birds) move (wings) lightly and quickly. 2 [I, T] (cause to) move about in a quick irregular way: curtains ~ing in the breeze. 3 [I] (of the heart) beat irregularly. **flutter** *n* 1 [C, usu sing] quick irregular movement. 2 [sing] state of nervous excitement.

flux /flʌks/ *n* [U] continuous change: *in a state of ~*.

fly[1] /flaɪ/ *v* (*pt* flew /fluː/, *pp* flown /fləʊn/) 1 [I] move through

the air as a bird does, or in an aircraft. 2 [T] control (an aircraft). 3 [I] move quickly: It's late. I must ~. 4 [T] raise (a flag). 5 (idm) **fly in the face of sth** be against sth; oppose. **fly into a 'passion, 'rage, 'temper, etc** become suddenly very angry. **flying 'saucer** *n* [C] spacecraft believed to have come from another planet. **'flying squad** *n* [C] group of police officers who are always ready to move quickly, eg to chase criminals. **flying 'start** *n* [C] very good beginning. **flying 'visit** *n* [C] very short visit.

fly[2] /flaɪ/ *n* [C] (*pl* flies) 1 insect with two wings. 2 natural or artificial fly used as a bait in fishing.

fly[3] /flaɪ/ *n* [C, usu pl] (*pl* flies) 1 buttoned opening on the front of a pair of trousers.

flyer = FLIER.

flyleaf /'flaɪliːf/ *n* [C] (*pl* -leaves /-liːvz/) blank page at the beginning or end of a book.

flyover /'flaɪəʊvə(r)/ *n* [C] bridge that carries one road over another.

foal /fəʊl/ *n* [C] young horse.

foam /fəʊm/ *n* [U] mass of small usu white air bubbles in a liquid. **foam** *v* [I] form or send out foam. **foam 'rubber** *n* [U] spongy rubber.

fob /fɒb/ *v* (-bb-) (phr v) **fob sb off (with sth)** trick sb into accepting sth of little or no value: He ~*bed me off with a weak excuse.*

focus /'fəʊkəs/ *n* [C] 1 point at which rays of light, heat, etc meet. 2 [usu sing] centre of interest: the ~ *of attention*. 3 (idm) **in/out of focus** giving/not giving a clear sharp picture. **focus** *v* (-s- or -ss-) 1 [I, T] adjust (a lens, etc) to give a clear sharp image. 2 [T] (on)/(concentrate (attention).

fodder /'fɒdə(r)/ *n* [U] hay, etc for farm animals.

foe /fəʊ/ *n* [C] (*fml* or *dated*) enemy.

foetus /'fiːtəs/ *n* [C] young human, animal or bird growing in the womb or egg.

fog /fɒg; *US* fɔːg/ *n* 1 [U] thick cloud of tiny drops of water in the air: I couldn't see through the ~. 2 [C, U] (area of) cloudiness on a photograph. **fog** *v* (-gg-) [I, T] cover (sth) or become covered with fog: The window has ~*ged up.* **'fog-bound** *adj* unable to travel or operate because of fog. **foggy** *adj* (-ier, -iest) not clear because of fog: a ~ *gy night.* **'fog-horn** *n* [C] instrument used for warning ships in fog. **'fog-lamp** *n* [C] powerful light on the front of a car for use in fog.

foil /fɔɪl/ n 1 [U] thin flexible sheet metal: tin ~. 2 [C] person or thing that contrasts with another.

foil /fɔɪl/ v [T] prevent (sb) from carrying out a plan.

foist /fɔɪst/ v (phr v) **foist sth on sb** force sb to accept sth not wanted.

fold /fəʊld/ v 1 [T] bend one part (of sth) back on itself: ~ a letter. 2 [I] be able to be folded: a ~ ing bed. 3 [I] (of a business) come to an end; fail. 4 (idm) **fold one's arms** cross one's arms over one's chest. **fold** n [C] 1 part that is folded. 2 line made by folding. **folder** n [C] holder, usu made of cardboard, for papers.

fold /fəʊld/ n [C] area surrounded by a wall where sheep are kept.

foliage /ˈfəʊlɪɪdʒ/ n [U] (fml) all the leaves of a tree or plant.

folk /fəʊk/ n 1 [U] people in general. 2 **folks** [pl] (infml) relatives: the ~ s at home. 3 [U] folk music. **folk-dance** n [C] (music for a) traditional popular dance. **folklore** /ˈfəʊklɔː(r)/ n [U] (study of the) traditional beliefs, stories, etc of a community. **folk-music** n [C] (also **folk-song** [C]) traditional popular music or song.

follow /ˈfɒləʊ/ v 1 [I] come or go after. 2 [T] go along (a road, etc). 3 [T] act according to: ~ her advice. 4 [T] engage in as a job or trade: ~ a career in law. 5 [T] take an interest in: ~ all the football news. 6 [I, T] understand (sth): I don't ~ (your meaning). 7 [I] be a necessary result: It ~ s from what you say that…. 8 [T] read a (text) while listening to it being spoken by sb else. 9 (idm) **as follows** (used to introduce a list). **follow in sb's footsteps** do what sb else has done earlier. **follow one's nose** act instinctively. **follow 'suit** do what sb else has just done. 10 (phr v) **follow sth through** carry out or continue sth to the end. **follow sth up** (a) take further action on sth: ~ up a suggestion. (b) investigate sth closely: ~ up a clue. **follower** n [C] supporter or admirer. **'follow-up** n [C] something done to continue what has already been done: ~-up visit.

following /ˈfɒləʊɪŋ/ adj next. **The ~ is about to be mentioned:** Answer the ~ questions. **following** n [sing] group of supporters. **following** prep after (sth); as a result of.

folly /ˈfɒlɪ/ n (pl -ies) 1 [U] foolishness. 2 [C] foolish act or idea.

fond /fɒnd/ adj 1 of/) having a great liking for sb/sth. 2 loving: a ~ embrace. 3 foolishly hoped: ~ belief/wish. **fondly** adv. **fondness** n [U].

fondle /ˈfɒndl/ v [T] touch lovingly.

font /fɒnt/ n [C] basin to hold water for baptism.

food /fuːd/ n 1 [U] something that can be eaten: a shortage of ~. 2 [C] particular kind of food: health ~ s. 3 (idm) **food for 'thought** something to think about seriously. **'foodstuff** n [C] substance used as food.

fool /fuːl/ n [C] 1 (derog) silly person. 2 (idm) **make a 'fool of oneself** behave foolishly. **fool** v 1 [I] behave foolishly: Stop ~ ing around! 2 [T] deceive. 3 [I] tease or joke. **fool** adj (infml derog) foolish: some ~ politician. **foolhardy** /-hɑːdɪ/ adj brave but foolish. **foolish** adj silly. **foolishly** adv. **foolishness** n [U]. **foolproof** /-pruːf/ adj that cannot go wrong: a ~proof plan.

foot /fʊt/ n (pl **feet** /fiːt/) 1 [C] lowest part of the leg, below the ankle. 2 [C] measure of length; 12 inches (0.3 metre). 3 [sing] lowest part: at the ~ of the stairs. 4 (idm) **fall/land on one's 'feet** recover quickly esp through good luck, after being in difficulties. **on foot** walking. **put one's 'feet up** rest. **put one's 'foot down** be firm in opposing sth. **put one's 'foot in it** say or do sth wrong. **foot** v (idm) **foot the 'bill** pay the bill. **'football** n 1 [C] large round or oval ball. 2 [U] outdoor game between two teams played with such a ball, esp association football. **footballer** n [C]. **football pools** n [pl] system of betting money on the results of football matches. **'foothill** n [C, usu pl] low hill at the foot(3) of a mountain. **'foothold** n [C] 1 firm place for the foot, eg when climbing. 2 (fig) position from which progress can be made. **'footnote** n [C] note at the bottom of a page. **footpath** n [C] path for people who are walking. **footprint** n [C, usu pl] mark made by a foot. **footstep** n [C, usu pl] sound or mark of a step taken when walking. **footwear** n [U] shoes, etc.

footing /ˈfʊtɪŋ/ n [sing] 1 secure placing of the feet. 2 relationship with others: on an equal ~.

for /fə(r); strong form fɔː(r)/ prep 1 (showing the person who will receive or gain from sth): a letter ~ you. 2 (showing the purpose or function): go ~ a walk ○ What's this machine ~? 3 (showing the destination, aim or reason): Is this the train ~ York? ○ books ~ children. 4 in order to help (sb/sth): What can I do ~ you? 5 as the price, reward or penalty of (sth): buy a book ~ £15. 6 to replace (sth): change one's car ~ a new one. 7 in support of (sb/sth): Are you ~ or against nuclear arms? 8 representing (sb/sth); meaning: Speak ~ yourself! ○ Red is ~ danger. 9 (after a v) in order to obtain (sth): pray ~ peace. 10 with regard to (sb/sth); concerning: anxious ~ his safety. 11 because of: famous ~ its church. 12 (showing distance or length of time): walk ~ three miles ○ stay ~ a few days. 13 (after an adj) considering (sb/sth): She's tall ~ her age. 14 (used for introducing phrases): It's impossible ~ me to continue.

forage /'fɒrɪdʒ; US 'fɔ:r/ v [I] (for)// search for sth.

foray /'fɒreɪ; US 'fɔ:reɪ/ n [C] sudden attack or rush: (fig the company's first ~ into the computer market.

forbear = FOREBEAR.

forbearance /fɔ:'beərəns/ n [U] (fml) patient self-control and forgiveness.

forbid /fə'bɪd/ v (pt forbade /fə'bæd; US fə'beɪd/ or pp /fə'bæd/, pp ~**den** /fə'bɪdn/) [Tn] 1 (to)// order (sb) not to do sth: I ~ you to go. 2 not allow: Smoking is ~ den. **forbidding** adj looking unfriendly; threatening.

force /fɔ:s/ n 1 [U] strength, power or violence. 2 [C, U] influence: economic ~ s. 3 [C, U] power that causes movement: the ~ of gravity. 4 [C] power of the wind, rain, etc: the ~ s of nature. 5 [C] group of soldiers, etc: the po'lice ~ ○ a sales ~. 6 [U] authority: the ~ of the law. 7 (idm) **bring sth/come into 'force** (cause a law, rule, etc to) come into operation. **in 'force** (a) (of people) in large numbers. (b) (of a law, etc) in operation. **force** v [Tn] 1 (to)// make (sb) do sth he/she does not want to do: ~ him to talk. 2 use physical strength to move (sth). 3 break (sth) open by using physical strength: ~ (open) a door. 4 produce with effort: ~ a smile. **forceful** /-fl/ adj (of a person or an argument, etc) strong; convincing. **forcefully** /-fəli/ adv. **forcible** /'fɔ:səbl/ adj done by physical force. **forcibly** adv.

forceps /'fɔ:seps/ n [pl] medical instrument used for holding things tightly.

ford /fɔ:d/ n [C] shallow place in a river where one can walk or drive across. **ford** v [T] cross (a river) at a ford.

fore /fɔ:(r)/ adj front: a cat's ~ legs. **fore** n (idm) **be/come to the fore** be/become important.

forearm /'fɔ:rɑ:m/ n [C] part of the arm from the elbow to the wrist.

forebear (also **forbear**) /'fɔ:-beə(r)/ n [C, usu pl] (fml) ancestor.

foreboding /fɔ:'bəʊdɪŋ/ n [C, U] strong feeling that danger or trouble is coming.

forecast /'fɔ:kɑ:st; US -kæst/ v (pt, pp ~ or ~**ed**) [T] say in advance (what is expected to happen). **forecast** n [C] statement of expected future events: weather ~.

forecourt /'fɔ:kɔ:t/ n [C] open area in front of a building.

forefather /'fɔ:fɑ:ðə(r)/ n [C, usu pl] ancestor.

forefinger /'fɔ:fɪŋgə(r)/ n [C] finger next to the thumb.

forefront /'fɔ:frʌnt/ n [sing] most forward or important position: in the ~ of space research.

foregone /'fɔ:gɒn; US -gɔ:n/ adj (idm) **a foregone conclusion** result that is certain to happen.

foreground /'fɔ:graʊnd/ n [sing] 1 nearest part of a view or picture: in the ~. 2 (fig) most noticeable position.

forehand /'fɔ:hænd/ adj, n [C] (stroke in tennis, etc) made with the palm of one's hand turned forward.

forehead /'fɒrɪd, also 'fɔ:hed; US 'fɔ:rɪd/ n [C] part of the face above the eyes.

foreign /'fɒrən; US 'fɔ:r-/ adj 1 (a) of, in or from a country that is not one's own. (b) concerning other countries: ~ policy. 2 (to) (fml) not natural to sb/sth: ~ to his nature. 3 (fml) coming from outside: a ~ body (eg a hair) in the eye. **foreigner** n [C] foreign person. **fo-reign ex'change** n [U] (system of buying and selling) foreign money.

foreman /'fɔ:mən/ n [C] (pl -**men** /-mən/, fem **forewoman** /-wʊmən/, pl -**women** /-wɪmɪn/) 1 worker who directs others. 2 leader of a jury.

foremost /'fɔ:məʊst/ adj most important.

forensic /fə'rensɪk; US -zɪk/ adj of or used in courts of law: ~ medicine.

forerunner /'fɔ:rʌnə(r)/ n [C] person or thing that prepares the way for the coming of another.

foresee /fɔːˈsiː/ v (pt foresaw /fɔːˈsɔː/, pp ~n /fɔːˈsiːn/) [T] see in advance: ~ difficulties. **foreseeable** /-əbl/ adj 1 that can be foreseen. 2 (idm) **in the foreseeable 'future** fairly soon.

forest /ˈfɒrɪst; US ˈfɔːr-/ n [C, U] large area of land covered with trees. **forestry** n [U] science and practice of planting and caring for forests.

forestall /fɔːˈstɔːl/ v [T] act before (sb) so as to prevent him/her from doing sth.

foretell /fɔːˈtel/ v (pt, pp foretold /fɔːˈtəʊld/) [T] (fml) tell (what will happen in the future).

forethought /ˈfɔːθɔːt/ n [U] careful planning for the future.

forever /fəˈrevə(r)/ adv 1 (also **for ever**) always: I'll love you ~ ! ○ (infml) It takes her ~ (ie a very long time) to get dressed. 2 constantly: He is ~ complaining.

forewarn /fɔːˈwɔːn/ v [T] (of)// warn (sb) of a possible danger or problem: ~ him of the danger.

foreword /ˈfɔːwɜːd/ n [C] short introduction to a book.

forfeit /ˈfɔːfɪt/ v [T] lose (sth) as a punishment for or as a result of an action. **forfeit** n [C] something forfeited.

forgave pt of FORGIVE.

forge[1] /fɔːdʒ/ n [C] place where metals are heated and shaped. **forge** v [T] 1 shape by heating and hammering. 2 (fig) form or make: ~ a friendship/link. 3 make a copy of (sth), in order to deceive: ~ banknotes. **forger** n [C] person who forges money, papers, etc. **forgery** /-əri/ n (pl -ies) 1 [U] forging of money, papers, etc. 2 [C] forged banknote, paper, etc.

forge[2] /fɔːdʒ/ v (phr v) **forge ahead** advance or progress quickly.

forget /fəˈget/ v (pt forgot /fəˈgɒt/, pp forgotten /fəˈgɒtn/) [I, T] 1 fail to remember (sth): Don't ~ to post the letters. 2 stop thinking about (sb/sth): Let's ~ our differences. **forgetful** /-fl/ adj in the habit of forgetting.

forgive /fəˈgɪv/ v (pt forgave /fəˈgeɪv/, pp ~n /fəˈgɪvn/) [T] stop being angry or bitter towards (sb) for (sth); stop blaming: She forgave him his rudeness. **forgivable** adj that can be forgiven. **forgiveness** n [U]. **forgiving** adj willing to forgive.

forgo /fɔːˈgəʊ/ v (pt forwent /-ˈwent/, pp -gone /-ˈgɒn; US -ˈgɔːn/) [T] do without (esp sth pleasant).

forgot pt of FORGET.

forgotten pp of FORGET.

fork /fɔːk/ n [C] 1 (a) instrument with points, for lifting food to the mouth. (b) gardening tool like this. 2 (a) place where a road, tree branch, etc divides into two parts. (b) either such part. **fork** v 1 [T] dig, lift with a fork. 2 [I] (of a road, etc) divide into two parts. 3 [I] (of a person) turn (left or right). 4 (phr v) **fork out (sth)** (infml) pay (money) unwillingly. **forked** adj divided into two or more parts. **fork-lift 'truck** n [C] small powerful vehicle for lifting heavy goods.

forlorn /fəˈlɔːn/ adj lonely and unhappy. **forlornly** adv.

form[1] /fɔːm/ n 1 [C, U] shape; appearance. 2 [C] kind or type: different ~ s of government. 3 [C, U] (grammar) spelling or pronunciation of a word: The plural ~ of 'goose' is 'geese'. 4 [C] printed paper with spaces to be filled in: application ~ s. 5 [C] (Brit) class in a school. 6 [U] general way in which sth is made or put together: ~ and content. 7 (idm) **on/off 'form** fit/unfit; performing well/badly. **formless** adj without shape.

form[2] /fɔːm/ v 1 [I, T] give shape to; make. 2 [I, T] (cause sth to) come into existence: ~ a government. 3 [T] be the material of (sth): It ~ s part of the course. 4 [I, T] be arranged or arrange in a certain order or shape: ~ a line.

formal /ˈfɔːml/ adj 1 (a) showing or expecting careful serious behaviour: a ~ dinner. (b) (of clothes or words) used in formal situations. 2 regular in design: ~ gardens. 3 official: a ~ declaration of war. **formality** /fɔːˈmælətɪ/ n (pl -ies) 1 [U] attention to rules. 2 [C] action required by custom: a legal ~ ity. **formalize** v [T] put (a plan, etc) into clear written form. **formally** adv.

format /ˈfɔːmæt/ n [C] size, shape or general arrangement of sth. **format** v (-tt-) [T] arrange (sth) in a particular format, usu for a computer.

formation /fɔːˈmeɪʃn/ n 1 [U] forming or shaping of sth. 2 [C, U] structure; arrangement.

formative /ˈfɔːmətɪv/ adj influencing the development of: a child's ~ years.

former /ˈfɔːmə(r)/ adj of an earlier period: the ~ president. **the former** pron the first mentioned of two. **formerly** adv in earlier times.

formidable /ˈfɔːmɪdəbl/ adj 1

causing fear: a ~ opponent. **2** difficult to deal with: a ~ task. **3** very impressive; excellent. **formidably** /-əblɪ/ adv.

formula /ˈfɔːmjʊlə/ n [C] (pl ~s or, in scientific use **-mulae** /-mjuːliː/) **1** rule, fact, etc shown in letters, signs or numbers: a chemical ~. **2** method or set of ideas to achieve sth: a peace ~. **3** fixed group of words used regularly: 'How d'you do' is a social ~. **4** list of substances and instructions for making sth.

formulate /ˈfɔːmjʊleɪt/ v [T] **1** create in a precise form: ~ a rule. **2** express exactly. **formulation** /ˌfɔːmjʊˈleɪʃn/ n [C, U].

forsake /fəˈseɪk/ v (pt **forsook** /fəˈsʊk/, pp ~**n** /fəˈseɪkən/) [T] (fml) abandon.

fort /fɔːt/ n [C] building for military defence.

forte /ˈfɔːteɪ; US fɔːrt/ n [C, usu sing] something sb does well: Singing is not my ~.

forth /fɔːθ/ adv **1** (fml) onwards. **2** (idm) **and (,so on and) 'so forth** and other things of the same kind.

forthcoming /ˌfɔːθˈkʌmɪŋ/ adj **1** about to happen or appear. **2** ready when needed: The money was not ~. **3** ready to be helpful.

fortieth ⇨ FORTY.

fortify /ˈfɔːtɪfaɪ/ v (pt, pp **-ied**) [T] **1** (against) strengthen (a place) against attack. **2** make stronger: cereal fortified with extra vitamins. **fortification** /ˌfɔːtɪfɪˈkeɪʃn/ n **1** [U] fortifying. **2** [C, usu pl] tower, wall, etc built for defence.

fortnight /ˈfɔːtnaɪt/ n [C] (esp Brit) two weeks. **fortnightly** adj, adv happening every fortnight.

fortress /ˈfɔːtrɪs/ n [C] large fort; castle.

fortuitous /fɔːˈtjuːɪtəs; US -ˈtuː-/ adj (fml) happening by chance.

fortunate /ˈfɔːtʃənət/ adj lucky. **fortunately** adv.

fortune /ˈfɔːtʃuːn/ n **1** [C, U] good or bad luck; chance. **2** [C] what will happen to sb in the future: tell sb's ~. **3** [C] large amount of money: cost a ~. **'fortune-teller** n [C] person who tells people's fortunes(2).

forty /ˈfɔːtɪ/ pron, adj, n [C] (pl **-ies**) **40**. **fortieth** /-tɪəθ/ pron, adj 40th. **fortieth** pron, n ⅟₄₀.

forum /ˈfɔːrəm/ n [C] place for public discussion.

forward¹ /ˈfɔːwəd/ adj **1** directed towards the front; at the front: ~ movements. **2** of the future: ~ planning. **3** (of plants or children) advanced in development. **4** too bold in one's manner. **forward**

n [C] attacking player in football, etc. **forward** v [T] **1** send (a letter, etc) to a new address. **2** send (goods) to a customer. **3** help to develop: ~ her career. **forwardness** n [U] state of being forward(4).

forward² /ˈfɔːwəd/ adv (also **forwards**) towards the front; towards the future: take a step ~. **forward-looking** adj having modern ideas.

forwent pt of FORGO.

fossil /ˈfɒsl/ n [C] (part or mark of) a prehistoric animal or plant hardened like rock. **fossilize** /-səlaɪz/ v [I, T] **1** (cause sth to) become a fossil. **2** (fig) (cause to) become fixed in ideas, attitudes, etc.

foster /ˈfɒstə(r); US ˈfɔː-/ v [T] **1** help (ideas, feelings) to grow or develop. **2** take care of (a child) without becoming his/her legal parent. **foster-** (in compound nouns) with a family connection through fostering(2): ~-parent/-child.

fought pt, pp of FIGHT.

foul /faʊl/ adj **1** having a bad smell or taste; dirty. **2** very unpleasant: a ~ temper. **3** (of language) obscene and offensive. **4** (of weather) stormy. **foul** n [C] (sport) action against the rules. **foul** v **1** [T] make (sth) dirty. **2** [I, T] (sport) commit a foul against (another player). **3** (phr v) **foul sth up** (infml) spoil sth. **foul 'play** n [U] **1** (sport) unfair play. **2** criminal violence that leads to murder.

found¹ pt, pp of FIND.

found² /faʊnd/ v **1** build; establish: ~ a hospital. **2** (usu passive) base: a novel ~ed on facts. **founder** n [C] person who establishes sth.

foundation /faʊnˈdeɪʃn/ n **1** [U] founding or establishing (of a school, organization, etc). **2** [C] organization that provides money for a charity, etc. **3** [C, usu pl] strong base under a building. **4** [C, U] on which an idea, etc is based.

founder /ˈfaʊndə(r)/ v [I] **1** (of a ship) fill with water and sink. **2** (fig) (of a plan, etc) fail.

foundry /ˈfaʊndrɪ/ n [C] (pl **-ies**) place where metal is melted and shaped into objects.

fount /faʊnt/ n [C] (of)‖ (rhet) source: the ~ of all wisdom.

fountain /ˈfaʊntɪn/ n [C] **1** structure in a pool that sends a jet of water into the air. **2** powerful jet of liquid. **'fountain-pen** n [C] pen with a container from which ink flows to the nib.

four /fɔː(r)/ pron, adj, n [C] **1** 4. **2**

(idm) **on all 'fours** with one's hands and knees on the ground.
fourth /fɔːθ/ *pron, adj* 1 4th. 2 (*US*) ⇨ QUARTER.
fourteen /ˌfɔːˈtiːn/ *pron, adj, n*[C] 14. **fourteenth** /ˌfɔːˈtiːnθ/ *pron, adj* 14th. **fourteenth** *pron, n*[C] ₁⁄₁₄.
fowl /faʊl/ *n* (*pl* **fowl** *or* ~s) 1 [C] domestic cock or hen. 2 [U] flesh of a bird, eaten as food.
fox /fɒks/ *n*[C] wild animal of the dog family with red fur and a bushy tail. **fox** *v*[T] confuse; trick. **'fox-hunting** *n*[U] sport in which a fox is hunted by hounds and people on horses.
foyer /ˈfɔɪeɪ; *US* ˈfɔɪər/ *n*[C] large entrance hall in a theatre.
fraction /ˈfrækʃn/ *n*[C] 1 division of a number, eg ½. 2 small part: *a ~ of a second.* **fractional** /-ʃənl/ *adj* very small.
fracture /ˈfræktʃə(r)/ *n*[C, U] breaking of sth, esp a bone. **fracture** *v*[I, T] break.
fragile /ˈfrædʒaɪl; *US* -dʒl/ *adj* 1 easily broken or destroyed. 2 (*infml*) weak; not healthy. **fragility** /frəˈdʒɪlətɪ/ *n*[U].
fragment /ˈfrægmənt/ *n*[C] small piece broken off; incomplete part. **fragment** /fræɡˈment/ *v*[I, T] break into pieces. **fragmentary** *adj* incomplete. **fragmentation** /ˌfrægmənˈteɪʃn/ *n*[U].
fragrance /ˈfreɪɡrəns/ *n*[C, U] sweet smell. **fragrant** /-grənt/ *adj* sweet-smelling.
frail /freɪl/ *adj* weak. **frailty** *n* (*pl* -ies) 1 [U] quality of being frail. 2 [C] fault in sb's character.
frame /freɪm/ *n*[C] 1 border in which a picture, window, etc is set. 2 main structure of a building, vehicle, etc that forms a support for its parts. 3 [usu *pl*] structure that holds the lenses of a pair of glasses. 4 [usu *sing*] human or animal body. 5 single photograph on a cinema film. 6 (idm) **a frame of 'mind** mood; state of one's mind. **frame** *v*[T] 1 put a frame(1) round. 2 express in words. 3 (*infml*) make (an innocent person) appear guilty of a crime. **'framework** *n*[C] 1 structure giving shape and support. 2 set of principles or ideas.
franchise /ˈfræntʃaɪz/ *n* 1 **the franchise** [*sing*] the right to vote. 2 [C] right to sell a product or service.
frank¹ /fræŋk/ *adj* showing thoughts and feelings openly. **frankly** *adv.* **frankness** *n*[U].
frank² /fræŋk/ *v*[T] mark (a letter) to show that postage has been paid.

frankfurter /ˈfræŋkfɜːtə(r)/ *n*[C] kind of small smoked sausage.
frantic /ˈfræntɪk/ *adj* 1 wildly afraid or anxious. 2 hurried but disorganized: *a ~ search.* **frantically** /-klɪ/ *adv.*
fraternal /frəˈtɜːnl/ *adj* brotherly. **fraternally** /-nəlɪ/ *adv.*
fraternity /frəˈtɜːnətɪ/ *n* (*pl* -ies) 1 [U] brotherly feeling. 2 [C] group of people with the same interests or job. 3 [C] (*US*) society of male university students.
fraternize /ˈfrætənaɪz/ *v*[I] (*with*)|| become friendly: ~ *with the enemy.* **fraternization** /ˌfrætənaɪˈzeɪʃn; *US* -nɪˈz-/ *n*[U].
fraud /frɔːd/ *n* 1 [C, U] (act of) deceiving sb illegally in order to gain money. 2 [C] person who deceives others. **fraudulent** /ˈfrɔːdjʊlənt; *US* -dʒʊ-/ *adj* obtained or done by fraud; deceitful.
fraught /frɔːt/ *adj* 1 *with*|| filled: ~ *with danger.* 2 worried or anxious.
fray /freɪ/ *v*[I, T] 1 (cause cloth, etc to) become worn, so that there are loose threads. 2 (*fig*) (cause sth to) become strained: ~*ed nerves.*
freak /friːk/ *n*[C] 1 very unusual act or event: *a ~ storm.* 2 person thought to be very abnormal. 3 (*infml*) person who is very interested in sth mentioned: *a jazz ~.* **freakish** *adj* strange; unusual.
freckle /ˈfrekl/ *n*[C, usu *pl*] small brown spot on the human skin. **freckled** *adj.*
free /friː/ *adj* (~r /-ə(r)/, ~st) 1 not in prison; allowed to move to where one wants. 2 not controlled by sb else, rules, a government, etc: *a ~ press.* 3 not fixed; loose: *the ~ end of a rope.* 4 not blocked; clear: *a ~ flow of water.* 5 *from/of*|| without sth, usu sth unpleasant: ~ *from pain/blame.* 6 costing nothing. 7 not including: *tax ~.* 8 (a) not being used: *a ~ seat.* (b) (of a person) not busy. 9 *with*|| giving sth readily: *He's ~ with his time.* 10 (idm) **free and easy** relaxed. **a free 'hand** permission to do what one wants: *get/have a ~ hand.* **free** *adv* 1 without payment. 2 no longer fixed; loose. 3 (idm) **make free with** sth treat sth with respect, as if it belongs to oneself. **free** *v*[T] make free. **free 'enterprise** *n*[U] operation of business and trade without government control. **'free-for-all** *n*[C] quarrel, etc in which everyone joins in. **'free-hand** *adj, adv* (drawn) by hand, without instruments. **'freelance** /-lɑːns; *US* -læns/ *n*[C], *adj,*

adv (done by a) writer, artist, etc who works for several employers. **'free-lance** *v* [I] work in this way. **freely** *adv* in a free manner; readily. **free-range** *adj* produced by hens kept in natural conditions. **free 'speech** *n* [U] right to express one's opinions in public. **free 'trade** *n* [U] system in which goods can be imported without taxes or other controls. **freeway** *n* [C] (*US*) motorway. **free 'will** *n* [U] 1 ability to decide freely what one does. 2 (belief in) one's power to choose one's actions, independently of God or fate.

freedom /'friːdəm/ *n* 1 [U] state of being free. 2 [C, U] (*of*/) right to act or speak freely: ~ *of worship*.

freeze /friːz/ *v* (*pt* **froze** /frəʊz/, *pp* **frozen** /'frəʊzn/) 1 [I, T] (*esp* of water) change into ice. 2 [I] (used with *it*) (of weather) be so cold that water turns into ice: *It's freezing today.* 3 [I] feel very cold. 4 [T] keep (food, etc) at a temperature below freezing-point: *frozen peas.* 5 [I, T] (cause a person or animal to) stop suddenly: ~ *with terror*. 6 [T] hold (prices, wages, etc) at a fixed level. 7 (idm) **freeze to 'death** die of cold. 8 (phr *v*) **freeze over/up** become covered/blocked with ice. **freeze** *n* [C] 1 period of freezing weather. 2 fixing of wages, prices, etc. **freezer** *n* [C] large refrigerator in which food is kept frozen. **'freezing-point** *n* [U, C] temperature at which a liquid, esp water, freezes.

freight /freɪt/ *n* [U] goods carried by ships, aircraft, etc. **freight** *v* [T] send or carry (goods). **freighter** *n* [C] ship or aircraft that carries freight.

French /frentʃ/ *n* 1 [U] the French language. 2 **the French** [pl] French people. **French** *adj* of France, its people or their language. **,French 'fries** *n* [pl] (*esp US*) chips. **,French 'window** *n* [C, usu pl] glass door that opens onto a garden or balcony.

frenzy /'frenzɪ/ *n* [sing, U] violent excitement. **frenzied** /'frenzɪd/ *adj*.

frequency /'friːkwənsɪ/ *n* (*pl* -ies) 1 [U] rate at which sth happens or is repeated. 2 [C] rate at which a radio wave vibrates.

frequent¹ /'friːkwənt/ *adj* happening often, frequent.

frequent² /frɪ'kwent/ *v* [T] (*fml*) go to (a place) often.

fresco /'freskəʊ/ *n* [C] (*pl* ~s or ~es /-kəʊz/) picture painted on a wall before the plaster is dry.

fresh /freʃ/ *adj* 1 new or different: *make a* ~ *start*. 2 newly made or produced; not stale: ~ *bread*. 3 (of food) not tinned or frozen. 4 (of water) not salty: ~ *water*. 5 (of weather) cool and windy. 6 (of colours) clear and bright. 7 not tired; strong again. 8 (*infml*) too bold with sb of the opposite sex. 9 *from/ out of/*) having just left a place: *students* ~ *from college*. **freshly** *adv* (usu with a *pp*) recently: ~*ly painted*. **freshness** *n* [U]. **'fresh-water** *adj* from, of, living in or containing fresh(4) water.

freshen /'freʃn/ *v* 1 [T] make (sth) fresh. 2 [I] (of the wind) become stronger. 3 (phr *v*) **freshen (oneself) up** wash and make oneself look clean and tidy.

fret¹ /fret/ *v* (-tt-) [I, T] (*about*/) (cause sb to) worry about sth. **fretful** /-fl/ *adj* worried or complaining. **fretfully** *adv*.

fret² /fret/ *n* [C] one of the metal ridges across the neck of a guitar, banjo, etc.

friar /'fraɪə(r)/ *n* [C] male member of a certain Christian group.

friction /'frɪkʃn/ *n* 1 [U] rubbing of one thing against another. 2 [C, U] disagreement between people.

Friday /'fraɪdɪ/ *n* [C, U, esp sing] the sixth day of the week, next after Thursday. (See examples of use at **Monday**).

fridge /frɪdʒ/ *n* [C] refrigerator.

fried *pt, pp* of **FRY**.

friend /frend/ *n* [C] 1 person whom one knows and likes, but who is not a relative. 2 helper or supporter: *a* ~ *of the arts*. 3 (idm) **be/make 'friends (with sb)** become a friend (of sb). **friendless** *adj* without any friends. **friendly** *adj* (-**ier**, -**iest**) 1 acting as a friend. 2 (of an argument, game, etc) not as a serious competition. **friendliness** *n* [C, U] friendly relationship. **friendship** *n* [C, U].

frieze /friːz/ *n* [C] band of decoration along the top of a wall.

frigate /'frɪɡət/ *n* [C] small fast warship.

fright /fraɪt/ *n* [U, C] feeling of sudden fear.

frighten /'fraɪtn/ *v* [T] fill (sb) with fear. **frightened** *adj* afraid. **frightening** *adj* causing fear. **frighteningly** *adv*.

frightful /'fraɪtfl/ *adj* 1 very unpleasant. 2 (*infml*) extreme; very bad. **frightfully** /-fəlɪ/ *adv* (*infml*) very.

frigid /'frɪdʒɪd/ *adj* 1 very cold. 2 (of a woman) having no sexual desire. **frigidity** /frɪ'dʒɪdətɪ/ *n* [U].

frigidly adv.

frill /frɪl/ n [C] 1 decorative border on a dress, etc. 2 [usu pl] (fig) unnecessary addition. **frilly** adj.

fringe /frɪndʒ/ n [C] 1 hair hanging over the forehead. 2 decorative edge of loose threads on a rug, etc. 3 edge: on the ~ of the forest/crowd.

frisk /frɪsk/ n 1 [I] jump and run about playfully. 2 [T] pass one's hands over (sb) to search for hidden weapons. **frisky** adj (-ier, -iest) lively.

fritter¹ /ˈfrɪtə(r)/ v (phr v) **fritter sth away** waste sth, esp one's money or time.

fritter² /ˈfrɪtə(r)/ n [C] piece of fried batter, with sliced fruit, meat, etc in it.

frivolous /ˈfrɪvələs/ adj not serious; silly. **frivolity** /frɪˈvɒlətɪ/ n (pl -ies) 1 [U] frivolous behaviour. 2 [C] frivolous act or comment. **frivolously** adv.

frizzy /ˈfrɪzɪ/ adj (of hair) having small tight curls.

fro /frəʊ/ adv (idm) **to and fro** ⇨ TO³.

frog /frɒg; US frɔːg/ n [C] small cold-blooded jumping animal that lives in water and on land. **'frogman** /-mən/ n [C] (pl -men) skilled underwater swimmer with a rubber suit and breathing apparatus.

frolic /ˈfrɒlɪk/ v (pt, pp ~ked) [I] play about in a lively way. **frolic** n [sing] lively enjoyable activity.

from /frəm; strong form frɒm/ prep 1 (showing the starting point): go ~ London to Oxford. 2 (showing the time at which sth starts): on holiday ~ 1 May. 3 (showing the sender or giver): a letter ~ my brother. 4 (showing the origin): quotations ~ Shakespeare. 5 (showing the distance between two places): 10 miles ~ the sea. 6 (showing a lower limit): Tickets cost ~ £3 to £12. 7 (showing the material from which sth is made): Wine is made ~ grapes. 8 (showing separation or removal): take the money ~ my purse. 9 (showing protection or prevention): save a boy ~ drowning ○ prevent sb ~ sleeping. 10 (showing the reason or cause): suffer ~ cold and hunger. 11 (showing change): ~ bad to worse. 12 considering (sth): reach a decision ~ the evidence.

front /frʌnt/ n 1 (esp the front) [sing] part or side that faces forward: the ~ of a building. 2 the front [sing] road beside the sea. 3 the front [sing] (in war) area where fighting takes place. 4 [sing] (often fake) appearance: put on a brave ~. 5 [C] boundary between cold and warm air. 6 [sing] (infml) thing or person that hides an illegal or secret activity. 7 [C] particular area of activity: on the financial ~. 8 (idm) in front in the most forward position; ahead. in front of (a) ahead of (sb/sth). (b) in the presence of (sb/sth). front v [I, T] have the front facing sth: hotels that ~ onto the sea. **frontage** /-ɪdʒ/ n [C] extent of a piece of land or building along its front. **frontal** adj of, from or in the front. the **front 'line** n [C] line of fighting that is nearest the enemy. **front-page** adj appearing on the front page of a newspaper.

frontier /ˈfrʌntɪə(r); US frʌnˈtɪər/ n [C] 1 (land near) the border between two countries. 2 [pl] extreme limit: the ~s of science.

frost /frɒst; US frɔːst/ n 1 [C, U] (period of) weather with temperature below freezing-point. 2 [U] white frozen water vapour on the ground, plants, etc. **frost** v 1 [T] cover with frost(2). 2 [T] give a rough surface to (glass) to make it opaque. 3 [T] (esp US) cover (a cake) with powdered sugar. 4 (phr v) **frost over/up** become covered with frost(2). **'frost-bite** n [U] injury to the fingers, toes, etc caused by extreme cold. **'frost-bitten** adj suffering from frost-bite. **frosty** adj (-ier, -iest) 1 cold with frost. 2 (fig) unfriendly: a ~y welcome.

froth /frɒθ; US frɔːθ/ n [U] 1 mass of small bubbles, eg on beer. 2 (derog) light but worthless talk, ideas, etc. **froth** v [I] have or produce froth. **frothy** adj (-ier, -iest) like or covered with froth.

frown /fraʊn/ v 1 [I] bring the eyebrows together (to express anger, thought, etc). 2 (phr v) **frown on/upon sth** disapprove of sth. **frown** n [C]: with a ~ on his face.

froze pt of FREEZE.

frozen pp of FREEZE.

frugal /ˈfruːgl/ adj 1 not wasteful; economical. 2 costing little; small: a ~ supper.

fruit /fruːt/ n 1 [C, U] part of a plant used as food, eg apple, banana. 2 [C] (botany) part of a plant or tree which contains the seeds. 3 (esp the fruits) [pl] result or reward of hard work, etc. **fruitful** adj (fig) producing good results. **fruitless** adj (fig) without success. **fruity** adj (-ier, -iest) 1 of or like fruit. 2 (infml) (of the voice) rich and deep.

fruition /fru:'ɪʃn/ *n* (idm) **come to fruition** (*fml*) (of hopes, plans, etc) be achieved or fulfilled.

frustrate /frʌ'streɪt; *US* 'frʌstreɪt/ *v* [T] **1** prevent (sb) from doing sth; upset or discourage. **2** prevent (plans) from being carried out. **frustrated** *adj* discouraged; not satisfied. **frustration** /frʌ'streɪʃn/ *n* [U, C].

fry /fraɪ/ *v* (*pt, pp* **fried** /fraɪd/) [I, T] cook in hot fat or oil. **'frying-pan** (*US* **'fry-pan**) *n* [C] **1** shallow pan used for frying food. **2** (idm) **out of the 'frying-pan into the 'fire** from a bad situation to a worse one.

ft *abbr* feet; foot.

fuck /fʌk/ *v* [I, T] (△ *sl*) **1** have sex with (sb). **2** (used for showing anger, annoyance, etc): *F~ (it)!* **3** (phr v) **fuck 'off** go away. **fuck** *n* [C] (△ *sl*) act of having sex. **,fuck-'all** *n* [U] (△ *sl*) nothing. **fucking** *adj, adv* (△ *sl*) (used for emphasis in expressions of anger, annoyance, etc).

fudge[1] /fʌdʒ/ *n* [U] soft brown sweet made of sugar, butter, milk, etc.

fudge[2] /fʌdʒ/ *v* [T] (*infml*) avoid speaking or acting firmly about (sth).

fuel /'fju:əl/ *n* [U] material, eg coal or oil, burned to produce heat or power. **fuel** *v* (**-ll-**; *US* **-l-**) [T] **1** supply with fuel. **2** make (a bad situation) worse: *to ~ inflation.*

fugitive /'fju:dʒətɪv/ *n* [C] (*from*)/ person who is escaping: *~ from famine.*

fulfil (*US* **fulfill**) /ful'fɪl/ *v* (**-ll-**) [T] **1** perform (a task, duty, promise, etc). **2** ~ **oneself** develop one's abilities and character fully. **fulfilment** *n* [U].

full /ful/ *adj* **1** holding as much or as many as possible: *a ~ bottle.* **2** having eaten enough. **3** complete: *give ~ details.* **4** plump: *a ~ fig-ure/face.* **5** (of clothes) wide and loose: *a ~ skirt.* **6** *of*// thinking only about sth: (*derog*) *He's ~ of himself.* **7** (idm) (at) **full speed/pelt/tilt** with great speed. **in full** completely. **to the 'full** as much as possible: *enjoy life to the ~.* **full** *adv* **1** exactly; directly: *hit him ~ in the face.* **2** very: *You knew ~ well that he was lying.* **,full-'board** *n* [U] hotel accommodation with all meals included. **,full-'length** *adj* **1** (of a picture, mirror, etc) showing the whole of a person. **2** not shortened. **,full 'moon** *n* [C] the moon appearing as a complete circle. **fullness** (also **fulness**)

n [U]. **,full-'scale** *adj* **1** (of drawings, plans, etc) of the same size as the object itself. **2** complete: *a ~ scale inquiry.* **,full'stop** (also **full point**) *n* [C] **1** mark (.) used esp at the end of a sentence. **2** (idm) **come to a full stop** stop completely. **,full-'time** *adj, adv* working all the normal hours. **fully** *adv* **1** completely. **2** at least: *The journey took ~ two hours.*

fumble /'fʌmbl/ *v* [I] use the hands awkwardly.

fume /fju:m/ *n* [C, usu pl] strong-smelling smoke or gas. **fume** *v* [I] **1** give off fumes. **2** (*fig*) be very angry.

fun /fʌn/ *n* [U] **1** (source of) enjoyment; pleasure. **2** playfulness. **3** (idm) **for 'fun** for amusement. **in 'fun** not seriously. **make fun of** sb/sth laugh at sb/sth unkindly. **'fun-fair** *n* [C] outdoor entertainment with machines to ride on, games, shows, etc.

function /'fʌŋkʃn/ *n* [C] **1** purpose of a thing or person. **2** formal social event. **function** *v* [I] operate or work: *The lift doesn't ~.* **functional** /-ʃənl/ *adj* **1** having a practical use, not decorative. **2** working; able to work.

fund /fʌnd/ *n* [C] **1** amount of money for a purpose. **2** supply of sth: *a large ~ of experience.* **fund** *v* [T] provide money for.

fundamental /,fʌndə'mentl/ *adj* very important; basic or essential. **fundamental** *n* [C, usu pl] basic rule or principle. **fundamentalism** /-təlɪzəm/ *n* [U] belief that everything in a holy book, eg the Bible or Koran, is true. **fundamentalist** *n* [C], *adj.* **fundamentally** /-təlɪ/ *adv.*

funeral /'fju:nərəl/ *n* [C] ceremony of burying or burning a dead person.

fungus /'fʌŋgəs/ *n* [C, U] (*pl* **-gi** /-gaɪ, also -dʒaɪ/ or ~ **es** /-gəsɪz/) plant without leaves that grows on decaying matter, eg old wood.

funnel /'fʌnl/ *n* [C] **1** tube that is wide at the top and narrow at the bottom, used for pouring liquids through. **2** chimney on a steam-engine or ship. **funnel** *v* (**-ll-**; *US* **-l-**) [I, T] pour through a funnel or narrow space.

funny /'fʌnɪ/ *adj* (**-ier, -iest**) **1** causing laughter; amusing. **2** strange. **funnily** *adv.* **'funny-bone** *n* [C] sensitive part of the elbow.

fur /fɜ:(r)/ *n* **1** [U] soft thick hair covering a cat, rabbit, etc. **2** [C] (garment made from an) animal skin with the fur on it. **3** [U] hard

grey covering on the inside of kettles, pipes, etc. **furry** *adj* (-ier, -iest) of, like or covered with fur.
furious /'fjʊərɪəs/ *adj* 1 very angry. 2 very strong; wild: *a ~ storm*. **furiously** *adv*.
furlong /'fɜːlɒŋ; *US* -lɔːŋ/ *n* [C] distance of 220 yards (201 metres).
furnace /'fɜːnɪs/ *n* [C] enclosed fireplace used eg for heating metals.
furnish /'fɜːnɪʃ/ *v* [T] 1 put furniture in. 2 (*fml*) provide. **furnishings** *n* [pl] furniture and fittings.
furniture /'fɜːnɪtʃə(r)/ *n* [U] large movable things, eg tables, chairs, etc in a house or office.
furrier /'fʌrɪə(r)/ *n* [C] person who prepares or sells fur clothing.
furrow /'fʌrəʊ/ *n* [C] 1 long mark cut into the ground by a plough. 2 wrinkle on the face. **furrow** *v* [T] make furrows in: *a ~ed brow*.
furry ⇨ FUR.
further /'fɜːðə(r)/ *adv* 1 at or to a greater distance in space or time: *It's not safe to go any ~*. 2 in addition; also: *F~, it has come to my attention...*. 3 to a greater degree. **further** *adj* 1 more distant in space or time. 2 additional; more: *~ information*. **further** *v* [T] help to advance. **furtherance** *n* [U] (*fml*) advancement. ,**further ed·u'cation** *n* [U] formal (but not university or polytechnic) education for people older than 16. **furthermore** *adv* in addition. **furthermost** *adj* most distant.
furthest /'fɜːðɪst/ *adj, adv* ⇨ FAR.
furtive /'fɜːtɪv/ *adj* done or behaving secretly so as not to be noticed. **furtively** *adv*. **furtiveness** *n* [U].
fury /'fjʊərɪ/ *n* [U, C] violent anger; rage.
fuse[1] /fjuːz/ *n* [C] short piece of wire that melts to break an electric circuit. **fuse** *v* [I, T] 1 (cause to) stop working because a fuse melts: *~ the lights*. 2 melt by means of heat; join by melting.
fuse[2] /fjuːz/ *n* [C] 1 cord, paper, etc that carries a spark to explode a firework or bomb. 2 (*US* also **fuze**) device in a bomb that makes it explode.
fuselage /'fjuːzəlɑːʒ; *US* -sə-/ *n* [C] body of an aircraft.
fusion /'fjuːʒn/ *n* [C, U] mixing or joining of different things into one.
fuss /fʌs/ *n* 1 [U, sing] unnecessary excited or anxious behaviour. 2 (*idm*) **make a fuss of sb** pay (too much) loving attention to sb. **fuss** *v* [I] be worried or excited esp

about small things. **fussy** *adj* (-ier, -iest) 1 (*about*)|| too concerned about unimportant details. 2 showing nervous excitement. 3 (of dress or style) decorated too much. **fussily** *adv*.
futile /'fjuːtaɪl; *US* -tl/ *adj* useless; unsuccessful: *a ~ attempt*. **futility** /fjuː'tɪlətɪ/ *n* [U].
future /'fjuːtʃə(r)/ *n* 1 **the future** [sing] the time that will come after the present: *in the ~*. 2 [C] what will happen to sb/sth: *The company's future is uncertain*. 3 [U] possibility of success: *There is no future in this job*. 4 (*idm*) **in future** from now onwards. **future** *adj* of or happening in the future.
futuristic /,fjuːtʃə'rɪstɪk/ *adj* looking very modern and strange.
fuzz /fʌz/ *n* [U] fluff. **fuzzy** *adj* (-ier, -iest) 1 (of hair) tightly curled. 2 (of cloth, etc) soft or fluffy. 3 not clear in shape or outline. **fuzzily** *adv*. **fuzziness** *n* [U].

G g

G, g /dʒiː/ *n* [C] (*pl* G's, g's /dʒiːz/) the seventh letter of the English alphabet.
g *abbr* gram(s): *500g*.
gabardine (also **gaberdine**) /'gæbədiːn, ,gæbə'diːn/ *n* 1 [C] strong cloth. 2 [C] raincoat made of this.
gabble /'gæbl/ *v* [I, T] talk or say (sth) too quickly to be understood clearly. **gabble** *n* [U] very fast talk.
gable /'geɪbl/ *n* [C] triangular part of an outside wall, between sloping roofs.
gad /gæd/ *v* (-dd-) (phr v) **gad about/around** (*infml*) go from one place to another in search of pleasure.
gadget /'gædʒɪt/ *n* [C] small machine or device. **gadgetry** *n* [U] gadgets.
Gaelic *n* [U], *adj* 1 /'geɪlɪk/ (language) of the Celtic people of Ireland. 2 /'gælɪk, also 'geɪlɪk/ (language) of the Celtic people of Scotland.
gaffe /gæf/ *n* [C] tactless remark or act.
gag /gæg/ *n* [C] 1 something put over sb's mouth to prevent him/her from speaking. 2 joke. **gag** *v* (-gg-) [T] put a gag(1) on (sb).
gaga /'gɑːgɑː/ *adj* (*infml*) senile.
gage (*US*) = GAUGE.

gaggle /'gægl/ n[C] 1 group of geese. 2 group of noisy people.

gaiety /'geɪəti/ n[U] cheerfulness; liveliness.

gaily /'geɪli/ adv happily; cheerfully.

gain¹ /geɪn/ v[I, T] 1 obtain (sth wanted or needed): ~ experience/ an advantage. 2 increase in (speed, weight, etc). 3 (of a clock or watch) go too fast: My watch ~s two minutes a day. 4 (idm) gain ground ⇨ GROUND¹. gain 'time obtain extra time by making excuses, thinking slowly, etc. 5 (phr v) gain on sb/sth come closer to sb/sth, eg in a race.

gain² /geɪn/ n[C, U] increase in amount or wealth. gainful /-fl/ adj providing money: ~ful employment.

gait /geɪt/ n[C] way of walking.

gala /'gɑːlə/ US 'geɪlə/ n[C] special public celebration or entertainment.

galaxy /'gæləksɪ/ n (pl -ies) 1[C] large group of stars. 2 the Galaxy [sing] the system of stars that contains our sun and planets, seen as a pale band in the sky. 3 (fig) group of people: a ~ of famous singers. galactic /gə'læktɪk/ adj.

gale /geɪl/ n[C] 1 very strong wind. 2 noisy outburst of laughter, etc.

gall¹ /gɔːl/ n[U] 1 = BILE. 2 impudent boldness. 'gall-bladder n[C] part of the body attached to the liver that stores bile. 'gall-stone n[C] hard mass that forms in the gall-bladder.

gall² /gɔːl/ v[T] annoy (sb).

gallant /'gælənt/ adj 1 brave. 2 (of a man) kind and polite to women. gallantly adv. gallantry n[U].

galleon /'gælɪən/ n[C] Spanish sailing-ship (15th to 17th centuries).

gallery /'gælərɪ/ n[C] (pl -ies) 1 room or building for showing works of art. 2 raised area along an inner wall of a hall or church. 3 highest seats in a theatre. 4 passage in a mine.

galley /'gælɪ/ n[C] 1 (formerly) long flat ship with sails and oars. 2 ship's kitchen.

gallivant /ˌgælɪ'vænt, 'gælɪvænt/ v (phr v) gallivant about (infml) travel for pleasure.

gallon /'gælən/ n[C] measure for liquids; four quarts (4.5 litres).

gallop /'gæləp/ n[C] fastest pace of a horse: at full ~. gallop v 1 [I, T] (cause a horse to) go at a gallop. 2 [I] (infml) hurry.

gallows /'gæləʊz/ n (usu with sing v) wooden framework on which criminals are put to death by hanging.

galore /gə'lɔː(r)/ adv in plenty: prizes ~.

galvanize /'gælvənaɪz/ v[T] 1 coat (iron) with zinc to protect it from rust. 2 (into) (fig) shock (sb) into action.

gambit /'gæmbɪt/ n[C] 1 opening move in chess, to produce an advantage later. 2 (fig) any first move.

gamble /'gæmbl/ v[I] 1 play games of chance for money. 2 (phr v) gamble on sth take a risk with sth. gamble n[C] risky attempt to win money or to be successful. gambler n[C] person who gambles. gambling n[U].

gambol /'gæmbl/ v (-ll- US also -l-) [I] jump about playfully.

game¹ /geɪm/ n 1 [C] form of play or sport with rules. 2 games [pl] sports, esp athletics competitions. 3 [C] single part of a match in tennis, etc. 4 [C] equipment, eg a board and dice, for playing a game. 5 [C] (infml) secret plan or trick. 6 [C] (infml) activity or business: Politics is a power ~. 7 [U] (flesh of) animals or birds hunted for sport or food. 8 (idm) give the 'game away carelessly reveal a secret. (be) off one's 'game (be) unable to play as well as usual. 'gamekeeper n[C] man employed to breed and protect game(7), eg pheasants.

game² /geɪm/ adj willing to do sth risky; brave. gamely adv.

gammon /'gæmən/ n[U] smoked or cured ham.

gamut /'gæmət/ n the gamut [sing] complete range (of sth).

gander /'gændə(r)/ n[C] male goose.

gang /gæŋ/ n[C, also sing with pl v] 1 organized group of criminals or workers. 2 group of young people, usu males. gang v (phr v) gang up (on sb) join together (against sb).

gangling /'gæŋglɪŋ/ adj (of a person) tall, thin and awkward.

gangrene /'gæŋɡriːn/ n[U] decay of a part of the body because blood has stopped flowing to it. gangrenous /'gæŋɡrɪnəs/ adj.

gangster /'gæŋstə(r)/ n[C] member of a gang of armed criminals.

gangway /'gæŋweɪ/ n 1 movable bridge from a ship to the land. 2 passage between rows of seats.

gaol (US usu **jail**) /dʒeɪl/ n[C] prison. gaol (US usu **jail**) v[T] put (sb) in gaol. gaoler (US usu **jailer**) n[C] person in charge of prisoners.

gap /gæp/ *n* [C] **1** empty space in sth or between two things. **2** unfilled period of time: ~ *between school and university.* **3** *(fig)* something missing; separation: ~*s in one's knowledge.*

gape /geɪp/ *v* [I] **1** stare with an open mouth, usu in surprise. **2** open wide: *a gaping hole.* **gape** *n* [C] open-mouthed stare.

garage /'gæra:ʒ, 'gæridʒ; *US* gə'ra:ʒ/ *n* [C] **1** building in which a car is kept. **2** place where cars are repaired. **garage** *v* [T] put (a car, van, etc) in a garage.

garbage /'gɑ:bɪdʒ/ *n* [U] *(esp US)* rubbish. **'garbage can** *n* [C] *(US)* dustbin.

garbled /'gɑ:bld/ *adj* incomplete and confused: *a ~ message.*

garden /'gɑ:dn/ *n* **1** [C, U] piece of private ground used for growing flowers, vegetables, etc. **2 gardens** [pl] public park. **garden** *v* [I] work in a garden. **'garden centre** *n* [C] place where garden plants, tools, etc are sold. **gardener** *n* [C] person who works in a garden. **gardening** *n* [U]. **garden party** *n* [C] formal social party in a garden.

gargle /'gɑ:gl/ *v* [I] wash the throat with liquid (without swallowing). **gargle** *n* **1** [C] liquid used for gargling. **2** [sing] act of gargling.

gargoyle /'gɑ:gɔɪl/ *n* [C] stone figure of an ugly creature on the roof of a church, etc, through which rain-water is carried away.

garish /'geərɪʃ/ *adj* unpleasantly bright. **garishly** *adv.*

garland /'gɑ:lənd/ *n* [C] circle of flowers or leaves as a decoration. **garland** *v* [T] put a garland on.

garlic /'gɑ:lɪk/ *n* [U] plant like a small onion, used in cooking.

garment /'gɑ:mənt/ *n* [C] *(fml)* article of clothing.

garnish /'gɑ:nɪʃ/ *v* [T] decorate (food). **garnish** *n* [C] something used to garnish.

garret /'gærət/ *n* [C] small room at the top of a house.

garrison /'gærɪsn/ *n* [C, also sing with pl v] group of soldiers living in a town or fort. **garrison** *v* [T] defend (a place) with a garrison.

garrulous /'gærələs/ *adj* *(fml)* talking too much.

garter /'gɑ:tə(r)/ *n* [C] elastic band worn round the leg to keep up a sock or stocking.

gas /gæs/ *n* *(pl* ~ **es;** *US* also ~ **ses)** **1** [C, U] substance like air. **2** [U] gas used for heating, cooking, etc. **3** [U] *(US infml)* petrol. **gas** *v* (**-ss-**) [T] kill (sb) with gas. **'gasbag**

n [C] *(infml derog)* person who talks too much. **gaseous** /'gæsɪəs, 'geɪsɪəs/ *adj* of or like gas. **'gas-fitter** *n* [C] worker who puts in gas pipes, heaters, cookers, etc. **'gaslight** *n* [C, U] light from burning gas. **'gasman** /-mæn/ *n* [C] *(pl* **-men** /-men/) *(infml)* official who reads gas meters and checks gas heaters, etc. **'gas mask** *n* [C] breathing apparatus to protect the wearer against poisonous gas. **'gas station** *n* [C] *(US)* petrol station. **gassy** *adj* (**-ier, -iest**) of or like gas; full of gas: ~*y beer.* **'gasworks** *n* [C] *(pl* **gasworks**) place where coal is made into gas.

gash /gæʃ/ *n* [C] *(in)//* long deep cut. **gash** *v* [T] make a gash in.

gasket /'gæskɪt/ *n* [C] soft flat piece of material between two metal surfaces to prevent oil, steam, etc from escaping.

gasoline (also **gasolene**) /'gæsəli:n/ *n* [U] *(US)* petrol.

gasp /gɑ:sp/ *v* **1** [I] breathe quickly, because of surprise, pain, etc; struggle for breath. **2** [T] say (sth) in a breathless way. **gasp** *n* [C] short quick breath.

gastric /'gæstrɪk/ *adj* of the stomach: ~ *ulcers.*

gastro-enteritis /,gæstrəʊ,entə'raɪtɪs/ *n* [U] painful swelling of the stomach and intestines.

gate /geɪt/ *n* [C] **1** movable barrier that closes an opening in a wall, fence, etc. **2** way out from an airport building to a plane. **3** (money paid by the) number of people attending a sports event. **'gatecrash** *v* [I, T] go to (a party) without being invited. **'gatecrasher** *n* [C]. **'gatepost** *n* [C] post on which a gate is hung. **'gateway** *n* [C] **1** opening with a gate. **2** [usu sing] *to// (fig)* means of reaching sth: *the ~ way to success.*

gâteau /'gætəʊ; *US* gæ'təʊ/ *n* [C] *(pl* ~ **x** or ~ **s)** large rich creamcake.

gather /'gæðə(r)/ *v* **1** [I, T] come or bring together. **2** [T] pick (flowers, fruit, etc). **3** [T] obtain gradually: ~ *information.* **4** [T] understand: *I* ~ *she's looking for a job.* **5** [T] increase in: ~ *speed.* **6** [T] draw (a garment) together in folds. **gathering** *n* [C] meeting.

gauche /gəʊʃ/ *adj* socially awkward.

gaudy /'gɔ:dɪ/ *adj* (**-ier, -iest**) *(derog)* too bright and showy. **gaudily** *adv.*

gauge (*US* also **gage**) /geɪdʒ/ *n* [C] **1** instrument for measuring sth: *a petrol* ~. **2** distance between the rails on a railway. **3** thickness of sth, esp sheet of metal or wire. **4** (fig) means of comparison; measure: *a ~ of her progress.* **gauge** *v* [T] **1** measure accurately. **2** (fig) estimate.

gaunt /gɔːnt/ *adj* (-er) very thin, as from illness or hunger. **gauntness** *n* [U].

gauntlet /ˈgɔːntlɪt/ *n* [C] strong glove with a wide covering for the wrist.

gauze /gɔːz/ *n* [U] thin net material, used eg on wounds.

gave *pt* of GIVE¹.

gawky /ˈgɔːkɪ/ *adj* (-ier, -iest) (esp of a tall person) awkward and clumsy. **gawkiness** *n* [U].

gawp /gɔːp/ *v* [I] (*infml*) stare rudely or stupidly.

gay /geɪ/ *adj* **1** homosexual. **2** happy; cheerful: *~ laughter/colours.* **gay** *n* [C] homosexual person.

gaze /geɪz/ *v* [I] (*at*)// look long and steadily. **gaze** *n* [sing] long steady look.

gazelle /gəˈzel/ *n* [C] small graceful antelope.

gazette /gəˈzet/ *n* [C] government newspaper with legal notices, news, etc.

gazump /gəˈzʌmp/ *v* [T] (*Brit infml derog*) (usu passive) increase the price of a house after accepting an offer from (a buyer).

GB /ˌdʒiː ˈbiː/ *abbr* Great Britain.

GCSE /ˌdʒiː siː es ˈiː/ *n* [C] (*Brit*) General Certificate of Secondary Education; examination in a particular subject taken by school pupils aged about 16.

GDR /ˌdʒiː diː ˈɑː(r)/ *abbr* German Democratic Republic (East Germany).

gear /gɪə(r)/ *n* **1** [C, U] set of toothed wheels working together in a machine: *The car has five ~s.* ○ *change ~.* **2** [U] equipment: *camping ~.* **3** [U] apparatus of wheels, levers, etc: *the 'landing-~ of an aircraft.* **gear** *v* (phr v) **gear sth to/towards sth** adapt or organize sth for a particular need: *The whole city is ~ed to the needs of tourists.* **gear (sb) up (for/to sth)** become or make sb ready (for sth). **'gearbox** *n* [C] case that contains the gears of a car or machine. **'gear-lever**, **'gear-stick** (*US* usu **'gearshift**) *n* [C] lever used for changing gear(s).

geese *pl* of GOOSE.

gelatine /ˈdʒelətiːn, -tɪn/ (also esp *US* **gelatin** /-tɪn/) *n* [U] clear tasteless substance, used for making jelly.

gelding /ˈgeldɪŋ/ *n* [C] male horse

whose sexual organs have been removed.

gelignite /ˈdʒelɪgnaɪt/ *n* [U] powerful explosive.

gem /dʒem/ *n* [C] **1** jewel. **2** (fig) person or thing that is highly valued.

gender /ˈdʒendə(r)/ *n* [C, U] **1** (*grammar*) grouping of nouns and pronouns into masculine, feminine and neuter. **2** (*fml*) grouping into male and female; sex.

gene /dʒiːn/ *n* [C] unit in a cell that controls heredity.

genealogy /ˌdʒiːnɪˈælədʒɪ/ *n* (*pl* -ies) **1** [U] study of family history. **2** [C] diagram showing the history of a family. **genealogical** /ˌdʒiːnɪəˈlɒdʒɪkl/ *adj*.

general /ˈdʒenrəl/ *adj* **1** affecting all or most of *~ interest.* **2** not specialized: *~ knowledge.* **3** not detailed: *~ impressions.* **4** (in titles) chief: *the Postmaster-'G~.* **5** (idm) **in 'general** usually. **general** *n* [C] army officer of very high rank. **general anaes'thetic** *n* [C] anaesthetic that affects the whole of one's body. **,general e'lection** *n* [C] election in which all the voters choose representatives for the national parliament. **generality** /ˌdʒenəˈrælətɪ/ *n* (*pl* -ies) **1** [C] general statement. **2** [U] quality of being general. **generally** *adv* **1** usually: *I ~ly get up early.* **2** by most people: *The plan was ~ly welcomed.* **3** in a general sense; not considering details: *~ly speaking.* **,general prac'titioner** *n* [C] doctor who treats patients with all kinds of illness in his/her surgery or in their homes. **,general 'strike** *n* [C] refusal to work by all or most workers.

generalize /ˈdʒenrəlaɪz/ *v* [I] make a general statement. **generalization** /ˌdʒenrəlaɪˈzeɪʃn; *US* -lɪˈz-/ *n* [C, U] (statement based on) generalizing.

generate /ˈdʒenəreɪt/ *v* [I] produce: *~ electricity.* **generative** /ˈdʒenərətɪv/ *adj* able to produce.

generator /ˈdʒenəreɪtə(r)/ *n* [C] machine that generates electricity.

generation /ˌdʒenəˈreɪʃn/ *n* **1** [C] all people born at about the same time. **2** [C] single stage in a family history. **3** [U] generating: *the ~ of heat.*

generic /dʒɪˈnerɪk/ *adj* (*fml*) shared by a whole group. **generically** /-klɪ/ *adv*.

generous /ˈdʒenərəs/ *adj* **1** giving freely: *He's ~ with his money.* **2** larger than normal. **generosity** /ˌdʒenəˈrɒsətɪ/ *n* [U]. **generously** *adv*.

genetic /dʒɪ'netɪk/ adj of genes or genetics. **genetically** /-klɪ/ adv. **genetics** n (with sing v) study of how characteristics are passed from one generation to the next.

genial /'dʒi:nɪəl/ adj kind and pleasant. **genially** adv.

genital /'dʒenɪtl/ adj of the reproductive organs of animals. **genitals** n [pl] external sex organs.

genius /'dʒi:nɪəs/ n 1 (a) [U] very great intelligence or ability. (b) [C] person with this. 2 [sing] exceptional natural ability: have a ~ for languages.

genocide /'dʒenəsaɪd/ n [U] killing of a nation or race of people.

genre /'ʒɑ:nrə/ n (fml) style or kind; class.

gent /dʒent/ n 1 [C] (infml or joc) gentleman. 2 **the Gents** (Brit infml) (usu with sing v) public toilet for men.

genteel /dʒen'ti:l/ adj polite, esp in an exaggerated way.

gentile /'dʒentaɪl/ n [C], adj (person who is) not Jewish.

gentle /'dʒentl/ adj (~r /-lə(r)/, ~st /-lɪst/) not rough or violent. **gentleness** n [U]. **gently** /-lɪ/ adv.

gentleman /'dʒentlmən/ n [C] (pl -men /-mən/) 1 man who is polite and behaves honourably. 2 (in polite use) any man. 3 (dated) man of wealth and social position. **gentlemanly** adv (fml or dated) of or like a gentleman(1).

gentry /'dʒentrɪ/ n **the gentry** [pl] people of high social class, just below the nobility.

genuine /'dʒenjʊɪn/ adj real; true. **genuinely** adv. **genuineness** n [U].

genus /'dʒi:nəs/ n [C] (pl **genera** /'dʒenərə/) division of animals or plants within a family(4).

geography /dʒɪ'ɒgrəfɪ/ n [U] 1 study of the earth's surface, climate, countries, population, etc. 2 arrangement of features in a particular region. **geographer** /-fə(r)/ n [C] expert in geography. **geographical** /dʒɪə'græfɪkl/ adj. **geographically** /-klɪ/ adv.

geology /dʒɪ'ɒlədʒɪ/ n [U] 1 study of the earth's rocks, crust, etc. 2 structure of rocks, etc, in a particular region. **geological** /dʒɪə'lɒdʒɪkl/ adj. **geologically** /-klɪ/ adv. **geologist** /dʒɪ'ɒlədʒɪst/ n [C] expert in geology.

geometry /dʒɪ'ɒmətrɪ/ n [U] study of lines, angles and figures and their relationships. **geometric** /dʒɪə'metrɪk/ (also **geometrical**) adj.

geranium /dʒə'reɪnɪəm/ n [C] garden plant with red, pink or white flowers.

geriatrics /dʒerɪ'ætrɪks/ n (with sing v) medical care of old people. **geriatric** adj.

germ /dʒɜ:m/ n 1 [C] very small living thing that can cause disease. 2 [sing] of/ beginning: the ~ of an idea.

German /'dʒɜ:mən/ n 1 [U] the German language. 2 [C] German person. **German** adj of Germany, its people or their language. **German 'measles** n [U] mild disease causing red spots all over the body.

germinate /'dʒɜ:mɪneɪt/ v [I, T] (cause seeds to) start growing. **germination** /ˌdʒɜ:mɪ'neɪʃn/ n [U].

gerund /'dʒerənd/ n [C] the -ing form of a verb when used as a noun (as in 'fond of swimming ').

gestation /dʒe'steɪʃn/ n [U] process or period of a baby or young animal being carried in the womb.

gesticulate /dʒe'stɪkjʊleɪt/ v [I] (fml) move one's hands and arms about to express oneself. **gesticulation** /dʒeˌstɪkjʊ'leɪʃn/ n [C, U].

gesture /'dʒestʃə(r)/ n 1 [C, U] movement of the hand or head to show an idea, feeling, etc. 2 (fig) action done to show one's feelings: a ~ of support/defiance.

get /get/ v (-tt-, pt, pp got /gɒt/; US pp **gotten** /'gɒtn/) 1 [T] obtain; gain: ~ a new car. 2 [T] receive: ~ a letter. 3 [T] fetch: G~ your coat. 4 [T] receive as a punishment: ~ six months, ie six months in prison. 5 [T] travel by (a bus, train, etc): ~ a plane to Rome. 6 [T] (begin to) suffer from: ~ flu/a headache. 7 [T] prepare (a meal). 8 [T] (a) capture: The police got the robber. (b) kill; punish: I'll ~ you for that! 9 [I, T] (cause to) become: ~ wet/dressed ○ ~ a box open ○ ~ your hair cut ○ He got (ie was) killed in a car accident. 10 [I] (a) reach the stage that is mentioned: ~ to know someone. (b) start doing sth: We soon got talking. 11 [T] cause sb/sth to do sth: I can't ~ her to understand. ○ He got me to help him with his homework. 12 [I, T] (cause to) move, sometimes with difficulty: ~ off the bus ○ We can't ~ the piano downstairs. ○ ~ a message to sb. 13 [I] to// arrive: ~ home early ○ What time did you ~ to London? 14 [T] (infml) understand: I don't ~ you. 15 [T] (infml) puzzle: That's got you! 16 [T] annoy: Loud pop music really ~s me.

17 (idm) **get into groove** ⇨ GROOVE. **get somewhere/anywhere/nowhere** (*infml*) achieve something/nothing: *I tried to persuade him but I got nowhere*, ie I failed. **get to grips** ⇨ GRIP. **18** (phr v) **get (sth) a'cross (to sb)** (cause sth to) be understood: *get a'head (of sb)* progress (beyond sb). **get a'long** = GET ON WITH (a). **get a'long (with sb)** = GET ON WITH sb. **get a'long (with sb)** (*infml*) criticize sb: *Stop ~ting at me!* **get at sb** (a) reach or get access to sth. (b) discover: *~ at the truth.* **be getting at sth** suggest sth indirectly: *What are you ~ting at?* **get a'way** (a) escape: *Two prisoners got away.* (b) have a holiday: *~ away for two weeks in France.* **get away with sth** do sth wrong and receive no punishment: *~ away with cheating.* **get by** survive: *~ by on a small salary.* **get sb 'down** (*infml*) make sb feel depressed. **get sth down** swallow sth with difficulty. **get down to sth** begin to do sth seriously: *~ down to work/business.* **get in** arrive: *The train got in late.* **get sb in** call sb to perform a service: *~ someone in to fix the TV.* **get sth in** obtain a supply of sth: *~ some coal in for the winter.* **get in with sb** (*infml*) become friendly with sb, usu to gain an advantage. **get into sth** (a) (cause oneself to be in a difficult situation: *~ into trouble.* (b) develop a habit: *~ into the habit of rising at 6 a.m.* ○ *Don't ~ into drugs!*, ie Don't start taking them!. (c) become interested in sth: *I can't ~ into this book.* (d) start sth: *~ into fight/conversation.* (e) start a career in: *~ into journalism.* **get sth 'off** (cause sb to) leave a place or start a journey: *~ the children off to school.* **get (sb) off (with sth)** (cause sb to) escape with little or no punishment: *She got off with just a fine.* **get on (with sb)** have a friendly relationship (with sb): *We don't ~ on.* ○ *Do you ~ on with your boss?* **get on (with sth)** (a) make progress: *How are you ~ting on with your new job?* (b) continue: *G~ on with your work.* **be getting on** (*infml*) (a) be elderly. (b) be late: *It's ~ting on, so I must go home.* **get 'out** (a) escape. (b) become known: *The secret got out.* **get out of sth/doing sth** avoid doing sth that one ought to do. **get over sth** (a) recover from sth: *I haven't yet got over my mother's death.* (b) overcome: *~ over one's shyness.* **get sth over (to sb)** make sth clear to

sb. **get sth over (with)** (*infml*) finish sth unpleasant: *I'm glad I've got my exams over with.* **get round sb** persuade sb to do sth, often by flattery, etc: *She knows how to ~ round her father.* **get round sth** avoid obeying a rule, etc but without breaking it. **get round to sth/doing sth** do sth, usu after a delay. **get through** use sth up: *~ through £100 a week.* **get through (sth)** be successful in (an exam, etc). **get 'through (to sb)** contact sb, esp by telephone. **get (sth) 'through to sb** succeed in making sb understand: *I just can't ~ through to them (that this is wrong).* **get to'gether (with sb)** meet: *~ together for a drink.* **get up** (a) get out of bed. (b) rise from a sitting, kneeling, etc position. **get up to sth** (a) reach: *~ up to page ten.* (b) do sth naughty, unexpected, etc: *What has been ~ting up to?* **'getaway** n [C] escape: *a fast ~away.* **'get-together** n [C] (*infml*) social meeting. **'get-up** n [C] (*infml*) set of clothes, esp an unusual one. **.get-up-and-'go** n [U] (*infml*) quality of being energetic.

geyser /'giːzə(r); US 'gaɪzər/ n [C] natural spring (1) sending up a column of hot water or steam.

ghastly /'gɑːstlɪ; US 'gæstlɪ/ adj (-ier, -iest) **1** causing horror: *a ~ accident.* **2** (*infml*) very bad: *a ~ mistake.* **3** very pale and ill.

ghetto /'getəʊ/ n [C] (pl ~s) often (derog) part of a town where a minority group or poor people live. **'ghetto blaster** n [C] (*infml*) large, powerful, portable radio and cassette player.

ghost /ɡəʊst/ n **1** [C] spirit of a dead person that appears to sb living. **2** [sing] (fig) small amount: *the ~ of a* (ie very little) *chance.* **3** (idm) **give up the 'ghost** die. **ghostly** adj of or like a ghost. **'ghost town** n [C] town that was once full of people but is now empty. **'ghost-writer** n [C] person who writes material for sb else but does not use his/her own name.

GI /ˌdʒiː 'aɪ/ n [C] soldier in the US army.

giant /'dʒaɪənt/ n [C] (fem ~ess) (in stories) enormous and very strong person. **giant** adj enormous.

gibberish /'dʒɪbərɪʃ/ n [U] meaningless talk; nonsense.

gibbon /'ɡɪbən/ n [C] long-armed ape.

gibe (also **jibe**) /dʒaɪb/ v [I] (at)// make fun of sb/sth. **gibe** (also **jibe**) n [C] comment that makes

giblets /'dʒɪblɪts/ n [pl] heart, liver, etc of a bird, taken out and usu cooked separately.

giddy /'gɪdɪ/ adj (-ier, -iest) having a feeling that everything is turning round and that one is going to fall. **giddiness** n [u].

gift /gɪft/ n [c] 1 something given freely; present. 2 natural ability: a ~ for languages. 3 (idm) **the gift of the 'gab** the ability to speak easily and persuasively. **gifted** adj talented.

gig /gɪg/ n [c] (infml) performance by pop or jazz musicians.

gigantic /dʒaɪ'gæntɪk/ adj very large.

giggle /'gɪgl/ v [ɪ] (at/) laugh lightly in a silly way. **giggle** n [c] 1 light silly laugh. 2 [sing] (infml) something done for amusement.

gild /gɪld/ v [T] cover with gold-leaf or gold paint.

gill¹ /gɪl/ n [c, usu pl] organ through which a fish breathes.

gill² /dʒɪl/ n [c] measure for liquids; one quarter of a pint (0.142 litre).

gilt /gɪlt/ n [u] material with which things are gilded.

gimmick /'gɪmɪk/ n [c] unusual thing or action used for attracting attention. **gimmicky** adj.

gin /dʒɪn/ n [u] strong colourless alcoholic drink.

ginger /'dʒɪndʒə(r)/ n [u] 1 (plant with a) hot-tasting spicy root used in cooking. 2 orange-brown colour. **ginger** v (phr v) **ginger sb/ sth up** make sb/sth more lively. **ginger-'ale**, **ginger-'beer** n [u] non-alcoholic drink flavoured with ginger. **'gingerbread** n [u] ginger-flavoured cake.

gingerly /'dʒɪndʒəlɪ/ adv with great care; hesitantly.

gingham /'gɪŋəm/ n [u] cotton cloth with a pattern of squares or stripes.

gipsy = GYPSY.

giraffe /dʒɪ'rɑːf; US dʒə'ræf/ n [c] African animal with a very long neck and legs.

girder /'gɜːdə(r)/ n [c] long strong piece of iron or steel used for supporting a floor, roof, bridge, etc.

girdle /'gɜːdl/ n [c] 1 belt round the waist to keep clothes in position. 2 corset. **girdle** v [T] (rhet) surround: a lake ~d with trees.

girl /gɜːl/ n [c] female child; daughter; young woman. **'girl-friend** n [c] 1 boy's or man's special female friend. 2 female friend. **Girl 'Guide** n [c] member of an organization for girls that aims to

develop practical skills and helpfulness. **girlhood** n [u] time of being a girl. **girlish** adj of, for or like a girl.

giro /'dʒaɪrəʊ/ n (pl ~s) 1 [u, c] system for transferring money directly from one bank or post-office account to another. 2 [c] (Brit) cheque issued by the government for a social security payment.

girth /gɜːθ/ n 1 [c, u] (fml) measurement round sth: the ~ of a tree. 2 [c] band round the body of a horse to keep the saddle in place.

gist /dʒɪst/ n **the gist** [sing] general meaning or main points: Tell me the ~ of what she said.

give /gɪv/ v (pt **gave** /geɪv/, pp **given** /gɪvn/) 1 [T] cause sb to have (sth): ~ her a cheque ○ Have you been ~n the books you need? 2 [T for/] pay (money) in exchange: I gave (her) £500 for the car. 3 [T] provide; supply: ~ a book giving information on schools. 4 [T] allow (to have): ~ her a week to decide. 5 [T] cause: ~ trouble ○ Does your back ~ you pain? 6 [T] utter (a laugh, groan, etc), 7 [T] express in words: ~ an account of one's journey ○ She gave a speech to parliament. 8 [T] perform (a play, etc) in public: ~ a poetry reading. 9 [T] perform (an action): ~ a wave ○ He gave the door a kick. 10 [T] provide (a party, meal, etc) as a host. 11 [ɪ] bend or stretch under pressure: The plank gave a little when I stepped on it. 12 (idm) **give and 'take** be tolerant and willing to compromise: You have to ~ and take in a marriage. **give ground** ⇨ GROUND¹. **give or take sth** (infml) plus or minus: It takes an hour to get to Hastings, ~ or take a few minutes. **give sb sth on a plate** ⇨ PLATE. 13 (phr v) **give sth away** give sth at no cost. **give sb/sth away** betray or reveal sth/sb: ~ away secrets. **give sth back (to sb), give sb back sth** return sth to sb: ~ the book back (to him) ○ ~ him back the book. **give 'in (to sb/ sth)** surrender. **give sth off** send out sth, eg smoke, a smell, etc. **give 'out (a)** (of supplies, sb's strength, etc) come to an end. (b) (of a motor, etc) stop working. **give sth out** distribute: give out prizes/leaflets. **give over (doing sth)** (infml) stop doing sth. **give sb up (a)** regard sb as hopeless: The doctors have ~n him up. (b) stop having a relationship with sb. **give (sth) up** stop trying to do sth: She has ~n up trying to change him. **give sth up (a)** stop doing or having sth: I've ~n up smoking. ○ I gave up my job. (b) allow sb else to have sth: *He gave up his seat to the old man.* **give sb/ oneself/sth up** surrender sb/ oneself/sth: *He gave himself up to the police.* **given** *adj* agreed: *at the ~n time.* **given** *prep* considering (sth): *He runs very fast for his size.* '**give-away** *n* [C] (*infml*) (a) thing given free of charge. (b) something that reveals a secret.

give² /gɪv/ *n* 1 [U] quality of bending and stretching under pressure: *This rope has too much ~ in it.* 2 (idm) **give and 'take** willingness to be tolerant and make compromises: *There must be ~ and take in a marriage.*

glacial /'gleɪsɪəl; *US* 'gleɪʃl/ *adj* of ice or the Ice Age.

glacier /'glæsɪə(r); *US* 'gleɪʃər/ *n* [C] mass of ice that moves slowly down a valley.

glad /glæd/ *adj* (~der, ~dest) 1 pleased. 2 (*dated*) causing joy: *~ news.* **gladden** /'glædn/ *v* [T] make glad. **gladly** *adv* happily; willingly: *I will ~ly help you.* **gladness** *n* [U].

glade /gleɪd/ *n* [C] (*rhet*) open space in a forest.

gladiator /'glædɪeɪtə(r)/ *n* [C] (in ancient Rome) man trained to fight at public shows in an arena.

glamour (*US* also **-or**) /'glæmə(r)/ *n* [U] 1 attractive and exciting charm. 2 attractive beauty with sex appeal. **glamorize** *v* [T] make (sth) seem more attractive and exciting than it really is. **glamorous** *adj*.

glance /glɑːns; *US* glæns/ *v* [I] 1 take a quick look. 2 (phr v) **glance off sth** hit sth and bounce off at an angle. **glance** *n* [C] 1 quick look. 2 (idm) **at a glance** at once.

gland /glænd/ *n* [C] (*anatomy*) organ that makes substances which the body uses or expels. **glandular** /-jʊlə(r); *US* -dʒʊlər/ *adj*.

glare /gleə(r)/ *v* [I] 1 (*at*) stare angrily or fiercely. 2 shine very brightly. **glare** *n* 1 [C] angry or fierce stare. 2 [U] very bright unpleasant light. **glaring** /'gleərɪŋ/ *adj* 1 very bright. 2 angry. 3 (*fig*) obviously bad: *a glaring mistake.*

glass /glɑːs; *US* glæs/ *n* 1 [U] hard transparent substance used in windows, mirrors, etc. 2 [C] a drinking container made of glass; its contents: *a ~ of milk.* 3 **glasses** [pl] two lenses in a frame worn in front of the eyes to help a person to see better. '**glasshouse** *n* [C] greenhouse. '**glassware** /-weə(r)/ *n* [U] objects made of glass. '**glassworks** *n* [C] (with sing or pl *v*) factory where glass is made. **glassy**

adj (-ier, -iest) 1 smooth and shiny. 2 (*fig*) with no expression: *a ~y stare.*

glaze /gleɪz/ *v* 1 [T] fit glass into: *~ a window.* 2 [T] cover with a thin shiny surface: *~ pottery.* 3 (phr v) **glaze over** (of the eyes) become dull and lifeless. **glaze** *n* [C, U] thin shiny coating. **glazier** /'gleɪzɪə(r); *US* -ʒər/ *n* [C] person who fits glass into windows, etc.

gleam /gliːm/ *n* [C] 1 beam of soft light. 2 (*fig*) brief sign of sth: *a ~ of hope.* **gleam** *v* [I] send out a gleam; shine softly.

glean /gliːn/ *v* [T] collect (facts, news, etc) in small quantities and with effort.

glee /gliː/ *n* [U] (*at*)// feeling of satisfied joy. **gleeful** /-fl/ *adj.* **gleefully** *adv.*

glen /glen/ *n* [C] narrow valley, esp in Scotland or Ireland.

glib /glɪb/ *adj* (~ber, ~best) (*derog*) speaking or spoken easily and confidently but not sincerely: *a ~ answer.* **glibly** *adv.* **glibness** *n* [U].

glide /glaɪd/ *v* [I] 1 move along smoothly and easily. 2 fly without engine power. **glide** *n* [C] gliding movement. **glider** *n* [C] aircraft without an engine. **gliding** *n* [U] sport of flying in gliders.

glimmer /'glɪmə(r)/ *v* [I] send out a weak unsteady light. **glimmer** *n* [C] 1 weak unsteady light. 2 (*fig*) small sign: *a ~ of interest.*

glimpse /glɪmps/ *n* [C] quick incomplete view: *catch a ~ of the secret papers.* **glimpse** *v* [T] have a glimpse of.

glint /glɪnt/ *v* [I] give out small flashes of light. **glint** *n* [C] flash of light.

glisten /'glɪsn/ *v* [I] (esp of wet surfaces) shine brightly.

glitter /'glɪtə(r)/ *v* [I] shine brightly with flashes of light: *~ing jewels.* **glitter** *n* [U] 1 bright sparkling light. 2 (*fig*) attractiveness; excitement: *the ~ of show business.*

gloat /gləʊt/ *v* [I] (*over*)// show selfish delight at one's own success or at sb else's failure. **gloatingly** *adv.*

global /'gləʊbl/ *adj* 1 of the whole world. 2 of the whole of a group of items. **globally** /-bəlɪ/ *adv.*

globe /gləʊb/ *n* 1 [C] a model of the earth. 2 **the globe** [sing] the earth.

globule /'glɒbjuːl/ *n* [C] (*fml*) tiny drop, esp of liquid.

gloom /gluːm/ *n* [U] 1 darkness. 2 sadness and hopelessness. **glo-**

omy *adj* (-ier, -iest) 1 dark. 2 depressed. **gloomily** /-ɪlɪ/ *adv*.

glorify /'glɔːrɪfaɪ/ *v* (*pt*, *pp* -**ied**) [T] 1 make (sb/sth) seem more important or impressive: *His cottage is just a glorified barn.* 2 praise and worship (God). **glorification** /ˌglɔːrɪfɪ'keɪʃn/ *n* [U].

glorious /'glɔːrɪəs/ *adj* 1 having or bringing glory: *a ~ victory.* 2 magnificent. **gloriously** *adv*.

glory /'glɔːrɪ/ *n* (*pl* -ies) 1 [U] fame and honour. 2 [U] praise and worship: *~ to God.* 3 [U] magnificent beauty: *the ~ of a sunset.* 4 [C] cause of honour or praise: *the glories of ancient Rome.* **glory** *v* (*pt*, *pp* -**ied**) [I] *in∥* take (too much) pleasure in sth.

gloss¹ /glɒs/ *n* [U, sing] 1 brightness or shine on a surface. 2 (*fig*) deceptively good appearance. **gloss** *v* (*phr v*) **gloss over** try to hide or ignore (a problem, fault, etc). **'gloss paint** *n* [U] paint that has a shiny surface. **glossy** (-ier, -iest) smooth and shiny: *~y magazines*, ie magazines printed on high-quality shiny paper with many coloured pictures.

gloss² /glɒs/ *n* [C] explanation of a word or phrase in a text. **gloss** *v* [T] give an explanation of.

glossary /'glɒsərɪ/ *n* [C] (*pl* -ies) alphabetical list of explanations of words.

glove /glʌv/ *n* [C] covering for the hand.

glow /gləʊ/ *v* [I] 1 send out light and heat without flames: *~ing coal.* 2 be warm or red in the face. 3 show bright strong colours. **glow** *n* [sing] glowing light: *the ~ of a sunset.* **glowing** *adj* giving praise; enthusiastic: *a ~ing report.*

glower /'glaʊə(r)/ *v* [I] (*at*)∥ look angrily.

glucose /'gluːkəʊs/ *n* [U] natural sugar found in fruit.

glue /gluː/ *n* [U, C] thick sticky liquid used for joining things. **glue** *v* [T] 1 join or stick with glue. 2 (*idm*) **glued to sth** (*infml*) constantly close to: *They were ~d to the television.* **'glue-sniffing** *n* [U] dangerous practice of breathing in the fumes of glue as a drug(2).

glum /glʌm/ *adj* (-**mer**, ~**mest**) sad; gloomy. **glumly** *adv*.

glut /glʌt/ *v* (-**tt**-) [T] supply with too much: *The market is ~ted with cheap apples.* **glut** *n* [C, usu sing] too great a supply.

glutton /'glʌtn/ *n* [C] 1 person who eats too much. 2 (*infml*) person who is always ready for more of sth difficult or unpleasant: *a ~*

for punishment. **gluttonous** /-tənəs/ *adj* very greedy. **gluttony** *n* [U] practice of eating too much.

glycerine /'glɪsəriːn/ (*US* **glycerin** /-rɪn/) *n* [U] thick colourless liquid used in eg medicines and explosives.

gm *abbr* gram(s).

gnarled /nɑːld/ *adj* (of trees) rough and twisted.

gnash /næʃ/ *v* [T] grind (one's teeth) together.

gnat /næt/ *n* [C] small fly with two wings that stings.

gnaw /nɔː/ *v* [I, T] 1 bite steadily at (sth). 2 (*fig*) affect (sb's mind or nerves) steadily: *guilt ~ing at his conscience.*

gnome /nəʊm/ *n* [C] 1 (in stories) small old man who lives under the ground. 2 model of such a man used as a decoration in a garden.

go¹ /gəʊ/ *v* (*3rd person sing present tense* **goes** /gəʊz/, *pt* **went** /went/, *pp* **gone** /gɒn*; US* gɔːn/) [I] 1 (a) move from one place to another: *go home/for a walk/on holiday/to the cinema.* (b) move; travel: *go five miles to get a doctor.* 2 leave: *It's time for us to go.* 3 extend; reach: *This road goes to London.* 4 *to∥* attend a place, esp regularly: *go to school/church.* 5 have as the usual position; be placed: *The book goes on the shelf.* 6 fit in: *This key won't go (in the lock).* 7 make progress: *How are things going?* ○ *The party went very well.* 8 work: *This clock doesn't go.* 9 (esp in commands) begin an activity: *One, two, three, go!* 10 make a certain sound: *The bell went at 3 p.m.* ○ *The clock goes 'tick-tock.'* 11 have a certain wording or tune: *How does the poem/song go?* 12 pass into or from the state that is mentioned; become: *go from bad to worse/go to sleep* ○ *go mad/blind.* 13 be in the state that is mentioned: *go hungry/armed.* 14 (a) be given, lost, used up, etc: *Supplies of coal went very quickly.* (b) (*to, for*)∥ be sold: *The car went to a dealer for £500.* 15 get worse; stop working: *My sight is going.* ○ *The car battery has gone.* 16 (of time) pass: *two hours to go before lunch.* 17 (*idm*) **'anything goes** (*infml*) anything is allowed. **be going to do sth** (a) intend; plan: *We're going to sell our house.* (b) be likely or about to happen: *It's going to rain.* **go and do sth** (*infml*) do sth foolish, wrong, etc: *That stupid girl went and lost her watch.* **go to seed** ⇨ SEED. **go to waste** ⇨ WASTE². **there goes sth**

(*infml*) (used for showing regret that sth has been lost): *There goes my chance of getting the job, ie I will certainly not get it.* **18** (phr v) **go a'bout** move from place to place. **go about sth** begin to do sth: *How do you go about writing a novel?* **go after sb/sth** try to win or obtain. **go against sb/sth** (a) oppose sb/sth: *Don't go against my wishes.* (b) be unfavourable to sb: *The verdict went against him.* **go a'head** proceed; take place: *The tennis match went ahead in spite of the bad weather.* **go a'long** proceed. **go a'long with sb/sth** (a) accompany sb. (b) agree with sb/sth: *Will they go along with the plan?* **go at sb/sth** (a) attack sb. (b) work hard at sth. **go a'way** (a) leave. (b) disappear: *Has the pain gone away?* **go 'back** (a) return. (b) extend backwards in space or time: *Our family goes back 300 years.* **go back on sth** fail to keep (a promise): *go back on one's word.* **go 'by** (of time) pass: *The days go by so slowly.* **'go by sth** be guided by sth: *I always go by what my doctor says.* **go 'down** (a) (of a ship, etc) sink. (b) (of the sun, moon, etc) set. (c) (of food) be swallowed. (d) (of the sea, wind, etc) become calm. (e) (of prices, the temperature, etc) become lower. **go 'down (in sth)** be written or recorded: *Her name will go down in history.* **go down well/badly (with sb)** (of a comment, performance, etc) be received well/badly (by sb). **go down with sb** become ill with an illness: *go down with flu.* **go for sb/sth** (a) fetch sb/sth. (b) attack sb: *The dog went for him.* (c) apply to: *What she said goes for me too.* (d) (*infml*) like. **go 'in** (a) enter. (b) (of the sun, moon, etc) disappear behind clouds. **go in for sth** (a) enter (a competition, etc). (b) have an interest in sth: *go in for golf.* **go into sth** (a) (of a car, etc) hit sth. (b) enter sth: *go into the Army.* (c) examine sth: *go into (the) details.* (d) begin to do sth: *go into a long explanation.* **go 'off** (a) explode; be fired. (b) (of food, etc) become unfit to eat: *The milk has gone off.* (c) proceed: *The party went off well.* **go off sb/sth** stop liking sb/sth. **go 'on** (a) (of time) pass. (b) (of a light, etc) be lit. (c) continue: *The meeting went on for hours.* (d) happen: *What's going on here?* **go 'on (about sb/sth)** talk about sth/sb for a long time. **go 'on (at sb)** criticize sb. **go on (with sth/doing sth)** continue sth. **go on to sth/to do sth** do or say sth next. **go 'out**

(a) go to parties, etc: *I don't go out much at weekends.* (b) (of a fire, light, etc) stop burning or shining. (c) become unfashionable. **go 'out (together)**, **go out with sb** (*infml*) have a romantic or sexual relationship with sb. **go over sth** examine sth carefully. **go 'round** be enough for everyone: *There aren't enough apples to go round.* (b) go by a longer route. **go round (to)** visit: *We're going round to see Sarah.* **go round with sb** be often in the company of sb. **go 'through** be successfully completed: *The deal didn't go through.* **go through sth** (a) discuss in detail. (b) examine: *go through the papers.* (c) suffer; endure. (d) use up (money). **go through with sth** complete sth, esp sth unpleasant or difficult. **go to/towards sth** be contributed to sth: *All profits go to charity.* **go 'under** (a) sink. (b) (*fig*) fail. **go 'up** (a) rise. (b) be built. (c) be destroyed in an explosion: *The petrol station went up in flames.* (d) (of prices) become higher. **go up with** climb sth. **go with sb** (a) accompany sb. (b) have sb as a girl-friend or boy-friend. **go together**, **go with sth** match: *Do green curtains go with a pink carpet?* **go without** (sth) endure the lack of: *go without food for four days.* **'go-ahead** *n* the go-ahead [sing] permission to do sth. **'go-ahead** *adj* willing to try new methods. **,go-'slow** *n* [C] industrial protest in which workers work slowly.

go² /gəʊ/ *n* (*pl* ~es /gəʊz/) **1** [C] person's turn to play in a game. **2** [C] attempt: *I can't lift this box.' 'Let me have a go.'* **3** [U] (*infml*) energy: *He's full of go.* **4** (idm) **be on the 'go** (*infml*) be very active or busy. **it's all 'go** (*infml*) it's very busy. **make a 'go of sth** (*infml*) make a success of sth.

goad /gəʊd/ *v* **1** [T] (*into*)// annoy (sb) continuously: *He ~ed me into an angry reply.* **2** (phr v) **goad sb on** urge sb to do sth. **goad** *n* [C] pointed stick for making cattle move.

goal /gəʊl/ *n* [C] **1** (a) (in football, hockey, etc) pair of posts between which the ball has to go in order to score. (b) point scored when the ball goes into the goal. **2** (*fig*) aim or purpose. **'goalkeeper** *n* [C] player who stands in the goal and tries to prevent the other team from scoring. **'goal-post** *n* [C] either of the two posts which form a goal(1).

goat /gəʊt/ *n* [C] **1** small horned animal with long hair. **2** (idm) **get**

sb's **'goat** (*infml*) annoy sb.

gobble¹ /'gɒbl/ *v* [I, T] eat (sth) quickly and greedily.

gobble² /'gɒbl/ *v* [I] *n* [C] (make the) sound of a male turkey.

go-between /'gəʊbɪtwiːn/ *n* [C] person who takes messages between two people who cannot meet.

goblet /'gɒblɪt/ *n* [C] glass, metal, etc drinking- cup with a stem but no handle.

goblin /'gɒblɪn/ *n* [C] (in fairy stories) small ugly mischievous creature.

god /gɒd/ *n* **1** [C] being that is believed to have power over nature and control over human affairs. **2** **God** [sing] (esp in Christianity, Judaism and Islam) the maker and ruler of the universe. **3** [C] person or thing that is greatly admired or loved. **4** **the gods** [pl] seats high up in a theatre. **5** (idm) **God willing** if everything goes as planned. **'godchild**, **'god-daughter**, **'godson** *n* [C] person for whom sb takes responsibility as a godparent. **goddess** /'gɒdɪs/ *n* [C] female god. **'godfather**, **'godmother**, **'godparent** *n* [C] person who promises when a child is baptized to see that he/she is brought up as a Christian. **'god-fearing** *adj* sincerely religious. **'godforsaken** *adj* (of places) sad and lonely. **godless** *adj* not believing in God; wicked. **godlike** *adj* like God or a god in some quality. **godly** *adj* (-ier, -iest) deeply religious. **godliness** *n* [U]. **'godsend** *n* [C] unexpected piece of good luck.

goggle /'gɒgl/ *v* [I] (*at*)/ look with wide round eyes. **goggles** *n* [pl] glasses worn to protect the eyes from water, wind, dust, etc.

going /'gəʊɪŋ/ *n* **1** [sing] departure. **2** [U] speed of working or travelling: *It was good ~ to get to York so quickly.* **going** (idm) **a ,going con'cern** a profitable business. **the ,going 'rate** the usual price or cost. **,goings-'on** *n* [pl] unusual events.

go-kart /'gəʊkɑːt/ *n* [C] small, low, open racing car.

gold /gəʊld/ *n* **1** [U] valuable yellow metal. **2** [U] jewellery, money, etc made of gold. **3** [U, C] bright yellow colour of gold. **4** [C] (*sport*) gold medal. **goldfish** *n* [C] (*pl* **goldfish**) small orange or red fish kept as a pet. **,gold 'foil**, **,gold-'leaf** [U] very thin sheet of gold(3). **,gold 'medal** *n* [C] prize given to the winner of a competition, esp a sports contest. **'gold-mine** *n* [C] **1** place where

gold is mined. **2** (*fig*) successful profitable business. **'gold-rush** *n* [C] rush to a place where gold has been discovered in the ground. **goldsmith** *n* [C] person who makes objects out of gold.

golden /'gəʊldən/ *adj* **1** of or like gold. **2** excellent: *a ~ opportunity*. **3** (idm) **a golden handshake** large amount of money given to a worker when he/she leaves a company. **golden jubilee** *n* [C] 50th anniversary. **,golden 'rule** *n* [C] very important rule of behaviour.

golf /gɒlf/ *n* [U] outdoor game in which players hit a small ball into a series of 9 or 18 holes. **'golf ball** *n* [C] ball used in golf. **'golf club** *n* [C] club for golfers; land where they play golf. **'golf-club** *n* [C] long stick used for hitting the ball in golf. **'golf-course** *n* [C] area of land where golf is played. **golfer** *n* [C] person who plays golf.

gone *pp* of GO¹.

gong /gɒŋ/ *n* [C] round piece of metal that gives a ringing sound when struck.

gonorrhoea (also **gonorrhea**) /ˌɡɒnəˈrɪə/ *n* [U] sexually transmitted disease.

good¹ /gʊd/ *adj* (**better** /'betə(r)/, **best** /best/) **1** of a high quality: *very ~ exam results*. **2** pleasant; enjoyable: *~ news/weather* ○ *a ~ time*. **3** able to do sth skilfully: *a ~ teacher* ○ *~ at languages*. **4** morally right or acceptable: *~ deeds*. **5** (esp of a child) well-behaved. **6** beneficial; suitable: *Milk is ~ for you.* **7** kind: *They were very ~ to her when she was ill.* **8** thorough: *a ~ sleep*. **9** good for sth (**a**) to be trusted for (the amount mentioned): *My credit is ~ for £500.* (**b**) valid for sth: *tickets ~ for three months.* (**c**) likely to last for a period of (time): *The car's ~ for a few months yet.* **10** (used in greetings and farewells): *G ~ morning/afternoon*. **11 a good... (a)** great in number, quantity, etc: *a ~ many people*. (**b**) not less than: *a ~ three miles to the station.* **12** (used in exclamations): *G ~ Heavens!* **13** (used as an expression of approval, agreement, etc): *'I've finished!' 'G~!'* **14** (idm) **a good deal** ⇨ DEAL¹. **a good 'job** (*infml*) a fortunate state of affairs. **a good many** ⇨ MANY. **all in good time** (sth will happen) after some time, but not now. **as good as** almost: *as ~ as finished*. **as good as gold** very well-behaved. **be a good thing** (**a**) be fortunate. (**b**) be a good idea. **do sb a good turn** do sth useful or helpful for sb. **for**

governor

good measure in addition to the amount already given. **good and** (*infml*) completely: *I won't go until I'm ~ and ready.* **good for 'sb, 'you, 'them, etc** (*infml*) (used for expressing approval and happiness at sb's success). **good 'grief** (*infml*) (used for expressing surprise or other strong feelings). **good 'luck** (used for wishing sb success). **have a good mind to do sth** be very willing to do sth. **have a good night** ⇨ NIGHT. **in good time** early. **make good** become successful. **'good-for-nothing** *n*[C], *adj* (person who is) worthless or lazy. **,Good 'Friday** *n*[U, C] the Friday before Easter Sunday. **,good-'humoured** *adj* friendly and cheerful. **,good-'looking** *adj* handsome; beautiful. **,good-'natured** *adj* kind and friendly. **,good 'sense** *n*[U] ability to act wisely. **,good-'tempered** *adj* not easily made angry.

good² /gʊd/ *n*[U] **1** that which is morally right or acceptable: ~ *and evil.* **2** that which gives a benefit or advantage: *It's for your own ~.* **3** (idm) **be no/not much 'good** be of no/not much value: *It's no ~ talking to them.* **do (sb) 'good** benefit sb: *Drinking the medicine will do you ~.* **for 'good** permanently. **up to no 'good** doing sth wrong.

goodbye /,gʊd'baɪ/ *interj, n*[C] (used when leaving or being left by sb).

goodness /'gʊdnɪs/ *n*[U] **1** quality of being good. **2** part of food that provides nourishment: *Brown bread is full of ~.* **3** (used in expressions of surprise, relief, annoyance, etc): *My ~! ◇ For goodness' sake!*

goods /gʊdz/ *n*[pl] **1** things for sale; movable property: *electrical ~.* **2** things carried by train: *a ~ train.* **3** (idm) **come up with/ deliver the 'goods** (*infml*) do what one has promised.

goodwill /,gʊd'wɪl/ *n*[U] **1** kind and friendly feeling. **2** (financial value of the) good reputation of a business.

goody /'gʊdɪ/ *n*[C] (*pl* **-ies**) (*infml*) **1** [usu pl] something pleasant, esp to eat. **2** hero of a book, film, etc.

goose /gu:s/ *n* (*pl* **geese** /gi:s/) **1** [C] water-bird larger than a duck. **2** [C] female of this. **3** [U] its meat. **'goose-flesh** *n*[U] (also **'goose-pimples** [pl]) small raised spots on the skin, caused by cold or fear.

gooseberry /'gʊzbərɪ; *US* 'gu:s-berɪ/ *n*[C] (*pl* **-ies**) (bush with a) green hairy sour berry.

gorge¹ /gɔ:dʒ/ *n*[C] narrow steep-sided valley.

gorge² /gɔ:dʒ/ *v*[I, T] ~ (**oneself**) (**on**) eat greedily.

gorgeous /'gɔ:dʒəs/ *adj* **1** (*infml*) giving pleasure; wonderful. **2** very attractive; magnificent. **gorgeously** *adv*.

gorilla /gə'rɪlə/ *n*[C] large powerful African ape.

gorse /gɔ:s/ *n*[U] evergreen bush with sharp thorns and yellow flowers.

gory /'gɔ:rɪ/ *adj* (**-ier, -iest**) involving blood and death: *a ~ film.*

gosh /gɒʃ/ *interj* (*infml*) (expressing surprise).

gosling /'gɒzlɪŋ/ *n*[C] young goose.

gospel /'gɒspl/ *n* **1** (*Bible*) (**a**) (**the Gospel** [sing] life and teaching of Jesus. (**b**) **Gospel** [C] any one of the first four books of the New Testament. **2** [U] the truth.

gossamer /'gɒsəmə(r)/ *n*[U] fine silky thread.

gossip /'gɒsɪp/ *n* **1** [U] informal talk about other people, esp about their private lives. **2** [C] person who likes gossip. **gossip** *v*[I] talk gossip.

got *pt, pp* of GET.

gotten (*US*) *pp* of GET.

gouge /gaʊdʒ/ *n*[C] tool with a sharp semicircular edge for cutting grooves in wood. **gouge** *v* **1** [T] make a hole in (sth) roughly. **2** (phr v) **gouge sth out** force sth out with a sharp tool or one's fingers.

goulash /'gu:læʃ/ *n*[C, U] stew of seasoned steak and vegetables.

gourd /gʊəd/ *n*[C] **1** (large hard-skinned fruit of **a**) kind of climbing plant. **2** bottle or bowl made from the dried skin of this fruit.

gourmet /'gʊəmeɪ/ *n*[C] expert in good food and drink.

gout /gaʊt/ *n*[U] disease that causes painful swellings in joints, esp toes and fingers.

govern /'gʌvn/ *v* **1** [I, T] rule (a country, city, etc). **2** [T] control or influence: *The law of supply and demand ~s the prices of goods.* **governing** /'gʌvənɪŋ/ *adj* having the power or right to govern: *the ~ing body of a school.*

governess /'gʌvənɪs/ *n*[C] woman who lives with a family and teaches the children at home.

government /'gʌvənmənt/ *n* **1** [C, also sing with pl v] group of people who govern a country or state. **2** [U] (method or system of) governing: *democratic ~.*

governor /'gʌvənə(r)/ *n*[C] **1** person who governs a province or (in the USA) a state. 2 head of an institution; member of a governing body: *a prison/school ~*.

gown /gaʊn/ *n* [C] 1 woman's long dress for special occasions. 2 loose usu black garment worn by judges, members of a university, etc.

GP /ˌdʒiː 'piː/ *abbr* general practitioner.

grab /græb/ *v* (-bb-) [I, T] take (sth) suddenly or roughly. **grab** *n* [C] 1 sudden attempt to grab sth. 2 (idm) **up for 'grabs** (*infml*) available for anyone to take.

grace /greɪs/ *n* 1 [U] simple beauty, esp in movement. 2 [U] extra time allowed to complete sth, pay money, etc: *give sb a week's ~*. 3 [U] goodwill. 4 [U, C] short prayer of thanks before or after a meal. 5 [U] God's kindness towards people. 6 (idm) **with (a) bad/good 'grace** unwillingly/willingly. **grace** *v* [T] (*fml*) 1 decorate. 2 give honour or dignity to: *The Queen is gracing us with her presence*. **graceful** /-fl/ *adj* having grace(1): *a ~ful dancer*. **gracefully** *adv*. **graceless** *adj* without grace(1); rude.

gracious /ˈɡreɪʃəs/ *adj* 1 polite; kind. 2 marked by luxury and leisure: *~ living*. **graciously** *adv*. **graciousness** *n* [U].

grade /greɪd/ *n* [C] 1 step or degree in quality, rank, etc: *different ~ s of pay*. 2 mark given for work in school. 3 (*US*) class in a school. 4 (*US*) gradient. 5 (idm) **make the 'grade** (*infml*) reach the required standard. **grade** *v* [T] arrange sth in grades; mark (schoolwork). **'grade school** *n* [C] (*US*) primary school.

gradient /ˈgreɪdɪənt/ *n* [C] degree of slope of a road, railway, etc.

gradual /ˈɡrædʒʊəl/ *adj* taking place slowly over a period of time; not sudden. **gradually** /-dʒʊli/ *adv*.

graduate¹ /ˈɡrædʒʊət/ *n* [C] 1 person with a university or college degree. 2 (*US*) person who has completed a course at an educational institution.

graduate² /ˈɡrædʒʊeɪt/ *v* 1 [I] (a) complete a course for a degree: *~ in law*. (b) (*US*) complete an educational course. 2 [T] divide into graded parts; mark into regular divisions for measurement. 3 [I] move on (from sth) to sth more difficult or important. **graduation** /ˌɡrædʒʊ'eɪʃn/ *n* 1 [U] (ceremony of) graduating at a university, etc. 2 [C] mark showing a measurement.

graffiti /grə'fiːtiː/ *n* [pl, U] drawings or writing on a wall.

graft¹ /ɡrɑːft; *US* græft/ *n* [C] 1 piece cut from a plant and fixed in another plant to form a new growth. 2 (*medical*) piece of skin, bone, etc transplanted to another body or another part of the same body. **graft** *v* [T] put on as a graft.

graft² /ɡrɑːft; *US* græft/ *n* [U] (*Brit*) hard work.

grain /greɪn/ *n* 1 (a) [U] seeds of food plants such as wheat and rice. (b) [C] single seed of such a plant. 2 [C] tiny hard piece: *~ s of sand*. 3 [C] (*fig*) very small amount: *a ~ of truth*. 4 [U, C] pattern of the lines of fibres in wood, etc. 5 (idm) **be/go against the 'grain** be undesirable or unusual. **take sth with a grain of salt** ⇨ SALT.

gram (also **gramme**) /græm/ *n* [C] metric unit of weight.

grammar /ˈɡræmə(r)/ *n* [C, U] (book that describes the) rules for forming words and making sentences. **grammarian** /ɡrə'meərɪən/ *n* [C] expert in grammar. **'grammar school** *n* [C] kind of British secondary school that provides academic courses. **grammatical** /ɡrə'mætɪkl/ *adj* of or correct according to the rules of grammar. **grammatically** /-klɪ/ *adv*.

gramophone /ˈɡræməfəʊn/ *n* [C] (*dated*) record-player.

granary /ˈɡrænərɪ/ *n* [C] (*pl* -ies) storehouse for grain.

grand /ɡrænd/ *adj* 1 magnificent or impressive: *a ~ palace*. 2 (usu *derog*) proud; important. 3 (*infml*) enjoyable: *We had a ~ time*. 4 full; final: *the ~ total*. **grand** *n* [C] 1 (*pl* grand) (*sl*) $1000; £1000. 2 grand piano. **grandly** *adv*. **grand 'piano** *n* [C] large piano with horizontal strings. **'grandstand** *n* [C] large building with rows of seats for people watching sports.

grand- (used in compound nouns to show family relationships). **'grandchild** (*pl* -children) **'granddaughter**, **'grandson** *n* [C] daughter or son of one's child. **'grandfather**, **'grandmother**, **'grandparent** *n* [C] father or mother of either of one's parents. **'grandfather clock** *n* [C] clock in a tall wooden case.

grand-dad (also **grandad**) /ˈɡrændæd/ *n* (*Brit infml*) grandfather.

grandeur /ˈɡrændʒə(r)/ *n* [U] greatness; magnificence.

grandiose /ˈɡrændɪəʊs/ *adj* (usu *derog*) planned on a large impressive scale.

grandma /ˈgrænmɑː/ n [C] (infml) grandmother.

grandpa /ˈgrænpɑː/ n [C] (infml) grandfather.

granite /ˈgrænɪt/ n [U] hard grey or red stone used for building.

granny (also **grannie**) /ˈgrænɪ/ n [C] (pl -ies) (infml) grandmother. **'granny flat** n [C] (infml) flat for an old person in a relative's house.

grant /grɑːnt/ v [T] 1 (fml) agree to give or allow: ~ sb's request. 2 (fml) agree (that sth is true). 3 (idm) **take sb/sth for 'granted** be so familiar with sb/sth that one no longer values him, her or it. **take sth for 'granted** accept sth as certain without discussion. **grant** n [C] something granted, esp money from the government.

granulated /ˈgrænjʊleɪtɪd/ adj (of sugar) in the form of grains, not fine powder.

granule /ˈgrænjuːl/ n [C] small grain(2).

grape /greɪp/ n [C] green or purple berry used for making wine. **'grape-vine** n 1 [C] kind of vine on which grapes grow. 2 [sing] (fig) unofficial way in which news is passed, eg in an office: heard about it on the ~-vine.

grapefruit /ˈgreɪpfruːt/ n [C] (pl **grapefruit** or ~s) large yellow fruit like an orange but usually not so sweet.

graph /grɑːf; US græf/ n [C] diagram showing the relationship of two changing quantities. **'graph paper** n [U] paper with small squares of equal size.

graphic /ˈgræfɪk/ adj 1 of visual symbols, eg lettering and drawings: ~ design. 2 (of descriptions) clear and detailed. **graphically** /-klɪ/ adv clearly: ~ally described. **graphics** n [pl] lettering, drawings, etc.

graphite /ˈgræfaɪt/ n [U] soft black substance used in pencils.

grapple /ˈgræpl/ v [I] (with)|| 1 hold and struggle with sb. 2 (fig) try to deal with a problem.

grasp /grɑːsp; US græsp/ v [T] 1 seize firmly with one's hand(s). 2 understand (sth) fully. 3 (phr v) **grasp at sth** try to seize sth: (fig) ~ at an opportunity. **grasp** n [C, usu sing] 1 firm grip. 2 understanding. **grasping** adj (derog) greedy for money.

grass /grɑːs; US græs/ n 1 [U] common wild short green plant eaten by cattle, etc. 2 [C] species of this plant. 3 [U] ground covered with grass: Don't walk on the ~. 4 [U] (sl) marijuana. 5 [C] (Brit sl)

person who grasses(2) on sb. 6 (idm) **(not) let the grass grow under one's feet** (not) delay in doing sth. **grass** v 1 [T] cover with grass. 2 [I] (Brit sl) tell the police about sb's criminal activities. **,grass 'roots** n [pl] ordinary people, esp in politics. **grassy** adj (-ier, -iest) covered with grass.

grasshopper /ˈgrɑːshɒpə(r); US ˈgræs-/ n [C] jumping insect that makes a chirping noise.

grate¹ /greɪt/ n [C] metal frame in a fireplace.

grate² /greɪt/ v 1 [T] rub (sth) into small pieces against a rough surface: ~d cheese. 2 [I] make a rough unpleasant noise by rubbing. 3 [I] (on)|| (fig) irritate: ~ on sb's nerves. **grater** n [C] device for grating food, etc. **grating** adj irritating.

grateful /ˈgreɪtfl/ adj feeling or showing thanks: I'm ~ to you for your help. **gratefully** /-fəlɪ/ adv.

gratify /ˈgrætɪfaɪ/ v (pt, pp -ied) [T] (fml) please or satisfy. **gratification** /ˌgrætɪfɪˈkeɪʃn/ n [U, C]. **gratifying** adj (fml) pleasing.

grating /ˈgreɪtɪŋ/ n [C] framework of bars across an opening, eg a window.

gratitude /ˈgrætɪtjuːd; US -tuːd/ n [U] being grateful; thankfulness: feel ~.

gratuitous /grəˈtjuːɪtəs; US -ˈtuː-/ adj (fml derog) not necessary; without reason: ~ violence on television. **gratuitously** adv.

gratuity /grəˈtjuːətɪ; US -ˈtuː-/ n [C] (pl -ies) 1 money given for a service done. 2 (Brit) money given to a retiring worker.

grave¹ /greɪv/ n [C] hole in the ground for a dead body. **'gravestone** n [C] stone over a grave. **'graveyard** n [C] cemetery.

grave² /greɪv/ adj (~r, ~st) serious: a ~ situation. **gravely** adv.

gravel /ˈgrævl/ n [U] small stones, used eg to make paths. **gravel** v (-ll-; US also -l-) [T] cover with gravel. **gravelly** /ˈgrævəlɪ/ adj 1 full of gravel. 2 (fig) (of a voice) deep and rough.

gravitate /ˈgrævɪteɪt/ v [I] towards|to|| move towards or be attracted to sb/sth. **gravitation** /ˌgrævɪˈteɪʃn/ n [U].

gravity /ˈgrævətɪ/ n [U] 1 force that attracts objects towards the centre of the earth. 2 seriousness: the ~ of the situation.

gravy /ˈgreɪvɪ/ n [U] juice that comes from meat while it is cooking.

gray (esp US) = GREY.

graze¹ /greɪz/ v 1 [I] (of cattle,

sheep, etc) eat grass. **2** [T] put (cattle, etc) in a field to eat grass.

graze² /greɪz/ *v* [T] **1** scrape the skin from (part of one's body). **2** touch or scrape lightly while passing. **graze** *n* [C] place where the skin has been scraped.

grease /griːs/ *n* [U] **1** soft animal fat. **2** thick oily substance. **grease** *v* [T] **1** put grease on. **2** (idm) **grease sb's palm** (*infml*) bribe sb. **like greased lightning** (*infml*) very fast. ˌgrease-proof 'paper *n* [U] paper that does not let grease pass through it. **greasy** *adj* (**-ier**, **-iest**) covered with grease. **greasily** *adv*.

great /greɪt/ *adj* **1** very large in size, quantity or degree: *of ~ importance.* **2** very able and famous: *a ~ artist.* **3** (*infml*) very enjoyable: *a ~ time on holiday.* **4** (*infml*) splendid: *What a ~ idea!* **5** healthy; fine: *I feel ~ today.* **6** (*infml*) (used for emphasis): *Look at that ~ big tree!* **7** (idm) **a great deal** ⇨ DEAL¹. **a great many** ⇨ MANY. ˌGreat 'Britain *n* [sing] England, Wales and Scotland. **greatly** *adv* (*fml*) very much. **greatness** *n* [U].

great- (used in compound nouns to show one further generation): *~ uncle* (ie the uncle of one's father or mother) ○ *ˌ~·grandson*, ie the grandson of one's son or daughter.

greed /griːd/ *n* [U] (*for*)|| strong desire for too much food, money, etc. **greedy** *adj* (**-ier**, **-iest**). **greedily** *adv*.

green¹ /griːn/ *adj* **1** of the colour of growing grass. **2** (of fruit) not yet ripe. **3** pale; looking ill. **4** (*infml*) inexperienced; easily fooled. **5** very envious: *~ with envy.* **6** (esp *politics*) concerned about protecting the environment. **7** (idm) **give sb/get the green 'light** (*infml*) give sb/get permission to do sth. ˌgreen 'belt *n* [C] area of open land round a city, where building is strictly controlled. ˌgreen 'fingers *n* [pl] (*infml*) skill in gardening. 'greengrocer *n* [C] (*Brit*) shopkeeper who sells fruit and vegetables. 'greenhouse *n* [C] glass building used for growing plants. 'greenhouse effect *n* [sing] slow warming of the earth's atmosphere, caused by increased carbon dioxide. **greenness** *n* [U].

green² /griːn/ *n* **1** [U, C] green colour. **2** greens [pl] green vegetables. **3** [C] area of land with grass growing: *the village ~.* **4** [C] smooth area of grass around a hole on a golf-course.

greenery /'griːnəri/ *n* [U] green leaves and plants.

greet /griːt/ *v* [T] **1** welcome. **2** (of

sights and sounds) be suddenly seen or heard by (sb). **greeting** *n* [C] first words used on seeing sb or writing to sb, eg *'Hello!'* or *'Dear Sir'*

gregarious /grɪ'geərɪəs/ *adj* **1** liking to be with other people. **2** living in groups.

grenade /grə'neɪd/ *n* [C] small bomb thrown by hand.

grew *pt* of GROW.

grey (also esp *US* **gray**) /greɪ/ *adj* **1** of the colour of black mixed with white. **2** having grey hair. **grey** *n* [U, C] grey colour. **grey** *v* [I] become grey. ˌgrey 'matter *n* [U] (*infml*) intelligence.

greyhound /'greɪhaʊnd/ *n* [C] thin dog able to run fast.

grid /grɪd/ *n* [C] **1** framework of bars: *a ˈcattle-~*, ie one placed at a gate to stop cattle from leaving a field. **2** (a) network of straight lines that cross each other to form squares. (b) network of squares on a map. **3** system of wires for supplying electricity.

grief /griːf/ *n* **1** [U] (*at/over*)|| great sorrow. **2** [C] event causing great sorrow. **3** (idm) **come to 'grief** end in failure; have an accident.

grievance /'griːvns/ *n* [C] (*against*)|| real or imagined cause for complaint.

grieve /griːv/ *v* (*fml*) **1** [I] feel grief. **2** [T] cause grief to (sb).

grill /grɪl/ *n* [C] **1** shelf in a cooker where food is cooked below direct heat. **2** food, esp meat, cooked in this way: *a mixed ~.* **grill** *v* **1** [I, T] cook (food) under or over direct heat. **2** [T] question (sb) severely.

grille (also **grill**) /grɪl/ *n* [C] framework of bars across an open space, eg at the counter of a bank.

grim /grɪm/ *adj* (**~mer**, **~mest**) **1** unpleasant: *~ news.* **2** serious; determined: *~-faced.* **grimly** *adv*.

grimace /grɪ'meɪs; *US* 'grɪməs/ *n* [C] ugly expression on the face. **grimace** *v* [I] make grimaces.

grime /graɪm/ *n* [U] dirt, esp on a surface. **grimy** *adj* (**-ier**, **-iest**).

grin /grɪn/ *v* (**-nn-**) [I] **1** smile broadly so as to show the teeth. **2** (idm) **grin and 'bear it** endure pain, disappointment, etc without complaining. **grin** *n* [C] act of grinning.

grind /graɪnd/ *v* (*pt, pp* **ground** /graʊnd/) [T] **1** crush to powder: *~ corn into flour.* **2** polish or sharpen by rubbing: *~ a knife.* **3** press or rub firmly: *~ one's teeth.* **4** (idm) **grind to a 'halt** stop slowly. **5** (phr v) **grind sb down** treat sb very cruelly or unfairly. **grind** *n* [sing] **1** act of grinding. **2** (*infml*) hard boring task. **grinder** *n* [C] person or thing that grinds. **'grindstone** *n* [C] round stone used for sharpening tools.

grip /grɪp/ *v* (**-pp-**) **1** [I, T] take and hold firmly. **2** [T] (*fig*) hold the attention of: *a ~ping film*. **grip** *n* **1** [sing] firm hold. **2** [C] thing that grips. **3** [C] (*US*) small bag for a traveller. **4** (*idm*) **come/get to grips with sth** begin to deal seriously with (a problem, etc).

grisly /'grɪzlɪ/ *adj* causing horror or terror.

gristle /'grɪsl/ *n* [U] tough tissue in meat.

grit /grɪt/ *n* [U] **1** tiny hard bits of stone, sand, etc. **2** courage and endurance. **grit** *v* (**-tt-**) [T] **1** spread grit on (esp icy roads). **2** (*idm*) **grit one's teeth** (**a**) keep one's jaws tightly together. (**b**) (*fig*) show courage and determination. **gritty** *adj* (**-ier, -iest**).

groan /grəʊn/ *v* [I] *n* [C] (make a) long deep sound of pain or distress: *She ~ed with pain.*

grocer /'grəʊsə(r)/ *n* [C] shopkeeper who sells food and goods for the home. **groceries** *n* [pl] things sold by a grocer.

groggy /'grɒgɪ/ *adj* (**-ier, -iest**) weak and unsteady after illness, etc.

groin /grɔɪn/ *n* [C] part of the body where the legs meet.

groom /gruːm/ *n* [C] **1** person who looks after horses. **2** bridegroom. **groom** *v* [T] **1** clean and brush (horses). **2** prepare (sb) for a particular job, etc. **groomed** *adj* neat and tidy: *a well-~ed young man.*

groove /gruːv/ *n* [C] **1** long narrow cut in a surface. **2** (*idm*) **get into/be stuck in a groove** become set in a particular way of life. **grooved** *adj* having grooves.

grope /grəʊp/ *v* [I] **1** search about with the hands as one does in the dark: *~ for one's glasses.* **2** [T] (*infml derog*) touch (sb) roughly to get sexual pleasure.

gross¹ /grəʊs/ *n* [C] (*pl* **gross**) 144.

gross² /grəʊs/ *adj* **1** very fat. **2** vulgar. **3** (of sth wrong) very clear: *~ injustice.* **4** total: *~ income*, ie before tax has been deducted. **gross** *v* [T] earn as a total amount. **grossly** *adv.* **grossness** *n* [U].

grotesque /grəʊ'tesk/ *adj* strange, ugly and unnatural. **grotesquely** *adv.*

grotto /'grɒtəʊ/ *n* [C] (*pl* **~es** *or* **~s**) cave.

ground¹ /graʊnd/ *n* **1 the**

ground [sing] solid surface of the earth: *fall to the ~*. **2** [U] area or distance on the earth's surface. **3** [U] soil: *stony/marshy ~*. **4** [C] piece of land used for a particular purpose: *a football ~ ○ a play~*. **5 grounds** [pl] land or gardens round a building: *the palace ~s*. **6** [U] (*fig*) area of interest, discussion, etc: *The programme covered a lot of ~*. ○ *Common ~ between the two sides*, ie points on which they can agree. **7** [C, esp pl] reason: *~s for divorce.* **8 grounds** [pl] small solid bits at the bottom of a liquid: *coffee-~s.* **9** (*idm*) **gain/make up ground** (**on sb/sth**) gradually catch up (with sb/sth): (*fig*) *gain ~ on one's competitors.* **get off the ground** (of a project) make a successful start. **give/lose 'ground** (**to sb/sth**) lose an advantage (over sb/sth). **hold/keep/stand one's 'ground** not change one's position, opinion, etc; not yield. **,ground 'floor** *n* [sing] (*Brit*) floor of a building at ground level. **groundless** *adj* without good reason: *~less fears.* **'groundsheet** *n* [C] waterproof sheet spread on the ground. **'groundwork** *n* [U] preparation for further study or work.

ground² /graʊnd/ *v* **1** [I, T] (cause a ship to) touch the sea bottom. **2** [T] force (an aircraft or pilot) to stay on the ground. **3** (*phr v*) **ground sb in sth** teach sb the basic principles of a subject. **ground sth on sth** base beliefs, etc on sth. **grounding** *n* [sing] teaching of the basic principles of a subject.

ground³ *pt, pp* of GRIND.

group /gruːp/ *n* [C, also sing with pl v] number of people or things together. **group** *v* [I, T] form into a group or groups.

grouse¹ /graʊs/ *n* [C] (*pl* **grouse**) small fat bird, shot for sport and food.

grouse² /graʊs/ *v* [I] (*infml*) complain; grumble. **grouse** *n* [C] complaint.

grove /grəʊv/ *n* [C] group of trees.

grovel /'grɒvl/ *v* (**-ll-**; *US* **-l-**) [I] (*derog*) show humility and respect towards sb, trying to gain his/her favour. **groveller** *n* [C] person who grovels.

grow /grəʊ/ *v* (*pt* **grew** /gruː/, *pp* **~n** /grəʊn/) **1** [I] increase in size. **2** [I, T] (cause to) develop: *Plants ~ from seeds.* ○ ... *a beard.* **3** (*usu* used with an adj) become: *~ older.* **4** (*phr v*) **grow on sb** become more attractive to sb: *The picture will ~ on you.* **grow out of sth** (**a**) become too big to wear sth. (b) become too old for sth: ~ *out of playing with toys.* **grow up** (a) become adult. (b) start to exist: *A warm friendship grew up between them.*

growl /graʊl/ v [I] n [C] (make a) low threatening sound: *The dog ~ed at the burglars.*

grown /grəʊn/ *adj* mature; adult. ,**grown 'up** *adj* adult; mature. '**grown-up** n [C]

growth /grəʊθ/ n 1 [U] growing; development. 2 [C] something growing: *three days' ~ of beard.* 3 [C] diseased formation, esp a lump, that grows in or on the body.

grub¹ /grʌb/ n 1 [C] first stage of an insect. 2 [U] (*sl*) food.

grub² /grʌb/ v (-bb-) [I] turn over soil, esp in order to find sth.

grubby /'grʌbɪ/ *adj* (-ier, -iest) dirty.

grudge /grʌdʒ/ v [T] be unwilling to give or accept: *I ~ paying so much for such bad goods.* **grudge** n [C] feeling of ill-will, envy, etc: *have a ~ against sb.* **grudging** *adj* unwilling. **grudgingly** *adv.*

gruelling (*US* **grueling**) /'gru:əlɪŋ/ *adj* very tiring.

gruesome /'gru:səm/ *adj* causing horror and disgust. **gruesomely** *adv.*

gruff /grʌf/ *adj* rough and unfriendly. **gruffly** *adv.* **gruffness** n [C]

grumble /'grʌmbl/ v [I] complain. **grumble** n [C] complaint.

grumpy /'grʌmpɪ/ *adj* (-ier, -iest) bad-tempered. **grumpily** *adv.*

grunt /grʌnt/ v [I] (a) (esp of pigs) make a low rough sound. (b) (of people) make a similar sound. **grunt** n [C] low rough sound.

guarantee /ˌgærən'ti:/ n [C] 1 promise, usu written, that certain conditions will be fulfilled: *The repairs to this watch are covered by the guarantee.* 2 promise to be responsible for the payment of a debt by another person. **guarantee** v [T] 1 give a guarantee for. 2 promise: *We cannot ~ that trains will arrive on time.*

guarantor /ˌgærən'tɔ:(r)/ n [C] (*law*) person who gives a guarantee(2).

guard /gɑ:d/ n 1 [U] state of readiness against attack: *a soldier on ~.* 2 [C] person who watches over sb or sth. 3 **the guard** [C, also sing with pl v] group of soldiers with the duty of protecting or escorting sb: *the ~ of honour.* 4 [C] (*Brit*) official in charge of a train. 5 [C] (esp in compounds) article de-

signed to protect: *fire-~.* **guard** v 1 [T] protect. 2 [T] watch (sb) to prevent escape. 3 (phr v) **guard against sth** use care to prevent sth: *~ against disease.* **guarded** *adj* not showing or saying too much.

guardian /'gɑ:dɪən/ n [C] person responsible for the care of a child. **guardianship** n [U] position of a guardian.

guerrilla (also **guerilla**) /gə'rɪlə/ n [C] fighter in an unofficial army that attacks in small groups.

guess /ges/ v 1 [I, T] give an answer or form an opinion about (sth) without clear knowledge. 2 [T] (*infml* esp *US*) suppose. **guess** n [C] 1 (*at*)] attempt to guess sth. 2 opinion formed by guessing. '**guesswork** n [U] guessing.

guest /gest/ n [C] 1 person staying at a house or a hotel. 2 person invited to a theatre, restaurant, etc, by sb else who pays. 3 performer taking part in a show. 4 (idm) **be my 'guest** (*infml*) please do. '**guest-house** n [C] small hotel.

guffaw /gə'fɔ:/ v [I] n [C] (give a) noisy laugh.

guidance /'gaɪdns/ n [U] help or advice.

guide /gaɪd/ n [C] 1 person who shows others the way. 2 person or thing that influences one's behaviour, etc. 3 (also '**guidebook**) book with information about a place. 4 book of information: *a ~ to plants.* 5 **Guide** Girl Guide. **guide** v [T] act as a guide to. ,**guided 'missile** n [C] missile that can be guided in flight. '**guide-line** n [C, usu pl] advice on how to do sth.

guild /gɪld/ n [C] society of people with similar jobs or interests.

guile /gaɪl/ n [U] deceit.

guillotine /'gɪləti:n/ n [C] 1 machine for cutting off the heads of criminals. 2 machine for cutting sheets of paper. 3 (*fig Brit politics*) time limit for a discussion in Parliament. **guillotine** v [T] use a guillotine on.

guilt /gɪlt/ n [U] 1 feeling of shame for having done wrong. 2 blame or responsibility for wrongdoing. **guilty** *adj* (-ier, -iest) 1 having done wrong. 2 feeling guilt. **guiltily** *adv.*

guinea /'gɪnɪ/ n [C] (esp formerly in Britain) 21 shillings (£1.05).

guinea-pig /'gɪnɪpɪg/ n [C] 1 short-eared animal like a big rat, often kept as a pet. 2 person used in an experiment.

guise /gaɪz/ n [C] (*fml*) outward appearance.

guitar /gɪ'tɑ:(r)/ n [C] musical instrument with six strings played with the fingers. **guitarist** n [C].

gulf /gʌlf/ n [C] **1** part of the sea almost surrounded by land: *the G~ of Mexico*. **2** (*between*)|| (*fig*) big difference in opinion.

gull /gʌl/ n [C] large sea-bird with long wings.

gullet /'gʌlɪt/ n [C] food passage from the mouth to the stomach.

gullible /'gʌləbl/ adj easily deceived.

gulp /gʌlp/ v [I,T] swallow quickly. **gulp** n [C] act of gulping.

gum¹ /gʌm/ n [C, usu pl] firm pink flesh around the teeth.

gum² /gʌm/ n **1** [U] sticky substance obtained from certain trees. **2** [U] chewing-gum. **3** [C] fruit-flavoured sweet. **gum** v (-**mm**-) [T] stick with gum; spread gum on. '**gumboot** n [C] rubber boot reaching the knee. **gummy** adj (-**ier**, -**iest**) sticky. '**gum-tree** n [C] eucalyptus tree.

gun /gʌn/ n [C] weapon that fires bullets or shells from a metal tube. **gun** v (-**nn**-) (phr v) **gun sb down** (*infml*) shoot sb, esp so as to kill him/her. **gun for sb** (*infml*) look for an opportunity to attack sb. '**gunboat** n [C] small warship with heavy guns. '**gunfire** n [U] shooting of guns. '**gunman** /-mən/ n [C] (*pl* -**men** /-mən/) man who uses a gun to rob or kill. **gunner** /'gʌnə(r)/ n [C] soldier who uses large guns. '**gunpoint** n (idm) **at gunpoint** under the threat of being shot. '**gunpowder** n [U] explosive powder. '**gunshot** n **1** [C] shot fired from a gun. **2** [U] range of a gun. '**gunsmith** n [C] person who makes and repairs guns.

gurgle /'gɜ:gl/ v [I] n [C] (make the) bubbling sound of flowing water.

gush /gʌʃ/ v [I] flow out suddenly: *blood ~ing from a wound*. **2** (*derog*) talk with too much enthusiasm. **gush** n [sing] sudden outburst. **gushing** adj.

gust /gʌst/ n [C] sudden rush of wind. **gusty** adj (-**ier**, -**iest**).

gut /gʌt/ n **1 guts** [pl] (*infml*) (**a**) stomach and intestines. (**b**) (*fig*) main parts of an engine, machine, etc. **2 guts** [pl] (*infml*) courage and determination. **3** [C] intestine. **4** [U] string made from the intestines of animals. **gut** v (-**tt**-) [T] **1** take the guts out of (a fish, etc). **2** destroy the inside of: *a house ~ted by fire*. **gut** adj based on feelings rather than thought: *a ~ reaction*.

gutter /'gʌtə(r)/ n **1** [C] channel under the edge of a roof, or at the side of a road, to carry away rainwater. **2 the gutter** [sing] (*fig*) poor state of life. **the 'gutter press** n [sing] (*derog*) newspapers that contain a lot of gossip and scandal.

guy¹ /gaɪ/ n [C] **1** (*infml*) man. **2** figure of a man dressed in old clothes burned in Britain on 5 November.

guy² /gaɪ/ n [C] rope used to keep a tent, etc, firmly in place.

guzzle /'gʌzl/ v [I, T] (*infml*) eat or drink greedily.

gym /dʒɪm/ n (*infml*) **1** [C] gymnasium. **2** [U] gymnastics. '**gym-shoe** n [C] plimsoll.

gymkhana /dʒɪm'kɑːnə/ n [C] public competition of horse-riding.

gymnasium /dʒɪm'neɪzɪəm/ n [C] hall with apparatus for physical exercise.

gymnast /'dʒɪmnæst/ n [C] expert in gymnastics.

gymnastics /dʒɪm'næstɪks/ n [pl] physical exercises to train the body or show how agile it is. **gymnastic** adj.

gynaecology (*US* **gynec-**) /ˌgaɪnɪ'kɒlədʒɪ/ n [U] study and treatment of disorders of the female reproductive system. **gynaecological** (*US* **gynec-**) /ˌgaɪnəkə'lɒdʒɪkl/ adj. **gynaecologist** (*US* **gynec-**) n [C] expert in gynaecology.

gypsy (also **gipsy**) /'dʒɪpsɪ/ n [C] (*pl* -**ies**) member of a travelling group of people who live in caravans.

gyrate /ˌdʒaɪ'reɪt; *US* 'dʒaɪreɪt/ v [I] move round in circles. **gyration** /dʒaɪ'reɪʃn/ n [C, U].

H h

H, h /eɪtʃ/ n [C] (*pl* **H's, h's** /'eɪtʃɪz/) the eighth letter of the English alphabet.

haberdasher /'hæbədæʃə(r)/ n [C] **1** (*Brit*) shopkeeper who sells cloth, pins, cotton, etc. **2** (*US*) shopkeeper who sells men's clothing. **haberdashery** n [U] goods sold by a haberdasher.

habit /'hæbɪt/ n **1** [C, U] person's usual action or behaviour: *Smoking is a bad ~*. **2** [C] long garment worn by a monk or nun. **3** (idm) **make a habit of (doing) sth** do sth regularly.

habitable /'hæbɪtəbl/ adj fit to be lived in.

habitat /'hæbɪtæt/ n [C] natural home of an animal or plant.

habitation /ˌhæbɪ'teɪʃn/ n [U] inhabiting: *houses fit for ~.*

habitual /hə'bɪtʃuəl/ adj 1 usual. 2 doing sth by habit: *a ~ smoker.* **habitually** adv.

hack¹ /hæk/ v [I, T] cut (sth) roughly. **'hack-saw** n [C] saw for cutting metal.

hack² /hæk/ n [C] person paid to do hard uninteresting work as a writer.

hacker /'hækə(r)/ n [C] person who uses the information in a company's computer system without permission.

hackneyed /'hæknɪd/ adj (of a phrase, etc) meaningless because used too often.

had pt, pp of HAVE.

haddock /'hædək/ n [C, U] (pl **haddock**) sea-fish used for food.

hadn't /'hædnt/ had not. ⇨ HAVE.

haemophilia (also esp US **hem-**) /ˌhiːmə'fɪlɪə/ n [U] disease that causes a person to bleed badly from even a small injury. **haemophiliac** (also esp US **hem-**) /-lɪæk/ n [C] person with haemophilia.

haemorrhage (also esp US **hem-**) /'hemərɪdʒ/ n [C, U] great flow of blood.

haemorrhoids (also esp US **hem-**) /'hemərɔɪdz/ n [pl] swollen veins inside the anus.

hag /hæg/ n [C] (derog) ugly old woman.

haggard /'hægəd/ adj looking tired, esp from worry.

haggis /'hægɪs/ n [C, U] Scottish food made from parts of a sheep and cooked in a sheep's stomach.

haggle /'hægl/ v [I] (over/about)/ argue about a price.

hail¹ /heɪl/ n 1 [U] frozen drops of rain. 2 [sing] (fig) something coming in great numbers and with force: *a ~ of bullets.* **hail** v 1 [I] (used with *it*) fall as hail. 2 [I, T] (fig) come or send down. **'hailstone** n [C] small ball of hail. **'hailstorm** n [C] storm with hail.

hail² /heɪl/ v 1 [T] call out to (sb), in order to attract attention. 2 [T] signal to (a taxi) to stop. 3 [T] recognize publicly the importance, etc of: *They ~ed him as their hero.* 4 [I] */from/* come from a place.

hair /heə(r)/ n 1 (a) [C] fine thread-like growth from the skin. (b) [U] mass of these, esp on the human head. 2 (idm) **(by) a hair's 'breadth** (by) a very small distance. **make one's hair stand on end** frighten one very much. **'haircut** n [C] act or style of cut-

ting the hair. **'hair-do** n [C] (pl -dos) (infml) act or style of arranging a woman's hair. **'hairdresser** n [C] person who cuts and styles hair. **'hair-grip** n [C] clip for holding the hair in place. **'hair-line** n [C] 1 edge of the hair above the forehead. 2 (fig) very thin line: *a ˌ~-line 'track.* **'hairpin** n [C] bent pin used for keeping the hair in place. **ˌhairpin 'bend** n [C] very sharp bend in a road. **'hair-raising** adj very frightening. **'hairstyle** n [C] way of arranging or cutting the hair. **hairy** adj (-ier, -iest) 1 of, like or covered with hair. 2 (sl) exciting but frightening. **hairiness** n [U].

hale /heɪl/ adj (idm) **hale and 'hearty** strong and healthy.

half /hɑːf; US hæf/ n (pl **halves** /hɑːvz; US hævz/) 1 one of two equal parts; ½. 2 a ticket or drink that is half the usual price or size: *Two halves* (ie children's fares) *to the station, please.* 3 one of two periods of time in a sports match, concert, etc. 4 (idm) **go 'halves (with sb)** share the cost of sth equally.

half² /hɑːf; US hæf/ adv 1 amounting to or forming a half: *~ an hour.* 2 (idm) **half past 'one, 'two,** etc, *(US)* **half after 'one, 'two,** etc thirty minutes after (any hour on the clock). **half** pron quantity that is a half: *H~ of the money is hers.* **ˌhalf-and-'half** adj half one thing and half another. **ˌhalf 'board** n [U] hotel accommodation with breakfast and evening meal included. **ˌhalf-'caste** (also **'half-breed**) n [C, adj] (person) with parents of different races. **ˌhalf-mast** n (idm) **at half-mast** (of a flag) half-way up a mast, as a sign of respect for a dead person. **ˌhalf-'term** n [C] short holiday in the middle of a school term. **ˌhalf-'time** n [U] interval between the two halves of a sports match. **ˌhalf-'way** adj, adv between and at an equal distance from two places. **'half-wit** n [C] foolish person. **ˌhalf-'witted** adj.

half³ /hɑːf; US hæf/ adv 1 to the extent of half: *~ full.* 2 partly: *~ cooked.* 3 (infml) nearly: *They felt ~ dead,* ie exhausted. 4 (idm) not **'half** (sl) very much: *'Do you like ice-cream?' 'Not ~.'* **ˌhalf-'baked** adj (infml) foolish. **ˌhalf-'hearted** adj showing little enthusiasm.

hall /hɔːl/ n [C] 1 space or passage inside the entrance of a house. 2 building or large room for meetings, concerts, meals, etc. 3 building for university students to live in: *a ~ of residence*.

hallelujah = ALLELUIA.

hallmark /'hɔ:lmɑ:k/ *n* [C] 1 mark stamped on gold or silver objects to show the quality of the metal. 2 (*fig*) particular feature. **hallmark** *v* [T] stamp a hallmark on.

hallo (also **hello**, **hullo**) /hə'ləʊ/ *n* [C], *interj* (*pl* ~s) (used in greeting, to attract sb's attention or to express surprise).

Hallowe'en /ˌhæləʊˈi:n/ *n* [U] 31 October, when children dress up as ghosts and witches.

hallucination /həˌlu:sɪˈneɪʃn/ *n* [C, U] seeing sth that is not actually present.

halo /'heɪləʊ/ *n* [C] (*pl* ~es) 1 circle of light round the head of a holy person in a picture. 2 circle of light round the sun or moon.

halt /hɔ:lt/ *v* [I, T] (cause sb/sth to) stop. **halt** *n* [sing, C] stop: *The train came to a ~ outside the station.*

halter /'hɔ:ltə(r)/ *n* [C] rope or leather strap put round a horse's head, for leading the horse.

halting /'hɔ:ltɪŋ/ *adj* slow and hesitating. **haltingly** *adv*.

halve /hɑ:v; *US* hæv/ *v* [T] 1 divide into two equal parts. 2 reduce by half: ~ *the cost*.

halves *pl* of HALF¹.

ham /hæm/ *n* 1 (a) [U] upper part of a pig's leg, salted and dried or smoked. (b) [U] meat from this. 2 [C] (*sl*) bad actor. 3 [C] (*infml*) amateur radio operator. **ham** *v* (-**mm**-) [I, T] (*sl*) act in an exaggerated way. ˌ**ham-ˈfisted** *adj* (*derog*) clumsy when using one's hands.

hamburger /'hæmbɜ:gə(r)/ *n* [C] flat round cake of minced meat, usu fried and eaten in a bread roll.

hamlet /'hæmlɪt/ *n* [C] small village.

hammer /'hæmə(r)/ *n* 1 [C] tool with a heavy metal head, used for hitting nails, etc. 2 [C] (in a piano) part that hits the strings. **hammer** *v* 1 [I, T] hit (sth) with a hammer. 2 [T] (*infml*) defeat (sb) completely. 3 (*phr v*) **hammer away at** sth work hard at sth. **hammer** sth **out** reach an agreement about sth through long discussion.

hammock /'hæmək/ *n* [C] bed made of cloth or rope net hung between two posts.

hamper¹ /'hæmpə(r)/ *v* [T] prevent the free movement or activity of (sb/sth).

hamper² /'hæmpə(r)/ *n* [C] large basket with a lid, used for carrying food.

hamster /'hæmstə(r)/ *n* [C] small

animal like a rat, kept as a pet.

hand¹ /hænd/ *n* 1 [C] part of the human arm below the wrist. 2 a **hand** [sing] help: *Can you give me a ~ with the washing-up?* 3 [C] pointer on a clock, dial, etc: *hour~.* 4 [C] worker: *a farm~.* 5 [C] set of cards dealt to a player in a card-game. 6 [sing] style of handwriting. 7 [sing] applause by clapping: *Give her a big ~.* 8 (idm) at **first/second ˈhand** directly/indirectly from the original person. at **ˈhand** near. by **ˈhand** (a) by a person, not a machine. (b) brought by a person, not sent by post. **change hands** ⇨ CHANGE. **hand in ˈhand** (a) holding each other's hand. (b) (*fig*) closely connected. **have/take a hand in** sth be partly responsible for sth. **have one's hands full** be very busy. **in ˈhand** (a) in one's possession and ready for use. (b) in control: *The situation is well in ~.* (c) being done: *the job in ~.* **in/out of sb's ˈhands** in/no longer in sb's control or care. **off/on one's ˈhands** no longer being/being one's responsibility. **on ˈhand** available. **on the ˈone hand… on the ˈother (hand)…** (used for showing two opposite points of view). **out of ˈhand** (a) out of control. (b) without further thought. **ˈhandbag** *n* [C] woman's bag for money, keys, etc. **ˈhandbook** *n* [C] book giving facts and instructions. **ˈhandbrake** *n* [C] brake in a car, van, etc operated by the driver's hand. **ˈhandcuff** *v* [T] put handcuffs on. **ˈhandcuffs** *n* [pl] metal rings joined by a chain, for fastening round a prisoner's wrists. **handful** *n* 1 [C] as much as can be held in one hand. 2 [sing] small number. 3 [sing] (*infml*) person or animal that is difficult to control. ˌ**hand-ˈpicked** *adj* carefully chosen. **ˈhandshake** *n* [C] shaking of sb's hand with one's own, as a greeting, etc. **ˈhandstand** *n* [C] balancing oneself on one's hands, with one's feet in the air. **ˈhandwriting** *n* [U] (style of) writing by hand.

hand² /hænd/ *v* 1 [T] give or pass with one's hand(s): *Please ~ me that book.* 2 (idm) **hand sb sth on a plate** ⇨ PLATE. 3 (phr v) **hand** sth **down** (to sb) pass (customs, knowledge, etc) to a later generation. **hand** sth **in** (to sb) bring or give sth to sb: ~ *in homework.* **hand** sth **on** (to sb) give sth to another person. **hand** sth **out** (to sb) (a) give sth to each person in a group. (b) give or offer freely. **hand** sb/sth **over** (to sb) give the responsibility for sb/sth to sb: ~ *a prisoner over to the authorities*. **'hand-out** *n* [C] 1 something, eg food or money, given freely. 2 sheet of information given out, eg by a teacher.

handicap /'hændɪkæp/ *n* [C] 1 disability in a person's body or mind. 2 condition that causes difficulty. 3 disadvantage given to a skilled competitor in a sport. **handicap** *v* (-pp-) [T] be or give a disadvantage to. **handicapped** *adj* having a handicap(1).

handicraft /'hændɪkrɑːft; -kræft/ *n* [C] work, eg pottery, that needs skill with the hands.

handiwork /'hændɪwɜːk/ *n* [U] 1 work done with the hands. 2 something done by a particular person.

handkerchief /'hæŋkətʃɪf/ *n* [C] square piece of cloth used for blowing one's nose.

handle /'hændl/ *n* [C] part of a cup, door, tool, etc, by which it is held. **handle** *v* 1 [T] touch with or hold in the hands. 2 [T] deal with: ~ *a situation*. 3 [I, T] (esp of a vehicle) operate or control in the way that is mentioned: *This car ~s well*. **'handlebars** *n* [pl] bar with a handle at each end for steering a bicycle, etc. **handler** *n* [C] person who trains an animal, eg a police dog.

handsome /'hænsəm/ *adj* 1 (esp of men) good-looking. 2 (of gifts, behaviour, etc) generous. **handsomely** *adv*.

handy /'hændɪ/ *adj* (-ier, -iest) 1 easy to handle or use. 2 easily reached; near. 3 clever with one's hands. 4 (idm) **come in 'handy** be useful. **handily** *adv*. **'handyman** *n* [C] (*pl* -men) person skilled at doing small repairs.

hang[1] /hæŋ/ *v* (*pt,pp* **hung** /hʌŋ/; in sense 2 ~**ed**) 1 [I, T] be supported or support (sth) from above. 2 [T] kill by hanging with a rope around the neck. 3 [T] stick (wallpaper) to a wall. 4 [I, T] (of meat) hang until ready to eat. 5 (phr v) **hang a'bout/a'round** stand, doing nothing definite. **hang back** be unwilling to do sth. **hang on(a)** hold sth tightly. (b) (*infml*) wait for a short time. **hang on to sth** (a) hold sth tightly. (b) (*infml*) keep sth. **hang up** put down a telephone receiver. **be/get hung 'up** (*sl*) feel very worried or nervous. **'hang-gliding** *n* [U] sport of flying while hanging from a large kite. **hanging** *n* 1 [U, C] death by hanging. 2 **hangings** [pl] curtains, etc hung on walls. **'hangman** *n* [C] (*pl* -men) man whose job is to hang

criminals. **'hang-up** *n* [C] (*sl*) feeling of worry about sth; inhibition.

hang[2] /hæŋ/ *n* (idm) **get the hang of sth** understand sth or how to do sth.

hangar /'hæŋə(r)/ *n* [C] building in which aircraft are kept.

hanger /'hæŋə(r)/ *n* [C] piece of wood, wire, etc with a hook, used for hanging up clothes: *a 'coat-~*. **,hanger-'on** *n* [C] (*pl* ~**s-on**) (*derog*) person who tries to be friendly, in the hope of personal gain.

hangover /'hæŋəʊvə(r)/ *n* [C] 1 unpleasant feeling after drinking too much alcohol on the previous night. 2 something left from an earlier time.

hanker /'hæŋkə(r)/ *v* [I] *after/ for//* have a strong desire for sth. **hankering** *n* [C].

hanky /'hæŋkɪ/ *n* [C] (*pl* -ies) (*infml*) handkerchief.

haphazard /,hæp'hæzəd/ *adj* without plan or order. **haphazardly** *adv*.

happen /'hæpən/ *v* [I] 1 (of an event) take place, usu by chance. 2 be or do by chance: *I ~ed to be out when he called.* 3 (phr v) **happen on sb/sth** (*fml*) find sb/sth by chance. **happening** *n* [C] event.

happy /'hæpɪ/ *adj* (-ier, -iest) 1 feeling or expressing pleasure. 2 (*fml*) pleased: *I shall be ~ to accept your invitation.* 3 (of words, behaviour, etc) well suited to the situation. 4 (used in greetings or to express good wishes): *H~ 'birthday!* 5 (idm) **a happy 'medium** a balance between extremes. **happily** *adv*. **happiness** *n* [U]. **,happy-go-'lucky** *adj* not worrying about the future.

harangue /hə'ræŋ/ *n* [C] long loud usu angry speech. **harangue** *v* [T] make a harangue to (sb).

harass /'hærəs; *US* hə'ræs/ *v* [T] trouble and annoy constantly. **harassment** *n* [U].

harbour (*US* -or) /'hɑːbə(r)/ *n* [C] place of shelter for ships. **harbour** *v* [T] 1 give shelter to. 2 hold in the mind: ~ *secret fears*.

hard[1] /hɑːd/ *adj* 1 firm and solid; not easy to bend, cut, etc: *as ~ as rock*. 2 difficult: *a ~ exam*. 3 needing or showing great effort: *~ work ◇ a ~ worker*. 4 causing unhappiness or pain: *I had a ~ childhood*. 5 (of the weather) severe: *a ~ winter*. 6 (of a person) showing no kindness; harsh. 7 (idm) **hard and 'fast** (of rules, etc) fixed. **hard 'at it** working hard. **hard 'facts** accurate information. **,hard 'luck** (used for showing sympathy for sb's misfortune). **,hard of 'hear-**

ing rather deaf. **'hardback** n [C] book with a stiff cover. **'hardboard** n [U] thin board made of very small pieces of wood pressed together. **hard 'cash** n [U] coins and notes, not a cheque. **,hard 'copy** n [U] information printed on paper from a computer. **'hard core** n [sing] central most involved members of a group. **,hard 'currency** n [C, U] money that is not likely to fall suddenly in value. **,hard 'drug** n [C] strong dangerous drug that is likely to lead to addiction. **,hard-'headed** adj practical; not influenced by feelings. **,hard-'hearted** adj not kind or caring. **,hard 'labour** n [U] (punishment of) heavy physical work. **,hard-'line** adj fixed in one's beliefs, etc. **,hard 'shoulder** n [C] hard surface at the side of a motorway, used in an emergency. **'hardware** n [U] 1 tools and equipment, eg pans and nails, for the home. 2 machinery that makes up a computer. **hard 'water** n [U] water that contains minerals that stop soap from lathering easily. **'hardwood** n [U] hard heavy wood, eg oak or beech.

hard² /hɑːd/ adv 1 with great effort: try/push ~. 2 heavily: raining ~. 3 with difficulty: my '~-earned money. 4 (idm) be hard 'put (to it) (to do sth) find it difficult to do sth. be hard to 'say be difficult to estimate. be hard 'up be short of money. hard 'done by unfairly treated. **hard on sb/sth** (fml) soon after sb/sth. **take sth hard** be very upset by sth. **,hard-'boiled** adj (of eggs) boiled until the yellow part (= YOLK) is hard. **hard-'pressed** adj in difficulties, because of lack of time or money. **,hard-'wearing** adj (of cloth) tough and lasting for a long time. **harden** /'hɑːdn/ v 1 [I, T] become or make hard, strong, etc. 2 [T] (to)|| make (sb) less sensitive to sth.

hardly /'hɑːdlɪ/ adv 1 only just; scarcely: I ~ know him. 2 not at all: You can ~ expect me to lend you money again. 3 almost no; almost not: ~ ever.

hardship /'hɑːdʃɪp/ n [C, U] (cause of) severe suffering.

hardy /'hɑːdɪ/ adj (-ier, -iest) able to endure cold, difficult conditions, etc. **hardiness** n [U].

hare /heə(r)/ n [C] fast-running animal, like a rabbit but larger, with long ears. **hare** v [I] run fast. **'hare-brained** adj foolish.

harem /'hɑːriːm; US 'hærəm/ n [C] (women living in the

separate women's part of a Muslim house.

hark /hɑːk/ v 1 [I] (arch) listen. 2 (phr v) **hark back (to sth)** mention again an earlier subject or event.

harm /hɑːm/ n [U] 1 damage; injury. 2 (idm) **out of harm's way** safe. **harm** v [T] cause harm to. **harmful** adj causing harm. **harmless** adj 1 not dangerous. 2 unlikely to annoy or upset people: ~ less fun.

harmonica /hɑːˈmɒnɪkə/ n [C] = MOUTH-ORGAN (MOUTH).

harmonize /'hɑːmənaɪz/ v [I, T] 1 come or bring into harmony: colours that ~ well. 2 (music) sing or play in harmony.

harmony /'hɑːmənɪ/ n (pl -ies) 1 [U] agreement of feelings, interests, etc: live together in perfect ~. 2 [C, U] pleasing combination of related things: the ~ of colours. 3 [C, U] pleasing combination of musical notes. **harmonious** /hɑːˈməʊnɪəs/ adj.

harness /'hɑːnɪs/ n [C, U] 1 set of leather straps for fastening a horse to a cart, etc. 2 similar arrangement for keeping sb/sth in place: a parachute ~. **harness** v [T] 1 put a harness on. 2 use a river, the sun's rays, etc) to produce power.

harp /hɑːp/ n [C] large upright musical instrument with vertical strings played with the fingers. **harp** v (phr v) **harp on (about)** sth talk about sth repeatedly or too much. **harpist** n [C] person who plays the harp.

harpoon /hɑːˈpuːn/ n [C] spear on a rope, used for catching whales. **harpoon** v [T] hit with a harpoon.

harpsichord /'hɑːpsɪkɔːd/ n [C] musical instrument like a piano, but with strings that are plucked mechanically.

harrowing /'hærəʊɪŋ/ adj very distressing.

harsh /hɑːʃ/ adj 1 unpleasantly rough or sharp. 2 cruel; severe: a ~ punishment. **harshly** adv. **harshness** n [U].

harvest /'hɑːvɪst/ n [C] 1 (a) (season for) cutting and gathering of crops. (b) quantity of crops gathered: a good wheat ~. 2 (fig) result of an action: reap the ~ of one's work. **harvest** v [T] gather (a crop).

has ⇨ HAVE.

hash /hæʃ/ n 1 [U] cooked chopped meat. 2 (idm) **make a hash of sth** (infml) do sth badly.

hashish /'hæʃiːʃ, 'hæʃɪʃ/ n [U]

hasn't 192

drug from the hemp plant.

hasn't /'hæznt/ has not. ⇨ HAVE.

hassle /'hæsl/ n [C, U] (*infml*) difficulty; trouble. **hassle** v [T] (*infml*) annoy (sb) by continually asking him/her to do sth.

haste /heist/ n [U] quickness of movement.

hasten /'heisn/ v 1 [I] be quick to do or say sth: I ~ to add that your child is safe. 2 [T] cause (sth) to happen earlier.

hasty /'heisti/ adj 1 made or done too quickly: a ~ meal. 2 (of a person) acting too quickly: too ~ in deciding to get married. **hastily** adv.

hat /hæt/ n [C] 1 covering for the head. 2 (idm) **take one's hat off to sb** show admiration for sb. **'hat trick** n [C] three similar successes made one after the other by one person.

hatch¹ /hætʃ/ v 1 [I, T] (cause to) come out of an egg: The chicks have ~ed ('out). 2 [T] prepare a plan, etc).

hatch² /hætʃ/ n [C] **(a)** opening in a floor, wall, etc. **(b)** movable cover over such an opening.

hatchback /'hætʃbæk/ n [C] car with a sloping door at the back that opens upwards.

hatchet /'hætʃit/ n [C] small axe.

hatchway /'hætʃwei/ n [C] = HATCH²a.

hate /heit/ v [T] 1 have a great dislike for. 2 (idm) **hate to do sth** be sorry: I ~ to trouble you. 3 (idm) **hate sb's 'guts** (*infml*) dislike sb very much. **hate** n [U] great dislike. **hateful** adj very unpleasant. **hatefully** adv.

hatred /'heitrid/ n [U] (for/of) hate.

haughty /'hɔːti/ adj (-ier, -iest) very proud; arrogant. **haughtily** adv. **haughtiness** n [U].

haul /hɔːl/ v [I, T] pull with effort. **haul** n [C] 1 act of hauling. 2 distance to be travelled. 3 quantity or amount gained. **haulage** n [U] transport of goods.

haunch /hɔːntʃ/ n [C, usu pl] part of the body between the waist and the thighs.

haunt /hɔːnt/ v [T] 1 (of ghosts and spirits) appear in (a place): a ~ed house. 2 visit often. 3 return repeatedly to the mind of: The memory still ~s me. **haunt** n [C] place visited often.

have¹ /hæv, əv, v; strong form hæv/ aux v (3rd person sing present tense **has** /həz, əz, s, z; strong form hæz/, pt **had** /həd, əd, d; strong form hæd/, pp **had** /hæd/) 1 (used for forming per-

fect tenses): I ~/I've finished. ○ She has/she's gone. 2 (idm) **had I, he, she, etc** if I, etc had: Had I known, ...

have² (Brit **have got**) /hæv/ v [T] 1 own or possess: He has/has got a house in London. ○ Has she (got)? Does she ~ blue eyes? 2 experience; keep in the mind: I ~ no doubt (is I am sure) that you are right. ○ H ~ you (got) any idea where he lives? 3 suffer from: ~ a headache. 4 (idm) **have it in for sb** (*infml*) want to be very unkind to sb. **have (got) to (do sth)** (showing obligation) must (do sth): I've got to go now. 5 (phr v) **have sth on** be wearing sth. **have sth on sb** (*infml*) have (information) to show that sb has done sth wrong.

have³ /hæv/ v [T] (always used in the negative and interrogative with do) 1 perform; take: ~ a swim/walk. 2 eat, drink, smoke, etc: ~ breakfast/a cigarette. 3 receive; experience: I've had a letter from my aunt. ○ ~ a good holiday. 4 give birth to; produce: to ~ a baby ○ (fig) ~ a good effect. 5 cause (sth to be done): You should ~ your hair cut. 6 suffer the results of: They had their house burgled. 7 allow: I won't ~ such behaviour here! 8 cause (sb) to come as a visitor: We're having friends round for dinner. 9 (*infml*) trick: You've been had! 10 (idm) **have 'had it** (*infml*) not be able to continue doing sth. **have it (that)** claim or say that: Rumour has it that .... 11 (phr v) **have sb 'on** (*infml*) play a trick on sb. **have sth 'out** cause sth to be removed: ~ a tooth out. **have sth 'out (with sb)** settle a disagreement with sb) by argument. **have sb 'up (for sth)** (*infml*) (esp passive) cause sb to appear in court for a crime: He was had up for robbery.

haven /'heivn/ n [C] place of safety or rest.

haven't /'hævnt/ have not. ⇨ HAVE.

haversack /'hævəsæk/ n [C] canvas bag usu carried over the shoulder.

havoc /'hævək/ n [U] widespread damage.

hawk /hɔːk/ n [C] 1 large bird that catches and eats small birds and animals. 2 (fig) person who favours the use of military force.

hay /hei/ n [U] grass cut and dried for use as animal food. **'hay fever** n [U] illness of the nose and throat, caused by pollen or dust. **'haystack** n large pile of hay firmly packed for storing. **'haywire** adj (idm) **go haywire** become disorganized or out of control.

hazard /'hæzəd/ n [C] (to)// danger; risk. **hazard** v [T] **1** put in danger; risk. **2** suggest or offer (a guess, etc). **hazardous** adj dangerous; risky.

haze /heiz/ n [U] **1** thin mist. **2** (fig) confusion in the mind.

hazel /'heizl/ n [C] bush with small edible nuts. **hazel** adj (esp of eyes) light yellowish brown.

hazy /'heizi/ adj (-ier, -iest) **1** misty. **2** not clear; vague: ~ *memories*. **hazily** adv. **haziness** n [U].

H-bomb /'eitʃ bɒm/ n [C] hydrogen bomb.

he /hi:/ pron (used as the subject of a v) **1** male person or animal mentioned earlier: *I spoke to John before he left.* **2** (male or female) person: *Anyone can learn a foreign language, if he wants to.*

head¹ /hed/ n **1** [C] part of the body that contains the eyes, nose, brain, etc. **2** [C] ability to think; mind: *The thought never entered my* ~. **3** [sing] natural talent: *a good* ~ *for figures.* **4** heads (with sing v) side of a coin with the head of a person on it. **5 a head** [sing] for each person: *dinner at £15 a* ~. **6** [C] something like a head: *the* ~ *of a pin/hammer.* **7** [C, usu sing] top: *at the* ~ *of the page.* **8** [C] more important end: *at the* ~ *of the table* ○ *the* ~ *of a bed,* ie where one's head rests. **9** [sing] leader; ruler: ~*s of government.* **10** [sing] front: *at the* ~ *of the queue.* **11** [sing] pressure of water or steam. **12** (idm) **above/over one's 'head** too difficult to understand. **bang/hit one's head against a brick wall** keep trying to do sth without any success. **bring sth/come to a 'head** bring sth to/reach the point at which action is essential. **go to one's 'head** (a) make one slightly drunk. (b) (of success) make one too confident. **have one's head screwed on** be sensible. **head 'first** (a) with one's head before the rest of one's body: *fall* ~ *first down the stairs.* (b) too quickly. **head over 'heels** (a) with the body rolling over in a forward direction. (b) (fig) completely: ~ *over heels in love.* **keep/lose one's 'head** stay calm/fail to stay calm in a crisis. **laugh, scream,** etc **one's head off** (infml) laugh, etc loudly. **put our/your/their 'heads together** discuss a plan, etc with other people. **'headache** n [C] **1** pain in the head. **2** (fig) problem. **'headland** n [C] high piece of land that sticks out into the sea.

'headlight (also **'headlamp**) n [C] bright light on the front of a vehicle. **'headline** n [C] **1** words printed in large letters above a newspaper story. **2 the headlines** [pl] main points of the news on radio or television. **head'master** (fem **head'mistress**) n [C] man/woman who is in charge of a school. **head-'on** adj, adv with the front parts hitting: *The cars crashed* ~-*on.* **'headphones** n [pl] receivers that fit over the ears, for listening to records, etc. **'headquarters** n (with sing or pl v) place from which an organization is controlled. **'head-rest** n [C] support for the head. **'headroom** n [U] clear space above a vehicle. **'headstone** n [C] stone that marks the head of a grave. **'headway** n (idm) **make headway** make progress.

head² /hed/ v **1** [T] (a) be at the front or top of: ~ *a procession/list.* (b) be in charge of: ~ *the government.* **2** [I] move in the direction that is mentioned: ~ *south/for home.* **3** [T] hit (the ball) with one's head in football. **4** (phr v) **head sb off** get in front of sb and make him/her change direction. **head sth off** prevent sth.

heading /'hedɪŋ/ n [C] words at the top of a page, as a title.

headlong /'hedlɒŋ; US -lɔ:ŋ/ adv, adj **1** with the head first. **2** quickly and foolishly: *rush* ~ *into a decision.*

headstrong /'hedstrɒŋ; US -strɔ:ŋ/ adj difficult to control; refusing advise.

heady /'hedi/ adj (-ier, -iest) **1** (of alcoholic drink) making one drunk. **2** (fig) exciting.

heal /hi:l/ v [I, T] become or make healthy again.

health /helθ/ n [U] **1** condition of the body or mind: *be in good/poor* ~. **2** freedom from illness. **healthy** adj (-ier, -iest) **1** having good health. **2** likely to produce good health: *a* ~*y climate.* **3** showing good health: *a* ~*y appetite* ○ (fig) ~*y profits.* **healthily** adv.

heap /hi:p/ n [C] **1** pile or mass of things or material: *a* ~ *of books/ sand.* **2 heaps** [pl] (infml) large quantity: ~*s of time.* **heap** v [T] put in a large pile: ~ *food on one's plate.*

hear /hɪə(r)/ v (pt, pp ~d /hɜ:d/) **1** [I, T] become aware of (sounds) with the ears. **2** [T] pay attention to: *You're not to go, do you* ~ *me?* **3** [I, T] be told about: *I* ~ *she's leaving.* **4** [T] try (a case) in a lawcourt. **5** (idm) ,**hear! 'hear!** (used for expressing agreement at a meeting).

6 (phr v) **hear from sb** receive a letter, news, etc from sb. **hear of sb/sth** know about: *I've never ~d of the place.* **not 'hear of sth** refuse to allow sth: *He wouldn't ~ of my walking home alone.* **hear sb out** listen to sb until they finish speaking.

hearing /'hɪərɪŋ/ *n* **1** [U] ability to hear. **2** [U] distance within which one can hear: *He's out of ~.* **3** [C] opportunity to defend one's opinion: *get a fair ~.* **4** [C] (*law*) trial of a case. **'hearing-aid** *n* [C] small device used for improving hearing.

hearsay /'hɪəseɪ/ *n* [U] rumour.

hearse /hɜːs/ *n* [C] car used for carrying the coffin to a funeral.

heart /hɑːt/ *n* [C] **1** organ that pumps blood through the body. **2** centre of a person's feelings, esp love. **3** centre of sth. **4** something shaped like a heart. **5** playing-card with red shapes like hearts. **6** (idm) **break sb's/one's 'heart** make sb/one feel very sad. **by 'heart** from memory: *learn/know a poem by ~.* **from the (bottom of one's) 'heart** sincerely. **not have the 'heart to do sth** not be cruel enough to do sth. **take/lose 'heart** become encouraged/discouraged. **take sth to 'heart** feel sth very deeply. **'heartache** *n* [U, C] great sadness. **'heart attack** *n* [C] sudden illness with irregular beating of the heart. **'heartbeat** *n* [C] pumping movement of the heart. **'heart-breaking** *adj* causing deep sadness. **'heart-broken** *adj* feeling deep sadness. **'heartburn** *n* [U] burning feeling in the chest, caused by indigestion. **'heartfelt** *adj* sincere. **heartless** *adj* without pity. **heartlessly** *adv.* **'heart-rending** *adj* causing deep sadness. **,heart-to-'heart** *n* [C] open honest talk about personal matters.

hearten /'hɑːtn/ *v* [T] encourage. **hearth** /hɑːθ/ *n* [C] (area in front of the) fireplace.

hearty /'hɑːtɪ/ *adj* (**-ier, -iest**) **1** happy and friendly: *a ~ welcome.* **2** loud and (too) cheerful. **3** (of a meal or appetite) big. **4** strong and healthy. **heartily** *adv* **1** in a hearty way. **2** very: *I'm heartily sick of this wet weather.*

heat¹ /hiːt/ *n* **1** [U] hotness. **2** hot weather. **3** [U] (*fig*) great anger or excitement. **4** [C] early stage in a competition. **5** (idm) **be on heat**, (*US*) **be in heat** (of female dogs, etc) be in a period of sexual excitement. **'heatwave** *n* [C] period of unusually hot weather.

heat² /hiːt/ *v* [I, T] become or make hot. **heated** *adj* angry; excited: *a ~ed argument.* **heater** *n* [C] device used for heating a room or water. **heating** *n* [U] system for heating a building.

heath /hiːθ/ *n* [C] area of open land covered with low shrubs, esp heather.

heathen /'hiːðn/ *n* [C] **1** (*dated*) person who does not believe in one of the world's main religions. **2** (*infml*) wild person.

heather /'heðə(r)/ *n* [U] low plant with small purple, pink or white flowers.

heave /hiːv/ *v* (*pt, pp* ~d; in sense **6 hove** /həʊv/) **1** [I, T] lift or pull (sth heavy) with great effort. **2** [T] throw (sth heavy). **3** [T] utter: *~ a sigh of relief.* **4** [I] rise and fall regularly. **5** [I] be sick; vomit. **6** (idm) **,heave 'to** (of a ship) stop. **heave** *n* [C] act of heaving.

heaven /'hevn/ *n* **1** [sing] place believed to be the home of God and of good people after death. **2** Heaven [sing] God. **3** [U, C] place or state of great happiness. **4** the heavens [pl] the sky. **5** (idm) **(Good) 'Heavens!** (used for showing surprise). **heavenly** *adj* **1** of or from heaven. **2** (*infml*) very pleasing. **,heavenly 'body** *n* [C] the sun or moon or a planet, etc.

heavy /'hevɪ/ *adj* (**-ier, -iest**) **1** having great weight. **2** of more than the usual amount, force, etc: *~ rain* ○ *a ~ smoker.* **2** a person who smokes a lot. **3** busy: *a very ~ day/schedule.* **4** (of work) needing a lot of effort. **5** (of food) difficult to digest. **6** (of writing, music, etc) difficult and dull. **7** sad: *a ~ heart.* **8** (idm) **,heavy 'going** difficult or boring. **make heavy weather of sth** make sth more difficult than it really is. **heavily** *adv.* drink/sleep heavily. **heaviness** *n* [U]. **heavy** *n* [C] (*pl* **-ies**) (*infml*) big strong man employed as a bodyguard, etc. **,heavy-'duty** *adj* strong enough for rough use, bad weather, etc. **,heavy 'industry** *n* [C] industry that produces metal, large machines, etc. **'heavyweight** *n* [C] **1** boxer weighing 79·3 kilograms or more. **2** important person.

heckle /'hekl/ *v* [I, T] interrupt (a speaker) at a meeting by shouting. **heckler** /'heklə(r)/ *n* [C].

hectare /'hekteə(r)/ *n* [C] metric measure of area; 10 000 square metres.

hectic /'hektɪk/ *adj* with a lot of busy activity and excitement: *lead* *a* ~ *life.*

he'd /hi:d/ **1** he had. ⇨ HAVE. **2** he would. ⇨ WILL¹, WOULD¹.

hedge /hedʒ/ *n* [C] **1** row of bushes between fields, gardens, etc. **2** (*fig*) defence: *a* ~ *against inflation.* **hedge** *v* [I, T] put a hedge round. **2** avoid giving a direct answer to a question. **3** (*idm*) ,**hedge one's 'bets** protect oneself against loss by supporting more than one course of action. **'hedgerow** *n* [C] row of bushes, etc forming a hedge.

hedgehog /'hedʒhɒg; *US* -hɔːg/ *n* [C] small animal covered with spines.

heed /hi:d/ *v* [T] (*fml*) give attention to. **heed** *n* [U] (*fml*) attention: *take ~ of/to his advice.* **heedless** *adj* (*of*)/ not giving attention to sth.

heel¹ /hi:l/ *n* [C] **1 (a)** back part of the human foot. **(b)** part of a sock or shoe that covers this. **2** raised part of a shoe under the back of the foot. **3** (*idm*) **at/on sb's 'heels** following sb closely. **come to 'heel (a)** obey. **(b)** (of a dog) come close behind its owner. ,**down at 'heel** untidy and poorly dressed. **heel** *v* [T] repair the heel of (a shoe).

heel² /hi:l/ *v* [I] (*over*)// (of a ship) lean over to one side.

hefty /'heftɪ/ *adj* (-**ier**, -**iest**) (*infml*) big; powerful.

heifer /'hefə(r)/ *n* [C] young cow.

height /haɪt/ *n* **1 (a)** [U, C] measurement from the bottom to top. **(b)** [U] being tall. **2** [C, U] distance of sth above ground or sea-level: *gain/lose ~.* **3** [C, esp pl] high place or area. **4** [sing] highest degree or main point of sth: *the ~ of folly/ summer.*

heighten /'haɪtn/ *v* [I, T] become or make higher or more intense.

heir /eə(r)/ *n* [C] person with the legal right to receive property, etc when the owner dies. **heiress** /'eərɪs, eə'res/ *n* [C] female heir. **heirloom** /'eəluːm/ *n* [C] valuable object that is passed from one generation to the next in a family.

held *pt, pp* of HOLD¹.

helicopter /'helɪkɒptə(r)/ *n* [C] aircraft with horizontal revolving blades (= ROTORS) on the top.

helium /'hiːlɪəm/ *n* [U] light colourless gas, used in balloons and airships.

hell /hel/ *n* **1** [sing] place believed to be the home of wicked people after death. **2** [U, C] place or state of great suffering or wickedness. **3** [U] (*sl*) (used for showing anger or for emphasis): *Who the ~ is he?* **4** (*idm*) **for the 'hell of it** (*infml*) just

for fun. **give sb 'hell** (*infml*) treat sb severely. **like 'hell (a)** (*infml*) (used for emphasis): *drive like ~,* ie very fast. **(b)** (*sl ironic*) not at all. **hellish** *adj* (*infml*) very unpleasant.

he'll /hi:l/ he will. ⇨ WILL¹.

hello = HALLO.

helm /helm/ *n* [C] **1** handle or wheel for moving the rudder of a boat. **2** (*idm*) **at the helm** in control.

helmet /'helmɪt/ *n* [C] protective covering for the head.

help¹ /help/ *v* **1** [I, T] do part of the work of (sb); be of use or service to (sb): *They ~ed me (to) lift the boxes.* ○ *H~! I'm stuck!* **2** [T] ~ **oneself/sb** (to) serve oneself/sb with food, drink, etc. **3** (*idm*) **can/ could not help (doing) sth** can/ could not prevent or avoid sth. **4** (*phr v*) **help (sb) 'out** help sb in a difficult situation. **helper** *n* [C] person who helps. **helping** *n* [C] serving of food.

help² /help/ *n* **1** [U] act of helping. **2** [C] person or thing that helps: *She's a great ~ to me.* **3** [C] person paid to do housework. **helpful** *adj* useful. **helpfully** *adv.* **helpfulness** *n* [U]. **helpless** *adj* needing the help of others; powerless. **helplessly** *adv.* **helplessness** *n* [U].

hem /hem/ *n* [C] edge of a piece of cloth, turned under and sewn. **hem** *v* (-**mm-**) **1** [T] make a hem on. **2** (*phr v*) **hem sb in** surround sb, so that he/she cannot move. **'hem-line** *n* [C] lower edge of a skirt or dress.

hemisphere /'hemɪsfɪə(r)/ *n* [C] **1** half a sphere. **2** half of the earth: *the Northern ~.*

hemo- = HAEMO-.

hemp /hemp/ *n* [U] **1** plant used for making rope and cloth. **2** drug made from this plant, eg cannabis.

hen /hen/ *n* [C] **1** adult female chicken. **2** female of any bird. **'henpecked** *adj* (*infml*) (of a man) ruled by his wife.

hence /hens/ *adv* (*fml*) **1** from now. **2** for this reason. **hence-forth** /,hens'fɔːθ/ (also **hence-forward**) *adv* (*fml*) from now on.

henchman /'hentʃmən/ *n* [C] (*pl* -**men**) faithful supporter who always obeys his leader's orders.

henna /'henə/ *n* [U] (plant producing a) reddish-brown dye.

her /hɜː(r)/ *pron* (used as the object of a *v* or *prep*) female person or animal mentioned earlier: *I love ~.* ○ *Give it to ~.* **her** *adj* belonging to her: *That's ~ book, not* yours. **hers** /hɜːz/ *pron* of or belonging to her: *Is that ~?*

herald /'herəld/ *n* [C] (formerly) person who delivered important messages. **herald** *v* [T] announce the approach of. **heraldry** /'herəldrɪ/ *n* [U] study of coats of arms.

herb /hɜːb; *US* ɜːrb/ *n* [C] plant whose leaves or seeds are used in medicine or to add flavour to food. **herbal** *adj* of herbs. **herbalist** *n* [C] person who grows or sells herbs for medical use.

herbaceous /hɜː'beɪʃəs; *US* ɜːr-/ *adj* (of a plant) having a soft stem. **her,baceous 'border** *n* [C] flowerbed with plants that flower every year.

herd /hɜːd/ *n* [C] group of animals, esp cattle, together. **herd** *v* [T] move (sb/sth) as a herd: *prisoners ~ed onto a train.* **herdsman** /-mən/ *n* [C] (*pl* -men) man who looks after a herd.

here /hɪə(r)/ *adv* 1 in, at or to this place: *I live ~.* ○ *Come ~.* 2 at this point: *H~ the speaker paused.* 3 (idm) **here and 'there** in various places. **here's to sb/sth** (used when drinking to the health or success of sb/sth). **neither ,here nor 'there** not connected with what is being discussed. **,herea'b-outs** *adv* (*fml*) near here. **,here'in** *adv* (*fml*) in this place or document. **,here'with** *adv* (*fml*) with this.

hereafter /,hɪər'ɑːftə(r); *US* -'æf-/ *adv* (*fml*) in future. **the hereafter** *n* [sing] life after death.

hereditary /hɪ'redɪtrɪ; *US* -terɪ/ *adj* passed on from parent to child. **heredity** /hɪ'redətɪ/ *n* [U] passing on of characteristics from parents to children.

heresy /'herəsɪ/ *n* [U, C] (*pl* -ies) (holding of a) belief that is completely different from what is generally accepted. **heretic** /'herətɪk/ *n* [C] person guilty of heresy. **heretical** /hɪ'retɪkl/ *adj*.

heritage /'herɪtɪdʒ/ *n* [C, usu sing] all the things that have been passed on over many years in a country.

hermit /'hɜːmɪt/ *n* [C] person who lives alone and simply, esp for religious reasons.

hernia /'hɜːnɪə/ *n* [C, U] condition in which the bowel comes through the wall of the abdomen.

hero /'hɪərəʊ/ *n* [C] (~es) 1 person admired for bravery or other good qualities. 2 main male character in a story, play, etc. **heroic** /hɪ'rəʊɪk/ *adj* of heroes; very brave. **heroically** /-klɪ/ *adv*.

heroics *n* [pl] talk or behaviour that is too grand. **heroine** /'herəʊɪn/ *n* [C] female hero. **heroism** /'herəʊɪzəm/ *n* [U] courage.

heroin /'herəʊɪn/ *n* [U] drug made from morphine.

herpes /'hɜːpiːz/ *n* [U] disease that causes blisters on the skin.

herring /'herɪŋ/ *n* [C] sea-fish used for food. **'herring-bone** *n* [U] V-shaped pattern.

hers ⇨ HER.

herself /hɜː'self/ *pron* 1 (used as a reflexive when the female doer of an action is also affected by it): *She 'hurt ~.* ○ *She 'bought ~ a new 'dress.* 2 (used for emphasis): *She told me the news ~.* 3 (idm) **(all) by her'self** (a) alone. (b) without help.

he's /hiːz/ 1 he is. ⇨ BE. 2 he has. ⇨ HAVE.

hesitant /'hezɪtənt/ *adj* tending to hesitate. **hesitancy** *n* [U].

hesitate /'hezɪteɪt/ *v* [I] be slow to speak or act because one is uncertain or unwilling. **hesitation** /,hezɪ'teɪʃn/ *n* [U, C].

heterogeneous /,hetərə'dʒiːnɪəs/ *adj* made up of different kinds.

heterosexual /,hetərə'sekʃʊəl/ *adj* sexually attracted to people of the opposite sex.

het up /,het'ʌp/ *adj* (*infml*) upset.

hexagon /'heksəgən; *US* -gɒn/ *n* [C] figure with six sides.

heyday /'heɪdeɪ/ *n* [sing] time of greatest success.

hiatus /haɪ'eɪtəs/ *n* [usu sing] space or pause where something is missing.

hibernate /'haɪbəneɪt/ *v* [I] (of animals) sleep during the winter. **hibernation** /,haɪbə'neɪʃn/ *n* [U].

hiccup (also **hiccough**) /'hɪkʌp/ *n* [C] 1 sudden stopping of the breath with a sharp sound. 2 (*infml*) small problem. **hiccup** *v* [I] give a hiccup(1).

hide[1] /haɪd/ *v* (*pt* **hid** /hɪd/, *pp* **hidden** /'hɪdn/) 1 [T] put or keep out of sight. 2 [I] get out of sight. **'hide-out** (*US* also **'hideaway**) *n* [C] hiding-place for people: *a terrorist ~out.* **'hiding** *n* [U] (idm) **,go into/come out of 'hiding** hide/show oneself. **in 'hiding** hidden. **'hiding-place** *n* [C] place where sb/sth is or could be hidden.

hide[2] /haɪd/ *n* [C] animal's skin.

hideous /'hɪdɪəs/ *adj* very ugly; horrible. **hideously** *adv*.

hiding[1] ⇨ HIDE[1].

hiding[2] /'haɪdɪŋ/ *n* [C] beating.

hierarchy /'haɪərɑːkɪ/ *n* [C] (*pl* -ies) organization with ranks of authority from lowest to highest.

hi-fi /ˈhaɪfaɪ/ adj, n [C] (infml) short for HIGH FIDELITY (HIGH¹).

high¹ /haɪ/ adj **1** (a) reaching far upwards: a ~ fence. (b) having the distance that is mentioned from the bottom to the top: The wall is six feet ~. **2** above the normal: a ~ price. **3** great; intense: a ~ degree of accuracy. **4** morally good: have ~ ideals. **5** very favourable: have a ~ opinion of her. **6** important: a ~ official. **7** (of a sound) not deep. **8** fully reached: ~ (ie the middle of) summer. **9** (of food) beginning to go bad. **10** (on)) (infml) under the influence of drugs. **11** (of a gear) allowing a faster speed. **12** (idm) **be/get on one's high 'horse** (infml) act proudly, thinking that one knows best. **high and 'dry** without help or support. **high time** right time for sth which has been delayed: It's ~ time you cleaned the car. **highbrow** n [C], adj (sometimes derog) (person) knowing a lot about intellectual matters. **high-class** adj of good quality. **High Com'missioner** n [C] representative of one Commonwealth country in another. **High 'Court** n [C] highest court for civil cases. **higher edu'cation** n [U] education at universities, polytechnics, etc. **high fi'delity** adj, n [C] (of) equipment that reproduces recorded sound almost perfectly. **high-'flier** n [C] person with the ambition and ability to be very successful. **high-'grade** adj of high quality. **high-'handed** adj using power without consideration for others. **the 'high jump** n [sing] sport of jumping over a high bar. **highlands** /-ləndz/ n [pl] mountainous part of a country. **high-'level** adj (of meetings, etc) involving important people. **the 'high life** n [sing] fashionable luxurious way of living. **high-'minded** adj having high ideals. **high-'powered** adj having great energy or ability. **high 'profile** ⇨ PROFILE. **'high-rise** adj (of a building) very tall. **'high school** n [C] (esp US) secondary school, for pupils aged about 15–18. **the high 'seas** n [pl] areas of the sea that do not belong to any particular country. **high 'season** n [U] time of year when a hotel, resort, etc has most visitors. **high-'spirited** adj lively; excited. **'high spot** n [C] outstanding, esp most pleasant, part of an activity. **high street** n [C] main street of a town. **high 'tea** n [U] (Brit) early evening meal. **high tech'nology** n [U] use

of the most modern methods and equipment. **high-'tech** adj (infml). **'highway** n [C] main public road. **'highwayman** n [C] (pl -men) (formerly) man who robbed travellers on roads.

high² /haɪ/ n [C] **1** high or highest level: Profits reached a new ~. **2** (infml) feeling of intense pleasure: on a ~.

high³ /haɪ/ adv at or to a high position.

highlight /ˈhaɪlaɪt/ n [C] **1** most interesting part of sth. **2** [usu pl] (a) light part of a picture. (b) light area in the hair. **highlight** v [T] give special attention to.

highly /ˈhaɪlɪ/ adv **1** to a great extent: a ~ amusing film. **2** very favourably: think ~ of sb. **highly-'strung** adj easily upset.

Highness /ˈhaɪnɪs/ n [C] title of a member of the royal family: His/ Her (Royal) ~.

hijack /ˈhaɪdʒæk/ v [T] take control of (esp an aircraft) by force. **hijacker** n [C].

hike /haɪk/ n [C], v [I] (go for a) long walk in the country. **hiker** n [C].

hilarious /hɪˈleərɪəs/ adj very amusing. **hilariously** adv. **hilarity** /hɪˈlærətɪ/ n [U] loud happy laughter.

hill /hɪl/ n [C] **1** area of high land, not as high as a mountain. **2** slope on a road, etc. **'hillside** n [C] side of a hill. **'hilltop** n [C] top of a hill. **hilly** adj having many hills.

hilt /hɪlt/ n [C] **1** handle of a sword. **2** (idm) **(up) to the 'hilt** completely: We support you to the ~.

him /hɪm/ pron (used as the object of a v or prep) male person or animal mentioned earlier: I love ~. ○ Give it to ~.

himself /hɪmˈself/ pron **1** (used as a reflexive when the male doer of an action is affected by it): He 'cut ~. **2** (used for emphasis): He told me the news ~. **3** (idm) **(all) by him'self** (a) alone. (b) without help.

hind¹ /haɪnd/ adj at the back: the ~ legs of a horse. **hind'quarters** n [pl] back parts of an animal with four legs.

hind² /haɪnd/ n [C] female deer.

hinder /ˈhɪndə(r)/ v [T] prevent the progress of: ~ sb from working. **hindrance** /ˈhɪndrəns/ n [C] person or thing that hinders.

hindsight /ˈhaɪndsaɪt/ n [U] understanding of an event after it has happened.

Hindu /ˌhɪnˈduː; US ˈhɪnduː/ n [C] person whose religion is Hinduism. **Hindu** *adj* of the Hindus. **Hinduism** /'hɪndu:ɪzəm/ *n* [U] Indian religion involving a caste system and belief in reincarnation.

hinge /hɪndʒ/ *n* [C] piece of metal on which a door, gate, etc swings. **hinge** *v* 1 [T] attach by a hinge. 2 (phr v) **hinge on sth** depend on sth: *Everything ~s on the result of these talks.*

hint /hɪnt/ *n* [C] 1 indirect suggestion. 2 slight trace: *a ~ of sadness in his voice.* 3 practical piece of advice: *helpful ~s.* **hint** *v* [I, T] *at/ ~* suggest (sth) indirectly.

hip /hɪp/ *n* [C] part on either side of the body above the legs and below the waist. **'hip-flask** *n* [C] small bottle for carrying brandy, etc in the pocket.

hippie (also **hippy**) /'hɪpɪ/ *n* [C] (*pl* **-ies**) person who rejects usual social standards.

hippo /'hɪpəʊ/ *n* [C] (*pl ~s*) (*infml*) short for HIPPOPOTAMUS.

hippopotamus /ˌhɪpə'pɒtəməs/ *n* [C] (*pl* **-muses** or **-mi** /-maɪ/) large African river animal with a thick skin.

hire /'haɪə(r)/ *v* [T] 1 obtain the use of (sth) in return for payment: *~ a car for a week.* 2 pay (sb) to do work. 3 (phr v) **hire sth out** allow the use of sth for a short time, in return for payment. **hire** *n* [U] hiring: *bicycles for ~.* **hire-'purchase** *n* [U] (*Brit*) agreement to pay small regular amounts for sth, having the use of it immediately.

his /hɪz/ *adj* belonging to him: *That's ~ book, not yours.* **his** *pron* of or belonging to him: *Is that ~?*

hiss /hɪs/ *v* [I, T] make a sound like that of a long 's', esp to show disapproval of (sb/sth). **hiss** *n* [C] hissing sound.

historian /hɪ'stɔ:rɪən/ *n* [C] person who studies history.

historic /hɪ'stɒrɪk; *US* -'stɔ:r-/ *adj* important in history: *a(n) ~ event.*

historical /hɪ'stɒrɪkl; *US* -'stɔ:r-/ *adj* of or concerning history: *~ studies/novels.* **historically** /-klɪ/ *adv.*

history /'hɪstrɪ/ *n* (*pl* **-ies**) 1 [U] study of past events. 2 [C] description of past events. 3 [C] past events or experiences of sb/sth: *his medical ~.* 4 (idm) **make/go down in 'history** be or do sth so important that it will be remembered.

hit /hɪt/ *v* (**-tt-**, *pt, pp* **hit**) [T] 1 (a) bring sth forcefully against: *He ~ me with a stick.* (b) come against with force: *The car ~ a tree.* 2 have

a bad effect on: *The new law will ~ the poor.* 3 reach; find: *~ the right road.* 4 (idm) **hit it'off** (*infml*) have a good relationship. **hit one's head against a brick wall** ⇨ HEAD¹. **hit the nail on the 'head** say the truth exactly. **hit the 'roof** (*infml*) suddenly become very angry. **hit the 'sack** (*infml*) go to bed. 5 (phr v) **hit back (at sb)** reply forcefully to an attack. **hit on/ upon sth** think of (a plan, solution, etc) unexpectedly. **hit out (at sb)** attack sb forcefully, esp with words. **,hit-and-'run** *adj* (of a road accident) caused by a driver who does not stop to help.

hit² /hɪt/ *n* [C] 1 act of hitting. 2 person or thing that is very popular; success: *Her new play is a great ~.* **'hit list** *n* [C] (*infml*) list of people to be killed or against whom an action is planned. **'hit man** *n* [C] (*infml esp US*) person who is paid to kill another person. **'hit parade** *n* [C] list of best-selling popular records.

hitch /hɪtʃ/ *v* 1 [I, T] get (free rides) in other people's cars: *~ round Europe.* 2 [T] fasten (sth) to sth with a loop or hook. 3 (phr v) **hitch sth up** pull (esp one's clothes) up quickly. **hitch** *n* [C] 1 small problem. 2 sudden pull or push. 3 kind of knot. **'hitch-hike** *v* [I] travel by obtaining free rides in other people's cars. **'hitch-hiker** *n* [C].

hitherto /ˌhɪðə'tu:/ *adv* (*fml*) until now.

HIV /ˌeɪtʃ aɪ 'vi:/ *abbr* virus that causes AIDS.

hive /haɪv/ *n* [C] 1 box for bees to live in. 2 (*fig*) place full of busy people: *a ~ of activity.* **hive** *v* (phr v) **hive sth off** make (part of an organization) independent.

HMS /ˌeɪtʃ em 'es/ *abbr* (used before the name of British warships) Her/His Majesty's Ship.

hoard /hɔ:d/ *n* [C] carefully guarded store of money, etc. **hoard** *v* [T] save and store.

hoarding /'hɔ:dɪŋ/ *n* [C] (*Brit*) large board on which advertisements are stuck.

hoarse /hɔ:s/ *adj* (*~r, ~st*) (of a voice) sounding rough. **hoarsely** *adv.* **hoarseness** *n* [U].

hoax /həʊks/ *n* [C] trick played on sb for a joke. **hoax** *v* [T] deceive with a hoax.

hob /hɒb/ *n* [C] flat heating surface on a cooker.

hobble /'hɒbl/ *v* [I] walk awkwardly, eg because one's feet hurt.

hobby /'hɒbɪ/ *n* [C] (*pl* **-ies**) activity done for pleasure during one's free time.

hobnail boot /'hɒbneɪl/ n [C] heavy boot with short nails in the sole.

hockey /'hɒkɪ/ n [U] team game played with curved sticks and a small ball.

hod /hɒd/ n [C] box with a long handle, used for carrying bricks.

hoe /həʊ/ n [C] garden tool with a long handle, used for loosening the soil. **hoe** v [I, T] use a hoe (on).

hog /hɒg; US hɔːg/ n [C] 1 castrated male pig. 2 (*infml*) selfish or greedy person. **hog** v (-gg-) [T] (*fig*) take more than one's fair share of (sth).

Hogmanay /'hɒgmaneɪ/ n [U] (*Scot*) New Year's Eve.

hoist /hɔɪst/ v [T] lift up, esp with ropes. **hoist** n 1 [C] machine with ropes and pulleys for lifting heavy things. 2 [sing] pulling or pushing up.

hold¹ /həʊld/ v (*pt, pp* held /held/) 1 [T] keep in one's hands, etc. 2 [T] keep in the position that is mentioned: H~ *your head up!* 3 [T] support: *That branch won't ~ you.* 4 [T] not allow to leave: H~ *the thief until the police come.* 5 [I] remain firm or unchanged: *How long will this fine weather ~? 6* [T] (of a car, etc) keep a grip on (a road). 7 [T] have room for; contain: *This barrel ~ s 25 litres.* 8 [T] defend against attack. 9 [T] own: ~ *shares.* 10 [T] have the position of: ~ *the post of Prime Minister.* 11 [T] keep (sb's attention or interest). 12 [T] have (a belief, opinion, etc). 13 [T] cause (a meeting) to take place. 14 [T] consider: *I ~ you responsible for the accident.* 15 (idm) **hold sb/sth at bay** ⇨ BAY³ **hold one's 'breath** stop breathing for a short time. **hold the 'fort** look after sth while others are away. **hold good** be true. **hold one's ground** ⇨ GROUND¹. **'hold it** (*infml*) (used for asking sb to wait, or not to move). **hold the 'line** keep a telephone connection open. **hold one's 'own (against sb)** not be defeated (by sb). **,hold one's 'tongue** not say anything. **there's no 'holding sb** sb cannot be prevented from doing sth. 16 (phr v) **hold sth against sb** allow sth bad to influence sb's opinion of sb. **hold 'back** be unwilling to act. **hold sb/sth back** (a) control sb/ sth: ~ *back the crowd.* (b) keep sth secret. **hold sb 'down** control the freedom of sb. **hold sth 'down** (a) keep sth at a low level: ~ *down prices.* (b) keep (a job) for some time. **hold 'forth (on sth)** speak

for a long time (about sth). **hold 'off** (of rain, etc) be delayed. **hold sb/sth off** resist (an attack). **hold off (doing) sth** delay sth. **hold 'on** (a) wait. (b) continue, even in difficulties. **hold sth on** keep sth in position. **hold on to sth** keep. **hold 'out** (a) last. (b) resist an attack. **hold sth out** offer sth. **hold out for sth** refuse to accept an offer, and continue to demand sth better. **hold sth over** postpone sth. **hold sb to sth** make sb keep (a promise). **hold sb/sth up** (a) suggest sb/sth as an example. (b) delay sth/sb: *Our flight was held up by fog.* **hold up sth** rob (a bank, etc) by force. **'hold-up** n [C] 1 delay, eg in traffic. 2 robbery by armed robbers.

hold² /həʊld/ n 1 [sing] act of holding. 2 [C] way of holding an opponent, eg in wrestling. 3 [C] something a person can hold, eg in climbing. 4 [sing] influence or power. 5 (idm) **catch, take, get hold of sb/sth** take sb/sth in one's hands. **get hold of sth** (*infml*) (a) find and use sth. (b) contact or find sb.

hold³ /həʊld/ n [C] part of a ship or aeroplane where cargo or luggage is stored.

holdall /'həʊldɔːl/ n [C] large soft bag, used when travelling.

holder /'həʊldə(r)/ n [C] 1 person who owns or possesses sth: *ticket-~.* 2 thing that supports or holds sth.

holding /'həʊldɪŋ/ n [C] something, eg land, that is owned.

hole /həʊl/ n 1 [C] hollow place or gap in a solid mass: *a ~ in the road/wall.* 2 [C] (a) small animal's home. (b) (*fig infml*) small dark unpleasant place. 3 [sing] (*sl*) difficult situation: *be in a ~.* 4 [C] place into which a ball must be hit in golf, etc. 5 (idm) **make a hole in sth** (*infml*) use a large part of (one's money, etc). **hole** v 1 [T] make a hole in (sth). 2 [I, T] (*out*)// (in golf, etc) hit (the ball) into a hole. 6 (phr v) **hole up** (*sl*) hide oneself.

holiday /'hɒlədeɪ/ n 1 [C] day(s) of rest from work. 2 (idm) **on 'holiday** having a holiday. **holiday** v [I] spend a holiday. **'holiday-maker** n [C] person on holiday.

holiness /'həʊlɪnɪs/ n [U] 1 being holy. 2 **His/Your Holiness** (title of the Pope).

hollow /'hɒləʊ/ *adj* 1 having empty space inside. 2 curving inwards; sunken: ~ *cheeks.* 3 (of sounds) echoing, as if coming from a hollow place. 4 (*fig*) false; unreal: ~ *words/pleasures.* **hol-**

low n [C] wide shallow hole. **hollow** /'hɒləʊ/ (*out*)// make a hollow in (sth): ~ *out a tree trunk to make a boat.*

holly /'hɒlɪ/ n [C, U] small evergreen tree with sharp-pointed leaves and red berries.

holocaust /'hɒləkɔːst/ n [C] large-scale destruction, esp of human lives.

holster /'həʊlstə(r)/ n [C] leather holder for a pistol.

holy /'həʊlɪ/ *adj* (**-ier, -iest**) 1 associated with God or religion. 2 pure and good: *live a ~ life.* **the Holy 'Spirit** (also **the Holy 'Ghost**) n [sing] (in Christianity) the Third Person of the Trinity.

homage /'hɒmɪdʒ/ n [U] (*fml*) expression of great respect.

home¹ /həʊm/ n 1 [C, U] place where one lives, esp with one's family. 2 [C] place for the care of old people or children. 3 [C] place where an animal or plant lives naturally. 4 [sing] place in which sth begins: *Greece is the ~ of democracy.* 5 [U] (in a race or game) finishing point. 6 (*idm*) **at home (a)** in the house, etc. (b) comfortable and relaxed: *Make yourself at ~!* **a ,home 'truth** unpleasant fact about sb the **,Home 'Counties** n [pl] the counties around London, eg Kent, Surrey, etc. **,home eco'nomics** n [U] (with sing v) study of food, budgets, etc for a home¹(1). **,home-'grown** *adj* (of food, etc) produced in one's own country, garden, etc. **,home 'help** n [C] person whose job is to help others with housework. **'homeland** n [C] 1 country in which one was born. 2 [usu pl] area reserved for black people in South Africa. **homeless** *adj* having no home. **,home-'made** *adj* made at home. the **'Home Office** n [sing] British government department dealing with the police, immigration, etc. **'homesick** *adj* sad because away from home. **'homesickness** n [U]. **homeward** *adj* going towards home. **homewards** *adv* towards home. **'homework** n [U] 1 work that a pupil does away from school. 2 (*fig*) work done to prepare for a meeting, discussion, etc.

home² /həʊm/ *adj* 1 of or connected with one's home. 2 in one's own country; not foreign: ~ *news.* 3 (*sport*) played on one's own ground: *a ~ match.*

home³ /həʊm/ *adv* 1 at, in or to one's home: *on her way ~.* 2 to the point aimed at: *drive a nail ~.* 3 (*idm*) **bring sth/come 'home to sb** make sth/become fully under-

stood. **home and 'dry** safe and successful. **'home-coming** n [C, U] arrival at home of sb who has been away for a long time.

home⁴ /həʊm/ v (*phr v*) **home in (on sth)** aim and move towards sth exactly.

homely /'həʊmlɪ/ *adj* (**-ier, -iest**) 1 (*approv* esp *Brit*) simple and plain. 2 (*US derog*) (of a person) not good-looking. **homeliness** n [U].

homeopathy /,həʊmɪ'ɒpəθɪ/ n [U] treatment of disease by giving small doses of drugs which in larger amounts would cause the same disease. **homeopathic** /,həʊmɪə'pæθɪk/ *adj*.

homicide /'hɒmɪsaɪd/ n [U] killing of one person by another. **homicidal** /,hɒmɪ'saɪdl/ *adj*.

homing /'həʊmɪŋ/ *adj* 1 (of a pigeon) having the ability to fly home. 2 (of a weapon) fitted with a device that guides it to the target.

homogeneous /,hɒmə'dʒiːnɪəs/ *adj* formed of parts of the same kind.

homogenized /hə'mɒdʒənaɪzd/ *adj* (of milk) treated so that the cream and the milk are evenly mixed.

homonym /'hɒmənɪm/ n [C] word spelt and pronounced like another word but with a different meaning, eg *bank¹* and *bank³*.

homosexual /,hɒmə'sekʃʊəl/ n [C], *adj* (person who is) sexually attracted to people of his/her own sex. **homosexuality** /,həʊmə-sekʃʊ'ælətɪ/ n [U].

honest /'ɒnɪst/ *adj* 1 (of a person) telling the truth; not cheating or stealing. 2 frank and sincere: *give an ~ opinion.* **honestly** *adv* 1 in an honest way. 2 (used for emphasis) really. **honesty** n [U].

honey /'hʌnɪ/ n 1 [U] sweet substance made by bees. 2 [C] (*infml* esp *US*) (used when talking to sb one likes or loves). **honeycomb** /-kəʊm/ n [C, U] wax structure made by bees for their honey and eggs. **honeysuckle** /-sʌkl/ n [U] climbing plant with sweet-smelling flowers.

honeymoon /'hʌnɪmuːn/ n [C] 1 holiday taken by a couple who have just got married. 2 (*fig*) pleasant time at the start of a new job, etc. **honeymoon** v [I] go on a honeymoon.

honk /hɒŋk/ v [I] n [C] (make the) sound of a car horn.

honorary /'ɒnərərɪ; *US* -rerɪ/ *adj* 1 (of a degree or rank) given as an honour. 2 (of a job) unpaid: ~ *president.*

honour (*US* -or) /'ɒnə(r)/ *n* **1** [U, sing] feeling of pride and pleasure: *a great ~ to be invited.* **2** [U] strong sense of right; reputation for good behaviour: *a man of ~.* **3** [U] great public respect. **4** [sing] person or thing that brings respect: *You are an ~ to your school.* **5** **honours** [pl] specialized university degree course; high level gained in this. **6** **your/his/her Honour** [sing] (title of respect to a judge). **honour** *v* [T] **1** give praise or respect to. **2** keep (an agreement).

honourable (*US* -nor-) /'ɒnərəbl/ *adj* **1** deserving or showing honour. **2** **the Honourable** (title given to certain high officials, etc). **honourably** *adv.*

hood /hʊd/ *n* [C] **1** covering for the head and neck, fastened to a coat. **2** folding cover of a car, pram, etc. **3** (*US*) car bonnet. **hooded** *adj* having a hood.

hoodwink /'hʊdwɪŋk/ *v* [T] deceive or trick sb.

hoof /huːf/ *n* [C] (*pl* ~s or **hooves** /huːvz/) hard bony part of the foot of a horse, etc.

hook /hʊk/ *n* [C] **1** curved piece of metal, plastic, etc used for catching hold of sth or for hanging sth on. **2** (in boxing) short blow with the elbow bent. **3** (idm) **off the 'hook** (a) (of a telephone receiver) not resting on the main part of the telephone. (b) (*infml*) no longer in a difficult situation: *let/get sb off the ~.* **hook** *v* [T] **1** fasten or catch with a hook. **2** make into the form of a hook: *~ one's foot round sth.* **hooked** *adj* **1** hook-shaped. **2** (idm) **be hooked on sth** be completely dependent on (drugs, etc).

hooligan /'huːlɪgən/ *n* [C] noisy violent young person. **hooliganism** *n* [U].

hoop /huːp/ *n* [C] circular band of wood or metal.

hooray = HURRAH.

hoot /huːt/ *n* [C] **1** cry of an owl. **2** sound of a car's horn. **3** shout of disapproval. **4** (idm) **not care/ give a hoot/two hoots** (*infml*) not care at all. **hoot** *v* [I] **1** make a hoot. **2** [T] sound (a horn). **hooter** *n* [C] (*esp Brit*) horn, siren, etc.

Hoover /'huːvə(r)/ *n* [C] (*P*) vacuum cleaner. **hoover** *v* [I, T] clean with a vacuum cleaner.

hooves *pl* of HOOF.

hop[1] /hɒp/ *v* (-**pp**-) [I] **1** (a) (of a person) jump on one foot. (b) (of an animal or bird) jump with all feet together. **2** (*infml*) move quickly or easily: *~ on a bus.* **3** (idm) **hop it** (*sl*) go away. **hop** *n* [C] **1** act of hopping; short jump. **2**

(*infml*) one stage in a long-distance flight.

hop[2] /hɒp/ *n* [C] climbing plant used to flavour beer.

hope /həʊp/ *n* **1** [C, U] desire and expectation that sth good will happen. **2** [C] person or thing on which hope is based. **3** (idm) **be beyond hope** have no chance of succeeding or recovering. **hope** *v* [I, T] desire and expect: *I ~ (that) you win.* **hopeful** *adj* having or giving hope. **hopefully** *adv* **1** in a hopeful way. **2** (used for expressing hope that sth will happen: *H~fully she'll be home soon.* **hopeless** *adj* **1** giving no hope. **2** (*at*)// (*infml*) not able to do sth: *~ less at maths.* **hopelessly** *adv.* **hopelessness** *n* [U].

horde /hɔːd/ *n* [C] very large crowd: *~s of football fans.*

horizon /hə'raɪzn/ *n* **1** **the horizon** [sing] the line at which the earth and sky seem to meet. **2** [C] (*fig*) limit of one's knowledge, experience, etc: *Travel broadens one's ~s.*

horizontal /ˌhɒrɪ'zɒntl/; *US* ˌhɔːr-/ *adj* flat or level. **horizontal** *n* [sing] horizontal line or position. **horizontally** /-təlɪ/ *adv.*

hormone /'hɔːməʊn/ *n* [C] substance produced in the body that encourages growth, etc.

horn /hɔːn/ *n* **1** (a) [C] hard pointed usu curved growth on the heads of cattle, deer, etc. (b) [U] substance that this is made of. **2** [C] musical instrument with a trumpet-shaped end: *a French '~.* **3** [C] device in a car, etc for making a warning sound. **horny** *adj* (-**ier**, -**iest**) **1** made of or like horn. **2** (*sl*) sexually excited.

hornet /'hɔːnɪt/ *n* [C] large wasp.

horoscope /'hɒrəskəʊp; *US* 'hɔːr-/ *n* [C] statement about sb's future based on the position of the stars and planets at the time of his/her birth.

horrendous /hɒ'rendəs/ *adj* very unpleasant or shocking: *~ colours/clothes.*

horrible /'hɒrəbl; *US* 'hɔːr-/ *adj* **1** causing horror: *a ~ crime.* **2** (*infml*) very unpleasant: *~ weather.* **horribly** *adv.*

horrid /'hɒrɪd; *US* 'hɔːrɪd/ *adj* (*infml*) very unpleasant; nasty.

horrific /hə'rɪfɪk/ *adj* horrifying. **horrifically** *adv.*

horrify /'hɒrɪfaɪ; *US* 'hɔːr-/ *v* (*pt, pp* -**ied**) [T] fill with horror: *horrified by his death.*

horror /'hɒrə(r); *US* 'hɔːr-/ *n* **1** [C, U] (something causing a) feeling of great fear or dislike. **2** [C] (*infml*) naughty mischievous child. **horror** *adj* intended to be frightening: *a ~ story/film*. '**horror-stricken** (also **-struck**) *adj* very shocked.

hors-d'oeuvre /ˌɔː'dɜːvrə; *US* ˈdɜːv/ *n* [C] food served at the beginning of a meal.

horse /hɔːs/ *n* [C] **1** large four-legged animal that people ride on or use for pulling carts, etc. **2** = VAULTING HORSE (VAULT²). **3** (idm) (**straight**) **from the horse's 'mouth** (of information) directly from the person concerned. **horse** *v* (phr v) **horse about/around** (*infml*) behave in a noisy playful way. '**horseplay** *n* [U] rough noisy fun or play. '**horsepower** *n* [U] unit for measuring the power of an engine. '**horseshoe** *n* [C] U-shaped metal shoe for a horse.

horseback /ˈhɔːsbæk/ *n* (idm) **on 'horseback** on horseback. **horseback** *adv*, *adj* (esp *US*): *~ riding*.

horticulture /ˈhɔːtɪkʌltʃə(r)/ *n* [U] science of growing flowers, fruit, and vegetables. **horticultural** /ˌhɔːtɪ'kʌltʃərəl/ *adj*.

hose¹ /həʊz/ (also '**hose-pipe**) *n* [C] flexible tube used for directing water onto a garden or a fire. **hose** *v* [Tn] (*down*)/ wash or water (sth) with a hose.

hose² /həʊz/ *n* [pl] stockings, socks, etc.

hosiery /ˈhəʊziəri; *US* ˈhəʊʒəri/ *n* [U] stockings, socks, etc.

hospice /ˈhɒspɪs/ *n* [C] hospital for people who are dying.

hospitable /hɒ'spɪtəbl, also 'hɒspɪtəbl/ *adj* **1** (*to/towards*)/ giving a kind welcome to guests. **2** (of places) pleasant to be in. **hospitably** *adv*.

hospital /ˈhɒspɪtl/ *n* [C] place where people are treated for illness or injuries. **hospitalize** *v* [Tn] put into hospital.

hospitality /ˌhɒspɪ'tælətɪ/ *n* [U] being kind and welcoming to guests.

host¹ /həʊst/ *n* [C] **1** person who entertains guests. **2** person who introduces guests on a radio or television programme. **host** *v* [Tn] act as a host at or to.

host² /həʊst/ *n* [C] large number: *a ~ of different reasons*.

hostage /ˈhɒstɪdʒ/ *n* [C] prisoner kept by a person who threatens to hurt or kill him/her unless certain demands are obeyed.

hostel /ˈhɒstl/ *n* [C] building in which students, homeless people, etc can live and eat.

hostess /ˈhəʊstɪs/ *n* [C] **1** female

host. **2** woman employed to welcome and entertain people at a night-club, etc.

hostile /ˈhɒstaɪl; *US* -tl/ *adj* (*to/towards*)/ **1** unfriendly. **2** of an enemy: *~ aircraft*.

hostility /hɒ'stɪlətɪ/ *n* **1** [U] unfriendly behaviour. **2 hostilities** [pl] (acts of) war.

hot /hɒt/ *adj* (**~ter**, **~test**) **1** having a high temperature. **2** producing a burning taste: *~ spices/curry*. **3** strong; fierce: *He has a ~ temper*, i.e gets angry quickly. **4** (of news) very recent. **5** (idm) be **in/get into hot 'water** (*infml*) be in/get into trouble. **hot 'air** (*infml*) meaningless talk. (be) **hot on sb's 'heels/'tracks/'trail** following sb closely. **not so 'hot** (*infml*) not good. **hot** *v* (**-tt-**) (phr v) **hot up** (*infml*) become more exciting or intense. ˌhot-'blooded *adj* easily angered; passionate. ˌhot 'dog *n* [C] hot sausage in a long bread roll. '**hotfoot** *adv* quickly and eagerly. '**hothead** *n* [C] person who acts too quickly, without thinking. ˌhot-'headed *adj*. '**hothouse** *n* [C] heated glass building for growing plants. '**hot line** *n* [C] direct telephone connection between heads of government. **hotly** *adv* **1** passionately. **2** closely: *~ly pursued*. ˌhot-'tempered *adj* easily angered.

hotel /həʊ'tel/ *n* [C] building where rooms and meals are provided for travellers. **hotelier** /-lɪə(r), -lɪeɪ; *US* ˌhəʊtel'jeɪ/ *n* [C] person who owns or manages a hotel.

hound /haʊnd/ *n* [C] hunting or racing dog. **hound** *v* [Tn] worry; pursue: *~ed by newspaper reporters*.

hour /ˈaʊə(r)/ *n* **1** [C] period of 60 minutes. **2** [C] time when it is exactly 1 o'clock, 2 o'clock, etc: *Trains leave on the ~*. **3 hours** [pl] fixed period of time for work, etc: *Office ~s are from 9 am to 5 pm*. **4** [C, usu sing] period of about an hour: *a long lunch ~*. **5** [C] distance that one can travel in an hour: *London is only two ~s away*. **6** (idm) **at the e,leventh 'hour** at the last possible moment.

hourly /ˈaʊəlɪ/ *adv* **1** once every hour. **2** according to the number of hours worked: *be paid ~*. **hourly** *adj* **1** done or happening every hour: *an ~ bus service*. **2** calculated by the hour.

house¹ /haʊs/ *n* [C] (*pl ~s* /ˈhaʊzɪz/) **1** (a) building made for people to live in. (b) [usu sing] people living in such a building:

Be quiet or you'll wake the whole ~! **2** building made for a purpose that is becoming: *an 'bpera-* ~ ○ *a* '*hen-* ~. **3** division of a school for competitions in sport, etc. **4** (usu **House**) (building used by) people who discuss or pass laws: *the ,H* ~ *s of 'Parliament* ○ *the ,H* ~ *of ,Repre'sentatives* ○ *a publishing* ~. **6** (usu **House**) important, esp royal, family. **7** (usu sing) audience in a theatre, etc: *a full* ~, ie a theatre with every seat occupied. **8** (idm) **bring the 'house down** (*infml*) make an audience laugh or clap loudly. **on the 'house** paid for by the pub, firm, etc. '**house-bound** *adj* not able to leave one's house. '**house-breaking** *n* [U] entering a building by force to commit a crime. '**housekeeper** *n* [C] person (esp a woman) whose job is to manage a household. '**housekeeping** *n* [U] **1** work of managing a household. **2** money allowed for this. '**house-master** (*fem* '**housemistress**) *n* [C] teacher in charge of a house(3) in a school. **the House of Lords** (*Brit*) the non-elected part of parliament. '**house-proud** *adj* giving great attention to the appearance of one's home. '**housewife** *n* [C] (*pl* **wives** /-waɪvz/) woman who works at home looking after her family, cleaning, cooking, etc. '**housework** *n* [U] work done in a house, eg cleaning and cooking.

house² /haʊz/ *v* [T] provide a house or room for.

household /ˈhaʊshəʊld/ *n* **1** [C] all the people living in a house. **2** (idm) **a ,household 'name/'word** name of sb/sth that is very well known.

housing /ˈhaʊzɪŋ/ *n* **1** [U] houses, flats, etc considered as a group. **2** [C] cover that protects a machine.

hove ⇨ **HEAVE**.

hovel /ˈhɒvl; *US* ˈhʌvl/ *n* [C] (*derog*) small dirty house or hut.

hover /ˈhɒvə(r); *US* ˈhʌvər/ *v* [I] **1** (of birds, etc) stay in the air in one place. **2** (of a person) wait about, in an uncertain manner. '**hovercraft** *n* [C] (*pl* **hovercraft**) vehicle that moves over land or water supported by air blown underneath it.

how /haʊ/ *adv* **1** (used in questions). (a) in what way: *H* ~ *is this word spelt?* (b) in what state of health: *H* ~ *are you?* (c) (used with an adj or adv) to what extent: *H* ~ *old is he?* **2** (used in exclamations to comment on extent): *H* ~ *hot it is!* **how** *conj* the way in which: *He told me* ~ *to get to the station.*

however /haʊˈevə(r)/ *adv* **1** to whatever extent: *He'll never succeed,* ~ *hard he tries.* **2** (used for commenting on a previously stated fact) although sth is, was, etc true: *She felt ill; she went to work,* ~. **3** (used in questions for showing surprise) how: *H* ~ *did you get here without a car?* **however** *conj* in any way: *H* ~ *I thought about the problem, I couldn't work out an answer.*

howl /haʊl/ *v* [I] *n* [C] (make a) long loud cry.

HQ /ˌeɪtʃ ˈkjuː/ *abbr* headquarters.

hr *abbr* (*pl* **hrs**) hour.

HRH /ˌeɪtʃ ɑː(r) ˈeɪtʃ/ *abbr* His/Her Royal Highness.

hub /hʌb/ *n* [C] **1** centre of a wheel. **2** (*fig*) central point of an activity. '**hub-cap** *n* [C] round metal cover over the hub of a car wheel.

hubbub /ˈhʌbʌb/ *n* [sing] loud confused noise.

huddle /ˈhʌdl/ *v* **1** [I, T] crowd together. **2** (phr v) **huddle up** curl one's body up into a small space, eg to keep warm. **huddle** *n* [C] number of people or things close together.

hue¹ /hjuː/ *n* [C] (*fml*) (shade of) colour.

hue² /hjuː/ *n* (idm) **hue and 'cry** loud angry public protest.

huff /hʌf/ *n* [sing] bad temper: *be in a* ~.

hug /hʌɡ/ *v* (**-gg-**) [T] **1** put one's arms round (sb) tightly, esp to show love. **2** keep close to: *The boat* ~ *ged the shore.* **hug** *n* [C] act of hugging(1): *give sb a* ~.

huge /hjuːdʒ/ *adj* very large. **hugely** *adv* very much.

hulk /hʌlk/ *n* [C] **1** broken old ship. **2** large awkward person or thing. **hulking** *adj* large and awkward.

hull /hʌl/ *n* [C] body of a ship.

hullo ⇨ **HALLO**.

hum /hʌm/ *v* (**-mm-**) **1** [I] make a sound like a bee. **2** [I, T] sing with closed lips: ~ *a tune.* **3** [I] be in a state of busy activity. **hum** *n* [C] humming sound.

human /ˈhjuːmən/ *adj* **1** of people. **2** showing the better qualities of people; kind. **human** (also **,human 'being**) *n* [C] person. **humanly** *adv* within human ability: *do all that is* ~ *ly possible.* **,human 'rights** *n* [pl] basic rights of freedom, equality, justice, etc.

humane /hjuːˈmeɪn/ *adj* **1** kind and caring towards others. **2** causing as little pain as possible: ~ *killing of animals.* **humanely** *adv*.

humanity /hju:'mænətɪ/ n [U] 1 human beings in general. 2 quality of being humane.

humble /'hʌmbl/ adj (~r, ~st) 1 having a modest opinion of oneself. 2 low in rank; unimportant. 3 (of things) poor in appearance: my ~ home. **humble** v [T] make humble. **humbly** adv.

humdrum /'hʌmdrʌm/ adj dull because ordinary.

humid /'hju:mɪd/ adj (esp of the air) damp. **humidity** /hju:'mɪdətɪ/ n [U] (degree of) dampness in the air.

humiliate /hju:'mɪlɪeɪt/ v [T] make (sb) feel ashamed or foolish. **humiliating** adj: a humiliating defeat. **humiliation** /hju:,mɪ-lɪ'eɪʃn/ n [C, U].

humility /hju:'mɪlətɪ/ n [U] quality of being humble(1).

humorist /'hju:mərɪst/ n [C] person who writes or tells jokes.

humorous /'hju:mərəs/ adj funny; amusing. **humorously** adv.

humour (US -or) /'hju:mə(r)/ n [U] (ability to cause or feel) amusement: a sense of ~. **humour** v [T] keep (sb) happy by doing what he/she wants.

hump /hʌmp/ n [C] round lump, esp on a camel's back. **hump** v [T] (infml) carry (sth heavy) with difficulty.

hunch /hʌntʃ/ n [C] (infml) idea based on feeling, not on thought. **hunch** v [T] bend (one's back and shoulders) into a rounded shape. **'hunchback** n [C] person with a rounded hump on his/her back. **'hunchbacked** adj.

hundred /'hʌndrəd/ pron, adj, n [C] 100: one, two, etc ~ ○ ~s of people. **hundredth** /-dθ/ pron, adj 100th. **hundredth** pron, n [C] ¹⁄₁₀₀.

hundredweight /'hʌndrədweɪt/ n [C] (pl **hundredweight**) measure of weight; one twentieth of one ton (50.8 kilograms).

hung pt, pp of HANG¹.

hunger /'hʌŋgə(r)/ n 1 [U] need or desire for food. 2 [sing for]// (fig) strong desire. **hunger** v (phr v) **hunger for/after sth** have a strong desire for sth. **'hunger strike** n [C] refusal to eat food as a protest.

hungry /'hʌŋgrɪ/ adj (-ier, -iest) feeling hunger. **hungrily** adv.

hunk /hʌŋk/ n [C] thick piece cut off sth: a ~ of bread.

hunt /hʌnt/ v [I, T] 1 chase (wild animals) for food or sport. 2 (for)// try to find sth. 3 (phr v) **hunt sb down** search for and find sb. **hunt**

n 1 [sing] act of hunting. 2 [C] group of people who hunt foxes. **hunter** n [C] person who hunts.

hurdle /'hɜ:dl/ n [C] 1 frame to be jumped over in a race. 2 (fig) difficulty to be overcome.

hurl /hɜ:l/ v [T] throw with force: (fig) ~ insults at sb.

hurly-burly /'hɜ:lɪ ˈbɜ:lɪ/ n [sing] noisy confused activity.

hurrah /hʊ'rɑ:/ (also **hurray**, **hooray** /hʊ'reɪ/) interj, n [C] (used for showing joy, approval, etc).

hurricane /'hʌrɪkən; US -keɪn/ n [C] storm with a violent wind.

hurry /'hʌrɪ/ v (pt, pp -ied) 1 [I, T] (make sb) move or do sth (too) quickly. 2 (phr v) **hurry up** (make sb) do sth more quickly: H~ up! It's late. **hurried** adj done (too) quickly. **hurriedly** adv. **hurry** n 1 [U] need to do sth quickly. 2 (idm) **in a 'hurry** (a) eager. (b) eager.

hurt /hɜ:t/ v (pt, pp hurt) 1 [I, T] cause injury or pain to: He ~ himself. ○ I've ~ my hand. 2 [T] cause pain to (a person or his/her feelings). 3 harm (sb): It wouldn't ~ (you) to say sorry. **hurt** n [C, U] injury or pain, esp to sb's feelings. **hurtful** adj. **hurtfully** adv.

hurtle /'hɜ:tl/ v [I] move violently or quickly.

husband /'hʌzbənd/ n [C] man to whom a woman is married.

hush /hʌʃ/ v 1 [I, T] become or make silent. 2 (phr v) **hush sth up** keep sth secret. **hush** n [U, sing] silence.

husk /hʌsk/ n [C] dry outer covering of seeds. **husk** v [T] remove the husks from.

husky¹ /'hʌskɪ/ adj (-ier, -iest) (of a voice) dry and rough. **huskily** adv.

husky² /'hʌskɪ/ n [C] (pl -ies) dog used for pulling sledges across snow.

hustle /'hʌsl/ v [T] 1 push roughly. 2 (into)// make (sb) act quickly: ~ sb into a decision. **hustle** n [U] busy lively activity. **hustler** /'hʌslə(r)/ n [C] (US sl) prostitute.

hut /hʌt/ n [C] small roughly-built house or shelter.

hutch /hʌtʃ/ n [C] cage for rabbits, etc.

hyacinth /'haɪəsɪnθ/ n [C] plant with sweet-smelling flowers, growing from a bulb.

hyaena = HYENA.

hybrid /'haɪbrɪd/ n [C] animal or plant produced from two different kinds.

hydrant /'haɪdrənt/ n [C] pipe connected to a water supply, esp in a street.

hydraulic /haɪˈdrɔːlɪk/ adj worked by the pressure of a liquid, esp water.

hydroelectric /ˌhaɪdrəʊɪˈlektrɪk/ adj using water-power to produce electricity.

hydrofoil /ˈhaɪdrəfɔɪl/ n [C] boat with fins that raise the hull out of the water.

hydrogen /ˈhaɪdrədʒən/ n [U] light colourless gas that combines with oxygen to form water. '**hydrogen bomb** n [C] extremely powerful bomb that explodes when the central parts (= NUCLEI) of hydrogen atoms join together.

hyena (also **hyaena**) /haɪˈiːnə/ n [C] wild animal with a laughing cry.

hygiene /ˈhaɪdʒiːn/ n [U] keeping oneself, etc clean, in order to prevent disease. **hygienic** /haɪˈdʒiːnɪk; US -dʒɪˈen-/ adj of hygiene; clean. **hygienically** adv.

hymn /hɪm/ n [C] song of praise to God.

hyperactive /ˌhaɪpə(r)ˈæktɪv/ adj very lively; unable to rest.

hypermarket /ˈhaɪpəmɑːkɪt/ n [C] (Brit) very large supermarket.

hyphen /ˈhaɪfn/ n [C] mark (-) used for joining two words or parts of words. **hyphenate** /ˈhaɪfəneɪt/ v [T] join with a hyphen.

hypnosis /hɪpˈnəʊsɪs/ n [U] state like deep sleep in which a person's actions may be controlled by another person. **hypnotic** /hɪpˈnɒtɪk/ adj. **hypnotism** /ˈhɪpnətɪzəm/ n [U] production of hypnosis. **hypnotist** /ˈhɪpnətɪst/ n [C]. **hypnotize** /ˈhɪpnətaɪz/ v [T] produce hypnosis in (sb).

hypochondriac /ˌhaɪpəˈkɒndrɪæk/ n [C] person who worries too much about his/her health.

hypocrisy /hɪˈpɒkrəsɪ/ n [C, U] (pl -ies) making oneself appear better than one really is. **hypocrite** /ˈhɪpəkrɪt/ n [C] person who makes himself/herself seem better than he/she really is. **hypocritical** /ˌhɪpəˈkrɪtɪkl/ adj.

hypodermic /ˌhaɪpəˈdɜːmɪk/ adj, n [C] (of a) needle used for injecting a drug into a person.

hypotenuse /haɪˈpɒtənjuːz; US -tənuːs/ n [C] longest side of a right-angled triangle.

hypothesis /haɪˈpɒθəsɪs/ n [C] (pl -theses /-siːz/) idea that is suggested as a possible explanation of facts. **hypothetical** /ˌhaɪpəˈθetɪkl/ adj not yet proved.

hysteria /hɪˈstɪərɪə/ n [U] 1 uncontrolled excitement. 2 disturbance of the nervous system, esp with emotional outbursts. **hysterical** /hɪˈsterɪkl/ adj. **hysterics** /hɪˈsterɪks/ n [pl] attack(s) of hysteria.

I i

I, **i**¹ /aɪ/ n [C] (pl **I's**, **i's** /aɪz/) 1 the ninth letter of the English alphabet. 2 Roman numeral for 1.

I² /aɪ/ pron (used as the subject of a v) person who is the speaker or writer.

ice¹ /aɪs/ n 1 [U] frozen water. 2 [C] portion of ice-cream. 3 (idm) **put sth on ice** delay action on (a plan, etc). **iceberg** /ˈaɪsbɜːg/ n [C] large mass of ice floating in the sea. '**icebox** n [C] 1 box with ice in, for keeping food cool. 2 (esp US) refrigerator. **ice-cream** /esp US ˈaɪskriːm/ n [C, U] (portion of) frozen flavoured creamy mixture. '**ice hockey** n [C] team game played on ice with sticks and a hard rubber disc. **ice 'lolly** n [C] flavoured ice on a stick. '**ice-skate** n [C] boot fitted with a thin metal blade for skating on ice. '**ice-skate** v [I] skate on ice.

ice² /aɪs/ v 1 [T] make very cold. 2 [T] cover with icing. 3 (phr v) **ice (sth) over/up** ice (sth) or become covered with ice.

icicle /ˈaɪsɪkl/ n [C] pointed piece of ice, formed when water freezes as it drips from roofs, etc.

icing /ˈaɪsɪŋ/ n [C] mixture of powdered sugar, flavouring, etc, used for decorating cakes.

icy /ˈaɪsɪ/ adj (-ier, -iest) 1 very cold. 2 covered with ice. 3 (fig) unfriendly: an ~ stare. **icily** adv.

I'd /aɪd/ 1 I had. ⇨ HAVE. 2 I would. ⇨ WILL¹, WOULD¹.

idea /aɪˈdɪə/ n 1 [C] plan or thought: That's a good ~! 2 [U, sing] picture in the mind. 3 [C] opinion or belief. 4 [U, sing] feeling that sth is probable: I've an ~ it will rain. 5 the idea [sing] the aim or purpose. 6 (idm) **get the i'dea** understand. **have no ~ not** know: He has no ~ how to manage people. **not have the first idea about sth** know nothing at all about sth.

ideal /aɪˈdɪəl/ adj 1 perfect: ~ weather. 2 existing only in the imagination: in an ~ world. **ideal** n [C] 1 [usu sing] person or thing considered perfect. 2 [usu pl] high

standard of behaviour. **ideally**
adv 1 in an ideal way: ~ *ly suited to*
the job. 2 if conditions were perfect.

idealist /aɪˈdɪəlɪst/ n [C] person
who has (often impractical)
ideals(2) and who tries to achieve
them. **idealism** n [U]. **idealistic**
/ˌaɪdɪəˈlɪstɪk/ adj.

idealize /aɪˈdɪəlaɪz/ v [T] think of
(sb/sth) as perfect. **idealization**
/aɪˌdɪəlaɪˈzeɪʃn/ n [U, C].

identical /aɪˈdentɪkl/ adj 1 the
same. 2 (to/with/) exactly alike: ~
twins. **identically** adv.

identify /aɪˈdentɪfaɪ/ v (pt, pp
-ied) 1 [T] show or prove who or
what (sb/sth) is: *Can you ~ the*
man who attacked you? 2 [T]
identify (oneself) with sb/sth be
associated with. **identify with sb**
understand the feelings of sb.
identification /aɪˌdentɪfɪˈkeɪʃn/
n [U] 1 act of identifying. 2 proof of
who a person is, eg a driving-
licence or passport.

identity /aɪˈdentətɪ/ n (pl -ies) 1
[C, U] who or what sb/sth is: *the ~*
of the thief. 2 [U] state of being the
same.

ideology /ˌaɪdɪˈɒlədʒɪ/ n [C, U] (pl
-ies) set of (political) beliefs.
ideological /ˌaɪdɪəˈlɒdʒɪkl/ adj.

idiocy /ˈɪdɪəsɪ/ n (pl -ies) 1 [U] extreme stupidity. 2 [C] very stupid
act, remark, etc.

idiom /ˈɪdɪəm/ n [C] group of
words with a meaning that is different from the meaning of all the
individual words: *'Pull your socks*
up' is an ~ meaning 'improve your
behaviour'. **idiomatic** /ˌɪdɪə-
ˈmætɪk/ adj (of language) natural
and correct.

idiosyncrasy /ˌɪdɪəˈsɪŋkrəsɪ/
n [C] (pl -ies) way of behaving that
is particular to a person. **idiosyn-**
cratic /ˌɪdɪəsɪŋkrˈætɪk/ adj.

idiot /ˈɪdɪət/ n [C] 1 (infml) fool. 2
(dated) person who is severely
mentally handicapped. **idiotic**
/ˌɪdɪˈɒtɪk/ adj very stupid.

idle /ˈaɪdl/ adj (~r, ~st) 1 (a) not
doing work. (b) in use: *The*
machines are lying ~. 2 lazy. 3
useless: ~ *gossip/promises.* **idle** v
1 [I] waste time. 2 [I] (of an engine)
run slowly in neutral gear. 3 (phr
v) **idle sth away** waste (time).
idleness n [U]. **idly** adv.

idol /ˈaɪdl/ n [C] 1 image of a god,
made of wood, stone, etc. 2 person
or thing that is greatly loved or
admired. **idolize** /ˈaɪdəlaɪz/ v [T]
worship (sb/sth) as an idol.

idyllic /ɪˈdɪlɪk; US aɪˈd-/ adj simple and very pleasant.

ie /ˌaɪ ˈiː/ abbr that is: *They ar-*

rived on the next day, ie Monday.

if /ɪf/ conj 1 on condition that: *She*
will help you if you ask her. 2
whether: *Do you know if he's work-*
ing today? 3 when: *If you mix yel-*
low and blue, you get green. 4 (used
after verbs or adjectives showing
feelings): *I'm sorry if I'm disturb-*
ing you. 5 although also: *The hotel*
was good value, if a little expen-
sive. 6 (idm) **if I were 'you** (used
for introducing advice): *If I were*
you, I'd look for a new job. **if 'only**
(used for expressing a strong
wish): *If only I were rich!* **if I** n [C] 1
uncertainty: *if he wins, but it's a*
big if. 2 (idm) **ifs and 'buts**
reasons for delay; uncertainty.

igloo /ˈɪɡluː/ n [C] (pl ~s) Eski-
mos' house made of blocks of
snow.

ignite /ɪɡˈnaɪt/ v [I, T] (cause sth
to) start to burn. **ignition**
/ɪɡˈnɪʃn/ n 1 [C] electrical apparatus that starts the engine of a
car, etc. 2 [U] process of igniting.

ignorant /ˈɪɡnərənt/ adj knowing little or nothing. **ignorance**
/-rəns/ n [U]. **ignorantly** adv.

ignore /ɪɡˈnɔː(r)/ v [T] take no
notice of.

ill /ɪl/ adj 1 sick. 2 bad: ~ *health/*
luck ○ ~ *feeling,* ie anger, jealousy, etc. 3 (idm) **be taken ill** become ill. **in ill** n (fml) 1 [U] harm;
evil. 2 [C, usp pl] difficulty. ill adv
1 badly: *an ~-written book.* 2 un-
favourably: *think ~ of sb.* 3
scarcely: *We can ~ afford the time.*
4 (idm) **ill at 'ease** uncomfortable; embarrassed. **ill-ad'vised**
adj unwise. **ill-'bred** adj badly
brought up. **ill-'natured** adj bad-
tempered. **ill-'treat** v [T] treat
cruelly. **ill-'treatment** n [U]. **ill**
'**will** n [U] unkind feeling.

I'll /aɪl/ I will. ⇨ WILL[1].

illegal /ɪˈliːɡl/ adj against the
law; not legal. **illegality**
/ˌɪlɪˈɡælətɪ/ n [U, C]. **illegally**
/-ɡəlɪ/ adv.

illegible /ɪˈledʒəbl/ adj difficult
or impossible to read.

illegitimate /ˌɪlɪˈdʒɪtɪmət/ adj 1
born to parents not married to
each other. 2 not allowed by the
law. **illegitimately** adv.

illicit /ɪˈlɪsɪt/ adj not allowed by
the law. **illicitly** adv.

illiterate /ɪˈlɪtərət/ n [C], adj
(person who is) unable to read or
write. **illiteracy** /-rəsɪ/ n [U].

illness /ˈɪlnɪs/ n 1 [U] state of being ill. 2 [C] specific kind of illness.

illogical /ɪˈlɒdʒɪkl/ adj not logical; not reasonable. **illogicality**
/ˌɪˌlɒdʒɪˈkælətɪ/ n [C, U]. **illogic-**
ally adv.

illuminate /ɪˈluːmɪneɪt/ v[T] 1 give light to. 2 decorate with lights. 3 (esp formerly) decorate (a book) with gold and bright colours. **illuminating** adj explaining sth clearly: an illuminating lecture. **illumination** /ɪˌluːmɪˈneɪʃn/ n 1 [U] lighting. 2 illuminations [pl] (Brit) bright colourful lights to decorate a town.

illusion /ɪˈluːʒn/ n[C] 1 false idea or belief. 2 something that a person wrongly believes to exist: an optical ~. **illusory** /ɪˈluːsərɪ/ adj based on an illusion.

illustrate /ˈɪləstreɪt/ v[T] 1 supply with pictures: ~ a book. 2 explain by using examples, diagrams, etc. **illustration** /ˌɪləˈstreɪʃn/ n 1 [C] picture or drawing. 2 [C] example. 3 [U] act of illustrating. **illustrative** /ˈɪləstrətɪv; US ɪˈlʌs-/ adj used as an example. **illustrator** n[C] person who draws pictures for books, etc.

illustrious /ɪˈlʌstrɪəs/ adj famous. **illustriously** adv.

I'm /aɪm/ I am. ⇨ BE.

image /ˈɪmɪdʒ/ n[C] 1 picture in the mind. 2 general impression that a person, company, etc gives to the public. 3 picture of sth seen in a mirror or through a camera. 4 copy of sth, esp in wood or stone. 5 (idm) be the (living/spitting) image of sb (infml) look exactly like sb. **imagery** n[U] use of figurative language to produce pictures in the mind.

imaginary /ɪˈmædʒɪnərɪ; US -əneri/ adj unreal.

imagine /ɪˈmædʒɪn/ v[T] 1 form a picture of (sth) in mind: Can you ~ life without electricity? 2 suppose (sth): I ~ he'll be there. **imaginable** adj that can be imagined. **imagination** /ɪˌmædʒɪˈneɪʃn/ n 1 [U, C] ability to form pictures or ideas in the mind, esp of interesting things. 2 [U] something experienced in the mind, not in real life. **imaginative** /ɪˈmædʒɪnətɪv; US -əneɪtɪv/ adj having or showing imagination(1).

imbalance /ˌɪmˈbæləns/ n[C] lack of equality or balance.

imbecile /ˈɪmbəsiːl; US -sl/ n[C] 1 (infml) fool. 2 (dated) person who is mentally handicapped. **imbecile** adj stupid; foolish.

imbue /ɪmˈbjuː/ v[T] with/ (fml) fill (sb) with a feeling, etc.

imitate /ˈɪmɪteɪt/ v[T] 1 copy the behaviour of. 2 copy the speech, actions, etc of. **imitative** /ˈɪmɪtətɪv; US -teɪtɪv/ adj following an example. **imitator** n[C].

imitation /ˌɪmɪˈteɪʃn/ n 1 [C] copy of the real thing. 2 [U] imitating. **imitation** adj not real; artificial: ~ jewels.

immaculate /ɪˈmækjʊlət/ adj clean; perfect. **immaculately** adv.

immaterial /ˌɪməˈtɪərɪəl/ adj (to/) 1 not important. 2 without physical substance.

immature /ˌɪməˈtjʊə(r); US -tʊər/ adj 1 not sensible in behaviour. 2 not fully developed. **immaturity** n[U].

immeasurable /ɪˈmeʒərəbl/ adj too large to be measured.

immediate /ɪˈmiːdɪət/ adj 1 happening or done at once: take ~ action. 2 nearest: in the ~ future.

immediately /ɪˈmiːdɪətlɪ/ adv 1 at once; without delay. 2 being nearest; directly: the years ~ after the war. **immediately** conj (esp Brit) as soon as: I recognized her ~ I saw her.

immense /ɪˈmens/ adj very large. **immensely** adv very much: I enjoyed the film ~ly. **immensity** n[U].

immerse /ɪˈmɜːs/ v[T] 1 (in/) put (sth) under the surface of a liquid. 2 ~ oneself (in) involve oneself deeply in sth: ~ oneself in one's work ○ ~d in thought. **immersion** /ɪˈmɜːʃn; US -ʒn/ n[U]. **im'mersion heater** n[C] electric heater in a water tank.

immigrant /ˈɪmɪɡrənt/ n[C] person who comes to live in another country. **immigration** /ˌɪmɪˈɡreɪʃn/ n[U] moving of people from one country to come to live in another country.

imminent /ˈɪmɪnənt/ adj likely to happen very soon. **imminently** adv.

immobile /ɪˈməʊbaɪl; US -bl/ adj unable to move; not moving. **immobility** /ˌɪməˈbɪlətɪ/ n[U]. **immobilize** /ɪˈməʊbəlaɪz/ v[T] make immobile.

immoral /ɪˈmɒrəl; US ɪˈmɔːrəl/ adj 1 not moral; wrong. 2 against usual standards of sexual behaviour. **immorality** /ˌɪməˈrælətɪ/ n[U].

immortal /ɪˈmɔːtl/ adj 1 living for ever. 2 that will be remembered for ever. **immortal** n[C] immortal being. **immortality** /ˌɪmɔːˈtælətɪ/ n[U]. **immortalize** /-təlaɪz/ v[T] give endless life or fame to: ~ized in a novel.

immune /ɪˈmjuːn/ adj 1 (to/ against/) that cannot be harmed by a disease: ~ to smallpox. 2 (to/) not affected by sth: ~ to criticism. 3 (from/) protected from sth: ~

from tax. **immunity** *n* [U]. **immunize** /ˈɪmjʊnaɪz/ *v* [T] (*against*)// make (sb) immune to a disease. **immunization** /ˌɪmjʊnaɪˈzeɪʃn; *US* -nɪˈz-/ *n* [U, C].

imp /ɪmp/ *n* [C] 1 little devil. 2 mischievous child.

impact /ˈɪmpækt/ *n* 1 [U] (force of the) hitting of one object against another: *The bomb exploded on ~*, ie when it hit sth. 2 [C, usu sing] (*on*)// strong effect on sb/sth: *the ~ of computers on industry.* **impact** /ɪmˈpækt/ *v* [T] press (sth) firmly in sth.

impair /ɪmˈpeə(r)/ *v* [T] damage; weaken: *Loud noise can ~ your hearing.*

impale /ɪmˈpeɪl/ *v* [T] (*on*)// pierce (sth) with a sharp-pointed object: *~d on a spear.*

impart /ɪmˈpɑːt/ *v* [T] (*fml*) give (information, etc).

impartial /ɪmˈpɑːʃl/ *adj* just; fair: *A judge must be ~.* **impartiality** /ˌɪmˌpɑːʃɪˈælətɪ/ *n* [U].

impassable /ɪmˈpɑːsəbl; *US* -ˈpæs-/ *adj* (of a road, etc) impossible to travel on.

impassioned /ɪmˈpæʃnd/ *adj* showing strong deep feeling: *an ~ appeal.*

impassive /ɪmˈpæsɪv/ *adj* showing no sign of feeling. **impassively** *adv.*

impatient /ɪmˈpeɪʃnt/ *adj* 1 showing a lack of patience. 2 very eager: *~ to leave school.* **impatience** /-ʃns/ *n* [U]. **impatiently** *adv.*

impeccable /ɪmˈpekəbl/ *adj* faultless. **impeccably** *adv.*

impede /ɪmˈpiːd/ *v* [T] get in the way of; hinder.

impediment /ɪmˈpedɪmənt/ *n* [C] 1 something that makes progress difficult. 2 physical defect, esp in speech.

impending /ɪmˈpendɪŋ/ *adj* about to happen: *~ disaster.*

impenetrable /ɪmˈpenɪtrəbl/ *adj* 1 that cannot be passed through. 2 impossible to understand.

imperative /ɪmˈperətɪv/ *adj* very urgent or important. **imperative** *n* [C] (*grammar*) verb form that expresses a command, eg *Go!* **imperatively** *adv.*

imperfect /ɪmˈpɜːfɪkt/ *adj* not perfect. **imperfect in the imperfect** [sing] (*grammar*) (verb in the) tense that shows incomplete action in the past, eg *was speaking.* **imperfection** /ˌɪmpəˈfekʃn/ *n* 1 [U] being imperfect. 2 [C] fault. **imperfectly** *adv.*

imperial /ɪmˈpɪərɪəl/ *adj* of an empire or its ruler. **imperialism**

n [U] (belief in a) political system of gaining economic or political control over other countries. **imperialist** *n* [C], *adj.* **imperially** *adv.*

impersonal /ɪmˈpɜːsənl/ *adj* 1 not influenced by human feelings: *a large ~ organization.* 2 not referring to any particular person. **impersonally** /-nəlɪ/ *adv.*

impersonate /ɪmˈpɜːsəneɪt/ *v* [T] pretend to be (another person). **impersonation** /ɪmˌpɜːsəˈneɪʃn/ *n* [C, U].

impertinent /ɪmˈpɜːtɪnənt/ *adj* not showing proper respect. **impertinence** /-nəns/ *n* [U, sing]. **impertinently** *adv.*

impervious /ɪmˈpɜːvɪəs/ *adj* (*to*)// 1 not allowing water, etc to pass through. 2 (*fig*) not influenced by sth: *~ to criticism.*

impetuous /ɪmˈpetʃʊəs/ *adj* acting quickly and without thinking.

impetus /ˈɪmpɪtəs/ *n* 1 [U, sing] something that encourages a process to develop more quickly: *give a fresh ~ to trade.* 2 [U] force with which sth moves.

impinge /ɪmˈpɪndʒ/ *v* [I] *on*// (*fml*) have an effect on sth.

implacable /ɪmˈplækəbl/ *adj* that cannot be changed or satisfied.

implant /ɪmˈplɑːnt; *US* -ˈplænt/ *v* [T] (*in/into*)// fix or put deeply into sb/sth: *~ ideas in sb's mind.*

implement[1] /ˈɪmplɪment/ *v* [T] carry out (a plan, idea, etc). **implementation** /ˌɪmplɪmenˈteɪʃn/ *n* [U].

implement[2] /ˈɪmplɪmənt/ *n* [C] tool or instrument.

implicate /ˈɪmplɪkeɪt/ *v* [T] (*in*)// show that (sb) is involved in a crime, etc.

implication /ˌɪmplɪˈkeɪʃn/ *n* 1 [C, U] something suggested or implied. 2 [U] act of implicating, esp in a crime.

implicit /ɪmˈplɪsɪt/ *adj* 1 implied, but not expressed directly. 2 unquestioning; complete: *~ trust.* **implicitly** *adv.*

implore /ɪmˈplɔː(r)/ *v* [T] ask or beg strongly: *They ~d her to stay.* **imploringly** *adv.*

imply /ɪmˈplaɪ/ *v* (*pt, pp* **-ied**) [T] 1 suggest that (sth) is true without actually saying it: *Are you ~ing that I stole your watch?* 2 suggest (sth) as a necessary result.

impolite /ˌɪmpəˈlaɪt/ *adj* not polite; rude. **impolitely** *adv.* **impoliteness** *n* [U].

import /ɪmˈpɔːt/ *v* [T] bring in (goods) from another country. **import** /ˈɪmpɔːt/ *n* 1 [U] (business

of) importing. **2** [C] something imported. **3** [U] (*fml*) importance. **importation** /,impɔ:'teiʃn/ *n* [U, C].
importer *n* [C] person, company, etc that imports goods.

important /im'pɔ:tnt/ *adj* **1** having a great effect or value: *an ~ decision.* **2** (of a person) having great influence or authority. **importance** /-tns/ *n* [U]. **importantly** *adv*.

impose /im'pəuz/ *v* **1** [T] (*on*)// put (a tax, penalty, etc) on sb/sth. **2** [T] (*on*)// try to make sb accept (an opinion, etc). **3** (phr v) **impose on sb** take advantage of sb unfairly. **imposing** *adj* large and impressive. **imposition** /,impə-'ziʃn/ *n* [U, C].

impossible /im'pɒsəbl/ *adj* **1** not possible. **2** very difficult to bear: *an ~ situation.* **impossibility** /im,pɒsə'biləti/ *n* [U, C]. **impossibly** *adv*.

impostor /im'pɒstə(r)/ *n* [C] person who pretends to be sb else, esp to deceive others.

impotent /'impətənt/ *adj* **1** powerless or helpless. **2** (of a man) unable to have sexual intercourse. **impotence** /-əns/ *n* [U].

impound /im'paund/ *v* [T] take possession of (sth) by law.

impoverish /im'pɒvəriʃ/ *v* [T] make poor.

impracticable /im'præktikəbl/ *adj* impossible to put into practice.

impractical /im'præktikl/ *adj* not sensible, useful or realistic.

imprecise /,impri'sais/ *adj* not exact or accurate.

impregnable /im'pregnəbl/ *adj* that cannot be entered by attack: *an ~ fort.*

impregnate /'impregneit; *US* im'preg-/ *v* [T] cause (one substance) to be filled in every part with another substance: *cloth ~d with perfume.*

impresario /,impri'sɑ:riəu/ *n* [C] (*pl ~s*) manager of a theatre or music company.

impress /im'pres/ *v* [T] **1** cause (sb) to feel admiration: *Her honesty ~ed me.* **2** *on*// fix (sth) in sb's mind: *~ on him the importance of hard work.* **3** press (sth) hard into a soft surface, leaving a mark.

impression /im'preʃn/ *n* [C] **1** lasting effect on sb's mind or feelings: *create a good ~.* **2** (unclear) idea or feeling: *My general ~ was that she seemed a nice woman.* **3** funny imitation of sb's behaviour or way of talking. **4** mark left by pressing. **5** (idm) **be under the impression that...** have the (usu

wrong) idea that... **impressionable** /-ʃənəbl/ *adj* easily influenced. **impressionism** /-ʃənizəm/ *n* [U] method of painting that gives a general impression(2) of sth by using the effects of colour and light.

impressive /im'presiv/ *adj* causing admiration: *an ~ building.* **impressively** *adv*.

imprint /im'print/ *v* [T] press (sth) onto a surface: (*fig*) *details ~ed on his memory.* **imprint** /'imprint/ *n* **1** mark made by pressing. **2** (*fig*) lasting effect.

imprison /im'prizn/ *v* [T] put in prison. **imprisonment** *n* [U].

improbable /im'prɒbəbl/ *adj* not likely to be true or to happen. **improbability** /im,prɒbə'biləti/ *n* [C, U] (*pl -ies*). **improbably** *adv*.

impromptu /im'prɒmptju:; *US* -tu:/ *adj, adv* (done) without preparation: *an ~ speech.*

improper /im'prɒpə(r)/ *adj* **1** wrong or incorrect: *~ use of a word/drug.* **2** not suitable for the purpose, situation, etc: *~ behaviour/dress.* **3** indecent: *make ~ suggestions.* **improperly** *adv*.

improve /im'pru:v/ *v* [I, T] become or make better. **improvement** *n* **1** [C, U] action or process of improving. **2** [C] change that improves sth: *home ~ments.*

improvise /'imprəvaiz/ *v* [I, T] **1** make (sth) from whatever is available, without preparation. **2** compose (music) or speak or act without preparation. **improvisation** /,imprəvai'zeiʃn/ *n* [U, C].

impudent /'impjudənt/ *adj* very rude and disrespectful. **impudence** /-əns/ *n* [U]. **impudently** *adv*.

impulse /'impʌls/ *n* **1** [C, U] sudden desire to do sth. **2** [C] sudden force: *an electrical ~.* **3** (idm) **on impulse** suddenly and without thought.

impulsive /im'pʌlsiv/ *adj* marked by sudden action without careful thought. **impulsively** *adv*. **impulsiveness** *n* [U].

impunity /im'pju:nəti/ *n* (idm) **with impunity** with freedom from punishment.

impure /im'pjuə(r)/ *adj* **1** mixed with sth else; not clean. **2** (*dated*) morally wrong. **impurity** *n* [C] (*pl -ies*).

in¹ /in/ *adv* **1** (to a position) within a particular area or space: *He opened the bedroom door and went in.* **2** at home or at a place of work: *Nobody was in when we called.* **3** (of trains, buses, etc) at the station. **4** (of the tide) at or towards its highest point on land. **5** (of letters) received: *Competition entries should be in by 31 May.* **6** fashionable; popular: *Miniskirts are in again.* **7** elected to office: *Labour came in after the war.* **8** (*sport*) (a) batting. (b) (of a ball) inside the line. **9** (idm) **be in for sth** (*infml*) be about to experience (esp sth unpleasant). **be/get in on sth** (*infml*) take part in. **be (well) 'in with sb** (*infml*) be (very) friendly with sb. **have (got) it 'in for sb** (*infml*) want to hurt or harm sb. **in-** *adj* **1** (*infml*) popular and fashionable: *the in-thing* ○ *the in-place.* **2** shared by a small group: *an in-joke.*

in² /ɪn/ *prep* **1** (showing place) within (sth); enclosed by (sth): *Rome is in Italy.* ○ *play in the street* ○ *lying in bed* ○ *a pen in his pocket.* **2** (showing movement): *Throw it in the fire.* **3** during (a period of time): *in June.* **4** after (a maximum length of time): *Lunch will be ready in an hour.* **5** forming the whole or part of (sth): *seven days in a week.* **6** (showing a ratio): *a slope of 1 in 5,* ie 20%. **7** wearing: *the woman in white.* **8** (showing surroundings): *go out in the cold.* **9** (showing a condition): *in a mess* ○ *in love.* **10** (showing form or arrangement): *a story in three parts.* **11** (showing the medium, means, etc): *speak in English* ○ *write in ink.* **12** with reference to: *lacking in courage* ○ *3 metres in length.* **13** (showing sb's occupation): *a career in journalism.* **14** (idm) **in that** because: *The chemical is dangerous in that it can kill.*

in³ /ɪn/ *n* (idm) **the ins and outs** (of sth) the details of (an activity, problem, etc).

inability /ˌɪnəˈbɪlətɪ/ *n* [U] (*to*)‖ lack of skill or power.

inaccessible /ˌɪnækˈsesəbl/ *adj* impossible to reach.

inaccurate /ɪnˈækjərət/ *adj* not correct. **inaccuracy** /-ərəsɪ/ *n* [U, C] (*pl* -ies). **inaccurately** *adv*.

inadequate /ɪnˈædɪkwət/ *adj* not (good) enough. **inadequately** *adv*.

inadmissible /ˌɪnədˈmɪsəbl/ *adj* that cannot be allowed in a law-court: ~ *evidence.*

inadvertent /ˌɪnədˈvɜːtənt/ *adj* done without thinking or accidentally. **inadvertently** *adv*.

inalienable /ɪnˈeɪlɪənəbl/ *adj* (*fml*) (of rights, etc) that cannot be taken away.

inane /ɪˈneɪn/ *adj* silly. **inanely** *adv*.

inanimate /ɪnˈænɪmət/ *adj* not living: *A rock is an ~ object.*

inapplicable /ɪnˈæplɪkəbl, also ˌɪnəˈplɪkəbl/ *adj* (*to*)‖ not applicable to sth.

inappropriate /ˌɪnəˈprəʊprɪət/ *adj* (*to/for*)‖ not suitable for sb/ sth. **inappropriately** *adv*.

inapt /ɪnˈæpt/ *adj* not suitable or relevant: ~ *remarks.*

inarticulate /ˌɪnɑːˈtɪkjʊlət/ *adj* **1** unable to express oneself clearly. **2** (of speech) not clear.

inasmuch as /ˌɪnəzˈmʌtʃ əz/ *conj* (*fml*) to the extent that; since.

inaudible /ɪnˈɔːdəbl/ *adj* not loud enough to be heard.

inaugural /ɪˈnɔːgjʊrəl/ *adj* of or for an inauguration: ~ *speech.*

inaugurate /ɪˈnɔːgjʊreɪt/ *v* [T] **1** introduce (a new official, etc) at a special ceremony. **2** start or open (an organization, exhibition, etc) with a special ceremony. **3** be the beginning of. **inauguration** /ɪˌnɔːgjʊˈreɪʃn/ *n* [C, U].

inborn /ˌɪnˈbɔːn/ *adj* (of a quality) existing in a person from birth.

inbred /ˌɪnˈbred/ *adj* **1** inborn. **2** having ancestors closely related to one another. **inbreeding** /ˈɪnbriːdɪŋ/ *n* [U] breeding among closely related people or animals.

in-built /ˌɪnˈbɪlt/ *adj* ⇨ BUILT-IN (BUILD).

Inc /ɪŋk/ *abbr* (*US*) Incorporated.

incalculable /ɪnˈkælkjʊləbl/ *adj* too great to be calculated.

incapable /ɪnˈkeɪpəbl/ *adj* (*of*)‖ not able: ~ *of telling a lie.*

incapacitate /ˌɪnkəˈpæsɪteɪt/ *v* [T] make (sb) unable to do sth. **incapacity** /-sətɪ/ *n* [U] inability.

incarcerate /ɪnˈkɑːsəreɪt/ *v* [T] (*fml*) put in prison. **incarceration** /ɪnˌkɑːsəˈreɪʃn/ *n* [U].

incarnation /ˌɪnkɑːˈneɪʃn/ *n* **1** [C] person that shows a particular quality. **2** [C, U] (instance of) being alive in human form.

incendiary /ɪnˈsendɪərɪ; *US* -dɪerɪ/ *adj* **1** causing fires: *an ~ bomb.* **2** causing violence: *an ~ speech.* **incendiary** *n* [C] (*pl* -ies) incendiary bomb.

incense¹ /ˈɪnsens/ *n* [U] substance that produces a pleasant smell when burnt.

incense² /ɪnˈsens/ *v* [T] make (sb) very angry.

incentive /ɪnˈsentɪv/ *n* [C, U] (*to*)‖ something that encourages sb to do sth.

incessant /ɪnˈsesnt/ *adj* not stopping; continual: *his ~ complaints.* **incessantly** *adv*.

incest /ˈɪnsest/ *n* [U] sexual intercourse between close relatives. **in-cestuous** /ɪnˈsestjʊəs; *US* -tʃʊəs/ *adj*.

inch /ɪntʃ/ *n* [C] **1** measure of length; one twelfth of a foot (2.54 centimetres). **2** small amount: *He escaped death by an* ~. **3** (idm) **every inch** all; completely. **within an inch of sth** very close to sth. **inch** *v* (phr v) **inch (sth) forward, past,** etc move (sth) slowly and carefully in the direction that is mentioned.

incidence /ˈɪnsɪdəns/ *n* [sing] number of times or way in which sth happens: *a high* ~ *of crime*.

incident /ˈɪnsɪdənt/ *n* [C] **1** event, esp of little importance. **2** event that includes or is likely to cause violence: *border* ~ *s*.

incidental /ˌɪnsɪˈdentl/ *adj* **1** small and unimportant: ~ *expenses*. **2** accompanying, but not an important part of sth: ~ *music for a film*. **incidentally** /-tlɪ/ *adv* (used for introducing sth extra that the speaker has just thought of).

incinerate /ɪnˈsɪnəreɪt/ *v* [T] burn (sth) completely. **incineration** /ɪnˌsɪnəˈreɪʃn/ *n* [U]. **incinerator** *n* [C] furnace, etc for burning rubbish.

incipient /ɪnˈsɪpiənt/ *adj* (*fml*) just beginning.

incision /ɪnˈsɪʒn/ *n* **1** [C] cuts, eg made by a surgeon. **2** [U] the act of cutting.

incisive /ɪnˈsaɪsɪv/ *adj* clear and exact; direct: ~ *questions*. **incisively** *adv*.

incisor /ɪnˈsaɪzə(r)/ *n* [C] any one of the front cutting teeth.

incite /ɪnˈsaɪt/ *v* [T] **1** encourage: ~ *workers to riot*. **2** create or cause: ~ *violence*. **incitement** *n* [U, C].

inclination /ˌɪnklɪˈneɪʃn/ *n* **1** [C, U] feeling that makes sb want to do sth; desire: *I have no* ~ *to leave*. **2** [C] tendency. **3** [U] angle of a slope.

incline[1] /ɪnˈklaɪm/ *v* **1** [I] *towards* || lean or slope towards. **2** [T] bend (the head, etc) forward. **3** [T] *towards* || (*fml*) persuade (sb) to do sth; influence. **4** [I] *to/towards* || (*fml*) have a tendency towards sth: *He* ~ *s to laziness*. **inclined** *adj* (*to*) || **1** wanting to behave in a particular way. **2** having a tendency to be/do sth: *She's* ~ *d to be depressed*.

incline[2] /ˈɪnklaɪm/ *n* [C] slope.

include /ɪnˈkluːd/ *v* [T] **1** have (sth) as part of a whole: *Prices* ~ *delivery*. **2** make (sb/sth) part of a larger group: ~ *Chris in the team*.

inclusion /ɪnˈkluːʒn/ *n* [U]. **in-clusive** /ɪnˈkluːsɪv/ *adj* including everything.

incognito /ˌɪnkɒgˈniːtəʊ; *US* ɪnˈkɒgnətəʊ/ *adj, adv* not using one's real name; in disguise: *travel* ~.

incoherent /ˌɪnkəʊˈhɪərənt/ *adj* not clear; not expressed clearly. **incoherence** /-əns/ *n* [U]. **incoherently** *adv*.

income /ˈɪnkʌm/ *n* [C, U] money received during a month, year, etc, esp as payment for work. **'income tax** *n* [U] tax on one's income.

incoming /ˈɪnkʌmɪŋ/ *adj* **1** coming in: ~ *mail*. **2** recently elected or appointed: *the* ~ *president*.

incomparable /ɪnˈkɒmprəbl/ *adj* too good, great, etc to have an equal.

incompatible /ˌɪnkəmˈpætəbl/ *adj* not able or suitable to exist together: *Smoking is* ~ *with good health*. **incompatibility** /ˌɪnkəmˌpætəˈbɪlətɪ/ *n* [U].

incompetent /ɪnˈkɒmpɪtənt/ *adj* not skilful enough to do sth. **incompetence** /-əns/ *n* [U].

incomplete /ˌɪnkəmˈpliːt/ *adj* not complete. **incompletely** *adv*.

incomprehensible /ɪnˌkɒmprɪˈhensəbl/ *adj* impossible to understand. **incomprehension** /-ˈhenʃn/ *n* [U] failure to understand sth.

inconceivable /ˌɪnkənˈsiːvəbl/ *adj* **1** (*infml*) very difficult to believe. **2** impossible to imagine.

inconclusive /ˌɪnkənˈkluːsɪv/ *adj* not leading to a definite decision or result: ~ *evidence*.

incongruous /ɪnˈkɒŋgrʊəs/ *adj* out of place: *Modern buildings look* ~ *in an old village*. **incongruity** /ˌɪnkɒŋˈgruːətɪ/ *n* [C, U] (*pl* **-ies**).

inconsiderate /ˌɪnkənˈsɪdərət/ *adj* not caring about the feelings of other people. **inconsiderately** *adv*.

inconsistent /ˌɪnkənˈsɪstənt/ *adj* (*with*) || not in harmony with sth; likely to change. **inconsistency** /-ənsɪ/ *n* [U, C] (*pl* **-ies**). **inconsistently** *adv*.

inconspicuous /ˌɪnkənˈspɪkjʊəs/ *adj* not very noticeable or obvious. **inconspicuously** *adv*.

incontinent /ɪnˈkɒntɪnənt/ *adj* unable to control one's bladder or bowels. **incontinence** /-əns/ *n* [U].

incontrovertible /ˌɪnkɒntrəˈvɜːtəbl/ *adj* so clear that it cannot be denied.

inconvenience /ˌɪnkənˈviːnɪəns/

n [C, U] (cause of) trouble, difficulty or discomfort. **inconvenience** *v* [T] cause inconvenience to. **inconvenient** /-ənt/ *adj* causing inconvenience. **inconveniently** *adv*.

incorporate /ɪnˈkɔːpəreɪt/ *v* [T] make (sth) part of a whole; include: ~ *your ideas in the new plan.* **incorporated** *adj* (US) formed into a legal organization(1). **incorporation** /ɪnˌkɔːpəˈreɪʃn/ *n* [U].

incorrect /ˌɪnkəˈrekt/ *adj* not correct; wrong. **incorrectly** *adv*. **incorrectness** *n* [U].

incorrigible /ɪnˈkɒrɪdʒəbl; US -ˈkɔːr-/ *adj* (of a person or bad behaviour) that cannot be corrected or improved.

increase[1] /ɪnˈkriːs/ *v* [I, T] become or make greater in number, quantity, etc. **increasingly** *adv* more and more: *increasingly difficult.*

increase[2] /ˈɪnkriːs/ *n* [C, U] amount by which sth increases.

incredible /ɪnˈkredəbl/ *adj* 1 impossible to believe. 2 (*infml*) wonderful; amazing. **incredibly** *adv*.

incredulous /ɪnˈkredjʊləs; US -dʒuːl-/ *adj* not believing; showing disbelief. **incredulity** /ˌɪnkrɪˈdjuːlətɪ; US -ˈduː-/ *n* [U]. **incredulously** *adv*.

increment /ˈɪnkrəmənt/ *n* [C] increase in money or value.

incriminate /ɪnˈkrɪmɪneɪt/ *v* [T] make (sb) appear to be guilty of wrongdoing.

incubate /ˈɪnkjʊbeɪt/ *v* [I, T] keep (eggs) warm until they hatch. **incubation** /ˌɪnkjʊˈbeɪʃn/ *n* 1 [U] hatching of eggs. 2 [C] (also **incubation period**) period between infection and the first appearance of a disease. **incubator** *n* [C] 1 apparatus for hatching eggs by artificial warmth. 2 apparatus for keeping alive small weak, esp premature, babies.

incumbent /ɪnˈkʌmbənt/ *adj* *on*|| (*fml*) necessary as a part of sb's duty. **incumbent** *n* [C] person holding an official position.

incur /ɪnˈkɜː(r)/ *v* (-rr-) [T] cause oneself to suffer (esp sth bad): ~ *large debts.*

incurable /ɪnˈkjʊərəbl/ *adj* impossible to cure. **incurable** *n* [C] person with an incurable disease. **incurably** *adv*.

incursion /ɪnˈkɜːʃn; US -ʒn/ *n* [C] (*fml*) sudden attack; invasion.

indebted /ɪnˈdetɪd/ *adj* very grateful: ~ *to him for his help.*

indecent /ɪnˈdiːsnt/ *adj* 1 likely to shock people; obscene. 2 unsuit-

able; not right. **indecency** /-nsɪ/ *n* [U]. **indecently** *adv*.

indecision /ˌɪndɪˈsɪʒn/ *n* [U] state of being unable to decide.

indecisive /ˌɪndɪˈsaɪsɪv/ *adj* 1 unable to make decisions. 2 not giving a certain result. **indecisively** *adv*.

indeed /ɪnˈdiːd/ *adv* 1 really; certainly: *'Did he complain?' 'I~ he did.'* 2 (used after *very* for making a statement stronger): *Thank you very much* ~. 3 (used for showing surprise, interest, etc): *'She thinks she got the job.' 'Does she ~!'*

indefensible /ˌɪndɪˈfensəbl/ *adj* impossible to defend: ~ *rudeness.*

indefinable /ˌɪndɪˈfaɪnəbl/ *adj* impossible to define or put in words.

indefinite /ɪnˈdefɪnət/ *adj* 1 not clear; vague. 2 having no fixed limit: *an* ~ *period of time.* **indefinite 'article** *n* [C] *a* or *an*. **indefinitely** *adv*: *The meeting was postponed* ~.

indelible /ɪnˈdeləbl/ *adj* impossible to rub out. **indelibly** *adv*.

indelicate /ɪnˈdelɪkət/ *adj* (*fml* often *euph*) rude or embarrassing.

indemnify /ɪnˈdemnɪfaɪ/ *v* (*pt, pp* -**ied**) [T] (promise to) pay (sb) for loss, damage, etc.

indemnity /ɪnˈdemnətɪ/ *n* (*pl* -**ies**) 1 [U] protection against damage or loss. 2 [C] payment for damage or loss.

indent /ɪnˈdent/ *v* [I, T] start (a line of writing) further in from the margin than the other lines. **indentation** /ˌɪndenˈteɪʃn/ *n* 1 [C, U] (act of) indenting. 2 [C] mark cut into the edge of sth: *the* ~ *ations of the coastline.*

independent /ˌɪndɪˈpendənt/ *adj* 1 self-governing: *an* ~ *nation.* 2 (*of*)| not needing money, etc from other people to live. 3 able to work alone; self-confident. **independent** *n* [C] politician who does not belong to a political party. **independence** /-əns/ *n* [U]: *independence from one's parents.* **independently** *adv*.

indescribable /ˌɪndɪˈskraɪbəbl/ *adj* impossible to describe. **indescribably** *adv*.

indestructible /ˌɪndɪˈstrʌktəbl/ *adj* impossible to destroy.

index /ˈɪndeks/ *n* [C] (*pl* ~**es** in sense 2 ~**es** or **indices** /ˈɪndɪsiːz/) 1 (**a**) list of names, subjects, etc in alphabetical order at the end of a book. (**b**) set of cards containing information, usu in alphabetical order (eg in a library): *a 'card* ~. 2 number that compares the level of prices, etc with that of a former time: *the cost-of-living ~.* **index** *v* [T] make an index for; enter in an index. '**index finger** *n* [C] finger next to one's thumb.

indicate /'ɪndɪkeɪt/ *v* 1 [T] show, esp by pointing; be a sign of. 2 [I, T] signal that one's vehicle is about to change direction. **indication** /,ɪndɪ'keɪʃn/ *n* 1 [U] indicating. 2 [C, U] remark, sign, etc that indicates sth. **indicative** /ɪn'dɪkətɪv/ *adj p*// showing or suggesting sth. **indicator** *n* [C] 1 something that gives information, eg a pointer on a machine. 2 flashing light on a vehicle showing that it is about to change direction.

indict /ɪn'daɪt/ *v* [T] (*for*)// (*law*) accuse (sb) officially of a crime: *~ed for murder.* **indictable** *adj* for which one can be indicted: *an ~able offence.* **indictment** *n* [C, U].

indifferent /ɪn'dɪfrənt/ *adj* 1 (*to*)// not interested in sth. 2 not very good: *an ~ meal.* **indifference** /-frəns/ *n* [U]. **indifferently** *adv*.

indigenous /ɪn'dɪdʒɪnəs/ *adj* (*to*)// belonging naturally to a place; native: *Kangaroos are ~ to Australia.*

indigestion /,ɪndɪ'dʒestʃən/ *n* [U] (pain from) difficulty in digesting food.

indignant /ɪn'dɪgnənt/ *adj* angry, esp at injustice. **indignantly** *adv*. **indignation** /,ɪndɪg'neɪʃn/ *n* [U].

indignity /ɪn'dɪgnɪtɪ/ *n* [C, U] (*pl* -ies) treatment causing shame or loss of respect.

indirect /,ɪndɪ'rekt, -daɪr-/ *adj* 1 not going in a straight line: *an ~ route.* 2 not mentioning sth directly: *an ~ answer.* 3 not immediate; secondary: *an ~ cause.* **indirectly** *adv*. ,**indirect 'object** *n* [C] (*grammar*) person or thing to whom or to which an action is done: *In 'Give him the book', 'him' is the ~ object.* ,**indirect 'speech** *n* [U] (*grammar*) reporting of what sb has said, without using his/her actual words: *In ~ speech, 'He said, "I will come."' becomes 'He said he would come.'* '**indirect tax** *n* [C] tax that is included in the price of certain goods.

indiscreet /,ɪndɪ'skri:t/ *adj* not cautious or careful. **indiscreetly** *adv*. **indiscretion** /,ɪndɪ'skreʃn/ *n* 1 [U] indiscreet behaviour. 2 [C] indiscreet remark or act.

indiscriminate /,ɪndɪ'skrɪmɪnət/ *adj* acting or done without careful thought: *~ praise.* **in-**

discriminately *adv*.

indispensable /,ɪndɪ'spensəbl/ *adj* absolutely necessary.

indisposed /,ɪndɪ'spəʊzd/ *adj* (*fml*) 1 ill. 2 unwilling: *~ to help.*

indisputable /,ɪndɪ'spju:təbl/ *adj* impossible to deny or question. **indisputably** *adv*.

indistinguishable /,ɪndɪ'stɪŋgwɪʃəbl/ *adj* (*from*)// impossible to identify as different: *~ from her sister.*

individual /,ɪndɪ'vɪdʒʊəl/ *adj* 1 single; separate. 2 of or for one person. **individual** *n* [C] any one human being. **individuality** /,ɪndɪ,vɪdʒʊ'æləti/ *n* [U] all the characteristics that make a person different from others. **individually** *adv*.

indoctrinate /ɪn'dɒktrɪneɪt/ *v* [T] (*with*)// (usu *derog*) fill (the mind of) a person with fixed beliefs or ideas. **indoctrination** /ɪn,dɒktrɪ'neɪʃn/ *n* [U].

indolent /'ɪndələnt/ *adj* (*fml*) lazy. **indolence** /-ləns/ *n* [U].

indoor /'ɪndɔ:(r)/ *adj* done or situated inside a building. **indoors** /,ɪn'dɔ:z/ *adv* in or into a building.

induce /ɪn'dju:s/ *v* [T] 1 persuade or influence. 2 cause. 3 cause (a woman) to begin childbirth by giving her drugs. **inducement** *n* [C, U] something, eg money, that encourages sb to do sth: *a pay rise as an ~ment to work harder.*

induction /ɪn'dʌkʃn/ *n* 1 [U, C] act of introducing sb to a new job. 2 [U] method of reasoning in which general laws are produced from particular facts. 3 [U] inducing of a pregnant woman.

indulge /ɪn'dʌldʒ/ *v* 1 [I] (*in*)// allow oneself to enjoy sth. 2 [T] satisfy (a desire). 3 [T] allow (sb) to have whatever he/she likes or wants. **indulgence** *n* 1 [C] something pleasant in which sb indulges. 2 [U] indulging. **indulgent** *adj* tending to indulge(3).

industrial /ɪn'dʌstrɪəl/ *adj* of industry. in,**dustrial 'action** *n* [U] refusing to work normally; striking. **industrialism** *n* [U] system in which large industries have an important part. **industrialist** *n* [C] owner of a large industrial company. **industrialize** *v* [I, T] develop (a country) with many industries. **industrially** *adv*.

industrious /ɪn'dʌstrɪəs/ *adj* hard-working; diligent.

industry /'ɪndəstri/ *n* (*pl* -ies) 1 [C, U] (branch of) manufacture or production of goods: *the steel ~.* 2

[U] (*fml*) quality of being hard-working.

inebriated /ɪˈniːbrɪeɪtɪd/ *adj* (*fml* or *joc*) drunk.

inedible /ɪnˈedəbl/ *adj* (*fml*) not suitable to be eaten.

ineffective /ˌɪnɪˈfektɪv/ *adj* not producing the results that one wants. **ineffectively** *adv*. **ineffectiveness** *n* [U].

ineffectual /ˌɪnɪˈfektʃuəl/ *adj* not producing the results that one wants: *an ~ attempt*. **ineffectually** *adv*.

inefficient /ˌɪnɪˈfɪʃnt/ *adj* 1 (of a person) wasting time, energy, etc. 2 (of a machine or process) not producing good results. **inefficiency** /-nsɪ/ *n* [U]. **inefficiently** *adv*.

ineligible /ɪnˈelɪdʒəbl/ *adj* (*for*)|| not having the suitable or necessary qualifications: *~ for the job*.

inept /ɪˈnept/ *adj* 1 (*at*) completely unskilful. 2 said or done at the wrong time. **ineptitude** /ɪˈneptɪtjuːd; US -tuːd/ *n* [U].

inequality /ˌɪnɪˈkwɒlətɪ/ *n* [C, U] (*pl* -ies) lack of equality; unfairness.

inert /ɪˈnɜːt/ *adj* 1 without power to move or act. 2 slow in mind or body.

inertia /ɪˈnɜːʃə/ *n* [U] 1 feeling of laziness. 2 (*physics*) tendency of an object to remain still or to continue moving unless another force acts on it.

inescapable /ˌɪnɪˈskeɪpəbl/ *adj* impossible to avoid.

inevitable /ɪnˈevɪtəbl/ *adj* 1 impossible to avoid. 2 (*infml*) familiar and expected: *a tourist with his ~ camera*. **inevitability** /ˌɪnˌevɪtəˈbɪlətɪ/ *n* [U]. **inevitably** *adv*.

inexact /ˌɪnɪɡˈzækt/ *adj* not exact or precise.

inexcusable /ˌɪnɪkˈskjuːzəbl/ *adj* too bad to be excused: *~ rudeness*.

inexpensive /ˌɪnɪkˈspensɪv/ *adj* not expensive.

inexperience /ˌɪnɪkˈspɪərɪəns/ *n* [U] (*in*)|| lack of experience. **inexperienced** *adj*.

inexplicable /ˌɪnɪkˈsplɪkəbl/ *adj* impossible to explain. **inexplicably** *adv*.

inextricable /ˌɪnɪkˈstrɪkəbl, ɪnˈekstrɪkəbl/ *adj* impossible to escape from or to separate.

infallible /ɪnˈfæləbl/ *adj* 1 never wrong: *Nobody is ~.* 2 never failing: *an ~ method.* **infallibility** /ɪnˌfæləˈbɪlətɪ/ *n* [U].

infamous /ˈɪnfəməs/ *adj* well-known as being wicked. **infamy** /ˈɪnfəmɪ/ *n* [C, U] (*pl* -ies) (in-stance of) infamous behaviour.

infancy /ˈɪnfənsɪ/ *n* [U] 1 state or period of being a young child. 2 (*fig*) early stage of development: *The project is still in its ~.*

infant /ˈɪnfənt/ *n* [C] young child.

infantile /ˈɪnfəntaɪl/ *adj* of an infant; childish: *~ behaviour.*

infantry /ˈɪnfəntrɪ/ *n* [U] (with sing or pl v) soldiers who fight on foot.

infatuated /ɪnˈfætʃueɪtɪd/ *adj* (*with*)|| filled with a foolish love for sb. **infatuation** /ɪnˌfætʃuˈeɪʃn/ *n* [U, C].

infect /ɪnˈfekt/ *v* [T] (*with*)|| 1 give a disease to (sb/sth). 2 (*fig*) influence the feelings or ideas of. **infection** /ɪnˈfekʃn/ *n* 1 [C] infectious disease. 2 [U] infecting: *danger of ~ion.* **infectious** /ɪnˈfekʃəs/ *adj* 1 (of a disease) caused by bacteria, etc that are passed from one person to another. 2 (*fig*) quickly influencing others: *~ious laughter.*

infer /ɪnˈfɜː(r)/ *v* (-rr-) [T] (*from*)|| reach (an opinion) from facts: *What can be ~red from the election results?* **inference** /ˈɪnfərəns/ *n* [C, U].

inferior /ɪnˈfɪərɪə(r)/ *adj* (*to*)|| low or lower in importance, quality, etc. **inferior** *n* [C] inferior person. **inferiority** /ɪnˌfɪərɪˈɒrətɪ; US -ˈɔːr-/ *n* [U]. **inferi'ority complex** *n* [C] feeling that one is inferior to others.

infernal /ɪnˈfɜːnl/ *adj* 1 of hell. 2 (*infml*) annoying.

inferno /ɪnˈfɜːnəʊ/ *n* [C] (*pl* ~s) 1 (place where there is a) large destructive fire. 2 place like hell.

infertile /ɪnˈfɜːtaɪl; US -tl/ *adj* not fertile: *~ land.*

infest /ɪnˈfest/ *v* [T] (*with*)|| (of rats, insects, etc) live in large numbers: *a dog ~ed with fleas.*

infidelity /ˌɪnfɪˈdelətɪ/ *n* [C, U] (*pl* -ies) (*fml*) (act of) disloyalty or being unfaithful, esp to one's wife/husband.

infighting /ˈɪnfaɪtɪŋ/ *n* [U] fierce competition between colleagues or rivals in an organization.

infiltrate /ˈɪnfɪltreɪt/ *v* [T] enter (sth) secretly to do harm, find information, etc. **infiltration** /ˌɪnfɪlˈtreɪʃn/ *n* [U]. **infiltrator** *n* [C].

infinite /ˈɪnfɪnət/ *adj* without limits; endless. **infinitely** *adv*.

infinitive /ɪnˈfɪnətɪv/ *n* [C] (*grammar*) basic form of a verb, without inflections, eg (in English used with or without *to*, eg 'let him go', 'allow him to go').

infinity /ɪnˈfɪnətɪ/ *n* [U] endless

distance, space or quantity.

infirm /ɪnˈfɜːm/ adj weak, esp from old age or illness. **infirmity** n [C, U] (pl -ies).

infirmary /ɪnˈfɜːmərɪ/ n [C] (pl -ies) hospital.

inflame /ɪnˈfleɪm/ v [T] make (sb/ sth) very angry or over-excited. **inflamed** adj (of a part of the body) red, hot and sore.

inflammable /ɪnˈflæməbl/ adj easily set on fire; that can burn easily.

inflammation /ˌɪnfləˈmeɪʃn/ n [C, U] condition in which a part of the body is red, swollen and sore.

inflammatory /ɪnˈflæmətrɪ; US -tɔːrɪ/ adj likely to make people angry or over-excited: ~ remarks.

inflate /ɪnˈfleɪt/ v [I, T] (of a tyre, balloon, etc) fill with air or gas. 2 [T] (fig) cause (sb's opinion of himself/herself) to become too great: an ~ d ego. 3 [I, T] increase the amount of money in (an economy). **inflation** /ɪnˈfleɪʃn/ n [U] 1 process of inflating or being inflated. 2 general rise in prices caused by an increase in the supply of money, credit, etc. **inflationary** /ɪnˈfleɪʃnrɪ; US -nerɪ/ adj of or causing inflation.

inflection (also **inflexion**) /ɪnˈflekʃn/ n [C, U] 1 (grammar) change in the form of a word to show a past tense, plural, etc. 2 rise and fall of the voice in speaking.

inflexible /ɪnˈfleksəbl/ adj 1 impossible to bend or turn. 2 (fig) refusing to change or be influenced. **inflexibility** /ˌɪnfleksəˈbɪlətɪ/ n [U]. **inflexibly** adv.

inflict /ɪnˈflɪkt/ v [T] (on)// force (sth unpleasant) on sb: ~ a defeat on the enemy. **infliction** /ɪnˈflɪkʃn/ n [C, U].

influence /ˈɪnfluəns/ n 1 [U] power to produce an effect. 2 [C] person, fact, etc that has this power: She's a bad ~ on me. 3 [U] ability to obtain favourable treatment from sb: Can you use your ~ to get me a job? 4 (idm) **under the ~** influence (fml or joc) drunk. **influence** v [T] have an influence on.

influential /ˌɪnfluˈenʃl/ adj having influence(3).

influenza /ˌɪnfluˈenzə/ n [U] (fml) infectious disease with fever, aches and a bad cold.

influx /ˈɪnflʌks/ n [C] arrival, esp in large numbers or quantities: an ~ of tourists.

inform /ɪnˈfɔːm/ v 1 [T] give knowledge to. 2 [I] against/on// (law) give information about sb

(to the police). **informant** /-ənt/ n [C] person who gives information. **informed** adj having or showing knowledge. **informer** n [C] person who informs(2) of a person.

informal /ɪnˈfɔːml/ adj 1 not formal or serious: ~ clothes, ie those worn when one is relaxing. 2 (of words) used when one can be friendly and relaxed. **informality** /ˌɪnfɔːˈmælətɪ/ n [U]. **informally** adv.

information /ˌɪnfəˈmeɪʃn/ n [U] (on/about// facts or knowledge given.

informative /ɪnˈfɔːmətɪv/ adj giving a lot of information.

infra-red /ˌɪnfrəˈred/ adj of the invisible, heat-giving rays below red in the spectrum.

infrequent /ɪnˈfriːkwənt/ adj not frequent; rare. **infrequency** /-kwənsɪ/ n [U]. **infrequently** adv.

infringe /ɪnˈfrɪndʒ/ v 1 [T] break (a rule, etc). 2 [I] on// limit or restrict unfairly: ~ on the rights of other people. **infringement** n [C, U].

infuriate /ɪnˈfjʊərɪeɪt/ v [T] make (sb) very angry.

infuse /ɪnˈfjuːz/ v 1 [T] (fml) fill (sb) with a quality: ~ the workers with energy ○ ~ energy into the workers. 2 [I, T] (of tea or herbs) soak in hot water to make a drink. **infusion** /ɪnˈfjuːʒn/ n [C, U] (liquid made by) infusing.

ingenious /ɪnˈdʒiːnɪəs/ adj 1 (of a person) very clever and skilful. 2 (of a thing) original and well-designed. **ingeniously** adv. **ingenuity** /ˌɪndʒɪˈnjuːətɪ; US -nuː-/ n [U].

ingot /ˈɪŋɡət/ n [C] (usu brick-shaped) piece of metal.

ingrained /ɪnˈɡreɪnd/ adj (of habits, etc) deeply fixed.

ingratiate /ɪnˈɡreɪʃɪeɪt/ v [T] (fml derog) ~ oneself (with) try to make oneself popular, so as to gain favours from sb. **ingratiating** adj.

ingratitude /ɪnˈɡrætɪtjuːd; US -tuːd/ n [U] lack of gratitude.

ingredient /ɪnˈɡriːdɪənt/ n [C] one of the parts of a mixture: the ~ s of a cake.

inhabit /ɪnˈhæbɪt/ v [T] live in (sth). **inhabitant** /-ənt/ n [C] person living in a place.

inhale /ɪnˈheɪl/ v [I, T] breathe in. **inhaler** n [C] device that produces a vapour to make breathing easier.

inherent /ɪnˈhɪərənt, -ˈher-/ adj (in)// existing as a natural and permanent part of sb/sth: ~ *weaknesses in a design.*

inherit /ɪnˈherɪt/ v [T] 1 receive (property, money, etc) after the death of the previous owner. 2 receive (qualities, etc) from ancestors. **inheritance** n 1 [U] inheriting. 2 [C] something inherited. **inheritor** n [C] person who inherits.

inhibit /ɪnˈhɪbɪt/ v [T] (*from*/) prevent or hinder. **inhibited** *adj* unable to relax and express one's feelings naturally. **inhibition** /ˌɪnhɪˈbɪʃn/ n [C, U] feeling of being unable to behave naturally.

inhospitable /ˌɪnhɒˈspɪtəbl/ *adj* not hospitable: *an ~ climate.*

inhuman /ɪnˈhjuːmən/ *adj* without kindness, pity, etc. **inhumanity** /ˌɪnhjuːˈmænəti/ n [C, U] (*pl* -ies).

inhumane /ˌɪnhjuːˈmeɪn/ *adj* not humane; cruel. **inhumanely** *adv*.

inimitable /ɪˈnɪmɪtəbl/ *adj* too good, clever, etc to imitate.

initial /ɪˈnɪʃl/ *adj* of or at the beginning. **initial** n [C, usu *pl*] first letter of a person's name. **initial** v (-ll-; *US* usu -l-) [I, T] sign (sth) with one's initials. **initially** /-ʃəli/ *adv* at the beginning.

initiate /ɪˈnɪʃɪeɪt/ v 1 (*fml*) make (sth) begin. 2 (*into*/) introduce (sb) into a club, group, etc. **initiate** /ɪˈnɪʃɪət/ n [C] person who has (just) been initiated into a group. **initiation** /ɪˌnɪʃɪˈeɪʃn/ n [U].

initiative /ɪˈnɪʃətɪv/ n 1 [C] action taken to solve a difficulty. 2 **the initiative** [sing] power or right to take action. 3 [U] ability to act without help: *do sth on one's own ~.* 4 (*idm*) **take the initiative** take the first step in a task.

inject /ɪnˈdʒekt/ v [T] 1 put sth into sb with a syringe: ~ *a drug into sb* ○ ~ *sb with a drug.* 2 (*into*/) (*fig*) introduce (sth new) into sth: ~ *new life into the team.* **injection** /ɪnˈdʒekʃn/ n [C, U].

injunction /ɪnˈdʒʌŋkʃn/ n [C] (*fml*) official order from a lawcourt.

injure /ˈɪndʒə(r)/ v [T] hurt; damage. **injured** *adj* wounded; offended. **the injured** n [*pl*] injured people.

injury /ˈɪndʒəri/ n (*pl* -ies) 1 [U] harm; damage. 2 [C] (a) harm to one's body. (b) damage to one's feelings.

injustice /ɪnˈdʒʌstɪs/ n 1 [U] unfairness. 2 [C] unfair act. 3 (*idm*) **do sb an in'justice** judge sb unfairly.

ink /ɪŋk/ n [U, C] coloured liquid for writing, printing, etc. **inky** *adj*

black.

inkling /ˈɪŋklɪŋ/ n [sing] vague idea.

inland /ˈɪnlənd/ *adj* inside a country: ~ *lakes.* **inland** /ˌɪnˈlænd/ *adv* towards the middle of a country. **the ˌInland 'Revenue** n [sing] (in Britain) government department that collects taxes.

in-laws /ˈɪnlɔːz/ n [*pl*] (*infml*) relatives by marriage.

inlet /ˈɪnlet/ n [C] strip of water reaching into the land.

inmate /ˈɪnmeɪt/ n [C] person living in a prison, hospital, etc.

inmost /ˈɪnməʊst/ *adj* 1 furthest inside. 2 (*fig*) most secret: ~ *thoughts.*

inn /ɪn/ n [C] small old hotel or pub, usu in the country. **'innkeeper** n [C] person who manages an inn.

innards /ˈɪnədz/ n [*pl*] 1 stomach and/or bowels. 2 any inner parts.

innate /ɪˈneɪt/ *adj* (of a quality, etc) existing in a person from birth. **innately** *adv*.

inner /ˈɪnə(r)/ *adj* 1 inside; near to the middle. 2 (of feelings) not expressed. **innermost** /-məʊst/ *adj* inmost: *her ~ most feelings.*

innings /ˈɪnɪŋz/ n [C] (*pl* innings) 1 (in cricket) time during which a team or player is batting. 2 (*idm*) **have had a good 'innings** (*Brit* *infml*) have had a long happy life. **inning** n [C] (in baseball) part of a game in which both teams bat.

innocent /ˈɪnəsnt/ *adj* 1 not guilty. 2 harmless: ~ *fun.* 3 knowing nothing of evil. 4 foolishly simple. **innocence** /-sns/ n [U]. **innocently** *adv*.

innocuous /ɪˈnɒkjuəs/ *adj* harmless: *an ~ remark.*

innovate /ˈɪnəveɪt/ v [I] make changes; introduce new things. **innovation** /ˌɪnəˈveɪʃn/ n 1 [U] innovating. 2 [C] new idea, method, etc. **innovative** /ˈɪnəvətɪv/ (also **innovatory** /ˌɪnəˈveɪtəri/) *adj*. **innovator** n [C] person who innovates.

innuendo /ˌɪnjuˈendəʊ/ n [C, U] (*pl* -es /-z/) unfavourable indirect reference.

innumerable /ɪˈnjuːmərəbl; *US* ɪˈnuː-/ *adj* too many to count.

inoculate /ɪˈnɒkjʊleɪt/ v [T] inject (sb) with a vaccine in order to prevent a disease: ~ *sb against cholera.* **inoculation** /ɪˌnɒkjʊˈleɪʃn/ n [C, U].

inoffensive /ˌɪnəˈfensɪv/ *adj* not giving offence; not rude.

inopportune /ɪnˈɒpətjuːn; *US* -tuːn/ *adj* (*fml*) not suitable or

convenient: *an ~ remark/time.* **inopportunely** *adv.*

inordinate /ɪnˈɔːdɪnət/ *adj (fml)* beyond normal limits; excessive. **inordinately** *adv.*

inorganic /ˌɪnɔːˈgænɪk/ *adj* not made of living substances: *Rocks and minerals are ~.*

input /ˈɪnpʊt/ *n* 1 [U] action of putting sth in. 2 [C] something that is put in, eg information into a computer. **input** *v* (-tt-, *pt, pp* **input** or ~ **ted**) [T] put (information) into a computer.

inquest /ˈɪnkwest/ *n* [C] official inquiry, esp about an unexpected death.

inquire (also **enquire**) /ɪnˈkwaɪə(r)/ *v* 1 [T] ask to be told (sth). 2 [I] *(about)* ask for information about sth: *~ about trains to Oxford.* 3 (phr v) **inquire after sb** ask about sb's health. **inquire into sth** try to find information about sth. **inquiring** *adj* showing an interest in learning: *an inquiring mind.*

inquiry (also **enquiry**) /ɪnˈkwaɪərɪ; *US* ˈɪnkwərɪ/ *n* (*pl* -ies) 1 [C] question; investigation. 2 [U] inquiring.

inquisition /ˌɪnkwɪˈzɪʃn/ *n* [C] *(fml)* severe and detailed investigation.

inquisitive /ɪnˈkwɪzətɪv/ *adj* (too) fond of inquiring into other people's affairs. **inquisitively** *adv.*

inroads /ˈɪnrəʊdz/ *n* [pl] 1 sudden attack (into a country, etc). 2 (idm) **make inroads into/on sth** gradually use, eat, etc more and more of sth: *make ~ into one's savings.*

insane /ɪnˈseɪn/ *adj* mad. **insanely** *adv.* **insanity** /ɪnˈsænətɪ/ *n* [U].

insatiable /ɪnˈseɪʃəbl/ *adj* impossible to satisfy.

inscribe /ɪnˈskraɪb/ *v* [T] write: *~ words on a tombstone ○ ~ a book with one's name.* **inscription** /ɪnˈskrɪpʃn/ *n* [C] words written on sth or cut in stone, etc.

inscrutable /ɪnˈskruːtəbl/ *adj* impossible to understand; mysterious.

insect /ˈɪnsekt/ *n* [C] kind of small animal with six legs, eg an ant or a fly. **insecticide** /ɪnˈsektɪsaɪd/ *n* [C, U] chemical used for killing insects.

insecure /ˌɪnsɪˈkjʊə(r)/ *adj* 1 not safe. 2 lacking confidence. **insecurely** *adv.* **insecurity** *n* [U].

insensible /ɪnˈsensəbl/ *adj (fml)* 1 unconscious. 2 *(of)//* unaware of sth. 3 *(to)//* not able to feel sth: *~ to*

pain. **insensibility** /ɪnˌsensəˈbɪlətɪ/ *n* [U].

insensitive /ɪnˈsensətɪv/ *adj* not sensitive. **insensitively** *adv.* **insensitivity** /ɪnˌsensəˈtɪvətɪ/ *n* [U].

inseparable /ɪnˈseprəbl/ *adj* impossible to separate: *~ friends.*

insert /ɪnˈsɜːt/ *v* [T] put or fit into sth: *~ a key in a lock.* **insert** /ˈɪnsɜːt/ *n* [C] something inserted, eg an advertisement put between the pages of a newspaper. **insertion** /ɪnˈsɜːʃn/ *n* [C, U].

inset /ˈɪnset/ *n* [C] small picture, map, etc within a larger one.

inshore /ˌɪnˈʃɔː(r)/ *adj, adv* (of sth at sea) close to the shore.

inside¹ /ˌɪnˈsaɪd/ *n* 1 [C, usu sing] part or surface nearest to the centre. 2 [sing] (also **insides** [pl]) *(infml)* stomach and bowels. 3 (idm) **inside 'out** (a) with the normal inner side on the outside. (b) thoroughly: *know sth ~ out.* **on the in'side** in an organization so that one can know secret information. **inside** *adj* 1 on or in the inside. 2 given or done by sb who is in an organization: *The robbery was an ~ job.* **insider** *n* [C] member of an organization who can obtain special information. **in‚sider 'dealing** (also **in‚sider 'trading**) *n* [U] buying or selling sth, esp business shares, with the help of information known only by people who work for the business.

inside² /ˌɪnˈsaɪd/ *prep* (esp *US* **inside of**) *prep* 1 on or to the inner side of sth/sb: *come ~ the house.* 2 (of time) in less than: *~ a year.* **inside** *adv* 1 on or to the inside, esp indoors: *go ~,* ie into the house. 2 *(sl)* in prison.

insidious /ɪnˈsɪdɪəs/ *adj* doing harm secretly. **insidiously** *adv.*

insight /ˈɪnsaɪt/ *n* [C, U] (instance of) understanding: *~s into his character.*

insignia /ɪnˈsɪgnɪə/ *n* [pl] symbols of rank or authority.

insignificant /ˌɪnsɪgˈnɪfɪkənt/ *adj* having little importance or value. **insignificance** /-kəns/ *n* [U]. **insignificantly** *adv.*

insincere /ˌɪnsɪnˈsɪə(r)/ *adj* not sincere. **insincerely** *adv.* **insincerity** /-ˈserətɪ/ *n* [U].

insinuate /ɪnˈsɪnjʊeɪt/ *v* [T] 1 suggest (sth) unpleasantly and indirectly. 2 *into//* *(fml)* place (oneself/sth) slowly and secretly in sth. **insinuation** /ɪnˌsɪnjʊˈeɪʃn/ *n* [C, U].

insipid /ɪnˈsɪpɪd/ *adj (derog)* 1 having almost no taste or flavour. 2 *(fig)* without interest or strength. **insipidly** adv.

insist /ɪnˈsɪst/ v [I, T] (on)// 1 demand (sth) strongly: ~ on going with sb ○ ~ that she (should) stop. 2 declare firmly: He ~s that he is innocent. **insistent** adj strongly insisting. **insistence** n [U].

insofar as /ˌɪnsəˈfɑːr əz/ = AS FAR AS (FAR[1]).

insolent /ˈɪnsələnt/ adj (to)) very rude. **insolence** /-əns/ n [U].

insoluble /ɪnˈsɒljʊbl/ adj 1 (of substances) impossible to dissolve. 2 (fig) (of problems, etc) impossible to solve.

insolvent /ɪnˈsɒlvənt/ n [C], adj (person who is) unable to pay debts. **insolvency** /-ənsɪ/ n [U].

insomnia /ɪnˈsɒmnɪə/ n [U] inability to sleep. **insomniac** /-nɪæk/ n [C] person who cannot go to sleep easily.

inspect /ɪnˈspekt/ v [T] examine carefully. **inspection** /ɪnˈspekʃn/ n [C, U]. **inspector** n [C] 1 official who inspects sth, eg schools. 2 (Brit) police officer above a sergeant in rank.

inspire /ɪnˈspaɪə(r)/ v [T] 1 fill (sb) with the ability or desire to do sth. 2 fill (sb) with feelings: ~ sb with confidence ○ ~ confidence in sb. **inspiration** /ˌɪnspəˈreɪʃn/ n 1 [U] influence producing creative ability; state of being inspired. 2 [C] person or thing that inspires. 3 [C] (infml) sudden good idea. **inspired** adj filled with or showing inspiration(1). **inspiring** adj.

instability /ˌɪnstəˈbɪlətɪ/ n [U] lack of stability.

install (US also **instal**) /ɪnˈstɔːl/ v [T] 1 put (machines, furniture, etc) in position. 2 (fml) put (sb) in a new job. 3 (fml) settle (oneself) in a place. **installation** /ˌɪnstəˈleɪʃn/ n [U, C].

instalment (US usu **-ll-**) /ɪnˈstɔːlmənt/ n [C] 1 one part of a story that appears over a period of time: a television series in six ~ s. 2 one part of a payment spread over a period of time.

instance /ˈɪnstəns/ n [C] 1 example; fact, occurrence, etc supporting a general truth. 2 (idm) **for instance** for example.

instant /ˈɪnstənt/ n [C, usu sing] 1 exact point of time. 2 moment: I'll be there in an ~. **instant** adj 1 coming or happening at once: an ~ success. 2 (of food) that can be made very quickly and easily: ~ coffee. **instantly** adv at once.

instantaneous /ˌɪnstənˈteɪnɪəs/ adj happening or done immediately. **instantaneously** adv.

instead /ɪnˈsted/ adv as an alter-

native: Bill was ill so I went ~. **instead of** prep as an alternative to (sb/sth); in place of: drink tea ~ of coffee.

instep /ˈɪnstep/ n [C] upper surface of the foot.

instigate /ˈɪnstɪgeɪt/ v [T] cause (sth) to begin or happen: ~ a strike/riot. **instigation** /ˌɪnstɪˈgeɪʃn/ n [U]. **instigator** n [C].

instil (US **instill**) /ɪnˈstɪl/ v (-ll-) [T] (in/into)) put (ideas, etc) into sb's mind.

instinct /ˈɪnstɪŋkt/ n [C, U] natural tendency to behave in a certain way. **instinctive** /ɪnˈstɪŋktɪv/ adj based on instinct: in ~ive fear of fire. **instinctively** adv.

institute /ˈɪnstɪtjuːt; US -tuːt/ n [C] (building of an) organization with a special purpose. **institute** v [T] (fml) start or establish (an inquiry, rule, etc).

institution /ˌɪnstɪˈtjuːʃn; US -tuːʃn/ n 1 [U] instituting. 2 [C] (building of an) organization with a social purpose, eg a school or hospital. 3 [C] established custom or practice. **institutional** /-ʃənl/ adj. **institutionalize** /-ʃənəlaɪz/ v [T] 1 make (sth) into an institution(3). 2 put (sb) in an institution(2) (with the result that he/she loses self-reliance).

instruct /ɪnˈstrʌkt/ v [T] 1 teach. 2 give orders to (sb): ~ the child not to go out. 3 (esp law) inform. **instructive** adj giving a lot of useful information. **instructor** n [C] teacher or trainer.

instruction /ɪnˈstrʌkʃn/ n 1 [U] instructing; teaching. 2 [C] order. 3 **instructions** [pl] information on how to do sth: follow the ~ s on a tin of paint.

instrument /ˈɪnstrəmənt/ n [C] 1 something used in performing an action, eg in scientific work. 2 apparatus for playing music, eg a violin or piano. **instrumental** /ˌɪnstrʊˈmentl/ adj 1 in)) responsible for sth; causing: You were ~ al in her promotion. 2 of or for musical instruments. **instrumentalist** /ˌɪnstrʊˈmentəlɪst/ n [C] person who plays a musical instrument.

insubordinate /ˌɪnsəˈbɔːdɪnət/ adj disobedient. **insubordination** /ˌɪnsəˌbɔːdɪˈneɪʃn/ n [U, C].

insufferable /ɪnˈsʌfrəbl/ adj unbearable: ~ behaviour.

insufficient /ˌɪnsəˈfɪʃnt/ adj not sufficient. **insufficiency** /-ʃnsɪ/ n [U]. **insufficiently** adv.

insular /ˈɪnsjʊlə(r); US -sələr/ adj 1 (derog) narrow-minded. 2 of an island. **insularity** /ˌɪnsjʊ-ˈlærətɪ; US -səˈl-/ n [U].

insulate /ˈɪnsjʊleɪt; US -səl-/ v [T] **1** cover (sth) to prevent heat, electricity, etc from escaping: ~d wires. **2** (fig) protect sb/sth from unpleasant effects. **insulation** /ˌɪnsjʊˈleɪʃn, US -səˈl-/ n [U] (materials used in) insulating.

insult /ɪnˈsʌlt/ v [T] be rude to (sb). **insult** /ˈɪnsʌlt/ n [C] rude remark or action. **insulting** adj.

insurance /ɪnˈʃɔːrəns; US -ˈʃʊər-/ n **1** [U] **(a)** agreement by a company or the state to pay money because of loss, illness, death, etc in return for regular payments. **(b)** money paid by or to a company, etc for this. **2** [C] (fig) protection against loss, failure, etc.

insure /ɪnˈʃɔː(r); US mˈʃʊər/ v [T] **1** protect (sb/sth) by insurance: ~ a car against fire/theft. **2** (US) = ENSURE.

insurgent /ɪnˈsɜːdʒənt/ adj rebellious. **insurgent** n [C] rebel soldier.

insurmountable /ˌɪnsəˈmaʊn-təbl/ adj (fml) (of problems or difficulties) impossible to solve or overcome.

insurrection /ˌɪnsəˈrekʃn/ n [C, U] rebellion.

intact /ɪnˈtækt/ adj undamaged; complete.

intake /ˈɪnteɪk/ n **1 (a)** [U] process of taking liquid, gas, etc into a machine, etc. **(b)** [C] place where liquid, etc enters. **2** [C, U] number of people taken in: last year's ~ of students.

intangible /ɪnˈtændʒəbl/ adj **1** impossible to understand clearly: an ~ air of sadness. **2** (commerce) (of a business asset) that has no physical existence: the ~ value of a good reputation.

integer /ˈɪntɪdʒə(r)/ n [C] (mathematics) whole number, eg 1, 3, 11.

integral /ˈɪntɪɡrəl/ adj necessary to make sth complete: an ~ part of the plan. **integrally** adv.

integrate /ˈɪntɪɡreɪt/ v **1** [T] (into/with)|| combine (sth) so that it becomes fully a part of sth else. **2** [I, T] (of people) mix or be together as one group. **integration** /ˌɪntɪˈɡreɪʃn/ n [U].

integrity /ɪnˈteɡrətɪ/ n [U] **1** honesty and goodness. **2** wholeness; unity.

intellect /ˈɪntəlekt/ n [U] power of the mind to reason. **intellectual** /ˌɪntɪˈlektʃʊəl/ adj **1** of the intellect. **2** of or interested in ideas, the arts, etc rather than practical matters. **intellectual** n [C] intellectual person. **intellec-**

tually adv.

intelligence /ɪnˈtelɪdʒəns/ n **1** [U] ability to learn, understand and think. **2 (a)** [U] information about enemies. **(b)** [sing] (with sing or pl v) people who collect such information. **intelligent** /-dʒənt/ adj clever. **intelligently** adv.

intelligible /ɪnˈtelɪdʒəbl/ adj that can be understood. **intelligibility** /ɪnˌtelɪdʒəˈbɪlətɪ/ n [U]. **intelligibly** adv.

intend /ɪnˈtend/ v [T] have as a purpose; mean: I ~ to leave soon.

intense /ɪnˈtens/ adj **1** extreme; very strong: ~ heat/anger. **2** (of a person) serious and very emotional. **intensely** adv. **intensify** /-sɪfaɪ/ v (pt, pp -ied) [I, T] become or make more intense. **intensification** /ɪnˌtensɪfɪˈkeɪʃn/ n [U]. **intensity** n [U] state of being intense; strength (of feeling, etc).

intensive /ɪnˈtensɪv/ adj concentrating effort, work, etc on one task; very thorough: an ~ search. **intensively** adv.

intent¹ /ɪnˈtent/ adj **1** showing fixed attention: an ~ look/gaze. **2** on|| determined to do sth: ~ on becoming manager. **intently** adv.

intent² /ɪnˈtent/ n **1** [U] (esp law) intention: shoot with ~ to kill. **2** (idm) **to all intents (and purposes)** in the important details; nearly.

intention /ɪnˈtenʃn/ n [C, U] aim; purpose. **intentional** /-ʃənl/ adj done on purpose. **intentionally** adv.

inter /ɪnˈtɜː(r)/ v (-rr-) [T] (fml) bury.

interact /ˌɪntərˈækt/ v [I] (with)|| **1** have an effect on each other. **2** (of people) communicate and work together. **interaction** /-ˈækʃn/ n [U, C]. **interactive** adj **1** interacting. **2** (computing) allowing a continuous exchange of information between a computer and a user.

intercept /ˌɪntəˈsept/ v [T] stop (sb/sth that is moving between two places). **interception** /-ˈsepʃn/ n [U].

interchange /ˌɪntəˈtʃeɪndʒ/ v [I, T] (cause to) change places with each other. **interchange** n **1** [C, U] (instance of) interchanging. **2** [C] place where roads join a motorway. **interchangeable** adj.

inter-city /ˌɪntəˈsɪtɪ/ adj (of fast transport) travelling between cities.

intercom /ˈɪntəkɒm/ n [C] system of communication using a microphone and loudspeaker, used eg in a building.

intercontinental /ˌɪntəˌkɒntr'nentl/ *adj* between continents: ~ *flights.*

intercourse /ˈɪntəkɔːs/ *n* [U] (*fml*) 1 ⇨ SEXUAL INTERCOURSE (SEXUAL). 2 dealings between people, nations, etc.

interest /ˈɪntrəst/ *n* 1 [U, sing (*in*)] desire to learn or know about sb/sth: *lose ~* ○ *take an ~ in art.* 2 [U] quality that causes concern or curiosity: *an idea of ~ to us.* 3 [C] something which one enjoys doing or learning about: *His great ~ is football.* 4 [C, usu pl] benefit: *It is in your ~(s)* (ie It is to your advantage) *to work hard.* 5 [U] money paid for the use of money: *borrow money at a high rate of ~.* 6 [C, usu pl] share in a business. 7 [C, usu pl] group of people in the same business, etc. 8 (idm) **in the interests of sth** for the sake of sth. **interest** *v* [T] make (sb) have or show interest(1). **interested** *adj* 1 (*in*)] showing interest(1) in sth: *be ~ed in history.* 2 personally involved. **interesting** *adj* holding one's attention.

interfere /ˌɪntəˈfɪə(r)/ *v* [I] 1 (*in*)] concern oneself with sb else's affairs without being asked to do so. 2 *with/*] (a) handle, touch, etc sth without permission, esp causing damage. (b) prevent sth from being done properly. 3 *with/*] (a) distract or hinder sb. (b) (*Brit euph*) touch or attack sb sexually. **interference** *n* [U] 1 interfering. 2 (*radio*) noise that prevents sound from being heard properly.

interim /ˈɪntərɪm/ *adj* existing only for a short time: ~ *arrangements.* **interim** *n* (idm) **in the interim** in the time between two events.

interior /ɪnˈtɪərɪə(r)/ *n* 1 [C] inner part; inside. 2 **the interior** [sing] inland part of a country or continent. **interior** *adj* 1 inside. 2 (*politics*) within a country.

interjection /ˌɪntəˈdʒekʃn/ *n* (*grammar*) word or phrase, eg *Oh!, Good heavens!* used for showing surprise, anger, etc.

interlock /ˌɪntəˈlɒk/ *v* [I, T] lock or join together.

interlude /ˈɪntəluːd/ *n* [C] short period of time between two parts of a play, etc or two events.

intermarry /ˌɪntəˈmærɪ/ *v* (*pt, pp* -**ied**) [I] (of people from different racial, religious, etc groups) marry each other. **intermarriage** /-ˈmærɪdʒ/ *n* [C].

intermediary /ˌɪntəˈmiːdɪərɪ; *US* -dɪerɪ/ *n* [C] (-**ies**) person who

passes information between two groups, esp to get agreement.

intermediate /ˌɪntəˈmiːdɪət/ *adj* 1 between two points or stages. 2 between elementary and advanced: *an ~ course.*

interminable /ɪnˈtɜːmɪnəbl/ *adj* (usu *derog*) lasting too long and therefore boring. **interminably** *adv.*

intermission /ˌɪntəˈmɪʃn/ *n* [C, U] interval in a play, etc; pause.

intermittent /ˌɪntəˈmɪtənt/ *adj* continually stopping and starting again: ~ *rain.* **intermittently** *adv.*

intern[1] /ɪnˈtɜːn/ *v* [T] put (sb) in prison, esp during a war. **internment** *n* [U].

intern[2] /ˈɪntɜːn/ *n* [C] (*US*) junior doctor at a hospital.

internal /ɪnˈtɜːnl/ *adj* 1 of or on the inside: ~ *injuries,* ie inside the body. 2 not foreign; domestic: ~ *trade.* **internally** *adv.*

international /ˌɪntəˈnæʃnəl/ *adj* of or existing between nations. **international** *n* [C] (**a**) sports match with teams from two countries. (**b**) person who plays in such a match. **internationally** *adv.*

interplay /ˈɪntəpleɪ/ *n* [U] way in which two or more things affect each other.

interpose /ˌɪntəˈpəʊz/ *v* (*fml*) 1 [T] place (sth) between two things. 2 [I] interrupt.

interpret /ɪnˈtɜːprɪt/ *v* 1 [T] explain (sth that is difficult to understand). 2 [T] *as/*] understand (sth) in a particular way: ~ *his silence as an expression of guilt.* 3 [I, T] give an immediate translation of (words spoken in another language). **interpretation** /ɪnˌtɜːprɪˈteɪʃn/ *n* [U, C] interpreting; explanation. **interpreter** *n* [C] person who interprets(3).

interrogate /ɪnˈterəgeɪt/ *v* [T] question (sb) closely and for a long time. **interrogation** /ɪnˌterəˈgeɪʃn/ *n* [C, U]. **interrogator** *n* [C].

interrogative /ˌɪntəˈrɒgətɪv/ *adj* (*grammar*) (used in questions): ~ *pronouns/adverbs* (eg *who, why*). **interrogative** *n* [C] interrogative word.

interrupt /ˌɪntəˈrʌpt/ *v* 1 [I, T] stop (sb) speaking by speaking oneself. 2 [T] break the continuity of: ~ *a journey.* **interruption** /-ˈrʌpʃn/ *n* [C, U].

intersect /ˌɪntəˈsekt/ *v* 1 [I, T] (of lines, roads, etc) meet and go across (each other). 2 [T] divide (sth) by going across it. **intersection** /-ˈsekʃn/ *n* 1 [U] intersecting. 2 [C] place where roads cross; crossroads.

intersperse /ˌɪntəˈspɜːs/ v [T] put (sth) between or among other things.

interval /ˈɪntəvl/ n [C] 1 (a) time between two events. (b) space between two things. 2 (Brit) short period of time between the parts of a play, film, etc.

intervene /ˌɪntəˈviːn/ v [I] (fml) 1 (in)// interfere and prevent sth happening. 2 (of time) come between. 3 (of events) happen so as to prevent or stop sth. **intervening** adj come between: in the intervening years. **intervention** /-'venʃn/ n [C, U].

interview /ˈɪntəvjuː/ n [C] (with)// meeting at which sb (eg sb applying for a job) is asked questions. **interview** v [T] ask (sb) questions in an interview. **interviewer** n [C] person who interviews sb.

intestate /ɪnˈtesteɪt/ adj (law) not having a will: die ~.

intestine /ɪnˈtestɪn/ n [C, esp pl] long tube from the stomach to the anus. **intestinal** adj.

intimacy /ˈɪntɪməsɪ/ n 1 [U] state of being intimate. 2 **intimacies** [pl] kisses or caresses.

intimate[1] /ˈɪntɪmət/ adj 1 having a very close relationship: They are ~ friends. 2 private and personal: ~ details of her life. 3 resulting from close study: an ~ knowledge of Greek. **intimately** adv.

intimate[2] /ˈɪntɪmeɪt/ v [T] (fml) make (sth) known; suggest. **intimation** /ˌɪntɪˈmeɪʃn/ n [C, U].

intimidate /ɪnˈtɪmɪdeɪt/ v [T] frighten (sb), esp by making threats. **intimidation** /ɪnˌtɪmɪˈdeɪʃn/ n [U].

into /ˈɪntə, before vowels ˈɪntuː/ prep 1 to a point within (sth): Come ~ the house. 2 to a point at which one hits (sb/sth): A lorry drove ~ a line of cars. 3 until a point during (sth): work long ~ the night. 4 (showing a change in form): Cut the paper ~ strips. 5 (showing a change to a condition or action): frighten sb ~ submission. 6 (used for expressing division in mathematics): 5 ~ 25 = 5. 7 (idm) be into sth (infml) be very interested in sth.

intolerable /ɪnˈtɒlərəbl/ adj too bad to be endured. **intolerably** adv.

intolerant /ɪnˈtɒlərənt/ adj not tolerant. **intolerance** /-əns/ n [U].

intonation /ˌɪntəˈneɪʃn/ n [C, esp pl] rise and fall of the voice in speak-

ing.

intoxicate /ɪnˈtɒksɪkeɪt/ v [T] (fml) 1 (of alcohol) make (sb) drunk. 2 (fig) excite (sb) greatly: ~d with success. **intoxication** /ɪnˌtɒksɪˈkeɪʃn/ n [U].

intransitive /ɪnˈtrænsətɪv/ adj (grammar) (of a verb) used without an object, eg rise in 'Smoke rises'.

in-tray /ˈɪntreɪ/ n [C] tray for holding letters, etc that are waiting to be read or answered.

intrepid /ɪnˈtrepɪd/ adj (esp rhet) brave: ~ explorers. **intrepidly** adv.

intricate /ˈɪntrɪkət/ adj with many small parts put together in a complicated way. **intricacy** /-kəsɪ/ n (pl -ies) 1 [U] being intricate. 2 [C, usu pl] something intricate. **intricately** adv.

intrigue /ɪnˈtriːg/ v 1 [T] make interested or curious: ~ sb with a story. 2 [I] make secret plans to do sth bad. **intrigue** /ˈɪntriːg, ɪnˈtriːg/ n 1 [U] making of secret plans to do sth bad. 2 [C] such a plan. **intriguing** adj very interesting, esp because unusual.

intrinsic /ɪnˈtrɪnsɪk, -zɪk/ adj (of a value or quality) belonging naturally. **intrinsically** /-klɪ/ adv.

introduce /ˌɪntrəˈdjuːs; US -'duːs/ v [T] 1 (to)// make (sb) known to sb else by giving each person's name to the other: I ~d Paul to Sarah. 2 bring in: ~ computers into schools. 3 announce and give (details of sth).

introduction /ˌɪntrəˈdʌkʃn/ n 1 [C, U] introducing of one person to another. 2 [C] (a) explanation at the beginning of a speech, book, etc. (b) textbook for people beginning to study a subject. 3 [U] bringing into use for the first time.

introductory /ˌɪntrəˈdʌktərɪ/ adj acting as an introduction(2).

introspection /ˌɪntrəˈspekʃn/ n [U] examining one's own thoughts, feelings, etc. **introspective** /-'spektɪv/ adj.

introvert /ˈɪntrəvɜːt/ n [C] person who is quiet and shy, and more interested in his/her own thoughts than in things outside himself/herself. **introverted** adj.

intrude /ɪnˈtruːd/ v [I] on// enter when not invited or wanted. **intruder** n [C] person who intrudes, esp in order to steal things. **intrusion** /ɪnˈtruːʒn/ n [C, U]. **intrusive** /ɪnˈtruːsɪv/ adj intruding.

intuition /ˌɪntjuːˈɪʃn; US -tuː-/ n (a) [U] ability to understand sth quickly without conscious thought. (b) [C] piece of knowledge gained by this ability. **intuitive** /ɪnˈtjuːɪtɪv; US -ˈtuː-/ *adj*. **intuitively** *adv*.

inundate /ˈɪnʌndeɪt/ *v*[T] 1 flood. 2 (*fig*) overwhelm: ~*d with replies*.

invade /ɪnˈveɪd/ *v*[T] 1 enter (a country) with armed forces in order to attack or occupy it. 2 (*fig*) crowd into: *Fans ~d the football pitch*. **invader** *n*[C]. **invasion** /ɪnˈveɪʒn/ *n*[C, U].

invalid[1] /ɪnˈvælɪd/ *adj* not valid: *an ~ argument/passport*. **invalidate** /ɪnˈvælɪdeɪt/ *v*[T]. **invalidation** /ɪnˌvælɪˈdeɪʃn/ *n*[U].

invalid[2] /ˈɪnvəlɪd, -liːd/ *n*[C] person who is weak or disabled because of illness or injury. **invalid** *v* (*phr v*) **invalid sb out (of sth)** make sb leave the army, navy, etc because he is ill.

invaluable /ɪnˈvæljuəbl/ *adj* having a value that is too high to be measured.

invariable /ɪnˈveərɪəbl/ *adj* never changing. **invariably** *adv* always: *He's invariably late*.

invasion ⇨ INVADE.

invective /ɪnˈvektɪv/ *n*[U] (*fml*) violent attack in words.

invent /ɪnˈvent/ *v*[T] 1 make or design (sth that did not exist before): *Who ~ed television?* 2 think of (sth untrue): ~ *an excuse*. **invention** /ɪnˈvenʃn/ *n* 1 [U] inventing. 2 [C] something invented. **inventive** *adj* having the ability to invent things. **inventor** *n*[C].

inventory /ˈɪnvəntrɪ; US -tɔːrɪ/ *n*[C] (*pl* -ies) detailed list, eg of goods or furniture.

inverse /ˌɪnˈvɜːs/ *adj* reversed in position, relation, etc. **inverse** /ˈɪnvɜːs/ *n* **the inverse** [sing] the direct opposite.

invert /ɪnˈvɜːt/ *v*[T] turn upside down or put in the opposite order. **inversion** /ɪnˈvɜːʃn; US ɪnˈvɜːrʒn/ *n*[C, U]. **inverted commas** *n*[pl] (*Brit*) = QUOTATION-MARKS (QUOTATION).

invest /ɪnˈvest/ *v* 1 [I, T] (*in*)// use (money) to buy business shares, property, etc in order to make more money: ~ (*money*) *in shares*. 2 [T] *in*// give (time, effort, etc) to a task: ~ *one's time in learning French*. 3 [I] *in*// (*infml*) buy sth expensive but useful: ~ *in a new car*. 4 [T] (*with*)// (*fml*) give power, a rank, etc to sb. **investment** *n* 1 [U] investing of money. 2 [C] amount of money invested. 3 [C] business in which money is invested. **investor** *n*[C].

investigate /ɪnˈvestɪgeɪt/ *v*[I, T]

examine (the facts about sth) in order to discover the truth: ~ *a murder*. **investigation** /ɪnˌvestɪˈgeɪʃn/ *n*[C, U]. **investigative** /-gətɪv; US -geɪtɪv/ *adj* of or concerned with investigating. **investigator** *n*[C].

investiture /ɪnˈvestɪtʃə(r); US -tʃʊər/ *n*[C] ceremony of giving sb power, a rank, etc.

inveterate /ɪnˈvetərət/ *adj* (*derog*) firmly fixed in a bad habit: *an ~ liar/smoker*.

invigilate /ɪnˈvɪdʒɪleɪt/ *v*[I, T] (*Brit*) watch over students in (an examination). **invigilation** /ɪnˌvɪdʒɪˈleɪʃn/ *n*[U]. **invigilator** *n*[C].

invigorate /ɪnˈvɪgəreɪt/ *v*[T] make (sb) feel more lively and healthy. **invigorating** *adj*: *an invigorating walk*.

invincible /ɪnˈvɪnsəbl/ *adj* too strong to be defeated.

inviolable /ɪnˈvaɪələbl/ *adj* (*fml*) that must not be violated: ~ *rights*.

inviolate /ɪnˈvaɪələt/ *adj* (*from*)// (*fml*) impossible to be harmed by sth.

invisible /ɪnˈvɪzəbl/ *adj* (*to*)// that cannot be seen. **invisibility** /ɪnˌvɪzəˈbɪlətɪ/ *n*[U]. **invisibly** *adv*.

invite /ɪnˈvaɪt/ *v*[T] 1 (*to/for*)// ask (sb) to go somewhere or to do sth: ~ *sb to/for dinner*. 2 ask for (questions, suggestions, etc). 3 encourage (sth bad): ~ *criticism*. **invitation** /ˌɪnvɪˈteɪʃn/ *n* 1 [U] inviting: *Admission is by invitation only*. 2 [C] request to go or come somewhere: *an invitation to a party*. **inviting** *adj* attractive. **invitingly** *adv*.

invoice /ˈɪnvɔɪs/ *n*[C] list of goods sold, with the prices charged. **invoice** *v*[T] send such a list to (sb) as a request for payment.

invoke /ɪnˈvəʊk/ *v*[T] (*fml*) 1 use (sth) as a reason for one's action. 2 call to (God or the law) for help. 3 make (sth) appear by magic. **invocation** /ˌɪnvəˈkeɪʃn/ *n*[C, U] prayer or appeal for help.

involuntary /ɪnˈvɒləntrɪ; US -terɪ/ *adj* done without intention: *an ~ movement*. **involuntarily** /-trəlɪ; US ɪnˌvɒlənˈterəlɪ/ *adv*.

involve /ɪnˈvɒlv/ *v*[T] 1 make (sth) a necessary condition or result: *The job ~d me/my living in London*. 2 include or affect. 3 *in*// make (sb/sth) take part in sth. **involved** *adj* 1 complicated. 2 (**a**) (*in*)// concerned with sth. (**b**) (*with*)// in a close personal relationship with sb. **involvement**

n [U, C].

invulnerable /ɪnˈvʌlnərəbl/ *adj* that cannot be hurt or damaged.

inward /ˈɪnwəd/ *adj* 1 inner: ~ *thoughts*. 2 turned towards the inside. **inward** (also **inwards**) *adv* 1 towards the inside. 2 into or towards the mind or spirit. **inwardly** *adv* in mind or spirit.

iodine /ˈaɪədiːn; *US* -daɪn/ *n* [U] dark blue liquid used in medicine and photography.

ion /ˈaɪən/ *n* [C] electrically charged particle. **ionize** *v* [I, T] change into ions.

iota /aɪˈəʊtə/ *n* [sing] very small amount.

IOU /ˌaɪ əʊ ˈjuː/ *n* [C] (*infml*) 'I owe you'; signed paper saying that one owes money.

IQ /ˌaɪ ˈkjuː/ *n* [C] measure of sb's intelligence: *have a high/low IQ*.

irate /aɪˈreɪt/ *adj* (*fml*) angry. **irately** *adv*.

iridescent /ˌɪrɪˈdesnt/ *adj* (*fml*) changing colour as light falls on it from different directions.

iris /ˈaɪrɪs/ *n* [C] 1 coloured part round the pupil of the eye. 2 tall plant with large bright flowers.

irk /ɜːk/ *v* [T] annoy. **irksome** /ˈɜːksəm/ *adj* annoying.

iron¹ /ˈaɪən; *US* ˈaɪərn/ *n* 1 [U] common hard metal, used in manufacturing and building: *an ~ bridge/gate*. 2 [C] implement with a flat base that can be heated to smooth clothes. 3 **irons** [pl] chains for a prisoner. 4 [U] (showing) determination: *have a will of ~/an ~ will*. 5 (idm) **have many, etc irons in the fire** be involved in many different activities at the same time. **the ˌIron ˈCurtain** *n* [sing] frontier separating the eastern European communist countries from the West. **ironmonger** /ˈaɪənmʌŋgə(r)/ *n* (*Brit*) dealer in tools and household goods.

iron² /ˈaɪən; *US* ˈaɪərn/ *v* 1 [I, T] make (clothes, etc) smooth with an iron(2). 2 (phr *v*) **iron sth out** remove (difficulties, etc). **ironing** *n* [U] 1 action of ironing clothes. 2 clothes that need to be ironed: *do the ~ing*. **ˈironing-board** *n* [C] board on which clothes are ironed.

ironic /aɪˈrɒnɪk/ (also **ironical** /-kl/) *adj* using or expressing irony. **ironically** /-klɪ/ *adv*.

irony /ˈaɪərənɪ/ *n* (*pl* **-ies**) 1 [U] saying the opposite of one's real meaning, in order to be amusing, emphatic, etc. 2 [U, C] event or situation that is unexpected.

irrational /ɪˈræʃənl/ *adj* not

guided by reason: *an ~ fear of water*. **irrationally** /-nəlɪ/ *adv*.

irreconcilable /ˌɪrekənˈsaɪləbl/ *adj* (*fml*) impossible to reconcile.

irregular /ɪˈregjələ(r)/ *adj* 1 uneven: *an ~ surface*. 2 against the normal rules. 3 (*grammar*) not having the usual endings or forms: ~ *verbs*. **irregularity** /ɪˌregjəˈlærətɪ/ *n* [C, U] (*pl* **-ies**). **irregularly** *adv*.

irrelevant /ɪˈreləvənt/ *adj* not relevant. **irrelevance** /-əns/ *n* [U].

irreparable /ɪˈrepərəbl/ *adj* (of damage, an injury, etc) too bad to be put right.

irreplaceable /ˌɪrɪˈpleɪsəbl/ *adj* impossible to replace if lost or damaged.

irrepressible /ˌɪrɪˈpresəbl/ *adj* impossible to hold back or control.

irreproachable /ˌɪrɪˈprəʊtʃəbl/ *adj* (*fml*) without fault or blame.

irresistible /ˌɪrɪˈzɪstəbl/ *adj* too strong, delightful, etc to be resisted. **irresistibly** *adv*.

irrespective /ˌɪrɪˈspektɪv/ **irrespective of** *prep* without considering (sb/sth): *buy it now, ~ of the cost*.

irresponsible /ˌɪrɪˈspɒnsəbl/ *adj* (of a person or action) without a proper sense of responsibility. **irresponsibility** /ˌɪrɪˌspɒnsəˈbɪlətɪ/ *n* [U]. **irresponsibly** *adv*.

irreverent /ɪˈrevərənt/ *adj* not showing respect, esp for holy things. **irreverence** /-əns/ *n* [U]. **irreverently** *adv*.

irrevocable /ɪˈrevəkəbl/ *adj* (*fml*) impossible to change; final: *an ~ decision*.

irrigate /ˈɪrɪgeɪt/ *v* [T] supply (land) with water. **irrigation** /ˌɪrɪˈgeɪʃn/ *n* [U].

irritable /ˈɪrɪtəbl/ *adj* easily annoyed. **irritability** /ˌɪrɪtəˈbɪlətɪ/ *n* [U]. **irritably** *adv*.

irritate /ˈɪrɪteɪt/ *v* [T] 1 annoy. 2 make (part of the body) sore. **irritation** /ˌɪrɪˈteɪʃn/ *n* [U, C].

is ⇔ BE.

Islam /ˈɪzlɑːm; *US* ˈɪslɑːm/ *n* 1 [U] Muslim religion, based on the teaching of the Prophet Muhammad. 2 [sing] all Muslims. **Islamic** /ɪzˈlæmɪk; *US* ɪsˈlɑːmɪk/ *adj*.

island /ˈaɪlənd/ *n* [C] 1 piece of land surrounded by water. 2 = TRAFFIC ISLAND (TRAFFIC). **islander** *n* [C] person living on an island.

isle /aɪl/ *n* [C] (esp in poetry and proper names) island.

isn't /ˈɪznt/ is not. ⇔ BE.

isolate /ˈaɪsəleɪt/ *v* [T] keep

separate from others. **isolated** adj far from others: an ~d cottage. **isolation** /ˌaɪsəˈleɪʃn/ n [U].

issue /ˈɪʃuː; ˈɪsjuː/ n 1 [C] subject for discussion. 2 [C] one of a regular series of a magazine, etc. 3 [U] supply and distribution of sth. 4 [sing] (fml) result. 5 [U] (law) children. 6 (idm) (**the matter, point**, etc) **at issue** (the matter, etc) being discussed. **issue** v (fml) 1 [T] make (sth) known: ~ a statement. 2 [T] supply or provide: ~ weapons. 3 [I] come out.

it /ɪt/ pron (used as the subject or object of a v or after a prep) 1 (a) animal or thing mentioned earlier: Where's my book. Have you seen it? (b) baby, esp one whose sex is not known. 2 (used for identifying a person): 'Who's that?' 'It's the postman.' 3 (used when the subject or object comes at the end of a sentence): It's nice to see you. 4 (used for saying something about time, distance or weather): It's 12 o'clock. ○ It's raining. 5 (used for emphasizing any part of a sentence): It was 'work that exhausted him. 6 (idm) **this/that is 'it** (a) this/that is what is required. (b) this/that is the reason. (c) this/that is the end: That's it, then—we've lost the match. **its** /ɪts/ adj of or belonging to a thing, animal or baby: its tail.

italic /ɪˈtælɪk/ adj (of printed letters) sloping forwards: This is ~ type. **italics** n [pl] italic letters.

itch /ɪtʃ/ n 1 [C, usu sing] feeling of irritation on the skin, causing a desire to scratch. 2 [sing] strong desire: have an ~ to travel. **itch** v 1 [I] have an itch(1). 2 [I] for/to/ (infml) feel a strong desire for sth: pupils ~ing for the lesson to end ○ ~ ing to tell her the news. **itchy** adj 1 having or producing irritation on the skin: an ~y shirt. 2 (idm) (**get/have) itchy feet** (infml) (feel a) restless desire to travel.

it'd /ˈɪtəd/ 1 it had. ⇨ HAVE. 2 it would. ⇨ WILL¹, WOULD¹.

item /ˈaɪtəm/ n [C] 1 single thing or unit in a list, etc. 2 single piece of news. **itemize** v [T] give or write every item of.

itinerant /ɪˈtɪnərənt/ adj (fml) travelling from place to place: an ~ preacher.

itinerary /aɪˈtɪnərəri; US -reri/ n [C] (pl -ies) plan for a journey.

it'll /ˈɪtl/ it will. ⇨ WILL¹.

its ⇨ IT.

it's /ɪts/ 1 it is. ⇨ BE. 2 it has. ⇨ HAVE.

itself /ɪtˈself/ pron 1 (used as a reflexive when the animal, thing etc

causing the action is also affected by it): My dog hurt ~. 2 (used for emphasis): The name ~ sounds foreign. 3 (idm) (**all) by it'self** (a) automatically. (b) alone.

ITV /ˌaɪ tiː ˈviː/ abbr Independent Television.

I've /aɪv/ I have. ⇨ HAVE.

ivory /ˈaɪvəri/ n 1 [U] creamy-white bone-like substance forming the tusks of elephants. 2 colour of ivory. 3 (idm) **an ivory 'tower** place where people stay away from the unpleasant realities of everyday life.

ivy /ˈaɪvi/ n [U] climbing evergreen plant with dark shiny leaves.

J j

J, j /dʒeɪ/ n [C] (pl **J's, j's** /dʒeɪz/) the tenth letter of the English alphabet.

jab /dʒæb/ v (-bb-) [I, T] push (sth pointed) with sudden force. **jab** n [C] 1 sudden strong push. 2 (infml) injection.

jabber /ˈdʒæbə(r)/ v [I, T] talk or say (sth) quickly and excitedly. **jabber** n [U] jabbering.

jack¹ /dʒæk/ n [C] 1 device for lifting sth heavy, esp a car. 2 playing-card between the ten and the queen.

jack² /dʒæk/ v (phr v) **jack sth in** (sl) stop (work, etc). **jack sth up** lift sth with a jack¹(1).

jacket /ˈdʒækɪt/ n [C] 1 short coat with sleeves. 2 outer cover round a tank, pipe, etc. 3 skin of a baked potato. 4 loose paper cover for a book.

jack-knife /ˈdʒæknaɪf/ n [C] (pl -**knives**) large pocket-knife with a folding blade. **jack-knife** v [I] (esp of an articulated lorry) bend sharply in the middle.

jackpot /ˈdʒækpɒt/ n [C] largest money prize to be won in a game.

Jacuzzi /dʒəˈkuːzi/ n [C] (P) bath with fast underwater currents of water.

jade /dʒeɪd/ n [U] hard, usu green, stone from which ornaments, etc are carved.

jaded /ˈdʒeɪdɪd/ adj tired and lacking energy, usu after too much of sth.

jagged /ˈdʒægɪd/ adj with a rough uneven edge.

jaguar /ˈdʒægjʊə(r)/ n [C] large spotted animal of the cat family, found in central America.

jail = GAOL.

jam[1] /dʒæm/ *n* [U] sweet food made by boiling fruit with sugar, eaten on bread.

jam[2] /dʒæm/ *v* (-mm-) 1 [T] push or squeeze into a space: ~ *clothes into a suitcase.* 2 [I, T] (of parts of a machine, etc) (cause to) become fixed; stick: *The window ~med.* 3 [T] block (a road or area). 4 [T] prevent (a radio message) from being heard by using a noise as interference. 5 (phr v) **jam sth on** operate (the brakes of a vehicle) suddenly and forcibly. **jam** *n* [C] 1 number of people, things, etc crowded together and preventing movement: *a traffic ~.* 2 (*infml*) difficult situation: *be in a ~.*

jangle /'dʒæŋgl/ *v* [I, T] (cause sth to) make an unpleasant noise like pieces of metal hitting one another. **jangle** *n* [sing] this noise.

janitor /'dʒænɪtə(r)/ *n* [C] (*US*) caretaker.

January /'dʒænjʊərɪ; *US* -jueri/ *n* [U, C] the first month of the year. (See examples of use at **April**.)

jar[1] /dʒɑː(r)/ *n* [C] (**a**) container, usu made of glass, with a wide top. (**b**) contents of this: *a ~ of honey.*

jar[2] /dʒɑː(r)/ *v* (-rr-) 1 [I] (*on*)// have an unpleasant effect on sb: *Her singing really ~s on my nerves.* 2 [I] (*with*)// disagree with sth; be unsuitable. 3 [T] give a sudden or painful shock to sb. **jarring** *adj*.

jargon /'dʒɑːgən/ *n* [U] special or technical words used by a particular group of people: *medical ~.*

jaundice /'dʒɔːndɪs/ *n* [U] disease that makes the skin and whites of the eyes yellow. **jaundiced** *adj* suspicious; bitter: *a ~d opinion.*

jaunt /dʒɔːnt/ *n* [C] short journey, made for pleasure: *go on a ~.* **jaunty** *adj* (**-ier, -iest**) cheerful and self-confident. **jauntily** *adv.*

javelin /'dʒævlɪn/ *n* [C] light spear for throwing.

jaw /dʒɔː/ *n* 1 [C] either of the bone structures containing the teeth: *the lower/upper ~.* 2 [sing] lower part of the face. 3 **jaws** [pl] mouth with its bones and teeth: (*fig*) *escape from the ~s of death.* 4 **jaws** [pl] part of a tool or machine that holds things tightly. '**jawbone** *n* [C] either of the two bones forming the lower jaw.

jazz /dʒæz/ *n* [U] music with a strong rhythm, of American Negro origin. **jazz** *v* 1 [T] play (music) in the style of jazz. 2 (phr v) **jazz sth up** make sth more lively. **jazzy** *adj* (**-ier, -iest**) (*infml*) 1 of

or like jazz. 2 bright or showy: *a ~y tie.*

jealous /'dʒeləs/ *adj* 1 feeling fear or bitterness at rivals in love: *a ~ husband.* 2 (*of*)// feeling bitterness and anger at sb's success, wealth, etc. 3 determined to protect what one has: *~ of one's rights.* **jealously** *adv.* **jealousy** *n* [U, C] (*pl* **-ies**).

jeans /dʒiːnz/ *n* [pl] trousers of strong cotton for informal wear.

Jeep /dʒiːp/ *n* [C] (*P*) small motor vehicle for driving over rough ground.

jeer /dʒɪə(r)/ *v* [I, T] (*at*)// laugh rudely at sb; mock. **jeer** *n* [C] jeering remark.

jelly /'dʒelɪ/ *n* (*pl* **-ies**) 1 [U, C] clear sweet soft fruit-flavoured food. 2 [U] kind of clear jam: *blackcurrant ~.* '**jellyfish** *n* [C] (*pl* **jellyfish** *or* **~es**) sea-animal with a soft clear body which can sting.

jeopardize /'dʒepədaɪz/ *v* [T] put in danger. **jeopardy** /-pədɪ/ *n* (idm) **in jeopardy** in danger of failure, loss, etc: *The success of our plan has been put in jeopardy.*

jerk /dʒɜːk/ *n* [C] 1 sudden forceful pull or movement. 2 (*infml derog*) foolish person. **jerk** *v* [I, T] pull or move (sth/sb) with a jerk. **jerky** *adj* (**-ier, -iest**) with sudden starts and stops.

jersey /'dʒɜːzɪ/ *n* [C] close-fitting knitted (esp woollen) garment for the upper body.

jest /dʒest/ *n* 1 [C] joke. 2 (idm) **in jest** in fun. **jest** *v* [I] (*fml*) joke.

jet[1] /dʒet/ *n* [C] 1 aircraft powered by a jet engine. 2 (**a**) strong narrow stream of gas, liquid, etc forced out of a small opening. (**b**) narrow opening from which this comes. **jet** *v* (-tt-) [I] travel by jet(1). '**jet engine** *n* [C] engine that is used on aircraft and sends out a jet of hot gases, etc at the back. '**jet lag** *n* [U] tiredness felt after a long flight to a place where the time is different. **the** '**jet set** *n* [sing] rich fashionable people who travel about the world.

jet[2] /dʒet/ *n* [U] hard black highly polished mineral. **jet-'black** *adj* of a deep shiny black colour.

jettison /'dʒetɪsn/ *v* [T] throw away (sth unwanted).

jetty /'dʒetɪ/ *n* [C] (*pl* **-ies**) stone wall or wooden platform built out into a sea, river, etc as a landing-place for boats.

Jew /dʒuː/ *n* [C] person of the Hebrew people or religion. **Jewish** *adj.*

jewel /'dʒuːəl/ *n* [C] 1 precious stone, eg a diamond. 2 small precious stone used in a watch. **3** (*fig*) person or thing that is greatly valued. **jeweller** (*US* **-l-**) *n* [C] person who sells, makes or repairs jewellery. **jewellery** (also **jewelry**) /-rı/ *n* [U] ornaments, eg rings and necklaces, esp made of gold, silver, etc.

jibe = GIBE.

jiffy /ˈdʒıfı/ *n* [C] (*pl* **-ies**) (*infml*) moment.

jig /dʒıg/ *n* [C] (music for a) quick lively dance. **jig** *v* (**-gg-**) **1** [I] dance a jig. **2** [I, T] move up and down with short quick movements.

jiggle /ˈdʒıgl/ *v* [I, T] (*infml*) move lightly and quickly from side to side or up and down.

jigsaw /ˈdʒıgsɔː/ *n* [C] (also **ˈjigsaw puzzle**) picture on cardboard or wood cut into irregular shapes that has to be fitted together again.

jilt /dʒılt/ *v* [T] suddenly leave (sb) with whom one has had a close relationship.

jingle /ˈdʒıŋgl/ *n* **1** [sing] gentle ringing sound of small bells, keys, etc. **2** [C] short simple rhyme or song, esp used in advertising. **jingle** *v* [I, T] (cause sth to) make a gentle ringing sound.

jinx /dʒıŋks/ *n* [C, usu sing] (person or thing thought to bring) bad luck.

jive /dʒaıv/ *n* (usu **the jive**) [sing] (dance to) a fast lively form of music with a strong beat. **jive** *v* [I] dance to jive music.

job /dʒɒb/ *n* [C] **1** regular paid occupation; employment. **2** piece of work. **3** difficult task: *Finding a flat to rent was quite a ~.* **4** [usu sing] duty or function: *It's not my ~ to do this.* **5** (*infml*) criminal act, esp theft. **6** (idm) **just the 'job** (*infml*) exactly what is wanted or needed. **make a bad, good, etc job of sth** do sth badly, well, etc. **jobless** *adj* unemployed. **job sharing** *n* [U] arrangement by which two people share a full-time job. **jockey¹** /ˈdʒɒkı/ *n* [C] professional rider in horse-races.

jockey² /ˈdʒɒkı/ *v* (phr v) **jockey for sth** try hard to gain (an advantage, favour, etc): ~ *for position*.

jog /dʒɒg/ *v* (**-gg-**) **1** [T] push or bump slightly. **2** [I] run slowly, esp for exercise. **3** (idm) **jog sb's memory** help sb to remember sth. **4** (phr v) **jog along/on** continue in a steady unexciting manner. **jog** *n* [sing] **1** slight push or bump. **2** slow run, esp for exercise. **jogger** *n* [C] person who jogs(2).

join /dʒɔın/ *v* **1** [T] fasten (one thing) to (another thing); connect.

2 [I, T] come together with (sb/sth): *The two roads ~ here.* ○ *Please ~ us for a drink.* **3** [T] become a member of: ~ *a club.* **4** (idm) **join 'forces (with sb)** come together to achieve a common purpose. **5** (phr v) **join in (sth)** take part in (an activity). **join** *n* [C] place where two things are joined.

joiner /ˈdʒɔınə(r)/ *n* [C] skilled worker who makes wooden window frames, doors, etc of buildings. **joinery** *n* [U] work of a joiner.

joint¹ /dʒɔınt/ *n* [C] **1** place where two bones are joined together. **2** place where two or more things are joined: *the ~ of a pipe.* **3** large piece of meat. **4** (*sl derog*) public place for drinking, gambling, etc. **5** (*sl*) cigarette containing marijuana.

joint² /dʒɔınt/ *adj* shared or done by two or more people: ~ *responsibility* ○ *a ~ account*, ie a bank account in the name of more than one person. **jointly** *adv*.

joist /dʒɔıst/ *n* [C] wood or steel beam supporting a floor or ceiling.

joke /dʒəʊk/ *n* [C] something said or done to cause amusement and laughter. **joke** *v* [I] tell jokes. **joker** *n* [C] **1** person who makes jokes. **2** extra playing-card used in certain card-games. **jokingly** *adv* in a joking manner.

jolly /ˈdʒɒlı/ *adj* (**-ier**, **-iest**) happy and cheerful. **jolly** *adv* (*Brit infml*) very: *a ~ good teacher.*

jolt /dʒəʊlt/ *v* [I, T] move with sudden jerky movements. **jolt** *n* [C, usu sing] sudden bump.

jostle /ˈdʒɒsl/ *v* [I, T] push roughly against (sb), usu in a crowd.

jot /dʒɒt/ *v* (**-tt-**) (phr v) **jot sth down** make a quick written note of sth. **jotter** *n* [C] notebook.

journal /ˈdʒɜːnl/ *n* [C] **1** magazine or newspaper. **2** daily record of events. **journalism** /-nəlızəm/ *n* [U] work of writing for newspapers, television or radio. **journalist** *n* [C] person whose profession is journalism.

journey /ˈdʒɜːnı/ *n* [C] (distance covered in) travelling to a place, usu by land. **journey** *v* [I] (*fml*) travel.

jovial /ˈdʒəʊvıəl/ *adj* happy and friendly.

joy /dʒɔı/ *n* **1** [U] great happiness. **2** [C] something that causes joy. **joyful** *adj* filled with or causing joy. **joyfully** *adv*. **joyous** *adj* (*rhet*) joyful. **joyously** *adv*.

jubilant /ˈdʒuːbılənt/ *adj* (*fml*) very happy, esp because of a success. **jubilation** /ˌdʒuːbɪˈleɪʃn/ *n* [U] great happiness, esp because of a success.

jubilee /ˈdʒuːbɪliː/ *n* [C] (celebration of a) special anniversary.

Judaism /ˈdʒuːdeɪɪzəm; *US* ·dɪzəm/ *n* [U] religion of the Jewish people; their culture.

judge /dʒʌdʒ/ *n* [C] 1 public officer with authority to decide cases in a lawcourt. 2 person that decides who has won a competition. 3 person able to give an opinion on the value of sth: *She's a good ~ of character.* **judge** *v* [I, T] 1 act as a judge in sth. 2 form an opinion about (sb/sth).

judgement (esp *law* **judgment**) /ˈdʒʌdʒmənt/ *n* 1 [C] opinion: *make a ~ of his character.* 2 [C, U] decision of a lawcourt or judge: *The court has still to pass ~,* ie give a decision. 3 [U] ability to make sensible decisions.

judicial /dʒuːˈdɪʃl/ *adj* of or by a lawcourt; of a judge or judgement.

judiciary /dʒuːˈdɪʃəri; *US* ·ʃieri/ *n* [C, also sing with pl v] (*pl* -ies) all the judges of a country.

judicious /dʒuːˈdɪʃəs/ *adj* (*fml*) showing or having good sense. **judiciously** *adv.*

judo /ˈdʒuːdəʊ/ *n* [U] Japanese sport of wrestling and self-defence.

jug /dʒʌg/ *n* [C] (*Brit*) (a) deep container for liquids, with a handle and a lip. (b) amount of liquid contained in this: *a ~ of milk.*

juggernaut /ˈdʒʌgənɔːt/ *n* [C] (*Brit*) very large lorry.

juggle /ˈdʒʌgl/ *v* [I, T] 1 keep (objects, esp balls) in the air by throwing and catching them. 2 (*with*) change the arrangement of (sth), esp to deceive: *juggling (with) the figures.* **juggler** *n* [C].

juice /dʒuːs/ *n* [U, C] liquid obtained from fruit, vegetables or meat. **juicy** *adj* (-ier, -iest) 1 containing a lot of juice. 2 (*infml*) interesting, esp because scandalous.

juke-box /ˈdʒuːkbɒks/ *n* [C] large coin-operated record-player.

July /dʒuˈlaɪ/ *n* [U, C] the seventh month of the year. (See examples of use at *April*).

jumble /ˈdʒʌmbl/ *v* [T] (*up*) mix (things) in a confused way. **jumble** *n* 1 [sing] confused or untidy group of things. 2 [U] (*Brit*) goods for a jumble sale. **'jumble sale** *n* [C] (*Brit*) sale of old unwanted goods to get money for a charity.

jumbo /ˈdʒʌmbəʊ/ *adj* (*infml*) very large. **jumbo** /ˈdʒʌmbəʊ/ *n* (*pl* ~**s**) (also **jumbo 'jet**) very large jet aircraft for passengers; Boeing 747.

jump /dʒʌmp/ *v* 1 [I] move quickly off the ground by using the force of the legs and feet: *~ up in the air.* 2 [T] pass over (sth) by jumping: *~ a wall.* 3 [I] move quickly and suddenly: *The loud bang made me ~.* 4 [I] rise suddenly by a large amount: *Prices ~ed by 60% last year.* 5 [T] (*infml*) attack suddenly. 6 (idm) **jump on the bandwagon** ⇨ BAND. **jump the gun** do sth too soon. **jump the queue** obtain sth without waiting for one's proper turn. **jump to con'clusions** come to a decision about sth too quickly. 7 (phr v) **jump at sth** accept (an opportunity, chance, etc) eagerly. **jumper** *n* [C].

jump² /dʒʌmp/ *n* [C] 1 act of jumping. 2 thing to be jumped over. 3 (*in*) sudden rise in amount: *a huge ~ in profits.* **jumpy** *adj* (-ier, -iest) (*infml*) nervous; anxious.

jumper /ˈdʒʌmpə(r)/ *n* [C] (*Brit*) = JERSEY.

junction /ˈdʒʌŋkʃn/ *n* [C] place where roads or railway lines meet.

juncture /ˈdʒʌŋktʃə(r)/ *n* (idm) **at this juncture** (*fml*) at this time.

June /dʒuːn/ *n* [U, C] the sixth month of the year. (See examples of use at *April*).

jungle /ˈdʒʌŋgl/ *n* [C, U] land in a tropical country, covered with thick forest.

junior /ˈdʒuːnɪə(r)/ *adj* 1 (*to*) lower in rank than sb. 2 **Junior** (esp *US*) (used of a son having the same name as his father). 3 (*Brit*) of or for children aged 7 to 11: *a ~ school.* **junior** *n* 1 [C] person with a lower rank. 2 [sing] person who is a certain number of years younger than sb else: *He is three years her ~.*

junk /dʒʌŋk/ *n* [U] old or unwanted things, usu of no value. **'junk food** *n* [U] (*infml derog*) food that is thought to be bad for one's health.

jurisdiction /ˌdʒʊərɪsˈdɪkʃn/ *n* [U] legal authority.

juror /ˈdʒʊərə(r)/ *n* [C] member of a jury.

jury /ˈdʒʊəri/ *n* [C, also sing with pl v] (*pl* -ies) 1 group of people in a lawcourt who decide whether the accused person is guilty or not guilty. 2 group of people who decide the winner of a competition.

just¹ /dʒʌst/ *adj* according to what is right and proper; fair: *a ~ decision.* **justly** *adv.*

just² /dʒʌst/ *adv* 1 a short time ago: *I've ~ had dinner.* 2 exactly:

It's ~ 2 o'clock. ○ *Put it ~ here.* **3 just as (a)** exactly as: *Leave everything ~ as you find it.* **(b)** at the same moment as: *She arrived ~ as I did.* **4** barely; scarcely: *I can only ~ reach the shelf.* **5** at this/that moment: *We're ~ leaving.* **6** *about/going to do sth/i/* (used for referring to the immediate future): *The clock is ~ going to strike 12.* **7** simply: *Why not ~ wait and see?* **8** only: *There is ~ one way of saving him.* **9** (used for calling attention): *J~ listen to me!* **10** (idm) **just about** almost. **just 'now (a)** at this moment: *I can't do it ~ now.* **(b)** only a short time ago: *I saw him ~ now.*

justice /ˈdʒʌstɪs/ *n* **1** [U] quality of being right and fair. **2** [U] the law and its administration: *a court of ~.* **3** [C] judge(1): *the Lord Chief J~.* ,**Justice of the 'Peace** *n* [C] magistrate.

justify /ˈdʒʌstɪfaɪ/ *v* (*pt, pp* **-ied**) [T] **1** show that (sth) is right or reasonable. **2** be a good reason for (sth). **justifiable** /ˌdʒʌstɪˈfaɪəbl/ *adj* that can be justified. **justifiably** *adv*. **justification** /ˌdʒʌstɪfɪˈkeɪʃn/ *n* [U, C] (*for*)|| acceptable reason.

jut /dʒʌt/ *v* (**-tt-**) (phr v) **jut out** stand out (from the surrounding surface).

juvenile /ˈdʒuːvənaɪl/ *n* [C] (*fml* or *law*) young person. **juvenile** *adj* (*fml* or *law*) of or suitable for young people. **2** (*derog*) immature or foolish. **juvenile de'linquent** *n* [C].

juxtapose /ˌdʒʌkstəˈpəʊz/ *v* [T] (*fml*) place side by side. **juxtaposition** /ˌdʒʌkstəpəˈzɪʃn/ *n* [U].

K k

K, k /keɪ/ *n* [C] (*pl* **K's, k's** /keɪz/) the eleventh letter of the English alphabet.

K /keɪ/ *abbr* (*computing*) kilobyte.

kaleidoscope /kəˈlaɪdəskəʊp/ *n* **1** [C] tube containing mirrors and small pieces of coloured glass, turned to produce changing patterns. **2** [sing] constantly and quickly changing pattern.

kangaroo /ˌkæŋɡəˈruː/ *n* [C] (*pl* ~ s) Australian animal that jumps along and carries its baby in a pouch.

karate /kəˈrɑːtɪ/ *n* [U] Japanese

system of fighting, using the hands and feet.

kebab /kɪˈbæb/ *n* [C] small pieces of meat cooked on a metal stick.

keel /kiːl/ *n* [C] wood or steel structure along the bottom of a ship. **keel** *v* (phr v) **keel over 1** (of a ship) capsize. **2** fall over sideways.

keen /kiːn/ *adj* **1 (a)** // having a strong interest in sth; enthusiastic or eager: *He's very ~ on tennis.* **(b)** *on*// fond of sb. **2** (of the senses, mind or feelings) strong; quick. **3** (of the wind) very cold. **keenly** *adv*.

keep¹ /kiːp/ *v* (*pt, pp* **kept** /kept/) **1** [I, T] (cause to) remain in a state or position: *K~ (them) quiet!* ○ *K~ off the grass!* **2** [I] (on) *doing/*/ continue doing sth; do sth repeatedly: *He ~ s (on) interrupting me.* **3** [T] continue to have (sth): *Here's £5 — you can ~ the change.* **4** [T] *from//* prevent (sb) from doing sth: *~ him from leaving.* **5** [T] delay or detain: *You're very late — what kept you?* **6** [T] own or manage: *~ a shop.* **7** [T] not tell (a secret). **8** [I] (of food) remain in good condition: *Milk doesn't ~ in hot weather.* **9** [I] be in the state of health that is mentioned: *Is she ~ ing well?* **10** [T] **(a)** make written entries in: *~ a diary.* **(b)** write a record of: *~ an account.* **11** [T] support (sb) with money, etc. **12** [T] fulfil: *~ a promise.* **13** (idm) **keep abreast of sth** ⇒ ABREAST. **keep sb at arm's length** refuse to let sb become friendly. **keep the ball rolling** ⇒ BALL¹. **keep sb/sth at bay** ⇒ BAY². **keep sb company** remain with sb, so that he/she is not alone. **keep count of sth** ⇒ COUNT². **keep one's 'distance (from sb/sth) (a)** not go too near to sb/sth. **(b)** not become friendly or involved with sb/sth. **keep an 'eye on sb/sth** make sure that sb/sth is safe. **keep one's fingers crossed** hope that sb will be successful: *Good luck with your exam — we're ~ ing our fingers crossed for you.* **keep one's ground** ⇒ GROUND¹. **keep one's 'hair/shirt on** (*inf/ml*) not become angry. **keep one's head** ⇒ HEAD¹. **keep one's head above water** stay out of debt or other difficulty. **keep sth in mind** ⇒ MIND¹. **keep sb in the dark** ⇒ DARK². **keep it 'up** continue to do good work. **keep one's 'mouth shut** not talk about a secret. **keep an open mind** ⇒ OPEN¹. **keep pace (with sb/sth)** move forward at the same speed (as sb/sth). **keep the 'peace (a)**

stop people fighting. (b) not make a disturbance in public. **keep quiet about sth**, **keep sth quiet** say nothing about sth. **keep a straight 'face** stop oneself from smiling and laughing. **keep a tight 'rein on sb/sth** control sb/sth firmly. **keep one's wits about one** ⇨ WIT. 14 (phr v) **keep at sth** continue to work at sth. **keep (sb/sth) away (from sb/sth)** (cause sb/sth) not to go near sb/sth. **keep sth back (from sb)** not tell (information, etc) (to sb). **keep sb 'down** repress or oppress (a people, etc). **keep sth 'down** not allow sth to grow or increase. **keep sth from sb** not tell sb about sth. **keep in with sb** remain friendly with sb. **keep sb on about sth** ⇨ ON¹. **keep 'on (at sb) (about sth)** continue talking (to sb) in an irritating way (about sth). **keep 'out (of sth)** not enter (a place). **keep out of sth** avoid sth. **keep to sth** (a) not wander from or leave sth: ~ *to the path* ○ (*fig*) ~ *to the point*. (b) follow or observe (a plan, schedule, promise, etc). **keep one self to one'self** avoid meeting people socially. **keep sth to one'self** not tell other people about sth. **keep sth up** (a) prevent sth from falling down. (b) cause sth to remain at a high level: ~ *prices up* ○ (*fig*) ~ *one's spirits up*. (c) continue sth: *Do you still* ~ *up* (ie *practise*) *your French?* (d) maintain (a house, garden, etc) in good condition. **keep 'up (with sb/sth)** move at the same speed (as sb/sth).

keep² /kiːp/ n 1 [U] (cost of food and other necessary things: *earn one's* ~. 2 (idm) **for 'keeps** (*infml*) for ever.

keeper /'kiːpə(r)/ n[C] 1 person who looks after animals in a zoo. 2 (esp in compounds) person who is in charge of sth: *a shop* ~.

keeping /'kiːpɪŋ/ n (idm) **in sb's keeping** in sb's care: *The keys are in his* ~. **in/out of keeping with sth** in/not in harmony with sth.

keepsake /'kiːpseɪk/ n[C] small present that reminds one of the giver.

kennel /'kenl/ n 1 [C] small hut for a dog. 2 **kennels** (with sing or pl v) place where dogs are bred, cared for, etc.

kept *pt*, *pp* of KEEP¹.

kerb (esp US **curb**) /kɜːb/ n[C] stone edge of a pavement.

kernel /'kɜːnl/ n[C] 1 inner part of a nut or seed. 2 (*fig*) most important part of a subject, etc.

kestrel /'kestrəl/ n[C] kind of

small hawk.

ketchup /'ketʃəp/ n[U] thick sauce made from tomatoes, vinegar, etc.

kettle /'ketl/ n[C] container with a spout, used for boiling water.

key¹ /kiː/ n[C] 1 piece of metal that locks or unlocks a door, etc. 2 [usu sing] (*to*)// (*fig*) something that provides the answer to a problem, etc: *Diet and exercise are the* ~ *to good health*. 3 set of answers to exercises. 4 lever or button to be pressed on a typewriter, piano, etc. 5 (*music*) set of related notes: *in the* ~ *of G*. **key** *adj* very important; essential: *a* ~ *position*. **'keyboard** n[C] set of keys(4) on a typewriter, computer, etc. **'keyboard** *v*[T] put (information) into a computer using a keyboard. **'keyhole** n[C] hole through which a key(1) is put. **'keynote** n[C] most important idea (of a speech, etc). **'key-ring** n[C] ring on which keys are kept.

key² /kiː/ *v*[T] (*in*)// (*computing*) type in (information) using a keyboard. **keyed up** *adj* excited or nervous.

kg *abbr* kilogram(s).

khaki /'kɑːkɪ/ *adj* brownish-yellow colour.

kibbutz /kɪ'bʊts/ n[C] (*pl* ~**im** /kɪbʊ'tsiːm/) communal farm or settlement in Israel.

kick¹ /kɪk/ *v* 1 [T] hit with the foot. 2 [I] move one's foot or feet suddenly and forcefully. 3 [I] (of a gun) move suddenly when fired. 4 (idm) **kick the 'bucket** (*sl*) die. **kick the habit** (*infml*) stop smoking, drinking alcohol, etc. 5 (phr v) **kick against sth** protest about (rules, authority, etc). **kick 'off** start. **kick sb out (of sth)** (*infml*) send sb away, esp forcefully. **'kick-off** n[C] start of a football match.

kick² /kɪk/ n 1 [C] act of kicking: *give sb a* ~. 2 [C] (*infml*) feeling of pleasure: *She gets her* ~ *s from skiing*. 3 [U, sing] (*infml*) strength.

kid¹ /kɪd/ n 1 [C] (*infml*) child or young person. 2 (a) [C] young goat. (b) [U] leather made from its skin.

kid² /kɪd/ *v* (**-dd-**) [I, T] (*infml*) deceive; pretend.

kidnap /'kɪdnæp/ *v* (**-pp-**; *US* **-p-**) [T] take (sb) away by force and illegally, esp in order to demand money. **kidnapper** n[C].

kidney /'kɪdnɪ/ n 1 [C] organ that removes waste products from the blood and produces urine. 2 [U, C] kidney(s) of certain animals used as food.

kill /kɪl/ *v* 1 (a) [I] cause death.

(b) [T] cause the death of: (fig infml) He'll ~ me (ie be very angry with me) if he finds me here. **2** [T] (infml) hurt: My feet are ~ing me. **3** [T] bring to an end: ~ sb's love. **4** (idm) **kill ,two 'birds with ,one 'stone** achieve two aims with one action. **kill** n **1** [C] act of killing. **2** [usu sing] animal(s) killed. **killer** n [C]. **killing** n **1** [C] act of killing. **2** (idm) **,make a 'killing** (infml) make a large profit quickly. **'killjoy** n [C] (derog) person who stops others enjoying themselves.

kiln /kɪln/ n [C] oven for baking pottery, bricks, etc.

kilo /'kiːləʊ/ n [C] (pl ~s) kilogram.

kilobyte /'kɪləbaɪt/ n [C] 1024 bytes of computer information.

kilogram (also **-gramme**) /'kɪləgræm/ n [C] metric unit of weight; 1000 grams.

kilometre (US **-meter**) /'kɪləmiːtə(r), kɪ'lɒmɪtə(r)/ n [C] metric unit of length; 1000 metres.

kilowatt /'kɪləwɒt/ n [C] unit of electrical power; 1000 watts.

kilt /kɪlt/ n [C] tartan skirt sometimes worn by Scotsmen.

kind[1] /kaɪnd/ n **1** [C] group with similar features; sort; type: two ~ s of fruit. **2** (idm) **in kind** (a) (of payment) in goods, not money. **(b)** (fig) in the same way. **a kind of** (infml) (used for showing uncertainty): I had a ~ of feeling this might happen.

kind[2] /kaɪnd/ adj friendly and thoughtful to others. **kind-'hearted** adj kind and gentle. **kindly** adj (-ier, -iest) (infml) kind. **kindly** adv **1** in a kind way. **2** (used in polite requests and for showing annoyance) please: K~ ly leave me alone! **3** (idm) **not take kindly to sb/sth** not like sb/sth. **kindness** n **1** [U] quality of being kind. **2** [C] kind act.

kindergarten /'kɪndəgɑːtn/ n [C] school for very young children.

kindle /'kɪndl/ v **1** [I, T] (cause sth to) start burning. **2** [T] (fig) arouse or stimulate (a feeling).

kindred /'kɪndrɪd/ adj (idm) **a kindred 'spirit** person whose interests, beliefs, etc are similar to one's own.

king /kɪŋ/ n [C] **1** (title of the) male ruler of a country. **2** the most important member of a group. **3** (in chess) the most important piece. **4** playing-card with a picture of a king. **'king-size** (also **-sized**) adj larger than normal: a ~-size bed.

kingdom /'kɪŋdəm/ n [C] **1** country ruled by a king or queen. **2** any one of the three divisions of the natural world: the animal, plant and mineral ~ s.

kink /kɪŋk/ n [C] **1** twist in a wire, hair, pipe, etc. **2** (usu derog) something strange or abnormal in sb's character. **kink** v [I, T] (cause sth to) form kinks(1). **kinky** adj (-ier, -iest) (infml) strange or abnormal, esp in sexual behaviour.

kiosk /'kiːɒsk/ n [C] small open-fronted shop where newspapers, sweets, etc are sold.

kipper /'kɪpə(r)/ n [C] salted herring, dried or smoked.

kiss /kɪs/ v [I, T] touch (sb) with one's lips to show affection or as a greeting. **kiss** n [C] touch given with the lips. **the kiss of 'life** n [sing] mouth-to-mouth way of helping sb to start breathing again.

kit /kɪt/ n [C] **1** set of tools or equipment: a first-aid ~. **2** [C, U] set of clothes and equipment, esp for a soldier or sportsman. **3** [C] set of pieces to be put together to make sth. **kit** v (-tt-) (phr v) **kit sb out/ up (with sth)** provide sb with necessary equipment, etc.

kitchen /'kɪtʃɪn/ n [C] room in which meals are cooked.

kite /kaɪt/ n [C] light framework covered with paper, cloth, etc, which flies in the wind.

kith /kɪθ/ n (idm) **,kith and 'kin** /kɪn/ friends and relations.

kitten /'kɪtn/ n [C] young cat.

kitty /'kɪtɪ/ n [C] (pl -ies) money collected by several people for a shared use.

kiwi /'kiːwiː/ n [C] **1** New Zealand bird that cannot fly. **2** Kiwi (infml) New Zealander.

km abbr (pl **km** or ~s) kilometre(s).

knack /næk/ n [sing] skill at doing a task.

knackered /'nækəd/ adj (Brit sl) very tired.

knead /niːd/ v [T] **1** press and stretch (bread dough) with the hands. **2** rub and press (muscles).

knee /niː/ n [C] **1** (a) joint in the middle of the leg. **(b)** part of the garment covering this. **2** (idm) **bring sb to his/her 'knees** force sb to give in. **'kneecap** n [C] small flat bone at the front of the knee. **,knee-'deep** adj deep enough to reach the knees.

kneel /niːl/ v (pt, pp **knelt** /nelt/ or esp US ~ed) [I] go down on one's knees.

knew pt of KNOW.

knickers /'nɪkəz/ n [pl] woman's or girl's underpants.

knick-knack /'nɪknæk/ n [C, esp pl] small ornament.

knife /naɪf/ n [C] (pl **knives** /naɪvz/) sharp blade with a handle, used for cutting. **knife** v [T] injure (sb) with a knife. '**knife-edge** n (idm) **on a knife-edge** (of an important situation or result) very uncertain.

knight /naɪt/ n [C] 1 man to whom the title 'Sir' has been given. 2 (formerly) soldier of noble birth. 3 chess piece. **knight** v [T] make (sb) a knight(1). **knighthood** /-hʊd/ n [C, U] rank of a knight.

knit /nɪt/ v (-tt-, pt, pp ~ **ted**; in sense 2, usu skip) [I, T] 1 make a (garment) by looping wool, etc on long needles. 2 (cause sth to) join firmly together: *a closely* ~ *family*. **knitting** n [U] material being knitted. '**knitting-needle** n [C] long thin rod, used for knitting.

knives pl of KNIFE.

knob /nɒb/ n [C] 1 (a) round handle of a door, drawer, etc. (b) round control button. 2 small round piece: *a* ~ *of butter*. **knobbly** /-blɪ/ adj (-ier, -iest) with many small hard lumps: ~*bly knees*.

knock¹ /nɒk/ v 1 (a) [T] hit sharply. (b) [I] make a noise by hitting sth: ~ *on the door*. 2 [T] (*infml*) criticize. 3 (phr v) **knock about with sb** (*infml*) be often in sb's company. **knock sb/sth about** hit sb/sth roughly. **knock sth back** (*infml*) drink sth quickly. **knock sb down** strike sb to the ground: *She was* ~*ed down by a bus.* **knock sth down** demolish (a building). **knock sth/sb down** (force sb to) reduce (a price). **knock off** (sth) (*infml*) stop (work): *When do you* ~ *off?* **knock sth off** (a) take sth from a price: ~ *£20 off the price*. (b) (*sl*) steal sth. **knock sb out** (a) make sb unconscious by hitting him/her. (b) make sb/oneself exhausted. **knock sb out (of sth)** eliminate sb (from a competition). **knock sth up** make sth quickly: ~ *up a meal*. **knocker** n [C] hinged metal device on a door, used for knocking(1b). ,**knock-'kneed** adj having knees that touch when walking. ,**knock-'on effect** n [C] indirect result of an action. '**knock-out** n [C] 1 blow that knocks a boxer out. 2 competition from which losers are eliminated. 3 (*infml*) person or thing that is very impressive.

knock² /nɒk/ n [C] 1 sound of knocking. 2 (*infml*) unfortunate experience.

knot¹ /nɒt/ n [C] 1 fastening made by tying pieces of string, rope, etc. 2 twisted piece; tangle. 3 hard round lump in wood. 4 small group of people. **knot** v (-tt-) 1 [I, T] make or form knots. 2 [T] fasten with a knot. **knotty** adj (-ier, -iest) 1 (of wood) full of knots. 2 difficult to solve: *a* ~ *ty problem.*

knot² /nɒt/ n [C, usu pl] unit of speed used by ships; one nautical mile (1·852 kilometres) per hour.

know /nəʊ/ v (*pt* **knew** /njuː; US nuː/, *pp* ~**n** /nəʊn/) 1 [I, T] have (sth) in one's mind. 2 [T] be acquainted with (sb). 3 [T] be familiar with (a place). 4 [T] recognize: *I'll* ~ *her when I see her.* 5 [T] understand and be able to use (a language, skill, etc). 6 [T] have personal experience of: *a man who has* ~*n poverty.* 7 (idm) **be known as sb/sth** be called or regarded as sb/sth. **know sb by sight** recognize sb without knowing him/her personally. **know one's own 'mind** know what one wants. 8 (phr v) **know about sth** have information about sth. **know of sb/ sth** have (only a little) information about sb/sth: *I* ~ *of the book but I've not read it.* '**know-how** n [C] (*infml*) practical knowledge or ability.

knowing /'nəʊɪŋ/ adj showing that one has information which is secret: *a* ~ *look.* **knowingly** adv 1 intentionally. 2 in a knowing way.

knowledge /'nɒlɪdʒ/ n 1 [U] understanding. 2 [U, sing] all that sb knows: *a* ~ *of French.* 3 [U] everything that is known; information. **knowledgeable** /-əbl/ adj well-informed.

known pp of KNOW.

knuckle /'nʌkl/ n [C] bone at the finger-joint. **knuckle** v (phr v) **knuckle under** (*infml*) be forced to accept sb's orders.

koala /kəʊ'ɑːlə/ n [C] Australian tree-climbing animal like a small bear.

Koran /kə'rɑːn; US -'ræn/ n **the Koran** [sing] the holy book of Muslims.

kosher /'kəʊʃə(r)/ adj (of food) fulfilling the requirements of Jewish law.

kowtow /ˌkaʊ'taʊ/ v [I] (*to*)// obey sb (too) humbly.

kph /ˌkeɪ piː 'eɪtʃ/ abbr kilometres per hour.

L *l*

L, l /el/ *n* [C] (*pl* **L's, l's** /elz/) **1** the twelfth letter of the English alphabet. **2** Roman numeral for 50.
L *abbr* **1** Lake. **2** (esp on electric plugs) live (connection).
l *abbr* **1** line. **2** litre(s).
Lab /læb/ *abbr* (*Brit politics*) Labour (Party).
lab /læb/ *n* [C] (*infml*) laboratory.
label /'leɪbl/ *n* [C] **1** piece of paper, cloth, etc fixed to sth to describe what it is, who owns it, etc. **2** (*fig*) word(s) describing sb/sth. **label** *v* (**-ll-**; *US* **-l-**) [T] **1** put a label on. **2** (*fig*) describe: *They ~led her (as) a liar.*
labor (*US*) = LABOUR. **labor union** (*US*) = TRADE UNION (TRADE[1]).
laboratory /lə'bɒrətrɪ; *US* 'læbrətɔːrɪ/ *n* [C] (*pl* **-ies**) room or building used for scientific experiments.
laborious /lə'bɔːrɪəs/ *adj* needing great effort. **laboriously** *adv*.
labour[1] (*US* **-or**) /'leɪbə(r)/ *n* **1** [U] (esp hard) work. **2** [C, usu pl] piece of work. **3** [U] workers as a group. **4** [U, sing] process of childbirth: *a woman in ~.* **5 Labour** [sing] (*Brit politics*) (with sing or pl v) the Labour Party. **the 'Labour Party** *n* [sing] (*Brit politics*) major political party, representing the interests of workers.
labour[2] (*US* **-or**) /'leɪbə(r)/ *v* [I] **1** work or try hard. **2** [I] do sth with difficulty and effort. **3** (idm) **~ the point** continue to repeat or explain sth already understood. **4** (phr v) **labour under sth** be deceived by (a mistaken idea). **labourer** (*US* **-bor-**) *n* [C] person who does heavy unskilled work.
labyrinth /'læbərɪnθ/ *n* [C] complicated network of winding paths, etc through which it is difficult to find one's way.
lace /leɪs/ *n* **1** [U] delicate decorative cloth with an open-work design of threads. **2** [C] cord for fastening shoes, etc. **lace** *v* [I, T] **1** fasten (sth) with a lace. **2** [T] (*with*)|| flavour or strengthen (a drink) with alcohol.
lacerate /'læsəreɪt/ *v* [T] (*fml*) cut or tear (the flesh). **laceration** /ˌlæsə'reɪʃn/ *n* [C, U].
lack /læk/ *v* [T] be without (sth/sb); have less than enough of. **2** (idm) **be 'lacking** not be available when needed. **be 'lacking in sth** not have enough of sth. **lack** *n* [U,

sing] absence or shortage (of sth needed): *a ~ of money.*
lackadaisical /ˌlækə'deɪzɪkl/ *adj* not showing enough interest or effort; unenthusiastic.
laconic /lə'kɒnɪk/ *adj* (*fml*) using few words. **laconically** /-klɪ/ *adv*.
lacquer /'lækə(r)/ *n* [U] **1** kind of transparent substance painted on metal or wood to give a hard glossy surface. **2** (*dated*) liquid spray to keep the hair in place. **lacquer** *v* [T] cover with lacquer.
lacy /'leɪsɪ/ *adj* (**-ier, -iest**) of or like lace(1).
lad /læd/ *n* [C] **1** boy; young man. **2** (*infml*) lively, daring or reckless man: *He's a bit of a ~.* **the lads** [pl] (*infml*) group of male friends: *He's gone out with the ~s.*
ladder /'lædə(r)/ *n* [C] **1** two lengths of wood with cross-pieces (= RUNGS), used for climbing. **2** fault in a woman's stocking, etc. **3** (*fig*) series of stages in an organization, sb's career, etc: *climb up the social ~.* **ladder** *v* [I, T] (of stockings, etc) (cause to) develop a ladder.
laden /'leɪdn/ *adj* (*with*)|| heavily loaded with goods.
ladle /'leɪdl/ *n* [C] large deep spoon for serving liquids. **ladle** *v* [T] serve with a ladle.
lady /'leɪdɪ/ *n* [C] (*pl* **-ies**) **1** (esp in polite use) woman. **2** woman who has good manners. **3** (esp formerly) woman of good family and social position. **4 Lady** (title of a) woman of noble rank. **5 the Ladies** [pl] (usu with sing v) (*Brit infml*) public toilet for women. **'ladylike** *adj* like or suitable for a lady; polite. **'ladyship** *n* (esp **Ladyship**) [C] (used as a title in speaking to or about a Lady): *her L~ship.*
lag[1] /læg/ *v* (**-gg-**) [I] (*behind*)|| go too slowly; go more slowly than others.
lag[2] /læg/ *v* (**-gg-**) [T] cover (pipes, etc) with material to prevent heat from escaping. **lagging** *n* [U] material used for this.
lager /'lɑːgə(r)/ *n* [C, U] (glass or bottle of) light pale beer.
lagoon /lə'guːn/ *n* [C] salt-water lake separated from the sea by sandbanks or coral reefs.
laid *pt, pp* of LAY[1].
lain *pp* of LIE[2].
lair /leə(r)/ *n* [C] home of a wild animal.
laity /'leɪətɪ/ *n* **the laity** [sing] (with sing or pl v) lay[3] people.
lake /leɪk/ *n* [C] large area of water surrounded by land.

lamb /læm/ n 1 (a) [C] young sheep. (b) [U] its meat. 2 [C] (*infml*) gentle or dear person.

lame /leɪm/ adj 1 unable to walk normally. 2 (of an excuse, etc) weak and unconvincing. 3 (idm) ,**lame 'duck** (a) person, organization, etc that is in difficulties and needs help. (b) (esp *US*) elected official in his/her final period of office. **lame** v [T] make lame. **lameness** n [U].

lament /lə'ment/ v [I, T] express great sorrow (for). **lament** n [C] song or poem expressing sorrow. **lamentable** /'læməntəbl/ adj unsatisfactory; regrettable. **lamentably** adv.

laminated /'læmɪneɪtɪd/ adj made by joining several thin layers together.

lamp /læmp/ n [C] apparatus for giving light. '**lamp-post** n [C] tall post supporting a street lamp. '**lampshade** n [C] cover placed round or over a lamp.

lance¹ /lɑːns; *US* læns/ n [C] long spearlike weapon formerly used by soldiers on horseback.

lance² /lɑːns; *US* læns/ v [T] cut open (a boil, etc) with a knife.

land¹ /lænd/ n 1 [U] solid dry part of the earth's surface. 2 [U] ground used for farming, etc: *work on the* '~. 3 (sometimes **lands**) [U, pl] property in the form of land. 4 [C] (*rhet*) country or nation. 5 (idm) **see, etc how the 'land lies** learn about the present situation. **landed** adj owning a lot of land. '**landlocked** adj (of a country) surrounded by other countries. '**landmark** n [C] 1 object easily seen and recognized from a distance. 2 (*fig*) important event, discovery, etc. '**landowner** n [C] person who owns (esp a large area of) land. '**landslide** n [C] 1 sliding of a mass of earth, rock, etc down the side of a mountain, etc. 2 (*fig*) victory by a very large majority in an election.

land² /lænd/ v 1 [I, T] (cause sb/ sth to) go on land from a ship. 2 [I, T] (of an aircraft) (cause to) come down to the ground. 3 [T] (*infml*) obtain: ~ *a job.* 4 (idm) **land on one's feet** ⇨ FOOT. 5 (idm) **land sb/oneself in sth** (*infml*) get sb/oneself into difficulties. **land up** (*infml*) reach a final position or situation: ~ *up in gaol.* **land sb with sth** (*infml*) give sb (an unwanted task, etc).

landing /'lændɪŋ/ n 1 act of coming to land: *a,crash-'landing.* 2 level area at the top of a set of stairs. 3 (also '**landing-place**) place where people and goods may

be landed from a ship, etc. '**landing-craft** n [C] flat-bottomed boat that brings soldiers, vehicles, etc ashore. '**landing-gear** n [U] = UNDERCARRIAGE. '**landing-stage** n [C] platform on which people and goods are landed from a boat.

landlady /'lændleɪdɪ/ n [C] (*pl* -**ies**) 1 woman from whom one rents a room, etc. 2 woman who owns or runs a public house or boarding-house.

landlord /'lændlɔːd/ n [C] 1 man from whom one rents land, a room, etc. 2 man who owns or runs a public house or boarding-house.

landscape /'lændskeɪp/ n [C] 1 scenery of an area of land. 2 picture showing a view of the countryside. **landscape** v [T] plan the appearance of (land) in a way that imitates attractive natural scenery.

lane /leɪn/ n [C] 1 narrow country road. 2 (in place names) narrow street: *Mill Lane.* 3 part of a road that is marked for a single line of traffic: *a four-* ~ *motorway.* 4 route regularly used by ships or aircraft. 5 marked part of track or water for each competitor in a race.

language /'læŋgwɪdʒ/ n 1 [U] system of sounds, words, etc used by humans to communicate thoughts and feelings. 2 [C] form of language used by a particular group, nation, etc: *the English* ~. 3 [U] manner of expressing oneself. 4 [U] words and phrases used by a particular group of people: *medical* ~. 5 [C, U] system of signs, symbols, etc: *a computer* ~ ○ *body* ~. '**language laboratory** n [C] room where foreign languages are learned using tape-recorders, etc.

languid /'læŋgwɪd/ adj (*fml*) (of a person) having no energy. **languidly** adv.

languish /'læŋgwɪʃ/ v [I] (*fml*) 1 be or become weak. 2 in// live and suffer in unpleasant conditions: ~ *in poverty.*

lank /læŋk/ adj 1 (of hair) straight and limp. 2 (of a person) tall and thin.

lanky /'læŋkɪ/ adj (-**ier**, -**iest**) unattractively tall and thin.

lantern /'læntən/ n [C] portable lamp with a transparent case for a candle or flame.

lap¹ /læp/ n [C] front part of a seated person from the waist to the knees: *a baby on his* ~.

lap² /læp/ n [C] one complete journey round a track or racecourse.

lap v (**-pp-**) [T] overtake (another competitor) to be one lap ahead.

lap³ /læp/ v (**-pp-**) 1 [T] (esp of animals) drink (sth) by taking it up with the tongue. 2 [I] (of water) make gentle splashing sounds. 3 (phr v) **lap sth up** (infml) receive (praise, news, etc) eagerly.

lapel /ləˈpel/ n [C] front part of the collar of a coat that is folded back.

lapse /læps/ n [C] 1 small error in behaviour, memory, etc. 2 passing of a period of time. **lapse** v [I] 1 (from, into)// change from good ways to bad ways: a ~d Catholic. 2 into// sink or pass gradually into sth: ~ into sleep. 3 (of time) pass. 4 (law) (of rights) be no longer valid because not used or continued.

larch /lɑːtʃ/ n [C] tall deciduous tree of the pine family with small cones.

lard /lɑːd/ n [U] fat of pigs, used in cooking.

larder /ˈlɑːdə(r)/ n [C] cupboard or small room for storing food.

large /lɑːdʒ/ adj (~r, ~st) 1 more than average or usual in size; big. 2 (idm) (as) **large as life** (joc) seen as sb really is. **by and large** on the whole; usually. **large** n (idm) **at large 1** (a) free. (b) in general: the country at ~. **largely** adv to a great extent; mainly. **'large-scale** adj 1 extensive: a ~ scale search. 2 drawn or made to a large scale.

lark¹ /lɑːk/ n [C] small songbird.

lark² /lɑːk/ n [C, usu sing] (infml) bit of fun. **lark** v [I] (about/around)// (infml) behave playfully or foolishly.

larva /ˈlɑːvə/ n [C] (pl ~ae /-viː/) insect in the first stage of its life.

larynx /ˈlærɪŋks/ n [C] (pl larynges /ləˈrɪndʒiːz/) box-like space at the top of the windpipe, containing the vocal cords that produce the voice. **laryngitis** /ˌlærɪnˈdʒaɪtɪs/ n [U] inflammation of the larynx.

lascivious /ləˈsɪvɪəs/ adj (fml) feeling, expressing or causing sexual desire.

laser /ˈleɪzə(r)/ n [C] device that produces an intense and highly controlled beam of light.

lash¹ /læʃ/ n [C] 1 (blow given with the) flexible part of a whip. 2 = EYELASH (EYE).

lash² /læʃ/ v 1 [I, T] strike (sb/sth) with or as if with a whip. 2 [I, T] (esp of an animal's tail) (cause to) move about violently. 3 [T] fasten tightly (with ropes, etc). 4 (phr v) **lash out** (against/at//) attack with blows or words. **(b)** (on)// (infml)

spend a lot of money freely.

lashings /ˈlæʃɪŋz/ n [pl] (Brit infml) plenty: ~s of cream.

lass /læs/ n [C] (esp Scot N Brit infml) girl.

lasso /læˈsuː/ n [C] (pl ~s or ~es) looped rope used for catching horses and cattle. **lasso** v [T] catch with a lasso.

last¹ /lɑːst; US læst/ adj 1 coming after all others: Friday is the ~ day of the week. 2 most recent; latest: ~ night. 3 only remaining; final: This is our ~ bottle of milk. 4 least likely or suitable: She's the ~ person to trust with a secret. 5 (idm) **be on one's/its last 'legs** be weak or in poor condition. **have the last 'laugh** be successful over one's critics, rivals, etc in the end. **have, etc the last 'word** make, etc the final remark that ends an argument. **in the/as a last re'sort** when everything else has failed. **the ˌlast 'ditch** the last effort to be made to avoid defeat: a ˌ~' ditch attempt. **the last straw** ⇨ STRAW. **the last 'word (in sth)** the most fashionable, modern, etc thing: This car is the ~ word in luxury. **last** n 1 the last person or thing that is last or mentioned last. 2 (idm) **at (long) 'last** after (much) delay. finally. **lastly** adv in the last place; finally.

last² /lɑːst; US læst/ adv 1 after all others. 2 most recently.

last³ /lɑːst; US læst/ v 1 [I] continue for a period of time. 2 [T] be enough (for): enough food to ~ two days. **lasting** adj continuing for a long time.

latch /lætʃ/ n [C] 1 small bar for fastening a door or gate. 2 spring lock on a door that needs a key to open it from the outside. **latch** v 1 [I, T] (cause to) be fastened with a latch. 2 (phr v) **latch on to sb** (infml) join sb and refuse to leave him/her.

late /leɪt/ adj (~r, ~st) 1 after the proper or usual time: The train is ~. 2 far on in time: in the ~ afternoon. 3 recent: the ~st news. 4 no longer alive: her ~ husband. 5 (idm) **at the 'latest** no later than a particular time. **late** adv 1 after the proper or usual time: get up ~. 2 far on in time: as ~ as the 1970's. **lately** adv recently.

latent /ˈleɪtnt/ adj existing but not yet active or developed: ~ talent.

lateral /ˈlætərəl/ adj of, at, from or to the side(s).

lathe /leɪð/ n [C] machine that shapes pieces of wood, metal, etc by turning them against a cutting tool.

lather /'lɑ:ðə(r); US 'læð-/ n [U] white foam produced by soap mixed with water. **lather** v 1 [I] form lather. 2 [T] cover with lather.

Latin /'lætɪn; US 'lætn/ adj, n [U] (of the) language of ancient Rome. ˌLatin A'merica n parts of Central and South America in which Spanish or Portuguese is the official language. ˌLatin A'merican n [C], adj.

latitude /'lætɪtjuːd; US -tuːd/ n 1 [U] distance north or south of the equator, measured in degrees. 2 [U] freedom of action or opinion.

latter /'lætə(r)/ adj near to the end of a period: the ~ part of her life. the **latter** pron the second mentioned of two. ˌlatter-'day adj modern. **latterly** adv recently.

lattice /'lætɪs/ n [C, U] framework of crossed (esp wooden) strips.

laugh /lɑːf; US læf/ v 1 [I] make the sounds and movements of the face that show lively amusement, happiness, etc. 2 (idm) **be no laughing matter** be serious. **laugh one's head off** ⇒ HEAD¹. 3 (phr v) **laugh at sb/sth** mock or ridicule sb/sth. **laugh** n [C] 1 act or sound of laughing. 2 (infml) amusing situation or person. **laughable** adj ridiculous. **laughably** adv. **laughing-stock** n [C, usu sing] person or thing that is made to appear foolish. **laughter** n [U] laughing.

launch¹ /lɔːntʃ/ v [T] 1 put (esp a newly-built ship) into the water. 2 send (a rocket, etc) high into the air. 3 begin (an activity): ~ a new business. 4 (phr v) **launch out into sth** begin sth with enthusiasm, boldness, etc: ~ out into a new career. **launch** n [C] act of launching sth. **'launching pad** n [C] base from which spacecraft, etc are launched.

launch² /lɔːntʃ/ n [C] large motor boat.

launder /'lɔːndə(r)/ v [T] (fml) wash and iron (clothes).

launderette /ˌlɔːn'dret, ˌlɔːndə'ret/ n [C] place where the public may wash and dry their clothes in coin-operated machines.

laundromat /'lɔːndrəmæt/ n [C] (P esp US) launderette.

laundry /'lɔːndrɪ/ n (pl -ies) 1 [C] place where clothes, etc are laundered. 2 [U] clothes, etc to be laundered.

laurel /'lɒrəl; US 'lɔːrəl/ n [C] evergreen shrub with smooth glossy leaves.

lava /'lɑːvə/ n [U] hot liquid rock that comes out of a volcano.

lavatory /'lævətrɪ; US -tɔːrɪ/ n [C] (pl -ies) toilet.

lavender /'lævəndə(r)/ n [U] 1 plant with sweet-smelling pale purple flowers. 2 pale purple colour.

lavish /'lævɪʃ/ adj 1 generous. 2 giving or producing in large quantities: a ~ meal. **lavish** v (phr v) **lavish sth on sb** give sth to sb generously. **lavishly** adv.

law /lɔː/ n 1 (a) [C] rule made by authority, esp a government. (b) (also the **law**) [U] system of such rules: Murder is against the ~. 2 [C] basic rule of action, eg in science: the ~ s of physics. 3 the **law** [sing] (infml) the police, etc. 4 (idm) **be a law unto one'self** ignore the usual rules and conventions of behaviour. **law and 'order** respect for the law. **law-abiding** adj obeying the law. **'law-court** n [C] place where legal cases are heard and judged. **lawful** adj 1 allowed by law. 2 recognized by law. **lawfully** adv. **lawless** adj not controlled by the law. **lawlessness** n [U]. **'lawsuit** n [C] non-criminal case in a lawcourt.

lawn /lɔːn/ n [C, U] area of closely-cut grass. **'lawn-mower** n [C] machine for cutting grass. ˌlawn 'tennis (fml) = TENNIS.

lawyer /'lɔːjə(r)/ n [C] person, esp a solicitor, who is trained and qualified in the law.

lax /læks/ adj not strict enough; careless. **laxity** n [U].

laxative /'læksətɪv/ n [C], adj (medicine, food or drink) that helps the bowels to empty.

lay¹ /leɪ/ v (pt, pp **laid** /leɪd/) 1 [T] put on a surface: ~ a book on the table. 2 [T] put in the correct position for a purpose: ~ the table, ie put knives, forks, plates, etc on it for a meal. 3 [T] (fml) cause (sth) to be less strong: ~ sb's fears. 4 [I, T] (of birds, insects, etc) produce (eggs). 5 [T] (△ sl) (esp passive) (of a man) have sex with (a woman). 6 (idm) **lay sth 'bare** reveal sth secret or hidden: ~ bare one's feelings. **lay the 'blame on sb** say that sb is responsible for a mistake, etc. **lay claim to sth** say that sth belongs to one. **lay down the 'law** say with authority what should be done. **lay down one's 'life** (rhet) sacrifice one's life. **lay a 'finger on sb** harm sb. **lay it 'on** ('thick) (infml) make one's feelings or experiences, seem greater than they really are. **lay sb 'low** make sb ill or weak. **lay oneself**

'open to sth behave so that one is likely to receive (criticism, etc). **lay sth 'waste** (*fml*) destroy sth completely. **7** (*phr v*) **lay into sb/ sth** (*infml*) attack sb/sth with words or blows. **lay 'off (sth)** (*infml*) stop doing or using sth harmful. **lay sb 'off** dismiss sb from work. **lay sth 'on** (a) supply (gas, water, etc) to a house. (b) (*infml*) provide sth: ~ *on a party*. **lay sb 'out** knock sb unconscious. **lay sth 'out** (a) spread sth out to be seen easily. (b) arrange sth in a planned way: *a well laid out garden*. **lay sb 'up** cause sb to stay in bed: *be laid up with flu*. **,laid-'back** *adj* (*sl*) happily relaxed and unworried. **'lay-off** *n* [C] act of dismissing a worker from a job. **'layout** *n* [C] way in which parts of sth are arranged according to a plan.

lay² *pt of* LIE².

lay³ /leɪ/ *adj* **1** of or by people who are not clergymen. **2** not professional. **'layman** /-mən/ *n* [C] lay person.

layabout /'leɪəbaʊt/ *n* [C] (*Brit infml*) lazy person who avoids work.

lay-by /'leɪ baɪ/ *n* [C] (*Brit*) area at the side of a road where vehicles may stop.

layer /'leɪə(r)/ *n* [C] thickness of some substance or material, often one of many, on a surface: *a ~ of dust* ○ *~s of clothing*.

layman ⇨ LAY³.

laze /leɪz/ *v* [I] be lazy; do nothing. **lazy** /'leɪzɪ/ *adj* (-ier, -iest) **1** unwilling to work. **2** showing a lack of activity. **lazily** *adv*. **laziness** *n* [U].

lb *abbr* (*pl* lb, lbs) pound (weight).

lead¹ /liːd/ *v* (*pt, pp* led /led/) **1** [T] (a) show (sb) the way, esp by going in front. (b) guide sb/sth by holding: ~ *a blind person*. **2** [T] influence the actions or opinions of: *What led you to this conclusion?* **3** [I] (of a road, etc) go somewhere or in a particular direction. **4** [I] *to// have sth as its result: a mistake that led to his death*. **5** [T] have a (certain kind of life): ~ *a miserable existence*. **6** [I, T] be in first place or ahead of (sb/sth). **7** [I, T] control or direct (sb/sth): ~ *a team of scientists*. **8** (idm) **lead sb astray** encourage sb to believe sth wrong or to do wrong. **lead the 'way** go first; show the way. **9** (*phr v*) **lead sb on** persuade sb to believe or do sth by making false promises, etc. **lead up to sth** prepare or introduce sth. **leader** *n* [C] person who leads. **leadership** *n* [U] position of being a leader; qualities of a

leader. **leading** *adj* most important. **,leading 'article** *n* [C] newspaper article giving the editor's opinion. **,leading 'question** *n* [C] question formed in such a way that it suggests the answer hoped for.

lead² /liːd/ *n* **1** [U, sing] guidance given by going first: *follow sb's ~*. **2** [sing] distance by which one competitor is in front: *a ~ of ten metres*. **3 the lead** [sing] first place or position: *take the ~*. **4** [C] (person playing the) main part in a play, etc. **5** [C] strap or cord for leading a dog. **6** [C] wire carrying electrical current. **7** [C] piece of information that might solve a crime or other problem.

lead³ /led/ *n* **1** [U] heavy soft greyish metal, used for water pipes, in roofing, etc. **2** [C, U] that part of a pencil which makes a mark. **leaden** /ledn/ *adj* **1** dull, heavy or slow. **2** dull grey.

leaf /liːf/ *n* (*pl* **leaves** /liːvz/) **1** [C] one of the (usu green and flat) parts of a plant growing from a stem. **2** [C] sheet of paper. **3** [U] metal, esp gold or silver, in the form of very thin sheets: *gold-~*. **4** [C] hinged, etc part of a table top. **5** (idm) **take a leaf out of sb's 'book** copy sb; behave in a similar way to sb. **leaf** *v* (*phr v*) **leaf through sth** turn over the pages of (a book, etc) quickly, without reading them closely. **leafy** *adj* (-ier, -iest).

leaflet /'liːflɪt/ *n* [C] printed sheet of paper.

league /liːg/ *n* [C] **1** group of people or countries that have joined together for a particular purpose. **2** group of sports clubs that play against each other. **3** (*infml*) group or class of people or things of different quality: *They're not in the same ~*. **4** (idm) **in league (with sb)** working together, esp secretly or to do wrong.

leak /liːk/ *n* [C] **1** (a) hole through which a liquid, gas, etc escapes. (b) liquid, etc that escapes. **2** (*fig*) instance of leaking(2): *a security ~*. **leak** *v* **1** [I] (a) (of a container) allow liquid or gas to pass through a hole. (b) (of liquid or gas) pass through a hole. **2** [T] make (secret information) publicly known. **leakage** /'liːkɪdʒ/ *n* [C, U] process of leaking; amount that leaks. **leaky** *adj* (-ier, -iest).

lean¹ /liːn/ *v* (*pt, pp* ~**t** /lent/ or esp *US* ~**ed** /liːnd/) **1** [I] be in a sloping position; bend. **2** [I, T] *against/on//* (cause sth to) rest in a sloping position against sth: ~ *a ladder against a wall*. **3** (*phr v*)

lean on sb (*infml esp US*) try to influence sb by threats. **lean (up)- on sb** depend on sb. **lean towards sth** have a tendency to approve of or support sth. **leaning** *n* [C] tendency; inclination: *political ~ings.*

lean² /liːn/ *adj* 1 (of a person or animal) thin and healthy. 2 (of meat) containing little fat. 3 not productive: ~ *years.*

leap /liːp/ *v* (*pt, pp* ~**t** /lept/ or *esp US* ~**ed** /liːpt/) [I, T] 1 jump. 2 move quickly in the direction that is mentioned: ~ *into the car.* 3 (*phr v*) **leap at sth** accept sth eagerly: *She ~ t at the chance.* **leap** *n* [C] 1 sudden jump. 2 sudden increase or change. 3 (idm) **by leaps and bounds** very quickly. **'leap-frog** *n* [U] game in which players jump over others' bent backs. **leap-frog** *v* (-gg-) [I, T] leap over (sb) in this way. **'leap year** *n* [C] one year in every four years, with an extra day (29 February).

learn /lɜːn/ *v* (*pt, pp* ~**t** /lɜːnt/ or *esp US* ~**ed** /lɜːnd/) 1 [I, T] gain knowledge or skill in (a subject or activity): ~ *Dutch* ○ ~ (*how to*) *swim.* 2 [T] fix in the memory: ~ *a poem.* 3 [I, T] (*of/about*)// become aware of sth: ~ *of his death.* **learned** /ˈlɜːnɪd/ *adj* having a lot of knowledge. **learner** *n* [C]. **learning** *n* [U] knowledge gained by study.

lease /liːs/ *n* [C] contract for the use of land, a building, etc in return for payment. **lease** *v* [T] give or obtain the use of (sth) in this way. **'leasehold** *n* [U], *adj* (land, etc) held on a lease.

leash /liːʃ/ *n* [C] = LEAD¹ 5.

least /liːst/ *adj* 1 *pron* smallest in size, amount, etc: *She gave (the) ~ of all towards the present.* **least** *adv* 1 to the smallest extent: *the ~ expensive hotel.* 2 (idm) **at least (a)** not less than: *at ~ three months.* **(b)** if nothing else is true: *at ~ she's reliable.* **not in the least** absolutely not; not at all. **not least** especially.

leather /ˈleðə(r)/ *n* [U] material from animal skins, used for making shoes, etc. **leathery** *adj* as tough as leather.

leave¹ /liːv/ *v* (*pt, pp* **left** /left/) 1 [I, T] go away from (a person or place). 2 [T] cause or allow (sb/sth) to remain in a certain condition: ~ *the window open.* 3 [T] forget or fail to take or bring: *I left my umbrella at home.* 4 [T] cause to remain as a result: *Blood ~ s a stain.* 5 [T] give (sth) through a will. 6 [T] give to (sb) the responsibility

for doing sth: *We left him to do the cooking.* 7 [T] (*mathematics*) have (a certain amount) remaining: 7 *from 10* ~ *s 3.* 8 (idm) **leave/let sb/ sth alone**/'be not interfere with or disturb sb/sth. **leave 'go/'hold (of sth)** stop holding sth. **leave it at 'that** (*infml*) say or do nothing more. **leave sb in the lurch** leave sb when he/she is in difficulty. **leave well alone** ⇨ WELL³. 9 (*phr v*) **leave sth behind** fail or forget to bring or take sb/sth. **leave off (doing) sth** (*infml*) stop (doing) sth. **leave sb/sth out** not include sb/sth.

leave² /liːv/ *n* [U] 1 time away from duty or work: *a few days ~.* 2 (*fml*) permission. 3 (idm) **take leave of one's 'senses** (*rhet* or *joc*) go mad.

leaves *pl* of LEAF.

lecherous /ˈletʃərəs/ *adj* (*derog*) having or showing strong sexual desire.

lectern /ˈlektən/ *n* [C] high sloping desk to hold a lecturer's notes, a book, etc.

lecture /ˈlektʃə(r)/ *n* [C] talk given for the purposes of teaching. **lecture** *v* 1 [I] give a lecture. 2 [T] scold or warn (sb). **lecturer** *n* [C] person who gives (college or university) lectures. **lectureship** *n* [C] position as a lecturer.

led *pt, pp* of LEAD¹.

ledge /ledʒ/ *n* [C] narrow shelf coming out from a wall, cliff, etc.

ledger /ˈledʒə(r)/ *n* [C] book in which a company's accounts are kept.

lee /liː/ *n* [sing] (*fml*) part of sth providing shelter against the wind.

leech /liːtʃ/ *n* [C] 1 small blood-sucking worm. 2 (*fig derog*) person who makes profit out of others.

leek /liːk/ *n* [C] vegetable with a white stem and long green leaves.

leer /lɪə(r)/ *n* [C, usu sing] unpleasant look that suggests sexual desire. **leer** *v* [I] (*at*)// look with a leer.

left¹ *pt, pp* of LEAVE¹. **left-'luggage office** *n* [C] (*Brit*) (at a railway station, etc) where one may leave one's luggage for a short time. **'left-overs** *n* [pl] food that remains uneaten after a meal.

left² /left/ *adj, adv* of, on or towards the side of the body that is towards the west when a person faces north. **left** *n* [U] left side or direction. **2 the Left** [sing] (with sing or pl v) **(a)** the left wing of a political party. **(b)** supporters of socialism in general. **'left-hand** *adj* of or on the left side. **left-**

'handed adj (of a person) using the left hand more easily or usually than the right. **leftist** n [C], adj (supporter) of socialism. the ˌleft-wing n [sing] (with sing or pl v) supporters of a more extreme form of socialism than others in their party. left-wing adj: ~-wing policies.

leg /leg/ n [C] 1 (a) one of the parts of the body of a person or animal, used for standing and walking. (b) this part of an animal used as food. (c) part of a garment that covers a person's leg(1a): a trouser ~. 2 support of a chair, table, etc. 3 one section of a journey. 4 (idm) **not have a ˌleg to 'stand on** (infml) have no evidence or reason for one's opinion or behaviour.

legacy /'legəsɪ/ n [C] (pl -ies) 1 money or property left to sb in a will(5). 2 (fig) something remaining as a result of sth: Famine was the ~ of the war.

legal /'liːgl/ adj 1 of or based on the law: my ~ adviser. 2 allowed by the law. **legality** /liː'gælətɪ/ n [U] state of being legal. **legally** /'liːgəlɪ/ adv.

legalistic /ˌliːgə'lɪstɪk/ adj (usu derog) strictly following the exact details of the law or a rule.

legalize /'liːgəlaɪz/ v [T] make legal.

legend /'ledʒənd/ n 1 (a) [C] old story, esp one that may not be true. (b) [U] such stories considered as a group. 2 [C] (infml) famous person or event: He has become a ~ in his own lifetime. 3 [C] explanatory words on a map, picture, etc. **legendary** /'ledʒəndrɪ; US -derɪ/ adj famous; known only in legends.

legible /'ledʒəbl/ adj clear enough to be read easily. **legibly** adv.

legion /'liːdʒən/ n [C] 1 division of an army, esp of the ancient Roman army. 2 large number of people. **legion** adj (rhet) very many. **legionary** /'liːdʒənərɪ; US -nerɪ/ n [C] (pl -ies) adj (member) of a legion(1).

legislate /'ledʒɪsleɪt/ v make laws. **legislation** /ˌledʒɪs'leɪʃn/ n [U] 1 action of making laws. 2 laws made. **legislator** n [C].

legislative /'ledʒɪslətɪv; US -leɪtɪv/ adj of the making of laws; having the duty or purpose of making laws: a ~ assembly.

legislature /'ledʒɪslətʃə(r) or 'ledʒɪsleɪtʃə(r)/ n [C, also sing with pl v] (fml) body of people with the power to make and change laws.

legitimate /lɪ'dʒɪtɪmət/ adj 1 allowed by law. 2 born of parents married to each other. 3 reasonable: a ~ excuse. **legitimacy** /-məsɪ/ n [U].

legless /'leglɪs; US 'liːʒər/ n [U] very drunk.

leisure /'leʒə(r); US 'liːʒər/ n [U] 1 free time. 2 (idm) **at one's 'leisure** when one is free and without hurrying. **leisured** adj having plenty of leisure. **leisurely** adj, adv without hurrying: a ~ly walk.

lemon /'lemən/ n 1 (a) [C, U] oval yellow fruit with a sour juice. (b) [C] tree on which this fruit grows. 2 [U] pale yellow colour.

lemonade /ˌlemə'neɪd/ n [C, U] sweet fizzy drink.

lend /lend/ v (pt, pp **lent** /lent/) [T] 1 (to)/ give the use of (sth) to sb for a short time: He lent him the money. ○ He lent it to him. 2 (to)/ (fml) contribute or add (sth) to sth: Her presence lent dignity to the occasion. 3 **lend itself to** be suitable for sth. 4 (idm) **lend (sb) a 'hand** give (sb) help.

length /leŋθ or leŋkθ/ n from 1 [U] measurement or extent from end to end. 2 [U, C] amount of time taken by sth. 3 [C] extent of sth used as a measurement: swim two ~s of the pool. 4 [C] piece of (sth): a ~ of wire. 5 (idm) **at length** (a) (fml) eventually. (b) in great detail. **go to any, some, great, etc 'lengths (to do sth)** be prepared to do anything, something, a lot, etc to achieve sth. **lengthen** v [I, T] (cause to) become longer. 'lengthways (also 'lengthwise) adv along the length of something. **lengthy** adj (-ier, -iest) very long.

lenient /'liːnɪənt/ adj not severe (esp in punishing people). **leniency** /-ənsɪ/ n [U]. **leniently** adv.

lens /lenz/ n [C] 1 piece of glass with one or more curved surfaces, for use in spectacles, cameras, etc. 2 part of the eye used for focusing light.

Lent /lent/ n [U] (in the Christian religion) the period of 40 weekdays before Easter.

lent pt, pp of LEND.

lentil /'lentl/ n [C] small bean-like seed eaten as food.

leopard /'lepəd/ n [C] large animal of the cat family with a yellow coat and dark spots. **leopardess** /ˌlepə'des/ n [C] female leopard.

leotard /'liːətɑːd/ n [C] close-fitting one-piece garment worn by acrobats, dancers, etc.

leper /'lepə(r)/ n [C] 1 person suffering from leprosy. **2** (*fig*) person who is rejected and avoided by others.

leprosy /'leprəsi/ *n* [U] kind of skin disease that causes loss of feeling and which can lead to the loss of fingers, toes, etc.

lesbian /'lezbiən/ *n* [C] homosexual woman. **lesbian** *adj* of or concerning lesbians.

less /les/ *adj, pron* not as much (as); a smaller amount (of): ~ *to do than I thought.* **less** *adv* 1 to a smaller extent; not so much (as): *It rains* ~ *here.* **2** (idm) **even/much/ still less** and certainly not. **less and less** at a continually decreasing rate. **no less (than)** as much (as). **less** *prep* before subtracting (sth); minus: £1000 *a month* ~ *tax.* **lessen** /'lesn/ *v* [I, T] (cause to) become less.

lesser /'lesə(r)/ *adj* 1 smaller. **2** (idm) **the lesser of two 'evils** the less harmful of two bad choices.

lesson /'lesn/ *n* [C] 1 period of time given to learning or teaching: *piano* ~*s.* **2** experience from which one can learn: *Let this be a* ~ *to you!*

lest /lest/ *conj* (*fml*) in order that (sth unpleasant that is mentioned) should not happen.

let /let/ *v* (*-tt-, pt, pp* **let**) [T] 1 allow (sb/sth) to: *We* ~ *him leave.* **2** allow to go or come in: ~ *sb into the house.* **3** (used as an imperative): *L* ~'s *go!* **4** allow sb to use (a house, room, etc) in return for regular payments. **5** (idm) **let alone** and certainly not: *We cannot even pay our bills,* ~ *alone make a profit.* **let sth/sb alone/be** ⇨ LEAVE¹. **let the 'cat out of the bag** tell a secret carelessly or by mistake. **let sth 'drop** do or say nothing more about sth. **let fly (at sb/sth)** attack (sb/sth) with blows or words. **let sth go, let 'go of sb/sth** stop holding sb/sth. **let oneself 'go (a)** no longer hold back one's feelings. **(b)** stop being tidy, careful, etc. **let one's 'hair down** (*infml*) relax after being formal. **let sb 'have it** (*sl*) get very angry with, punish, etc sb. **let sb know (about sth)** tell sb about sth. **let off 'steam** (*infml*) release energy or anger and become less excited. **let the 'side down** not give the other members of one's group the help, support, etc they expect. **let sleeping dogs 'lie** leave sth alone. **let sth 'slide** allow sth to become neglected, less organized, etc. **let sth slip (a)** miss or not take (an opportunity, etc). **(b)** accidentally reveal (a secret). **let us 'say** for

example. **let well alone** ⇨ WELL³. **6** (phr v) **let sb down** disappoint sb. **let sth down (a)** make (clothes) longer. **(b)** allow air to escape from (a tyre, etc). **let sb/oneself in for sth** cause sb/oneself to suffer (difficulty, hard work, etc). **let sb in on/into sth** (*infml*) allow sb to share (a secret). **let sb off** (with sth) not punish sb severely. **let sb off** (sth) allow sb not to do (an unpleasant task). **let sth off** explode sth. **let 'on** (*infml*) tell a secret: *Don't* ~ *on that you know.* **let sth out (a)** make (a garment) looser or larger. **(b)** utter (a shout, scream, etc). **let 'up** become less strong; stop: *The rain began to* ~ *up.* **'let-down** *n* [C] disappointment. **'let-up** *n* [C, U] reduction in strength, intensity, etc.

lethal /'li:θl/ *adj* causing death.

lethargy /'leθədʒi/ *n* [U] lack of energy or interest. **lethargic** /lə'θɑ:dʒɪk/ *adj.*

let's let us. ⇨ LET 3.

letter /'letə(r)/ *n* 1 [C] written message sent to sb. **2** [C] written or printed sign representing a sound. **'letter-bomb** *n* [C] small bomb sent to sb in an envelope. **'letter-box** *n* [C] 1 (*Brit*) hole in a door for letters. **2** box in the street or at a post office into which letters are posted. **lettering** *n* [U] letters or words, esp with reference to their style and size.

lettuce /'letis/ *n* [C, U] garden plant with crisp green leaves, eaten in salads.

leukaemia (*US* **-kem-**) /luː'kiːmɪə/ *n* [U] disease in which there are too many white blood cells.

level¹ /'levl/ *adj* 1 having a horizontal surface; flat. **2** (*with*)|| at the same height, position, etc as another; equal: *Wales drew* ~ *early in the game*, ie made the score equal. **3** (idm) **do one's level 'best** do all that one can. **,level-'crossing** *n* [C] place where a road crosses a railway at the same level. **,level-'headed** *adj* sensible; calm.

level² /'levl/ *n* 1 [C] line or surface parallel with the horizon. **2** [C] position on a scale of quantity, strength, value, etc: *a high* ~ *of output.* **3** [U] position in rank or authority: *talks at management* ~.

level³ /'levl/ *v* (**-ll-**; *US* **-l-**) [T] 1 make (sth) level. **2** demolish (a building, etc). **3** (*at*)|| aim (a weapon or criticism) at sb. **4** (phr v) **level off/out (a)** (of an aircraft) become horizontal. **b)** (*fig*) become level after rising or falling: *Prices*

~led off. level with sb (*infml*) speak honestly to sb.

lever /'li:və(r)/ n [C] 1 bar that turns on a fixed point used to lift things. 2 handle used to operate a machine. 3 (*fig*) means by which influence may be used. lever v [T] move with a lever: *L~ it into position.* leverage /-ərɪdʒ/ n [U] 1 power of a lever. 2 (*fig*) power.

levity /'levətɪ/ n [U] (*fml*) lack of seriousness.

levy /'levɪ/ v (*pt, pp -ied*) [T] demand or collect (a payment) by authority: ~ *a tax.* levy n [C] (*pl -ies*) sum of money that is levied.

lewd /ljuːd; *US* luːd/ *adj* treating sexual matters in an indecent way: ~ *jokes*.

liability /ˌlaɪə'bɪlətɪ/ n (*pl -ies*) 1 [U] state of being liable. 2 liabilities [pl] debts that must be paid. 3 [C] (*infml*) person or thing that causes difficulties or problems: *An old car is a ~*.

liable /'laɪəbl/ *adj* 1 *to/* likely to do sth: ~ *to make mistakes.* 2 *to/* likely to suffer sth: *be ~ to flu in winter.* 3 responsible by law: ~ *for debts.*

liaise /lɪ'eɪz/ v [I] work together; inform each other.

liaison /lɪ'eɪzn; *US* 'lɪəzɒn/ n 1 [U] working association between different groups. 2 [C] sexual relationship between unmarried people.

liar /'laɪə(r)/ n [C] person who tells lies.

libel /'laɪbl/ n [U, C] (publishing of a) written statement that damages sb's reputation. libel v (*-ll-; US -l-*) [T] publish a libel against. libellous (*US libelous*) /-bələs/ *adj*.

liberal /'lɪbərəl/ *adj* 1 tolerant of the beliefs or behaviour of others. 2 giving or given generously: *a ~ supply.* 3 (of education) giving a wide general knowledge. liberalism n [U] liberal opinions. liberalize /'lɪbrəlaɪz/ v [T] free from restrictions: ~ *shop opening hours.* liberally *adv.* the 'Liberal Party n [sing] (*Brit politics*) former political party, now part of the Social and Liberal Democrats.

liberate /'lɪbəreɪt/ v [T] (*fml*) set free. liberated *adj* free in social and sexual matters. liberation /ˌlɪbə'reɪʃn/ n [U].

liberty /'lɪbətɪ/ n (*pl -ies*) 1 [U] (*fml*) state of being free. 2 [C, U] (*fml*) right to do as one chooses. 3 (*idm*) at liberty free. take the liberty of doing sth do sth without permission.

library /'laɪbrərɪ; *US* -brerɪ/ n [C] (*pl -ies*) (room or building for a)

collection of books, records, etc. librarian /laɪ'breərɪən/ n [C] person in charge of a library.

lice *pl* of LOUSE.

licence (*US* license) /'laɪsns/ n [C, U] (official paper giving) permission to do, own, etc sth.

license (also licence) /'laɪsns/ v [T] give a licence to. licensee /ˌlaɪsn'siː/ n [C] person who has a licence, esp to sell alcohol.

lick /lɪk/ v [T] 1 move the tongue over: *The dog ~ed its paw.* 2 (*infml*) defeat. 3 (of waves or flames) touch lightly. 4 (idm) lick one's lips ⇨ LIP. lick n 1 [C] act of licking. 2 [sing] small amount (of paint, etc).

licorice (*US*) = LIQUORICE.

lid /lɪd/ n [C] 1 movable cover of a container. 2 = EYELID (EYE).

lie¹ /laɪ/ v (*pt, pres p lying*) [I] tell a lie. lie n [C] statement that one knows to be untrue.

lie² /laɪ/ v (*pt lay* /leɪ/, *pp lain* /leɪn/, *pres p lying*) [I] 1 have or put one's body in a flat position on a surface. 2 be at rest on a surface. 3 be or remain in a state that is mentioned: *machines lying idle.* 4 be situated: *The town ~s on the coast.* 5 be spread out to view; extend: *The valley lay before us.* 6 (of abstract things) be found: *It does not ~ within my power to help you.* 7 (idm) lie in 'wait (for sb) be hidden, waiting to surprise sb. lie 'low (*infml*) keep quiet or hidden. not take sth lying 'down refuse to accept an insult, unfair treatment, etc without protesting. 8 (*phr v*) lie behind sth be the reason for sth. lie down move into a horizontal position on a bed, etc in order to sleep or rest. lie with sb (*fml*) be sb's duty or responsibility: *The final decision ~s with the director.* lie n [sing] 1 way sth lies. 2 (idm) the ,lie of the 'land (a) natural features of an area. (b) (*fig*) the state of affairs. 'lie-down n [sing] (*infml*) short rest. 'lie-in n [sing] (*infml*) stay in bed later than one's usual time in the morning.

lieutenant /lef'tenənt; *US* luː't-/ n [C] junior officer in the army or navy.

life /laɪf/ n (*pl* lives /laɪvz/) 1 [U] ability to function and grow that makes animals and plants different from rocks, metals, etc. 2 [U] living things: *Is there ~ on Mars?* 3 [U] state of human existence: *He expects a lot from ~*. 4 [C] person: *Many lives were lost.* 5 [C] period between birth and death: *She spent her whole ~ in Canada.*

6 [U] (also **life sentence**) (*infml*) punishment of being in prison for the rest of one's life or a very long time. **7** [U] business, pleasure and social activities of the world: *Join the navy and see ~!* **8** [U] liveliness, activity, energy: *full of ~.* **9** [C, U] way of living: *city ~.* **10** [C] biography: *a ~ of Dante.* **11** [U] living model, used as the subject in art: *a portrait drawn from ~.* **12** [C] period during which sth continues to exist or function: *a battery with a ~ of three years.* **13** (idm) **come to 'life** become lively or active. **for the 'life of one** (*infml*) however hard one tries. **the life and soul of the party** (*infml*) the most lively and amusing person at a party. **not on your 'life** (*infml*) certainly not. **take one's life in one's hands** put oneself in danger of being killed. **take sb's 'life** kill someone. **'lifebelt** (also **'lifebuoy**) *n* [C] floating ring for sb who has fallen into the water to hold onto. **'lifeboat** *n* [C] boat built to save people in danger at sea. **life cycle** *n* [C] (*biology*) series of stages of development an animal or plant goes through during its life: *the ~ cycle of a frog.* **'life-guard** *n* [C] expert swimmer employed to rescue other swimmers in danger. **'lifejacket** *n* [C] jacket worn to keep a person afloat in water. **lifeless** *adj* **1** dead. **2** not lively; dull. **'lifelike** *adj* exactly like a real person or thing: *a ~like painting.* **'lifeline** *n* [C] **1** rope used for saving life. **2** (*fig*) something on which one's life depends. **'lifelong** *adj* lasting throughout one's life. **'life-size(d)** *adj* of the same size as the person or thing represented. **'life-span** *n* [C] length of time that sth is likely to live, continue, or function. **'life-style** *n* [C] way of living. **'lifetime** *n* [C] length of time that sb is alive.

lift /lɪft/ *v* **1** [T] raise to a higher level. **2** [T] make more cheerful: *The news ~ed her spirits.* **3** [I] (of clouds, fog, etc) disappear. **4** [T] end (a ban or other restriction). **5** [T] (*infml*) steal. **6** (idm) **not lift a finger** (*infml*) not give any help. **7** (phr v) **lift off** (of a spacecraft) rise up from the ground. **lift** *n* **1** [sing] act of lifting. **2** [C] device for moving people or goods from one floor of a building to another. **3** [C] free ride in a vehicle: *a ~ to the station.* **4** [sing] feeling of great happiness. **'lift-off** *n* [C, U] act of launching a spacecraft into the air.

ligament /'lɪgəmənt/ *n* [C] band of strong tissue that holds bones together.

light¹ /laɪt/ *n* **1** [U] brightness by which things are seen: *the ~ of the sun.* **2** [C] something, esp an electric lamp, that gives light. **3** [C] (something used to produce a) flame. **4** [U] understanding. **5** [sing] way in which sth/sb is thought about: *see things in a good ~,* ie favourably. **6** (idm) **bring sth/come to 'light** make sth/become known. **cast/shed/throw light on sth** make sth clearer. **in the light of sth** considering sth: *in the ~ of this news.* **light at the end of the tunnel** success, happiness, etc after a period of difficulty. **'light bulb** = BULB 1. **'lighthouse** *n* [C] tower containing a powerful light for warning ships. **'light-year** *n* [C] distance that light travels in one year. **2** [usu pl] (*infml*) a very long time.

light² /laɪt/ *adj* **1** (of a place) bright; not dark: *a ~ room.* **2** pale: *~-blue eyes.*

light³ /laɪt/ *v* (*pt, pp* **lit** /lɪt/ or **lighted**) **1** [I, T] (cause sth to) begin burning. **2** [T] turn on (an electric light). **3** [T] provide (sth) with light: *a castle lit by coloured lights.* **4** (phr v) **light up** (*infml*) begin to smoke a cigarette, etc. **light (sth) up** (cause sb's face, etc to) become bright. **light sth up** cause light to shine on sth: *The fire lit up the whole sky.* **lighting** *n* [U] equipment or quality of lights in a room, street, etc.

light⁴ /laɪt/ *adj* **1** easy to lift or move; not heavy. **2** of less than the usual amount, force, etc: *~ rain.* **3** gentle: *a ~ touch.* **4** easy to perform: *~ work.* **5** not serious or difficult: *~ reading.* **6** not severe: *a ~ attack of flu.* **7** (of food) easy to digest. **8** (of sleep) not deep. **9** (of drinks) low in alcohol. **10** (idm) **make light of sth** treat sth as unimportant. **,light-'fingered** *adj* (*infml*) in the habit of stealing, eg from sb's pockets. **,light-'headed** *adj* feeling slightly faint. **,light-'hearted** *adj* cheerful. **,light 'industry** *n* [C] industry that produces small consumer goods or parts. **lightly** *adv* **1** in a light manner. **2** not seriously. **3** (idm) **get off 'lightly** (*infml*) avoid severe punishment. **lightness** *n* [U]. **'lightweight** *n* [C] **1** boxer weighing between 59 and 61 kilograms. **2** (*infml*) person of little importance.

light⁵ /laɪt/ *v* (*pt, pp* **lit** /lɪt/ or **lighted**) (*fml*) (phr v) **light on/**

upon sb/sth find sb/sth suddenly by chance.

lighten[1] /'laɪtn/ v [I, T] (cause sth to) become lighter in weight.

lighten[2] /'laɪtn/ v [I, T] (cause sth to) become brighter.

lighter /'laɪtə(r)/ n [C] device for lighting cigarettes, etc.

lightning /'laɪtnɪŋ/ n [U] flash of bright light in the sky, produced by electricity. **lightning** adj very quick, brief or sudden: at ~ speed. **'lightning conductor** (US **lightning rod**) n [C] metal wire that goes from the top of a building to the ground, to prevent damage by lightning.

like[1] /laɪk/ v [T] 1 find (sb/sth) pleasant; be fond of. 2 be unwilling: I didn't ~ to stop you. 3 (used with should or would to express a wish or choice): Would you ~ a cup of tea? ○ I'd ~ to think about it. 4 (idm) **if you like** (used as a polite form of agreement or suggestion). **not like the look/sound of sth** have a bad impression of what one has seen/heard of sth. **likeable** (also **likable**) adj pleasant. **likes** n [pl] (idm) **likes and 'dislikes** things one does and does not like.

like[2] /laɪk/ prep 1 similar to (sb/ sth): a hat ~ mine. 2 typical of (sb/ sth): It's just ~ him to be rude. 3 in the manner of (sb/sth): behave ~ children ○ drink ~ a fish. 4 for example: sports, ~ football and hockey. 5 (idm) **like 'anything** (infml) very fast, much, etc. **like** conj (infml) 1 in the same manner as: No one sings ~ she did. 2 (esp US) as if.

like[3] /laɪk/ adj similar. **like** n [sing] person or thing that is like another: Music, painting and the ~. **like-'minded** adj having the same opinions, attitudes, etc.

likelihood /'laɪklɪhʊd/ n [U] probability.

likely /'laɪklɪ/ adj (-ier, -iest) 1 that is expected; probable: ~ to rain. 2 (idm) a **'likely story** (ironic) (used for showing disbelief about what sb has said). **likely** adv 1 (idm) as **'likely as 'not, most/very 'likely** (very) probably. **not 'likely** (infml) certainly not.

liken /'laɪkən/ v [T] to// (fml) compare (sb/sth) to another.

likeness /'laɪknɪs/ n [C, U] (instance of) being similar in appearance: a family ~.

likewise /'laɪkwaɪz/ adv similarly; also.

liking /'laɪkɪŋ/ n (idm) **have a liking for sth** be fond of sth. **to sb's liking** (fml) giving sb satis-

faction.

lilac /'laɪlək/ n 1 [C] shrub with sweet-smelling pale purple or white flowers. 2 [U] pale purple colour.

lilt /lɪlt/ n [sing] pleasant rise and fall of the voice when speaking. **lilting** adj.

lily /'lɪlɪ/ n [C] (pl -ies) plant that grows from a bulb and has large usu white flowers.

limb /lɪm/ n [C] 1 leg, arm or wing. 2 main branch of a tree. 3 (idm) **out on a 'limb** (infml) alone and without supporters.

limber /'lɪmbə(r)/ v (phr v) **limber 'up** exercise one's muscles before a race, etc.

limbo /'lɪmbəʊ/ n (idm) **in limbo** in an uncertain state: The company is in ~.

lime[1] /laɪm/ n [U] white substance used in making cement. **'limestone** n [U] kind of rock containing lime.

lime[2] /laɪm/ n [C] tree with sweet-smelling yellow flowers.

lime[3] /laɪm/ n [C] (tree producing a) fruit like a lemon but more acid.

limelight /'laɪmlaɪt/ n the **limelight** [sing] position of receiving a lot of public attention.

limerick /'lɪmərɪk/ n [C] humorous poem with five lines.

limit /'lɪmɪt/ n [C] 1 point or line that may not or cannot be passed. 2 greatest amount allowed or possible. 3 (idm) **(be) the limit** (sl) as much as one can bear. **off 'limits** (US) = OUT OF BOUNDS (BOUNDS). **within 'limits** up to a reasonable point: You are free to spend money, within ~ s. **limit** v [T] keep within a limit. **limitation** /ˌlɪmɪ'teɪʃn/ n 1 [U] limiting. 2 [C] condition or fact that limits; weakness. **limited** adj 1 restricted; few or small. 2 (of a company) having members who are liable for its debts only up to the amount they have provided. **limitless** adj without limits.

limousine /'lɪməziːn/ n [C] large luxurious car with the driver's seat separated from the passengers in the back.

limp[1] /lɪmp/ v [I] walk unevenly. **limp** n [sing] limping walk.

limp[2] /lɪmp/ adj not stiff or firm. **limply** adv. **limpness** n [U].

linchpin /'lɪntʃpɪn/ n [C] 1 bar passed through the end of an axle to keep the wheel in position. 2 (fig) person or thing that is essential to an organization, plan, etc.

line[1] /laɪn/ n 1 [C] (a) long narrow mark on a surface. (b) mark like this on skin: the ~ s on his face. 2 [C] limit; boundary: ~ s *marking a tennis court.* **3** [C] series of connected military defences. **4** [C] row of people or things: *customers standing in* a ~. **5** [C, usu sing] series of people, esp of the same family. **6** [C] (a) row of words on a page. (b) lines [pl] words spoken by an actor. **7** [C] (*infml*) short letter. **8** [C] length or thread, rope or wire. **9** [C] telephone connection: *Our firm has 20* ~ s. **10** [C] railway. **11** lines [pl] overall shape; outline. **12** [C] course of action, behaviour or thought: *a new* ~ *of research.* **13** [sing] direction or course: *the* ~ *of gunfire.* **14** [C] system of transport: *a 'shipping* ~. **15** [sing] (a) department of activity; kind of business: *a job in the banking* ~. (b) kind of product: *a new* ~ *in coats.* **16** (idm) in line for sth likely to get sth. in line with sth in accordance with sth. (put sth) on the 'line (*infml*) put (sth) at risk. on the right 'lines following a way that is likely to succeed. out of 'line (with sb/sth) (a) not forming a straight line with sb/sth. (b) unacceptably different from others. **'line-drawing** *n* [C] drawing done with a pen, pencil, etc. **'line-printer** *n* [C] (*computing*) high-speed printer that prints a complete line of text at a time.

line² /laɪn/ *v* [T] **1** mark with lines: ~*d paper.* **2** form a line along: *a road* ~*d with trees.* **3** (phr v) **line (sb) up** (cause people to) form a line. **line sth up** (*infml*) arrange or organize sth. **'line-up** *n* [C] **1** line of people formed for inspection, etc. **2** set of people or things arranged for a purpose.

line³ /laɪn/ *v* [T] **1** cover the inside surface of sth with material: *fur*-~*d gloves.* **2** (idm) **line one's (own) pocket(s)** make a lot of money for oneself, esp dishonestly.

linear /'lɪnɪə(r)/ *adj* **1** of or in lines. **2** of length: ~ *measurement.*

linen /'lɪnɪn/ *n* [U] (cloth for making) sheets, table-cloths, etc.

liner¹ /'laɪnə(r)/ *n* [C] large passenger or cargo ship.

liner² /'laɪnə(r)/ *n* (in compounds) something put inside sth to protect it: *bin*-~*s.*

linesman /'laɪnzmən/ *n* [C] (*pl* **-men**) (*sport*) official who says whether a ball has gone outside the limits during a game.

linger /'lɪŋgə(r)/ *v* [I] stay for a long time; be slow to leave or disappear. **lingering** *adj* long; remaining: *a* ~ *illness.*

lingerie /'lænʒəri:; *US* ,lɑ:ndʒə'reɪ/ *n* [U] (*fml*) women's underwear.

linguist /'lɪŋgwɪst/ *n* [C] **1** person who knows several foreign languages well. **2** person who studies linguistics. **linguistic** /lɪŋ-'gwɪstɪk/ *adj* of language or linguistics. **linguistics** *n* (with sing v) study of language.

liniment /'lɪnɪmənt/ *n* [C, U] liquid for rubbing on parts of the body which ache.

lining /'laɪnɪŋ/ *n* [C, U] layer of material used to cover the inside surface of sth: *a fur* ~.

link /lɪŋk/ *n* [C] **1** connection. **2** one ring or loop of a chain. **link** *v* **1** [T] join; connect. **2** (phr v) **link (sth) up (with sth)** connect (sth) to another thing.

lino /'laɪnəʊ/ *n* [U] (*infml*) short for LINOLEUM.

linoleum /lɪ'nəʊlɪəm/ *n* [U] strong, smooth, shiny floor-covering.

lint /lɪnt/ *n* [U] soft cotton material, used for putting on wounds.

lion /'laɪən/ *n* [C] **1** large strong flesh-eating animal of the cat family. **2** (idm) the **'lion's share (of sth)** the largest part of sth. **lioness** *n* [C] female lion.

lip /lɪp/ *n* **1** [C] either of the fleshy edges of the mouth. **2** [C] edge of a jug, cup, etc. **3** [U] (*sl*) rude disrespectful talk. **4** (idm) **lick/smack one's lips** (*infml*) show that one is looking forward eagerly to sth enjoyable. **one's lips are sealed** one will not tell a secret to others. **'lip-read** *v* (*pt, pp* **'lip-read** /-red/) [I, T] understand (sb's speech) by watching the movements of his/her lips. **'lip-reading** *n* [U]. **'lip-service** *n* (idm) **give/pay 'lip-service to sth** say that one supports sth while not doing so in reality. **'lipstick** *n* [C, U] (stick of) colouring for the lips.

liqueur /lɪ'kjʊə(r); *US* lɪ'kɜ:r/ *n* [C, U] strong (usu sweet) alcoholic drink.

liquid /'lɪkwɪd/ *n* [C, U] substance, eg water or oil, that flows freely but which is not a gas. **liquid** *adj* **1** in the form of a liquid. **2** clear and looking wet: ~ *blue eyes.* **3** (of sounds) clear and flowing. **4** (*finance*) easily changed into cash: ~ *assets.*

liquidate /'lɪkwɪdeɪt/ *v* [T] **1** (*infml*) get rid of (sb), esp by killing. **2** (*finance*) close down (an unsuccessful business company). **liquidation** /,lɪkwɪ'deɪʃn/ *n* [U].

liquidize /'lɪkwɪdaɪz/ *v* [T] crush (fruit, vegetables, etc) into liquid. **liquidizer** (esp *US* **blender**) *n* [C] electric device for liquidizing food.

liquor /'lɪkə(r)/ n [U] (esp *US*) strong alcoholic drink.

liquorice /'lɪkərɪs, -ɪʃ/ n [U] black substance used as a sweet or in medicine.

lisp /lɪsp/ v [I, T] pronounce /s/ as /θ/; say in a lisping way. **lisp** n [sing] lisping way of speaking.

list¹ /lɪst/ n [C] set of names, things, etc written down in order. **list** v [T] make a list of; put on a list.

list² /lɪst/ v [I] (of a ship) lean over to one side. **list** n [sing] listing position.

listen /'lɪsn/ v [I] 1 (*to*) try to hear sb/sth; pay attention: *L∼ carefully to what I'm saying.* 2 (*to*) do what sb advises; believe sb: *I warned you, but you wouldn't ∼.* 3 (phr v) **listen 'in (to sth)** (a) listen to a radio programme. (b) listen secretly to a conversation. **listener** n [C].

listless /'lɪstlɪs/ adj too tired to show interest. **listlessly** adv. **listlessness** n [U].

lit pt, pp of LIGHT³,⁵.

liter (*US*) = LITRE.

literacy /'lɪtərəsɪ/ n [U] ability to read and write.

literal /'lɪtərəl/ adj 1 taking the basic or usual meaning of a word. 2 giving one word for each original word: *a ∼ translation.* **literally** adv 1 (*infml*) (used loosely for intensifying meaning): *I was ∼ly bored to tears.* 2 word for word: *translate ∼ly.*

literary /'lɪtərərɪ; *US* 'lɪtərerɪ/ adj of literature or authors.

literate /'lɪtərət/ adj 1 able to read and write. 2 well-educated; cultured.

literature /'lɪtrətʃə(r); *US* -tʃʊər/ n [U] 1 writings valued as works of art. 2 writings on a particular subject. 3 (*infml*) printed material giving information; leaflets.

lithe /laɪð/ adj (*fml*) (of a person, his/her body, etc) able to bend easily.

litigation /ˌlɪtɪ'geɪʃn/ n [U] process of making or defending a non-criminal case in a law-court.

litre /'liːtə(r)/ n [C] metric unit of capacity, used for measuring liquids.

litter /'lɪtə(r)/ n 1 [U] bits of paper, bottles, etc left lying about. 2 [C] all the young born to an animal at one time. **litter** v [T] make (a place) untidy with litter. **'litterbin** n [C] container for rubbish.

little¹ /'lɪtl/ adj 1 small: ∼ *cups.* 2 (of distance or time) short: *wait a ∼ while.* 3 not important: *a ∼ mis-*

little² /'lɪtl/ adj (**less, least**) a small amount (of sth): not enough: *I have very ∼ time to spare.* **little** pron [U], n a small amount: *I understood ∼ of what she said.* **little** adv 1 not much; only slightly: *I slept very ∼ last night.* ○ *Little does she know* (ie He doesn't know) *what trouble he's in.* 2 (idm) **,little by 'little** gradually. **,little wonder** ⇨ WONDER.

little³ /'lɪtl/ pron, adj a small amount (of sth); some but not much: *a ∼ sugar.* **a little** adv to some extent: *a ∼ afraid.*

live¹ /lɪv/ v 1 [I] be alive. 2 [I] remain alive: *The doctors don't think he'll ∼.* 3 [I] have one's home: ∼ *in Leeds.* 4 [I, T] lead one's life in the way that is mentioned: ∼ *happily.* 5 [I] enjoy life fully. 6 (idm) **live be,yond/with,in one's 'means** spend more/less than one earns or can afford. **live from ,hand to 'mouth** have just enough money and food for living. **live it 'up** (*infml*) live in a lively extravagant way. 7 (phr v) **live sth 'down** live in such a way that (a past bad action) is forgotten. **live for sth** regard sth as the aim of one's life. **live in/out** (of a worker or student) live at/away from the place of work or study. **live off sb** obtain money for one's needs from sb. **live on** continue to live or exist. **live on sth** (a) have sth as one's main food. (b) depend on (an amount of money) to provide for one's needs. **live through sth** experience sth and survive: ∼ *through two wars.* **live together** live as if married. **live up to sth** be as good as (a high standard): ∼ *up to my expectations.* **live with sb** live with sb as if married. **live with sth** accept and endure (sth unpleasant).

live² /laɪv/ adj 1 having life. 2 burning or glowing: ∼ *coals.* 3 not yet exploded or lit: *a ∼ bomb.* 4 (of a wire) carrying electricity. 5 (of a broadcast) happening while it is being heard or seen. 6 of great interest or importance: *a ∼ issue.*

liveable /'lɪvəbl/ adj fit to live in; tolerable.

livelihood /'laɪvlɪhʊd/ n [C, usu sing] way in which one earns one's money.

lively /'laɪvlɪ/ adj (**-ier, -iest**) 1 full of life and energy. 2 (of colours) bright. **liveliness** n [U].

liven /'laɪvn/ v (phr v) **,liven (sb/ sth) 'up** (cause sb/sth to) become lively.

liver /'lɪvə(r)/ n 1 [C] large organ

in the body that cleans the blood. 2 [U] animal's liver as food.

lives pl of LIFE.

livestock /'laɪvstɒk/ n [U] farm animals.

livid /'lɪvɪd/ adj 1 (infml) extremely angry. 2 bluish-grey.

living /'lɪvɪŋ/ adj 1 alive. 2 being used still: a ~ language. 3 (idm) **be the living image of sb** ⇨ IMAGE. **within/in living 'memory** at a time remembered by people still alive. **the living** n [pl] people who are now alive.

living² /'lɪvɪŋ/ n 1 [sing] way in which one earns one's money. 2 [U] manner of life: a low standard of ~. **'living-room** n [C] room in a house for general use.

lizard /'lɪzəd/ n [C] small four-legged reptile with a long tail.

load /ləʊd/ n 1 [C] thing that is carried. 2 [U] (esp in compounds) quantity that can be carried: coach-~s of tourists. 3 [C] amount of work that an engine, etc is required to do. 4 [C] (fig) weight of responsibility, worry, etc. 5 **loads (of)** [pl] (infml) plenty of (sth): ~s of money. **load** v 1 [I, T] put (a load) in or on (sth/sb): ~ cargo on-to a ship. 2 [T] (a) put ammunition into (a gun). (b) put a film) into (a camera). **loaded** adj 1 carrying a load. 2 (sl) very rich. 3 (idm) a **loaded 'question** question intended to trap sb.

loaf¹ /ləʊf/ n (pl **loaves** /ləʊvz/) [C] mass of shaped and baked bread.

loaf² /ləʊf/ v [I] (about/around)// (infml) spend time lazily.

loan /ləʊn/ n 1 [C] something, esp money, lent. 2 [U] lending. 3 (idm) **on loan** borrowed. **loan** v [T] (esp US or Brit fml) lend.

loath (also **loth**) /ləʊθ/ adj to// (fml) unwilling to do sth.

loathe /ləʊð/ v [T] dislike strongly. **loathing** n [U] disgust. **loathsome** /-səm/ adj disgusting.

loaves pl of LOAF¹.

lob /lɒb/ v (-bb-) [I, T] send or strike (a ball) in a high curve. **lob** n [C] ball that is lobbed.

lobby /'lɒbɪ/ n (pl **-ies**) 1 [C] entrance-hall of a hotel, theatre, etc. 2 [C, also sing with pl v] group of people who try to influence politicians: the anti-nuclear ~. **lobby** v (pt, pp **-ied**) [I, T] try to persuade (a politician) to support or oppose a proposed law, etc.

lobe /ləʊb/ n [C] lower soft part of the ear.

lobster /'lɒbstə(r)/ n [C] shellfish with eight legs and two claws. 2 [U] its flesh as food.

local /'ləʊkl/ adj 1 of a particular place: ~ news. 2 affecting only a part, not the whole, of the body: a ~ anaes'thetic. **local** n [C] 1 (usu pl) person who lives in a particular place. 2 (Brit infml) local public house. **locally** adv.

locality /ləʊ'kælətɪ/ n [C] (pl **-ies**) district; place.

localize /'ləʊkəlaɪz/ v [T] keep (sth) inside a particular area: a ~ disease.

locate /ləʊ'keɪt; US 'ləʊkeɪt/ v [T] 1 find out the exact position of. 2 (usu passive) establish in a place: Our offices are ~d in Paris. **location** /ləʊ'keɪʃn/ n 1 [C] position. 2 (idm) **on location** (of a film) photographed in natural surroundings, not in a studio.

loch /lɒk/ n [C] (Scot) lake: L~ Ness.

lock¹ /lɒk/ n 1 [C] device for fastening a door, etc. 2 [C] enclosed section of a canal, in which the water level can be raised or lowered. 3 (idm) **lock, stock and 'barrel** including everything. **'locksmith** n [C] person who makes and mends locks.

lock² /lɒk/ v [I, T] 1 fasten with a lock. 2 (cause to) become fixed. 3 (phr v) **lock sth away** store sth safely in a locked place. **lock sb in/out** keep (sb, eg a prisoner, or oneself) inside/outside a place by locking the door. **lock (sth) up** make (a house, etc) safe by locking the doors. **lock sb up** put sb in prison, a psychiatric hospital, etc.

lock³ /lɒk/ n [C] portion of hair that naturally hangs together.

locker /'lɒkə(r)/ n [C] small cupboard for storing clothes, luggage, etc.

locket /'lɒkɪt/ n [C] small case for a picture, etc, worn on a chain round one's neck.

locomotive /ˌləʊkəməʊtɪv/ n [C] (fml) railway engine.

locust /'ləʊkəst/ n [C] winged insect that flies in large groups and destroys crops.

lodge¹ /lɒdʒ/ n [C] 1 small house, esp at the entrance to the grounds of a large house. 2 country house or cabin: a hunting ~.

lodge² /lɒdʒ/ v 1 [I] live for payment in sb's house. 2 [T] provide (sb) with a place to live for payment. 3 [I, T] in// (cause to) enter and become fixed in sth: The bullet (was) ~d in his arm. 4 [T] make (a statement, etc) officially: ~ a complaint. **lodger** n [C] person who pays to live in sb's house.

lodging /'lɒdʒɪŋ/ n 1 [U] place to stay. 2 **lodgings** [pl] room or rooms rented for living in.

loft /lɒft; US lɔːft/ n [C] room or space under the roof of a house, used for storing things.

lofty /'lɒftɪ; US 'lɔːftɪ/ adj (**-ier, -iest**) **1** (of thoughts, etc) noble. **2** (rhet) very high. **3** (derog) proud.

log¹ /lɒg; US lɔːg/ n [C] length of a tree-trunk that has fallen or been cut down.

log² /lɒg; US lɔːg/ n [C] **1** official record of the journey of a ship or plane. **2** registration document of a motor vehicle. **log** v (**-gg-**) [T] **1** enter (facts) in a log. **2** (idm) **log in/on** start using a computer system by giving a particular word or number. **log out/off** finish using a computer system by giving a particular word or number.

loggerheads /'lɒgəhedz/ n (idm) **at loggerheads (with sb)** quarrelling with sb.

logic /'lɒdʒɪk/ n [U] **1** science or method of organized reasoning. **2** sensible reasoning: *There's no ~ in what he says.* **logical** /'lɒdʒɪkl/ adj in accordance with logic. **logically** /-klɪ/ adv.

loins /lɔɪnz/ n [pl] lower part of the body between the waist and the legs.

loiter /'lɔɪtə(r)/ v [I] stand about idly.

loll /lɒl/ v [I] **1** rest or sit lazily. **2** (phr v) **loll out** (of the tongue) hang loosely.

lollipop /'lɒlɪpɒp/ n [C] large boiled sweet or piece of frozen fruit juice on a stick.

lolly /'lɒlɪ/ n (pl **-ies**) (Brit) **1** (infml) lollipop. **2** [U] (sl) money.

lone /ləʊn/ adj (usu rhet) without others near; solitary.

lonely /'ləʊnlɪ/ adj (**-ier, -iest**) **1** sad because one does not have any friends. **2** (of places) not often visited. **loneliness** n [U].

lonesome /'ləʊnsəm/ adj (esp US) lonely.

long¹ /lɒŋ; US lɔːŋ/ adj (**~er** /-ŋgə(r)/, **~est** /-ŋgɪst/) **1** having a great or a given extent in space or time: *a ~ journey* ○ *800 metres ~.* **2** (idm) **go a long way** ⇨ FAR¹. **in the long run** eventually; ultimately. **long in the 'tooth** (joc) (of a person) old. **not by a long chalk/shot** not at all. **long-'distance** adj, adv travelling or operating between distant places. **'long drink** n [C] drink, esp non-alcoholic drink, served in a tall glass. **'long-range** adj of or for a long period of time or distance: *a ~-range weather forecast.* **long-'sighted** adj only able to see distant objects clearly.

adj of or for a long period of time. **'long wave** n [U] radio wave with a wavelength of more than 1000 metres. **long-'winded** adj (of talking or writing) too long; boring.

long² /lɒŋ; US lɔːŋ/ n **1** [U] long time: *This won't take ~.* ○ *I hope to see you before ~,* ie soon. **2** (idm) **the long and (the) 'short of it** all that need be said about it.

long³ /lɒŋ; US lɔːŋ/ adv (**~er** /-ŋgə(r)/, **~est** /-ŋgɪst/) **1** for a long time: *Were you in Rome long?* ○ *I shan't be ~, I will come soon.* **2** at a distant time: *~ ago.* **3** (of duration) throughout: *all day ~.* **4** (idm) **as/so long as** on condition that; provided that. **no/any/much 'longer** after a certain point in time. **long-playing 'record** n [C] record that plays for 20 - 30 minutes on each side. **long-'standing** adj that has existed for a long time: *a ~-standing arrangement.* **long-'suffering** adj patiently bearing problems and difficulties.

long⁴ /lɒŋ; US lɔːŋ/ v [I] **for; to//** want sth very much: *~ for the holidays.* **longing** adj, n [C, U] (having) a strong wish. **longingly** adv.

longitude /'lɒndʒɪtjuːd; US -tuːd/ n [U] distance east or west of Greenwich in Britain, measured in degrees.

loo /luː/ n [C] (pl **~s**) (Brit infml) toilet.

look¹ /lʊk/ v **1** [I] (*at*)// use one's eyes to see sth/sb. **2** (usu used with an adj) seem to be; appear: *~ sad.* **3** [I] face a particular direction: *The house ~s east.* **4** [I, T] pay attention to (sth): *L~ where you're going!* **5** (usu imperative) appear as beautiful, attractive, etc as possible. **look daggers at sb** look very angrily at sb. **look down one's 'nose at sb/sth** treat sb/sth with contempt. **'look 'here** (used for expressing a protest or for asking sb to pay attention). **look like sb/sth, look as if** have the appearance of sb/sth; seem probable: *She ~ed as if she was asleep.* ○ *It ~s like rain.* **look 'sharp** hurry up. **never/not look 'back** (infml) continue to be successful. **not be much to 'look at** (infml) not have an attractive appearance. **not look one'self** not have one's usual healthy appearance. **6** (phr v) **look 'after sb/sth** take care of sb/sth. **look a'head** think about what is going to happen in the future. **look at sth** examine or consider sth: *I'll ~ at your proposal tomorrow.* **look 'back (on sth)** think about sth in the past. **look down on sb/sth** (*infml*) consider sb/sth inferior to oneself; despise. **look for sb/sth** try to find sb/sth. **look forward to sth** think about sth that will happen in the future with pleasure. **look 'in (on sb)** make a short visit to sb's house. **look into sth** investigate or examine sth. **look 'on** watch. **look on sb as sth** consider sb/sth to be sth. **look 'out** be careful. **look out for sb/sth** watch for sb/sth. **look out onto sth** (of a room, etc) overlook sth. **look over sth** inspect or examine sth. **look round sth** visit (a place or building). **look through sth** examine or read sth quickly. **look to sb for sth/to do sth** rely on sb to provide or do sth. **look 'up** (*infml*) become better. **look sb 'up** (*infml*) find sb's home and visit him/her. **look sth up** search for sth in a reference book. **look up to sb** admire or respect sb. **look** *interj* (used for making sb listen to what one is going to say). **'look-in** *n* (idm) (**not**) **give sb/get a look-in** (*infml*) (not) give sb/have a chance to take part in sth. **'look-out** *n* [C] 1 place from which sb watches carefully. 2 person who watches for danger. 3 (idm) **be 'sb's lookout** (*infml*) be sb's responsibility: *If you want to waste your money, that's your ~out.*

look² /lʊk/ *n* 1 [C, usu sing] act of looking: *Take a ~ at this.* 2 [C] expression or appearance: *I don't like the ~ of him.* 3 **looks** [pl] person's (attractive) appearance: *She's got her father's good ~s.*

loom¹ /luːm/ *n* [C] machine for weaving cloth.

loom² /luːm/ *v* [I] appear in an unclear, often threatening, way: *The outline of a ship ~ed through the fog.* ○ (*fig*) *Her problems ~ed large in her mind.*

loop /luːp/ *n* [C] 1 shape produced by a curve crossing itself. 2 string, wire, etc in such a shape. **loop** *v* 1 [I, T] form into a loop. 2 [T] fasten with a loop.

loophole /'luːphəʊl/ *n* [C] way of escape from a legal restriction: *tighten up ~s in the law.*

loose /luːs/ *adj* (~r, ~st) 1 freed from control; not tied up: *The dog is too dangerous to be set ~.* 2 not firmly fixed: *a ~ tooth.* 3 not fastened together: *~ sheets of paper.* 4 (of clothes) not tight. 5 not exact: *a ~ translation.* 6 (*dated*) immoral. 7 (idm) **at a loose 'end**, (*US* also) **at loose ends** having nothing to do. **come/work 'loose** (of a fastening, etc) become unfas-

tened. **loosely** *adv.* **loosen** /'luːsn/ *v* [I, T] become or make loose or looser.

loot /luːt/ *n* [U] goods taken from an enemy in war or stolen by thieves. **loot** *v* [I, T] take loot (from).

lop /lɒp/ *v* (**-pp-**) [T] cut (branches, etc) off (a tree).

lop-sided /,lɒp 'saɪdɪd/ *adj* with one side lower than the other.

lord /lɔːd/ *n* 1 [C] male ruler. 2 **(the) Lord** [sing] God; Jesus. 3 (a) [C] nobleman. (b) **the Lords** [sing] (with sing or pl *v*) (members of the House of Lords. ⇨ HOUSE¹). 4 **Lord** [C] (*Brit*) (title of certain high officials): *L~ Mayor.* 5 [C] (used in exclamations of surprise, etc): *Good L~!* **lordly** *adj* proud; arrogant. **lordship** *n* [C] (title of a) Lord.

lorry /'lɒrɪ; *US* 'lɔːrɪ/ *n* [C] (*pl* -ies) large strong motor vehicle for transporting goods.

lose /luːz/ *v* (*pt*, *pp* **lost** /lɒst; *US* lɔːst/) 1 [T] become unable to find: *~ one's keys.* 2 [T] have (sth) taken away from one by accident, death, etc: *~ one's job.* 3 [T] no longer have or keep: *~ interest in sth* ○ *~ weight.* 4 [I, T] fail to win: *~ a game.* 5 [I, T] (of a clock or watch) go too slowly by (an amount of time). 6 *~ oneself in* become so interested in sth that one is unaware of anything else. 7 [T] (*infml*) be no longer understood by (sb): *I'm afraid you've lost me.* 8 [T] waste (time or an opportunity). 9 (idm) **lose count of sth** ⇨ COUNT. **lose 'face** lose one's reputation (and feel ashamed). **lose ground** ⇨ GROUND¹. **lose one's head** ⇨ HEAD¹. **lose heart** ⇨ HEART. **lose one's 'heart to sb** fall in love with sb. **lose sight of sth/sb** (a) no longer be able to see sb/sth. (b) fail to consider or remember sth. **lose touch (with sb)** no longer write to, telephone or visit sb. **lose one's 'way** become lost. **lose weight** ⇨ WEIGHT. 10 (phr *v*) **lose 'out** be unsuccessful. **loser** *n* [C].

loss /lɒs; *US* lɔːs/ *n* 1 [U] act or fact of losing; failure to keep: *~ of blood.* 2 [C] (a) person or thing lost: *heavy ~s of life.* (b) money lost in business. 3 (idm) **at a 'loss** uncertain what to do or say.

lost¹ /lɒst/ *pt*, *pp* of LOSE.

lost² /lɒst; *US* lɔːst/ *adj* 1 unable to find one's way. 2 that cannot be found. 3 (idm) **a lost 'cause** plan, project, etc that is certain to fail.

lot¹ /lɒt/ *pron* **a lot, lots** (*infml*) large number or amount. **a lot of** (also (*infml*)**lots of**) *adj* a large number or amount of (sb/sth): a ~ of people. **the 'lot** n [sing] (with sing or pl v) (infml) the whole (of sb/sth).

lot² /lɒt/ adv **a lot** (infml) 1 (used with an adj and adv) considerably; much: I feel a ~ better. 1 (used with a v) (a) a great amount. (b) often.

lot³ /lɒt/ n 1 [C, also sing with pl v] group or set of people or things: the next ~ of students. 2 [C] object to be sold at an auction. 3 [C] piece of land. 4 [sing] person's fate. 5 (idm) **cast/draw 'lots** make a choice by lot.

loth = LOATH.

lotion /ˈləʊʃn/ n [C, U] liquid used to clean or improve the condition of skin or hair.

lottery /ˈlɒtəri/ n [C] (pl -ies) way of giving prizes to the buyers of numbered tickets chosen by chance.

loud /laʊd/ adj 1 producing a lot of sound. 2 (of colours) unpleasantly bright. **loud** adv in a loud manner. **loudly** adv. **loudness** n [U]. **'loud'speaker** n [C] part of a radio, etc that changes electrical signals into sound.

lounge /laʊndʒ/ v [I] sit or stand in a lazy way. **lounge** n [C] 1 (Brit) comfortable sitting-room. 2 large waiting-room at an airport. **'lounge bar** n [C] (Brit) room in a pub or hotel that is smarter and more expensive than other bars.

louse /laʊs/ n [C] (pl **lice** /laɪs/) small insect that lives on the bodies of animals and human beings.

lousy /ˈlaʊzi/ adj (-ier, -iest) 1 (infml) very bad: a ~ holiday. 2 covered with lice.

lout /laʊt/ n [C] rough ill-mannered man or boy. **loutish** adj.

lovable /ˈlʌvəbl/ adj easy to love; deserving love.

love /lʌv/ n 1 [U] strong liking or affection. 2 [U] strong affection and sexual attraction: He's in ~. 3 [U, sing] strong liking for sth: a ~ of books. 4 [C] person or thing that is loved. 5 [U] (in tennis) nil. 6 (idm) **give/send sb one's 'love** give/send warm friendly greetings to sb. **make love (to sb)** have sexual intercourse with sb. **there's little/no 'love lost between A and B** A and B dislike each other. **love** v [T] 1 have love for: ~ one's wife. 2 like a lot: I ~ cakes. **'love-affair** n [C] romantic (usu sexual) relationship.

lovely /ˈlʌvli/ adj (-ier, -iest) 1 beautiful: a ~ woman. 2 very pleasant: a ~ holiday. **loveliness**

n [U].

lover /ˈlʌvə(r)/ n [C] 1 partner in a sexual relationship outside marriage. 2 person who is fond of sth mentioned: a ~ of music.

loving /ˈlʌvɪŋ/ adj feeling or showing love. **lovingly** adv.

low¹ /ləʊ/ adj 1 not high: a ~ wall. 2 below the usual level: ~ prices. 3 below others in importance or quality. 4 vulgar; dishonest: keep ~ company. 5 (of a sound) deep. 6 not loud. 7 not strong; weak or unhappy: feel ~. 8 unfavourable: have a ~ opinion of him. 9 (of a gear) allowing a slower speed. 10 (idm) **at a low 'ebb** in a poor or bad state. **be/run 'low (on sth)** (of supplies) be/become almost finished. **'low-down** n [sing] **give sb/get the low-down on sb/ sth** (infml) tell sb/be told the full facts about sb/sth. **'low-down** adj (infml) dishonest. **'low-'key** (also **,low-'keyed)** adj not intense; controlled. **'lowlands** /ˈləʊləndz/ n [pl] flat low-lying land. **lowness** n [U]. **low 'profile** ⇒ PROFILE. **,low-'spirited** adj depressed.

low² /ləʊ/ adv at or to a low level: aim/shoot ~.

low³ /ləʊ/ n [C] low or lowest level: Shares reached a new ~ yesterday.

lower /ˈləʊə(r)/ adj at or being the bottom part: the ~ lip. **lower** v 1 [T] let or bring down: ~ a flag. 2 [I, T] (cause to) become less in amount or quantity: ~ the price. 3 ~ oneself behave in such a way that causes people to respect one less. **,lower 'class** n [C] social class below middle class. **the ,lower-'class** adj.

lowly /ˈləʊli/ adj (-ier, -iest) (dated) humble.

loyal /ˈlɔɪəl/ adj (to)) faithful to sb/sth: ~ supporters ○ ~ to one's country. **loyally** adv. **loyalty** n [C, U] (pl -ies) 1 [U] being loyal. 2 [C, usu pl] connection that makes a person faithful to sb/sth.

lozenge /ˈlɒzɪndʒ/ n [C] 1 small sweet containing medicine. 2 diamond-shaped figure.

LP /ˌel ˈpiː/ abbr long-playing (record). ⇒ LONG³.

Ltd abbr Limited. = LIMITED 2 (LIMIT).

lubricate /ˈluːbrɪkeɪt/ v [T] put oil on or in (a machine), so that its parts will move easily. **lubrication** /ˌluːbrɪˈkeɪʃn/ n [U].

lucid /ˈluːsɪd/ adj (fml) 1 easy to understand; clear. 2 able to think and speak clearly. **lucidity** /luːˈsɪdəti/ n [U]. **lucidly** adv.

luck /lʌk/ n [U] 1 chance, thought

of as a force that causes good or bad things to happen to people. **2** good fortune. **3** (idm) be **down on one's 'luck** (*infml*) have a period of misfortune. **be in/out of 'luck** be fortunate/unfortunate. **lucky** *adj* (-ier, -iest) having, bringing or resulting from good luck. **luckily** *adv*.

lucrative /'lu:krətɪv/ *adj* profitable.

ludicrous /'lu:dɪkrəs/ *adj* causing laughter; very foolish. **ludicrously** *adv*.

lug /lʌg/ *v* (-gg-) [T] carry or drag with great effort.

luggage /'lʌgɪdʒ/ *n* [U] bags, suitcases, etc taken on a journey.

lukewarm /ˌlu:k'wɔ:m/ *adj* **1** (of a liquid) only slightly warm. **2** (*fig*) not enthusiastic.

lull /lʌl/ *v* [T] cause to become calm: ~ *a baby to sleep.* **lull** *n* [C, usu sing] interval of calm.

lullaby /'lʌləbaɪ/ *n* [C] (*pl* -ies) song to make a young child go to sleep.

lumbago /lʌm'beɪgəʊ/ *n* [U] pain in the lower back.

lumber[1] /'lʌmbə(r)/ *n* [U] **1** (esp *Brit*) unwanted old furniture. **2** (esp *US*) = TIMBER 1. **lumber** *v* [T] (*with*)|| (*infml*) give sth/sb unwanted to (sb): *They've ~ed me with the washing-up again.* '**lumberjack** *n* [C] man whose job is to cut down trees or produce timber.

lumber[2] /'lʌmbə(r)/ *v* [I] move in a heavy clumsy way.

luminous /'lu:mɪnəs/ *adj* giving out light; that can be seen in the dark.

lump[1] /lʌmp/ *n* [C] **1** hard mass, esp without a regular shape: *a ~ of coal.* **2** swelling or bump. **3** (idm) **have a lump in one's throat** have a tight feeling in one's throat, caused by some strong emotion. **lump** *v* [T] (*together*)|| treat (different people or things) in the same way. '**lump sum** *n* [C] larger sum of money given as one payment instead of as several smaller amounts. **lumpy** *adj* (-ier, -iest).

lump[2] /lʌmp/ *v* (idm) **lump it** (*infml*) accept sth unpleasant or unwanted.

lunacy /'lu:nəsɪ/ *n* [U] madness.

lunar /'lu:nə(r)/ *adj* of the moon.

lunatic /'lu:nətɪk/ *n* [C] **1** (*infml*) wildly foolish person. **2** (*dated*) person who is mad. **lunatic** *adj* (*infml*) wildly foolish. '**lunatic asylum** *n* [C] (*dated*) psychiatric hospital.

lunch /lʌntʃ/ *n* [C, U] meal eaten in the middle of the day. **lunch** *v* [I] (*fml*) eat lunch.

luncheon /'lʌntʃən/ *n* [C, U] (*fml*) = LUNCH.

lung /lʌŋ/ *n* [C] either of the two breathing organs in the chest.

lunge /lʌndʒ/ *n* [C], *v* [I] (make a) sudden forward movement.

lurch[1] /lɜ:tʃ/ *n* [C, usu sing] sudden movement, esp to one side. **lurch** *v* [I] move along with a lurch.

lure /lʊə(r)/ *n* [C, usu sing] something that attracts: *the ~ of adventure.* **lure** *v* [T] attract; tempt: ~ *sb into a trap.*

lurid /'lʊərɪd/ *adj* **1** having unpleasantly bright colours. **2** (*fig*) shocking and unpleasant: ~ *details of the murder.*

lurk /lɜ:k/ *v* [I] stay hidden, esp when waiting to attack.

luscious /'lʌʃəs/ *adj* having a very sweet pleasant taste.

lush /lʌʃ/ *adj* (of plants, trees, etc) growing thickly and strongly.

lust /lʌst/ *n* [C] **1** strong sexual desire. **2** (*for*)|| strong desire for sth. **lust** *v* [I] *after/for*|| having a strong desire for sb/sth. **lustful** *adj*.

lustre (*US* **luster**) /'lʌstə(r)/ *n* [U] **1** soft brightness of a shining surface. **2** (*fig*) glory.

lusty /'lʌstɪ/ *adj* healthy and strong.

luxuriant /lʌg'zʊərɪənt/ *adj* growing thickly and strongly. **luxuriance** /-əns/ *n* [U]. **luxuriantly** *adv*.

luxurious /lʌg'zʊərɪəs/ *adj* very comfortable and expensive. **luxuriously** *adv*.

luxury /'lʌkʃərɪ/ *n* (*pl* -ies) **1** [U] great comfort, esp in expensive surroundings: *a life of ~.* **2** [C] thing that is expensive and enjoyable, but not essential.

lying ⇨ LIE[1,2].

lynch /lɪntʃ/ *v* [T] put (sb) to death by hanging, without a lawful trial.

lyric /'lɪrɪk/ *adj* (of poetry) expressing direct personal feelings. **lyric** *n* **1** lyric poem. **2** **lyrics** [pl] words of a song. **lyrical** /-kl/ *adj* **1** = LYRIC. **2** very enthusiastic. **lyrically** /-klɪ/ *adv*.

M *m*

M, m /em/ *n* [C] (*pl* **M's, m's** /emz/) **1** the thirteenth letter of the English alphabet. **2** Roman numeral for 1000. **3** motorway:

take the M1 to London.

m *abbr* **1** metre(s). **2** mile(s). **3** million.

ma /maː/ *n* [C] (*infml*) mother.

ma'am /mæm *or rarely* maːm/ *n* [sing] (used as a polite from of address) madam.

mac /mæk/ *n* [C] (*Brit infml*) short for MACINTOSH.

macabre /məˈkɑːbrə/ *adj* connected with death, and so causing fear.

macaroni /ˌmækəˈrəʊni/ *n* [U] pasta in the form of short hollow tubes, cooked by boiling.

mace¹ /meɪs/ *n* [C] ornamental stick carried by an official as a sign of authority.

mace² /meɪs/ *n* [U] dried covering of nutmegs, used as a spice.

Mach /mɑːk, mæk/ *n* [U] ratio of the speed of an aircraft, etc to the speed of sound: *M ~ 2*, ie twice the speed of sound.

machete /məˈtʃeti, -ˈʃeti/ *n* [C] broad heavy knife.

machine /məˈʃiːn/ *n* [C] **1** device that uses power to perform a particular task. **2** group of people that control an organization: *the party ~.* **machine** *v* [T] make with a machine. **ma'chine-gun** *n* [C] gun that fires continuously while the trigger is pressed. **ma,chine-'readable** *adj* (of information) in a form that a computer can understand. **machinery** *n* [U] **1** machines. **2** moving parts of a machine. **3** system of methods or organization: *the ~ of government.* **ma'chine tool** *n* [C] tool for cutting or shaping materials, driven by a machine. **machinist** *n* [C] person who operates a machine.

macho /ˈmætʃəʊ/ *adj* (*infml esp derog*) (of a man or his behaviour) having or showing a strong interest in male strength, pride, etc.

mackerel /ˈmækrəl/ *n* [C] (*pl* mackerel) striped sea-fish, eaten as food.

mackintosh /ˈmækɪntɒʃ/ *n* [C] (*Brit*) coat made of rainproof material.

mad /mæd/ *adj* (~**der**, ~**dest**) **1** mentally ill. **2** (*infml*) very foolish; crazy. **3** *about//* very enthusiastic about sth/sb: *He's ~ about football.* **4** (*at*)// (*infml*) angry with sb: *You're driving me ~!* **5** (*infml*) very excited: *in a ~ rush.* **6** (idm) **like 'mad** (*infml*) very much, quickly, etc. **mad 'keen (on sb/sth)** (*infml*) very enthusiastic about sb/sth. **madly** *adv* **1** in a mad manner: *rush about ~.* **2** (*infml*) extremely: *~ly in love.* **'madman, 'madwoman** *n* [C] person who is mad(1). **madness** *n* [U].

madam /ˈmædəm/ *n* **Madam** [sing] (*fml*) (used as a polite way of addressing a woman).

madden /ˈmædn/ *v* [T] make (sb) very angry.

made *pt, pp* of MAKE¹.

Madonna /məˈdɒnə/ *n* **1** the **Madonna** [sing] Mary, the mother of Jesus Christ. **2 madonna** [C] picture or statue of Mary.

madrigal /ˈmædrɪɡl/ *n* [C] song for several singers without any instruments.

maestro /ˈmaɪstrəʊ/ *n* [C] (*pl* ~**s** or -**stri** /-striː/) great musical composer, conductor or teacher.

magazine /ˌmæɡəˈziːn; *US* ˈmæɡəziːn/ *n* [C] **1** weekly or monthly paper-covered publication with articles, stories, etc. **2** place in a gun for holding cartridges.

magenta /məˈdʒentə/ *adj, n* [U] bright purplish red (dye).

maggot /ˈmæɡət/ *n* [C] creature like a short worm that is the young of a fly or other insect.

magic /ˈmædʒɪk/ *n* [U] **1** art of changing things or controlling events by supernatural forces. **2** art of performing tricks with mysterious results. **3** (*fig*) mysterious charm: *the ~ of the circus.* **magic** *adj* **1** used in or using magic. **2** (*sl*) wonderful. **magical** /-kl/ *adj* mysterious and wonderful. **magically** /-klɪ/ *adv*. **magician** /məˈdʒɪʃn/ *n* [C] person who is skilled in magic(2).

magistrate /ˈmædʒɪstreɪt/ *n* [C] official who acts as a judge in the lowest courts.

magnanimous /mæɡˈnænɪməs/ *adj* (*fml*) generous. **magnanimity** /ˌmæɡnəˈnɪmətɪ/ *n* [U]. **magnanimously** *adv*.

magnate /ˈmæɡneɪt/ *n* [C] wealthy and powerful person, esp in business.

magnesium /mæɡˈniːzɪəm; *US* mæɡˈniːʒəm/ *n* [U] silver-white metal.

magnet /ˈmæɡnɪt/ *n* [C] **1** piece of iron or steel that attracts other metal objects. **2** (*fig*) person or thing that has a powerful attraction. **magnetic** /mæɡˈnetɪk/ *adj* **1** having the qualities of a magnet. **2** (*fig*) having a powerful attraction. **magnetically** /-klɪ/ *adv*. **magnetic 'north** *n* [U] direction to which the needle on a compass points. **magnetic 'tape** *n* [U, C] tape on which sound or vision can be recorded. **magnetism** /ˈmæɡnɪtɪzəm/ *n* **1** power of magnets. **2** (*fig*) great personal attraction. **magnetize** *v* [T] make magnetic.

magnificent /mæg'nɪfɪsnt/ *adj* extremely good or beautiful; splendid. **magnificence** /-sns/ *n* [U]. **magnificently** *adv*.

magnify /'mægnɪfaɪ/ *v* (*pt, pp* -ied) [T] **1** make (sth) appear larger. **2** (*fml*) exaggerate: ~ *the dangers*. **magnification** /ˌmægnɪfɪ'keɪʃn/ *n* [U] power or act of magnifying. **'magnifying glass** *n* [C] lens for making objects appear larger.

magnitude /'mægnɪtjuːd; *US* -tuːd/ *n* [U] **1** (*fml*) size. **2** (degree of) importance.

magpie /'mægpaɪ/ *n* [C] noisy black-and-white bird that likes to collect bright objects.

mahogany /mə'hɒgənɪ/ *n* [U] dark-brown wood used for furniture.

maid /meɪd/ *n* [C] woman servant.

maiden /'meɪdn/ *n* [C] (*arch*) young unmarried woman. **maiden** *adj* first: *a ship's ~ voyage.* **2** (of an older woman) unmarried. **'maiden name** *n* [C] woman's family name before her marriage.

mail /meɪl/ *n* [U] **1** official system of collecting, transporting and delivering letters and parcels. **2** letters, parcels, etc sent or delivered by post. **mail** *v* [T] (esp *US*) send by post. **'mailbox** *n* [C] (*US*) = LETTERBOX (LETTER). **'mailman** /-mæn/ *n* [C] (*US*) = POSTMAN (POST¹). **'mail order** *n* [U] system of buying and selling goods by post. **'mailshot** *n* [C] (**a**) advertisement sent to possible customers by post. (**b**) act of sending these.

maim /meɪm/ *v* [T] injure (sb) so seriously that some part of the body cannot be used.

main¹ /meɪn/ *adj* **1** most important; chief: *the ~ purpose of the meeting.* **2** (idm) **in the main** generally. **'mainframe** *n* [C] large powerful computer which can be used by several people at the same time. **'mainland** *n* [sing] large mass of land, considered without its islands. **mainly** *adv* chiefly. **'mainspring** *n* [C] **1** chief spring in a clock or watch. **2** (*fml/fig*) chief motive or reason. **'mainstay** *n* [C] chief support; foundation. **'mainstream** *n* [sing] group of commonly accepted opinions about a subject.

main² /meɪn/ *n* [C] **1** large pipe supplying water or gas, or large wire supplying electricity, to a building. **2 the mains** source of

supply of water, gas or electricity to a building.

maintain /meɪn'teɪn/ *v* [T] **1** cause to continue; keep in existence: ~ *peaceful relations.* **2** support (sb) with money. **3** keep in good condition: ~ *a car.* **4** state firmly: ~ *one's innocence.* **maintenance** /'meɪntənəns/ *n* [U] **1** maintaining or being maintained. **2** (*Brit*) money that one is legally required to pay to support sb.

maisonette /ˌmeɪzə'net/ *n* [C] flat on two floors that is part of a larger building.

maize /meɪz/ *n* [U] tall plant that bears large yellow seeds on a long head.

majesty /'mædʒəstɪ/ *n* (*pl* -ies) **1** **Majesty** [C] (used when speaking to or about a king or queen): *Good morning, Your M~.* ○ *His M~.* **2** [U] grandness; dignity. **majestic** /mə'dʒestɪk/ *adj.* **majestically** /-klɪ/ *adv.*

major¹ /'meɪdʒə(r)/ *adj* (more) important; chief: *a ~ road.* **major** *v* [I] **in//** study sth as the main subject at college or university: ~ *in French.*

major² /'meɪdʒə(r)/ *n* [C] army officer between a captain and a colonel.

majority /mə'dʒɒrətɪ; *US* -'dʒɔːr-/ *n* (*pl* -ies) **1** [sing] (with sing or pl v) greater number; most. **2** [C] number by which votes for one side are more than those for the other side: *win by a ~ of 9 votes.* **3** [sing] legal age of becoming an adult.

make¹ /meɪk/ *v* (*pt, pp* **made** /meɪd/) **1** [T] construct, produce or prepare; bring into existence: ~ *bread* ○ ... *a lot of noise.* **2** [T] cause: ~ *trouble.* **3** [T] cause to be or become: *The news made her happy.* **4** [T] (**a**) cause sth to happen: *Can you ~ this door shut?* (**b**) cause sb to do sth: ~ *sb jump.* **5** [T] elect; appoint: *They made me the manager.* **6** [T] prove to be: *She will ~ a brilliant doctor.* **7** [T] earn; acquire: ~ *a profit.* **8** [T] reckon (to be); calculate: *What do you ~ the time?* **9** [T] add up to; equal: *Two and two ~ four.* **10** [T] reach (a place or a speed): ~ *the station on time.* **11** [I] behave as if about to do sth: *She made (as if) to hit him.* **12** (idm) **make** (**sth**) **'do, make do with sth** manage with sth which is not really adequate. **'make it** (*infml*) be successful; achieve one's goal. **make up ground** ⇨ GROUND¹. **13** (phr v) **make after sb/sth** chase sb/sth. **make for sb/sth** (**a**) move towards sb/sth. (b) help to cause: *Does exercise ~ for good health?* **make A into B** change A to B: *~ water into wine.* **make sth of sb/sth** understand: *What do you ~ of this sentence?* **make 'off** (*infml*) hurry away, esp to escape. **make off with sth** steal sth and escape with it. **make 'out** (*infml*) manage: *How are you ~ing out in your new job?* **make sth out** (a) write out: *~ out a cheque.* (b) manage to see or read: *I can't ~ out his writing.* **make sb/sth out** (in negative sentences and questions) understand: *I just can't ~ her out.* **make out that**, **make oneself/sb/sth out to be** claim to be: *He ~ s himself out to be cleverer than he is.* **make (sb/oneself) up** put cosmetics on the face. **make sth up** (a) complete: *We need £5 to ~ up the sum.* (b) invent, esp to deceive: *a made-up story.* (c) compose: *Bodies are made up of cells.* (d) make (material, cloth, etc) into clothes. (e) prepare a bed for use. **make up (for sth)** compensate for. **make up to sb** be pleasant to sb in order to get sth. **make it up to sb** compensate sb for a loss, etc. **make (it) 'up(with sb)** end a dispute or disagreement. **make-believe** *n* [U] pretending: *a world of make-believe.* **make-up** *n* 1 [U] cosmetics. 2 [sing] a person's character and personality: *There is no jealousy in his ~-up.* (b) parts, people, etc that form sth: *the ~ up of the new committee.*

make² /meɪk/ *n* [C] 1 named kind of product: *a ~ of car.* 2 (idm) on the 'make (*infml*) trying to gain an advantage for oneself.

maker /ˈmeɪkə(r)/ *n* 1 [C] person who makes sth: *a film-~.* 2 the/our Maker [sing] God.

makeshift /ˈmeɪkʃɪft/ *adj* used for a time because there is nothing better.

making /ˈmeɪkɪŋ/ *n* (idm) be the making of sb cause sb to succeed or develop well. have the makings of sth have the qualities needed to become sth.

maladjusted /ˌmæləˈdʒʌstɪd/ *adj* unable to behave acceptably and deal satisfactorily with other people. **maladjustment** /-mənt/ *n* [U].

malaria /məˈleərɪə/ *n* [U] serious fever caught from mosquito bites.

male /meɪl/ *adj* 1 of the sex that does not give birth. 2 (of a plant) having flowers with parts that produce pollen. 3 (of part of a device) having a part that sticks out and can be put into a hollow part.

male *n* [C] male person or animal.

male 'chauvinist *n* [C] (*derog*) man who believes men are superior to women.

malevolent /məˈlevələnt/ *adj* (*fml*) wishing to do evil or cause harm to others. **malevolence** /-ləns/ *n* [U]. **malevolently** *adv*.

malformation /ˌmælfɔːˈmeɪʃn/ *n* [U, C] (state of having a) badly formed or shaped part of the body. **malformed** /-ˈfɔːmd/ *adj*.

malfunction /ˌmælˈfʌŋkʃn/ *v* [I] (*fml*) (of a machine) fail to work properly. **malfunction** *n* [C, U].

malice /ˈmælɪs/ *n* [U] desire to harm other people. **malicious** /məˈlɪʃəs/ *adj*. **maliciously** *adv*.

malignant /məˈlɪgnənt/ *adj* 1 having a great desire to harm others. 2 (of a disease) serious and likely to cause death. **malignantly** *adv*.

mall /mæl, mɔːl/ *n* [C] (esp US) street or covered area with shops, closed to traffic.

malleable /ˈmælɪəbl/ *adj* 1 (of metals) that can be beaten or pressed into new shapes. 2 (*fig*) (of a person, his/her character, etc) easily influenced or changed.

mallet /ˈmælɪt/ *n* [C] hammer with a wooden head.

malnutrition /ˌmælnjuːˈtrɪʃn; *US* -nuː-/ *n* [U] condition caused by a lack of (the right kind of) food.

malt /mɔːlt/ *n* [U] grain, esp barley, used for making beer, whisky, etc.

maltreat /ˌmælˈtriːt/ *v* [T] (*fml*) treat roughly or cruelly. **maltreatment** *n* [U].

mamba /ˈmæmbə/ *n* [C] black or green poisonous snake.

mamma /ˈmɑːmə/ *n* [C] (*US infml*) mother.

mammal /ˈmæml/ *n* [C] any of the kind of animal of which the female feeds her young with milk from her body.

mammoth /ˈmæməθ/ *n* [C] large hairy kind of elephant, now extinct. **mammoth** *adj* (*infml*) extremely large.

man¹ /mæn/ *n* (*pl* **men** /men/) 1 [C] adult male human being. 2 [C] human being: *All men must die.* 3 [U] the human race: *the origins of ~.* 4 [C, usu pl] male person under the authority of sb else: *officers and men.* 5 [C] husband, male lover, etc: *~ and wife.* 6 [C] male person with the qualities of strength, courage, etc associated with men: *Don't give up - be a ~!* 7 [C] piece used in chess, etc. 8 (idm) **be one's own 'man** be able to decide matters independently of others. **the ,man in the 'street** the average person. **,man to 'man** frankly; openly. **to a 'man** all, without exception. **'manhole** n [C] opening in a street through which sb enters an underground drain, etc. **manhood** n [U] state or qualities of being a man. **,man·'made** adj not naturally made; artificial. **'manpower** n [U] number of people available for work. **'man·slaughter** n [U] crime of killing sb unintentionally.

man² /mæn/ v (-nn-) [T] supply with people for service or operation: ~ a boat.

manacle /'mænəkl/ n [C, usu pl] one of a pair of chains for tying a prisoner's hands or feet. **manacle** v [T] tie up (sb) with manacles.

manage /'mænɪdʒ/ v 1 [T] be in charge of (sth); run or control. 2 [I, T] (a) succeed in doing (sth): *How did the prisoners ~ to escape?* (b) [I] succeed in living, esp with little money: *I can only just ~ on my wages.* **manageable** adj that can be dealt with.

management /'mænɪdʒmənt/ n 1 [U] control and organization of a business, etc: *problems caused by bad ~*. 2 [C, also sing with pl v] people who manage a business, etc: *workers and ~*. 3 [U] (fml) skilful treatment.

manager /'mænɪdʒə(r)/ n [C] person who organizes a business, sports team, etc. **manageress** /,mænɪdʒə'res/ n [C] woman who is in charge of a shop or restaurant. **managerial** /,mænə-'dʒɪərɪəl/ adj of managers.

mandate /'mændeɪt/ n [C, usu sing] authority given to a government, trade union, etc by the people who support it. **mandatory** /'mændətərɪ; US -tɔːrɪ/ adj (fml) required by law.

mandolin /'mændəlɪn, ,mæn-də'lɪn/ n [C] musical instrument with eight metal strings.

mane /meɪn/ n [C] long hair on the neck of a horse or lion.

maneuver = MANOEUVRE.

manful /'mænfl/ adj brave; determined. **manfully** adv.

manger /'meɪndʒə(r)/ n [C] long open box from which horses or cattle can feed.

mangle /'mæŋgl/ v [T] (usu passive) cut up, crush or damage (sth) greatly.

mango /'mæŋgəʊ/ n [C] (pl ~es or ~s) (tropical tree producing a) fruit with yellow flesh.

mangy /'meɪndʒɪ/ adj (-ier, -iest) with patches of hair, fur, etc missing; shabby.

manhandle /'mænhændl/ v [T] 1 move by physical strength. 2 treat (sb) roughly.

mania /'meɪnɪə/ n 1 [C, U] (for)// extreme enthusiasm for sth: *a ~ for motor bikes.* 2 [U] mental illness. **maniac** /-nɪæk/ n [C] 1 mad person. 2 person with an extreme enthusiasm for sth. **maniacal** /mə'naɪəkl/ adj.

manicure /'mænɪkjʊə(r)/ n [C, U] care of the hands and finger-nails. **manicure** v [T] care for (sb's) hands and finger-nails. **manicurist** n [C].

manifest /'mænɪfest/ adj (fml) clear and obvious. **manifest** v [T] (fml) show clearly: *The disease ~ed itself.* **manifestation** /,mænɪfe'steɪʃn/ n [C, U]. **manifestly** adv.

manifesto /,mænɪ'festəʊ/ n [C] (pl ~s or ~es) public statement of principles and plans, esp of a political party.

manifold /'mænɪfəʊld/ adj (fml) of many different kinds. **manifold** n [C] pipe with several openings that connect with other parts.

manipulate /mə'nɪpjʊleɪt/ v [T] 1 handle with skill. 2 control or influence, esp in a clever and selfish way. **manipulation** /mə,nɪp-jʊ'leɪʃn/ n [C, U]. **manipulative** /mə,nɪp-/lətɪv; US -leɪtɪv/ adj.

mankind /,mæn'kaɪnd/ n [U] the human race.

manly /'mænlɪ/ adj (-ier, -iest) (approv) (of a man) having the qualities or appearance expected of a man. **manliness** n [U].

manner /'mænə(r)/ n 1 [sing] (fml) way in which sth is done or happens: *in a friendly ~*. 2 [sing] person's way of behaving towards others: *I don't like your ~*. 3 **manners** [pl] (polite) social behaviour: *good ~*. 4 (idm) **all manner of** sb/sth (fml) every kind of sb/sth. **in a manner of speaking** to some extent; if considered in a certain way. **-mannered** (in compound adjectives) having manners of the kind stated: *,well-'~ed.*

mannerism /'mænərɪzəm/ n [C] peculiar habit of behaviour or speech.

manoeuvre (*US* **maneuver**) /mə'nuːvə(r)/ n 1 [C] (a) movement performed with skill. (b) (fig) clever plan to achieve one's own purpose. 2 **manoeuvres** [pl] large-scale training by soldiers. **manoeuvrable** (*US* **maneuverable**) adj that can be manoeuvred easily. **manoeuvre** (*US* **maneuver**) v 1 [I, T] turn skilfully. 2 [T] guide (sth) skilfully.

manor (also **manor house**) /'mænə(r)/ n [C] large country house with a surrounding estate.

mansion /'mænʃn/ n [C] large grand house.

mantelpiece /'mæntlpiːs/ n [C] shelf above a fireplace.

mantle /'mæntl/ n 1 (a) loose sleeveless cloak. (b) (fig) covering: a ~ of snow. 2 [sing] (of) (rhet) the responsibilities of an important job: take on the ~ of supreme power.

manual /'mænjʊəl/ adj, done with or controlled by the hands. **manual** n [C] book giving practical information or instructions. **manually** adv.

manufacture /,mænjʊ-'fæktʃə(r)/ v [T] make (goods) in large quantities using machinery. **manufacture** n [U] activity of manufacturing. **manufacturer** n [C].

manure /mə'njʊə(r)/ n [U] animal waste matter spread over the soil to help plants to grow.

manuscript /'mænjʊskrɪpt/ n [C] 1 author's handwritten or typed work. 2 old handwritten book.

many /'meni/ adj, pron 1 a large number of people or things: ~ people ○ ~ of the students. 2 **many a** (used with a singular noun) a large number of: ~ a mother, ie many mothers. 3 (idm) **a good/great many** very many. **have had one too 'many** (infml) be slightly drunk.

map /mæp/ n [C] 1 drawing on paper, etc of (part of) the earth's surface. 2 (idm) **put sth on the 'map** cause sth to be considered important. **map** v (-pp-) [T] make a map of.

mar /mɑː(r)/ v (-rr-) [T] (fml) spoil: a mistake that ~red his career.

marathon /'mærəθən; US -θɒn/ n [C] long-distance running race (about 42 kilometres or 26 miles). **marathon** adj (fig) very long and needing a lot of effort: a ~ speech lasting five hours.

marauding /mə'rɔːdɪŋ/ adj going about searching for things to steal or people to attack. **marauder** /-də(r)/ n [C].

marble /'mɑːbl/ n 1 [U] kind of hard stone, used, when cut and polished, for building and sculpture. 2 (a) [C] small ball of glass used by children in games. (b) **marbles** [pl] game played with these.

March /mɑːtʃ/ n [U, C] the third month of the year. (See examples of use at April.)

march /mɑːtʃ/ v 1 [I] walk as soldiers do, with regular steps. 2 [T] cause (sb) to march: They ~ed the prisoner away. **march** n 1 [C] action of marching. 2 [C] piece of music for marching to. 3 [C] act of walking from one place to another by many people, esp as a protest. 4 [sing] (of) (fig) the steady progress of sth: the ~ of time.

marchioness /,mɑː'ʃə'nes/ n [C] 1 wife of a marquis. 2 woman with the same rank as a marquis.

mare /meə(r)/ n [C] female horse or donkey.

margarine /,mɑː'dʒə'riːn; US 'mɑːrdʒəriːn/ n [U] food like butter, made from animal or vegetable fats.

margin /'mɑːdʒɪn/ n [C] 1 blank space round the writing or printing on a page. 2 edge or border. 3 (a) amount of votes, time etc by which sth is won: a ~ six votes. (b) amount of space, time, etc allowed for success or safety. **marginal** /-nl/ adj very small: a ~al increase. **marginally** /-nəli/ adv.

marijuana /,mærɪ'wɑːnə, ,mærɪ'wænə/ n [U] dried leaves and flowers of Indian hemp, usu smoked as a drug.

marina /mə'riːnə/ n [C] small harbour for yachts and pleasure-boats.

marinade /,mærɪ'neɪd/ n [C, U] mixture of wine, herbs, etc in which meat or fish is soaked before being cooked. **marinade** (also **marinate** /'mærɪneɪt/) v [T] soak (food) in a marinade.

marine /mə'riːn/ adj 1 of, or found in, the sea: ~ life. 2 of ships, sea-trade, etc. **marine** n [C] soldier trained to fight on land or sea.

mariner /'mærɪnə(r)/ n [C] (dated or fml) sailor.

marionette /,mærɪə'net/ n [C] puppet moved by strings.

marital /'mærɪtl/ adj of marriage.

maritime /'mærɪtaɪm/ adj 1 of the sea or shipping. 2 near the sea.

mark /mɑːk/ n [C] 1 (a) stain, spot, etc esp that spoils the appearance of sth: dirty ~s on my new shirt. (b) spot or area on the body by which sth/sb may be clearly known: a birth~. 2 written or printed symbol: punctuation ~s. 3 visible sign: ~s of old age ○ a ~ of respect. 4 number or letter to show the quality of sb's work or behaviour: top ~s. 5 **Mark** model or type of a machine, etc: a M~ 2 Ford Escort. 6 (idm) **be quick/slow off the 'mark** be fast/slow to act or to understand sth. ,make one's 'mark (in sth) become famous or successful in sth. 'up to the 'mark equal to the required standard.

mark² /mɑːk/ v 1 [I, T] (cause sth to) have a mark: You've ~ed the table. ○ The carpet ~s easily. 2 [T] be a sign of: This cross ~s the place where she died. ○ His death ~ed the end of an era. 3 [T] give marks(4) to. 4 [T] put a written symbol on: documents ~ed 'secret' 5 [T] (fml) pay attention to: M~ my words, ie You will find that what I say is correct. 6 [T] be a feature of: qualities that ~ a leader. 7 [T] (sport) stay close to (an opposing player). 8 (idm) mark 'time pass one's time doing sth uninteresting until one can do sth more exciting. 9 (phr v) mark sth down/up lower/increase the price of sth. mark sth off/out separate sth by marking a boundary line. mark sb out for sth choose sb to receive sth special. marked adj easily seen; clear: a ~ed improvement. markedly /'mɑːkɪdlɪ/ adv. marker n [C] 1 person or tool that makes marks. 2 person who marks examination, etc papers. 3 flag, post, etc that marks a place. marking n [C, usu pl] pattern of marks, eg colours of an animal's skin. 'mark-up n [C, usu sing] amount that a seller adds to a price.

market /'mɑːkɪt/ n 1 [C] (public place for a) gathering of people for buying and selling goods. 2 [C, usu sing] state of trade: The coffee ~ was steady. 3 [sing, U] (for)// demand: a good ~ for cars. 4 [C] area in which goods may be sold: foreign ~. 5 the market [sing] buyers and sellers. 6 (idm) in the market for sth (infml) interested in buying sth. on/onto the 'market offered for sale: a product not yet on the ~. ○ new goods coming onto the ~. market v [T] offer for sale, esp by advertising, etc. marketable adj. ,market 'garden n [C] (Brit) farm where vegetables and fruit are grown for sale. marketing n [U] part of business concerned with the advertising, selling and distribution of goods. 'market-place n 1 [C] open area in a town where a market is held. 2 the market-place [sing] activity of buying and selling. ,market re'search n [C] study of what people buy and why.

marksman /'mɑːksmən/ n [C] (pl -men /-mən/) person skilled in shooting accurately.

marmalade /'mɑːməleɪd/ n [U] kind of jam made from oranges.

maroon¹ /mə'ruːn/ adj, n [C] (of a) brownish red.

maroon² /mə'ruːn/ v [T] leave (sb) in a place from which he/she cannot escape.

marquee /mɑː'kiː/ n [C] very large tent.

marquis (also marquess) /'mɑːkwɪs/ n [C] (in the UK) nobleman next in rank above an earl and below a duke.

marriage /'mærɪdʒ/ n [U, C] legal union of a man and woman as husband and wife. marriageable adj old enough or suitable for marriage.

marrow¹ /'mærəʊ/ n [C, U] very large oval vegetable with white flesh and stripy green skin.

marrow² /'mærəʊ/ n [U] soft fatty substance that fills the inside of bones.

marry /'mærɪ/ v (pt, pp -ied) 1 [I, T] take (sb) as a husband or wife. 2 [T] join as husband and wife: Which priest is going to ~ them? 3 [T] (off)// find a suitable partner for (sb): They married (off) their daughter to a rich banker. married adj 1 (to)// having a husband or wife. 2 of marriage: married life.

marsh /mɑːʃ/ n [C, U] (area of) low-lying wet land. marshy adj (-ier, -iest).

marshal¹ /'mɑːʃl/ n [C] 1 officer of very high rank in the air force or army. 2 official who organizes a public event, eg a motor race. 3 (US) officer with duties similar to a sheriff's.

marshal² /'mɑːʃl/ v (-ll-; US -l-) [T] 1 arrange (sb/sth) in proper order. 2 lead or guide (people) carefully.

marsupial /mɑː'suːpɪəl/ adj, n [C] (of an) animal, eg a kangaroo, the female of which has a pouch on its body to hold its young.

martial /'mɑːʃl/ adj (fml) of war, soldiers, etc. martial 'arts n [pl] fighting sports such as judo and karate. ,martial 'law n [U] government by army officers.

martin /'mɑːtɪn/ US -tn/ n [C] bird of the swallow family.

martyr /'mɑːtə(r)/ n [C] person who dies or suffers for his/her (esp religious) beliefs. martyr v [T] cause (sb) to suffer as a martyr. martyrdom /'mɑːtədəm/ n [U, C] martyr's suffering or death.

marvel /'mɑːvl/ n [C] wonderful thing: the ~s of modern science. marvel v (-ll-; US -l-) [T] at// (fml) be very surprised at sth. marvellous (US -velous) /'mɑːvələs/

adj excellent; wonderful. **marvellously** (*US* **-velously**) *adv.*

Marxism /ˈmɑːksɪzəm/ *n* [U] political and economic theory of Karl Marx, on which Communism is based. **Marxist** /-sɪst/ *n* [C], *adj.*

marzipan /ˈmɑːzɪpæn/ *n* [U] thick paste of crushed almonds, sugar, etc.

mascara /mæˈskɑːrə; *US* -ˈskærə/ *n* [U] colour for darkening the eyelashes.

mascot /ˈmæskət, -skɒt/ *n* [C] thing, animal or person thought to bring good luck.

masculine /ˈmæskjʊlɪn/ *adj* 1 of or like men. 2 (*grammar*) of a particular class of nouns, pronouns, etc. **masculinity** /ˌmæskjʊˈlɪnətɪ/ *n* [U] quality of being masculine.

mash /mæʃ/ *v* [T] crush (cooked potatoes, etc) to a soft mass. **mash** *n* [U] (*infml*) mashed potatoes.

mask /mɑːsk; *US* mæsk/ *n* [C] covering for (part of) the face worn to hide or protect it: (*fig*) *His behaviour is really a ~ for his shyness.* **mask** *v* [T] cover or hide. **masked** *adj* wearing a mask: *~ed robbers.*

masochism /ˈmæsəkɪzəm/ *n* [U] mental disorder of gaining (esp sexual) pleasure from one's own pain. **masochist** /-kɪst/ *n* [C]. **masochistic** /ˌmæsəˈkɪstɪk/ *adj.*

mason /ˈmeɪsn/ *n* [C] person who builds in or works with stone. **masonry** /-sənrɪ/ *n* [U] stone used in building.

masquerade /ˌmɑːskəˈreɪd; *US* ˌmæsk-/ *v* [I] (*as*)// pretend to be sb/sth: *~ as a police officer.* **masquerade** *n* [C] false show.

Mass (also **mass**) /mæs/ *n* [C, U] (esp in the Roman Catholic Church) service based on the last meal of Jesus Christ when people share bread and sometimes wine.

mass /mæs/ *n* 1 [C] quantity of matter without a regular shape: *a ~ of earth.* 2 [C] large number: *a ~ of tourists.* 3 [U] (*physics*) amount of matter in an object. 4 **the masses** [pl] ordinary working people. **mass** *v* [I, T] form into a large group: *The general ~ed his troops for the attack.* **the ˌmass 'media** *n* [pl] television, radio, newspapers, etc. **ˌmass-proˈduce** *v* [T] make (goods) in very large quantities. **ˌmass proˈduction** *n* [U].

massacre /ˈmæsəkə(r)/ *n* [C] cruel killing of a large number of people. **massacre** *v* [T] kill a large number of (people) cruelly.

massage /ˈmæsɑːʒ; *US* məˈsɑːʒ/ *n* [C, U] (act of) rubbing and pressing sb's body, esp to lessen pain or stiffness. **massage** *v* [T] give massage to.

masseur /mæˈsɜː(r)/ *n* [C] (*fem* **masseuse** /mæˈsɜːz/) person whose job is to give massage.

massive /ˈmæsɪv/ *adj* extremely large. **massively** *adv.*

mast /mɑːst; *US* mæst/ *n* [C] 1 long upright post used to support a ship's sails. 2 tall structure for aerials.

master[1] /ˈmɑːstə(r); *US* ˈmæs-/ *n* [C] 1 man who has others working for him. 2 male head of a household. 3 captain of a ship. 4 male owner of a dog, horse, etc. 5 (esp *Brit*) male schoolteacher. 6 **Master** holder of the second (in Scotland the first) university degree: *a M~ of 'Arts/ Sciences.* 7 great artist. 8 *of*// (*fml*) person who is very skilled in sth. 9 film, tape, etc from which copies can be made: *the ~ copy.* **master** *adj* 1 having professional skill: *a ~ carpenter.* 2 including everything: *a ~ plan.* **ˈmastermind** *v* [T] plan or direct (a scheme) cleverly. **ˈmastermind** *n* [C] extremely clever person. **ˌMaster of 'Ceremonies** *n* [C] person in charge of an important social occasion, who introduces guests, etc. **ˈmasterpiece** *n* [C] something, eg a painting, done with very great skill.

master[2] /ˈmɑːstə(r); *US* ˈmæs-/ *v* [T] 1 gain control of. 2 gain great skill in: *~ a foreign language.*

masterful /ˈmɑːstəfl; *US* ˈmæs-/ *adj* able to control others. **masterfully** /-fəlɪ/ *adv.*

masterly /ˈmɑːstəlɪ; *US* ˈmæs-/ *adj* very skilful.

mastery /ˈmɑːstərɪ/ *n* [U] 1 great skill or knowledge. 2 complete control.

masturbate /ˈmæstəbeɪt/ *v* [I] gain sexual pleasure by stroking or rubbing one's own genital organs. **masturbation** /ˌmæstəˈbeɪʃn/ *n* [U].

mat[1] /mæt/ *n* [C] 1 piece of material used for covering part of a floor. 2 small piece of material put under a vase, hot dish, etc to protect a table. **mat** *v* (-**tt**-) [I, T] (cause) to become twisted in a thick mass: *~ted hair.*

mat[2] = **MATT**.

matador /ˈmætədɔː(r)/ *n* [C] bullfighter whose task is to kill the bull.

match[1] /mætʃ/ *n* [C] short piece of wood, etc with a head that burns when rubbed against a rough surface. **ˈmatchbox** *n* [C] box for holding matches.

match² /mætʃ/ *n* **1** [C] game in which people or teams compete against each other: *a football ~.* **2** [sing] person equal to sb else in skill, etc: *He's no ~ for her in tennis.* **3** [C] marriage: *They made a good ~.* **4** [sing] thing that combines with another: *The carpets and curtains are a perfect ~.*
match *v* **1** [I, T] combine well with (sth): *The carpets and the curtains ~ perfectly.* **2** [T] (**a**) be equal to (sb). (**b**) find (sb/sth) equal to another. **matchless** *adj* (*fml*) without an equal. '**matchmaker** *n* [C] person who likes trying to arrange marriages or relationships for others.
mate /meɪt/ *n* [C] **1** friend, companion or person one works or lives with: *He's gone out with his ~ s.* ○ *a flat-~.* **2** (*Brit sl*) (used for addressing a man). **3** (in the merchant navy) officer below a captain. **4** either of a pair of male and female animals. **5** worker's helper: *a plumber's ~.* **mate** *v* [I, T] (*with*)‖ (of birds or animals) join sexually to produce young.
material /məˈtɪəriəl/ *n* **1** [C, U] substance from which sth else is or can be made. **2** [U, C] cloth. **3** [U] information to be used in writing a book, etc: *~ for a newspaper article.* **material** *adj* **1** of or having physical substance; not spiritual. **2** of the body; of physical needs: *~ comforts.* **3** (*esp law*) important: *~ evidence.*
materialism /məˈtɪəriəlɪzəm/ *n* [U] (*usu derog*) belief that only money, possessions, etc are important. **materialist** /-lɪst/ *n* [C]. **materialistic** /məˌtɪəriəˈlɪstɪk/ *adj.*
materialize /məˈtɪəriəlaɪz/ *v* [I] **1** become a reality; happen. **2** take material form; become able to be seen.
maternal /məˈtɜːnl/ *adj* **1** of or like a mother. **2** related through the mother's side of the family: *a ~ grandfather.*
maternity /məˈtɜːnəti/ *n* [U] being a mother. **maternity** *adj* of or for women who are giving birth: *a ~ hospital* ○ *~ leave,* ie absence from work.
math /mæθ/ *n* (*US*) (with sing *v*) short for MATHEMATICS.
mathematics /ˌmæθəˈmætɪks/ *n* (with sing *v*) study of numbers. **mathematical** /-ɪkl/ *adj.* **mathematically** /-klɪ/ *adv.* **mathematician** /ˌmæθəməˈtɪʃn/ *n* [C] student of or expert in mathematics.
maths /mæθs/ *n* (*Brit*) (with sing

v) short for MATHEMATICS.
matinée (*US* also **matinee**) /ˈmætɪneɪ, ˈmætɪneɪ; *US* ˌmætnˈeɪ/ *n* [C] afternoon performance of a play or film.
matriarch /ˈmeɪtrɪɑːk/ *n* [C] woman who rules a family or group of people. **matriarchal** /ˌmeɪtrɪˈɑːkl/ *adj.*
matriculate /məˈtrɪkjuleɪt/ *v* [I] be admitted as a student to a university. **matriculation** /məˌtrɪkjuˈleɪʃn/ *n* [U].
matrimony /ˈmætrɪməni; *US* -məʊni/ *n* [U] (*fml*) state of being married. **matrimonial** /ˌmætrɪˈməʊnɪəl/ *adj.*
matron /ˈmeɪtrən/ *n* [C] **1** (formerly) woman in charge of the nurses in a hospital. **2** woman who manages the domestic affairs of a school. **3** middle-aged married woman with a serious appearance. **matronly** *adj* of or like a matron(3).
matt (also **mat** (*US* also **matte**) /mæt/ *adj* (of surfaces) not shiny.
matter¹ /ˈmætə(r)/ *n* **1** [C] affair or subject: *an important business ~.* **2** [U] physical substance of which sth is made: *The universe is composed of ~.* **3** [U] substance or material of the kind that is mentioned: *reading ~,* ie books, newspapers, etc. **4** (idm) **as a matter of fact** (used for emphasis) in reality. **for 'that matter** (used for showing that sth is also true for another situation). (**as**) **a matter of 'course** (as) a regular or usual habit. (**be**) **the matter (with sb/sth)** (*infml*) the reason for unhappiness, pain, etc: *What's the ~ with her?* ○ *Is anything the ~?* **a matter of 'hours, 'minutes, etc** not more than a few hours, etc. **a matter of o'pinion** subject on which there is disagreement. (**be**) **a matter of (doing) sth** (be) a question or situation that depends on sth else: *Teaching isn't just a ~ of good communication.* **no matter who, what, etc** it is not important who, etc: *Don't believe him, no ~ what he says.* ,**matter-of-'fact** *adj* showing no feeling or imagination.
matter² /ˈmætə(r)/ *v* [I] be important: *It doesn't ~.*
matting /ˈmætɪŋ/ *n* [U] rough woven material used as a floor covering.
mattress /ˈmætrɪs/ *n* [C] large thick cloth case filled with feathers, etc, for sleeping on.
mature /məˈtjʊə(r); *US* -ˈtʊər/ *adj* **1** fully grown or developed. **2** (of a person or his/her behaviour)

sensible, esp because of age and experience. **3** (of wine or cheese) having reached its full flavour. **mature** v [I, T] become or make mature. **maturity** n [U].

maul /mɔːl/ v [T] hurt by rough or cruel handling: ~ed by a lion.

mausoleum /ˌmɔːsəˈliːəm/ n [C] large stone building containing a grave.

mauve /məʊv/ adj, n [U] (of a) pale purple colour.

maxim /ˈmæksɪm/ n [C] saying that expresses a general truth or rule of behaviour.

maximize /ˈmæksɪmaɪz/ v [T] make as large as possible.

maximum /ˈmæksɪməm/ n [C, usu sing] (pl maxima /-mə/) largest possible amount: the ~ load a lorry can carry. **maximum** adj as large as possible: make ~ use of the room.

May /meɪ/ n [U, C] the fifth month of the year. (See examples of use at **April**).

may /meɪ/ modal v (neg **may not**, rare contracted form **mayn't** /meɪnt/, pt **might** /maɪt/, neg **might not**, rare contracted form **mightn't** /ˈmaɪtnt/) **1** (used for showing possibility): This coat ~ be Sarah's. ○ He ~ have (ie Perhaps he has) forgotten to come. **2** (fml) (used for asking permission): M~ I sit down? **3** (used for expressing a wish): M~ you both be very happy!

maybe /ˈmeɪbiː/ adv perhaps.

mayonnaise /ˌmeɪəˈneɪz; US ˈmeɪəneɪz/ n [U] thick creamy sauce made from eggs, oil and vinegar, and eaten with salads.

mayor /meə(r); US ˈmeɪər/ n [C] head, usu elected yearly, of a city or town council. **mayoress** /meəˈres; US ˈmeɪərəs/ n [C] **1** woman who is a mayor. **2** mayor's wife.

maze /meɪz/ n [C] system of paths, arranged like a puzzle, in which one must find one's way.

MC /ˌem ˈsiː/ abbr **1** Master of Ceremonies. **2** (US) Member of Congress.

MD /ˌem ˈdiː/ abbr Doctor of Medicine.

me /miː/ pron (used as the object of a v or prep) person who is the speaker or writer: Don't hit me. ○ Give it to me.

meadow /ˈmedəʊ/ n [C, U] field of grass.

meagre (US **meager**) /ˈmiːgə(r)/ adj (too) small in quantity: a ~ income. **meagrely** adv. **meagreness** n [U].

meal¹ /miːl/ n [C] **(a)** occasion when food is eaten. **(b)** food that is eaten.

meal² /miːl/ n [U] roughly crushed grain: oat~.

mean¹ /miːn/ v (pt, pp ~t /ment/) [T] **1** (of words, sentences, etc) have as an explanation: What does this word ~? **2** (of signs or symbols) represent: A green light ~s 'go'. **3** result in: This will ~ more work. **4** have as a purpose; intend: What do you ~ by coming (ie Why did you come) so late? ○ Sorry, I ~t to tell you earlier. ○ Don't laugh! I ~ it!, ie I am serious. **5** be important to sb: Your friendship ~s a lot to me. **6** (idm) **be meant to** be supposed to; be expected to: You're ~t to pay before you come in. **mean 'business** be serious in one's intentions. '**mean well** have good intentions, but not the ability, etc to carry them out.

meaning n **1** [U, C] what is understood by a word, sentence, etc. **2** [U] purpose: My life has lost all ~ing. **meaningful** adj full of meaning; significant. **meaningless** adj without meaning.

mean² /miːn/ adj **1** ungenerous; selfish. **2** unkind. **3** (esp US) bad-tempered; vicious. **4** (idm) **no mean** (approv) (a) very good (performer, achievement, etc): He's no mean tennis player. **meanness** n [U].

mean³ /miːn/ n [C] (mathematics) quantity between two extremes; average. **mean** adj.

meander /miˈændə(r)/ v [I] **1** (of a river, etc) follow a winding course. **2** wander about.

means¹ /miːnz/ n (with sing or pl v) **1** method: find a ~ of improving the standard of education. **2** (idm) **by 'all means** (fml) yes, of course. **by means of sth** (fml) by using sth. **by 'no means** (fml) not at all.

means² /miːnz/ n [pl] money; wealth: a man of ~, ie a rich man. '**means test** n [C] official inquiry that considers how much money sb has, before the state gives him/her support.

meant pt, pp of **MEAN¹**.

meantime /ˈmiːntaɪm/ n (idm) **in the 'meantime** meanwhile. **meantime** adv meanwhile.

meanwhile /ˈmiːnwaɪl; US -hwaɪl/ adv in the time between two events; at the same time.

measles /ˈmiːzlz/ n (with sing v) infectious disease, marked by small red spots on the skin.

measure /ˈmeʒə(r)/ v [T] **1** find the size, length, degree, etc of: ~ a piece of wood. **2** be of the size, length, etc that is mentioned: The *room ~s* 5 metres across. **3** (phr v) **measure sth out** give a measured quantity of sth. **measure up (to sth)** reach the required or expected standard. **measured** *adj* careful. **measurement** *n* **1** [U] measuring. **2** [C] length, width, etc that is measured.

measure² /'meʒə(r)/ *n* **1** (a) [U, C] standard or system used in measuring. (b) [C] unit in such a system: *The metre is a ~ of length.* **2** [C] device, eg a ruler, marked with standard units: *a tape-~.* **3** [sing] *of*|| way of seeing the extent of sth: *a ~ of his anger.* **4** [sing] *of*|| (*fml*) degree of sth; some: *a ~ of success.* **5** [C, usu pl] action taken to achieve a purpose: *The government is taking ~s to reduce crime.* **6** (idm) **made-to-measure** (of clothing) specially made for a person after taking measurements. **get/take the measure of sb** judge sb's character or abilities.

meat /miːt/ *n* **1** [U, C] flesh of animals, used as food. **2** [U] (*fig*) substance: *There's not much ~ in his argument.* **meaty** *adj* (**-ier, -iest**).

mechanic /mɪ'kænɪk/ *n* [C] worker skilled in using or repairing machines. **mechanical** *adj* **1** of, connected with or produced by machines. **2** done without thought; automatic. **mechanically** -klɪ/ *adv.*

mechanics /mɪ'kænɪks/ *n* **1** (with sing v) science of motion and force; science of machinery. **2** **the mechanics** [pl] (a) working parts (of sth). (b) (*fig*) processes by which sth is done.

mechanism /'mekənɪzəm/ *n* [C] **1** working parts of sth. **2** (*fig*) way of getting sth done.

mechanize /'mekənaɪz/ *v* [T] change (a process, factory, etc) so that it is run by machines, rather than people. **mechanization** /ˌmekənaɪ'zeɪʃn; *US* -nɪ'z-/ *n* [U].

medal /'medl/ *n* [C] small round flat piece of metal, given as an honour for bravery or as a prize. **medallist** (*US* **medalist**) /'medəlɪst/ *n* [C] person who has won a medal, esp in sport.

medallion /mɪ'dæliən/ *n* [C] large medal or similar piece of jewellery.

meddle /'medl/ *v* [I] (*derog*) take part in sth that does not concern one. **meddler** *n* [C].

media /'miːdɪə/ *n* **the media** [pl] television, radio, newspapers, etc.

mediaeval = MEDIEVAL.

mediate /'miːdɪeɪt/ *v* [I] (*between*)|| act so as to obtain an agreement between two quarrelling

groups. **mediation** /ˌmiːdɪ'eɪʃn/ *n* [U]. **mediator** *n* [C].

medic /'medɪk/ *n* [C] (*infml*) medical student or doctor.

medical /'medɪkl/ *adj* **1** of the science of medicine. **2** of the treatment of diseases using medicine. **medical** *n* [C] examination of the body to check one's health. **medically** -klɪ/ *adv.*

Medicare /'medɪkeə(r)/ *n* [U] *US* government scheme providing medical care, esp for old people.

medication /ˌmedɪ'keɪʃn/ *n* [C, U] medicine used for curing a disease.

medicinal /mə'dɪsɪnl/ *adj* (used for) healing.

medicine /'medsn; *US* 'medɪsn/ *n* **1** [U] science of the prevention and cure of disease. **2** [C, U] liquid, tablets, etc used to treat disease. **3** (idm) **a dose/taste of one's own medicine** treatment of the same kind that one has given sb else. **'medicine-man** *n* [C] = WITCHDOCTOR (WITCH).

medieval (also **mediaeval**) /ˌmedɪ'iːvl; *US* ˌmiːd-/ *adj* of the Middle Ages, about AD 600 - 1400.

mediocre /ˌmiːdɪ'əʊkə(r)/ *adj* not very good. **mediocrity** /ˌmiːdɪ'ɒkrətɪ/ *n* [U, C] (*pl* **-ies**).

meditate /'medɪteɪt/ *v* [I] (*on*)|| think deeply and seriously about sth. **meditation** /ˌmedɪ'teɪʃn/ *n* [U, C].

medium /'miːdɪəm/ *n* [C] (*pl* **media** /'miːdɪə/ or ~**s**; in sense 4 ~**s**) **1** means by which sth is expressed or communicated: *an effective advertising ~.* **2** something that is in the middle between two extremes. **3** substance or surroundings in which sth exists. **4** person who claims to communicate with dead people. **medium** *adj* in the middle between two extremes. **'medium wave** *n* [U] radio wave with a wavelength of between 100 and 1000 metres.

meek /miːk/ *adj* gentle and patient. **meekly** *adv.* **meekness** *n* [U].

meet¹ /miːt/ *v* (*pt, pp* **met** /met/) **1** [I, T] come together with (sb): *Let's ~ again soon.* **2** [I, T] be introduced to (sb). **3** [T] (*fig*) experience (sth unpleasant): *~ one's death.* **4** [T] go to a place and await the arrival of. **5** [I, T] come into contact with (sth): *Their hands met.* **6** [T] fulfil (a demand); satisfy: *~ sb's wishes.* **7** [T] pay: *~ all expenses.* **8** (idm) **meet sb half-way** make a compromise with sb. **there is more to sb/sth than**

meets the eye sb/sth is more complicated, interesting, etc than one might at first think. **9 (phr v) meet with sb** (US) meet sb, esp for discussion. **meet with sth** experience sth: ~ *with difficulties/an accident.*

meet² /miːt/ *n* [C] **1** (esp Brit) gathering of riders and hounds for fox-hunting. **2** (esp US) gathering of competitors for a sporting test.

meeting /'miːtɪŋ/ *n* [C] coming together of people, esp for discussion.

megaphone /'megəfəʊn/ *n* [C] funnel-shaped device used to make sb's voice sound louder.

melancholy /'melənkɒlɪ/ *n* [U] deep sadness that lasts for a long time. **melancholic** /,melən'kɒlɪk/ *adj.* **melancholy** *adj* sad.

mellow /'meləʊ/ *adj* **1** fully ripe in flavour or taste. **2** soft and rich in colour. **3** made wise and kind by age. **mellow** *v* [I, T] (cause to) become mellow. **mellowness** *n* [U].

melodrama /'melədrɑːmə/ *n* [C, U] (a) story, play, etc that is exciting and full of strong feeling. (b) event, behaviour, etc that is like this. **melodramatic** /,melədrə'mætɪk/ *adj.* **melodramatically** /-klɪ/ *adv.*

melody /'melədɪ/ *n* [C] (*pl* **-ies**) tune or song. **melodic** /mɪ'lɒdɪk/ *adj* of melody. **melodious** /mɪ'ləʊdɪəs/ *adj* having a pleasant tune.

melon /'melən/ *n* [C] large round juicy fruit with a hard skin.

melt /melt/ *v* [I, T] (cause to) become liquid through heating: *The sun ~ ed the snow.* **2** [I] (*away*)|| become smaller; disappear. **3** [I, T] (cause sb, sb's feelings, etc to) become less hard and more sympathetic. **4** (phr v) **melt sth down** melt (a metal object) in order to use the metal again. **'meltdown** *n* [C] melting of the overheated centre of a nuclear reactor, causing the escape of radioactivity. **'melting-pot** *n* [C] **1** place where large numbers of people from different countries live together. **2** (idm) **in the melting-pot** likely to be changed.

member /'membə(r)/ *n* [C] **1** person belonging to a group, club, etc. **2** (*fml*) part of the body; limb. **,Member of 'Parliament** *n* [C] elected representative in the House of Commons. **membership** *n* **1** [U] state of being a member(1). **2** [sing] (with sing or pl v) (number of) members.

membrane /'membreɪn/ *n* [C, U]

piece of soft thin skin-like tissue.

memento /mɪ'mentəʊ/ *n* [C] (*pl* ~ **s** or ~ **es**) thing that is kept as a reminder of a person or event.

memo /'meməʊ/ *n* [C] (*pl* ~ **s**) (*infml*) short for MEMORANDUM.

memoir /'memwɑː(r)/ *n* **memoirs** [pl] person's written account of his/her own life.

memorable /'memərəbl/ *adj* deserving to be remembered; remarkable. **memorably** *adv.*

memorandum /,memə'rændəm/ *n* [C] (*pl* **-da** /də/ or ~ **s**) informal written (esp business) communication.

memorial /me'mɔːrɪəl/ *n* [C] something, eg a stone monument, that reminds people of an event or person.

memorize /'meməraɪz/ *v* [T] learn (sth) well enough to remember it exactly.

memory /'memərɪ/ *n* (*pl* **-ies**) **1** [C, U] ability of the mind to remember: *He's got a good ~.* **2** [C] something remembered: *memories of childhood.* **3** [U] period over which the memory goes back. **4** [U] what is remembered about sb after his/her death. **5** [C] part of a computer where information is stored. **6** (idm) **in memory of sb** in order that people will remember sb.

men *pl* of MAN¹.

menace /'menəs/ *n* **1** [C, U] danger; threat. **2** [sing] (*infml*) annoying person or thing. **menace** *v* [T] threaten. **menacingly** *adv.*

menagerie /mɪ'nædʒərɪ/ *n* [C] collection of wild animals; zoo.

mend /mend/ *v* **1** [T] return (sth worn out or broken) to good condition. **2** [I] return to good health. **3** (idm) **mend one's 'ways** improve one's behaviour. **mend** *n* **1** [C] part that has been mended. **2** (idm) **on the 'mend** (*infml*) returning to good health.

menial /'miːnɪəl/ *adj* (usu *derog*) (of work) not interesting or important.

meningitis /,menɪn'dʒaɪtɪs/ *n* [U] serious illness causing inflammation of the outer part of the brain and spinal cord.

menopause /'menəpɔːz/ *n* **the menopause** [sing] gradual stopping of a woman's menstruation usu about the age of 50.

menstruate /'menstrʊeɪt/ *v* [I] (*fml*) (of a woman) have a flow of blood from her uterus every month. **menstrual** /-strʊəl/ *adj.* **menstruation** /,menstrʊ'eɪʃn/ *n* [U].

mental /'mentl/ *adj* **1** of or in the mind: *a ~ illness* ○ *make a ~ note* *of sth*, ie try to remember it. **2** of or concerned with illness of the mind: *a ~ patient/hospital.* **3** (*infml derog*) mad. **mentally** /-təlɪ/ *adv* in the mind: *~ly ill.*

mentality /men'tælətɪ/ *n* (*pl -ies*) **1** [C] way of thinking. **2** [U] (*fml*) ability of the mind.

menthol /'menθɒl/ *n* [U] solid white substance obtained from peppermint, used medically and as a flavouring.

mention /'menʃn/ *v* **1** [T] speak or write about (sth/sb) briefly. **2** (*idm*) **don't 'mention it** (used for showing that thanks are not necessary). **not to mention** (used for giving emphasis) and also. **mention** *n* [C, U] brief reference.

menu /'menju:/ *n* [C] list of food that can be ordered in a restaurant.

MEP /ˌem i: 'pi:/ *abbr* Member of the European Parliament.

mercantile /'mɜːkəntaɪl; *US* -ti:l, -tɪl/ *adj* (*fml*) of trade, commerce or merchants.

mercenary /'mɜːsɪnərɪ; *US* -nerɪ/ *adj* interested only in making money. **mercenary** *n* [C] (*pl -ies*) soldier paid to fight in a foreign army.

merchandise /'mɜːtʃəndaɪz/ *n* [U] (*fml*) goods bought and sold.

merchant /'mɜːtʃənt/ *n* [C] person who buys and sells goods in large quantities. **merchant** *adj* concerned with trade, rather than being part of the armed forces: *the ~ navy.* ˌ**merchant 'bank** *n* [C] bank that provides (esp large) commercial loans and finance for industry.

mercury /'mɜːkjʊrɪ/ *n* [U] heavy silver-coloured metal, usu in liquid form. **mercurial** /mɜː-'kjʊrɪəl/ *adj* (*fml*) (of a person or his/her moods) lively and often changing.

mercy /'mɜːsɪ/ *n* (*pl -ies*) **1** [U] kindness or forgiveness shown to sb one has the power to punish. **2** [C] (event that is a) piece of good fortune. **3** (*idm*) **at the mercy of sb/sth** without defence against sb/sth. **merciful** *adj* having or showing mercy. **mercifully** *adv.* **merciless** *adj* showing no mercy. **mercilessly** *adv.*

mere /mɪə(r)/ *adj* nothing more than; only: *She's a ~ child.* **merely** *adv* only; simply.

merge /mɜːdʒ/ *v* **1** [I, T] join together to make one thing: *The two companies ~d.* **2** [I] (*into*)// fade or change gradually into sth: *Day ~d into night.* **merger** *n* [C] joining together of two compa-

nies, etc.

meridian /mə'rɪdɪən/ *n* [C] imaginary circle round the earth, passing through the North and South Poles.

meringue /mə'ræŋ/ *n* (a) [U] baked mixture of the whites of egg and sugar. (b) [C] cake made of this.

merit /'merɪt/ *n* **1** [U] quality deserving praise; worth. **2** [C, usu pl] fact, quality, etc that deserves praise; advantage. **merit** *v* [T] (*fml*) deserve.

mermaid /'mɜːmeɪd/ *n* [C] (in stories) woman with a fish's tail instead of legs.

merry /'merɪ/ *adj* (*-ier, -iest*) **1** (*dated*) happy and cheerful. **2** (*infml*) slightly drunk. **merrily** *adv.* **merriment** *n* [U]. ˈ**merry-go-round** *n* [C] = ROUNDABOUT 2.

mesh /meʃ/ *n* [C, U] (piece of) material made of a net of wire, thread, etc with small holes. **mesh** *v* [I] (of toothed wheels) fit together closely: (*fig*) *Their opinions don't really ~.*

mesmerize /'mezməraɪz/ *v* [T] hold the attention of (sb) completely.

mess¹ /mes/ *n* **1** [C, usu sing] dirty or untidy state. **2** [sing] difficult or confused situation: *My life's in a ~.* **mess** *v* (*infml*) (*phr v*) **mess about/around** (a) behave in a foolish way. (b) do things without a definite plan. **mess sb about/around** treat sb badly. **mess sth up** make sth untidy. (b) do sth badly; spoil. **messy** *adj* (*-ier, -iest*).

mess² /mes/ *n* [C] room or building in which soldiers eat their meals.

message /'mesɪdʒ/ *n* **1** [C] piece of information sent to sb. **2** [sing] central idea that a writer, politicians, book, etc tries to communicate. **3** (*idm*) **get the 'message** (*infml*) understand what sb has been trying to tell one. **messenger** /'mesɪndʒə(r)/ *n* [C] person who takes a message to sb.

messiah /mɪ'saɪə/ *n* **1** [C] new religious leader expected to save the world. **2 the Messiah** [sing] Jesus Christ.

met *pt, pp* of MEET¹.

metabolism /mə'tæbəlɪzəm/ *n* [U] process in the body by which food is used to supply energy. **metabolic** /ˌmetə'bɒlɪk/ *adj.*

metal /'metl/ *n* [C, U] any of a kind of mineral substance such as tin, iron or gold. **metallic** /mɪ'tælɪk/ *adj.*

metaphor /'metəfə(r)/ *n* [C, U]

(example of the) use of words to show sth different from the literal meaning, as in 'She has a heart of stone'. **metaphorical** /ˌmetə-'fɒrɪk(l); US -'fɔːr-/ adj. **metaphorically** /-klɪ/ adv.

mete /miːt/ v (phr v) **mete sth out (to sb)** (fml) give (esp punishment) to sb.

meteor /'miːtɪə(r)/ n [C] small piece of matter that moves through space into the earth's atmosphere, becoming bright as it burns. **meteoric** /ˌmiːtɪ'ɒrɪk; US -'ɔːr-/ adj 1 of meteors. 2 (fig) very fast: a ~ ic rise to fame. **meteorite** /'miːtɪəraɪt/ n [C] a meteor that has fallen to earth.

meteorology /ˌmiːtɪə'rɒlədʒɪ/ n [U] study of the weather and the earth's atmosphere. **meteorological** /-rə'lɒdʒɪkl/ adj. **meteorologist** n [C] expert in meteorology.

meter¹ /'miːtə(r)/ n [C] device that measures sth: a gas ~.

meter² (US) = METRE.

method /'meθəd/ n 1 [C] way of doing sth. 2 [U] organized system. **methodical** /mɪ'θɒdɪkl/ adj acting an organized system; careful. **methodically** /-klɪ/ adv.

methodology /ˌmeθə'dɒlədʒɪ/ n [C, U] (pl -ies) set of methods.

meticulous /mɪ'tɪkjʊləs/ adj showing great care and attention to detail **meticulously** adv.

metre¹ /'miːtə(r)/ n [C] metric unit of length. **metric** /'metrɪk/ adj of the metric system. **metrication** /ˌmetrɪ'keɪʃn/ n [U] changing to the metric system. the 'metric system n [sing] decimal measuring system based on the metre, kilogram etc.

metre² /'miːtə(r)/ n [C, U] pattern of stressed and unstressed syllables in poetry.

metropolis /mə'trɒpəlɪs/ n [C] main or capital city of a region or country. **metropolitan** /ˌmetrə'pɒlɪtən/ adj.

mettle /'metl/ n [U] 1 ability or will to carry on bravely. 2 (idm) **put sb on his/her mettle** encourage or force sb to do his/her best.

mews /mjuːz/ n [C] (pl mews) street of stables, converted into houses or flats.

miaow /miː'aʊ/ n [C] sound made by a cat. **miaow** v [I] make this sound.

mice pl of MOUSE.

mickey /'mɪkɪ/ n (idm) **take the mickey (out of sb)** (infml) tease sb.

micro /'maɪkrəʊ/ n [C] (pl ~s)

(infml) short for MICROCOMPUTER.

microbe /'maɪkrəʊb/ n [C] tiny living being, esp one that causes disease.

microchip /'maɪkrəʊtʃɪp/ n [C] small piece of material that has a complicated electronic circuit on it.

microcomputer /ˌmaɪkr-əʊkəm'pjuːtə(r)/ n [C] small home or business computer.

microcosm /'maɪkrəʊkɒzəm/ n [C] something that represents a large system on a small scale.

microfilm /'maɪkrəʊfɪlm/ n [C, U] film on which extremely small photographs are stored. **microfilm** v [T] photograph (sth) using such film.

microphone /'maɪkrəfəʊn/ n [C] instrument which makes sound louder or broadcasts it.

microscope /'maɪkrəskəʊp/ n [C] instrument that makes very small objects appear larger. **microscopic** /ˌmaɪkrə'skɒpɪk/ adj 1 very small. 2 of or using a microscope.

microwave (also ˌmicrowave 'oven) /'maɪkrəweɪv/ n [C] kind of oven that cooks food very quickly using very short electric waves.

mid- /mɪd/ prefix in the middle of: ~-morning ◇ ~-air (ie in the sky).

midday /ˌmɪd'deɪ/ n [U] 12 o'clock in the middle of the day.

middle /'mɪdl/ n the **middle** [sing] position at an equal distance from two or more points. **middle** adj in the middle. **middle 'age** n [U] period between youth and old age. **ˌmiddle-'aged** adj. the ˌMiddle 'Ages n [pl] (in European history) period from about AD 600 to 1400. the ˌmiddle 'class n [C] social class between the lower and upper classes; business and professional people. **ˌmiddle-'class** adj. the ˌMiddle 'East n [sing] countries from Egypt to Iran. **'middleman** n [C] (pl -men /-men/) trader who buys goods from a producer and sells them. **ˌmiddle-of-the-'road** adj moderate; avoiding extremes.

middling /'mɪdlɪŋ/ adj of average quality.

midge /mɪdʒ/ n [C] small winged insect.

midget /'mɪdʒɪt/ n [C] extremely small person. **midget** adj very small.

Midlands /'mɪdləndz/ n the **Midlands** (with sing or pl v) central inland counties of England.

midnight /'mɪdnaɪt/ n [U] 12 o'clock in the middle of the night.

midriff /'mɪdrɪf/ n [C] middle

part of the body, between the waist and the chest.

midst /mɪdst/ n (idm) **in the midst of sth** in the middle of sth.

midway /ˌmɪdˈweɪ/ adj, adv halfway: ~ *between Paris and Rome.*

midwife /ˈmɪdwaɪf/ n [C] (pl -**wives** /-waɪvz/) person, esp a woman, who helps women in childbirth. **midwifery** /ˈmɪdwɪfərɪ; *US* -waɪf-/ n [U] profession and work of a midwife.

might[1] /maɪt/ *modal v* (*neg* **might not**, contracted form **mightn't** /ˈmaɪtnt/) **1** (used for showing slight possibility): *He ~ be at home, but I doubt it.* **2** (used for asking permission): *M~ I make a suggestion?* **3** (used for making polite requests or appeals): *You ~ at least offer to help!*

might[2] *pt of* MAY.

might[3] /maɪt/ n [U] strength or power. **mighty** adj (-**ier**, -**iest**) *fml* **1** powerful. **2** great: *the ~y oceans.* **mightily** adv. **mighty** (*infml* esp *US*) very: *~y good.*

migraine /ˈmiːɡreɪn, ˈmaɪɡreɪn/ n [U, C] very painful headache.

migrate /maɪˈɡreɪt; *US* ˈmaɪɡreɪt/ v [I] (*from, to*)) **1** move from one place to go to live in another. **2** (of birds, etc) go from one part of the world to another regularly each year. **migrant** /ˈmaɪɡrənt/ n [C] person or bird, etc that migrates. **migration** /maɪˈɡreɪʃn/ n [C, U]. **migratory** /ˈmaɪɡrətrɪ, maɪˈɡreɪtərɪ; *US* ˈmaɪɡrətɔːrɪ/ adj.

mike /maɪk/ n [C] (*infml*) short for MICROPHONE.

mild /maɪld/ adj **1** gentle; not severe: *a ~ punishment/climate.* **2** not sharp or strong in flavour. **mildly** adv. **mildness** n [U].

mildew /ˈmɪldjuː; *US* -duː/ n [U] tiny fungus forming a white coating on plants, leather, food, etc in warm and damp conditions.

mile /maɪl/ n [C] unit of distance; 1760 yards (1.6 kilometres). **mileage** /-ɪdʒ/ n 1 [C, U] distance travelled, measured in miles. **2** [U] (*fig infml*) benefit or advantage: *The unions are getting a lot of ~ out of the manager's mistakes.* **milestone** /ˈmaɪlstəʊn/ n [C] **1** stone at the side of a road showing the distance to a place. **2** (*fig*) important event in history. **milometer** (also **mileometer**) /maɪˈlɒmɪtə(r)/ n [C] device in a car, etc that records the number of miles travelled.

militant /ˈmɪlɪtənt/ n [C], adj (person) supporting the use of strong methods, esp force, to achieve one's aims. **militancy**

/-tənsɪ/ n [U].

military /ˈmɪlɪtrɪ; *US* -terɪ/ adj of or for soldiers or war. **the military** n (with sing or pl v) soldiers; the army.

militate /ˈmɪlɪteɪt/ v [I] (*against*)) (*fml*) have a great influence to prevent sth.

militia /mɪˈlɪʃə/ n [C, also sing with pl v] force of people trained to be soldiers in an emergency.

milk /mɪlk/ n [U] **1** white liquid produced by female mammals as food for their young. **2** milk-like juice of some trees and plants: *coconut ~.* **milk** v [I, T] obtain milk from (a cow, etc). **2** [T] (*fig*) obtain money, information, etc dishonestly from. **milkman** /-mən/ n [C] man who delivers milk to homes. **milk shake** n [C] milk drink with flavouring mixed into it. **milky** adj (-**ier**, -**iest**) **1** of or like milk. **2** (of tea, coffee, etc) made with a lot of milk. **the Milky 'Way** n [sing] = GALAXY **2**.

mill[1] /mɪl/ n [C] **1** (building with) machinery for crushing grain into flour. **2** small machine for crushing sth: *a pepper-~.* **3** factory: *a paper-~.* **4** (idm) **put sb/go through the 'mill** (cause sb to) experience great difficulties, very hard training, etc. **miller** n [C] person who owns or runs a mill. **millstone** n [C] **1** either of a pair of circular stones between which grain is crushed. **2** (*fig*) difficult problem or responsibility: *His debts are a ~ stone round his neck.*

mill[2] /mɪl/ v [I [T] put through a machine for grinding. **2** (phr v) **mill about/around** move aimlessly in a disorganized group.

millennium /mɪˈlenɪəm/ n (pl -**nia** /-nɪə/ or ~**s**) **1** [C] period of 1000 years. **2 the millennium** [sing] future time of great happiness.

millepede (also **millipede**) /ˈmɪlɪpiːd/ n [C] small worm-like creature with many legs.

millet /ˈmɪlɪt/ n [U] **(a)** tall cereal plant grown for its small seeds. **(b)** these seeds, used as food.

milli- /ˈmɪlɪ/ prefix (in the metric system) one thousandth part of: *'~ metre.*

milliner /ˈmɪlɪnə(r)/ n [C] maker or seller of women's hats. **millinery** n [U] (business of making or selling) women's hats.

million /ˈmɪljən/ pron, adj, n [C] **1** one thousand thousand (1,000,000). **2** (*infml*) a lot: *~s of things to do.* **millionaire** /ˌmɪljəˈneə(r)/ n [C] (*fem* **millionairess** /ˌmɪljəˈneəres/) person who has a million pounds, dollars, etc; very rich person. **millionth** *pron, adj* 1,000,000th. **millionth** *pron,* n [C] $\frac{1}{1,000,000}$.

millipede = MILLEPEDE.

milometer ⇨ MILE.

mime /maɪm/ n (a) [U] (in the theatre, etc) use of only expressions of the face and gestures to tell a story. (b) [C] actor in such a drama. **mime** v [I, T] act (sth) using mime.

mimic /'mɪmɪk/ v (pt, pp ~ked) [T] 1 copy (sb/sth) in a mocking or amusing way. 2 (of things) look very like (sth). **mimic** n [C] person who mimics others. **mimicry** n [U] mimicking.

minaret /ˌmɪnə'ret/ n [C] tall thin tower of a mosque, from which people are called to prayer.

mince /mɪns/ v 1 [T] cut (meat, etc) into very small pieces. 2 (idm) **not mince one's 'words** speak plainly, esp when criticizing sb/sth. **mince** n [U] minced meat. '**mincemeat** n [U] 1 mixture of currants, raisins, etc used as a filling for pastry. 2 (idm) **make mincemeat of sb** defeat sb completely in a fight or argument.

mind[1] /maɪnd/ n 1 [U] part of a person's brain where one's thoughts are. *The idea never entered my ~.* ○ *She has a brilliant ~,* ie She is very clever. 2 [U] memory: *My ~ has gone blank!* 3 [C] person considered for his/her ability to think: *one of the greatest ~s this century.* 4 (idm) **be in two 'minds about sth** feel doubtful about sth. **be/take a load/weight off sb's mind** remove a cause of worry from sb. **be on one's mind, have sth on one's mind** (cause sb to) worry about sth. **be out of one's 'mind** (*infml*) be mad. **bear/keep sth in 'mind** remember sth. **bring/call sth to mind** cause sth to be remembered. **have a (good) mind to do sth** (*infml*) have a (strong) desire to do sth. **in one's mind's 'eye** in one's imagination. **make up one's 'mind** reach a decision. **put/set/turn one's 'mind to sth** give one's attention to sth. **take one's mind off sth** help one not to think about sth. **to 'my mind** in my opinion.

mind[2] /maɪnd/ v 1 [I, T] feel annoyed at (sth): *Do you ~ if I (ie May I please) open the windows?* 2 [T] take care of: *~ the baby.* 3 [I, T] *you don't fall!* 4 (idm) **mind one's 'own 'business** not interfere in other people's affairs. **mind one's step** ⇨ STEP[1]. ,**mind 'you, mind**

please note: *She's still ill, ~ you, but at least she's getting better.* ,**never 'mind** don't worry. 5 (phr v) ,**mind 'out** (*infml*) be careful. **minder** n [C] person who looks after sb/sth: *a 'child-~er.*

mindful /'maɪndfl/ *adj of*|| (*fml*) giving thought to sth.

mindless /'maɪndlɪs/ *adj* 1 not needing thought. 2 (*derog*) having no purpose; stupid.

mine[1] /maɪn/ *pron* of or belonging to me: *Is this book yours or ~?*

mine[2] /maɪn/ n [C] 1 deep holes, tunnels, etc made in the earth, from which coal, etc is taken. 2 bomb used at sea or hidden in the ground. 3 (idm) **a mine of information** rich source of knowledge. **mine** v [I, T] (*for*)|| dig (coal, etc) from mine(s). 2 [T] lay mines(2) in (sth). '**mine-detector** n [C] device for finding mines(2). '**minefield** n [C] 1 area of land or sea where mines(2) have been laid. 2 very dangerous situation. **miner** n [C] person who works in an underground mine(1). '**minesweeper** n [C] ship used for clearing the sea of mines(2).

mineral /'mɪnərəl/ n [C, U] natural substance (eg coal or gold) taken from the earth. **mineral** *adj* of or containing minerals. '**mineral water** n [U] water that naturally contains a mineral, esp one thought to be good for one's health.

mineralogy /ˌmɪnə'rælədʒɪ/ n [U] scientific study of minerals. **mineralogist** n [C] student of or expert in mineralogy.

mingle /'mɪŋgl/ v [I, T] *with*|| mix.

mini- /'mɪnɪ/ *prefix* of small size, length, etc: *a '~bus.*

miniature /'mɪnətʃə(r); US 'mɪnɪətʃʊər/ *adj* (of a copy or model) much smaller than the normal size. **miniature** n [C] very small painting of a person. **miniaturize** v [T] make a smaller version of.

minimal /'mɪnɪml/ *adj* smallest in amount or degree.

minimize /'mɪnɪmaɪz/ v [T] reduce to the smallest possible amount or degree.

minimum /'mɪnɪməm/ n [C, usu sing] (*pl* **minima** /-mə/) smallest possible amount, degree, etc. **minimum** *adj* as small as possible: *the ~ age.*

mining /'maɪnɪŋ/ n [U] process of getting coal, metals, etc from the earth.

minion /'mɪnɪən/ n [C] (*derog*) worker, esp one who obeys orders very readily.

minister /ˈmɪnɪstə(r)/ n [C] 1 person at the head of a government department. 2 Christian clergyman. **minister** v [I] to/i (fml) give help or service to sb/sth. **ministerial** /ˌmɪnɪˈstɪərɪəl/ adj.

ministry /ˈmɪnɪstrɪ/ n (pl -ies) 1 [C] government department. 2 [C] work of a minister(2). 3 **the ministry** [sing] work of being a clergyman: enter the ~, ie become a clergyman.

mink /mɪŋk/ n (a) [C] small fierce animal. (b) [U] valuable fur of this animal.

minor /ˈmaɪnə(r)/ adj less important; smaller: ~ problems ○ a ~ illness. **minor** n [C] (law) person below the age of full legal responsibility.

minority /maɪˈnɒrətɪ; US -ˈnɔːr-/ n (pl -ies) 1 [C] (a) [also sing with pl v] smaller number or part, esp of votes. (b) small group of people of a different race, religion, etc from the rest. 2 [U] (law) state or time of being a minor.

minster /ˈmɪnstə(r)/ n [C] large or important church.

minstrel /ˈmɪnstrəl/ n [C] (in the Middle Ages) travelling singer.

mint¹ /mɪnt/ n 1 [U] plant whose leaves are used for flavouring. 2 [U, C] short for PEPPERMINT.

mint² /mɪnt/ n 1 [C] place where coins are made. 2 [sing] (infml) very large amount of money: make/earn a ~. 3 (idm) **in mint condition** (as if) new. **mint** v [T] make (a coin) by stamping metal.

minuet /ˌmɪnjuˈet/ n [C] (music for a) slow graceful dance.

minus /ˈmaɪnəs/ prep 1 less: 15 ~ 6 equals 9. 2 below zero: ~ 3 degrees Celsius. 3 (infml) without. **minus** adj negative. **minus** (also **minus sign**) n [C] mathematical sign (-).

minute¹ /ˈmɪnɪt/ n 1 (a) [C] one sixtieth part of an hour. (b) [sing] very short time: I'll be with you in a ~. 2 [C] one sixtieth part of a degree of an angle. 3 **minutes** [pl] record of what is said and decided at a meeting. 4 (idm) **the minute/moment (that)** as soon as. **minute** v [T] record in the minutes(3).

minute² /maɪˈnjuːt; US -ˈnuːt/ adj (-r, -st) very small. **minutely** adv.

minutiae /maɪˈnjuːʃɪ; US mɪˈnuː-/ n [pl] very small details.

miracle /ˈmɪrəkl/ n 1 (a) [C] welcome event that does not follow the known laws of nature. (b) [sing] (infml fig) remarkable event: It's a ~ we weren't all killed. 2 [C] of/I wonderful example of sth: a

~ of modern science. **miraculous** /mɪˈrækjʊləs/ adj.

mirage /ˈmɪrɑːʒ, mɪˈrɑːʒ/ n [C] something seen that does not really exist, esp a pool of water in the desert.

mire /ˈmaɪə(r)/ n [U] soft muddy ground.

mirror /ˈmɪrə(r)/ n [C] piece of glass that one can look in and see oneself. **mirror** v [T] show exactly as in a mirror.

misadventure /ˌmɪsədˈventʃə(r)/ n [C, U] (fml) (piece of) bad luck.

misappropriate /ˌmɪsəˈprəʊprɪeɪt/ v [T] take and use wrongly: ~ sb's money.

misbehave /ˌmɪsbɪˈheɪv/ v [I] behave badly. **misbehaviour** (US -ior) n [U].

miscalculate /ˌmɪsˈkælkjʊleɪt/ v [I, T] calculate (amounts, etc) wrongly. **miscalculation** /ˌmɪskælkjʊˈleɪʃn/ n [C, U].

miscarriage /ˌmɪsˈkærɪdʒ, ˈmɪskærɪdʒ/ n [C, U] giving birth to a baby before it has developed enough to stay alive. **miscarriage of justice** n [C] incorrect legal decision.

miscarry /ˌmɪsˈkærɪ/ v (pt, pp -ied) [I] 1 (of a woman) have a miscarriage. 2 (of a plan, etc) fail.

miscellaneous /ˌmɪsəˈleɪnɪəs/ adj of various kinds.

miscellany /mɪˈseləni; US ˈmɪsəleɪnɪ/ n [C] (pl -ies) collection of things of various kinds.

mischance /ˌmɪsˈtʃɑːns; US -ˈtʃæns/ n [C, U] (fml) (piece of) bad luck.

mischief /ˈmɪstʃɪf/ n [U] 1 behaviour (esp of children) that is bad, but not serious. 2 (idm) **do sb/oneself a 'mischief** (infml joc) hurt sb/oneself. **mischievous** /ˈmɪstʃɪvəs/ adj 1 filled with or fond of mischief. 2 harmful. **mischievously** adv.

misconceive /ˌmɪskənˈsiːv/ v [T] (fml) (esp passive) have a wrong understanding of. **misconception** /-ˈsepʃn/ n [C, U].

misconduct /ˌmɪsˈkɒndʌkt/ n (fml) bad (esp immoral) behaviour.

misdeed /ˌmɪsˈdiːd/ n [C, usu pl] (fml) wicked act; crime.

miser /ˈmaɪzə(r)/ n [C] person who loves money and spends as little as possible. **miserly** adj.

miserable /ˈmɪzrəbl/ adj 1 very unhappy. 2 causing unhappiness: ~ weather. 3 poor in quality: earn a ~ wage. **miserably** adv.

misery /ˈmɪzərɪ/ n (pl -ies) 1 [U, C] great suffering or unhappiness. **2** [C] (*Brit infml*) person who is always complaining.

misfire /ˌmɪsˈfaɪə(r)/ v [I] **1** (of a gun, etc) fail to work properly. **2** (*fig infml*) (of a plan, etc) fail to have the intended effect.

misfit /ˈmɪsfɪt/ n [C] person who is not well suited to his/her surroundings.

misfortune /ˌmɪsˈfɔːtʃuːn/ n [C, U] (instance of) bad luck.

misgiving /ˌmɪsˈɡɪvɪŋ/ n [U, C, esp pl] (*fml*) (feeling of) doubt or suspicion.

misguided /ˌmɪsˈɡaɪdɪd/ adj wrong or foolish in one's opinions or actions.

mishap /ˈmɪshæp/ n [C, U] unlucky (but usu not serious) accident.

misjudge /ˌmɪsˈdʒʌdʒ/ v [T] form a wrong opinion or estimate of: ~ sb/sb's character.

mislay /ˌmɪsˈleɪ/ v (*pt, pp* **mislaid** /-ˈleɪd/) [T] put (sth) down and forget where it is.

mislead /ˌmɪsˈliːd/ v (*pt, pp* **misled** /-ˈled/) [T] cause (sb) to have a wrong idea or impression about sth.

mismanage /ˌmɪsˈmænɪdʒ/ v [T] manage badly. **mismanagement** n [U].

misprint /ˈmɪsprɪnt/ n [C] mistake in printing.

misrepresent /ˌmɪsˌreprɪˈzent/ v [T] give a false account of. **misrepresentation** /-ˌzenˈteɪʃn/ n [C, U].

Miss /mɪs/ n [C] (title for an unmarried woman): M~ *Smith*.

miss /mɪs/ v **1** [I, T] fail to hit, catch, etc (sth aimed at): ~ *the ball/the train*. **2** [T] fail to see, hear, etc. **3** [T] feel unhappy at the absence of: *I'll ~ you when you go.* **4** (phr v) **miss sb/sth out** not include sb/sth. **miss 'out (on sth)** lose an opportunity to gain a benefit from sth. **miss** n [C] **1** failure to hit, catch, etc. **2** (idm) **give a 'miss** not do sth; not go somewhere. **missing** adj that cannot be found; lost.

missile /ˈmɪsaɪl; *US* ˈmɪsl/ n [C] **1** explosive weapon sent through the air: *nuclear ~s*. **2** object or weapon thrown or fired.

mission /ˈmɪʃn/ n [C] **1** (work done by) group of people sent abroad: *a trade ~ to China.* **2** special work or duty: *her ~ in life.* **3** place where missionaries work. **missionary** /ˈmɪʃənri; *US* -neri/ n [C] (*pl* -ies) person sent to another country to preach his/her religion.

misspell /ˌmɪsˈspel/ v (*pt, pp* ~**t** /-ˈspelt/ or esp *US* ~**ed**) [T] spell

wrongly. **misspelling** n [U, C].

misspent /ˌmɪsˈspent/ adj used wrongly or foolishly: *his ~ youth.*

mist /mɪst/ n [U, C] (a) cloud of very fine drops of water in the air, less thick than fog: *hills covered in ~.* (b) (*fig*) something that confuses: *lost in the ~s of time.* **mist** v (phr v) **ˌmist 'over** become covered with mist: *His glasses ~ed over.* **misty** adj (-ier, -iest) (a) full of or covered with mist: *a ~y morning.* (b) (*fig*) not clear: *a ~y old photograph.*

mistake /mɪˈsteɪk/ n [C] **1** wrong act, idea or opinion. **2** (idm) **by miˈstake** as a result of carelessness, etc. **mistake** v (*pt* **mistook** /mɪˈstʊk/, *pp* ~**n** /mɪˈsteɪkən/) [T] **1** have or get a wrong idea about. **2** *for//* wrongly suppose that (sb/sth) is sb/sth else: *People often ~ Jill for her twin sister.* **mistaken** adj wrong; not correct: *~n beliefs.* **mistakenly** adv.

mistletoe /ˈmɪsltəʊ/ n [U] evergreen plant with white berries, used as a Christmas decoration.

mistress /ˈmɪstrɪs/ n [C] **1** woman in a position of authority. **2** female owner of a dog, horse, etc. **3** (esp *Brit*) female schoolteacher. **4** woman who has a sexual relationship with a man to whom she is not married.

mistrust /ˌmɪsˈtrʌst/ v [T] feel no confidence in. **mistrust** n [U] lack of confidence. **mistrustful** adj.

misty ⇨ MIST.

misunderstand /ˌmɪsˌʌndəˈstænd/ v (*pt, pp* -**stood** /-ˈstʊd/) [T] understand wrongly: *He ~stood the instructions and got lost.* **misunderstanding** n [C, U] failure to understand correctly, esp when this causes argument.

misuse /ˌmɪsˈjuːz/ v [T] **1** use wrongly: ~ *one's time.* **2** treat (sb/sth) badly: *He felt ~d by the company.* **misuse** /ˌmɪsˈjuːs/ n [C, U].

mitigate /ˈmɪtɪɡeɪt/ v [T] (*fml*) make less severe or painful. **mitigating** adj making (sth) seem less serious: *There were ~ing circumstances to explain her bad behaviour.* **mitigation** /ˌmɪtɪˈɡeɪʃn/ n.

mitre (*US* **miter**) /ˈmaɪtə(r)/ n [C] tall pointed hat worn by bishops.

mitten /ˈmɪtn/ (also **mitt** /mɪt/) n [C] kind of glove that covers the four fingers together and the thumb separately.

mix /mɪks/ v **1** [I, T] put (different substances or things) together to make one new substance or thing: ~ *flour and water to make paste* ○ *Oil and water don't ~.* **2** [I] (of people) come or be together socially: *He finds it hard to ~.* **3** (idm) **be/get mixed 'up in sth** (*infml*) be/become involved in sth bad. **4** (phr v) **mix sb/sth up** confuse sb/ sth with sb/sth else: *I got her ~ed up with her sister.* **mix sb/sth up** set of different substances to be mixed together: *a 'cake ~.* **mixed** *adj* **1** of different kinds. **2** for people of both sexes: *a ~ ed school.* **mixer** *n* [C] thing or person that mixes. **'mix-up** *n* [C] (*infml*) confused situation.

mixture /'mɪkstʃə(r)/ *n* [C] something made by mixing: *a ~ of fear and sadness.*

mm *abbr* (*pl* **mm** or **~s**) millimetre(s).

moan /məʊn/ *v* [I] **1** make a long low sound of pain. **2** (*about*) (*infml*) complain: *He's always ~ing about having no money.* **moan** *n* [C].

moat /məʊt/ *n* [C] deep wide ditch filled with water, round a castle.

mob /mɒb/ *n* [C] **1** noisy disorganized crowd. **2** (*sl*) group of criminals. **mob** *v* (-**bb**-) [T] gather round (sb) in great numbers to attack or admire: *a film star ~bed by his fans.*

mobile /'məʊbaɪl; *US* -bl/ *adj* that can move or be moved easily from place to place. **mobile** *n* [C] ornamental hanging structure with parts that move freely in currents of air. **mobility** /məʊˈbɪlətɪ/ *n* [U].

mobilize /'məʊbɪlaɪz/ *v* [I, T] (cause to) become organized or ready for service, eg in war.

moccasin /'mɒkəsɪn/ *n* [C] soft leather shoe.

mock¹ /mɒk/ *v* [I, T] laugh at (sb/ sth); make (sb/sth) appear foolish: *a ~ing smile.* **mockery** *n* [U] act of mocking. **1** [sing] very bad example: *a ~ of justice.* **3** (idm) **make a mockery of sth** make sth appear foolish.

mock² /mɒk/ *adj* not real: *a ~ battle.*

modal (also **modal au'xiliary**) /'məʊdl/ *n* [C] (*grammar*) verb that is used with another verb, eg *can*, *may* or *should.*

mode /məʊd/ *n* [C] (*fml*) way in which sth is done.

model¹ /'mɒdl/ *n* [C] **1** small-scale copy: *a ~ of the new airport.* **2** design or kind of product: *This car is our latest ~.* **3** person or thing of the best kind: *a ~ wife.* **4** person who poses for an artist or photographer. **5** person who wears and shows new clothes to possible buyers: *a fashion ~.*

model² /'mɒdl/ *v* (-**ll**-; *US* -**l**-) [I, T] make a model(1) of sth in clay, etc. **2** [I, T] show (clothes, etc) to possible buyers by wearing them. **3** [T] *on//* take as an example for one's actions: *He ~ s himself on his uncle.*

moderate¹ /'mɒdərət/ *adj* not extreme; limited. **moderate** *n* [C] person who has moderate opinions, esp in politics. **moderately** *adv* not very: *only ~ly successful.*

moderate² /'mɒdəreɪt/ *v* [I] (cause to) become less violent or extreme.

moderation /ˌmɒdəˈreɪʃn/ *n* [U] **1** quality of being moderate. **2** (idm) **in moderation** not excessively: *drink whisky in ~.*

modern /'mɒdn/ *adj* **1** of the present or recent times. **2** new; upto-date. **modernize** /'mɒdənaɪz/ *v* [I, T] bring (sth) up to date. **modernization** /ˌmɒdənaɪˈzeɪʃn; *US* -nɪˈz-/ *n* [U].

modest /'mɒdɪst/ *adj* **1** having a not too high opinion of oneself. **2** moderate; not large: *a ~ salary.* **3** not sexually improper; shy: *~ behaviour.* **modestly** *adv*. **modesty** *n* [U].

modify /'mɒdɪfaɪ/ *v* (*pt, pp* -**ied**) [T] **1** change slightly. **2** make less severe, etc: *~ one's demands.* **3** (*grammar*) (esp of an adj or adv) make the sense of (a word) less general: *In the phrase 'the red car', 'red' ~ies 'car'.* **modification** /ˌmɒdɪfɪˈkeɪʃn/ *n* [C, U].

module /'mɒdjuːl; *US* -dʒuːl/ *n* [C] **1** standard part used in a building. **2** independent unit of a spacecraft. **3** independent unit in a course of study: *the biology ~ in the science course.* **modular** /-jʊlə(r); *US* -dʒʊ-/ *adj*.

mohair /'məʊheə(r)/ *n* [U] (cloth from the) fine hair from a type of goat.

Mohammedan = **MUHAMMADAN** (**MUHAMMAD**).

moist /mɔɪst/ *adj* slightly wet. **moisten** /'mɔɪsn/ *v* [I, T] become or make moist. **moisture** /'mɔɪstʃə(r)/ *n* [U] tiny drops of water on a surface, etc.

molar /'məʊlə(r)/ *n* [C] large back tooth, used for grinding and chewing food.

mold (*US*) = **MOULD**.

molder (*US*) = **MOULDER**.

mole¹ /məʊl/ *n* [C] small dark spot on the skin.

mole² /məʊl/ *n* [C] **1** small grey furry animal that lives in tunnels. **2** (*infml*) employee who secretly gives information to another organization, etc. **'molehill** *n* [C] small pile of earth thrown up by a mole.

molecule /'mɒlɪkjuːl/ n [C] smallest group of atoms that a particular substance can consist of. **molecular** /mə'lekjʊlə(r)/ adj.

molest /mə'lest/ v [T] 1 trouble or annoy. 2 attack (usu a woman or child) sexually.

mollusc (US also **mollusk**) /'mɒləsk/ n [C] any of a class of animals, eg oysters and snails, that have a soft body and usu a hard shell.

molt (US) = MOULT.

molten /'məʊltən/ adj melted: ~ rock/steel.

moment /'məʊmənt/ n 1 [C] very short period of time. 2 [sing] exact point in time. 3 [U] (fml) importance: a matter of great ~. 4 (idm) **the moment (that)** ⇨ MINUTE¹. **momentary** /-mantri/ adj lasting for a moment. **momentarily** /US ˌməʊmən'terəlɪ/ adv 1 for a very short time. 2 (esp US) very soon.

momentous /mə'mentəs, məʊ'm-/ adj very important.

momentum /mə'mentəm, məʊ'm-/ n [U] 1 (physics) quantity of motion of a moving object. 2 (fig) force that increases speed with which a process is happening: The demands for reform are slowly gathering ~.

monarch /'mɒnək/ n [C] king, queen, emperor or empress. **monarchy** n (pl -ies) 1 [U] system of rule by a monarch. 2 [C] country ruled by a monarch.

monastery /'mɒnəstrɪ; US -terɪ/ n [C] (pl -ies) building in which monks live.

monastic /mə'næstɪk/ adj of monks or monasteries.

Monday /'mʌndɪ/ n [U, C] the second day of the week; next after Sunday: They're coming on ~. ◇ last/next ~ ◇ The museum is closed on ~s, ie every Monday.

monetary /'mʌnɪtrɪ; US -terɪ/ adj of money.

money /'mʌnɪ/ n [U] 1 coins and printed paper accepted when buying and selling. 2 wealth. 3 (idm) **get one's money's worth** get full value for the money one has spent. **'money box** n [C] box used for saving coins.

mongrel /'mʌŋɡrəl/ n [C] dog of mixed breed.

monitor /'mɒnɪtə(r)/ n [C] 1 device used to watch or test sth: a heart ~. 2 person who listens to foreign radio broadcasts to screen information. 3 television screen used to check or choose what is

broadcast. 4 screen or other device used for checking the operation of a computer. 5 pupil with certain duties in a school. **monitor** v [T] listen to, watch or test the progress, operation, etc of.

monk /mʌŋk/ n [C] member of a male religious community living in a monastery.

monkey /'mʌŋkɪ/ n [C] 1 small long-tailed tree-climbing animal. 2 (infml) lively mischievous child. **monkey** v (phr v) **monkey about/around** (infml) behave mischievously.

mono /'mɒnəʊ/ adj, n [U] (of) sound that needs only one loudspeaker: a recording in ~.

monochrome /'mɒnəkrəʊm/ adj having only one colour or black and white.

monocle /'mɒnəkl/ n [C] framed lense for one eye.

monogamy /mə'nɒɡəmɪ/ n [U] practice of being married to only one person at a time. **monogamous** /-məs/ adj.

monogram /'mɒnəɡræm/ n [C] two or more letters (esp a person's initials) combined in one design.

monologue (US also **monolog**) /'mɒnəlɒɡ; US -lɔːɡ/ n [C] long speech by one person, eg in a play.

monopoly /mə'nɒpəlɪ/ n [C] (pl -ies) right of one person or organization to be the only supplier of a product, etc: (fig) A good education should not be the ~ of the rich. **monopolize** v [T] get or keep complete control of.

monorail /'mɒnəʊreɪl/ n [U] railway system using a single rail.

monosyllable /'mɒnəsɪləbl/ n [C] word with only one syllable. **monosyllabic** /ˌmɒnəsɪ'læbɪk/ adj.

monotonous /mə'nɒtənəs/ adj uninteresting, because unchanging: a ~ voice. **monotonously** adv. **monotony** /-tənɪ/ n [U].

monsoon /ˌmɒn'suːn/ n [C] wind which blows in the region of the Indian Ocean, bringing heavy rains in the summer.

monster /'mɒnstə(r)/ n [C] 1 large ugly frightening (esp imaginary) creature. 2 cruel or evil person. 3 thing that is extremely large: The new house is a real ~.

monstrous /'mɒnstrəs/ adj 1 of a large size and strange ugly shape. 2 shocking or wrong. **monstrosity** /mɒn'strɒsətɪ/ n [C] (pl -ies) large very ugly building, etc. **monstrously** adv.

month /mʌnθ/ n [C] one of the twelve divisions of the year; period of about four weeks.

monthly adj, adv **1** done once a month. **2** valid for one month. **monthly** n [C] (pl -**ies**) magazine published once a month.

monument /'mɒnjʊmənt/ n [C] **1** building, statue, etc to remind people of a person or event. **2** very old interesting building. **monumental** /ˌmɒnjʊ'mentl/ adj **1** of a monument. **2** very large and impressive. **3** very great: a ~ failure.

moo /muː/ n [C] long deep sound made by a cow. **moo** v [I] make this sound.

mood[1] /muːd/ n [C] **1** state of one's feelings: in a good ~, ie happy. **2** state of being angry or impatient. **moody** adj (-**ier**, -**iest**) having moods that often change; bad-tempered. **moodily** adv.

mood[2] /muːd/ n [C] (grammar) any of the three sets of verb forms which show that sth is certain, possible, doubtful, etc: the subjunctive ~.

moon[1] /muːn/ n **1** the moon [sing] the body that moves round the earth and shines at night. **2** [C] body that moves round a planet other than the earth. **3** (idm) **over the 'moon** (infml) extremely happy. **'moonbeam** n [C] ray of moonlight. **'moonlight** n [U] light of the moon. **'moonlight** v (pt, pp -**lighted**) [I] have a second job, esp at night, in addition to one's main job.

moon[2] /muːn/ v [I] (about/around)/ wonder about aimlessly.

moor[1] /mɔː(r); US mʊər/ n [C, U pl] open uncultivated high land, esp covered with heather: walk on the ~ s. **'moorland** /-lənd/ n [U, C] land consisting of moor.

moor[2] /mɔː; US mʊər/ v [I, T] fasten (a boat, etc) to the land or a fixed object with ropes, etc. **mooring** n **1 moorings** [pl] ropes, anchors, etc, used to moor a boat. **2** [C] place where a boat is moored.

moose /muːs/ n [C] (pl **moose** (US)) kind of very large deer.

mop /mɒp/ n [C] **1** bundle of strings, cloth, etc fastened to a long handle, used for cleaning floors. **2** mass of thick untidy hair. **mop** v (-**pp-**) **1** [T] wipe with or as with a mop. **2** (phr v) **mop sth up** wipe (a liquid) from a surface with a cloth.

mope /məʊp/ v [I] feel very unhappy.

moped /'məʊped/ n [C] kind of motor cycle with a small engine.

moral[1] /'mɒrəl; US 'mɔːr-/ adj **1** concerning principles of right and wrong: a drop in ~ standards. **2** good and honest in behaviour.

morally adv. ˌmoral 'support n [U] encouragement or sympathy.

moral[2] /'mɒrəl; US 'mɔːr-/ n **1** [C] lesson that a story or experience teaches. **2 morals** [pl] principles or standards of behaviour.

morale /mə'rɑːl; US -'ræl/ n [U] state of confidence, enthusiasm, etc of a person or group.

morality /mə'rælətɪ/ n (pl -**ies**) **1** [U] principles of good or right behaviour. **2** [C] particular system of morals.

moralize /'mɒrəlaɪz; US 'mɔːr-/ v [I] (about/on)/ esp derog) talk or write critically about right and wrong behaviour.

morbid /'mɔːbɪd/ adj having an unhealthy interest in death. **morbidly** adv.

more /mɔː(r)/ adj, pron a greater or additional number or amount (of): I need ~ time. ○ ~ people ○ Please tell me ~. **more** adv **1** (used for forming comparatives of adjectives and adverbs): ~ expensive ○ talk ~ quietly. **2** to a greater extent: You need to sleep ~. **3** again: I'll go there once ~. **4** (idm) **more and 'more** increasingly. **more or 'less** (a) almost. (b) about: £20, ~ or less.

moreover /mɔː'rəʊvə(r)/ adv (fml) in addition; besides.

morgue /mɔːg/ n [C] (esp US) building in which dead bodies are kept before a funeral.

morning /'mɔːnɪŋ/ n [C, U] **1** time of the day between sunrise and noon or before a midday meal. **2** (idm) **in the 'morning** during the morning of the next day: see him in the ~. **'morning dress** n [U] clothes worn by a man on very formal occasions, eg weddings.

moron /'mɔːrɒn/ n [C] (infml) very stupid person. **moronic** /mə'rɒnɪk/ adj.

morose /mə'rəʊs/ adj sad, bad-tempered and silent. **morosely** adv.

morphine /'mɔːfiːn/ n [U] drug made from opium, used for relieving pain.

Morse (also ˌMorse 'code) /mɔːs/ n [U] system of sending messages using short and long sounds, etc to represent letters.

morsel /'mɔːsl/ n [C] (of)/ small piece, esp of food.

mortal /'mɔːtl/ adj **1** that must die. **2** causing death: a ~ wound. **3** extreme: in ~ fear. **mortal** n [C] human being. **mortality** /mɔː'tælətɪ/ n [U] **1** state of being mortal. **2** number or rate of deaths. **mortally** /-təlɪ/ adv resulting in death: ~ly wounded. 2 greatly: ~ly offended.

mortar¹ /'mɔːtə(r)/ n [U] mixture of lime, sand and water, used to hold bricks, etc together in building.

mortar² /'mɔːtə(r)/ n [C] 1 cannon that fires shells at high angles. 2 strong bowl in which substances are crushed.

mortgage /'mɔːɡɪdʒ/ n [C] (a) arrangement to borrow money to buy a house, etc. (b) sum of money borrowed for this. **mortgage** v [T] give a bank, etc the right to own (one's house) in return for money lent.

mortify /'mɔːtɪfaɪ/ v (pt, pp -ied) [T] (usu passive) cause (sb) to be very ashamed or embarrassed. **mortification** /ˌmɔːtɪfɪ'keɪʃn; n [U].

mortuary /'mɔːtʃərɪ; US 'mɔːtʃʊərɪ/ n [C] (pl -ies) building in which dead bodies are kept before a funeral.

mosaic /məʊ'zeɪk/ n [C, U] picture or pattern made by placing together small pieces of coloured glass or stone.

Moslem = MUSLIM.

mosque /mɒsk/ n [C] building in which Muslims worship.

mosquito /məs'kiːtəʊ/ n (pl ~es) small flying insect that sucks blood.

moss /mɒs; US mɔːs/ n [U] (thick mass of a) small green or yellow plant that grows on damp surfaces. **mossy** adj (-ier, -iest).

most /məʊst/ adj, pron 1 greatest in number, amount or extent: Who will get the ~ votes? ○ He ate the ~. 2 more than half of sb/sth: M~ people must pay the new tax. 3 (idm) **at (the) most** not more than. **most** adv 1 (used for forming superlatives of adjectives and adverbs): the ~ expensive car. 2 to the greatest extent: Children need ~ sleep. 3 very: a ~ interesting talk. 4 (idm) **most likely** ⇨ LIKELY. **mostly** adv mainly; generally.

motel /məʊ'tel/ n [C] motorist's hotel.

moth /mɒθ; US mɔːθ/ n [C] winged insect, similar to the butterfly that flies mainly at night. **'mothball** n [C] small ball of a strong-smelling substance, for keeping moths out of clothes. **'moth-eaten** adj 1 eaten by moths. 2 (fig) old; worn out.

mother /'mʌðə(r)/ n [C] 1 female parent. 2 head of a female religious community. **mother** v [T] 1 care for as a mother does. 2 protect too much. **'mother coun-**

try n [C] country in which one was born. **motherhood** n [U]. **'mother-in-law** n [C] (pl ~s-in-law) mother of one's wife or husband. **motherly** adv of or like a mother. **mother 'tongue** n [C] first language that one learns as a child.

motif /məʊ'tiːf/ n [C] theme or pattern in music or art.

motion /'məʊʃn/ n 1 [U] (manner of) moving. 2 [C] particular movement: signal with a ~ of the hand. 3 [C] formal suggestion to be discussed and voted on at a meeting. 4 (idm) **go through the motions** (infml) do sth without being sincere or serious. **put/set sth in 'motion** start sth moving or operating. **motion** v [I, T] to// signal to sb by a movement of the hand. **motionless** adj not moving.

motivate /'məʊtɪveɪt/ v [T] 1 be the reason for (sb's action). 2 cause (sb) to want to do sth. **motivation** /ˌməʊtɪ'veɪʃn/ n [C, U].

motive /'məʊtɪv/ n [C] reason that causes sb to act in a certain way.

motor /'məʊtə(r)/ n [C] 1 device that changes power into movement: an electric ~. 2 (Brit dated or joc) car. **motor** adj 1 having a motor: ~ vehicles. 2 of vehicles: ~ racing. **motor** v [I] (dated Brit) travel by car. **'motor bike** n [C] (infml) = MOTORCYCLE. **motorcade** /'məʊtəkeɪd/ n [C] procession of motor cars. **'motor car** n [C] (Brit fml) = CAR. **'motor cycle** n [C] kind of large heavy bicycle that is driven by an engine. **motorist** n [C] person who drives a car. **motorize** v [T] (usu passive) fit with an engine. **'motor-scooter** n [C] = SCOOTER 1. **'motorway** n [C] wide road for fast traffic.

motto /'mɒtəʊ/ n [C] (pl ~es) short sentence or phrase used as a rule of behaviour (eg 'Live each day as it comes').

mould¹ /məʊld/ n [C] shaped container, into which a soft or liquid substance is poured so that it sets in that shape. **mould** v [T] 1 shape in a mould. 2 (fig) influence: ~ sb's character.

mould² /məʊld/ n [U] fine furry growth of fungi on old food, etc. **mouldy** adj (-ier, -iest).

moulder /'məʊldə(r)/ v [I] crumble to dust; decay slowly.

moult /məʊlt/ v [I] 1 (of a bird) lose feathers. 2 (of a dog or cat) lose hair.

mound /maʊnd/ n [C] 1 small hill. 2 pile or heap.

mount¹ /maʊnt/ v [I, T] go up; climb: slowly ~ the stairs. 2 [I, get on (a horse); provide (sb) with a horse. **3** [I] increase: ~*ing costs.* **4** [T] fix in position: ~ *pictures,* eg in an album. **5** [T] organize; start: ~ *an exhibition.* **mount** n[C] horse on which sb rides.

mount² /maʊnt/ n[C] (used in place names) mountain.

mountain /'maʊntɪn; US -ntn/ n **1** [C] mass of very high rock with steep sides. **2** [sing] very large amount: *a ~ of work.* **3** (idm) **make a mountain out of a molehill** make an unimportant matter seem important. **mountaineer** /ˌmaʊntɪ'nɪə(r); US -ntn-/ n[C] person who is skilled at climbing mountains. **mountaineering** n[U]. **mountainous** adj **1** having many mountains. **2** huge: ~*ous waves.*

mourn /mɔːn/ v[I, T] (*for*)// feel or show sorrow for sb/sth, esp sb's death. **mournful** adj sad. **mourning** n[U] **1** (expression of) sorrow, esp for sb's death. **2** black clothes, worn as a sign of sorrow at sb's death.

mouse /maʊs/ n[C] (*pl* **mice** /maɪs/) **1** small furry animal with a long tail. **2** shy timid person. **3** (*computing*) small hand-held device used to choose a particular computer operation. **mousy** /'maʊsɪ/ adj (**-ier, -iest**) (*derog*) **1** (esp of hair) dull brown. **2** (of people) timid; shy.

mousse /muːs/ n[U, C] dish made from cream and eggs, flavoured with fruit or chocolate.

moustache /mə'stɑːʃ/ (*US* **mustache** /'mʌstæʃ/) n[C] hair allowed to grow on the upper lip.

mouth¹ /maʊθ/ n[C] (*pl* ~**s** /maʊðz/) **1** opening through which animals take in food. **2** opening: *the ~ of the cave.* **mouthful** n **1** [C] amount put into the mouth. **2** [sing] (*infml joc*) word or phrase that is too long or difficult to say. **'mouth-organ** n[C] musical instrument played by passing it along the lips while blowing or sucking air. **'mouthpiece** n[C] **1** part of a musical instrument, telephone, etc that is placed in or near the mouth. **2** person, newspaper, etc that expresses the opinions of others. **mouthwatering** adj (*approv*) (of food) looking or smelling delicious.

mouth² /maʊð/ v[I, T] say (sth) by moving one's lips but not making any sound.

movable /'muːvəbl/ adj that can be moved.

move¹ /muːv/ v **1** [I, T] (cause to) change place or position: *Don't ~* while I'm taking the photo. **2** [I] (*from, to*)// go from one house to live in another: *They are ~ing (house) soon.* **3** [I] make progress: *The company has ~d ahead of the competition.* **4** [T] cause (sb) to have strong feelings, esp in a mood of pity: ~*d by a sad film.* **5** [T] suggest formally at a meeting. **6** (idm) **move 'house** move(2). **7** (phr v) **move in/out** take possession of a new/ leave one's old house. **move off** (esp of a vehicle) start.

move² /muːv/ n[C] **1** change of place or position, esp in a board game: *It's your ~!* **2** action done to achieve a purpose: ~*s to end the strike.* **3** (idm) **get a 'move on** (*infml*) hurry up. **make a 'move** (**a**) start a journey. (**b**) take action. **on the 'move** moving.

movement /'muːvmənt/ n [C, U] (act of) moving. **2** [C, also sing with pl v] group of people with a shared set of aims or principles: *the peace ~.* **3** [C] one of the main sections of a piece of music.

movie /'muːvɪ/ n (esp *US*) **1** [C] cinema film. **2 the movies** [pl] the cinema.

mow /məʊ/ v (*pt* ~**ed**, *pp* ~**n** /məʊn/ *or* ~**ed**) [T] **1** cut (grass, etc), esp with a lawn-mower. **2** (phr v) **mow sb down** kill (people) in large numbers. **mower** n[C] = LAWN-MOWER (LAWN).

MP /ˌem 'piː/ *abbr,* n[C] (esp *Brit*) Member of Parliament.

mpg /ˌem piː 'dʒiː/ *abbr* miles per gallon.

mph /ˌem piː 'eɪtʃ/ *abbr* miles per hour.

Mr /'mɪstə(r)/ *abbr* (title for a man).

Mrs /'mɪsɪz/ *abbr* (title for a married woman).

Ms /mɪz/ *abbr* (title for a married or unmarried woman).

Mt *abbr* Mount²: *Mt Everest.*

much¹ /mʌtʃ/ adj, *pron* **1** a large amount or quantity (of sth): *I haven't got ~ money.* ○ *There's too ~ salt in this pie.* ○ *How ~ is it?,* ie What does it cost?. **2** (idm) **not much of a** not a good (sth): *It isn't ~ of a car.*

much² /mʌtʃ/ adv **1** to a great degree: *work ~ harder* ○ *He isn't in the office ~,* ie often: *I would very much ~ like to come.* **2** (idm) **much as** although: *M~ as I want to stay, I must go now.* **much the 'same** in about the same condition.

muck /mʌk/ n[C] **1** manure; dung. **2** (*infml*) dirt. **muck** v (phr v) **muck about/around** (*Brit infml*) behave in an aimless silly way. **muck in** (*Brit infml*) share tasks with others: *If we all muck in we'll soon get the job done.* **muck sth up** (*infml esp Brit*) (**a**) make sth dirty. (**b**) do sth badly. **mucky** *adj* (**-ier, -iest**).

mucous /'mju:kəs/ *adj* of or covered with mucus. **,mucous 'membrane** *n* [C] moist skin that lines parts of the body such as the nose and mouth.

mucus /'mju:kəs/ *n* [U] sticky liquid produced by the mucous membrane eg in the nose.

mud /mʌd/ *n* [U] soft wet earth. **muddy** *adj* (**-ier, -iest**). **'mud-guard** *n* [C] curved cover over a wheel on a bicycle, etc.

muddle /'mʌdl/ *n* [C, usu sing] state of confusion or untidiness. **muddle** *v* 1 [T] put into disorder, confuse or mix up. 2 (phr *v*) **mud-dle along** (*derog*) live or exist with no clear purpose or plan. **muddle through** (esp *joc*) achieve one's aims, even though one doesn't really know how to do things.

muesli /'mju:zlɪ/ *n* [U] breakfast food of grain, nuts, dried fruit, etc.

muffle /'mʌfl/ *v* [T] 1 make (sound) quieter and less easily heard. 2 wrap or cover for warmth. **muffler** *n* [C] 1 (*dated*) scarf worn round the neck for warmth. 2 (*US*) silencer.

mug[1] /mʌg/ *n* [C] (**a**) straight-sided fairly large drinking cup with a handle. (**b**) contents of this. 2 (*sl*) face.

mug[2] /mʌg/ *n* [C] (*sl*) person who is easily deceived.

mug[3] /mʌg/ *v* (**-gg-**) [T] (*infml*) attack and rob violently. **mugger** *n* [C]. **mugging** *n* [C, U].

muggy /'mʌgɪ/ *adj* (**-ier, -iest**) (of weather) unpleasantly warm and damp.

Muhammad /mə'hæmɪd/ *n* prophet and founder of Islam. **Muhammadan** (also **Muham-medan**, **Mohammedan**) /-ən/ *adj, n* [C] Muslim.

mulberry /'mʌlbrɪ; *US* -berɪ/ *n* [C] (**a**) (purple or white fruit of a) tree with broad dark-green leaves.

mule /mju:l/ *n* [C] animal that is half donkey and half horse. **mul-ish** *adj* stubborn.

mull[1] /mʌl/ *v* [T] make (wine) into a hot drink with sugar, spices, etc.

mull[2] /mʌl/ (phr *v*) **mull sth over** think about sth carefully: *Give me time to ~ my decision over. ~ over what to do.*

multilateral /,mʌltɪ'lætərəl/ *adj* involving two or more countries, groups of people, etc.

multinational /,mʌltɪ'næʃnəl/

adj involving many countries. **multinational** *n* [C] very large company with offices in many countries.

multiple /'mʌltɪpl/ *adj* having or involving many parts or in-dividuals. **multiple** *n* [C] (*mathematics*) quantity that contains another quantity an exact number of times: *28 is a ~ of 7.* **multiple choice** *adj* (of examination ques-tions) with several possible ans-wers shown from which one must choose the correct one. **,multiple scle'rosis** /sklə'rəusɪs/ *n* [U] serious disease of the nervous sys-tem that causes loss of control of bodily movements.

multiply /'mʌltɪplaɪ/ *v* (*pt, pp* **-ied**) [I, T] 1 add (a number) to itself the number of times that is mentioned: *6 multiplied by 5 is 30.* 2 increase in number or quantity. 3 breed: *Rabbits ~ quickly.* **multi-plication** /,mʌltɪplɪ'keɪʃn/ *n* [U, C].

multitude /'mʌltɪtju:d; *US* -tu:d/ *n* [C] (*fml*) large number of people or things.

mum[1] /mʌm/ *n* [C] (*infml*) mother.

mum[2] /mʌm/ *adj* 1 silent. 2 (idm) **mum's the 'word** (*Brit infml*) say nothing about this.

mumble /'mʌmbl/ *v* [I, T] speak or say (sth) unclearly.

mummify /'mʌmɪfaɪ/ *v* (*pt, pp* **-ied**) [T] preserve (a dead body) by treating it with oils and wrapping it in cloth.

mummy[1] /'mʌmɪ/ *n* [C] (*pl* **-ies**) (used by children) mother.

mummy[2] /'mʌmɪ/ *n* [C] (*pl* **-ies**) dead body that has been mum-mified: *an Egyptian ~.*

mumps /mʌmps/ *n* (with sing *v*) contagious disease with painful swellings in the neck.

munch /mʌntʃ/ *v* [I, T] chew (sth) with a lot of movement of the jaw.

mundane /mʌn'deɪn/ *adj* ordin-ary and unexciting.

municipal /mju:'nɪsɪpl/ *adj* of a town or city with its own local government. **municipality** /mju:,nɪsɪ'pælətɪ/ *n* [C] (*pl* **-ies**) town or city with its own local government.

munitions /mju:'nɪʃnz/ *n* [pl] military supplies, esp bombs and guns.

mural /'mjʊərəl/ *n* [C] picture painted on a wall.

murder /'mɜ:də(r)/ *n* 1 [C, U] (in-stance of the) crime of deliberately killing sb. 2 [U] (*fig infml*) very difficult or unpleasant experience: *Climbing that hill was ~.* **murder**

v [T] kill unlawfully and deliberately. **murderer** *n* [C] person guilty of murder. **murderess** *n* [C] woman guilty of murder. **murderous** /-rəs/ *adj* intending or likely to murder: *a ~ous attack.*

murky /'mɜːkɪ/ *adj* (-**ier**, -**iest**) unpleasantly dark: *~ streets.*

murmur /'mɜːmə(r)/ *n* [C] **1** low continuous unclear sound. **2** quietly spoken word(s). **3** quiet complaint. **murmur** *v* **1** [I] make a murmur. **2** [T] say in a low voice.

muscle /'mʌsl/ *n* **1** [C, U] (one of the pieces of) elastic tissue in the body that can be tightened to produce movement. **2** [U] (*fig*) power. **muscle** *v* (*phr v*) **muscle in (on sth)** (*infml derog*) join in sth when one has no right to do so, for one's own advantage.

muscular /'mʌskjʊlə(r)/ *adj* **1** of the muscles. **2** having large strong muscles.

museum /mju:'zɪəm/ *n* [C] building in which objects of art, history or science are shown.

mushroom /'mʌʃrʊm; *US* -ruːm/ *n* [C] fungus of which some kinds can be eaten. **mushroom** *v* [I] spread or grow in number quickly.

music /'mju:zɪk/ *n* [U] (**a**) art of arranging sounds of voices and instruments in a pattern, esp to give a pleasing effect. (**b**) sounds so made: *a piece of ~.* (**c**) written signs representing these sounds. **musical** /-kl/ *adj* **1** of music. **2** fond of or skilled in music. **musical** *n* [C] play or film with songs and usu dancing. **musically** /-klɪ/ *adv.*

musician /mju:'zɪʃn/ *n* [C] person skilled in playing music; writer of music.

Muslim /'mʊzlɪm; *US* 'mʌzləm/ (also **Moslem** /'mɒzləm/) *n* [C] person whose religion is Islam. **Muslim** (also **Moslem**) *adj* of Muslims or Islam.

muslin /'mʌzlɪn/ *n* [U] thin fine cotton cloth.

mussel /'mʌsl/ *n* [C] kind of edible shellfish with a black shell.

must /məst; strong form mʌst/ *modal v* (*neg* **must not**, *contracted form* **mustn't** /'mʌsnt/) **1** (used for expressing obligation): *You ~ finish your work before you go.* ○ *Visitors ~ not feed the birds.* **2** (used for showing strong probability): *You ~ be* (ie I am sure that you are) *tired after your journey.* **must** *n* [C] (*infml*) thing that must be done, seen, etc: *If you like her acting then her new film is a ~.*

mustache (*US*) = MOUSTACHE.

mustard /'mʌstəd/ *n* [U] yellow substance made from the seeds of a plant, used to flavour food.

muster /'mʌstə(r)/ *v* [I, T] gather together.

musty /'mʌstɪ/ *adj* (-**ier**, -**iest**) smelling stale, mouldy and damp.

mutation /mju:'teɪʃn/ *n* [C, U] (instance of) change in a living thing that causes a new kind of thing to develop.

mute /mju:t/ *adj* silent. **mute** *n* [C] **1** (*dated*) dumb person. **2** object used to lessen the sound of a musical instrument. **muted** *adj* quiet; gentle; not bright: *~d colours.*

mutilate /'mju:tɪleɪt/ *v* [T] damage or injure by breaking, tearing or cutting off a necessary part. **mutilation** /ˌmju:tɪ'leɪʃn/ *n* [C, U].

mutiny /'mju:tɪnɪ/ *n* [C, U] (*pl* -**ies**) rebellion against authority, esp by sailors. **mutineer** /ˌmju:tɪ'nɪə(r)/ *n* [C] person who takes part in a mutiny. **mutinous** /-nəs/ *adj* taking part in a mutiny; refusing to obey. **mutiny** *v* (*pt, pp* -**ied**) [I] take part in a mutiny.

mutter /'mʌtə(r)/ *v* [I, T] speak or say in a low quiet unclear voice; grumble. **mutter** *n* [C, usu *sing*] muttered speech or sound.

mutton /'mʌtn/ *n* [U] meat from a sheep.

mutual /'mju:tʃʊəl/ *adj* **1** felt or done by each towards the other: *~ affection.* **2** shared by two or more people: *our ~ friend/interests.* **mutually** /-əlɪ/ *adv.*

muzzle /'mʌzl/ *n* [C] **1** (**a**) nose and mouth of an animal. (**b**) guard placed over this to prevent the animal from biting. **2** open end of a firearm. **muzzle** *v* [T] **1** put a muzzle on (a dog, etc). **2** (*fig*) prevent from expressing opinions freely.

my /maɪ/ *adj* **1** belonging to me: *Where's my hat?* **2** (used as a form of address): *Yes, my dear.* **3** (used in exclamations): *My goodness!*

myopia /maɪ'əʊpɪə/ *n* [U] inability to see clearly objects that are far away. **myopic** /-'ɒpɪk/ *adj.*

myriad /'mɪrɪəd/ *n* [C] extremely large number: *a ~ of stars.*

myrrh /mɜː(r)/ *n* [U] sweet-smelling, bitter-tasting substance used for making incense and perfumes.

myself /maɪ'self/ *pron* **1** (used as a reflexive when the speaker or writer is also the person affected by the action): *I've cut ~.* **2** (used for emphasis): *I said so ~.* **3** (*idm*) (**all**) **by my'self** (**a**) alone. (**b**) without help.

mysterious /mɪ'stɪərɪəs/ *adj* 1 hard to understand or explain: *her ~ disappearance.* 2 keeping things secret: *He's been very ~ and not told anyone his plans.* **mysteriously** *adv.*

mystery /'mɪstərɪ/ *n* (*pl* -**ies**) 1 [C] something that cannot be understood or explained: *Her disappearance is a real ~.* 2 [U] quality of being secret or puzzling.

mystic /'mɪstɪk/ (also **mystical** /'mɪstɪkl/) *adj* of hidden meaning or spiritual power. **mystic** *n* [C] person who practises mysticism. **mysticism** /'mɪstɪsɪzəm/ *n* [U] searching for secret religious understanding by prayer and meditation.

mystify /'mɪstɪfaɪ/ *v* (*pt, pp* -**ied**) [T] make confused through lack of understanding; puzzle.

mystique /mɪ'stiːk/ *n* [C, usu sing] quality of mystery associated with a person or thing: *Computers are surrounded by a certain ~.*

myth /mɪθ/ *n* 1 (a) [C] story about gods and goddesses, etc passed down from ancient times: *one of many ~s about the creation of the world.* (b) [U] such stories considered as a group. 2 [C] imaginary or invented story. **mythical** /-ɪkl/ *adj* 1 of or existing in myths. 2 not real; imaginary.

mythology /mɪ'θɒlədʒɪ/ *n* [U] 1 group of myths: *Greek ~.* 2 study of myths. **mythological** /ˌmɪθə'lɒdʒɪkl/ *adj* of or in mythology or myths.

N n

N, n /en/ *n* [C] (*pl* **N's, n's** /enz/) the fourteenth letter of the English alphabet.

N *abbr* 1 north(ern): *N Yorkshire.* 2 (esp on electric plugs) neutral (connection).

nab /næb/ *v* (-**bb**-) [T] (*Brit infml*) catch (sb) doing wrong.

nag¹ /næg/ *v* (-**gg**-) [I, T] (*at*)// find fault with (sb); constantly criticize.

nag² /næg/ *n* [C] (*infml*) old horse.

nail /neɪl/ *n* [C] 1 small thin pointed piece of metal, hit with a hammer, eg to hold pieces of wood together. 2 layer of hard substance at the end of a finger or toe. **nail** *v* [T] 1 fasten with a nail. 2

(*infml*) catch (sb). 3 (*phr v*) **nail sb down** force sb to say clearly what he/she plans to do.

naive (also **naïve**) /naɪ'iːv/ *adj* natural and innocent in behaviour, esp because of inexperience. **naively** *adv.* **naivety** *n* [U].

naked /'neɪkɪd/ *adj* 1 without clothes on. 2 without the usual covering: *a ~ light.* 3 (idm) **with the naked 'eye** without the use of a telescope, microscope, etc. **nakedly** *adv.* **nakedness** *n* [U].

name /neɪm/ *n* 1 [C] word(s) by which a person or thing is known: *My ~ is Tim.* 2 [sing] general opinion that people have of sb/sth; reputation: *a ~ for being lazy.* 3 [C] famous person: *the big ~s in show business.* 4 (idm) **in the name of sb/sth (a)** on behalf of sb/sth. **(b)** by the authority of sth: *I arrest you in the ~ of the law.* **make a 'name for oneself** become well known. **take sb's name in vain** talk disrespectfully about sb. **name** *v* [T] 1 (*after, US for*)// give a name to: *The child was ~d after his father.* 2 give the name(s) of. 3 state; choose: *~ the day for the party.* '**name-dropping** *n* [U] mentioning the names of famous people that one knows or pretends to know. **nameless** *adj* 1 having no name. 2 not to be mentioned or described: *~less horrors.* '**namesake** *n* [C] person with the same name as another.

namely /'neɪmlɪ/ *adv* that is to say: *Only one child was missing, ~ John.*

nanny /'nænɪ/ *n* [C] (*pl* -**ies**) woman employed to look after young children.

nanny-goat /'nænɪ gəʊt/ *n* [C] female goat.

nap¹ /næp/ *n* [C] short sleep. **nap** *v* (-**pp**-) [I] have a nap.

nap² /næp/ *n* [U] surface of cloth, etc made of soft hairs usu brushed in one direction.

napalm /'neɪpɑːm/ *n* [U] petrol jelly used in bombs.

nape /neɪp/ *n* [C, usu sing] back of the neck.

napkin /'næpkɪn/ *n* [C] piece of cloth or paper used at meals for protecting one's clothes and wiping one's hands and lips.

nappy /'næpɪ/ *n* [C] (*pl* -**ies**) piece of cloth or padding folded round a baby's bottom to absorb waste matter.

narcissus /nɑː'sɪsəs/ *n* [C] (*pl* ~**es** /nɑː'sɪsəsɪz/ or **narcissi** /nɑː'sɪsaɪ/) one of several kinds of spring flower, eg daffodil.

narcotic /nɑːˈkɒtɪk/ n [C], adj (kind of drug) producing sleep.

narrate /nəˈreɪt; US ˈnæreɪt/ v[T] tell (a story). **narration** /nəˈreɪʃn/ n [C, U]. **narrator** n [C] person who narrates.

narrative /ˈnærətɪv/ n 1 [C] story. 2 [U] story-telling.

narrow /ˈnærəʊ/ adj 1 small in width: a ~ road. 2 small; limited: a ~ circle of friends. 3 with only a small margin: a ~ escape. 4 not accepting new ideas: a ~ mind. **narrow** v [I, T] become or make narrow. **narrowly** adv not just: ~ly escape. **narrow-'minded** adj not ready to consider the opinions of others. **narrowness** n [U].

nasal /ˈneɪzl/ adj of, for or in the nose.

nasturtium /nəˈstɜːʃəm; US næ-/ n [C] garden plant with red, orange or yellow flowers.

nasty /ˈnɑːstɪ; US ˈnæ-/ adj (-ier, -iest) 1 unpleasant; disgusting: a ~ smell. 2 unkind; spiteful: a ~ person. 3 painful; serious: a ~ injury. **nastily** adv. **nastiness** n [U].

nation /ˈneɪʃn/ n [C] large community of people living in a particular country under one government. **nation-'wide** adj, adv over the whole of a nation.

national /ˈnæʃnəl/ adj 1 of the (whole) nation: local and ~ news. 2 owned, controlled or supported by the State. **national** n [C] citizen of a particular nation. ˌnational 'anthem n [C] official song of a nation. ˌNational 'Health Service n [sing] (in Britain) public service that provides medical care, paid for by taxation. **nationalism** n [U] 1 love of and support for one's own nation. 2 feeling that one's country should be politically independent. **nationalist** adj, n [C]. **nationally** adv. ˌnational 'service n [U] period of compulsory service in the armed forces.

nationality /ˌnæʃəˈnælətɪ/ n [U, C] (pl -ies) membership of a particular nation: a person with French ~.

nationalize /ˈnæʃnəlaɪz/ v[T] transfer (a company) from private to State ownership. **nationalization** /ˌnæʃnəlaɪˈzeɪʃn; US -lɪˈz-/ n [U].

native /ˈneɪtɪv/ n [C] 1 person born in a place or country. 2 (esp offensive) local inhabitant, not an immigrant. 3 animal or plant which occurs naturally in a place. **native** adj 1 of the place of one's birth: my ~ city. 2 (of an animal or plant) found naturally in a certain area.

nativity /nəˈtɪvətɪ/ n the Nativity [sing] birth of Jesus Christ.

NATO /ˈneɪtəʊ/ n [sing] North Atlantic Treaty Organization; military association of several countries.

natural /ˈnætʃrəl/ adj 1 of or concerned with nature(1), not people: the earth's ~ resources, eg coal, oil and gas. 2 of the basic character of a living thing: It's ~ for a bird to fly. 3 born with a certain skill: a ~ artist. 4 as expected; normal: It's only ~ you're upset. 5 not exaggerated or self-conscious. **natural** n [C] person with a natural skill in sth: That dancer is a ~. ˌnatural 'history n [U] study of plants and animals.

naturalist /ˈnætʃrəlɪst/ n [C] person who studies plants and animals.

naturalize /ˈnætʃrəlaɪz/ v[T] make (sb from another country) a citizen of a country. **naturalization** /ˌnætʃrəlaɪˈzeɪʃn; US -lɪˈz-/ n [U].

naturally /ˈnætʃrəlɪ/ adv 1 as a skill from birth: She's ~ musical. 2 of course: N~, I'll help you. 3 in a normal way: behave ~. 4 without artificial help.

nature /ˈneɪtʃə(r)/ n 1 [U] the whole universe and every created (not man-made) thing: Animals and plants are all part of ~. 2 [U] simple life without civilization: go back to ~. 3 [C, U] typical qualities of sb/sth: It's her ~ to be kind. ○ the ~ of language. 4 [sing] kind; type; sort: changes of that ~.

naught /nɔːt/ n (arch) 1 nothing. 2 (idm) ˌcome to 'naught fail: All his plans came to ~.

naughty /ˈnɔːtɪ/ adj (-ier, -iest) 1 (esp of a child) disobedient; bad. 2 mildly indecent; shocking. **naughtily** adv. **naughtiness** n [U].

nausea /ˈnɔːsɪə; US ˈnɔːʒə/ n [U] feeling of sickness. **nauseate** /ˈnɔːsɪeɪt; US ˈnɔːʒ-/ v [T] make (sb) feel nausea. **nauseous** adj.

nautical /ˈnɔːtɪkl/ adj of ships or the sea. ˌnautical 'mile n [C] measure of distance at sea; about 6080 feet (1852 metres).

naval /ˈneɪvl/ adj of a navy.

nave /neɪv/ n [C] long central part of a church.

navel /ˈneɪvl/ n [C] small hollow in the middle of the belly.

navigable /ˈnævɪgəbl/ adj (of a river, etc) wide and deep enough for ships to travel on.

navigate /ˈnævɪgeɪt/ v [I, T] direct and control the course of (a ship, aircraft, car, etc). **naviga-**

tion /ˌnævɪˈgeɪʃn/ n [U]. **navigator** n [C].

navy /ˈneɪvɪ/ n [C] country's force of ships and their crews. ˌnavy **blue** adj dark blue.

NB /ˌen ˈbiː/ abbr note carefully.

near¹ /nɪə(r)/ adj 1 at a short distance in space or time; not far: The house is ~ (to) the station. 2 closely related: ~ relations. 3 (idm) a **near 'thing** a situation in which failure or disaster is only just avoided. **near** υ [I, T] come closer to (sth): The ship is ~ing land. **nearness** n [U]. **'nearside** adj, n [sing] (on the) side nearest the kerb. **ˌnear-'sighted** = SHORT-SIGHTED (A) (SHORT).

near² /nɪə(r)/ prep with only a short distance or time between: Bradford is ~ Leeds. **near** adv 1 at a short distance away. 2 (idm) nowhere **'near** far from. **near 'by** adv at a short distance from sth/sth: They live ~ by. **'nearby** adj not far away. **nearly** adv 1 almost; very close to. 2 (idm) not **nearly** far from: not ~ly enough money.

neat /niːt/ adj 1 tidy; arranged carefully. 2 cleverly and skilfully done: a ~ answer to the problem. 3 (infml) splendid: a ~ idea. 4 (of an alcoholic drink) not mixed with water. **neatly** adv. **neatness** n [U].

necessary /ˈnesəsərɪ; US -serɪ/ adj that is needed; that must be; essential: Have you made the ~ arrangements? **necessarily** /ˌnesəˈserəlɪ/ adv as a necessary result: Tall men aren't ~ly strong.

necessitate /nɪˈsesɪteɪt/ υ [T] (fml) make (sth) necessary.

necessity /nɪˈsesɪtɪ/ n (pl -ies) 1 [U] state of being necessary; need. 2 [C] something necessary: Food is a ~ of life.

neck /nek/ n [C] 1 (a) part of the body that joins the head to the shoulders. (b) part of a garment round this. 2 narrow neck-shaped part of sth: the ~ of a bottle. 3 (idm) **ˌneck and 'neck** level in a race. **risk/save one's 'neck** risk/save one's life. **up to one's neck in sth** very deeply involved in sth. **neck** υ [I] (infml) (of couples) hug and kiss each other. **necklace** /ˈnekləs/ n [C] decorative string of beads, jewels, etc worn round the neck. **'necktie** n [C] (dated or US) = TIE² 1.

nectar /ˈnektə(r)/ n [U] sweet liquid collected by bees from plants.

née /neɪ/ adj (used after the name of a woman to give her family name before she married): Mrs Jane Smith, ~ Brown.

need¹ /niːd/ modal υ (pres tense all persons **need**, neg **need not** or **needn't** /ˈniːdnt/) (used for showing what has to be done): You ~n't finish that work today.

need² /niːd/ υ [T] 1 require; want: That dog ~s a bath. 2 (used for showing what has to be done): You ~ to work harder!

need³ /niːd/ n 1 [sing, U] circumstances in which sth is necessary: There's a ~ for more engineers. ○ There's no ~ to start yet. 2 needs [pl] necessary things: My ~s are few. 3 [U] poverty; misfortune: in ~. 4 (idm) **if need be** if necessary.

needless adj 1 unnecessary. 2 (idm) **needless to 'say** as you already know. **needlessly** adv.

needy adj (-ier, -iest) very poor.

needle /ˈniːdl/ n [C] 1 small pointed piece of steel, with a hole at the top for thread, used in sewing. 2 = KNITTING-NEEDLE (KNIT). 3 the pointed hollow end of a syringe used for giving injections. 4 stylus used in playing records. **needle** υ [T] (infml) annoy. **'needlework** n [U] sewing; embroidery.

negation /nɪˈgeɪʃn/ n [U] (fml) act of denying or refusing.

negative /ˈnegətɪv/ adj 1 (of words, answers, etc) showing or meaning 'no' or 'not'. 2 not helpful or encouraging: ~ criticism. 3 (mathematics) less than zero. 4 of the kind of electric charge carried by electrons. **negative** n [C] 1 word or statement that means 'no' or 'not'. 2 film with light and dark areas reversed. 3 (idm) **in the 'negative** (of an answer) meaning 'no'. **negatively** adv.

neglect /nɪˈglekt/ υ [T] 1 give not enough care or attention to: ~ one's work. 2 fail or forget to do sth: He ~ed to write. **neglect** n [U] neglecting or being neglected. **neglectful** adj (fml) in the habit of neglecting sb/sth.

négligé (also **negligee**) /ˈneglɪʒeɪ; US ˌneglɪˈʒeɪ/ n [C] woman's thin light dressing-gown.

negligent /ˈneglɪdʒənt/ adj not giving proper care to sth. **negligence** /-dʒəns/ n [U]. **negligently** adv.

negligible /ˈneglɪdʒəbl/ adj of little importance or size.

negotiable /nɪˈgəʊʃɪəbl/ adj 1 that can be settled by discussion. 2 (of a cheque, etc) that can be exchanged for cash or passed to sb else for cash. 3 (of roads, rivers, etc) that can be crossed or passed along.

negotiate /nɪˈgəʊʃɪeɪt/ υ 1 [I, T]

try to come to (an agreement) by discussion. 2 [T] get past or over (an obstacle). **negotiation** /nɪ,gəʊʃɪ'eɪʃn/ n [C, U]. **negotiator** n [C] person who negotiates.

Negress /'niːgres/ n [C] (sometimes *offensive*) Negro woman or girl.

Negro /'niːgrəʊ/ n [C] (pl ~es) sometimes *offensive*) member of the race of black people that originally came from Africa.

neigh /neɪ/ v [I] n [C] (make the) cry of a horse.

neighbour (US -or) /'neɪbə(r)/ n [C] 1 person who lives in a house, etc near another. 2 person, thing or country that is next to or near another. **neighbourhood** n [C] 1 district; nearby area. 2 (idm) in the **neighbourhood of** approximately. **neighbouring** adj near to sth: ~ing towns. **neighbourliness** n [U] friendliness. **neighbourly** adj friendly.

neither /'naɪðə(r), 'niːðə(r)/ adj, pron not one nor the other of two: N~ boy is to blame. ○ I chose ~ of them. **neither** adv, conj 1 not either; also not: She doesn't like Mozart and ~ do I. ○ I've never been to Paris and ~ has she. 2 (idm) **neither ... nor** not ... and not: N~ his sister nor his brother was invited.

neon /'niːɒn/ n [U] colourless gas used in electric lights.

nephew /'nevjuː, 'nefjuː/ n [C] son of one's brother(-in-law) or sister(-in-law).

nepotism /'nepətɪzəm/ n [U] giving of special favour to one's relatives.

nerve /nɜːv/ n 1 [C] thread-like part of the body that carries messages and feelings between the brain and other parts of the body. 2 **nerves** [pl] (*infml*) condition of being worried, easily excited, etc: He has ~s of steel, ie He's not easily worried. 3 [U] boldness; courage: lose one's ~. 4 [sing] disrespect and rudeness; impudence: She had the ~ to say I was cheating! 5 (idm) **get on sb's 'nerves** (*infml*) annoy sb. '**nerve-racking** adj causing great worry.

nervous /'nɜːvəs/ adj 1 of the nerves(1). 2 worried and rather afraid; tense. ,**nervous 'breakdown** n [C] mental illness that causes depression, tiredness and weakness. **nervously** adv. **nervousness** n [C]. '**nervous system** n [C] all the nerves in the body of a person or animal.

nervy /'nɜːvɪ/ adj (*infml Brit*) nervous(2).

nest /nest/ n [C] 1 place made by a bird for its eggs. 2 group of similar things (esp tables) fitting one inside another. **nest** v [I] make or use a nest. '**nest-egg** n [C] sum of money saved for future use.

nestle /'nesl/ v 1 [I] settle comfortably and warmly in a soft place: ~ (down) among the cushions. 2 [T] push (one's head, etc) lovingly against sth: She ~d her head on his shoulder.

nestling /'nestlɪŋ/ n [C] bird that is too young to leave its nest.

net[1] /net/ n [C, U] (piece of) loose open material of knotted string, wire, etc: fishing-~s. **net** v (-tt-) [T] catch (as if) with a net. '**netball** n [U] team game in which a ball is thrown through a net on the top of a post. '**network** n [C] 1 complex system of roads, etc crossing each other. 2 closely linked group of people. 3 group of radio or television stations.

net[2] (also **nett**) /net/ adj remaining when nothing more is to be taken away: ~ profit. **net** v (-tt-) [T] gain (sth) as a net profit.

netting /'netɪŋ/ n [U] string, wire, etc knotted into a net.

nettle /'netl/ n [C] common wild plant with leaves that sting.

network ⇨ NET[1].

neurology /njʊə'rɒlədʒɪ; US nʊ-/ n [U] study of nerves and their diseases. **neurologist** n [C] expert in neurology.

neurosis /njʊə'rəʊsɪs; US nʊ-/ n [C] (pl -oses /-əʊsiːz/) nervous or mental illness causing depression or abnormal behaviour.

neurotic /njʊə'rɒtɪk; US nʊ-/ adj abnormally sensitive and anxious. **neurotic** n [C] neurotic person.

neuter /'njuːtə(r)/ adj (*grammar*) neither masculine nor feminine in gender. **neuter** v [T] remove the sex organs of (an animal).

neutral /'njuːtrəl; US 'nuː-/ adj 1 not supporting either side in an argument, war, etc. 2 having no clear or strong qualities: a dull ~ colour. 3 (of a gear) in which the engine is not connected to the wheels. **neutral** n 1 [C] neutral person, country, etc. 2 [U] neutral position of gears. **neutrality** /nju:'træləti; US nuː-/ n [U] state of being neutral(1). **neutralize** v [T] take away the effect of: ~ize a poison.

neutron /'njuːtrɒn; US 'nuː-/ n [C] tiny particle of matter inside an atom, with no electric charge.

never /'nevə(r)/ adv at no time:

I've ~ been to Wales.

nevertheless /ˌnevəðə'les/ *adv, conj (fml)* in spite of this: *He was old and poor, but ~ he was happy.*

new /njuː; *US* nuː/ *adj* 1 not existing before; made, introduced, etc recently: *a ~ film.* 2 existing, but only now seen, discovered, etc: *learn ~ words.* 3 *(to)//* unfamiliar with sth: *I'm ~ to this town.* 4 changed from the previous one: *get a ~ job.* 5 beginning again: *start a ~ life.* 6 (idm) **new blood** ⇒ BLOOD. **a new lease of 'life** new energy or desire to live. **new-** *prefix* (forming compound adjs) recently: *~-born.* **'newcomer** *n* [C] person who has recently arrived in a place. **newly** *adv* recently: *a ~ly married couple.* **'newly-weds** *n* [pl] recently married couple. **new 'moon** *n* [C] the moon appearing as a thin crescent. **newness** *n* [U]. **new 'year** *n* [U, C] first few days of January.

news /njuːz; *US* nuːz/ *n* 1 [U] report(s) of recent events: *Here's some good ~!* 2 **the news** [sing] regular programme reporting on recent events on radio or television. **'newsagent** (*US* **'news-dealer**) *n* [C] shopkeeper who sells newspapers, etc. **'newsflash** *n* [C] short piece of important news on television or radio. **'newspaper** /'njuːˌspeɪpə(r); *US* 'nuːz-/ *n* [C] printed publication, issued daily or weekly, with news, advertisements, etc.

newt /njuːt; *US* nuːt/ *n* [C] small lizard-like animal that can live in water or on land.

next /nekst/ *adj* 1 coming immediately after in order, space or time: *the ~ name on the list.* 2 the one immediately following: *~ Thursday.* **next** *adv* after this or that: *What are you going to do ~?* **,next 'door** *adv* in or into the next house. **next of 'kin** /'kɪn/ *n* (with sing or pl v) closest relatives. **next** *to prep* 1 at the side of: *Come and sit ~ to me.* 2 almost: *say ~ to nothing* ○ *in ~ to no time.*

NHS /ˌen eɪtʃ 'es/ *abbr* (*Brit*) National Health Service.

nib /nɪb/ *n* [C] metal point of a pen.

nibble /'nɪbl/ *v* [I, T] take tiny bites of (sth). **nibble** *n* [C] act of nibbling.

nice /naɪs/ *adj* (~r, ~st) 1 pleasant: *a ~ day.* 2 kind; friendly. 3 *(ironic)* bad: *You've got us into a ~ mess!* 4 needing care; subtle: *a ~ distinction.* 5 (idm) **nice and ...** *(infml)* (used before adjectives) pleasantly: *It's ~ and quiet here.*

nicely *adv* 1 in a nice way. 2 *(infml)* very well: *The patient is doing ~ly,* ie making good progress. **niceness** *n* [U].

nicety /'naɪsətɪ/ *n* [C, usu pl] (*pl* **-ies**) small distinction: *niceties of meaning.*

niche /niːʃ, nɪtʃ/ *n* [C] 1 hollow place in a wall, eg for a statue. 2 *(fig)* suitable position, job, etc.

nick¹ /nɪk/ *n* [C] 1 small cut. 2 (idm) **in good, bad, etc 'nick** (*Brit sl*) in good, bad, etc condition. **in the ,nick of 'time** only just in time. **nick** *v* [T] make a small cut in (sth).

nick² /nɪk/ *n* **the nick** [sing] (*Brit sl*) prison or police station. **nick** *v* [T] (*Brit*) 1 *(sl)* arrest. 2 *(infml)* steal.

nickel /'nɪkl/ *n* 1 [U] hard silver-white metal. 2 [C] coin of the US or Canada worth five cents.

nickname /'nɪkneɪm/ *n* [C] informal name used instead of sb's real name. **nickname** *v* [T] give a nickname to.

nicotine /'nɪkətiːn/ *n* [U] poisonous oily substance found in tobacco.

niece /niːs/ *n* [C] daughter of one's brother(-in-law) or sister (-in-law).

night /naɪt/ *n* 1 [C, U] time of darkness between sunset and sunrise. 2 (idm) **at/by night** during the night. **have a good/bad 'night** sleep well/badly. **,night and 'day, ,day and 'night** all the time. **'night-club** *n* [C] club open until late at night for drinking, dancing, entertainment, etc. **'night-dress** (also *infml* **nightie** /'naɪtɪ/) *n* [C] garment worn by a woman or girl in bed. **'nightfall** *n* [U] time when darkness comes. **'night-life** *n* [U] entertainment, eg bars and discos, available at night. **nightly** *adj, adv* (happening, done, etc) at night or every night. **'nightmare** *n* [C] 1 frightening dream. 2 *(infml)* very frightening or unpleasant experience. **'night-watchman** *n* [C] (*pl* **-men**) man employed to guard a building at night.

nightingale /'naɪtɪŋgeɪl; *US* -tŋg-/ *n* [C] small bird that sings sweetly.

nil /nɪl/ *n* [U] nothing.

nimble /'nɪmbl/ *adj* (~r, ~st) 1 able to move quickly and neatly; agile. 2 *(fig)* (of the mind) able to think quickly; sharp. **nimbly** *adv*.

nine /naɪn/ *pron, adj, n* [C] 9.

ninth /naɪnθ/ *pron, adj, n* 9th.

ninth *pron, n* [C] ⅑.

nineteen /ˌnaɪn'tiːn/ *pron, adj,*

n [C] 19. **nineteenth** /ˌnaɪn'tiːnθ/ *pron, adj* 19th. **nineteenth** *pron, n* [C] ¹⁄₁₉.

ninety /'naɪntɪ/ *pron, adj, n* [C] (*pl* -**ies**) 90. **ninetieth** /'naɪntɪəθ/ *pron, adj* 90th. **ninetieth** *pron, n* [C] ¹⁄₉₀.

nip /nɪp/ *v* (-**pp**-) 1 [T] press hard (eg between one's finger and thumb or with one's teeth). 2 [I] (*infml*) move quickly; hurry: *I'll just ~ along to the shops.* 3 (*idm*) **nip sth in the bud** stop sth in its early development. **nip** *n* [C] 1 [usu sing] sharp pinch or bite. 2 small drink (esp of spirits). 3 (*idm*) **a 'nip in the air** sharp feeling of cold.

nipple /'nɪpl/ *n* [C] 1 round point of the breast. 2 something like a nipple, eg on a baby's bottle.

nippy /'nɪpɪ/ *adj* (-**ier**, -**iest**) (*infml*) 1 cold. 2 quick: *a ~ little car.*

nit /nɪt/ *n* [C] 1 egg of a parasitic insect. 2 (*infml esp Brit*) = NITWIT.

nitrogen /'naɪtrədʒən/ *n* [U] gas that forms about four-fifths of the earth's atmosphere.

nitro-glycerine (also *esp US* -**glycerin**) /ˌnaɪtrəʊ 'glɪsəriːn; *US* -rɪn/ *n* [U] powerful explosive.

nitwit /'nɪtwɪt/ *n* [C] (*infml*) stupid person.

No (also **no**) *abbr* (*pl ~* s) number.

no /nəʊ/ *adj* 1 not any; not one: *She had no money.* 2 (used for showing that sth is not allowed): *No smoking.* 3 (used for showing an opposite): *He's no fool,* ie He is intelligent. **no** *interj* (used when refusing, disagreeing, denying, etc): *'Would you like a drink?' 'No thanks.'* **no** *adv* not: *He's feeling no better.* **no** *n* [C] (*pl ~* es) 1 person who votes 'no'. 2 word or answer of 'no'. **ˌno-claims** *n* [C] reduction from an insurance fee because no claim has been made. **ˌno-go area** *n* [C] place where some people are not allowed to go. **'no man's land** *n* [U] (in war) ground between two opposing armies. **no one** = NOBODY.

nobility /nəʊ'bɪlətɪ/ *n* 1 [U] quality of being noble; noble birth or rank. 2 **the nobility** [sing] (with sing or pl *n*) people of noble birth or rank.

noble /'nəʊbl/ *adj* (*~* r, *~* st) 1 of high rank or birth. 2 having an excellent moral character: *a ~ leader.* 3 impressive in appearance, size, etc. **noble** *n* [C] person of noble rank or birth. **'nobleman** (*fem* **'noblewoman**) *n* [C] person of noble birth or rank. **nobly** *adv.*

nobody /'nəʊbədɪ/ (also **no one** /'nəʊwʌn/) *pron* not anybody; no person: *N~ came to see me.* **nobody** *n* [C] (*pl* -**ies**) unimportant person.

nocturnal /nɒk'tɜːnl/ *adj* of, in or active in the night: *Owls are ~.*

nod /nɒd/ *v* (-**dd**-) 1 [I, T] move (one's head) down and then up, in agreement or as a greeting. 2 (*phr v*) **nod off** (*infml*) fall asleep. **nod** *n* [C, usu sing] act of nodding.

noise /nɔɪz/ *n* [C, U] sound, esp when loud or unpleasant. **noisy** *adj* (-**ier**, -**iest**) making a lot of noise. **noisily** *adv.*

nomad /'nəʊmæd/ *n* [C] member of a tribe that wanders from place to place. **nomadic** /nəʊ'mædɪk/ *adj.*

nominal /'nɒmɪnl/ *adj* 1 existing in name only; not in fact: *the ~ ruler of the country.* 2 very small: *a ~ rent.* 3 (*grammar*) of a noun. **nominally** /-nəlɪ/ *adv.*

nominate /'nɒmɪneɪt/ *v* [T] suggest officially that (sb) should be chosen for a position. **nomination** /ˌnɒmɪ'neɪʃn/ *n* [C, U].

nominee /ˌnɒmɪ'niː/ *n* [C] person who has been nominated.

non- /nɒn/ *prefix* not. **ˌnoncom'missioned** *adj* not having a commission(4) in the armed forces. **ˌnon-com'mittal** /kə'mɪtl/ *adj* not expressing an opinion or decision clearly. **ˌnoncon'formist** *n* [C], *adj* (person) who does not think or behave like other people. **ˌnon-'fiction** *n* [U] writing that describes real people and events. **ˌnon-'stick** *adj* (of pans) covered with a material that prevents food from sticking during cooking. **ˌnon-'stop** *adj, adv* without a stop: *a ~ stop train.*

nonchalant /'nɒnʃələnt/ *adj* not showing interest or enthusiasm. **nonchalance** /-ləns/ *n* [U]. **nonchalantly** *adv.*

nondescript /'nɒndɪskrɪpt/ *adj* ordinary; uninteresting.

none /nʌn/ *pron* not one; not any: *N~ of them has/have come back yet.* **none** *adv* 1 **none the** not at all: *~ the worse for this experience.* 2 **none too** not very: *~ too happy.* **ˌnone the 'less** *adv* in spite of this: *She may be ill but she does the work done ~ the less.*

nonentity /nɒ'nentətɪ/ *n* [C] (*pl* -**ies**) unimportant person.

nonplussed /ˌnɒn'plʌst/ *adj* very surprised and puzzled.

nonsense /'nɒnsns; *US* -sens/ *n* 1 [U] meaningless words. 2 [U, sing] foolish talk, ideas, etc. **nonsensical** /nɒn'sensɪkl/ *adj* stupid; foolish.

noodle /'nuːdl/ n [C, usu pl] long thin strip made of flour or water or flour and eggs, eaten with sauces, etc.

nook /nʊk/ n [C] **1** sheltered quiet place. **2** (idm) every ,nook and 'cranny everywhere.

noon /nuːn/ n [U] 12 o'clock in the middle of the day.

no-one, no one = NOBODY.

noose /nuːs/ n [C] loop of a rope that becomes tighter when the rope is pulled.

nor /nɔː(r)/ conj, adv (used after *neither* or *not*) and not: *Neither Chris ~ his sister wanted to come.* ○ *He can't see, ~ can he hear.*

norm /nɔːm/ n [C] usual or expected way of behaving.

normal /'nɔːml/ adj usual or regular. **normal** n [U] usual state or level. **normality** /nɔː'mælətɪ/ (also esp US **normalcy** /'nɔːmlsɪ/) n [U] state of being normal. **normally** /-məlɪ/ adv.

north /nɔːθ/ n [sing] **1** the north point of the compass, to the left of a person facing the sunrise. **2** the North part of a particular country towards the north. **north** adj **1** in or towards the north. **2** (of winds) from the north. **north** adv towards the north. **,north-'east** n [sing], adj, adv (region, direction, etc) midway between north and east. **,north-'eastern** adj. **northerly** /'nɔːðəlɪ/ adj, adv **1** in or towards the north. **2** (of winds) from the north. **northern** /'nɔːðən/ adj of the north part of the world or a particular country. **northerner** n [C] person born or living in the northern part of a country. **northward** /'nɔːθwəd/ adj towards the north. **northward(s)** adv. **,north-'west** n [sing], adj, adv (region, direction, etc) midway between north and west. **,north-'western** adj.

Nos abbr numbers.

nose¹ /nəʊz/ n **1** [C] part of the face above the mouth for breathing and smelling. **2** front part, eg of an aircraft. **3** [sing] **(a)** sense of smell. **(b)** for|| (infml) ability to find sth: *a ~ for a good story.* **4** (idm) get up sb's 'nose (sl) annoy sb. poke/stick one's nose into sth (infml) interfere in sth that does not concern one. under sb's nose (infml) directly in front of sb. 'nosebleed n [C] bleeding from the nose. 'nosedive n [C], v[I] (make a) sharp vertical drop in an aircraft: *(fig) Prices have taken a ~ dive.*

nose² /nəʊz/ v **1** [I, T] (cause to) go forward slowly in a particular direction. **2** (phr v) nose about/around pry into sb's affairs, etc: *He's always been nosing around in my desk.*

nosey (also **nosy**) /'nəʊzɪ/ adj (-ier, -iest) (infml derog) too interested in other people's private lives. Nosey 'Parker n [C] (Brit infml derog) nosey person.

nostalgia /nɒ'stældʒə/ n [U] desire for sth that one has known in the past. **nostalgic** /-dʒɪk/ adj of, feeling or causing nostalgia.

nostril /'nɒstrəl/ n [C] either of the two openings into the nose.

not /nɒt/ (also contracted form **-n't** /nt/) adv **1** (used for forming the negative): *She did ~ see him.* ○ *He warned me ~ to be late.* ○ *Don't be late!* **2** (idm) not only . . . (but) also (used to emphasize the addition of sth/sb): *She's ~ only my sister but also my best friend.* 'not that although one is not suggesting that: *I asked him to visit me - ~ that I like him, you understand.*

notable /'nəʊtəbl/ adj deserving to be noticed. **notable** n [C] important person. **notably** adv particularly.

notary /'nəʊtərɪ/ n [C] (pl -ies) **,notary 'public** official with authority to witness documents.

notation /nəʊ'teɪʃn/ n [C, U] system of signs or symbols representing numbers, musical notes, etc.

notch /nɒtʃ/ n [C] V-shaped cut. **notch** v [T] **1** make a notch in. **2** (phr v) notch sth up achieve; win: *~ up a victory.*

note /nəʊt/ n **1** [C] short written record to help the memory: *take ~s at a lecture.* **2** [C] short letter: *Leave a ~ about it on his desk.* **3** [C] short explanation of a word, etc in a book. **4** [C] piece of paper money: *'bank ~s.* **5** [C] **(a)** single musical sound. **(b)** sign representing this. **6** [sing] quality or tone, esp of voice: *a ~ of bitterness in his voice.* **7** [U] importance: *a family of ~.* **8** (idm) take note of sth pay attention to sth. note v[T] **1** notice. **2** (down)|| record in writing. 'notebook n [C] small book for writing notes(1). noted adj famous. 'note paper n [C] paper for writing letters on. noteworthy adj deserving to be noted; remarkable.

nothing /'nʌθɪŋ/ pron **1** not anything: *I've had ~ to eat since lunch.* ○ '*You've hurt your arm.*' '*It's ~.*', ie It is not important, serious, etc. **2** (idm) for 'nothing **(a)** free: *He did the job for ~.* **(b)** with no good result; to no purpose. have nothing to 'do with sb/sth not concern oneself with sb/sth. **'nothing but** only: ~ *but the best.* **nothing (else)'for it (but)** no other action except: *There's* ~ *for it but to work late tonight.* **nothing like** (*infml*) (a) not at all like: *She's* ~ *like her sister.* (b) absolutely not: *This is* ~ *like as good.*

notice /'nəʊtɪs/ n 1 [C] (written or printed) news or information. 2 [U] warning: *give her a month's* ~ *to leave* ○ *at short* ~, ie with little warning. 3 (idm) **bring sth/come to sb's notice** (cause sth to) be seen, heard, etc by sb. **take no notice of sb/sth** pay no attention to sb/sth. **notice** *v* [I, T] see or observe (sb/sth). **noticeable** *adj* easily noticed. **noticeably** *adv.*

notify /'nəʊtɪfaɪ/ *v* (*pt, pp* **-ied**) [T] (*of*)/ tell (sb) about sth; inform: ~ *the police of the accident.* **notification** /ˌnəʊtɪfɪ'keɪʃn/ *n* [U, C].

notion /'nəʊʃn/ *n* [C] idea; opinion.

notorious /nəʊ'tɔːrɪəs/ *adj* well-known for sth bad: *a* ~ *murderer.* **notoriety** /ˌnəʊtə'raɪətɪ/ *n* [U] state of being notorious. **notoriously** *adv.*

nougat /'nuːɡɑː, 'nʌɡət; US 'nuːɡət/ *n* [U] hard sweet made of sugar, nuts, etc.

nought /nɔːt/ *n* [C] the figure 0.

noun /naʊn/ *n* [C] (*grammar*) word that is the name of a thing, quality, person, etc and can be the subject or object of a verb.

nourish /'nʌrɪʃ/ *v* [T] 1 keep alive and healthy with food. 2 (*fml fig*) allow to grow stronger. **nourishment** *n* [U] food.

novel¹ /'nɒvl/ *n* [C] long written story. **novelist** /'nɒvəlɪst/ *n* [C] writer of novels.

novel² /'nɒvl/ *adj* new and unusual: *a* ~ *idea.*

novelty /'nɒvltɪ/ *n* (*pl* **-ies**) 1 [U] quality of being novel². 2 [C] something unusual or new. 3 [C] small cheap toy or decoration.

November /nəʊ'vembə(r)/ *n* [U, C] the eleventh month of the year. (See examples of use at *April*).

novice /'nɒvɪs/ *n* [C] 1 person who is new and inexperienced in a job, activity, etc. 2 person training to become a monk or nun.

now /naʊ/ *adv* 1 (a) at the present time: *Where are you living* ~? (b) immediately: *Start writing* ~. 2 (used for attracting attention, etc): *N*~ *stop quarrelling and listen!* 3 (idm) **(every) now and then/again** sometimes: *He visits me every* ~ *and then.* **now** *conj* (*that*)/ because of the fact (that): *N*~

(that) you're here, let's begin.

nowadays /'naʊədeɪz/ *adv* at the present time: *She doesn't go out much* ~.

nowhere /'nəʊweə(r); US -hweər/ *adv* 1 not anywhere: *There is* ~ *interesting to visit in this town.* 2 (idm) **get nowhere** ⇨ GET.

noxious /'nɒkʃəs/ *adj* (*fml*) harmful; poisonous.

nozzle /'nɒzl/ *n* [C] shaped end of a hose through which liquid is directed.

nuance /'njuːɑːns; US 'nuː-/ *n* [C] small difference in meaning, opinion, colour, etc.

nuclear /'njuːklɪə(r); US 'nuː-/ *adj* of a nucleus; using nuclear energy. **,nuclear 'energy** *n* [U] extremely powerful form of energy produced by the splitting of the nuclei of atoms. **,nuclear re'actor** *n* [C] device that produces nuclear energy.

nucleus /'njuːklɪəs; US 'nuː-/ *n* [C] (*pl* **nuclei** /-klɪaɪ/) 1 (a) (*physics*) central part of an atom. (b) (*biology*) central part of a cell. 2 central part, around which other parts are grouped: *These books form the* ~ *of the library.*

nude /njuːd; US nuːd/ *adj* without clothes on. **nude** *n* 1 [C] nude person, esp in paintings, etc. 2 (idm) **in the nude** without clothes on. **nudism** /-ɪzəm/ *n* [U] practice of not wearing clothes. **nudist** *n* [C]. **nudity** *n* [U].

nudge /nʌdʒ/ *v* [T] push gently, esp with one's elbow. **nudge** *n* [C] gentle push.

nugget /'nʌɡɪt/ *n* [C] 1 lump of metal, esp gold. 2 (*fig*) interesting piece of information.

nuisance /'njuːsns; US 'nuː-/ *n* [C, usu sing] annoying person, thing, situation, etc.

null /nʌl/ *adj* (idm) **null and void** having no legal effect. **nullify** /'nʌlɪfaɪ/ *v* (*pt, pp* **-ied**) [T] make (sth) have no effect.

numb /nʌm/ *adj* unable to feel: ~ *with cold/shock.* **numb** *v* [T] make numb. **numbness** *n* [U].

number /'nʌmbə(r)/ *n* 1 symbol or word for a quantity: *3, 13 and 103 are* ~ *s.* 2 quantity or amount: *a large* ~ *of people* ○ *A* ~ *of* (ie several) *books are missing.* 3 issue of a magazine. 4 dance, song, tune, etc. **number** *v* [T] 1 give a number to: ~ *the pages.* 2 amount to: *The crowd* ~ *ed over 3000.* 3 among// include: *I* ~ *her among my friends.*

numeral /'njuːmərəl; US 'nuː-/ *n* [C] figure or symbol representing a number.

numerate /'nju:mərət; *US* 'nu:-/ *adj* having a good basic ability in mathematics.

numerical /nju:'merɪkl; *US* 'nu:-/ *adj* of or expressed in numbers. **numerically** /-klɪ/ *adv*.

numerous /'nju:mərəs; *US* 'nu:-/ *adj* (*fml*) very many: on ~ *occasions*.

nun /nʌn/ *n* [C] member of a female religious community, living in a convent. **nunnery** *n* [C] (*pl* -ies) convent.

nurse /nɜ:s/ *n* [C] person who cares for ill or injured people, esp in a hospital. **nurse** *v* [T] 1 care for (people who are ill, etc). 2 feed (a baby) with milk from the breast. 3 give special care to: ~ *young plants*. 4 have in the mind: ~ *feelings of revenge*. **nursing** *n* [U] profession or work of a nurse(1). **'nursing-home** *n* [C] small, usu private, hospital.

nursery /'nɜ:sərɪ/ *n* [C] (*pl* -ies) 1 place where young children are cared for while their parents are at work. 2 place where young plants are grown. **'nursery rhyme** *n* [C] poem or song for young children. **'nursery school** *n* [C] school for children from 2 or 3 to 5 years old.

nurture /'nɜ:tʃə(r)/ *v* [T] (*fml*) 1 care for and educate (a child). 2 encourage the growth of.

nut /nʌt/ *n* [C] 1 fruit with a hard shell round a part (= KERNEL) that can be eaten. 2 small piece of metal with a threaded hole for screwing onto a bolt. 3 (*sl derog*) mad person. 4 (*idm*) **off one's nut** (*sl*) mad. **'nut-case** *n* [C] (*sl*) mad person. **'nutcrackers** *n* [pl] device for cracking open the shells of nuts. **'nutshell** *n* (*idm*) **(put sth) in a nutshell** (say sth) in very few words. **nutty** *adj* (-ier, -iest) 1 tasting of nuts. 2 (*sl*) mad.

nutmeg /'nʌtmeg/ *n* [U, C] (powder from crushing a) sweet-smelling seed of an E Indian tree, used as a flavouring.

nutrient /'nju:trɪənt; *US* 'nu:-/ *n* [C] substance needed by plants and animals for life and growth.

nutrition /nju:'trɪʃn; *US* nu:-/ *n* [U] process of supplying and receiving healthy food. **nutritional** /-ʃənl/ *adj*. **nutritious** /-ʃəs/ *adj* of (high) value as food.

nuts /nʌts/ *adj* (*sl*) crazy; mad.

nuzzle /'nʌzl/ *v* [I, T] press or rub (sb/sth) gently with one's nose, esp to show affection.

nylon /'naɪlɒn/ *n* [U] very strong artificial material, used in clothes,

rope, etc.

nymph /nɪmf/ *n* [C] (in Greek and Roman stories) goddess living in rivers, trees, etc.

O *o*

O, o /əʊ/ *n* [C] (*pl* O's, o's /əʊz/) 1 the fifteenth letter of the English alphabet. 2 (eg in saying telephone numbers) zero.

oaf /əʊf/ *n* [C] awkward or stupid person.

oak /əʊk/ *n* (a) [C] large tree with tough hard wood. (b) [U] wood of this tree.

OAP /ˌəʊ eɪ 'pi:/ *abbr* (*Brit infml*) old-age pensioner.

oar /ɔ:(r)/ *n* 1 [C] long pole with a flat blade, for rowing a boat. 2 (*idm*) **put/stick one's 'oar in** (*infml*) interfere.

oasis /əʊ'eɪsɪs/ *n* [C] (*pl* oases /-si:z/) place with water and plants in a desert.

oath /əʊθ/ *n* [C] (*pl* ~s /əʊðz/) 1 solemn promise or declaration. 2 swear-word. 3 (*idm*) **be on/under 'oath** (in a lawcourt) have promised to tell the truth.

oats /əʊts/ *n* [pl] (grain from a) cereal plant grown as food. **'oatmeal** *n* [U] crushed oats.

obedient /ə'bi:dɪənt/ *adj* doing what one is told to do. **obedience** /-əns/ *n* [U]. **obediently** *adv*.

obelisk /'ɒbəlɪsk/ *n* [C] tall pointed stone pillar.

obese /əʊ'bi:s/ *adj* (*fml*) (of people) very fat. **obesity** *n* [U].

obey /ə'beɪ/ *v* [I, T] do what one is told to do by (sb).

obituary /ə'bɪtʃʊərɪ; *US* -tʃʊerɪ/ *n* [C] (*pl* -ies) report of a person's death in a newspaper, etc.

object¹ /'ɒbdʒɪkt/ *n* [C] 1 thing that can be seen or touched. 2 (*of*) person or thing to which an action, feeling, etc is directed: *an ~ of pity*. 3 purpose: *Our ~ is to win*. 4 (*grammar*) noun, phrase, etc towards which the action of a verb is directed, for example *him* and *the money* in: *Give him the money*. 5 (*idm*) **money, etc is no object** money, etc is not a problem.

object² /əb'dʒekt/ *v* [I] (*to*/*!*) say that one is against sth; protest.

objection /əb'dʒekʃn/ *n* 1 [C, U] statement or feeling of dislike or opposition. 2 [C] reason for disliking sth. **objectionable** /-ʃənəbl/ *adj* very unpleasant. **objection-**

ably adv.

objective /əb'dʒektɪv/ adj 1 not influenced by personal feelings: an ~ report. 2 (philosophy) having existence outside the mind; real. **objective** n[C] thing aimed at; purpose. **objectively** adv in an objective(1) manner. **objectivity** /ˌɒbdʒek'tɪvəti/ n[U].

obligation /ˌɒblɪ'geɪʃn/ n[C, U] 1 something that ought to be done; duty. 2 (idm) **be under no obligation to do sth** not have to do sth. **obligatory** /ə'blɪgətri; US -tɔːri/ adj that is required by law or custom.

oblige /ə'blaɪdʒ/ v 1 [T] to/(usu passive) require (sb) to do (sth): They were ~d to sell the house. 2 [I, T] do sth as a favour for (sb): Could you ~ me by closing the door? 3 (idm) **much obliged, I'm much obliged to you** (dated) thank you. **obliging** adj willing to help. **obligingly** adv.

oblique /ə'bliːk/ adj 1 sloping. 2 (fig) indirect: an ~ reference. **obliquely** adv.

obliterate /ə'blɪtəreɪt/ v[T] remove all traces of; destroy. **obliteration** /əˌblɪtə'reɪʃn/ n[U].

oblivion /ə'blɪvɪən/ n[U] state of being unaware of sth or of being forgotten.

oblivious /ə'blɪvɪəs/ adj of/to/ not aware of sth: ~ of the news ○ ~ to his problems.

oblong /'ɒblɒŋ; US 'ɒblɔːŋ/ n[C], adj (figure) with four straight sides and angles of 90°, longer than it is wide.

obnoxious /əb'nɒkʃəs/ adj very unpleasant.

oboe /'əʊbəʊ/ n[C] wooden instrument that one blows into to make sound. **oboist** n[C] oboe player.

obscene /əb'siːn/ adj shocking and offensive, esp sexually. **obscenely** adv. **obscenity** n[C, U](pl -ies) (instance of) obscene language or behaviour.

obscure /əb'skjʊə(r)/ adj 1 not easily seen or understood. 2 not well-known: an ~ poet. **obscure** v[T] make (sth) obscure(1): a hill ~d by fog. **obscurely** adv. **obscurity** n[U] state of being obscure.

observance /əb'zɜːvəns/ n 1 [U] keeping of a law, custom, festival, etc. 2 [C] part of a religious ceremony.

observant /əb'zɜːvənt/ adj quick at noticing things.

observation /ˌɒbzə'veɪʃn/ n 1 [U] observing: a doctor's ~ of a patient. 2 [U] ability to notice things:

keen powers of ~. 3 [C] remark. 4 (idm) **under obser'vation** being carefully watched, esp in a hospital or by the police.

observatory /əb'zɜːvətri; US -tɔːri/ n[C] (pl -ies) building in which scientists watch and study the stars, etc.

observe /əb'zɜːv/ v[T] 1 watch carefully. 2 (fml) obey (a rule, law, etc). 3 (fml) celebrate (a festival, birthday, etc). 4 (fml) comment, say. **observer** n[C] 1 person who observes. 2 person who attends a meeting to listen and watch but not to take part.

obsess /əb'ses/ v[T] (usu passive) fill the mind of (sb), so that he/she finds it difficult to think about other things: be ~ed by the fear of death. **obsession** /əb'seʃn/ n 1 [U] state of being obsessed. 2 [C] something (esp unreasonable) that fills sb's mind. **obsessive** adj of an obsession.

obsolescent /ˌɒbsə'lesnt/ adj becoming out of date. **obsolescence** /-'lesns/ n[U].

obsolete /'ɒbsəliːt/ adj no longer used; out of date.

obstacle /'ɒbstəkl/ n[C] (usu fig) something that stops progress or makes it difficult: an ~ to world peace.

obstetrics /əb'stetrɪks/ n (with sing v) branch of medicine concerned with childbirth. **obstetrician** /ˌɒbstə'trɪʃn/ n[C] doctor trained in obstetrics.

obstinate /'ɒbstənət/ adj 1 not willing to change one's opinion or chosen course of action. 2 difficult to remove or destroy: ~ stains. **obstinacy** /-nəsi/ n[U]. **obstinately** adv.

obstreperous /əb'strepərəs/ adj noisy and difficult to control: a class full of ~ children.

obstruct /əb'strʌkt/ v[T] 1 block: ~ a road. 2 prevent the progress of; put difficulties in the way of: ~ justice. **obstruction** /-kʃn/ n 1 [U] obstructing. 2 [C] something that obstructs. **obstructive** adj intending to obstruct.

obtain /əb'teɪn/ v[T] (fml) get: Where can I ~ the book? **obtainable** adj.

obtrusive /əb'truːsɪv/ adj very noticeable in an unpleasant way: a modern house which is ~ in an old village. **obtrusively** adv.

obtuse /əb'tjuːs/ adj 1 (fml derog) slow to understand; stupid. 2 (of an angle) between 90° and 180°. **obtusely** adv. **obtuseness** n[U].

obverse /'ɒbvɜːs/ n (usu sing) (fml) 1 main or front side of a coin,

etc. 2 opposite.
obvious /'ɒbvɪəs/ *adj* easily seen or understood; clear. **obviously** /-nəlɪ/ *adv.*

occasion /ə'keɪʒn/ *n* 1 [C] time at which a particular event happens. 2 [C] special event or celebration. 3 [U, sing] (*fml*) time that provides a reason for sth to happen: *I have had no ~ to visit them recently.* 5 (idm) **on oc'casion** sometimes. **occasion** *v* [T] (*fml*) cause.
occasional /ə'keɪʒənl/ *adj* happening sometimes, but not regularly: *an ~ drink/visit.* **occasionally** /-nəlɪ/ *adv.*
occidental /ˌɒksɪ'dentl/ *adj* (*fml*) of the countries of the West, ie Europe and America.
occult /ɒ'kʌlt; *US* ə'-/ *n* **the occult** [sing] supernatural or magical powers, practices, etc. **occult** *adj.*
occupant /'ɒkjʊpənt/ *n* [C] person who lives or works in a house or room. **occupancy** /-pənsɪ/ *n* [U] act or period of being an occupant.
occupation /ˌɒkjʊ'peɪʃn/ *n* 1 [C] job or profession. 2 [C] activity that fills one's time. 3 [U] action of taking possession of a country. **occupational** /-ʃənl/ *adj* of or connected with sb's job.
occupy /'ɒkjʊpaɪ/ *v* (*pt, pp* **-pied**) [T] 1 live in (a house, etc); be in. 2 take possession of (a country, town, etc). 3 fill (eg time, space or sb's mind). 4 hold or fill (a position). 5 ~ **oneself** be busy. **occupier** *n* [C] person who lives in a house or room.

occur /ə'kɜː(r)/ *v* (**-rr-**) [i] 1 happen: *The accident ~red in the rain.* 2 be found; exist: *Poverty ~s in every country.* 3 *to* (of an idea, etc) come into (sb's mind): *It never ~red to me that I should tell you.* **occurrence** /ə'kʌrəns/ *n* 1 [C] event. 2 [U] (*fml*) fact of sth happening.
ocean /'əʊʃn/ *n* **Ocean** [C] one of the very large areas of sea on the earth's surface: *the Pacific O~.* **oceanic** /ˌəʊʃɪ'ænɪk/ *adj.*
o'clock /ə'klɒk/ *adv* (used after numbers in telling the time) the hour mentioned: *It's 5 ~.*
octagon /'ɒktəgən; *US* -gɒn/ *n* [C] flat figure with eight sides and eight angles. **octagonal** /ɒk'tægənl/ *adj.*
octane /'ɒkteɪn/ *n* [U] a substance found in petrol used as a measure of its quality.
octave /'ɒktɪv/ *n* [C] (*music*) space between a note and the next note of the same name above or below it.

October /ɒk'təʊbə(r)/ *n* [U, C] the tenth month of the year. (See examples of use at *April*).
octopus /'ɒktəpəs/ *n* [C] sea-animal with a soft body and eight arms (= TENTACLES).
odd /ɒd/ *adj* 1 strange; unusual. 2 (of numbers) that cannot be divided by 2: *1, and 5 are ~ numbers.* 3 missing its pair or set: *an ~ sock/ shoe.* 4 a little more than (the number mentioned): *30~ years.* 5 (idm) **odd man/one 'out** person or thing that is different from the others in a group. **oddity** *n* (*pl* **-ies**) 1 [U] quality of being odd(1). 2 [C] strange or unusual thing or person. **odd 'jobs** *n* [pl] small jobs of various kinds. **odd 'job man** *n* [C] person paid to do odd jobs. **oddly** *adv* strangely.
oddment /'ɒdmənt/ *n* [C] something left over.
odds /ɒdz/ *n* [pl] 1 probability or chance that sth will or will not happen: *The ~ are (ie It is probable that) she'll win.* 2 (idm) **be at odds** be disagreeing. **it makes no 'odds** it is unimportant. **odds and 'ends** *n* [pl] (*Brit infml*) small articles of various kinds.
ode /əʊd/ *n* [C] (usu long) poem expressing noble feelings.
odious /'əʊdɪəs/ *adj* (*fml*) extremely unpleasant.
odour (*US* **odor**) /'əʊdə(r)/ *n* [C] (*fml*) smell.
oesophagus /i:'sɒfəgəs/ *n* [C] (*medical*) tube through which food passes from the mouth to the stomach.

of /əv/; strong form ɒv/ *prep* 1 belonging to (sb/sth): *a friend of mine ○ the lid of the box.* 2 coming from; living in (a place): *the miners of Wales.* 3 created by: *the works of Shakespeare.* 4 done about: *a picture of sb.* 5 (showing the material used for making sth): *a dress of silk.* 6 (showing a relationship): *a lover of music ○ the support of the voters.* 7 (showing a measure or time that is contained): *40 litres of petrol ○ a bottle of lemonade.* 8 (showing a part): *a member of the team.* 9 (showing distance in space or time): *20 kilometres south of Paris.* 10 (used in dates): *the first of May.* 11 (showing a cause): *die of cancer.* 12 (showing relief, separation, etc): *rob sb of sth.* 13 (*dated*) usually in: *go for a walk of an evening.*
off /ɒf/ *adv, prep* 1 at or to a point distant in space or time; away: *The town is still 5 miles ~.* 2 (showing removal or separation): *take one's hat ~.* 3 starting a journey: *He's ~ to France today.* 4

(*infml*) cancelled: *The wedding is* ~. **5** disconnected: *The electricity is* ~. **6** not being used: *The radio is* ~. **7** (of food in a restaurant) no longer available: *The soup is* ~. **8** away from work: *take the day* ~. **9** (idm) **off and 'on, ,on and 'off** sometimes.

off² /ɒf; US ɔːf/ *adj* **1** (*infml*) impolite or unfriendly: *He can be a bit* ~ *sometimes*. **2** (of food) no longer fresh: *The milk is* ~. **3** (*infml*) not as good as usual: *an* ~*-day*. **4** having little activity: *the* '~*-seas-on*. **5** (idm) **on the 'off-chance** with the slight possibility: *I went to his house on the* ~*-chance (that he'd be at home)*.

off³ /ɒf; US ɔːf/ *prep* **1** down or away from: *fall* ~ *a ladder* ○ *take a packet* ~ *the shelf* ○ (*fig*) *We're getting* ~ *the subject*. **2** (esp of a road) extending from: *a lane* ~ *the main road*. **3** at some distance from: *a house* ~ *the high street*. **4** (*infml*) not wanting or needing: ~ *one's food* ○ *He's* ~ *drugs now*.

offal /'ɒfl; US ɔːf/ *n* [U] inside parts of an animal used as food.

offence (*US* **-ense**) /ə'fens/ *n* **1** [C] breaking of a rule; crime. **2** [C] (cause of) hurting sb's feelings: *I didn't mean to give* ~, ie He is easily upset.

offend /ə'fend/ *v* **1** [T] hurt the feelings of; upset. **2** [T] displease: *ugly buildings that* ~ *the eye*. **3** [I] *against*|| (*fml*) do wrong to sth. **offender** *n* [C] person who breaks the law. **offending** *adj* causing a problem or difficulty.

offensive /ə'fensɪv/ *adj* **1** very unpleasant; insulting: ~ *language*. **2** (*fml*) used for attacking: ~ *weapons*. **offensive** *n* [C] **1** strong military attack. **2** (idm) **go on/take the offensive** start to attack. **offensively** *adv*. **offensiveness** *n* [U].

offer /'ɒfə(r); US ɔːf-/ *v* **1** [I] present (sth) to be accepted or refused: *They* ~*ed him a good job*. **2** [I, T] show that one is willing to do or give (sth): *I* ~*ed to go first*. **3** (*fml*) provide: *The job* ~*s good chances of promotion*. **offer** *n* [C] **1** statement offering to do or give sth. **2** something offered. **offering** *n* [C] something offered, esp to God.

offhand /,ɒf'hænd; US ɔːf-/ *adj* (of behaviour, etc) careless; impolite. **offhand** *adv* without previous thought: *I can't give you an answer* ~.

office /'ɒfɪs; US ɔːfɪs/ *n* **1** [C] room or building used as a place of

business, written work, etc. **2** [C] room or building used for a particular purpose: *a ticket* ~. **3** **Office** [sing] (building of a) government department: *The Foreign O~*. **4** [C, U] (work of an) important position of authority: *the* ~ *of president*.

officer /'ɒfɪsə(r); US ɔːf-/ *n* [C] **1** person in command in the armed forces: *an* ~ *in the navy*. **2** person with authority: *a customs* ~. **3** policeman or policewoman.

official /ə'fɪʃl/ *adj* **1** of a position of authority or trust. **2** said, done, etc with authority: *an* ~ *statement*. **official** *n* [C] person who holds an office(4). **officialdom** /-dəm/ *n* [U] (with sing or pl v) (*fml often derog*) officials as a group. **officially** /-ʃəlɪ/ *adv* in an official manner; formally.

officiate /ə'fɪʃɪeɪt/ *v* [I] (*at*) (*fml*) perform official duties at a ceremony.

officious /ə'fɪʃəs/ *adj* (*derog*) too eager to give orders. **officiously** *adv*. **officiousness** *n* [U].

offing /'ɒfɪŋ; US ɔːf-/ *n* (idm) **in the offing** (*infml*) likely to happen soon.

off-licence /'ɒf laɪsns/ *n* [C] (*Brit*) shop where alcoholic drinks are sold to be taken away.

off-peak /,ɒf 'piːk; US ɔːf/ *adj* in or used at a time that is less busy: ~ *travel*.

off-putting /,ɒf 'pʊtɪŋ; US ɔːf/ *adj* (esp *Brit infml*) causing dislike; unpleasant: *His manner is very* ~.

offset /'ɒfset; US ɔːf-/ *v* (**-tt-**, *pt*, *pp* **offset**) [T] balance (sth): *increase prices to* ~ *higher costs*.

offshoot /'ɒfʃuːt; US ɔːf-/ *n* [C] stem or branch growing from a main stem: (*fig*) *the* ~ *of a large organization*.

offshore /,ɒf'ʃɔː(r); US ɔːf-/ *adj*, *adv* **1** away from the shore: ~ *breezes*. **2** at a distance out to sea: *an* ~ *oil rig*.

offside /,ɒf'saɪd; US ɔːf-/ *adj*, *adv* (*sport*) (of a player) in a position in front of the ball, which is against the rules. **offside** *adj*, *n* [sing] (on the) side furthest away from the kerb.

offspring /'ɒfsprɪŋ; US ɔːf-/ *n* [C] (*pl* **offspring**) (*fml*) a person's child or children; young of animals.

off-white /,ɒf 'waɪt; US ɔːf 'hwaɪt/ *adj* not pure white, but with a slight grey or yellow colour.

often /'ɒfn, also 'ɒftən; US ɔːfn/ *adv* **1** many times; frequently: *We* ~ *go there*. **2** in many instances:

Old houses are ~ damp. **3** (idm) as ,often as 'not, more ,often than 'not very frequently. ,every so 'often sometimes.

ogle /ˈəʊgl/ *v* [I, T] (*at*)// (*derog*) look at (sb) with great sexual interest.

ogre /ˈəʊgə(r)/ *n* **1** (in stories) cruel frightening giant who eats people. **2** (*fig*) very frightening person: *Our teacher is a real ~.* **ogress** /ˈəʊgres/ female ogre.

oh /əʊ/ *interj* (used for showing surprise, fear, etc): *Oh dear!*

oil /ɔɪl/ *n* **1** [U] several thick slippery liquids that burn easily, used for fuel, food, etc. **2 oils** [pl] oil-colours. oil *v* [T] put oil on or into. '**oil-colour** *n* [C, U] paint made by mixing colouring matter in oil. '**oilfield** *n* [C] area where oil is found in the ground or under the sea. '**oil-painting** *n* [C] picture painted in oil-colours. '**oil rig** *n* [C] structure for drilling for oil. '**oilskin** *n* [C, U] (coat, etc made of) cloth treated with oil to make it waterproof. '**oil-slick** *n* [C] layer of oil on the sea, etc. '**oil well** *n* [C] hole drilled into the ground or seabed. **oily** *adj* (**-ier, -iest**) **1** of or like oil; covered with oil. **2** (*derog*) unpleasantly polite and flattering.

ointment /ˈɔɪntmənt/ *n* [C, U] smooth oily paste rubbed on the skin, esp to help it heal.

OK (also **okay**) /ˌəʊˈkeɪ/ *adj, adv* (*infml*) all right; satisfactory: *Was your holiday OK?* **OK** *interj* (*infml*) (used for showing agreement): *OK, I'll do it.* **OK** *v* [T] (*infml*) agree to; approve of: *I'll OK the plan if you make a few changes.* **OK** *n* [C] (*infml*) agreement; permission: *give a plan the OK.*

old /əʊld/ *adj* **1** of a particular age: *He's 40 years ~.* ○ *How ~ are you?* **2** having lived for a long time: *an ~ man.* **3** having been in existence or use for a long time: *~ shoes.* **4** belonging to past times: *~ habits.* **5** known for a long time: *an ~ friend.* **6** former: *~ boys/girls, ie former pupils.* **7** (idm) (**be) an old hand** (at sth) be very experienced in sth. **old 'hat** old-fashioned. **an old 'wives' tale** traditional (often foolish) belief. **the old** *n* [pl] old people. ,**old age 'pension** *n* [C] money paid regularly by the State to people above a certain age. ,**old-age 'pensioner** *n* [C] person who receives such money. ,**old-'fash-ioned** *adj* **1** out of date. **2** believing in old ways, etc. **old 'maid** *n* [C] (*infml derog*) unmarried woman thought to be too old for marriage. **old 'master** *n* [C] (picture by an)

important painter of the past.

olden /ˈəʊldən/ *adj* (*arch*) of a past age: *in the ~ days.*

olive /ˈɒlɪv/ *n* **1** [C] (tree of S Europe with a) small fruit, eaten raw or used for making cooking oil. **2** [U] yellowish-green colour. '**olive-branch** *n* [C] symbol of a wish for peace.

ombudsman /ˈɒmbʊdzmən/ also -mæn/ *n* [C] (*pl* -**men** /-mən/) person appointed by a government to consider complaints about public organizations.

omelette /ˈɒmlɪt/ *n* [C] eggs beaten together and fried.

omen /ˈəʊmen/ *n* [C] sign of sth good or bad in the future.

ominous /ˈɒmɪnəs/ *adj* suggesting that sth bad will happen. **ominously** *adv*.

omission /əˈmɪʃn/ *n* **1** [U] act of omitting. **2** [C] something omitted.

omit /əˈmɪt/ *v* (**-tt-**) [T] **1** not include; leave out. **2** *to*// (*fml*) fail to do sth: *I ~ted to mention his age.*

omnibus /ˈɒmnɪbəs/ *n* [C] **1** book containing several stories, esp by the same writer. **2** radio or television programme which contains two or more similar programmes previously broadcast separately. **3** (*dated fml*) bus.

omnipotent /ɒmˈnɪpətənt/ *adj* (*fml*) having unlimited power. **omnipotence** /-təns/ *n* [U].

omniscient /ɒmˈnɪsɪənt/ *adj* (*fml*) knowing everything. **omniscience** /-əns/ *n* [U].

omnivorous /ɒmˈnɪvərəs/ *adj* (*fml*) (of animals) eating meat and plants.

on[1] /ɒn/ *adv* **1** (showing continued activity or progress): *They wanted the band to play on.* **2** (showing movement forward in space or time): *walk on to the bus-stop* ○ *from that day on,* ie from then until now. **3** (of clothes) being worn: *Put your coat on.* ○ *He had nothing on.* **4** connected: *The electricity is on.* **5** being used: *The radio is on.* **6** planned to take place: *Is the strike still on?* ○ *What's on at the cinema?* ○ *Have you got anything* (ie any plans) *on for this evening?* **7** in or into a large vehicle: *get on the bus.* **8** with the stated part in front: *crash head-on.* **9** (idm) **be 'on** (*infml*) be acceptable: *Such bad behaviour isn't on.* **be/go/keep on about sth** (*infml*) talk in a boring way about sth. **on and off** ⇨ OFF[1]. ,**on and 'on** without stopping.

on[2] /ɒn/ *prep* **1** (in or into a position) covering, touching or forming part of (a surface): *a picture on the wall.* **2** supported by; attached to: *a roof on the house.* **3** in or into (a large vehicle): *on the train.* **4** being carried by; in the possession of: *Have you got any money on you?* **5** (used for showing a time): *on Sunday* ○ *on 1 May.* **6** at or immediately after the time of: *on arriving home.* **7** about: *a lecture on Bach.* **8** (showing membership of a group): *on the committee.* **9** by means of; using: *Most cars run on petrol.* ○ *speak on the telephone.* **10** (showing direction): *to march on Rome.* **11** very close to: *a town on the coast.* **12** (showing a reason): *arrested on a charge of theft.* **13** supported financially by: *live on a student grant.* **14** (showing the money concerned): *a tax on beer.* **15** (showing an activity or state): *go to Paris on business* ○ *on fire, is burning.*

once /wʌns/ *adv* **1** on one occasion only; (for) one time: *I've only been there* ~. **2** at some time in the past; formerly: *She* ~ *lived in Zambia.* **3** (idm) **at 'once (a)** immediately; without delay. **(b)** at the same time: *Don't all speak at* ~! ,**once and for 'all** now and for the last time. ,**once in a blue 'moon** (*infml*) very rarely. (every) ,**once 'more** again. ,**one or 'two** a few. ,**once 'up on sb** (*infml*) having an advantage over sb. **one** *n* [C] the number 1. ,**one-** '**off** *n* [C], *adj* (thing) made or happening only once. ,**one-'sided** *adj* **1** (esp of ideas) unfair: *a ,*~*sided 'argument.* **2** (esp in sport) with opposing players of unequal abilities. ,**one-parent 'family** *n* [C] family in which one parent brings up a child or children on his/her own. '**one-time** *adj* former. ,**one-to-'one** *adj, adv* between only two people: *a* ~*-to-~ relationship.* ,**one-'way** *adj, adv* (allowing movement) in one direction only: *a* ~*way street.*

one² /wʌn/ *pron* **1** (used instead of

a noun): *I forgot to bring a pen. Can you lend me* ~? ○ ○ **The** *blue hat is the* ~ *I like best.* ○ *The small car is just as fast as the big* ~. **2** *of*‖ (showing inclusion in a group): *He is not* ~ *of my customers.* **3** (*fml*) any person: *O* ~ *cannot always find the time for reading.* ,**one a'nother** each other: *They don't like* ~ *another.*

onerous /'ɒnərəs, 'əʊn-/ *adj* (*fml*) needing effort; difficult.

oneself /wʌn'self/ *pron* **1** (used as a reflexive when people in general cause and are also affected by an action): *wash* ~. **2** (used as emphasis): *One could arrange it all* ~. **3** (idm) **(all) by one'self (a)** alone. **(b)** without help.

ongoing /'ɒngəʊɪŋ/ *adj* continuing: ~ *research.*

onion /'ʌnɪən/ *n* [C, U] round vegetable with a strong smell and flavour, used in cooking.

onlooker /'ɒnlʊkə(r)/ *n* [C] person who watches sth happening.

only¹ /'əʊnlɪ/ *adj* **1** with no other(s) of the same group: *Jane was the* ~ *person able to do it.* **2** (*infml*) best: *He's the* ~ *person for the job.*

only² /'əʊnlɪ/ *adv* **1** and no one or nothing else: *I* ~ *saw 'Mary.* **2** (idm) **only 'just** almost not: *We* ~ *just caught the train.* **only too** ⇨ **TOO.**

only³ /'əʊnlɪ/ *conj* (*infml*) except that; but: *I'd love to come,* ~ *I have to work.*

onrush /'ɒnrʌʃ/ *n* [sing] (*fml*) sudden strong movement.

onset /'ɒnset/ *n* [sing] start (esp of sth unpleasant).

onshore /ɒn'ʃɔː(r)/ *adj, adv* towards the shore: ~ *winds.*

onslaught /'ɒnslɔːt/ *n* [C] (*on*)‖ fierce attack on sb/sth.

onto (also *on to*) /'ɒntə/ *prep* **1** to a position on: *climb* ~ *a horse.* **2** (idm) **be onto sb** pursue sb who is doing sth illegal. **be onto sth** have information that could lead to discovering sth important.

onus /'əʊnəs/ *n* [sing] (*fml*) duty or responsibility: *The* ~ *is on you.*

onward /'ɒnwəd/ *adj* forward: *an* ~ *movement.* **onward** (also **onwards**) *adv: move* ~*s.*

ooze /uːz/ *v* **1** [I] (of thick liquids) come or flow out slowly. **2** [I, T] allow (sth) to come out in this way: (*fig*) *She* ~*d charm.* **ooze** *n* [U] soft liquid mud.

opacity /əʊ'pæsətɪ/ *n* [U] (*fml*) quality of being opaque.

opal /'əʊpl/ *n* [C] bluish-white or milky-white semi-precious stone.

opaque /əʊ'peɪk/ *adj* **1** not allowing light to pass through. **2** (of language, writing, etc) not easily understood.

open¹ /'əʊpən/ adj **1** not closed: *leave the door ~*. **2** not enclosed: *~ fields*. **3** ready for business: *Are the shops ~ yet?* **4** spread out; unfolded: *The flowers were all ~*. **5** not fastened: *an ~ shirt*. **6** not covered: *an ~ car*, ie with no roof. **7** public; free to all. **8** known to all: *an ~ secret*. **9** willing to talk; honest. **10** not finally decided: *leave the matter ~*. **11** ~|| (a) willing to receive: *~ to new ideas*. (b) likely to receive: *~ to criticism*. **12** (idm) **have/keep an open 'mind** be willing to consider new ideas. **in the open air** outside (a building, etc). **with open 'arms** with great affection or enthusiasm. **the open** *n* [sing] **1** the open air. **2** (idm) **bring sth/be/come (out) in(to) the open** make (sth secret) known publicly: *bring the truth out into the ~* ◦ *a problem which is out in the ~*. ,**open-'air** *adj* taking place outside. ,**open-and-'shut** *adj* easily decided. ,**open 'cheque** *n* [C] cheque that is not crossed and may be exchanged for cash. ,**open-'ended** *adj* without any limits set in advance. ,**open-'handed** *adj* generous. **openly** *adv* not secretly. ,**open-'minded** *adj* willing to consider new ideas. **openness** *n* [U] honesty. ,**open-'plan** *adj* with no dividing walls. '**open-work** *n* [U] pattern with spaces between threads, etc.

open² /'əʊpən/ *v* **1** [I, T] become open: *The door ~ed.* ◦ *Please ~ a window.* **2** [T] make an opening in or a passage through: *~ a new road through the forest.* **3** [I, T] (cause to) spread out; unfold: *~ a book.* **4** [T] start: *~ a bank account.* **5** [I, T] (cause) to be ready for business: *When does the bank ~?* **6** (idm) **open one's/sb's eyes** make one/sb realize (sth). **open 'fire** start shooting. **7** (phr v) **open up** (*infml*) talk freely and openly. **open (sth) up** (cause sth to) be available for development, business, etc: *~ up possibilities.* **opener** /'əʊpnə(r)/ *n* [C] (usu in compounds) thing that opens: *tin-~er.*

opening /'əʊpnɪŋ/ *n* [C] **1** way in or out; open space. **2** [usu sing] beginning. **3** [sing] process of becoming or making open: *the ~ of the new library.* **4** position in a business company, etc that is not filled. **opening** *adj* first: *her ~ words.*

opera /'ɒprə/ *n* [C] musical play in which most of the words are sung. **operatic** /,ɒpə'rætɪk/ *adj*.

operate /'ɒpəreɪt/ *v* **1** [I, T] (cause sth to) work: *~ a machine.* **2** [I] have or produce an effect. **3** [I, T] do business; direct. **4** [I] perform a surgical operation. **operable** /'ɒpərəbl/ *adj* that can be treated by an operation(3). '**operating-theatre** *n* [C] room in a hospital for operations(3).

operation /,ɒpə'reɪʃn/ *n* **1** [U] working: *the ~ of the controls.* **2** [C] planned activity: *a rescue ~.* **3** [C] (*medical*) cutting of the body to remove a diseased or injured part. **4** [C] business company. **5** [C, usu pl] planned military movement. **6** (idm) **in(to) operation** in(to) a state of working or being used: *put our plans into ~.* **operational** /-ʃənl/ *adj* (*fml*) **1** of, for or used in operations. **2** ready for use.

operative /'ɒpərətɪv; US -reɪt'-/ *adj* (*fml*) operating; in use: *The law becomes ~ in July.* **operative** *n* [C] (*fml*) worker.

operator /'ɒpəreɪtə(r)/ *n* [C] person who works sth, esp a telephone switchboard.

operetta /,ɒpə'retə/ *n* [C] short light musical comedy.

opinion /ə'pɪnɪən/ *n* **1** [C] judgement or belief about sb/sth, esp one not based on fact or knowledge: *In my ~, the price is too high.* ◦ *his ~ of the new manager.* **2** [U] beliefs or views of a group of people: *public ~.* **3** [C] professional judgement or advice: *a doctor's ~.* **opinionated** /-eɪtɪd/ *adj* having opinions that one is not willing to change.

opium /'əʊpɪəm/ *n* [U] drug made from poppy seeds.

opponent /ə'pəʊnənt/ *n* [C] person who is against another in a fight, argument or game.

opportune /'ɒpətjuːn; US -tuːn/ *adj* (*fml*) **1** (of time) suitable for a purpose. **2** (of an action) coming at the right time.

opportunism /,ɒpə'tjuːnɪzəm; US -'tuːn-/ *n* [U] (*fml derog*) taking advantage of good opportunities, sometimes against the interests of others. **opportunist** /-ɪst/ *n* [C].

opportunity /,ɒpə'tjuːnətɪ; US -'tuːn-/ *n* [C, U] (*pl* -ies) favourable time or chance to do sth.

oppose /ə'pəʊz/ *v* [T] show one's strong disagreement with (sb/sth). **opposed** *adj* **1** to|| strongly against sth: *He is ~ed to our plans.* **2** (idm) **as opposed to** in contrast to.

opposite /'ɒpəzɪt/ *adj* **1** facing: *the house ~ (to) mine.* **2** complete-

ly different; contrary: *in the ~ di-*
rection. **opposite** *prep, adv* on the
other side of; facing: *~ the station*
○ *the person sitting ~.* **opposite**
n[C] word or thing that is completely different. **one's opposite**
number *n*[C] person occupying
the same position as oneself, but
in a different group, etc: *the*
President's ~ number from
France.

opposition /ˌɒpəˈzɪʃn/ *n* 1 [U]
state or action of opposing: *strong*
~ to the new law. 2 [sing, also sing
with pl *v*] **(a)** people who oppose
sb. **(b)** the **Opposition** (esp *Brit*)
political parties opposing the
government.

oppress /əˈpres/ *v* [T] 1 rule or
treat unjustly or cruelly. 2 make
(sb) feel uncomfortable, unhappy,
etc: *~ed by the heat.* **oppression**
/əˈpreʃn/ *n* [U, c]. **oppressive** *adj*
1 unjust; cruel. 2 hard to bear; uncomfortable: *~ive heat.* **oppress-**
or *n* [C] cruel or unjust leader or
ruler.

opt /ɒpt/ *v* 1 [T] *to//* choose to do
sth: *He ~ed to go to Paris.* 2 (phr *v*)
opt for sth choose to do sth. **opt**
for that plan. opt out (of sth) choose
not to take part (in sth).

optic /ˈɒptɪk/ *adj* (*fml*) of the
eyes: *the ~ nerve.* **optical** /-kl/
adj of the sense of sight. **optical**
il'lusion *n*[C] something by
which the eyes are deceived. **op-**
tician /ɒpˈtɪʃn/ *n* [C] person who
makes or sells glasses and contact
lenses.

optimism /ˈɒptɪmɪzəm/ *n* [U] belief that good things will happen.
optimist /-mɪst/ *n* [C]. **optimis-**
tic /ˌɒptɪˈmɪstɪk/ *adj*.

optimize /ˈɒptɪmaɪz/ *v* [T] make
as effective or favourable as possible.

optimum /ˈɒptɪməm/ *adj* (*fml*)
most favourable; best: *the ~ price.*

option /ˈɒpʃn/ *n* 1 [U] right or
freedom to choose. 2 [C] something that may be chosen. **option-**
al /-ʃənl/ *adj* that may be chosen
or not chosen.

opulent /ˈɒpjʊlənt/ *adj* (*fml*)
showing signs of great wealth. **op-**
ulence /-ləns/ *n* [U].

or /ɔː(r)/ *conj* 1 (introducing an alternative): *Is it green or blue?* ○ *Do*
you want tea, coffee or milk? 2 if
not; otherwise: *Turn the heat*
down or the cake will burn. 3 in
other words: *It weighs one pound,*
or about 450 grams. 4 (idm) **or**
'else (*infml*) (used as a threat) or
something bad will happen: *Do it,*
or else I'll hit you! **or so** about: *We*
stayed there an hour or so.

oral /ˈɔːrəl/ *adj* 1 spoken, not
written: *an ~ test.* 2 of, by or for
the mouth: *~ medicine.* **oral** *n* [C]
a spoken examination. **orally**
adv.

orange /ˈɒrɪndʒ; *US* ˈɔːr-/ *n* [C]
round thick-skinned juicy red-
dish-yellow fruit. **orange** *adj* red-
dish-yellow in colour.

orang-utan (also **orang-outan**
/ɔːˌræŋuːˈtæn; *US* əˌræŋəˈtæn/
(also **orang-outang** /-uːˈtæŋ/)
n[C] large ape with long arms.

oration /ɔːˈreɪʃn/ *n* [C] (*fml*) formal public speech.

orator /ˈɒrətə(r); *US* -ɔːr-/ *n* [C]
(*fml*) person who makes formal
public speeches. **oratory**
/ˈɒrətrɪ; *US* ˈɔːrətɔːrɪ/ *n* [U] art of
skilful public speaking.

orbit /ˈɔːbɪt/ *n* [C] 1 path of eg a
planet or satellite round the earth,
sun, etc. 2 (*fig*) area of influence.
orbit *v* [I, T] move in an orbit
round (sth). **orbital** /-tl/ *adj*.

orchard /ˈɔːtʃəd/ *n* [C] piece of
land on which fruit trees are
grown.

orchestra /ˈɔːkɪstrə/ *n* [C, also
sing with pl *v*] group of people
playing different musical instruments together. **orchestral**
/ɔːˈkestrəl/ *adj*. **orchestrate**
/-streɪt/ *v* [T] 1 arrange (music) to
be played by an orchestra. 2 organize carefully to bring about a
result. **orchestration** /ˌɔːkɪ-
streɪʃn/ *n* [C, U].

orchid /ˈɔːkɪd/ *n* [C] plant with
flowers of brilliant colours and
unusual shapes.

ordain /ɔːˈdeɪn/ *v* [T] 1 make (sb)
a member of the clergy. 2 (*fml*) (of
God, the law, etc) order.

ordeal /ɔːˈdiːl, ˈɔːdiːl/ *n* [C] difficult or painful experience.

order[1] /ˈɔːdə(r)/ *n* 1 [U] way in
which things are arranged in relation to one another: *names in*
alphabetical ~ ○ *arranged in ~ of*
size. 2 [U] condition in which
everything is carefully arranged.
3 [U] condition of working properly: *The machine is out of ~.* 4 [U]
(condition of) obedience to laws. 5
[C] command given with authority. 6 [C] **(a)** request to supply
goods: *Send the shop your ~ for*
books. **(b)** goods supplied: *Your ~*
will arrive tomorrow. 7 [C] written
instruction (esp to a bank or post
office) to pay money. 8 [U] system
of rules for a public meeting: *a*
point of ~. 9 [C] (*fml*) kind; sort:
skills of the highest ~. 10 [C]
(badge, etc worn by) group of
people who are specially ho-
noured: *~s and medals.* 11 (idm)

in 'order as it should be: *Your passport is in ~.* **in the order of** (*fml*) about: *It will cost in the ~ of £60.* **in order that** (*fml*) so that. **in order to do sth with** to be capable of doing sth. **on 'order** asked for, but not yet supplied. **take (holy) orders** become a member of the clergy.

order² /'ɔːdə(r)/ *v* 1 [T] command: *He ~ed the soldiers to attack.* 2 [I, T] ask for sb to supply (sth): *to ~ a new carpet.* 3 [T] (*fml*) arrange. 4 (*phr v*) **order sb about** keep telling sb what to do in an unkind way.

orderly /'ɔːdəlɪ/ *adj* 1 well-arranged; tidy. 2 well-behaved; peaceful: *an ~ crowd.* **orderliness** *n* [U]. **orderly** *n* (*pl* **-ies**) attendant in a hospital.

ordinal /'ɔːdɪnl; *US* -dənl/ (also **,ordinal 'number**) *n* [C] number, eg *first, second* and *third,* showing order in a series.

ordinary /'ɔːdnrɪ; *US* 'ɔːrd-ənerɪ/ *adj* 1 normal; usual. 2 (idm) **out of the 'ordinary** unusual. **ordinarily** /-rəlɪ; *US* ,ɔːrd-n'erəlɪ/ *adv* usually.

ordination /,ɔːdɪ'neɪʃn; *US* ,ɔːd-n'eɪʃn/ *n* [C, U] ceremony of making a person a member of the clergy.

ore /ɔː(r)/ *n* [U, C] rock or earth from which metal can be obtained.

organ¹ /'ɔːgən/ *n* [C] 1 part of an animal body or plant that has a particular purpose: *The eye is the ~ of sight.* 2 organization which serves a special purpose: *Parliament is an organ of government.* 3 (*fml*) newspaper, etc that supplies information.

organ² /'ɔːgən/ *n* [C] large musical instrument from which sounds are produced by air forced through pipes. **organist** *n* [C] player of an organ.

organic /ɔː'gænɪk/ *adj* 1 of, found in or formed by living things. 2 (of food, etc) produced without using chemicals. 3 (*fml*) made of related parts. **organically** /-klɪ/ *adv.*

organism /'ɔːgənɪzəm/ *n* [C] 1 (usu very small) living being. 2 (*fml*) system with parts dependent on each other.

organization /,ɔːgənaɪ'zeɪʃn; *US* -nɪ'z-/ *n* 1 [C] group of people, eg in a club or business, with a particular purpose. 2 [U] act of organizing.

organize /'ɔːgənaɪz/ *v* [T] 1 make preparations for: *~ a party.* 2 arrange in a system that works well: *~ one's time.*

orgasm /'ɔːgæzəm/ *n* [C] point of feeling greatest sexual pleasure.

orgy /'ɔːdʒɪ/ *n* [C] (*pl* **-ies**) wild party with a lot of drinking and sexual activity.

orient /'ɔːrɪənt/ *n* **the Orient** [sing] (*fml* or *rhet*) counties of the (Far) East, eg China and Japan. **oriental** /,ɔːrɪ'entl/ *adj* of or from the Orient.

orientate /'ɔːrɪənteɪt/ (esp *US* **orient** /'ɔːrɪent/) *v* 1 [T] (usu passive) direct (sth) towards a particular purpose: *Our company is ~d towards exports.* 2 **~ oneself** make oneself familiar with one's surroundings. **orientation** /,ɔːrɪən'teɪʃn/ *n* [U, C].

orifice /'ɒrɪfɪs/ *n* [C] (*fml*) outer opening, esp in the body.

origin /'ɒrɪdʒɪn/ *n* 1 [C, U] starting-point. 2 [C, esp pl] person's parents, background, etc: *of Polish ~.*

original /ə'rɪdʒənl/ *adj* 1 first or earliest. 2 (a) (usu *approv*) newly created; fresh: *~ designs.* (b) able to produce new ideas: *an ~ thinker.* 3 not copied. **original** *n* **the original** [C] the earliest form of sth, from which copies can be made. **originality** /ə,rɪdʒə-'næletɪ/ *n* [U] quality of being original(2). **originally** /-nəlɪ/ *adv* 1 in an original(2) way. 2 from or in the beginning: *His shirt was ~ly white.*

originate /ə'rɪdʒɪneɪt/ *v* [I, T] (*fml*) begin. **originator** *n* [C].

ornament /'ɔːnəmənt/ *n* 1 [C] object that is beautiful rather than useful. 2 [U] (*fml*) decoration. **ornament** /-ment/ *v* [T] decorate. **ornamental** /,ɔːnə'mentl/ *adj.*

ornate /ɔː'neɪt/ *adj* having a lot of decoration. **ornately** *adv.*

ornithology /,ɔːnɪ'θɒlədʒɪ/ *n* [U] study of birds. **ornithologist** *n* [C].

orphan /'ɔːfn/ *n* [C] child whose parents are dead. **orphan** *v* [T] cause to be an orphan. **orphanage** /'ɔːfənɪdʒ/ *n* [C] place where orphans live.

orthodox /'ɔːθədɒks/ *adj* (having opinions that are) generally accepted. **orthodoxy** *n* [U, C] (*pl* **-ies**).

orthography /ɔː'θɒɡrəfɪ/ *n* [U] (*fml*) (study or system of) spelling.

orthopaedics (also **-pedics**) /,ɔːθə'piːdɪks/ *n* (with *sing v*) branch of medicine that deals with problems and diseases of bones. **orthopaedic** (also **-pedic**) *adj.*

oscillate /'ɒsɪleɪt/ *v* [I] (*fml*) 1 move regularly from one position to another and back again. 2 (*fig*) keep changing between extremes of feeling or opinion. **oscillation** /ˌɒsɪˈleɪʃn/ *n* [C, U] (*fml*).

ostensible /ɒˈstensəbl/ *adj* (*fml*) given (as a reason, etc) though perhaps not the real one. **ostensibly** *adv*.

ostentation /ˌɒstenˈteɪʃn/ *n* [U] (*derog*) show of wealth, importance, etc in order to impress people. **ostentatious** /-ˈʃəs/ *adj*.

ostracize /ˈɒstrəsaɪz/ *v* [Tn] refuse to talk to, meet, etc (sb); exclude.

ostrich /ˈɒstrɪtʃ/ *n* [C] very large African bird with a long neck and long legs but not able to fly.

other /ˈʌðə(r)/ *adj* 1 (person or thing) additional to that already mentioned: *Tim, John and two ~ students were there.* 2 the second of two: *Pull the cork out with your ~ hand.* 3 remaining: *The ~ teachers are from Brunei.* **others** *pron* 1 people or things that are additional to or different from those already mentioned. 2 the remaining people or things in a group: *I went swimming while the ~s played tennis.* **other than** *prep* except: *She never speaks to me ~ than to ask for something.*

otherwise /ˈʌðəwaɪz/ *adv* 1 (*fml*) in a different way. 2 in other respects; apart from that: *The rent is high, but ~ the room is satisfactory.* **otherwise** *conj* if not: *We must run, ~ we'll be late.*

otter /ˈɒtə(r)/ *n* [C] fur-covered animal that lives in rivers and eats fish.

ouch /aʊtʃ/ *interj* (used for expressing sudden pain): *Ouch! That hurt!*

ought /ɔːt/ *modal v* (*neg* **ought not** *or* **oughtn't** /ˈɔːtnt/) *to*|| 1 (used for showing duty or obligation): *You ~ to say you're sorry.* 2 (used for showing advice): *You ~ to see a doctor about that cough.* 3 (used for showing probability): *She started early, so she ~ to be here by now.*

ounce /aʊns/ *n* 1 [C] unit of weight; one sixteenth of a pound (28.35 grams). 2 [sing] (*infml*) small amount.

our /ɑː(r), ˈaʊə(r)/ *adj* belonging to us: *~ house.* **ours** /ɑːz, ˈaʊəz/ *pron* of or belonging to us: *That's ~s.*

ourselves /ɑːˈselvz, ˌaʊəˈselvz/ *pron* 1 (used as a reflexive when I and others cause and are affected by an action): *We dried ~.* 2 (used for emphasis): *We saw the crash ~.* 3 (*idm*) **(all) by our'selves (a)** alone. **(b)** without help.

oust /aʊst/ *v* [Tn] (*from*)|| (*fml*) force (sb) to leave a job, etc.

out /aʊt/ *adv* 1 away from or not inside a place: *come ~ for some fresh air.* 2 not at home or at a place of work: *I phoned her but she was ~.* 3 (showing distance away from land, a town, etc): *The boats were all ~ at sea.* 4 not hidden or covered: *The secret is ~.* 5 no longer fashionable: *Short skirts are ~.* 6 (of the tide) away from the shore. 7 on strike: *The teachers are ~ again.* 8 (of fire, lights, etc) no longer burning. 9 to the end; completely: *I'm tired ~.* 10 clearly and loudly: *shout ~.* 11 (showing a mistake): *I'm ~ in my calculations.* 12 (*sport*) **(a)** no longer batting. **(b)** (of a ball) outside the line. 13 (*idm*) **be out to do sth** be trying to do sth: *I'm not ~ to change the world!* **out-and-'out** *adj* complete. **out of** *prep* 1 (situated) at a distance from: *Fish cannot live ~ of water.* 2 (moving) away from: *walk ~ of the room.* 3 (showing a motive or cause): *They helped us ~ of kindness.* 4 from among: *in nine cases ~ of ten.* 5 by using: *made ~ of wood.* 6 without: *~ of breath.* 7 not in the condition mentioned: *~ of order.* 8 having (sth) as its origin: *a story ~ of books.* 9 at a certain distance from: *a mile ~ of Hull.*

outboard /ˈaʊtbɔːd/ *adj* fixed to the outside of a boat: *~ motor.*

outbreak /ˈaʊtbreɪk/ *n* [C] sudden appearance or start: *the ~ of war.*

outbuilding /ˈaʊtbɪldɪŋ/ *n* [C] building separate from the main building.

outburst /ˈaʊtbɜːst/ *n* [C] sudden strong expression, esp of anger.

outcast /ˈaʊtkɑːst; *US* -kæst/ *n* [C] person sent away from home or society.

outcome /ˈaʊtkʌm/ *n* [C, usu sing] effect or result.

outcrop /ˈaʊtkrɒp/ *n* [C] (*geology*) layer of rock that sticks out of the ground.

outcry /ˈaʊtkraɪ/ *n* [C] (*pl* **-ies**) strong public protest.

outdated /ˌaʊtˈdeɪtɪd/ *adj* no longer in use.

outdo /ˌaʊtˈduː/ *v* (*3rd pers sing pres t* **-does** /-ˈdʌz/, *pt* **-did** /-ˈdɪd/, *pp* **-done** /-ˈdʌn/) [Tn] do more or better than: *She tries to ~ her friends at games.*

outdoor /ˈaʊtdɔː(r)/ *adj* done or situated outside a building. **outdoors** /ˌaʊtˈdɔːz/ *adv* out or outside a building.

outer /'aʊtə(r)/ adj 1 of or for the outside: ~ *walls*. 2 farther from the inside: *the* ~ *suburbs*. **outermost** adj farthest from the inside. ,outer 'space = SPACE 5.

outfit /'aʊtfɪt/ n [C] 1 clothing or equipment needed for a purpose. 2 (*infml*) organization. **outfitter** n [C] shop or shopkeeper selling clothes.

outflank /,aʊt'flæŋk/ v [T] go round the side of (an enemy) in order to attack.

outgoing /,aʊt'gəʊɪŋ/ adj 1 leaving: *the* ~ *president*. 2 friendly. **outgoings** n [pl] amount of money spent.

outgrow /,aʊt'grəʊ/ v (pt **-grew** /-'gruː/, pp **-grown** /-'grəʊn/) [T] 1 grow too big for (esp one's clothes). 2 stop doing (bad habits, etc) as one grows older.

outhouse /'aʊthaʊs/ n [C] (pl ~**s** /-haʊzɪz/) small building next to the main building.

outing /'aʊtɪŋ/ n [C] short journey for pleasure.

outlandish /aʊt'lændɪʃ/ adj (esp *derog*) strange; shocking: ~ *clothes*. **outlandishly** adv.

outlaw /'aʊtlɔː/ n [C] (esp formerly) person who has broken the law and is hiding to avoid being caught. **outlaw** v [T] declare to be illegal: ~ *the sale of guns*.

outlay /'aʊtleɪ/ n [C] amount of money spent on sth.

outlet /'aʊtlet/ n [C] 1 way out for water, etc. 2 (*fig*) way of showing one's feelings, using one's energy, etc: *sport is an* ~ *for energy*.

outline /'aʊtlaɪn/ n [C] 1 line showing the shape (of sth). 2 statement of the main facts: *an* ~ *of the plan*. **outline** v [T] give a short general description of.

outlive /,aʊt'lɪv/ v [T] live longer than: ~ *one's children*.

outlook /'aʊtlʊk/ n [C] 1 person's way of looking at life; attitude. 2 what seems likely to happen.

outlying /'aʊtlaɪɪŋ/ adj far from a centre or city: ~ *villages*.

outmoded /,aʊt'məʊdɪd/ adj no longer fashionable.

outnumber /,aʊt'nʌmbə(r)/ v [T] be greater in number than.

out of date ⇨ DATE[1].

outpatient /'aʊtpeɪʃnt/ n [C] person who goes to a hospital for treatment, but does not stay there.

outpost /'aʊtpəʊst/ n [C] 1 (soldiers at an) observation post far from the main army. 2 distant settlement.

output /'aʊtpʊt/ n [sing] 1 quantity of goods, etc produced. 2 something that is got out, eg information from a computer.

outrage /'aʊtreɪdʒ/ n 1 [C, U] (act of) great violence. 2 [C] act that shocks public opinion. 3 [U] strong anger. **outrage** v [T] shock greatly. **outrageous** /aʊt'reɪdʒəs/ adj 1 very shocking. 2 very unusual. **outrageously** adv.

outright /'aʊtraɪt/ adv 1 openly and honestly: *I told him* ~ *what I thought*. 2 not gradually; immediately: *be killed* ~. 3 clearly and completely: *He won* ~. **outright** adj without any doubt; clear: *the* ~ *winner*.

outset /'aʊtset/ n (idm) **at/from the outset** at/from the beginning.

outshine /,aʊt'ʃaɪn/ v (pt, pp **outshone** /-'ʃɒn/) [T] (*fig*) be much better than: *She* ~ *s all her friends at games*.

outside /,aʊt'saɪd/ n [C, usu sing] outer side or surface: *the* ~ *of the house*. **outside** /'aʊtsaɪd/ adj 1 of, on or facing the outer side. 2 not connected with a group, etc: ~ *help*. 3 very small: *an* ~ *chance*. **outside** adv on or to the outside; in the open air: *Please wait* ~. **outside** (also esp US **outside of**) prep 1 on or to a place on the outside of: ~ *the bank*. 2 not within the limits of: ~ *my areas of responsibility*. 3 except for: *no interests* ~ *his work*.

outsider /,aʊt'saɪdə(r)/ n [C] 1 person who is not a member of or not accepted by a group of people. 2 horse, team, etc that is not expected to win a competition.

outsize /'aʊtsaɪz/ adj (esp of clothing) larger than the standard sizes.

outskirts /'aʊtskɜːts/ n [pl] outer areas of a city or town.

outsmart /,aʊt'smɑːt/ v [T] defeat (sb) by being cleverer than him/her.

outspoken /,aʊt'spəʊkən/ adj saying freely what one thinks.

outstanding /,aʊt'stændɪŋ/ adj 1 much better than others; excellent. 2 easily noticed. 3 not yet paid or done. **outstandingly** adv.

outstay /,aʊt'steɪ/ v (idm) **outstay one's welcome** stay too long as a guest.

outstrip /aʊt'strɪp/ v (**-pp-**) [T] do better than; be bigger than: *Demand is* ~*ping production*.

outward /'aʊtwəd/ adj 1 (of a journey) going out: *the* ~ *flight*. 2 of or on the outside: *an* ~ *appearance*. **outward** (also **outwards**) adv towards the outside; away from home. **outwardly** adv on the surface; apparently.

outweigh /,aʊt'weɪ/ v [T] be more important than.

outwit /ˌaʊt'wɪt/ v (-tt-) [T] defeat (sb) by being cleverer than him/her.

outworn /ˌaʊt'wɔːn/ adj no longer useful; old-fashioned.

oval /'əʊvl/ n [C], adj (shape) like an egg.

ovary /'əʊvərɪ/ n [C] (pl -ies) (anatomy) either of the two organs in female animals that produce eggs.

ovation /əʊ'veɪʃn/ n [C] enthusiastic expression of approval by clapping and cheering.

oven /'ʌvn/ n [C] enclosed box-like space in which food is cooked or heated.

over¹ /'əʊvə(r)/ prep 1 resting on and covering: spill oil ~ one's clothes. 2 in or to a position higher than but not touching: They held an umbrella ~ her. 3 (a) from one side of (sth) to the other: a bridge ~ the river. (b) on the far side of. (c) so as to cross (sth): jump ~ the wall. 4 in or across every part or most parts of: travel all ~ Africa. 5 more than: wait for ~ an hour. 6 (showing control, command, etc): rule ~ an empire. 7 while doing, eating, etc: discuss it ~ lunch. 8 because of: an argument ~ money. 9 by means of: hear it ~ the radio/ telephone. 10 (idm) ,over and a'bove in addition to. over one's 'head ⇔ HEAD¹.

over² /'əʊvə(r)/ adv 1 outwards and downwards from an upright position: knock a vase ~. 2 from one side to another side: turn a page ~. 3 across (a road, open space, etc): Take this letter ~ to the post office. 4 (esp US) again: do it ~. 5 remaining: the food left ~. 6 in addition; more: children of 14 and ~. 7 ended: The meeting is ~. 8 so as to cover: paint sth ~. 9 (idm) (all) over a'gain once more. ,over and ,over a'gain many times.

over³ /'əʊvə(r)/ n [C] (in cricket) series of six balls bowled in succession by the same bowler.

over- prefix 1 across; above: ~ land ○ ~ head. 2 too much: ~ eat ○ ~ work.

overall¹ /ˌəʊvər'ɔːl/ adj, adv including everything: the ~ cost.

overall² /'əʊvərɔːl/ n 1 [C] (Brit) loose coat worn over other clothing to protect it. 2 **overalls** [pl] (Brit) one-piece garment covering the body and legs, worn over other clothing to protect it.

overawe /ˌəʊvər'ɔː/ v [T] (usu passive) cause (sb) to feel great respect or fear.

overbalance /ˌəʊvə'bæləns/ v [I]

fall over.

overbearing /ˌəʊvə'beərɪŋ/ adj (derog) forcing others to do what one wants. **overbearingly** adv.

overboard /'əʊvəbɔːd/ adv over the side of a ship into the water.

overcast /ˌəʊvə'kɑːst; US 'əʊvərkæst/ adj (of the sky) covered with cloud.

overcharge /ˌəʊvə'tʃɑːdʒ/ v [I, T] charge (sb) too high a price.

overcoat /'əʊvəkəʊt/ n [C] thick warm coat.

overcome /ˌəʊvə'kʌm/ v (pt -came /-'keɪm/, pp -come) [T] 1 defeat. 2 make weak: ~ by/with sadness.

overcrowded /ˌəʊvə'kraʊdɪd/ adj with too many people in a place. **overcrowding** /-dɪŋ/ n [U].

overdo /ˌəʊvə'duː/ v (3rd pers sing pres t -does /-'dʌz/, pt -did /-'dɪd/, pp -done /-'dʌn/) 1 [T] do (sth) too much; exaggerate. 2 (idm) **over'do** it work, etc too hard.

overdose /'əʊvədəʊs/ n [C, usu sing] too much of a drug.

overdraft /'əʊvədrɑːft; US -dræft/ n [C] amount of money by which a bank account is overdrawn.

overdrawn /ˌəʊvə'drɔːn/ adj 1 (of a person) having an overdraft. 2 (of an account) having more money taken out than it contains.

overdrive /'əʊvədraɪv/ n [C, U] device providing an extra gear above the normal top gear in a car.

overdue /ˌəʊvə'djuː; US -'duː/ adj not paid, arrived, returned, etc by the right or expected time.

overflow /ˌəʊvə'fləʊ/ v [I, T] 1 flow over the edges of (sth): The river has ~ed it banks. 2 go beyond the limits of (a room, etc). **overflow** /'əʊvəfləʊ/ n [C] 1 [usu sing] something that overflows. 2 pipe for letting out extra water, etc.

overgrown /ˌəʊvə'grəʊn/ adj covered with plants that are growing thickly in an uncontrolled way.

overhang /ˌəʊvə'hæŋ/ v (pt, pp -hung /-'hʌŋ/) [I, T] hang over or stand out over (sth). **overhang** /'əʊvəhæŋ/ n [C, usu sing] part that overhangs.

overhaul /ˌəʊvə'hɔːl/ v [T] examine thoroughly and repair any faults: ~ the engine. **overhaul** /'əʊvəhɔːl/ n [C, usu sing] thorough examination, etc.

overhead /'əʊvəhed/ adj raised above the ground: ~ wires. **overhead** /ˌəʊvə'hed/ adv above one's head: aircraft flying ~.

overheads /ˈəʊvəhedz/ n [pl] regular business expenses, eg rent, salaries and insurance.

overhear /ˌəʊvəˈhɪə(r)/ v (pt, pp **-heard** /-ˈhɜːd/) [T] hear (what sb is saying) without him/her knowing.

overjoyed /ˌəʊvəˈdʒɔɪd/ adj extremely happy.

overland /ˈəʊvəlænd/ adj, adv across the land; by land (not by sea or air).

overlap /ˌəʊvəˈlæp/ v (-pp-) [I, T] partly cover (sth) by going over its edge: (fig) These two subjects ~. **overlap** /ˈəʊvəlæp/ n [C, U] part that overlaps.

overleaf /ˌəʊvəˈliːf/ adv on the other side of the page.

overload /ˌəʊvəˈləʊd/ v [T] 1 put too great a weight on. 2 put too great an electric current through.

overlook /ˌəʊvəˈlʊk/ v [T] 1 have a view of (a place) from above. 2 fail to notice; miss. 3 allow to pass without punishing: ~ a fault.

overmanned /ˌəʊvəˈmænd/ adj having more workers than are needed. **overmanning** /-nɪŋ/ n [U].

overnight /ˌəʊvəˈnaɪt/ adv 1 during or for the night: stay ~. 2 (infml) very quickly; suddenly: become a success ~. **overnight** /ˈəʊvənaɪt/ adj: an ~ bag.

overpass /ˈəʊvəpɑːs; US /ˈəʊvəpæs/ n [C] (esp US) bridge that carries one road over another.

overpower /ˌəʊvəˈpaʊə(r)/ v [T] defeat by greater strength. **overpowering** adj too strong; very powerful: an ~ing smell.

overrate /ˌəʊvəˈreɪt/ v [T] have too good an opinion of.

overreach /ˌəʊvəˈriːtʃ/ v [T] ~ oneself fail by trying to achieve more than is possible.

over-react /ˌəʊvərɪˈækt/ v [I] behave too strongly as a result of sth.

override /ˌəʊvəˈraɪd/ v (pt **-rode** /-ˈrəʊd/, pp **-ridden** /-ˈrɪdn/) [T] 1 take no notice of (sb's opinion, etc). 2 be more important than. **overriding** adj more important than anything else.

overrule /ˌəʊvəˈruːl/ v [T] decide against (sth already decided) by using one's higher authority.

overrun /ˌəʊvəˈrʌn/ v (pt **-ran** /-ˈræn/, pp **-run**) 1 [T] spread over and occupy: a house ~ by insects. 2 [I, T] continue beyond (a time limit): The meeting might ~.

overseas /ˌəʊvəˈsiːz/ adj, adv (at, to or from places) across the sea.

oversee /ˌəʊvəˈsiː/ v (pt **-saw** /-ˈsɔː/, pp **-seen** /-ˈsiːn/) [T] watch over (work) to see that it is done

properly. **overseer** /ˈəʊvəsɪə(r)/ n [C].

overshadow /ˌəʊvəˈʃædəʊ/ v [T] 1 cause (sth) to be shaded. 2 (fig) cause to seem less important or happy.

overshoot /ˌəʊvəˈʃuːt/ v (pt, pp **-shot** /-ˈʃɒt/) [T] go further or beyond (a place aimed at).

oversight /ˈəʊvəsaɪt/ n [C, U] careless failure to notice sth.

oversleep /ˌəʊvəˈsliːp/ v (pt, pp **-slept** /-ˈslept/) [I] sleep longer than one intended to.

overspill /ˈəʊvəspɪl/ n [U] (esp Brit) people from a crowded city who are moved to better houses elsewhere.

overstep /ˌəʊvəˈstep/ v (-pp-) [T] go beyond (the normal accepted limit).

overt /ˈəʊvɜːt; US /əʊˈvɜːrt/ adj (fml) done or shown openly: ~ hostility. **overtly** adv.

overtake /ˌəʊvəˈteɪk/ v (pt **-took** /-ˈtʊk/, pp **-taken** /-ˈteɪkən/) 1 [I, T] come level with and pass (a moving vehicle or person). 2 [T] (of unpleasant events) come to (sb) suddenly and unexpectedly.

overthrow /ˌəʊvəˈθrəʊ/ v (pt **-threw** /-ˈθruː/, pp **-thrown** /-ˈθrəʊn/) [T] remove (a government, ruler, etc) from power. **overthrow** /ˈəʊvəθrəʊ/ n [C].

overtime /ˈəʊvətaɪm/ n [U], adv (time spent at work) in addition to one's usual working hours.

overtone /ˈəʊvətəʊn/ n [C, usu pl] something suggested but not expressed openly.

overture /ˈəʊvətjʊə(r)/ n 1 [C] musical introduction to an opera, etc. 2 (idm) **make overtures to sb** try to begin a friendly relationship with sb.

overturn /ˌəʊvəˈtɜːn/ v 1 [I, T] turn over. 2 [T] decide against (sth already decided) by using one's higher authority. 3 [T] remove (a government, etc) from power.

overview /ˈəʊvəvjuː/ n [C] short general description.

overweight /ˌəʊvəˈweɪt/ adj (of people) too heavy; fat.

overwhelm /ˌəʊvəˈwelm; US /-ˈhwelm/ v [T] 1 (usu passive) cause (sb) to feel helpless or embarrassed: ~ed by sorrow. 2 defeat, esp by force of numbers.

overwork /ˌəʊvəˈwɜːk/ v 1 [I, T] (cause sb to) work too hard. 2 [T] use (a word) too much.

overwrought /ˌəʊvəˈrɔːt/ adj nervous, anxious and upset.

ovulate /ˈɒvjʊleɪt/ v [I] (medical) produce an egg (= ovum) from an ovary. **ovulation** /ˌɒvjʊˈleɪʃn/

n [U].

ovum /ˈəʊvəm/ *n* [C] (*pl* **ova** /ˈəʊvə/) (*biology*) female egg-cell that can develop into a new individual.

ow /aʊ/ *interj* (used for showing pain): *Ow! That hurt!*

owe /əʊ/ *v* [T] **1** have to pay (money) back to (sb): *I ~ him £10.* **2** to/I recognize sb/sth as the cause of (sth): *She ~ s her success to hard work.* **3** feel grateful to (sb).

owing /ˈəʊɪŋ/ *adj* still to be paid. **owing to** *prep* because of.

owl /aʊl/ *n* [C] night-flying bird that eats small animals.

own¹ /əʊn/ *adj, pron* **1** belonging to the person mentioned: *his ~ room* ○ *a room of his ~.* **get one's own back (on sb)** (*infml*) harm sb in return for him/her harming one. **(all) on one's own** (**a**) alone. (**b**) without help.

own² /əʊn/ *v* [T] **1** possess: *~ a house.* **2** (phr v) **own up (to sth)** (*infml*) admit that one is to blame for sth. **owner** *n* [C]. **ownership** *n* [U].

ox /ɒks/ *n* [C] (*pl ~en* /ˈɒksn/) fully grown castrated bull.

oxygen /ˈɒksɪdʒən/ *n* [U] gas without colour, taste or smell, present in the air and necessary for life.

oyster /ˈɔɪstə(r)/ *n* [C] kind of shellfish. **'oyster-catcher** *n* [C] wading sea-bird.

oz *abbr* (*pl oz or ozs*) ounce(s).

ozone /ˈəʊzəʊn/ *n* [U] **1** form of oxygen. **2** (*infml*) fresh air at the seaside.

P *p*

P, p /piː/ *n* [C] (*pl* **P's**, **p's** /piːz/) the sixteenth letter of the English alphabet.

p *abbr* (*Brit*) **1** (*infml*) penny; pence. **2** (*pl* **pp**) page.

pa /pɑː/ *n* [C] (*infml*) father.

pace /peɪs/ *n* **1** [C] (length of a) single step in walking or running. **2** [sing] speed, esp of walking or running. **3** [U] rate of progress. **pace** *v* **1** [I, T] walk (across sth) with slow or regular steps. **2** [T] set a speed for (a runner). **3** (phr v) **pace sth off/out** measure sth by taking regular steps. **'pacemaker** *n* [C] device placed on the heart to make weak or irregular heartbeats stronger.

pacifism /ˈpæsɪfɪzəm/ *n* [U] belief

that all war is wrong. **pacifist** /-ɪst/ *n* [C].

pacify /ˈpæsɪfaɪ/ *v* (*pt, pp* **-ied**) [T] make (sb who is angry) calm. **pacification** /ˌpæsɪfɪˈkeɪʃn/ *n* [U].

pack¹ /pæk/ *n* [C] **1** number of things wrapped or tied together for carrying. **2** (*esp US*) packet(1). **3** group of wild animals: *a ~ of wolves.* **4** group of people or things: *a ~ of fools/lies.* **5** complete set of playing-cards.

pack² /pæk/ *v* **1** [I, T] put (things) into (a container): *~ clothes in a bag.* **2** [T] cover or protect (sth) with material, to prevent damage: *glass ~ed in paper.* **3** [I, T] (*into*)/(*T*) fill (a space) with people or things: *Crowds ~ed (into) the theatre.* **4** (phr v) **pack sth in** (*infml*) stop doing sth. **pack sb off** (*infml*) send sb away. **pack up** (*infml*) (**a**) finish one's work. (**b**) (of a machine) stop working properly. **pack (sth) up** put (one's possessions) into cases and leave. **packed** *adj* full of people.

package /ˈpækɪdʒ/ *n* [C] **1** number of things wrapped together; parcel. **2** (*US*) packet(1). **3** (also **'package deal**) set of suggestions offered together. **package** *v* [T] make into or put in a package, eg for selling. **'package holiday/ tour** *n* [C] holiday/tour in which travel, accommodation, etc are organized by a travel agent.

packet /ˈpækɪt/ *n* **1** [C] small container: *a ~ of cigarettes.* **2** [sing] (*infml*) large amount of money.

packing /ˈpækɪŋ/ *n* [U] **1** process of packing goods. **2** materials used for packing, to avoid damage to goods.

pact /pækt/ *n* [C] agreement.

pad¹ /pæd/ *n* [C] **1** thick piece of soft material, to prevent damage or give shape to sth. **2** number of sheets of paper fastened together. **3** flat surface from which spacecraft are launched or helicopters take off. **4** (*sl*) one's home. **5** soft fleshy part under the foot of a dog, fox, etc.

pad² /pæd/ *v* (**-dd-**) **1** [T] fill or cover with pads(1). **2** (phr v) **pad sth out** make (eg a book) longer by adding unnecessary parts. **padding** *n* [U] **1** soft material used to pad sth. **2** unnecessary material in a book, etc.

pad³ /pæd/ *v* (**-dd-**) (phr v) **pad about, along, etc** walk in the direction that is mentioned softly and steadily.

paddle¹ /ˈpædl/ *n* [C] short pole with a broad blade at one end or both ends, used to move a small boat through water. **paddle** v [I, T] move (a boat) with a paddle.

paddle[2] /ˈpædl/ v [I] walk with bare feet in shallow water. **paddle** n [sing] act of paddling.

paddock /ˈpædək/ n [C] small field where horses are kept.

paddy (also **'paddy-field**) /ˈpædɪ/ n [C] (pl **-ies**) field where rice is grown.

padlock /ˈpædlɒk/ n [C] lock with a curved bar that forms a loop when closed. **padlock** v [T] fasten with a padlock.

paediatrics /ˌpiːdɪˈætrɪks/ n (with sing v) branch of medicine concerned with children. **paediatrician** /ˌpiːdɪəˈtrɪʃn/ n [C] doctor who specializes in paediatrics.

pagan /ˈpeɪɡən/ n [C] person who does not believe in any religion or any of the world's main religions. **pagan** adj of or relating to pagans. **paganism** n [U].

page[1] /peɪdʒ/ n [C] **(a)** one side of a piece of paper in a book, etc. **(b)** both sides of such a piece of paper.

page[2] (also **'page-boy**) /peɪdʒ/ n [C] **(a)** boy servant. **(b)** boy attendant at a wedding.

pageant /ˈpædʒənt/ n [C] **1** public entertainment in which historical events are acted. **2** grand display. **pageantry** n [U] grand display.

pagoda /pəˈɡəʊdə/ n [C] religious building in India and E Asia, with several floors.

paid pt, pp of PAY[1].

pail /peɪl/ n [C] bucket.

pain /peɪn/ n **1** [U] suffering in body or mind: cry with ~. **2** [C] feeling of suffering in a particular part of the body: a ~ in her leg. **3** [C] (infml) annoying or boring person or thing. **4** (idm) **a pain in the neck** (infml) annoying or boring person or thing. **pain** v [T] cause pain to. **pained** adj unhappy and upset: a ~ed look. **painful** adj causing pain. **painless** adj not causing pain.

pains /peɪnz/ n [pl] (idm) **take (great)/be at pains to do sth** make a great effort to do sth. **'painstaking** adj very careful; thorough.

paint /peɪnt/ n **1** [U] coloured liquid that is put on a surface. **2 paints** [pl] set of tubes of paint. **paint** v [I, T] make a picture (of) with paint: ~ flowers. **2** [T] cover with paint: ~ the door. **3** [T] (fig) describe in clear words. **4** (idm) **paint the 'town red** (infml) go out and enjoy a lively time. **painting** n **1** [U] action or skill of painting. **2** [C] painted picture. **'paintwork** n [U] painted surface.

painter /ˈpeɪntə(r)/ n [C] **1** person who paints pictures. **2** worker who paints buildings, etc.

pair /peə(r)/ n [C] **1** two things of the same kind: a ~ of shoes. **2** [C] object made of two parts joined together: a ~ of trousers/scissors. **3** [C, also sing with pl v] two people closely connected, eg a married couple. **pair** v [I, T] (off)// form a pair or pairs: ~ (off) a pile of socks.

pajamas (US) = PYJAMAS.

pal /pæl/ n [C] (infml) friend.

palace /ˈpælɪs/ n [C] large splendid house, esp the home of a king, queen or president.

palaeontology /ˌpælɪɒnˈtɒlədʒɪ/ (also esp US **paleon-** /ˌpeɪl-/) n [U] study of fossils. **palaeontologist** (also esp US **paleon-**) /-dʒɪst/ n [C].

palatable /ˈpælətəbl/ adj **1** pleasant to taste. **2** (fig) acceptable: The truth is not always very ~.

palate /ˈpælət/ n [C] **1** top part of the inside of the mouth. **2** [usu sing] sense of taste.

palatial /pəˈleɪʃl/ adj like a palace; very large and splendid: a ~ hotel.

palaver /pəˈlɑːvə(r); US ·ˈlæv-/ n [U, sing] (infml) unnecessary trouble; fuss.

pale[1] /peɪl/ adj (~r, ~st) **1** (of a person or his/her face) having little colour; white. **2** (of a colour) not bright: ~ blue eyes. **pale** v [I] **1** become pale. **2** become less important in comparison with sth: Compared to your problems mine ~ into insignificance. **paleness** n [U].

pale[2] /peɪl/ n (idm) **be yond the 'pale** considered unacceptable: Your remarks are beyond the ~.

paleo- = PALAEO-.

palette /ˈpælət/ n [C] board on which an artist mixes colours.

paling /ˈpeɪlɪŋ/ n [C] fence made of pointed pieces of wood.

pall[1] /pɔːl/ v [I] become uninteresting, because experienced too often.

pall[2] /pɔːl/ n [C] **1** cloth spread over a coffin. **2** [usu sing] (fig) dark or heavy covering: a ~ of smoke. **'pallbearer** n [C] person who walks beside or helps to carry the coffin at a funeral.

pallet /ˈpælɪt/ n [C] large flat frame for carrying heavy goods, lifted by a fork-lift truck.

pallid /ˈpælɪd/ adj pale; looking ill. **pallor** /ˈpælə(r)/ n [U].

palm[1] /pɑːm/ n [C] inner surface of the hand. **palm** v (phr v) **palm sth off (on sb)** (infml) get rid of sth unwanted by persuading sb to accept it: She always ~s off her old *clothes on me.*

palm² (also **'palm-tree**) /pɑːm/ *n* [C] tree growing in warm climates, with no branches and a mass of large leaves at the top.

palmist /'pɑːmɪst/ *n* [C] person who claims to be able to tell sb's future by looking at his/her palm. **palmistry** *n* [U] skill of a palmist.

palpable /'pælpəbl/ *adj* (*fml*) clear to the mind; obvious. **palpably** /-əblɪ/ *adv.*

palpitate /'pælpɪteɪt/ *v* [I] 1 (of the heart) beat very fast and irregularly. 2 tremble with fear. **palpitation** /ˌpælpɪ'teɪʃn/ *n* [U, C, usu *pl*].

paltry /'pɔːltrɪ/ *adj* (**-ier, -iest**) very small; worthless.

pamper /'pæmpə(r)/ *v* [T] be too kind to.

pamphlet /'pæmflɪt/ *n* [C] small book with a paper cover.

pan¹ /pæn/ *n* [C] 1 metal container with a handle, used for cooking: *a frying-~*. 2 bowl-shaped container: *a toilet ~*. **pan** *v* (**-nn-**) 1 [I] (*for*)// wash gravel in a dish in order to find gold. 2 [T] (*infml*) criticize strongly. 3 (phr v) **pan out** (*fig*) (of events) develop; turn out: *How did things ~ out?*

pan² /pæn/ *v* (**-nn-**) [I, T] (*cinema*) turn (a camera, etc) to follow a moving object.

panacea /ˌpænə'sɪə/ *n* [C] something that will put right all diseases or troubles.

panache /pæ'næʃ; *US* pə-/ *n* [U] confident stylish manner.

pancake /'pænkeɪk/ *n* [C] thin cake of batter fried on both sides.

pancreas /'pæŋkrɪəs/ *n* [C] part of the body that produces substances which help in the digestion of food.

panda /'pændə/ *n* [C] large bear-like black and white animal from China.

pandemonium /ˌpændɪ-'məʊnɪəm/ *n* [U] wild and noisy disorder.

pander /'pændə(r)/ *v* (phr v) **pander to sb/sth** try to satisfy (a weak or bad desire or sb having one): *newspapers that ~ to the public's interest in violence.*

pane /peɪn/ *n* [C] sheet of glass in a window.

panel /'pænl/ *n* [C] 1 flat part of the surface of a door, etc, raised above or sunk below the surrounding area. 2 board for controls and instruments. 3 group of speakers who answer questions, esp on a radio or television programme. **panel** *v* (**-ll-**; *US* **-l-**) [T] decorate with panels(1). **panell-**

ing (*US* **-l-**) *n* [U] series of panels(1) on a wall, etc.

pang /pæŋ/ *n* [C] sudden strong feeling of pain, guilt, etc.

panic /'pænɪk/ *n* [U, C] sudden uncontrollable feeling of great fear. **panic** *v* (**-ck-**) [I] feel panic. **panicky** *adj* (*infml*) of or feeling panic. **'panic-stricken** *adj* filled with panic.

pannier /'pænɪə(r)/ *n* [C] one of a pair of bags on either side of the back wheel of a bicycle.

panorama /ˌpænə'rɑːmə; *US* -'ræmə/ *n* [C] view of a wide area. **panoramic** /-'ræmɪk/ *adj.*

pansy /'pænzɪ/ *n* [C] (*pl* **-ies**) 1 small flowering plant. 2 (*infml derog*) effeminate man; homosexual.

pant /pænt/ *v* [I] breathe with short quick breaths. **pant** *n* [C] short quick breath.

panther /'pænθə(r)/ *n* [C] leopard, esp a black one.

panties /'pæntɪz/ *n* [pl] (*infml*) short close-fitting underpants worn by women or girls.

pantomime /'pæntəmaɪm/ *n* [C, U] funny play for children, based on a fairy-tale, with music and dancing, esp at Christmas.

pantry /'pæntrɪ/ *n* [C] (*pl* **-ies**) small room in a house where food is kept.

pants /pænts/ *n* [pl] 1 (*Brit*) men's underpants; women's or girls' knickers. 2 (esp *US*) trousers.

papa /pə'pɑː; *US* 'pɑːpə/ *n* [C] (*dated infml*) (used by children) father.

papacy /'peɪpəsɪ/ *n* **the papacy** [sing] position or authority of the Pope. **papal** /'peɪpl/ *adj* of the Pope.

paper /'peɪpə(r)/ *n* 1 [U] substance in thin sheets used for writing, printing or drawing on or wrapping things in. 2 [C] newspaper. 3 **papers** [pl] official documents. 4 [C] set of examination questions. 5 [C] academic article or essay. **paper** *v* [T] put wallpaper on. **'paperback** *n* [C] book with a thin cardboard cover. **'paper-boy, 'paper-girl** *n* [C] boy/girl who delivers newspapers to people's houses. **'paper-clip** *n* [C] piece of bent wire, used to hold sheets of paper together. **'paperweight** *n* [C] small heavy object put on top of loose papers to keep them in place. **'paperwork** *n* [U] writing letters and reports, filling in forms, etc.

paprika /'pæprɪkə; *US* pə'priːkə/ *n* [U] red powder of a sweet pepper, used in cooking.

par /pɑː(r)/ *n* **1** [sing] (in golf) average number of hits. **2** (idm) **below 'par** (*infml*) less well, efficient, etc than usual. **on a par with sb/sth** equal in quality, importance, etc to sb/sth.

parable /'pærəbl/ *n* [C] (esp in the Bible) simple story that teaches a moral lesson.

parachute /'pærəʃuːt/ *n* [C] umbrella-shaped apparatus by which sb may fall slowly and safely to the ground from an aircraft. **parachute** *v* [I, T] drop from an aircraft using a parachute. **parachutist** *n* [C] person who drops from an aircraft using a parachute.

parade /pə'reɪd/ *n* [C] **1** formal gathering of soldiers, eg for inspection. **2** procession. **parade** *v* **1** [I, T] gather (soldiers) for inspection, etc. **2** [I] walk in a procession. **3** [T] show, in order to attract attention: ~ *one's wealth*.

paradise /'pærədaɪs/ *n* **1** [U] heaven. **2** [C, usu sing, U] place or state of perfect happiness.

paradox /'pærədɒks/ *n* [C] statement which seems to contain two opposite facts but is or may be true. **paradoxical** /,pærə-'dɒksɪkl/ *adj*. **paradoxically** /-klɪ/ *adv*.

paraffin /'pærəfɪn/ *n* [U] oil obtained from petroleum, used as a fuel.

paragon /'pærəgən; *US* -gɒn/ *n* [C] (*of*) person who is a perfect example of a quality: *She is a ~ of virtue.*

paragraph /'pærəgrɑːf; *US* -græf/ *n* [C] division of a piece of writing, started on a new line.

parakeet /'pærəkiːt/ *n* [C] small long-tailed parrot.

parallel /'pærəlel/ *adj* **1** (of lines) always at the same distance from each other. **2** (*fig*) similar. **parallel** *n* **1** [C, U] person or thing that is exactly similar to another. **2** [C] comparison or similarity: *draw a ~ between A and B.* **parallel** *v* [T] be equal or similar to.

parallelogram /,pærə'leləgræm/ *n* [C] (*geometry*) four-sided figure with its opposite sides parallel to each other.

paralyse (*US* -**lyze**) /'pærəlaɪz/ *v* [T] **1** affect with paralysis. **2** (*fig*) prevent from moving or working normally: *The city was ~d by the railway strike.*

paralysis /pə'ræləsɪs/ *n* [U] **1** loss of feeling in or control of part of the body. **2** (*fig*) inability to move or work normally. **paralytic** /,pærə'lɪtɪk/ *adj* **1** suffering from paralysis. **2** (*Brit sl*) very

drunk. **paralytic** *n* [C] person suffering from paralysis.

parameter /pə'ræmɪtə(r)/ *n* [C, usu pl] limit that affects how sth operates.

paramilitary /,pærə'mɪlɪtrɪ; *US* -terɪ/ *adj* (of a military force) organized like but not part of an official army.

paramount /'pærəmaʊnt/ *adj* (*fml*) having the greatest importance.

paranoia /,pærə'nɔɪə/ *n* [U] mental illness in which sb believes that other people want to harm him/her. **paranoid** /'pærənɔɪd/ *n* [C], *adj* (person) suffering from paranoia.

parapet /'pærəpɪt, -pet/ *n* [C] low protective wall at the edge of a roof, bridge, etc.

paraphernalia /,pærəfə'neɪlɪə/ *n* [U] many small articles of different kinds.

paraphrase /'pærəfreɪz/ *v* [T] *n* [C] (give a) restatement of (sth written or spoken) in different words.

parasite /'pærəsaɪt/ *n* [C] **1** animal or plant that lives on and gets food from another. **2** (*fig*) person supported by others, giving nothing in return. **parasitic** /,pærə'sɪtɪk/ *adj*.

parasol /'pærəsɒl; *US* -sɔːl/ *n* [C] umbrella used for giving shade from the sun.

paratroops /'pærətruːps/ *n* [pl] soldiers trained to drop from an aircraft using parachutes. **paratrooper** /-pə(r)/ *n* [C].

parcel /'pɑːsl/ *n* [C] something wrapped up for carrying and sending by post. **parcel** *v* (-**ll**-; *US* -**l**-) (phr v) **parcel sth out** divide sth into parts. **parcel sth up** wrap sth up into a parcel.

parched /pɑːtʃt/ *adj* **1** very dry, because of a lack of water. **2** (*infml*) very thirsty.

parchment /'pɑːtʃmənt/ *n* [U] (a) material made from animal skin for writing on. (b) kind of paper like this.

pardon /'pɑːdn/ *n* [C, U] **1** (act of) forgiveness. **2** freeing sb from punishment for a crime. **pardon** *v* [T] forgive. **pardon** *interj* (used for asking sb to repeat sth that has not been fully heard). **pardonable** *adj* that can be forgiven.

pare /peə(r)/ *v* [T] **1** cut away the outer part, edge or skin of. **2** (phr v) **pare sth down** reduce sth.

parent /'peərənt/ *n* [C] father or mother. **parental** /pə'rentl/ *adj*.

parenthesis /pə'renθəsɪs/ *n* [C] (*pl* -**eses** /-əsiːz/) (a) additional sentence or phrase within another sentence, marked off by dashes, commas or brackets. (b) [usu pl] round brackets () used for this.

parish /'pærɪʃ/ n [C] area that has its own church and clergyman. **parishioner** /pə'rɪʃənə(r)/ n [C] person (esp a church-goer) who lives in a parish.

parity /'pærətɪ/ n [U] (fml) state of being equal.

park /pɑːk/ n [C] public garden or area of ground for public use. **park** v [I, T] stop and leave (a vehicle) in a place for a time. **'parking-meter** n [C] device into which one puts money to pay for parking near it for a time. **'parkland** n [U] open area of grass and trees.

parliament /'pɑːləmənt/ n [C, also sing with pl v] group of people that make the laws of a country. **parliamentary** /ˌpɑːlə'mentrɪ/ adj.

parlour (US -lor) /'pɑːlə(r)/ n [C] 1 (formerly) sitting-room. 2 (esp US) shop: an ice-tream ~.

parochial /pə'rəʊkɪəl/ adj 1 (fml) of a parish. 2 (fig derog) narrow; limited: a ~ attitude. **parochially** adv.

parody /'pærədɪ/ n (pl -ies) 1 [C, U] (piece of) writing intended to amuse by imitating the style of sb else. 2 [C] bad imitation: a ~ of justice. **parody** v (pt, pp -ied) [T] make a parody(1) of.

parole /pə'rəʊl/ n [U] setting a prisoner free before his/her term of imprisonment is finished, after he/she has made a promise to behave well. **parole** v [T] set (a prisoner) free on parole.

paroxysm /'pærəksɪzəm/ n [C] (fml) sudden attack or burst of anger, pain, etc.

parquet /'pɑːkeɪ; US pɑːr'keɪ/ n [C] floor covering made of wooden blocks.

parrot /'pærət/ n [C] tropical bird with a curved beak and brightly-coloured feathers. **parrot** v [T] repeat (the words or actions of sb else) without thinking.

parry /'pærɪ/ v (pt, pp -ied) [T] turn aside or avoid (a blow, question, etc). **parry** n [C] act of parrying.

parsimonious /ˌpɑːsɪ'məʊnɪəs/ adj (fml derog) very careful in spending money.

parsley /'pɑːslɪ/ n [U] small plant with curly leaves used for flavouring and decorating food.

parsnip /'pɑːsnɪp/ n [C, U] plant with a long yellow root, cooked as a vegetable.

parson /'pɑːsn/ n [C] parish

priest. **parsonage** /-ɪdʒ/ n [C] parson's house.

part /pɑːt/ n [C] 1 (of)|| some but not all: We spent (a) ~ of our holiday in Paris. 2 piece of a machine: spare ~s. 3 area of a country, town, etc. 4 one of a number of (equal) divisions. 5 [usu sing] person's share in an activity; actor's role in a play, film, etc. 6 (music) melody for a particular voice or instrument. 7 (idm) **for the 'most part** mainly; usually. **for 'my, 'his/'her, etc part** as far as I, etc am concerned. **in 'part** to some extent. **on sb's part** made or done by sb. **take part (in sth)** have a share, with others, in sth. **take sb's part** support sb, eg in an argument. **part** adv partly. **partly** adv to some extent; not completely. **,part of 'speech** [C] (grammar) one of the classes of words, eg noun or verb. **,part-'time** adj, adv working only a part of the day or week.

part² /pɑːt/ v [I, T] separate: The clouds ~ed. ○ ~ two people. 2 [T] separate (the hair on the head) along a line and comb the hair away from it. 3 (idm) **part 'company (with sb/sth)** (a) go different ways; separate after being together. (b) disagree with sb. 4 (phr v) **part with sth** give away sth: She'll never ~ with the family jewels. **parting** n 1 [U, C] leaving. 2 [C] line where the hair is parted.

partake /pɑː'teɪk/ v (pt -took /-'tʊk/, pp -taken /-'teɪkən/) [I] (of) in|| (fml) eat or drink (sth); have a share in (sth).

partial /'pɑːʃl/ adj 1 not complete: only a ~ success. 2 (towards)|| unfairly showing favour to one person or side. 3 to|| liking sth very much: He's (rather) ~ to cakes. **partiality** /ˌpɑːʃɪ'ælətɪ/ n 1 [U] being partial(2). 2 [C, usu sing] fondness. **partially** /'pɑːʃəlɪ/ adv not completely; partly.

participate /pɑː'tɪsɪpeɪt/ v [I] (in)|| take part or become involved in an activity. **participant** /-pənt/ n [C] person who participates. **participation** /pɑːˌtɪsɪ'peɪʃn/ n [U].

participle /'pɑːtɪsɪpl/ n [C] (grammar) form of a verb: 'Hurrying' and 'hurried' are the present and past ~s of 'hurry'.

particle /'pɑːtɪkl/ n [C] 1 very small piece. 2 (grammar) part of speech, eg an article or adverb.

particular /pə'tɪkjʊlə(r)/ adj 1 relating to one, not others: in this ~ case. 2 special: of ~ interest. 3

(about)|| giving too much attention to details; not easily satisfied. 4 (idm) in par'ticular most of all: *I like these flowers in ~.* par'ticular *n* [C, usu pl] piece of information; detail. particularly *adv* especially.

partisan /ˌpɑːtɪˈzæn; US ˈpɑːrtɪzn/ *n* [C] 1 enthusiastic esp uncritical supporter of a person, cause, etc. 2 member of an unofficial armed force in a country occupied by enemy soldiers. partisan *adj* uncritically supporting a person, cause, etc.

partition /pɑːˈtɪʃn/ *n* 1 thin wall between rooms in a house, office, etc. 2 division of a country into parts. partition *v* 1 [T] divide into parts. 2 (phr v) partition sth off separate sth with a partition.

partner /ˈpɑːtnə(r)/ *n* [C] 1 person who takes part in an activity, with others, esp in a business. 2 either of two people dancing, playing tennis, etc together. 3 person one is married to or one has a sexual relationship with. partner *v* [T] be the partner of. partnership *n* 1 [U] state of being a partner. 2 [C] business owned by two or more people.

partook *pt* of PARTAKE.

partridge /ˈpɑːtrɪdʒ/ *n* [C] game bird with brown feathers, a plump body and a short tail.

party /ˈpɑːtɪ/ *n* [C] (*pl* -ies) 1 social gathering: *a birthday ~.* 2 group of people with the same political aims. 3 group of people doing sth together: *a ~ of tourists.* 4 (*law*) person or people forming one side in an agreement, etc. 5 (idm) be (a) party to sth be involved in or support sth. the ˌparty 'line *n* [sing] the official views of a political party.

pass¹ /pɑːs; US pæs/ *v* 1 [I, T] move towards and beyond (sb/sth): *~ the house.* 2 [I, T] (cause to) go or move in the direction that is mentioned: *He ~ed through Oxford on his way to London.* 3 [T] give (sth) to sb: *Please ~ me the butter.* 4 [I, T] (*sport*) kick, hit, etc (the ball, etc) to a player on one's own side. 5 [I] change (from one state to another). 6 (a) [I] (of time) go by; be spent. (b) [T] spend (time). 7 [I] come to an end: *wait for the storm to ~.* 8 (a) [I, T] reach the required standard in (an examination). (b) [T] examine (sb) and declare to have reached the required standard. 9 [T] approve (a new law) by voting. 10 [I] be allowed: *I don't like it but I'll let it ~.* 11 [T] give (an official opinion):

~ *(a) sentence on a prisoner.* 12 (idm) pass the time of 'day (with sb) greet sb and have a short conversation with him/her. pass 'water (*fml*) urinate. 13 (phr v) pass a'way (*euph*) die. pass by sb/sth go past sb/sth. pass sb/sth by pay no attention to sb/sth. pass for sb/sth be accepted as sb/sth: *He could ~ for a Frenchman.* pass 'off (of an event) take place and be completed. pass sb/sth off as sb/sth present sb/sth falsely as another. pass 'on = PASS AWAY. pass sth on (to sb) give sth to sb else. pass 'out faint. pass sb over not choose sb for a job. pass over sth ignore sth. pass sth up not take advantage of sth. ˌpasser-'by *n* [C] (*pl* passers-by) person who is going past sb/sth.

pass² /pɑːs; US pæs/ *n* [C] 1 success in an examination. 2 paper or card giving permission to travel, enter a building, etc. 3 (*sport*) act of kicking, hitting, etc the ball to a player on one's own side. 4 narrow way through a range of mountains. 5 (idm) make a pass at sb (*infml*) try to interest sb sexually. 'password *n* [C] secret word or phrase that one must know to be allowed to enter a building, use a computer, etc.

passable /ˈpɑːsəbl; US ˈpæs-/ *adj* 1 (of a road, etc) open to traffic. 2 fairly good, but not excellent. passably /-əblɪ/ *adv*.

passage /ˈpæsɪdʒ/ *n* 1 [C] narrow way through sth; corridor. 2 [C, usu sing] way through sth: *clear a ~ through the crowd.* 3 [U] action or process of passing: *the ~ of time.* 4 [C] (cost of a) journey by ship. 5 [C] short section of a book, speech, etc.

passenger /ˈpæsɪndʒə(r)/ *n* [C] person travelling in a bus, train, aircraft, etc other than the crew.

passing /ˈpɑːsɪŋ; US ˈpæsɪŋ/ *adj* lasting for a short time: *a ~ thought.* passing *n* [U] 1 process of going by. 2 (a) (*fml*) end. (b) (*euph*) death. 3 (idm) in passing briefly, while talking or writing about sth else.

passion /ˈpæʃn/ *n* 1 [U, C] strong feeling, esp of love, hate or anger. 2 [U] very strong sexual love. 3 [sing] *for*|| strong liking: *a ~ for books.* passionate /ˈpæʃənət/ *adj* showing passion. passionately *adv*.

passive /ˈpæsɪv/ *adj* 1 not showing one's feelings, eg not resisting, when people do things to one. 2 (*grammar*) of the verb form used when the subject of a sentence is

affected by the action, as in 'She *was bitten* by a dog'. **the passive** *n* [sing] passive(2) form of a verb.
passively *adv.* **passiveness** *n* [U].
Passover /'pɑːsəʊvə(r); US 'pæs-/ *n* [U] Jewish religious festival.

passport /'pɑːspɔːt; US 'pæs-/ *n* [C] 1 official document to be carried by a traveller abroad. 2 (*fig*) something that makes sth possible: *a ~ to success*.

past¹ /pɑːst; US pæst/ *adj* 1 of the time before the present; gone by in time: *in ~ years*. 2 (*grammar*) (of a verb form) showing a state or action in the past: *the ~ tense* ○ *a ~ participle*. **past** *n* [sing] 1 **the past** (things that happened in) the time before the present. 2 person's (esp bad) past life.

past² /pɑːst; US pæst/ *prep* 1 of (time) later than; after: *~ midnight*. 2 on the far side of; from one side to the other of: *She walked ~ the church.* 3 beyond the interest or ability of: *I'm ~ caring* (ie I no longer care) *what happens.* 4 (idm) **past it** (*infml*) too old to do what one could once do. **past sth** from one side to the other of sth. **'past** *adv* from one side to the other of sth.

pasta /'pæstə; US 'pɑːstə/ *n* [U] dried paste made from flour, eggs and water and cut into various shapes.

paste /peɪst/ *n* 1 [C, U] mixture of powder and a liquid. 2 [U] mixture of flour and water, used eg for sticking paper to a wall. 3 [U] (esp in compounds) mixture of meat or fish for spreading on bread: *fish ~.* **paste** *v* [T] stick (sth) to (sth else) with paste(2).

pastel /'pæstl; US pæ'stel/ *adj* light and soft in colour. **pastel** *n* [C] (a) crayon of coloured chalk. (b) picture drawn with pastels.

pasteurize /'pɑːstʃəraɪz; US 'pæs-/ *v* [T] heat (esp milk) in order to remove bacteria.

pastille /'pæstɪl; US pæ'stiːl/ *n* [C] small flavoured sweet to be sucked, esp one containing medicine for a sore throat.

pastime /'pɑːstaɪm; US 'pæs-/ *n* [C] something done to pass the time pleasantly.

pastor /'pɑːstə(r); US 'pæs-/ *n* [C] Christian clergyman in charge of a church.

pastoral /'pɑːstərəl; US 'pæs-/ *adj* 1 of the work of a clergyman. 2 of (esp peaceful) country life or the countryside.

pastry /'peɪstrɪ/ *n* (*pl* -ies) (a) [U] mixture of flour, fat and water baked in an oven and used for pies, etc. (b) [C] usually sweet article of food in which this is used.

pasture /'pɑːstʃə(r); US 'pæs-/ *n* [C, U] (area of) land covered with grass for cattle.

pasty¹ /'peɪstɪ/ *adj* (-ier, -iest) pale; looking unhealthy: *a ~ white skin.*

pasty² /'pæstɪ/ *n* [C] (*pl* -ies) piece of pastry folded round a filling of meat, etc.

pat¹ /pæt/ *v* (-tt-) [T] tap gently with one's open hand. **pat** *n* [C] 1 gentle tap with the open hand. 2 small shaped mass of butter.

pat² /pæt/ *adj* too quickly and easily given: *a ~ answer.*

patch /pætʃ/ *n* [C] 1 small piece of material put over a hole or damaged place. 2 part of a surface that is different from the rest. 3 pad worn to protect an injured eye. 4 small area of ground: *a 'cabbage ~.* 5 (idm) **not be a patch on sb/sth** (*infml*) not be nearly as good as sb/sth. **patch** *v* [T] 1 put a patch(1) on. 2 (phr v) **patch sth up** (a) repair sth quickly. (b) settle (a quarrel). **'patchwork** *n* 1 [U] material in which different small pieces of cloth are sewn together. 2 [C, usu sing] pattern made up of many different items. **patchy** *adj* (-ier, -iest) uneven in quality.

pâté /'pæteɪ; US pɑː'teɪ/ *n* [U] rich paste of meat or fish.

patent¹ /'peɪtnt, also 'pætnt; US 'pætnt/ *adj* clear; obvious. **patently** *adv* clearly.

patent² /'pætnt, also 'peɪtnt; US 'pætnt/ *n* [C] (official document giving sb the) right to be the only person to make or sell a new invention. **patent** *adj* protected by a patent. **patent** *v* [T] obtain a patent for. **patent 'leather** *n* [U] leather with a hard shiny surface.

paternal /pə'tɜːnl/ *adj* 1 of or like a father. 2 related through the father's side of the family: *my ~ grandfather.* **paternally** *adv.*

paternity /pə'tɜːnətɪ/ *n* [U] being a father.

path /pɑːθ; US pæθ/ *n* [C] (*pl* ~s /pɑːðz; US pæðz/) 1 (also **'pathway**) way or track made for or by people walking. 2 line along which sth moves.

pathetic /pə'θetɪk/ *adj* 1 causing one to feel pity or sadness: *a ~ sight.* 2 (*infml*) inadequate: *a ~ attempt.* **pathetically** /-klɪ/ *adv.*

pathology /pə'θɒlədʒɪ/ *n* [U] study of diseases. **pathological** /,pæθə'lɒdʒɪkl/ *adj* 1 of pathology. 2 of or caused by (mental) illness. 3 (*infml*) unreasonable. **pathologist** *n* [C] expert in pathology.

pathos /'peɪθɒs/ *n* [U] (*fml*) quality that causes pity or sadness.

patience /ˈpeɪʃns/ *n* [U] 1 ability to accept delay, annoyance or suffering without complaining. 2 ability to wait calmly. 3 card-game for one player.

patient /ˈpeɪʃnt/ *adj* having or showing patience. **patiently** *adv*.

patient[2] /ˈpeɪʃnt/ *n* [C] person receiving medical treatment.

patio /ˈpætɪəʊ/ *n* [C] (*pl* ~s) paved area next to a house where people can sit, eat, etc outdoors.

patriarch /ˈpeɪtrɪɑːk; US ˈpæt-/ *n* [C] 1 male head of a family or tribe. 2 **Patriarch** (in Eastern Churches) high-ranking bishop. **patriarchal** /ˌpeɪtrɪˈɑːkl; US ˌpæt-/ *adj*.

patriot /ˈpeɪtrɪət; US ˈpeɪt-/ *n* [C] person who loves his/her country and is ready to defend it. **patriotic** /ˌpætrɪˈɒtɪk; US ˌpeɪt-/ *adj*. **patriotically** /-klɪ/ *adv*. **patriotism** *n* [U].

patrol /pəˈtrəʊl/ *v* (-ll-) [I, T] go round (an area or building) to protect or guard it. **patrol** *n* 1 [U] act of patrolling: *soldiers on ~*. 2 [C] person or group on patrol.

patron /ˈpeɪtrən/ *n* [C] 1 person who gives money or other support to sb or an activity: *a wealthy ~ of the arts*. 2 (*fml*) regular customer at a shop, etc. **patronage** /ˈpætrənɪdʒ; US ˈpeɪt-/ *n* [U] 1 support given by a patron: *her ~ age of the arts* ◇ *his ~ age of the shop*. 2 right to appoint sb to an important job. **patron 'saint** *n* [C] saint believed to give special protection to a particular group of people or place.

patronize /ˈpætrənaɪz; US ˈpeɪt-/ *v* [T] 1 treat (sb) in a way that shows one thinks (sb) is inferior to oneself. 2 (*fml*) be a regular customer of. **patronizing** *adj*.

patter[1] /ˈpætə(r)/ *v* [I] *n* [sing] (make) the sound of quick light steps or taps.

patter[2] /ˈpætə(r)/ *n* [U] fast talk, eg of entertainers or salespeople.

pattern /ˈpætn/ *n* [C] 1 arrangement of lines, shapes, etc, esp regularly repeated as a decorative design. 2 way in which something happens or is arranged: *the usual ~ of events*. 3 design or instructions from which sth is to be made: *a knitting ~*. **pattern** *v* [T] *on/ ~* (usu passive) use sth/sb as a model for (sth/sb): *The tax system is ~ed on the one used in Sweden.* **patterned** *adj* decorated with a pattern.

paucity /ˈpɔːsətɪ/ *n* [sing] (*fml*) small amount; lack.

paunch /pɔːntʃ/ *n* [C] fat stomach.

pauper /ˈpɔːpə(r)/ *n* [C] very poor person.

pause /pɔːz/ *n* [C] short stop or interval in action or speech: *a ~ in the conversation*. **pause** *v* [I] make a pause: *He ~d a minute before finishing his speech.*

pave /peɪv/ *v* 1 [T] cover (a path, etc) with flat stones or bricks. 2 (idm) **,pave the 'way (for sth)** create a situation in which sth can happen. **'paving stone** *n* [C] flat piece of stone used for making pavements.

pavement /ˈpeɪvmənt/ *n* [C] paved path at the side of a road for people to walk on.

pavilion /pəˈvɪlɪən/ *n* [C] 1 (*Brit*) building next to a sports ground, used by players and spectators. 2 large tent used for an exhibition for a short time.

paw /pɔː/ *n* [C] animal's foot with claws. **paw** *v* 1 [I, T] (*at/*)) (of an animal) feel or scratch (sth) with the paws. 2 [T] (of people) touch roughly or rudely.

pawn[1] /pɔːn/ *n* [C] 1 least valuable chess piece. 2 (*fig*) unimportant person used by others for their own advantage.

pawn[2] /pɔːn/ *v* [T] leave (an object) with a pawnbroker in exchange for money lent. **'pawnbroker** *n* [C] person who lends money in exchange for articles left with him/her, which he/she can sell if one does not pay the money back.

pay[1] /peɪ/ *v* (*pt, pp* **paid** /peɪd/) 1 [I, T] give (money) to (sb) for goods, services, etc: *~ him for the bread*. 2 [T] give (what is owed): *~ the rent*. 3 [I, T] have a good result; be profitable: *It ~ s to be honest.* 4 [T] give or make: *~ attention to sth* ◇ *~ a visit*. 5 (idm) **pay lip-service to 'sth** ⇒ LIP. **pay through the 'nose (for sth)** pay too much money for sth. **pay one's way** provide for oneself with money that one has earned. **put 'paid to sth** destroy or ruin sth. 6 (phr v) **pay sb back (sth)** return (money) to sb that one has borrowed from him/her. **pay sb back (for sth)** punish sb for doing sth unpleasant to one. **pay for sth** suffer or be punished for sth. **pay off** (*infml*) be successful. **pay sb off** (a) pay sb's wages and dismiss him/her. (b) (*infml*) give money to sb to prevent him/her from doing sth. **pay sth off** pay (money owed) in full. **pay sth out** (a) pay (a large sum of money). (b) allow (rope) to move freely through one's hands.

pay up pay in full the money that is owed. **,paid-'up** adj having paid in full the money to belong to a club, political party, etc. **payable** adj that must or may be paid. **payee** /peɪ'iː/ n [C] person to whom money is to be paid. **payer** n [C] person who pays. **payment** n 1 [U] paying or being paid. 2 [C] amount of money (to be) paid. **'pay-off** n [C] (infml) 1 act of paying sb, eg to prevent him/her from doing sth. 2 result or reward.

pay² /peɪ/ n [U] money paid for regular work. **'payload** n [C] amount carried in an aircraft or other vehicle. **'pay-packet** n [C] envelope containing wages. **'pay phone** n [C] coin-operated telephone. **'payroll** n [C] list of people employed and paid by a company.

PE /ˌpiː 'iː/ abbr physical education: a PE lesson at school.

pea /piː/ n [C] round green seed eaten as a vegetable.

peace /piːs/ n 1 [U] state of freedom from war. 2 **the peace** [sing] freedom from violence and disorder in a country: break/disturb the ~. 3 [U] freedom from quarrelling; friendliness. 4 [U] state of calm or quiet; freedom from worry: be at ~ with oneself. 5 (idm) **make one's peace with sb** end a quarrel with sb, esp by apologizing. **peaceable** adj avoiding fighting or quarrelling. **peaceful** adj 1 not involving war or violence. 2 quiet; calm. **peacefully** adv. **peacefulness** n [U]. **'peacetime** n [U] time when a country is not at war.

peach /piːtʃ/ n [C] round juicy fruit with soft yellowish-red skin. **peach** adj yellowish-red in colour.

peacock /'piːkɒk/ n [C] large male bird with blue and green tail feathers.

peahen /'piːhen/ n [C] female of a peacock.

peak /piːk/ n [C] 1 pointed top of a mountain. 2 highest point, stage, etc: Sales reached a new ~ in May. 3 pointed front part of a cap. **peak** adj at its highest level; busiest: ~ hours. **peak** v [I] reach a peak. **peaked** adj having a peak.

peal /piːl/ n [C] 1 loud ringing of bells. 2 loud burst of sound: ~ s of laughter|thunder. **peal** v [I] (of bells) ring loudly.

peanut /'piːnʌt/ n 1 [C] nut that grows underground in a thin shell. 2 **peanuts** [pl] (sl) very small amount of money.

pear /peə(r)/ n [C] sweet juicy rounded fruit that becomes

narrower towards the stalk.

pearl /pɜːl/ n [C] small hard round silvery-white jewel that grows inside an oyster.

peasant /'peznt/ n [C] 1 (in some countries) person who works on the land. 2 (infml derog) person with rough uneducated manners. **peasantry** n [sing] (with sing or pl v) all the peasants of a country.

peat /piːt/ n [U] partly decayed plant material, used in gardening or as a fuel. **peaty** adj.

pebble /'pebl/ n [C] small stone made smooth and round by water. **pebbly** adj.

peck /pek/ v 1 [I, T] (of a bird) strike with the beak. 2 [T] (infml) kiss lightly and quickly. **peck** n [C] 1 stroke, mark or wound made by pecking. 2 (infml) light quick kiss.

peckish /'pekɪʃ/ adj (infml) slightly hungry.

peculiar /pɪ'kjuːliə(r)/ adj 1 odd or strange. 2 (infml) unwell. 3 (to)// belonging only to a particular person, time, place, etc: an accent ~ to the West of the country. **peculiarity** /pɪˌkjuːliˈærətɪ/ n (pl -ies) 1 [C] strange or unusual quality, habit, etc. 2 [C] something peculiar(3). 3 [U] being peculiar. **peculiarly** adv 1 oddly. 2 especially.

pedagogue (US -gog) /'pedəgɒg/ n [C] 1 (arch or fml) teacher. 2 (derog) very strict teacher. **pedagogy** /'pedəgɒdʒɪ/ n [U] (fml) study of the methods of teaching. **pedagogic** /ˌpedəˈgɒdʒɪk/ (also **pedagogical** /-ɪkl/) adj. **pedagogically** /-ɪklɪ/ adv.

pedal /'pedl/ n [C] lever that drives or controls a machine (eg a bicycle) when pressed down by the foot. **pedal** v (-ll-; US also -l-) [I, T] use a pedal; move by using pedals.

pedant /'pednt/ n [C] (derog) person who values small details and formal rules too highly. **pedantic** /pɪ'dæntɪk/ adj. **pedantically** /-klɪ/ adv.

peddle /'pedl/ v (-ll-) [I, T] go from house to house trying to sell (goods). **peddler** n [C] 1 (US = **PEDLAR**). 2 person who sells illegal drugs.

pedestal /'pedɪstl/ n [C] 1 base of a pillar, for a statue. 2 (idm) **put sb on a 'pedestal** admire sb greatly, without noticing his/her faults.

pedestrian /pɪ'destriən/ n [C] person who walks. **pedestrian** adj 1 not interesting; dull. 2 of or for pedestrians. **pe,destrian 'crossing** n [C] special place marked on a road where vehicles must stop to allow pedestrians to cross.

pediatrics (US) = PAEDIATRICS.

pedigree /'pedɪgriː/ n (a) [C] line of ancestors of an animal or person. (b) [U] quality of having descended from a known line of ancestors of the same breed. **pedigree** adj (of an animal) descended from a known line of ancestors of the same breed.

pedlar /'pedlə(r)/ n [C] person who goes from house to house trying to sell goods.

pee /piː/ v [I] (sl) urinate. **pee** n (sl) 1 [U] urine. 2 [sing] act of urinating.

peek /piːk/ v [I] n [C] (at)|| (take a) quick look at sth.

peel /piːl/ v 1 [T] take the skin off (fruit or vegetables): ~ the potatoes. 2 [I] come off in strips or flakes: The paint is ~ing. 3 (phr v) **peel (sth) off** (infml) remove (one's clothes). **peel** n [U] skin of fruit, etc: lemon ~.

peep¹ /piːp/ v [I] n [sing] (at)|| (take a) quick, often secret, look at sth.

peep² /piːp/ n 1 [C] short high sound. 2 [sing] (infml) sound made by sb, esp sth said.

peer¹ /pɪə(r)/ n [C] 1 (in Britain) (esp male) member of the nobility: Dukes and earls are ~s. 2 [usu pl] person of about the same age and interests as oneself. **peerage** n 1 the **peerage** [sing] all the peers(1). 2 [C] rank of a peer(1). **peeress** n [C] 1 female peer(1). 2 wife of a peer(1). '**peer group** n [C] group of people of about the same age and interests.

peer² /pɪə(r)/ v [I] (at)|| look closely or carefully at (sth), as if unable to see well.

peeved /piːvd/ adj (infml) annoyed. **peevish** /'piːvɪʃ/ adj easily annoyed; bad-tempered. **peevishly** adv.

peg /peg/ n [C] 1 short thin piece of wood, metal or plastic, used to hang things on or for fastening sth. 2 = CLOTHES-PEG (CLOTHES). **peg** v (-gg-) 1 [T] fasten with pegs. 2 [T] (usu passive) fix or keep at a particular level: Pay increases have been ~ged at five per cent. 3 (phr v) **peg out** (infml) die.

pejorative /pɪ'dʒɒrətɪv/, US ·'dʒɔːr-/ adj (fml) expressing criticism.

Pekinese /ˌpiːkɪ'niːz/ n [C] small dog with short legs and long silky hair.

pelican /'pelɪkən/ n [C] large water-bird with a big beak for storing fish to eat. ˌ**pelican 'crossing** n [C] (in Britain) place where pedestrians wanting to cross the road press a button that operates

traffic-lights to stop the traffic.

pellet /'pelɪt/ n [C] 1 small tightly-packed ball of soft material. 2 small metal ball, fired from a gun.

pelmet /'pelmɪt/ n [C] strip of wood, cloth, etc above a window to hide a curtain-rail.

pelt¹ /pelt/ v 1 [T] (with)|| throw sth at (sb). 2 [I] (down)|| (of rain) fall very heavily. (idm) **(at) full pelt** ⇨ FULL.

pelt² /pelt/ n [C] animal's skin with the fur on it.

pelvis /'pelvɪs/ n [C] (anatomy) basin-shaped framework of bones at the lower end of the main part of the human body. **pelvic** /·vɪk/ adj.

pen¹ /pen/ n [C] instrument for writing with ink. **pen** v (-nn-) [T] (fml) write (a letter, etc.). '**pen-friend** n [C] person in another country that one writes to but may never have met. '**penknife** n [C] (pl -knives) small knife with folding blades. '**pen-name** n [C] name used by a writer instead of his/her real name.

pen² /pen/ n [C] small enclosed piece of land for keeping farm animals in. **pen** v (-nn-) [T] (up/in)|| shut up (as if) in a pen.

penal /'piːnl/ adj of the punishment of criminals: reform of the ~ system.

penalize /'piːnəlaɪz/ v [T] (usu passive) 1 punish (sb) for breaking a rule or law. 2 cause (sb) to suffer a disadvantage.

penalty /'penltɪ/ n [C] (pl -ies) 1 punishment for doing wrong: the 'death ~. 2 (sport) disadvantage to a player or team for breaking a rule. 3 disadvantage or inconvenience suffered as a result of an action or situation. '**penalty kick** n [C] (in football) free kick at the goal by the attackers.

penance /'penəns/ n [U, C] punishment that one makes oneself suffer to show that one is sorry for a wrong action.

pence pl of PENNY.

penchant /'pɒnʃɒn; US 'pentʃɒnt/ n [sing] for|| (fml) liking for sth.

pencil /'pensl/ n [C] instrument containing a thin stick of graphite for writing or drawing. **pencil** v (-ll-; US -l-) 1 [T] write or draw with a pencil. 2 (phr v) **pencil sth in** include sth now, although it might be changed in the future.

pendant /'pendənt/ n [C] piece of jewellery that hangs from a chain worn round the neck.

pending /'pendɪŋ/ adj (fml) 1 waiting to be decided. 2 about to

happen. pending *prep* (*fml*) until.
pendulum /ˈpendjʊləm; US
-dʒʊləm/ *n* [C] weight hung so
that it can swing freely, esp in a
clock.
penetrate /ˈpenɪtreɪt/ *v* 1 [I, T]
make a way into or through (sth):
The snow ~d the holes in his shoes.
2 [T] (*fig*) see into or through: ~
the disguise. **penetrating** *adj* 1 (of
a sound) loud and clear. 2 able to
see and understand
quickly.
penetration /ˌpenɪˈtreɪʃn/ *n* [U].
penguin /ˈpeŋgwɪn/ *n* [C] black
and white Antarctic sea-bird with
wings like flippers used for swimming.
penicillin /ˌpenɪˈsɪlɪn/ *n* [U] antibiotic medicine.
peninsula /pəˈnɪnsjʊlə; US
-nsələ/ *n* [C] area of land almost
surrounded by water. **peninsular**
adj.
penis /ˈpiːnɪs/ *n* [C] sex organ of a
male animal.
penitent /ˈpenɪtənt/ *adj* feeling
or showing sorrow for having
done wrong. **penitence** /-təns/
n [U].
penitentiary /ˌpenɪˈtenʃərɪ/ *n* [C]
(*pl* **-ies**) (*US*) prison.
pennant /ˈpenənt/ *n* [C] long narrow pointed flag, used on a ship
for signalling, etc.
penniless /ˈpenɪlɪs/ *adj* without
any money.
penny /ˈpenɪ/ *n* [C] (*pl* **pence**
/pens/ or **pennies**) 1 (since 1971)
British coin worth one hundredth
of a pound. 2 (before 1971) British
coin worth one twelfth of a shilling. 3 (idm) **the penny (has) dropped** (esp *Brit infml*) the meaning
of a remark has at last been understood: *I had to explain the problem
to him several times before the ~
dropped.*
pension[1] /ˈpenʃn/ *n* [C, U] money
paid regularly to sb who is above a
certain age, disabled, widowed,
etc. **pension** *v* (phr v) **pension sb
off** dismiss sb from work and pay
him/her a pension. **pensionable**
adj giving sb the right to receive a
pension. **pensioner** *n* [C] person
receiving a pension, esp because
he/she has retired from work.
pension[2] /ˈpɒnsɪɒn/ *n* [C] small
private hotel, esp in France.
pensive /ˈpensɪv/ *adj* thinking
deeply about sth. **pensively** *adv.*
pentagon /ˈpentəgən; US -gɒn/ *n*
1 [C] flat shape with five sides and
five angles. 2 **the Pentagon** [sing]
(with sing or pl v) the headquarters of the US Defense Department. **pentagonal** /penˈtægənl/
adj.

pentathlon /penˈtæθlən/ *n* [C]
sports contest in which each competitor takes part in five events.
penthouse /ˈpenthaʊs/ *n* [C]
house or flat built on the roof of a
tall building.
pent up /ˌpent ˈʌp/ *adj* (of feelings) not expressed: ~ *anger.*
penultimate /penˈʌltɪmət/ *adj*
next to and before the last one.
penury /ˈpenjʊrɪ/ *n* [U] (*fml*) being extremely poor. **penurious**
/prɪˈnjʊərɪəs; US -ˈnʊr-/ *adj.*
people /ˈpiːpl/ *n* 1 [pl] persons in
general: *How many ~ were at the
party?* 2 [C] nation; race: *the ~s of
Asia.* 3 [pl] persons who live in a
particular place: *the ~ of London.*
4 **the people** [pl] ordinary persons without special rank or position. **people** *v* [T] fill with people.
pep /pep/ *n* [U] (*infml*) energy;
liveliness. **pep** *v* (-**pp-**) (phr v) **pep
sb/sth up** (*infml*) make sb/sth
(feel) more lively or energetic.
'**pep pill** *n* [C] pill taken to make
one feel happier or livelier. '**pep
talk** *n* [C] talk intended to encourage the listeners to work
harder, try to win, etc.
pepper /ˈpepə(r)/ *n* 1 [U] hot-tasting powder made from the dried
berries of certain plants, used for
flavouring food. 2 [C] hollow
rounded vegetable: *green ~s.* **pepper** *v* [T] 1 put pepper on food. 2
(*with/*)// hit (sb/sth) repeatedly
with small objects. ,**peppercorn**
'**rent** *n* [C] very low rent.
peppermint /ˈpepəmɪnt/ *n* (**a**)
[U] kind of mint grown for its
strong-tasting oil. (**b**) [C] sweet flavoured with this oil.
per /pə(r); strong form pɜː(r)/
prep for each: *£60 ~ day.* ,**per
'annum** /ˈænəm/ *adv* for each
year. ,**per 'cent** *adv* for or in each
hundred: *a five ~ cent wage increase.* ,**per 'se** /ˌpɜː ˈseɪ/ *adv* by
or of itself.
perambulator /pəˈræm-
bjʊleɪtə(r)/ *n* [C] (*Brit fml*) pram.
perceive /pəˈsiːv/ *v* [T] (*fml*) become aware of (sth); see or understand.
percentage /pəˈsentɪdʒ/ *n* 1 [C]
rate, number or amount in each
hundred. 2 [also sing with pl v]
proportion: *pay a ~ of one's earnings in tax.*
perceptible /pəˈseptəbl/ *adj*
(*fml*) that can be seen or noticed: *a
~ change in colour.* **perceptibly**
adv.
perception /pəˈsepʃn/ *n* (*fml*) 1
[U] ability to perceive. 2 [C] way of
seeing or understanding sth.
perceptive /pəˈseptɪv/ *adj* (*fml*)

perch[1] /pɜːtʃ/ *n* [C] 1 place, eg a branch, where a bird rests. 2 (*infml*) high seat or position. **perch** *v* 1 [I] (of a bird) rest or stay. 2 [I] sit, esp on sth high or narrow. 3 [I, T] be or put in a high or dangerous position.

perch[2] /pɜːtʃ/ *n* [C] (*pl* **perch**) kind of freshwater fish, eaten as food.

percolate /ˈpɜːkəleɪt/ *v* 1 [I, T] (of water) (cause to) pass slowly through (coffee). 2 [I] *through*|| (eg of news) spread or become known gradually through a group of people. **percolator** *n* [C] coffee pot in which boiling water percolates through crushed coffee beans.

percussion /pəˈkʌʃn/ *n* [U] musical instruments, eg drums, played by being struck.

peremptory /pəˈremptərɪ/; US ˈperəmptɔːrɪ/ *adj* (*fml*) showing that one expects to be obeyed immediately. **peremptorily** /-trəlɪ; US -tɔːrəlɪ/ *adv*.

perennial /pəˈrenɪəl/ *adj* 1 lasting for ever or for a long time. 2 constantly recurring: *a ~ problem*. 3 (of a plant) living for more than two years. **perennial** *n* [C] perennial plant. **perennially** *adv*.

perfect[1] /ˈpɜːfɪkt/ *adj* 1 without fault; excellent: *~ weather*. 2 the best of its kind; ideal: *the ~ example*. 3 having everything needed; complete: *a ~ set of teeth*. 4 exact: *The dress is a ~ fit*. 5 (*infml*) total: *a ~ stranger*. 6 (*grammar*) of a tense formed with *have* and a past participle, eg *I have eaten*. **perfectly** *adv* in a perfect way; completely.

perfect[2] /pəˈfekt/ *v* [T] make perfect. **perfectible** *adj* that can be perfected.

perfection /pəˈfekʃn/ *n* [U] 1 making perfect. 2 being perfect: *The part of 'Macbeth' suited him to ~*. **perfectionist** /-ʃənɪst/ *n* [C] person who is not satisfied with anything less than perfection.

perfidious /pəˈfɪdɪəs/ *adj* (*fml*) disloyal; deceitful.

perforate /ˈpɜːfəreɪt/ *v* [T] 1 make a hole through. 2 make a row of small holes in (esp paper) so that it will tear easily. **perforation** /ˌpɜːfəˈreɪʃn/ *n* [C, U].

perform /pəˈfɔːm/ *v* 1 [T] do (a piece of work): *a ~ a task*. 2 [I, T] act (a play), play (music) or sing to an audience. 3 [I] work or function in the way that is mentioned: *This new car ~s well*. **performance** *n* 1 [U] process or manner of performing. 2 [C] performing of a play,

concert, etc. **performer** *n* [C] person who sings, acts, etc in front of an audience.

perfume /ˈpɜːfjuːm; US pərˈfjuːm/ *n* [C, U] (liquid having a) sweet smell. **perfume** /pəˈfjuːm/ *v* [T] give a sweet smell to.

perfunctory /pəˈfʌŋktərɪ/ *adj* (*fml*) done quickly, without care or interest. **perfunctorily** /-trəlɪ; US -tərəlɪ/ *adv*.

perhaps /pəˈhæps, also præps/ *adv* it may be (that); possibly: *P~ the weather will improve tomorrow*.

peril /ˈperəl/ *n* (*fml*) 1 [U] great danger. 2 [C] something that causes danger. **perilous** *adj*. **perilously** *adv*.

perimeter /pəˈrɪmɪtə(r)/ *n* [C] (length of the) outer edge of a shape or a closed area, eg an airfield.

period /ˈpɪərɪəd/ *n* [C] 1 length of time. 2 (time allowed for a) lesson at school. 3 monthly flow of blood from a woman's womb. 4 (esp US) full stop. **periodic** /ˌpɪərɪˈɒdɪk/ *adj* occurring at (esp regular) intervals. **periodical** /-kl/ *n* [C] magazine that is published at regular intervals. **periodically** /-klɪ/ *adv* at regular intervals; occasionally.

peripatetic /ˌperɪpəˈtetɪk/ *adj* (*fml*) going from place to place, esp to work.

periphery /pəˈrɪfərɪ/ *n* [C] (*pl* -ies) (*fml*) outer edge. **peripheral** /-əl/ *adj* (*fml*) of or on the outer edge: (*fig*) ~ *topics*.

periscope /ˈperɪskəʊp/ *n* [C] instrument with mirrors, for seeing things at a higher level, used esp in submarines.

perish /ˈperɪʃ/ *v* [I] 1 (*fml*) be destroyed; die. 2 decay or rot. **perishable** *adj* (of food) likely to go bad quickly. **perishables** *n* [pl] perishable food. **perishing** *adj* (*infml* esp *Brit*) extremely cold.

perjure /ˈpɜːdʒə(r)/ *v* ~ *oneself* tell a lie in a court of law. **perjury** *n* [C].

perk[1] /pɜːk/ *v* (*phr v*) **perk** (*sb*) *up* become or make sb/sth more cheerful or lively. **perky** *adj* (-ier, -iest) lively; confident.

perk[2] /pɜːk/ *n* [C, usu *pl*] (*infml*) money, goods, etc given by one's employer in addition to one's pay.

perm /pɜːm/ *n* [C] (*infml*) putting of artificial curls into the hair. **perm** *v* [T] give a perm to.

permanent /ˈpɜːmənənt/ *adj* lasting for a long time or for ever. **permanence** /-nəns/ *n* [U]. per-

manently adv.
permeate /'pɜːmɪeɪt/ v [I, T] (through)|| (fml) enter and spread to every part of sth. **permeable** /'pɜːmɪəbl/ adj (fml) that can be permeated.
permissible /pə'mɪsəbl/ adj (fml) that is allowed. **permissibly** /-əblɪ/ adv.
permission /pə'mɪʃn/ n [U] act of allowing.
permissive /pə'mɪsɪv/ adj allowing great freedom of behaviour, esp in sexual matters: the ~ society. **permissiveness** n [U].
permit /pə'mɪt/ v (-tt-) [T] (fml) allow. **permit** /'pɜːmɪt/ n [C] official written paper that allows sb to do sth.
permutation /ˌpɜːmjuːˈteɪʃn/ n [C] (fml) way in which a number of things are arranged.
pernicious /pə'nɪʃəs/ adj (fml) very harmful.
pernickety /pə'nɪkətɪ/ adj (infml often derog) worrying too much about small unimportant things.
perpendicular /ˌpɜːpənˈdɪkjʊlə(r)/ adj 1 upright. 2 at an angle of 90° (to another line or surface). **perpendicular** n [C, U] perpendicular line or position.
perpetrate /'pɜːpɪtreɪt/ v [T] (fml) be guilty of (a crime, etc). **perpetrator** n [C].
perpetual /pə'petʃʊəl/ adj 1 never ending. 2 frequently repeated: their ~ complaints. **perpetually** /-tʃʊəlɪ/ adv.
perpetuate /pə'petʃʊeɪt/ v [T] (fml) cause to continue. **perpetuation** /pəˌpetʃʊ'eɪʃn/ n [U].
perplex /pə'pleks/ v [T] make (sb) feel puzzled or confused, because he/she does not understand sth: They were all ~ed by her behaviour ○ a ~ing problem. **perplexity** /-ətɪ/ n [U] state of feeling perplexed.
per se ⇨ PER.
persecute /'pɜːsɪkjuːt/ v [T] treat (sb) cruelly or unfairly, esp because of his/her religious or political beliefs. **persecution** /ˌpɜːsɪ'kjuːʃn/ n [C, U]. **persecutor** n [C].
persevere /ˌpɜːsɪ'vɪə(r)/ v [I] (in/with)|| continue doing (sth), esp in spite of difficulties: You need to ~ with your studies if you want to pass your exams. **perseverance** n [U].
persist /pə'sɪst/ n [I] 1 (in/with)|| continue to do sth in a firm way: He will ~ in thinking I don't like him. 2 continue to exist: Fog will ~ in most areas. **persistence** n [U]. **persistent** adj continuing;

repeated: ~ent warnings/attacks. **persistently** adv.
person /'pɜːsn/ n [C] (pl **people** /'piːpl/ or, in formal use **persons**) 1 man or woman: You're just the ~ we need. 2 (grammar) any of the three classes of personal pronouns: the first ~, ie I, we ○ the second ~, ie you ○ the third ~, ie he, she, it, they. 3 (idm) **in 'person** actually present; oneself: The actress will be there in ~.
personable /'pɜːsənəbl/ adj having a pleasant appearance or manner: a ~ young woman.
personage /'pɜːsənɪdʒ/ n [C] (fml) important or famous person.
personal /'pɜːsənl/ adj 1 of or belonging to a particular person: ~ belongings. 2 not of one's professional life; private: receive a ~ phone call at work. 3 critical of a person: ~ remarks. 4 of the body: ~ cleanliness. **personally** /'pɜːsənəlɪ/ adv 1 giving one's own opinion: P~ly, I think you're crazy! 2 doing sth oneself. 3 privately. **personal 'pronoun** n [C] (grammar) pronoun I, she, you, etc.
personality /ˌpɜːsə'nælətɪ/ n (pl -ies) 1 [C, U] person's character: a strong ~. 2 [C] famous person, esp from entertainment, sport, etc: a television ~.
personify /pə'sɒnɪfaɪ/ v (pt, pp -ied) [T] 1 represent (sth) as a person. 2 be a good example of (a quality): She ~ kindness. **personification** /pəˌsɒnɪfɪ'keɪʃn/ n [U, C].
personnel /ˌpɜːsə'nel/ n 1 [pl] all the people who work in an organization. 2 [U] department in a company, etc that deals with employees and their problems: a ~ manager.
perspective /pə'spektɪv/ n 1 [U] art of drawing things so as to give the impression of distance, size, etc. 2 [C] (fig) way of thinking about sth. 3 (idm) **in perspective** in a way in which the importance of sth is seen in relation to other things: get/see one's problems in ~.
Perspex /'pɜːspeks/ n [U] (P) strong plastic used instead of glass.
perspire /pə'spaɪə(r)/ v [I] (fml) sweat. **perspiration** /ˌpɜːspə'reɪʃn/ n [U].
persuade /pə'sweɪd/ v [T] 1 cause (sb) to do sth, by discussion, reasoning, etc: They ~d him to try again. 2 (fml) cause (sb) to believe sth; convince.
persuasion /pə'sweɪʒn/ n 1 [U] act of persuading. 2 [C] set of beliefs.

persuasive /pəˈsweɪsɪv/ adj able to persuade: *She can be very ~ when she wants.* **persuasively** adv.

pert /pɜːt/ adj cheeky; disrespectful: *a ~ reply.* **pertly** adv. **pertness** n [U].

pertain /pəˈteɪn/ v [I] *to/l* (fml) be connected with or belong to sth.

pertinent /ˈpɜːtɪnənt/ US /ˈpɜːtənənt/ adj (fml) relevant.

perturb /pəˈtɜːb/ v [T] (fml) make (sb) very worried.

peruse /pəˈruːz/ v [T] (fml) read, esp carefully. **perusal** n [C, U].

pervade /pəˈveɪd/ v [T] (fml) spread through every part of.

pervasive /pəˈveɪsɪv/ adj present or felt everywhere.

perverse /pəˈvɜːs/ adj 1 (of a person) deliberately continuing to do sth wrong or unreasonable. 2 (of behaviour) unreasonable. **perversely** adv. **perversity** n [U].

perversion /pəˈvɜːʃn; US -ʒn/ n 1 [U] changing (sth) from what it should be: *the ~ of truth.* 2 [C, U] unnatural sexual action or desire.

pervert¹ /pəˈvɜːt/ v [T] 1 turn (sth) away from its proper use: *~ the course of justice.* 2 cause (sb) to turn away from what is right or (esp sexually) natural.

pervert² /ˈpɜːvɜːt/ n [C] person whose (esp sexual) behaviour is unnatural and harmful.

pessimism /ˈpesɪmɪzəm/ n [U] belief that bad things will happen. **pessimist** /-mɪst/ n [C]. **pessimistic** /ˌpesɪˈmɪstɪk/ adj.

pest /pest/ n [C] 1 insect or animal that destroys plants, food, etc. 2 (infml) annoying person, esp a child.

pester /ˈpestə(r)/ v [T] annoy or bother constantly.

pesticide /ˈpestɪsaɪd/ n [C, U] chemical substance used for killing pests, esp insects.

pestle /ˈpesl/ n [C] stick with a thick end used for crushing things in a bowl (= MORTAR²(2)).

pet /pet/ n [C] 1 tame animal, eg a cat or dog, kept as a companion. **pet** v (-tt-) 1 [T] treat lovingly, esp by stroking. 2 [I] kiss and touch each other. **'pet name** n [C] name used instead of one's real name by one's friends and family.

petal /ˈpetl/ n [C] coloured leaf-like division of a flower.

peter /ˈpiːtə(r)/ v (phr v) **peter out** gradually come to an end.

petition /pəˈtɪʃn/ n [C] 1 written request to a government, etc, signed by many people. 2 (law) request to a court of law for some legal ac-

tion to be taken. **petition** v [I, T] (fml) make a formal request to (sb).

petrify /ˈpetrɪfaɪ/ v (pt, pp -ied) 1 [T] (usu passive) frighten (sb) greatly. 2 [I, T] change into stone.

petrol /ˈpetrəl/ n [U] liquid obtained from petroleum, used as a fuel in motor vehicles. **'petrol station** n [C] place beside a road where petrol and oil are sold and put into cars, etc.

petroleum /pəˈtrəʊliəm/ n [U] mineral oil that forms underground.

petticoat /ˈpetɪkəʊt/ n [C] thin skirt-like garment, worn under a skirt or dress.

petty /ˈpeti/ adj (-ier, -iest) 1 small and unimportant: *~ details.* 2 concerned with unimportant matters; not generous: *~ jealousies.* **pettiness** n [U]. **petty 'cash** n [U] money kept in an office for small payments. **petty 'officer** n [C] senior non-commissioned officer in the navy.

petulant /ˈpetjʊlənt/ US -tʃʊ-/ adj bad-tempered in a childish way. **petulance** /-ləns/ n [U]. **petulantly** adv.

pew /pjuː/ n [C] long bench-like seat with a back, in a church.

pewter /ˈpjuːtə(r)/ n [U] grey metal made by mixing tin with lead.

phallus /ˈfæləs/ n [C] image of the penis. **phallic** /ˈfælɪk/ adj.

phantom /ˈfæntəm/ n [C] 1 ghost. 2 unreal or imagined thing.

pharaoh /ˈfeərəʊ/ n [C] king of ancient Egypt.

pharmaceutical /ˌfɑːməˈsjuːtɪkl; US -ˈsuː-/ adj of the making of drugs and medicines.

pharmacist /ˈfɑːməsɪst/ n [C] person trained to make and sell medicines.

pharmacy /ˈfɑːməsi/ n (pl -ies) 1 [U] (study of the) preparation of drugs and medicines. 2 [C] (part of a) shop where medicines are sold.

phase /feɪz/ n [C] 1 stage of development. 2 shape that the moon appears to have at a particular time. **phase** v 1 [T] plan or develop in phases. 2 (phr v) **phase sth in/out** begin/stop using sth gradually.

PhD /ˌpiː eɪtʃ ˈdiː/ abbr Doctor of Philosophy.

pheasant /ˈfeznt/ n 1 [C] long-tailed bird often shot for food. 2 [U] its meat.

phenomenal /fəˈnɒmɪnl/ adj enormous; very unusual: *~ success.* **phenomenally** /-nəli/ adv: *~ly successful.*

phenomenon /fə'nɒmɪnən/ *US* ·non/ *n* [C] (*pl* -mena /-mɪnə/) 1 fact or event known to exist, experienced by the senses. 2 remarkable or unusual person, thing, etc.

philanthropy /fɪ'lænθrəpɪ/ *n* [U] giving of money and other help to people in need. **philanthropic** /ˌfɪlən'θrɒpɪk/ *adj*. **philanthropist** /fɪ'lænθrəpɪst/ *n* [C].

philately /fɪ'lætəlɪ/ *n* [U] hobby of collecting postage stamps.

philistine /'fɪlɪstaɪn/ *US* -sti:n/ *n* [C] person who dislikes good art, music, etc.

philosopher /fɪ'lɒsəfə(r)/ *n* [C] 1 person who studies or teaches philosophy. 2 (*infml*) person who thinks deeply about things.

philosophy /fɪ'lɒsəfɪ/ *n* (*pl* -ies) 1 [U] study of the nature and meaning of existence, how people should live, etc. 2 [C] system of thought. **philosophical** /ˌfɪlə'sɒfɪkl/ *adj* 1 of philosophy. 2 having a calm courage in failure, disappointments, etc. **philosophically** /-klɪ/ *adv*. **philosophize** /-faɪz/ *v* [I] talk or think like a philosopher.

phlegm /flem/ *n* [U] 1 thick semi-liquid substance that forms in the nose and throat. 2 (*dated fml*) calmness. **phlegmatic** /fleg'mætɪk/ *adj* slow to show feelings; calm. **phlegmatically** /-klɪ/ *adv*.

phobia /'fəʊbɪə/ *n* [C] strong fear or dislike.

phone /fəʊn/ *n* [C], *v* [I, T] short for TELEPHONE. '**phone book** [C] ⇨ TELEPHONE DIRECTORY (TELE-PHONE). '**phone-box** (also '**phone booth**) *n* [C] = TELEPHONE-BOX (TELEPHONE). '**phone-in** [C] radio or television programme in which telephoned questions and answers from the public are broadcast. '**phone number** = TELEPHONE NUMBER (TELEPHONE).

phonetic /fə'netɪk/ *adj* (*linguistics*) of the sounds of human speech. **phonetically** /-klɪ/ *adv*. **phonetician** /ˌfəʊnɪ'tɪʃn/ *n* [C] expert in phonetics. **phonetics** *n* (with *sing* v) study of speech sounds.

phoney (also **phony**) /'fəʊnɪ/ *adj* (-ier, -iest) (*infml derog*) false; pretended. **phoney** (also **phony**) *n* [C] phoney person or thing.

phonology /fə'nɒlədʒɪ/ *n* [U] (*linguistics*) (study of the) system of speech sounds, esp in a particular language: *English* ~. **phonological** /ˌfəʊnə'lɒdʒɪkl/ *adj*.

phosphorescence /ˌfɒsfə'resns/ *n* [U] production of a faint glow or

light without heat, esp in the dark. **phosphorescent** /-'resnt/ *adj* glowing in the dark.

phosphorus /'fɒsfərəs/ *n* [U] pale yellow waxlike poisonous substance that gives out light.

photo /'fəʊtəʊ/ *n* [C] (*pl* ~s) (*infml*) short for PHOTOGRAPH. ˌ**photo 'finish** *n* [C] finish in a race in which the leading competitors are so close together that a photograph is needed to show the winner.

photocopy /'fəʊtəʊkɒpɪ/ *n* [C] (*pl* -ies) photographic copy. **photocopy** *v* (*pt, pp* -ied) make a photocopy (of). **photocopier** /-ɪə(r)/ *n* [C] machine for photocopying documents, etc.

photogenic /ˌfəʊtəʊ'dʒenɪk/ *adj* looking attractive in photographs.

photograph /'fəʊtəgrɑːf; *US* -græf/ *n* [C] picture recorded by the action of light on film in a camera. **photograph** *v* [T] take a photograph of. **photographer** /fə'tɒgrəfə(r)/ *n* [C] person who takes photographs, esp as a job. **photographic** /ˌfəʊtə'græfɪk/ *adj*. **photography** /fə'tɒgrəfɪ/ *n* [U] art or process of taking photographs.

phrasal /'freɪzl/ *adj* in the form of a phrase. ˌ**phrasal 'verb** *n* [C] group of two or more words with a single meaning, consisting of a verb and an adverb and/or preposition: '*Blow up' and 'look forward to' are ~ verbs*.

phrase /freɪz/ *n* [C] 1 short group of words. 2 (*grammar*) group of words without a verb that form part of a sentence. **phrase** *v* [T] express in words in the way that is mentioned: *a badly ~d example*. '**phrase-book** *n* [C] book containing common foreign expressions and their translations.

phraseology /ˌfreɪzɪ'ɒlədʒɪ/ *n* [U] choice or style of words.

physical /'fɪzɪkl/ *adj* 1 of the body: ~ *exercise* ○ ~ *education*, eg gymnastics, athletics and games. 2 of things that can be touched or seen: *the* ~ *world*. 3 of the laws of nature: *a* ~ *impossibility*. 4 of the natural features of the world: ~ *geography*. **physically** /-klɪ/ *adv*.

physician /fɪ'zɪʃn/ *n* [C] doctor, esp one not specializing in surgery.

physicist /'fɪzɪsɪst/ *n* [C] student of or expert in physics.

physics /'fɪzɪks/ *n* [U] scientific study of matter and energy.

physiology /ˌfɪzɪ'ɒlədʒɪ/ *n* [U] scientific study of how animals' bodies and plants function. **phy-**

siological /ˌfɪziə'lɒdʒɪkl/ adj.

physiologist n [U] student of or expert in physiology.

physiotherapy /ˌfɪziəʊ'θerəpɪ/ n [U] medical treatment by means of exercises, rubbing, heat, etc. **physiotherapist** n [C].

physique /fɪ'ziːk/ n [C] general appearance and size of a person's body.

piano /pɪ'ænəʊ/ n [C] (pl ~s) large musical instrument in which metal strings are struck by hammers operated by pressing black and white keys. **pianist** /'pɪənɪst/ n [C] person who plays the piano.

piccolo /'pɪkələʊ/ n [C] (pl ~s) small flute.

pick¹ /pɪk/ v [T] 1 choose. 2 break (flowers, vegetables, etc) from a plant, etc and collect: ~ strawberries. 3 take up, esp with one's fingers. 4 remove small pieces of unwanted matter from: ~ one's teeth. 5 deliberately cause (a fight or quarrel). 6 open (a lock) without a key. 7 make (a hole) in sth by pulling at it. 8 (of birds) take up (grain, etc) in the beak. 9 (idm) **pick and 'choose** choose slowly and carefully. **pick sb's 'brains** ask sb questions to get information that one can use. **pick holes in sth** find faults in sth. **pick sb's 'pocket** steal money, etc from sb's pocket. 10 (phr v) **pick at sth** eat (food) in very small amounts. **pick on sb** choose sb unfairly for punishment, etc: He's always ~ing on me. **pick sb/sth out** (a) choose sb/sth carefully. (b) see sb/sth clearly in a large group. **pick up** (a) become better, improve. (b) start again. **pick sb up** (a) stop to collect sb in a car. (b) (infml derog) talk to sb one does not know, esp to try to start a sexual relationship. (c) catch or arrest sb. **pick sth up** (a) take hold of and lift up sth. (b) learn (a skill, foreign language, etc). (c) catch (an illness). (d) collect. (e) receive (a radio signal). **picker** n [C] person or thing that picks fruit, etc. **pickings** n [pl] money or profits that can be (easily) gained: rich **pickpocket** n [C] person who steals from people's pockets. **'pick-up** n [C] 1 part of a record-player that holds the needle. 2 small van or truck with low sides. 3 (infml derog) person who is picked up (b).

pick² /pɪk/ n [sing] 1 choice: take your ~. 2 **the pick of sth** the best of sth.

pick³ /pɪk/ n (also **pickaxe** (US **pickax**) /'pɪkæks/) n [C] large

tool with an iron bar having two sharp ends, used for breaking up roads, rocks, etc.

picket /'pɪkɪt/ n [C] worker or group of workers standing outside a place of work esp during a strike to try to persuade others not to enter. **picket** v [I, T] be or place a picket (at): ~ a factory.

pickle /'pɪkl/ n 1 (a) [U] salt water or vinegar, etc for keeping meat, etc in good condition. (b) [C, U] vegetables kept in pickle. 2 [sing] (infml) difficult or unpleasant situation: in a ~. **pickle** v [T] preserve in pickle. **pickled** adj (infml) drunk.

picnic /'pɪknɪk/ n [C] informal meal eaten outdoors. **picnic** v (-ck-) [I]. **picnicker** n [C] person who is having a picnic.

pictorial /pɪk'tɔːrɪəl/ adj of or using pictures.

picture /'pɪktʃə(r)/ n 1 [C] (a) painting, drawing, or photograph, esp as a work of art. (b) photograph. (c) what is seen on a television screen. 2 (Brit dated) (a) [C] cinema film. (b) **the pictures** [pl] cinema: go to the ~. 3 [C] image in the mind. 4 [C] description of what sth is like. 5 (idm) **be/put sb in the 'picture** know/cause sb to know all the facts about a situation. **be the picture of health, happiness,** etc look very healthy, happy, etc. **get the ' picture** (infml) understand a situation. **picture** v [T] 1 imagine: He ~d himself as a rich man. 2 make a picture of.

picturesque /ˌpɪktʃə'resk/ adj 1 attractive to look at: a ~ fishing village. 2 (of language) interesting, because very descriptive.

pidgin /'pɪdʒɪn/ n [C] language that is a mixture of other languages, used esp for business purposes.

pie /paɪ/ n [C, U] meat or fruit covered with pastry and baked in a dish.

piebald /'paɪbɔːld/ adj (of a horse) having black and white patches of irregular shape.

piece¹ /piːs/ n [C] 1 part or bit of sth. 2 part of which sth is made. 3 single item or example of sth: a ~ of furniture ○ a ~ of news/advice. 4 single work of art, music, etc. 5 small object used in a board game: a chess ~. 6 coin: a ten-pence ~. 7 (idm) **give sb a piece of one's ' mind** (infml) tell sb angrily what one thinks, esp about his/her bad behaviour. **go to 'pieces** lose control of oneself. **in one 'piece** unharmed, eg after a dangerous experience. **a piece of cake** (*infml*) very easy. **'piece-work** *n* [U] work paid for by the amount done and not by the hours worked.

piece² /piːs/ *v* (phr v) **piece sth together** put the parts of sth together to make it complete.

piecemeal /'piːsmiːl/ *adv* one (part) at a time: *work done* ~ . **piecemeal** *adj* done in parts.

pier /pɪə(r)/ *n* [C] 1 structure of wood, iron, etc built out into the sea, esp with places of entertainment on it. 2 pillar supporting a bridge, etc.

pierce /pɪəs/ *v* 1 [I, T] (of sharp instruments) go into or through (sth), making a hole in it. 2 [T] (*fig*) (of sound or light) force a way into or through. **piercing** *adj* 1 (of sound) sharp and unpleasant. 2 (of eyes) searching. 3 (of the wind) cold and very strong. **piercingly** *adv*.

piety /'paɪətɪ/ *n* [U] strong religious beliefs and behaviour.

pig /pɪg/ *n* [C] 1 fat short-legged animal without fur, kept on farms for its meat. 2 (*infml derog*) greedy, dirty or rude person. 3 (idm) **make a 'pig of oneself** (*infml*) eat or drink too much. **piggy** *n* [C] (*pl* -ies) (*infml*) (used by children) little pig. **'piggy bank** *n* [C] small container, esp one shaped like a pig, used by children for saving money in. **pig'headed** *adj* refusing to change one's opinion or actions; stubborn. **'pigsty** *n* [C] 1 small building for pigs. 2 (*infml*) very dirty or untidy room or house. **'pigtail** *n* [C] length of plaited hair that hangs down from the back of the head.

pigeon /'pɪdʒɪn/ *n* [C] 1 grey bird of the dove family. 2 (*infml*) responsibility: *That's not my* ~ . **'pigeon-hole** *n* [C] one of a series of small open box-like sections for letters or messages. **pigeon-hole** *v* [T] 1 put strictly into a particular class or group. 2 put aside; avoid dealing with. **'pigeon-toed** *adj* having toes that turn inwards.

piglet /'pɪglɪt/ *n* [C] young pig.

pigment /'pɪgmənt/ *n* 1 [C, U] colouring matter for making dyes or paint. 2 [U] natural colouring matter in the skin, hair, etc. **pigmentation** /ˌpɪgmenˈteɪʃn/ *n* [U] natural colouring.

pigmy = PYGMY.

pike¹ /paɪk/ *n* [C] (*pl* pike) large freshwater fish.

pike² /paɪk/ *n* [C] long wooden spear, formerly used by soldiers.

pilchard /'pɪltʃəd/ *n* [C] small

sea-fish eaten as food.

pile¹ /paɪl/ *n* [C] 1 quantity of things lying one upon another: *a* ~ *of papers*. 2 [usu pl] (*infml*) a lot: ~ *s of work*. 3 (idm) **make a 'pile** (*infml*) earn a lot of money. **pile** *v* 1 [T] make a pile(1) of things: ~ *the books on the table*. 2 [T] load (sth) with sth: *The table was* ~ *d high with boxes*. 3 [I] *into/out of/* enter/ leave (a car, etc) in a disorganized way. 4 (phr v) **pile up** (a) increase in quantity: *The work is* ~ *ing up*. (b) (of vehicles) crash into each other. **'pile-up** *n* [C] road crash involving several vehicles.

pile² /paɪl/ *n* [C] heavy column of wood, metal or concrete pushed into the ground as a foundation for a building, etc.

pile³ /paɪl/ *n* [U] soft surface of threads or loops on a carpet or cloth.

piles /paɪlz/ *n* [pl] = HAEMORRHOIDS.

pilfer /'pɪlfə(r)/ *v* [I, T] steal (esp sth of small value).

pilgrim /'pɪlgrɪm/ *n* [C] person who makes a journey to a holy place. **pilgrimage** /-ɪdʒ/ *n* [C, U] journey made by a pilgrim.

pill /pɪl/ *n* 1 [C] small round piece of medicine. 2 **the pill** [sing] pill taken regularly as a form of birth-control.

pillage /'pɪlɪdʒ/ *v* [I, T] (*fml*) steal things violently from (sb/sth), as in a war.

pillar /'pɪlə(r)/ *n* [C] 1 tall upright post of stone, etc, used as a support for part of a building. 2 active and important member. **'pillar-box** *n* [C] tall round container in the street, in which letters are posted.

pillion /'pɪlɪən/ *n* [C] seat for a passenger behind the driver of a motor cycle.

pillory /'pɪlərɪ/ *v* (*pt, pp* -ied) [T] (*fml*) attack (sb) with words in public.

pillow /'pɪləʊ/ *n* [C] soft cushion used for supporting the head in bed. **pillow** *v* [T] rest (one's head) on a pillow. **'pillowcase** (also **'pillowslip**) *n* [C] cloth cover for a pillow.

pilot /'paɪlət/ *n* [C] 1 person trained to operate the controls of an aircraft. 2 person who guides a ship into or out of a harbour. **pilot** *adj* used for testing sth: *a* '~ *scheme*. **pilot** *v* [T] act as a pilot of; guide. **'pilot-light** *n* [C] small flame that burns all the time on a gas cooker, etc and lights a larger burner.

pimp /pɪmp/ *n* [C] man who controls prostitutes, finds customers for them and makes a profit from them.

pimple /'pɪmpl/ n [C] small sore spot on the skin. **pimply** adj.

pin¹ /pɪn/ n [C] short thin pointed piece of metal with a round head, used for fastening things together. '**pincushion** n [C] small cushion used for sticking pins in when they are not being used. '**pinpoint** v [T] discover or describe exactly. **,pins and 'needles** n [pl] tingling feeling in a limb. '**pinstripe** adj (of cloth) with very narrow stripes.

pin² /pɪn/ v (-nn-) [T] 1 fasten with a pin. 2 hold (sb/sth) firmly so that one cannot move. 3 on// put (esp blame or one's hopes) on sb/sth. 4 (phr v) **pin sb down** make sb agree to do sth which they have been trying to avoid doing: Try and ~ him down to (giving you) an answer. **pin sth down** describe sth exactly: The nature of beauty is difficult to ~ down. '**pin-up** n [C] picture of an attractive person, eg a film star, for pinning on a wall.

pinafore /'pɪnəfɔː(r)/ n [C] loose sleeveless garment worn over a dress to keep it clean.

pincer /'pɪnsə(r)/ n 1 **pincers** [pl] tool used for holding things tightly and pulling out nails. 2 [C] curved claw of a shellfish.

pinch /pɪntʃ/ v 1 [T] press tightly between the thumb and finger or two surfaces. 2 [I] be too tight: These shoes ~. 3 [T] (infml) steal. **pinch** n 1 [C] act of pinching. 2 [C] amount held between the thumb and finger: a ~ of salt. 3 **the pinch** [sing] suffering caused by not having enough money: feel the ~. 4 (idm) **at a 'pinch** if necessary. **take sth with a pinch of salt** ⇨ SALT.

pine¹ /paɪn/ n 1 [C] (also '**pine tree**) evergreen tree with needle-shaped leaves. 2 [U] its pale soft wood.

pine² /paɪn/ v [I] (for; to)// 1 be very unhappy because sb has gone away or has died: ~ for one's lover. 2 have a strong desire for sth that is unlikely to happen.

pineapple /'paɪnæpl/ n [C, U] large juicy tropical fruit with sweet yellow flesh.

ping /pɪŋ/ v [I] n [C] (make a) short sharp high-sounding ringing noise.

ping-pong /'pɪŋpɒŋ/ n [U] = TABLE TENNIS (TABLE).

pinion¹ /'pɪnɪən/ v [T] prevent (sb) from moving, esp by holding or tying his/her arms.

pinion² /'pɪnɪən/ n [C] small cog-wheel.

pink /pɪŋk/ adj of a pale red colour. **pink** n 1 [U] pale red colour. 2 [C] garden plant with sweet-smelling flowers. 3 (idm) **in the pink** in very good health.

pinnacle /'pɪnəkl/ n [C] 1 pointed stone decoration on a roof. 2 high pointed rock. 3 [usu sing] (fig) highest point: the ~ of her career.

pinpoint ⇨ PIN¹.

pin-stripe ⇨ PIN¹.

pint /paɪnt/ n [C] 1 measure for liquids; one eighth of a gallon (0.568 litre). 2 this quantity of milk or beer.

pioneer /,paɪə'nɪə(r)/ n [C] 1 person who is one of the first to go into a new land or area. 2 person who is the first to study a new area of knowledge. **pioneer** v [T] be a pioneer in.

pious /'paɪəs/ adj having or showing a deep belief in God and religion. **piously** adv.

pip¹ /pɪp/ n [C] small seed, eg of an apple, orange or grape.

pip² /pɪp/ n **the pips** [pl] short high-pitched sounds on the radio used for giving the exact time.

pip³ /pɪp/ v (-pp-) 1 (idm) **pip sb at the post** just beat sb in a competition, etc.

pipe¹ /paɪp/ n 1 [C] tube through which liquids or gases can flow. 2 [C] narrow tube with a bowl at one end, used for smoking tobacco. 3 [C] musical instrument consisting of a tube with holes. 4 **pipes** [pl] = BAGPIPES. '**pipe-dream** n [C] impossible idea or plan. '**pipeline** n 1 [C] system of connected pipes, usu underground, for carrying oil or gas. 2 (idm) **in the 'pipeline** being prepared; about to happen.

pipe² /paɪp/ v 1 [T] carry (water, gas, etc) in pipes. 2 [I, T] play a tune (as) on a pipe¹(3)'(4). 3 (phr v) **pipe down** be less noisy; stop talking. **pipe up** (infml) suddenly begin to speak. **piped music** n [U] recorded music played continuously in large shops, stations, etc.

piper /'paɪpə(r)/ n [C] person who plays a pipe¹(3) or bagpipes.

piping /'paɪpɪŋ/ n [U] 1 pipe; system of pipes¹(1). **piping** adj (of a voice) high-pitched. **piping 'hot** adj (of food, etc) very hot.

piquant /'piːkənt/ adj 1 having a pleasantly sharp taste. 2 pleasantly exciting to the mind. **piquancy** /-ənsɪ/ n [U]. **piquantly** adv.

pique /piːk/ n [U] annoyance and bitterness because one's pride has been hurt. **pique** v [T] (usu passive) hurt the pride of.

313 place

piracy /'paɪərəsɪ/ n [U] 1 robbery by pirates. 2 pirating of books, etc.

piranha /pɪ'rɑːnə/ n [C] small tropical American freshwater fish that eats meat.

pirate /'paɪərət/ n [C] 1 (esp formerly) person who robs other ships at sea. 2 person who takes and uses sb else's book, video, etc illegally. **pirate** v [T] illegally use or copy (sb else's book, video, etc).

pirouette /ˌpɪru'et/ n [C] ballet-dancer's fast turn on the toes or ball of the foot. **pirouette** v [I] perform a pirouette.

piss /pɪs/ v (△ sl) 1 [I] pass urine. 2 (phr v) **piss off** (esp Brit) go away. those n (△ sl) 1 (idm) **take the piss (out of sb)** make fun (of sb). **pissed** adj (Brit △ sl) drunk.

pistol /'pɪstl/ n [C] small gun held in one hand.

piston /'pɪstən/ n [C] round plate or short cylinder that moves up and down inside a tube, used in engines, pumps, etc.

pit /pɪt/ n 1 [C] large, usu deep, hole in the ground. 2 [C] large hole in the ground from which minerals are dug out: a *gravel-~*. 3 [C] coal-mine. 4 [C] natural hollow in an animal body: *the ~ of the stomach*, ie where fear is thought to be felt. 5 [C] hollow mark left on the skin after smallpox. 6 [C] space in front of the stage for the orchestra. 7 **the pits** [pl] (in motor racing) place near a race-track where cars stop for fuel, etc during a race. 8 (idm) **be the pits** (infml) be the worst example of sth. **pit** v (-tt-) 1 [T] mark with pits(5) or holes. 2 (phr v) **pit sb/sth against** sb test (sb or esp sb's wits) in a competition or fight with sb.

pitch¹ /pɪtʃ/ n 1 [C] area of ground with lines marked for playing football, cricket, etc. 2 [U] degree of highness or lowness of a sound. 3 [sing] degree or level: *The excitement reached a high ~*. 4 [C] (esp Brit) place where a street trader does business. 5 [sing] talk used by a salesman/saleswoman to sell things: *a clever sales ~*.

pitch² /pɪtʃ/ v 1 [T] throw in the direction that is mentioned. 2 [I, T] (cause sb/sth to) fall heavily esp forwards or outwards. 3 [I] (of a ship or aircraft) move up and down on the water or in the air. 4 [T] set up (a tent). 5 [T] (in music) set in a certain pitch¹(2). 6 [T] express (sth) at a particular level. 7 (phr v) **pitch in** (a) start work energetically. (b) offer help or sup-

port. **pitch into sb** (infml) attack sb violently. **pitched 'battle** n [C] intense violent fight. **'pitchfork** n [C] long-handled fork for lifting hay, etc.

pitch³ /pɪtʃ/ n [U] black substance that is sticky when hot and hard when cold, used for making roofs, etc waterproof. **pitch-'black** adj completely black.

pitcher¹ /'pɪtʃə(r)/ n [C] 1 (esp Brit) large jug with two handles. 2 (US) jug.

pitcher² /'pɪtʃə(r)/ n [C] (in baseball) player who throws the ball to the batter.

piteous /'pɪtɪəs/ adj (fml) arousing or deserving pity: *a ~ cry*. **piteously** adv.

pitfall /'pɪtfɔːl/ n [C] hidden or unexpected difficulty or danger.

pith /pɪθ/ n [U] soft white substance under the skin of oranges, etc and in the stems of some plants. **pithy** adj (-ier, -iest) 1 short, but full of meaning: ~ *remarks*. 2 full of pith. **pithily** adv.

pitiable /'pɪtɪəbl/ adj 1 deserving or arousing pity. 2 causing disrespect; worthless. **pitiably** adv.

pitiful /'pɪtɪfl/ adj 1 arousing pity. 2 causing disrespect; worthless: *a ~ attempt*. **pitifully** adv.

pitiless /'pɪtɪlɪs/ adj showing no pity or mercy; cruel. **pitilessly** adv.

pittance /'pɪtns/ n [usu sing] very small amount of money.

pity /'pɪtɪ/ n 1 [U] feeling of sorrow for the sufferings or troubles of others. 2 [sing] something that is sad and unfortunate: *It's a ~ (that) the weather isn't better*. 3 (idm) **more's the 'pity** (infml) unfortunately. **take 'pity on sb** help sb because one feels sorry for him/her. **pity** v (pt, pp -ied) [T] feel pity for.

pivot /'pɪvət/ n 1 central pin or point on which sth turns. 2 (fig) central or most important person or thing. **pivot** v [I] turn (as) on a pivot. **pivotal** adj.

pixie (also **pixy**) /'pɪksɪ/ n [C] (pl -ies) small elf or fairy.

pizza /'piːtsə/ n [C, U] flat round piece of dough covered with tomatoes, cheese, etc and baked in an oven.

placard /'plækɑːd/ n [C] large notice that is shown publicly.

placate /plə'keɪt/ US /'pleɪkeɪt/ v [T] cause (sb) to stop feeling angry.

place¹ /pleɪs/ n 1 [C] city, town, village, etc: *Canada is a big ~*. 2 [C] building or area used for a particular purpose: *a 'meeting-~*. 3

[C] particular area or position in space occupied by sb/sth. 4 [C] seat or position kept for or occupied by sb. 5 [sing] rank in society's role or duty. 6 [C] position of employment; opportunity to study: *get a ~ at university*. 7 [C] usual or correct position: *Put everything away in the right ~*. 8 [C, usu sing] (in a competition or race) position among the winners. 9 [sing] numbered step in an argument: *in the first ~*. 10 [C, usu sing] (*infml*) home: *come to my ~*. 11 **Place** [sing] (*esp Brit*) (used as part of the name of a short street or square). 12 [C] setting with knife, fork, etc for one person at a table: *lay/set a ~*. 13 (idm) **all 'over the place** (*infml*) (a) everywhere. (b) in an untidy state. **in/out of place** (a) in/not in the usual or correct position. (b) suitable/unsuitable: *His remarks were out of ~*. **in place of sb/sth** as an alternative to sb/sth: *Machines can do this job in ~ of people*. **put sb in his/her 'place** show sb that he/she is not as important as he/she thinks. **take 'place** happen. **take the place of sb/sth** perform the function of sb/sth; be used instead of; replace.

place² /pleɪs/ *v* [T] 1 put in a certain place. 2 appoint (sb) to a position; put (responsibility, etc) on sb. 3 put (an order for goods, etc) with a business company. 4 remember (sb) exactly: *I know her face, but I can't ~ her*. **placement** *n* [U] action of placing sb/sth.

placenta /pləˈsentə/ *n* [C] (*pl* -tae /-tiː/ or ~s) (*anatomy*) organ in the womb during pregnancy, through which the foetus is fed.

placid /ˈplæsɪd/ *adj* calm; not easily angered. **placidly** *adv*.

plagiarize /ˈpleɪdʒəraɪz/ *v* [T] take (the words, ideas, etc of sb else) and use them as if they were one's own. **plagiarism** /-rɪzəm/ *n* [C, U].

plague /pleɪg/ *n* 1 [C, U] disease that spreads quickly and kills many people. 2 [C] (*fig*) cause of great trouble, disaster, etc: *a ~ of locusts*. **plague** *v* [T] (*with/*) (*infml*) annoy continually with sth: *~d him with questions*.

plaice /pleɪs/ *n* [C, U] (*pl* plaice) flat-fish eaten as food.

plaid /plæd/ *n* [C, U] (long piece of) woollen cloth with a pattern of coloured stripes or squares.

plain¹ /pleɪn/ *adj* 1 not decorated; ordinary and simple. 2 easy to see, hear or understand. 3 (of people or their words or actions) honest and

direct. 4 not beautiful or good-looking: *a ~ girl*. 5 (idm) **plain 'sailing** action that is easy and simple to do. **plain** *adv* absolutely; clearly. **plain-clothes** *adj* (*esp* of a police officer) wearing ordinary clothes, not a uniform. **plainly** *adv*. **plainness** *n* [U]. **plain-,spoken** *adj* very honest and direct in one's speech.

plain² /pleɪn/ *n* [C] large area of flat land.

plaintiff /ˈpleɪntɪf/ *n* [C] (*law*) person who brings a legal action against sb.

plaintive /ˈpleɪntɪv/ *adj* sounding sad. **plaintively** *adv*.

plait /plæt/ *v* [T] twist (esp lengths of hair) under and over one another to make one rope-like length. **plait** *n* [C] length of sth, esp hair, that has been plaited.

plan /plæn/ *n* [C] 1 arrangement for doing sth, considered in advance: *make ~s for the holidays*. 2 diagram of the parts of a system, machine, etc. 3 outline drawing of a building, town, garden, etc. **plan** *v* (**-nn-**) [I, T] make a plan of or for (sth). **planner** *n* [C] person who plans, esp how land is to be used in a town.

plane¹ /pleɪn/ *n* [C] 1 = AEROPLANE. 2 (*geometry*) flat surface. 3 (*fig*) level of thought, existence, etc. **plane** *adj* completely flat.

plane² /pleɪn/ *n* [C] flat-bottomed tool with a sharp blade, used for making wood smooth. **plane** *v* [T] make smooth with a plane.

plane³ /pleɪn/ *n* (also **'plane-tree**) *n* [C] tree with broad leaves and thin bark.

planet /ˈplænɪt/ *n* [C] one of the large round natural objects, eg the Earth or Mars, that move round a star, esp the sun. **planetary** /-trɪ/ *adj*.

plank /plæŋk/ *n* [C] long flat piece of wood. **planking** *n* [U] planks, esp as a floor.

plankton /ˈplæŋktən/ *n* [U] very small plants and animals that live near the surface of the sea.

plant /plɑːnt; *US* plænt/ *n* 1 [C] living thing that grows in the earth, with a stem, leaves and roots. 2 [U] machinery used in an industrial process. 3 [C] factory.

plant² /plɑːnt; *US* plænt/ *v* [T] 1 put (plants, seeds, etc) in (a garden, etc). 2 put (sth) firmly in position. 3 (*on/*) (*infml*) hide (stolen goods) on sb to make him/her seem guilty. 4 (*infml*) cause (sb) to join a group secretly, as a spy. **planter** *n* [C] person who works on a plantation.

plantation /plæn'teɪʃn/ *n* [C] area of land planted with trees or crops, eg sugar-cane or tea.

plaque¹ /plɑːk; *US* plæk/ *n* [C] flat piece of stone, metal, etc fixed on a wall as an ornament or memorial.

plaque² /plɑːk; *US* plæk/ *n* [U] (*medical*) harmful substance that forms on the teeth.

plasma /'plæzmə/ *n* [U] clear liquid part of blood, in which the cells are carried.

plaster /'plɑːstə(r); *US* 'plæs-/ *n* 1 [U] mixture of lime, sand, water, etc that becomes hard when dry, used for covering walls and ceilings. 2 [U] (also **plaster of Paris**) white paste that becomes very hard when dry, used for holding broken bones in place: *Her leg is still in ~.* 3 [C, U] (small strip of) fabric that can be stuck to the skin to protect a small wound. **plaster** *v* [T] 1 cover (a wall, etc) with plaster(1). 2 cover thickly: *hair ~ed with oil.* **'plaster cast** *n* [C] 1 mould made with plaster(2) to hold a broken bone in place. 2 copy of a small statue made of plaster(2). **plastered** *adj* (*sl*) drunk. **plasterer** /-rə(r)/ *n* [C] person whose job is to put plaster(1) on walls and ceilings.

plastic /'plæstɪk/ *n* [U, C] light, chemically produced material that can be formed into different shapes. **plastic** *adj* 1 (of goods) made of plastic. 2 (of materials) easily shaped. **plasticity** /plæ'stɪsəti/ *n* [U]. **plastic 'surgery** *n* [U] repairing or replacing injured or damaged skin on the body.

plasticine (also **Plasticine**) /'plæstɪsiːn/ *n* [U] (*P*) soft coloured substance like clay, used by children for making models.

plate /pleɪt/ *n* 1 [C] (a) shallow usu round dish from which food is eaten. (b) contents of this. 2 [U] gold or silver articles, eg spoons and dishes. 3 [C] flat thin sheet of metal or glass. 4 [C] (a) sheet of metal from which the pages of a book are printed. (b) book illustration printed separately from the text. 5 (idm) **hand/give sb sth on a 'plate** give sb sth without him/her making any effort. **on one's 'plate** (*infml*) to deal with or do: *I've got a lot on my ~ at the moment.* **plate** *v* [T] cover (another metal) with a thin layer of gold, silver, etc. **plate 'glass** *n* [U] clear glass made in large thick sheets.

plateau /'plætəʊ; *US* plæ'təʊ/ *n* [C] (*pl* ~s or **-eaux** /-təʊz/) 1 large area of high level ground. 2

state of no change or development: *prices have reached a ~.*

platform /'plætfɔːm/ *n* [C] 1 raised surface beside the track at a railway station. 2 flat raised surface for speakers or performers. 3 main aims and plans of a political party, esp as stated before an election.

plating /'pleɪtɪŋ/ *n* [U] (esp thin) covering of gold, silver, etc.

platinum /'plætɪnəm/ *n* [U] very valuable greyish white metal, used for jewellery, etc.

platitude /'plætɪtjuːd; *US* -tuːd/ *n* [C] (*fml*) statement that is obviously true but not at all new or interesting.

platonic /plə'tɒnɪk/ *adj* (of love or friendship between two people) close and deep, but not sexual.

platoon /plə'tuːn/ *n* [C] small group of soldiers, commanded by a lieutenant.

platter /'plætə(r)/ *n* [C] 1 large shallow dish for serving food. 2 (*arch Brit*) flat wooden dish.

platypus /'plætɪpəs/ *n* [C], **duck-billed 'platypus** small Australian animal with a duck-like beak, which lays eggs and feeds its young on milk.

plausible /'plɔːzəbl/ *adj* seeming to be right or reasonable. **plausibly** *adv*.

play¹ /pleɪ/ *n* 1 [U] activity done for amusement, esp by children. 2 [U] (manner of) playing of a game or sport. 3 [C] story written to be performed by actors. 4 [U] light quick movement: *the ~ of sunlight on water.* 5 [U] (space for) free and easy movement: *a lot of ~ in the rope.* 6 (idm) **bring sth/come into 'play** (cause sth to) have an influence or effect. **a play on 'words** = PUN. **'play-act** *v* [I] make a show of feelings that one does not really have. **'playboy** *n* [C] rich (esp young) man who spends his time enjoying himself. **'playground** *n* [C] area of land where children can play. **'playgroup** *n* [C] informal kind of school for children below school age. **'playhouse** *n* [C] = THEATRE. **'playmate** *n* [C] friend with whom a child plays. **'play-pen** *n* [C] small portable enclosure in which a baby can play. **'plaything** *n* [C] 1 toy. 2 (*fig*) person treated for amusement only and without care. **'playwright** /'pleɪraɪt/ *n* [C] person who writes plays.

play² /pleɪ/ *v* 1 [I] amuse oneself with toys, games, etc. 2 [I, T] (*at*)// pretend to be sb/sth. 3 [I, T] take part in (a game or sport); compete against (sb) in a game. 4 [T] (in cricket, football, etc) hit and send (the ball). 5 [I, T] (a) move (a piece) in chess. (b) put (a playing-card) face upwards on the table. 6 [I, T] perform on (a musical instrument). 7 [T] cause (a record, record-player, etc) to produce sound. 8 [T] perform (a drama) on the stage; act the role of. 9 [T] (infml) behave in the way that is mentioned: ~ *the fool*, ie act foolishly ○ ~ *(it) safe*. 10 [T] (on)// do (sth) that causes other people to laugh at sb: ~ *a joke/trick on sb*. 11 [T] direct or aim: ~ *water on a burning building*. 12 [I] move quickly and lightly: *sunlight* ~*ing on the lake*. 13 (idm) play 'ball (infml) co-operate. **play sth by 'ear** work out how to deal with sth as it happens, without making plans in advance: *We'll* ~ *it by ear depending on the weather*. **play one's 'cards right** act in the most effective way to get sth that one wants. **play it 'cool** (infml) act calmly, not get excited. **play for 'time** try to gain time by delaying. **play the 'game** behave fairly and honestly. **play gooseberry** (infml) be the unwanted third person when two lovers want to be alone together. **play hell with sth** (infml) have a bad, esp damaging, effect on sth. **play into sb's 'hands** do sth that gives (one's opponent) an advantage. **play a part (in sth)** be involved or have an effect in sth. **play second 'fiddle (to sb)** have a less important position than sb in an activity. 14 (phr v) **play a'long (with sb/sth)** pretend to agree or co-operate with sb/sth. **play at sth** (a) do sth with little seriousness or interest. (b) **what sb is playing at** (showing anger) what sb is doing. **play sth 'back** allow the material recorded on a tape to be heard or seen. **play sth 'down** try to make sth appear less important. **play sth off against sb else** cause two people to fight or argue with each other, esp for one's own advantage. **play on sth** try to use (another's feelings or weaknesses) for one's own advantage. **play (sb) up** cause (sb) pain or trouble. **play sth up** try to make sth appear more important. **play up to sb** behave so as to win the favour of sb. **play with sth** consider (an idea, etc) with little seriousness. '**play-back** n [U] playing-back of recorded sound or pictures. '**playing-card** n [C] any of a set of 52 thin pieces of card-

board used for various games. '**playing-field** n [C] large area of grass on which people play sports. '**play-off** n [C] further match between two players who are level, to decide the winner.

player /'pleɪə(r)/ n [C] 1 person who plays a game. 2 person who plays a musical instrument: *a* '*trumpet* ~. 3 actor.

playful /'pleɪfl/ adj 1 fond of playing. 2 not serious. **playfully** adv. **playfulness** n [U].

plaza /'plɑːzə; US 'plæzə/ n [C] open square or market-place.

PLC (also **plc**) /ˌpiː el 'siː/ abbr (Brit) Public Limited Company.

plea /pliː/ n [C] 1 (fml) serious request: ~*s for mercy*. 2 (law) statement made by sb in court, saying whether he/she is guilty or not.

plead /pliːd/ v (pt, pp ~ed; US **pled** /pled/) 1 [I] (with)// make repeated requests to sb. 2 [T] (law) state officially in court that one is (guilty or not guilty). 3 [I] for// (law) (of a lawyer) speak to a lawcourt on behalf of sb. 4 [T] offer as an excuse.

pleasant /'pleznt/ adj 1 giving pleasure; enjoyable. 2 friendly. **pleasantly** adv. **pleasantness** n [U].

pleasantry /'plezntrɪ/ n [C] (pl -ies) (fml) polite friendly remark.

please /pliːz/ interj (used when one is politely making a request): *Come in,* ~. **please** v 1 [I, T] make (sb) happy and satisfied. 2 [I] choose or want: *He does as he* ~*s*. **pleased** adj happy or satisfied: *She was very* ~ *with her exam results*. **pleasing** adj giving pleasure, pleasant.

pleasure /'pleʒə(r)/ n 1 [U] feeling of happiness or enjoyment. 2 [C] something that gives happiness or enjoyment: *It's a* ~ *helping you*. **pleasurable** /-ərəbl/ adj (fml) giving enjoyment. **pleasurably** adv. '**pleasure-boat** n [C] boat used for pleasure only.

pleat /pliːt/ n [C] pressed or stitched fold in cloth. **pleat** v [T] make pleats in.

plebeian /plɪ'biːən/ n [C], adj (derog) (member) of the lower social classes.

plectrum /'plektrəm/ n [C] (pl ~s or -tra /-trə/) small piece of plastic, metal, etc for plucking the strings of a guitar, etc.

pled (US) pt, pp of PLEAD.

pledge /pledʒ/ n [C] 1 solemn promise. 2 something valuable left with sb to be kept until the giver has done what he/she has to do. 3 something given as a sign of love.

pledge /v/ [T] 1 promise solemnly to give or do (sth). 2 decide definitely that (one/sb) will do sth: *The government has ~d itself to fight poverty.*

plenary /'pliːnərɪ/ *adj* (of a meeting) attended by all who have the right to attend: *a ~ session.*

plentiful /'plentɪfl/ *adj* in large quantities: *a ~ supply.* **plentifully** *adv.*

plenty /'plentɪ/ *pron* (of/) as much as or more than is needed: *There's ~ of time before the train goes.*

pleurisy /'plʊərəsɪ/ *n* [U] serious illness with inflammation of the lining of the chest and lungs.

pliable /'plaɪəbl/ *adj* 1 easily bent or shaped. 2 (*fig*) easily influenced. **pliability** /plaɪə'bɪlɪtɪ/ *n* [U].

pliant /'plaɪənt/ *adj* 1 bending easily. 2 (*fig*) easily influenced.

pliers /'plaɪəz/ *n* [pl] tool used for holding small things or for bending or cutting wire.

plight /plaɪt/ *n* [sing] (*fml*) serious and difficult situation.

plimsoll /'plɪmsəl/ *n* [C] light rubber-soled canvas shoe.

Plimsoll line /'plɪmsəl/ *n* [C] line on the side of a ship to show how far it may legally go down in the water when loaded.

plinth /plɪnθ/ *n* [C] square base on which a column or statue stands.

plod /plɒd/ *v* (**-dd-**) 1 walk slowly with heavy steps. 2 work steadily but slowly. **plodder** *n* [C] person who works steadily but slowly.

plonk[1] /plɒŋk/ *v* [T] (*down*) (*infml*) put (sth) heavily and carelessly: *P~ it (down) on the chair.*

plonk[2] /plɒŋk/ *n* [U] (*infml* esp *Brit*) cheap wine of poor quality.

plop /plɒp/ *n* [C] sound of an object dropping smoothly into water. **plop** *v* (**-pp-**) [I] drop with or make a plop.

plot[1] /plɒt/ *n* [C] small piece of land. **plot** *v* (**-tt-**) [T] 1 mark (the position or course of a ship or aircraft) on a map. 2 make (a line) by joining points on a graph.

plot[2] /plɒt/ *n* [C] 1 secret plan made by several people, esp to do sth wrong. 2 events in the story of a film, novel, etc. **plot** *v* (**-tt-**) [I, T] plan secretly to do (sth wrong). **plotter** *n* [C].

plough (*US* **plow**) /plaʊ/ *n* [C] large farming tool for breaking and turning over soil. **plough** (*US* **plow**) *v* 1 [I, T] break up and turn over (soil) with a plough. 2 (*phr v*)

plough sth back put (profits) into the business that produced them. **plough into sth** crash forcefully into sth. **plough (one's way) through sth** make slow and difficult progress through sth.

ploy /plɔɪ/ *n* [C] something said or done to gain an advantage.

pluck /plʌk/ *v* [T] 1 remove (sth) by pulling; pick: *~ flowers/fruit.* 2 pull the feathers off (a hen, etc). 3 (*at/*) take hold of and pull (sth). 4 sound (the strings of a musical instrument) by pulling them and letting them go. 5 (*idm*) **pluck up 'courage** make an effort to be brave. **pluck** *n* [U] courage. **plucky** *adj* (**-ier, -iest**) brave.

plug /plʌg/ *n* [C] 1 piece of rubber or plastic that fits tightly into a hole in a wash-basin or bath. 2 device with metal pins for connecting a piece of equipment to the electricity supply. 3 (*infml*) piece of favourable publicity for a product on radio or television. **plug** *v* (**-gg-**) [T] 1 block or fill (a hole) with sth. 2 (*infml*) give a plug(3) to. 3 (*phr v*) **plug away (at sth)** work hard and steadily at sth. **plug sth in** connect (sth) to the electricity supply with a plug(2). **plug-hole** *n* [C] hole in a wash-basin, bath, etc into which a plug(1) fits.

plum /plʌm/ *n* [C] round sweet smooth-skinned fruit with a stone in the middle. **plum** *adj* (*infml*) considered good and desirable: *a ~ job.*

plumage /'pluːmɪdʒ/ *n* [U] feathers on a bird's body.

plumb /plʌm/ *v* [T] 1 (try to) understand (sth) completely. 2 (*idm*) **plumb the depths of sth** reach the lowest point of sth. **plumb** *adv* exactly: *~ in the middle.* **'plumb-line** *n* [C] piece of string with a weight tied to one end, used esp for testing whether a wall is vertical.

plumber /'plʌmə(r)/ *n* [C] person whose job is to fit and repair water-pipes.

plumbing /'plʌmɪŋ/ *n* [U] 1 system of water-pipes, tanks, etc in a building. 2 work of a plumber.

plume /pluːm/ *n* [C] 1 feather, esp one that is large and brightly coloured. 2 something feather-shaped that rises into the air: *a ~ of smoke.*

plummet /'plʌmɪt/ *v* [I] fall quickly or steeply: *House prices have ~ed.*

plump[1] /plʌmp/ *adj* full and rounded in shape. **plump** *v* (*phr v*) **plump up** cause (sth) to become full and rounded: *~ up the cush-*

ions. **plumpness** n [U].

plump² /plʌmp/ v (phr v) **plump (oneself/sb/sth) down** (cause sb/ sth to) fall or drop suddenly and heavily. **plump for sb/sth** choose sb else's property. **plump** n [C, usu sing] (sound of a) sudden heavy fall.

plunder /'plʌndə(r)/ v [I, T] steal (goods) from a place, esp during a war. **plunder** n [U] 1 action of plundering. 2 goods that have been plundered.

plunge /plʌndʒ/ v [I, T] move suddenly and forcefully forwards and/or downwards: *The car ~d into the river.* *He ~d his hands into his pockets.* **plunge** n 1 [C, usu sing] act of plunging. 2 (idm) **take the 'plunge** finally decide to do sth bold. **plunger** n [C] part of a machine that moves up and down.

pluperfect /ˌpluː'pɜːfɪkt/ n **the pluperfect** [sing] (*grammar*) verb form which expresses an action that is completed before a particular time in the past, formed in English with *had* and a past participle.

plural /'plʊərəl/ n [usu sing], adj (*grammar*) (form of a word) used for referring to more than one: *The ~ of 'child' is 'children'.*

plus /plʌs/ prep 1 with the addition of: *One ~ two equals three.* 2 above zero. 3 (*infml*) as well as; with. **plus** adj above zero; positive. **plus** (also **plus sign**) n [C] mathematical sign (+). 2 (*infml*) favourable addition.

plush /plʌʃ/ adj smart, expensive and comfortable.

plutonium /pluː'təʊniəm/ n [U] (*chemistry*) radioactive element used in nuclear reactors and weapons.

ply¹ /plaɪ/ n [U] 1 thickness of wool, rope, etc, measured by the number of threads in it. 2 thickness of plywood, measured by the number of layers in it. '**plywood** n [U] board made by gluing together thin layers of wood.

ply² /plaɪ/ v (*pt, pp* **plied**) 1 [I, T] (of ships, etc) go regularly along a route: *ferries that ~ between the islands.* 2 (idm) **ply one's 'trade** work at a (skilled) job. 3 (phr v) **ply sb with sth** (a) keep giving sb (food and drink). (b) keeping asking sb (questions).

PM /ˌpiː'em/ abbr (*infml* Brit): Prime Minister.

pm /ˌpiː'em/ abbr after noon.

pneumatic /njuː'mætɪk/ adj 1 worked by compressed air: *a ~ drill.* 2 filled with air: *a ~ tyre.* **pneumatically** /-klɪ/ adv.

pneumonia /njuː'məʊniə/ n [U] serious illness with inflammation of the lungs.

PO /ˌpiː'əʊ/ abbr 1 Post Office. 2 postal order.

poach¹ /pəʊtʃ/ v 1 [I, T] catch (animals) without permission on sb else's property. 2 [T] (*fig*) take from sb/sth dishonestly; steal. **poacher** n [C].

poach² /pəʊtʃ/ v [T] cook (fish, or an egg) without its shell) in water that is boiling gently.

pock /pɒk/ n [C] '**pock-mark** small hollow mark on the skin caused by smallpox. '**pock-marked** adj having marks left after (esp) smallpox.

pocket /'pɒkɪt/ n [C] 1 (a) small bag in an article of clothing, for carrying things. (b) container like this, eg inside a car-door or suitcase. 2 small separate group or area: *~ s of resistance.* 3 [usu sing] money that one has for spending: *within reach of everyone's ~,* ie that everyone can afford. 4 (idm) **out of 'pocket** having spent an amount of one's own money. **pocket** v [T] 1 put into one's pocket. 2 keep or take for oneself, esp dishonestly. **pocket** adj small enough to fit into one's pocket: *a ~ calculator.* '**pocket-book** n [C] small notebook. '**pocket-money** n [U] money given to a child every week by his/her parents.

pod /pɒd/ n [C] long green part of a plant, in which peas or beans grow. **pod** v (**-dd-**) [T] take (peas, etc) out of pods.

podgy /'pɒdʒɪ/ adj (**-ier, -iest**) (of a person) short and fat.

poem /'pəʊɪm/ n [C] piece of writing arranged in lines, usu with a regular rhythm and often with a pattern of rhymes.

poet /'pəʊɪt/ n [C] writer of poems. ˌPoet 'Laureate /'lɒrɪət; *US* 'lɔːr-/ n [C] poet appointed to the British Royal Household to write poems for special occasions.

poetic /pəʊ'etɪk/ (also **poetical** /-ɪkl/) adj 1 graceful and pleasing. 2 of poetry. **poetically** /-klɪ/ adv.

poetry /'pəʊɪtrɪ/ n 1 poems. 2 graceful quality: *the ~ of dance.*

poignant /'pɔɪnjənt/ adj causing deep sadness: *~ memories.* **poignancy** /-jənsɪ/ n [U]. **poignantly** adv.

point¹ /pɔɪnt/ n 1 [C] sharp end: *the ~ of a pin/pencil.* 2 [C] narrow piece of land that extends into the sea. 3 [C] point in writing or printing; full stop or marker of decimals. 4 [C] particular position in space or time. 5 [C] state or degree of progress or temperature: *'boil-*

ing-~. 6 [C] one of the 32 marks on a compass. 7 [C] unit of measurement or scoring: *We won the game by six ~ s.* 8 [C] single idea: *the main ~ s of a story.* 9 **the point** [sing] main idea: *come to/get to the ~ ○ see/miss the ~ of a joke.* 10 [T] purpose; reason: *There's no ~ in going now.* 11 [C] particular feature: *Tidiness is not his strong ~.* 12 [C] electrical socket. 13 **points** [pl] (*Brit*) movable rails by which a train can move from one track to another. 14 (idm) **beside the 'point** not relevant. **make a point of doing sth** make a special effort to do sth. **on the point of doing sth** just about to do sth. **a point of 'view** opinion about sth. **take sb's 'point** understand and accept what sb is saying. **to the 'point** relevant.

point² /pɔɪnt/ *v* 1 [I] (*at/to*)// direct attention to sb/sth; show the position of sb/sth, eg by using one's finger. 2 [T] *at/to* aim or direct (sth) towards sb/sth: *~ a gun at sb.* 3 [T] fill in the joints of (brickwork, etc) with cement. 4 (phr v) **point sth out** direct attention to sth. **pointed** *adj* 1 having a sharp end. 2 (*fig*) directed against a particular person: *~ remarks.* **pointedly** *adv.*

point-blank /ˌpɔɪnt 'blæŋk/ *adj, adv* 1 (of a shot) (aimed or fired) from a very close position. 2 (*fig*) directly and rather rudely: *He refused ~.*

pointer /'pɔɪntə(r)/ *n* [C] 1 stick used for pointing to things. 2 thin piece of metal, plastic, etc that points to numbers on a dial or scale. 3 piece of advice. 4 shorthaired hunting dog.

pointless /'pɔɪntlɪs/ *adj* with no sense or purpose; useless. **pointlessly** *adv.*

poise /pɔɪz/ *n* [U] 1 balanced control of movement. 2 (*fig*) quiet confident self-control. **poise** *v* [I, T] be or keep balanced. **poised** *adj* 1 (*to; for*)// ready for action. 2 (*fig*) having poise(2).

poison /'pɔɪzn/ *n* [C] substance causing death or serious illness if absorbed by a living thing. **poison** *v* [T] 1 give poison to; put poison in. 2 (*fig*) spoil or ruin. **poisonous** *adj.*

poke /pəʊk/ *v* [I, T] 1 push sharply with a stick, etc. 2 put or move with a sharp push: *P~ your head out of the window.* 3 (idm) **poke 'fun at sb** make sb appear foolish. **poke one's nose into sth** ⇨ NOSE¹. **poke** *n* [C] act of poking.

poker¹ /'pəʊkə(r)/ *n* [C] strong

metal rod used for moving coal in a fire.

poker² /'pəʊkə(r)/ *n* [U] card-game played for money.

poky /'pəʊki/ *adj* (-ier, -iest) (*infml derog*) too small.

polar /'pəʊlə(r)/ *adj* 1 of or near the North or South Pole. 2 (*fml*) directly opposite. **'polar bear** *n* [C] white bear living near the North Pole. **polarity** /pə'lærəti/ *n* [U] (*fml*) state of having two opposite qualities or tendencies.

polarize /'pəʊləraɪz/ *v* [I, T] (cause people or views to) form into two groups which are completely opposite to each other: *an issue that ~ d opinions.* **polarization** /ˌpəʊləraɪ'zeɪʃn; US -rɪ'z-/ *n* [U].

pole¹ /pəʊl/ *n* [C] 1 either of the two ends of the Earth's axis: *the North/South P~.* 2 either of the ends of a magnet or the points of an electric battery. 3 (idm) **be 'poles apart** having completely different opinions or beliefs.

pole² /pəʊl/ *n* [C] long thin piece of wood or metal. **'pole-vault** *n* [C] jump over a very high bar, using a long pole.

polecat /'pəʊlkæt/ *n* [C] small fur-covered animal with an unpleasant smell.

police /pə'liːs/ *n* (**the**) **police** [pl] (members of an) official organization whose job is to keep public order, prevent and solve crime, etc. **police** *v* [T] keep order in (a place) (as) with police. **po'lice force** *n* [C] police of a country or region. **po'liceman**, **po'lice-officer**, **po'licewoman** *n* [C] member of a police force. **po'lice station** *n* [C] office of a local police force.

policy /'pɒləsi/ *n* [C] (*pl* -ies) 1 plan of action; statement of aims: *the Government's foreign ~.* 2 written insurance contract.

polio /'pəʊliəʊ/ *n* [U] serious infectious disease of the spinal cord, often causing paralysis.

polish /'pɒlɪʃ/ *v* [I, T] 1 make smooth and shiny by rubbing. 2 (*up*)// (*fig*) improve. 3 (phr v) **polish sth off** finish sth quickly. **polish** *n* 1 [C] substance used for polishing. 2 [sing] action of polishing. 3 [U] (*fig*) quality of fineness. **polished** *adj* skilled and controlled; fine.

polite /pə'laɪt/ *adj* having good manners. **politely** *adv.* **politeness** *n* [U].

politic /'pɒlətɪk/ *adj* (*fml*) (of actions) sensible; wise.

political /pə'lɪtɪkl/ *adj* 1 of the State; of government. 2 of politics;

of political parties. 3 (of people) interested in politics. **politically** /-klɪ/ adv.

politician /ˌpɒlɪˈtɪʃn/ n [C] person who takes part in politics.

politics /ˈpɒlətɪks/ n 1 [also sing with pl v] activities of government; political affairs. 2 [pl] political views. 3 (with sing v) study of government.

polka /ˈpɒlkə; US ˈpəʊlkə/ n [C] (music for a) lively dance.

poll /pəʊl/ n 1 [C] survey of public opinion. 2 [C] election. 3 [sing] number of votes given. **poll** v [T] 1 receive (a certain number of votes). 2 ask (sb) his/her opinions in a poll(1). **'polling-booth** also **'polling-station** n [C] place where voters go to vote. **poll tax** n [sing] (infml) = COMMUNITY CHARGE (COMMUNITY).

pollen /ˈpɒlən/ n [U] fine powder formed on flowers that fertilizes other flowers.

pollinate /ˈpɒləneɪt/ v [T] make fertile with pollen. **pollination** /ˌpɒləˈneɪʃn/ n [U].

pollute /pəˈluːt/ v [T] make dirty or impure: ~d water. **pollution** /pəˈluːʃn/ n [U].

polo /ˈpəʊləʊ/ n [U] ball game played on horseback with long-handled hammers. **'polo neck** n [C] round turned-over collar.

polyester /ˌpɒlɪˈestə(r); US ˈpɒliːestər/ n [U] artificial fabric used for making clothes.

polygamy /pəˈlɪɡəmɪ/ n [U] practice of having more than one wife at the same time.

polygon /ˈpɒlɪɡən; US -ɡɒn/ n [C] figure with five or more straight sides.

polystyrene /ˌpɒlɪˈstaɪriːn/ n [U] light plastic material, used for making containers, etc.

polytechnic /ˌpɒlɪˈteknɪk/ n [C] college for advanced education, esp in scientific and technical subjects.

polythene /ˈpɒlɪθiːn/ n [U] plastic material used for waterproof packaging, etc.

polyunsaturated /ˌpɒliːʌnˈsætʃəreɪtɪd/ adj (esp of vegetable fats) having a chemical structure that does not help cholesterol to form in the blood.

pomegranate /ˈpɒmɪɡrænɪt/ n [C] thick-skinned round fruit with a reddish centre full of seeds.

pomp /pɒmp/ n [U] solemn, magnificent display, esp at a public ceremony.

pompous /ˈpɒmpəs/ adj full of self-importance. **pomposity** /pɒmˈpɒsətɪ/ n [U]. **pompously**
adv.

poncho /ˈpɒntʃəʊ/ n [C] (pl ~s) piece of cloth with a hole for the head, worn as a cloak.

pond /pɒnd/ n [C] small area of water.

ponder /ˈpɒndə(r)/ v [I, T] think about (sth) carefully.

ponderous /ˈpɒndərəs/ adj (fml) 1 slow and awkward. 2 (of speech or writing) serious and dull. **ponderously** adv.

pong /pɒŋ/ v [I] n [C] (Brit infml) (make a) strong unpleasant smell.

pontoon¹ /pɒnˈtuːn/ n [C] flat-bottomed boat or structure, esp supporting a bridge.

pontoon² /pɒnˈtuːn/ n [U] (Brit) kind of card-game.

pony /ˈpəʊnɪ/ n [C] (pl -ies) small horse. **'pony-tail** n [C] hair tied at the back of the head so that it hangs down.

poodle /ˈpuːdl/ n [C] small dog with thick curling hair.

pool¹ /puːl/ n [C] 1 small area of water. 2 small amount of liquid on a surface: a ~ of blood. 3 = SWIMMING-POOL (SWIM).

pool² /puːl/ n 1 [C] common supply of goods, services or people, shared among many: a typing ~. 2 [U] (esp US) game similar to snooker. 3 **the pools** [pl] = FOOTBALL POOLS (FOOT). **pool** v [T] put into a common supply; share.

poor /pɔː(r); US pʊər/ adj 1 having very little money. 2 small in quantity: a ~ crop. 3 low in quality: ~ soil. 4 deserving pity: P~ Lisa is ill. **poorness** n [U].

poorly /ˈpɔːlɪ; US ˈpʊərlɪ/ adj (infml) not well. **poorly** adv in a poor manner, badly.

pop¹ /pɒp/ n 1 [C] short sharp explosive sound. 2 [U] (infml) fizzy drink. **pop** adv with a pop.

pop² /pɒp/ n [C] (infml) father.

pop³ /pɒp/ n [U] (infml) modern popular music with a strong rhythm: a ~ singer/group.

pop⁴ /pɒp/ v (-pp-) 1 [I, T] (cause to) make a short sharp explosive sound. 2 [I] come or go quickly in the direction mentioned: She's just ~ped out to the shops. 3 (phr v) **pop up** appear unexpectedly. **'popcorn** n [U] dried maize heated until it bursts open. **'pop-eyed** adj with eyes wide open with surprise.

pope /pəʊp/ n [C] head of the Roman Catholic Church.

poplar /ˈpɒplə(r)/ n [C] tall straight thin tree.

poppy /ˈpɒpɪ/ n [C] (pl -ies) plant with large red flowers.

populace /ˈpɒpjʊləs/ n the pop-

ulace [sing] (*fml*) (ordinary) people in a country.

popular /ˈpɒpjʊlə(r)/ *adj* 1 liked or enjoyed by many people. 2 (of beliefs) held by many people. 3 of or for ordinary people, not experts. **popularity** /ˌpɒpjʊˈlærəti/ *n* [U]. **popularize** *v* [T] make popular. **popularly** *adv*.

populate /ˈpɒpjʊleɪt/ *v* [T] (usu passive) live in (an area) as its population.

population /ˌpɒpjʊˈleɪʃn/ *n* [C] (number of) people living in a particular country, city, etc.

porcelain /ˈpɔːsəlɪn/ *n* [U] (articles made of) fine china.

porch /pɔːtʃ/ *n* [C] covered entrance to a building.

porcupine /ˈpɔːkjupaɪn/ *n* [C] animal with long pointed spikes on its back.

pore[1] /pɔː(r)/ *n* [C] tiny opening in the skin, through which sweat passes.

pore[2] /pɔː(r)/ *v* (phr v) **pore over** sth study sth carefully.

pork /pɔːk/ *n* [U] meat from a pig.

porn /pɔːn/ *n* [U] (*infml*) short for PORNOGRAPHY.

pornography /pɔːˈnɒɡrəfi/ *n* [U] books, films, etc that show sexual activity in order to cause sexual excitement. **pornographic** /ˌpɔːnəˈɡræfɪk/ *adj*.

porous /ˈpɔːrəs/ *adj* allowing liquid or air to pass through.

porpoise /ˈpɔːpəs/ *n* [C] sea-animal like dolphin.

porridge /ˈpɒrɪdʒ/ *US* /ˈpɔːr-/ *n* [U] soft food made by heating crushed oats in water or milk.

port[1] /pɔːt/ *n* [C] 1 harbour. 2 town or city with a harbour.

port[2] /pɔːt/ *n* [U] left side of a ship or aircraft when it is facing forward.

port[3] /pɔːt/ *n* [U] strong sweet dark-red wine of Portugal.

portable /ˈpɔːtəbl/ *adj* that can be carried.

porter /ˈpɔːtə(r)/ *n* [C] 1 person whose job is to carry luggage, etc at a railway station. 2 person whose job is to be on duty at the entrance of a hotel, etc.

portfolio /pɔːtˈfəʊliəʊ/ *n* [C] (pl ~s) 1 flat case for carrying papers, drawings. 2 set of business shares owned. 3 position and duties of a minister of state.

porthole /ˈpɔːthəʊl/ *n* [C] window in the side of a ship or aircraft.

portion /ˈpɔːʃn/ *n* [C] 1 part or share of sth. 2 amount of food for one person. **portion** *v* (phr v) **portion sth out** divide sth into shares.

portly /ˈpɔːtli/ *adj* (-ier, -iest) stout; fat.

portmanteau /pɔːtˈmæntəʊ/ *n* [C] (pl ~s or ~x /-təʊz/) large oblong leather case for clothes.

portrait /ˈpɔːtreɪt, also -trɪt/ *n* [C] 1 picture of a person. 2 description in words.

portray /pɔːˈtreɪ/ *v* [T] 1 make a picture. 2 describe in words. 3 act the part of, in a play. **portrayal** *n* [C, U].

pose /pəʊz/ *v* 1 [I] (*for*)// sit or stand in a particular position, to be photographed, drawn, etc. 2 [I] *as*// pretend to be sb. 3 [T] cause (a difficulty or problem). 4 [T] (*fml*) ask (a question). **pose** *n* [C] 1 position when being photographed, drawn, etc. 2 unnatural way of behaving. **poser** *n* [C] difficult question.

posh /pɒʃ/ *adj* (*infml*) smart; expensive.

position /pəˈzɪʃn/ *n* 1 [C, U] place where sb/sth is. 2 [C] way in which sb/sth is placed; posture: *lie in a comfortable ~* . 3 [C] opinion or attitude. 4 [C] situation; condition: *I am not in a ~* (ie I am unable) *to help you*. 5 [C] (*fml*) job. 6 [C] place or rank in relation to others. 7 (idm) **in position** in the right or proper place. **position** *v* [T] place.

positive /ˈpɒzətɪv/ *adj* 1 clear and definite: ~ *proof*. 2 [C] (of a person) certain and confident: *I'm ~ he's here*. 3 useful; helpful. 4 (*mathematics*) (of a number) more than zero. 5 of the kind of electric charge carried by protons. 6 (*infml*) complete; real: *a ~ pleasure*. **positively** *adv* definitely; really.

possess /pəˈzes/ *v* [T] 1 have; own. 2 (esp passive) (esp of a feeling) control (sb's mind): *~ed by jealousy*. **possessor** *n* [C] (*fml*) owner.

possession /pəˈzeʃn/ *n* 1 [U] possessing; ownership. 2 [C, esp pl] thing that one owns.

possessive /pəˈzesɪv/ *adj* 1 unwilling to share what one owns. 2 (*grammar*) of or showing possession: *'Yours' is a ~ pronoun*. **possessively** *adv*. **possessiveness** *n* [U].

possibility /ˌpɒsəˈbɪləti/ *n* (pl -ies) 1 [U] state of being possible; likelihood. 2 [C] something that may happen.

possible /ˈpɒsəbl/ *adj* 1 that can be done; that can exist. 2 reasonable; acceptable. **possible** *n* [C] person or thing that might be chosen. **possibly** *adv* 1 perhaps. 2 reasonably: *I'll come as soon as I ~*

can.

post¹ /pəʊst/ n 1 [U] official system of collecting, transporting and delivering letters and parcels. 2 [C, U] (one collection or delivery of) letters, parcels, etc. **post** v [T] send by post. **'post-box** n [C] box into which letters are put for collection. **'postcard** n [C] card for sending messages by post without an envelope. **'post-code** n [C] group of letters and numbers used as part of an address, to make sorting and delivery easier. **post-'haste** adv (fml) very quickly. **'postman** /-mən/ (pl -men) n [C] person whose job is to collect and deliver letters, etc. **'postmark** n [C] official mark on a letter, etc, giving the place and date of posting. **'post-office** n [C] building where postal business takes place. **'post-office box PO box** n [C] numbered place in a post office where letters are kept for collection.

post² /pəʊst/ n 1 [C] upright piece of wood, metal, etc supporting or marking sth. 2 [sing] place where a race finishes. **post** v [T] 1 fix (a notice) in a public place. 2 make known by means of a posted notice.

post³ /pəʊst/ n [C] 1 job. 2 place where sb, esp a soldier, is on duty. **post** v [T] 1 send (sb) to a job, esp abroad. 2 put (a guard, soldier, etc) on duty.

postage /'pəʊstɪdʒ/ n [U] amount charged for the sending of a letter, etc by post. **'postage stamp** n [C] = STAMP¹ 1.

postal /'pəʊstl/ adj of the post¹(1). **'postal order** n [C] written form for money, to be cashed at a post office.

post-date /ˌpəʊst'deɪt/ v [T] write on (esp a cheque) a date later than the actual date of writing.

poster /'pəʊstə(r)/ n [C] large printed notice or picture.

posterior /pɒ'stɪərɪə(r)/ adj (fml) placed nearer or at the back.

posterity /pɒ'sterətɪ/ n [U] (fml) future generations.

postgraduate /ˌpəʊst'grædʒʊət/ adj (of studies, etc) after gaining a first degree. **postgraduate** n [C] person doing such studies.

posthumous /'pɒstjʊməs; US 'pɒstʃəməs/ adj happening after death. **posthumously** adv.

post-mortem /ˌpəʊst 'mɔːtəm/ n [C] 1 medical examination to find the cause of death. 2 (infml) review of an event after it has happened.

postpone /pə'spəʊn/ v [T] arr-

ange for (sth) to happen at a later time than originally planned: The match was ~d because of the rain. **postponement** n [C, U].

postscript /'pəʊsskrɪpt/ n [C] extra message written at the end of a letter.

posture /'pɒstʃə(r)/ n 1 [U] way of standing, sitting, etc. 2 [C] attitude of mind.

posy /'pəʊzɪ/ n [C] (pl -ies) small bunch of flowers.

pot¹ /pɒt/ n 1 [C] (a) round container, esp one used for cooking things in. (b) contents of this. 2 [U] (sl) marijuana. 3 **pots** [pl] (infml) large amount: ~s of money. 4 (idm) go to 'pot (infml) be spoilt or ruined. take ,pot 'luck accept whatever is available, without any choice. **,pot-'bellied** adj (infml) having a fat stomach. **'pot-hole** n [C] 1 deep hole worn in rock by water. 2 hole in a road made by rain and traffic. **'pot-shot** n [C] carelessly aimed shot.

pot² /pɒt/ v (-tt-) [T] plant in a flowerpot. **potted** adj 1 (of cooked meat or fish) put into a pot to preserve it. 2 (of a book, etc) in a short simplified form.

potassium /pə'tæsɪəm/ n [U] soft silver-white metal.

potato /pə'teɪtəʊ/ n [C, U] (pl ~es) round vegetable, with a brown or red skin, that grows underground.

potent /'pəʊtnt/ adj powerful: ~ arguments/drugs. **potency** /-tnsɪ/ n [U]. **potently** adv.

potential /pə'tenʃl/ adj that may come into existence, action or use. **potential** n [U] qualities that exist and can be developed. **potentiality** /pəˌtenʃɪ'ælətɪ/ n [C, U] (pl -ies) (fml) power or quality that can be developed. **potentially** /-ʃəlɪ/ adv.

potion /'pəʊʃn/ n [C] drink of medicine, poison, or magical liquid.

potter¹ /'pɒtə(r)/ v (phr v) **potter about/around** work in an unhurried relaxed way, doing small unimportant tasks.

potter² /'pɒtə(r)/ n [C] person who makes pottery. **pottery** n (pl -ies) 1 [U] (pots, etc made of) baked clay. 2 [C] place where pottery is made.

potty¹ /'pɒtɪ/ adj (-ier, -iest) (Brit infml) foolish or mad.

potty² /'pɒtɪ/ n [C] (pl -ies) pot that young children use as a toilet.

pouch /paʊtʃ/ n [C] 1 small bag carried in the pocket or on the belt. 2 bag-like pocket of skin, on eg a kangaroo.

poultry /ˈpəʊltrɪ/ n 1 [pl] hens, ducks, etc. 2 [U] meat of these.

pounce /paʊns/ v [I] (on/)] 1 make a sudden downward attack on sb/ sth. 2 (fig) seize sth eagerly: She ~d on the chance to go abroad.

pound¹ /paʊnd/ n [C] 1 unit of money in Britain; 100 pence. 2 unit of money of various other countries, eg Ireland. 3 measure of weight; 16 ounces (0.454 kilogram).

pound² /paʊnd/ n [C] place where lost dogs and cats are kept until claimed by their owners.

pound³ /paʊnd/ v 1 [I, T] strike (sth) heavily and repeatedly. 2 [T] crush to powder; break to pieces. 3 [I] (of sb's heart) beat heavily.

pour /pɔː(r)/ v 1 [I, T] (cause a liquid to) flow in a continuous stream. 2 [I] (of rain) fall heavily. 3 [I] come or go in a continuous stream: In summer tourists ~ into London. 4 (idm) **pour cold water on sth** ⇒ COLD¹. 5 (phr v) **pour sth out** tell sth freely and fully: ~ out one's troubles.

pout /paʊt/ v [I] push one's lips forward, in annoyance. **pout** n [C, usu sing] act of pouting.

poverty /ˈpɒvətɪ/ n [U] state of being poor. **'poverty-stricken** adj extremely poor.

powder /ˈpaʊdə(r)/ n [C, U] (substance in the form of a) mass of fine dry particles. **powder** v [T] put (esp sweet-smelling) powder on. **powdered** adj in the form of a powder. **'powder-room** n [C] women's toilet in a hotel, etc. **powdery** adj of or like powder.

power /ˈpaʊə(r)/ n 1 [U] (in people) ability to do or act. 2 [C] (also powers) [pl] particular ability of the body or mind: the ~ of speech. 3 [U] strength. 4 [C] (a) control over others. (b) political control: The Conservative Party came to ~ in 1979. 5 [C, U] legal right; authority. 6 [C] person, country, etc with great authority or influence: a world ~. 7 [U] energy or force that can be used to do work: nuclear ~. **power** v [T] supply power to: ~ed by electricity. **'power-station** n [C] building where electricity is produced.

powerful /ˈpaʊəfl/ adj having or producing great power. **powerfully** adv.

powerless /ˈpaʊəlɪs/ adj without power; unable: ~ to act. **powerlessness** n [U].

pp abbr pages.

PR /ˌpiː ˈɑː(r)/ abbr public relations.

practicable /ˈpræktɪkəbl/ adj

that can be done or used: ~ ideas.

practicability /ˌpræktɪkəˈbɪlətɪ/ n [U].

practical /ˈpræktɪkl/ adj 1 concerned with actually doing sth rather than theory. 2 suitable for the purpose for which it was made: ~ clothing for wearing in bad weather. 3 (of a person) clever at doing and making things. 4 (of a person) sensible. **practicality** /ˌpræktɪˈkælətɪ/ n [C, U] (pl -ies). **practical 'joke** n [C] trick played on sb. **practically** /-klɪ/ adv 1 almost: ~ no time left. 2 in a practical manner.

practice /ˈpræktɪs/ n 1 [U] actual doing of sth: put a plan into ~. 2 [C, U] regularly repeated exercise to improve one's skill. 3 [C, U] usual way of doing sth; procedure or custom: standard ~. 1 [C] (a) work of a doctor or lawyer. (b) (place of) business of a doctor or lawyer. 5 (idm) **in/out of 'practice** having/not having spent time doing practice.

practise (US -ice) /ˈpræktɪs/ v 1 [I, T] do (sth) repeatedly or regularly to improve one's skill: ~ the piano. 2 [T] make (sth) part of one's behaviour by doing it regularly. 3 [I, T] (as)) work as a doctor or lawyer. 4 [T] do actively: ~ one's religion. 5 (idm) **practise what one 'preaches** do what one advises others to do. **practised** adj experienced; skilled.

practitioner /prækˈtɪʃənə(r)/ n [C] 1 person who practises a skill or art. 2 person who practises a profession, esp medicine.

pragmatic /prægˈmætɪk/ adj concerned with practical results; sensible and realistic.

prairie /ˈpreərɪ/ n [C] large area of flat grass-covered land in North America.

praise /preɪz/ v [T] 1 say that one approves of and admires (sb/sth). 2 worship (God). **praise** n [U] expression of praise. **'praiseworthy** adj deserving praise.

pram /præm/ n [C] four-wheeled carriage for a baby, pushed by hand,.

prance /prɑːns; US præns/ v [I] 1 (of a horse) jump about on its back legs. 2 move in a happy or exaggerated way.

prank /præŋk/ n [C] mischievous trick.

prattle /ˈprætl/ v [I] talk for a long time about unimportant things. **prattle** n [U] unimportant chatter.

prawn /prɔːn/ n [C] edible shellfish like a large shrimp.

pray /preɪ/ v [I] 1 speak to God, to give thanks or to ask for help. 2 (*infml*) hope very strongly: *I just ~ he won't get hurt.*

prayer /preə(r)/ n 1 [U] praying. 2 [C] words used in praying. 3 [C] form of religious worship.

preach /priːtʃ/ v 1 [I, T] give a religious talk in a church service. 2 [T] try to persuade people to accept (sth). 3 [I] give unwanted advice on morals. **preacher** n [C].

preamble /priːˈæmbl/ n [C, U] introduction, esp to a formal document.

precarious /prɪˈkeəriəs/ adj not steady or safe; uncertain. **precariously** adv.

precaution /prɪˈkɔːʃn/ n [C] action taken in advance to avoid danger or trouble: *take ~s against illness.* **precautionary** adj.

precede /prɪˈsiːd/ v [T] come or go before in time, place or order. **preceding** adj existing or coming before.

precedence /ˈpresɪdəns/ n [U] (*fml*) right to come before sb/sth in importance: *take ~ over all others.*

precedent /ˈpresɪdənt/ n [C, U] (*fml*) earlier decision or action that is taken as a rule for the future: *set a ~.*

precinct /ˈpriːsɪŋkt/ n 1 [C] (*Brit*) area of a town with a special use: *a shopping ~.* 2 [C] division of a city, county, etc. 3 **precincts** [pl] space enclosed by outer walls or boundaries of a university, church, etc.

precious /ˈpreʃəs/ adj 1 of great value. 2 (*derog*) (of language, style, etc) unnaturally polite or fine. **precious** adv (*infml*) very: *~ little time.*

precipice /ˈpresɪpɪs/ n [C] very steep cliff.

precipitate /prɪˈsɪpɪteɪt/ v [T] 1 (*fml*) cause (an event) to happen more quickly: *Illness ~d her death.* 2 (*chemistry*) cause (solid matter) to separate from a liquid. **precipitate** n [C, U] (*chemistry*) solid matter that has been precipitated(2). **precipitate** /prɪˈsɪpɪtət/ adj too hurried. **precipitation** /prɪˌsɪpɪˈteɪʃn/ n [U] 1 precipitating. 2 being hurried. 3 fall of rain, snow, etc.

precipitous /prɪˈsɪpɪtəs/ adj (*fml*) dangerously high or steep.

précis /ˈpreɪsiː; US preˈsiː/ n [C] (*pl* **précis** /-iːz/) short statement of the main points of a speech or piece of writing.

precise /prɪˈsaɪs/ adj 1 stated clearly and accurately. 2 exact. 3 showing care about small details.

precisely adv 1 exactly. 2 (used for showing agreement) you are right.

precision /prɪˈsɪʒn/ n [U] exactness and accuracy.

preclude /prɪˈkluːd/ v [T] (*from*)// (*fml*) prevent (sth) from happening.

precocious /prɪˈkəʊʃəs/ adj (of a child) having developed intelligence earlier than is normal. **precociously** adv. **precociousness** n [U].

preconceived /ˌpriːkənˈsiːvd/ adj (of an opinion) formed in advance, before gaining enough knowledge. **preconception** /-ˈsepʃn/ n [C] preconceived idea.

precursor /ˌpriːˈkɜːsə(r)/ n [C] (*fml*) something that comes before and leads to sth more important.

predatory /ˈpredətrɪ; US -tɔːrɪ/ adj (of animals) killing other animals for food. **predator** /-tə(r)/ n [C] predatory animal.

predecessor /ˈpriːdɪsesə(r); US ˈpredə-/ n [C] person who had a job or position before sb else.

predestined /ˌpriːˈdestɪnd/ adj decided in advance (by God or by fate).

predicament /prɪˈdɪkəmənt/ n [C] difficult or unpleasant situation.

predicate /ˈpredɪkət/ n [C] (*grammar*) part of a statement that says sth about the subject, eg 'is short' in 'Life is short'.

predicative /prɪˈdɪkətɪv; US ˈpredɪkeɪtɪv/ adj (*grammar*) coming after a verb.

predict /prɪˈdɪkt/ v [T] say in advance that (sth) will happen. **predictable** adj that can be predicted. **prediction** /-ˈdɪkʃn/ n 1 [U] predicting. 2 [C] something predicted.

predispose /ˌpriːdɪˈspəʊz/ v [T] (*fml*) influence (sb) in the way that is mentioned in advance. **predisposition** /-dɪspəˈzɪʃn/ n [C].

predominant /prɪˈdɒmɪnənt/ adj (*fml*) more powerful, important or noticeable. **predominance** /-nəns/ n [U]. **predominantly** adv mainly.

predominate /prɪˈdɒmɪneɪt/ v [I] (*fml*) 1 have control or power. 2 be greater in numbers, strength, etc.

pre-eminent /ˌpriːˈemɪnənt/ adj (*fml*) best of all. **pre-eminence** /-nəns/ n [U]. **pre-eminently** adv.

preen /priːn/ v 1 [I, T] (of a bird) clean and smooth (its feathers) with its beak. 2 (*fig*) ~ oneself (of a person) tidy oneself.

prefabricated /ˌpriːˈfæbrɪkeɪtɪd/ adj (of a building) made in parts that have been produced in advance in a factory and fitted together later.

preface /'prefɪs/ n [C] introduction to a book. **preface** v [T] (with)// (fml) begin by saying or doing sth.

prefect /'pri:fekt/ n [C] **1** older pupil who has authority over younger pupils. **2** (in France) chief administrative officer of an area.

prefer /prɪ'fɜ:(r)/ v (-rr-) [T] **1** like better: I ~ tea to coffee. **2** (idm) **prefer 'charges** (law) make an accusation (against sb). **preferable** /'prefrəbl/ adj more desirable or suitable. **preferably** adv.

preference /'prefrəns/ n **1** [U, sing] (for)// liking for sth (more than sth else). **2** [C] thing that is liked better. **3** [U] favour shown to one person, group, etc.

preferential /,prefə'renʃl/ adj giving or receiving preference(3): get ~ treatment.

prefix /'pri:fɪks/ n [C] syllable, eg pre- or un-, placed in front of a word to change its meaning. **prefix** v [T] add a prefix to.

pregnant /'pregnənt/ adj **1** having a baby or young animal in the womb. **2** (fig) full of (unexpected) meaning: a ~ 'pause. **pregnancy** /-nənsɪ/ n [C, U] (pl -ies).

prehistoric /,pri:hɪ'stɒrɪk; US -tɔ:rɪk/ adj of the time before recorded history. **prehistory** /,pri:'hɪstrɪ/ n [U].

prejudge /,pri:'dʒʌdʒ/ v [T] (fml) decide or form an opinion about (sth) before knowing all the facts.

prejudice /'predʒodɪs/ n **1** [C, U] unfair dislike of sb/sth. **2** [U] (law) harm. **prejudice** v [T] **1** cause (sb) to have a prejudice(1). **2** cause harm to; weaken. **prejudicial** /,predʒʊ'dɪʃl/ adj.

prelate /'prelət/ n [C] high-ranking clergyman.

preliminary /prɪ'lɪmɪnərɪ; US -nerɪ/ adj coming first: a ~ study/ report. **preliminary** n [C] (pl -ies) (usu pl) preliminary action, etc.

prelude /'prelju:d/ n [C] **1** action, event, etc that acts as an introduction to another. **2** introductory piece of music.

premarital /,pri:'mærɪtl/ adj before marriage: ~ sex.

premature /'premətjʊə(r); US ,pri:mə'tʊər/ adj happening before the proper or expected time: ~ birth. **prematurely** adv.

premeditated /,pri:'medɪteɪtɪd/ adj planned or considered in advance: ~ murder.

premier /'premɪə(r); US 'pri:mɪə(r)/ n [C] head of the

government. **premier** adj first in importance, position, etc. **premiership** n [U].

première /'premɪeə(r); US prɪ'mɪər/ n [C] first public performance of a play or film.

premise /'premɪs/ n [C] (fml) statement on which reasoning is based.

premises /'premɪsɪz/ n [pl] building with its land, considered as a piece of property: The company is looking for larger ~.

premium /'pri:mɪəm/ n [C] **1** money paid for an insurance policy. **2** additional payment. **'Premium Bond** n [C] (Brit) government savings certificate that gives a chance of a cash prize.

premonition /,premə'nɪʃn, ,pri:-/ n [C] feeling that sth unpleasant is going to happen.

preoccupation /,pri:ɒkjʊ'peɪʃn/ n **1** [U] being preoccupied. **2** [C] something that a person thinks about all the time.

preoccupy /,pri:'ɒkjʊpaɪ/ v (pt, pp -ied) [T] take all the attention of (sb).

preparation /,prepə'reɪʃn/ n **1** [U] preparing: work done without ~. **2** [C, usu pl] arrangement for a future event. **3** [C] mixture that has been prepared for use as medicine, food, etc.

preparatory /prɪ'pærətrɪ; US -tɔ:rɪ/ adj preparing for sth. **pre'paratory school** n [C] **1** (in Britain) private school for pupils up to the age of 13. **2** (in the US) (usu private) school that prepares students for college.

prepare /prɪ'peə(r)/ v [I, T] get or make (sb/sth) ready. **2** (idm) **be prepared to do sth** be willing to do sth.

preposition /,prepə'zɪʃn/ n [C] (grammar) word, eg in, from or to, often placed before a noun or pronoun to show place, direction, etc. **prepositional** /-ʃənl/ adj.

preposterous /prɪ'pɒstərəs/ adj completely unreasonable; ridiculous. **preposterously** adv.

prerogative /prɪ'rɒgətɪv/ n [C] right or privilege of a particular person or group.

Presbyterian /,prezbɪ'tɪərɪən/ n [C], adj (member of a) Church governed by officials of equal rank.

prescribe /prɪ'skraɪb/ v [T] **1** order the use of: ~ medicine. **2** (fml) state with authority (what must be done).

prescription /prɪ'skrɪpʃn/ n [C] (a) doctor's written in for a medicine. (b) this r

[U] act of prescribing.

prescriptive /prɪˈskrɪptɪv/ adj (fml) making rules or giving orders.

presence /ˈprezns/ n [U] 1 being present in a place. 2 person's appearance and manner.

present¹ /ˈpreznt/ adj 1 being in this/that place: Were you ~ at the meeting when the news was announced? 2 existing or happening now: the ~ government. 3 (grammar) (of a verb form) showing an action or state in the present: the ~ tense ○ a ~ participle. **present** n 1 the present [sing] now. 2 (idm) at 'present now.

present² /ˈpreznt/ n [C] something given; gift.

present³ /prɪˈzent/ v [T] 1 (with, to)// give (sth) to (sb), esp formally: ~ her with a book ○ ~ it to her. 2 (to)// introduce (sb) to sb, esp of higher rank. 3 offer for consideration. 4 ~ oneself (a) appear or attend. (b) (of an opportunity) occur: The opportunity may not ~ itself again. 5 show or reveal. 6 show (eg a play) to the public. 7 introduce (a programme) on radio or television. **presenter** n [C] person who introduces (a programme) on radio or television.

presentable /prɪˈzentəbl/ adj fit to appear or be shown in public. **presentably** adv.

presentation /ˌprezn'teɪʃn; US ˌpriːzen-/ n 1 [C] presenting. 2 [U] way in which sth is presented; appearance. 3 [C] something that is presented.

presently /ˈprezntli/ adv 1 soon: I'll see you ~. 2 (esp US) now.

preservative /prɪˈzɜːvətɪv/ n [C], adj (substance) used for preserving sth, esp food.

preserve /prɪˈzɜːv/ v [T] 1 keep in an unchanged condition. 2 keep safe from harm or danger. 3 keep (food) from decay, eg by drying or freezing. **preservation** /ˌprezə'veɪʃn/ n [U]. **preserve** n [C, usu pl, U] preserved fruit; jam.

preside /prɪˈzaɪd/ v [I] (over/at)// be in charge of a formal meeting.

presidency /ˈprezɪdənsi/ n [pl -ies) 1 the presidency [sing] position of being a president. 2 [C] term of office as a president.

president /ˈprezɪdənt/ n [C] 1 elected head of state in the US and some other republics. 2 head of a government department, company, etc. **presidential** /ˌprezɪ'denʃl/ adj.

press¹ /pres/ v 1 [T] push firmly against. 2 [T] make (sth) flat and smooth by using a hot iron. 3 [T]

use force or weight to get juice out of (fruit). 4 try repeatedly to persuade (sb); urge. 5 [I] (esp of a crowd) move in the direction that is mentioned by pushing: The crowd ~ed forward. 6 (idm) be pressed for sth have barely enough of sth: be ~ed for time. 7 (phr v) press for sth make repeated and urgent requests for sth. press on (with sth) continue doing sth in a determined way. **pressing** adj urgent: ~ing business.

press² /pres/ n 1 [C, usu sing] act of pressing. 2 [C] machine for pressing sth. 3 the press [sing] (with sing or pl) (writers for) newspapers. 4 [sing] treatment given by newspapers, etc: The film got a good ~. 'press conference n [C] meeting at which a politician, etc answers reporters' questions.

pressure /ˈpreʃə(r)/ n 1 [C, U] (force produced by) pressing: the ~ of her hand on his head. 2 [C, U] (force of) the weight of a gas: air ~. 3 [U] force or strong persuasion. 4 [U] worry caused by a lot of difficulties in one's life or work: The ~ of work is making her ill. 'pressure-cooker n [C] airtight pot in which food is cooked quickly by steam. 'pressure group n [C] organized group of people who try to persuade the government, etc to act in a certain way.

pressurize /ˈpreʃəraɪz/ v [T] 1 (into)// use forceful influence to make (sb) do sth. 2 keep (a cabin in an aircraft, etc) at a constant air pressure.

prestige /pre'stiːʒ/ n [U] respect or admiration caused by success, status, etc. **prestigious** /-'stɪdʒəs/ adj having or bringing prestige.

presumably /prɪˈzjuːməbli; US -'zuː-/ adv one may presume that.

presume /prɪˈzjuːm; US -'zuːm/ v 1 [T] suppose to be true. 2 [I] (fml) be bold enough to do sth; dare: I wouldn't ~ to advise you.

presumption /prɪˈzʌmpʃn/ n 1 [C] something presumed. 2 [U] (fml) too bold or disrespectful behaviour.

presumptuous /prɪˈzʌmptʃuəs/ adj acting without the necessary authority; too bold.

presuppose /ˌpriːsə'pəʊz/ v [T] (fml) 1 accept as true in advance. 2 require as a condition. **presupposition** /-ˈsʌpə'zɪʃn/ n [C, U].

pretence (US **-tense**) /prɪ'tens/ n [C, U] act of pretending sth: a ~

of grief.

pretend /prɪˈtend/ *v* [I, T] behave in a way that is intended to make people believe (that sth is true) when in reality it is not.

pretension /prɪˈtenʃn/ *n* [C, U, esp pl] claim to possess a skill or great importance.

pretentious /prɪˈtenʃəs/ *adj* claiming great importance. **pretentiously** *adv.* **pretentiousness** *n* [U].

pretext /ˈpriːtekst/ *n* [C] reason that is not true.

pretty /ˈprɪti/ *adj* (-ier, -iest) pleasing and attractive: *a ~ girl.* **prettily** *adv.* **prettiness** *n* [U]. **pretty** *adv* 1 quite; fairly: *I'm ~ sure he came back.* 2 (idm) **pretty well** almost.

prevail /prɪˈveɪl/ *v* [I] (*fml*) 1 exist or happen generally. 2 win. 3 (phr v) **prevail on/upon sb to do sth** persuade sb to do sth. **prevailing** *adj* 1 most usual. 2 (of winds) most frequent.

prevalent /ˈprevələnt/ *adj* (*fml*) existing generally; common. **prevalence** /-ləns/ *n* [U].

prevent /prɪˈvent/ *v* [T] stop (sb) from doing sth; stop (sth) from happening. **prevention** /-ˈvenʃn/ *n* [U]. **preventive** *adj* intended to prevent: *~ ive medicine.*

preview /ˈpriːvjuː/ *n* [C] showing of a film, play, etc in private before it is shown to the public. **preview** *v* [T] give a preview of.

previous /ˈpriːvɪəs/ *adj* coming before: *the ~ day.* **previously** *adv.*

prey /preɪ/ *n* [U] animal, bird, etc killed by another for food. **prey** *v* 1 (idm) **prey on sb's 'mind** trouble sb greatly. **prey on sth** hunt and catch (an animal, etc) as prey.

price /praɪs/ *n* 1 [C] sum of money for which sth is sold or bought. 2 [sing] what must be done or experienced to obtain sth: *a small ~ to pay for freedom.* **price** *v* [T] fix the price of. **priceless** *adj* 1 extremely valuable. 2 (*infml*) very funny.

prick¹ /prɪk/ *v* 1 [T] make a small hole in (sth) with sth with a sharp point. 2 [I, T] (cause to) feel a sharp pain in the skin. 3 (idm) **prick up one's 'ears** (a) (of a horse, dog, etc) raise its ears. (b) (of a person) suddenly listen carefully.

prick² /prɪk/ *n* [C] 1 small hole caused by pricking. 2 pain caused by pricking. 3 (△ *sl*) (a) penis. (b) (*derog*) stupid man.

prickle /ˈprɪkl/ *n* [C] 1 small sharp point growing on a plant or on the skin of an animal. 2 prick-

ing feeling on the skin. **prickle** *v* [I, T] give or have a pricking feeling. **prickly** *adj* (-ier, -iest) 1 covered with prickles. 2 (*infml*) easily angered.

pride /praɪd/ *n* 1 [U] (a) feeling of satisfaction that one gets from doing sth well. (b) [sing] object of this: *Their daughter was their ~ and joy.* 2 [U] self-respect. 3 [U] too high an opinion of oneself. 4 [C] group of (esp) lions. **pride** *v* (phr v) **pride oneself on sth** be pleased and satisfied about sth.

priest /priːst/ *n* [C] clergyman of the Christian Church, esp of the Roman Catholic Church. **the priesthood** *n* [sing] position of being a priest.

prig /prɪg/ *n* [C] (*derog*) very moral person who disapproves of others' behaviour. **priggish** *adj.*

prim /prɪm/ *adj* (~ **mer**, ~ **mest**) easily shocked by anything rude: *~ and proper.*

primary /ˈpraɪməri; *US* -meri/ *adj* 1 first in time or order of development. 2 most important. **primarily** /ˈpraɪmərəli; *US* praɪˈmerəli/ *adv* mainly. **primary** *n* [C] (*pl* -ies) (in the US) election in which voters choose candidates for a coming election. **primary 'colour** *n* [C] red, yellow or blue. **'primary school** *n* [C] 1 (in Britain) school for children of 5-11 years. 2 (in the US) part of an elementary school, for children of (usu) 6-9 years.

primate¹ /ˈpraɪmeɪt/ *n* [C] member of the most highly developed group of mammals, including humans, apes and monkeys.

primate² /ˈpraɪmeɪt/ *n* [C] archbishop.

prime¹ /praɪm/ *adj* 1 most important. 2 of the best quality. **prime 'minister** *n* [C] chief minister in a government.

prime² /praɪm/ *n* [sing] best part: *in the ~ of life.*

prime³ /praɪm/ *v* [T] 1 cover (wood) with primer. 2 supply (sb) with information in advance.

primer /ˈpraɪmə(r)/ *n* [C] special paint put on before the main layer.

primeval (also **-aeval**) /praɪˈmiːvl/ *adj* very ancient.

primitive /ˈprɪmɪtɪv/ *adj* 1 of or at an early stage of social development: *~ tribes.* 2 simple; old-fashioned. **primitively** *adv.*

primrose /ˈprɪmrəʊz/ *n* [C] wild plant with pale yellow flowers in spring.

prince /prɪns/ *n* [C] 1 male member of a royal family, esp the son of a king or queen. 2 male royal ruler of a small country. **princely** *adj* 1 of or for a prince. 2 generous.

princess /prɪn'ses/ *n* [C] 1 female member of a royal family, esp the daughter of a king or queen. 2 wife of a prince.

principal /'prɪnsəpl/ *adj* most important; main. **principal** *n* [C] 1 head of a college or school. 2 [usu sing] money lent, on which interest is paid. **principally** /-plɪ/ *adv* mainly.

principality /ˌprɪnsɪ'pælətɪ/ *n* [C] (*pl* -**ies**) country ruled by a prince.

principle /'prɪnsəpl/ *n* 1 [C] basic general truth: *the ~ of justice.* 2 [C, U] rule for personal behaviour. 3 [idm] **in principle** concerning the basic idea, but perhaps not the details. **on principle** because of one's beliefs.

print[1] /prɪnt/ *v* 1 [T] (a) make letters, etc on (paper) by pressing ink-covered shapes on it. (b) make (books, etc) in this way. 2 [I, T] write with letters that are not joined together. 3 [T] make (a photograph) from a negative film. **printer** *n* [C] 1 person or company that prints books, etc. 2 machine, eg attached to a computer, for printing. **printout** *n* [C, U] printed paper produced from a computer, etc.

print[2] /prɪnt/ *n* 1 [U] letters, words, etc in printed form. 2 [C] mark left on a surface: *finger ~ s.* 3 [C] picture made by printing from an ink-covered surface. 4 [C] photograph printed from a negative. 5 [idm] **in/out of print** (of a book) available/no longer available.

prior /'praɪə(r)/ *adj* earlier in time, order or importance: *a ~ engagement.* '**prior to** *prep* before.

priority /praɪ'ɒrətɪ; *US* -'ɔːr-/ *n* (*pl* -**ies**) 1 [U] (right of) being more important. 2 [C] something that is (considered) more important than others.

prise (also esp *US* **prize**) /praɪz/ *v* [T] use force to open or remove (sth).

prism /'prɪzəm/ *n* [C] transparent block of glass that separates light into the colours of the rainbow.

prison /'prɪzn/ *n* [C, U] building in which criminals are kept as a punishment. **prisoner** *n* [C] person kept in prison. **prisoner of 'war** *n* [C] soldier caught by the enemy in war.

privacy /'prɪvəsɪ, 'praɪv-/ *n* [U] state of being alone and undisturbed.

private /'praɪvɪt/ *adj* 1 of or for

the use of one person or group, not the public. 2 not to be told or shown to others; secret. 3 not concerned with one's work; personal. 4 not organized or paid for by the government; independent: *a ~ school.* 5 (of a place) quiet; away from people. **private** *n* 1 [C] soldier of the lowest rank. 2 [idm] **in private** with no one else present. **privately** *adv.*

privatize /'praɪvɪtaɪz/ *v* [T] transfer (a company) from State to private ownership. **privatization** /ˌpraɪvɪtaɪ'zeɪʃn; *US* -tɪ'z-/ *n* [U].

privet /'prɪvɪt/ *n* [U] evergreen bush often used for garden hedges.

privilege /'prɪvɪlɪdʒ/ *n* 1 [C, U] special right or advantage available only to a particular person or group. 2 [C] opportunity that gives one great pleasure: *a ~ to hear him sing.* **privileged** *adj* having privileges.

prize[1] /praɪz/ *n* [C] something given for winning a competition, doing good work, etc. **prize** *adj* winning or likely to win a prize: *~ cattle.* **prize** *v* [T] value highly.

prize[2] (esp *US*) = PRISE.

pro[1] /prəʊ/ *n* [idm] the **pros and 'cons** /'kɒnz/ arguments for and against.

pro[2] /prəʊ/ *n* [C] (*pl* ~ s) (*infml*) short for PROFESSIONAL.

pro- /prəʊ/ *prefix* supporting: *pro-American.*

probability /ˌprɒbə'bɪlətɪ/ *n* (*pl* -**ies**) 1 [U, sing] likelihood: *There is little ~ that you will win.* 2 [C] (most) probable event or result. 3 [idm] **in all proba'bility** very probably.

probable /'prɒbəbl/ *adj* likely to happen or be true. **probably** *adv.*

probation /prə'beɪʃn; *US* prəʊ-/ *n* [U] 1 system of officially checking the behaviour of sb who has committed a crime rather than sending him/her to prison: *a ~ officer,* ie person whose job is to watch and help people on probation. 2 testing of sb's abilities, etc to find out if he/she is suitable.

probe /prəʊb/ *v* [I, T] 1 investigate (sth) closely. 2 examine (sth) with a probe(1). **probe** *n* [C] 1 long thin metal instrument for examining a wound, etc. 2 (*into*)) careful investigation into sth. 3 spacecraft used for investigating.

problem /'prɒbləm/ *n* [C] something that is difficult to deal with or understand. **problematic** /ˌprɒblə'mætɪk/ *adj* full of problems.

procedure /prə'siːdʒə(r)/ *n* [C, U]

usual or proper way of doing sth.
procedural adj.

proceed /prə'si:d; US prəʊ-/ v [I]
1 (to)// continue; go on. 2 (fml)
move or go in the direction that is
mentioned.

proceedings /prə'si:dɪŋz/ n [pl]
(fml) 1 legal action against sb. 2
what takes place at a meeting, etc.

proceeds /'prəʊsi:dz/ n [pl] money obtained from sth; profits.

process /'prəʊses; US 'prɒses/ n
1 [C] series of actions carried out
in order to do or achieve sth. 2 [C]
method, esp one used in industry
to make sth. 3 (idm) **in the
process of doing sth** actually still
doing sth. **process** v [T] 1 treat
(food) in order to preserve it. 2 develop (a photographic film). 3 deal
with: ~ *an application.* 4 analyse
(information) using a computer.

procession /prə'seʃn/ n [C] line
of people, vehicles, etc moving along, esp as part of a ceremony.

proclaim /prə'kleɪm/ v [T] (fml)
make known officially or publicly.
proclamation /,prɒklə'meɪʃn/ n
1 [C] something that is pro-
claimed. 2 [U] act of proclaiming.

procure /prə'kjʊə(r)/ v [T] (fml)
obtain.

prod /prɒd/ v (-dd-) 1 [I, T] push
(sb/sth) with one's finger or a pointed object. 2 [T] (fig) urge (sb) to do
sth. **prod** n [C].

prodigal /'prɒdɪgl/ adj (fml derog) spending money wastefully.

prodigious /prə'dɪdʒəs/ adj enormous; wonderful. **prodigious-
ly** adv.

prodigy /'prɒdɪdʒɪ/ n [C] (pl -ies)
person who is unusually able or
clever.

produce /prə'dju:s; US -'du:s/
v [T] 1 cause (sth) to occur. 2 make;
manufacture. 3 bring out to be
looked at. 4 organize (eg a play or
film) for the stage, television, etc.
produce /'prɒdju:s; US -du:s/
n [U] things that have been
produced, esp by farming.

producer /prə'dju:sə(r); US
-'du:-/ n [C] 1 person who
produces(4) a play, film, etc. 2 person, company, etc that produces
goods.

product /'prɒdʌkt/ n [C] 1 something produced(2). 2 result. 3
(mathematics) number obtained
by multiplying two numbers
together.

production /prə'dʌkʃn/ n 1 [U]
process of producing. 2 [U] quantity produced. 3 [C] play, film, etc
that is produced(4).

productive /prə'dʌktɪv/ adj 1
producing goods or crops in large

quantities. 2 achieving a lot; useful: *a ~ meeting.* **productively**
adv.

productivity /,prɒdʌk'tɪvətɪ/
n [U] rate of producing goods: *P~
has fallen sharply.*

profane /prə'feɪn; US prəʊ-/ adj
(fml) 1 showing disrespect for
holy things. 2 shocking: ~ *language.* 3 not spiritual; secular.
profane v [T] (fml) treat with disrespect. **profanely** adv. **profan-
ity** /prə'fænətɪ; US prəʊ-/ n [C, U]
(pl -ies) (instance of) profane behaviour or language.

profess /prə'fes/ v [T] (fml) 1
claim (sth), often falsely: *I don't ~
to be an expert.* 2 state openly. 3
have as one's religion. **professed**
adj 1 (falsely) claimed. 2 self-
declared.

profession /prə'feʃn/ n [C] 1 occupation, esp one needing special
knowledge, eg medicine or law. 2
public statement.

professional /prə'feʃənl/ adj 1
of a profession(1). 2 having or
showing a high standard of work.
3 doing as a job what others do as
a hobby: *a ~ actor.* **professional**
n [C] professional person.
professionalism n [U] skill or
qualities of a professional.
professionally /-ʃənəlɪ/ adv.

professor /prə'fesə(r)/ n [C] university teacher of the highest
grade. **professorial** /,prɒfɪ-
'sɔ:rɪəl/ adj. **professorship** n [C]
position of a professor.

proffer /'prɒfə(r)/ v [T] (fml) offer.

proficient /prə'fɪʃnt/ adj skilled.
proficiency /-nsɪ/ n [U]. **profi-
ciently** adv.

profile /'prəʊfaɪl/ n [C] 1 side
view of the human face. 2 brief
biography. 3 (idm) a ,high/low
'profile a way of behaving that at-
tracts/does not attract attention.

profit /'prɒfɪt/ n 1 [C, U] money
gained in business, etc. 2 [U] (fml)
advantage gained from sth. **profit**
v [I] *from/by//* gain an advantage
or benefit from sth. **profitable** adj
1 bringing profit. 2 (fig) useful: *a
~ discussion.* **profitably** adv.

profound /prə'faʊnd/ adj (fml) 1
deep; very great: *a ~ effect.* 2
having or showing great knowledge or thought. **profoundly** adv
deeply.

profuse /prə'fju:s/ adj (fml) in
great quantity. **profusely** adv.
profusion /-'fju:ʒn/ n [sing, U]
(fml) very large quantity: *a ~ of
flowers ○ flowers growing in ~.*

program /'prəʊgræm; US -grəm/
n [C] 1 set of instructions for a

computer. 2 (*US*) = PROGRAMME.

program *v* (**-mm-**; *US* also **-m-**) [T] 1 give a set of instructions to (a computer). 2 (*US*) = PROGRAMME.

programmer /'prəugræmə(r)/ *US* also **programer** *n* [C] person who writes programs for a computer.

programme /'prəugræm/ *n* [C] 1 television or radio broadcast. 2 plan of what is to be done: *a ~ of modernization.* 3 list of items in eg a concert or course of study. **programme** *v* [T] plan or control.

progress /'prəugres; *US* 'prɒg-/ *n* [U] 1 forward movement. 2 improvement; development. 3 (idm) **in progress** happening; being done. **progress** /prə'gres/ *v* [I] make progress.

progression /prə'greʃn/ *n* 1 process of progressing. 2 [C] set or series.

progressive /prə'gresɪv/ *adj* 1 favouring new, modern ideas: *~ policies.* 2 taking place by a series of small changes over a period of time. **progressive** *n* [C] person with progressive(1) ideas. **progressively** *adv.*

prohibit /prə'hɪbɪt; *US* prəu-/ *v* [T] (*fml*) 1 forbid from doing sth. 2 prevent.

prohibition /,prəuhɪ'bɪʃn; *US* ,prəuə'bɪʃn/ *n* 1 [U] prohibiting. 2 [C] order that forbids sth.

prohibitive /prə'hɪbɪtɪv; *US* prəu-/ *adj* 1 (of prices) so high that one cannot afford to buy. 2 that prohibits. **prohibitively** *adv.*

project[1] /'prɒdʒekt/ *n* [C] (plan for a) scheme or undertaking.

project[2] /prə'dʒekt/ *v* 1 [T] plan. 2 [T] estimate, using known facts: *~ the population growth.* 3 [T] (*on(to)*) cause (light, a film, etc) to appear on a screen or surface. 4 [T] make known (sb/sth/oneself) to others in a way that creates a good impression. 5 [I] stick out from a surface.

projectile /prə'dʒektaɪl/ *n* [C] object fired from a gun or thrown.

projection /prə'dʒekʃn/ *n* 1 [U] projecting. 2 [C] something that sticks out from a surface. 3 [C] estimate that is based on known facts.

projector /prə'dʒektə(r)/ *n* [C] apparatus for projecting pictures onto a screen.

proletariat /,prəulɪ'teəriət/ *n* **the proletariat** [sing] (with sing or pl *v*) the working class.

proliferate /prə'lɪfəreɪt; *US* prəu-/ *v* [I] increase rapidly in numbers. **proliferation** /prə,lɪfə'reɪʃn; *US* prəu-/ *n* [U].

prolific /prə'lɪfɪk/ *adj* (of a

writer, artist, etc) producing many works.

prologue (*US* also **-log**) /'prəulɒg; *US* -lɔːg/ *n* [C] 1 introduction to a play, poem, etc. 2 act or event that leads to sth.

prolong /prə'lɒŋ; *US* -'lɔːŋ/ *v* [T] make (sth) last longer. **prolonged** *adj* continuing for a long time.

promenade /,prɒmə'nɑːd; *US* -'neɪd/ *n* [C] paved area for walking next to the beach at a seaside town.

prominent /'prɒmɪnənt/ *adj* 1 (of a person) famous and important. 2 noticeable or important. 3 sticking out. **prominence** *n* 1 [U] being prominent. 2 [C] (*fml*) part or place that sticks out. **prominently** *adv.*

promiscuous /prə'mɪskjuəs/ *adj* (*derog*) having sexual relations with many people. **promiscuity** /,prɒmɪ'skjuːətɪ/ *n* [U]. **promiscuously** *adv.*

promise /'prɒmɪs/ *n* 1 [C] written or spoken statement to do sth. 2 [U] sign of future success or good results: *His work shows great ~.* **promise** *v* 1 [I, T] make a promise (to). 2 [T] make (sth) seem likely: *It ~ s to be a hot day.* **promising** *adj* likely to succeed.

promontory /'prɒməntrɪ; *US* -tɔːrɪ/ *n* [C] (*pl* **-ies**) point of high land that stretches out into the sea.

promote /prə'məut/ *v* [T] 1 give (sb) a higher position or rank. 2 help the progress of; encourage or support. 3 advertise. **promoter** *n* [C] person who organizes or supports sth.

promotion /prə'məuʃn/ *n* [C, U] 1 (instance of) promoting. 2 advertising or other activity to increase the sales of sth.

prompt[1] /prɒmpt/ *adj* done or acting without delay: *a ~ reply.* **promptly** *adv.* **promptness** *n* [U].

prompt[2] /prɒmpt/ *v* 1 [T] cause (sb) to do sth. 2 [I] [T] remind (an actor) of the words that he/she has forgotten. **prompt** *n* [C] action of prompting(2). **prompter** *n* [C] person who prompts actors.

prone /prəun/ *adj* 1 (*to*) likely to be affected by sth: *~ to infection* ○ *accident-~.* 2 lying flat, face downwards.

prong /prɒŋ; *US* prɔːŋ/ *n* [C] thin pointed part of a fork.

pronoun /'prəunaun/ *n* [C] (*grammar*) word, eg *hers* or *it* used instead of a noun.

pronounce /prə'nauns/ *v* [T] 1 make the sound of (a word or letter). 2 (*fml*) state officially. **pro-**

nounced *adj* very noticeable.
pronouncement *n* [C] formal official statement.

pronunciation /prəˌnʌnsɪˈeɪʃn/ *n* 1 [U] way in which a language is spoken. 2 [C] way in which a word is spoken.

proof¹ /pruːf/ *n* 1 [C, U] something that shows that sth is true or is a fact. 2 [U] testing. 3 [C, esp pl] trial copy of sth printed. 4 [U] standard of strength of alcoholic drink.

proof² /pruːf/ *adj* (in compounds) that can resist sth or protect against sth mentioned: *bullet-~ glass* ○ *water-~*.

prop¹ /prɒp/ *n* [C] 1 support used to keep sth up. 2 (*fig*) person or thing that supports another. **prop** *v* (**-pp-**) [T] support or keep in position.

prop² /prɒp/ *n* [C, usu pl] object, eg piece of furniture, used on stage.

propaganda /ˌprɒpəˈɡændə/ *n* [U] information spread in order to influence people's opinions.

propagate /ˈprɒpəɡeɪt/ *v* 1 [I, T] (of plants) increase in number. 2 [T] (*fml*) spread: *~ ideas.* **propagation** /ˌprɒpəˈɡeɪʃn/ *n* [U].

propel /prəˈpel/ *v* (**-ll-**) [T] move or push forward; drive. **propeller** *n* [C] blades that turn, to move a ship, helicopter, etc.

propensity /prəˈpensəti/ *n* [C] (*pl* **-ies**) (*for*/*to*)) (*fml*) natural tendency to do sth.

proper /ˈprɒpə(r)/ *adj* 1 correct or suitable. 2 socially respectable. 3 real; true: *We've not had a ~ holiday in years.* 4 itself: *There is a small hall and the concert hall ~.* **properly** *adv* correctly. **'proper name** (also **'proper noun**) *n* [C] (*grammar*) name of a particular person, place, etc, written with a capital letter.

property /ˈprɒpəti/ *n* (*pl* **-ies**) 1 [U] things owned; possession(s). 2 [C, U] area of land and buildings. 3 [C, esp pl] special quality: *the chemical properties of the metal.*

prophecy /ˈprɒfəsi/ *n* (*pl* **-ies**) 1 [U] power of saying what will happen in the future. 2 [C] statement that tells what will happen in the future.

prophesy /ˈprɒfəsaɪ/ *v* (*pt, pp* **-ied**) [I, T] say (what will happen in the future).

prophet /ˈprɒfɪt/ *n* [C] 1 person who says what will happen in the future. 2 person who teaches religion and claims that his/her teaching comes directly from God.

prophetic /prəˈfetɪk/ *adj.*

propitious /prəˈpɪʃəs/ *adj* (*fml*) favourable.

proportion /prəˈpɔːʃn/ *n* 1 [C] part or share. 2 [U] relation of one thing to another in quantity, size, etc. 3 **proportions** [pl] size: *trade of substantial ~s.* 4 (idm) **in proportion to** sth relative to sth: *paid in ~ to the work done.* **proportional** *adj* having the same proportion.

proposal /prəˈpəʊzl/ *n* [C] 1 plan or scheme. 2 offer of marriage.

propose /prəˈpəʊz/ *v* 1 [T] suggest. 2 [T] intend or plan. 3 [I, T] (*to*)) make an offer of (marriage) to sb.

proposition /ˌprɒpəˈzɪʃn/ *n* [C] 1 statement that expresses a judgement or opinion. 2 suggested offer, esp in business. 3 (*infml*) matter to be dealt with. **proposition** *v* [T] suggest sexual intercourse to.

proprietary /prəˈpraɪətri; US -teri/ *adj* made by a particular company and sold under a trade name.

proprietor /prəˈpraɪətə(r)/ *n* [C] (*fem* **-tress** /-trɪs/) owner of a business.

propriety /prəˈpraɪəti/ *n* [U] (*fml*) being correct in one's social or moral behaviour.

propulsion /prəˈpʌlʃn/ *n* [U] propelling force.

pro rata /ˌprəʊ ˈrɑːtə/ *adv, adj* (*fml*) according to the share of each.

prosaic /prəˈzeɪɪk/ *adj* uninteresting; dull.

proscribe /prəˈskraɪb/; US prəʊ-/ *v* [T] forbid by law.

prose /prəʊz/ *n* [U] ordinary written or spoken language, not poetry.

prosecute /ˈprɒsɪkjuːt/ *v* [I, T] bring a criminal charge against (sb) in a lawcourt. **prosecution** /ˌprɒsɪˈkjuːʃn/ *n* 1 [C, U] (instance of) prosecuting. 2 **the prosecution** [sing] (with sing or pl v) lawyer(s) that prosecute sb in a lawcourt. **prosecutor** *n* [C] (esp US).

prospect¹ /ˈprɒspekt/ *n* 1 [U] (*of*//) reasonable hope of sth happening. 2 [C] something that is going to happen soon. 3 **prospects** [pl] chances of success.

prospect² /prəˈspekt; US ˈprɒs-/ *v* [I] (*for*//) search for oil, gold, etc. **prospector** *n* [C].

prospective /prəˈspektɪv/ *adj* wanting or likely to be or do.

prospectus /prəˈspektəs/ *n* [C] printed leaflet giving details of a business, college, etc.

prosper /'prɒspə(r)/ v [I] succeed, esp financially. **prosperity** /prɒ'sperəti/ n [U] success or wealth. **prosperous** /'prɒspərəs/ adj successful; rich.

prostitute /'prɒstɪtju:t; US -tu:t/ n [C] person who offers himself/ herself for sexual intercourse for money. **prostitute** v [T] use (oneself or one's abilities) unworthily, esp to earn money. **prostitution** /,prɒstɪ'tju:ʃn; US -'tu:ʃn/ n [U].

prostrate /'prɒstreɪt/ adj lying on the ground, face downwards. **prostrate** /prɒ'streɪt; US 'prɒstreɪt/ v ~ **oneself** lie on the ground, face downwards.

protagonist /prə'tægənɪst/ n [C] 1 (fml) main person in a play or real event. 2 (leading) supporter of a movement, idea, etc.

protect /prə'tekt/ v [T] keep safe from harm, injury, etc. **protection** /prə'tekʃn/ n 1 [U] protecting. 2 [C] something that protects. **protective** adj 1 intended to protect. 2 (towards)|| (of people) wishing to protect sb. **protector** n [C] person or thing that protects.

protectorate /prə'tektərət/ n [C] country that is controlled and protected by a more powerful country.

protégé /'prɒtɪʒeɪ; US ˌprəʊtɪ'ʒeɪ/ n [C] person helped and guided by sb important and influential.

protein /'prəʊti:n/ n [C, U] body-building substance essential to good health.

protest[1] /'prəʊtest/ n [C, U,] statement or action that shows strong disapproval or disagreement.

protest[2] /prə'test/ v 1 [I, T] (about/against/at)|| show one's strong disapproval or disagreement of sb/sth. 2 [T] declare firmly, against opposition: He ~ed his innocence. **protester** n [C].

Protestant /'prɒtɪstənt/ n [C], adj (member) of any of the Christian groups that separated from the Roman Catholic Church in the 16th century.

protocol /'prəʊtəkɒl; US -kɔ:l/ n [U] system of rules of behaviour at formal occasions.

proton /'prəʊtɒn/ n [C] tiny particle of matter inside an atom, with a positive electric charge.

prototype /'prəʊtətaɪp/ n [C] first example, eg of an aircraft, from which others are developed.

protracted /prə'træktɪd; US prəʊ-/ adj lasting for a long time.

protractor /prə'træktə(r); US prəʊ-/ n [C] instrument for measuring and drawing angles.

protrude /prə'tru:d; US prəʊ-/ v [I, T] (cause to) stick out. **protrusion** /-tru:ʒn/ n [C, U].

protuberance /prə'tju:bərəns; US prəʊ'tu:-/ n [C] (fml) swelling; bulge.

proud /praʊd/ adj 1 having a feeling of satisfaction from doing sth well or owning sth. 2 having self-respect. 3 having too high an opinion of oneself. **proudly** adv.

prove /pru:v/ v (pp ~ d; US ~ n /'pru:vn/) 1 [T] show to be true. 2 be seen or found to be: The attempts ~ d to be useless.

proverb /'prɒvɜ:b/ n [C] well-known short saying that states the truth or gives advice, eg It takes two to make a quarrel. **proverbial** /prə'vɜ:bɪəl/ adj 1 of or expressed in a proverb. 2 widely known.

provide /prə'vaɪd/ v 1 [T] (for)|| give (sth) to sb; supply. 2 (phr v) **provide for sb** supply sb with the things that he/she needs. **provide for sth** make arrangements that can be carried out if sth occurs. **provided** /prə'vaɪdɪd/ (also **providing** /prə'vaɪdɪŋ/) conj (that)|| on condition that.

providence /'prɒvɪdəns/ n [U] the care and kindness of God or fate. **providential** /,prɒvɪ'denʃl/ adj (fml) fortunate.

province /'prɒvɪns/ n 1 [C] main administrative division of a country. 2 **the provinces** [pl] the parts of a country except the capital. 3 [sing] (fml) area of knowledge or responsibility. **provincial** adj 1 of a province(1) or the provinces(2). 2 narrow or old-fashioned. **provincial** n [C] person from the provinces(2).

provision /prə'vɪʒn/ n 1 [U] act of providing. 2 [U] (for)|| preparation for future needs. 3 **provisions** [pl] food supplies. 4 [C] conditions in a legal document.

provisional /prə'vɪʒənl/ adj for the present time only and likely to be changed in the future. **provisionally** /-nəlɪ/ adv.

provocation /,prɒvə'keɪʃn/ n 1 [U] provoking. 2 [C] something that provokes.

provocative /prə'vɒkətɪv/ adj 1 intended to cause anger, argument, etc. 2 intended to cause sexual desire. **provocatively** adv.

provoke /prə'vəʊk/ v [T] 1 make angry. 2 cause (a feeling or reaction).

prow /praʊ/ n [C] pointed front part of a ship.

prowess /'praʊɪs/ n [U] (fml) great skill or ability.

prowl /praʊl/ v [I, T] (about/

around)|| go about (a place) quietly, looking for food, or to steal, etc. **prowl** *n* (idm) **be on the prowl** be prowling.

proximity /prɒkˈsɪmətɪ/ *n* [U] (*fml*) nearness.

proxy /ˈprɒksɪ/ *n* (*pl* **-ies**) 1 [U] authority to act for another person, esp to vote. 2 [C] person given this authority.

prude /pruːd/ *n* [C] (*derog*) person easily shocked by sexual matters. **prudish** *adj*.

prudent /ˈpruːdnt/ *adj* careful and sensible. **prudence** /-dns/ *n* [U]. **prudently** *adv*.

prune[1] /pruːn/ *n* [C] dried plum.

prune[2] /pruːn/ *v* [T] 1 cut off some of the branches of (a tree or bush) to encourage further growth. 2 (*fig*) take out unnecessary parts from.

pry /praɪ/ *v* (*pt*, *pp* **pried** /praɪd/) [I] (*into*)|| try to find out about sb's private affairs.

PS /ˌpiː ˈes/ *abbr* (at the end of a letter) postscript.

psalm /sɑːm/ *n* [C] religious song or poem, esp one of those in the Bible.

pseudonym /ˈsjuːdənɪm; *US* ˈsuːdənɪm/ *n* [C] name that sb, esp a writer, uses, instead of his/her real name.

psyche /ˈsaɪkɪ/ *n* [C] human soul or mind.

psychedelic /ˌsaɪkɪˈdelɪk/ *adj* 1 (of drugs) causing sb to see sth that isn't there. 2 having very bright colours and strange patterns.

psychiatry /saɪˈkaɪətrɪ; *US* sɪ-/ *n* [U] study and treatment of mental illness. **psychiatric** /ˌsaɪkɪˈætrɪk/ *adj*. **psychiatrist** *n* [C] doctor trained in psychiatry.

psychic /ˈsaɪkɪk/ *adj* 1 having strange powers such as being able to see into the future. 2 (also **psychical** /-kɪkl/) (**a**) of the soul or mind, not the body. (**b**) of conditions, etc outside physical laws.

psychoanalysis /ˌsaɪkəʊəˈnæləsɪs/ *n* [U] method of treating some mental illnesses by looking at and discussing the effects of events in the patient's life as possible causes. **psychoanalyse** /ˌsaɪkəʊˈænəlaɪz/ *v* [T] treat (sb) using psychoanalysis. **psychoanalyst** /ˌsaɪkəʊˈænəlɪst/ *n* [C] person who practises psychoanalysis.

psychology /saɪˈkɒlədʒɪ/ *n* [U] study of the mind and how it functions. **psychological** /ˌsaɪkəˈlɒdʒɪkl/ *adj*. **psychologist** *n* [C] student of or expert in psychology.

psychopath /ˈsaɪkəʊpæθ/ *n* [C] person suffering from a severe mental disorder who may behave violently. **psychopathic** /ˌsaɪkəʊˈpæθɪk/ *adj*.

pt *abbr* 1 part. 2 pint. 3 point. 4 port.

PTO /ˌpiː tiː ˈəʊ/ *abbr* (at the bottom of a page, etc) please turn over.

pub /pʌb/ *n* [C] building where alcoholic drinks are sold and drunk.

puberty /ˈpjuːbətɪ/ *n* [U] stage at which a person becomes physically able to have children.

pubic /ˈpjuːbɪk/ *adj* of or near the sexual organs.

public /ˈpʌblɪk/ *adj* 1 of or for people in general. 2 of or provided by the government: *money* ○ *a ~ library*. 3 known to many people; not secret. 4 (idm) **in the public 'eye** often seen on television and mentioned in newspapers, etc. **public** *n* 1 **the public** [sing] (with *sing* or *pl* *v*) (**a**) people in general. (**b**) particular section of the community: *the reading ~*. 2 (idm) **in public** not in private; openly. **ˌpublic 'bar** *n* [C] (*Brit*) bar in a pub or hotel that is plainer and cheaper than a lounge bar. **ˌpublic 'company** **ˌpublic 'limited company** *n* [C] business company that sells shares in itself to the public. **ˌpublic con'venience** *n* [C] (*Brit*) toilet which the public may use. **ˌpublic 'house** *n* [C] (*fml*) = PUB. **publicly** *adv*. **ˌpublic re'lations** *n* 1 [U] work of obtaining good public opinion of an organization. 2 [pl] relationship between an organization and the public. **ˌpublic 'school** *n* [C] (in Britain) private secondary school for fee-paying pupils.

publication /ˌpʌblɪˈkeɪʃn/ *n* 1 [U] act of publishing sth. 2 [C] book, magazine, etc.

publicity /pʌbˈlɪsətɪ/ *n* [U] 1 information that attracts public attention to sth; advertising. 2 state of being known to the public.

publicize /ˈpʌblɪsaɪz/ *v* [T] make known to the public.

publish /ˈpʌblɪʃ/ *v* [T] 1 print and offer (a book, etc) for sale to the public. 2 make known to the public. **publisher** *n* [C] person or company that publishes(1) books, etc.

pucker /ˈpʌkə(r)/ *v* [I, T] (cause to) form small folds or wrinkles.

pudding /ˈpʊdɪŋ/ *n* [C, U] 1 sweet food eaten at the end of a meal. 2 sweet or savoury food made with flour and baked, boiled or steamed.

puddle /'pʌdl/ n [C] small pool of water, esp rain.

puff /pʌf/ v 1 [I, T] (of smoke, steam, etc) (cause to) come out in puffs. 2 [I, T] smoke (a pipe, cigarette, etc) in puffs. 3 [I] breathe loudly and quickly. 4 (phr v) **puff (sth) out/up** swell. **puffed** adj (infml) breathing with difficulty.

puff /pʌf/ n [C] short light blowing of air, smoke, etc. **puff 'pastry** n [U] type of pastry which is light and flaky. **puffy** adj (-ier, -iest) swollen.

puffin /'pʌfɪn/ n [C] N Atlantic sea-bird with a large brightly-coloured beak.

pull¹ /pʊl/ v 1 [I, T] use force on (sth) in order to move it towards one or to a different position: ~ the cart up the hill. ○ ~ the plug out. 2 [T] remove by using force: ~ (out/a) tooth. 3 [T] damage by using too much force: ~ a muscle. 4 (idm) **pull faces/a face** ⇨ FACE. **pull a 'fast one (on sb)** (infml) gain an advantage (over sb) by a trick. **pull one's finger out** ⇨ FINGER. **pull sb's 'leg** (infml) make fun of sb by making him/her believe sth untrue. **pull one's 'socks up** (infml) try to improve one's work or behaviour. **pull sth to 'pieces** criticize sth strongly. **pull one's weight** do one's fair share of the work. 5 (phr v) **pull away** (of a vehicle) begin to move forward. **pull sth down** destroy (eg an old building). **pull in (a)** (of a train) enter a station. **(b)** (of a vehicle) move in (towards sth) and stop. **pull sth off** (infml) succeed in sth. **pull out** (of a vehicle) move out or sideways. **pull (sb/sth) out (of sth)** (cause sb/sth to) withdraw from sth: ~ out of a race. **pull over** (of a vehicle) move a vehicle to one side and stop. **pull (sb) through** (help sb to) recover from an illness. **pull together** work together in an organized way. **pull oneself together** get control of one's feelings. **pull up** (of a vehicle) stop. **pull sb up** (infml) criticize sb for making mistakes.

pull² /pʊl/ n 1 [C] act of pulling. 2 [sing] force or attraction: the ~ of the river current. 3 [U] (infml) influence. 4 [sing] prolonged effort: a hard ~ to the top of the hill.

pullet /'pʊlɪt/ n [C] young hen.

pulley /'pʊlɪ/ n [C] device with a wheel and rope, used for lifting things.

pullover /'pʊləʊvə(r)/ n [C] knitted garment for the upper body,

pulled on over the head.

pulp /pʌlp/ n [U] 1 soft fleshy inner part of fruit. 2 soft mass of other material, esp wood fibre used for making paper. **pulp** v [T] make into pulp(2).

pulpit /'pʊlpɪt/ n [C] raised enclosed platform in a church, from which a clergyman speaks.

pulsate /pʌl'seɪt; US 'pʌlseɪt/ v [I] move or shake with a strong regular action. **pulsation** /-'seɪʃn/ n [C, U].

pulse¹ /pʌls/ n 1 [C, usu sing] regular beating of the arteries as the blood is pumped through them. 2 [sing] regular beat in music. **pulse** v [I] move or beat with a strong regular action.

pulverize /'pʌlvəraɪz/ v [T] 1 crush to a powder. 2 destroy completely.

puma /'pjuːmə/ n [C] large brown American animal of the cat family.

pump /pʌmp/ n [C] machine for forcing liquid, gas or air into, out of or through sth. **pump** v 1 [T] force (air, gas, etc) to move in a particular direction: The heart ~s blood around the body. 2 [I] work like a pump; beat. 3 [T] (infml) try to get information from (sb) by asking him/her questions repeatedly.

pumpkin /'pʌmpkɪn/ n [C, U] large round orange-yellow fruit, used as a vegetable.

pun /pʌn/ n [C] humorous use of words that sound the same or have two meanings, eg 'The soldier laid down his arms'. **pun** v (-nn-) [I] make a pun.

punch¹ /pʌntʃ/ v [T] hit hard with one's fist. **punch** n 1 [C] blow given with the fist. 2 [U] (infml fig) force or power. **'punch-up** n [C] fight with the fists.

punch² /pʌntʃ/ n [C] tool for cutting holes in sth. **punch** v [T] make a hole in (sth) with a punch.

punch³ /pʌntʃ/ n [U] drink made of wine or spirits mixed with sugar, lemon, spice, etc.

punctual /'pʌŋktʃʊəl/ adj happening or doing sth at exactly the right time. **punctuality** /ˌpʌŋktʃʊ'æləti/ n [U]. **punctually** adv.

punctuate /'pʌŋktʃʊeɪt/ v 1 [I, T] put full stops, commas, etc into (a piece of writing). 2 [T] (with/by)) (usu passive) interrupt at intervals. **punctuation** /ˌpʌŋktʃʊ'eɪʃn/ n [U] (practice of putting) marks such as full stops and commas in a piece of writing.

puncture /'pʌŋktʃə(r)/ n [C]

small hole made by a sharp point in a tyre. **puncture** v [I, T] (cause a tyre to) get a puncture.

pungent /'pʌndʒənt/ adj having a sharp or strong taste or smell.

punish /'pʌnɪʃ/ v [T] 1 cause (sb) to suffer in some way for doing wrong. 2 (infml) treat roughly. **punishing** adj that makes one very tired or weak. **punishment** n 1 [U] punishing. 2 [C] way of punishing sb.

punitive /'pjuːnɪtɪv/ adj (fml) intended as punishment; harsh or severe.

punk /pʌŋk/ n 1 [U] (also punk 'rock) loud violent rock music first appearing in the late 1970s and associated with protest against conventional attitudes. 2 [C] (also punk 'rocker) young person who likes punk rock, wears strange clothes and metal chains and has brightly coloured hair.

punnet /'pʌnɪt/ n [C] small square basket used as a container for fruit.

punt /pʌnt/ n [C] long shallow flat-bottomed boat moved along by a long pole. **punt** v [I] move in a punt.

punter /'pʌntə(r)/ n [C] (Brit infml) 1 person who bets money on horse-races. 2 customer.

puny /'pjuːnɪ/ adj (-ier, -iest) small and weak.

pup /pʌp/ n [C] 1 = PUPPY. 2 young of various animals, eg seals.

pupil[1] /'pjuːpl/ n [C] person being taught.

pupil[2] /'pjuːpl/ n [C] round opening in the centre of the eye, through which the light passes.

puppet /'pʌpɪt/ n [C] 1 doll that can be made to move by wires or that fits over sb's hand so that the fingers can move it. 2 person or group whose actions are controlled by another.

puppy /'pʌpɪ/ n [C] (pl -ies) young dog.

purchase /'pɜːtʃəs/ v [T] (fml) buy. **purchase** n (fml) 1 [U] buying. 2 [C] something bought. **purchaser** n [C] person who buys sth.

pure /pjʊə(r)/ adj (~r, ~st) 1 not mixed with any other substance. 2 not containing harmful substances; clean. 3 without evil or sin. 4 (of sounds) clear. 5 complete; sheer: *They met by ~ chance.* 6 concerned with theory only; not practical: *~ science.* **purely** adv completely; only.

purée /'pjʊəreɪ/ US pjʊə'reɪ/ n

[U, C] vegetables, fruit, etc mashed or blended to a smooth thick liquid.

purgatory /'pɜːgətrɪ/ US -tɔːrɪ/ n [U] 1 (in Roman Catholic teaching) place after death in which the soul has to be purified by suffering. 2 (fig) very unpleasant experience of suffering.

purge /pɜːdʒ/ v [T] 1 (of/from)|| remove (unwanted people) from a political party, etc): *~ a party of extremists* ○ *~ extremists from the party.* 2 (of/from)|| make (sb) clean or free of impurity. **purge** n [C] act of purging(1).

purify /'pjʊərɪfaɪ/ v (pt, pp -ied) [T] make pure. **purification** /ˌpjʊərɪfɪˈkeɪʃn/ n [U].

purist /'pjʊərɪst/ n [C] person who pays great attention to correctness.

puritan /'pjʊərɪtən/ adj, n [C] 1 (usu derog) (of a) person who is very strict in morals. 2 **Puritan** (of a) member of a former Protestant group who wanted simpler forms of church ceremony. **puritanical** /ˌpjʊərɪˈtænɪkl/ adj (usu derog).

purity /'pjʊərətɪ/ n [U] state of being pure.

purl /pɜːl/ n [U] stitch made by knitting into the back of a stitch. **purl** v [I, T] knit (sth) in this stitch.

purple /'pɜːpl/ adj having the colour of red and blue mixed together.

purpose /'pɜːpəs/ n 1 [C] reason for which sth is done or made. 2 [U] (fml) ability to form plans and carry them out. 3 (idm) **on purpose** deliberately. **purposeful** adj showing purpose(2).

purr /pɜː(r)/ v [I] (of a cat) make a low vibrating sound expressing pleasure. **purr** n [C] purring sound.

purse[1] /pɜːs/ n [C] 1 small bag for money. 2 sum of money given as a prize. 3 (US) handbag.

purse[2] /pɜːs/ v [T] draw (the lips) together in tiny folds.

purser /'pɜːsə(r)/ n [C] officer responsible for a ship's accounts, stores, etc.

pursue /pə'sjuː; US -'suː/ v [T] (fml) 1 follow (sb) in order to catch him/her. 2 go on steadily with: *~ one's studies.* **pursuer** n [C].

pursuit /pə'sjuːt; US -'suːt/ n (fml) 1 [U] act of pursuing. 2 [C, usu pl] occupation; hobby.

purvey /pə'veɪ/ v [T] (fml) supply (sth, esp food). **purveyor** n [C].

pus /pʌs/ n [U] thick yellowish liquid formed in an infected wound.

push[1] /pʊʃ/ v 1 [I, T] use force on

(sth) in order to move it forward, away or to a different position: ~ *a bike up the hill* ○ ~ *the plug in.* **2** [T] (*infml*) try to make (sb) do sth that he/she does not want to do. **3** [I, T] (*for*)∥ (*infml*) try to obtain sth from (sb) forcefully: ~ *sb for payment.* **4** [T] (*infml*) sell (illegal drugs). **5** (*idm*) **be pushed for sth** (*infml*) not have enough of sth: *be* ~ *ed for time.* **6** (*phr v*) **push sb around** (*infml*) order sb to do things unfairly and roughly. **push off** (*infml*) go away. **'push-bike** *n* [C] (*infml*) bicycle operated by pedals. **'push-button** *adj* operated by pushing a button. **'push-chair** *n* [C] small chair on wheels for a small child. **pusher** *n* [C] (*infml*) person who sells illegal drugs.

push² /pʊʃ/ *n* [C, usu sing] **1** act of pushing. **2** great effort or attack. **3** (*idm*) **give sb/get the push** (*infml*) dismiss sb/be dismissed from one's job.

pussy /'pʊsɪ/ *n* [C] (*pl* **-ies**) (also **'pussy-cat**) (used by children) cat.

put /pʊt/ *v* (*pt*, *pp* ~, *pres part* ~**ting**) [T] **1** move to a certain place or position: *She* ~ *the book on the table.* ○ (*fig*) *They* ~ *the blame on me.* **2** write or mark: ~ *his name on the form.* **3** cause to be in a certain state: ~ *sth right*, ie correct sth. **4** (*a*) (*to*)∥ offer: ~ *a proposal to a client.* (*b*) express: ~ *sth politely.* **5** (*idm*) **put one's cards on the table** ⇨ CARD. **put the clock back** ⇨ CLOCK. **put one's oar in** ⇨ OAR. **put sth right** ⇨ RIGHT¹. **put sb/sth to 'rights** ⇨ RIGHT¹. **6** (*phr v*) **put sth a'bout** cause (rumours, etc) to pass from one person to another. **put sth a'cross (to sb)** communicate sth well. **put sth a'side (a)** lay down: ~ *aside a book.* (*b*) save (esp money). (*c*) pay no attention to; ignore: ~ *one's disagreements aside.* **put sth at sth** estimate: *I* ~ *the possible cost at £500.* **put sth a'way** put sth in its usual place: ~ *the cup away in the cupboard.* **put sth 'back (a)** replace: ~ *the book back on the shelf.* (*b*) move the hands of (a clock) back to show the correct time. (*c*) cause a delay to: ~ *the meeting back by one hour.* **put sb 'down (a)** allow to get off (eg a bus). (*b*) (*infml*) make sb seem foolish. **put sth down (a)** set or place on a surface. (*b*) land (an aircraft). (*c*) stop sth by force: ~ *down a rebellion.* (*d*) write down. (*e*) kill (a sick animal). **put sth down to sth** regard sth as being caused by sth: *I* ~ *his failure down to laziness.* **put**

sth forward (a) suggest; propose: ~ *forward a new idea.* (*b*) move the hands of (a clock) forward to show the correct time. **put sth in (a)** perform; do: ~ *in an hour's work.* (*b*) install; fit: ~ *a new bath in.* **put (sb/sth) in for sth** attempt to win a competition, get a job, etc: ~ *a painting in for the competition.* **put sb off (a)** distract sb from sth: *Don't* ~ *me off when I'm trying to concentrate.* (*b*) cause sb to dislike or lose interest in sth/sb. **put sth off (a)** switch off: ~ *the television off.* (*b*) postpone. **put sth 'on (a)** cover oneself with (clothes): ~ *a coat on.* (*b*) apply (paint, make-up, etc). (*c*) operate (sth): ~ *on the television.* (*d*) arrange; provide: ~ *on extra trains.* (*e*) organize (a performance, etc): ~ *on a play.* (*f*) grow heavier or fatter: ~ *on a stone (in weight).* **put sb out (a)** cause to be upset or offended. (*b*) cause inconvenience to sb: *I hope my visit won't* ~ *you out.* **put sth out (a)** extinguish: ~ *out the lights.* (*b*) issue; broadcast: ~ *out a warning.* **put sth over** = PUT STH ACROSS. **put sb through** connect by telephone. **put up sth** offer (resistance, etc): ~ *up a fight.* **put sb up** give sb food and lodging. **put sth up (a)** raise: ~ *one's hand up.* (*b*) build, construct: ~ *a tent up.* (*c*) increase: ~ *up the rent.* (*d*) supply (a sum of money). **put 'up (at...)** obtain food and lodging (at a place): ~ *up at a hotel.* **put sb up to sth** urge sb to do sth wrong. **put sb up with sb/sth** endure; tolerate: ~ *up with bad behaviour.* **'put-down** *n* humiliating remark.

putrefy /'pjuːtrɪfaɪ/ *v* (*pt*, *pp* **-ied**) [I] decay. **putrefaction** /ˌpjuːtrɪ'fækʃn/ *n* [U].

putrid /'pjuːtrɪd/ *adj* rotten and bad-smelling.

putt /pʌt/ *v* [I, T] (in golf) hit (the ball) gently along the ground.

putty /'pʌtɪ/ *n* [U] soft paste used for fixing glass in window frames.

puzzle /'pʌzl/ *n* [C] **1** question that is difficult to answer. **2** problem or toy designed to test a person's knowledge or skill: *a crossword* ~. **puzzle** *v* **1** [T] (of something that is difficult to understand) confuse (sb): *I'm* ~*ed by his not replying to my letter.* **2** [I] (*over*)∥ think deeply about sth in order to understand it. **3** (*phr v*) **puzzle sth out** find the answer to sth by thinking hard.

PVC /ˌpiː/ *vi*: 'siː/ *n* [U] kind of plastic.

pygmy (also **pigmy** /'pɪgmɪ/) n [C] (pl -ies) **1** Pigmy member of an African race of very short people. **2** very small person or animal.

pyjamas /pə'dʒɑːməz; US -'dʒæm-/ n [pl] loose-fitting jacket and trousers for sleeping in.

pylon /'paɪlən; US -lɒn/ n [C] tall steel structure for carrying electric cables.

pyramid /'pɪrəmɪd/ n [C] **1** structure with a square base and sloping sides meeting at a point, esp one built in ancient Egypt. **2** pile of objects in the shape of a pyramid.

pyre /'paɪə(r)/ n [C] high pile of wood for burning a dead body on.

python /'paɪθn; US -θɒn/ n [C] large snake that kills animals by twisting its body tightly round them.

Q q

Q, q /kjuː/ n [C] (pl **Q's, q's** /kjuːz/) the seventeenth letter of the English alphabet.

quack[1] /kwæk/ v [I] n [C] (make the) sound of a duck.

quack[2] /kwæk/ n [C] (infml) person dishonestly claiming to have medical knowledge.

quad /kwɒd/ n [C] **1** short for QUADRANGLE 2. **2** short for QUADRUPLET.

quadrangle /'kwɒdræŋgl/ n [C] **1** flat figure with four sides. **2** open square area with buildings round it.

quadruped /'kwɒdrʊped/ n [C] four-footed animal.

quadruple /'kwɒdrʊpl; US kwɒ'druːpl/ adj consisting of four parts. **quadruple** n [C] number four times as great. **quadruple** v [I, T] multiply (sth) by four.

quadruplet /'kwɒdrʊplet; US kwɒ'druːp-/ n [C] one of four babies born to the same mother at one time.

quagmire /'kwægmaɪə(r), also kwɒg-/ n [C] area of soft wet ground.

quail[1] /kweɪl/ n [C] small game bird.

quail[2] /kweɪl/ v [I] (fml) be very afraid.

quaint /kweɪnt/ adj pleasing because unusual or old-fashioned. **quaintly** adv.

quake /kweɪk/ v [I] shake; tremble.

qualification /ˌkwɒlɪfɪ'keɪʃn/ n **1** [C] training, test, diploma, etc that qualifies(1) a person. **2** [U, C] statement that modifies or limits sth: accept an offer with ~s. **3** [U] qualifying.

qualify /'kwɒlɪfaɪ/ v (pt, pp -ied) **1** [I, T] have or give the qualities, training, etc that are necessary or suitable for sth: She'll ~ as a doctor next year. **2** [T] make (a statement) less general or extreme. **qualified** adj **1** have the necessary qualifications. **2** limited: qualified approval.

qualitative /'kwɒlɪtətɪv; US -teɪt-/ adj of or concerned with quality.

quality /'kwɒlɪtɪ/ n (pl -ies) **1** [U, C] (high) standard of goodness. **2** [C] typical part of the nature of sb/sth: Kindness is not one of her qualities.

qualm /kwɑːm/ n [C] feeling of doubt about whether what one is doing is right.

quandary /'kwɒndərɪ/ n [C] (pl -ies) state of not being able to decide what to do.

quantitative /'kwɒntɪtətɪv; US -teɪt-/ adj of or concerned with quantity.

quantity /'kwɒntɪtɪ/ n [C, U] (pl -ies) (esp large) amount or number.

quarantine /'kwɒrəntiːn; US 'kwɔːr-/ [U] period when a person or animal is separated from others to prevent the spread of a disease. **quarantine** v [T] put in quarantine.

quarrel /'kwɒrəl; US 'kwɔːrəl/ n [C] **1** angry argument. **2** reason to disagree with sb/sth. **quarrel** v (-ll-; US -l-) [I] **1** argue angrily. **2** with// disagree with sb. **quarrelsome** /-səm/ adj often causing arguments.

quarry[1] /'kwɒrɪ; US 'kwɔːrɪ/ n [C] place (not underground) where stone, slate, etc is dug. **quarry** v (pt, pp -ied) [T] dig (stone, etc) from a quarry.

quarry[2] /'kwɒrɪ; US 'kwɔːrɪ/ n [C, usu sing] (pl -ies) hunted animal or bird.

quart /kwɔːt/ n [C] measure for liquids; two pints (1.14 litres).

quarter /'kwɔːtə(r)/ n **1** [C] one of four equal parts of sth;¼. **2** [C] 15 minutes: a ~ to four (US): a ~ of four ○ a ~ past six (US): a ~ after six. **3** [C] period of three months. **4** [C] part of a town or city: the business ~. **5** [C] person or group from which help or information may come. **6** **quarters** [pl] accommodation, esp for soldiers: married ~s. **quarter** v [T] 1 divide into four parts. 2 provide (sb) with lodgings. **quarter 'final** n [C] one of four matches in a competition, whose winners play in the semifinals. **'quartermaster** n [C] army officer in charge of stores and accommodation.

quarterly /'kwɔːtəlɪ/ adj, adv (happening or produced) every three months. **quarterly** n [C] (pl -ies) quarterly magazine.

quartet /kwɔː'tet/ n [C] (music for) four players or singers.

quartz /kwɔːts/ n [U] hard mineral used eg in making very accurate clocks.

quash /kwɒʃ/ v [T] put an end to; reject: ~ a revolt/an appeal.

quaver /'kweɪvə(r)/ v 1 [I] (of the voice or a sound) shake; tremble. 2 [T] say or sing in a shaking voice. **quaver** n [C, usu sing] trembling sound.

quay /kiː/ n [C] landing-place for loading and unloading ships.

queasy /'kwiːzɪ/ adj (-ier, -iest) feeling one is going to be sick.

queen /kwiːn/ n [C] 1 (title of the) female ruler of a country. 2 wife of a king. 3 woman considered as the best or most important in some way. 4 (in chess) the most powerful piece. 5 playing-card with a picture of a queen. 6 egg-producing female of bees, ants, etc. **queen 'mother** n [C] mother of a ruling king or queen.

queer /kwɪə(r)/ adj 1 strange; unusual. 2 (sl derog) homosexual. 3 (dated infml) unwell. **queer** n [C] (sl derog) homosexual man.

quell /kwel/ v [T] put an end to; defeat.

quench /kwentʃ/ v [T] 1 satisfy (one's thirst) by drinking. 2 put out (a fire).

query /'kwɪərɪ/ n [C] (pl -ies) question. **query** v (pt, pp -ied) [T] 1 express doubt about. 2 ask.

quest /kwest/ n [C] (fml) long search.

question¹ /'kwestʃən/ n 1 [C] sentence that asks for information, an answer, etc. 2 [C] matter that needs to be discussed; problem. 3 [U] doubt: His honesty is beyond ~. 4 (idm) in 'question being discussed. out of the 'question impossible. 'question mark n [C] mark (?) at the end of a question.

question² /'kwestʃən/ v [T] 1 ask (sb) questions. 2 express one's doubts about. **questionable** adj that can be doubted.

questionnaire /ˌkwestʃə'neə(r)/ n [C] list of questions to be ans-

wered to get information.

queue /kjuː/ n [C] line of people, vehicles, etc waiting for sth. **queue** v [I] wait in a queue.

quibble /'kwɪbl/ v [I] argue about small unimportant points. **quibble** n [C] argument about a small matter.

quiche /kiːʃ/ n [C] open pastry tart with a savoury filling of eggs, cheese, etc.

quick /kwɪk/ adj 1 moving fast; done in a short time. 2 easily excited: a ~ temper. 3 enthusiastic and intelligent: He's ~ at (learning) languages. 4 (idm) be quick off the mark ⇨ MARK¹. quick on the uptake ⇨ UPTAKE. **quick** adv quickly. **quick** n [sing] soft tender flesh below the finger-nails. **quickly** adv. **quickness** n [U]. **,quick-'witted** adj able to think and act quickly; clever.

quicken /'kwɪkən/ v [I, I] become or make quicker.

quicksand /'kwɪksænd/ n [U, C] loose wet deep sand into which people or things will sink.

quid /kwɪd/ n [C] (pl quid) (Brit infml) pound in money.

quiet /'kwaɪət/ adj 1 with little noise. 2 without excitement or trouble: a ~ life. 3 gentle. 4 (of colours) not bright. **quiet** n 1 [U] state of being quiet. 2 (idm) on the quiet secretly. **quieten** /-tn/ v [I, T] become or make quiet. **quietly** adv. **quietness** n [U].

quill /kwɪl/ n [C] 1 (a) large feather. (b) pen made from this. 2 spine of a porcupine.

quilt /kwɪlt/ n [C] thick bed-covering of cloth filled with soft material. **quilted** adj having two layers of cloth padded with soft material.

quin /kwɪn/ (US quint /kwɪnt/) n [C] (infml) short for QUINTUPLET.

quinine /kwɪ'niːn; US 'kwaɪ-naɪn/ n [U] bitter liquid used to treat fevers such as malaria.

quintet /kwɪn'tet/ n [C] (music for) five players or singers.

quintuplet /'kwɪntjuːplet; US kwɪn'tuːpliːt/ n [C] one of five babies born to the same mother at one time.

quip /kwɪp/ n [C] clever or amusing remark. **quip** v (-pp-) [I] make a quip.

quirk /kwɜːk/ n [C] 1 person's strange habit or action. 2 strange happening; accident.

quit /kwɪt/ v (-tt-, pt, pp quit or, in British use ~ted) 1 [T] (infml) stop (doing sth). 2 [I, T] leave (a job or place).

quite /kwaɪt/ adv 1 to some extent; fairly: ~ *hot*. **2** completely: *She played* ~ *brilliantly!* **3** (used for showing agreement): *Q~ (so)*. **4** (idm) **quite a/an** an unusual: *There's ~ a story about how they met.*

quiver[1] /'kwɪvə(r)/ v [I, T] (cause to) tremble slightly. **quiver** n [C] quivering movement.

quiver[2] /'kwɪvə(r)/ n [C] container for carrying arrows.

quiz /kwɪz/ n [C] (pl ~zes) game in which people are asked questions to test their knowledge. **quiz** v (-zz-) [T] ask (sb) questions.

quizzical /'kwɪzɪkl/ adj in a questioning manner, esp when amused. **quizzically** /-klɪ/ adv.

quoit /kɔɪt; US kwɔɪt/ n **1** [C] ring, eg of rubber, thrown onto a small post in a game. **2 quoits** (with sing v) game in which this is done.

quota /'kwəʊtə/ n [C] limited number or share that is officially allowed.

quotation /kwəʊ'teɪʃn/ n **1** [C] group of words quoted. **2** [U] quoting. **3** [C] cost of work to be done. **quo'tation-marks** n [pl] punctuation marks (' ' or " ") used at the beginning and end of a quotation(1).

quote /kwəʊt/ v **1** [I, T] repeat in speech or writing (words used by another person). **2** [T] give (eg a reference) to support a statement. **3** [T] state (an amount) as the price of. **quote** n (*infml*) **1** [C] short for QUOTATION. **2** short for QUOTATION. **3. quotes** [pl] short for QUOTATION MARKS (QUOTATION).

quotient /'kwəʊʃnt/ n [C] (*mathematics*) number obtained by dividing one number by another.

R r

R, r /ɑː(r)/ n [C] (pl **R's, r's** /ɑːz/) the eighteenth letter of the English alphabet.

rabbi /'ræbaɪ/ n [C] Jewish spiritual leader; teacher of Jewish law.

rabbit /'ræbɪt/ n [C] small long-eared animal that lives in a hole in the ground. **rabbit** v [I] on/off (*infml*) talk aimlessly for a long time.

rabble /'ræbl/ n [C] disorderly noisy crowd. **'rabble-rousing** adj encouraging excitement or violence in a disorderly crowd.

rabid /'ræbɪd/ adj **1** suffering from rabies. **2** (*fig*) (of feelings or opinions) violent or extreme: *a* ~ *Conservative*.

rabies /'reɪbiːz/ n [U] serious fatal disease causing madness in animals (esp dogs) and people.

race[1] /reɪs/ n [C] **1** competition of speed, eg in running. **2** competition or rivalry: *the arms* ~. **race** v [I, T] **1** (*against*) take part in a race against (sb). **2** (cause to) go very fast. **3** own or train (eg a horse) to race. **'racecourse** n [C] ground where horses are raced against each other. **'racehorse** n [C] horse that is trained to run in races. **'race-track** n [C] **1** track round which runners, cars, etc race. **2** (*US*) racecourse.

race[2] /reɪs/ n [C, U] any of several large divisions of human beings with the same physical characteristics, eg colour of skin. **2** [C] main division of animals or plants: *the human* ~, ie people. **3** [C] group of people with the same history, language, etc. **'race relations** n [pl] relations between people of different races in the same community.

racial /'reɪʃl/ adj of race(1). **racialism** (also **racism** /'reɪsɪzəm/) n [U] belief that one's own race is best; unfair treatment of other races. **racialist** (also **racist** /'reɪsɪst/) adj, n [C]. **racially** adv.

rack[1] /ræk/ n **1** framework with bars, pegs, etc for holding things or hanging things on. **2** shelf over the seats in a train, aeroplane, etc for light luggage.

rack[2] /ræk/ v **1** [T] cause great suffering or pain to. **2** (idm) **rack one's 'brains** try very hard to think of sth.

rack[3] /ræk/ n (idm) **go to ,rack and 'ruin** become ruined or fall to pieces by being neglected.

racket[1] (also **racquet**) /'rækɪt/ n [C] **1** bat with a round or oval stringed frame, used for hitting the ball in tennis, etc. **2 rackets** (also **racquets**) (with sing v) game played with a ball in a court with four walls.

racket[2] /'rækɪt/ n (*infml*) **1** [sing] loud noise. **2** [C] dishonest way of getting money. **racketeer** /,rækə'tɪə(r)/ n [C] person involved in a racket(2).

racy /'reɪsɪ/ adj (-ier, -iest) lively, amusing and perhaps about sex. **racily** adv. **raciness** n [U].

radar /'reɪdɑː(r)/ n [U] equipment or system for showing the position of solid objects on a screen by using radio waves.

radiant /'reɪdɪənt/ adj 1 sending out rays of light or heat. 2 (of a person) showing great joy; bright: ~ beauty. **radiance** /-əns/ n [U]. **radiantly** adv.

radiate /'reɪdɪeɪt/ v [I, T] 1 send out rays of (light or heat). 2 (fig) send out (sth): He ~s confidence.

radiation /,reɪdɪ'eɪʃn/ n [U] 1 (sending out of) heat, energy, etc in the form of rays. 2 radioactivity.

radiator /'reɪdɪeɪtə(r)/ n [C] 1 apparatus, esp a set of pipes, used for heating a room. 2 device for cooling the engine of a vehicle.

radical /'rædɪkl/ adj 1 basic. 2 (of a person) complete and thorough. 3 favouring thorough political changes. **radical** n [C] person with radical(3) opinions. **radically** /-klɪ/ adv.

radii pl of RADIUS.

radio /'reɪdɪəʊ/ n (pl ~s) 1 [U] (a) process of sending and receiving messages, etc through the air by electrical waves. (b) broadcasting by these means. 2 [C] apparatus for receiving radio broadcasts. **radio** v [I, T] send a message to (sb) by radio.

radioactive /,reɪdɪəʊ'æktɪv/ adj sending out energy in the form of rays that can be harmful. **radioactivity** /-æk'tɪvətɪ/ n [U].

radiography /,reɪdɪ'ɒgrəfɪ/ n [U] production of X-ray photographs. **radiographer** /-fə(r)/ n [C] person trained in radiography.

radiology /,reɪdɪ'ɒlədʒɪ/ n [U] study of radiation and X-rays, esp as used in medicine. **radiologist** n [C].

radish /'rædɪʃ/ n [C] sharp-tasting red or white root of a small plant, eaten raw in salads.

radium /'reɪdɪəm/ n [U] radioactive chemical element used in the treatment of some diseases.

radius /'reɪdɪəs/ n [C] (pl radii /-dɪaɪ/) 1 (length of a) straight line from the centre of a circle to the side. 2 circular area measured from a central point: within a two-mile ~ of the factory.

raffia /'ræfɪə/ n [U] soft fibre from the leaves of a kind of palm-tree, used for making mats, etc.

raffle /'ræfl/ n [C] way of getting money (esp for charity) by selling numbered tickets that may win prizes. **raffle** v [T] offer as a prize in a raffle.

raft /rɑːft; US ræft/ n [C] flat floating structure of logs fastened together, used as a boat.

rafter /'rɑːftə(r); US 'ræf-/ n [C] large sloping piece of wood that

supports a roof.

rag¹ /ræg/ n 1 [C] piece of old cloth. 2 **rags** [pl] old, worn or torn clothes. 3 [C] (infml derog) newspaper.

rag² /ræg/ n [C] amusing lively public event held by students to collect money for charity. **rag** v (-gg-) [T] (infml) make fun of; tease.

rage /reɪdʒ/ n 1 [U, C] (outburst of) extreme anger. 2 (idm) (be) all the 'rage (infml) (be) very fashionable. **rage** v [I] 1 be extremely angry. 2 (eg of storms) be very violent.

ragged /'rægɪd/ adj 1 (a) (of clothes) old and torn. (b) (of people) wearing badly worn or torn clothes. 2 rough; uneven. **raggedly** adv.

ragtime /'rægtaɪm/ n [U] popular 1920s jazz music.

raid /reɪd/ n [C] 1 sudden attack on an enemy position. 2 sudden unexpected visit by the police, eg to arrest people. **raid** v [T] make a raid on. **raider** n [C].

rail /reɪl/ n 1 [C] bar or rod of wood or metal, eg as part of a fence. 2 [C] bar or rod used for hanging things on: a towel ~. 3 [C, esp pl] steel bar on which trains run. 4 [U] railway: travel by ~. **rail** v (phr v) **rail sth in/off** surround/separate sth with rails. **railing** n [C, esp pl] fence made with rails. **railroad** n [C] (US) railway. **railway** n [C] 1 track on which trains run. 2 system of such tracks, with the trains, etc.

rain /reɪn/ n [U] water falling in drops from the clouds. **rain** v 1 [I] (used with it) fall as rain: It ~ed all day. 2 (phr v) **rain (sth) down** (cause sth to) flow or come down in large quantities. **rain sth off** (usu passive) prevent (an event) from taking place because of rain.

rainbow /'reɪnbəʊ/ n [C] curve of many colours seen in the sky when the sun shines through rain. **'raincoat** n [C] light waterproof coat. **'rainfall** n [U] amount of rain that falls in a certain area during a particular time. **'rain forest** n [C] thick forest in tropical areas with heavy rainfall.

rainy /'reɪnɪ/ adj (-ier, -iest) 1 having a lot of rain. 2 (idm) for a ,rainy 'day (of money) for a time when one might need it.

raise /reɪz/ v [T] 1 move to a higher level; lift. 2 (a) increase the amount of: ~ sb's hopes, ie make sb more hopeful. (b) increase the loudness of: ~ one's voice. 3 cause to appear or arise: ~ doubts. 4

cause to be heard. 5 bring up for attention or discussion: ~ *a new point*. 6 bring or collect together: ~ *an army/money*. 7 (a) grow (crops); breed (sheep, etc). (b) look after (a child) until he/she is fully grown. 8 (idm) raise 'hell/the 'roof (*infml*) become very angry. raise n [C] (*US*) increase in wages.

raisin /'reɪzn/ n [C] dried sweet grape.

rake /reɪk/ n [C] long-handled gardening tool with a row of prongs at the end. rake v 1 [I, T] level sth with a rake. 2 [T] collect or move with a rake. (phr v) rake sth in (*infml*) earn a lot of money: *She's really raking it in!* rake sth up remind people of (sth unpleasant that happened in the past). 'rake-off n [C] (*infml*) (usu dishonest) share of profits.

rally /'rælɪ/ n [C] (*pl* -ies) 1 large gathering of people for a particular (esp political) purpose. 2 driving competition on public roads. 3 long series of hits in tennis, etc. rally v (*pt, pp* -ied) [I, T] 1 (cause to) come together to make new efforts. 2 (cause to) recover health, strength, etc. 3 (phr v) rally round come together to help sb/sth in a time of need.

ram /ræm/ n [C] 1 uncastrated male sheep. 2 = BATTERING-RAM (BATTER¹). ram (-mm-) [T] 1 crash against (sth) heavily. 2 push very forcefully.

ramble /'ræmbl/ n [C] (long) pleasant walk in the countryside. ramble v [I] 1 go on a ramble. 2 (*fig*) talk or write in a wandering confused way. 3 (of a plant) grow wildly. rambler n [C]. rambling adj 1 (esp of buildings) extending in many directions irregularly. 2 (of speech or writing) confused and badly ordered.

ramification /ˌræmɪfɪ'keɪʃn/ n [C, usu pl] (*fml*) 1 result or consequence (of sth) that makes it more complicated: *the ~s of the new system*. 2 part of a complicated structure.

ramp /ræmp/ n [C] sloping way from one level to another.

rampage /ræm'peɪdʒ/ v [I] rush around wildly or violently. rampage n (idm) be/go on the 'rampage rampage.

rampant /'ræmpənt/ adj (eg of disease or crime) growing or spreading uncontrollably.

rampart /'ræmpɑːt/ n [C] wide bank of earth built to defend a fort, etc.

ramshackle /'ræmʃækl/ adj (of a house or vehicle) almost collaps-

ing.

ran *pt* of RUN¹.

ranch /rɑːntʃ; *US* ræntʃ/ n [C] large farm, esp in the US, where cattle are raised. rancher n [C] person who owns or manages a ranch.

rancid /'rænsɪd/ adj (of fatty foods) tasting or smelling bad because of staleness.

rancour (*US* -cor) /'ræŋkə(r)/ n [U] (*fml*) deep long-lasting bitterness. rancorous /-kərəs/ adj.

random /'rændəm/ adj done, chosen, etc without a definite plan or pattern. random n (idm) at 'random in a random way. randomly adv.

randy /'rændɪ/ adj (-ier, -iest) (*infml esp Brit*) sexually excited.

rang *pt* of RING¹.

range¹ /reɪndʒ/ n 1 [C] connected line of mountains, hills, etc. 2 [C] group or series of similar things; variety: *sell a wide ~ of books*. 3 [C] limits between which sth varies. 4 (a) [U] distance within which one can see or hear. (b) [U, sing] distance to which a gun, missile, etc can be fired: *shot him at close ~*. 5 [C] area of ground with targets for shooting at.

range² /reɪndʒ/ v 1 [I] vary between limits: *Prices ~ from £70 to £100*. 2 [I] (over)/(*fig*) include, cover: *a talk ranging over many subjects*. 3 [T] (*fml*) put in a line.

ranger /'reɪndʒə(r)/ n person who patrols a forest or large park.

rank¹ /ræŋk/ n 1 [C, U] position in the army, navy, etc. 2 [U] position in an organization or in society. 3 [C] line of things: *a taxi ~*. 4 the ranks [pl] ordinary soldiers, not officers. rank v [I, T] be or put in a certain position or class: *among the world's best*. the rank and 'file n [sing] (with sing or pl v) ordinary members of an organization, not its leaders.

rank² /ræŋk/ adj 1 (of plants) growing too thickly. 2 smelling or tasting bad. 3 (of sth bad) complete.

rankle /'ræŋkl/ v [I] cause lasting bitterness or anger.

ransack /'rænsæk; *US* ræn'sæk/ v [T] search (a place) thoroughly leaving it very untidy.

ransom /'rænsəm/ n [C] money paid to set a prisoner free. ransom v [T] get the freedom of (sb) by paying a ransom.

rant /rænt/ v [I] talk loudly and violently.

rap /ræp/ n [C] 1 (sound of) a light quick blow. 2 (idm) take the rap for sth (*infml*) be punished, esp for sth one has not done. **rap** v (-pp-) [I, T] hit (sth) lightly and quickly.

rape /reɪp/ v [T] commit the crime of forcing (a woman) to have sexual intercourse against her will. **rape** n [C, U] 1 act of raping. 2 (fig) spoiling or destruction. **rapist** n [C].

rapid /'ræpɪd/ adj moving with great speed; fast. **rapidity** /rə'pɪdətɪ/ n [U]. **rapidly** adv. **rapids** n [pl] part of a river where a steep slope causes the water to flow fast.

rapport /ræ'pɔː(r); US -'pɔːrt/ n [U, sing] close relationship and understanding.

rapt /ræpt/ adj so deep in thought that one is not aware of other things.

rapture /'ræptʃə(r)/ n 1 [U] (fml) great joy. 2 (idm) **go into raptures about/over** sth show great happiness or enthusiasm about sth. **rapturous** adj: rapturous applause.

rare¹ /reə(r)/ (~r, ~st) not common. **rarely** adv not often. **rareness** n [U].

rare² /reə(r)/ adj (of meat) lightly done.

rarefied /'reərɪfaɪd/ adj 1 (of air) containing less oxygen and less dense than usual. 2 (fig) very grand; exclusive.

raring /'reərɪŋ/ adj to// very eager to do sth.

rarity /'reərətɪ/ n (pl -ies) 1 [U] rareness. 2 [C] something uncommon or unusual.

rascal /'rɑːskl; US 'ræskl/ n [C] 1 naughty child. 2 dishonest person.

rash¹ /ræʃ/ adj acting or done without careful thought. **rashly** adv. **rashness** n [U].

rash² /ræʃ/ n 1 [C] area of tiny red spots on the skin, caused by illness. 2 [sing] (fig) sudden large number: a ~ of strikes.

rasher /'ræʃə(r)/ n [C] thin slice of bacon.

rasp /rɑːsp; US ræsp/ n 1 [sing] unpleasant rough sound. 2 [C] tool used for making metal or wood smoother. **rasp** v [I, T] say (sth) in an unpleasant rough voice. **rasping** adj.

raspberry /'rɑːzbrɪ; US 'ræzberɪ/ n [C] (pl -ies) 1 (bush with a) sweet red berry. 2 (infml) noise made by putting one's tongue out and blowing, to show disapproval.

rat /ræt/ n [C] 1 animal like, but larger than, a mouse. 2 (infml) unpleasant or disloyal person. 3 (idm) **the 'rat race** endless competition for success. **rat** v (-tt-) [I] (on)// (infml) reveal sb's secret; betray. **ratty** adj (-ier, -iest) (Brit infml) irritable.

rate¹ /reɪt/ n [C] 1 one amount in relation to another: a ~ of 3 miles per hour ○ the 'birth ~. 2 measure of cost or quality: postage ~s ○ a first-~ job. 3 speed. 4 **rates** [pl] (formerly in Britain) local tax on buildings. 5 (idm) **at 'any rate** whatever happens. **at 'this/'that rate** if this/that continues. **'ratepayer** n [C] (formerly in Britain) person who has to pay rates.

rate² /reɪt/ v [T] 1 consider in the way that is mentioned: He is generally ~d as one of the best players. 2 regard as; consider: ~ sb as a friend. 3 (esp infml) deserve.

rather /'rɑːðə(r); US 'ræ-/ adv 1 to some extent: They were ~ surprised. 2 (idm) **or rather** more exactly: last night, or ~ early this morning. **would rather... (than)** prefer to: I'd ~ walk than go by bus.

ratify /'rætɪfaɪ/ v (pt, pp -ied) [T] give one's formal approval to (an agreement). **ratification** /ˌrætɪfɪ'keɪʃn/ n [U].

rating /'reɪtɪŋ/ n 1 [C, U] grade or position of quality. 2 [pl] figures showing the popularity of television programmes. 3 [C] (esp Brit) (in the navy) non-commissioned sailor.

ratio /'reɪʃɪəʊ/ [i] [C] (pl -s) relationship between two amounts: The ~ of men to women was 3 to 1.

ration /'ræʃn/ n 1 [C] fixed quantity, esp of food, allowed to one person. 2 **rations** [pl] supplies of food. **ration** v [T] 1 limit (sb) to a ration. 2 limit supplies of.

rational /'ræʃnəl/ adj 1 able to reason. 2 sensible. **rationally** /-ʃnəlɪ/ adv.

rationale /ˌræʃə'nɑːl; US -'næl/ n [sing] logical reasons on which a course of action, belief, practice, etc is based.

rationalize /'ræʃnəlaɪz/ v 1 [I, T] think and offer reasons for (sth that seems unreasonable). 2 [T] organize (a system or industry) more efficiently, so as to reduce waste. **rationalization** /ˌræʃnəlaɪ'zeɪʃn; US -lɪ'z-/ n [C, U].

rattle /'rætl/ v 1 [I, T] (cause to) make short sharp sounds. 2 [T] (infml) make (sb) nervous. 3 (phr v) **rattle along, off,** etc move in the direction that is mentioned with a rattling sound. **rattle sth off** repeat sth quickly and without much thought. **rattle** n [C] 1 rattling sound. 2 baby's toy that produces a rattling sound. '**rattlesnake** n [C] poisonous American snake that makes a rattling noise with its tail.

ratty ⇨ RAT.

raucous /'rɔːkəs/ adj loud and rough. **raucously** adv.

ravage /'rævɪdʒ/ v [T] damage badly; destroy. **the ravages** n [pl] damaging effects: the ~ s of time.

rave /reɪv/ v [I] 1 talk wildly or angrily. 2 about// (infml) talk with great admiration about sth. **rave** adj (infml) full of great praise: a ~ review. **raving** adv, adj completely (mad).

raven /'reɪvn/ n [C] large black bird like a crow. **raven** adj (of hair) glossy and black.

ravenous /'rævənəs/ adj very hungry. **ravenously** adv.

ravine /rə'viːn/ n [C] deep narrow steep-sided valley.

ravish /'rævɪʃ/ v [T] (fml) (esp passive) fill with delight. **ravishing** adj very beautiful.

raw /rɔː/ adj 1 uncooked. 2 in the natural state: ~ materials. 3 (of people) not yet trained or experienced. 4 (of skin) sore and painful. 5 (of the weather) cold and wet.

ray /reɪ/ n [C] 1 narrow line of light, heat, etc. 2 (fig) small sign: a ~ of hope.

rayon /'reɪɒn/ n [U] smooth silk-like material.

raze (also **rase**) /reɪz/ v [T] destroy (a building, town, etc) completely.

razor /'reɪzə(r)/ n [C] instrument with a sharp blade, used for shaving.

Rd abbr road.

re- /riː/ prefix again: refill ○ re-examine.

reach /riːtʃ/ v 1 [T] arrive at: ~ London ○ (fig) ~ an agreement. 2 [I, T] stretch out (one's hand or arm) to touch or take (sth): He ~ ed for his gun. ○ Can you ~ the book on the top shelf? 3 [I, T] go as far as (sth): Their land ~ es (down to) the river. 4 [T] communicate with (sb), esp by telephone. **reach** n 1 [U] distance that one can reach: Medicines should be kept out of ~ of children. 2 [C, usu pl] part of a river.

react /rɪ'ækt/ v 1 (to) behave differently as a result of sth. 2 against// behave in a certain way in opposition to sth. 3 (with)// (chemistry) have an effect on (another substance).

reaction /rɪ'ækʃn/ n 1 [C, U] response to an earlier action or activity. 2 [U] opposition to (esp political) changes. 3 [C] (chemistry) change caused in a substance by the effect of another. **reactionary** /-ʃənrɪ; US -ʃənerɪ/ n [C], adj (pl -ies) (person) opposed to (esp political) changes.

reactor /rɪ'æktə(r)/ n [C] = NUCLEAR REACTOR (NUCLEAR).

read /riːd/ v (pt, pp read /red/) 1 [I, T] (a) look at and understand (sth written or printed): ~ a book. (b) say aloud the words of (a book, etc). 2 [I] have the words or sense mentioned: The sign ~ s 'No Entry'. ○ Her reports always ~ well. 3 [T] understand: ~ sb's thoughts. 4 [T] (of measuring instruments) show (an amount, etc). 5 [T] study (a subject) at university. 6 (idm) ,read between the 'lines find a meaning that is not openly expressed. **readable** adj that is easy or pleasant to read.

reader /'riːdə(r)/ n [C] 1 person who reads. 2 book that gives students practice in reading. 3 (in Britain) senior university teacher. **readership** n [sing] number of readers of a newspaper, etc.

reading /'riːdɪŋ/ n 1 [U] (a) act of reading. (b) book, etc to be read: light (ie not serious) ~. 2 [C] amount, etc shown by a measuring instrument. 3 [C] way in which sth is understood: My ~ of the situation is... 4 [C] (Brit) (in Parliament) one of three stages of debate before a bill's(2) becomes law.

ready /'redɪ/ adj (-ier, -iest) 1 for/ to// prepared and fit for action or use: ~ for action ○ ~ to eat. 2 willing. 3 to// on the point of doing sth: She looked ~ to collapse. 4 quick: a ~ answer. 5 easily available. **readily** adv 1 without hesitation. 2 easily. **readiness** n [U]. **ready** adv already: ~ cooked. **ready in** n (idm) at the '**ready** ready for action or use. ,**ready-'made** adj ready to use or wear immediately.

real /rɪəl/ adj 1 existing as a fact. 2 true or actual. '**real estate** n [U] (esp US law) property, consisting of land and buildings.

realism /'rɪəlɪzəm/ n [U] 1 acceptance of the facts of a situation. 2 (in art and literature) showing of things as they are in real life. **realist** n [C]. **realistic** /,rɪə'lɪstɪk/ adj.

reality /rɪ'ælətɪ/ n (pl -ies) 1 [U] real existence. 2 [C] something actually seen or experienced: the realities of war. 3 (idm) **in re'ality** in actual fact.

realize /'rɪəlaɪz/ v [T] 1 be fully aware of; understand. 2 (fml) make (eg plans or fears) real. 3

(fml) be sold for. **realization**
/ˌrɪəlaɪˈzeɪʃn; US -lɪˈz-/ *n* [U].

really /ˈrɪəlɪ/ *adv* 1 in reality; truly. 2 very. 3 (used for showing interest, surprise, etc).

realm /relm/ *n* [C] 1 *(fml)* kingdom. 2 *(fig)* area of activity or interest.

reap /riːp/ *v* 1 [I, T] cut and gather (a crop, esp grain). 2 [T] *(fig)*
obtain, esp as a result of hard
work.

rear[1] /rɪə(r)/ *n* 1 **the rear** [sing]
back part. 2 (idm) **bring up the
'rear** be or come last. **rear** *adj*
back. **the 'rearguard** /-ɡɑːd/ [C] soldiers protecting the back part of an
army.

rear[2] /rɪə(r)/ *v* 1 [T] **(a)** look after
(a child) until he/she is fully
grown. **(b)** breed and look after
(sheep, etc). 2 [I] *(up)// (*of a horse)
raise itself on its back legs. 3 [T]
raise (one's head).

reason[1] /ˈriːzn/ *n* 1 [C, U] fact or
situation that explains why sth
happens; cause. 2 [U] power of the
mind to understand, etc. 3 [sing]
good sense: *lose one's ~*, ie go mad.
4 (idm) **within reason** sensible
and fair.

reason[2] /ˈriːzn/ *v* 1 [I] use one's
power to think, understand, etc. 2
[T] state (sth) after careful
thought. 3 (phr v) **reason with sb**
argue with sb in order to persuade
him/her. **reasoning** *n* [U] reaching
conclusions by using one's
reason.

reasonable /ˈriːznəbl/ *adj* 1 fair;
sensible. 2 not too expensive.
reasonably *adv* 1 quite. 2 in a
reasonable way.

reassure /ˌriːəˈʃɔː(r); US -ˈʃʊər/
v [T] remove (sb's) worries. **reas-
surance** *n* [U, C].

rebate /ˈriːbeɪt/ *n* [C] part of tax,
rent, etc paid back.

rebel[1] /ˈrebl/ *n* [C] 1 person who
fights against the government. 2
person who opposes authority. **re-
bel**[2] /rɪˈbel/ *v* (**-ll-**) [I] 1 *(against)//*
fight against the government. 2
oppose authority. **rebellion**
/rɪˈbeljən/ *n* [C, U] (act of) rebell-
ing. **rebellious** *adj*.

rebound /rɪˈbaʊnd/ *v* [I] 1 bounce
back after hitting sth. 2 *(on)// (*have
unexpected and unpleasant effects on the doer. **rebound** /ˈriː-
baʊnd/ *n* (idm) **on the 'rebound**
while still affected by sadness, disappointment, etc of a broken relationship.

rebuff /rɪˈbʌf/ *n* [C] unkind refusal or answer. **rebuff** *v* [T] give a
rebuff to.

rebuke /rɪˈbjuːk/ *v* [T] *(fml)* speak

severely to (sb) for doing sth
wrong: *He was ~d for being late.*
rebuke *n* [C, U].

recall /rɪˈkɔːl/ *v* [T] 1 remember.
2 order to return or be returned.
recall / also ˈriːkɔːl/ *n* 1 [sing]
order to return. 2 [U] ability to remember.

recap /ˈriːkæp/ *v* (**-pp-**) [I, U]
(infml) short for RECAPITULATE.

recapitulate /ˌriːkəˈpɪtʃuleɪt/
v [I, T] repeat the main points of.
recapitulation /ˌriːkəpɪtʃʊ-
ˈleɪʃn/ *n* [C, U].

recede /rɪˈsiːd/ *v* [I] 1 move away
or back. 2 slope backwards.

receipt /rɪˈsiːt/ *n* 1 [C] written
statement that one has received
money or goods. 2 **receipts** [pl]
money received by a business. 3
[U] *(fml)* act of receiving sth.

receive /rɪˈsiːv/ *v* [T] 1 get or accept (sth sent or given). 2 experience; suffer: *~d severe injuries in the crash.* 3 accept as a
member or visitor. 4 change
(broadcast signals) into sounds or
pictures. **receiver** /-ə(r)/ *n* 1 part of a
telephone that is held to the ear. 2
radio or television set. 3 person
who receives sth, esp stolen goods.
4 **Receiver** official appointed to
look after the affairs of a bankrupt
company.

recent /ˈriːsnt/ *adj* that happened, began, etc a short time ago.
recently *adv* not long ago.

receptacle /rɪˈseptəkl/ *n* [C] *(fml)*
container.

reception /rɪˈsepʃn/ *n* 1 [C] formal party. 2 [C] welcome: *be given
a warm ~*. 3 [U] part of a hotel,
office, etc where visitors are received. 4 [U] quality of radio or
television signals received. **recep-
tionist** /-ʃənɪst/ *n* [C] person employed to receive and deal with
visitors to a hotel, office building,
etc.

receptive /rɪˈseptɪv/ *adj* willing
to consider new ideas.

recess /rɪˈses; US ˈriːses/ *n* 1
[C, U] period of time when work is
stopped. 2 [C] area of a room
where part of a wall is set back. 3
[C, usu pl] *(fig)* secret or hidden
part.

recession /rɪˈseʃn/ *n* 1 [C, U]
period of less economic activity. 2
[U] act of receding.

recipe /ˈresəpɪ/ *n* [C] 1 set of instructions for preparing a food
dish. 2 *(fig)* way of achieving sth: *a
~ for disaster.*

recipient /rɪˈsɪpɪənt/ *n* [C] *(fml)*
person who receives sth.

reciprocal /rɪˈsɪprəkl/ *adj* given
and received in return: *~ trade*

agreements. **reciprocally** /-klɪ/ *adv*.

reciprocate /rɪ'sɪprəkeɪt/ *v* [I, T] (*fml*) give and receive (sth) in return.

recital /rɪ'saɪtl/ *n* [C] performance of music or poetry by one person or a small group.

recite /rɪ'saɪt/ *v* [T] **1** say (eg a poem) aloud from memory. **2** give a list of (names, facts, etc). **recitation** /ˌresɪ'teɪʃn/ *n* [C, U].

reckless /'reklɪs/ *adj* not caring about danger or the effects of sth. **recklessly** *adv*. **recklessness** *n* [U].

reckon /'rekən/ *v* [T] **1** (*infml*) think; consider: *I ~ we ought to go now*. **2** calculate roughly; guess. **3** add up. **4** (*phr v*) **reckon on sth** depend on sth happening. **reckon with sth/sb** (**a**) deal with sb/sth. (**b**) consider sb/sth as important: *a force to be ~ed with*, ie that cannot be ignored. **reckoning** *n* [U] **1** calculation. **2** final punishment: *the day of '~ing*.

reclaim /rɪ'kleɪm/ *v* [T] **1** ask for (sth) to be given back. **2** make (land) suitable for use. **reclamation** /ˌreklə'meɪʃn/ *n* [U].

recline /rɪ'klaɪn/ *v* [I] (*fml*) lie back or down.

recluse /rɪ'kluːs/ *n* [C] person who lives alone and avoids other people.

recognize /'rekəgnaɪz/ *v* [T] **1** know again (sb/sth that one has seen, heard, etc before). **2** accept as real or true: *refuse to ~ a new government*. **3** be prepared to admit: *~ one's faults*. **4** show thankfulness towards (sb) by giving him/her a special honour. **recognition** /ˌrekəg'nɪʃn/ *n* [U]. **recognizable** *adj*.

recoil /rɪ'kɔɪl/ *v* [I] **1** move back suddenly in fear, dislike, etc. **2** (of a gun) move back quickly when fired. **recoil** /'riːkɔɪl/ *n* [U, sing].

recollect /ˌrekə'lekt/ *v* [I, T] remember (sth). **recollection** /-'lekʃn/ *n* **1** [C] something remembered. **2** [U] act or power of remembering.

recommend /ˌrekə'mend/ *v* [T] **1** praise (sb/sth) as suitable for a job/purpose. **2** suggest or advise: *I ~ leaving/you leave early*. **recommendation** /-men'deɪʃn/ *n* [C, U].

recompense /'rekəmpens/ *v* [T] (*fml*) reward (sb) for work; repay (sb) for losses or harm. **recompense** *n* [sing, U] (*fml*) reward or repayment.

reconcile /'rekənsaɪl/ *v* [T] **1** cause (people) to become friends again, esp after quarrelling. **2**

cause (two things) to agree when they seem to be opposed to each other. **3** ~ **oneself to** accept sth unpleasant. **reconciliation** /ˌrekən,sɪlɪ'eɪʃn/ *n* [U, C].

reconnaissance /rɪ'kɒnɪsns/ *n* [C, U] (act of) reconnoitring.

reconnoitre (*US* **-ter**) /ˌrekə'nɔɪtə(r)/ *v* [I, T] get information about the strength, etc of (an enemy position) or features of (an area).

record /'rekɔːd; *US* 'rekərd/ *n* [C] **1** written account of facts, events, etc. **2** known facts about sb's character or past. **3** the best yet done: *a new world ~ in the 100 metres ○ ~ profits*. **4** round flat piece of plastic on which sound has been recorded. **5** (*idm*) **off the 'record** unofficial and not for publication. **on 'record** officially noted. **'record-player** *n* [C] machine for producing sound from records(4).

record /rɪ'kɔːd/ *v* **1** [T] write down for future use or reference. **2** [T, I] keep (sound or pictures) on tape, disc, etc to be heard or seen later. **3** [T] (of a measuring instrument) show on a scale.

recorder /rɪ'kɔːdə(r)/ *n* [C] **1** machine for recording sounds or pictures. **2** musical instrument played by blowing into one end. **3** (*Brit*) judge in certain law-courts.

recording /rɪ'kɔːdɪŋ/ *n* [C] sounds or pictures recorded on a tape or disc.

recount /rɪ'kaʊnt/ *v* [T] (*fml*) give a description of; tell.

re-count /ˌriː'kaʊnt/ *v* [T] count (esp votes) again. **re-count** /'riːkaʊnt/ *n* [C] second count.

recoup /rɪ'kuːp/ *v* [T] get back (esp money).

recourse /rɪ'kɔːs/ *n* (*idm*) **have recourse to sth** (*fml*) use sth in order to help one.

recover /rɪ'kʌvə(r)/ *v* **1** [I] (*from*)|| become well again after an illness, etc. **2** [T] get back (sth lost or stolen). **3** [T] get control of (oneself, one's emotions, etc) again. **recovery** /rɪ-/ *n* [U, sing].

recreation /ˌrekrɪ'eɪʃn/ *n* [C, U] (form of) play or amusement or way of spending one's free time.

recrimination /rɪˌkrɪmɪ'neɪʃn/ *n* [C, usu pl, U] (act of) accusing and blaming each other.

recruit /rɪ'kruːt/ *n* [C] new member of a society, etc, esp the army. **recruit** *v* [I, T] get (sb) as a recruit. **recruitment** *n* [U].

rectangle /'rektæŋgl/ *n* [C] four-sided shape with four right angles. **rectangular** /rek'tæŋgjʊlə(r)/ *adj*.

rectify /ˈrektɪfaɪ/ v (pt, pp **-ied**) [T] put right: ~ an error.

rector /ˈrektə(r)/ n [C] clergyman in charge of a parish. **rectory** /ˈrektərɪ/ n [C] (pl **-ies**) rector's house.

rectum /ˈrektəm/ n [C] (anatomy) lower end of the large intestine.

recuperate /rɪˈkuːpəreɪt/ v [I] (from)|| (fml) become strong again after an illness, etc. **recuperation** /rɪˌkuːpəˈreɪʃn/ n [U].

recur /rɪˈkɜː(r)/ v (-rr-) [I] happen again. **recurrence** /rɪˈkʌrəns/ n [C, U] repetition. **recurrent** /rɪˈkʌrənt/ adj.

recycle /ˌriːˈsaɪkl/ v [T] treat (sth already used) so that it can be used again.

red /red/ adj (~**der**, ~**dest**) 1 of the colour of blood. 2 (of the face) redder than usual, because of embarrassment or anger. 3 (of hair) reddish-brown. 4 **Red** (infml) Communist. 5 (idm) red 'herring something irrelevant that takes attention away from the main point. ¸red 'tape unnecessary official rules that delay. red n 1 [C, U] red colour. 2 [U] red clothes: dressed in ~. 3 **Red** [C] (infml) Communist. 4 (idm) in the 'red having debts. 'redhead [C] person with red(3) hair. ¸red 'hot adj so hot that it glows red.

redden /ˈredn/ v [I, T] become or make red.

redeem /rɪˈdiːm/ v [T] 1 buy (sth back) by payment. 2 make (sth unpleasant) less bad: a film with no ~ing features. **redemption** /rɪˈdempʃn/ n [U].

redouble /ˌriːˈdʌbl/ v [T] increase greatly: ~ one's efforts.

redress /rɪˈdres/ v [T] 1 (fml) put (a wrong) right again. 2 (idm) redress the 'balance make things equal again. **redress** n [U] (fml) money, etc that puts right a wrong.

reduce /rɪˈdjuːs; US -ˈduːs/ v [T] 1 make less or smaller. 2 (to)|| (usu passive) bring (sb) to a certain condition: He was ~d to tears. **reduction** /rɪˈdʌkʃn/ n 1 [C, U] (instance of) reducing: ~s in price. 2 [C] small copy of a picture, map, etc.

redundant /rɪˈdʌndənt/ adj 1 dismissed from a job because no longer needed. 2 not needed. **redundancy** /-dənsɪ/ n [C, U] (pl **-ies**).

reed /riːd/ n [C] 1 grass-like plant growing near water. 2 (in some wind instruments) piece of wood or metal that vibrates to produce sound.

reef /riːf/ n [C] line of rocks, sand, etc just below or above the surface of the sea.

reek /riːk/ n [sing] strong unpleasant smell. **reek** v [I] (of)|| smell unpleasantly of sth.

reel¹ /riːl/ n [C] 1 cylinder on which thread, wire, film, etc is wound. 2 length of thread, film, etc on one reel. **reel** v 1 [T] in/out/| wind (sth) on/off a reel. 2 (phr v) reel sth off say sth quickly without a pause.

reel² /riːl/ v [I] 1 move unsteadily; sway. 2 (fig) (of the mind) be confused.

refectory /rɪˈfektrɪ/ n [C] (pl **-ies**) dining-hall, eg in a college.

refer /rɪˈfɜː(r)/ v (-rr-) 1 [I] to|| (a) talk about sth/sb; mention. (b) be about sb/sth; concern. 2 [I] to|| look at (eg a book) for information. 3 [T] to|| send (sb/sth) to sb/sth for help, advice, etc.

referee /ˌrefəˈriː/ n [C] 1 (sport) person who controls a game. 2 person who gives a reference(3).

reference /ˈrefərəns/ n 1 [C, U] (act of) referring. 2 [C] note, etc telling where information may be found. 3 [C] statement about sb's character and abilities. 4 (idm) in/ with reference to sth (esp commerce) about sth. 'reference book n [C] book, eg a dictionary or an encyclopedia, looked at for finding information.

referendum /ˌrefəˈrendəm/ n (pl **-da** /-də/ or **-dums**) n [C] direct vote by all the people on a political question.

refine /rɪˈfaɪn/ v [T] 1 make pure. 2 improve (sth) by removing errors. **refined** adj 1 well educated and polite. 2 made pure. **refinement** n 1 [U] refining. 2 [U] good education and politeness. 3 [C] improvement; clever addition. **refinery** /-ərɪ/ n [C] (pl **-ies**) place where oil, sugar, etc is refined.

reflate /ˌriːˈfleɪt/ v [I, T] increase the amount of money in (an economy). **reflation** /riːˈfleɪʃn/ n [U].

reflect /rɪˈflekt/ v 1 [T] throw back (an image, heat, sound, etc). 2 [T] (fig) show the nature of; express: The book faithfully ~s his ideas. 3 [I] (on)|| think deeply about sth. 4 (phr v) reflect on sb/ sth cause sb/sth to be considered in the way that is mentioned. **reflector** n [C] something that reflects heat, light or sound.

reflection /rɪˈflekʃn/ n 1 [C] reflected image, eg in a mirror. 2 [U] reflecting of light, heat, etc. 3 [C, U] deep thought: on ~, ie after thinking very carefully.

reflex /'ri:fleks/ [C] (also **'reflex action**) sudden unintended movement, eg sneezing, made in response to sth.

reflexive /rɪ'fleksɪv/ n [C], adj (grammar) (word) showing that the action of the verb is performed on the subject: a ~ verb ○ In 'I cut myself', 'myself' is a ~ pronoun.

reform /rɪ'fɔːm/ v [I, T] become or make better in behaviour; improve. **reform** n [C, U] change or improvement in a law or social system. **reformer** n [C] person who supports reform.

re-form /ˌriː 'fɔːm/ v [I, T] form again: The army ~ed and attacked.

reformation /ˌrefə'meɪʃn/ n 1 [C, U] improvement, esp in behaviour. **2 the Reformation** [sing] 16th century religious movement that led to the establishment of Protestant Churches.

refract /rɪ'frækt/ v [T] bend (a ray of light) where it enters water, glass, etc. **refraction** /-kʃn/ n [U].

refrain[1] /rɪ'freɪn/ v [I] (from)// (fml) not do sth.

refrain[2] /rɪ'freɪn/ n [C] lines of a song that are repeated.

refresh /rɪ'freʃ/ v [T] **1** give new strength to. **2** (idm) **refresh one's memory** remind oneself of facts by referring to notes, etc. **re'fresher course** n [C] course providing teaching on new developments, etc. **refreshing** adj **1** giving new strength. **2** (fig) welcome and interesting because unusual. **refreshment** n **1** (fml) refreshing. **2 refreshments** [pl] food and drink.

refrigerate /rɪ'frɪdʒəreɪt/ v [T] make (food) cool or cold in order to freeze or preserve it. **refrigeration** /rɪˌfrɪdʒə'reɪʃn/ n [C]. **refrigerator** n [C] cupboard in which food is kept cold.

refuel /ˌriː'fjuːəl/ v (-ll-; US -l-) [I, T] (cause to) be filled with more fuel.

refuge /'refjuːdʒ/ n [C, U] (place giving) protection from danger.

refugee /ˌrefju'dʒiː/ n [C] person forced to leave his/her country, esp because of political or religious beliefs.

refund /'riːfʌnd/ n [C] repayment. **refund** /rɪ'fʌnd/ v [T] pay back (money).

refusal /rɪ'fjuːzl/ n [C, U] (instance of) refusing.

refuse[1] /rɪ'fjuːz/ v [I, T] not give, accept or do (sth): ~ permission ○ ~ to help.

refuse[2] /'refjuːs/ n [U] waste material; rubbish.

regain /rɪ'geɪn/ v [T] get back; recover: ~ one's strength.

regal /'riːgl/ adj of or fit for a king or queen; royal or splendid.

regalia /rɪ'geɪlɪə/ n [U] traditional ceremonial clothes and symbols, eg of a king or queen.

regard[1] /rɪ'gɑːd/ v [T] as// think about (sb/sth) in the way that is mentioned: She is ~ed as the best teacher in the school. **regarding** (also **as regards**) prep concerning; about.

regard[2] /rɪ'gɑːd/ n **1** [U] attention; concern: with no ~ for safety. **2** [U] respect: have a high ~ for sb. **3 regards** [pl] kind wishes. **4** (idm) **in/with regard to sth** concerning sth; about. **regardless (of)** adv paying no attention (to sb/sth).

regatta /rɪ'gætə/ n [C] meeting for boat races.

regency /'riːdʒənsɪ/ n (pl -ies) **1** [C] (period of) office of a regent. **2 the Regency** [sing] period 1810-20 in Britain.

regenerate /rɪ'dʒenəreɪt/ v [I, T] give new strength or life to (sb/sth). **regeneration** /rɪˌdʒenə'reɪʃn/ n [U].

regent /'riːdʒənt/ n [C] person who rules instead of a king or queen who is too young, ill, etc.

reggae /'reɡeɪ/ n [U] West Indian popular music and dance.

regime /reɪ'ʒiːm/ n [C] (system of) government.

regiment /'redʒɪmənt/ n [C] army unit commanded by a colonel. **regiment** v [T] organize strictly. **regimental** /ˌredʒɪ'mentl/ adj.

region /'riːdʒən/ n **1** [C] large area or part. **2** [C] division of a country. **3** (idm) **in the region of** sth about sth; approximately. **regional** adj.

register /'redʒɪstə(r)/ n [C] **1** (book containing a) list of names, etc. **2** range of the voice or a musical instrument. **register** v **1** [I] put one's name on a list. **2** [T] record (sth) on an official list. **3** [I, T] (of measuring instruments) show (an amount). **4** [T] show (one's feelings) on one's face. **5** [T] send (a letter, etc) by special post, paying extra for compensation if it is lost.

registrar /ˌredʒɪ'strɑː(r)/ n [C] keeper of official records.

registration /ˌredʒɪ'streɪʃn/ n [U] registering; recording. **regi'stration number** n [C] numbers and letters on a vehicle used to identify it.

registry office /'redʒɪstrɪ/ n [C] place where non-religious marriages can take place and where births, marriages and deaths are officially recorded.

regret¹ /rɪˈgret/ v (-tt-) [T] be sorry or sad about: *Later, I ~ted my decision to leave.* **regrettable** *adj* that is to be regretted. **regrettably** *adv.*

regret² /rɪˈgret/ n [U, C] feeling of being sorry at the loss of sth or because of sth one has done. **regretful** *adj* sad; sorry.

regular /ˈregjʊlə(r)/ *adj* 1 happening, coming, etc repeatedly at times or places that are the same distance apart: ~ *breathing.* 2 evenly arranged. 3 usual or normal. 4 (*grammar*) (of verbs, nouns, etc) having normal inflections. 5 belonging to the permanent armed forces: *a* ~ *soldier.* **regular** *n* [C] 1 regular soldier. 2 (*infml*) regular customer. **regularity** /ˌregjʊˈlærətɪ/ n [U]. **regularly** *adv* at regular times or intervals.

regulate /ˈregjʊleɪt/ v [T] 1 control, using rules. 2 adjust (a machine) to get the desired result.

regulation /ˌregjʊˈleɪʃn/ n 1 [C, usu pl] rule or order. 2 [U] regulating. **regulation** *adj* as required by rules: ~ *clothes.*

rehabilitate /ˌriːəˈbɪlɪteɪt/ v [T] help (sb who has been imprisoned or ill) live a normal life again. **rehabilitation** /ˌriːəˌbɪlɪˈteɪʃn/ n [U].

rehearse /rɪˈhɜːs/ v [I, T] practise (a play, music, etc) for public performance. **rehearsal** n [C, U].

reign /reɪn/ n [C] (period of) rule of a king or queen. **reign** v [I] 1 be king or queen. 2 (*fig*) exist strongly: *Silence ~ed.*

reimburse /ˌriːɪmˈbɜːs/ v [T] pay back to (sb) (money that he/she has spent or lost). **reimbursement** n [U, C].

rein /reɪn/ n [C, usu pl] long narrow strap for controlling a horse.

reincarnate /ˌriːɪnˈkɑːneɪt/ v [T] (usu passive) bring back (a soul after death) in another body. **reincarnation** /ˌriːɪnkɑːˈneɪʃn/ n [U, C].

reindeer /ˈreɪndɪə(r)/ n [C] (*pl* **reindeer**) large deer with antlers, living in northern regions.

reinforce /ˌriːɪnˈfɔːs/ v [T] make stronger by adding material, etc. **reinforcement** n 1 [U] reinforcing. 2 **reinforcements** [pl] extra soldiers sent to reinforce an army.

reinstate /ˌriːɪnˈsteɪt/ v [T] put (sb) into his/her former job or position. **reinstatement** n [U].

reiterate /riːˈɪtəreɪt/ v [T] (*fml*) repeat several times. **reiteration**

/riːˌɪtəˈreɪʃn/ n [C, U].

reject /rɪˈdʒekt/ v [T] 1 refuse to accept. 2 send back or throw away as not good enough. **reject** /ˈriːdʒekt/ n [C] something rejected. **rejection** /rɪˈdʒekʃn/ n [U, C].

rejoice /rɪˈdʒɔɪs/ v [I] (*fml*) feel or show great joy. **rejoicing** n [U] happiness; joy.

rejuvenate /rɪˈdʒuːvəneɪt/ v [T] make young or strong again. **rejuvenation** /rɪˌdʒuːvəˈneɪʃn/ n [U].

relapse /rɪˈlæps/ v [I] return to one's bad ways or bad health. **relapse** n [C].

relate /rɪˈleɪt/ v 1 [I, T] (*to*)// (cause) to be connected to sth. 2 [I] (*to*)// be able to understand and talk to sb easily. 3 [T] (*fml*) tell (a story). **related** *adj* of the same family or kind.

relation /rɪˈleɪʃn/ n 1 [C] member of one's family. 2 [U] connection. 3 **relations** [pl] contacts or dealings between people, countries, etc. 4 (idm) **in relation to sth** (*fml*) with reference to sth. **relationship** n [C] 1 connection. 2 feelings or friendship between one person or group and another. 3 close emotional or sexual friendship.

relative /ˈrelətɪv/ *adj* 1 considered in relation to sth else. 2 *to//* (*fml*) with reference to sth. **relative** n [C] member of one's family. **relative 'clause** n [C] (*grammar*) clause joined to the rest of a sentence by a relative pronoun or adverb. **relatively** *adv* moderately; quite: ~ *cheap food.* **relative 'pronoun** n [C] (*grammar*) pronoun that joins a clause to the rest of a sentence eg *who* in *the woman who came.*

relax /rɪˈlæks/ v 1 [I, T] become or make less worried or tight and more calm. 2 [T] let (rules, etc) become less strict. **relaxation** /ˌriːlækˈseɪʃn/ n 1 [U, C] (form of) recreation. 2 [U] relaxing. **relaxed** *adj* less worried; calm.

relay /ˈriːleɪ/ n 1 (a) [C, U] group of people that replace others to keep sth going continuously. (b) '**relay race** [C] race in which each member of a team runs, swims, etc one part of the total distance. 2 [C] electrical device that receives signals and sends them on. **relay** /also rɪˈleɪ/ v (*pt, pp* ~ed) [T] receive or pass on (a message or broadcast).

release /rɪˈliːs/ v [T] 1 set free. 2 allow (news, etc) to be made known; make available. 3 move from a fixed position: ~ *the brake.*

release *n* 1 [U, C] releasing. 2 [C] new record, film, etc that has been released(2).

relegate /'relɪgeɪt/ *v* [T] put into a lower or less important position. **relegation** /ˌrelɪ'geɪʃn/ *n* [U].

relent /rɪ'lent/ *v* [I] become less strict or harsh. **relentless** *adj* constant; harsh.

relevant /'reləvənt/ *adj* connected with what is being discussed. **relevance** /-vəns/ *n* [U]. **relevantly** *adv.*

reliable /rɪ'laɪəbl/ *adj* that may be relied on. **reliability** /rɪˌlaɪə'bɪlətɪ/ *n* [U]. **reliably** *adv.*

reliant /rɪ'laɪənt/ *adj on/upon* dependent on sb/sth. **reliance** /-əns/ *n* [U] dependence.

relic /'relɪk/ *n* [C] 1 something remaining from an earlier time. 2 part of the body or sth that belonged to a holy person and is deeply respected.

relief¹ /rɪ'liːf/ *n* 1 [U, sing] lessening or ending of pain, worry, etc: ~ *of suffering.* 2 [U] help given to people in need. 3 [C] person taking over another's duty.

relief² /rɪ'liːf/ *n* [U, C] (method of) carving, etc in which the design stands out from a flat surface. **re'lief map** *n* [C] map showing the height of hills, etc by shading or colour.

relieve /rɪ'liːv/ *v* [T] 1 lessen or remove (pain or trouble): *medicine to ~ the pain.* 2 take over the duties of. 3 introduce variety or interest into. 4 (phr v) **relieve sb of** sth (*fml*) take (a responsibility or job) away from sb: *He was ~d of his duties.* **relieved** *adj* no longer anxious.

religion /rɪ'lɪdʒən/ *n* 1 [U] belief in and worship of God or gods. 2 [C] particular system of faith and worship based on such belief.

religious /rɪ'lɪdʒəs/ *adj* 1 of religion. 2 (of a person) believing in and practising a religion. **religiously** *adv* regularly.

relinquish /rɪ'lɪŋkwɪʃ/ *v* [T] (*fml*) give up; surrender: ~ *one's duties.*

relish /'relɪʃ/ *v* [T] enjoy: *I don't* ~ *the idea of getting up so early.* **relish** *n* 1 [U] great enjoyment. 2 [C] sauce, etc added to food to give it more flavour.

reluctant /rɪ'lʌktənt/ *adj* unwilling. **reluctance** /-təns/ *n* [U]. **reluctantly** *adv.*

rely /rɪ'laɪ/ *v* (*pt, pp* **-ied**) [I] *on/* depend on sb/sth; trust.

remain /rɪ'meɪn/ *v* 1 (usu used with an adj) continue to be: ~

silent. 2 [I] be still present after other people/things have gone or been dealt with: *Not much* ~*ed of the house after the fire.* ○ *She* ~*ed in the house after her friends had left.* 3 [I] be still to be done: *There are only a couple of jobs* ~*ing now.*

remainder /-də(r)/ *n* [sing, also sing with pl v] part that remains.

remains *n* [pl] 1 parts that are left. 2 (*fml*) dead body.

remand /rɪ'mɑːnd; *US* -'mænd/ *v* [T] send (an accused person) from a law-court back to prison, to be tried later. **remand** *n* (idm) **on remand** being remanded.

remark /rɪ'mɑːk/ *v* [I, T] (*on*)// say or write sth, esp as a comment: *They all* ~*ed on his youth.* **remark** *n* [C] something said; comment. **remarkable** *adj* worth noticing or unusual. **remarkably** *adv.*

remedial /rɪ'miːdɪəl/ *adj* providing a remedy.

remedy /'remədɪ/ *n* [C, U] (*pl* **-ies**) 1 way of putting sth right. 2 cure. **remedy** *v* (*pt, pp* **-ied**) [T] put (sth wrong) right.

remember /rɪ'membə(r)/ *v* [I, T] have or keep (sth) in the memory; bring back to one's memory. 2 [T] give money, etc to. 2 (phr v) **remember sb to sb** pass greetings from one person to another. **remembrance** /-brəns/ *n* (*fml*) 1 [U] remembering. 2 [C] something given or kept to remind one of sb/sth.

remind /rɪ'maɪnd/ *v* [T] 1 cause (sb) to remember sth: *R~ me to buy some more milk, will you?* 2 *of/* cause sb to think about sb/sth similar: *He* ~*s me of his brother.* **reminder** *n* [C] something, eg a letter, that causes a person to remember sth.

reminisce /ˌremɪ'nɪs/ *v* [I] (*about*)// talk with enjoyment about the past. **reminiscences** *n* [pl] remembered experiences. **reminiscent** *adj of/* reminding one of sth.

remission /rɪ'mɪʃn/ *n* 1 [U, C] shortening of the time spent in prison, because of good behaviour. 2 [U] forgiveness.

remit /rɪ'mɪt/ *v* (*-tt-*) [T] (*fml*) 1 send (money) by post. 2 cancel (a payment or punishment). **remittance** *n* [C] sum of money remitted.

remnant /'remnənt/ *n* [C] small part that remains.

remonstrate /'remənstreɪt; *US* rɪ'mɒnstreɪt/ *v* [I] (*with/*) (*fml*) protest to sb about sth: ~*d with him about being late again.*

remorse /rɪˈmɔːs/ n [U] strong sorrow for having done wrong. **remorseful** adj. **remorseless** adj 1 without pity. 2 unpleasant and not stopping.

remote /rɪˈməʊt/ adj (~r, ~st) 1 (from)|| far away from places where people live. 2 far away in time or space. 3 (from)|| not connected with sth. 4 (of a person) unfriendly; not interested in others. 5 very small: a ~ possibility. **re‚mote con'trol** n [U] control of an apparatus from a distance by radio or electrical signals. **remotely** adv to a very small degree. **remoteness** n [U].

remove /rɪˈmuːv/ v [T] 1 take away or off. 2 get rid of: ~ stains/doubts. 3 dismiss from a job. **removal** n 1 [U] removing. 2 [C] moving furniture, etc to a different home. **removed** adj from|| different from sth. **remover** n [C, U]: a stain ~er.

remunerate /rɪˈmjuːnəreɪt/ v [T] (fml) pay (sb) for work done. **remuneration** /rɪˌmjuːnəˈreɪʃn/ n [C, U]. **remunerative** /-ərətɪv; US -əreɪtɪv/ adj profitable.

renaissance /rɪˈneɪsns; US ˈrenəsɑːns/ n 1 **the Renaissance** [sing] renewed interest in art and literature in Europe in the 14th-16th centuries. 2 [C] any similar renewed interest.

renal /ˈriːnl/ adj (anatomy) of the kidneys.

render /ˈrendə(r)/ v [T] (fml) 1 cause to be: The shock ~ed him speechless. 2 give: a reward for services ~ed. 3 perform. 4 translate. **rendering** n [C] performance.

rendezvous /ˈrɒndɪvuː/ n [C] (pl rendezvous /-vuːz/) 1 (place chosen for) a meeting. 2 place where people often meet. **rendezvous** v [I] meet at a rendezvous.

rendition /renˈdɪʃn/ n [C] (fml) performance.

renegade /ˈrenɪɡeɪd/ n [C] person who abandons his/her political or religious beliefs and joins a different group.

renew /rɪˈnjuː; US -ˈnuː/ v [T] 1 begin again: ~ a friendship. 2 put sth new of the same kind to take the place of. 3 put new strength into. 4 make (sth) last for a further period of time; extend: ~ a passport. **renewal** n [C, U].

renounce /rɪˈnaʊns/ v [T] (fml) 1 declare formally that one will no longer have anything to do with (sth): ~ one's faith. 2 formally give up (eg a rank or right).

renovate /ˈrenəveɪt/ v [T] put back (eg an old building) into good condition. **renovation** /ˌrenəˈveɪʃn/ n [C, U].

renown /rɪˈnaʊn/ n [U] (fml) fame. **renowned** adj famous.

rent¹ /rent/ n [U, C] money paid regularly for the use of a building, television, etc. **rent** v [T] 1 pay rent for the use of (sth). 2 (out)|| allow (sth) to be used in return for payment of rent. **rental** n [C] amount of rent paid.

rent² /rent/ n [C] torn place in a cloth, etc.

renunciation /rɪˌnʌnsɪˈeɪʃn/ n [U] (fml) act of renouncing sth.

reorganize /ˌriːˈɔːɡənaɪz/ v [I, T] organize (sth) in a new way. **reorganization** /ˌriːˌɔːɡənaɪˈzeɪʃn; US -nɪˈz-/ n [U, C].

Rep abbr (US) Republican.

rep¹ /rep/ n [C] (infml) short for REPRESENTATIVE 2.

rep² /rep/ n [U] (infml) short for REPERTORY.

repair /rɪˈpeə(r)/ v [T] put (sth damaged or badly worn) back into good condition; mend. **repair** n 1 [C, U] (act or result of) repairing: His car is under ~ (ie being repaired) at the moment. 2 (idm) in **good/bad re'pair** in a good/bad condition.

reparation /ˌrepəˈreɪʃn/ n [C] (fml) money given or sth done to compensate for loss or damage.

repatriate /ˌriːˈpætrieɪt; US -ˈpeɪt-/ v [T] send (sb) back to his/her own country. **repatriation** /ˌriːˌpætriˈeɪʃn; US -ˌpeɪt-/ n [U].

repay /rɪˈpeɪ/ v (pt, pp repaid /rɪˈpeɪd/) [T] 1 pay back (money). 2 give in return for: How can I ~ your kindness? **repayment** n [C, U].

repeal /rɪˈpiːl/ v [T] end (a law) officially. **repeal** n [U].

repeat /rɪˈpiːt/ v 1 [T] say or do again. 2 ~ oneself say or do sth that was said or done before. **repeat** n [C] act of repeating; sth repeated. **repeated** adj done again and again. **repeatedly** adv.

repel /rɪˈpel/ v (-ll-) [T] 1 drive back or away. 2 cause a feeling of great dislike. **repellent** adj causing great dislike. **repellent** n [C, U] substance that repels insects.

repent /rɪˈpent/ v [I, T] (of)|| (fml) be sorry about (sth wrong one has done). **repentance** n [U]. **repentant** adj.

repercussion /ˌriːpəˈkʌʃn/ n [C, usu pl] far-reaching indirect effect.

repertoire /ˈrepətwɑː(r)/ n [C] all the plays, songs, etc that an actor or musician can perform.

repertory /'repətrɪ; US -tɔːrɪ-/ n [U] performance of several plays for a short time using the same actors: a ~ *company*.

repetition /,repɪ'tɪʃn/ n [C, U] (act of) repeating. **repetitive** /rɪ'petətɪv/ adj having repeated actions.

rephrase /,riː'freɪz/ v [T] say again, using different words.

replace /rɪ'pleɪs/ v [T] 1 put back in its place. 2 take the place of. 3 put a new thing in the place of (an old, broken, etc one). **replacement** n 1 [U] replacing. 2 [C] person or thing that replaces another.

replay /,riː'pleɪ/ v [T] 1 play a (drawn sports match) again. 2 play (sth recorded) again on a tape-recorder, etc. **replay** /'riː'pleɪ/ n [C] replayed match.

replenish /rɪ'plenɪʃ/ v [T] (fml) get a further supply of; fill again.

replica /'replɪkə/ n [C] exact copy.

reply /rɪ'plaɪ/ v (pt, pp **-ied**) [I, T] give (sth) as an answer. **reply** n [C] (pl **-ies**) act of replying; what is replied.

report[1] /rɪ'pɔːt/ n 1 [C] account of sth heard, seen, done, etc. 2 [C] (*Brit*) written statement about a pupil's work and behaviour. 3 [C, U] talk that is not fully proved; rumours. 4 [C] (fml) sound of an explosion.

report[2] /rɪ'pɔːt/ v 1 [I, T] give an account of (sth heard, seen, done, etc), esp for a newspaper. 2 [T] (*to*)// make a complaint about (sb) to sb in authority. 3 [I] *to*/*for*// go to sb and say that one has come or that one is ready for work. **reported speech** n [U] = INDIRECT SPEECH (INDIRECT). **reporter** n [C] person who reports news for a newspaper or on radio or television.

repose /rɪ'pəʊz/ v [I] (fml) rest or lie. **repose** n [U] (fml) rest.

reprehensible /,reprɪ'hensəbl/ adj (fml) deserving blame; very bad.

represent /,reprɪ'zent/ v [T] 1 act or speak officially on behalf of (sb): ~ *the Queen*. 2 be a picture or sculpture of; show. 3 be a sign or example of. 4 [T] describe in a particular way. 5 (fml) correspond to; be the result of: *This figure ~ s an increase of 10%.* **representation** /,reprɪzen'teɪʃn/ n [U, C].

representative /,reprɪ'zentətɪv/ n [C] 1 person who represents(1) sb or a group of people. 2 person whose job is to go to different shops, etc in a particular area to sell a company's products and get orders. **representative** adj 1 typical. 2 of government in which a small number of people make decisions for a larger group.

repress /rɪ'pres/ v [T] keep back; control: ~ *one's emotions/a nation*. **repression** /rɪ'preʃn/ n [U]. **repressive** adj harsh or cruel.

reprieve /rɪ'priːv/ v [T] delay or cancel punishment, esp execution. **reprieve** n [C] 1 order for the delay or cancelling of punishment, esp execution. 2 (fig) delay of an unpleasant event.

reprimand /'reprɪmɑːnd; US -mænd/ v [T] express strong official disapproval of. **reprimand** n [C].

reprisal /rɪ'praɪzl/ n [C, U] (act of) doing harm to a person or group that has wronged or hurt oneself.

reproach /rɪ'prəʊtʃ/ v [T] (*for*)// find fault with (sb) for a wrong action. **reproach** n 1 [U] reproaching. 2 [C] word, etc of reproach. 3 (idm) **above/beyond reproach** perfect.

reproduce /,riːprə'djuːs; US -'duːs/ v 1 [T] make a copy of (a picture). 2 [I, T] produce young of (oneself). **reproduction** /-'dʌkʃn/ n [C, U]. **reproductive** /-'dʌktɪv/ adj of or for reproduction of young.

reproof /rɪ'pruːf/ n [C, U] (fml) (remark expressing) blame or disapproval. **reprove** /rɪ'pruːv/ v [T] (fml) express disapproval of; blame.

reptile /'reptaɪl; US -tl/ n [C] cold-blooded egg-laying animal, eg a lizard or snake. **reptilian** /rep'tɪlɪən/ adj.

republic /rɪ'pʌblɪk/ n [C] country with a system of government by elected representatives and with an elected president, not a king or queen. **republican** adj of or supporting the principles of a republic. **republican** n [C] 1 person favouring republican government. 2 **Republican** (*US*) member of the Republican party.

repudiate /rɪ'pjuːdɪeɪt/ v [T] (fml) refuse to accept; refuse to have anything more to do with. **repudiation** /rɪ,pjuːdɪ'eɪʃn/ n [U].

repugnant /rɪ'pʌgnənt/ adj (fml) causing a feeling of strong dislike. **repugnance** /-nəns/ n [U].

repulse /rɪ'pʌls/ v [T] (fml) 1 (fml) drive back (an enemy). 2 (fig) refuse to accept. **repulsion** /rɪ'pʌlʃn/ n [U] 1 strong feeling of dislike. 2 (*physics*) tendency of objects to move away from each other. **repulsive** *adj* causing strong dislike.

reputable /'repjʊtəbl/ *adj* having a good reputation.

reputation /ˌrepjʊ'teɪʃn/ *n* [C, U] general opinion about the qualities, abilities, etc of sb/sth.

repute /rɪ'pjuːt/ *n* [U] (*fml*) 1 reputation. 2 good reputation: *a doctor of ~*. **reputed** *adj* generally believed (to be), but with some doubt. **reputedly** *adv*.

request /rɪ'kwest/ *n* 1 [C, U] act of politely asking for sth: *make a ~ for more money*. 2 [C] something asked for. **request** *v* [Tn] (*fml*) ask for (sth) politely.

require /rɪ'kwaɪə(r)/ *v* [Tn] 1 need: *My car ~ s some attention*. 2 (*fml*) (usu passive) order; demand: *You are ~ d to pay the fine*. **requirement** *n* [C] something needed.

requisite /'rekwɪzɪt/ *adj* (*fml*) (something) needed for a purpose.

rescue /'reskjuː/ *v* [T] save or bring away from danger or harm. **rescue** *n* [C, U] (act of) saving from danger.

research /rɪ'sɜːtʃ; *US* 'riːsɜːtʃ/ *n* [U, C] detailed study to discover new facts, etc. **research** /rɪ'sɜːtʃ/ *v* [I, T] do research (on sth). **researcher** *n* [C].

resemble /rɪ'zembl/ *v* [T] be like; be similar to. **resemblance** *n* [C, U] (instance of) likeness.

resent /rɪ'zent/ *v* [T] feel bitter and angry about: *~ his success*. **resentful** *adj*. **resentment** *n* [U, C].

reservation /ˌrezə'veɪʃn/ *n* 1 [C, U] limiting condition; doubt: *I have a few ~ s about the plan*. 2 [C] arrangement to keep sth, eg a seat in a train, for sb. 3 [C] area of land kept separate for a particular group of people to live in.

reserve /rɪ'zɜːv/ *v* [T] 1 keep for special use or a later occasion. 2 arrange to have the use of: *~ a seat on a train*. **reserve** *n* 1 [C] supply kept for use when needed. 2 **reserves** [pl] military forces kept back for use when needed. 3 [C] land kept for a particular purpose: *a nature ~*. 4 [C] person who plays if another player cannot. 5 [U] state of being reserved. 6 (idm) **in re'serve** available for use if needed. **reserved** *adj* slow to show one's feelings or opinions; shy.

reservoir /'rezəvwɑː(r)/ *n* [C] artificial lake where water is stored.

reside /rɪ'zaɪd/ *v* [I] (*fml*) 1 make one's home. 2 *in//* be present in sth.

residence /'rezɪdəns/ *n* (*fml*) 1 [C] (esp large or impressive) house. 2 [U] state of residing. 3 (idm) **in 'residence** living in a particular place.

resident /'rezɪdənt/ *n*, *adj* (person) living in a place. **residential** /ˌrezɪ'denʃl/ *adj* 1 having houses, not offices or factories. 2 requiring a person to live where he/she works or studies.

residue /'rezɪdjuː; *US* -duː/ *n* [C] small amount that remains after most has been taken or used. **residual** /rɪ'zɪdjʊəl/ *adj* remaining.

resign /rɪ'zaɪn/ *v* [I, T] give up (one's job, position, etc). 2 (phr v) **resign oneself to sth** accept sth unpleasant without complaining. **resigned** *adj* accepting sth unpleasant without complaining.

resignation /ˌrezɪg'neɪʃn/ *n* 1 [C, U] (act or formal written statement of) resigning. 2 [U] state of being resigned.

resilient /rɪ'zɪliənt/ *adj* 1 able to spring back quickly to its original shape. 2 (*fig*) able to recover quickly from illness, defeat, etc. **resilience** /-əns/ *n* [U].

resin /'rezɪn; *US* 'rezn/ *n* [C, U] 1 sticky substance that is produced by some trees. 2 similar manmade plastic substance.

resist /rɪ'zɪst/ *v* [T] 1 oppose; use force against. 2 be undamaged or unharmed by. 3 succeed in not accepting: *~ temptation*. **resistance** *n* 1 [U, sing] (act or action) of resisting. (b) opposing force: *wind ~ance*. 2 **the resistance** [sing] (with sing or pl v) secret organization that opposes the enemy in a country controlled by the enemy. **resistant** *adj* showing resistance.

resistor /rɪ'zɪstə(r)/ *n* [C] device that reduces the power in an electric circuit.

resolute /'rezəluːt/ *adj* (*fml*) determined; firm. **resolutely** *adv*.

resolution /ˌrezə'luːʃn/ *n* 1 [C] formal decision at a meeting. 2 [C] firm decision: *a New Year ~ to give up smoking*. 3 [U] quality of being resolute. 4 [U] (*fml*) act of resolving(2).

resolve /rɪ'zɒlv/ *v* [T] (*fml*) 1 decide firmly. 2 find an answer to (a problem, etc). **resolve** *n* [C, U] resolution(2)(3).

resonant /'rezənənt/ *adj* (of a sound) resounding; strong. **resonance** /-nəns/ *n* [U].

resort /rɪ'zɔːt/ *v* [I] *to//* make use of sth for help, esp when nothing else is available. **resort** *n* [C] popular holiday centre: *a 'seaside ~*.

resound /rɪ'zaʊnd/ *v* [I] 1 (of a

sound) be heard loudly and clearly; produce echoes. **2** *(with)/|* (of a place) be filled with sound. **resounding** *adj* loud and clear: ~ *ing cheers.* **2** very great: *a* ~ *ing success.*

resource /rɪˈsɔːs, -ˈzɔːs; US 'riːsɔːs/ *n* [C, usu pl] **1** supply of raw materials, etc that a country can use to bring wealth. **2** thing that can be used for help when needed. **resourceful** *adj* good at solving difficulties. **resourcefully** *adv.*

respect /rɪˈspekt/ *n* **1** [U] admiration. **2** [U] consideration: *show* ~ *for her wishes.* **3** [C] detail: *In some* ~ *s, I agree with you.* **4** **respects** [pl] *(fml)* polite greetings. **5** (idm) **with respect to sth** *(fml)* concerning sth; about. **respect** *v* [T] show respect for; treat with consideration.

respectable /rɪˈspektəbl/ *adj* **1** socially acceptable. **2** of a fairly large size: *a* ~ *income.* **respectability** /rɪˌspektəˈbɪlətɪ/ *n* [U]. **respectably** *adv.*

respectful /rɪˈspektfl/ *adj* showing respect. **respectfully** *adv.*

respective /rɪˈspektɪv/ *adj* of, for or belonging to each one separately. **respectively** *adv* in the order mentioned.

respiration /ˌrespəˈreɪʃn/ *n* [U] *(fml)* breathing. **respiratory** /ˈrespɪrətrɪ, rɪˈspaɪərətrɪ; US -tɔːrɪ/ *adj* of or for breathing.

respite /ˈrespaɪt, -pɪt/ *n* [U, sing] short rest from sth unpleasant.

resplendent /rɪˈsplendənt/ *adj* *(fml)* very bright; splendid.

respond /rɪˈspɒnd/ *v* [I] *(to)/|* **1** answer sb/sth. **2** act in answer to sb/sth. **3** react favourably to sth: ~ *to treatment.*

response /rɪˈspɒns/ *n* **1** [C] answer. **2** [C, U] action done in answer to sth.

responsibility /rɪˌspɒnsəˈbɪlətɪ/ *n* *(pl -ies)* **1** [U] being responsible. **2** [C] something for which sb is responsible; duty.

responsible /rɪˈspɒnsəbl/ *adj* **1** *(for)/|* having to look after or do sth as a duty: ~ *for cleaning the car.* **2** *(to)/|* having to report to sb and having to explain one's actions to him/her. **3** *(for)/|* being the cause of sth bad: *Who's* ~ *for this mess?* **4** trustworthy. **5** (of a job) having important duties. **responsibly** *adv.*

responsive /rɪˈspɒnsɪv/ *adj* quick to react to sth, eg by showing one's feelings.

rest¹ /rest/ *n* **1** [C, U] (period of) sleep or not being active. **2** [C] support for an object: *an 'arm-* ~ *.* **3** [C]

(*music*) (sign making) a pause. **4** (idm) **at 'rest (a)** not moving. **(b)** free from worry. **restful** *adj* giving rest; peaceful. **restless** *adj* always moving; unable to be still or quiet. **restlessly** *adv.*

rest² /rest/ *v* **1** [I, T] (allow to) have a rest. **2** [I, T] *on/against/|* lean (sth) on sth. **3** [I] *on/|* (of sb's eyes) be directed at sb/sth. **4** (idm) **rest assured** *(fml)* be certain. **rest on one's laurels** be satisfied with one's successes and do nothing more. **5** [I] *on/|* depend on sth. **rest with sb** be the responsibility of sb.

rest³ /rest/ *n* the rest **1** [sing] the remaining part. **2** [pl] the others.

restaurant /ˈrestrɒnt; US -tərɒnt/ *n* [C] place where meals can be bought and eaten.

restitution /ˌrestɪˈtjuːʃn; US -ˈtuː-/ *n* [U] *(fml)* giving back sth stolen, etc to its owner or paying money for damage.

restive /ˈrestɪv/ *adj* *(fml)* unable to be controlled; unable to be still.

restoration /ˌrestəˈreɪʃn/ *n* **1** [U] restoring. **2** **the Restoration** [sing] period just after 1660 in Britain.

restorative /rɪˈstɔːrətɪv/ *adj* bringing back health and strength. **restorative** *n* [C] restorative food, medicine, etc.

restore /rɪˈstɔː(r)/ *v* [T] **1** *(fml)* give back. **2** bring back to a former state or position. **3** bring back into use. **4** repair (an old building, picture, etc) so that it is like the original. **restorer** *n* [C] person who restores(4) things.

restrain /rɪˈstreɪn/ *v* [T] hold back from movement or action; keep under control. **restrained** *adj* controlled; calm. **restraint** /rɪˈstreɪnt/ *n* **1** [C, U] something that restrains. **2** [U] quality of being restrained.

restrict /rɪˈstrɪkt/ *v* [T] put a limit on. **restriction** /rɪˈstrɪkʃn/ *n* [C, U]. **restrictive** *adj.*

result /rɪˈzʌlt/ *n* **1** [C, U] something that happens because of an action or event. **2** [C] final score in a game; marks in an examination. **3** [C] answer to a mathematical calculation. **result** *v* [I] *(from)/|* happen as a result of an action or event. **2** (phr v) **result in sth** cause sth; bring about. **resultant** *adj* *(fml)* happening as a result.

resume /rɪˈzjuːm; US -ˈzuːm/ *v* **1** [I, T] begin (sth) again after stopping. **2** [T] *(fml)* occupy again: ~ *one's seat.*

résumé /ˈrezjuːmeɪ; US ˌrezuːˈmeɪ/ *n* [C] summary.

resumption /rɪˈzʌmpʃn/ n [U, sing] (fml) act of resuming.

resurrect /ˌrezəˈrekt/ v [T] bring back into use. **resurrection** /ˌrezəˈrekʃn/ n 1 [U] act of resurrecting. 2 **the Resurrection** [sing] (a) (in Christianity) coming back to life of Jesus after his death. (b) coming back to life of all dead people at the end of the world.

resuscitate /rɪˈsʌsɪteɪt/ v [T] (fml) bring back to consciousness. **resuscitation** /rɪˌsʌsɪˈteɪʃn/ n [U].

retail /ˈriːteɪl/ n [U] selling of goods to the public. **retail** adv by retail. **retail** v [I, T] be sold or sell retail. **retailer** n [C] person who sells goods to the public; shopkeeper.

retain /rɪˈteɪn/ v [T] (fml) 1 keep in place. 2 obtain the services of (esp a lawyer) by payment. **retainer** n [C] 1 fee paid to a lawyer. 2 reduced rate paid to reserve a flat, etc when one is absent from it. 3 (arch) servant.

retaliate /rɪˈtælieɪt/ v [I] repay an injury, insult, etc with a similar one. **retaliation** /rɪˌtæliˈeɪʃn/ n [U].

retard /rɪˈtɑːd/ v [T] (fml) make slow or late. **retarded** adj slow in mental development.

retch /retʃ/ v [I] try to vomit but without bringing up anything.

retention /rɪˈtenʃn/ n [U] (fml) act of retaining.

retentive /rɪˈtentɪv/ adj (of the memory) able to remember things well.

reticent /ˈretɪsnt/ adj saying little; not saying all that is known. **reticence** /-sns/ n [U].

retina /ˈretɪnə/ US /ˈretənə/ n [C] (pl ~s or -ae /-niː/) part of the eye at the back of the eyeball, sensitive to light.

retinue /ˈretɪnjuː/ US /ˈretənuː/ n [C, also sing with pl v] group of people travelling with an important person.

retire /rɪˈtaɪə(r)/ v 1 (a) [I] (from)// give up one's regular work, esp because of age. (b) [T] cause (sb) to do this. 2 [I] (fml) go away, esp to somewhere quiet. 3 [I] (fml) go to bed. **retired** adj having retired from work. **retirement** n [U] **retiring** adj avoiding meeting people or talking.

retort /rɪˈtɔːt/ v [T] answer quickly or angrily with a **retort**. **retort** n [C, U] quick or angry reply.

retrace /rɪˈtreɪs/ v [T] go back over: ~ one's steps, ie return the way one came.

retract /rɪˈtrækt/ v [I, T] 1 take back (a statement, offer, etc). 2 draw (sth) in or back: A cat can ~ its claws. **retractable** adj. **retraction** /rɪˈtrækʃn/ n [C, U].

retread /ˈriːtred/ n [C] tyre that has been given a new outer surface.

retreat /rɪˈtriːt/ v [I] (esp of an army) go back. **retreat** n [C, U] 1 act of retreating. 2 (place for) a period of quiet and rest.

retribution /ˌretrɪˈbjuːʃn/ n [U] (fml) deserved punishment.

retrieve /rɪˈtriːv/ v [T] (fml) 1 find and bring back. 2 put right. **retrieval** n [U] act of retrieving. **retriever** n [C] dog trained to find and bring back shot birds, etc.

retrograde /ˈretrəɡreɪd/ adj (fml) going back to an earlier worse condition.

retrogression /ˌretrəˈɡreʃn/ n [U] (fml) going back to an earlier worse condition. **retrogressive** /-ˈɡresɪv/ adj.

retrospect /ˈretrəspekt/ n (idm) **in retrospect** looking back on a past event. **retrospective** adj 1 looking back on the past. 2 (eg of a law or payment) applying to the past.

return¹ /rɪˈtɜːn/ v 1 [I] (a) come or go back: ~ home. (b) go back to an earlier state. 2 [T] give, send or put back: ~ damaged goods to the shop. 3 [T] elect (sb) to parliament. 4 [T] state officially: The jury ~ed a verdict of guilty.

return² /rɪˈtɜːn/ n 1 [C, U] act of returning. 2 [C, esp pl] profit on an investment. 3 [C] official report or statement: fill in one's tax ~. 4 [C] (also **return 'ticket**) ticket for a journey to a place and back again. 5 (idm) **in return (for sth)** in exchange or as a payment for sth.

reunion /ˌriːˈjuːnɪən/ n 1 [C] meeting of former friends, colleagues, etc who have not seen one another for a long time. 2 [U] coming together again after a separation.

Rev (also **Revd**) abbr Reverend.

rev /rev/ v (-vv-) [I, T] (up)// increase the speed of (an engine): ~ the car (up).

reveal /rɪˈviːl/ v [T] 1 make known: ~ a secret. 2 allow to be seen.

revel /ˈrevl/ v (-ll-; US -l-) (phr v) **revel in sth** enjoy sth very much.

revelation /ˌrevəˈleɪʃn/ n 1 [U] making known of sth secret. 2 [C] something (esp surprising) that is revealed.

revenge /rɪˈvendʒ/ n [U] punishment or injury done in return for harm that one has suffered. **revenge** *v* [T] ~ **oneself (on)** punish or hurt sb in return for harm that one has suffered.

revenue /'revənju:; *US* -ənu:/ *n* [U, C] income, especially as received by the government.

reverberate /rɪ'vɜ:bəreɪt/ *v* [I] (of sound) echo again and again. **reverberation** /rɪ,vɜ:bə'reɪʃn/ *n* 1 [C, U] reverberating sound. 2 [C, usu pl] (*fig*) continuing powerful effect.

revere /rɪ'vɪə(r)/ *v* [T] (*fml*) have great respect for.

reverence /'revərəns/ *n* [U] great respect.

Reverend /'revərənd/ *n* [C] (title of a) clergyman.

reverent /'revərənt/ *adj* feeling or showing reverence. **reverently** *adv*.

reversal /rɪ'vɜ:sl/ *n* [C, U] (instance of) reversing.

reverse /rɪ'vɜ:s/ *adj* opposite in position or order. **reverse** *n* 1 **the reverse** [sing] the opposite. 2 [U] control used for making a vehicle move backwards: *put the car into* ~ *(gear)*. 3 [C] back side of a coin, etc. **reverse** *v* 1 [T] turn (sth) the other way round. 2 [T] make (sth) the opposite of what it was: ~ *a decision.* 3 [I, T] (cause a vehicle to) move backwards. 4 (idm) **reverse the 'charges** (*Brit*) make a telephone call that will be paid for by the person receiving the call.

revert /rɪ'vɜ:t/ *v* [I] *to*|| go back to a former state, owner or kind of behaviour.

review /rɪ'vju:/ *v* 1 [T] consider or examine again: ~ *the past/a decision.* 2 [I, T] write a review(2) of (a new book, film, etc). 3 [T] inspect formally (troops, etc). **review** *n* 1 [C, U] (act of) reviewing(1). 2 [C] article in a newspaper, etc that gives an opinion of a new book, film, etc. 3 [C] inspection of military forces. **reviewer** *n* [C] person who writes reviews /2.

revise /rɪ'vaɪz/ *v* 1 [T] examine (sth) again and correct or improve it. 2 [I, T] (*for*)|| go over (work already done) to prepare for an examination. **revision** /rɪ'vɪʒn/ *n* 1 [C, U] (act of) revising. 2 [C] corrected version.

revitalize /ri:'vaɪtəlaɪz/ *v* [T] put new life or strength into.

revive /rɪ'vaɪv/ *v* [I, T] 1 come or bring back to consciousness. 2 come or bring into use again: ~ *old customs.* **revival** *n* [C, U]

revoke /rɪ'vəʊk/ *v* [T] (*fml*) cancel or withdraw (a law, permission, etc).

revolt /rɪ'vəʊlt/ *v* 1 [I] (*against*)|| fight against a government or authority; rebel. 2 [T] cause (sb) to feel horror or disgust. **revolt** *n* [C, U] rebellion. **revolting** *adj* extremely unpleasant.

revolution /,revə'lu:ʃn/ *n* 1 [C, U] complete change in the system of government, esp by force. 2 [C] (*fig*) complete change in conditions or ways of doing things: *the computer* ~. 3 [C] one complete movement in a circle. **revolutionary** *adj* 1 of a revolution(1). 2 completely different: *a* ~ *ary idea.* **revolutionary** *n* [C] (*pl* -ies) person who begins or supports a revolution(1). **revolutionize** /-ʃənaɪz/ *v* [T] cause great changes in.

revolve /rɪ'vɒlv/ *v* 1 [I] (*around*)|| go round sth in a circle. 2 (phr v) **revolve around sb/sth** have sb/sth as its main subject: *The story* ~ *s around the old man.*

revolver /rɪ'vɒlvə(r)/ *n* [C] small gun with a revolving container for bullets.

revue /rɪ'vju:/ *n* [C] theatrical entertainment with dances, songs and jokes.

revulsion /rɪ'vʌlʃn/ *n* [U, sing] feeling of disgust or horror.

reward /rɪ'wɔ:d/ *n* [C, U] something given in return for work or services or for bringing back stolen property. **reward** *v* [T] give reward to. **rewarding** *adj* giving satisfaction.

rewind /,ri:'waɪnd/ *v* (*pt, pp* rewound /,ri:'waʊnd/) [T] cause (a tape, film, etc) to go back to the beginning.

rhapsody /'ræpsədi/ *n* [C] (*pl* -ies) 1 piece of music in irregular form. 2 expression of great delight.

rhetoric /'retərɪk/ *n* [U] 1 (art of) using words impressively in speech and writing. 2 (*derog*) fine-sounding language that is insincere or meaningless. **rhetorical** /rɪ'tɒrɪkl; *US* -'tɔ:r-/ *adj* 1 (of a question) asked only for effect, not to get an answer. 2 intended to impress or persuade.

rheumatism /'ru:mətɪzəm/ *n* [U] disease causing pain and stiffness in the muscles and joints. **rheumatic** /ru:'mætɪk/ *adj, n* [C].

rhino /'raɪnəʊ/ *n* [C] (*pl* ~s) (*infml*) short for RHINOCEROS.

rhinoceros /raɪ'nɒsərəs/ *n* [C] large heavy thick-skinned animal with one or two horns on its nose.

rhododendron /,rəʊdə'dendrən/ *n* [C] evergreen bush with large flowers.

rhubarb /'ru:bɑ:b/ *n* [U] (garden

plant with) thick reddish stems that are cooked and eaten like fruit.

rhyme /raɪm/ v [I] (of words or lines of a poem) end with the same sound: *'Fall'* ~*s with 'wall'*. **rhyme** n 1 [U] (use of) rhyming words at the end of lines in poetry. 2 [C] word that rhymes with another word. 3 [C] short rhyming poem.

rhythm /'rɪðəm/ n 1 [C, U] regular pattern of beats or movements. 2 [C] (*fig*) regular pattern of changes: *the* ~ *of the tides*. **rhythmic(al)** /'rɪðmɪk(l)/ *adj*.

rib /rɪb/ n [C] 1 one of the curved bones that go from the backbone to the chest. 2 raised line in knitting. **ribbed** *adj* having ribs(2).

ribbon /'rɪbən/ n [C, U] long narrow piece of cloth.

rice /raɪs/ n [U] (plant with) white grain that is cooked and eaten.

rich /rɪtʃ/ *adj* 1 having a lot of money or property. 2 beautiful and splendid: ~ *clothes*. 3 *in*// having a lot of sth: *soil* ~ *in minerals*. 4 (of food) containing a lot of fat, oil, eggs, etc. 5 (of colours or sounds) pleasantly deep, full or strong. **rich** n 1 **the rich** [pl] rich people. 2 **riches** [pl] wealth. **richly** *adv*. **richness** n [U].

rickety /'rɪkɪtɪ/ *adj* likely to break or collapse.

rickshaw /'rɪkʃɔ:/ n [C] two-wheeled carriage pulled by a man.

ricochet /'rɪkəʃeɪ, US ˌrɪkə'ʃeɪ/ v (*pt, pp* -t- or -tt-) [I] (of a bullet) hit a surface and bounce away from it at an angle. **ricochet** n [C].

rid /rɪd/ v (-dd-, *pt, pp* **rid**) 1 [T] *of*// (*fml*) make free of sth unpleasant or unwanted. 2 (idm) **be/get rid of sb/sth** be/become free of sb/ sth; remove or throw away.

riddance /'rɪdns/ n (idm) **good riddance** (said when one is glad that sb has left): *He's finally gone and good riddance to him!*

ridden *pp* of **RIDE**[1].

riddle[1] /'rɪdl/ n [C] 1 difficult or amusing question or statement. 2 mysterious person, thing or situation.

riddle[2] /'rɪdl/ v [T] *with*// (esp passive) make many holes in (*a body* ~*d with bullets*.

ride[1] /raɪd/ v (*pt* **rode** /rəʊd/, *pp* **ridden** /'rɪdn/) 1 [I, T] travel on (a horse, bicycle, etc) controlling its movements. 2 [I] travel in a bus or other vehicle. 3 [T] float on: *a ship riding the waves*. 4 (phr v) **ride up** (of an article of clothing) move upwards. **rider** n [C] person who rides a horse, bicycle, etc.

2 additional remark following a statement.

ride[2] /raɪd/ n [C] 1 journey on a horse or bicycle or in a car, etc. 2 (idm) **take sb for a 'ride** (*infml*) deceive sb.

ridge /rɪdʒ/ n [C] 1 long narrow piece of high land. 2 raised line where two sloping surfaces meet.

ridicule /'rɪdɪkju:l/ n [U] making sb/sth appear foolish. **ridicule** v [T] make (sb/sth) appear foolish.

ridiculous /rɪ'dɪkjʊləs/ *adj* very foolish; absurd. **ridiculously** *adv*.

rife /raɪf/ *adj* (esp of sth bad) widespread; common.

rifle[1] /'raɪfl/ n [C] gun with a long barrel, fired from the shoulder.

rifle[2] /'raɪfl/ v [T] search thoroughly in order to steal sth.

rift /rɪft/ n [C] 1 split or crack. 2 (*fig*) disagreement.

rig[1] /rɪg/ v (-gg-) [T] 1 fit (a ship) with masts, sails, etc. 2 (phr v) **rig sb out** provide sb with a particular kind of clothes. **rig sth up** make sth quickly out of the available materials. **rig** n [C] 1 way that a ship's masts, sails, etc are arranged. 2 equipment for a special purpose: *an 'bil* ~. **rigging** n [C] ropes, etc that support a ship's masts and sails.

rig[2] /rɪg/ v (-gg-) [T] arrange dishonestly for one's own advantage: ~ *an election*.

right[1] /raɪt/ *adj* 1 (of behaviour) just; morally good. 2 correct: *the* ~ *answer*. 3 most suitable: *the* ~ *person for the job*. 4 healthy: *Do you feel all* ~*?* ○ *in one's* ~ *mind*, ie mentally normal. 5 on or at the side of sb that is towards the east when one faces north: the right 'track ⇨ **TRACK**. **put/set sth right** correct sth. **right angle** n [C] angle of 90°. **'right-angled** *adj*. **rightly** *adv* justly; correctly. **rightness** n [U].

right[2] /raɪt/ *adv* 1 exactly: *Put it* ~ *in the middle*. 2 completely: *Go* ~ *to the end of the road*. 3 correctly. 4 (idm) **'right away** without delay. **right 'now** at this moment.

right[3] /raɪt/ n 1 [U] what is good, just, true, etc. 2 [C, U] moral or legal authority; thing one may do or have by law: *You have no* ~ *to be here*. ○ *basic political* ~*s*. 3 (idm) **be in the 'right** behave correctly. **by 'rights** according to what is proper or just. **in one's own 'right** because of a personal claim or qualification. **put/set sb/ sth to 'rights** put sth in order. **,right of 'way** n 1 [U] (in road traffic) right to go first. 2 [C] (right to use a) path that goes across private land.

right[4] /raɪt/ v [T] make right or

upright: ~ *a wrong* ○ *The ship* ~*ed herself.*

right⁵ /raɪt/ *adj, adv,* of, on or towards the side of the body that is towards the east when a person faces north. **right** *n* 1 [U] right side or direction. 2 **the Right** [sing] (with sing or pl *v*) the right wing of a political party or group. **'right-hand** *adj* of or on the right side. **right-'handed** *adj* (of a person) using the right hand more easily or usually than the left. **right-hand 'man** *n* [C] main helper and supporter. **the ,right 'wing** *n* [sing] (with sing or pl *v*) conservative political group or party. **,right-'wing** *adj.*

righteous /'raɪtʃəs/ *adj* (doing what is) morally right. **righteously** *adv.* **righteousness** *n* [U].

rightful /'raɪtfl/ *adj* according to a legal or moral claim: *the ~ owner.* **rightfully** *adv.*

rigid /'rɪdʒɪd/ *adj* 1 stiff; that cannot be bent. 2 strict; not changing. **rigidity** /rɪ'dʒɪdətɪ/ *n* [U]. **rigidly** *adv.*

rigorous /'rɪgərəs/ *adj* 1 careful and detailed. 2 strict; severe. **rigorously** *adv.*

rigour (*US* -or) /'rɪgə(r)/ *n* (*fml*) 1 [U] strictness; severity. 1 **rigours** [pl] severe conditions.

rim /rɪm/ *n* [C] edge of sth circular: *the ~ of a cup.* **rim** *v* (-mm-) [T] be the rim of.

rind /raɪnd/ *n* [C, U] hard outer covering of certain fruits, cheese or bacon.

ring¹ /rɪŋ/ *v* (*pt* **rang** /ræŋ/, *pp* **rung** /rʌŋ/) 1 [I, T] (of a bell) (cause to) sound clearly. 2 [I, T] telephone. 3 [I] (*for*)// cause a bell to sound to call sb/sth. 4 [T] (*with*)// be filled with sounds. 5 (used with an *adj*) produce a certain effect: *Her words rang true.* 6 (idm) ring a 'bell (*infml*) remind one of sth. 7 (phr v) ring 'off (*Brit*) end a telephone conversation. ring out sound loudly and clearly. ring sb up telephone sb. ring *n* 1 [C] sound of a bell. 2 [sing] particular quality: *a ~ of truth.* 3 [C] (*Brit infml*) telephone call.

ring² /rɪŋ/ *n* [C] 1 small circular metal band worn on a finger. 2 circular band of any kind of material. 3 circle: *The children stood in a ~.* 4 group of people working together: *a 'spy ~.* 5 circular enclosure for circus performances: *a 'circus ~.* 6 roped area for a boxing match. **ring** *v* (*pt, pp* -**ed**) [T] 1 surround. 2 make a circular mark round. **'ringleader** *n* [C] person who leads others in doing sth

wrong. **'ring road** *n* [C] road round a town.

ringlet /'rɪŋlɪt/ *n* [C, esp pl] long hanging curl of hair.

rink /rɪŋk/ *n* [C] specially prepared area of ice for skating.

rinse /rɪns/ *v* [T] wash in clean water. **rinse** *n* 1 [C] act of rinsing. 2 [C, U] liquid for colouring the hair.

riot /'raɪət/ *n* 1 [C] noisy violent behaviour by a crowd. 2 [sing] bright display: *a ~ of colour.* 3 (idm) **run 'riot** ⇨ RUN¹. **riot** *v* [I] take part in a riot(1). **rioter** *n* [C]. **riotous** *adj* disorderly; wild.

rip /rɪp/ *v* (-pp-) 1 [I, T] pull or tear (sth) quickly and with force. 2 (phr v) **rip sb off** (*sl*) charge sb too much money. **rip** *n* [C] long cut; torn place. **'rip-cord** *n* [C] cord that opens a parachute. **'rip-off** *n* [C] (*sl*) act of charging sb too much money.

ripe /raɪp/ *adj* (~**r**, ~**st**) 1 (fully grown and) ready to be eaten: ~ *apples/cheese.* 2 fully developed. 3 *for*// ready for sth. **ripeness** *n* [U].

ripen /'raɪpən/ *v* [I, T] become or make ripe.

ripple /'rɪpl/ *n* [C] 1 very small wave or movement on the surface of water. 2 short sound of quiet laughter, etc. **ripple** *v* [I, T] move in ripples.

rise¹ /raɪz/ *v* (*pt* **rose** /rəʊz/, *pt* ~**n** /'rɪzn/) [I] 1 come or go up wards. 2 (*fml*) (a) stand up. (b) get out of bed. 3 (of the sun, moon, etc) appear above the horizon. 4 increase: *Prices have continued to ~.* 5 slope upwards: *rising ground.* 6 get stronger: *The wind is rising.* 7 reach a higher rank. 8 (*fml*) rebel. 9 (of a river) start. 10 (idm) **rise to the oc'casion** show that one is able to deal with a difficulty successfully. **rising** *n* [C] armed rebellion.

rise² /raɪz/ *n* 1 [sing] upward movement or progress: *his ~ to power.* 2 [C] increase. 3 [C] (*Brit*) increase in wages. 4 [C] small hill. 5 (idm) **give rise to sth** cause.

risk /rɪsk/ *n* 1 [C, U] possibility of meeting danger, suffering loss, etc. 2 [C] person or thing insured or considered to be a source of danger. 3 (idm) **at one's own risk** agreeing to make no claims for loss or injury. **at 'risk** in danger. **risk one's 'neck** ⇨ NECK. **run the risk of sth, take a 'risk** do sth that involves the possibility of danger. **risk** *v* [T] 1 put (sth) in danger. 2 take the chance of (sth bad) happening: ~ *getting wet.* 3 (idm) **risk one's neck** ⇨ NECK.

risotto 358

risky *adj* (**-ier, -iest**) dangerous.

risotto /rɪ'zɒtəʊ/ *n* [C, U] (*pl* ~s) Italian dish of rice with meat, cheese, onions, etc.

rissole /'rɪsəʊl/ *n* [C] small flat cake of minced meat, fish, etc.

rite /raɪt/ *n* [C] traditional, esp religious, ceremony.

ritual /'rɪtʃʊəl/ *n* [C, U] 1 system of rites. 2 series of actions regularly followed. **ritual** *adj* of or done as a ritual.

rival /'raɪvl/ *n* [C] person one is competing with. **rival** *v* (**-ll-**; *US* also **-l-**) [T] be a rival of. **rivalry** *n* [C, U] (*pl* **-ies**) competition.

river /'rɪvə(r)/ *n* [C] large natural stream of water flowing to the sea.

rivet /'rɪvɪt/ *n* [C] metal pin or bolt used for fastening pieces of metal together. **rivet** *v* [T] 1 fasten with rivets. 2 (*fig*) attract and strongly hold the attention of. **riveting** *adj* extremely interesting.

road /rəʊd/ *n* 1 [C] specially prepared hard way between places for vehicles. 2 (*idm*) **on the road to sth** the way of reaching sth: *on the ~ to success.* '**roadblock** *n* [C] barrier placed across the road, esp by the police. '**roadhog** *n* [C] careless driver. '**roadworks** *n* [pl] repairs to the road. '**roadworthy** *adj* (of a vehicle) fit to be driven on roads.

roam /rəʊm/ *v* [I, T] wander about with no clear purpose.

roar /rɔː(r)/ *n* [C] deep loud sound (like that) made by a lion. **roar** *v* 1 (a) [I] make such deep loud sounds. (b) [T] express in this way. 2 [I] laugh noisily. **roaring** *adj* (*infml*) 1 noisy. 2 very good: *do a ~ing trade.* **roaring** *adv* very: *~ing drunk.*

roast /rəʊst/ *v* [I, T] cook (esp meat) in an oven or over a fire. **roast** *adj* that has been roasted. **roast** *n* [C] large piece of roasted meat.

rob /rɒb/ *v* (**-bb-**) [T] steal sth from (sb or a place). **robber** *n* [C] person who robs. **robbery** *n* [C, U] (*pl* **-ies**) (instance of) robbing.

robe /rəʊb/ *n* [C] long loose garment.

robin /'rɒbɪn/ *n* [C] small brown bird with a red breast.

robot /'rəʊbɒt/ *n* [C] machine that can do certain human tasks automatically.

robust /rəʊ'bʌst/ *adj* strong; healthy. **robustly** *adv*. **robustness** *n* [U].

rock¹ /rɒk/ *n* 1 (a) [U] solid part of the earth's crust. (b) [C, U] mass of rock. 2 [C] large stone. 3 [C]

(*Brit*) hard stick-shaped sweet. 4 (*idm*) **on the 'rocks** (a) (of a marriage) likely to fail soon. (b) (of a drink) with ice. ,rock-'bottom *n* [U] lowest point. **rockery** *n* [C] (*pl* **-ies**) part of a garden with small rocks and plants.

rock² /rɒk/ *v* 1 [I, T] move gently backwards and forwards or from side to side. 2 [T] (*fig*) shock greatly. 3 (*idm*) **rock the 'boat** spoil a calm situation. **rocker** *n* 1 [C] either of the curved pieces of wood on which a rocking-chair rests. 2 = ROCKING-CHAIR. 3 (*idm*) **off one's rocker** (*sl*) mad. '**rocking-chair** *n* [C] chair fitted with rockers.

rock³ (also '**rock music**) /rɒk/ *n* [U] modern popular music with a strong beat, played on electric guitars, etc. ,rock **and 'roll** (also ,rock 'n' 'roll) *n* [U] earlier (and usu simpler) form of this.

rocket /'rɒkɪt/ *n* [C] 1 tube-shaped device filled with fast-burning fuel that is used to launch a missile or spacecraft. 2 firework that shoots high into the air. **rocket** *v* [I] increase quickly and suddenly: *Prices are ~ing.*

rocky /'rɒkɪ/ (**-ier, -iest**) *adj* 1 of rock; full of rocks. 2 (*infml*) unsteady: *The table is ~.*

rod /rɒd/ *n* [C] long thin straight piece of wood, metal, etc: *a 'fishing~.*

rode *pt* of RIDE¹.

rodent /'rəʊdnt/ *n* [C] small animal, eg a rat or squirrel, with strong front teeth.

rodeo /rəʊ'deɪəʊ; *US* 'rəʊdɪəʊ/ *n* [C] (*pl* ~s) (in the US) contest of skill in catching cattle with a rope, riding wild horses, etc.

roe¹ /rəʊ/ *n* [C] mass of fish eggs, eaten as food.

roe² /rəʊ/ *n* [C] small kind of deer. '**roebuck** *n* [C] male roe.

rogue /rəʊg/ *n* [C] dishonest or criminal person. **roguish** *adj* mischievous; playful.

role (also **rôle**) /rəʊl/ *n* [C] 1 actor's part in a play. 2 function or importance of sb/sth.

roll¹ /rəʊl/ *v* 1 [I, T] move along by turning over and over. 2 [I] move in a rolling motion: *The clouds ~ed away.* 3 [I, T] (cause to) move from side to side: *The ship was ~ing heavily.* 4 [T] (*up*)) make into a ball or tube: *~ up a carpet.* 5 [T] make flat, by rolling a rounded object over it: *~ a lawn.* 6 [I] make a long deep sound: *The thunder ~ed in the distance.* 7 (phr v) **roll in** (*infml*) come or arrive in large quantities. **roll up** (*infml*) arrive.

roll² /rəʊl/ n [C] **1** something made into a tube: a ~ of film. **2** rolling movement. **3** small rounded portion of bread for one person. **4** official list of names. **5** long deep sound: the ~ of drums.

roller /'rəʊlə(r)/ n [C] tube-shaped object for pressing, smoothing, etc. '**roller-skate** n [C] shoe with small wheels for moving over flat surfaces. '**roller-skate** v [I] move along by means of roller-skates.

rolling /'rəʊlɪŋ/ adj **1** rising and falling gently: ~ hills/waves. **2** (idm) **be 'rolling in it** (infml) have a lot of money. '**rolling-pin** n [C] cylinder of wood, etc for flattening pastry.

Roman /'rəʊmən/ n [C], adj (citizen) of Rome, esp ancient Rome. ,**Roman** '**Catholic** n [C], adj (member) of the Christian Church that has the Pope as its leader. ,**Roman** '**Catholicism** n [U]. ,**Roman** '**numeral** n [C] letter, eg V, L or M, or group of letters, eg IV, used to represent a number.

romance /rəʊ'mæns/ n **1** [C, U] love affair. **2** [C] story of love, adventure, etc. **3** [U] romantic(3) quality.

romantic /rəʊ'mæntɪk/ adj **1** not practical; very imaginative. **2** of or having feelings of love. **3** of or suggesting love, adventure and excitement: a ~ journey. **romantic** n [C] romantic person. **romantically** /-klɪ/ adv. **romanticism** /rəʊ'mæntɪsɪzəm/ n [U] romantic feelings, attitudes, etc. **romanticize** /rəʊ'mæntɪsaɪz/ v [I, T] make (sb/sth) seem more romantic, interesting, etc than it really is.

romp /rɒmp/ v [I] (esp of children) play noisily and roughly. **romp** n [C].

roof /ruːf/ n [C] **1** top covering of a building, car, etc. **2** upper part: the ~ of the mouth. **roof** v [I] fit with a roof. **roofing** n [U] material for roofs. '**roof-rack** n [C] metal frame fixed on top of a car, used for carrying large objects.

rook¹ /rʊk/ n [C] large black bird like a crow. **rookery** /-ərɪ/ n [C] (pl -ies) group of trees where rooks nest.

rook² /rʊk/ v [T] (sl) cheat.

rook³ /rʊk/ n = CASTLE 2.

room /ruːm, rʊm/ n **1** [C] part of a building with its own walls, ceiling and door. **2** [U] amount of empty or available area in sth; (enough) space: Is there ~ for me in the car? **3** [U] (fig) opportunity or scope: ~ for improvement. **roomy** adj (-ier, -iest) having

plenty of space.

roost /ruːst/ n [C] place on which a bird rests. **roost** v [I] (of a bird) settle down for sleep.

rooster /'ruːstə(r)/ n [C] (esp US) adult male chicken; cock.

root¹ /ruːt/ n **1** [C] part of a plant that is in the soil and takes in water and food from the soil. **2** **roots** [pl] (connections with the) place in which one grew up. **3** [C] base of a hair, tooth, etc. **4** [C] (fig) source; basis: Is money the ~ of all evil? **5** [C] (grammar) form of a word on which other forms are based. **6** (idm) **take root** become established.

root² /ruːt/ v **1** [I, T] (cause to) form roots. **2** [T] cause to stand unmoving: ~ed to the spot by fear. **3** [T] (usu passive) (of ideas, etc) fix firmly: deeply ~ed feelings. **4** (phr v) **root sth out** destroy sth completely.

rope /rəʊp/ n [C, U] **1** (piece of) thick strong cord. **2** [pl] usual way of doing sth: show sb the ~s. **rope** v [T] **1** fasten with a rope. **2** (phr v) **rope sb in to do sth** persuade sb to take part in an activity. **rope sth off** enclose or separate with ropes. **ropy** (also **ropey**) adj (-ier, -iest) (Brit infml) poor in quality, health, etc.

rosary /'rəʊzərɪ/ n [C] (pl -ies) **1** string of beads used for counting prayers. **2** series of prayers counted in this way.

rose¹ pt of RISE¹.

rose² /rəʊz/ n **1** [C] (bush with thorns producing a) colourful sweet-smelling flower. **2** [U] pink-ish-red colour.

rosé /'rəʊzeɪ, US rəʊ'zeɪ/ n [U] pink wine.

rosette /rəʊ'zet/ n [C] small rose-shaped badge made of ribbons.

roster /'rɒstə(r)/ n [C] (esp US) list of people's names and their duties.

rostrum /'rɒstrəm/ n [C] (pl -s or -tra /-trə/) raised platform for a public speaker.

rosy /'rəʊzɪ/ adj (-ier, -iest) **1** deep pink. **2** (fig) hopeful; cheerful: a ~ future.

rot /rɒt/ v (-tt-) [I, T] (cause to) decay. **rot** n **1** [U] decay. **2** (fig) situation in which things are getting worse. **3** (dated infml) nonsense.

rota /'rəʊtə/ n [C] (Brit) list of people who are to do things in turn.

rotary /'rəʊtərɪ/ adj moving round a central point.

rotate /rəʊ'teɪt; US 'rəʊteɪt/ v [I, T] **1** (cause to) move round a central point. **2** (cause to) take turns or come in succession: ~ **crops**. **rotation** /-'teɪʃn/ n 1 [C] rotating: *the rotation of the Earth*. 2 [C] one complete turn.

rotor /'rəʊtə(r)/ n [C] rotating part of a machine, esp on a helicopter.

rotten /'rɒtn/ adj 1 decayed. 2 (*infml*) very bad; very unpleasant.

rouge /ruːʒ/ n [U] red powder for colouring the cheeks.

rough¹ /rʌf/ adj 1 (of a surface) not level or smooth. 2 not gentle; behaving violently. 3 stormy: *a ~ sea*. 4 not exact; not in detail: *a ~ guess/sketch*. 5 (idm) **'rough and ,ready** not perfect or carefully made. **rough** adv in uncomfortable conditions out of doors: *live/sleep ~*. **rough** n 1 [U] rough surface. 2 (idm) **in 'rough** not complete; unfinished. **roughly** adv 1 in a rough manner. 2 approximately: *It will cost ~ ly £100*. **roughness** n [U].

rough² /rʌf/ v 1 (idm) **'rough it** (*infml*) live without the normal comforts. 2 (phr v) **rough sb up** (*infml*) attack sb physically.

roughen /'rʌfn/ v [I, T] become or make rough.

roulette /ruː'let/ n [U] gambling game played with a small ball on a revolving wheel.

round¹ /raʊnd/ adj 1 shaped like a circle or a ball. 2 going and returning: *a ~ trip*. 3 (of a number) expressed to the nearest 10, 100, etc. **roundly** adv forcefully. **roundness** n [U]. **,round-'shouldered** adj with the shoulders bent forward.

round² /raʊnd/ adv 1 to face the opposite way: *Turn your chair ~*. 2 with a return to the starting point: *The hands of a clock go ~*. 3 in a circle: *A crowd gathered ~*. ○ *spin ~*. 4 from one place, person, etc to another: *Please pass these papers ~*. 5 not by the direct route: *a long way ~*. 6 to sb's house: *Come ~ and see me*.

round³ /raʊnd/ n [C] 1 series of events: *the next ~ of talks*. 2 regular series of events: *a postman's ~*. 3 (a) stage in a competition. (b) (in golf) one game. (c) (in boxing) stage in a game. 4 set of drinks bought for everyone one is with. 5 sandwich made from two whole slices of bread. 6 bullet.

round⁴ /raʊnd/ prep 1 with a circular movement about: *The earth moves ~ the sun*. 2 surrounding: *a wall ~ the house*. 3 to or at a point on the other side of: *walk ~ the corner*. 4 to or at various points in: *look ~ the shop*. 5 near: *I've never seen him ~ here*.

round⁵ /raʊnd/ v [T] 1 go round: *~ a corner*. 2 make round. 3 (phr v) **round sth off** complete sth satisfactorily. **round sth up** (a) bring sth together; *~ up cattle*. (b) increase sth to the nearest whole number.

roundabout /'raʊndəbaʊt/ n [C] 1 road junction where vehicles must go round a circle. 2 (at a fair, etc) revolving circular platform with wooden horses, etc on which children ride. **roundabout** adj indirect: *a ~ route*.

rounders /'raʊndəz/ n (with sing v) team game played with a bat and a ball.

rouse /raʊz/ v 1 [I, T] (*fml*) wake (sb) up. 2 [T] cause (sb) to be more active, interested, etc: *a rousing speech*.

rout /raʊt/ v [T] defeat completely. **rout** n [C] complete defeat.

route /ruːt; US ruː/ n [C] way from one place to another. **route** v [T] send by a certain route.

routine /ruː'tiːn/ n [C, U] regular way of doing things. **routine** adj 1 regular or normal. 2 uninteresting.

row¹ /rəʊ/ n [C] 1 line of people or things. 2 (idm) **in a row** one after another without interruption: *She's been to the cinema two evenings in a ~*.

row² /rəʊ/ v [I, T] move (a boat) through the water with oars. **row** n [C] journey in a rowing boat. **'rowing-boat** n [C] boat moved along by oars.

row³ /raʊ/ n 1 [C] noisy argument. 2 [U, sing] loud noise. **row** v [I] quarrel noisily.

rowdy /'raʊdɪ/ adj (-ier, -iest) rough and noisy. **rowdy** n [C] (pl -ies) (*dated derog*) rowdy person.

royal /'rɔɪəl/ adj of, suitable for or belonging to a king or queen. **royal** n [C, usu pl] (*infml*) member of the royal family. **,royal 'blue** adj deep bright blue. **royalist** n [C] person who supports (rule by) a king or queen. **royally** adv splendidly.

royalty /'rɔɪəltɪ/ n (pl -ies) 1 [U] royal person or people. 2 [C] payment to an author, etc for every copy of a book sold, etc.

RSVP /ˌɑːr es viː 'piː/ abbr (on an invitation) please reply.

rub /rʌb/ v (-bb-) 1 [I, T] move (sth) backwards and forwards on the surface of (sth else). 2 [T] cause to be in the condition that is mentioned, by rubbing: *~ the surface dry*. 3 (idm) **rub it in** (*infml*) remind sb of sth unpleasant. **rub sb**

up the wrong way (*infml*) annoy sb. 4 (phr v) **rub sb/sth down** (sb or an animal) with a towel to make dry and clean. **rub sth down** make sth smooth by rubbing. **rub sth in** force (ointment, etc) into the skin by rubbing. **rub sth off** remove by rubbing, esp with the hands: *R~ the dirt off your trousers.* **rub sth out** remove (pencil marks, etc) by using a rubber¹(2). **rub** *n* [C] act of rubbing.

rubber¹ /'rʌbə(r)/ *n* 1 [U] strong elastic substance used for making tyres, etc. 2 [C] piece of rubber for removing pencil marks. **,rubber 'band** [C] thin circular strip of rubber, used for keeping papers, etc together.

rubber² /'rʌbə(r)/ *n* [C] match of (the best of) three games at bridge, etc.

rubbish /'rʌbɪʃ/ *n* [U] 1 waste material. 2 nonsense. **rubbishy** *adj* (*infml*) worthless.

rubble /'rʌbl/ *n* [U] bits of broken stone, rocks or bricks.

ruby /'ru:bɪ/ *n* [C] (*pl* **-ies**) dark red precious stone.

rucksack /'rʌksæk/ *n* [C] large bag carried on the back by walkers and climbers.

rudder /'rʌdə(r)/ *n* [C] flat hinged piece at the back of a boat or aircraft, used for steering.

ruddy¹ /'rʌdɪ/ *adj* (**-ier, -iest**) 1 (of sb's face) red and healthy. 2 red.

ruddy² /'rʌdɪ/ *adj, adv* (*Brit sl*) (used to add force to an expression: *You're a ~ fool!*

rude /ru:d/ *adj* (**~r, ~st**) 1 not polite. 2 not decent; vulgar. 3 unexpected and violent: *a ~ reminder.* 4 (*dated*) roughly made. **rudely** *adv.* **rudeness** *n* [U].

rudiments /'ru:dɪmənts/ *n* [pl] first simple stages of a subject. **rudimentary** /ˌru:dɪ'mentrɪ/ *adj* 1 simple; basic. 2 undeveloped.

ruffian /'rʌfɪən/ *n* [C] (*dated*) violent lawless man.

ruffle /'rʌfl/ *v* [T] 1 make uneven. 2 (*fig*) upset or annoy.

rug /rʌg/ *n* [C] 1 thick floor mat (smaller than a carpet). 2 small blanket.

Rugby /'rʌgbɪ/ *n* [U] kind of football played with an oval ball that may be kicked or carried.

rugged /'rʌgɪd/ *adj* 1 uneven; rocky. 2 strong-looking; hard: *a ~ face.*

rugger /'rʌgə(r)/ *n* [U] (*infml esp Brit*) Rugby.

ruin /'ru:ɪn/ *v* [T] 1 destroy or spoil. 2 cause (sb) to lose all his/her money. **ruin** *n* 1 [U] destruc-

tion. 2 [C] destroyed building, etc: *The house is in ~s.* 3 [U] cause of financial collapse: *Drink was his ~.* **ruined** *adj* partly destroyed. **ruinous** *adj* causing ruin.

rule /ru:l/ *n* 1 [C] statement of what one must or must not do. 2 [C] usual way sth happens. 3 [U] government: *under foreign ~.* 4 (idm) **as a 'rule** usually. **rule of thumb** rough practical way of measuring or judging. **rule** *v* 1 [I, T] have authority (over); govern. 2 [I, T] give as a decision: *She ~d that the evidence could not be accepted.* ○ *The judge ~d in his favour.* 3 [T] draw (a line) with a ruler. 4 (idm) **rule the 'roost** be the leader. 5 (phr v) **rule sth out** declare that sth cannot be considered or is not possible. **ruler** *n* [C] 1 person who rules. 2 straight piece of wood, plastic, etc used in drawing straight lines or for measuring. **ruling** *n* [C] official decision.

rum /rʌm/ *n* [U] alcoholic drink made from sugar-cane.

rumble /'rʌmbl/ *v* [T] *n* [C] (make a) deep heavy continuous sound.

rummage /'rʌmɪdʒ/ *v* [I] turn things over carelessly while looking for sth.

rumour (*US* **-or**) /'ru:mə(r)/ *n* [C, U] (piece of) information spread by being talked about but not certainly true. **rumoured** (*US* **-ored**) *adj* reported as a rumour.

rump /rʌmp/ *n* 1 [C] animal's buttocks. 2 **,rump 'steak** [C, U] (piece of) beef cut from near the rump.

rumple /'rʌmpl/ *v* [T] make (sth) creased or untidy.

rumpus /'rʌmpəs/ *n* [sing] noisy quarrel or disturbance.

run /rʌn/ *v* (**-nn-**, *pt* **ran** /ræn/, *pp* **run**) 1 [I] (of people and animals) move quickly, faster than when walking. 2 [T] cover (a certain distance) by running. 3 (a) [I] practise running as a sport. (b) [I, T] take part in (a running race). 4 [I, T] move quickly in the specified direction: *The car ran down the hill.* 5 [I] go forward with a continuous motion: *The train ran past the signal.* 6 [I] (of buses, etc) travel on a particular route. 7 [I] extend in the direction that is mentioned: *The road ~s east.* 8 [T] control or manage: *~ a hotel.* 9 [I] continue: *The play ran for six months.* 10 [I, T] (cause sth) to operate: *The heater ~s on electricity.* 11 [T] pass: *~ a comb through one's hair.* 12 [T] transport: *I'll ~ you home.* 13 [I *for/*] (esp *US*) compete for an elected office: ~ *for president.* 14 [I, T] (cause liquid to) flow: *a river that ~s into the sea.* 15 [I] (of colours) spread. 16 (usu used with adj) become: *Supplies are ~ning low.* 17 [T] publish in a newspaper, etc. 18 [T] bring into a country illegally and secretly: ~ *drugs.* 19 [I] be a regular feature of: *Red hair ~s in the family.* 20 (idm) **run amok** rush about wildly (doing great damage). **run its course** ⇨ COURSE[1]. **'run for it** run in order to escape from sb/sth. **run 'high** (of feelings) be very excited. **run 'riot/'wild** behave in a very free and uncontrolled way. **run the risk of** ⇨ RISK. **run to seed** ⇨ SEED. **run short (of sth)** use up most of one's supply (of sth). **run to waste** ⇨ WASTE[2]. 21 (phr v) **run across sb** meet sb unexpectedly. **run after sb** (a) chase sb. (b) try to get the attention of sb: *She's always ~ning after men.* **run a'long** go away. **run a'way (from sb/sth)** leave sb/sth; escape. **run a'way with one** (of a feeling) control one completely. **run away/off with sb** go away secretly with (a lover). **run (sth) down** (a) (cause to) lose power or stop functioning. (b) (cause to) stop functioning: *The company is being ~ down.* **run sb/sth down** (a) hit and injure sb/sth with a vehicle. (b) criticize sb/sth unfairly. **run into sb/sth** (a) meet sb/sth unexpectedly. (b) experience (difficulties) unexpectedly. **run sth off** produce (copies). **run out** become no longer valid. **run out (of sth)** (a) have no more of sth left. (b) (of supplies) come to an end. **run sb over** (of a vehicle) knock down and pass over sb. **run through sth** (a) practise or rehearse sth. (b) read or examine sth quickly. **run to sth** (a) reach (an amount, enough for, etc). (b) (of money) be enough for sth. **run sth up** (a) raise (a flag). (b) cause (a bill, etc) to grow quickly: ~ *up big debts.* **run up against sth** experience (difficulties) unexpectedly. **'runaway** *adj* 1 who has run away. 2 out of control. **'runaway** *n* [C] runaway child. **,run-'down** *adj* 1 tired, esp from working too hard. 2 in bad condition. **'run-up** *n* [sing] period leading to an event.

run[2] /rʌn/ *n* 1 [C] act of running on foot. 2 [C] journey in a car, train, etc. 3 [C] series of performances. 4 [C] period; succession: *a ~ of bad luck.* 5 [sing] sudden great demand. 6 [C] (enclosed) space for domestic animals. 7 [C]

point scored in cricket or baseball. 8 (idm) **on the 'run** trying to escape. **,run-of-the-'mill** *adj* ordinary.

rung[1] *pp* of RING[1].

rung[2] /rʌŋ/ *n* [C] step on a ladder.

runner /'rʌnə(r)/ *n* [C] 1 person or animal that runs. 2 smuggler: *a 'gun-~.* 3 thin strip on which sth slides or moves: *the ~s of a sledge.* **,runner 'bean** *n* [C] climbing plant with a long flat green bean container, eaten as a vegetable. **,runner-'up** (*pl* ,runners-'up) *n* [C] person who finishes second in a race.

running /'rʌnɪŋ/ *n* [U] 1 action or sport of running. 2 management or operation. 3 (idm) **make the 'running** set the pace or standard. **'running** *adj* 1 continuous: *a ~ battle.* 2 in succession: *win three times ~.* 3 (of water) flowing.

runny /'rʌnɪ/ *adj* (**-ier, -iest**) (*infml*) 1 more liquid than usual. 2 (of the eyes or nose) producing liquid.

runway /'rʌnweɪ/ *n* [C] surface along which aircraft take off and land.

rupture /'rʌptʃə(r)/ *n* [C] 1 (*fml*) instance of the ending of friendly relations. 2 breaking or bursting of part of the body; hernia. **rupture** *v* [I, T] 1 (*fml*) end. 2 (cause (oneself) to) have a rupture(2).

rural /'rʊərəl/ *adj* in or of the countryside.

ruse /ruːz/ *n* [C] trick.

rush[1] /rʌʃ/ *v* 1 [I, T] (cause to) go or come or do sth quickly. 2 [T] force (sb) to do sth too quickly. 3 [T] attack (sth) suddenly with great force. 4 (idm) **be rushed off one's feet** be extremely busy. **rush** *n* 1 [C, U] rapid movement; sudden advance. 2 [sing] sudden demand. 3 [sing, U] (period of) great activity: *the Christmas ~.* **'rush-hour** *n* [C] busy period when many people are travelling to or from work.

rush[2] /rʌʃ/ *n* [C] marsh plant with a long thin stem.

rusk /rʌsk/ *n* [C] hard dry biscuit given to babies.

rust /rʌst/ *n* [U] reddish-brown coating formed on metal by the action of water and air. **rust** *v* [I, T] (cause to) become covered in rust. **rusty** *adj* (**-ier, -iest**) 1 covered with rust. 2 showing lack of recent practice: *His piano-playing is a bit ~y.*

rustle /'rʌsl/ *v* 1 [I, T] (cause to) make a gentle light sound (like dry leaves blown by the wind). 2 [T] (*US*) steal (cattle or horses). 3 (phr

v) **rustle sth up** provide quickly: ~ *up a meal.* **rustle** *n* [C, U] rustling sound.

rut /rʌt/ *n* [C] 1 deep track made by a wheel in soft ground. 2 fixed (and boring) way of living: *be in a ~.* **rutted** *adj* having ruts(1).

ruthless /'ruːθlɪs/ *adj* without pity; cruel. **ruthlessly** *adv.*

rye /raɪ/ *n* [U] (grain of a) kind of cereal plant used for making flour and whisky.

S s

S, s /es/ *n* [C] (*pl* **S's, s's** /'esɪz/) the nineteenth letter of the English alphabet.

S *abbr* south(ern): *S Yorkshire.*

Sabbath /'sæbəθ/ *n* **the Sabbath** [sing] the day of rest, Sunday for Christians, Saturday for Jews.

sabotage /'sæbətɑːʒ/ *n* [U] deliberate damaging of an enemy's or rival's equipment, plans, etc. **sabotage** *v* [T] secretly damage or spoil (a machine, a car, sb's plans, etc). **saboteur** /ˌsæbə'tɜː(r)/ *n* [C] person who commits sabotage.

sabre (*US* **saber**) /'seɪbə(r)/ *n* [C] heavy sword with a curved blade.

saccharin /'sækərɪn/ *n* [U] very sweet substance used in place of sugar.

sachet /'sæʃeɪ; *US* sæ'ʃeɪ/ *n* [C] small paper or plastic pack for holding sugar, shampoo, etc.

sack[1] /sæk/ *n* [C] (contents of a) large bag of strong material for carrying coal, potatoes, etc. **'sackcloth** (also **sacking**) *n* [U] material for making sacks. **'sackful** *n* [C] amount held by a sack.

sack[2] /sæk/ *v* [T] (*infml esp Brit*) dismiss (sb) from a job. **the sack** *n* [sing] dismissal from a job: *give sb/get the ~.*

sack[3] /sæk/ *v* [T] steal or destroy property in (a captured city, etc).

sacrament /'sækrəmənt/ *n* [C] Christian ceremony, eg baptism or confirmation. **sacramental** /ˌsækrə'mentl/ *adj.*

sacred /'seɪkrɪd/ *adj* 1 connected with religion or with God: *a ~ shrine.* 2 (*to*)|| treated with great respect: *In India the cow is a ~ animal.* 3 very important; solemn: *a ~ promise/duty.*

sacrifice /'sækrɪfaɪs/ *n* 1 [U, C] (*to*)|| offering of sth valuable to a god. 2 (a) [U] giving up of sth valuable for a good purpose. (b) [C]

thing given up in this way: *make ~ s.* **sacrifice** *v (to)*|| 1 [I, T] make a sacrifice(1). 2 [T] give (sth) up as a sacrifice(2): ~ *a career to have a family.* **sacrificial** /ˌsækrɪ'fɪʃl/ *adj.*

sacrilege /'sækrɪlɪdʒ/ *n* [C, usu sing, U] disrespectful treatment of sth sacred. **sacrilegious** /ˌsækrɪ'lɪdʒəs/ *adj.*

sad /sæd/ *adj* (~**der**, ~**dest**) unhappy or causing sorrow: *a ~ person/song.* **sadden** *v* [I, T] become or make sad: ~ *dened by his death.* **sadly** *adv* 1 in a sad way: *smile ~ly.* 2 unfortunately: *S~ly, we have no more money.* **sadness** *n* [U, C].

saddle /'sædl/ *n* [C] 1 seat for a rider on a horse, bicycle, etc. 2 ridge of high land rising to a high point at each end. 3 (idm) **in the 'saddle** (a) on a horse. (b) (*fig*) in control. **saddle** *v* [T] 1 put a saddle on (a horse). 2 (phr v) **saddle sb with sth** give sb an unpleasant task, etc: ~*d with cleaning the car.* **'saddle-bag** *n* [C] bag attached to a saddle.

sadism /'seɪdɪzəm/ *n* [U] (getting sexual pleasure from) cruelty to other people. **'sadist** *n* [C] person who practises sadism. **sadistic** /sə'dɪstɪk/ *adj.*

sae /ˌes en 'iː/ *abbr* stamped addressed envelope, usually sent to sb when you want a reply.

safari /sə'fɑːrɪ/ *n* [C, U] journey to hunt or watch wild animals, esp in Africa: *on ~ in Kenya.*

safe[1] /seɪf/ *adj* (~**r**, ~**st**) 1 (*from*)|| free from danger and harm: ~ *from attack.* 2 not likely to cause damage, loss, etc: *a ~ speed.* 3 not hurt: *The plane crashed but the pilot is ~.* 4 (of a place, etc) giving protection from danger, harm, etc. 5 careful: *a ~ driver.* 6 (idm) **(as) safe as 'houses** very safe. **for/in safe 'keeping** to be/being kept safely. **safe and 'sound** unharmed. **safely** *adv.* **safeness** *n* [U].

safe[2] /seɪf/ *n* [C] very strong box with a lock, for keeping valuable objects.

safeguard /'seɪfgɑːd/ *n* [C] (*against*)|| something that prevents harm, damage, etc. **safeguard** *v* [T] (*against*)|| protect or guard.

safety /'seɪftɪ/ *n* [U] state of being safe; freedom from danger. **'safety-belt** *n* [C] = SEAT-BELT (SEAT). **'safety-pin** *n* [C] pin used for fastening things, covered by a guard so it doesn't hurt anybody. **'safety-valve** *n* [C] 1 valve which lets gas, liquid, etc escape if the pressure gets too high. 2 (fig) non-violent way of showing anger, etc.

sag /sæg/ v (-gg-) [I] 1 sink or curve down under weight or pressure. 2 hang unevenly.

saga /'sɑːgə/ n [C] 1 long story full of adventures about people who lived a long time ago. 2 long story, esp about a family.

sage[1] /seɪdʒ/ n [C] (fml) wise man. **sage** adj wise.

sage[2] /seɪdʒ/ n [U] herb used for flavouring food.

said pt, pp of SAY.

sail[1] /seɪl/ n 1 [C, U] strong cloth used for catching the wind and moving a boat along. 2 [sing] trip on a boat: go for a ~. 3 [C] arm of a windmill. 4 (idm) **set sail (from/to/for)** begin a journey by boat.

sail[2] /seɪl/ v 1 travel on water in a ship, yacht, etc. 2 [I] begin a voyage. 3 [T] travel in a boat across (a sea or ocean). 4 [I, T] control (a boat or ship): Can you ~ (a yacht)? 5 (phr v) **sail through** (sth) pass (an examination, etc) easily. **sailing** n [U] sport of sailing boats: go ~ing. **'sailing-boat** (also **'sailing-ship**) n [C] boat or ship that uses sails. **sailor** n [C] member of a ship's crew; seaman.

saint /seɪnt or, before names sənt/ n [C] person recognized as holy by the Christian Church because he/she performed miracles, etc. **saintly** adj (-ier, -iest) of or like a saint; holy.

sake /seɪk/ n (idm) **for goodness', Heavens', etc sake** (used before or after an order or request to express anger, etc): For goodness' ~ hurry up! **for the sake of** 1 for the benefit of: for the ~ of her children. 2 in order to get or keep sth: for the ~ of peace.

salad /'sæləd/ n [C, U] (a) sliced raw vegetables, eg lettuce, cucumber, tomatoes. (b) food served with salad: a cheese ~. **'salad dressing** n [U] sauce of oil, vinegar, etc put on salads.

salami /sə'lɑːmɪ/ n [U] sausage salted and flavoured.

salary /'sælərɪ/ n [C] (pl -ies) (weekly or monthly) payment for a job. **salaried** adj receiving a salary.

sale /seɪl/ n 1 [U, C] selling or being sold. 2 [C] period when goods are sold at a lower price than usual: buy a dress in the ~ s. 3 (idm) **for sale** intended to be sold. **on sale** (of goods in shops, etc) offered for people to buy. **salesman** n [C] (pl -men) **'salesperson** (pl -people) **'saleswoman** (pl

-women) person who sells goods. **'salesmanship** n [U] skill in selling goods.

saline /'seɪlaɪn; US -liːn/ adj containing salt.

saliva /sə'laɪvə/ n [U] natural liquid produced in the mouth when one chews.

sallow /'sæləʊ/ adj (of sb's skin or face) having an unhealthy yellow colour.

salmon /'sæmən/ n (pl salmon) 1 (a) [C] large fish often fished as sport. (b) [U] its flesh eaten as food. 2 [U] orange-pink colour of its flesh.

salmonella /ˌsælmə'nelə/ n [U] type of bacteria that causes food poisoning.

salon /'sælɒn; US sə'lɒn/ n [C] shop where hairdressers and beauticians work.

saloon /sə'luːn/ n 1 [C] public room in a ship, hotel, etc. 2 (US) bar. 3 (also **saloon-car**) car for four or five people without a large door at the back. **sa'loon bar** = LOUNGE BAR (LOUNGE).

salt /sɔːlt/ n 1 [U] common white substance obtained from mines and sea-water, used to flavour food. 2 [C] chemical compound of a metal and an acid. 3 (idm) **the salt of the 'earth** honest decent person. **take sth with a grain/pinch of salt** not necessarily believe all of sth. **salt** v [T] put salt in or on (food). **'salt-cellar** n [C] small container for salt. **salty** adj (-ier, -iest).

salute /sə'luːt/ n [C] greeting or sign of respect, eg (in the armed forces) the raising of the hand to the forehead. **salute** v [I, T] 1 give (sb) a salute. 2 honour or praise.

salvage /'sælvɪdʒ/ n [U] 1 saving of property from loss. 2 property saved, eg a wrecked ship. 3 (saving of) waste material that can be used again. **salvage** v [T] save from loss, wreckage, etc.

salvation /sæl'veɪʃn/ n [U] 1 saving or being saved from sin. 2 thing or person that prevents loss, disaster, etc.

same /seɪm/ adj 1 **the same** not different; identical: He's the ~ age as his wife. 2 exactly like the one mentioned: My car is the ~ as yours. **the same** pron 1 the same thing: I bought a red dress and then she bought the ~. 2 (idm) **all/just the same** nevertheless; in spite of this: She's quite old, but very lively all the ~. **be all the same to** ⇨ ALL³. **same here** I feel the same; I agree: 'I feel hot.' 'S~ here.' **the same** adv in the same way: *The two words are pronounced the* ~. **sameness** *n* [U] being the same; lack of variety.

sample /'sɑ:mpl; *US* 'sæmpl/ *n* [C] one of a number of things, or part of a whole, used for showing what the rest is like: *wallpaper* ~*s.* **sample** *v* [T] test a part of: ~ *our new wine.*

sanatorium /ˌsænə'tɔ:rɪəm/ *n* (*pl* ~**s** or **-ria** /-rɪə/) place for treating people who are or have been ill.

sanctimonious /ˌsæŋktɪ'məʊnɪəs/ *adj* (*derog*) showing that one feels morally better than others. **sanctimoniously** *adv.*

sanction /'sæŋkʃn/ *n* 1 [U] permission; approval. 2 [C] action taken to make sb or a country obey a law: *economic* ~*s.* **sanction** *v* [T] permit, allow.

sanctity /'sæŋktətɪ/ *n* [U] holiness.

sanctuary /'sæŋktʃʊərɪ; *US* -ʊerɪ/ *n* (*pl* **-ies**) 1 [C] holy place, eg a church. 2 [C, U] (place offering) protection from arrest, attack, etc: *be offered* ~. 3 [C] area where it is forbidden to kill birds, animals, etc.

sand /sænd/ *n* 1 [U] (mass of) fine grains of crushed rock, eg on the sea-shore, in deserts, etc. 2 [C, usu pl] area of sand. **sand** *v* [T] 1 smooth with sandpaper: ~ (*down*) *the wood.* 2 cover with sand. **'sandbag** *n* [C] bag filled with sand, used for stopping bullets, water, etc. Take *v* [T] fill or protect with sandbags. **'sand-castle** *n* [C] pile of sand like a castle, usu made by a child on the beach. **'sand-dune** = DUNE. **'sandpaper** *n* [U] strong paper with sand glued to it, used for rubbing surfaces smooth. **'sandstone** /U] rock formed from sand. **sandy** *adj* (**-ier**, **-iest**) 1 like or covered with sand. 2 (of hair) yellowish-red.

sandal /'sændl/ *n* [C] type of open shoe attached to the foot by straps.

sandwich /'sænwɪdʒ; *US* -wɪtʃ/ *n* [C] two slices of bread with meat, salad, etc between them: *a cheese* ~. **sandwich** *v* [T] put (sb/sth) between two other people or things.

sane /seɪn/ *adj* (~**r**, ~**st**) 1 having a healthy mind. 2 sensible: *a* ~ *policy.* **sanely** *adv.*

sang *pt* of SING.

sanitary /'sænɪtrɪ; *US* -terɪ/ *adj* 1 free from dirt that might cause disease; clean: ~ *conditions.* 2 of or concerned with protecting health: ~ *measures.* **'sanitary towel** *n* [C] pad of cotton wool, used by a woman during her period(3).

sanitation /ˌsænɪ'teɪʃn/ *n* [U] system of protecting people's health, esp removing sewage.

sanity /'sænətɪ/ *n* [U] the quality of being sane; health of mind.

sank *pt* of SINK³.

sap¹ /sæp/ *n* [U] liquid in a plant that carries food to all its parts. **'sapling** *n* [C] young tree.

sap² /sæp/ *v* (**-pp-**) [T] weaken sb/ sth by taking away (strength, confidence, etc).

sapphire /'sæfaɪə(r)/ *n* [C] bright blue precious stone. **sapphire** *adj* bright blue in colour.

sarcasm /'sɑ:kæzəm/ *n* [U] (use of) ironic remarks, intended to hurt sb's feelings. **sarcastic** /sɑ:'kæstɪk/ *adj.* **sarcastically** /-klɪ/ *adv.*

sardine /sɑ:'di:n/ *n* [C] 1 small fish, often sold in tins in oil or tomato sauce. 2 (idm) **like sardines** pressed tightly together.

sari /'sɑ:rɪ/ *n* [C] dress worn by Indian women made of a long piece of cloth wrapped round the body.

sarong /sə'rɒŋ; *US* -'rɔ:ŋ/ *n* [C] long piece of cloth worn as a skirt in Indonesia.

sash /sæʃ/ *n* [C] long piece of cloth worn round the waist or over the shoulder.

ˌsash-'window /ˌsæʃ 'wɪndəʊ/ *n* [C] window with two frames that slide up and down.

sat *pt, pp* of SIT.

Satan /'seɪtn/ *n* the Devil. **Satanic** /sə'tænɪk/ *adj.*

satchel /'sætʃəl/ *n* [C] bag with a long strap for carrying school books.

satellite /'sætəlaɪt/ *n* [C] 1 (a) small body, eg a moon, that moves round a planet. (b) artificial object, eg a spacecraft, that moves round a planet. 2 (*fig*) country that depends on another stronger country. **satellite television** *n* [U] television programmes transmitted to people's homes by satellite and received by a large dish-shaped aerial.

satin /'sætɪn; *US* 'sætn/ *n* [U] silk material that is shiny on one side.

satire /'sætaɪə(r)/ *n* 1 [U] making a person, idea, etc seem foolish or wicked, esp in a book, play, etc. 2 [C] book, play, etc that does this: *a* ~ *on snobbery.* **satirical** /sə'tɪrɪkl/ *adj.* **satirize** /'sætəraɪz/ *v* [T] make fun of (sb/ sth) using satire.

satisfaction /ˌsætɪs'fækʃn/ *n* 1 [U] feeling of being contented: *get* ~ *from one's work.* 2 [C] something that makes sb contented. 3

satisfactory 366

[U] compensation or apology.
satisfactory /ˌsætɪsˈfæktərɪ/ *adj*
good enough (but not very good):
~ *progress.* **satisfactorily**
/-tərəlɪ/ *adv.*

satisfy /ˈsætɪsfaɪ/ *v* (*pt, pp* -**ied**)
[T] 1 give (sb) what he/she wants
or needs; make contented: *enough
food to* ~ *us.* 2 fulfil (a desire, need,
etc). 3 give (sb) proof; convince: ~
the police of my innocence. **satisfied** *adj* contented.

saturate /ˈsætʃəreɪt/ *v* [T] 1
make (sb/sth) completely wet. 2
(usu pass) fill completely. **sat-
urated** *adj* 1 very wet. 2 (of butter,
oils, etc) containing chemicals formed in a way thought to be harmful to one's health. **saturation**
/ˌsætʃəˈreɪʃn/ *n* [U].

Saturday /ˈsætədɪ/ *n* [U, C] the
seventh day of the week, next after
Friday. (See examples of use at
Monday).

sauce /sɔːs/ *n* 1 [C, U] liquid served with food to give it flavour. 2
[U] (*infml*) disrespectful talk.
saucy *adj* (-**ier**, -**iest**) disrespectful. **saucily** *adv.*

saucepan /ˈsɔːspən; *US* -pæn/
n [C] deep cooking pot with a lid
and a handle.

saucer /ˈsɔːsə(r)/ *n* [C] small shallow dish on which a cup stands.

sauna /ˈsɔːnə, *also* ˈsaʊnə/ *n* [C]
(period of sitting in a) very hot
room filled with steam.

saunter /ˈsɔːntə(r)/ *v* [I] walk in a
leisurely way; stroll. **saunter**
n [sing] leisurely walk.

sausage /ˈsɒsɪdʒ; *US* ˈsɔːs-/ *n*
[C, U] mixture of chopped meat,
flavouring, etc inside a tube of
thin skin.

savage /ˈsævɪdʒ/ *adj* 1 wild and
fierce: *a* ~ *animal.* 2 cruel or vicious: ~ *criticism.* 3 (*offensive*) primitive; not civilized. **savage** *n* [C]
(*offensive*) member of a primitive
tribe. **savage** *v* [T] attack fiercely;
~*d by a dog.* **savagely** *adv.* **sav-
agery** *n* [U] savage behaviour.

save /seɪv/ *v* 1 [T] (*from*)// make
or keep safe from harm, loss, etc:
~ *sb's life.* 2 [I, T] (*up*) *for sth*) keep
(esp money) for future use: ~ (*up*)
for a new car. ○ *S~ some cake for
me!* 3 [T] make unnecessary: *That
will* ~ *you a lot of trouble.* 4 [T] (in
football, etc) stop (the ball) going
into the net. 5 (idm) **save (one's)
face** avoid losing one's dignity.
save one's 'neck ⇒ NECK. **save**
n [C] (in football, etc) act of stopping a goal being scored. **saving**
n 1 [C] amount saved: *a saving of £5.*
2 **savings** [pl] money saved.
'savings account *n* [U] bank acc-

ount in which interest is paid on
money saved.

saviour (*US* -**or**) /ˈseɪvɪə(r)/ *n* [C]
1 person who saves sb from dan-
ger. 2 **the Saviour** Jesus Christ.

savour (*US* -**or**) /ˈseɪvə(r)/ *n* [C,
U] taste or flavour. **savour** *v* [T]
enjoy the taste of: ~ *the wine* ○
(*fig*) ~ *one's freedom.*

savoury (*US* -**ory**) /ˈseɪvərɪ/ *adj*
having a salty taste; not sweet. **savoury** *n* [C] (*pl* -**ies**) savoury dish.

saw¹ *pt* of SEE.

saw² /sɔː/ *n* [C] tool which has a
long blade with sharp teeth, for
cutting wood, metal, etc. **saw** *v* (*pt*
~**ed**, *pp* ~**n** /sɔːn/; *US* ~**ed**) 1
[I, T] cut (sth) with a saw. 2 [I] capable of being sawn: *Wood* ~ *s easily.* 3 (phr v) **saw sth up** cut sth
into pieces with a saw. **'sawdust**
n [U] tiny pieces of wood falling
from wood as it is sawn. **'sawmill**
n [C] factory where wood is sawn.

saxophone /ˈsæksəfəʊn/ *n* [C]
curved metal musical instrument,
often used for jazz.

say /seɪ/ *v* (*pt, pp* **said** /sed/) [T] 1
utter (a word, remark, etc); tell
(sth) to sb in words. 2 (of something printed) give information: *It
~ s here that she was killed.* 3 make
(sth) clear by words, gestures, etc:
What does this poem ~ to you? 4
give an opinion. 5 suppose or suggest: *I'd ~ this can't be done.* 6
(idm) **go without saying** be very
obvious. **you can say that again**
(*infml*) I agree. **that is to say** ⇒
THAT¹. **say** *n* 1 [U, sing] power to
decide: *a ~ in what happens.* 2
(idm) **have one's say** express
one's opinion. **saying** *n* [C] remark often made; well-known
phrase.

scab /skæb/ *n* [C] 1 dry crust that
forms over a wound. 2 (*infml derog*) worker who refuses to join a
strike.

scaffold /ˈskæfəʊld/ *n* [C] 1
framework of poles and boards
round a building for workers to
stand on. 2 platform on which
criminals are executed. **scaffold-
ing** /ˈskæfəʊldɪŋ/ *n* [U] (poles,
boards, etc for a) scaffold(1).

scald /skɔːld/ *v* [T] burn with hot
liquid or steam. **scald** *n* [C] injury
to one's skin from hot liquid or
steam. **scalding** *adj* very hot.

scale¹ /skeɪl/ *n* 1 [C] one of the
thin pieces of hard material that
cover fish, snakes, etc. 2 [U] (*Brit*)
chalky substance left inside kettles, water-pipes, etc. **scale** *v* [T]
remove the scales from (a fish).
scaly *adj* (-**ier**, -**iest**).

scale² /skeɪl/ *n* 1 [C] regular

series of marks, used for measuring. 2 [C] system of grading people or things: *a salary ~*. 3 [C] relation between a map, diagram, etc and the thing that it represents. 4 [C, U] relative size, extent, etc: *riots on a large ~*. 5 [C] (*music*) series of notes arranged in order of pitch. **scale** *v* (phr v) **scale sth up/down** increase/decrease sth.

scale³ /skeɪl/ *v* [T] climb up (a cliff, wall, etc).

scales /skeɪlz/ *n* [pl] instrument for weighing: *weigh oneself on the bathroom ~*.

scallop /'skɒləp/ *n* [C] shellfish with two fan-shaped shells.

scalp /skælp/ *n* [C] skin and hair on top of the head. **scalp** *v* [T] cut the scalp off (sb).

scalpel /'skælpəl/ *n* [C] small light knife used by surgeons.

scamper /'skæmpə(r)/ *v* [I] run quickly like a child or small animal.

scampi /'skæmpi/ *n* [pl] large prawns.

scan /skæn/ *v* (-nn-) 1 [T] examine closely: *~ the horizon*. 2 [T] look at quickly but not thoroughly: *~ the newspapers*. 3 [T] (*medical*) examine (sb's body) with a scanner. 4 [I] (of poetry) have a regular rhythm. 5 [T] (*computing*) search through (data) to find a certain item. **scan** *n* [C] act of scanning. **scanner** *n* [C] machine which uses X-rays, etc to make a picture of the inside of the body.

scandal /'skændl/ *n* 1 [C, U] action or behaviour that offends or shocks people. 2 [U] talk which damages a person's reputation. **scandalize** /-dəlaɪz/ *v* [T] morally offend or shock. **scandalous** *adj*.

scant /skænt/ *adj* (*fml*) hardly enough. **scantily** *adv* **scanty** *adj* (-ier, -iest) very small in size or amount.

scapegoat /'skeɪpɡəʊt/ *n* person blamed for the wrong acts of another.

scar /skɑː(r)/ *n* [C] 1 mark left on the skin by a wound that has healed. 2 (*fig*) mental suffering after a bad experience. **scar** *v* (-rr-) [T] leave a scar on (sb).

scarce /skeəs/ *adj* (~r, ~st) 1 less than is needed; hard to obtain. 2 (*fig*) rarely seen: *~ enough food*. **scarcely** *adv* almost not; barely: *~ enough food*. **scarcity** *n* [C, U] (*pl* -ies) (instance of) being scarce.

scare /skeə(r)/ *v* 1 [T] frighten. 2 [I] become afraid: *He ~s easily*. **scare** *n* [C] feeling or state of fear. **'scarecrow** *n* [C] figure dressed in old clothes, to scare birds away from crops. **scary** /'skeəri/ *adj*

(-ier, -iest) (*infml*) frightening.

scarf /skɑːf/ *n* [C] (*pl* **scarves** /skɑːvz/ *or* ~s) piece of material worn round the neck or over the hair.

scarlet /'skɑːlət/ *n* [U], *adj* bright red. **,scarlet 'fever** *n* [C] serious disease causing red marks on the skin.

scathing /'skeɪðɪŋ/ *adj* (of criticism, etc) harsh; scornful. **scathingly** *adv*.

scatter /'skætə(r)/ *v* 1 [I, T] (cause to) move in various directions. 2 [T] put or throw in various directions: *~ seed*. **'scatter-brain** *n* [C] person who cannot concentrate for long or forgets quickly. **'scatter-brained** *adj*. **scattered** *adj* not close together.

scavenge /'skævɪndʒ/ *v* [I, T] 1 search for or eat (decaying flesh). 2 look among rubbish for food, etc. **scavenger** *n* [C] animal, bird or person that scavenges.

scenario /sɪ'nɑːrɪəʊ; *US* -'nær-/ *n* [C] (*pl* ~s) 1 written outline of a play, film, etc. 2 imagined series of future events.

scene /siːn/ *n* [C] 1 place where an event happens: *the ~ of the crime*. 2 incident in real life: *~s of horror during the fire*. 3 emotional outburst: *make a ~*. 4 view, esp part of an act in a play. 5 place represented on the stage of the theatre. 7 (idm) **behind the scenes** (a) behind the stage. (b) in secret. **on the scene** present. **scenery** *n* [U] 1 natural features of an area, eg mountains. 2 painted canvas, etc used on the stage of a theatre. **scenic** /'siːnɪk/ *adj* having beautiful natural scenery.

scent /sent/ *n* 1 [C, U] smell, esp a pleasant one. 2 [U] (esp *Brit*) perfume. 3 [C] smell left by an animal. 4 [U] sense of smell, esp in dogs. 5 (idm) **on the scent of sb/sth** likely to find sb/sth. **scent** *v* [T] 1 (a) discover (sth) by the sense of smell. (b) (*fig*) suspect the presence of (sth): *~ danger*. 2 give (sth) a certain scent: *~ed paper*.

sceptic (*US* **sk-**) /'skeptɪk/ *n* [C] person who doubts that a statement, theory, etc is true. **sceptical** *adj*. **scepticism** /'skeptɪsɪzəm/ *n* [U] sceptical attitude.

sceptre (*US* **-er**) /'septə(r)/ *n* [C] rod carried by a ruler as a symbol of power.

schedule /'ʃedjuːl; *US* 'skedʒʊl/ *n* [C, U] 1 list of planned events, times for doing things, etc: *production ~s on/behind ~*, ie on time/ not on time. 2 (*US*) = TIMETABLE scheme 368

(TIME¹). **schedule** v [T] include (sth) in a schedule.

scheme /skiːm/ n [C] **1** ordered arrangement: *a 'colour ~.* **2** plan of work: *a ~ for raising money.* **3** secret or dishonest plan. **scheme** v [T] make (esp secret) plans. **schemer** n [C] person who schemes dishonestly.

schizophrenia /ˌskɪtsəʊˈfriːnɪə/ n [U] illness in which the mind becomes separated from actions. **schizophrenic** /-ˈfrenɪk/ adj, n (person) with schizophrenia.

scholar /ˈskɒlə(r)/ n [C] **1** person who knows a lot about an academic subject. **2** student who is awarded money to attend school or university. **scholarly** adj. **scholarship** n (a) [U] knowledge of an academic subject. (b) [C] payment given to a scholar(2).

school¹ /skuːl/ n **1** [C] place where children or adults learn (sth): *All children should go to* (ie attend) *~.* ○ *primary/secondary ~* ○ *a driving ~.* **2** [C] (US) college or university. **3** [U] (a) attendance at a school: *Is she old enough for ~?* (b) time when teaching is being done in a school: *S~ starts at 9 am.* **4 the school** [sing] all the pupils in a school. **5** [C] department of a university: *medical ~.* **6** [C] group of artists, thinkers, etc: *the Dutch ~ of painting.* **school** v [T] train; control. **schooling** n [U] education. **school-leaver** n [C] person who has recently left school. **'schoolmaster 'schoolmistress** n [C] teacher in a school.

school² /skuːl/ n [C] large number of fish swimming together.

schooner /ˈskuːnə(r)/ n [C] **1** sailing-ship with two or more masts. **2** tall drinking-glass.

science /ˈsaɪəns/ n (a) [U] organized knowledge obtained by observation and testing of facts. (b) [C, U] branch of such knowledge, eg physics. **science 'fiction** n [U] fiction dealing with future scientific discoveries, imaginary worlds, etc. **scientific** /ˌsaɪənˈtɪfɪk/ adj. **scientifically** /-klɪ/ adv. **scientist** /ˈsaɪəntɪst/ n [C] expert in one of the sciences.

scintillating /ˈsɪntɪleɪtɪŋ; US -təl-/ adj lively and witty.

scissors /ˈsɪzəz/ n [pl] instrument with two blades, used for cutting paper, cloth, etc: *a pair of ~.*

scoff /skɒf/ v [I] *(at)* say disrespectful things (of).

scold /skəʊld/ v [I, T] express anger, blame, etc: *~ a child for being naughty.*

scone /skɒn; US skəʊn/ n [C] small cake made with fat and flour and eaten with butter.

scoop /skuːp/ n [C] **1** small, short-handled shovel for picking up grain, flour, etc. **2** piece of news obtained by one newspaper, etc before its rivals. **scoop** v [T] **1** make (a hole, etc) with, or as if with, a scoop. **2** (phr v) **scoop sth out/up** lift with, or as if with, a scoop.

scooter /ˈskuːtə(r)/ n [C] **1** (also **'motor-scooter**) motor bike with a small engine and a shield for the driver's legs. **2** toy vehicle with two wheels, moved by pushing one foot against the ground.

scope /skəʊp/ n **1** [U] opportunity: *~ for improvement.* **2** [sing] range of things being dealt with, studied, etc.

scorch /skɔːtʃ/ v **1** (a) [T] burn the surface of (sth) by dry heat. (b) [I] be burned in this way. **2** [T] cause (a plant) to dry up and die. **scorch** n [C] brown mark, esp on cloth, made by dry heat.

score¹ /skɔː(r)/ n [C] **1** (record of) points, goals, etc in a game. **2** cut or scratch on a surface. **3** copy of written music. **4** (dated) twenty. **5** (idm) **on that score** as far as that is concerned. **pay/settle an old score** have one's revenge.

score² /skɔː(r)/ v **1** [I, T] (a) keep a record of the points, goals, etc in a game. (b) gain (points, goals, etc) in a game. **2** [T] make a cut or scratch on (a surface). **3** [I, T] achieve (a success). **4** [T] write (music): *~d for the piano.* **scorer** n **1** person who keeps a score¹(1). **2** player who scores goals, etc.

scorn /skɔːn/ n [U] feeling that a person or thing deserves no respect. **scorn** v [T] **1** feel or show scorn for (sb/sth). **2** refuse proudly: *~ sb's advice.* **scornful** adj. **scornfully** adv.

scorpion /ˈskɔːpɪən/ n [C] small animal with claws and a poisonous sting in its tail.

Scot /skɒt/ n [C] person from Scotland.

Scotch /skɒtʃ/ n [C, U] (type or glass of) Scottish whisky.

scot-free /ˌskɒtˈfriː/ adj unpunished: *escape ~.*

Scots /skɒts/ adj Scottish.

Scottish /ˈskɒtɪʃ/ adj of Scotland or its people.

scoundrel /ˈskaʊndrəl/ n [C] person without moral principles.

scour /ˈskaʊə(r)/ v [T] clean (a surface) by rubbing with a rough pad, etc. **scour** n [sing] act of scouring. **scourer** n [C] pad of stiff nylon or wire used for scouring

screw

pots.

scour² /'skaʊə(r)/ *v* [T] search carefully: ~ *the area for the thief.*

scourge /skɜːdʒ/ *n* [C] cause of great suffering: *the ~ of war.*

scout /skaʊt/ *n* [C] 1 person, ship or aircraft sent out to get information about the enemy. 2 Scout member of an organization for boys that aims to develop practical skills and helpfulness. 3 (phr v) **scout about/around** look for sb/sth in different places.

scowl /skaʊl/ *n* [C] angry or bad-tempered look. **scowl** *v* [I] *(at)/* look (at sb/sth) with a scowl.

scrabble /'skræbl/ *v* (phr v) **scrabble about (for sth)** feel with one's fingers to find sth.

scraggy /'skrægɪ/ *adj* (-ier, -iest) *(derog)* thin and bony.

scram /skræm/ *v* (-mm-) [I] *(sl)* go away quickly.

scramble /'skræmbl/ *v* 1 [I] climb or crawl, often with difficulty. 2 [T] beat and cook (eggs). 3 [T] mix up (a telephone conversation, etc) so that it is impossible to understand. 4 [I] **scramble for sth** compete with others for sth: ~ *for the best seats.* **scramble** *n* 1 [sing] walk or climb over rough ground. 2 [sing] rough struggle: *a ~ for seats.* 3 [C] motorbike race over rough ground.

scrap¹ /skræp/ *n* 1 [C] small piece: *a ~ of paper* ○ *(fig) ~s of information.* 2 [U] unwanted objects: ~ *metal.* **scrap** *v* (-pp-) [T] throw away (sth useless). '**scrapbook** *n* [C] book of blank pages on which newspaper cuttings, etc are pasted. '**scrap-heap** *n* [C] 1 pile of scrap. 2 (idm) **on the scrap-heap** no longer wanted. **scrappy** *adj* (-ier, -iest) not well organized.

scrap² /skræp/ *n* [C] *(infml)* fight, esp between children. **scrap** *v* (-pp-) [I] fight; quarrel.

scrape /skreɪp/ *v* 1 [T] **(a)** make (a surface) clean or level by pulling a hard tool across it. **(b)** *(from/off/away)//* remove (mud, paint, etc) in this way. 2 [T] damage or injure by rubbing: ~ *one's arm on the wall.* 3 [I] rub against sth: *The branch ~d against the side of the car.* 4 [T] make by scraping: ~ *(out) a hole.* 5 (idm) **scrape (the bottom of) the 'barrel** use the least satisfactory thing or person because nothing better is available. 6 (phr v) **scrape sth together/up** get (esp a sum of money) with difficulty: ~ *up enough to pay the gas bill.* **scrape** *n* [C] 1 act or sound of scraping. 2 mark, wound, etc made by scraping. 3 *(infml)* difficult situation.

scratch¹ /skrætʃ/ *v* 1 **(a)** [I, T] make lines on (a surface) with sth sharp, eg a nail. **(b)** [T] make (a line, etc) by scratching. 2 [I, T] rub (the skin), esp with one's nails, to stop itching. 3 (idm) **scratch the surface** study, discuss, etc a matter not very thoroughly. 4 (phr v) **scratch sth away, off, etc** remove sth by scratching.

scratch² /skrætʃ/ *n* 1 [C] mark, cut or sound made by scratching. 2 [sing] act of scratching(2). 3 (idm) **(start sth) from 'scratch** (begin sth) at the beginning. **up to scratch** good enough. **scratchy** *adj* 1 making the skin itch. 2 (of a record) sounding bad because of scratches.

scrawl /skrɔːl/ *v* [I, T] 1 write quickly or carelessly. 2 make meaningless marks. **scrawl** *n* [C, sing] (piece of) untidy handwriting.

scream /skriːm/ *v* 1 **(a)** [I] give a long sharp cry of fear, pain, anger, etc. **(b)** [T] shout (sth) in this way. 2 [I] (of the wind, machines, etc) make a loud, high noise. 3 (idm) **scream one's head off** ⇨ HEAD¹. **scream** *n* [C] loud sharp cry or noise.

screech /skriːtʃ/ *v* 1 [I] make a harsh, piercing sound. 2 [T] shout (sth) in this way. 3 [I] scream (as if) in anger or pain. **screech** *n* [sing] screeching cry or sound: *a ~ of brakes.*

screen /skriːn/ *n* 1 [C] upright framework, used for dividing a room, stopping heat or light, etc. 2 [C] anything that hides or protects sb/sth: *a ~ of trees around the house.* 3 [C] white surface on which films, etc are shown. 4 [C] surface on a television, etc on which the picture appears. 5 [sing] the cinema industry. 6 [C] frame with fine wire netting. **screen** *v* [T] 1 shelter or protect (sb/sth) with a screen. 2 examine (sb/sth) for defects, diseases, etc. 3 show (a film etc) on a screen. '**screenplay** *n* [C] script for a film.

screw /skruː/ *n* [C] 1 metal pin with a spiral groove cut round its length, used to fasten things together. 2 action of turning; turn. 3 propeller of a ship. 4 *(Brit △ sl)* sexual intercourse. 5 (idm) **have a screw loose** *(Brit sl)* be mad or eccentric. **screw** *v* 1 [T] fasten with a screw. 2 [T] twist round; tighten by twisting: ~ *the lid on.* 3 [I, T] *(Brit △ sl)* have sexual intercourse with (sb). 4 (phr v) **screw sth up (a)** twist (a part of the face):

~ed up her eyes in the bright sunshine. (b) twist (paper) into a ball. (c) (sl) do sth badly. 'screwdriver n [C] tool for turning a screw(1). ,screwed-'up adj (sl) upset and confused.

scribble /'skrɪbl/ v [I, T] **1** write carelessly: ~ (a note) on an envelope. **2** make meaningless marks on paper, etc. scribble n [I, sing] careless handwriting. **2** [C] something scribbled.

scribe /skraɪb/ n [C] person who made copies in writing before printing was developed.

script /skrɪpt/ n **1** [C] written form of a play, speech, film, etc. **2** [U] handwriting. **3** [U] system of writing. script v [T] write a script for (a film, etc). 'script-writer n [C] person who writes scripts for radio, films, etc.

scripture /'skrɪptʃə(r)/ n **1** Scripture [U] (also the Scriptures) [pl] the Bible. **2** scriptures [pl] holy writings of a religion. scriptural adj.

scroll /skrəʊl/ n [C] **1** (a) roll of paper for writing on. (b) ancient book written on such a roll. **2** design like a scroll, cut in stone. scroll v [I, T] (of data on a computer screen) move slowly up or down; cause (such data) to move in this way.

scrounge /skraʊndʒ/ v [I, T] (infml often derog) get (money, food, etc) by persuading sb to give it to one rather than by working for it: ~ (£10) off a friend. scrounger n [C].

scrub¹ /skrʌb/ v (-bb-) **1** [T] clean (a surface) by rubbing hard, esp with a stiff brush; remove (dirt) in this way. **2** [T] (infml) cancel. scrub n [sing] act of scrubbing. 'scrubbing-brush n [C] stiff brush for scrubbing floors, etc.

scrub² /skrʌb/ n [U] (land covered with) low trees and bushes.

scruff /skrʌf/ n (idm) the scruff of the neck the back of the neck.

scruffy /'skrʌfi/ adj (-ier, -iest) (infml) dirty and untidy. scruff n [C] (infml) dirty or untidy person.

scruple /'skru:pl/ n [C, U] (doubt caused by a) feeling that one is doing wrong: have no ~s about doing sth.

scrupulous /'skru:pjʊləs/ adj **1** paying great attention to small details. **2** very honest. scrupulously adv.

scrutinize /'skru:tɪnaɪz/ v [T] examine carefully and thoroughly.

scrutiny /'skru:tɪnɪ/ n (pl -ies) [C, U] careful and thorough exam-

ination.

scuff /skʌf/ v **1** [I, T] drag (one's feet) along the ground when walking. **2** [T] mark or scrape (one's shoes, a surface).

scuffle /'skʌfl/ v [I] take part in a rough struggle. scuffle n [C].

sculpt = SCULPTURE.

sculptor /'skʌlptə(r)/ (fem sculptress) n [C] person who makes sculptures.

sculpture /'skʌlptʃə(r)/ n **1** [U] art of making figures, statues, etc in stone, wood. **2** [C, U] (piece of) such work. sculpture (also sculpt /skʌlpt/) v [I, T] make (a sculpture).

scum /skʌm/ n **1** [U] froth that forms on the surface of some liquids; layer of dirt on water. **2** [pl] (fig derog) people regarded as worthy of contempt.

scurry /'skʌrɪ/ v (pt, pp -ied) [I] run with short quick steps. scurry n [U, sing] movement or sound of scurrying.

scythe /saɪð/ n [U] tool with a long handle and a curved blade, used for cutting grass, etc. scythe v [I, T] cut (as if) with a scythe.

sea /siː/ n **1** the sea [U] salt water that covers most of the earth's surface. **2** [C] (in proper names) particular area of the sea, sometimes surrounded by land **3** [sing] movement of the sea: a heavy/ calm ~. **4** [sing] large amount (of sth) covering a large area: a ~ of corn. **5** (idm) at sea (a) on a ship, etc on the sea. (b) unable to cope or understand. by sea in a ship. go to sea become a sailor. put to sea leave port on a ship, etc. 'seaboard n [C] coastal region. 'seafaring /-feərɪŋ/ adj, n [U] (of) work or voyages on the sea. 'seafood n [U] fish, shellfish, etc from the sea used as food. 'sea front n [C, U] part of a town facing the sea. 'seagoing adj (of ships) built for crossing the sea. 'seagull n [C] = GULL. 'sea-horse n [C] small fish with a head like a horse. sea-legs n [pl] ability to travel on a ship without being seasick. 'sea-level n [sing] level of the sea used as a basis for measuring the height of land. 'sea-lion n [C] large seal. 'seaman n [C] sailor. 'seamanship n [U] skill in controlling a ship. 'sea-shore n [U] land close to the sea. 'seasick adj feeling sick from the motion of a ship. 'seaside n [U] place by the sea, esp a holiday resort. 'seaward adj, adv towards the sea. 'seaweed n [U] plant growing in the sea, esp on rocks at its edge. 'seaworthy adj (of a ship) fit for a voyage.

seal[1] /siːl/ *n* [C] sea-animal with flippers. **'sealskin** *n* [U] skin of a seal, used for clothing.

seal[2] /siːl/ *n* [C] **1 (a)** piece of wax, etc stamped with a design, attached to a document to show that it is genuine, or to a letter, etc to stop it coming open. **(b)** piece of metal, etc with a design used for stamping a seal on wax, etc. **2** something that prevents gas, liquid, etc escaping through a hole, etc. **3** (idm) **seal of approval** formal approval. **seal** *v* [T] **1** put a seal(1a) on. **2** stick or fasten tightly. **3** (*fml*) settle; decide: ~ *a bargain* ○ ~ *sb's fate*. **4** (phr v) **seal sth off** prevent anyone from entering or leaving (an area, etc): *Police* ~*ed off the building.*

seam /siːm/ *n* [C] **1** line where two edges, eg of cloth, are joined or sewn together. **2** layer of coal, etc in a mine.

seance /'seɪɑːns/ *n* [C] meeting where people try to talk to the spirits of the dead.

search /sɜːtʃ/ *v* [I, T] examine or look at (sb/sth) carefully to find sth: ~ (*her pockets*) *for money.* **search** *n* [C] **1** act of searching. **2** (idm) **in search of** searching for. **searching** *adj* **(a)** (of a look) taking in all the details. **(b)** (of a test, etc) thorough. **'searchlight** *n* [C] powerful light that can be turned in any direction. **'search-party** *n* [C] group of people formed to search for sb/sth. **'search-warrant** *n* [C] official document allowing a building, etc to be searched by police, etc.

season /'siːzn/ *n* [C] **1** division of the year made according to its kind of weather, ie spring, summer, autumn and winter. **2** period when something typically happens: *the rainy* ~. **3** (idm) **in/out of season** (of fruit, etc) available/not available. **season** *v* [T] **1** make suitable for use: ~*ed wood* ○ (*fig*) *a* ~*ed* (ie experienced) *politician.* **2** flavour (food) with salt, pepper, etc. **seasonable** /-əbl/ *adj* **(a)** (of weather) expected at the time of year. **(b)** (of help, etc) coming at the right time. **seasonal** *adj* happening during a particular season: ~ *trade.* **seasonally** *adv.* **seasoning** *n* [U] herb, spice, etc used to season food. **'season-ticket** *n* [C] ticket that can be used many times within a stated period of time.

seat /siːt/ *n* [C] **1** something used for sitting on, eg a chair. **2** part of a chair, etc on which one sits. **3** place where one pays to sit in a

vehicle, hall etc: *There are no* ~*s left for the concert.* **4** the buttocks; the clothing covering them: *the* ~ *of his trousers.* **5** place where an activity goes on: *the* ~ *of government.* **6** place as a member of a council, parliament, etc. **7** (idm) **have/take a** ~ sit down. **seat** *v* [T] **1** (*fml*) make (sb) sit: *please be seated,* ie sit down. **2** have seats for: *The cinema* ~*s 200.* **'seat-belt** *n* [C] strap fastened across a passenger in a car or aircraft. **seating** *n* [U] seats.

secateurs /'sekətɜːz/ *n* [pl] strong scissors used in the garden for cutting twigs, etc.

secede /sɪ'siːd/ *v* [I] *from*/ (of a group) withdraw (from an organization, etc). **secession** /sɪ'seʃn/ *n* [C, U] (instance of) seceding.

secluded /sɪ'kluːdɪd/ *adj* not visited by many people; isolated. **seclusion** /sɪ'kluːʒn/ *n* [U] being secluded; privacy.

second[1] /'sekənd/ *adj* **1** next after the first: *the* ~ *person to come.* **2** additional; another: *a* ~ *pair of shoes.* **3** (idm) **second to none** as good as the best: *As a writer, she's* ~ *to none.* **second** *adv* in the second place: *come (in)* ~ *in a race.* **,second-'best** *n, adj* next after the best. **,second-'class** *adj, adv* of or by a class not as good as the best. **,second-'hand** *adj* **(a)** previously owned by somebody else. **(b)** (of news, etc) obtained from a source other than the origin. **secondly** *adv* (in giving a list) as second item, etc; furthermore. **,second 'nature** *n* [U] habit that has become instinctive. **,second-'rate** *adj* not of the best quality. **,second 'thoughts** *n* [pl] different decision reached after further thought.

second[2] /'sekənd/ *n* **1 the second** [sing] person or thing after the first: *the* ~ *to leave.* **2** [C, usu pl] manufactured item not of the best quality and thus sold cheaper. **3 seconds** [pl] second helping of food. **4** [C] (*Brit*) university examination result of the class next after the highest.

second[3] /'sekənd/ *n* [C] **1** sixtieth part of a minute or of a degree(3). **2** (*infml*) short time; moment: *Wait a* ~*!* **'second hand** *n* [C] hand on a watch or clock recording seconds.

second[4] /'sekənd/ *v* [T] (in a debate) formally support (a proposal). **seconder** *n* person who seconds a motion at a meeting.

second[5] /sɪ'kɒnd/ *v* [T] move (sb) from his/her normal duties to special duties. **secondment** *n* [U].

secondary /'sekəndrɪ/ adj 1 (of a school or education) for children over eleven. 2 less important: of ~ interest. 3 developing from something else: a ~ infection.

secrecy /'si:krəsɪ/ n [U] keeping secrets; state of being secret.

secret /'si:krɪt/ adj 1 (to be kept from the knowledge or view of others: ~ information. 2 not declared or admitted: a ~ admirer. 3 (of places) quiet and unknown; secluded. **secret** n [C] 1 something that is secret. 2 unknown cause or explanation: the ~ of her success. 3 mystery: the ~ s of nature. 4 (idm) **in secret** secretly. **secret 'agent** n [C] member of a secret service; spy. **secretly** adv. **secret 'service** n [C] government department concerned with spying.

secretariat /ˌsekrə'teərɪət/ n [C] department concerned with running a large organization.

secretary /'sekrətrɪ; US -rəterɪ/ n [C] 1 employee who types letters, makes arrangements and appointments, etc. 2 official of a society, club, etc in charge of the correspondence, records, etc. **secretarial** /ˌsekrə'teərɪəl/ adj. **Secretary of State** n (a) [C] (Brit) head of a government department. (b) [sing] (US) head of the Foreign Affairs department.

secrete /sɪ'kri:t/ v [T] 1 (of the body) produce (a liquid, eg saliva). 2 hide: ~ money in a drawer. **secretion** /sɪ'kri:ʃn/ n 1 [U] process of secreting(1). 2 [C] liquid produced in the body.

secretive /'si:krətɪv/ adj liking to hide one's thoughts or keep things secret. **secretively** adv.

sect /sekt/ n [C] group of people sharing the same (esp religious) beliefs. **sectarian** /sek'teərɪən/ adj of a sect.

section /'sekʃn/ n [C] 1 one of the parts into which something is or can be divided. 2 department of an organization, etc. 3 view or drawing of something seen as if cut through from top to bottom. **sectional** (a) made in sections(1). (b) of sections of a community, etc.

sector /'sektə(r)/ n [C] 1 branch of industry, etc): the private/public ~. 2 division of an area, esp for control of military operations.

secular /'sekjʊlə(r)/ adj not religious or spiritual: ~ education.

secure /sɪ'kjʊə(r)/ adj 1 free from worry, doubt, etc. 2 certain: a ~ job. 3 (from/against)|| safe. 4 unlikely to break, fall, etc; fastened tightly: a ~ grip. **secure** v [T] 1 close tightly: ~ all the doors. 2

(from/against)|| make safe. 3 (fml) succeed in getting: ~ a job. **securely** adv.

security /sɪ'kjʊərətɪ/ n (pl -ies) 1 [U] safety, freedom from danger or worry. 2 [U] measures to prevent attacks, spying, etc: tight ~ at the airport. 3 [C, U] something valuable used as a guarantee, eg that a loan will be repaid. 4 [C, usu pl] document showing ownership of property.

sedan /sɪ'dæn/ n (US) = SALOON 3.

sedate /sɪ'deɪt/ adj calm and dignified. **sedately** adv.

sedation /sɪ'deɪʃn/ n [U] treatment using sedatives.

sedative /'sedətɪv/ n [C], adj (medicine) used to calm the nerves or make sb sleep.

sedentary /'sedntrɪ; US -terɪ/ adj 1 (of work) done sitting down. 2 (of people) spending much of their time seated.

sediment /'sedɪmənt/ n [U] matter (eg sand) that settles to the bottom of a liquid. **sedimentary** /-'mentrɪ/ adj.

seduce /sɪ'dju:s/ v [T] 1 persuade (sb) to have sexual intercourse. 2 persuade (sb) to do wrong. **seduction** /sɪ'dʌkʃn/ n [C, U]. **seductive** /sɪ'dʌktɪv/ adj very attractive.

see¹ /si:/ v (pt saw /sɔ:/, pp ~ n /si:n/) 1 [I] (often with can, could) have the power of sight: If you shut your eyes you can't ~. 2 [T] (often with can, could) become aware of (sb/sth) by using the eyes: He couldn't ~ her in the crowd. 3 [T] watch (a film, TV programme, etc): What did you ~ at the theatre last night? 4 [T] (imperative) look at: S ~ page 4. 5 [T] understand: He didn't ~ the joke. 6 [T] find out; learn: I'll go and ~ if she's there. 7 [T] consult; visit: ~ a doctor. 8 [T] meet: I don't ~ her often now. 9 [T] ensure; check: ~ that the windows are shut. 10 [T] escort (sb): Will you ~ him home? 11 (idm) let me see I'm trying to find/remember (sth). (you) see (you) understand: She couldn't come, (you) see, because she was ill. (not) see eye to 'eye with sb (not) agree with sb. ,see for one'self check sth to be convinced. see how the 'land lies see what the situation is like. ,seeing is 'believing one needs to actually see something to believe it exists or happens. see the 'light (a) begin to understand. (b) accept a (religious) belief. see 'red become very angry. see 'sense become reasonable. be 'seeing

things think one sees things that are not really there. **12** (phr v) **see about sth** deal with sth. **see sb about sth** take advice. **see sth in sb/sth** find sb/sth interesting or attractive. **see sb off** go to a railway station, etc with sb who is leaving. **see through sb/sth** not be deceived by. **see sth through** continue sth until it is finished. **see to sth** attend to sth.

see² /siː/ *n* [C] (*fml*) district for which a bishop is responsible; bishop's position.

seed /siːd/ *n* **1** [C] part of a plant from which a new plant can grow. **2** [U] quantity of these for planting, etc. **3** [C, usu pl] origin of a development, etc: *the ~s of doubt.* **4** [C] (esp in tennis) seeded(4) player. **5** (idm) **go/run to seed (a)** (of a plant) stop flowering as seed is produced. **(b)** (of a person) begin to look untidy, scruffy, old, etc. **seed** *v* **1** [I] (of a plant) produce seed. **2** [T] sow (soil, etc) with seed. **3** [T] (esp in tennis) list competitors according to who is most likely to win. **seedless** *adj* having no seeds. **seedling** *n* [C] young plant grown from a seed.

seedy /siːdɪ/ *adj* (**-ier, -iest**) **1** looking worn, shabby, neglected, etc. **2** (*infml*) unwell: *feel ~.* **seediness** *n* [U].

seek /siːk/ *v* (*pt, pp* **sought** /sɔːt/) (*fml*) **1** [I, T] look for (sb/sth). **2** [T] ask for: *~ advice.* **3** [T] (*fml*) try: *~ to end the conflict.*

seem /siːm/ *v* [I] give the appearance of being or doing sth: *This book ~s interesting.* **seeming** *adj* appearing to be sth, but perhaps not really so: *her ~ing friendliness.* **seemingly** *adv.*

seemly /siːmlɪ/ *adj* (**-ier, -iest**) (of behaviour) proper or correct.

seen *pp* of **SEE¹**.

seep /siːp/ *v* [I] (of liquids) come slowly through sth: *water ~ing through the cracks.* **seepage** /-ɪdʒ/ *n* [U] process of seeping; liquid that seeps.

see-saw /siːsɔː/ *n* **1** [C] long plank supported in the middle, with a person sitting at each end, rising and falling in turn. **2** [sing] up-and-down or to-and-fro movement. **see-saw** *v* [I] move up and down.

seethe /siːð/ *v* [I] **1** be very excited, agitated or angry: *~ing (with rage) at his behaviour.* **2** (of a liquid) move and bubble as if boiling.

segment /segmənt/ *n* [C] **1** part of something, esp of a circle, marked off or cut off. **2** section of an orange, lemon, etc.

segregate /segrɪgeɪt/ *v* [T] put (people of a different race, etc) apart from the rest of the community. **segregation** /segrɪgeɪʃn/ *n* [U].

seismic /saɪzmɪk/ *adj* of earthquakes.

seize /siːz/ *v* **1** [T] take hold of (sb/sth) suddenly and with force. **2** [I, T] see and use (an opportunity, etc): *~ a chance to get revenge.* **3** (phr v) **seize up** (of machinery) become stuck and stop working.

seizure /siːʒə(r)/ *n* **1** [C, U] (act of) seizing. **2** [C] sudden attack of illness.

seldom /seldəm/ *adv* not often; rarely.

select /sɪˈlekt/ *v* [T] choose the most suitable, best, etc. **select** *adj* **1** carefully chosen. **2** (of a meeting, etc) limited to people of a certain type: *a ~ audience.* **selection** /-kʃn/ *n* **1** [U] choosing. **2** [C] group of selected things; number of things from which to select. **selective** *adj* **(a)** affecting certain things only. **(b)** tending to choose carefully.

self /self/ *n* (*pl* **selves** /selvz/) *n* [C, U] one's own nature; one's personality.

self- /self-/ *prefix* of, to or by oneself or itself. **self-as'sured** *adj* confident. **self-'catering** *adj* (of holiday accommodation) with no meals provided, so one must cook for oneself. **self-'centred** *adj* thinking too much about oneself. **self-'confident** *adj* confident in one's own ability. **self-'confidence** *n* [U]. **self-'conscious** *adj* nervous or embarrassed because one is aware of being watched by others. **self-'consciousness** *n* [U]. **self-con'tained** *adj* **(a)** (of a person) not depending on others; not showing one's feelings. **(b)** (esp of a flat) having no shared facilities. **self-con'trol** *n* [U] control of one's own feelings, behaviour, etc. **self-de'fence** *n* [U] defence of one's own body, property, etc. **self-em'ployed** *adj* working independently, not for an employer. **self-es'teem** *n* [U] good opinion of oneself, one's abilities, etc. **self-'evident** *adj* obvious; without need for proof. **self-'help** *n* [U] using one's own efforts, resources, etc to achieve things, without the help of others. **self-im'portant** *adj* (*derog*) having too high an opinion of oneself. **self-im'portance** *n* [U] (*derog*). **self-in'dulgent** *adj* (derog) too willing to allow oneself what one enjoys a lot. ,self-in'dulgence n [U]. ,self-'interest n [U] (concern for) one's own personal advantage. ,self-'pity n [U] (usu derog) pity for oneself. ,self-re'liant adj not depending on others. ,self-re'liance n [U]. ,self-re'spect n [U] feeling that one need not be ashamed of one's character, abilities, etc. ,self-'righteous adj convinced that one's behaviour, beliefs are better than other people's. ,self-'sacrifice n [U] giving up things one has or wants, esp to help others. 'self-same adj identical. ,self-'satisfied adj (derog) too pleased with oneself and one's achievements. ,self-'service n [U] system in which buyers collect goods themselves and pay at a special desk. ,self-suf'ficient adj able to fulfil one's own needs. ,self-'willed adj determined to do what one wants; stubborn.

selfish /'selfɪʃ/ adj (derog) thinking mainly of oneself and one's own needs, not of others. selfishly adv. selfishness n [U].

sell /sel/ v (pt, pp sold /səʊld/) 1 [I, T] give (sth) to sb in exchange for money. 2 [T] keep stocks for sale: Do you ~ needles? 3 [I] be sold; find buyers: Does this book ~ well? 4 [T] cause (sth) to be sold: Scandals ~ newspapers. 5 [T] persuade sb to accept (sth) as good, useful, true, etc: ~ sb an idea. 6 [T] ~ oneself (a) present oneself, one's ideas, etc in a way which is attractive to others. (b) accept money, etc for doing something bad. 7 (idm) sell sb/sth short not recognize the true value of sth/sb. sell one's soul (to the devil) do sth dishonourable for money. 8 (phr v) sell sth off sell cheaply. sell out (a) sell all of sth, eg tickets. (b) be disloyal. sell up sell one's house, business, etc, eg when retiring.

Sellotape /'seləʊteɪp/ n [U] (Brit P) thin, clear, sticky plastic tape used for joining, mending, etc things: mend a torn map with S~.

selves pl of SELF.

semantics /sɪ'mæntɪks/ n [U] study of the meanings of words.

semaphore /'seməfɔː(r)/ n [U] system of sending signals by holding two flags in various positions. semaphore v [I, T] send a (message) by semaphore.

semblance /'sembləns/ n [sing, U] appearance: create a/some ~ of order.

semen /'siːmən/ n [U] whitish li-

quid containing sperm, produced by male animals.

semi- /'semɪ-/ prefix half; partially: ~-literate. 'semicircle n [C] half a circle. 'semicolon n [C] the punctuation mark (;). 'semiconductor n [C] substance that conducts electricity under certain conditions. ,semi-de'tached adj (of a house) joined to another by a shared wall. ,semi'final n [C] either of two matches before the final.

seminar /'semɪnɑː(r)/ n [C] small group of students meeting for study.

senate /'senɪt/ n [C, also sing with pl v] 1 upper house of the law-making assembly in the US, France, etc. 2 governing council of some universities. senator (also Senator) n [C] member of a senate(1).

send /send/ v (pt, pp sent /sent/) [T] 1 cause to go or be taken: ~ a letter. 2 cause to move quickly: The explosion sent them running. 3 make sb enter a particular state: ~ sb to sleep. 4 (idm) send sb one's love ⇨ LOVE. 5 (phr v) send away for sth write and ask for sth to be sent to one by post. send sb away tell sb to leave. send for sb/sth ask or order that sb should come, or sth be brought send off for sth = SEND AWAY FOR STH. send sth out (a) give out: The sun ~s out light. (b) produce: plants that ~ out shoots. send sb/sth up (infml) make sb/sth seem funny. 'send-off n [C] act of saying goodbye to sb.

senile /'siːnaɪl/ adj weak in body or mind as a result of old age. senility /sɪ'nɪlətɪ/ n [U].

senior /'siːnɪə(r)/ adj 1 (to) higher in rank; older. 2 Senior (of a parent) having the same name as one's child. senior n 1 [sing] person who is a certain number of years older than sb else: He is three years her ~. 2 [C, usu pl] older school pupil. ,senior 'citizen n [C] person over the age of retirement; old-age pensioner. seniority /ˌsiːnɪ'ɒrətɪ/ n [U] condition of being senior.

sensation /sen'seɪʃn/ n 1 [C, U] ability to feel; feeling. 2 [C, U] (cause of a) state of great excitement, surprise, etc. sensational adj (a) causing or intended to cause a sensation(2). (b) (infml) wonderful; very good.

sense /sens/ n 1 [C] power (sight, hearing, smell, taste and touch) by which a person is conscious of things. 2 [pl] ability to think reasonably: take leave of one's ~s, ie become mad. **3** [sing] understanding of the nature or value of sth: *a ~ of humour.* **4** [C] vague feeling: *a ~ of dread.* **5** [U] good practical judgement: *There's no ~ in doing that.* **6** [C] meaning of a word, etc. **7** (idm) **make sense (a)** have a meaning that can be understood. **(b)** be sensible. **make sense of sth** understand sth. **sense** *v* [T] become aware of; feel: *~ danger.*

senseless /'senslɪs/ *adj* **1** foolish. **2** unconscious. **senselessly** *adv.* **senselessness** *n* [U].

sensibility /ˌsensə'bɪlətɪ/ *n* [C, usu pl] ability to feel and receive delicate impressions.

sensible /'sensəbl/ *adj* **1** having or showing good sense(5); practical: *a ~ person/idea.* **2** ~ *of sth/ (fml)* aware of sth. **sensibly** *adv.*

sensitive /'sensətɪv/ *adj* **1** (*to*)// easily hurt or damaged (by sth): *~ skin ○ ~ to light.* **2** easily offended or upset: *~ about his baldness.* **3** (*approv*) having or showing delicate feeling or understanding: *a ~ friend.* **4** (of instruments) able to record very small changes. **5** requiring great care: *a ~ issue.* **sensitivity** *n* [U] quality or degree of being sensitive.

sensitize /'sensɪtaɪz/ *v* [T] (*to*)// make sensitive.

sensual /'senʃʊəl/ *adj* **1** of the pleasures of the senses(1). **2** enjoying physical, esp sexual, pleasures. **sensuality** /ˌ-'ælətɪ/ *n* [U] enjoyment of sensual pleasures.

sensuous /'senʃʊəs/ *adj* affecting or giving pleasure to the senses(1). **sensuously** *adv.* **sensuousness** *n* [U].

sent *pt, pp* of SEND.

sentence /'sentəns/ *n* **1** [C] (*grammar*) group of words that express a statement, question, etc. **2** [C, U] (statement of the) punishment given by a lawcourt. **sentence** *v* [T] state that sb is to have a certain punishment: *~ sb to death.*

sentiment /'sentɪmənt/ *n* **1** [U, C, usu pl] (expression of an) attitude or opinion. **2** [U] (usu *derog*) (display of) emotional feelings. **3** sentiments [pl] opinion.

sentimental /ˌsentɪ'mentl/ *adj* **1** emotional. **2** (usu *derog*) feeling or causing too much emotion. **sentimentality** /ˌ-'tælətɪ/ *n* [U] the quality of being very sentimental. **sentimentally** *adv.*

sentry /'sentrɪ/ *n* [C] (*pl* -ies) soldier keeping guard.

separate[1] /'seprət/ *adj* **1** divided; not joined: *~ rooms.* **2** different: *on three ~ occasions.* **separately**

adv.

separate[2] /'sepəreɪt/ *v* **1** [I, T] (cause to) come apart; divide. **2** [I] stop living together as husband and wife. **separation** /ˌ-'reɪʃn/ *n* **1** [U] separating or being separated. **2** [C] period of living apart from sb. **3** [U, sing] (*law*) legal agreement by a married couple to live apart.

September /sep'tembə(r)/ *n* [U, C] ninth month of the year. (See examples of use at *April*).

septic /'septɪk/ *adj* infected with harmful germs: *a ~ wound.*

sepulchre (*US* **sepulcher**) /'seplkə(r)/ *n* [C] (*arch*) tomb, esp one cut in rock.

sequel /'siːkwəl/ *n* [C] **1** thing that happens as a result of an earlier event. **2** film, etc continuing the story of an earlier one.

sequence /'siːkwəns/ *n* [C, U] succession of events, actions, etc.

sequin /'siːkwɪn/ *n* [C] small shiny disc sewn on to dresses, etc for decoration.

serene /sɪ'riːn/ *adj* calm and peaceful. **serenely** *adv.* **serenity** /sɪ'renətɪ/ *n* [U].

sergeant /'sɑːdʒənt/ *n* [C] **1** non-commissioned army officer of middle rank. **2** police officer below an inspector in rank.

serial /'sɪərɪəl/ *n* [C] story, etc broadcast or published in parts. **serial** *adj* of or forming a series. **serialize** /ˌ-aɪz/ *v* [T] produce (a story, etc) in parts for the television, a magazine, etc. **'serial number** *n* [C] number identifying an item in series, eg on a banknote.

series /'sɪəriːz/ *n* [C] (*pl* **series**) group of related things, events, etc, occurring one after the other.

serious /'sɪərɪəs/ *adj* **1** not funny; thoughtful: *a ~ face.* **2** (of books, music, etc) intended to make people think. **3** important because of possible danger: *a ~ illness.* **4** (*about*)// sincere: *Are you ~ about this plan?* **seriously** *adv.* **seriousness** *n* [U].

sermon /'sɜːmən/ *n* [C] speech on religious or moral matters, esp one given in a church.

serpent /'sɜːpənt/ *n* [C] (*dated* or *poet*) snake.

serrated /se'reɪtɪd/ *adj* having a row of teeth(2) on the edge.

serum /'sɪərəm/ *n* (*pl* ~s *or* **sera** /'sɪərə/) *n* [C, U] (dose of) liquid which fights disease, injected into a person's blood.

servant /'sɜːvənt/ *n* [C] person who works in sb's household for wages.

serve /sɜːv/ *v* **1** [I, T] work for

(sb), esp as a servant. 2 [I, T] perform duties (for): ~ *on a committee.* 3 [I, T] (a) give food to (sb) at a meal. (b) attend to (customers) in a shop. 4 [T] provide (sb/sth) with sth needed: *This bus ~s our area.* 5 [I] (*for/as sth*)// be suitable for a purpose: *This room ~s as a study.* 6 [T] spend (a period of time) in prison: ~ *a life sentence.* 7 [T] (*law*) deliver (an official order, etc). 8 [I, T] (in tennis, etc) begin to play by hitting the ball to one's opponent. 9 (idm) **serve sb right** (of a misfortune, etc) be deserved by sb. **serve** *n* [C] act of serving(8). **server** *n* person who serves(8). **serving** *n* [C] amount of food for one person.

service /'sɜːvɪs/ *n* 1 [U] performing duties: *ten years' ~ in the army.* 2 [U] work done by a vehicle: *This car has given good ~*, ie has been reliable. 3 [U] serving customers in hotels, restaurants, etc. 4 [C] system or business that meets public needs: *a 'bus ~.* 5 [C, usu pl] thing done to help others. 6 [C] department of government. 7 [C] branch of the armed forces. 8 [C] form of religious worship or prayer. 9 [C] complete set of plates, etc. 10 [C, U] maintenance or repair of a car, machine, etc after sale. 11 [C] (in tennis) act or manner of serving the ball. 12 (idm) **at your service** ready to help you. **of service** useful or helpful. **service** *v* [T] maintain (a car, machine, etc) after sale. **serviceable** *adj* fit for use. **'service charge** *n* [C] additional charge on a bill for service in a restaurant, etc. **'serviceman** /-mən/ *n* [C] (*pl* **-men** /-mən/, *fem* **servicewoman** /-wʊmən/, *pl* **-women** /-wɪmɪn/) person serving in the armed forces. **'service station** *n* [C] = PETROL STATION (PETROL).

serviette /ˌsɜːvɪ'et/ *n* = NAPKIN.

session /'seʃn/ *n* [C] 1 meeting or series of meetings of a parliament, lawcourt, etc. 2 year or term at school or university. 3 period spent in one activity: *a re'cording ~.*

set¹ /set/ *n* 1 [C] group of things of the same kind that belong together. 2 [C] television or radio receiver. 3 [C, also sing with pl v] group of people who spend a lot of time together or have similar interests. 4 [C] scenery for a play, film, etc. 5 [C] division of a tennis match. 6 [C] act of styling hair.

set² /set/ *v* (*-tt-, pt, pp* **set, -tt-**) 1 [T] move, put or place in a position: ~ *a tray down on the table.* 2 [T]

cause (sb/sth) to be in a specified state: ~ *a prisoner free.* 3 [T] cause (sb/sth) to begin doing sth: ~ *sb thinking.* 4 [T] present or impose (a task, etc): ~ *an examination.* 5 [T] adjust (sth) so that it is ready for use: ~ *the controls.* 6 [T] arrange plates, knives, forks, etc on a table ready for a meal. 7 [T] fix; arrange: ~ *a date for the wedding.* 8 [T] fix one thing firmly in another. 9 [I, T] (cause to) become firm or solid: *The cement has ~.* 10 [T] put in a certain state or position: ~ *a broken bone,* ie put it in the right position to mend. 11 [T] (*to*)// provide music for (words, a poem, etc). 12 [I] (of the sun or moon) go down. 13 (idm) **set an 'example** offer a good standard for others to follow. **set 'eyes on** see. **set 'foot in** enter. **set 'light/'fire to sth, set sth on 'fire** cause sth to start burning. **set one's 'heart on sth** want sth very much. **set one's mind to sth** ⇨ MIND¹. **set sth right** ⇨ RIGHT¹. **set sb/sth to rights** ⇨ RIGHT³. **set sail** begin a voyage. **set the 'scene** describe a place where sth is about to happen. **set sb's 'teeth on edge** (esp of a sharp sound or taste) annoy or displease sb. 14 (phr v) **set about sb** attack sb. **set about** begin sth. **set sb back** (*infml*) cost sb. **set sb/sth back** delay the progress of sb/sth. **set sth back (from)** place sth at a slight distance, eg from a road. **set in** start and seem likely to continue. **set off** begin a journey, etc. **set sth off** (a) cause (a bomb, etc) to explode. (b) cause (sth) to begin. (c) make (sth) look attractive: *This colour ~s off her eyes.* **set on sb** attack. **set out to do sth** have sth as an aim. **set sth out** (a) arrange. (b) express in an orderly way: ~ *out one's ideas in an essay.* **set to** begin doing sth. **set sth up** (a) place sth in position. (b) establish (a business, etc). **set (oneself) up as** (a) go into business as. (b) claim to be. **'set-back** *n* [C] something that delays progress or development. **'set-up** *n* [C] (*infml*) structure of an organization.

set³ /set/ *adj* 1 (*infml*) ready: ~ *to go.* 2 (*on*)// determined: *She's ~ on winning.* 3 unmoving; not changing, fixed: *a ~ grin* ○ ~ *ideas about sth.* 4 (idm) **set in one's ways** unwilling to change one's habits. **set book** *n* [C] book fixed for study at school, university, etc.

set-square /'set skweə(r)/ *n* [C]

triangular instrument used for drawing lines at certain angles.

settee /se'ti:/ n [C] = SOFA.

setter /'setə(r)/ n [C] breed of long-haired dog.

setting /'setɪŋ/ n 1 [C] place in which sth is fixed. 2 [C] surroundings: *a rural ~*. 3 [C] height, speed, etc at which a machine, etc is or can be set. 4 [sing] descent (of the sun, etc).

settle /'setl/ v 1 [I, T] make one's permanent home in a place. 2 [I] come to rest: *The bird ~d on a branch.* 3 [I, T] make (sb/oneself) comfortable: *~d (back) in the chair.* 4 [I, T] pay (a debt). 5 [I, T] (cause to) become calm: *~ sb's nerves.* 6 [T] make an agreement about: *~ an argument.* 7 [I, T] (cause to) sink to a lower level: *dust settling on the floor* ○ *The rain ~d the dust.* 8 (phr v) **settle down** sit or lie comfortably. **settle (down) to sth** begin to give one's attention to sth. **settle for sth** accept sth that is not quite what you want. **settle (sb) in** (help sb to) become established in a new house, job, etc. **settle on sb/sth** decide to have sb/sth. **settled** *adj* not changing: *~d weather.* **settler** n [C] person who settles permanently in a place.

settlement /'setlmənt/ n 1 [C, U] (instance of) settling a dispute, debt, etc. 2 [C] (statement of) property given to a person. 3 [U, C] process of settling people in a place; place where they settle.

seven /'sevn/ *pron, adj,* n [C] 7. **seventh** /'sevnθ/ *pron, adj* 7th. **seventh** *pron,* n [C] ⅐.

seventeen /ˌsevn'ti:n/ *pron, adj,* n [C] 17. **seventeenth** /ˌsevn'ti:nθ/ *pron, adj* 17th. **seventeenth** *pron,* n [C] ⅟₁₇.

seventy /'sevntɪ/ *pron, adj,* n [C] 70. **seventieth** /'sevntɪəθ/ *pron, adj* 70th. **seventieth** *pron,* n [C] ⅟₇₀.

sever /'sevə(r)/ v 1 [T] cut (a part of sth from the rest): *~ a limb from the body.* 2 [T] (fig) end: *~ relations with sb.*

several /'sevrəl/ *adj, pron* three or more; some, but not many.

severe /sɪ'vɪə(r)/ *adj* 1 stern; strict: *~ discipline.* 2 very bad, difficult, intense, etc: *a ~ storm.* **severely** *adv.* **severity** /sɪ'verətɪ/ n 1 [U] quality of being severe. 2 **severities** [pl] severe treatment or experiences.

sew /səʊ/ v (*pt* ~**ed**, *pp* ~**n** /səʊn/) [I, T] 1 make stitches with a needle and thread; fasten (cloth, etc) with stitches. 2 (phr v) **sew sth up (a)** join or mend sth by sew-

ing. **(b)** (*infml*) settle sth.

sewage /'su:ɪdʒ/ n [U] waste matter from homes, factories, etc carried away by sewers.

sewer /'su:ə(r)/ n [C] underground pipe that carries sewage and rain-water away.

sewn *pt* of SEW.

sex /seks/ n 1 [U] state of being male or female. 2 [C] group of all male or all female people. 3 [U] (sexual activity leading to and including) sexual intercourse. **sexy** *adj* (-ier, -iest) sexually attractive. **sexily** *adv.* **sexiness** n [U].

sexism /'seksɪzəm/ n [U] prejudice against people (esp women) because of their sex. **sexist** *adj,* n [C].

sextant /'sekstənt/ n [C] instrument for measuring the altitude of the sun, etc.

sexton /'sekstən/ n [C] person who takes care of a church, churchyard, etc.

sexual /'sekʃʊəl/ *adj* of sex or the sexes. **sexual intercourse** n [U] physical union of two people often leading to the production of offspring. **sexuality** /-'ælətɪ/ n [U] sexual nature or characteristics; sexual attraction. **sexually** *adv.*

shabby /'ʃæbɪ/ *adj* (-ier, -iest) 1 in poor condition; poorly dressed. 2 (of behaviour) unfair; mean. **shabbily** *adv.*

shack /ʃæk/ n [C] small, crudely built shed or house.

shackle /'ʃækl/ n [C, usu pl] 1 one of a pair of metal rings linked by a chain, for fastening a prisoner's wrists or ankles. 2 (fig) anything that prevents freedom of action. **shackle** v [T] 1 put shackles on (sb). 2 (fig) prevent (sb) from acting freely.

shade /ʃeɪd/ n 1 [U] (place where there is) slight darkness; shelter from direct rays of light: *sit in the ~.* 2 [C] thing that reduces light: *a 'lamp~.* 3 **shades** [pl] (*infml*) sun-glasses. 4 [C] (depth of) colour: *four ~s of blue.* 5 [C] slight difference: *~s of meaning.* 6 **a shade** [sing] a slight amount: *a ~ warmer.* **shade** v 1 [T] keep direct light from: *~ one's eyes.* 2 [T] cover (a light) to reduce brightness. 3 [T] darken (parts of a drawing, etc). 4 [I] change gradually: *green shading into blue.*

shadow /'ʃædəʊ/ n 1 [C, U] (area of) shade caused by something which cuts out light: *the ~ of the tree on the grass.* 2 [C] dark area: *~s under the eyes.* 3 [U] shaded part of a picture. 4 **shadows** [pl] partial darkness. 5 [sing] a slight

trace of (sth): *not a ~ of doubt*.
shadow *v* [T] follow closely and watch the movements of (sb). **shadowy** *adj* 1 full of shade or shadow. 2 not clear; mysterious.
shady /ˈʃeɪdɪ/ *adj* (**-ier**, **-iest**) 1 giving shade from sunlight; situated in the shade. 2 (*infml*) not entirely honest: *a ~ character*.
shaft /ʃɑːft; *US* ʃæft/ *n* 1 long thin rod forming the body of an arrow, spear, etc. 2 handle of an axe or other tool. 3 either of two poles between which a horse is fastened to a cart, etc. 4 long passage going down, eg for entering a coal-mine. 5 rod joining parts of a machine. 6 ray of light, etc.
shaggy /ˈʃægɪ/ *adj* (**-ier**, **-iest**) 1 (of hair) rough and untidy. 2 covered with rough, coarse hair.
shake[1] /ʃeɪk/ *v* (*pt* **shook** /ʃʊk/, *pp* ~**n** /ˈʃeɪkən/) 1 [I, T] (cause to) move quickly from side to side, up and down, etc. 2 [I] (of sb's voice) tremble. 3 [T] trouble; shock: *We were ~n by his death*. 4 (idm) **shake hands** (**with sb**), **shake sb's hand** take sb's hand and move it up and down as a greeting. **shake one's head** move one's head from side to side to indicate 'no' or to show doubt, etc. 5 (phr v) **shake sb/sth off** free oneself from sb/sth. **shake sth up** mix well by shaking. **'shake-up** *n* [C] major reorganization of a company, etc. **shakily** /-əlɪ/ *adv*. **shaky** *adj* (**-ier**, **-iest**) (a) (of a person) weak and trembling. (b) not firm and steady.
shake[2] /ʃeɪk/ *n* [C, usu sing] act of shaking.
shale /ʃeɪl/ *n* [U] soft rock that splits easily.
shall /ʃəl; strong form ʃæl/ *modal v* (*neg* **shall not**, *contracted form* **shan't** /ʃɑːnt/, *pt* **should** /ʃʊd/, *neg* **should not**, *contracted form* **shouldn't** /ˈʃʊdnt/) 1 (used to express the future tense): *We ~/ We'll arrive tomorrow.* 2 (*fml*) (used to express obligation or determination): *You ~ have a new bike for your birthday, I promise.* ○ *You shan't beat me so easily next time.* 3 (used to express offers or suggestions): *S~ I open the window?* 4 (used to express commands): *You '~ go with her.*
shallot /ʃəˈlɒt/ *n* [C] kind of small onion.
shallow /ˈʃæləʊ/ *adj* 1 not deep: *a ~ river*. 2 (*derog*) not serious: *a ~ thinker*. **shallowness** *n* [U]. **shallows** *n* [pl] shallow place in a river, etc.
sham /ʃæm/ *v* (**-mm-**) [I, T]

pretend (to be or to have): *~ ill-ness*. **sham** *n* 1 [C] person who shams; something intended to deceive. 2 [U] pretence. **sham** *adj* not real; pretended: *a ~ fight*.
shamble /ˈʃæmbl/ *v* [I] walk without lifting one's feet properly. **shamble** *n* [sing] shambling walk.
shambles /ˈʃæmblz/ *n* [sing] scene of disorder or confusion.
shame /ʃeɪm/ *n* 1 [U] sad feeling resulting from guilt, failure, bad behaviour, etc: *feel ~ at having told a lie*. 2 [U] ability to feel shame: *He has no ~*. 3 [U] dishonour: *bring ~ on one's family*. 4 [sing] something to be regretted: *It's/What a ~ you can't come*. 5 (idm) **put sb/sth to shame** be far superior to sb/sth. **shame** *v* 1 cause (sb) to feel shame(1). 2 bring shame(2) on (sb). 3 (phr v) **shame sb into/out of doing sth** cause sb to do/not to do sth by making him/her feel shame. **shamefaced** /ˌʃeɪmˈfeɪst/ *adj* looking ashamed. **shameful** *adj* causing shame; very bad. **shamefully** /-əlɪ/ *adv*. **shameless** *adj* having or showing no shame(2).
shampoo /ʃæmˈpuː/ *n* (a) [U, C] (type of) liquid, etc for washing the hair. (b) [C] act of washing the hair. **shampoo** *v* [T] wash (hair) with shampoo.
shamrock /ˈʃæmrɒk/ *n* [C, U] small plant with three leaves on each stem, the national emblem of Ireland.
shandy /ˈʃændɪ/ *n* [C, U] drink of beer mixed with lemonade.
shan't shall not. ⇨ **SHALL**.
shanty town /ˈʃæntɪ taʊn/ *n* [C], *n* [C] town or part of a town where poor people live in very bad conditions.
shape /ʃeɪp/ *n* 1 [C, U] outer form or outline: *a round ~*. 2 [U] (*infml*) condition; state: *She's in good ~*. 3 (idm) **get/put sth into shape** put sth into an orderly state. **take shape** take on a definite form. **shape** *v* 1 [T] give a shape to: (*fig*) *~ sb's character*. 2 [I] (*up*)// develop: *Our plans are shaping up well*. **shapeless** *adj* having no definite shape. **shapely** *adj* (**-ier**, **-iest**) (esp of a person) having a pleasing shape.
share /ʃeə(r)/ *n* 1 [C] part of something divided among several people. 2 [U, sing] person's part of sth received, done, etc by several people: *your ~ of the blame*. 3 [C] one of the equal parts into which the capital of a company is divided and which people buy as a way of

investing money. **share** v 1 [T] (*out*)// give a share (of sth) to others. 2 [I, T] (*with*)// have or use (sth) with another or others: ~ *a house with sb.* 3 [I, T] have a share; participate: ~ (*in*) *sb's joy.* '**shareholder** n [C] owner of shares(3). '**share-out** n [sing] act of sharing(1); distribution.

shark /ʃɑːk/ n [C] 1 large and dangerous fish. 2 (*infml derog*) person who cheats to gain money.

sharp /ʃɑːp/ adj 1 having a fine cutting edge or point: *a ~ knife.* 2 well-defined; clear: *a ~ outline.* 3 (of bends, etc) changing direction suddenly. 4 sudden: *a ~ rise/fall.* 5 (of sounds) shrill. 6 (of tastes) sour and slightly stinging. 7 causing a cutting or piercing feeling: *a ~ wind/pain.* 8 quickly aware of things; alert: ~ *eyes.* 9 harsh: ~ *words.* 10 (*music*) (a) (of an acceptable note) half a tone¹(5) higher than the preceding note. (b) higher than the true or acceptable note. 11 (*infml*) fashionable; smart: *a ~ dresser.* **sharp** n [C] (*music*) sharp(10) note. **sharp** adv 1 punctually: *at seven (o'clock) ~.* 2 abruptly: *turn ~ left.* 3 (*music*) higher than the true or acceptable note. **sharpen** v [I, T] (cause to) become sharp. **sharpener** n device that sharpens. **sharply** adv. **sharpness** n [U].

shatter /ˈʃætə(r)/ v 1 [I, T] break suddenly into small pieces. 2 [T] shock: ~ *ed by the bad news.* 3 [T] (*infml*) (usu passive) tire.

shave /ʃeɪv/ v 1 [I, T] cut (hair) off the face, etc with a razor or shaver. 2 [T] (*infml*) pass very close to (sth), almost touching. 3 (phr v) **shave sth off** (sth) remove (a thin layer) from a surface. **shave** n [C] act of shaving the face. **shaven** /ˈʃeɪvn/ adj shaved. **shaver** n [C] electric razor. **shavings** n [pl] thin pieces of wood which have been shaved off.

shawl /ʃɔːl/ n [C] large piece of material worn over a woman's shoulders or head or wrapped round a baby.

she /ʃiː/ pron (used as the subject of a v) female person or animal mentioned earlier: *My sister says ~ is going.*

sheaf /ʃiːf/ n [C] (pl **sheaves** /ʃiːvz/) 1 corn, etc tied into a bundle after it has been cut. 2 bundle of papers, etc tied together.

shear /ʃɪə(r)/ v (pt ~ **ed**, pp **shorn** /ʃɔːn/ or ~ **ed**) [T] cut the wool off (a sheep) with shears. **shears** n [pl] large instrument like scissors: *a pair of ~.*

sheath /ʃiːθ/ n [C] (pl ~ **s** /ʃiːðz/) 1 cover for a blade. 2 = CONDOM.

sheathe /ʃiːð/ v [T] put into a sheath(1).

sheaves pl of SHEAF.

shed¹ /ʃed/ n [C] small building, usually of wood, used for storing things, etc.

shed² /ʃed/ v (pt, pp shed, **-dd-**) [T] 1 let (leaves, etc) fall: *Flowers ~ their petals.* 2 (of blood) allow to pour out: ~ *tears,* ie cry. 3 take or throw off: ~ *one's clothes.* 4 send out: ~ *light.*

she'd /ʃiːd/ v 1 she had. ⇨ HAVE. 2 she would. ⇨ WILL¹, WOULD¹.

sheep /ʃiːp/ n [C] (pl **sheep**) grass-eating animal kept for food and for its wool. '**sheepdog** n [C] dog trained to look after sheep. '**sheepskin** n [C, U] (rug or coat of) sheep's skin with the wool on it. **sheepish** adj (feeling) foolish or embarrassed because of a fault.

sheer /ʃɪə(r)/ adj 1 complete: ~ *nonsense.* 2 (of cloth, etc) thin and light. 3 very steep: *a ~ drop.* **sheer** adv very steeply.

sheet /ʃiːt/ n [C] 1 rectangular piece of cotton cloth, used on a bed. 2 flat thin piece of a material: *a ~ of glass/paper.* 3 wide expanse (of water, ice, etc). '**sheet music** n [U] music printed on single sheets.

sheikh (also **sheik**) /ʃeɪk/ n [C] Arab chief or ruler.

shelf /ʃelf/ n [C] 1 flat piece of wood, etc attached to a wall, etc for things to stand on. 2 piece of rock like a shelf on a cliff face or underwater.

shell /ʃel/ n [C] 1 hard outer covering of eggs, nuts and some animals, eg snails. 2 outside walls of an unfinished building, ship, etc. 3 metal case filled with explosive, to be fired from a large gun. 4 (idm) **come out of one's shell** become less shy, quiet, etc. **shell** v [T] 1 take the shell(1) off. 2 fire shells(3) at. 3 (phr v) **shell out** (*infml*) pay. '**shellfish** n [C, U] (pl **shellfish**) sea animal(s), eg crabs, lobsters, with a shell(1).

she'll /ʃiːl/ she will. ⇨ WILL¹.

shelter /ˈʃeltə(r)/ n 1 [U] condition of being protected, eg from rain or danger. 2 [C] building, etc that gives shelter. **shelter** v 1 [I] give shelter to; protect. 2 [I] find a place that gives shelter: ~ *from the rain under a tree.*

shelve¹ /ʃelv/ v [T] 1 put (books, etc) on a shelf. 2 (*fig*) delay dealing with (a problem, project, etc).

shelve² /ʃelv/ v [I] (of land) slope gently.

shelves 380

shelves pl of SHELF.

shepherd /ˈʃepəd/ (fem **shepherdess** /ˌʃepəˈdes/, US 'sepərdis/) n [C] person who takes care of sheep. **shepherd** v [T] guide (people) like sheep. **shepherd's pie** n [C, U] dish of finely chopped meat with mashed potato on top.

sheriff /ˈʃerɪf/ n [C] (US) chief law officer in a county.

sherry /ˈʃerɪ/ n [U] yellow or brown wine from Spain, Cyprus, etc.

shied pt, pp of SHY².

shield¹ /ʃiːld/ n [C] 1 piece of metal, etc carried to protect the body when fighting. 2 drawing or model of a shield showing a coat of arms. 3 thing that protects sb operating a machine. **shield** v [T] protect.

shift¹ /ʃɪft/ n [C] 1 change of place, character, etc. 2 (period worked by a) group of workers which starts work as another group finishes.

shift² /ʃɪft/ v 1 [I, T] (cause to) change position or direction. 2 (infml) remove: ~ a stain.

shifty /ˈʃɪftɪ/ adj (-ier, -iest) not to be trusted. **shiftiness** n [U].

shilling /ˈʃɪlɪŋ/ n [C] (before 1971) British coin worth one twentieth of a pound.

shimmer /ˈʃɪmə(r)/ v [I] shine with a soft wavering light.

shin /ʃɪn/ n [C] front part of the leg below the knee. **shin** v (-nn-) (phr v) **shin up** (sth) climb (sth) fast.

shine /ʃaɪn/ v (pt, pp **shone** /ʃɒn/ or, in sense 3 ~ d) 1 [I] give out or reflect light. 2 [I] (in/at/) show great ability: She ~ s in English. 3 [T] (infml) polish: ~ shoes. **shine** n [sing, U] brightness; polished appearance: Give your shoes a ~. **shiny** adj (-ier, -iest) shining; bright.

shingle /ˈʃɪŋɡl/ n [U] area of small pebbles on a sea-shore. **shingly** /-ɡlɪ/ adj.

ship¹ /ʃɪp/ n [C] 1 large boat for passengers or cargo. 2 (infml) aircraft or spacecraft. **'shipmate** n [C] person belonging to the same crew. **'shipshape** adj tidy; in good order. **'shipwreck** n [C, U] loss or destruction of a ship at sea. **'shipwreck** v [T] (usu passive) cause to suffer shipwreck. **'shipyard** n [C] place where ships are built.

ship² /ʃɪp/ v (-pp-) [T] transport or send, esp in a ship. **shipment** n 1 [C] goods shipped. 2 [U] action of shipping. **shipper** n [C] person who arranges for goods to be shipped. **shipping** n [U] all the ships of

a country, port, etc.

shirk /ʃɜːk/ v [I, T] try to avoid (work, duty, etc), esp through laziness. **shirker** n [C].

shirt /ʃɜːt/ n [C] men's garment for the upper part of the body, with sleeves.

shirty /ˈʃɜːtɪ/ adj (-ier, -iest) (infml) annoyed; angry.

shit /ʃɪt/ n (△ sl) 1 [U] solid waste matter passed from the bowels. 2 [sing] act of emptying the bowels. 3 [C] (derog) unpleasant person. 4 (idm) **not give a shit (about sb/ sth)** not care at all. **shit** v (-tt-, pt, pp **shitted** or **shat** /ʃæt/) (△ sl) pass solid waste matter from the bowels. **shit** interj (△ sl) (used for showing anger or annoyance). **shitty** adj (-ier, -iest) (△ sl) nasty; disgusting.

shiver /ˈʃɪvə(r)/ v [I] tremble, esp with cold or fear. **shiver** n [C] act of shivering. **shivery** adj.

shoal¹ /ʃəʊl/ n [C] great number of fish swimming together.

shoal² /ʃəʊl/ n [C] shallow place in the sea.

shock¹ /ʃɒk/ n 1 [C] violent blow, caused by a crash, explosion, etc. 2 [C] effect caused by an electric current passing through the body. 3 [U, C] (condition or feeling caused by a) sudden very great surprise, fear, worry, etc. **shock** v [T] cause a shock(3) to. **shocking** adj (a) causing a shock(3): ~ ing behaviour. (b) (infml) very bad.

shod pt, pp of SHOE.

shoddy /ˈʃɒdɪ/ adj (-ier, -iest) of poor quality: ~ work.

shoe /ʃuː/ n [C] 1 outer covering of leather, etc for the foot which does not reach above the ankle. 2 (idm) **in sb's shoes** in sb's position. **shoe** v (pt, pp **shod** /ʃɒd/) fit (a horse) with horseshoes. **'shoelace** n [C] cord for fastening a shoe. **'shoe-string** n [C] (idm) **on a shoestring** with a very small amount of money.

shone pt, pp of SHINE.

shoo /ʃuː/ interj said to make animals or people, esp children, go away. **shoo** v [T] make (animals, etc) go away by saying 'shoo'.

shook pt of SHAKE¹.

shoot¹ /ʃuːt/ v (pt, pp **shot** /ʃɒt/) 1 (a) [I, T] aim and fire with a gun, bow and arrow, etc. (b) [T] kill or wound in this way. 2 [I, T] (cause to) move suddenly or quickly: Pain shot up his arm. 3 [I, T] photograph or film (an object or scene). 4 [I] (in football) try to score a goal. 5 [I] (of a plant) send out new buds, leaves, etc. 6 (idm) **shoot one's mouth off** (infml) talk indiscreetly. '**shooting-star** n [C] meteor.

shoot² /ʃuːt/ n [C] **1** young growth on a plant. **2** group of people shooting animals or birds for sport.

shop /ʃɒp/ n [C] **1** (esp *Brit*) (part of a) building where goods are sold. **2** workshop(1). **3** (idm) **talk shop** talk about one's work. **shop** v (-**pp-**) **1** [I] go to the shops to buy things: ~ *for presents.* **2** [T] (*Brit sl*) give information about (sb), eg to the police. **3** (phr v) **shop around** search carefully for goods giving best value. '**shop assistant** n [C] person serving in a shop. ,**shop-'floor** n [sing] area in a factory where goods are made. '**shopkeeper** n [C] owner of a (small) shop. '**shoplifter** n [C] person who steals things from shops. '**shoplifting** n [U]. ,**shop-'steward** n [C] official of a branch of a trade union elected by the workers. **shopper** n [C]. **shopping** n [U] **1** act of shopping: *go* ~ *ping.* **2** goods bought from shops.

shore¹ /ʃɔː(r)/ n [C] stretch of land along the edge of the sea or a lake.

shore² /ʃɔː(r)/ v (phr v) **shore sth up** support (sth) with a wooden beam, etc.

shorn pp of **SHEAR.**

short¹ /ʃɔːt/ adj **1** having a small extent in space or time: *a* ~ *journey.* **2** below the average height. **3** less than the required amount: *get* ~ *change.* **4** (of/i) (**a**) not having enough of sth: ~ *of money.* (**b**) distant from: *five miles* ~ *of our destination.* **5** on/i (*infml*) lacking in a certain quality: ~ *on tact.* **6** (*with/i*) speaking harshly to sb: *I was a little* ~ *with her.* **7** (idm) **for short** as an abbreviation. **in short** briefly. **in the short term** ⇨ **TERM. little/nothing short of** almost. **short cut** (**a**) route taken to shorten a journey, etc. (**b**) way of doing sth more quickly, efficiently, etc. '**shortbread** n [U] crumbly biscuit made with a lot of butter. ,**short-'change** v [T] cheat, esp by giving too little change. ,**short-'circuit** n [C] electrical fault causing current to flow the wrong way. ,**short-'circuit** v [I, T] (cause to) have a short-circuit. '**shortcoming** n [C] (usu pl) failure to reach the required standard; fault. '**shortfall** n [C] amount less than is needed. '**shorthand** n [U] system of writing quickly using special symbols. ,**short-'handed** adj not having enough workers, helpers, etc. '**short-list** n [C] list of candidates (eg for a job) selected from a larger group, from which the fi-

nal choice is to be made. '**short-list** v [T]. **short-lived** adj lasting for a short time. **shortness** n [U]. **short sight** n [U] inability to see distant objects clearly. ,**short-'sighted** adj (**a**) suffering from short sight. (**b**) (*fig*) not thinking about what may happen in the future. ,**short-'tempered** adj easily annoyed. ,**short-'term** adj of or for a short period of time. ,**short 'wave** n [U] radio wave with a wavelength of less than 100 metres.

short² /ʃɔːt/ adv **1** abruptly: *stop* ~. **2** (idm) **go short (of)** not have enough of sth. **short of** except: *do anything* ~ *of murder.*

short³ /ʃɔːt/ n [C] **1** small drink of strong alcohol. **2** short film.

shortage /'ʃɔːtɪdʒ/ n [C, U] lack of sth; state of not having enough.

shorten /'ʃɔːtn/ v [I, T] (cause to) become shorter: ~ *a dress.*

shortly /'ʃɔːtlɪ/ adv **1** soon: *We leave* ~. **2** crossly; curtly: *speak* ~ *to sb.*

shot /ʃɒt/ n [C] **1** act of firing a gun, etc; sound of this. **2** throw, kick, stroke, etc in certain games: *a* ~ *at goal.* **3** attempt; try: *a* ~ *at solving the problem.* **4** person who shoots with the stated degree of skill: *a poor* ~. **5** photograph; single part of a film. **6** (*infml*) injection of a drug, etc. **7** (idm) **like a 'shot** very quickly. **a shot in the 'arm** something that gives fresh energy to sb/sth. **a shot in the 'dark** answer, etc that is risked in the hope that it may be right. **not by a long shot** ⇨ **LONG². 'shotgun** n [C] gun used for shooting birds and animals. '**shot-put** n [sing] contest in which athletes throw a heavy metal ball as far as possible.

should¹ /ʃəd; strong form ʃʊd/ modal v (neg **should not**, contracted form **shouldn't** /'ʃʊdnt/) **1** (used to express obligation): *You* ~ *leave now.* **2** (used to express a conclusion that is not certain): *We* ~ *arrive before dark.* **3** (used in a *that* clause after certain *adjs*): *We're sorry that you* ~ *have been given so much trouble.* **4** (used to suggest the consequence of an event): *If she* ~ *come back, please tell me.* **5** (*fml*) (used to express purpose): *He put flowers in the room so that it* ~ *look nice.* **6** (used to give an opinion or advice): *You* ~ *stop smoking.* **7** (used to make polite requests): *I* ~ *like to make a phone call, please.* **8** (used with question words to express lack of interest, disbelief, etc): *How* ~ *I know?*

should² pt of **SHALL.**

shoulder /ˈʃəʊldə(r)/ n 1 [C] (a) part of the body where a person's arm or animal's front leg is attached. (b) part of a garment which covers this. 2 **shoulders** [pl] upper part of the back. 3 [C] anything resembling a human shoulder in shape or position. 4 (idm) **shoulder to 'shoulder** (a) side by side. (b) working, fighting, etc together. **shoulder** v [T] carry (sth) on the shoulder: (fig) ~ the responsibility. 2 push (sb/sth) with one's shoulder: ~ed sb aside. '**shoulder-blade** n [C] either of the flat bones of the upper back.

shouldn't /ˈʃʊdnt/ should not. ⇨ SHOULD[1].

shout /ʃaʊt/ n [C] loud call or cry. **shout** v [I, T] speak, say or call in a loud voice: Don't ~ at me! ○ ~ (out) orders. 2 (phr v) **shout sb down** shout in order to prevent sb being heard. **shouting** n [U] shouts.

shove /ʃʌv/ v 1 [I, T] push roughly. 2 (phr v) **shove over/up** (infml) move, esp to make more room: S~ over so I can sit down. **shove** n [C] strong push.

shovel /ˈʃʌvl/ n [C] tool like a spade, used for moving coal, sand, etc. **shovel** v (-ll-; US -l-) [T] lift or move (sth) with a shovel.

show[1] /ʃəʊ/ n 1 [C] any of various kinds of public entertainment, eg in the theatre, on television, etc. 2 [C] collection of things for public display. 3 [C, U] outward appearance: Her glory is all ~. 4 [U] splendid or impressive display: all the ~ of the circus. 5 [C, usu sing] (infml) effort: put up a good ~. 6 (idm) for 'show only done to impress others: She does it for ~. on 'show being displayed. a **show of 'hands** raising of hands to vote for or against (sth). '**show business** n [U] business of entertaining the public. '**show-down** n [C] final settlement of a quarrel, etc. '**show-jumping** n [U] riding of horses over fences as a competition. **showroom** n [C] place where goods, etc are put on display. **showy** adj (-ier, -iest) intended to attract attention.

show[2] /ʃəʊ/ v (pt ~ed, pp ~n /ʃəʊn/) 1 [T] cause to be seen: ~ your ticket at the gate. 2 [I, T] be visible; allow (sth) to be seen: Black doesn't ~ the dirt. 3 [T] point to; indicate: S~ me which one you want. 4 [T] direct; guide: S~ her in. 5 [T] express: He ~ed me great kindness. 6 [T] give evidence of: She ~ed great courage. 7 [T] make clear; explain: She ~ed me how to

do it. 8 (idm) **go to 'show** serve to prove or demonstrate. **show one's 'face** appear before people. **show one's 'hand** reveal one's intentions. 9 (phr v) **show off** try to impress people with one's wealth, ability, etc. **show up** (a) become visible: The lines ~ed up in the light. (b) arrive: All the guests ~ed up. **showing** n 1 [C] act of displaying. 2 [sing] performance: the company's poor ~ing. '**show-off** n [C] person who shows off.

shower /ˈʃaʊə(r)/ n [C] 1 brief fall of rain. 2 (a) (room or cabinet containing a) device which sprays water from above for people to wash under. (b) act of washing the body with this: have a ~. 3 fall of a large number of things: a ~ of stones. **shower** v 1 [I] fall in a shower. 2 [T] (with, on, upon)|| (a) cause (a lot of sth) to fall (on sb). (b) give (a lot of sth) to (sb): ~ sb with praise. **showery** adj (of the weather) with frequent showers of rain.

shown pt, pp of SHOW[2].

shrank pt of SHRINK.

shrapnel /ˈʃræpnəl/ n [U] fragments of exploded shell.

shred /ʃred/ n [C] 1 [esp pl] piece torn or broken from sth. 2 (fig) very small amount: not one ~ of proof. **shred** v (-dd-) [T] cut or tear into shreds.

shrewd /ʃruːd/ adj having or showing sound judgement and common sense: a ~ guess. **shrewdly** adv.

shriek /ʃriːk/ v 1 [I] scream in a shrill voice. 2 [T] say (sth) with a shrill scream. **shriek** n [C] shrill scream.

shrill /ʃrɪl/ adj (of sounds, etc) high-pitched; piercing. **shrillness** n [U].

shrimp /ʃrɪmp/ n [C] small shellfish, pink when boiled.

shrine /ʃraɪn/ n [C] 1 tomb, etc where holy relics are kept. 2 any place associated with a deeply respected person, activity, etc.

shrink /ʃrɪŋk/ v (pt **shrank** /ʃræŋk/ or **shrunk** /ʃrʌŋk/, pp **shrunk**) 1 [I, T] (cause to) become smaller: My shorts shrank in the wash. 2 (phr v) **shrink (back/away) from sth/sb** move back out of fear, disgust, etc. **shrink from sth** be reluctant to do sth. **shrinkage** /-ɪdʒ/ n [U] process or amount of shrinking. **shrunken** /ˈʃrʌŋkən/ adj having shrunk.

shrivel /ˈʃrɪvl/ v (-ll-; US -l-) [I, T] (up)|| (cause to) shrink and wrinkle through heat, frost, or old age.

shroud /ʃraʊd/ n [C] 1 cloth wrapped round a dead body. 2 (fig) thing that covers and hides: a ~ of mist. **shroud** v [T] (usu passive) cover and hide: ~ed in mystery.

shrub /ʃrʌb/ n [C] plant with a woody stem, lower than a tree. **shrubbery** n [C, U] (pl -ies) place planted with shrubs.

shrug /ʃrʌg/ v (-gg-) 1 [I, T] lift (one's shoulders) slightly to express doubt, etc. 2 (phr v) **shrug sth off** treat sth as unimportant. **shrug** n [C] act of shrugging.

shrunk pt, pp of SHRINK.

shrunken ⇨ SHRINK.

shudder /ˈʃʌdə(r)/ v [I] tremble with fear, cold, etc. **shudder** n [C] shuddering movement.

shuffle /ˈʃʌfl/ v 1 [I] walk without lifting one's feet properly. 2 [I, T] move (oneself or one's feet) because of restlessness, boredom, etc. 3 [T] mix up (playing cards) to change their order. **shuffle** n 1 [sing] shuffling walk. 2 [C] change of positions.

shun /ʃʌn/ v [T] (-nn-) avoid.

shunt /ʃʌnt/ v 1 [I, T] move (trains, etc) from one track to another. 2 [T] move (sb/sth) to a different place.

shush /ʃʊʃ/ interj be quiet.

shut /ʃʌt/ v (pt, pp ~, -tt-) 1 [T] move (a door, etc) into a position where it blocks an opening; close. (b) [I] (of a door, etc) become closed: The window won't ~. 2 [I, T] (cause a shop, etc) to stop operating temporarily: When does the baker's shut? 3 [T] fold together: ~ a book. 4 (idm) **shut one's eyes to** deliberately ignore. **shut up 'shop** close a business; stop trading, etc. 5 (phr v) **shut (sth) down** (cause a factory, etc to) stop working. **shut sth off** stop the supply of (gas, water, etc). **shut sb/ sth off** keep sb/sth separate. **shut (sth) up** (a) close and secure the doors and windows of (a house, etc). (b) put away for safety. **shut (sb) up** (infml) (cause sb to) stop talking. **'shut-down** n [C] process of closing (a factory, etc).

shutter /ˈʃʌtə(r)/ n [C] 1 movable cover for a window. 2 device that opens to admit light through the lens of a camera. **shuttered** adj with shutters closed.

shuttle /ˈʃʌtl/ n [C] 1 aircraft, bus, etc that travels regularly between two places. 2 device for carrying thread in a sewing machine, etc. **shuttle** v [I, T] (cause sth to) move or travel backwards and forwards. **'shuttlecock** n [C] cork with feathers in it, used in badminton.

shy¹ /ʃaɪ/ adj 1 (of people) timid and uncomfortable in the presence of others. 2 (of animals) easily frightened. **shyly** adv. **shyness** n [U].

shy² /ʃaɪ/ v (pt, pp **shied** /ʃaɪd/) 1 [I] (of a horse) turn aside in fear. 2 (phr v) **shy away from sth** avoid sth that is feared.

Siamese 'twins /ˌsaɪəmiːz 'twɪnz/ n [pl] twins born with their bodies joined together.

sibilant /ˈsɪbɪlənt/ adj, n (like or produced with a) hissing sound.

sibling /ˈsɪblɪŋ/ n [C] (fml) brother or sister.

sick /sɪk/ adj 1 ill: care for ~ people in hospital. 2 likely to vomit: feel ~. 3 (idm) **(of)** (infml) bored with (sb/sth); no longer patient with (sb/sth): I'm ~ of this job. 4 (at/ about)} (infml) very annoyed or upset: We're ~ about losing. 5 (infml) cruel or offensive: ~ jokes. 6 (idm) **worried sick** very worried. **the sick** n [pl] the sick people. **'sick-leave** n [U] permission to be absent from work, etc because of illness.

sicken /ˈsɪkən/ v 1 [T] cause to feel disgusted: Violence ~s him. 2 [I] (for)} begin to be ill. **sickening** adj disgusting.

sickle /ˈsɪkl/ n [C] short tool with a curved blade for cutting grass.

sickly /ˈsɪklɪ/ adj (-ier, -iest) 1 often ill. 2 looking ill: a ~ complexion. 3 causing or likely to cause distaste or sickness: a ~ atmosphere.

sickness /ˈsɪknɪs/ n 1 [C, U] (kind of) illness or disease. 2 [U] feeling that one is about to vomit.

side¹ /saɪd/ n [C] 1 flat surface of an object. 2 any surface that is not the top, bottom, front or back. 3 either surface of a piece of paper, etc. 4 edge or boundary: the ~ of the bed. 5 left or right part of a body: a pain in one's ~. 6 part of an object away from the central line: the sunny ~ of the street. 7 (a) either of two opposing groups of people (in games, politics, etc). (b) opinion of such a group. 8 aspect: study all ~s of a problem. 9 (idm) **get on the right/wrong side of sb** please/displease sb. **on/from all 'sides** in/from all directions. **on the 'big, 'small, etc ~** slightly too big, small, etc. **put sth on to one 'side** postpone dealing with sth. **side by 'side** close together. **take 'sides (with sb)** support sb in a dispute. **'sideboard** n [C] cupboard with drawers for holding plates, etc. **'sideburns, 'side-**

boards *n* [pl] hair on a man's face in front of the ears. **'side-effect** *n* [C] indirect effect of a drug, etc. **'sidelight** *n* [C] either of a pair of two small lights at the front of a car. **'sideline** *n* [C] (**a**) line forming the edge of a football pitch, etc. (**b**) occupation that is not one's main work. **'sidelong** *adj* to or from the side: *a* ~ *glance*. **'sideroad** *n* [C] minor road. **'side-step** *v* (-pp-) [I, T] (**a**) make (a blow, etc) by stepping to one side. (**b**) (*fig*) avoid answering (a question). **'side-track** *v* [T] turn sb's attention away from more important matters. **sidewalk** *n* (*US*) ⇔ PAVEMENT. **'sideways** *adv* to or from the side.

side² /saɪd/ *v* (phr v) **side with** support (sb) in an argument, etc.

siding /'saɪdɪŋ/ *n* [C] short railway track off the main lines.

siege /siːdʒ/ *n* [C, U] **1** (act of) surrounding a city, etc with armed forces to capture it. **2** (idm) **lay siege to** surround in this way.

sieve /sɪv/ *n* [C] frame with wire netting through which sand, flour, etc are passed to separate coarse grains from fine grains. **sieve** *v* [T] pass through a sieve.

sift /sɪft/ *v* **1** [T] put through a sieve. **2** [I, T] (*fig*) examine carefully: ~ *(through) the evidence*.

sigh /saɪ/ *v* **1** [I] take a deep breath, expressing sadness, tiredness, relief, etc. **2** [T] express with sighs. **sigh** *n* [C] act or sound of sighing.

sight /saɪt/ *n* **1** [U] ability to see. **2** [U] act of seeing: *our first* ~ *of land*. **3** [U] range within which sth/sb can be seen: *out of* ~. **4** (**a**) [C] thing seen or worth seeing. (**b**) **sights** [pl] famous buildings, etc of a place: *the* ~*s of London*. **5** [C] device that helps one aim a gun, etc. **6 a sight** [sing] (*infml*) sth/sb that looks ridiculous, dirty, etc. **7** (idm) **at/on sight** as soon as sb/sth is seen. **in 'sight** (**a**) able to be seen. (**b**) near: *The end of the war is in* ~. **,sight for sore 'eyes** something very pleasing to see. **sight** *v* [T] manage to see, esp by coming near. **sighted** *adj* able to see. **sighting** *n* [C] instance of sb/ sth being sighted. **'sightseeing** *n* [U] seeing the sights(4b) of a place.

sign /saɪn/ *n* [C] **1** mark or symbol used to represent sth. **2** notice, board, etc that gives a warning, directions, advertises a business, etc. **3** thing that shows that sb/sth exists or is present: *the* ~*s of suffering on her face*. **4** movement of

the hand, head, etc to show sth. **5** (idm) **a ,sign of the 'times** event, etc typical of its period. **sign** *v* **1** [I, T] write one's name on (a document, letter, etc). **2** (phr v) **sign sth away** give away (property, etc) by signing a document. **sign off** (**a**) end (a letter, etc) with a signature. (**b**) end a broadcast. **sign on** officially register as unemployed. **sign** (**sb**) **on/up** (cause sb to) sign an agreement to work for sb. **'signpost** *n* [C] post placed at a road junction to give directions.

signal /'sɪgnəl/ *n* [C] **1** gesture, light, etc that sends a message or instruction: *A red light is a danger* ~. **2** event which causes sth: *His speech was the* ~ *for applause*. **3** device which gives information to train drivers. **4** message sent or received by radio waves. **signal** *v* (-ll-; *US* -l-) [I, T] send (sth) by signal; send a signal to. **'signal-box** *n* [C] building beside a railway, from which signals(3) are controlled.

signatory /'sɪgnətrɪ; *US* -tɔːrɪ/ *n* [C] (*pl* -ies) person, country, etc that has signed an agreement.

signature /'sɪgnətʃə(r)/ *n* [C] person's name written by himself/ herself. **'signature tune** *n* brief tune that introduces a broadcast or performer.

significance /sɪg'nɪfɪkəns/ *n* [U] meaning; importance. **significant** *adj* **1** having a special meaning; important. **2** full of meaning: *a* ~ *look*. **significantly** *adv*.

signify /'sɪgnɪfaɪ/ *v* (*pt, pp* -ied) **1** [T] (**a**) be a sign of. (**b**) make known (one's intentions, views, etc). **2** [I] (*fml*) be of importance; matter.

silence /'saɪləns/ *n* [U, C] **1** condition or period of being silent. **2** condition or period of not speaking or answering. **3** (idm) **in silence** silently. **silence** *v* [T] make (sb/sth) silent. **silencer** *n* [C] device for reducing the noise of a petrol engine, gun, etc.

silent /'saɪlənt/ *adj* **1** making no or little sound. **2** saying little or nothing. **3** (of a letter(2)) written but not pronounced. **silently** *adv*.

silhouette /ˌsɪluː'et/ *n* [C] dark outline of sth/sth against a lighter background. **silhouette** *v* [T] (*usu passive*) show as a silhouette: *trees* ~*d against the sky*.

silicon /'sɪlɪkən/ *n* [U] non-metallic substance found combined with oxygen in quartz, etc. **silicon chip** *n* [C] microchip made of silicon.

silk /sɪlk/ *n* [U] (material made

from) fine, soft thread from the cocoons of certain insects. **silken** *adj* soft and smooth or shiny like silk. **'silkworm** *n* [C] caterpillar that spins silk. **silky** *adj* (**-ier, -iest**) soft, shiny or smooth like silk.

sill /sɪl/ *n* [C] flat shelf at the base of a window.

silly /'sɪlɪ/ *adj* (**-ier, -iest**) showing little thought or good sense; foolish. **silliness** *n* [U].

silt /sɪlt/ *n* [U] sand, mud, etc left behind by moving water. **silt** *v* (phr v) **silt (sth) up** (cause sth to) become blocked with silt.

silver /'sɪlvə(r)/ *n* [U] **1** shiny white precious metal. **2** articles, coins, etc of silver. **3** the colour of silver. **silver** *adj* made of or looking like silver. **silver 'jubilee** *n* [C] 25th anniversary of an important event. **silver 'medal** *n* [C] prize given to the person who comes second in a competition. **silver-'plated** *adj* (of spoons, dishes, etc) coated with silver. **'silversmith** *n* [C] person who makes or sells silver articles. **silver 'wedding** *n* [C] 25th anniversary of a wedding. **silvery** *adj* like silver.

similar /'sɪmɪlə(r)/ *adj* resembling (sb/sth); alike. **similarly** *adv*. **similarity** /ˌsɪmɪ'lærətɪ/ *n* (*pl* **-ies**) **1** [U] state of being similar. **2** [C] similar feature, characteristic, etc.

simile /'sɪmɪlɪ/ *n* [U, C] (use of) description of one thing as being like another, eg *as brave as a lion*.

simmer /'sɪmə(r)/ *v* **1** [I, T] (cause to) boil gently. **2** [I] *with//* be almost unable to control (an emotion): *~ ing with anger*. **3** (phr v) **simmer down** become calm (after being angry).

simple /'sɪmpəl/ *adj* **1** easily understood; not difficult: *a ~ problem*. **2** plain: *~ food*. **3** not highly developed: *~ forms of life*. **4** not having many parts. **5** open and straightforward: *as ~ as a child*. **6** easily deceived. **7** (*infml*) not having normal intelligence. **simply** *adv* **1** in a simple(1)(2) way. **2** absolutely. **3** only: *She's simply here to help.*

simplicity /sɪm'plɪsətɪ/ *n* [U] **1** being simple. **2** (idm) be **sim,plicity it'self** be very easy.

simplify /'sɪmplɪfaɪ/ *v* (*pt, pp* **-ied**) [T] make simpler. **simplification** /ˌsɪmplɪfɪ'keɪʃn/ *n* [C, U].

simulate /'sɪmjʊleɪt/ *v* [T] pretend to be, have or feel: *~ interest*. **simulation** /ˌ/ *n* [C, U].

simultaneous /ˌsɪml'teɪnɪəs; US

,saɪm-/ *adj* happening or done at the same time. **simultaneously** *adv*.

sin /sɪn/ *n* **1** [U] breaking of God's laws. **2** [C] offence against such a law. **sin** *v* (**-nn-**) [I] commit a sin; do wrong. **sinful** /-fl/ *adj* wrong; wicked. **sinfulness** *n* [U]. **sinner** /'sɪnə(r)/ *n* [C].

since /sɪns/ *prep* (with perfect tenses) after a stated time in the past: *I haven't seen him ~ Tuesday.* **since** *conj* **1** from the time when: *How long is it ~ you were here?* **2** because, as: *S~ I have no money, I can't buy it.* **since** *adv* (with perfect tenses) from a stated time in the past onwards: *I met her last summer and haven't seen her ~.*

sincere /sɪn'sɪə(r)/ *adj* **1** (of feelings, etc) genuine: *~ friendship.* **2** (of people) not deceiving others; honest. **sincerely** *adv.* **sincerity** /sɪn'serətɪ/ *n* [U].

sinew /'sɪnjuː/ *n* [C, U] tendon. **sinewy** *adj* muscular; tough.

sing /sɪŋ/ *v* (*pt* **sang** /sæŋ/, *pp* **sung** /sʌŋ/) **1** [I, T] make musical sounds with the voice; speak words to a tune. **2** [I] make a humming or ringing sound. **singer** *n* [C]. **singing** *n* [U].

singe /sɪndʒ/ *v* [I, T] (cause sth to) be blackened by burning. **singe** *n* [C] slight burn on cloth, etc.

single /'sɪŋgl/ *adj* **1** one only: *a ~ apple.* **2** not married. **3** for the use of one person: *a ~ bed.* **4** (*Brit*) (of a ticket) for a journey to a place but not back. **single** *n* **1** singles [U] game with one person on each side. **2** [C] single ticket. **3** [C] record with only one short piece of music on each side. **single** *v* (phr v) **single sb/sth out** select sb/sth from a group, eg for special attention. **,single 'file** *n* [U] line of people, vehicles, etc one following another. **,single-'handed** *adj* (done) by one person without help. **,single-'minded** *adj* giving all one's attention, energy, etc to one aim. **,single 'parent** *n* [C] parent caring for a child on his/ her own. **singly** /'sɪŋglɪ/ *adv* by one; not in a group.

singsong /'sɪŋsɒŋ/ *n* **1** [C] gathering at which people sing songs together. **2** [sing] way of speaking with a rising and falling rhythm.

singular /'sɪŋgjʊlə(r)/ *adj* **1** (*grammar*) referring to one person: *a ~ verb.* **2** (*fml*) (**a**) outstanding. (**b**) unusual; strange. **singular** *n* [usu sing] (word in a singular form. **singularly** *adv* (*fml*) very; remarkably.

sinister /'sɪnɪstə(r)/ adj suggesting evil: a ~ place.

sink¹ /sɪŋk/ n [C] fixed basin with taps and a drain, usually in a kitchen.

sink² /sɪŋk/ v (pt sank /sæŋk/, pp sunk /sʌŋk/) 1 [I, T] (cause to) go down below the surface of a liquid or sth soft. 2 [I] (of the sun, etc) go down below the horizon. 3 [I, T] (cause to) become lower: She sank to the ground. 4 [I] lose value, strength, etc. 5 [T] make by digging: ~ a well. 6 (phr v) sink in/into (a) (of liquids) go deep into another substance. (b) (of words, etc) be understood. sink sth into sth invest (money) in sth.

sinuous /'sɪnjʊəs/ adj curving; twisting.

sinus /'saɪnəs/ n [C] space in the skull behind the nose.

sip /sɪp/ v (-pp-) [I, T] drink in very small quantities. sip n [C] act of sipping; quantity sipped.

siphon /'saɪfən/ n [C] 1 tube curved in such a way that liquid can flow up through it and then down. 2 bottle from which soda-water can be forced out by the pressure of gas in it. siphon v (phr v) siphon sth off/out draw (liquid) out through a siphon. siphon sth off transfer sth, often illegally.

sir /sɜː(r)/ n (also **Sir**) [sing] 1 (fml) (used as a polite way of addressing a man). 2 (used before the name of a knight or baronet).

sire /'saɪə(r)/ n [C] male parent of an animal. sire v [T] (esp of horses) be the sire of.

siren /'saɪərən/ n [C] device for producing a loud noise (as a warning, etc).

sirloin /ss:lɔɪn/ n [C, U] best part of loin of beef.

sister /'sɪstə(r)/ n [C] 1 daughter of the same parents as oneself or another person. 2 (Brit) senior hospital nurse. 3 female member of a religious society. 4 (used esp by feminist women) fellow woman. **sisterhood** n [C] group of women living together in a religious society, etc. 2 [U] state of being sisters. **sisterly** adj of or like a sister.

sit /sɪt/ v (pt, pp sat /sæt/, -tt-) 1 (a) [I] rest on one's buttocks with the body upright. (b) [I, T] (cause to) take up such a position: ~ (down) on the chair. 2 [I] (of Parliament, a lawcourt, etc) hold a meeting. 3 [I, T] (for)/(for) be a candidate for (an examination). 4 [I] (for)/(for) pose for a portrait, etc. 5 (idm) sit on the 'fence not decide between two opposite beliefs, courses of action,

etc. sit 'tight (a) remain in position. (b) refuse to take action, etc. 6 (phr v) **sit around** sit doing nothing, unable or unwilling to do anything. **sit back** relax and do nothing: ~ back and watch television. **sit in** occupy a building, etc as a protest. **sit in on sth** attend (a discussion, etc) as an observer. **sit on** (a) be a member of (a committee, etc). (b) take no action on (sth). **sit up** not go to bed until later than usual. **sit (sb) up** (cause to) take a sitting position. '**sit-in** n [C] act of occupying a building, etc as a protest.

site /saɪt/ n [C] place where sth is, happens or is done. **site** v [T] position; place.

sitting /'sɪtɪŋ/ n [C] 1 time during which Parliament, a law court, etc meets. 2 act of posing for a portrait or photograph. 3 period in which a group of people eat a meal. 4 (idm) ,sitting 'duck easy target. '**sitting-room** n [C] room in a house for general use.

situate /'sɪtjʊeɪt; US 'sɪtʃueɪt/ v [T] (usu passive) place: a house ~d near the church. **situated** adj (of a person) in the stated circumstances: I'm badly ~d at the moment.

situation /,sɪtjʊ'eɪʃn/ n [C] 1 circumstances at a certain time. 2 position of a town, building, etc. 3 (fml) paid job.

six /sɪks/ pron, adj, n [C] 1 6. 2 (idm) at sixes and sevens (infml) in confusion. **sixth** /sɪksθ/ pron, adj 6th. **sixth** pron, n [C] ⅙.

sixteen /,sɪks'tiːn/ pron, adj, n [C] 16. **sixteenth** /,sɪks'tiːnθ/ pron, adj 16th. **sixteenth** pron, n [C] ⅟₁₆.

sixty /'sɪksti/ pron, adj, n [C] (pl -ies) 60. **sixtieth** /'sɪkstɪəθ/ pron, adj 60th. **sixtieth** pron, n [C] ⅟₆₀.

size /saɪz/ n 1 [U, C] degree of largeness. 2 [C] standard measurement of clothing: ~ five shoes. **size** v 1 [T] arrange according to size. 2 (phr v) **size sb/sth up** (infml) form a judgement of sb/sth. **sizeable** /-əbl/ adj fairly large.

sizzle /'sɪzl/ v [I] n [C] (infml) (make) the hissing sound of sth cooking in fat.

skate /skeɪt/ n [C] 1 boot with a steel blade attached to the sole for moving over ice. 2 roller-skate. 3 (idm) **get/put one's 'skates on** (infml) hurry up. **skate** v 1 [I] move on skates. 2 (idm) be **skating on thin 'ice** be doing sth risky. 3 (phr v) **skate over/round sth** not deal with sth directly. '**skateboard** n [C] short, narrow board with small wheels attached, for standing and riding on for fun. **skater** n [C].

skeleton /'skelɪtn/ n [C] 1 bony framework supporting a body. 2 framework of a building, etc. 3 outline of a plan, etc. 4 smallest number needed to provide a service, etc: a ~ staff. 5 (idm) **skeleton in the 'cupboard** secret about which one is ashamed. **'skeleton key** n [C] key that opens several different locks.

sketch /sketʃ/ n [C] 1 rough quickly-made drawing. 2 short description. 3 short humorous play. **sketch** v 1 [I, T] make a sketch. 2 (phr v) **sketch sth out** give a rough plan of sth. **sketchy** adj (-ier, -iest) not done thoroughly; lacking detail.

skewer /'skju:ə(r)/ n [C] pointed wood or metal pin for holding meat together during cooking. **skewer** v [T] push a skewer into (sth).

ski /ski:/ n [C] long narrow strip of wood, etc attached to special boots for moving over snow. **ski** v (pt, pp **skied**, pres part ~**ing**) [I] move on skis: go ~ing. **skier** n [C].

skid /skɪd/ n [C] sideways slipping movement, eg of a car on ice. **skid** v (-dd-) [I] (of a car, etc) move or slip sideways.

skies pl of SKY.

skilful (US **skillful**) /'skɪlfl/ adj having or showing skill: a ~ player. **skilfully** adv.

skill /skɪl/ n [C, U] 1 ability to do sth well. 2 experience of needing skill: a ~ed job. 2 experienced; trained: ~ed workers.

skim /skɪm/ v (-mm-) 1 [T] remove matter from the surface of (a liquid). 2 [I, T] move lightly over (a surface), barely touching it. 3 [I, T] (through) read (sth) quickly.

skin /skɪn/ n 1 [U] outer covering of the body of a person or animal. 2 [C, U] skin removed from an animal's body. 3 [C, U] outer covering of a fruit. 4 [C, U] thin layer on the surface of some liquids, eg boiled milk. 5 (idm) **by the skin of one's 'teeth** by a narrow margin. **get under sb's 'skin** (infml) (a) annoy sb. (b) interest or attract sb. **be no skin off sb's nose** (infml) not matter to sb. **be skin and 'bone(s)** (infml) be very thin. **skin** v (-nn-) take the skin off. **,skin-'deep** adj (of beauty, feelings, etc) not deep or lasting. **'skinflint** n [C] miser. **'skinhead** n [C] young person with very short hair, esp one who is violent. **,skin-'tight** adj (of clothing) fitting very close to the

body. **skinny** adj (-ier, -iest) thin.

skint /skɪnt/ adj (Brit infml) having no money.

skip /skɪp/ v (-pp-) 1 [I] jump lightly and quickly. 2 [I] jump over a rope swung under the feet as one jumps. 3 [I, T] leave quickly or secretly: ~ the country. 4 [I] move quickly or casually. 5 [T] miss out: ~ part of the book. 6 [T] not attend (a meeting, etc). **skip** n [C] skipping movement.

skip /skɪp/ n [C] large metal container for rubbish, etc.

skipper /'skɪpə(r)/ n [C] captain of a ship or team. **skipper** v [I, T] act as captain.

skirt /skɜːt/ n [C] woman's outer garment that hangs from the waist. **skirt** v 1 [T] be or go round the edge of (sth): a wood ~ing the field. 2 [I] avoid (a topic, etc). **'skirting-board** n [U] board attached to the wall of a room, near the floor.

skittles /skɪtlz/ n [U] game played by throwing a ball at a group of bottle-shaped wooden pins.

skulk /skʌlk/ v [I] hide or move around, trying not to be seen.

skull /skʌl/ n [C] bony framework of the head.

skunk /skʌŋk/ n [C] small N American animal that sends out a strong smell when attacked.

sky /skaɪ/ n [U, C, usu sing] (pl **skies** /skaɪz/) the space above the earth, where we see clouds, the sun, moon and stars. **,sky-'high** adj (infml) very high. **'skylark** n [C] small bird that sings as it flies high in the sky. **'skylight** n [C] window in a sloping roof. **'skyline** n [C, usu sing] outline of buildings, hills, etc against the sky. **'skyscraper** n [C] very tall building.

slab /slæb/ n [C] thick flat piece of stone, etc.

slack /slæk/ adj 1 not tight: a ~ rope. 2 giving little care, attention or energy to a task. 3 not busy or active: Trade is ~. **slack** v [I] 1 be lazy or careless in one's work. 2 (phr v) **slack off/up** reduce one's activities or speed. **slackness** n [U].

slack /slæk/ **the slack** n [U] 1 slack part of a rope. 2 (idm) **take up the slack** tighten a rope, etc.

slacken /'slækən/ v [I, T] 1 (cause to) become slack. 2 (off/up) (cause to) become slower, less active, etc.

slag /slæg/ n 1 [U] waste matter remaining when metal has been extracted from ore. 2 [C] (Brit derog sl) immoral woman. **slag** v

(-gg-) (phr v) **slag sb off** (*Brit sl*) say offensive things about sb. **'slag-heap** *n* [C] hill of slag.

slam /slæm/ *v* (**-mm-**) **1** [I, T] shut with great force. **2** [T] throw or knock with great force: ~ *a book against the wall.* **3** [T] (*infml*) criticize. **slam** *n* [C] noise of sth being slammed.

slander /'slɑːndə(r)/ *n* [U, C] (offence of) saying sth false that damages sb's reputation. **slander** *v* [T] say sth false about (sb). **slanderous** *adj.*

slang /slæŋ/ *n* [U] words, phrases, etc used in very informal conversation, not suitable for formal situations. **slang** *v* [T] attack (sb) using angry or rude words.

slant /slɑːnt/ *v* **1** [I, T] (cause to) lean in a certain direction; slope. **2** [T] often *derog*) present (information, etc) from a particular point of view. **slant** *n* [C] **1** slope. **2** (*infml*) point of view.

slap /slæp/ *v* (**-pp-**) **1** strike with the palm of the hand. **2** place (sth) with a slapping noise: ~ *paint onto the wall.* **slap** *n* [C] **1** blow with the palm of the hand. **2** (idm) **a slap in the 'face** insult; snub. **slap** (also **slap-'bang**) *adv* (*infml*) straight: *The car ran ~ into the wall.*

slapdash /'slæpdæʃ/ *adj, adv* (done or doing things) in a careless way.

slapstick /'slæpstɪk/ *n* [U] comedy in which people fall over, knock each other down, etc.

slap-up /'slæpʌp/ *adj* (*Brit infml*) (of a meal) first-class.

slash /slæʃ/ *v* **1** [I, T] cut (sth) with sweeping strokes. **2** (*infml*) reduce greatly: ~ *prices.* **slash** *n* [C] **1** act of slashing. **2** long cut.

slat /slæt/ *n* [C] thin, narrow piece of wood, metal, etc.

slate /sleɪt/ *n* **1** [U] blue-grey rock that splits easily into thin, flat layers. **2** [C] thin piece of this used for making roofs. **slate** *v* [T] (*infml*) criticize severely.

slaughter /'slɔːtə(r)/ *n* [U] **1** killing of animals, esp for food. **2** killing of many people at once. **slaughter** *v* [T] **1** kill (animals or people) in great numbers. **2** (*infml*) defeat completely. **'slaughterhouse** *n* [C] place where animals are killed for food.

slave /sleɪv/ *n* [C] **1** person who is owned by and forced to work for another. **2** person controlled by a habit, etc: *a ~ to drink.* **slave** *v* [I] work hard: ~ *away in the kitchen.* **slavery** *n* [U] **1** being a slave. **2** system of using slaves.

slaver /'slævə(r)/ *v* [I] (*over*)) **1** let saliva run from one's mouth. **2** (*usu derog*) show great eagerness, desire, etc.

slavish /'sleɪvɪʃ/ *adj* (*derog*) lacking originality or independence: *a ~ copy.* **slavishly** *adv.*

slay /sleɪ/ *v* (*pt* **slew** /sluː/, *pp* **slain** /sleɪn/) [T] (*fml or US*) kill violently.

sledge /sledʒ/ (also **sled** /sled/) *n* [C] vehicle with strips of wood or metal instead of wheels, used on snow.

sledge hammer /'sledʒ hæmə(r)/ *n* [C] heavy hammer with a long handle.

sleek /sliːk/ *adj* **1** smooth and shiny: ~ *hair.* **2** *often*|| (*derog*) looking well-fed and wealthy.

sleep[1] /sliːp/ *n* **1** [U] condition when the body is at rest with the eyes closed, mostly at night. **2** [sing] period of sleep. **3** (idm) **go to 'sleep** begin to sleep. **put to 'sleep (a)** make (sb) fall asleep, esp by using an anaesthetic. **(b)** kill (an animal) esp because it is ill. **sleepless** *adj* without sleep.

sleep[2] /sliːp/ *v* (*pt, pp* **slept** /slept/) **1** [I] be in a state of sleep. **2** [T] have enough beds, etc for: *a flat that ~ s six.* **3** (idm) **sleep like a 'log/'top** (*infml*) sleep well. **sleep 'tight** (*infml*) (used to wish sb a good night's sleep). **4** (phr v) **sleep around** have sexual intercourse with a lot of people. **sleep in** sleep later than one ought to. **sleep sth off** recover from (drunkenness, etc) by sleeping. **sleep on sth** leave a problem, etc to the next day. **sleep through sth** not be woken by a (noise). **sleep with sb** have sexual intercourse with sb. **sleeper** *n* [C] **1** person who sleeps. **2** beam of wood, etc supporting the rails of a railway track. **3** (berth in a) sleeping-car. **'sleeping-bag** *n* [C] bag with warm lining for sleeping in. **'sleeping-car** *n* [C] railway coach fitted with beds. **'sleeping-pill** *n* [C] pill containing a drug that helps sb to sleep. **sleepy** *adj* (**-ier, -iest**) **1** needing or ready for sleep. **2** (of places, etc) without much activity: *a ~ little town.* **sleepily** *adv.*

sleet /sliːt/ *n* [U] falling snow mixed with rain. **sleet** *v* (used with *it*) fall as sleet: *It's ~ ing outside.*

sleeve /sliːv/ *n* [C] **1** part of a garment that covers the arm. **2** stiff envelope for a record. **3** (idm) **have sth up one's sleeve** have a secret idea, plan, etc.

sleigh /sleɪ/ *n* [C] sledge, esp one pulled by a horse.

sleight /slaɪt/ *n* (idm) ˌsleight of 'hand skill with one's hands in performing tricks, etc.

slender /'slendə(r)/ *adj* 1 narrow but quite long. 2 (of people) slim. 3 small: *have a ~ chance*. **slenderness** *n* [U].

slept *pt, pp* of SLEEP².

slice /slaɪs/ *n* [C] 1 thin flat piece cut off sth, esp bread or meat. 2 (*infml*) part or share: *a ~ of the credit.* 3 utensil with a wide blade for cutting or lifting, eg cooked fish. 4 (idm) **a ˌslice of 'life** a portrayal of life as it really is, eg in a novel. **slice** *v* 1 [T] (*up*)// cut into pieces. 2 [I] *into*/*through*// cut *into*/ *through*: *a knife slicing through butter.*

slick /slɪk/ *adj* 1 smooth and slippery. 2 done (too) smoothly and efficiently. 3 (*usu derog*) (of people) doing things in a slick(2) way.

slide¹ /slaɪd/ *n* 1 [sing] act of sliding(1). 2 [C] smooth slope down which things can slide or on which children may play. 3 [C] picture on photographic film projected onto a screen. 4 [C] glass plate on which sth is examined under a microscope.

slide² /slaɪd/ *v* (*pt, pp* **slid** /slɪd/) [I, T] 1 (cause to) move smoothly over a polished or slippery surface. 2 (cause to) move quietly or without being noticed. 3 (idm) **let sth 'slide** neglect sth. **'slide-rule** *n* [C] ruler with a part that slides in a groove, used for making calculations.

slight¹ /slaɪt/ *adj* 1 not serious or important: *a ~ headache.* 2 frail-looking; slender. 3 (idm) **not in the 'slightest** not at all. **slightly** *adv* 1 to a small degree: *feel ~ly better.* 2 slenderly: *a ~ly built boy.* **slightness** *n* [U].

slight² /slaɪt/ *v* [T] treat without proper respect, etc. **slight** *n* [C] act of slighting. **slightingly** *adv*.

slim /slɪm/ *adj* (**-mer, -mest**) 1 (*approv*) not fat or thick; slender. 2 small: *a ~ chance of success.* **slim** *v* (**-mm-**) [I] eat less, etc to reduce one's weight. **slimmer** *n* [C] person who is slimming. **slimness** *n* [U].

slime /slaɪm/ *n* [U] 1 soft thick sticky substance. 2 sticky substance produced by snails, etc. **slimy** *adj* (**-ier, -iest**) 1 of or like slime. 2 (*infml*) dishonestly flattering, friendly, etc: *a ~ young man.*

sling /slɪŋ/ *n* [C] band of material looped round an object, eg a broken arm, to support or lift it. **sling** *v* (*pt, pp* **slung** /slʌŋ/) [T] (*infml*) throw with force: *We slung him out of the bar.*

slink /slɪŋk/ *v* (*pt, pp* **slunk** /slʌŋk/) [I] move as if one does not want to be seen or is ashamed.

slip¹ /slɪp/ *n* 1 [C] act of slipping; false step. 2 [C] slight error. 3 [C] loose sleeveless garment worn under a dress. 4 = PILLOWCASE (PILLOW). 5 [C] small piece of paper. 7 (idm) **give sb the 'slip** (*infml*) escape from sb. **a 'slip of a boy, girl**, etc a slightly-built boy, etc.

slip² /slɪp/ *v* (**-pp-**) 1 [I] slide accidentally and (almost) fall: *He ~ped (over) in the mud.* 2 [I, T] (cause to) move quietly and quickly, without being seen: *He ~ped the coin into his pocket.* 3 [I] move, escape, fall, etc, eg by being difficult to hold: *The plate ~ped from my hand.* 4 [I, T] put (clothing, etc) on, esp easily and quickly: *~ on a coat.* 5 (idm) **let sth slip (a)** not use (an opportunity, etc). (b) accidentally reveal (a secret, etc). **slip one's 'memory**/**'mind** (of sb's name, etc) be forgotten. 6 (phr v) **slip up** (*infml*) make a mistake. **'slip-road** *n* [C] road for joining or leaving a motorway. **'slip-stream** *n* [C] stream of air from the engine of an aircraft. **'slip-up** *n* [C] (*infml*) mistake.

slipper /'slɪpə(r)/ *n* [C] loose-fitting soft shoe worn in the house.

slippery /'slɪpərɪ/ *adj* (**-ier, -iest**) 1 (of a surface) smooth, wet, difficult to hold or move on without slipping. 2 (*infml*) (of people) not to be trusted. 3 (*infml*) (of problems, etc) difficult to deal with. 4 (idm) **the slippery 'slope** (*infml*) course of action that easily leads to disaster, etc.

slipshod /'slɪpʃɒd/ *adj* not done or not doing things carefully; careless.

slit /slɪt/ *n* [C] long narrow cut, tear or opening. **slit** *v* (**-tt-**, *pt, pp* **~**) [T] make a slit in.

slither /'slɪðə(r)/ *v* [I] slide unsteadily.

sliver /'slɪvə(r)/ *n* [C] long thin piece of sth: *a ~ of glass.*

slob /slɒb/ *n* [C] (*infml derog*) dirty, untidy, lazy person.

slog /slɒg/ *v* (**-gg-**) [I] 1 (*infml*) 1 work hard: *~ (away) at sth.* 2 walk with difficulty: *~ up the hill.* **slog** *n* [sing, U] (*infml*) period of slogging; hard work.

slogan /'sləʊgən/ *n* [C] easily remembered phrase used in advertising.

slop /slɒp/ v (-pp-) **1** [I] (of liquids) spill over the edge of a container. **2** [T] cause to spill: *Don't ~ the water all over the floor!* **3** (phr v) **slop about/around** (of liquids) move around esp in a container. **slop** *n* splashes dirty waste water.

slope /sləʊp/ *n* **1** [C, U] slanting line. **2** [C] area of rising or falling ground. **slope** *v* **1** [I] have a slope. **2** (phr v) **slope off** (*Brit sl*) go away, esp to avoid doing work, etc.

sloppy /'slɒpɪ/ *adj* (-ier, -iest) **1** not doing things or done with care: ~ *work*. **2** (*infml*) too sentimental: *a ~ love story*. **3** (of clothes) loose and fitting badly. **4** wet and dirty. **sloppily** *adv* in a sloppy(1)(2) way. **sloppiness** *n* [U].

slosh /slɒʃ/ *v* **1** [I, T] (cause to) splash about: ~ *water all over the floor.* **2** [T] (*sl*) hit. **sloshed** (*sl*) drunk.

slot /slɒt/ *n* [C] **1** narrow opening: *put a coin in the ~.* **2** groove into which sth fits. **3** (*infml*) suitable place in a plan, schedule, etc: ~ *s for advertisements on television.* **slot** *v* (-tt-) [T] make a slot; place in a slot.

sloth /sləʊθ/ *n* **1** [U] laziness. **2** [C] S American animal that lives in trees and moves very slowly. **slothful** *adj*.

slouch /slaʊtʃ/ *v* [I] stand, sit or move in a lazy way. **slouch** *n* **1** [sing] slouching posture, walk, etc. **2** (idm) **be no slouch at sth** be very good at sth.

slovenly /'slʌvnlɪ/ *adj* untidy; dirty. **slovenliness** *n* [U].

slow[1] /sləʊ/ *adj* **1** taking a long time; not fast: *a ~ vehicle.* **2** not quick to learn: *a ~ child.* **3** not acting immediately. **4** not interesting or lively: *a very ~ film.* **5** (of a watch or clock) showing a time later than the true time. **6** (idm) **slow off the mark** ⇨ MARK[1]. **slow on the uptake** ⇨ UPTAKE. **'slowcoach** *n* [C] (*infml*) person who moves, works, etc slowly. **slowly** *adv*. **slowness** *n* [U].

slow[2] /sləʊ/ *adv* **1** slowly: ~ *moving.* **2** (idm) **go 'slow** (of workers) work slowly as a protest.

slow[3] /sləʊ/ *v* [I, T] (*down/up*)|| (cause to) go, move, etc at a slower speed. **'slow-down** *n* [C] reduction of speed, activity, etc.

sludge /slʌdʒ/ *n* [U] (anything resembling) thick greasy mud.

slug[1] /slʌg/ *n* [C] creature like a snail but without a shell.

slug[2] /slʌg/ *v* (-gg-) [T] (*US infml*) hit hard.

slug[3] /slʌg/ *n* [C] (esp *US*) bullet.

sluggish /'slʌgɪʃ/ *adj* slow-moving; not alert or lively. **sluggishly** *adv*.

sluice /slu:s/ *n* [C] (also **'sluice-gate**) device for controlling the flow of water in a canal, etc. **sluice** *v* [T] wash or rinse with water.

slum /slʌm/ *n* [C] (house in an) area of dirty, over-crowded buildings. **slum** *v* (-mm-) [I] (also **slum it**) choose or be forced to live cheaply or in poor conditions. **slummy** *adj*.

slumber /'slʌmbə(r)/ *v* [I] (*fml*) sleep, sleep peacefully. **slumber** *n* [U] **slumbers** [pl] sleep.

slump /slʌmp/ *v* [I] **1** fall heavily. **2** (of prices, trade, etc) fall steeply. **slump** *n* [C] fall in prices, trade, etc.

slung *pt, pp* of SLING.

slur /slɜ:(r)/ *v* (-rr-) [T] **1** join (sounds, words) together so that they are not clear. **2** damage sb's reputation. **slur** *n* [C] damaging remark: *a ~ on her name.*

slush /slʌʃ/ *n* [U] **1** melting, dirty snow. **2** (*infml* usu *derog*) silly sentimental speech or writing. **'slush fund** *n* [C] money used for bribes. **slushy** *adj* (-ier, -iest).

slut /slʌt/ *n* [C] (*derog offensive*) sexually immoral woman. **sluttish** *adj*.

sly /slaɪ/ *adj* doing things or done in secret; deceitful. **sly** *n* (idm) **on the 'sly** secretly. **slyly** *adv*. **slyness** *n* [U].

smack[1] /smæk/ *n* [C] **1** (sound of a) blow given with the open hand. **2** (*infml*) loud kiss. **smack** *v* [T] **1** strike with the open hand. **2** (idm) **smack one's lips** ⇨ LIP. **smack** *adv* suddenly and forcefully: *run ~ into a wall.*

smack[2] /smæk/ *v* (phr v) **smack of sth** have a slight flavour or suggestion of sth.

small /smɔ:l/ *adj* **1** less than average or usual in size; little: *a ~ house.* **2** young: ~ *children.* **3** not doing things on a large scale: ~ *businesses.* **4** unimportant; slight: *a ~ problem.* **5** (idm) **feel 'small** feel ashamed, humiliated, etc. **a small 'fortune** a large sum of money. **the 'small hours** the three or four hours after midnight. **small wonder** ⇨ WONDER. **small** *n* [sing] the slender part of sth: *the ~ of the back.* **small 'arms** *n* [pl] weapons carried in the hand. **'smallholding** *n* [C] (*Brit*) piece of land less than 50 acres in size used for farming. **small-'minded** *adj* mean and selfish. **smallness** *n* [U]. **'smallpox** *n* [U] contagious disease that leaves permanent scars on the skin. '**small talk** n [U] talk about everyday social matters.

smart¹ /smɑːt/ adj 1 clean and neat; well-dressed: a ~ appearance/person. 2 fashionable: a ~ restaurant. 3 (esp US) clever: a ~ answer. 4 quick or hard: a ~ pace ○ a ~ slap. **smarten** /'smɑːtn/ v (phr v) **smarten (oneself/sb/sth) up** make (oneself/sb/sth) smarter. **smartly** adv. **smartness** n [U].

smart² /smɑːt/ v [I] (feel a) sharp pain: The smoke made my eyes ~.

smash /smæʃ/ v 1 [I, T] break violently into small pieces: ~ a cup on the floor. 2 [I] into, through, etc|| move with great force into, through, etc: They ~ed into the wall. 3 [T] hit (sb/sth) very hard. 4 [T] (infml) defeat or destroy. **smash** n 1 [sing] act or sound of smashing. 2 [C] (in tennis, etc) hard, downward stroke. 3 [C] (also **smash 'hit**) (infml) play, song, etc that is suddenly very successful. 4 = SMASH-UP. **smash** with a smash: drive ~ into the wall. **smashing** adj (Brit infml) very good. '**smash-up** n [C] car crash.

smattering /'smætərɪŋ/ n [sing of|| slight knowledge of esp a language: a ~ of French.

smear /smɪə(r)/ v 1 [T] cover (a surface) with (sth oily or sticky): ~ mud on the wall. 2 [T] (fig) harm (sb or sb's reputation). **smear** n [C] 1 mark made by smearing. 2 (fig) remark, etc that smears(2). 3 small amount of a substance taken from the body, to be tested for disease.

smell¹ /smel/ n 1 [U] ability to notice (sth/sb) by using the nose. 2 [C, U] anything that is smelled. 3 [C] bad smell: What a ~! 4 [C, usu sing] act of smelling: Have a ~ of this. **smelly** adj (-ier, -iest) (infml) having a bad smell.

smell² /smel/ v (pt, pp **smelt** /smelt/ or **smelled**) 1 [T] (often with can, could) notice (sth/sb) by using the sense of smell: Can you ~ gas? 2 [I, T] (with sth) to test sth by its smell: ~ the flowers. 3 [I] have the sense of smell: Can birds ~? 4 [I] (a) (of|| give out a smell: ~ good/of soap. (b) have a bad smell: Your feet ~. 5 (idm) **smell a 'rat** (infml) notice that sth is wrong.

smile /smaɪl/ n [C] expression of the face with the corners of the mouth turned up, showing amusement, pleasure, etc. **smile** v [I] give a smile. **smilingly** adv.

smirk /smɜːk/ v [I] n [C] (give a) silly self-satisfied smile.

smithereens /ˌsmɪðə'riːnz/ n [pl] (idm) **smash, break, etc sth (in-**

to smithereens smash, etc sth into tiny pieces.

smitten /'smɪtn/ adj (with)|| 1 feeling an (emotion) deeply. 2 suddenly very attracted to: I'm rather ~ with her.

smock /smɒk/ n [C] loose shirtlike garment.

smog /smɒg/ n [U] mixture of fog and smoke.

smoke¹ /sməʊk/ n 1 [U] usu white, grey or black vapour produced by sth burning. 2 [C] act of smoking a cigarette, etc. 3 (idm) **go up in 'smoke (a)** be completely burned. **(b)** result in failure. '**smoke-screen** n [C] **(a)** cloud of smoke made to hide sth which is happening. **(b)** (fig) explanation, etc designed to hide one's real intentions. **smoky** adj (-ier, -iest).

smoke² /sməʊk/ v 1 [I] give out smoke. 2 [I, T] breathe smoke from a cigarette, pipe, etc. 3 [T] preserve (meat or fish) with smoke. 4 (phr v) **smoke sb/sth out** fill a place with smoke to drive sb/sth out. **smoker** n [C] person who smokes. **smoking** n [U] activity of smoking a cigarette, etc.

smooth /smuːð/ adj 1 having an even surface: ~ skin. 2 (of movement) free from bumping, etc: a ~ ride. 3 (of a liquid) free from lumps. 4 free from difficulties, problems, etc. 5 free from harshness in sound or taste. 6 (usu derog) (of a person) polite and flattering. **smooth** v 1 [T] make smooth. 2 (phr v) **smooth sth over** make problems, etc seem less important. **smoothly** adv. **smoothness** n [U].

smother /'smʌðə(r)/ v 1 [I, T] (cause to) die by not being able to breathe. 2 [T] (in/with)|| cover: a cake ~ed in cream. 3 [T] put out (a fire) by covering it: (fig) ~ a yawn.

smoulder (US **smol-** /'sməʊldə(r)/ v [I] burn slowly without flame: ~ing ashes ○ (fig) Hate ~ed within her.

smudge /smʌdʒ/ n [C] dirty mark. **smudge** v 1 [T] make a smudge on. 2 [I] (of ink, etc) become blurred.

smug /smʌg/ adj (-ger, -gest) too pleased with oneself. **smugly** adv. **smugness** n [U].

smuggle /'smʌgl/ v [T] take (goods, people, etc) illegally or secretly into or out of a place or country: ~ drugs into the country ○ ~ a letter into prison. **smuggler** /'smʌglə(r)/ n [C]. **smuggling** n [U].

smut /smʌt/ n 1 [C] (mark made by a) bit of dirt, soot, etc. 2 [U] indecent or vulgar stories, etc. **smutty** adj.

snack /snæk/ n [C] small quick meal, usu eaten instead of or between main meals.

snag /snæg/ n [C] 1 hidden or unexpected difficulty. 2 sharp or rough piece that sticks out. **snag** v (-gg-) [T] catch on a snag(2).

snail /sneɪl/ n [C] small, slow-moving animal with a soft body, no limbs and a spiral shell.

snake /sneɪk/ n [C] 1 long, thin legless reptile. 2 (fig) person likely to deceive others. 3 (idm) **a snake in the 'grass** person who pretends to be a friend but who is really an enemy. **snake** v [I] follow a twisting path.

snap /snæp/ v (-pp-) 1 [I, T] (cause to) break suddenly with a sharp noise. 2 [I, T] open or close with a sudden sharp noise: ~ shut. 3 [I, T] say sth in a sharp voice: ~ orders. 4 [I] (of dogs, etc) shut the jaws quickly: The dog ~ped at her ankles. 5 [T] take a photograph of. 6 (idm) **snap one's 'fingers** make a clicking noise with one's fingers to attract attention, etc. **snap 'out of it** (infml) get out of a (bad, unhappy, etc) mood. 7 (phr v) **snap at sb** speak harshly to sb. **snap at sth** try to catch with the teeth: (fig) ~ at the chance to go on holiday. **snap sth up** buy sth eagerly. **snap** n [C] 1 act or sound of snapping. 2 sudden short period of (usu cold) weather. 3 (also 'snapshot) photograph, usu one quickly taken. **snap** adj done suddenly, without warning: a ~ decision. **snappy** adj (-ier, -iest) (a) irritable. (b) fashionable. (c) lively.

snare /sneə(r)/ n [C] 1 trap for catching small animals and birds. 2 situation which traps sb. **snare** v [T] catch in a snare.

snarl[1] /snɑːl/ v 1 [I] (of dogs, etc) show the teeth and growl. 2 [I, T] speak or say in an angry voice. **snarl** n [C] act or sound of snarling.

snarl[2] /snɑːl/ v (infml) (phr v) **snarl (sth) up** (cause to) become confused or tangled: The traffic was ~ed up. **'snarl-up** n [C] (infml) confused or tangled state, esp of traffic.

snatch /snætʃ/ v 1 [I, T] (try to) take suddenly: ~ the child from her father. 2 [T] get quickly: ~ a kiss. **snatch** n 1 [sing] act of snatching. 2 [C, usu pl] short piece: ~es of conversation.

sneak /sniːk/ v 1 [I] go quietly and secretly: ~ past sb. 2 [T] take secretly: ~ money from the box. 3

[I] tell sb in authority about things sb else has done wrong. **sneak** n [C] person who sneaks(3). **sneakers** n [pl] (US) plimsolls. **sneaking** adj (a) secret: a ~ing respect for sb. (b) vague: a ~ing suspicion. **sneaky** adj (infml derog) done or acting in a secret sly way.

sneer /snɪə(r)/ v [I] (at)// show contempt by looks or words. **sneer** n [C] sneering look, smile, etc.

sneeze /sniːz/ n [C] uncontrollable outburst of air from the nose and mouth when one has a cold, etc. **sneeze** v [I] make a sneeze. 2 (idm) **not to be 'sneezed at** (infml) worth having.

sniff /snɪf/ v 1 [I] (a) [I] draw air in through the nose, producing a sound. (b) [I, T] (at)// do this in order to smell (sth): ~ (at) the roses. 2 (phr v) **sniff at sth** (usu passive) show contempt for sth: Her offer is not to be ~ed at. **sniff sb out** discover sb. **sniff** n [C] act or sound of sniffing.

snigger /'snɪgə(r)/ n [C] quiet or secret laugh. **snigger** v [I] (at)// laugh in this way.

snip /snɪp/ v (-pp-) [I, T] cut sharply (with scissors, etc) in short quick strokes. **snip** n [C] 1 act of snipping. 2 (Brit infml) bargain: It's a ~ at only £10.

snipe /snaɪp/ v [I] 1 shoot from a hiding-place. 2 (fig) criticize. **sniper** n [C].

snippet /'snɪpɪt/ n [C] small item of news, information, etc: ~s of gossip.

snivel /'snɪvl/ v (-ll-; US -l-) [I] cry or complain in a miserable way.

snob /snɒb/ n [C] person who respects social position or wealth too much. **snobbery** n [U] behaviour of a snob. **snobbish** adj.

snog /snɒg/ v (-gg-) [I] (Brit infml) kiss and cuddle.

snooker /'snuːkə(r)/ n [U] game played with 15 red balls and 7 of other colours on a billiard-table. **snooker** v [T] place (sb) in a difficult position.

snoop /snuːp/ v [I] (about/ around)// take an interest in other people's affairs, etc without their knowledge or permission, usu to find fault.

snooze /snuːz/ v [I] n [C] (infml) (take) a short sleep, esp during the day.

snore /snɔː(r)/ v [I] breathe noisily while sleeping. **snore** n [C] sound of snoring.

snorkel /'snɔːkl/ n [C] tube that

allows a swimmer to breathe air while under water. **snorkel** *v* (-ll-; *US* -l-) [I] swim with a snorkel.

snort /snɔːt/ *v* 1 [I] force air out loudly through the nose. 2 [I] (*at*)// express (anger, etc) by snorting. **snort** *n* [C] act or sound of snorting.

snout /snaʊt/ *n* [C] nose of an animal, esp a pig.

snow¹ /snəʊ/ *n* [U] frozen water falling from the sky in soft, white flakes or a mass of this on the ground, etc. **'snowball** *n* [C] ball of snow for throwing in play. **'snowball** *v* [I] grow quickly in size, importance, etc. **'snow-drift** *n* [C] snow blown into heaps by the wind. **'snowdrop** *n* [C] type of small white spring flower growing from a bulb. **'snowman** *n* [C] figure of a man made from snow. **'snow-plough** (*US* -plow) *n* [C] device for pushing snow off roads, etc. **'snowstorm** *n* [C] heavy fall of snow, esp with a strong wind.

snow² /snəʊ/ *v* 1 [I] (used with *it*) fall as snow: *It ~ed all day.* 2 (phr v) **snow sb in/up** (usu passive) prevent sb from going outside because of heavy snow. **snow sb under** (usu passive) be far too much or too many: *He is ~ed under with work.* **snowy** *adj* (-ier, -iest).

snub /snʌb/ *v* (-bb-) [T] ignore or treat (sb/sth) rudely or with contempt. **snub** *n* [C] snubbing words or behaviour.

snub nose /'snʌb nəʊz/ *n* [C] short, turned-up nose. **'snub-nosed** *adj.*

snuff¹ /snʌf/ *n* [U] powdered tobacco that is sniffed into the nose.

snuff² /snʌf/ *v* 1 [T] (*out*)// put out (a candle) by pinching the burning part. 2 (idm) **snuff it** (*Brit infml*) die. 3 (phr v) **snuff sth out** put an end to sth.

snug /snʌg/ *adj* (-gg-) 1 warm and comfortable. 2 tight-fitting: *a ~ jacket.* **snugly** *adv.*

snuggle /'snʌgl/ *v* [I] (*up/down*)// lie or get close (to sb) for warmth or affection.

so¹ /səʊ/ *adv* 1 to such a (great) extent: *not so big as I thought.* 2 very: *I'm so glad to see you.* 3 (idm) **so much for 'sb/sth** nothing further needs to be said or done about sb/sth. **,so much 'so that** to such an extent that.

so² /səʊ/ *adv* 1 in this or that way: *Kick the ball so.* 2 (used to replace a phrase): *'Is he coming?' 'I think so.'* 3 (used to express agreement): *'It's Friday today, not Thursday.' 'So it is.'* 4 also: *You are young and so am I.* 5 (idm) **and 'so on** and

other things of the same kind. **so as to** with the intention of: *He drove fast so as not to be late.* **so that (a)** in order that: *Hurry up and finish so that we can go home early.* **(b)** with the result that: *Nothing was heard from her, so that people thought she was dead.* **so-and-so** *n* səʊ/ *n* (*infml*) **1** some person or other. **2** contemptible person: *That so-and-so lied to me.* **'so-called** *adj* wrongly described like this: *Her so-called friends refused to help her.*

so³ /səʊ/ *conj* 1 that is why: *He was hurt so I helped him.* 2 (*infml*) (indicating purpose): *I gave you a map so you wouldn't get lost.* 3 (used to introduce the next part of a story): *So she went and told the police.* 4 (idm) **so what?** (*infml*) and what does it matter?: *'She's lying about it.' 'So what?'*

soak /səʊk/ *v* 1 (a) [I] become completely wet by being in a liquid. (b) [T] cause sth to absorb as much liquid as possible: ~ *the bread in milk.* 2 [T] (of a liquid) make (sth) completely wet: *The rain ~ed (through) his coat.* 3 (phr v) **soak sth up** take in a (liquid): *Paper ~ s up water.* **soak** *n* [C] act of soaking. **soaked, soaking** *adj* very wet.

soap /səʊp/ *n* 1 [U] substance made of fat or oil, etc, used for washing. 2 [C] (*infml*) = SOAP OPERA. **soap** *v* [T] apply soap to. **'soap opera** *n* [C, U] radio or television drama dealing with people's everyday lives. **soapy** *adj* (-ier, -iest).

soar /sɔː(r)/ *v* [I] 1 (of birds, etc) fly or go high up in the air. 2 (*fig*) rise rapidly: ~ *ing prices.*

sob /sɒb/ *v* (-bb-) 1 [I] draw in the breath in short irregular bursts when crying. 2 (phr v) **sob sth out** tell sth while crying. **sob** *n* [C] act or sound of sobbing. **'sob-story** *n* [C] (usu *derog*) sad story intended to gain sympathy.

sober /'səʊbə(r)/ *adj* 1 not drunk. 2 serious and responsible: *a ~ person.* **sober** *v* 1 [I, T] (cause to) become sober(2). 2 (phr v) **sober sb up** make sb sober(1). **soberly** *adv.*

soccer /'sɒkə(r)/ *n* [U] association football.

sociable /'səʊʃəbl/ *adj* liking company or friendly. **sociably** *adv.*

social /'səʊʃl/ *adj* 1 of relations between people and communities: ~ *customs.* 2 of or in society: *one's ~ equals.* 3 for companionship or recreation: *a '~ club.* 4 (of animals, etc) living in groups. 5

(*infml*) sociable. **Social and Liberal 'Democrats** *n* [pl] British political party formed in 1988 from a merger between the Social Democratic Party and the Liberal Party. **social 'science** *n* [C, U] subjects concerning people within society, eg sociology, economics. **social se'curity** *n* [U] government payments to help the unemployed, disabled, etc. **'social worker** *n* [C] person employed to provide help and advice on health, housing, social security, etc. **socially** *adv*.

socialism /'səʊʃəlɪzəm/ *n* [U] political and economic theory that land, industries, etc should be owned by the state. **socialist** *adj*, *n* [C].

socialize /'səʊʃəlaɪz/ *v* [I] mix socially with others.

society /sə'saɪətɪ/ *n* (*pl* -ies) 1 [U] system in which people live in organized communities. 2 [C, U] social community. 3 [U] (*fml*) company: *in the ~ of her friends*. 4 [U] wealthy, fashionable people in a place, country, etc. 5 [C] organization of people with a common interest: *a drama ~*.

sociology /ˌsəʊsɪ'ɒlədʒɪ/ *n* [U] study of the nature and growth of society and social behaviour. **sociologist** *n* [C] expert in sociology. **sociological** /-'lɒdʒɪkl/ *adj*.

sock¹ /sɒk/ *n* [C] covering of wool, cotton, etc for the foot and ankle.

sock² /sɒk/ *n* [C] (*infml*) hard blow, esp with the fist. **sock** *v* [T] give (sb) such a blow.

socket /'sɒkɪt/ *n* [C] hollow in which sth fits or turns.

sod /sɒd/ *n* [C] (*Brit* △ *sl*) 1 (used as a term of abuse) person: *You rotten ~!* 2 thing that causes difficulty.

soda /'səʊdə/ *n* 1 [U] substance used for making soap, glass, etc. 2 soda-water. **'soda-water** *n* [U] water containing a gas to make it bubble.

sodden /'sɒdn/ *adj* very wet.

sodium /'səʊdɪəm/ *n* [U] chemical element, a silver-white metal.

sofa /'səʊfə/ *n* [C] large seat with raised ends and back for two or more people.

soft /sɒft/ *adj* 1 not hard or stiff: *a ~ pillow*. 2 (of surfaces) smooth and delicate: *~ skin*. 3 (of light or colours) not bright or glaring. 4 (of sounds) not loud. 5 (of outlines) not clear; indistinct. 6 (of answers, words, etc) not angry; gentle. 7 easy: *a ~ job*. 8 (*on*)/*(too)* kind and gentle: *Don't be too ~ on the class*. 9 (*infml derog*) weak and

lacking in courage. 10 (*infml*) foolish. 11 (idm) **have a soft 'spot for** be very fond of. **soft-'boiled** *adj* (of eggs) boiled for a short time so that the yellow part (= YOLK) stays soft. **'soft drink** *n* [C] drink with no alcohol. **'soft drug** *n* [C] drug not likely to cause addiction. **soft-'hearted** *adj* (too) kind and caring. **softly** *adv*. **softness** *n* [U]. **soft-'pedal** *v* (-ll-; *US* -l-) [I, T] (*infml*) make (an issue, etc) seem less important. **soft-'soap** *v* [T] (*infml*) persuade (sb) to do (sth) using flattery. **'software** *n* [U] data, programmes, etc used when operating a computer.

soften /'sɒfn/ *v* 1 [I, T] (cause to) become soft. 2 [T] make (sth) easier to accept: *try to ~ the shock*. 3 (phr v) **soften (sb) up** (*infml*) make (sb) less opposed to (sth).

soggy /'sɒgɪ/ *adj* (-ier, -iest) very wet or heavy with water. **sogginess** *n* [U].

soil /sɔɪl/ *n* [C, U] upper layer of earth in which plants grow. **soil** *v* [I, T] (cause to) become dirty.

sojourn /'sɒdʒən; *US* səʊ'dʒɜːrn/ *n* [C] (*fml*) temporary stay in a place.

solace /'sɒlɪs/ *n* [C, U] (*fml*) (thing that gives) comfort or relief from grief, etc.

solar /'səʊlə(r)/ *adj* of the sun: *~ power*. **the 'solar system** *n* [usu sing] the sun and its planets.

sold *pt*, *pp* of SELL.

solder /'səʊldə(r)/ *n* [U] type of metal which melts easily, used for joining harder metals, etc. **solder** *v* [T] join with solder. **'soldering-iron** *n* [C] tool used for this work.

soldier /'səʊldʒə(r)/ *n* [C] member of an army. **soldier** *v* (phr v) **soldier 'on** continue in spite of difficulties.

sole¹ /səʊl/ *n* [C, U] (*pl* **sole** or *~* s) flat sea-fish used for food.

sole² /səʊl/ *n* [C] bottom surface of a human foot, shoe, etc. **sole** *v* [T] put a sole on (a shoe, etc).

sole³ /səʊl/ *adj* 1 one and only: *the ~ owner*. 2 not shared: *have ~ responsibility*. **solely** /'səʊlɪ/ *adv* alone; only.

solemn /'sɒləm/ *adj* 1 done in a serious, formal way: *a ~ promise*. 2 serious-looking: *a ~ face*. **solemnly** *adv*. **solemnness** *n* [U]. **solemnity** /sə'lemnətɪ/ *n* (*pl* -ies) (*fml*) 1 [U] seriousness. 2 [C, usu pl] solemn ceremony.

solicit /sə'lɪsɪt/ *v* 1 [I, T] (*for*)/*(fml)* ask or beg for earnestly. 2 [I, T] (of a prostitute) offer sex (to sb) for money.

solicitor /sə'lɪsɪtə(r)/ *n* [C] (*Brit*

lawyer who prepares legal documents, advises clients, etc.

solid /'sɒlɪd/ *adj* 1 not in the form of a liquid or gas: *Water becomes ~ when it freezes.* 2 not hollow. 3 strongly and firmly made. 4 that can be depended on: *~ arguments.* 5 of the same substance throughout: *~ gold.* 6 in complete agreement: *The workers were ~ on this issue.* 7 continuous: *sleep ten hours ~.* 8 having length, breadth and thickness. **solid** *n* [C] 1 hard body or substance. 2 figure with length, breadth and thickness. **solidly** *adv.* **solidity** /sə'lɪdətɪ/ *n* [U].

solidarity /ˌsɒlɪ'dærətɪ/ *n* [U] unity resulting from shared interests.

solidify /sə'lɪdɪfaɪ/ *v* (*pt, pp* -**ied**) [I, T] (cause to) become solid or firm.

solitary /'sɒlɪtrɪ; *US* -terɪ/ *adj* 1 (living) alone; lonely. 2 only one: *a ~ visitor.* 3 remote.

solitude /'sɒlɪtjuːd; *US* -tuːd/ *n* [U] being alone.

solo /'səʊləʊ/ *n* (*pl* ~s) piece of music, dance, etc (to be) performed by one person: *a clarinet ~.* **solo** *adj, adv* 1 by oneself: *a ~ flight.* 2 of or performed as a solo: *music for ~ flute.* **soloist** *n* person who gives a solo.

solstice /'sɒlstɪs/ *n* [C] time at which the sun is furthest north or south of the equator.

soluble /'sɒljʊbl/ *adj* 1 that can be dissolved in liquid. 2 able to be solved. **solubility** *n* [U].

solution /sə'luːʃn/ *n* 1 (a) [C] answer to a question, difficulty, etc. (b) [U] process of finding this. 2(a) [U] process of dissolving a solid in liquid. (b) [C, U] liquid that results from this.

solve /sɒlv/ *v* [T] find the answer to (a problem, etc). **solvable** *adj*.

solvent /'sɒlvənt/ *adj* having enough money to pay one's debts. **solvent** *n* [C, U] liquid able to dissolve another substance. **solvency** *n* [U] being solvent.

sombre (*US* **somber**) /'sɒmbə(r)/ *adj* 1 dark-coloured or dull: *~ colours.* 2 serious and sad: *a ~ mood.* **sombrely** *adv.* **sombreness** *n* [U].

some¹ /sʌm weak form səm/ *adj* 1 an unspecified number or amount of: *Have ~ milk.* ○ *~ children.* 2 unknown or not named: *She's living at ~ place in Surrey.* 3 approximately: *~ twenty years ago.* 4 large amount of: *for ~ time.*

some² /sʌm/ *pron* 1 an unspecified number or amount: *S~ of these books are quite useful.* 2 part

of an amount or number: *S~ of the guests didn't stay for long, but most did.* ○ *S~ people have very bad manners.*

somebody /'sʌmbədɪ/ (also **someone** /'sʌmwʌn/) *pron* 1 an unknown or unnamed person: *There's ~ at the door.* 2 an important person: *She really thinks she's ~.*

somehow /'sʌmhaʊ/ *adv* 1 in some way; by some means: *We'll get there ~.* 2 for some reason: *S~ I just don't think she'll come back.*

someone = SOMEBODY.

somersault /'sʌməsɔːlt/ *n* [C] rolling jump in which a person's feet go over his/her head before he/she lands on the ground. **somersault** *v* [I] turn a somersault.

something /'sʌmθɪŋ/ *pron* 1 an unknown or unnamed thing: *I want ~ to eat.* 2 a significant thing: *I'm sure she knows ~ about this.* 3 (idm) **or something** (*infml*) or another thing similar to the one mentioned: *She caught flu or something.* **something like a 'sb/sth** (a) rather similar to sb/sth. (b) approximately sb/sth.

sometime /'sʌmtaɪm/ *adv* at an unspecified point in time: *~ in May.*

sometimes /'sʌmtaɪmz/ *adv* occasionally: *I ~ receive letters from him.*

somewhat /'sʌmwɒt/ *adv* quite; rather: *I was ~ surprised.*

somewhere /'sʌmweə(r); *US* -hweər/ (*US* **someplace**) *adv* 1 in, at or to an unknown or unnamed place: *It must be ~ near here.* 2 (idm) **get somewhere** ⇨ GET.

son /sʌn/ *n* 1 [C] male child of a parent. 2 (used as a form of address by an older man to a younger man or boy): *What's your name, ~?* **'son-in-law** *n* (*pl* '**sons-in-law**) husband of one's daughter.

sonata /sə'nɑːtə/ *n* [C] music for one or two instruments, usu with three or four parts.

song /sɒŋ/ *n* 1 [C] poem set to music, intended to be sung. 2 [U] singing. 3 (idm) **for a song** (*infml*) at a very low price. **a song and 'dance** an unnecessary fuss.

sonic /'sɒnɪk/ *adj* relating to sound or the speed of sound.

sonnet /'sɒnɪt/ *n* [C] poem containing 14 lines with 10 syllables each.

soon /suːn/ *adv* 1 not long after the present time or the time mentioned: *We shall ~ be home.* **2** early: *How ~ can you be ready?* **3** (idm) **as 'soon as 'soon as** at the moment that: *He left as ~ as he heard the news.* **no sooner... than** immediately when or after: *No ~er had she arrived than she had to leave again.* **the 'sooner the 'better** as quickly as possible. **sooner... than** rather than: *I would ~er die than marry you.*

soot /sʊt/ *n* [U] black powder left on surfaces by smoke. **sooty** *adj* (**-ier, -iest**) covered with or black with soot.

soothe /suːð/ *v* [T] **1** make (sb) quiet and calm. **2** make (pains, etc) less severe. **soothing** *adj*.

sop /sɒp/ *n* [C] something offered to please sb who is angry, disappointed, etc.

sophisticated /səˈfɪstɪkeɪtɪd/ *adj* **1** having or showing experience of the world and cultured. **2** complicated and refined: *~ weapons.* **sophistication** /səˌfɪstɪˈkeɪʃn/ *n* [U].

soppy /ˈsɒpɪ/ *adj* (**-ier, -iest**) (*infml*) very sentimental.

soprano /səˈprɑːnəʊ/ *n* [C] (*pl* *~s*) *adj* (music for or singer with the) highest singing voice of women.

sorcerer /ˈsɔːsərə(r)/ (*fem* **sorceress** /-ɪs/) *n* [C] person who practises witchcraft. **sorcery** *n* [U] witchcraft.

sordid /ˈsɔːdɪd/ *adj* **1** (of places, etc) dirty and poor. **2** (of people, behaviour, etc) showing selfishness, meanness, etc. **sordidly** *adv*. **sordidness** *n* [U].

sore /sɔː(r)/ *adj* **1** (of a part of the body) hurting when touched or used. **2** (*fml*) serious: *in ~ need.* **3** (esp *US infml*) angry: *feel ~.* **4** (idm) **a ,sore 'point** subject that makes one feel angry or ashamed whenever it is mentioned. **stand/ stick out like a sore 'thumb** be very noticeable. **sore** *n* [C] painful infected area on the skin. **sorely** *adv* greatly: *~ needed.* **soreness** *n* [U].

sorrow /ˈsɒrəʊ/ *n* [C, U] (cause of) sadness; regret. **sorrow** *v* [I] (*at/ over*)) feel sadness, grief, etc. **sorrowful** *adj*.

sorry /ˈsɒrɪ/ *adj* **1** feeling regret or sadness: *She was ~ for her past crimes.* **2** feeling sympathy or pity (for sb): *I do feel ~ for him.* **3** (used to express mild regret, etc): *I'm ~, but I don't agree.* **4** (**-ier, -iest**) poor and causing pity: *in a ~ state.* **sorry** *interj* **1** (used for apologizing, etc): *Sorry! Did I hurt you?* **2** (used for asking sb to repeat what

one has not heard).

sort¹ /sɔːt/ *n* **1** [C] group of people or things that are alike in some way. **2** (idm) **out of 'sorts** feeling unwell or angry. **sort of** to some extent: *~ of pleased that it happened.*

sort² /sɔːt/ *v* **1** [T] (*out*))] arrange in groups: *~ (out) the good and bad apples.* **2** (phr v) **sort sth out** (a) put sth in good order. (b) deal with or solve: *~ out a problem.*

SOS /ˌes əʊ ˈes/ *n* [sing] urgent message for help sent by radio, etc.

so-so /ˈsəʊsəʊ/ *adj, adv* (*infml*) average; neither very well nor very badly: *'How are you feeling?' 'So-so.'*

soufflé /ˈsuːfleɪ; *US* suːˈfleɪ/ *n* [C, U] dish of eggs, milk, cheese etc beaten together and baked in the oven.

soul /səʊl/ *n* **1** [C] spiritual part of a person, believed to exist after death. **2** [C, U] emotional and intellectual energy: *put ~ into one's work.* **3** [sing] perfect example of: *the ~ of discretion.* **4** [C] person: *not a ~ to be seen.* **5** = SOUL MUSIC (SOUL). **'soul-destroying** *adj* (of work) very dull. **soulful** *adj* showing deep feeling. **soulfully** *adv*. **soulless** *adj* having no gentle, kindly feelings. **'soul music** *n* [U] popular modern Black American music. **'soul-searching** *n* [U] examination of one's mind and conscience.

sound¹ /saʊnd/ *adj* **1** in good condition; healthy: *a ~ body.* **2** careful and accurate: *a ~ worker.* **3** showing good sense: *a ~ policy.* **4** thorough; deep: *be a ~ sleeper.* **sound** *adv* deeply: *~ asleep.* **soundly** *adv* in a deep or thorough manner. **soundness** *n* [U].

sound² /saʊnd/ *n* **1** [C, U] that which is heard: *the ~ of drums.* **2** [C] impression or idea sth stated gives: *I don't like the ~ of this.* **'sound barrier** *n* [C] point at which an aircraft's speed equals that of sound. **'sound effects** *n* [pl] sounds other than speech or music used in a film, play, etc. **'soundproof** *adj* not allowing sound to pass through. **'sound-proof** *v* [T] make (a room, etc) sound-proof. **'sound-track** *n* [C] music, etc used in a cinema film.

sound³ /saʊnd/ *v* **1** [I] give a certain impression: *His story ~s genuine.* **2** [I, T] (cause to) produce a sound. **3** [T] give a signal by making a sound: *~ the alarm.* **4** [T] pronounce: *Don't sound the 'b' in 'dumb'.* **5** (phr v) **sound off** (*infml*) talk loudly or boastfully.

sound¹ /saʊnd/ v [I, T] measure the depth (of the sea, etc) with a weighted line. 2 (phr v) **sound sb out** (**about/on sth**) try to learn what sb's views, opinions, etc are.

soup /suːp/ n [U] 1 liquid food made by cooking meat, vegetables, etc together in water. 2 (idm) **in the 'soup** (*infml*) in difficulties.

sour /'saʊə(r)/ adj 1 having a sharp taste. 2 not fresh: ~ *milk.* 3 bad-tempered. 4 (idm) **go/turn 'sour** become unpleasant or difficult. **sour** v [I, T] (cause) to become sour. **sourly** adv. **sourness** n [U].

source /sɔːs/ n [C] place from where sth comes: the ~ of a river/ belief.

south /saʊθ/ n [sing] 1 the south point of the compass, to the right of a person facing the sunrise. 2 **the South** part of a particular country towards the south. **south** adj 1 in or towards the south. 2 (of winds) from the south. **south** adv towards the south. **south-'east** n [sing], adj, adv (region, direction, etc) midway between south and east. **south-'eastern** adj. **southerly** /'sʌðəli/ adj, adv 1 in or towards the south. 2 (of winds) from the south. **southern** /'sʌðən/ adj of the south part of the world or a particular country. **southerner** n [C] person born or living in the southern part of a country. **southward** /'saʊθwəd/ adj towards the south. **southward(s)** adv. **south-'west** n [sing], adj, adv (region, direction, etc) midway between south and west. **south-'western** adj.

souvenir /ˌsuːvəˈnɪə(r)/ n [C] thing kept as a reminder of a person, place or event.

sovereign /'sɒvrɪn/ n [C] king or queen. **sovereign** adj 1 (of power) unlimited. 2 (of a nation or ruler) independent and self-governing. **sovereignty** /'sɒvrəntɪ/ n [U] power to govern.

Soviet /'saʊvɪət/ adj of the USSR or its people.

sow¹ /saʊ/ n [C] adult female pig.

sow² /saʊ/ v (pt ~**ed**, pp ~**n** /saʊn/ or ~**ed**) [T] 1 place (seed) in or on soil; plant (land) with seed. 2 spread or introduce (feelings, etc): ~ *discontent.*

soya bean /'sɔɪə biːn/ n [C] type of bean grown as food and for its oil.

spa /spɑː/ n [C] (place with a) spring of mineral water.

space /speɪs/ n 1 [C, U] distance between objects: a narrow ~ be-

tween the chairs. 2 [C, U] area of land: the wide open ~ s. 3 [U] unoccupied area; room(2): There's not enough ~ here. 4 [U] expanse in which all things exist, move, etc: stare into ~. 5 [U] (also **outer 'space**) the universe outside the earth's atmosphere. 6 [C] period of time: within the ~ of a day. **space** v [T] (out)// put regular spaces between. **'space-age** adj very modern. **'spacecraft**, **'spaceship** n [C] vehicle for travelling in space. **'space station** n [C] large artificial satellite used as a base for operations in space(5).

spacious /'speɪʃəs/ adj having a lot of space. **spaciousness** n [U].

spade /speɪd/ n [C] 1 long-handled tool with a flat blade and sharp edge for digging. 2 playing-card with black figures shaped like leaves. **'spadework** n [U] hard work done as preparation.

spaghetti /spə'getɪ/ n [U] long thin string-like pieces of pasta.

span /spæn/ n [C] 1 distance or part between the supports of an arch. 2 time from beginning to end: the ~ of a person's life. **span** v (-nn-) [T] 1 form a bridge over (sth). 2 (esp of time) last: a life ~ ning fifty years.

spaniel /'spænɪəl/ n [C] breed of dog with long drooping ears.

spank /spæŋk/ v [T] slap (esp a child) on the buttocks as a punishment. **spank** n [C].

spanner /'spænə(r)/ (US **wrench**) n [C] tool for holding and turning nuts onto bolts, etc.

spar /spɑː(r)/ v (-rr-) [I] (*with*)// 1 practise boxing. 2 argue, usu in a friendly way.

spare¹ /speə(r)/ adj 1 (a) additional to what is needed: two ~ chairs. (b) (of time) free from work. 2 (of people) thin. **spare** (also **spare 'part**) n [C] part of a machine, etc used for replacing a damaged or worn part. **spare tyre** n [C] tyre carried in a vehicle to be used as a replacement should one of those in use be punctured.

spare² /speə(r)/ v [T] 1 (be able to) give (money, time, etc) for a purpose: Can you ~ me a few minutes? 2 not use, give, spend, etc: No expense was ~ d, ie A lot of money was spent. 3 (decide to) not hurt, damage or destroy: ~ a prisoner's life. 4 (idm) **spare a 'thought for** consider (sb/sth) when making a decision. **sparing** adj not wasteful. **sparingly** adv.

spark /spɑːk/ n [C] 1 tiny glow produced by sth burning or an electric current being broken. 2

[usu sing] (fig) sign of sth: *not a ~ of decency in him*. **spark** v **1** [I] give out sparks. **2** (phr v) **spark sth off** be the immediate cause of sth. **'spark-plug** (also **'sparking-plug**) n [C] device for lighting the fuel in an engine.

sparkle /'spɑːkl/ v [I] send out flashes of light: (fig) *Her conversation ~d.* **sparkle** n [C, U] act of sparkling: (fig) *a performance lacking in ~*. **sparkling** /'spɑːklɪŋ/ adj.

sparrow /'spærəʊ/ n [C] common small brownish-grey bird.

sparse /spɑːs/ adj not crowded or thick: *~ population*. **sparsely** adv. **sparseness** n [U].

spasm /'spæzəm/ n **1** [C, U] sudden uncontrollable tightening of a muscle. **2** [C] sudden burst (of energy, etc). **spasmodic** adj **spæz-ˈmɒdɪk/ adj 1** done or happening at irregular intervals. **2** caused or affected by spasms. **spasmodically** adv.

spastic /'spæstɪk/ n [C], adj (person) physically disabled because of damage to the nervous system.

spat pt, pp of SPIT².

spate /speɪt/ n [sing] large number coming all at once: *a ~ of robberies*.

spatial /'speɪʃl/ adj of or concerning space. **spatially** adv.

spatter /'spætə(r)/ v [I, T] splash in drips. **spatter** n [sing] shower.

spatula /'spætjʊlə/ n [C] tool with a flat flexible blade used for mixing and spreading.

spawn /spɔːn/ n [U] eggs of fish and frogs. **spawn** v [I, T] **1** produce (eggs). **2** (fig) produce in large quantities.

speak /spiːk/ v (pt spoke /spəʊk/, pp spoken /'spəʊkən/) **1** v say things; talk: *I was ~ing to her about my plans.* **2** [I] be able to use (a language): *~ French.* **3** [I] make a speech. **4** [T] make known; express: *~ the truth.* **5** [I] express ideas, feelings, etc without words: *Actions ~ louder than words.* **6** (idm) on **'speaking terms** know sb well enough to speak to him/ her. **speak one's 'mind** express one's opinion openly. **7** (phr v) **speak for sb (a)** give sb's views, etc. **(b)** give evidence for sb. **speak out (a)** express (an opinion, etc) openly and boldly. **speak up (a)** speak more loudly. **(b)** speak out. **speaker** n [C] **1** person who makes speeches. **2** person who speaks a particular language: *a French ~er.* **3** short for LOUDSPEAKER.

spear /spɪə(r)/ n [C] weapon with a metal point on a long shaft.

spear v [T] pierce with a spear. **'spearhead** n [C] person or group who leads an attack. **'spearhead** v [T] lead (an attack), etc.

spearmint /'spɪəmɪnt/ n [U] kind of mint used for flavouring.

special /'speʃl/ adj **1** of a particular kind; not common. **2** of or for a certain person or purpose. **3** exceptional in amount, degree, etc: *~ treatment.* **special** n [C] **1** thing not of the usual type: *a television ~ about the elections.* **2** (US infml) reduced price in a shop. **specialist** n [C] person who is an expert in a particular subject, profession, etc. **specially** adv particularly.

speciality /ˌspeʃɪˈælətɪ/ (esp US **specialty** /'speʃəltɪ/) n [C] **1** sb's special interest, skill, subject, etc. **2** thing for which a person, company, etc is well known.

specialize /'speʃəlaɪz/ v [I] (in)// limit one's study, profession, etc to a particular thing: *~ in modern history.* **specialization** /-ˈzeɪʃn; US -lɪˈz-/ n [U].

species /'spiːʃiːz/ n [C] (pl **species**) group of animals with certain characteristics and able to breed with each other.

specific /spəˈsɪfɪk/ adj **1** detailed and precise: *~ instructions.* **2** relating to one particular thing, etc: *for a ~ purpose.* **specifically** /-klɪ/ adv.

specification /ˌspesɪfɪˈkeɪʃn/ n [C, usu pl] details, etc of the design and materials needed for sth.

specify /'spesɪfaɪ/ v (pt, pp -ied) [T] state (details, materials, etc) clearly and precisely.

specimen /'spesɪmɪn/ n [C] **1** thing or part of a thing taken as an example of a class or a whole: *a ~ of her work.* **2** thing to be tested for disease, etc.

speck /spek/ n [C] small spot; tiny piece (of dirt, etc).

speckle /'spekl/ n [C] small spot, esp one of many, on feathers, etc. **speckled** adj.

spectacle /'spektəkl/ n **1** [C] grand public display, performance, etc. **2** [C] interesting or impressive sight. **3** [pl] (fml) glasses.

spectacular /spekˈtækjʊlə(r)/ adj very impressive or remarkable. **spectacularly** adv.

spectator /spekˈteɪtə(r)/ n [C] person watching a show, game, etc.

spectrum /'spektrəm/ n [usu sing] (pl **-tra** /-trə/) **1** image of a band of colours as seen in a rainbow. **2** (fig) wide range: *a ~ of opinions.*

speculate /'spekjuleɪt/ v 1 [I, T] form opinions without having complete knowledge. 2 [I] buy and sell goods, shares, etc, hoping to make a profit but risking loss. **speculation** /-'leɪʃn/ n [C, U]. **speculative** adj.

sped pt, pp of SPEED.

speech /spiːtʃ/ n 1 [U] power, act or way of speaking. 2 [C] talk given to an audience: make a ~. **speechless** adj unable to speak, eg because of deep feeling.

speed /spiːd/ n 1 [U] quickness of movement: move with great ~. 2 [C, U] rate at which sb/sth moves: a ~ of 10 kilometres an hour. (idm) (at) full speed ⇨ FULL. **speed** v (pt, pp sped /sped/ in sense 2 ~ed) 1 [I] go quickly. 2 drive faster than the speed allowed by law. 3 (phr v) speed (sth) up (cause to) go faster: ~ up production. **speedometer** /spiːˈdɒmɪtə(r)/ n instrument showing the speed of a vehicle, etc. **'speedway** n [C, U] (track used for) racing motorbikes. **speedy** adj (-ier, -iest) quick.

spell¹ /spel/ n [C] (condition produced by) words supposed to have magic power: (fig) under the ~ of a fascinating man. **'spellbound** adj with the attention held (as if) by a spell.

spell² /spel/ n [C] 1 period of time: a ~ in prison. 2 period spent in a certain activity: a ~ at the wheel, ie driving.

spell³ /spel/ v (pt, pp spelt /spelt/ or spelled /speld/) 1 [I, T] name or write the letters of (a word). 2 [T] (of letters) form (words) when in a particular order: C-A-T ~s cat. 3 [T] result in: Does laziness always ~ failure? 4 (phr v) spell sth out make sth easy to understand. **spelling** n 1 [U] (a) ability to spell. (b) action of spelling. 2 [C] way in which a word is spelt.

spend /spend/ v (pt, pp spent /spent/) 1 [I, T] (on) pay out (money) for goods, services, etc. 2 [T] pass (time): ~ a week in hospital. 3 [T] use (time, etc) for a purpose: ~ one's energy cleaning the house. 4 (idm) spend a 'penny (infml euph) go to the toilet. **'spendthrift** n [C] person who wastes money. **spent** adj used up.

sperm /spɜːm/ n [U] male sex cell which fertilizes a female egg.

spew /spjuː/ v [I, T] (cause to) come out in a stream.

sphere /sfɪə(r)/ n [C] 1 completely round solid object. 2 range of interests, activities, influence, etc. **spherical** /'sferɪkl/ adj round in shape.

spice /spaɪs/ n 1 [C, U] substance, eg nutmeg, used for flavouring food. 2 [U] (fig) interest or excitement: add ~ to a story. **spice** v [T] add spice to. **spicy** adj (-ier, -iest) 1 containing spice. 2 (fig) exciting, esp because slightly rude.

spick /spɪk/ adj (idm) **spick and 'span** bright, clean and tidy.

spider /'spaɪdə(r)/ n [C] small eight-legged creature, esp one that spins a web to trap insects. **spidery** adj (of handwriting) with long thin strokes.

spied pt, pp of SPY.

spike /spaɪk/ n [C] 1 sharp point. 2 metal point attached to the sole of a running shoe, etc. 3 pointed cluster of flowers or grain on a single stem. **spike** v [T] pierce with a spike. **spiky** adj (-ier, -iest).

spill /spɪl/ v (pt, pp spilt /spɪlt/ or ~ed) [I, T] 1 (cause liquid or powder to) run over the side of the container. 2 (idm) spill the 'beans (infml) reveal a secret.

spin /spɪn/ v (pt spun /spʌn/ or span /spæn/, pp spun, -nn-) 1 [I, T] (cause to) go round and round quickly. 2 [I, T] form (thread) by twisting wool, cotton, etc. 3 [T] form by means of threads: Spiders ~ webs. 4 [T] (infml) compose (a story). 5 (phr v) spin sth out make sth last as long as possible. **spin** n 1 [C, U] spinning action. 2 [C] short ride in a car. 3 (idm) in a (flat) 'spin in a state of panic or confusion. **'spin-drier** n [C] device that spins clothes to dry them. **'spin-off** n [C] product, etc resulting indirectly from another process.

spinach /'spɪnɪdʒ/ n [U] plant with large green leaves, cooked and eaten as a vegetable.

spinal /'spaɪnl/ adj (anatomy) of the spine(1).

spindle /'spɪndl/ n [C] 1 thin rod for winding thread by hand in spinning. 2 bar on which part of a machine turns. **spindly** /'spɪndlɪ/ adj (-ier, -iest) long and thin.

spine /spaɪn/ n [C] 1 = BACKBONE (BACK³). 2 sharp point on some animals and plants, eg the cactus. 3 part of the cover of a book where the pages are joined together. **'spine-chilling** adj very frightening. **spineless** adj (derog) cowardly. **spiny** adj (-ier, -iest) having spines(2).

spinster /'spɪnstə(r)/ n [C] (sometimes derog) unmarried woman.

spiral /'spaɪərəl/ n [C] 1 curve winding round a central point: *A snail's shell is a ~.* 2 [usu sing] continuous increase or decrease. **spiral** adj having a spiral form. **spiral** v (-ll-; US -l-) [I] 1 move in a spiral. 2 increase or decrease.

spire /spaɪə(r)/ n [C] pointed tower, esp of a church.

spirit /'spɪrɪt/ n 1 [C, U] person's thoughts and feelings or soul. 2 [C] being without a body; ghost. 3 [C] person: *What a generous ~!* 4 [U] courage or liveliness: *act with ~.* 5 [sing] mental attitude; state of mind: *It depends on the ~ in which it was done.* 6 [U] real meaning: *obey the ~, not the letter, of the law.* 7 **spirits** [pl] state of mind: *in high ~s,* ie cheerful. 8 [C, usu pl] strong alcoholic drink, esp whisky. 9 (idm) **in spirit** in one's thoughts. **spirit** v (phr v) **spirit sth/sb away/off** take sth/sb quickly or mysteriously. **spirited** adj 1 lively, brave, etc. 2 having the mood stated: *high-/low-spirited.*

spiritual /'spɪrɪtʃuəl/ adj 1 of the spirit(1) or soul. 2 religious. **spiritual** n [C] religious song as originally sung by black slaves in the US. **spiritually** adv.

spit¹ /spɪt/ n [C] 1 metal spike which holds meat, etc for roasting. 2 narrow point of land jutting out into the sea, etc.

spit² /spɪt/ v (pt, pp **spat** /spæt/, -tt-) 1 [I] send liquid from the mouth. 2 [T] (out)/(a) send (liquid, food, etc) from the mouth. (b) shout angrily: *~ (out) a command.* 3 [I] (used with *it*) rain lightly. 4 (idm) **be the spitting image of sb** ⇨ IMAGE. **spit** n [U] saliva.

spite /spaɪt/ n [U] 1 desire to annoy, offend or cause pain: *do sth out of ~.* 2 (idm) **in spite of** without being prevented by (the conditions mentioned): *They went out in ~ of the rain.* **spite** v [T] annoy, offend, etc out of spite. **spiteful** adj.

splash /splæʃ/ v 1 (a) [I] (of liquid) move or fall in drops. (b) [T] make (sb/sth) wet by throwing (liquid): *~ water on the floor.* 2 [T] display: *~ his name all over the newspapers.* 3 (phr v) **splash out (on sth)** (infml) spend a lot of money (on sth). **splash** n [C] sound or act of, or mark made by, splashing.

spleen /spliːn/ n [C] organ that controls the quality of the blood in the body.

splendid /'splendɪd/ adj 1 magnificent: *a ~ view.* 2 (infml) excellent: *a ~ performance.* **splen-**

didly adv.

splendour (US **-dor**) /'splendə(r)/ n [U] quality of being splendid or magnificent.

splice /splaɪs/ v [T] join (two pieces of a rope, wood, etc) together.

splint /splɪnt/ n [C] piece of wood, etc strapped to an arm, etc to keep a broken bone in position.

splinter /'splɪntə(r)/ n [C] sharp piece of wood, glass, etc broken from a larger piece. **splinter** v [I, T] break into splinters. **splinter group** n [C] (esp in politics) group that has separated from a larger one.

split /splɪt/ v (pt, pp **split**, -tt-) 1 [I, T] divide (sth) along its length. 2 [T] divide into separate or opposing parts: *Arguments ~ the group.* 3 [I, T] (open)/(cause to) open suddenly: *The box ~ (open).* 4 [T] share: *~ the profits.* 5 [I] (esp US sl) leave: *Let's ~!* 5 (idm) **split 'hairs** make (too) fine distinctions in an argument, etc. **split one's 'sides** laugh very much. 6 (idm) **split up** end a marriage or relationship. **split** n [C] crack or tear made by splitting. 2 [C] act of splitting. 3 [C] separation or division. 4 **the splits** [pl] act of sitting with the legs stretched in opposite directions. **,split perso'nality** n [C] mental disorder in which one person seems to have two distinct personalities. **split 'second** n [C] very short moment.

splutter /'splʌtə(r)/ v 1 [I, T] speak (words) in a quick confused way, eg because of excitement. 2 [I] make a spitting sound: *The fire ~ed.* **splutter** n [C] spluttering sound.

spoil /spɔɪl/ v (pt, pp ~t or ~ed) 1 [T] harm the value or pleasure of: *Rain ~ed our holiday.* 2 [T] harm the character of (esp a child) by lack of discipline. 3 [I] (of food, etc) become bad. **spoils** n [pl] (fml) stolen goods, profit, etc. **'spoilsport** n [C] person who ruins others' enjoyment.

spoke¹ /spəʊk/ n [C] rod connecting the centre of a wheel to the edge.

spoke² pt of SPEAK.

spoken pp of SPEAK.

spokesman /'spəʊksmən/ (pl -men /-mən/) **spokesperson** (pl -people) **spokeswoman** (pl -women) n [C] person speaking as the representative of a group, etc.

sponge /spʌndʒ/ n 1 [C] simple sea-animal with a body full of holes, able to absorb water easily. 2 [C, U] piece of one of these, or sth

similar, used for cleaning or wiping. 3 [C, U] sponge-cake.
sponge *v* 1 [T] wipe with a sponge. 2 [I] (*infml*) take (esp money) without giving anything in return: ~ *money off/from one's friends.* '**sponge-cake** *n* [C, U] soft light cake. **spongy** *adj* (**-ier, -iest**).

sponsor /'spɒnsə(r)/ *n* [C] 1 person, company, etc that pays for an event. 2 person who takes responsibility for another. **sponsor** *v* [T] 1 act as a sponsor. 2 pay (sb) money if they do (sth) for charity. **sponsorship** *n* [U].

spontaneous /spɒn'teɪnɪəs/ *adj* done, happening, etc naturally and not planned: *a ~ offer of help.* **spontaneity** /ˌspɒntə'neɪətɪ/ *n* [U]. **spontaneously** *adv.*

spoof /spuːf/ *n* [C] (*infml*) humorous copy.

spooky /'spuːkɪ/ *adj* (**-ier, -iest**) (*infml*) frightening.

spool /spuːl/ *n* [C] reel for thread, film, tape, etc.

spoon /spuːn/ *n* [C] utensil with a shallow bowl on a handle, used for putting food, eg soup, into the mouth. **spoon** *v* [T] take with a spoon. '**spoon-feed** *v* [T] give (sb) too much help, teaching, etc.

sporadic /spə'rædɪk/ *adj* occurring only occasionally. **sporadically** /-klɪ/ *adv.*

spore /spɔː(r)/ *n* [C] seed of some plants, eg mushrooms.

sport /spɔːt/ *n* 1 [C, U] activity done for amusement or exercise, usu according to rules. 2 **sports** [pl] meeting for athletic contests: *school ~ s.* 3 [C] (*infml*) unselfish, kind person. **sport** *v* [T] have or wear proudly: *~ a new beard.* **sporting** *adj* 1 of or interested in sport. 2 showing fairness. 3 (*idm*) **a sporting chance** a reasonable chance of success. '**sports car** *n* [C] car designed for high speeds. '**sportsman, sportswoman** *n* [C] person who takes part in sport. '**sportsmanship** *n* [U] quality of being fair and generous, esp in sport. **sporty** *adj* (**-ier, -iest**) good at or fond of sports.

spot /spɒt/ *n* [C] 1 small esp round mark of a different colour from the surface it is on. 2 dirty mark. 3 small red inflamed mark on the skin. 4 place: *the ~ where she died.* 5 (*infml*) small amount: *a ~ of tea.* 6 (*idm*) **in a (tight) 'spot** (*infml*) in a difficult situation. **on the 'spot (a)** at the place where one is needed. **(b)** immediately: *killed on the ~.* **spot** *v* (**-tt-**) [T] 1 (usu passive) mark with spots. 2 see (sb). **spotted** *adj* marked with

spots. **spotless** *adj* completely clean. **spotty** *adj* (**-ier, -iest**) having spots, esp on the skin.

spotlight /'spɒtlaɪt/ *n* [C] (lamp used for sending a) strong light directed at a particular place. **spotlight** *v* [T] 1 direct a spotlight at. 2 (*fig*) direct attention at: *~ a problem.*

spouse /spaʊs/ *n* [C] (*fml* or *law*) husband or wife.

spout /spaʊt/ *n* [C] 1 pipe through which liquid pours: *a ~ on a teapot.* 2 (*idm*) **up the 'spout** (*infml*) ruined. **spout** *v* 1 [I, T] (cause liquid to) come out with great force. 2 [T] (*infml*) speak (eg verse) loudly and for a long time.

sprain /spreɪn/ *v* [T] injure (a joint) by twisting violently: *~ an ankle.* **sprain** *n* [C] injury caused in this way.

sprang *pt* of SPRING².

sprawl /sprɔːl/ *v* [I] 1 sit or lie with one's arms and legs spread carelessly. 2 (of plants, towns) spread over an area. **sprawl** *n* [C, U] sprawling position or area: *urban ~.*

spray¹ /spreɪ/ *n* [C] small branch of a tree or plant, esp for decoration.

spray² /spreɪ/ *n* 1 [U] liquid sent through the air in tiny drops. 2 [C, U] liquid, eg perfume, in the form of tiny drops. 3 [C] device that turns liquid into tiny drops. **spray** *v* 1 [T] put (liquid) on (sth), using a spray. 2 [I] (of a liquid) come out in tiny drops.

spread /spred/ *v* (*pt, pp* **spread**) 1 [T] extend the surface of sth by unfolding it: *The bird ~ its wings.* 2 [T] put (a substance) on (a surface): *~ butter on bread.* 3 [I, T] (cause to) become more widely known, felt, etc: *~ disease.* 4 [I] extend over an area or period of time. **spread** *n* 1 [usu sing] extent or width. 2 [C] (*infml*) a lot of food on a table. 4 [U, C] paste for spreading on bread, etc. '**spread-eagle** *v* [T] put (sb) in a position with arms and legs in the form of a cross. '**spreadsheet** *n* [C] computer program for displaying and changing rows of figures.

sprightly /'spraɪtlɪ/ *adj* (**-ier, -iest**) lively and active. **sprightliness** *n* [U].

spring¹ /sprɪŋ/ *n* 1 [C] (place where there is) water coming up from the ground. 2 [C] length of coiled wire which returns to its shape after being pulled or pressed. 3 [C] act of jumping. 4 [U] elastic quality. **springy** *adj* (**-ier,**

-iest).

spring² /sprɪŋ/ v (pt **sprang** /spræŋ/, pp **sprung** /sprʌŋ/) 1 [I] jump or move suddenly: ~ (up) from one's chair ○ The door sprang open. 2 (idm) **spring a 'leak** (of a boat, etc) begin to leak. 4 (phr v) **spring from sth** have sth as a source or origin. **spring sth on sb** produce suddenly as a surprise: She sprang the news on me. **spring up** grow or rise quickly.

spring³ /sprɪŋ/ n [C, U] season of the year between winter and summer, when plants begin to grow. ,**spring-'clean** v [T] clean (a house, etc) thoroughly. ,**spring-'cleaning** n [U].

sprinkle /'sprɪŋkl/ v [T] scatter (liquid, dust, etc) on to (a surface). **sprinkler** /-klə(r)/ n [C] device for sprinkling water, eg on grass. **sprint** /sprɪnt/ v [I] run at full speed. **sprint** n [C] fast run. **sprinter** n [C].

sprout /spraʊt/ v [I, T] produce (leaves, etc) or begin to grow: (fig) houses sprouting (up) on the edge of town. **sprout** n [C] 1 new part of a plant. 2 = BRUSSELS SPROUT.

sprung pp of SPRING².

spun pp of SPIN.

spur /spɜː(r)/ n [C] 1 sharp-toothed wheel on the heel of a rider's boot, used to make the horse go faster. 2 (fig) thing that encourages sb to try or work harder. 3 (idm) **on the spur of the moment** suddenly and without thinking. **spur** v (-rr-) [T] (-rr-) encourage (sb) to make greater efforts, etc.

spurn /spɜːn/ v [T] reject or refuse (sb, an offer, etc).

spurt /spɜːt/ v [I, T] (cause liquids, etc to) come out in a sudden burst. 2 [I] make a sudden effort in a race, contest, etc. **spurt** n [C] 1 sudden burst of energy, speed, etc. 2 sudden rush of liquid, etc.

sputter /'spʌtə(r)/ v [I] make a series of spitting sounds.

spy /spaɪ/ n [C] (pl -ies) 1 person who tries to get secret information, esp about an enemy, for his/her government. 2 person who secretly watches and reports on others. **spy** v (pt, pp -ied) 1 [I, T] (on)// watch (sb) secretly. 2 [T] (fml or joc) catch sight of.

squabble /'skwɒbl/ v [I] (have) a noisy quarrel, usu about sth unimportant.

squad /skwɒd/ n [C, also sing with pl v] small group of people working as a team: a football ~.

squadron /'skwɒdrən/ n [C, also sing with pl v] group of soldiers, military aircraft, warships, etc.

squalid /'skwɒlɪd/ adj 1 dirty and unpleasant. 2 morally bad. **squalidly** adv.

squall /skwɔːl/ n [C] 1 sudden violent wind. 2 loud cry, esp from a baby. **squall** v [I] cry noisily.

squalor /'skwɒlə(r)/ n [U] squalid state.

square¹ /skweə(r)/ adj 1 having the shape of a square²(1). 2 forming a right angle: ~ corners. 3 equal to a square with sides of a stated length: six metres ~. 4 honest; fair: ~ dealings. 5 having paid all bills, etc. 6 (idm) **a square meal** a satisfying meal. **be (all) square (with sb)** (a) have equal points. (b) not owing anything to sb. **square** adv squarely. **squarely** adv 1 so as to form a right angle. 2 directly: I looked her ~ly in the eye. 3 honestly. **squareness** n [U].

square root n [C] number which multiplied by itself gives a specified result: The ~ root of 4 is 2.

square² /skweə(r)/ n [C] 1 shape or area with four equal sides and four right angles. 2 anything having the shape of a square. 3 four-sided open area, eg in a town. 4 result when a number is multiplied by itself. 5 (idm) **back to square one** back to one's starting-point.

square³ /skweə(r)/ v 1 [T] make square. 2 [T] make straight or level. 3 [T] multiply (a number) by itself. 4 [I, T] with// (infml) be or make consistent with: ~ the theory with the facts. 5 [T] (infml) bribe. 6 (phr v) **square sth off** mark off in squares. **square up (with sb)** pay (sb) the money one owes, esp before leaving a restaurant.

squash¹ /skwɒʃ/ v 1 [T] press flat; crush. 2 [I, T] squeeze or crowd: ~ ten people into a car. 3 [T] defeat (a rebellion, etc). 4 [T] reject (a proposal, etc). **squash** n 1 [sing] crowd of people squashed together. 2 [U, C] drink made from fruit juice.

squash² /skwɒʃ/ n [U] game played with rackets and a rubber ball in a walled court.

squat /skwɒt/ v (-tt-) [I] 1 sit with one's legs bent under the body. 2 occupy empty buildings, land, etc without permission. **squat** adj short and thick. **squat** n [C] place occupied by squatters. **squatter** n [C] person who squats(2).

squaw /skwɔː/ n [C] North American Indian woman.

squawk /skwɔːk/ v [I] 1 (esp of birds) make a loud harsh cry. 2 (*infml*) complain loudly. **squawk** n [C].

squeak /skwiːk/ v [I, T] n [C] (make) a short shrill noise or cry. **squeaky** *adj* (-ier, -iest).

squeal /skwiːl/ n [C] shrill noise or cry, longer and louder than a squeak. **squeal** v [I] 1 make a squeal. 2 (*sl*) reveal secret information, esp to the police about a partner in crime.

squeamish /ˈskwiːmɪʃ/ *adj* 1 easily made sick. 2 easily shocked, offended, etc. **squeamishly** *adv*. **squeamishness** n [U].

squeeze /skwiːz/ v 1 [T] press from opposite sides, or from all sides: ~ a sponge. 2 [T] (*from/out of*)// get (water, juice, etc) out of sth by pressing hard. 3 [I, T] force (sb/sth/oneself) into or through a small space: ~ *into the back seat*. 4 (phr v) **squeeze sth out of sb** get (information, etc) by force. **squeeze** n [C] act of squeezing. 2 [sing] condition of being squeezed. 3 [C] (*infml*) period of financial difficulty.

squelch /skweltʃ/ v [I] make a sucking sound as when feet are lifted from mud. **squelch** n [C] squelching sound.

squid /skwɪd/ n [C, U] sea-animal with ten long arms round the mouth.

squint /skwɪnt/ v [I] 1 have eyes that look in different directions at once. 2 look at sth with half-shut eyes. **squint** n [sing] squinting position of the eyes.

squirm /skwɜːm/ v [I] 1 move by twisting the body about. 2 feel embarrassment or shame. **squirm** n [C] squirming movement.

squirrel /ˈskwɪrəl/ n [C] small bushy-tailed animal with red or grey fur.

squirt /skwɜːt/ v (a) [T] force (liquid, powder, etc) out in a thin stream. (b) [I] (of liquid, powder, etc) be forced out in this way. **squirt** n [C] thin stream or jet of liquid, powder, etc.

St *abbr* 1 saint(1). 2 street.

stab /stæb/ v (-bb-) 1 [T] strike or wound with a pointed weapon. 2 (idm) **stab sb in the ˈback** betray sb. **stab** n [C] 1 stabbing blow. 2 sudden sharp pain. 3 attempt: *have a ~ at sth.* **stabbing** adj (of pain) very sharp and sudden.

stable[1] /ˈsteɪbl/ adj (~r, ~st) not likely to move or change. **stability** /stəˈbɪlətɪ/ n [U]. **stabilize** /ˈsteɪbəlaɪz/ v [I, T] (cause to) become stable. **stabilizer** n [C] per-

son or thing that stabilizes.

stable[2] /ˈsteɪbl/ n [C] building in which horses are kept. **stable** v [T] put (a horse) in a stable.

stack /stæk/ n [C] 1 (usu neat) pile: *a ~ of books.* 2 pile of hay, straw, etc stored in the open. 3 tall chimney or group of chimneys. 4 **stacks of sth** [pl] (*infml*) large number of sth. **stack** v [T] make into a stack.

stadium /ˈsteɪdɪəm/ (*pl* ~s or **-dia** /-dɪə/) n [C] enclosed area of land for sports, with seats for spectators.

staff /stɑːf/ n 1 [C] strong stick used as a support when walking. 2 [C] group of assistants working together under a manager. 3 [U] people in authority in an organization, eg the teachers in a school. 4 [C] group of senior army officers. **staff** v [T] provide with staff(2)(3).

stag /stæg/ n [C] male deer.

stage /steɪdʒ/ n 1 [C] raised platform on which actors perform plays. 2 **the stage** [sing] acting as a profession. 3 [usu sing] (*fig*) place where events occur. 4 period or step in development, growth, etc: *at an early ~ in her life.* 5 part of a journey. 6 (idm) **be/go on the ˈstage** become an actor. **stage** v [T] produce a performance of (a play, etc). **ˈstage-coach** n [C] horse-drawn vehicle which was used to carry passengers. **ˈstage-manager** n [C] person in charge of a theatre stage.

stagger /ˈstægə(r)/ v 1 [I] walk unsteadily. 2 [T] (of news, etc) shock deeply. 3 [T] arrange (events, etc) so that they do not happen together. **stagger** n [sing] staggering movement.

stagnant /ˈstægnənt/ adj 1 (of water) not moving and often smelling bad. 2 (*fig*) not developing.

stagnate /stægˈneɪt/ v [I] 1 become dull through doing nothing, etc. 2 become stagnant(1). **stagnation** /-ʃn/ n [U].

staid /steɪd/ adj (of appearance, behaviour, etc) dull, quiet and serious. **staidly** adv. **staidness** n [U].

stain /steɪn/ v 1 (a) [T] make coloured patches or dirty marks on sth. (b) [I] become stained. 2 [T] colour (wood, fabric, etc). **stain** n 1 [U] liquid used for colouring wood, etc. 2 [C] stained place. 3 [C] thing that harms sb's reputation, etc. **stained ˈglass** n [U] coloured glass, often used to make patterns in windows. **stainless** adj (esp of steel) that does not rust.

stair /steə(r)/ n 1 **stairs** [pl] series of fixed steps leading from one floor of a building to another: *a flight of ~ s.* 2 [C] one of a series of steps: *sitting on the bottom ~.* 'staircase, 'stairway n [C] set of stairs inside a building.

stake /steɪk/ n 1 [C] strong pointed wooden post driven into the ground. 2 [C, usu pl] sum of money risked or gambled. 3 [C] part-ownership and interest in a company: *I have a ~ in the company's success.* 4 (idm) **at stake** being risked. **stake** v [T] 1 support with a stake. 2 risk (money, etc). 3 (idm) **stake a claim** declare that one owns sth, has certain rights, etc. 4 (phr v) **stake sth out** (esp *US infml*) (esp of the police) watch (a place) continuously and secretly.

stale /steɪl/ adj 1 (of food, etc) not fresh. 2 no longer interesting because too well-known. 3 (of athletes, musicians, etc) not able to perform well because of too much practice, etc. **staleness** n [U].

stalemate /'steɪlmeɪt/ n [C, U] 1 position in chess in which no further move can be made. 2 stage in an argument, etc in which no further discussion seems possible.

stalk[1] /stɔ:k/ n [C] part of a plant supporting a flower, leaves or fruit.

stalk[2] /stɔ:k/ v 1 [I] walk with slow stiff strides, esp in a proud way. 2 [T] hunt (wild animals, etc) by following them quietly and gradually moving closer: *~ deer.* **stalker** n [C] person who stalks animals.

stall /stɔ:l/ n [C] 1 compartment for one animal in a stable. 2 table or small open shop, etc from which things are sold in the street. 3 **stalls** [pl] seats in a theatre nearest the stage. **stall** v 1 [I, T] (cause an engine, etc to) stop because of lack of power. 2 [I, T] (cause an aircraft to) become out of control through loss of speed. 3 [I] delay.

stallion /'stælɪən/ n [C] male horse, esp one used for breeding.

stamina /'stæmɪnə/ n [U] energy and strength to work hard, run long distances, etc.

stammer /'stæmə(r)/ v 1 [I] repeat certain sounds rapidly when speaking, because of a speech defect, fear, etc. 2 [T] (*out*)(*I*) say (sth in this way): *~ (out) an apology.* **stammer** n [sing] (tendency to) stammering speech.

stamp[1] /stæmp/ n [C] 1 small piece of printed paper stuck on envelopes, documents, etc to show

that postage, duty, etc has been paid. 2 device with which a mark is stamped on a surface. 3 word(s), design, etc made by stamping on a surface. 4 act of stamping with the foot. 'stamp album n [C] book for keeping postage stamps collected as a hobby.

stamp[2] /stæmp/ v 1 [I, T] put (one's foot) down with force on (the ground, etc). 2 [T] *A on B; B with A*// print (a design, the date, etc) on (paper or another surface). 3 [T] put a postage stamp on (a letter, etc). 4 (on) [T] make an impression on: *~ one's personality on sth.* 5 (phr v) **stamp sth out** put an end to or destroy (a rebellion, etc).

stampede /stæm'pi:d/ n [C] sudden rush of people or animals, eg through fear, excitement. **stampede** v [I, T] (cause to) move in a stampede.

stance /stæns/ n [C] 1 way of standing, esp when striking the ball in golf, cricket, etc. 2 attitude, opinion: *her ~ on nuclear arms.*

stand[1] /stænd/ n 1 [sing] stationary condition or position: *come to a ~.* 2 [C] piece of furniture on which things are placed: *a music ~.* 3 [C] table, kiosk, etc where things are sold or shown. 4 [C] building where people stand or sit to watch sports contests, etc. 5 [C] (period of) resistance to attack: *make a ~.* 6 (*US*) = WITNESS-BOX (WITNESS). **standpoint** n [C] point of view.

stand[2] /stænd/ v (pt, pp **stood** /stʊd/) 1 [I] have, take or keep an upright position; support one's body on one's feet. 2 [I] have a stated height: *She ~ s five foot six.* 3 [T] place in an upright position: *~ the ladder against the wall.* 4 [I] be in a certain place: *the house ~ s on the corner.* 5 [I] remain unchanged: *My decision ~ s.* 6 [I] pay for: *~ sb a meal.* 7 [I] (*for*)// be a candidate in an election: *~ for parliament.* 8 (idm) **stand a chance** have a chance of succeeding, etc. **stand firm/fast** not change one's views, etc. **stand one's ground** ⇨ GROUND[1]. **stand on one's own (two) feet** be independent. **stand out like a sore thumb** ⇨ SORE. **stand to reason** be obvious to everyone. 9 (phr v) **stand by** (a) be present without doing anything. (b) be ready for action. **stand by sb** support sb. **stand by sth** be faithful to (a promise, etc). **stand down** resign from a job, etc; withdraw. **stand for sth** (a) represent: *PO ~ s for Post Office.* (b) (*infml*) tolerate: *She doesn't ~ for* *disobedience*. **stand in (for sb)** take the place of sb. **stand out (a)** be easily seen. **(b)** continue to resist: ~ *out against the enemy*. **stand sb up** (*infml*) not keep an appointment. **stand up for sb/sth** support sb/sth. **stand up to sb** resist sb. **stand up to sth** remain in good condition in spite of (hard use, etc). **stand-by** *n* **(a)** [U] state of readiness. **(b)** [C] person or thing (to be) used as a substitute. **stand-in** *n* [C] person who takes the place of sb else. **stand-offish** *adj* (of people) reserved and unfriendly.

standard /'stændəd/ *n* [C] **1** thing used as a measure. **2** (normal or expected) level of quality: *the ~ of her school work*. **3** special flag. **standard** *adj* of the normal or usual kind: ~ *sizes of paper*. **standardize** /US -daiz/ *v* [T] make (sth) conform to a fixed standard of size, shape, quality, etc. **'standard lamp** *n* [C] tall lamp with a base on the floor. **standard of 'living** *n* [C] level of comfort, wealth, etc enjoyed by sb.

standing /'stændɪŋ/ *n* [U] **1** rank or reputation. **2** length of existence: *debts of long* ~. **standing** *adj* permanent and established: *a* ~ *army*.

stank *pt* of STINK.

stanza /'stænzə/ *n* [C] group of lines in a poem.

staple[1] *n* [C] small piece of bent wire for holding sheets of paper together. **staple** *v* [T] fasten or secure with a staple. **stapler** *n* [C] device for putting in staples.

staple[2] *n* [C] main article or product. **staple** *adj* forming the main part (of sth): *Their ~ diet is rice*.

star /stɑ:(r)/ *n* [C] **1** large ball of burning gas seen as a point of light in the sky at night. **2** figure with five or more points resembling a star, often used to show quality. **3** famous singer, actor, etc. **4** body in the sky thought to influence one's fate: *born under a lucky* ~. **star** *v* (**-rr-**) **(a)** [I] be the main actor in a film, etc. **(b)** [T] (of a film, etc) have (sb) as the main actor. **'stardom** /'stɑ:dəm/ *n* [U] status of being a star(3). **'starfish** *n* [C] sea animal shaped like a star. **starry** *adj*.

starboard /'stɑ:bəd/ *n* [U] right side of a ship or aircraft when it is facing forward.

starch /stɑ:tʃ/ *n* [U] **1** white, tasteless food substance found in potatoes, rice, etc. **2** this substance used for stiffening cotton clothes,

etc. **starch** *v* [T] make stiff with starch. **starchy** *adj* (**-ier**, **-iest**).

stare /steə(r)/ *v* [I] (*at*)// look for a long time with great attention. **stare** *n* [C] staring look.

stark /stɑ:k/ *adj* **1** desolate and bare: *a* ~ *landscape*. **2** obvious; clear: *in* ~ *contrast*. **stark** *adv* completely: ~ *naked*.

starling /'stɑ:lɪŋ/ *n* [C] common small bird with dark shiny feathers.

starry ⇔ STAR.

start[1] /stɑ:t/ *n* **1** [C, usu sing] beginning of a journey, activity, etc. **2 the start** [sing] place where a race begins. **3** [U, C] time or distance by which one starts in front of competitors.

start[2] /stɑ:t/ *v* **1** [I] (*out*)// begin a journey. **2** [I, T] begin (to do sth). **3** [I, T] (*up*)// (cause an engine, etc to) begin running: *The car won't ~*. **4** [T] bring into existence, originate: ~ *a business*. **5** (*idm*) **start the ball rolling** ⇔ START¹. **(phr v) start off (on sth)** cause sb to begin saying, doing, etc sth. **start off (to do sth)** (*infml*) begin. **starter** *n* [C] **1** device to start an engine. **2** first course of a meal. **3** person who starts a race. **4** (*idm*) **for 'starters** first of all.

startle /'stɑ:tl/ *v* [T] give a shock or surprise to.

starve /stɑ:v/ *v* **1** [I, T] (cause to) suffer or die from hunger. **2** [I] (*infml*) be hungry: *I'm starving*. **3** [T] (usu passive) not allow sb to have sth needed: *children ~d of love*. **starvation** /-'veɪʃn/ *n* [U].

state[1] /steɪt/ *n* **1** [C] condition of a person or thing: *a poor ~ of health*. **2** (also **State**) [C] country. **3** (also **State**) [C] organized political community forming part of a larger country: *Ohio is a ~ in America*. **4** (esp **the State**) [U] government of a country. **5** [U] very formal ceremony: *buried in ~*. **state** *adj* of the state(4). **2** of or for ceremony: *a ~ visit*. **stately** *adj* (**-ier**, **-iest**) dignified.

state[2] /steɪt/ *v* [T] express in words, esp fully, clearly and formally. **statement** *n* [C] **1** formal account of events, views, etc. **2** financial report: *a bank ~*.

statesman /'steɪtsmən/ *n* [C] (*pl* **-men**) person taking an important part in state affairs. **'statesmanship** *n* [U] skill and wisdom in managing state affairs.

static /'stætɪk/ *adj* not moving. **static** *n* [U] **1** atmospheric disturbance affecting radio broadcasts. **2** (also ,**static elec'tricity**) electricity which collects on the surface of objects.

station /'steɪʃn/ n [C] 1 building, etc where a service is organized: *a 'bus ~*. 2 stopping-place for trains. 3 broadcasting company. **station** v [T] put (eg troops) at a certain place. **'station-wagon** n [C] (*US*) = ESTATE CAR (ESTATE).

stationary /'steɪʃənrɪ/ adj not moving: *~ traffic*.

stationer /'steɪʃnə(r)/ n [C] person who sells stationery. **stationery** /'steɪʃnrɪ/; *US* -nerɪ/ n [U] paper, envelopes, etc for writing.

statistics /stə'tɪstɪks/ n 1 [pl] information shown as numbers. 2 [U] the science of collecting and explaining statistics. **statistical** /-kl/ adj. **statistically** /-klɪ/ adv. **statistician** /ˌstætɪ'stɪʃn/ n [C] expert in statistics.

statue /'stætjuː/ n [C] figure of a person, animal, etc in wood, stone, bronze, etc. **statuette** /ˌstætʃʊ'et/ n [C] small statue.

stature /'stætʃə(r)/ n [U] 1 (person's) size or height. 2 (*fig*) importance gained from achievement or ability.

status /'steɪtəs/ n [U] person's legal, social or professional position. **'status symbol** n [C] item showing sb's importance, wealth, etc, eg a large car.

status quo /ˌsteɪtəs kwəʊ/ n [C] existing state of affairs.

statute /'stætjuːt/ n [C] law passed by Parliament. **statutory** /-trɪ/; *US* -tɔːrɪ/ adj fixed or required by statute.

staunch /stɔːntʃ/ adj (of a supporter, etc) loyal. **staunchly** adv.

stave /steɪv/ v (*pt, pp* ~d or **stove** /stəʊv/) (phr v) **stave sth in** break or make a hole in sth. **stave sth off** (*pt, pp* ~d) delay (danger, etc).

stay /steɪ/ v 1 [I] be or remain in the same place or condition: *~ at home ~ sober*. 2 [I] live temporarily: *~ at a hotel*. 3 [T] stop or delay: *~ the progress of the disease*. 4 (idm) **stay clear of sb/sth** ⇨ CLEAR¹. **stay put** remain where one/it is. 5 (phr v) **stay up** not go to bed. **stay** n [C] 1 period of being or living in a place: *a long ~ in hospital*. 2 (*law*) stopping or delay: *a ~ of execution*. **'staying-power** n [U] = STAMINA.

steadfast /'stedfɑːst; *US* -fæst/ adj firm and unchanging. **steadfastly** adv.

steady /'stedɪ/ adj (-ier, -iest) 1 firmly fixed or supported; not moving: *hold the ladder ~*. 2 even and regular: *a ~ speed*. 3 reliable:

a ~ worker. 4 unchanging: *a ~ purpose*. **steady** adv steadily. **steady** v (-ied) [I, T] make or become steady. **steadily** adv in a regular way.

steak /steɪk/ n [C, U] (thick slice of) meat or fish.

steal /stiːl/ v (*pt* **stole** /stəʊl/, *pp* **stolen** /'stəʊlən/) 1 [I, T] (*from*) take (sb's property) without permission. 2 [T] obtain by surprise or by a trick: *~ a kiss*. 3 [I] move secretly and quietly. 4 (idm) **steal the show** attract the most attention.

stealth /stelθ/ n [U] behaving in a quiet or secret way. **stealthy** adj (-ier, -iest).

steam /stiːm/ n [U] 1 mist which rises from boiling water. 2 power obtained from steam. 3 (idm) **run out of steam** become exhausted. **steam** v 1 [I] give out steam. 2 [I] move, work, etc by steam power. 3 [T] cook by steam. 4 (phr v) **steam up** (cause to) become misty with steam. **'steam-engine** n [C] engine driven by steam. **steamer** n [C] 1 steamship. 2 vessel in which food is steamed. **'steam-roller** n [C] heavy vehicle used for flattening new roads. **steamy** adj.

steel /stiːl/ n [U] hard metal made from iron and carbon, used for knives, machinery, etc. **steel** v [T] not allow (oneself) to feel pity, etc: *~ oneself (against a cry for help)*.

steep /stiːp/ adj 1 (of a slope) rising or falling sharply. 2 (*infml*) too high: *~ prices*. **steeply** adv. **steepness** n [U].

steep² /stiːp/ v 1 [I, T] soak in liquid. 2 (phr v) **steep sb/oneself in sth** give (sb/oneself) a thorough knowledge of sth.

steeple /'stiːpl/ n [C] high tower with a spire above a church. **'steeplechase** n [C] race for horses or athletes with obstacles such as fences and ditches. **'steeplejack** n [C] person who repairs steeples, tall chimneys, etc.

steer /stɪə(r)/ v [I, T] 1 direct the course of (a boat, car, etc). 2 (idm) **steer clear of sb/sth** ⇨ CLEAR¹. **'steering-wheel** n [C] wheel used for steering a car.

stem¹ /stem/ n [C] (a) part of a plant coming up from the roots. (b) part like a stem, eg on a wine glass. **stem** v (-mm-) (phr v) **stem from sth** have sth as an origin.

stem² /stem/ v [T] (-mm-) stop (the flow of liquid, etc).

stench /stentʃ/ n [C] unpleasant smell.

stencil /'stensl/ n [C] 1 thin sheet of metal, etc with letters or designs cut in it. **2** letters, etc made by putting ink, etc through holes on a stencil. stencil *v* (-ll-; *US* -l-) [I, T] produce (letters, etc) with a stencil.

step¹ /step/ *n* [C] **1 (a)** act of stepping once. **(b)** distance covered by doing this. **2** way or sound of walking: *heard her ~ on the stair.* **3** one of a series of actions to do sth: *take ~s to help her.* **4** flat place for the foot when going from one level to another. **5 steps** [pl] step-ladder. **6** (idm) **in/out of step (with)** (a) putting/not putting one's feet down at the same time as others. **(b)** agreeing/not agreeing with. **mind/watch one's** step behave carefully. **step by 'step** gradually. '**step-ladder** *n* [C] folding ladder with steps.

step² /step/ *v* (-pp-) [I] **1** move the foot, as in walking. **2** *in, out, up, etc*∥ move in the stated direction by stepping. **3** (idm) '**step on it** (*infml*) go faster or hurry. ,**step out of 'line** do sth different from what is expected. **4** (phr v) **step aside**, **step down** resign from a position or job, esp so sb else may have it. **step in** become involved (in sth) so as to help. **step sth up** increase sth. '**stepping-stone** *n* [C] **1** one of a series of stones used to cross a stream, etc. **2** (*fig*) stage towards achieving sth.

step- /step/ *prefix* related as a result of remarriage: '*~ daughter.*

stereo /'steriəʊ/ *adj* using sound that gives a natural effect by using two loudspeakers. **stereo** *n* **1** [U] stereo sound: *in ~.* **2** [C] stereo record-player, radio, etc.

stereotype /'steriətaip/ *n* [C] fixed idea of what sb/sth is like.

sterile /'sterail; *US* 'sterəl/ *adj* **1** not able to produce babies or young. **2** (of land) not able to produce crops. **3** (*fig*) having no result: *a ~ argument.* **4** free from germs. **sterility** /stə'riləti/ *n* [U]. **sterilize** /'sterəlaiz/ *v* [T] make sterile(1)(4).

sterling /'stɜːlɪŋ/ *n* [U] British money. **sterling** *adj* (*fml*) of good character, quality, etc.

stern¹ /stɜːn/ *adj* severe, strict or serious. **sternly** *adv*.

stern² /stɜːn/ *n* [C] rear end of a ship.

steroid /'steroid, 'stɪəroid/ *n* [C] powerful chemical produced in the body or taken as a drug.

stethoscope /'steθəskəʊp/ *n* [C] instrument for listening to the beating of the heart, etc.

stew /stjuː/ *v* [T] cook slowly in water or juices in a closed pan, etc.

stew *n* [C, U] (dish of) stewed meat, etc. **2** (idm) **in a stew** (*infml*) nervous or excited.

steward /'stjʊəd; *US* 'stuːəd/ *n* [C] **1** (also **stewardess** /,stjʊə'des; *US* ,stuːə'des/) person who attends to the passengers in a ship or on an airliner. **2** person responsible for organizing a race-meeting, dance, etc.

stick¹ /stɪk/ *n* [C] **1** small thin piece of wood. **2** rod of wood: *a 'walking-~.* **3** slender piece of chalk, etc). **4** (idm) **give sb 'stick** (*infml*) punish or criticize sb.

stick² /stɪk/ *v* (*pt, pp* **stuck** /stʌk/) **1** [I, in, T] in, into, through, *etc*∥ push (sth) pointed in, into, etc: *~ the knife into the cheese.* **2** [I, T] (cause) to be fastened, esp with glue. **3** [T] (*infml*) put (sth) in some position, esp quickly or carelessly: *S~ it in the bag.* **4** [I] be or become fixed in one place and not move: *The key stuck in the lock.* **5** [T] (*infml*) tolerate: *I can't ~ it.* **6** (idm) **stick one's neck out** take risks. **stick one's nose into sth** ⇨ NOSE¹. **stick one's oar in** ⇨ OAR. **stick out like a sore thumb** ⇨ SORE. **stick to one's guns** (*infml*) refuse to change one's opinions, actions, etc. **stuck in a groove** ⇨ GROOVE. **7** (phr v) **stick around** (*infml*) not go away. **stick at sth** keep on with sth. **stick by sb** continue to support sb. **stick sth out** (cause) to project: *~ one's tongue out.* **stick it/sth out** (*infml*) continue to the very end. **stick to sb/sth** be faithful to (a friend, one's ideals, etc). **stick up** stand above a surface. **stick up for sb/sth** defend or support sb/sth. **sticker** *n* [C] sticky label. '**sticking-plaster** *n* [C, U] = PLASTER 3. '**stick-in-the-mud** *n* [C] (*infml*) person who resists change. **sticky** *adj* (-ier, -iest) **1** like or covered with glue. **2** (*infml*) difficult: *a ~ situation.*

stiff /stɪf/ *adj* **1** not easily bent, folded, etc: *~ cardboard.* **2** hard to stir, move, etc: *a ~ paste.* **3** difficult: *a ~ climb.* **4** (of manners, etc) formal; not friendly. **5** strong: *a ~ breeze.* **6** (idm) **a stiff upper lip** ability to keep calm in spite of trouble, etc. **stiff** *adv* (*infml*) extremely: *bored ~.* **stiffly** *adv*. **stiffness** *n*.

stiffen /'stɪfn/ *v* [I, T] become or make difficult to bend, move, etc.

stifle /'staifl/ *v* **1** [I, T] (cause to) have difficulty breathing. **2** [T] stop from happening: *~ a yawn.*

stigma /'stɪɡmə/ *n* [C, U] mark of shame.

stile /stail/ *n* [C] step used to

climb over a fence, etc.

still¹ /stɪl/ *adj* **1** without movement or sound. **2** (of a drink) not bubbly. **still** *v* [T] make calm or silent. **'stillborn** *adj* **1** (of a child) dead at birth. **2** (*fig*) (of an idea, etc) having no result.

still² /stɪl/ *adv* **1** up to now or the time mentioned: *She is ~ busy.* **2** even: *Tom is tall, but Mary is ~ taller.* **3** nevertheless: *It's raining. Still, we must go shopping.*

still³ /stɪl/ *n* [C] apparatus for making whisky, brandy, etc.

stilt /stɪlt/ *n* [C] one of two poles with a support for the foot, used for walking raised above the ground.

stilted /'stɪltɪd/ *adj* (of speech, behaviour, etc) stiff and unnatural.

stimulant /'stɪmjʊlənt/ *n* [C] drink, drug, etc that increases bodily or mental activity.

stimulate /'stɪmjʊleɪt/ *v* [T] **1** excite or arouse: *~ interest.* **2** encourage (sb/sth) to develop. **stimulating** *adj*. **stimulation** /ˌstɪmjʊ'leɪʃn/ *n* [U].

stimulus /'stɪmjʊləs/ *n* [C] (*pl* -li /-laɪ/) something that stimulates: *a ~ to hard work.*

sting¹ /stɪŋ/ *n* [C] **1** sharp, often poisonous organ of some insects, eg bees. **2** wound caused by this. **3** sharp pain.

sting² /stɪŋ/ *v* (*pt, pp* stung /stʌŋ/) [I, T] **1** wound with a sting. **2** cause sudden sharp pain (to): (*fig*) *a stinging attack.*

stingy /'stɪndʒɪ/ *adj* (-ier, -iest) (*infml*) unwilling to spend or give money, etc. **stingily** /-əlɪ/ *adv.* **stinginess** *n* [U].

stink /stɪŋk/ *v* (*pt* stank /stæŋk/ or stunk /stʌŋk/, *pp* stunk) [I] **1** have an unpleasant smell. **2** (*infml*) be very bad, dishonest, etc. **3** (*phr v*) **stink sth out** fill (a place) with a bad smell. **stink** *n* **1** [C] unpleasant smell. **2** [sing] (*sl*) trouble; fuss.

stint /stɪnt/ *v* [I, T] **~ on sth; ~ sb (of sth)**‖ give (sb/oneself) only a small amount of (sth). **stint** *n* [C] fixed amount of work, etc.

stipulate /'stɪpjʊleɪt/ *v* [T] state as a necessary condition. **stipulation** /-'leɪʃn/ *n* [U].

stir /stɜː(r)/ *v* (-rr-) [I T] **1** mix (a liquid) by moving a spoon, etc round and round in it. **2** [I, T] (cause to) move. **3** [T] (*up*)‖ excite or arouse: *speakers ~ ring up the crowd.* **4** [I] (*sl*) cause trouble between people. **stir** *n* [sing] excitement or confusion. **stirring** *adj* exciting.

stirrup /'stɪrəp/ *n* [C] one of two

metal loops attached to a horse's saddle which support the rider's feet.

stitch /stɪtʃ/ *n* **1** [C] **(a)** single passing of a needle and thread through cloth, etc to join or decorate or through skin to close a wound. **(b)** one turn of the wool round the needle in knitting. **2** [C] the thread, etc used for one stitch. **3** [sing] pain in the side caused by running. **4** (*idm*) **not have a 'stitch on/not be wearing a 'stitch** be naked. **in 'stitches** (*infml*) unable to stop laughing. **stitch** *v* [I, T] put stitches in (sth).

stoat /stəʊt/ *n* [C] small brown furry animal, larger than a rat.

stock /stɒk/ *n* **1** [C, U] goods available for sale or use. **2** [C, U] supply of sth. **3** [U] = LIVESTOCK. **4** [C, usu pl, U] share in a company, issued in fixed amounts, bought as a way of investing money. **5** [U] liquid in which bones, etc have been cooked, used for soup, etc. **6** (*idm*) **in/out of stock** available/ not available. **take stock of** sth review (a situation). **stock** *adj* not interesting because used too often: *a ~ phrase.* **'stockbroker** *n* [C] person who buys and sells stock(4). **'stock exchange** *n* [C] place where stocks(4) are bought and sold. **'stock-market** *n* [C] (business done at the) stock exchange. **'stockpile** *v* [T] buy large quantities (of sth) and keep for use in the future. **'stockpile** *n* [C]. **ˌstock-'still** *adv* not moving. **'stock-taking** *n* [U] counting stock(1) in a shop, etc.

stock² /stɒk/ *v* [T] **1** supply with or have a stock'(1) (of sth). **2** (*phr v*) **stock up (on sth)** get supplies of sth.

stockade /stɒ'keɪd/ *n* [C] tall strong fence, built for defence.

stockings /'stɒkɪŋz/ *n* [pl] pair of tight-fitting coverings for a woman's foot and leg.

stocky /'stɒkɪ/ *adj* (-ier, -iest) (of people) short, strong and solid-looking. **stockily** *adv.*

stodge /stɒdʒ/ *n* [U] (*sl*) heavy solid food. **stodgy** *adj* (-ier, -iest) **1** heavy and solid. **2** dull.

stoic /'stəʊɪk/ *n* [C] person who suffers without complaint. **stoical** *adj.* **stoically** /-klɪ/ *adv.* **stoicism** /'stəʊɪsɪzəm/ *n* [U] patient suffering, etc.

stoke /stəʊk/ *v* (*phr v*) **stoke (sth) up** put coal, etc on the fire of (an engine, etc). **stoker** *n* [C].

stole¹ /stəʊl/ *n* [C] long strip of cloth, etc worn over the shoulders.

stole² pt of STEAL.

stolen pp of STEAL.

stomach /'stʌmək/ n 1 [C] bag-like organ in the body where food is digested. 2 [C] front part of the body. 3 [U] wish: have no ~ for an argument. **stomach** v [T] tolerate.

stone /stəʊn/ n 1 [U] solid mineral substance that is not metallic; rock. 2 [C] piece of rock. 3 [C] jewel. 4 [C] hard seed of some fruits, eg the cherry. 5 [C] (pl **stone**) unit of weight, 14 pounds (6.35 kilograms). 6 [C] piece of hard matter formed in a body organ. 7 (idm) **a stone's throw** a short distance. **stone** v [T] 1 throw stones at. 2 take the stone out of (fruit). **the 'Stone Age** n [sing] period in history when tools, etc were made of stone. **stoned** adj (infml) 1 drunk. 2 under the influence of drugs. ,stone-'deaf adj completely deaf.

stony /'stəʊnɪ/ adj (-ier, -iest) 1 having a lot of stones: a ~ path. 2 hard and unsympathetic. **stonily** /-əlɪ/ adv.

stood pt, pp of STAND².

stool /stuːl/ n [C] small seat without a back.

stoop /stuːp/ v 1 [I] bend the body forward and down. 2 (phr v) **stoop to sth** lower one's standards to do (sth wrong). **stoop** n [sing] stooping position.

stop¹ /stɒp/ n [C] 1 act of stopping: come to a ~. 2 place at which buses, etc stop regularly. 3 = FULL STOP. 4 (idm) **put a stop to sth** stop sth from happening.

stop² /stɒp/ v (-pp-) 1 [T] put an end to (movement, progress, etc). 2 [T] prevent: ~ her (from) leaving. 3 [I] cease moving, working, etc: The engine ~ped. 4 [I] come to a rest: Where does the bus ~? 5 [T] refuse to give (sth normally given): ~ a cheque. 6 [I] (infml) stay. 7 (phr v) **stop off** make a short break in a journey. **stop over** stop at a place and stay overnight. **stopcock** n [C] valve to regulate the flow of water through a pipe. **stopgap** n [C] temporary substitute. **stopover** n [C] short stay. **stoppage** /-pɪdʒ/ n [C] period when work is stopped. **stopper** n [C] object that fits into an opening. 'stop-press n [U] late news added to a newspaper.

storage /'stɔːrɪdʒ/ n [U] (space used for) storing goods.

store /stɔː(r)/ n 1 [C] quantity of sth kept for use as needed. 2 place where goods are stored. 3 (esp a large) shop. 4 (idm) **in store (a)** kept ready for use. **(b)** likely to happen: What's in ~ for us today? **set great/not much store by** think sth is very/not very important, etc. **store** v [T] 1 (up)// collect and keep for future use. 2 put (eg furniture) in a warehouse, etc to keep it safe.

storey /'stɔːrɪ/ n [C] floor in a building.

stork /stɔːk/ n [C] large, long-legged wading bird.

storm /stɔːm/ n [C] 1 period of very strong winds, rain, etc. 2 violent show of feeling: a ~ of anger. 3 (idm) **take by storm** capture by violent attack. **storm** v 1 [T] capture (a place) by violent attack. 2 [I] speak, move, etc angrily. **stormy** adj (-ier, -iest).

story¹ /'stɔːrɪ/ n [C] (pl -ies) 1 account of past or imaginary events. 2 news report. 3 (infml) lie.

story² (US) = STOREY.

stout /staʊt/ adj 1 strong and thick. 2 (of a person) slightly fat. 3 (fml) determined and brave. **stout** n [U] strong dark beer. **stoutly** adv.

stove /stəʊv/ n [C] closed apparatus burning wood, coal, etc used for cooking, etc.

stow /stəʊ/ v [T] (away)// pack, esp carefully and out of sight. 'stowaway n [C] person who hides on a ship or aircraft to avoid paying.

straddle /'strædl/ v [T] sit or stand across (sth) with the legs on either side.

straight¹ /streɪt/ adj 1 not bent or curved: a ~ line. 2 level. 3 in good order; tidy. 4 (of a person) honest and open. 5 (of alcoholic drinks) without water. 6 (sl) heterosexual. 7 (idm) **keep a straight face** not smile. **straightness** n [U].

straight² /streɪt/ adv 1 not in a curve; in a straight line: walk ~. 2 by a direct route and without delay: Come ~ home. 3 honestly, clearly: Tell her ~ what you think. 4 (idm) **go 'straight** stop committing crimes. **straight a'way** adv immediately.

straight³ /streɪt/ n [C] straight part of sth, esp a race-course.

straighten /'streɪtn/ v [I, T] make or become level, tidy, etc.

straightforward /ˌstreɪt'fɔːwəd/ adj 1 honest. 2 easy to understand or do. **straightforwardly** adv.

strain¹ /streɪn/ n 1 [C, U] (force causing) condition of being stretched: put ~ on a rope. 2 (a) [C, U] severe test of one's patience, tolerance, etc: a ~ on our relations. **(b)** [U] distress, worry, etc caused by this. **3** [C, U] damage caused by stretching a muscle too much.

strain² /streɪn/ v **1** [I, T] make the greatest possible effort: ~ *(every muscle) to move it.* **2** [T] injure a (muscle, etc) by stretching it too much. **3** [T] pass (liquid) through a sieve, cloth, etc. **4** [T] force (sth) beyond a normal or acceptable limit: ~ *one's authority.* **strained** *adj* forced and unnatural. **strainer** *n* [C] sieve.

strain³ /streɪn/ *n* [C] type (of a virus, insect, etc).

strait /streɪt/ *n* **1** [C] narrow stretch of water connecting two seas. **2** **straits** [pl] trouble: *in terrible* ~*s.*

strait-jacket /'streɪt dʒækɪt/ *n* [C] jacket with long sleeves tied round a violent person to prevent movement.

strait-laced /,streɪt 'leɪst/ *adj* morally strict or serious.

strand /strænd/ *n* [C] **1** one of the threads, etc twisted together into a rope or cloth. **2** (*fig*) line of development in a story, etc.

stranded /'strændɪd/ *adj* in a helpless position, unable to move, etc.

strange /streɪndʒ/ *adj* **1** not familiar, unknown. **2** unusual; odd: *What ~ ideas you have!* **strangely** *adv.* **strangeness** *n* [U]. **stranger** *n* [C] **1** person one does not know. **2** person in a new or unfamiliar place.

strangle /'stræŋgl/ *v* [T] kill by squeezing the throat. **'stranglehold** *n* [C, usu sing] tight grip: *They have a ~ hold on the economy.* **strangler** *n* [C].

strap /stræp/ *n* [C] strip of leather, plastic, etc used for fastening or support. **strap** *v* (-pp-) [T] fasten or hold in place with a strap. **strapping** *adj* (of people) big and strong.

strata *pl* of STRATUM.

strategic /strə'tiːdʒɪk/ *adj* **1** of or by strategy. **2** suitable for a particular purpose. **strategically** /-klɪ/ *adv.*

strategy /'strætədʒɪ/ *n* [C] **1** general plan of action. **2** [U] (skill in) planning and managing, esp armies in war. **strategist** *n* [C] person skilled in strategy.

stratosphere /'strætəsfɪə(r)/ *n* [sing] layer of the atmosphere between about 10 and 60 km above the earth.

stratum /'strɑːtəm/ *n* [C] (*pl* -ta /-tə/) **1** horizontal layer of rock, etc in the earth. **2** social division or class.

straw /strɔː/ *n* **1** [U] dry, cut stalks of wheat, barley, etc. **2** [C] single stalk of straw. **3** [C] thin tube through which liquid is sucked up. **4** (idm) **the last/final straw** new event, etc that finally makes sth intolerable.

strawberry /'strɔːbrɪ; *US* -berɪ/ *n* [C] (*pl* -ies) (plant with) small juicy red fruit with tiny seeds on its surface.

stray /streɪ/ *v* [I] move away (from the right path, etc). **stray** *n* [C] strayed animal or person. **stray** *adj* **1** having strayed: *a ~ dog.* **2** isolated; not part of a group.

streak /striːk/ *n* [C] **1** long thin line. **2** bad quality in sb's character: *a ~ of cruelty.* **3** brief period: *a ~ of good luck.* **streak** *v* **1** [T] mark with streaks. **2** [I] move very fast. **streaky** *adj* (-ier, -iest) marked with streaks.

stream /striːm/ *n* [C] **1** small river. **2** steady flow (of people, liquid, things, etc): *a ~ of abuse.* **3** group of pupils with the same level of ability. **4** (idm) **with/against the stream** with/against the majority. **stream** *v* [I] **1** flow as a stream. **2** float in the wind: *with her long hair ~ing.* **streamer** *n* [C] long narrow ribbon of paper. **'streamline** *v* [T] **1** give a smooth shape to (a car, etc) so that it moves easily, etc. **2** make more efficient, simple, etc. **'streamlined** *adj.*

street /striːt/ *n* [C] **1** road with houses on one or both sides. **2** (idm) **streets ahead of** (*infml*) far ahead of. **up one's street** (*infml*) in one's area of interest, etc. **'streetcar** *n* [C] (*US*) = TRAM.

strength /streŋθ/ *n* **1** [U] quality or degree of being strong. **2** [C] way in which sb/sth is strong, effective, etc: *Her intelligence is one of her ~ s.* **3** [U] number of people available: *The army is below ~.* **4** (idm) **on the strength of** because of: *buy it on the ~ of his advice.* **strengthen** *v* [I, T] become or make strong(er).

strenuous /'strenjʊəs/ *adj* using or needing great effort. **strenuously** *adv.* **strenuousness** *n* [U].

stress /stres/ *n* **1** (a) [U] condition caused by anxiety, too much work, etc. (b) [C] something causing stress. **2** [U] emphasis: *put ~ on the need to improve.* **3** [C, U] extra force used when speaking a particular word or syllable. **stress** *v* [T] put stress or emphasis on.

stretch /stretʃ/ *v* **1** [T] make wider, longer or tighter by pulling. 2 [I] (be able to) be stretched. 3 [I, T] straighten (the body, a limb, etc) to full length. 4 [I] extend over an area: *fields ~ing for miles*. 5 [T] use (one's powers) fully. 6 (idm) **stretch one's legs** go for a walk. 7 (phr v) **stretch (oneself) out** lie at full length. **stretch** *n* 1 [C] act of stretching. 2 [U] ability to stretch, eg of a rope. 3 [C] continuous expanse of land, etc or period of time: *ten hours at a ~*. **stretchy** *adj* (-ier, -iest).

stretcher /'stretʃə(r)/ *n* [C] frame covered with canvas for carrying a wounded person.

stricken /'strɪkən/ *adj* (*by/with*)/ affected or overcome by sth bad: *~ with terror*.

strict /strɪkt/ *adj* 1 requiring obedience to rules, etc or severe. 2 (a) exactly defined: *the ~ sense of a word*. (b) complete: *in ~ secrecy*. **strictly** *adv.* **strictness** *n* [U].

stride /straɪd/ *v* (*pt* **strode** /strəʊd/, *pp* rarely **stridden** /'strɪdn/) 1 [I] walk with long steps. 2 (phr v) **stride over/ across sth** cross sth with one step. **stride** *n* [C] 1 long step. 2 (idm) **take sth in one's stride** do, accept, etc sth without difficulty.

strident /'straɪdnt/ *adj* (esp of a voice) loud and insistent: *~ protests*.

strife /straɪf/ *n* [U] state of conflict.

strike¹ /straɪk/ *v* (*pt, pp* **struck** /strʌk/) 1 [T] hit. 2 [T] attack. 3 [T] produce (a light) by striking: *~ a match*. 4 [T] discover (gold, etc) by mining, drilling, etc. 5 [I, T] (cause to) sound: *The clock struck (four)*. 6 [I] (of workers) stop working as a protest, etc. 7 [T] give a stated impression: *She ~ s me as a clever girl*. 8 [T] reach: *~ a bargain*. 9 [T] produce by stamping: *~ a medal*. 10 [T] cause to be (ill, etc) suddenly: *struck dumb*. 10 (idm) **strike camp** remove tents, etc. **strike a 'chord with sb** be regarded by sb with sympathy. **strike it rich** become suddenly rich. 12 (phr v) **strike sth off** remove sth, eg from a list. **strike out (a)** aim wild blows. **(b)** follow a new path. **strike up** begin.

strike² /straɪk/ *n* [C] 1 act of stopping work as a protest. 2 act of finding (oil, etc) in the earth. 3 (idm) **be (out) on 'strike** be striking(6).

striking /'straɪkɪŋ/ *adj* attracting attention, beautiful.

string¹ /strɪŋ/ *n* 1 [C, U] (length of) fine cord for tying things, etc. 2 [C] stretched piece of cord or wire,

e.g. on a violin. 3 **the strings** [pl] the players of string instruments in an orchestra. 4 [C] series of things threaded on a string: *a ~ of beads*. 5 [C] series of things: *a ~ of accidents*. 6 (idm) **with no 'strings (attached)** (*infml*) (of help, etc) given without conditions. **stringy** *adj* (-ier, -iest) like string.

string² /strɪŋ/ *v* (*pt, pp* **strung** /strʌŋ/) [T] 1 put a string or strings on (a violin, tennis racket, etc). 2 put (pearls, etc) on a thread or string. 3 (*up*)// tie or hang on a string, etc. 4 (phr v) **string along (with sb)** accompany sb for a while. **string sb along** mislead sb. **string (sb/sth) out** (cause to) be spread at intervals in a line. **strung up** *adj* (of a person) tense and nervous.

stringent /'strɪndʒənt/ *adj* (of rules, etc) strict. **stringently** *adv*.

strip /strɪp/ *v* (-pp-) 1 [I, T] take off (clothes, coverings, parts, etc). 2 [T] *of*// take (sth) from sb: *~ sb of his liberty*. 3 [T] (*down*)// remove parts of (eg an engine) for servicing, etc. **strip** *n* long narrow piece (of material, land, etc). 'strip cartoon = COMIC STRIP (COMIC). **stripper** *n* [C] person who performs a strip-tease. 'strip-tease *n* [C, U] entertainment in which a person undresses in front of an audience.

stripe /straɪp/ *n* [C] 1 long narrow band on a surface that is different in colour, material, etc. 2 (often a v-shaped) badge worn on a uniform, showing rank. **striped** *adj* having stripes(1). **stripy** *adj*.

strive /straɪv/ *v* (*pt* **strove** /strəʊv/, *pp* **striven** /'strɪvn/) [I] (*fml*) 1 try very hard: *~ to succeed*. 2 struggle.

strode *pt* of STRIDE.

stroke¹ /strəʊk/ *n* [C] 1 (act of striking) a blow. 2 one of a series of repeated movements, eg in swimming. 3 act of hitting the ball, eg in tennis, cricket. 4 (mark made by a) single movement of a pen or brush. 5 sound made by a bell. 6 sudden bursting of a blood vessel in the brain. 7 *of*// piece of (luck, misfortune, etc). 8 (idm) **at a 'stroke** with one action; immediately.

stroke² /strəʊk/ *v* [T] pass the hand gently over (a surface). **stroke** *n* [usu sing] act of stroking.

stroll /strəʊl/ *n* [C] quiet unhurried walk. **stroll** *v* [I] walk slowly, esp for pleasure. **stroller** *n* [C] 1 person who strolls. 2 (*US*) pushchair.

strong /strɒŋ; US strɔːŋ/ adj (~**er** /-ŋgə(r)/, ~**est** /-ŋgɪst/) **1** (a) having great power. (b) not easily hurt, broken, changed, etc. **2** able to resist influence: a ~ will. **3** (a) having a great effect on the senses: a ~ smell. (b) having a lot of flavour: ~ coffee. **4** (of a drink) containing a lot of alcohol. **5** having the stated number: an army 2000 ~. **6** (idm) going '**strong** continuing with energy; in good health. **strong on sth** good at sth. '**stronghold** n [C] **1** fort. **2** (fig) place where a cause has strong support. **strongly** adv.

strove pt of STRIVE.

struck pt, pp of STRIKE¹.

structural /'strʌktʃərəl/ adj of a structure, esp the framework. **structurally** adv.

structure /'strʌktʃə(r)/ n **1** [C, U] way in which the parts of sth are put together, etc. **2** [C] thing made of parts, esp a building. **structure** v [T] plan or organize.

struggle /'strʌgl/ v [I] **1** (a) fight. (b) move violently: ~ to get free. **2** make great efforts: ~ to earn a living. **struggle** n **1** [C] fight. **2** [usu sing] thing needing great effort.

strum /strʌm/ v [I, T] (on)) play (a guitar, etc) unskilfully.

strung pt, pp of STRING².

strut¹ /strʌt/ n [C] piece of wood or metal to strengthen a framework.

strut² /strʌt/ v (-tt-) [I] walk in a proud, angry, etc way.

stub /stʌb/ n [C] **1** short remaining end of a pencil, cigarette, etc. **2** piece of a cheque left in the book. **stub** v (-bb-) **1** [T] hit (one's toe) against sth. **2** (phr v) **stub out** extinguish (esp a cigarette) by pressing.

stubble /'stʌbl/ n [U] **1** stalks of corn, etc, left in the ground after harvest. **2** short growth of beard. **stubbly** /'stʌblɪ/ adj.

stubborn /'stʌbən/ adj **1** having a strong will; (too) determined. **2** difficult to move, remove, cure, etc: a ~ cough. **stubbornly** adv. **stubbornness** n [U].

stubby /'stʌbɪ/ adj (-ier, -iest) short and thick.

stuck¹ pt, pp of STICK².

stuck² /stʌk/ adj unable to move or continue. **2** with// (infml) having sb/sth one does not want: ~ with sb all day. **3** (idm) **get stuck in (to sth)** (infml) begin sth (doing) enthusiastically.

stud¹ /stʌd/ n [C], n **1** small fastener for collars, etc. **2** nail on the sole of a boot, etc. **stud** v (-dd-) [T] (usu

passive) set (jewels, etc) in a surface.

stud² /stʌd/ n [C] **1** place where a number of horses are kept for breeding. **2** (infml △) young man regarded as a good sexual partner.

student /'stjuːdnt; US 'stuː-/ n [C] **1** (Brit) person who is studying at a college or university. **2** any person who studies.

studio /'stjuːdiəʊ/ n [C] (pl ~ s) **1** workroom of a painter, photographer, etc. **2** room(s) where films, or radio or television programmes are made.

studious /'stjuːdiəs; US 'stuː-/ adj **1** liking study. **2** careful. **studiously** adv.

study¹ /'stʌdɪ/ n (pl -ies) **1** [U] (also studies [pl]) process of learning sth. **2** [C] investigation into a subject: a ~ of the country's problems. **3** [C] book, etc resulting from research. **4** [C] room used for reading, writing, etc. **5** [C] (a) sketch, etc made for practice. (b) piece of music played as an exercise.

study² /'stʌdɪ/ v (pt, pp -ied) **1** [I, T] give time and attention to learning (sth). **2** [T] examine carefully.

stuff¹ /stʌf/ n [U] **1** material of which sth is made. **2** things, possessions: Put your ~ in your room. **3** (idm) **do one's 'stuff** show what one can do.

stuff² /stʌf/ v [I] **1** fill sth tightly with sth. **2** [T] put flavoured food into (a bird, etc) before cooking. **3** [T] fill the skin of (a dead animal, etc) with material to give it the original shape. **4** [I, T] (infml) fill (oneself) with food. **5** (idm) **get 'stuffed** (Brit infml) (used for expressing anger, scorn, etc). **stuffing** n [U] **1** material for stuffing cushions, etc. **2** food used to stuff(2) a bird, etc.

stuffy /'stʌfɪ/ adj (-ier, -iest) **1** (of a room) not having enough fresh air. **2** (infml) (of people) formal and dull. **stuffiness** n [U].

stumble /'stʌmbl/ v [I] **1** hit the foot against sth and (almost) fall. **2** make a mistake or mistakes as one speaks. **3** (phr v) **stumble across/ on/upon sth** find sth unexpectedly. **stumble** n [C] act of stumbling. '**stumbling-block** n [C] something that prevents progress.

stump /stʌmp/ n [C] **1** part of a tree left in the ground after the rest has been cut down, etc. **2** anything left after the main part has been cut or broken off. **3** (in cricket) one of the three upright pieces of wood at which the ball is aimed.

stump v [I] 1 walk with stiff heavy movements. 2 [T] (*infml*) be too difficult for. **stumpy** adj (-ier, -iest) short and thick.

stun /stʌn/ v (-nn-) [T] 1 make unconscious by a blow. 2 (a) shock. (b) make a very good impression. **stunning** adj very attractive.

stung pt, pp of STING².

stunk pp of STINK.

stunt¹ /stʌnt/ n [C] 1 thing done to attract attention. 2 dangerous thing done as entertainment. '**stunt man**, '**stunt woman** n [C] person employed to do stunts(2) in a film, etc.

stunt² /stʌnt/ v [T] stop or slow the growth of.

stupendous /stju:ˈpendəs; US stu:-/ adj amazingly large, good, etc. **stupendously** adv.

stupid /ˈstju:pɪd; US ˈstu:-/ adj unintelligent; foolish. **stupidity** /ˈpɪdətɪ/ n [C, U]. **stupidly** adv.

stupor /ˈstju:pə(r); US ˈstu:-/ n [C, U] condition of being almost unconscious from shock, drink, etc.

sturdy /ˈstɜ:dɪ/ adj (-ier, -iest) strong and solid. **sturdily** /-əlɪ/ adv.

stutter /ˈstʌtə(r)/ v [I, T] n = STAMMER.

sty¹ /staɪ/ n [C] (pl -ies) = PIGSTY (PIG).

sty² (also **stye**) /staɪ/ n [C] (pl sties or styes) inflamed swelling of the eyelid.

style /staɪl/ n 1 [C, U] manner of writing, speaking, doing sth, etc. 2 [U] superior quality of sth. 3 [C, U] fashion in dress. 4 [C] design or type. 5 (idm) (**not/more**) **sb's style** (not) what sb likes: *Big cars are not my ~.* **style** v [T] design or arrange (hair, etc). **stylish** adj fashionable. **stylist** n [C] person who styles hair or clothes. **stylistic** /-ˈlɪstɪk/ adj of literary style. **stylize** v [T] treat in a fixed simplified style.

stylus /ˈstaɪləs/ n [C] needle used for reproducing sound from records.

suave /swɑ:v/ adj (sometimes derog) having smooth polite manners.

sub /sʌb/ n [C] (*infml*) 1 short for SUBMARINE. 2 substitute, esp in cricket or football.

subconscious /ˌsʌbˈkɒnʃəs/ adj of thoughts, fears, etc in the mind, which one is not aware of but which influence one's actions. **the subconscious** n [sing] subconscious thoughts, etc. **subconsciously** adv.

subcontinent /ˌsʌbˈkɒntɪnənt/ n [C] large land mass forming part of a continent.

subdivide /ˌsʌbdɪˈvaɪd/ v [I, T] divide again into smaller parts. **subdivision** /-dɪˈvɪʒn/ n [C, U].

subdue /səbˈdju:; US -ˈdu:/ v [T] 1 bring under control. 2 make quieter or softer: *~d lighting.*

subject¹ /ˈsʌbdʒɪkt/ n [C] 1 thing (to be) talked or written about etc: *the ~ of the book.* 2 branch of knowledge. 3 (*grammar*) noun or phrase which comes before a verb and which performs the action of that verb or is described by it, eg *book in The book is green.* 4 member of a state(2).

subject² /səbˈdʒekt/ v [T] 1 bring (a nation, person) under one's control. 2 (to) cause to experience: *~ sb to criticism.* **subjection** /-ʃn/ n [U].

subject³ /ˈsʌbdʒɪkt/ adj (to)// 1 having to obey: *~ to the law.* 2 depending on: *~ to confirmation.* 3 often having, suffering, etc sth: *~ to frequent colds.*

subjective /səbˈdʒektɪv/ adj 1 influenced by personal feelings. 2 (*philosophy*) having no existence outside the mind; imaginary. **subjectively** adv. **subjectivity** /ˌsʌbdʒekˈtɪvətɪ/ n [U].

sublet /ˌsʌbˈlet/ v (-tt-, pt, pp **sublet**) [I, T] (of a tenant) rent a house, flat, etc) to sb else.

sublime /səˈblaɪm/ adj of the greatest and highest kind. **sublimely** adv.

submarine /ˌsʌbməˈri:n; US ˈsʌbməri:n/ n [C] ship which can operate under water.

submerge /səbˈmɜ:dʒ/ v [I, T] (cause to) go under water. 2 [T] cover completely. **submersion** /səbˈmɜ:ʃn/ n [U] submerging or being submerged.

submission /səbˈmɪʃn/ n 1 [U] accept sb's power over one. 2 [U, C] (act of) presenting (sth) for consideration.

submissive /səbˈmɪsɪv/ adj accepting the authority of others; obedient. **submissively** adv. **submissiveness** n [U].

submit /səbˈmɪt/ v (-tt-) 1 [I] (to)// accept the power of sb over one. 2 [T] put forward (an idea, etc) for consideration etc.

subordinate /səˈbɔ:dɪnət; US -dənət/ adj 1 lower in rank. 2 of less importance. **subordinate** n [C] person who is subordinate to sb. **subordinate** /səˈbɔ:dɪneɪt/ v [T] (to)// treat as less important.

subscribe /səbˈskraɪb/ v 1 [I, T] agree to pay (a sum of money) to a cause, etc. 2 [I] (*to*)// take (a newspaper, etc) regularly. 3 (phr v) **subscribe to** sth share an opinion, etc). **subscriber** *n* [C]. **subscription** /səb'skrɪpʃn/ *n* 1 [C] subscribing. 2 [C] money paid to charity, for receiving a magazine, for belonging to a club, etc.

subsequent /'sʌbsɪkwənt/ *adj* (*to*)// following. **subsequently** *adv* afterwards.

subservient /səb'sɜːvɪənt/ *adj* giving too much respect. **subservience** /-əns/ *n* [U]. **subserviently** *adv*.

subside /səb'saɪd/ *v* [I] 1 (of water, etc) return to the normal level. 2 (of land or a building) sink lower. 3 become less strong, active, loud, etc. **subsidence** /səb'saɪdns, 'sʌbsɪdns/ *n* [C, U] (instance of) subsiding(2).

subsidiary /səb'sɪdɪərɪ; US -dɪərɪ/ *adj* of less importance: *a ~ role*. **subsidiary** *n* [C] (*pl* -ies) company controlled by another.

subsidy /'sʌbsɪdɪ/ *n* [C] (*pl* -ies) money granted, esp by a government, to help an industry, theatre, etc. **subsidize** /'sʌbsɪdaɪz/ *v* [T] give a subsidy to.

subsist /səb'sɪst/ *v* [I] (continue to) stay alive, esp with little food and money. **subsistence** *n* [U] (means of) subsisting.

substance /'sʌbstəns/ *n* 1 [C, U] (particular kind of) matter. 2 [U] most important part or real meaning of sth. 3 [U] importance, significance: *a speech with little ~*.

substantial /səb'stænʃl/ *adj* 1 large: *a ~ amount*. 2 solidly built. **substantially** *adv* 1 greatly. 2 essentially.

substantiate /səb'stænʃɪeɪt/ *v* [T] prove (a claim, etc) by giving facts.

substitute /'sʌbstɪtjuːt/ *n* [C] person or thing taking the place of another. **substitute** *v* [I, T] (*for*)// serve or use as a substitute. **substitution** /ˌsʌbstɪ'tjuːʃn/ *n* [C, U].

subsume /səb'sjuːm; US -suːm/ *v* [T] (*fml*) include.

subterfuge /'sʌbtəfjuːdʒ/ *n* [C, U] clever or dishonest trick(s).

subterranean /ˌsʌbtə'reɪnɪən/ *adj* = UNDERGROUND 1.

subtitle /'sʌbtaɪtl/ *n* [C] 1 secondary title of a book, etc. 2 [usu pl] words printed on a film, translating the dialogue, giving the dialogue for deaf viewers, etc.

subtle /'sʌtl/ *adj* 1 difficult to perceive or describe: *a ~ difference*. 2 clever: *a ~ plan*. 3 good at seeing and describing subtle differences, etc. **subtlety** *n* [U, C] (*pl* -ies).

subtly /'sʌtlɪ/ *adv*.

subtract /səb'trækt/ *v* [T] (*from*)// take (a number, etc) away from (another number, etc). **subtraction** /-ʃn/ *n* [C, U].

suburb /'sʌbɜːb/ *n* [C] residential area of a town away from the centre. **suburban** /sə'bɜːbən/ *adj*. **suburbia** /sə'bɜːbɪə/ *n* [U] (life lived by people in) suburbs.

subvert /səb'vɜːt/ *v* [T] destroy the authority of (a government, etc). **subversion** /-ʃn/ *n* [U]. **subversive** *adj* trying to subvert.

subway /'sʌbweɪ/ *n* [C] 1 pedestrian tunnel beneath a road, etc. 2 (*US*) underground railway.

succeed /sək'siːd/ *v* 1 [I] (*in*)// do what one is trying to do or do well: *~ in winning the race*. 2 [T] come next after: *~ sb as president*. 3 [I] (*to*)// have the right to sth when sb dies.

success /sək'ses/ *n* 1 [U] achievement of one's aims, fame, wealth, etc. 2 [C] person or thing that succeeds. **successful** *adj*. **successfully** *adv*.

succession /sək'seʃn/ *n* 1 [U] coming of one thing after another. 2 [C] series of things following one another. 3 (idm) in suc'cession one after the other. **successive** *adj* coming one after the other. **successor** *n* [C] person or thing that follows another.

succinct /sək'sɪŋkt/ *adj* expressed briefly and clearly. **succinctly** *adv*. **succinctness** *n* [U].

succulent /'sʌkjʊlənt/ *adj* 1 (of fruit and meat) juicy and delicious. 2 (of plants) thick and fleshy.

succumb /sə'kʌm/ *v* [I] (*to*)// (*fml*) stop resisting (temptation, illness, etc).

such /sʌtʃ/ *adj* 1 of the specified kind: *~ countries as France*. 2 (a) so great: *Don't be in ~ a hurry*. (b) to a certain degree (of importance, badness, etc): *~ a boring speech*. **such** *pron* 1 person or thing of a specified kind: *S~ were her words. His behaviour was ~ that everyone disliked him*. 2 (idm) as such as the word is usually understood. **such as** for example. 'such-and-such *pron, adj* (thing) of an unspecified type. **suchlike** /'sʌtʃlaɪk/ *pron, adj* (things) of the same kind.

suck /sʌk/ *v* 1 [I, T] draw (liquid) into the mouth using the lips. 2 [T] hold (a sweet, etc) in the mouth and lick with the tongue. 3 [T] draw strongly: *The current ~ed her under the water*. 4 [T] (of a pump, etc) draw (liquid, air, etc) out of sth. **suck** n[C] act of sucking. **sucker** n[C] **1** organ of some animals that holds on to a surface by suction. **2** rubber disc sticking to a surface by suction used for attaching sth, etc. **3** (*infml*) person easily deceived. **4** *for*|| person who likes sb/sth: ~ *er for old films*.

suckle /'sʌkl/ v[T] feed with milk from the breast.

suction /'sʌkʃn/ n[U] process of causing a vacuum, esp so that two surfaces stick together.

sudden /'sʌdn/ adj happening unexpectedly and quickly. **suddenly** adv. **suddenness** n[U].

suds /sʌdz/ n[pl] mass of bubbly or soapy water.

sue /sju:/ US su:/ v[I, T] make a legal claim against (sb).

suede /sweɪd/ n[U] soft leather with one rough side.

suet /'su:ɪt/ (*Brit* also 'sju:ɪt/ n[U] hard animal fat used in cooking.

suffer /'sʌfə(r)/ v **1** [I] (*from/with*)|| feel pain, sorrow, etc. **2** [T] experience (sth unpleasant). **3** [T] tolerate: ~ *fools*. **4** [I] become worse: *Her work* ~*ed when she was ill.* **suffering** n[U] (also **sufferings**) [pl] pain of body or mind.

suffice /sə'faɪs/ v[I] (*fml*) be enough.

sufficient /sə'fɪʃnt/ adj enough. **sufficiency** /-nsɪ/ n[sing] sufficient quantity. **sufficiently** adv.

suffix /'sʌfɪks/ n[C] syllable, eg -*able*, placed after a word to change its meaning.

suffocate /'sʌfəkeɪt/ v[I, T] **1** (cause sb to) have difficulty in breathing. **2** (cause sb to) die from not being able to breathe. **suffocation** /,sʌfə'keɪʃn/ n[U].

sugar /'ʃʊgə(r)/ n[U] sweet substance obtained from various plants. **sugar** v[T] sweeten with sugar. **'sugar-cane** n[C] tall tropical grass from which sugar is made. **sugary** adj **1** containing sugar; sweet. **2** too sentimental.

suggest /sə'dʒest; US səg'dʒ-/ v[T] **1** put forward for consideration. **2** bring (an idea) into the mind. **suggestion** /-tʃn/ n **1** [U] suggesting. **2** [C] idea, plan, etc that is suggested. **suggestive** adj making sb think sth, esp sth indecent. **suggestively** adv.

suicide /'su:ɪsaɪd (also *Brit* 'sju:ɪ-/ n **1** [C, U] deliberately killing oneself: *commit* ~. **2** [C] person who does this. **3** [U] (*fig*) action that is very harmful to one's welfare. **suicidal** adj likely to lead to suicide or great misfortune. **2** wanting to commit suicide.

suit¹ /su:t (also *Brit* sju:t/ n[C] **1**

jacket and trousers (or skirt) of the same material. **2** garment or set of clothes for a special purpose. **3** any of the four sets of playing cards (spades, hearts, diamonds, clubs). **'suitcase** n[C] case for carrying clothes, etc when travelling.

suit² /su:t (also *Brit* sju:t/ v **1** [I, T] be convenient or acceptable (for). **2** [T] (esp of clothes) look attractive on (sb): *That hat* ~ *s you.* **3** (*infml*) ~ **oneself** do as one wants. **suitable** /-əbl/ adj right for a purpose. **suitably** adv. **suitability** n[U]. **suited** adj suitable or appropriate.

suite /swi:t/ n[C] **1** set of matching pieces of furniture. **2** set of rooms, eg in a hotel. **3** piece of music in three or more parts.

sulk /sʌlk/ v[I] be silent as a result of a bad temper. **sulky** adj (-ier, -iest).

sullen /'sʌlən/ adj silent and badtempered. **sullenly** adv. **sullenness** n[U].

sulphur (*US* **sulfur**) /'sʌlfə(r)/ n[U] yellow element that burns with a bright flame. **sulphuric** /sʌl'fjʊərɪk/ adj.

sultan /'sʌltən/ n[C] ruler of certain Muslim countries.

sultana /sʌl'tɑːnə/ n[C] kind of small seedless raisin.

sultry /'sʌltrɪ/ adj (-ier, -iest) **1** (of the weather) unpleasantly hot and humid. **2** (of a woman) sensual and attractive.

sum /sʌm/ n[C] **1** calculation in arithmetic. **2** amount of money. **3** total obtained by adding together numbers or amounts. **sum** v (-**mm**-) (*phr v*) **sum** (sth) **up** give a summary of sb/sth. **sum sth/sb up** form an opinion of sb/sth.

summary /'sʌmərɪ/ n[C] (*pl* -**ies**) brief account of the main points of sth. **summary** adj **1** done without delay: *a* ~ *execution.* **2** giving the main points only; brief. **summarize** /-raɪz/ v[T] give a summary of.

summer /'sʌmə(r)/ n[C, U] warmest season of the year. **summery** adj like or suitable for summer.

summit /'sʌmɪt/ n[C] **1** highest point. **2** meeting of two or more heads of government.

summon /'sʌmən/ v[T] **1** order (sb to come. **2** (*up*)|| find a quality) within oneself: ~ (*up*) *all one's courage.*

summons /'sʌmənz/ n[C] order to appear in a lawcourt. **summons** v[T] order (sb) to appear in a law-court.

sun /sʌn/ n 1 the sun [sing] the star round which the earth moves and which gives it warmth and light. 2 (also the sun) [sing, U] light and warmth from the sun. 3 [C] any star, esp one with planets moving around it. 4 (idm) under the 'sun (anywhere) in the world. sun v (-nn-) ~ oneself lie in the sun. sunbathe v [I] expose one's body to sunlight. 'sunbeam n [C] ray of sunshine. 'sunburn n [U] painful red skin caused by exposure to the sun. sunburnt adj suffering from sunburn. 'sunglasses n [pl] glasses with dark lenses to protect the eyes from the sun. 'sunlight n [U] light of the sun. sunny adj (-ier, -iest) 1 bright with sunlight. 2 cheerful. 'sunrise n [U] dawn. 'sunshade n [C] shade like an umbrella to keep off the sun. 'sunshine n [U] light of the sun. 'sunstroke n [U] illness caused by too much exposure to the sun. 'suntan n [C] browning of the skin by exposure to sunlight.

Sunday /'sʌndɪ/ n [U, C] the first day of the week, next after Saturday. (See examples of use at *Monday*).

sundry /'sʌndrɪ/ adj various. **sundries** n [pl] various small items.

sung pp of SING.

sunk pt, pp of SINK².

sunken /'sʌŋkən/ adj 1 that has sunk to the bottom of the sea. 2 (of cheeks, etc) hollow. 3 lower than the surrounding area.

super /'suːpə(r), 'sjuː-/ adj (*infml*) excellent.

superb /suː'pɜːb, 'sjuː-/ adj excellent. **superbly** adv.

superficial /ˌsuːpə'fɪʃl, ˌsjuː-/ adj 1 of or on the surface only. 2 not thorough or deep: a ~ knowledge. **superficiality** /ˌsuːpəˌfɪʃɪ'ælətɪ/ n [U]. **superficially** adv.

superfluous /suː'pɜːfluəs, sjuː-/ adj more than is needed or wanted. **superfluously** adv.

superhuman /ˌsuːpə'hjuːmən, ˌsjuː-/ adj exceeding normal human power, size, etc.

superimpose /ˌsuːpərɪm'pəʊz, ˌsjuː-/ v [T] (*on*)// put (sth) on top of sth else.

superintend /ˌsuːpərɪn'tend, ˌsjuː-/ v [I, T] watch and control (work, etc). **superintendent** n [C] 1 person who superintends. 2 senior police officer.

superior /suː'pɪərɪə(r), sjuː-/ adj 1 high(er) in rank, importance, quality, etc. 2 (*derog*) showing that one thinks one is better than others. **superior** n [C] person of higher rank. **superiority** /suːˌpɪərɪ'ɒrətɪ; US -'ɔːr-/ n [U].

superlative /suː'pɜːlətɪv, sjuː-/ adj 1 of the highest degree or quality. 2 (*grammar*) of adjectives or adverbs, expressing the highest degree, eg *best, worst, most*. **superlative** n [C] superlative form of an adjective or adverb.

supermarket /'suːpəmɑːkɪt, 'sjuː-/ n [C] large self-service store selling food, household goods, etc.

supernatural /ˌsuːpə'nætʃrəl, ˌsjuː-/ adj magical, etc, not explained by the laws of science.

superpower /'suːpəpaʊə(r), 'sjuː-/ n [C] one of the most powerful nations in the world.

supersede /ˌsuːpə'siːd/ v [T] take the place of.

supersonic /ˌsuːpə'sɒnɪk, ˌsjuː-/ adj (able to travel) faster than the speed of sound.

superstar /'suːpəstɑː(r)/ n [C] very famous entertainer.

superstition /ˌsuːpə'stɪʃn, ˌsjuː-/ n [C, U] (idea, practice, etc based on) belief in magic, etc. **superstitious** adj.

supervise /'suːpəvaɪz, 'sjuː-/ v [I, T] manage and control (workers, etc). **supervision** /ˌsuːpə'vɪʒn/ n [U] supervising. **supervisor** n [C] person who supervises.

supper /'sʌpə(r)/ n [C, U] last meal of the day.

supple /'sʌpl/ adj easily bent; not stiff. **suppleness** n [U].

supplement /'sʌplɪmənt/ n [C] 1 something added to improve or complete sth else. 2 additional section of a book, newspaper, etc. **supplement** v [T] (*with*)// make an addition to. **supplementary** /ˌsʌplɪ'mentrɪ; US -terɪ/ adj additional.

supply /sə'plaɪ/ v (pt, pp -ied) [T] 1 provide (sth needed or asked for): ~ gas to a house ○ ~ sb with food. 2 fulfil (a need). **supply** n (pl -ies) 1 [U] supplying. 2 [C, esp pl] thing supplied or available: *food supplies*. **supplier** n [C] person or company that supplies goods, etc.

support /sə'pɔːt/ v [T] 1 bear the weight of. 2 provide (sb) with what is necessary to live: ~ a family. 3 approve of. 4 be a fan of (a team, etc). 5 help to prove (a theory, etc). **support** n 1 [U] supporting. 2 [C] person or thing that supports. 3 [U] people who support a party, team, etc. **supporter** n [C]. **supportive** adj giving encouragement, help, etc.

suppose /sə'pəʊz/ v [T] **1** accept as a fact: *Let us ~ (that) the news is true.* **2** guess or think: *Do you ~ he's gone?* **3** (idm) **be supposed to (a)** be expected or required to do sth (by law, etc): *You're not ~d to leave early.* **(b)** (*infml*) be allowed to: *You're now ~d to leave early.* **supposedly** /-ɪdlɪ/ *adv* according to what is supposed(2). **supposing** *conj* if.

supposition /ˌsʌpə'zɪʃn/ n **1** [U] supposing. **2** [C] thing supposed; guess.

suppress /sə'pres/ v [T] **1** put an end to: *~ a revolt.* **2** prevent from being known: *~ the truth.* **suppression** /-ʃn/ n [U].

supreme /su:'pri:m, sju:-, sə-/ *adj* **1** highest in rank or authority. **2** greatest. **supremacy** /su:'preməsɪ/ n [U]. **supremely** *adv.*

surcharge /'sɜːtʃɑːdʒ/ n [C] payment additional to the usual charge.

sure /ʃɔː(r); US ʃʊər/ *adj* **1** free from doubt, confident that one is right: *I think he's coming but I'm not quite ~.* **2** reliable: *a ~ cure for colds.* **3** to// certain to do sth: *He's ~ to be late.* **4** (idm) **be sure to** don't fail to. **make sure (of sth/that ...) (a)** find out whether sth is definitely so. **(b)** make certain that sth happens. **sure** *adv* (*infml esp US*) certainly: *It ~ is cold!* **2** (idm) **sure enough** as was expected: *I said he would be late and ~ enough, he was.* **surely** *adv* **1** certainly. **2** (used for expressing hope, certainty, etc): *Surely not!* **surety** /'ʃʊərətɪ/ n (pl -ies) [C, U] **1** (money etc given as a) guarantee that sb will pay his/her debts, etc. **2** person responsible for the conduct or debt(s) of another.

surf /sɜːf/ n [U] (white foam on) waves breaking on the shore. **'surfboard** n [C] long narrow board used for surfing. **surfing** n [U] sport of riding on top of the waves using a board.

surface /'sɜːfɪs/ n **1** [C] the outside of any object, etc. **2** [sing] top of a liquid. **3** [sing] (*fig*) outward appearance: *She was angry, in spite of her calm ~.* **surface** *adj.* **surface** v [T] **1** give a surface to: *~ the roads.* **2** [I] (of a submarine, etc) come to the surface: (*fig*) not ~ (ie get out of bed) *until noon.* **'surface mail** n [U] letters sent by land or sea.

surfeit /'sɜːfɪt/ n [sing] too much of sth, esp of food and drink.

surge /sɜːdʒ/ v [I] **1** move forward or upward like waves. **2** (of a feeling) become suddenly strong.

surge n [C] **1** forward or upward movement. **2** sudden increase.

surgeon /'sɜːdʒən/ n [C] doctor who performs surgical operations.

surgery /'sɜːdʒərɪ/ n (pl -ies) **1** [U] treatment of injuries and diseases by cutting into the body. **2** [C] place where a doctor, dentist, etc sees his/her patients.

surgical /'sɜːdʒɪkl/ *adj* of, by or for surgery. **surgically** /-klɪ/ *adv.*

surly /'sɜːlɪ/ *adj* (-ier, -iest) bad-tempered and unfriendly. **surliness** n [U].

surmount /sə'maʊnt/ v **1** [T] overcome (a difficulty, etc). **2** (idm) **be surmounted by** (*fml*) have on the top: *a church ~ed by a tower.*

surname /'sɜːneɪm/ n [C] name shared by all the members of a family.

surpass /sə'pɑːs/ v [T] (*fml*) do or be better than.

surplus /'sɜːpləs/ n [C] amount of money, etc that is needed.

surprise /sə'praɪz/ n [U, C] **1** (usu pleasant feeling caused by) sth sudden or unexpected. **2** (idm) **take sb by surprise** surprise sb by happening unexpectedly. **surprise** v [T] **1** cause (sb) to feel surprise. **2** discover suddenly: *~ a burglar.* **surprised** *adj* experiencing surprise. **surprising** *adj.* **surprisingly** *adv.*

surrender /sə'rendə(r)/ v **1** [I, T] (*oneself*) (to)// stop fighting against (an enemy, etc). **2** [T] give up possession of. **3** (phr v) **surrender (oneself) to** allow (a habit, etc) to control one's actions. **surrender** n [U, C] act of surrendering.

surround /sə'raʊnd/ v [T] be or go all round, enclose. **surround** n [C] (usu decorative) edge. **surrounding** *adj.* **surroundings** n [pl] everything around sb/sth.

surveillance /sɜː'veɪləns/ n [U] close watch kept on sb suspected of doing wrong, etc: *under ~.*

survey /sə'veɪ/ v [T] **1** look at or study the whole of. **2** measure and make a map of (an area of land, etc). **3** examine the condition of (a building, etc). **survey** /'sɜːveɪ/ n [C] **1** general view or study. **2** (map or record of the) measuring of land. **3** examination of the condition of (a building, etc). **surveyor** /sə'veɪə(r)/ n [C] person who surveys(2)(3).

survival /sə'vaɪvl/ n **1** [U] surviving. **2** [C] thing that has survived from an earlier time.

survive /sə'vaɪv/ v [I, T] continue to live or exist (after or longer than): ~ *an accident* ○ *She* ~ *d her husband.* **survivor** *n* [C] person who has survived.

susceptible /səˈseptəbl/ *adj* 1 to// easily affected by: ~ *to cold.* 2 easily influenced. **susceptibility** /səˌseptəˈbɪlətɪ/ *n* [U].

suspect /səˈspekt/ *v* [T] 1 think that sth is possible: *We* ~ *that he's dead.* 2 feel doubt about: ~ *the truth of her statement.* 3 *of*// feel that sb is guilty of sth: ~ *sb of lying.* **suspect** /ˈsʌspekt/ *n* [C] person suspected of doing wrong, etc. **suspect** /ˈsʌspekt/ *adj* not to be relied on or trusted.

suspend /səˈspend/ *v* [T] 1 (*from*)// hang: ~ *a lamp from the ceiling.* 2 delay: ~ *judgement.* 3 (*from*)// stop (sb) performing his/ her duties, etc for a time: *They* ~ *ed the two boys from school.* **suspenders** /səˈspendəz/ *n* [pl] 1 (*Brit*) short elastic strap for holding up stockings or socks. 2 (*US*) = BRACE 3.

suspense /səˈspens/ *n* [U] uncertainty or worry about what may happen.

suspension /səˈspenʃn/ *n* [U] 1 suspending. 2 springs, etc that support a car so the driver cannot feel bumps in the road. **su'spension bridge** *n* [C] bridge hanging on steel cables attached to towers.

suspicion /səˈspɪʃn/ *n* 1 (**a**) [U] suspecting: *arrested on* ~ *of murder.* (**b**) [C] feeling that sth is wrong, sb has done wrong, etc. 2 [sing] slight suggestion: *a* ~ *of sadness.* **suspicious** *adj* having or causing suspicion. **suspiciously** *adv.*

sustain /səˈsteɪn/ *v* [T] 1 (*fml*) support (weight). 2 keep alive or in existence. 3 suffer: ~ *an injury.*

sustenance /ˈsʌstɪnəns/ *n* (*fml*) (nourishing quality of) food or drink.

swab /swɒb/ *n* [C] piece of cotton wool, etc used for cleaning wounds, taking a sample for testing, etc. **swab** *v* (**-bb-**) [T] clean (a wound, etc) with a swab.

swagger /ˈswæɡə(r)/ *v* [I] walk or behave in a boastful way. **swagger** *n* [sing] swaggering walk or manner.

swallow[1] /ˈswɒləʊ/ *n* [C] small bird with a forked tail.

swallow[2] /ˈswɒləʊ/ *v* 1 [I, T] cause (food, etc) to go down the throat. 2 [T] (*up*)// use completely: *earnings* ~ *ed up by bills.* 3 [T] (*infml*) accept (an insult, etc) without complaining. 4 [T] (*infml*) believe too easily: *I'm not* ~ *ing that story!* 5 [T] not express (a feeling).

swallow *n* [C] act of swallowing or amount swallowed.

swam *pt* of SWIM.

swamp /swɒmp/ *n* [C, U] (area of) soft wet land. **swamp** *v* [T] 1 flood with water. 2 (*fig*) overwhelm: ~ *ed with requests.* **swampy** *adj* (**-ier, -iest**) having swamps.

swan /swɒn/ *n* [C] large white long-necked water-bird. **swan** *v* (**-nn-**) [I] (*around/off*)// go or pass time aimlessly or irresponsibly. **'swan-song** *n* [C] last performance or last work of a musician, poet, etc.

swank /swæŋk/ *v* [I] behave or speak in a boastful way. **swank** *n* (*infml derog*) 1 [U] swanking behaviour or talk. 2 [C] person who swanks. **swanky** *adj* (**-ier, -iest**) fashionable or expensive.

swap (also **swop**) /swɒp/ *v* (**-pp-**) [I, T] (*with*)// (*infml*) exchange sth for sth else: ~ *seats with sb.* **swap** *n* [C] act of swapping or sth swapped.

swarm /swɔːm/ *n* [C] large number of insects, etc. **swarm** [I] 1 move in large numbers: *a crowd* ~ *ing through the gate.* 2 (*phr v*) **swarm with sb/sth** be crowded with sb/sth: *beaches* ~ *ing with people.*

swat /swɒt/ *v* (**-tt-**) [T] strike or kill with a flat object.

sway /sweɪ/ *v* 1 [I, T] (cause to) move from side to side. 2 [T] influence. **sway** *n* [U] 1 swaying movement. 2 (*fml*) control, influence.

swear /sweə(r)/ *v* (*pt* **swore** /swɔː(r)/, *pp* **sworn** /swɔːn/) 1 [I] (*at*)// use offensive or rude words. 2 [T] say or promise solemnly or definitely: ~ *to tell the truth.* 3 [I, T] make a solemn promise. 4 (*phr v*) **swear by sth** have great confidence in sth. **swear sb in** introduce sb formally to a new position, etc. **'swear-word** *n* [C] rude or offensive word.

sweat /swet/ *n* 1 [U] moisture which comes through the skin when one is hot, nervous etc. 2 **a sweat** [sing] state of sweating. 3 [U] (*infml*) hard work. **sweat** *v* [I] 1 produce sweat. 2 be worried or nervous. 3 [I] (*infml*) (**a**) work very hard. (**b**) be very worried. **'sweat blood** (*infml*) be very worried. **'sweat-shirt** *n* [C] long-sleeved cotton sweater. **sweaty** *adj* (**-ier, -iest**) (causing sb/sth to be) damp with sweat.

sweater /ˈswetə(r)/ *n* [C] knitted garment (usu of thick wool) for the upper body.

swede /swiːd/ *n* [C, U] kind of yellow turnip.

sweep[1] /swiːp/ v (pt, pp **swept** /swept/) 1 [I, T] clean or clear (dust, dirt, etc) using a brush, broom, etc. 2 [T] carry or move quickly. 3 [I, T] pass over quickly: *A huge wave swept (over) the deck.* 4 [I] move in a proud way. 5 [I] lie in a curve: *The coast ~ s northwards.* 6 (idm) **sweep sb off his/her feet** fill sb with passion or enthusiasm. **sweep sth under the carpet** hide sth embarrassing or scandalous. **sweeper** n [C] person or thing that sweeps. **sweeping** adj 1 having a wide effect: ~ *changes.* 2 too general: *a ~ statement.*

sweep[2] /swiːp/ n 1 [C] act of sweeping. 2 [C] sweeping movement. 3 [sing, U] (fig) range: *the broad ~ of a novel.* 4 [C] long curve on a road, river, etc. 5 = CHIMNEY-SWEEP (CHIMNEY).

sweet /swiːt/ adj 1 tasting like sugar. 2 pleasant or attractive: *a ~ face.* 3 lovable: *a ~ little boy.* 4 fresh and pure: *the ~ smell of the countryside.* 5 smelling pleasant: *Don't the roses smell ~!* 6 (idm) **a sweet tooth** a liking for things that taste sweet. **sweet** n [C] 1 small piece of sth sweet, eg boiled sugar, chocolate, etc. 2 dish of sweet food. **'sweet corn** n [U] type of maize with sweet seeds. **sweeten** v [I, T] become or make sweet. **sweetener** n [C] substance used to sweeten sth. **'sweetheart** n [C] (dated) one of a pair of lovers. **sweetly** adv. **sweetness** n [U]. **'sweet-talk** v [T] (into)// persuade sb by flattery, etc.

swell /swel/ v (pt **swelled** /sweld/, **swollen** /'swəʊlən/ or **swelled**) [I, T] 1 (cause to) become greater in volume, thickness, etc: *a swollen ankle.* 2 (cause to) curve outwards. **swell** n [U, sing] slow rise and fall of the sea's surface. **swelling** n [C] swollen place on the body.

swelter /'sweltə(r)/ v [I] be uncomfortably warm.

swept pt, pp of SWEEP[1].

swerve /swɜːv/ v [I, T] change direction suddenly: *The car ~ d to avoid her.* **swerve** n [C] swerving movement.

swift[1] /swɪft/ adj quick, prompt: *a ~ reply.* **swiftly** adv. **swiftness** n [U].

swift[2] /swɪft/ n [C] small bird similar to a swallow.

swig /swɪg/ v (-gg-) [T] (infml) drink in large amounts.

swill /swɪl/ v [T] 1 rinse by pouring large amounts of water, etc over. 2 (infml) drink in large

amounts: ~ *tea.* **swill** n [U] waste food for pigs.

swim /swɪm/ v (pt **swam** /swæm/, pp **swum** /swʌm/, **-mm-**) 1 [I] move the body through the water using arms, legs, fins, etc. 2 [T] cross by swimming: ~ *the English Channel.* 3 [I] (in/with)// be covered with liquid). 4 [I] seem to turn round and round: *His head swam.* **swim** n [C] 1 act or period of swimming: *go for a ~.* 2 (idm) **in/out of the swim** be aware/unaware of what is happening. **swimmer** n [C] person who swims. **'swimming-bath, 'swimming-pool** n [C] pool for swimming in. **'swimming-costume, 'swim-suit** n [C] garment worn by women and girls for swimming. **'swimming-trunks** n [pl] shorts worn by boys and men for swimming.

swindle /'swɪndl/ v [T] get (money, etc) from (sb) by cheating. **swindle** n [C] act of swindling. **swindler** n [C] person who gets money, etc by swindling.

swing /swɪŋ/ v (pt, pp **swung** /swʌŋ/) [I, T] 1 move backwards and forwards from a fixed end: ~ *one's arms.* 2 (cause to) turn: ~ *round the corner.* 3 (cause to) change from one view, etc to another: *a speech that ~ s the voters.* 4 (idm) **swing into a'ction** act quickly. **swing** n 1 [C] swinging movement. 2 [U, sing] strong rhythm. 3 [C] change from one view, etc to another. 4 [C] seat hanging from a bar, etc for swinging on. 5 (idm) **go with a'swing** be lively and enjoyable. **swings and 'roundabouts** (infml esp Brit) a situation in which there are gains and losses.

swingeing /'swɪndʒɪŋ/ adj (esp Brit) large in amount, etc, severe.

swipe /swaɪp/ v [T] (sl) 1 hit hard. 2 steal. **swipe** n [C] swinging blow.

swirl /swɜːl/ v [I, T] (cause air, water, etc to) move or flow with twists and turns: *dust ~ ing about the room.* **swirl** n [C] swirling movement.

swish /swɪʃ/ v [I, T] (cause to) move through the air with a hissing sound. **swish** n [sing] act of swishing. **swish** adj (infml) fashionable or expensive.

switch /swɪtʃ/ n [C] 1 device for making and breaking an electrical circuit: *a 'light-~.* 2 change: *a ~ from gas to electricity.* **switch** v 1 [I, T] (cause to) change: ~ *to using gas.* 2 [I, T] (cause to) exchange positions: ~ *the two batteries (round).* 3 (phr v) **switch sth on/**

off start/stop an appliance, etc using a switch(1). **'switchboard** n[C] panel of switches for connecting telephone calls.

swivel /'swɪvl/ v (-ll-; *US* -l-) [I, T] (cause to) turn (as if) on a central point: ~ *(round) in one's chair.*

swollen pp of SWELL.

swoop /swu:p/ v[I] descend suddenly with a rush: *(fig) Police ~ed (on the house) at dawn.* **swoop** n[C] 1 swooping movement. 2 sudden attack.

swop = SWAP.

sword /sɔ:d/ n[C] weapon with a long steel blade fixed in a handle. **'swordfish** n[C] large sea-fish with a long upper jaw.

swore pt of SWEAR.

sworn¹ pp of SWEAR.

sworn² /swɔ:n/ adj extreme: ~ *friends/enemies.*

swum pp of SWIM.

swung pt, pp of SWING.

syllable /'sɪləbl/ n[C] unit into which a word can be divided, usu containing a vowel: *'Table' has two ~ s.* **syllabic** /sɪ'læbɪk/ adj.

syllabus /'sɪləbəs/ n[C] list of subjects, etc in a course of study.

syllogism /'sɪlədʒɪzəm/ n[C] logical argument in which a conclusion is drawn from two statements.

symbol /'sɪmbl/ n[C] sign, mark, object, etc that represents sth: *The dove is a ~ of peace.* **symbolic** /sɪm'bɒlɪk/ adj of or used as a symbol. **symbolically** adv. **symbolism** /'sɪmbəlɪzəm/ n[U] (use of) symbols. **symbolize** /'sɪmbəlaɪz/ v[T] be a symbol of.

symmetry /'sɪmətrɪ/ n[U] 1 exact match in size and shape of the two halves. 2 balance. **symmetric** /sɪ'metrɪk/ (also **symmetrical** /-ɪkl/) adj.

sympathetic /ˌsɪmpə'θetɪk/ adj 1 feeling or showing sympathy: ~ *looks.* 2 (of a person) pleasant, likeable. **sympathetically** /-klɪ/ adv.

sympathize /'sɪmpəθaɪz/ v[I] *(with/)/* feel or express sympathy. **sympathizer** n[C] person who supports a cause, party, etc.

sympathy /'sɪmpəθɪ/ n (pl -ies) 1 [U] (capacity for) sharing or understanding the feelings of others. 2 **sympathies** [pl] feelings of agreement.

symphony /'sɪmfənɪ/ n[C] (pl -ies) long musical composition, usu in three or four parts, for an orchestra.

symptom /'sɪmptəm/ n[C] 1 change in the body that is a sign of illness. 2 sign, usu of sth bad: ~ *s of*

discontent. **symptomatic** /-'mætɪk/ adj being a symptom.

synagogue /'sɪnəgɒg/ n[C] building used by Jews for religious worship and teaching.

synchronize /'sɪŋkrənaɪz/ v [I, T] (cause to) happen, operate, etc at the same time, speed, etc: ~ *watches.*

syndicate /'sɪndɪkət/ n[C] group of people or companies that join together for business. **syndicate** /'sɪndɪkeɪt/ v[T] publish (articles, etc) in many newspapers, etc through a central agency.

syndrome /'sɪndrəʊm/ n[C] *(medical)* set of symptoms which are a sign of an illness, etc.

synonym /'sɪnənɪm/ n word with the same meaning as another. **synonymous** /sɪ'nɒnɪməs/ adj.

synopsis /sɪ'nɒpsɪs/ n[C] (pl -opses /-si:z/) summary or outline of a book, play, etc.

syntax /'sɪntæks/ n[U] *(linguistics)* (rules for) making sentences out of words and phrases. **syntactic** /sɪn'tæktɪk/ adj of syntax.

synthesis /'sɪnθəsɪs/ n[U, C] (pl -theses /-si:z/) combining of separate parts to make a single whole. **synthetic** /sɪn'θetɪk/ adj artificial, not natural: ~ *fabric.* **synthesize** /'sɪnθəsaɪz/ v[T] make by combining. **synthetically** /-klɪ/ adv.

syphilis /'sɪfɪlɪs/ n[U] serious venereal disease.

syphon = SIPHON.

syringe /sɪ'rɪndʒ/ n[C] device with a needle for injecting liquids into the body, etc. **syringe** v[T] clean (sth) or inject liquid with a syringe.

syrup /'sɪrəp/ n[U] thick sweet liquid.

system /'sɪstəm/ n 1 [C] group of parts working together. 2 [C] ordered set of ideas, action: a ~ *of government.* 3 [U] orderly way of doing sth. **systematic** /ˌsɪstə'mætɪk/ adj based on order, following a fixed plan. **systematically** /-klɪ/ adv.

T t

T, t /ti:/ n[C] (pl **T's, t's** /ti:z/) the twentieth letter of the English alphabet. **'T-shirt** n[C] short-sleeved shirt like a vest.

ta /tɑ:/ interj *(Brit infml)* thank you.

tab /tæb/ *n* [C] small piece of cloth, paper, etc attached to sth, used for fastening, pulling, etc.

tabby /'tæbı/ *n* [C] (*pl* -ies) (also **'tabby-cat**) cat with grey or brown fur and dark stripes.

table /'teibl/ *n* [C] 1 piece of furniture with a flat top on legs. 2 list of facts or figures arranged in columns or rows. **table** *v* [T] present officially for discussion: **'table-cloth** *n* [C] cloth for covering a table, esp during meals. **'table-spoon** *n* [C] large spoon for serving food. **tablespoonful** *n* [C] amount contained in a tablespoon. **'table tennis** *n* [U] indoor game in which a small light ball is hit over a low net on a table.

tablet /'tæblıt/ *n* [C] 1 small hard piece of medicine. 2 small bar of soap. 3 flat piece of stone, etc with words cut into it.

tabloid /'tæbloıd/ *n* [C] newspaper with small pages, short news articles and many pictures.

taboo /tə'bu:; *US* tæ'bu:/ *n* [C, U] (*pl* ~s) something that is forbidden because of a strong religious or social custom. **taboo** *adj* forbidden by taboo.

tabulate /'tæbjuleıt/ *v* [T] arrange (facts, figures, etc) in a table(2). **tabulation** /,tæbju-'leıʃn/ *n* [U].

tacit /'tæsıt/ *adj* understood without being said: ~ *agreement*. **tacitly** *adv*.

tack /tæk/ *n* 1 [C] small flat-headed nail. 2 [U, sing] (*fig*) course of action: *change* ~. 3 [C] long loose stitch. **tack** *v* [T] fasten with loose stitches.

tackle /'tækl/ *v* 1 [T] deal with (a problem, piece of work, etc). 2 [T] (*about*)|| speak to (sb) frankly about sth. 3 [I, T] (in football, etc) try to take the ball away from (sb). 4 [T] seize or attack (eg a thief). **tackle** *n* 1 [C] act of tackling(3). 2 [U] equipment needed for a certain sport. 3 [U] set of ropes and pulleys for lifting weights, etc.

tacky /'tækı/ *adj* (*infml*) in poor taste: ~ *jewellery*.

tact /tækt/ *n* [U] skill of not offending people by saying or doing the right thing. **tactful** *adj* having or showing tact. **tactfully** *adv*. **tactless** *adj*. **tactlessly** *adv*.

tactic /'tæktık/ *n* 1 [C, usu pl] method of achieving an aim. 2 **tactics** [also sing with pl v] art of arranging and moving armies in a battle. **tactical** *adj* of tactics: *a* ~*al move*. **tactician** /tæk'tıʃn/ *n* [C] expert in tactics.

tadpole /'tædpəul/ *n* [C] small creature that grows into a frog or toad.

tag /tæg/ *n* 1 [C] small piece of cloth, paper, etc attached to sth to show its cost, owner, etc. 2 [U] game in which one child chases and tries to touch another. **tag** *v* (-gg-) 1 [T] fasten a tag to. 2 (phr v) **tag along/after/behind** follow sb closely.

tail /teıl/ *n* [C] 1 long movable part at the end of the body of an animal, bird, etc. 2 something like a tail in its shape or position: *the* ~ *of an aircraft*. 3 (*infml*) person employed to follow sb. 4 **tails** [pl] side of a coin without a ruler's head on it. **tail** *v* 1 [T] follow (sb) closely. 2 (phr v) **tail off/away** become gradually less or quieter. **'tail-back** *n* [C] long line of traffic reaching back along a road. **tail-less** *adj*. **'tail-light** *n* [C] red light at the back of a car, bus, etc. **'tail-wind** *n* [C] wind blowing from behind.

tailor /'teılə(r)/ *n* [C] maker of men's clothes, eg coats and jackets. **tailor** *v* [T] 1 cut out and sew: *a well-* ~ *ed suit*. 2 make or fit for a purpose. **,tailor-'made** *adj* 1 made to fit a particular person. 2 (*fig*) perfectly suitable: *She is* ~*-made for the job.*

taint /teınt/ *v* [T] spoil by adding a bad quality. **taint** *n* [sing] trace of a bad quality.

take[1] /teık/ *v* (*pt* **took** /tuk/, *pp* ~**n** /'teıkən/) 1 [T] get, hold or grasp: ~ *her hand* ○ *She took him in her arms*. 2 [T] carry (sth/sb) or cause (sb) to go from one place to another: *T~ an umbrella with you.* ○ *She took a friend home.* 3 [T] remove and use, esp without permission or by mistake; steal: *Who has* ~*n my bicycle?* 4 [T] obtain from a certain source: *This line is* ~*n from a poem by Keats.* 5 [T] capture, gain possession of: ~ *a town (in war)* ○ *He took first prize.* 6 [T] accept; receive: ~ *advice* ○ *Will you* ~ *£450 for the car?* 7 [T] receive (esp a newspaper) regularly: *He* ~*s The Times.* 8 [T] eat or drink: *Do you* ~ *sugar in your tea?* 9 [T] have enough space for: *The car* ~*s five people.* 10 [T] be able to endure sth; bear: *He can't* ~ *being criticized.* 11 [T] react to (sb/sth) in the way stated: *She took her mother's death very badly*, ie was made very unhappy by it. 12 [T] experience (a feeling, etc): ~ *pleasure in being cruel.* 13 [T] consider (to be): *What do you* ~ *this to be?* 14 [T] need;

require: *The work took four hours.*
15 [T] wear (a particular size in clothes or shoes): *What size shoes do you ~?* **16** [T] do (an examination, etc): *~ a driving test.* **17** [T] make a written record of: *~ notes* ○ *~ the names of the volunteers.* **18** [T] make (a photograph). **19** [T] test; measure: *The doctor took my temperature.* **20** [T] be in charge of: *~ a class, course, etc.* **21** [T] have the desired effect: *The smallpox injection did not ~.* **22** [T] use (a means of transport, a road, etc): *a bus into town* ○ *~* (ie turn into) *the first road on the left.* **23** [T] (used with nouns to show that a specific action is being performed): *~ a bath/walk/holiday.* **24** (idm) **take sth** ⇨ **COURSE**¹. **take heart** ⇨ HEART. **25** (phr v) **take sb aback** shock and surprise sb. **take after sb** be like (one's mother or father) in appearance or character. **take sth apart** separate the parts of (a machine, etc). **take sth away (a)** subtract: *T ~ 5 from 10, and that leaves 5.* **(b)** buy (a meal) at a restaurant and take it somewhere else to eat. **take sb/sth back (a)** admit that sb one has said is wrong. **(b)** agree to receive sb/sth back: *This shop only ~s goods back if you have your receipt.* **take sb back (to sth)** cause sb to remember (sth). **take sth down (a)** make a written record of sth. **(b)** take (a structure) to pieces. **take sb in** deceive: *Don't be ~n in by him.* **take sth in (a)** do (work) at home for payment: *~ in washing.* **(b)** make (a garment) tighter by altering the seams. **(c)** include: *The trip took in several cities.* **(d)** see, hear and understand; pay attention to: *I couldn't ~ in everything she said.* **take 'off (a)** (of an aircraft) leave the ground. **(b)** (of a project, etc) become successful quickly. **take sb off** (*infml*) imitate: *She's good at taking off her teachers.* **take sth off (sth) (a)** remove (clothes, etc): *~ off one's hat.* **(b)** withdraw (a train, etc) from service. **(c)** deduct: *~ 50p off (the price).* **(d)** take (time) as a break from work: *~ a week off to go on holiday.* **take on sth** begin to have (a quality, appearance, etc). **take sth on** decide to do (work, etc). **take sb on (a)** accept sb as an opponent. **(b)** employ sb. **take sb/ sth on** (of a vehicle, aircraft, etc) allow (passengers, fuel, cargo) to be loaded. **take sb out** accompany sb to a social event: *~ her out to*

dinner. **take sth out (a)** remove or extract (a part of the body): *~ out a tooth.* **(b)** obtain (an official document) for payment: *~ out a licence.* **take it out of sb** (*infml*) exhaust: *That run really took it out of me.* **take it/sth out on sb** (*infml*) show one's anger, irritation, etc by being unkind to sb. **take over (from sb)** accept (sb's) duties, responsibilities, etc. **take sth 'over** take control of: *~ over another business.* **take to sth (a)** start an activity; begin to do sth: *took to cycling ten miles a day.* **(b)** use as a means of escape: *~ to the woods to avoid capture.* **take to sb/sth** begin to like. **take sth up (a)** raise; lift: *took up a knife.* **(b)** shorten (a skirt, etc). **(c)** start (an activity); begin to do: *took up cycling, chess.* **(d)** continue (sth unfinished). **(e)** occupy (time or space): *This table ~s up half the room.* **(f)** accept (an offer). **take up with sb** begin to spend time in company of sb; become friendly with sb. **take sth up with sb** speak or write to sb about sth. **take sth upon oneself** assume (responsibility) for sth. **be taken with sb/sth** find sb/sth interesting or attractive. **'take-away** *n* [C] **(a)** restaurant from which food is taken to be eaten somewhere else. **(b)** meal bought from such a restaurant: *go for a ~away.* **'take-off** *n* [C] start of a flight, when an aircraft leaves the ground. **'take-over** *n* act of taking over (a business, etc).

take² /teɪk/ *n* [C] period of filming without stopping.

taker /'teɪkə(r)/ *n* [C] person who accepts an offer.

takings /'teɪkɪŋz/ *n* [pl] amount of money that a shop, theatre, etc receives.

talcum powder /'tælkəm/ *n* [U] perfumed powder for the skin.

tale /teɪl/ *n* [C] **1** story: *~ s of adventure.* **2** report or account. **3** lie.

talent /'tælənt/ *n* [C, U] natural ability to do sth well: *have a ~ for music.* **talented** *adj* having talent; skilled.

talk¹ /tɔːk/ *v* **1** [I] say things; speak to give information: *He was ~ing to a friend.* **2** [I] have the power of speech: *Can the baby ~ yet?* **3** [T] discuss: *We ~ed politics all evening.* **4** [I] gossip. **5** [I] give secret information, esp unwillingly: *Has the prisoner ~ed yet?* **6** (phr v) **talk down to sb** speak to sb in a way that shows one thinks one is more important, cleverer, etc than him/her. **talk sb into/out of sth** persuade sb to do/not to do sth.

talk sth over discuss sth. **talk-ative** /'tɔ:kətɪv/ adj liking to talk a lot. **talker** n [C]. **'talking-point** n [C] subject for discussion. **'talking-to** n [sing] angry talk to criticize sb.

talk¹ /tɔ:k/ n 1 [C, U] conversation. 2 [U] gossip or rumour. 3 [C] informal speech. 4 **talks** [pl] formal discussions.

tall /tɔ:l/ adj 1 of more than average height. 2 of the height that is mentioned: *Tim is six feet ∼.* 3 (idm) **a tall 'order** task that is difficult to do. **a tall 'story** story that is difficult to believe.

tally /'tælɪ/ n [C] (pl **-ies**) record of money spent, points scored in a game, etc. **tally** v (pt, pp **-ied**) [I] be exactly the same; correspond.

talon /'tælən/ n [C] curved claw of a bird, eg an eagle.

tambourine /ˌtæmbə'ri:n/ n [C] small shallow drum with metal discs round the edge, shaken or hit with the hand.

tame /teɪm/ adj (∼r, ∼st) 1 (of animals) trained to live with people; not wild or fierce: *a ∼ monkey.* 2 (of a person) easily controlled: *Her husband is a ∼ little man.* 3 dull: *The film has a rather ∼ ending.* **tame** v [T] make tame: *∼ a lion.* **tamely** adv. **tameness** n [U]. **tamer** n [C] person who tames animals: *a lion-∼r.*

tamper /'tæmpə(r)/ v [I] *with//* interfere with or change sth without authority.

tampon /'tæmpɒn/ n [C] long piece of cotton wool put inside a woman's vagina to collect blood during her period(3).

tan /tæn/ n 1 [C] brown colour of the skin from sunlight. 2 [U] yellowish brown colour. **tan** v (**-nn-**) 1 [T] make (animal skins) into leather. 2 [I, T] (cause to) go brown from sunlight. 3 (idm) **tan sb's hide** (*infml*) beat sb hard.

tandem /'tændəm/ n 1 bicycle for two riders. 2 (idm) **in 'tandem** working closely together.

tandoori /tæn'dʊərɪ/ n [C, U] (dish of meat, etc in the) style of Indian cooking using a clay oven.

tang /tæŋ/ n [C, usu sing] strong sharp taste, flavour or smell.

tangent /'tændʒənt/ n 1 [C] straight line that touches a curve but does not cross it. 2 (idm) **go off at a 'tangent** change suddenly from one line of thought, action, etc to another.

tangerine /ˌtændʒə'ri:n; *US* 'tændʒəri:n/ n [C] kind of small sweet orange.

tangible /'tændʒəbl/ adj 1 (*fml*)

that can be known by touch. 2 clear and definite: *∼ proof.* **tangibly** adv.

tangle /'tæŋgl/ n 1 [C] confused mass of string, hair, etc. 2 [sing] confused state: *in a ∼.* **tangle** v 1 [I, T] (cause to) become twisted into a confused mass: *∼d hair.* 2 [I] *with//* become involved in a fight or quarrel with sb.

tango /'tæŋgəʊ/ n [C] (pl ∼s) (music for a) South American dance.

tank /tæŋk/ n [C] 1 large container for liquid or gas. 2 armoured fighting vehicle with guns.

tankard /'tæŋkəd/ n [C] large metal mug for beer.

tanker /'tæŋkə(r)/ n [C] ship, lorry, etc that carries large quantities of liquid or gas.

tantalize /'tæntəlaɪz/ v [T] tease (sb) by offering sth that he/she wants and then not allowing him/her to have it.

tantamount /'tæntəmaʊnt/ adj *to//* having the same effect as sth.

tantrum /'tæntrəm/ n [C] outburst of bad temper, esp by a child.

tap¹ /tæp/ n 1 [C] device for controlling the flow of liquid or gas from a pipe or container. 2 (idm) **on tap** available when needed. **tap** v (**-pp-**) [T] 1 draw (liquid) from (sth). 2 obtain sth from: *∼ a country's resources.* 3 listen secretly to (a telephone).

tap² /tæp/ v [I, T] n [C] (hit (sb/sth) with a) quick light blow: *∼ sb on the shoulder.* **'tap-dancing** n [U] dancing in which one makes tapping steps on the floor with special shoes.

tape /teɪp/ n 1 (a) [C, U] (piece of a) narrow strip of material. (b) [C] piece of this stretched across the finishing line of a race-track. 2 [U, C] = MAGNETIC TAPE (MAGNET). **tape** v [T] 1 fasten with tape. 2 record (sound, etc) on magnetic tape. 3 (idm) **have sb/sth taped** (*infml esp Brit*) understand sb/sth fully. **'tape-measure** n [C] strip of cloth or thin metal, marked for measuring things. **'tape-recorder** n [C] apparatus for recording and playing sound on magnetic tape.

taper¹ /'teɪpə(r)/ v 1 [I, T] (cause to) become narrower at one end. 2 [I] *off//* become less.

taper² /'teɪpə(r)/ n [C] long thin candle.

tapestry /'tæpəstrɪ/ n [C, U] (pl **-ies**) (piece of) heavy cloth with a picture or pattern woven into it, used for covering walls.

tar /tɑ:(r)/ n [U] thick black sticky

substance, hard when cold, used for making roads, preserving wood, etc. **tar** v (**-rr-**) 1 [T] cover with tar. 2 (idm) **tarred with the same 'brush** having the same faults.

tarantula /təˈræntjʊlə; *US* -tʃələ/ *n* [C] large hairy poisonous spider.

target /ˈtɑːgɪt/ *n* 1 [C] something aimed at in shooting. 2 [C] person or thing at which criticism is aimed. 3 [C, U] result aimed at: *achieve a sales ~*. **target** v [T] aim.

tariff /ˈtærɪf/ *n* [C] 1 tax on goods coming into a country. 2 list of prices for rooms, meals, etc in a hotel.

Tarmac /ˈtɑːmæk/ *n* [U] 1 (P) mixture of tar and broken stones for making road surfaces. 2 **tarmac** area covered with this, esp at an airport.

tarnish /ˈtɑːnɪʃ/ *v* 1 [I, T] (esp of metal surfaces) (cause to) lose brightness: *Brass ~es easily.* 2 [T] lessen the quality of (sb's reputation).

tarpaulin /tɑːˈpɔːlɪn/ *n* [C, U] (sheet or covering of) heavy waterproof cloth.

tart¹ /tɑːt/ *n* [C] small esp uncovered piece of pastry containing jam or fruit.

tart² /tɑːt/ *adj* 1 sharp-tasting. 2 (*fig*) bitter: *a ~ reply.* **tartly** *adv.* **tartness** *n* [U].

tart³ /tɑːt/ *n* [C] (*sl derog*) sexually immoral girl or woman. **tart** v (phr v) **tart sb/sth up** (*infml derog*) dress or decorate sb/sth in a cheap showy way.

tartan /ˈtɑːtn/ *n* [C, U] (woollen cloth with a) pattern of coloured stripes crossing each other, esp of a Scottish clan.

tartar /ˈtɑːtə(r)/ *n* [U] hard chalklike substance that forms on one's teeth.

task /tɑːsk; *US* tæsk/ *n* 1 [C] piece of (esp hard or unpleasant) work that has to be done. 2 (idm) **take sb to task** criticize sb. '**task force** *n* [C] group of people organized for a special (esp military) purpose. **taskmaster** (*fem* '**taskmistress**) *n* [C] person who is strict in making others work hard.

tassel /ˈtæsl/ *n* [C] bunch of threads tied at one end, hanging as decoration from sth.

taste¹ /teɪst/ *n* 1 [U] ability to recognize a food or drink in the mouth. 2 [sing] flavour of sth as sweet, salty, etc: *Sugar has a sweet ~.* 3 [sing] small quantity. 4 [U] ability to make a (good) choice about what is beautiful, pleasing, etc: *Your choice of colours shows*

good ~. 5 [C, U] personal liking. 6 (idm) **in good/bad taste** suitable/offensive. **a taste of one's own medicine** ⇨ MEDICINE. **tasteful** *adj* showing good taste(4). **tastefully** *adv.* **tasteless** *adj* 1 (of food) having no flavour. 2 showing bad taste(4). **tastelessly** *adv.* **tasty** *adj* (**-ier, -iest**) having a pleasant flavour.

taste² /teɪst/ *v* 1 [T] be aware of (a taste). 2 [I] (*of/i*) have a certain taste: *~ bitter/sweet.* 3 [T] test the taste of: *She ~d the soup.* 4 [T] (*fig*) experience: *~ freedom/success.*

tatters /ˈtætəz/ *n* [pl] (idm) **in tatters** (a) (of clothes) torn and old. (b) (*fig*) ruined. **tattered** *adj* ragged.

tattoo¹ /təˈtuː; *US* tæˈtuː/ *v* [T] mark (a picture or pattern) on (sb's skin) by pricking and putting in colouring. **tattoo** *n* [C] (*pl ~s*) tattooed picture or pattern.

tattoo² /təˈtuː; *US* tæˈtuː/ *n* [C] (*pl ~s*) public entertainment with music, marching, etc by soldiers.

taught *pt, pp* of TEACH.

taunt /tɔːnt/ *v* [T] say unkind or insulting words to (sb) in order to upset him/her. **taunt** *n* [C] taunting remark.

taut /tɔːt/ *adj* tightly stretched. **tautly** *adv.* **tautness** *n* [U].

tautology /tɔːˈtɒlədʒɪ/ *n* [C, U] (*pl -ies*) unnecessary repeating of the same thing in different ways. **tautological** /ˌtɔːtəˈlɒdʒɪkl/ *adj.*

tavern /ˈtævən/ *n* [C] (*arch*) public house; inn.

tawny /ˈtɔːnɪ/ *adj* brownish-yellow.

tax /tæks/ *n* [C, U] money that has to be paid to a government for public purposes. **tax** *v* [T] 1 put a tax on. 2 require (sb) to pay a tax. 3 make great demands on: *~ sb's patience.* **taxable** *adj* that can be taxed: *~able income.* **taxation** /tækˈseɪʃn/ *n* [U] (system of) raising money by taxes. ˌ**tax-'free** *adj* on which tax need not be paid. '**taxpayer** *n* [C] person who pays taxes, esp income tax.

taxi /ˈtæksɪ/ *n* [C] (also 'taxi-cab) car with a driver which may be hired. **taxi** *v* [I] (of an aircraft) move along the ground before or after flying. '**taxi rank** *n* [C] place where taxis wait to be hired.

tea /tiː/ *n* 1 (a) [U] (dried leaves of a) bush grown in China, India, etc. (b) [C, U] drink made by pouring boiling water on these leaves. 2 [C, U] drink made like tea from the leaves of other plants: *mint ~.* 3 [C, U] (a) light afternoon meal. (b) early evening meal. '**tea-bag** *n* [C] small paper bag containing tea-leaves. **'tea-caddy** /-kædɪ/ (pl **-dies**) n [C] small tin in which tea is kept. **'tea-chest** n [C] large light wooden box in which tea is packed. **'teacup** n [C] cup from which tea is drunk. **'teapot** n [C] container in which tea is made and served. **'tea-service** (also **'tea-set** n [C] set of cups, plates, etc for serving tea. **'teaspoon** n [C] small spoon for stirring tea. **'teaspoonful** n [C] amount contained in a teaspoon. **'tea-strainer** n [C] device for pouring tea through to stop tea-leaves going into a cup. **'tea-time** n [U] time at which tea is served. **'tea-towel** (also **'tea-cloth**) n [C] cloth used for drying washed dishes and cutlery.

teach /tiːtʃ/ v (pt, pp **taught** /tɔːt/) [I, T] give instruction to (sb); give sb (knowledge, skill, etc): *He taught them art.* ○ *a child (how) to swim.* **teacher** n [C] person who teaches, esp in a school. **teaching** n 1 [U] work of a teacher: *earn a living by ~ing.* **2** [C, usu pl] idea or belief that is taught: *the ~ings of Jesus.*

teak /tiːk/ n [U] strong hard wood of a tall Asian tree.

team /tiːm/ n [C, also sing with pl v] **1** group of people playing on the same side in a game: *a football ~.* **2** group of people working together: *a ~ of surgeons.* **team** v [I] *up (with)//* work together (with sb). **team 'spirit** n [U] loyal feeling between members of a team helping one another to do well. **'teamwork** n [U] organized co-operation.

tear¹ /tɪə(r)/ n 1 [C, usu pl] drop of salty liquid coming from the eye when one cries. **2** (idm) **in 'tears** crying. **'tear-drop** n [C] single tear. **tearful** adj crying or likely to cry. **tearfully** adv. **'tear-gas** n [U] gas that stings the eyes. **'tear-jerker** n [C] (infml) story, film, etc likely to make people cry.

tear² /teə(r)/ v (pt **tore** /tɔː(r)/, pp **torn** /tɔːn/) **1** [T] pull apart or to pieces: ~ *a sheet of paper.* **2** [I] remove by pulling forcefully: ~ *a page out of a book.* **3** [I] move fast; hurry: *We tore home.* **5** [T] destroy the peace of: *a country torn by civil war.* **6** (idm) **be torn between A and B** be unable to choose between two things or people. **7** (phr v) **tear sth down** destroy (a building). **tear sth up** pull (a piece of paper) into small bits. **tear** n [C] hole made by tearing. **'tearaway** n [C] violent

youth.

tease /tiːz/ v [I, T] make fun of (sb) playfully or unkindly. **tease** n [C] person who is fond of teasing. **teaser** n [C] (infml) difficult question.

teat /tiːt/ n [C] **1** animal's nipple. **2** rubber end on a baby's feeding-bottle.

tech /tek/ n [C] (infml) short for TECHNICAL COLLEGE (TECHNICAL).

technical /'teknɪkl/ adj **1** of or concerning detailed practical knowledge of an industrial or scientific subject. **2** of a particular subject: *the ~ terms of physics.* **3** of or showing technique. **4** in a strict legal sense. **'technical college** n [C] (in Britain) college that teaches practical subjects. **technicality** /ˌteknɪˈkælətɪ/ n [C] (pl **-ies**) technical point or detail, sometimes one of no real importance. **technically** /-klɪ/ adv.

technician /tekˈnɪʃn/ n [C] person with a practical, mechanical or industrial skill.

technique /tekˈniːk/ n **1** [C] method of doing sth that needs skill. **2** [U] skill in art, music, etc.

technocrat /'teknəkræt/ n [C] (usu derog) scientist or technician who manages a company, a country's resources, etc.

technology /tekˈnɒlədʒɪ/ n [U] study and use of science for practical tasks in industry, business, etc. **technological** /ˌteknəˈlɒdʒɪkl/ adj. **technologist** n [C] expert in technology.

teddy bear /'tedɪ beə(r)/ n [C] soft furry toy bear.

tedious /'tiːdɪəs/ adj long and boring: *a ~ lecture* ○ ~ *work.* **tediously** adv.

tee /tiː/ n [C] **1** (in golf) flat area from which a player starts at each hole. **2** piece of wood, plastic, etc on which a golf ball is placed before it is hit. **tee** v (phr v) **tee off** hit the ball from a tee. **tee (sth) up** put a golf ball on the tee.

teem¹ /tiːm/ v [I] *with* have sth in great numbers: *The river was ~ing with fish.*

teem² /tiːm/ v [I] (used with *it*) (of rain) fall very heavily.

teenage /'tiːneɪdʒ/ adj for people in their teens: ~ *fashions.*

teenager /'tiːneɪdʒə(r)/ n [C] person in his/her teens.

teens /tiːnz/ n [pl] years of a person's age from 13 to 19: *girls in their ~s.*

teeter /'tiːtə(r)/ v [I] stand or move unsteadily.

teeth pl of TOOTH.

teethe /tiːð/ v [I] (of a baby) grow

its first teeth. **'teething troubles** *n* [pl] problems that occur when first using a new system.

teetotal /ti:'təʊtl; *US* 'ti:təʊtl/ *adj* never drinking alcohol. **tee-totaller** *n* [C].

telecommunications /ˌtelɪkə-ˌmjuːnɪ'keɪʃnz/ *n* [pl] communications over long distances, using radio, telephone, satellites, etc.

telegram /'telɪgræm/ *n* [C] message sent by telegraph.

telegraph /'telɪgrɑːf; *US* -græf/ *n* [U] method of sending messages to a distant place by means of electrical or radio signals. **telegraph** *v* [I, T] send a telegram. **telegraphic** /ˌtelɪ'græfɪk/ *adj*.

telepathy /tɪ'lepəθɪ/ *n* [U] communication of thoughts from one mind to another without using speech, writing, etc. **telepathic** /ˌtelɪ'pæθɪk/ *adj*.

telephone /'telɪfəʊn/ *n* [C, U] (instrument used in the) system of sending and hearing sounds over a distance by wire and radio. **telephone** *v* [I, T] send (a message) or speak to (sb) by telephone. **'telephone-box** (also **'telephone booth**) *n* [C] small covered or enclosed structure containing a public telephone. **'telephone directory** *n* [C] list of names with telephone numbers and addresses. **'telephone exchange** *n* [C] place where telephone connections are made. **'telephone number** *n* [C] number given to a particular telephone and used in dialling to call it.

telephonist /tɪ'lefənɪst/ *n* [C] person whose job is to make telephone connections in an office or at a telephone exchange.

telephoto lens /ˌtelɪ'fəʊtəʊ lenz/ *n* [C] special lens that produces a large clear picture of a distant object being photographed.

telescope /'telɪskəʊp/ *n* [C] long tube-shaped instrument with lenses, for making distant objects appear nearer and larger. **telescope** *v* [I, T] become or make shorter by sliding one section within another: *When the trains collided, the first two carriages (were) ~d.* **telescopic** /ˌtelɪ'skɒpɪk/ *adj*.

teletext /'telɪtekst/ *n* [U] computerized service providing information on television screens.

television /'telɪvɪʒn/ *n* 1 [U] system of sending and receiving pictures and sounds over a distance by radio waves. 2 [C] (also **'television set**) apparatus for receiving such pictures and sounds.

televise /'telɪvaɪz/ *v* [T] broadcast on television.

telex /'teleks/ *n* 1 [U] system of sending typed messages round the world by telephone lines. 2 [C] message sent by telex. **telex** *v* [T] send (a message) to (sb) by telex.

tell /tel/ *v* (*pt, pp* told /təʊld/) 1 [T] make (sth) known to (sb) in words: *I told her my name.* 2 [T] order; advise: *I told them to go.* 3 [I, T] know (sth) definitely: *How can you ~ which key to use?* 4 [T] give information to. 5 [I] (*on*)// have an unpleasant effect on sb: *All this hard work is ~ing on him.* 6 [I] (*infml*) reveal a secret: *You promised not to ~.* 7 (idm) **all told** with all the people or things counted. **I 'told you so** (*infml*) I warned you that this would happen. **tell tales (about sb)** make known sb's mistakes, etc. **tell the 'time** read the time from a clock, etc. 8 (phr v) **tell A and B apart** be able to see the difference between A and B. **tell sb off** speak angrily to sb who has done sth wrong. **tell on sb** (*infml*) inform against sb: *John told on his sister.* **teller** *n* [C] 1 person who receives and pays out money in a bank. 2 person who counts votes. **telling** *adj* effective: *a ~ing argument.*

tell-tale /'telteɪl/ *n* [C] person who tells sb's secrets, etc. **tell-tale** *adj* that makes sth known: *a ~ blush.*

telly /'telɪ/ *n* [C, U] (*pl -ies*) (*infml*) short for TELEVISION.

temerity /tɪ'merətɪ/ *n* [U] (*fml*) rashness or boldness: *He had the ~ to call me a liar.*

temp /temp/ *n* [C] (*infml*) person, esp a secretary, employed for a short time.

temper /'tempə(r)/ *n* 1 [C] state of the mind: *in a good/bad ~.* 2 [sing, U] angry state of mind: *in a ~.* 3 (idm) **keep/lose one's temper** succeed/fail in controlling one's anger. **temper** *v* [T] make less extreme: *justice ~ed with mercy.* **-tempered** /-tempəd/ (forming compound adjectives) having a certain temper: *a 'bad-tempered man.*

temperament /'temprəmənt/ *n* [U, C] person's character shown in the way he/she thinks, feels and behaves. **temperamental** /ˌtemprə'mentl/ *adj* 1 having frequent changes of temper: *Children are often ~.* 2 caused by temperament. **temperamentally** /-təlɪ/ *adv*.

temperate /'tempərət/ *adj* 1 moderate in behaviour, drinking alcohol, etc. 2 (of climate) free from extremes of heat and cold.

temperature /'temprətʃə(r)/ US 'tempərtʃuər/ n 1 [C, U] degree of heat or cold. 2 (idm) **have a 'temperature** be ill and have a body temperature that is higher than normal.

tempest /'tempɪst/ n [C] (fml) violent storm. **tempestuous** /tem'pestʃuəs/ adj stormy, violent: (fig) a tempestuous love-affair.

temple¹ /'templ/ n [C] building used in the worship of a god or gods, esp in the Hindu and Buddhist religions.

temple² /'templ/ n [C] flat part on each side of the forehead.

tempo /'tempəʊ/ n [C] (pl ~s; in sense 2 tempi /'tempiː/) 1 rate of movement or activity: the ~ of city life. 2 speed at which music is played.

temporal /'tempərəl/ adj (fml) 1 of, or existing in, time. 2 of earthly, not spiritual, affairs.

temporary /'tempərərɪ; US -pərəri/ adj lasting for only a short time. **temporarily** /'tempərərəlɪ; US ˌtempə'rerəlɪ/ adv.

tempt /tempt/ v [T] 1 (try to) persuade (sb) to do sth, esp sth wrong or unwise: Nothing could ~ her to tell lies. 2 attract (sb) to do sth. **temptation** /temp'teɪʃn/ n 1 [U] tempting. 2 [C] sth that tempts. **tempting** adj attractive: a ~ing offer.

ten /ten/ pron, adj, n [C] 10. **tenth** pron, adj 10th. **tenth** pron, n [C] ¹⁄₁₀.

tenable /'tenəbl/ adj 1 (of an opinion) that can be reasonably defended. 2 (of an office or position) that can be held for the stated time.

tenacious /tɪ'neɪʃəs/ adj very determined to get or keep sth. **tenacity** /tɪ'næsətɪ/ n [U].

tenant /'tenənt/ n [C] person who pays rent for the use of a building, land, etc. **tenancy** /-ənsɪ/ n (pl -ies) 1 [C] use of land, etc as a tenant. 2 [C] length of time as a tenant.

tend¹ /tend/ v [I] to// be likely: He ~ s to make too many mistakes.

tend² /tend/ v [T] (fml) take care of: shepherds ~ ing their flocks.

tendency /'tendənsɪ/ n [C] (pl -ies) 1 way a person or thing is likely to be or behave: a ~ to get fat. 2 direction in which sth moves or changes: an increasing ~ for parents to help at school.

tender¹ /'tendə(r)/ adj 1 gentle; kind. 2 painful when touched; sensitive. 3 easily hurt or damaged. 4 (of meat) easily cut or chewed; not tough. **tenderly** adv. **tenderness** n [U].

tender² /'tendə(r)/ v 1 [T] (fml) offer or present: He ~ed his resignation. 2 [I] (for)// make an offer to do work at the stated price: ~ for the construction of the new motorway. **tender** n [C] statement of the price to do work.

tendon /'tendən/ n [C] strong cord that joins a muscle to a bone.

tenement /'tenəmənt/ n [C] large building, esp in a poor part of a city, divided into flats.

tenet /'tenɪt/ n [C] (fml) principle; belief.

tenner /'tenə(r)/ n [C] (Brit infml) £10 (note).

tennis /'tenɪs/ n [U] game for two or four players who hit a ball across a net with a racket. **'tennis court** n [C] marked area on which tennis is played.

tenor /'tenə(r)/ n [C] 1 (a) (music for or singer with the) highest normal adult male voice. (b) (of instruments) with a range of the tenor voice: a ~ saxophone. 2 (fml) general meaning.

tenpin bowling /ˌtenpɪn 'bəʊlɪŋ/ n [U] game in which a ball is rolled towards ten bottle-shaped objects, in order to knock them down.

tense¹ /tens/ adj (~r, ~st) 1 stretched tightly. 2 nervous and worried. **tense** v [I, T] become or make tense: He ~d his muscles. **tensely** adv.

tense² /tens/ n [C] (grammar) verb form that shows the time of the action: the present/past/future ~.

tension /'tenʃn/ n 1 [U] state or degree of being stretched: the ~ of the rope. 2 [U] mental, emotional or nervous strain. 3 [C, U, usu pl] conditions when feelings or relations are tense: political ~ (s). 4 [U] electrical power: high ~ cables.

tent /tent/ n [C] shelter made of canvas, etc and supported by poles and ropes.

tentacle /'tentəkl/ n [C] long thin part of certain creatures (eg an octopus) used for feeling, holding, etc.

tentative /'tentətɪv/ adj made or done to test sth; not definite: make a ~ offer. **tentatively** adv.

tenterhooks /'tentəhʊks/ n (idm) (be) on 'tenterhooks be in a state of anxious waiting.

tenth ⇨ TEN.

tenuous /'tenjʊəs/ adj very slight; weak: a ~ relationship.

tepid /'tepɪd/ adj slightly warm.

term /tɜːm/ n 1 [C] fixed period of time: *the president's ~ of office.* 2 [C] division of the school or university year: *end-of-~ exams.* 3 [C] word or phrase with a special meaning: *technical ~.* 4 **terms** [pl] (a) conditions of an agreement. (b) conditions of sale or payment. **terms** [pl] way of expression: *I'll explain this in general ~ first.* 6 (idm) **be on good, friendly, bad 'terms with** have a good, etc relationship with sb. **come to terms with sb** learn to accept (sth unpleasant or difficult). **in the 'long/ 'short term** over a long/short period of time. **in terms of sth** concerning sth: *in ~ s of economics.* **term** *v* [T] call or name.

terminal /'tɜːmɪnl/ adj of or being an illness that will cause death and cannot be cured. **terminal** *n* [C] 1 building for passengers or goods, esp at an airport or port. 2 device used for putting information into a computer and obtaining information from it. **terminally** /-nəlɪ/ adv.

terminate /'tɜːmɪneɪt/ *v* [I, T] come or bring to an end. **termination** /ˌtɜːmɪ'neɪʃn/ n [U, C] ending: *the termination of a contract.*

terminology /ˌtɜːmɪ'nɒlədʒɪ/ n [U, C] (pl -ies) special words and expressions used in a particular subject.

terminus /'tɜːmɪnəs/ n [C] (pl -ni /-naɪ/ or ~ es) station or stop at the end of a railway line or bus route.

termite /'tɜːmaɪt/ n [C] ant-like insect that eats wood.

terrace /'terəs/ n [C] 1 long row of houses joined together. 2 flat area beside a house. 3 one of a series of level step-like areas of ground on a hillside. 4 wide steps where spectators may stand at a football ground, etc. **terrace** *v* [T] form into terraces: *~ d houses.*

terrain /tə'reɪn, 'terem/ n [C, U] area of land: *hilly ~.*

terrestrial /tə'restrɪəl/ adj 1 of or living on the land. 2 of the earth.

terrible /'terəbl/ adj 1 causing great fear or trouble: *a ~ war/ accident.* 2 hard to bear; extreme: *~ toothache.* 3 (infml) very bad: *What ~ food!* **terribly** adv (infml) extremely: *terribly busy.*

terrier /'terɪə(r)/ n [C] kind of small lively dog.

terrific /tə'rɪfɪk/ adj (infml) 1 very great: *a ~ storm.* 2 wonderful. **terrifically** /-klɪ/ adv extremely.

terrify /'terɪfaɪ/ *v* (pt, pp -ied) [T] fill with fear: *I'm terrified of dogs.*

territorial /ˌterə'tɔːrɪəl/ adj of land or territory.

territory /'terətrɪ; US -tɔːrɪ/ n [C, U] (pl -ies) 1 (area of) land under the control of a ruler, country, etc: *Spanish ~.* 2 area of land claimed and defended by one person or animal. 3 area for which sb is responsible.

terror /'terə(r)/ n (a) [U] very great fear. (b) [C] something that causes this. **terrorism** /-rɪzəm/ n [U] use of violence for political purposes. **terrorist** adj, n [C]. **terrorize** *v* [T] fill with terror by threats or violence.

terse /tɜːs/ adj using few, often unfriendly, words. **tersely** adv. **terseness** n [U].

test /test/ n [C] 1 examination or trial of the qualities of a person or thing: *a driving-~ ◇ a blood ~.* 2 examination of a person's knowledge or ability. **test** *v* [T] examine and measure the qualities of (sb/ sth) or the knowledge or abilities of (sb). **'test match** n [C] international cricket or rugby match. **'test-tube** n [C] small glass tube, closed at one end, used in chemical experiments.

testament /'testəmənt/ n [C] (fml) 1 (to/) thing that clearly shows or proves sth. 2 **Testament** either of the two main divisions of the Bible: *the New T~.*

testicle /'testɪkl/ n [C] either of the two glands of the male sex organ that produce sperm.

testify /'testɪfaɪ/ *v* (pt, pp -ied) [I, T] 1 make a formal statement, esp in a law-court. 2 (to/) (fml) show that (sth) is true.

testimonial /ˌtestɪ'məʊnɪəl/ n [C] 1 formal written statement of sb's character, abilities, etc. 2 thing given to sb to show honour or thanks.

testimony /'testɪmənɪ; US -məʊnɪ/ n [U, C] (pl -ies) formal statement of truth, esp in a law-court.

tetanus /'tetənəs/ n [U] serious disease, caused by infection of a cut, causing muscles to become stiff.

tête-à-tête /ˌteɪt ɑː 'teɪt/ n [C] private conversation between two people.

tether /'teðə(r)/ n [C] rope or chain to which an animal is tied. **tether** *v* [T] fasten with a tether.

text /tekst/ n 1 main printed part of a book. 2 [C] original words of a speaker, author, etc. 3 [C] book, play, etc that is studied. 4 [C] short passage of the Bible, etc as the subject of a sermon. '**textbook** n [C] book giving instruction in a subject.

textual /'tekstʃʊəl/ adj (fml) of or in a text.

textile /'tekstaɪl/ n [C, esp pl] woven cloth.

texture /'tekstʃə(r)/ n [C, U] way a surface or cloth feels or looks, eg how rough or smooth it is.

than /ðən rare strong form ðæn/ conj, prep 1 (used for introducing the second part of a comparison): Sylvia is taller ~ me. 2 (used after more or less and before expressions of time, distance, etc): It cost more ~ £100. ○ It's less ~ a mile to the station.

thank /θæŋk/ v 1 [T] express one's gratitude to. 2 (idm) ,**no**, '**thank you** (used for refusing an offer politely). '**thank you** (used for expressing gratitude or accepting an offer). **thankful** adj grateful. **thankfully** adv. **thankless** adj not likely to be rewarded with thanks: a ~ less task. **thanks** n [pl] 1 (expressions of) gratitude. 2 (idm) **thanks to sb/sth** because of sb/sth. **thanks** interj (infml) thank you. '**thanksgiving** n [C, U] 1 expression of gratitude, esp to God. 2 **Thanksgiving** (**Day**) holiday in the USA and Canada.

that¹ /ðæt/ adj, pron (pl **those** /ðəʊz/) 1 (being) the person or thing mentioned, known or understood, esp one more distant than another: Look at ~ man standing there. ○ Those are nice hats. 2 (idm) **that is** (**to say**) (used for giving more exact details of sth). **that** adv to that degree; so: The film wasn't ~ bad.

that² /ðət/ rare strong form ðæt/ conj (used for introducing various clauses): She said ~ she would come.

that³ /ðət/ rare strong form ðæt/ relative pronoun 1 (as the subject of a verb): You're the only person ~ can help me. 2 (as the object of the verb, but often omitted): The pen ~ you gave me is a nice one.

thatch /θætʃ/ n [C, U] roof covering of dried straw, reeds, etc. **thatch** v [T] cover (a roof, etc) with a thatch.

thaw /θɔː/ v 1 [I, T] (of snow or ice) (cause to) melt. 2 [T] cause to become liquid or soft again: ~ frozen food. 3 [I] (fig) become friendlier and less formal. **thaw** n [C, usu sing] (weather causing) thawing.

the /ðə, ðɪ; strong form ðiː/ definite article 1 (used for referring to a particular thing): T~ sky was

blue. ○ Please close ~ window. 2 all the people, things, etc of the stated kind: T~ dog is a popular pet. 3 (used for referring to a group or nationality): ~ rich ○ ~ French. 4 (used before certain geographical names): ~ Mediterranean ○ ~ Atlantic (Ocean). 5 (used with musical instruments): play ~ piano. 6 (used with a unit of measure): every: paid by ~ hour. 7 (used with a superlative): ~ best day of your life. **the** adv (used in comparisons for showing a connection): T~ more I read, ~ less I understand.

theatre (US **theater**) /'θɪətə(r)/ n 1 [C] building in which plays are performed. 2 **the theatre** [sing] work of acting in, producing, etc plays. 3 [C] hall or room for lectures. 4 [C] = OPERATING-THEATRE (OPERATE). '**theatre-goer** n [C] person who frequently sees plays at the theatre. **theatrical** /θɪˈætrɪkl/ adj 1 of or for the theatre. 2 not natural; showy.

theft /θeft/ n [C, U] (act or instance of) stealing.

their /ðeə(r)/ adj belonging to them: They have lost ~ dog. **theirs** /ðeəz/ pron of or belonging to them: That dog is ~, not ours.

them /ðəm; strong form ðem/ pron 1 (used as the object of a v or prep) people, animals or things mentioned earlier: Give ~ to me. ○ Did you eat all of ~? 2 (infml) him or her: If someone comes in, ask ~ to wait.

theme /θiːm/ n [C] 1 subject of a talk, book, etc. 2 repeated tune in a piece of music. '**theme park** n [C] park which has swings, roundabouts, etc which are based on a single idea. '**theme song** n [C] song often repeated in a musical play, film, etc.

themselves /ðəmˈselvz/ pron 1 (used as a reflexive when the people or animals doing an action are also affected by it): They hurt ~. 2 (used for emphasis): They ~ have often made that mistake. 3 (idm) **by them'selves** (a) alone. (b) without help.

then /ðen/ adv 1 at that time: I was still unmarried ~. 2 next; after that: We stayed in Rome and ~ in Naples. 3 in that case; therefore: 'It isn't here.' 'T~ it must be in the car.' 4 and also: There's the soup to heat, then there's the bread to butter.

thence /ðens/ adv (arch or fml) from there.

theology /θɪˈɒlədʒɪ/ n [U] study of religion and God. **theologian**

/ˌθɪəˈləʊdʒən/ n [C]. **theological**
/ˌθɪəˈlɒdʒɪkl/ adj.

theorem /ˈθɪərəm/ n [C] mathematical statement that can be proved by reasoning.

theory /ˈθɪərɪ/ n (pl -ies) 1 [C] set of reasoned ideas intended to explain facts or events: *Darwin's ~ of evolution.* 2 [U] general principles of sth, contrasted with practice. **theoretical** /ˌθɪəˈretɪkl/ adj.

therapeutic /ˌθerəˈpjuːtɪk/ adj of or for the curing of a disease.

therapy /ˈθerəpɪ/ n [U] treatment of illness. **therapist** n [C].

there¹ /ðeə(r)/ adv 1 in, at or to that place: *We'll soon be ~.* 2 at that point in a story, etc: *Don't stop ~!* 3 (used for calling attention to sth): *T~'s the bell for lunch.* 4 (idm) **,there and 'then** at that place and time. **there** interj 1 (used for expressing triumph, dismay, encouragement, etc): *T~! You've woken the baby!* 2 (used for comforting a child): *T~, ~! You'll soon feel better.*

there² /ðeə(r); strong form ðeə(r)/ adv (used as the subject of a verb, esp be): *T~'s a man at the door.*

thereabouts /ˈðeərəbaʊts/ adv near that place, number, year, etc.

thereafter /ˌðeərˈɑːftə(r); US -ˈæf-/ adv (fml) after that.

thereby /ˌðeəˈbaɪ/ adv (fml) by that means.

therefore /ˈðeəfɔː(r)/ adv for that reason.

thereupon /ˌðeərəˈpɒn/ adv (fml) immediately; because of that.

thermal /ˈθɜːml/ adj 1 of or caused by heat. 2 (of clothes) designed to keep the wearer warm in cold weather.

thermometer /θəˈmɒmɪtə(r)/ n [C] instrument for measuring temperature.

Thermos (also **'Thermos flask**) /ˈθɜːməs/ n [C] (P) type of vacuum flask.

thermostat /ˈθɜːməstæt/ n [C] device that automatically keeps a building, engine, etc at an even temperature.

thesaurus /θɪˈsɔːrəs/ n [C] (pl ~es or -ri /-raɪ/) book of words grouped together according to their meanings.

these ⇨ THIS.

thesis /ˈθiːsɪs/ n [C] (pl **theses** /ˈθiːsiːz/) 1 statement or theory supported by arguments. 2 long piece of writing on a subject, done as part of a university degree.

they /ðeɪ/ pron (used as the subject of a v) 1 people, animals or things mentioned earlier. 2 people in general: *They ~ say we're going to*

have a hot summer. 3 (infml) (used instead of he or she): *If anyone comes late, ~'ll have to wait.*

they'd /ðeɪd/ 1 they had. ⇨ HAVE. 2 they would. ⇨ WILL¹, WOULD¹.

they'll /ðeɪl/ they will. ⇨ WILL¹.

they're /ðeə(r)/ they are. ⇨ BE.

they've /ðeɪv/ they have. ⇨ HAVE.

thick /θɪk/ adj 1 having a great or the stated distance between opposite surfaces: *a ~ slice of bread ◦ a wall 2 feet ~.* 2 having a large number of things close together: *~ hair ◦ a ~ forest.* 3 (of a liquid) containing little water; not flowing easily. 4 difficult to see through: *a ~ fog.* 5 (infml) stupid. **thick** adv 1 thickly: *spread the butter too ~.* 2 (idm) **,thick and 'fast** quickly and in large numbers. **thick** n (idm) **in the thick of sth** in the part of sth in which there is the most activity. **,through ,thick and 'thin** under good and bad conditions. **thicken** v [I, T] become or make thick: *~ en the soup.* **thickly** adv. **thickness** n 1 [U] quality or degree of being thick: *4 centimetres in ~ ness.* 2 [C] layer. **,thick'set** adj having a broad solid-looking body. **,thick-'skinned** adj not sensitive to criticism, etc.

thicket /ˈθɪkɪt/ n [C] mass of trees or bushes growing closely together.

thief /θiːf/ n [C] (pl **thieves** /θiːvz/) person who steals. **thieve** /θiːv/ v [I, T] steal (sth).

thigh /θaɪ/ n [C] part of the human leg between the knee and the hip.

thimble /ˈθɪmbl/ n [C] small cap of metal or plastic worn over the end of the finger to protect it when sewing.

thin /θɪn/ adj (~ner, ~nest) 1 having a small distance between opposite surfaces. 2 not fat. 3 (of a liquid) containing a lot of water: *~ soup.* 4 having a small number of things widely separated: *~ hair. The audience is rather ~ tonight.* 5 easy to see through: *a ~ mist.* 6 weak; feeble: *a ~ excuse.* 7 (idm) **the thin end of the 'wedge** sth that seems unimportant but is likely to lead to more important and often harmful things. **thin** adv thinly: *cut the bread too ~.* **thin** v (-nn-) [I, T] become or make thin. **thinly** adv. **thinness** n [U].

thing /θɪŋ/ n 1 [C] any unnamed object: *What is that ~ on the table?* 2 **things** [pl] (a) personal possessions, clothes, etc: *Bring your swimming ~ s.* (b) general state of one's life: How are ~s? **3** [C] task or action. **4** [C] subject: There's another ~ I want to ask you about. **5** [C] (used of a person or animal): She's a sweet little ~. **6 the thing** [sing] **(a)** what is most suitable: A holiday will be just the ~ for you. **(b)** what is fashionable or popular. **7** (idm) **for 'one thing** (used for introducing a reason). **have a thing about sb/sth** (infml) have very strong feelings, esp dislike, about sb/sth. **the ,thing 'is** the question to be considered is.

think /θɪŋk/ v (pt, pp **thought** /θɔːt/) **1** [I] use the mind to form opinions, make decisions, etc. **2** [T] have as an opinion; believe or consider: Do you ~ it's going to rain? **3** [T] imagine: I can't ~ why he came. **4** [T] have a plan or intention: I ~ I'll go for a swim. **5** (idm) **think a'loud** speak one's thoughts as they come. **think better of (doing) sth** decide against (doing) sth after thinking further about it. **think highly, a lot, a lit-tle, etc of sb/sth** have a good, bad, etc opinion of sb/sth: I don't ~ much (ie I have a low opinion) of our new teacher. **think nothing of sth** consider sth to be usual or easy. **6** (phr v) **think about sth** consider sth carefully. **think of sth (a)** consider sth. **(b)** have sth as a possible plan: We're ~ing of going to Venice. **(c)** imagine sth: Just ~ of the cost! **(d)** remember sth: I can't ~ of her name. **think sth out/through** consider sth carefully and thoroughly. **think sth over** consider sth carefully before reaching a decision. **think sth up** invent or devise (a plan, etc). **think n** [sing] act of thinking.

thinker /'θɪŋkə(r)/ n [C] person who thinks: a great ~.

thinking /'θɪŋkɪŋ/ n [U] thought; opinion. **thinking** adj intelligent and thoughtful.

third /θɜːd/ pron, adj 3rd. **third** pron, n [C] ⅓. **the ,third de'gree** n [sing] long hard questioning; use of torture. **thirdly** adv. **,third 'party** n [C] person other than the two main people involved: ~ party in'surance, ie covering cost for damage or injury to another person or his/her property. **the ,third 'person** n [sing] (grammar) set of pronouns, eg she, it, they and verb forms, eg is, used by a speaker to refer to the people or things spoken about. **,third-'rate** adj of very poor quality. **the ,Third 'World** n [sing] the developing countries of the world in Africa, Asia and South America.

thirst /θɜːst/ n **1** [U, sing] feeling caused by a desire or need to drink. **2** [sing] (fig) strong desire: a ~ for revenge. thirsty adj (-ier, -iest) feeling or causing thirst.

thirteen /,θɜː'tiːn/ pron, adj, n [C] 13. **thirteenth** /,θɜː'tiːnθ/ pron, adj 13th. **thirteenth** pron, n [C] ¹⁄₁₃.

thirty /'θɜːti/ pron, adj, n [C] (pl -ies) 30. **thirtieth** /'θɜːtiəθ/ pron, adj 30th. **thirtieth** pron, n [C] ¹⁄₃₀.

this /ðɪs/ adj, pron (pl **these** /ðiːz/) **1** (being) the person or thing nearby, named or understood: Look at ~ box. **2** (infml) a certain: Then ~ man came in. **this** adv to this degree: It was about ~ high.

thistle /'θɪsl/ n [C] wild plant with prickly leaves and esp purple flowers.

thong /θɒŋ/ n [C] narrow strip of leather used esp as a fastening.

thorn /θɔːn/ n **1 (a)** [C] sharp pointed growth on the stem of a plant. **(b)** [C, U] tree or shrub with thorns. **2** (idm) **a thorn in one's flesh/side** person or thing that constantly annoys one. **thorny** adj (-ier, -iest) **1** having thorns. **2** (fig) difficult: a ~y problem.

thorough /'θʌrə; US 'θɜːrəʊ/ adj **1** done completely and carefully. **2** (of a person) doing work carefully, with attention to detail. **'thoroughgoing** adj complete: a ,~ going re'vision. **thoroughly** adv. **thoroughness** n [U].

thoroughbred /'θʌrəbred/ n [C], adj (animal, esp a horse) of pure breed.

thoroughfare /'θʌrəfeə(r)/ n [C] (fml) public road or street.

those pl of THAT¹.

though /ðəʊ/ conj **1** in spite of the fact that: They bought the car, even ~ they couldn't really afford it. **2** and yet; but: It's possible, ~ un-likely. **though** adv however: I expect you're right ... I'll ask him, ~.

thought¹ pt, pp of THINK.

thought² /θɔːt/ n **1** [C] idea or opinion produced by thinking. **2** [U] (power or process of) thinking. **3** [U] particular way of thinking: modern scientific ~. **4** [U, C] care; consideration. **5** (idm) **second 'thoughts** change of opinion after further thinking. **thoughtful** adj **1** thinking deeply. **2** caring for other people; kind. **thoughtfully** adv. **thoughtless** adj not caring for other people; selfish. **thought-**

lessly *adv*.

thousand /'θaʊznd/ *pron, adj, n* [C] **1** 1000. **2** (also **thousands** [pl]) (*infml*) great number: *A ~ thanks.* **thousandth** /'θaʊznθ/ *pron, adj* 1000th. **thousandth** *pron, n* [C] 1/1000.

thrash /θræʃ/ *v* 1 [T] beat with a stick, whip, etc. 2 [T] defeat thoroughly in a game, etc. 3 [I] move violently: *He ~ed about in the water.* 4 (phr v) **thrash sth out** discuss (a problem) thoroughly and come to an answer. **thrashing** *n* [C] 1 beating. 2 defeat.

thread /θred/ *n* 1 [C, U] (length of) cotton, silk, wool, etc used in sewing. 2 [C] (*fig*) line of thought connecting parts of a story. 3 [C] raised spiral line round a screw or bolt. **thread** *v* [T] 1 put a thread through the hole in (a needle). 2 put (beads, etc) on a thread. 3 pass (film, tape, etc) into position on a machine. 4 (idm) **thread one's way through (sth)** go carefully through (sth). **'threadbare** /-beə(r)/ *adj* (of cloth) worn.

threat /θret/ *n* 1 [C, U] statement of an intention to punish or harm sb. 2 [C] likely cause of danger: *He is a ~ to society.* 3 [C, usu sing] sign of coming trouble, danger, etc.

threaten /'θretn/ *v* 1 [T] make a threat or threats against (sb); use (sth) as a threat: *They ~ed to kill all the passengers.* 2 [I, T] give warning of: *Black clouds ~ rain.* 3 [I] (of oth bel) seem likely to happen: *Danger ~ed.* 4 [T] be a threat to. **threatening** *adj*, **threateningly** *adv*.

three /θriː/ *pron, adj, n* [C] 3. **three-di'mensional** *adj* having length, breadth and depth.

thresh /θreʃ/ *v* [T] beat (corn, wheat, etc) to separate the grains from the rest of the plant.

threshold /'θreʃhəʊld/ *n* [C] (*fml*) 1 piece of wood or stone forming the bottom of a doorway. 2 (*fig*) point of beginning sth: *on the ~ of a new career.*

threw *pt* of THROW.

thrift /θrɪft/ *n* [U] careful use of money. **thrifty** *adj* (**-ier, -iest**).

thrill /θrɪl/ *n* [C] 1 (a) sudden feeling of great excitement, fear, etc. (b) something causing this. **thrill** *v* [T] cause (sb) to feel a thrill. **thriller** *n* [C] book, play or film full of excitement and esp about crime.

thrive /θraɪv/ *v* (*pt* **thrived** or **throve** /θrəʊv/, *pp* **thrived** or **thriven** /'θrɪvn/) [I] grow well and strong; prosper: *a thriving business.*

throat /θrəʊt/ *n* [C] 1 passage in the neck through which food and air pass into the body. 2 front part of the neck.

throb /θrɒb/ *v* (**-bb-**) [I] (of the heart, pulse, etc) beat, esp more quickly and strongly than usual. **throb** *n* [C].

throes /θrəʊz/ *n* (idm) **in the throes of sth** busily involved in sth.

thrombosis /θrɒm'bəʊsɪs/ (*pl* **-ses** /-siːz/ *n* [C, U] (formation of a) small thick mass of blood in a blood vessel or the heart.

throne /θrəʊn/ *n* 1 [C] special chair used by a king or queen in official ceremonies. 2 **the throne** [sing] position of being king or queen.

throng /θrɒŋ; *US* θrɔːŋ/ *n* [C] (*fml*) large crowd of people. **throng** *v* [I, T] go to or be present in (a place) in a large crowd.

throttle /'θrɒtl/ *v* [T] seize (sb) by the throat to stop him/her breathing. **throttle** *n* [C, C] valve controlling the flow of fuel into an engine.

through /θruː/ *prep* 1 from one end or side (of) to the other: *The train went ~ the tunnel.* *The River Thames flows ~ London.* 2 from the beginning to the end of: *She won't live ~ the night.* 3 (*US*) up to and including; until: *Monday ~ Thursday.* 4 by means of; because of: *arrange insurance ~ a bank.* *The accident happened ~ lack of care.* 5 past (a barrier): *smuggle drugs ~ customs.* **through** *adv* 1 from one side of sth to the other: *It's very crowded in here—can you get ~?* 2 from the beginning to the end of sth. 3 past a barrier: *The ambulance drove straight ~.* 4 (*Brit*) connected by telephone: *I tried to ring you but I couldn't get ~.* 5 (idm) **,through and 'through** completely. 6 (phr v) **be through (with sb/sth)** have finished (a relationship, etc) with sb/sth: *Keith and I are ~.* **through** *adj* allowing a direct journey: *a ~ train.*

throughout /θruː'aʊt/ *prep, adv* 1 in or into every part of (sth): *They're sold ~ the world.* 2 during (the whole period of time): *I watched the film and cried ~.*

throw /θrəʊ/ *v* (*pt* **threw** /θruː/, *pp* **~n** /θrəʊn/) 1 [I, T] send (sth) through the air with some force, esp by moving the arm. 2 [T] move (a part of the body) suddenly and forcefully: *~ up one's hands in horror.* 3 [T] *on/off/) put* (clothes) on/off quickly or carelessly. 4 [T] cause to fall to the ground: *The horse threw him.* 5 [T] *(fig)* direct: *She threw me an angry look.* ○ *The trees threw long shadows on the grass.* 6 [T] shape (pottery) on a potter's wheel. 7 [T] *(infml)* confuse: *The interruptions threw him.* 8 [T] cause to be in a certain state: *Hundreds were ~ n out of work.* 9 [T] operate (a switch). 10 [T] arrange (a party). 11 (idm) **throw cold water on sth** ⇨ COLD[1]. **throw a fit** ⇨ FIT[3]. **throw sb in at the deep end** *(infml)* ask sb to do sth new and difficult for which he/she is unprepared. **throw in the sponge/towel** admit defeat. **throw light on sth** ⇨ LIGHT[1]. **throw one's weight about** try to make people obey one's orders because one considers oneself important. 12 (phr v) **throw sth away** (a) get rid of sth unwanted. (b) waste (an opportunity, etc). **throw sth in** include sth extra, without increasing the price. **throw oneself into sth** become involved in (an activity) with enthusiasm. **throw sb/sth off** become free from sth/sb. **throw oneself on sb/sth** *(fml)* depend completely on sb/sth for help, etc: *~ oneself on the mercy of others.* **throw sb out** force (a trouble-maker) to leave. **throw sth out** reject (a plan, etc). **throw sth together** make or produce sth quickly. **throw sb up** vomit. **throw sth up** (a) leave (one's job). (b) bring (sth) to notice. **throw** *n* [C] 1 act of throwing. 2 distance thrown. **thrower** *n* [C].

thru *(US)* = THROUGH.

thrush /θrʌʃ/ *n* [C] kind of singing bird with a brown back and a spotted breast.

thrust /θrʌst/ *v* *(pt, pp* **thrust)** [I, T] push (sth/sb) suddenly and forcefully. **thrust** *n* 1 [C] act of thrusting. 2 [U] forward-moving force of an engine. 3 [U] *(fig)* main meaning or point.

thud /θʌd/ *n* [C] dull sound of a heavy object hitting sth softer. **thud** *v* **(-dd-)** [I] strike or fall with a thud.

thug /θʌɡ/ *n* [C] violent and dangerous person.

thumb /θʌm/ *n* [C] 1 short thick finger set apart from the other four. 2 (idm) **thumbs 'up/'down** expression of approval/disapproval. **under sb's 'thumb** under sb's control. **thumb** *v* [I, T] *(through)*// turn over the pages of (a book, etc) quickly. 2 (idm) **thumb a 'lift** ask for a free ride from passing motorists by signall-

ing with one's thumb. **'thumb-nail** *n* [C] nail at the tip of the thumb. **'thumb-nail** *adj* briefly written: *a ~ nail sketch.* **'thumb-tack** *n* [C] *(US)* drawing-pin.

thump /θʌmp/ *v* 1 [I, T] hit (sb/sth) with one's fist; strike heavily. 2 [I] beat heavily: *His heart ~ ed with excitement.* **thump** *n* [C] (noise of a) heavy blow.

thunder /'θʌndə(r)/ *n* [U] **(a)** loud noise that follows a flash of lightning. (b) loud noise like thunder: *the ~ of guns.* **thunder** *v* 1 [I] (used with *it*) sound with thunder: *It's been ~ ing all night.* 2 [I] make a loud noise like thunder. 3 [T] say in a loud angry voice. **'thunder-bolt** *n* [C] 1 flash of lightning with a crash of thunder. 2 *(fig)* sudden terrible event. **'thunderclap** *n* [C] crash of thunder. **'thunderous** *adj* very loud: *~ ous applause.* **'thunderstorm** *n* [C] storm of lightning, thunder and heavy rain.

Thursday /'θɜːzdɪ/ *n* [U, C] the fifth day of the week, next after Wednesday. (See examples of use at *Monday*).

thus /ðʌs/ *adv* *(fml)* 1 in this way. 2 as a result of this.

thwart /θwɔːt/ *v* [T] *(fml)* prevent (sb or his/her plans) from succeeding.

thyme /taɪm/ *n* [U] kind of herb used in cooking.

thyroid /'θaɪrɔɪd/ **thyroid 'gland** *n* [C] gland in the neck that affects the body's growth.

tiara /tɪ'ɑːrə/ *n* [C] small crown for a woman.

tic /tɪk/ *n* [C] sudden unconscious moving of the muscles, esp in the face.

tick[1] /tɪk/ *n* [C] 1 light repeated sound of a clock or watch. 2 *(infml)* moment: *I'll be with you in a ~.* 3 mark showing that sth is correct or has been dealt with. **tick** *v* 1 [I] (of a clock, etc) make ticks(1). 2 [T] *(off)*// put a tick(3) next to. 3 (idm) **what makes sb 'tick** *(infml)* the reasons for sb's behaviour. 4 (phr v) **tick sb off** *(infml)* speak angrily to sb because he/she has done sth wrong. **tick over** work or operate steadily.

tick[2] /tɪk/ *n* [C] small blood-sucking insect.

ticket /'tɪkɪt/ *n* [C] 1 printed piece of card or paper which shows that payment has been made to travel on a bus, enter a cinema, etc. 2 piece of card or paper giving the price or size of sth. 3 official notice of an offence against traffic laws.

tickle /'tɪkl/ *v* 1 [T] touch (part of

sb's body) lightly, esp so as to cause laughter. 2 [I, T] have or cause an itching feeling (in). 3 [T] please or amuse. **tickle** n [C] act or feeling of tickling. **ticklish** adj 1 (of a person) sensitive to tickling. 2 (infml) (of a problem) needing to be dealt with carefully.

tidal /'taɪdl/ adj of or caused by tides. **tidal 'wave** n [C] very large ocean wave.

tide /taɪd/ n 1 (a) [C, U] regular rise and fall in the level of the sea. (b) [U] water moved by this: *Beware of strong ~ s.* 2 [C, usu sing] direction in which opinions, events, etc seem to move. **tide** v (phr v) **tide sb over (sth)** help sb through (a difficult period). **'tide-mark** n [C] highest point reached by a tide on a beach.

tidings /'taɪdɪŋz/ n [pl] (arch or joc) news: *glad ~.*

tidy /'taɪdɪ/ adj (-ier, -iest) 1 neat; orderly: *a ~ room/girl.* 2 (infml) fairly large: *a ~ sum of money.* **tidily** adv. **tidiness** n [U]. **tidy** v (pt, pp -ied) [I, T] make (sth/sb) tidy: *~ (up) the room.*

tie¹ /taɪ/ v (pres part **tying** /taɪɪŋ/) 1 [T] fasten or bind with string, rope, etc: *A label was ~d to the handle. ~ (up) a parcel.* 2 [T] arrange (string, etc) to form a knot or bow: *~ one's shoe-laces.* 3 [I] be fastened: *Does this dress ~ in front?* 4 [I, T] make the same score (in): *The two teams ~ d.* 5 (phr v) **tie sb down** limit sb's freedom. **tie in (with sth)** agree or be consistent with sth. **tie sb up** (a) bind sb with rope so that he/she cannot move or escape. (b) (infml) (usu passive) cause sb to be very busy: *I'm ~ d up now; can you come back later?* **tie sth up** do sth with (eg money) so that it cannot be used for other purposes.

tie² /taɪ/ n [C] 1 band of material worn round the neck under the collar of a shirt and tied at the front. 2 something, eg cloth or wire, used for fastening. 3 (fig) something that unites: *family ~ s.* 4 something that limits one's freedom. 5 equal score in a game, etc. **'tie-breaker** n [C] way of deciding the winner when competitors have the same score.

tier /tɪə(r)/ n [C] one of a number of rows (esp seats) rising one behind the other.

tiff /tɪf/ n [C] slight quarrel.

tiger /'taɪgə(r)/ n [C] large fierce animal of the cat family, yellowish with black stripes. **tigress** /'taɪgrɪs/ n [C] female tiger.

tight /taɪt/ adj 1 firmly fastened

or held: *a ~ knot.* 2 (a) fitting closely: *These shoes are too ~.* (b) made so that sth cannot get in or out: *'air~ 'water~.* 3 fully stretched: *a ~ belt.* 4 with things or people arranged closely: *(fig) a ~ schedule.* 5 (money) difficult to obtain. 6 (sl) drunk. 7 (infml) unwilling to spend money. 8 (idm) **in a tight corner/spot** in a difficult situation. **tight** adv tightly: *The bags are packed ~.* **tighten** v [I, T] (cause to) become tighter: *~ (up) the screws.* **tight-'fisted** adj (infml) unwilling to spend money. **tightly** adv. **tightness** n [U]. **'tightrope** n [C] tightly stretched high rope on which acrobats perform. **tights** n [pl] close-fitting clothing covering the hips, legs and feet.

tile /taɪl/ n [C] 1 thin usu square piece of baked clay or other material for covering roofs, walls and floors. 2 (idm) **on the 'tiles** (infml) enjoying oneself wildly away from home. **tiled** adj.

till¹ = UNTIL.

till² /tɪl/ n [C] drawer or box for money in a shop, bank, etc.

till³ /tɪl/ v [T] prepare and use (land) for growing crops.

tiller /'tɪlə(r)/ n [C] handle used for turning the rudder of a boat.

tilt /tɪlt/ v [I, T] (cause to) come into a sloping position (as if) by lifting one end. **tilt** n [C] 1 sloping position. 2 (idm) **at full tilt** ⇨ FULL.

timber /'tɪmbə(r)/ n 1 [U] (a) wood prepared for use in building, etc. (b) trees suitable for this. 2 [C] large piece of wood used in building a ship or house. **timbered** adj.

time¹ /taɪm/ n 1 [U] (the passing of) all the days, years, etc of the past, present and future: *The world exists in space and ~.* 2 [U] portion or measure of time: *Is there ~ for another cup of tea?* 3 [U] point of time: *The ~ is 2 o'clock.* 4 [U, C] period of time taken to do sth: *The winner's ~ was 11 seconds.* 5 [U] point or period of time: *It's 'lunch- ~. ◇ It's ~ for us to go now.* 6 [C] occasion: *He failed the exam three ~ s.* 7 [C] often [pl] period of time; age: *in prehistoric ~ s.* 8 [U] (music) speed of a piece of music: *beat ~.* 9 (idm) **ahead of one's 'time** having ideas that are too advanced for the period in which one lives. **all the 'time** during the whole period. **at 'all times** always. **at 'one time** in the past. **at a 'time** separately. **at 'times** sometimes. **behind the 'times** old-fashioned. **do 'time** (sl) go to prison. **for the time 'being** for a short time, until some other arrangement is made. **from time to 'time** occasionally. **have no time for sb/sth** dislike sb/sth. **have the ,time of one's 'life** (*infml*) be extremely excited or happy. **in 'time** eventually. **on 'time** not late or early; punctual(ly). **take one's 'time** not hurry. **,time after 'time, ,time and (time) a'gain** repeatedly. **'time bomb** *n* [C] bomb set to explode at a certain time. **'time-limit** *n* [C] period of time during which sth must be done. **times** *prep* multiplied by: *5* ~ *2 is 10.* **times** *n* [pl] (used for showing multiplication): *This book is three* ~*s as long as that one.* **'time-scale** *n* [C] period of time in which events take place. **'time-sharing** *n* [U] 1 use of a computer for different operations by two or more people at the same time. 2 arrangement in which a holiday home is owned by several people who use it for a short time each year. **'time-signal** *n* [C] signal broadcast on the radio that gives the exact time of day. **'time-switch** *n* [C] switch that can be set to operate automatically at a certain time. **'timetable** *n* [C] 1 list showing the times at which trains, buses, etc depart or arrive. 2 list showing the times at which the various subjects are taught at school.

time² /taɪm/ *v* [T] 1 choose the time or moment for: *She* ~*d her journey so that she arrived early.* 2 measure the time taken by or for. **timer** *n* [C] person or device that times sth. **timing** *n* [U] (skill in) choosing the best moment to do sth.

timely /'taɪmlɪ/ *adj* (-**ier**, -**iest**) occurring at just the right time.

timid /'tɪmɪd/ *adj* shy and not brave or self-confident. **timidity** /tɪ'mɪdətɪ/ *n* [U]. **timidly** *adv*.

tin /tɪn/ *n* 1 [U] soft white metal. 2 [C] (*Brit*) metal container for food: *a* ~ *of beans.* **tin** *v* (-**nn-**) [T] put (food) in tins(2): ~*ned peaches.* **tin 'foil** *n* [U] very thin sheets of metal, used for wrapping food in. **tinny** *adj* (-**ier**, -**iest**) 1 of or like tin. 2 (of a sound) light high and unpleasant. **'tin-opener** *n* [C] (*Brit*) tool for opening tins of food.

tinge /tɪndʒ/ *v* [T] (**with**)|| 1 add a small amount of colour to. 2 (*fig*) affect slightly: *admiration* ~*d with envy.* **tinge** *n* [C, usu sing] small amount: *a* ~ *of sadness in her voice.*

tingle /'tɪŋgl/ *v* [I] have a slight

pricking feeling in one's skin: (*fig*) ~ *with excitement.* **tingle** *n* [C, usu sing] tingling feeling.

tinker /'tɪŋkə(r)/ *v* [I] (**with**)|| work in a casual or not an expert way, esp trying to mend or improve sth.

tinkle /'tɪŋkl/ *v* [I] make a light ringing sound. **tinkle** *n* [C] 1 tinkling sound. 2 (*Brit infml*) telephone call.

tinsel /'tɪnsl/ *n* [U] strip or thread of shiny material used as a Christmas decoration.

tint /tɪnt/ *n* [C] (esp pale) shade of colour. **tint** *v* [T] give a tint to.

tiny /'taɪnɪ/ *adj* (-**ier**, -**iest**) extremely small.

tip¹ /tɪp/ *n* [C] 1 pointed or thin end of sth: *the* ~*s of one's fingers.* 2 small piece put at the end: *a stick with a rubber* ~. 3 (*idm*) **on the tip of one's 'tongue** just about to be remembered or spoken. **the tip of the 'iceberg** small sign of a much larger problem. **tip** *v* (-**pp-**) [T] fit with a tip(2): ~*ped cigarettes.* **'tiptoe** *n* (*idm*) **on 'tiptoe** on the tips of one's toes: *stand on* ~ *to see over sb's head* ◇ *walk on* ~ *toe so as not to be heard.* **'tiptoe** *v* [I] walk quietly: *She* ~*toed out.* **,tip'top** *adj* (*infml*) excellent.

tip² /tɪp/ *v* (-**pp-**) 1 [I, T] (**a**) (cause sth to) lean on one side. (**b**) (**over**)|| (cause sth to) turn or fall over. 1 [T] (esp *Brit*) empty (sth), esp quickly. **tip** *n* [C] 1 public place where rubbish is put. 2 (*infml*) very untidy place.

tip³ /tɪp/ *n* [C] 1 small amount of money given to sb who has done a service. 2 small useful piece of advice. **tip** *v* (-**pp-**) 1 [I, T] give a tip(1) to sb: ~ *the waiter.* 2 (**phr v**) **tip sb off** (*infml*) give secret information to sb as a warning. **'tip-off** *n* [C] piece of secret information.

tipple /'tɪpl/ *v* [C] (*infml*) alcoholic drink.

tipsy /'tɪpsɪ/ *adj* (-**ier**, -**iest**) (*infml*) slightly drunk.

tire¹ /'taɪə(r)/ *v* [I, T] (cause to) become tired: *The long walk* ~*d them* (*out*). **tired** *adj* 1 feeling that one needs rest or sleep. 2 *of*|| bored with sth: *I'm* ~*d of watching television.* **tiredness** *n* [U]. **tireless** *adj* not getting tired easily. **tiresome** *adj* annoying or boring.

tire² (*US*) = **TYRE**.

tissue /'tɪʃuː/ *n* 1 [U, C] mass of cells in an animal body: *nerve* ~. 2 [U] (also **'tissue-paper**) thin soft paper, used esp for wrapping. 3 [C] piece of soft paper used as a handkerchief. 4 [C] (*fig*) connected series: *a* ~ *of lies.*

tit[1] /tɪt/ n [C] small bird of various kinds.

tit[2] /tɪt/ n (idm) **tit for 'tat** /tæt/ something unpleasant done to sb in return for sth unpleasant he/ she has done to one.

tit[3] /tɪt/ n [C] (△ sl) woman's breast.

titbit /'tɪtbɪt/ n [C] **1** small tasty piece of food. **2** small piece of gossip, etc.

titillate /'tɪtɪleɪt/ v [T] excite (sb), esp sexually.

title /'taɪtl/ n **1** [C] name of a book, play, picture, etc. **2** [C] word, eg Lord, Mrs or Professor, used for showing sb's rank, occupation or profession. **3** [C] (sports) position of champion. **4** [U, C] (law) right to own sth. **titled** adj having a title of nobility: a ~d lady. **'title-deed** n [C] document proving a title(4). **'title-role** n [C] part in a play, etc that is used as the title.

titter /'tɪtə(r)/ v [I] give a nervous or silly little laugh. **titter** n [C].

TNT /ˌti: en 'ti:/ n [U] powerful explosive.

to[1] /tə, tu or tu:; strong form tu:/ prep **1** in the direction of: walk to the shops. **2** reaching the point of; towards: rise to power. **3** as far as: The dress reaches to her ankles. **4** until and including: from Monday to Friday. **5** (of time) before: It's ten (ie minutes) to three. **6** (introducing the direct object): Give it to Peter. **7** belonging to: the key to the door. **8** (showing a comparison or ratio): I prefer walking to climbing. We won by 6 goals to 3.

to[2] /tə, tu or tu:; strong form tu:/ (used before the simple form of a v to form the infinitive) **1** (used as the object): He wants to go. **2** (used for showing purpose or result): They came (in order) to help me. **3** (used instead of the whole infinitive): 'Will you come?' 'I hope to.'

to[3] /tu:/ adv **1** (of a door) into a closed position: Push the door to. **2** (idm) **to and 'fro** backwards and forwards.

toad /təʊd/ n [C] animal like a frog.

toadstool /'təʊdstu:l/ n [C] kind of fungus, esp one that is poisonous.

toast[1] /təʊst/ n [U] sliced bread made brown by heating. **toast** v [I, T] (cause bread to) become brown by heating. **2** [T] warm (esp oneself) in front of a fire. **toaster** n [C] electric device for toasting bread.

toast[2] /təʊst/ v [T] wish happiness, success, etc to (sb) by drink-

ing wine, etc: ~ the bride and bridegroom. **toast** n [C] act of toasting; person toasted: propose/ drink a ~.

tobacco /tə'bækəʊ/ n [U] (plant having) leaves that are dried and used for smoking in cigarettes, pipes, etc. **tobacconist** /tə'bækənɪst/ n [C] shop or person that sells tobacco, cigarettes, etc.

toboggan /tə'bɒgən/ n [C] long narrow board used for travelling on snow. **toboggan** v [I] use a toboggan.

today /tə'deɪ/ adv, n [U] **1** (on) this day. **2** (at) this present time: the young people of ~.

toddle /'tɒdl/ v [I] (esp of a young child) walk with short unsteady steps. **toddler** n [C] small child that has just learned to walk.

to-do /tə'du:/ n [C, usu sing] (pl ~s) (infml) state of excitement, confusion or annoyance.

toe /təʊ/ n [C] **1** (a) any of the five movable parts at the end of the foot. (b) front part of a sock, shoe, etc. **2** (idm) **on one's 'toes** ready for action. **toe** v (idm) **toe the 'line** obey orders. **'toe-nail** n [C] hard layer covering the end of a toe.

toffee /'tɒfɪ; US 'tɔ:fɪ/ n [C, U] (piece of) hard sticky sweet made by heating sugar, butter, etc.

together /tə'geðə(r)/ adv **1** with each other: They went for a walk ~. **2** so as to be joined to each other: Tie the ends ~. **3** at the same time: All his troubles happened ~. **4** in agreement. **5** (idm) **get it to'gether** (sl) get things organized or under control. **together with** in addition to. **togetherness** n [U] feeling of friendliness or love.

toil /tɔɪl/ v [I] (away)|| (fml) work long or hard. **toil** n [U] (fml) long or hard work.

toilet /'tɔɪlɪt/ n [C] (room containing a) bowl used for receiving and taking away waste matter from the body. **'toilet-paper** n [U] paper used for cleaning oneself after passing waste matter from one's body. **toiletries** n [pl] things, eg soap and toothpaste, used in washing and taking care of one's body. **'toilet-roll** n [C] roll of toilet paper.

token /'təʊkən/ n [C] **1** sign or mark: a ~ of my affection. **2** round flat piece of metal used instead of a coin. **3** card with a voucher that can be exchanged for goods: a book ~. **token** adj small; not serious: ~ one-day strikes.

told pt, pp of TELL.

tolerate /'tɒləreɪt/ v [T] **1** allow (sth that one disagrees with or dis-

likes): *I won't ~ such behaviour.* 2 endure (sb/sth unpleasant) without protesting: *~ heat/noise.*
tolerable /-rəbl/ *adj* that can be tolerated; fairly good. **tolerably** *adv* fairly. **tolerance** /-rəns/ *n* [U] willingness or ability to tolerate sb/sth: *religious/racial tolerance.*
tolerant /-rənt/ *adj* showing tolerance. **toleration** /ˌtɒlə-ˈreɪʃn/ *n* [U] action or practice of tolerating sb/sth.

toll[1] /təʊl/ *n* [C] 1 money used for the use of a road, bridge, etc. 2 loss or damage caused by sth: *the death-~* (ie the number of people killed) *in the earthquake.*

toll[2] /təʊl/ *v* [I, T] (of a bell) ring slowly and repeatedly. **toll** *n* [sing] tolling sound.

tomato /təˈmɑːtəʊ; *US* -meɪ-/ *n* [C] (*pl* -es) (plant with a) soft red fruit eaten raw or cooked as a vegetable.

tomb /tuːm/ *n* [C] place, esp with a stone monument, where a dead body is buried. **tombstone** *n* [C] stone monument over a tomb.

tomboy /ˈtɒmbɔɪ/ *n* [C] lively young girl who enjoys rough noisy games.

tom-cat /ˈtɒm kæt/ *n* [C] male cat.

tomorrow /təˈmɒrəʊ/ *adv, n* [U] 1 (on) the day after today. 2 (in) the near future.

ton /tʌn/ *n* 1 [C] measure of weight; 2240 pounds (1.016 tonnes) in Britain, 2000 pounds (0.907 tonnes) in the USA. **2 tons** [pl] (*infml*) a lot: *~s of money.*

tone[1] /təʊn/ *n* 1 [C] quality of sound: *the sweet ~(s) of a piano.* 2 [C] signal on a telephone line: *the engaged ~.* 3 [sing] general quality or character: *the serious ~ of the article.* 4 [C] shade of colour. 5 [C] (*music*) one of the five larger differences in pitch between one note and the next. **tone-'deaf** *adj* not able to recognize different musical notes.

tone[2] /təʊn/ *v* 1 [T] give a particular tone of sound or colour to. 2 (*phr v*) **tone (sth) down** (cause sth to) become less forceful or intense. **tone in (with sth)** (of colours, etc) fit in well with sth. **tone (sth) up** (cause sth to) become stronger or more intense: *Exercise ~s up the body.*

tongs /tɒŋz/ *n* [pl] instrument with two movable arms joined at one end, used for picking up and holding things.

tongue /tʌŋ/ *n* 1 [C] (a) movable organ in the mouth, used in talking, tasting, licking, etc. (b) (*fig*) way of speaking: *He has a sharp ~,* ie He often speaks harshly or angrily. 2 [C] (*fml*) language. 3 [C, U] tongue of an ox, etc used as food. 4 [C] thing shaped like a tongue, eg the leather flap in a shoe. 5 (*idm*) **with one's tongue in one's 'cheek** saying sth that one does not intend to be taken seriously. **'tongue-tied** *adj* unable to speak because of shyness or nervousness. **'tongue-twister** *n* [C] word or phrase that is difficult to say.

tonic /ˈtɒnɪk/ *n* 1 [C, U] medicine that gives strength or energy. 2 [C] something that makes one feel healthier or happier. 3 [C, U] tonic water. **'tonic water** *n* [C, U] mineral water flavoured with quinine.

tonight /təˈnaɪt/ *adv, n* [U] (during the) evening or night of today.

tonnage /ˈtʌnɪdʒ/ *n* [U, C] amount of cargo a ship can carry.

tonne /tʌn/ *n* [C] metric unit of weight; 1000 kilograms.

tonsil /ˈtɒnsl/ *n* [C] either of the two small organs at the back of the throat. **tonsillitis** /ˌtɒnsɪˈlaɪtɪs/ *n* [U] painful swelling of the tonsils.

too /tuː/ *adv* 1 in addition; also: *She plays the guitar and sings ~.* 2 to a higher degree than is allowed or desirable: *You're driving ~ fast!* 3 (*idm*) **all/only too** very: *only ~ pleased to help.*

took *pt* of TAKE[1].

tool /tuːl/ *n* [C] instrument held in the hand and used for working on sth.

toot /tuːt/ *n* [C] short sound from a horn. **toot** *v* [I, T] (cause sth to) make a toot.

tooth /tuːθ/ *n* (*pl* teeth /tiːθ/) 1 [C] hard white bony structure in the mouth, used for biting and chewing. 2 [C] tooth-like part, eg on a comb or saw. 3 **teeth** [pl] (*infml*) effective force: *The present law must be given more teeth.* 4 (*idm*) **get one's teeth into sth** (*infml*) become involved with sth with great energy and concentration. **in the teeth of sth** in spite of sth. **toothache** *n* [U] pain in a tooth or teeth. **'tooth-brush** *n* [C] brush for cleaning one's teeth. **toothed** /tuːθt/ *adj* having teeth. **toothless** *adj.* **'toothpaste** *n* [C] paste for cleaning one's teeth. **'toothpick** *n* [C] short pointed piece of wood, etc, used for removing food from between one's teeth.

top[1] /tɒp/ *n* 1 [C] highest part or point: *at the ~ of the hill.* 2 [C] upper surface: *the ~ of the table.* 3

[sing] highest or most important position. **4** [C] cover: *a pen ~*. **5** [C] (esp woman's) garment covering the upper part of the body. **6** (idm) **at the top of one's 'voice** as loudly as one can. **from ,top to 'bottom** completely. **get on top of sb** (*infml*) (of work) cause sb too much worry. **on top of sth** (a) able to deal with or control sth. (b) in addition to sth. **on ,top of the 'world** very happy: *He feels on ~ of the world today.* **,over the 'top** (esp *Brit infml*) unacceptably extreme or exaggerated. **top 'brass** (*sl*) senior officers or officials. **top 'dog** (*sl*) person, group, etc in the highest or most important position. **top** *adj* highest in position, rank, degree, etc: *a room on the ~ floor ○ at ~* (ie the fastest) *speed.* **,top 'hat** *n* [C] man's tall formal black or grey hat. **,top-'heavy** *adj* too heavy at the top. **topless** *adj* (of a woman) having the breasts bare. **'topmost** *adj* highest. **,top 'secret** *adj* needing to be kept completely secret. **'topsoil** *n* [U] layer of soil nearest the surface.

top² /tɒp/ *v* (**-pp-**) [T] **1** provide a top for: *a cake ~ped with icing.* **2** be higher than: *Exports have ~ped £100 million.* **3** come first in. **4** (phr v) **top (sth) up** fill up (a partly empty container): *~ up with petrol ○ ~ up a drink.*

top³ /tɒp/ *n* [C] toy that spins on its pointed end.

topic /'tɒpɪk/ *n* [C] subject for discussion or study. **topical** *adj* of present interest: *~al issues.*

topple /'tɒpl/ *v* [I, T] (cause to) fall over: (*fig*) *The crisis ~d the government.*

torch /tɔːtʃ/ *n* [C] **1** (*Brit*) small electric light held in the hand. **2** piece of wood soaked in oil, etc for carrying as a light. **'torchlight** *n* [U] light of torch or torches: *a ~ light procession.*

tore *pt* of TEAR².

torment /'tɔːment/ *n* (**a**) [U] extreme pain or suffering. (**b**) [C] cause of this. **torment** /tɔː'ment/ *v* [T] **1** cause torment to. **2** annoy. **tormentor** /tɔː'mentə(r)/ *n*.

torn *pp* of TEAR².

tornado /tɔː'neɪdəʊ/ *n* [C] (*pl ~es*) violent destructive storm with circular winds.

torpedo /tɔː'piːdəʊ/ *n* [C] (*pl ~es*) tube-shaped bomb that travels underwater and is used for destroying ships. **torpedo** /v/ [T] attack and destroy (as if) with a torpedo.

torrent /'tɒrənt; *US* 'tɔːr-/ *n* **1** violently rushing stream of water. **2** (*fig*) violent outburst: *a ~ of*

abuse. **torrential** /tə'renʃl/ *adj* like a torrent: *~ial rain.*

torso /'tɔːsəʊ/ *n* [C] (*pl ~s*) main part of the human body without arms or legs.

tortoise /'tɔːtəs/ *n* [C] slow-moving animal with a hard shell. **'tortoiseshell** *n* [U] hard yellow and brown shell of some turtles, used for making ornaments.

tortuous /'tɔːtʃuəs/ *adj* **1** full of bends; winding. **2** not direct; complicated.

torture /'tɔːtʃə(r)/ *v* [T] cause extreme pain to (sb), as a punishment or to force him/her to say sth. **torture** *n* **1** [U] act of torturing. **2** [C, U] extreme pain. **torturer** *n* [C].

Tory /'tɔːrɪ/ *n* [C] (*pl -ies*) *adj* (member) of the Conservative Party.

toss /tɒs; *US* tɔːs/ *v* **1** [T] throw lightly or carelessly. **2** [T] move (one's head) suddenly and quickly. **3** [I, T] move restlessly from side to side: *I kept ~ing and turning all night.* **4** [T] mix gently: *~ a salad.* **5** [I, T] decide sth by throwing (a coin) and guessing which side will be on top when it falls: *Let's ~ to see who goes first.* **toss** *n* [C] act of tossing: *with a ~ of her head.* **'toss-up** *n* [sing] even chance.

tot¹ /tɒt/ *n* [C] **1** very small child. **2** small amount of alcoholic drink.

tot² /tɒt/ *v* (**-tt-**) (phr v) **tot sth up** (*infml*) add up (numbers).

total /'təʊtl/ *n* **1** [C] complete number or amount. **2** (idm) **in 'total** altogether. **total** *adj* complete. **total** /v (**-ll-**; *US also* **-l-**) [T] **1** count the total of. **2** reach a total of: *The number of visitors ~led 15 000.* **totality** /təʊ'tælətɪ/ *n* [U] (*fml*) whole amount. **totally** *adv* completely: *~ly blind.*

totalitarian /ˌtəʊtælɪ'teərɪən/ *adj* of a system of government in which there is only one political party and no other parties are allowed.

totter /'tɒtə(r)/ *v* [I] **1** walk or move unsteadily. **2** shake as if about to fall.

touch¹ /tʌtʃ/ *v* **1** [I, T] put one's fingers or hand lightly on (sth): *The dish is hot—don't ~ (it)!* **2** [I, T] be or come together with (sth else) so that there is no space between: *The two wires ~ed.* **3** [T] eat or drink: *He hasn't ~ed any food for two days.* **4** [T] (usu passive) cause (sb) to feel sympathy, sadness, etc: *We were greatly ~ed by your thoughtfulness.* **5** [T] equal in excellence: *No one can ~ him as an* actor. 6 (idm) **touch wood** touch sth made of wood to avoid bad luck. 7 (phr v) **touch down** (on an aircraft) land. **touch sth off** cause (esp sth violent) to start. **touch on/upon sth** mention sth briefly. **touch sth up** improve sth by making small changes. '**touch-down** n [C] landing of an aircraft. **touched** adj 1 thankful. 2 slightly mad. **touching** adj causing sympathy, sadness, etc.

touch² /tʌtʃ/ n 1 [C, usu sing] act of touching. 2 [U] sense of feeling. 3 [sing] way sth feels when touched: *The material has a velvety ~*. 4 [C] small detail: *put the finishing ~es to the project*. 5 [sing] slight quantity: *a ~ of frost in the air*. 6 [sing] manner of doing sth: *Her work shows that professional ~*. 7 [U] (in football) part of the pitch outside the sidelines: *The ball is in ~*. 8 (idm) in/out of 'touch (with sb) in/not in communication with sb. **touch-and-go** adj uncertain; risky.
touchy /'tʌtʃi/ adj (-ier, -iest) easily offended.

tough /tʌf/ adj 1 not easily cut or broken. 2 (of meat) difficult to cut and chew. 3 able to endure hardship; strong. 4 difficult: *a ~ problem*. 5 very firm; severe: *~ laws to deal with terrorism*. 6 unfortunate: *~ luck*. **toughen** /'tʌfn/ v [I, T] become or make tough. **toughness** n [U].
toupee /'tuːpeɪ; US tuː'peɪ/ n [C] small wig worn on a bald part of a man's head.

tour /tʊə(r)/ n [C] 1 journey during which many places are visited: *a round-the-world ~*. 2 brief visit: *a ~ of the palace*. **tour** v [I, T] make a tour of or in (a place). **tourism** /'tʊərɪzəm/ n [U] business of providing hotels, special trips, etc for tourists. **tourist** n [C] person who visits places for pleasure.

tournament /'tɔːnəmənt; US 'tɜːrn-/ n [C] series of games or contests: *a chess ~*.
tourniquet /'tʊənɪkeɪ; US 'tɜːrnɪkət/ n [C] bandage twisted tightly round an injured arm or leg to stop it bleeding.
tout /taʊt/ v 1 [I, T] try to get people to buy (one's goods or services), esp in an annoyingly direct way. 2 [T] (*Brit*) sell (tickets for sports matches, etc) at very high prices. **tout** n [C] person who touts.

tow /taʊ/ v [T] pull (a vehicle, etc) with a rope, chain, etc. **tow** n 1 [C] act of towing sth. 2 (idm) **in tow**

(*infml*) following closely behind. **on tow** being towed. '**tow-path** n [C] path along the bank of a canal or river.

towards /tə'wɔːdz; *US* tɔːrdz/ (also **toward** /tə'wɔːd; *US* tɔːrd/) prep 1 in the direction of: *walk ~ the door*. 2 moving closer to achieving (sth): *steps ~ unity*. 3 in relation to: *friendly ~ tourists*. 4 just before: *~ the end of the 19th century*. 5 for the purpose of: *The money will go ~ a new car*.

towel /'taʊəl/ n [C] piece of cloth for drying one's hands or body. **towelling** ((*US*)-l-) n [U] thick soft cloth used for making towels.

tower /'taʊə(r)/ n [C] 1 tall narrow (part of a) building. 2 (idm) **a ,tower of 'strength** person who can be relied on to give a lot of help or support. **tower** v [I] *above/over*| be much higher than sb/sth. '**tower block** n [C] (*Brit*) very tall block of flats or offices. **towering** adj very tall; very great.

town /taʊn/ n 1 (a) [C] place with many buildings and houses, larger than a village. (b) [C, also sing with pl v] all the people who live in a town. 2 [U] main business or shopping area of a town. 3 [U] main town or city of an area. 4 [U] towns and cities in general: *~ life*. 5 (idm) **go to 'town** (*infml*) do sth with great energy or enthusiasm. **(out) on the 'town** enjoying oneself by visiting places of entertainment, esp at night. **,town 'clerk** n [C] official in charge of town or city records. **,town 'council** n [C] group of officials who govern a town. **,town 'hall** n [C] buildings with the offices of the town's local government. **township** /'taʊnʃɪp/ n [C] (in South Africa) a town or suburb where black citizens live.

toxic /'tɒksɪk/ adj (*fml*) poisonous.

toy /tɔɪ/ n [C] thing for children to play with. **toy** v (phr v) **toy with sth** (a) think about (an idea, etc) but not seriously. (b) handle or move sth carelessly: *~ with a pencil*.

trace /treɪs/ v [T] 1 find (sth) after looking for it with great effort: *I cannot ~ the letter*. 2 describe the development of; find the origin of. 3 copy (sth) by drawing on transparent paper placed over it. **trace** n 1 [C, U] mark, sign, etc showing that sb/sth has been present in a place: *~s of an ancient civilization* ○ *disappear without ~*. 2 [C] very small amount: *~s of poison in his blood*. **tracing** n [C] copy of a

drawing, etc made by tracing(3).
'**tracing-paper** n [U] transparent paper used for making tracings.
trachea /trəˈkɪə; US ˈtreɪkɪə/ n [C] (pl ~s or, in scientific use, ~e /-kiːiː/) (anatomy) windpipe.
track /træk/ n [C] 1 path or rough road. 2 series of marks left by a moving vehicle, person or animal. 3 railway line. 4 course or circuit for racing. 5 piece of music or song on a record or tape. 6 (idm) **hot on sb's tracks** ⇨ HOT. **in one's 'tracks** (infml) where one is; suddenly: stop him in his ~s. **keep/lose track of sb/sth** keep/fail to keep oneself informed about sb/sth. **make 'tracks** leave a place. **on the right/wrong 'track** thinking in a correct/incorrect way. **track** v 1 [T] follow the track(2) of. 2 (phr v) **track sb/sth down** find sb/sth by searching. **tracker** n [C]. '**track record** n [C] past achievements of a person or organization. '**track suit** n [C] loose warm suit worn by athletes, etc during training.
tract¹ /trækt/ n [C] 1 large area of land. 2 system of connected parts in an animal body: the reˈspiratory ~.
tract² /trækt/ n [C] short article on a religious, political or moral subject.
traction-engine /ˈtrækʃn ˌendʒɪn/ n [C] large vehicle powered by steam, formerly used for pulling heavy loads.
tractor /ˈtræktə(r)/ n [C] motor vehicle used for pulling farm machinery.
trade¹ /treɪd/ n 1 (a) [U] business of buying, selling or exchanging goods or services. (b) [C] business of a particular kind: She's in the book ~. 2 [U, C] job, esp needing training and skill with the hands: He's a carpenter by ~. '**trade mark** n [C] word or symbol used on a product by a manufacturer. '**trade name** n [C] name given by a manufacturer to a product. '**tradesman** n [C] person, eg a shopkeeper, who sells goods. ˌtrade 'union n [C] organization of workers, formed to protect their interests and get better working conditions. ˌtrade-'unionist n [C] member of a trade union.
trade² /treɪd/ v 1 [I] buy, sell or exchange goods or services. 2 [T] (for) exchange (sth) for another. 3 (phr v) **trade sth in** give (a used article) in part payment for sth new. **trade on sth** take unfair advantage of sth. **trader** n [C].
tradition /trəˈdɪʃn/ n (a) [C] cus-

tom, belief or practice passed down from one generation to the next. (b) [U] (passing on of such) customs, etc. **traditional** /-ʃənl/ adj. **traditionally** adv.
traffic /ˈtræfɪk/ n [U] 1 vehicles moving along a road. 2 movement of ships or aircraft along a route. 3 business of moving people or goods from one place to another. 4 illegal trade. **traffic** v (-ck-) [I] (in)// trade, esp in illegal goods, eg drugs. **trafficker** n [C]. '**traffic island** n [C] raised area for pedestrians in the middle of a busy road. '**traffic jam** n [C] situation in which vehicles cannot move freely and come to a stop. '**traffic-light** n [C, usu pl] set of coloured lights that control the flow of traffic at a road junction. '**traffic warden** n [C] person whose job is to control the parking of cars in a town.
tragedy /ˈtrædʒədɪ/ n (pl -ies) 1 [C, U] terrible event that causes great sadness. 2 (a) [C] serious play with a sad ending. (b) [U] such plays considered as a group.
tragic /ˈtrædʒɪk/ adj 1 very sad or terrible: a ~ accident. 2 of or in the style of tragedy(2). **tragically** /-klɪ/ adv.
trail /treɪl/ n [C] 1 mark, track, etc left by sb/sth. 2 path, esp through rough country. **trail** v 1 [I, T] (cause sth to) be dragged along behind. 2 [I] walk or move slowly, esp behind others. 3 [I] lose in a game, etc. 4 [I] (of plants) grow along the ground or hang down loosely. 5 [T] follow the trail of; track. 6 (idm) **hot on sb's trail** ⇨ HOT. **trailer** n [C] 1 vehicle pulled by another one. 2 series of short pieces from a new film, shown to advertise it.
train¹ /treɪn/ n [C] 1 line of carriages or trucks joined together and pulled by an engine along a railway. 2 series of connected things: a ~ of thought. 3 part of a long dress that rests on the ground. 4 number of people or animals moving in a line.
train² /treɪn/ v 1 [I, T] receive or give teaching, practice or exercise: ~ a football team. 2 [T] aim; point: ~ a gun on the enemy. 3 [T] cause to grow in a certain direction: ~ roses up a wall. **trainee** /treɪˈniː/ n [C] person being trained. **trainer** n [C] 1 person who trains eg athletes or animals. 2 [usu pl] strong sports shoe. **training** n [U] preparation; practice.
traipse /treɪps/ v [I] (infml) walk

in a tired way.

trait /treɪt, treɪ/ n [C] particular quality or characteristic.

traitor /ˈtreɪtə(r)/ n [C] person who betrays his/her country, friends, etc.

tram /træm/ n [C] passenger vehicle powered by electricity that runs on rails set in the road.

tramp /træmp/ v 1 [I] walk with heavy or noisy steps. 2 [I, T] walk across (an area) for a long distance: ~ *over the hills*. **tramp** n [C] 1 person with no house or job and who wanders from place to place. 2 long walk.

trample /ˈtræmpl/ v 1 [I, T] (on)) tread heavily on (sth) so as to destroy it. 2 [I] *on//* treat sb or his/her rights or feelings in a harsh uncaring way.

trampoline /ˈtræmpəli:n/ n [C] strong cloth held by springs in a frame, on which gymnasts jump up and down.

trance /trɑ:ns/ *US* træns/ n [C] sleep-like condition of the mind.

tranquil /ˈtræŋkwɪl/ *adj* (of sth) calm; quiet. **tranquillity** (*US* also -l-) /træŋˈkwɪləti/ n [U] calm quiet state. **tranquillize** (*US* also -l-) /v [T] make calm, esp by drugs. **tranquillizer** (*US* also -l-) n drug for making an anxious person feel calm. **tranquilly** *adv.*

transact /trænˈzækt/ v [T] (*fml*) conduct or carry out (business). **transaction** /-ˈzækʃn/ n 1 [U] transacting. 2 [C] piece of business. 3 **transactions** [pl] written records of the meetings of an academic society.

transatlantic /ˌtrænzət'læntɪk/ *adj* of travelling or communications across the Atlantic Ocean.

transcend /trænˈsend/ v [T] (*fml*) go beyond: ~ *human knowledge.*

transcontinental /ˌtrænzˌkɒntɪˈnentl/ *adj* crossing a continent.

transcribe /trænˈskraɪb/ v [T] 1 copy in writing. 2 write in a special form: ~ *d in phonetic symbols.* 3 arrange (a piece of music) so that it can be played by a different instrument, etc. **transcript** /ˈtrænskrɪpt/ n [C] written copy. **transcription** /-ˈskrɪpʃn/ n [U, C].

transfer¹ /trænsˈfɜ:(r)/ v (-rr-) 1 [I, T] move from one place, job etc to another: *He was ~red to the sales department.* 2 [T] give the possession of (sth) to sb else. **transferable** *adj* that can be transferred(2): *This ticket is not ~able.* **transference** /ˈtrænsfərəns/ *US* trænsˈfɜ:rəns/ n [U].

transfer² /ˈtrænsfɜ:(r)/ n 1 [C, U] (instance of) transferring. 2 [C] design that can be transferred from one surface to another.

transfix /trænsˈfɪks/ v [T] (*fml*) (usu passive) make (sb) unable to move, think or speak because of fear, astonishment, etc.

transform /trænsˈfɔ:m/ v [T] change completely the appearance or character of them. **transformation** /ˌtrænsfəˈmeɪʃn/ n [C, U]. **transformer** n [C] apparatus that changes the voltage of an electric current.

transfusion /trænsˈfju:ʒn/ n [C, U] act or process of putting one person's blood into another person's body.

transgress /trænzˈgres/ v [I, T] (*fml*) go beyond (a moral limit); do wrong. **transgression** /-ˈgreʃn/ n [C, U].

transient /ˈtrænzɪənt/ *US* ˈtrænʃnt/ *adj* lasting for only a short time.

transistor /trænˈzɪstə(r)/ -ˈsɪst-/ n [C] 1 small electronic device used in radios, etc. 2 small radio with transistors. **transistorized** /-təraɪzd/ *adj* having transistors.

transit /ˈtrænzɪt, -sɪt/ n [U] travelling or taking of people or goods from one place to another: *goods damaged in ~.*

transition /trænˈzɪʃn/ n [C, U] (instance of) changing from one state to another. **transitional** /-ʃənl/ *adj.*

transitive /ˈtrænsətɪv/ *adj* (*grammar*) (of a verb) used with a direct object, eg *washed* in 'He washed the cups'.

transitory /ˈtrænsɪtrɪ; *US* -tɔ:rɪ/ *adj* lasting for only a short time.

translate /trænzˈleɪt/ v 1 [I, T] put (sth written or spoken) into a different language: ~ *(the book) from French into Russian.* 2 [T] (*in to//*) express (sth) in a more definite form: ~ *ideas into practice.* **translation** /-ˈleɪʃn/ n [C, U]. **translator** n [C].

translucent /trænzˈlu:snt/ *adj* allowing light to pass through, but not transparent.

transmission /trænzˈmɪʃn/ n 1 [U] transmitting. 2 [C] television or radio broadcast. 3 [C] parts of a vehicle that pass power to the wheels.

transmit /trænzˈmɪt/ v (-tt-) [T] 1 send electronically by radio waves. 2 send or pass from one person to another. **transmitter** n [C] device that transmits radio or television signals.

transparent /trænsˈpærənt/ *adj*

1 that can be seen through: *Glass is ~.* 2 easily understood; obvious. **transparency** /-'rænsɪ/ *n* (*pl* -ies) 1 [U] state of being transparent. 2 [C] small piece of photographic film in a frame. **transparently** *adv*.

transplant /træns'plɑːnt; *US* -'plænt/ *v* 1 [T] take up (a plant) from one place and plant it in another. 2 [T] move (a body organ or piece of skin or hair) from one person or part of the body to another. 3 [I, T] (*fig*) move to another place. **transplant** /'trænsplɑːnt; *US* -plænt/ *n* [C] instance of transplanting(2): *a heart ~.*

transport /træn'spɔːt/ *v* [T] move (goods or people) from one place to another. **transport** /'trænspɔːt/ *n* [U] 1 (also esp *US* **transportation** /ˌtrænspɔː-'teɪʃn/) (system of) transporting. 2 means of transport; vehicle. **transporter** *n* [C] large vehicle used for carrying cars.

transpose /træn'spəʊz/ *v* [T] 1 cause (two or more things) to change places. 2 (*music*) put into a different key/(5). **transposition** /ˌtrænspə'zɪʃn/ *n* [C, U].

transverse /'trænzvɜːs/ *adj* (*fml*) lying or placed across. **transversely** *adv*.

transvestite /trænz'vestaɪt/ *n* [C] person who enjoys wearing the clothes of the opposite sex.

trap /træp/ *n* [C] 1 device for catching animals. 2 (*fig*) plan for catching or deceiving sb. 3 light two-wheeled carriage. 4 (*sl*) mouth. **trap** *v* (-pp-) [T] 1 keep (sb) in a place from which he/she cannot move or escape. 2 catch (an animal) in a trap. 3 trick or deceive. **'trap'door** *n* [C] small door in a floor or ceiling. **trapper** *n* [C] person who catches animals.

trapeze /trə'piːz; *US* træ-/ *n* [C] bar hung from two ropes, used by acrobats for swinging on.

trash /træʃ/ *n* [U] 1 (*infml*) material, writing, etc of very low quality. 2 (*US*) rubbish. **'trashcan** *n* [C] (*US*) dustbin. **trashy** *adj* (-ier, -iest) (*infml*) of very low quality.

trauma /'trɔːmə; *US* 'traumə/ *n* 1 [U] emotional shock producing a lasting harmful effect. 2 [C] (*infml*) very upsetting unpleasant experience. **traumatic** /trɔː'mætɪk; *US* trau-/ *adj*.

travel /'trævl/ *v* (-ll-; *US* -l-) 1 [I, T] make a journey through (an area). 2 [T] cover (a distance) in travelling. 3 [I] move or go: *Light*

~s faster than sound. **travel** *n* 1 [U] travelling: *space ~.* 2 **travels** [pl] journeys, esp abroad. **'travel agent** *n* [C] person whose job is to make arrangements for travel. **travelled** (*US* -l-) *adj* having travelled to many places: *a well-~ writer.* **traveller** (*US* -l-) *n* [C] 1 person on a journey. 2 travelling salesman. **'traveller's cheque** *n* [C] cheque that can be exchanged abroad for the money of the country one is in.

traverse /trə'vɜːs/ *v* [T] (*fml*) go across or over.

travesty /'trævəstɪ/ *n* (*pl* -ies) very bad imitation or representation of sth: *a ~ of justice.*

trawl /trɔːl/ *v* [I, U] fish with a large wide net dragged along the bottom of the sea. **trawler** *n* [C] ship that is used for trawling.

tray /treɪ/ *n* [C] flat piece of wood, plastic, etc, used for carrying things, esp food.

treacherous /'tretʃərəs/ *adj* 1 disloyal or deceitful. 2 dangerous: *~ tides.* **treacherously** *adv*. **treachery** /-tʃərɪ/ *n* [U, C] (*pl* -ies).

treacle /'triːkl/ *n* [U] thick sticky liquid made from sugar. **treacly** *adv*.

tread /tred/ *v* (*pt* **trod** /trɒd/, *pp* **trodden** /'trɒdn/) 1 [I] set one's foot down; step. 2 [T] press or crush with one's feet. 3 [T] make (a path) by walking. 4 (idm) **,tread on sb's 'toes** (*infml*) offend sb. **,tread 'water** keep oneself upright in water by moving one's legs up and down. **tread** *n* 1 [sing] manner or sound of walking. 2 [C, U] pattern of raised lines on a tyre. 3 [C] upper surface of a step or stair.

treason /'triːzn/ *n* [U] betraying one's country, eg by helping its enemies. **treasonable** /-zənəbl/ *adj* of or being treason.

treasure /'treʒə(r)/ *n* 1 [U] (store of) gold and silver, jewels, etc. 2 [C] very valuable object or person. **treasure** *v* [T] value highly. **treasurer** *n* [C] person in charge of the money, bills, etc of an organization. **'treasure trove** /trəʊv/ *n* [U] treasure found hidden and claimed by no one.

treasury /'treʒərɪ/ *n* **the Treasury** [sing] (with sing or pl *v*) government department that controls public money.

treat /triːt/ *v* [T] 1 act or behave towards: *They ~ their children badly.* 2 consider; deal with: *~ it as a joke.* 3 give medical care to: *~ a patient.* 4 put a special substance

on: ~ *crops with insecticide*. 5 give
(sb/oneself) food, entertainment,
etc at one's own expense. treat
n [C] 1 sth special that gives great
pleasure. 2 act of treating(5) sb.
treatise /'triːtɪz, -tɪs/ *n* [C] long
formal written work on one subject.
treatment /'triːtmənt/ *n* [C, U]
(way of) treating a person or
thing: *medical ~*.
treaty /'triːtɪ/ *n* [C] (*pl* -ies) formal agreement between coun-
tries: *a peace ~*.
treble[1] /'trebl/ *adj*, *n* [C] three
times as much or as many (as): *He
earns ~ my salary*. **treble** *v* [I, T]
become or make treble.
treble[2] /'trebl/ *n* [C] (music for or
by) boy with the highest singing
voice. **treble** *adj* high-pitched: *a
~ recorder*.
tree /triː/ *n* [C] tall plant with a
wooden trunk and branches. **tree-
less** *adj* without trees.
trek /trek/ *v* (-kk-) [I] *n* [C] (make
a) long hard journey, esp on foot.
trellis /'trelɪs/ *n* [C] light wooden
framework used for supporting
climbing plants.
tremble /'trembl/ *v* [I] 1 shake
uncontrollably (from fear or cold).
2 shake slightly: *The leaves ~ d in
the breeze*. 3 be very anxious: *She
~ d at having to make a decision*.
tremble *n* [C] shaking: *a ~ in her
voice*.
tremendous /trɪ'mendəs/ *adj* 1
very great; enormous: *a ~ explosion*. 2 (*infml*) very good.
tremendously *adv*.
tremor /'tremə(r)/ *n* [C] shaking
or trembling: *earth ~s*.
trench /trentʃ/ *n* [C] long narrow
channel dug in the ground, eg for
drainage or to protect soldiers.
trend /trend/ *n* [C] general
change or development: *the ~
towards smaller families*. '**trend-
setter** *n* [C] person that starts a
new fashion or trend. **trendy** *adj*
(-ier, -iest) (*infml*) very fashionable.
trespass /'trespəs/ *v* [I] (*on*) go
on sb's private land without his/
her permission. **trespass** *n* [U, C]
trespassing. **trespasser** *n* [C].
trestle /'tresl/ *n* [C] wooden
structure with legs, used for supporting a flat surface. ,**trestle-
table** *n* [C] table supported on
trestles.
trial /'traɪəl/ *n* 1 [C, U] examination in a law-court before a judge
(and jury) to decide if sb is guilty
or innocent. 2 [C, U] (act of) testing
how good sth is. 3 [C] cause of
worry or difficulty. 4 (*idm*) **on**

'**trial** (a) being tried in a law-
court. (b) being tested and examined. ,**trial and 'error** trying various methods and learning from
one's failures. ,**trial 'run** *n* [C]
first test of sth to see how good it
is.
triangle /'traɪæŋgl/ *n* [C] figure
with three straight sides and three
angles. **triangular** /traɪ'æŋ-
gjʊlə(r)/ *adj*.
tribe /traɪb/ *n* [C] group of people
of the same race, customs, language, etc living together under
the rule of a chief. **tribal** *adj*.
'**tribesman** *n* [C] male member of
a tribe.
tribunal /traɪ'bjuːnl/ *n* [C] group
of officials with the authority to
settle certain kinds of problems.
tributary /'trɪbjʊtrɪ; *US* -terɪ/
n [C] (*pl* -ies) river or stream that
flows into a larger river.
tribute /'trɪbjuːt/ *n* [C, U] something done, said or given to show
respect or admiration: *pay ~ to
her courage*.
trick /trɪk/ *n* [C] 1 clever or skilful action intended to entertain
people: *conjuring ~s*. 2 action
done in order to deceive sb or
make him/her appear foolish: *play
a ~ on sb*. 3 clever way of doing
sth. 4 (cards played in) one round
of a game. 5 (*idm*) **do the 'trick**
(*infml*) succeed in doing what is
needed or wanted. **trick** *v* [T] deceive: *He was ~ ed into giving
away all his money*. **trickery** [U]
deception; cheating. **tricky** *adj*
(-ier, -iest) 1 difficult to deal with:
a ~ y position. 2 (of a person) deceitful.
trickle /'trɪkl/ *v* [I] flow in a thin
stream: *Tears ~ d down her cheek*.
trickle *n* [C] slow or thin flow: *a ~
of blood*.
tricycle /'traɪsɪkl/ *n* [C] three-
wheeled cycle.
tried *pt, pp* of TRY[1].
trifle /'traɪfl/ *n* 1 [C] thing of little
value or importance. 2 [C, U] sweet
dish made of cream, cake, jelly,
etc. 3 (*idm*) **a trifle** (*fml*) slightly:
They felt a ~ sad. **trifle** *v* [I] (*with*)||
treat sb/sth lightly or disrespect-
fully. **trifling** *adj* unimportant.
trigger /'trɪgə(r)/ *n* [C] lever that
is pulled to fire a gun. **trigger** *v* [T]
(*off*)|| be the cause of (a sudden ev-
ent or reaction).
trill /trɪl/ *n* [C] 1 vibrating sound
of the voice or of a bird singing. 2
(*music*) quick repeated playing of
two different notes. **trill** *v* [I, T]
sound or sing with a trill.
trilogy /'trɪlədʒɪ/ *n* [C] (*pl* -ies)
group of three related books,

plays, etc.

trim /trɪm/ *adj* (~ **mer**, ~ **mest**) (*approv*) 1 neat and tidy. 2 slim.

trim *v* (-**mm**-) /T/ 1 make neat by cutting. 2 decorate esp the edge of.

trim *n* 1 *C*, usu *sing*) act of cutting. 2 (idm) **in (good) trim** in good condition. **trimming** *n* (c, usu *pl*) (a) decoration or addition. (b) usual accompaniment: *roast beef with all the trimmings*, ie vegetables, sauce, etc.

Trinity /'trɪnətɪ/ *n* the Trinity [sing] (in Christianity) union of Father, Son and Holy Spirit as one God.

trinket /'trɪŋkɪt/ *n* [C] small ornament, etc of little value.

trio /'triːəʊ/ *n* [C] (*pl* ~ **s**) 1 group of three. 2 (music for) a group of three players or singers.

trip /trɪp/ *v* (-**pp**-) 1 [I] (*over/up*)) catch one's foot on sth and fall over. 2 [T] (a) (*up*)// cause (sb) to do this. (b) cause (sb) to make a mistake. 3 [I] move with quick light steps. **trip** *n* [C] 1 (usu short) journey, esp for pleasure. 2 (*sl*) experience caused by taking a drug causing hallucinations. 3 fall. **tripper** *n* [C] person making a trip(1).

tripartite /ˌtraɪ'pɑːtaɪt/ *adj* (*fml*) having three parts or groups.

tripe /traɪp/ *n* [U] 1 stomach of a cow or ox used as food. 2 (*sl*) nonsense.

triple /'trɪpl/ *adj* having three parts; involving three groups. **triple** *v* [I, T] become or make three times as much or as many.

triplet /'trɪplɪt/ *n* [C] one of three children born to the same mother at one time.

triplicate /'trɪplɪkeɪt/ *n* (idm) **in 'triplicate** having three identical copies, one of which is the original.

tripod /'traɪpɒd/ *n* [C] stand with three legs, eg for a camera.

trite /traɪt/ *adj* uninteresting and not original.

triumph /'traɪʌmf/ *n* (a) [C] great achievement or success. (b) [U] feeling of joy and satisfaction resulting from this. **triumph** *v* [I] (*over*)// win a victory over sb/sth. **triumphal** /traɪ'ʌmfl/ *adj* of or for a triumph. **triumphant** /traɪ'ʌmfnt/ *adj* joyful because one has triumphed. **triumphantly** *adv*.

trivia /'trɪvɪə/ *n* [pl] trivial things.

trivial /'trɪvɪəl/ *adj* having little importance. **triviality** /ˌtrɪvɪ-'ælətɪ/ *n* [C, U] (*pl* -**ies**). **trivialize** *v* [T] make (sth) seem trivial.

trod *pt* of TREAD.

trodden *pp* of TREAD.

trolley /'trɒlɪ/ *n* [C] 1 small cart on wheels that is pushed by hand. 2 small table on wheels for serving food.

trombone /trɒm'bəʊn/ *n* [C] brass musical instrument with a sliding tube. **trombonist** *n* [C].

troop /truːp/ *n* 1 **troops** [pl] soldiers. 2 [C] group of people or animals. **troop** *v* [I] move in a group. **trooper** *n* [C] soldier in an armoured or cavalry unit.

trophy /'trəʊfɪ/ *n* [C] (*pl* -**ies**) 1 prize given for winning a competition. 2 something kept as a reminder of a victory or success.

tropic /'trɒpɪk/ *n* 1 (a) [C, usu *sing*] line around the world, either north or south of the equator. (b) **the tropics** [pl] parts of the world between these two lines, with a hot climate. 2 (idm) **tropic of Cancer** /'kænsə(r)/ line around the world at 23°27' north. **tropic of Capricorn** /'kæprɪkɔːn/ line around the world at 23°27' south. **tropical** *adj* of the tropics.

trot /trɒt/ *v* (-**tt**-) 1 [I] (esp of a horse) move fairly quickly, at a speed faster than a walk but slower than a gallop. 2 [I] run with short steps. 3 (*phr v*) **trot sth out** (*infml derog*) repeat or produce sth in a boring way: ~ *out the same old excuses*. **trot** *n* 1 [sing] trotting speed. 2 (idm) **on the 'trot** (*infml*) one after the other.

trouble /'trʌbl/ *n* 1 [C, U] (situation causing) worry, pain or difficulty: *You shouldn't have any* ~ *finding the house*. 2 [U] inconvenience; bother: *I don't want to be any* ~ *to you*. 3 [C, U] unrest; fighting, etc: *the* ~ *s in Northern Ireland*. 4 [U] illness: *have back* ~. 5 [U] faulty operation of a machine: *engine* ~. 6 (idm) **get into 'trouble (a)** have serious difficulties. (b) do sth deserving punishment. **get sb into 'trouble** (*infml*) make (an unmarried woman) pregnant. **take the 'trouble to do sth** do sth that requires effort. **trouble** *v* 1 [T] cause worry to. 2 [T] (*fml*) (used in requests) cause inconvenience to: *I'm sorry to* ~ *you, but could you tell me the way to the station?* 3 [I] (*fml*) make an effort; bother. **troubled** *adj* worried. **'trouble-maker** *n* [C] person who causes trouble. **troublesome** *adj* annoying.

trough /trɒf/ *US* trɔːf/ *n* [C] 1 long narrow container for animals to feed or drink from. 2 low area between two waves. 3 area of low air pressure.

troupe /truːp/ n [C, also sing with pl v] group of actors, dancers, etc.

trousers /'trauzəz/ n [pl] two-legged outer garment reaching from the waist to the ankles: *a pair of ~.*

trout /traut/ n [C] (*pl* trout) kind of freshwater fish.

trowel /'trauəl/ n [C] 1 small garden tool with a curved blade. 2 small tool with a flat blade, used for spreading cement, etc.

truant /'truːənt/ n [C] child who stays away from school without permission: *play* (ie be a) *~.* **truancy** /-ənsɪ/ n [U].

truce /truːs/ n [C] agreement for the stopping of fighting for a time.

truck¹ /trʌk/ n [C] 1 (*Brit*) open railway wagon for carrying goods. 2 (*esp US*) lorry.

truck² /trʌk/ n (idm) **have no truck with sb** (*fml*) refuse to deal with sb.

trudge /trʌdʒ/ v [I] walk slowly or with difficulty. **trudge** n [C, usu sing] long tiring walk.

true /truː/ adj (~r, ~st) 1 in agreement with facts or reality. 2 real: *my ~ feelings for you.* 3 faithful; loyal: *a ~ friend.* 4 exact: *a ~ copy.* 5 (idm) **come 'true** (of a hope, dream) really happen. **true to sth** being or acting as one would expect from sth: *~ to life, is realistic.* **true** n (idm) **out of 'true** not in its exact position: *The door is out of ~.*

truly /'truːlɪ/ adv 1 really: *a ~ brave action.* 2 sincerely: *feel ~ grateful.* 3 truthfully.

trump /trʌmp/ n 1 [C] card of a suit that is chosen to have a higher value in a game. 2 (idm) **turn/ ,come up 'trumps** (*infml*) be unexpectedly helpful or generous. **trump** v [T] beat (a card) by playing a trump. 2 (phr v) **trump sth up** (usu passive) invent a (false accusation): *~ed-up charges.* **'trump-card** n [C] (*fig*) most powerful way of gaining an advantage over others.

trumpet /'trʌmpɪt/ n [C] brass musical instrument with a long curved tube, widening into a bell-like end. **trumpet** v 1 [I, T] declare (sth) loudly. 2 [I] (of an elephant) make a loud noise. **trumpeter** n [C] trumpet player.

truncate /trʌŋ'keɪt; US 'trʌŋkeɪt/ v [T] shorten (sth) by cutting off the top or end.

truncheon /'trʌntʃən/ n [C] short thick stick carried as a weapon by a police officer.

trundle /'trʌndl/ v [I, T] roll or move heavily.

trunk /trʌŋk/ n 1 [C] main stem of a tree. 2 [C] large box for storing or transporting clothes, etc. 3 [C] long nose of an elephant. 4 [C, usu sing] body apart from the head, arms and legs. 5 **trunks** [pl] shorts worn by men or boys for swimming. 6 [C] (*US*) boot of a car. **'trunk-call** n [C] (*Brit dated*) long-distance telephone call. **'trunk-road** n [C] important main road.

truss /trʌs/ v [T] 1 tie or bind firmly. 2 tie the legs and wings of (a chicken, etc) before cooking. **truss** n [C] 1 padded belt worn by sb suffering from a hernia. 2 framework supporting a roof, bridge, etc.

trust /trʌst/ n 1 [U] strong belief in the honesty, goodness, strength of sb/sth. 2 [U] responsibility. 3 [C] (arrangement for the) holding and managing of money for others: *money kept in a ~.* 4 (idm) **take sth on trust** believe sth without proof. **trusting** adj ready to trust others. **trustingly** adv. **trustworthy** adj dependable. **trusty** adj (-ier, -iest) (*arch* or *joc*) dependable; faithful.

trust² /trʌst/ v 1 have or put trust¹(1) in: *You can ~ me.* 2 depend on (sb) to do or use sth properly: *You can't ~ young children with matches.* 3 (*fml*) hope: *I ~ you are well.*

trustee /trʌ'stiː/ n [C] person who is responsible for managing a trust¹(3).

truth /truːθ/ n (pl ~s /truːðz/) 1 [U] quality or state of being true: *There's no ~ in what he says.* 2 [U] that which is true: *tell the ~.* 3 [C] fact that is accepted as true: *scientific ~s.* **truthful** adj 1 (of a person) telling the truth. 2 (of statements) true. **truthfully** adv. **truthfulness** n [U].

try¹ /traɪ/ v (*pt, pp* tried) 1 [I] make an attempt: *He tried to escape.* 2 [T] use, do or test (sth) to see if it is satisfactory, enjoyable, etc: *Have you tried this new soap?* 3 [T] examine and decide (a case) in law-court: *He was tried for murder.* 4 [T] be very tiring or difficult to bear for (sb/sth): *You're ~ing my patience!* 5 (idm) **try one's hand at sth** attempt to do sth. 6 (phr v) **try sth on** (a) put on (a garment) to see if it fits and how it looks. (b) (*infml*) behave in a deceitful or improper way to see if it will be tolerated: *Stop ~ing it on!* **try sth out** test sth to see if it is satisfactory or useful. **tried** adj that has proved to be good. **trying**

adj difficult to deal with; annoying.

try² /traɪ/ *n* [C] (*pl* **-ies**) 1 attempt. 2 (in Rugby football) points scored by a player touching the ball down behind the line of the opponents' goal.

tsar /zɑː(r)/ *n* [C] (before 1917) emperor of Russia. **tsarina** /zɑːˈriːnə/ *n* [C] (before 1917) empress of Russia or wife of the tsar.

tsetse fly /ˈtsetsɪ flaɪ/ *n* [C] tropical African fly that can cause serious disease by its bite.

T-shirt ⇨ T, t.

tub /tʌb/ *n* [C] 1 open round container. 2 bath.

tuba /ˈtjuːbə; US ˈtuːbə/ *n* [C] large deep-sounding brass musical instrument.

tubby /ˈtʌbɪ/ *adj* (**-ier, -iest**) (*infml*) short and fat.

tube /tjuːb; US tuːb/ *n* 1 [C] long hollow pipe of rubber, plastic, etc, esp for carrying liquids. 2 [C] soft metal or plastic container for pastes, paints, etc. 3 **the tube** [U, sing] (*Brit*) (in London) underground railway. 4 [C] hollow tube-shaped organ in the body. **tubing** *n* [U] tubes. **tubular** /ˈtjuːbjʊlə(r); US ˈtuː-/ *adj* in the form of a tube.

tuber /ˈtjuːbə(r); US ˈtuː-/ *n* [C] short thick rounded part of an underground stem on eg a potato.

tuberculosis /tjuːˌbɜːkjʊˈləʊsɪs; US tuː-/ *n* [U] serious infectious disease that affects esp the lungs.

TUC /ˌtiː juː ˈsiː/ *n* **the TUC** [sing] Trades Union Congress; association of representatives of British trade unions.

tuck /tʌk/ *v* 1 [T] push the loose ends of (sth) into sth else so that it is tidy: *He ~ed his shirt into his trousers.* 2 [T] put (sth) in a tidy, comfortable or hidden position. 3 (*phr v*) **tuck in** (*infml*) eat food eagerly. **tuck sb up** make (esp a child) comfortable in bed by pulling the sheets and blankets tight. **tuck** *n* 1 [C] narrow flat fold sewn into a garment. 2 [U] (*Brit infml*) food, esp sweets, as eaten by children: *a school ~-shop.*

Tuesday /ˈtjuːzdɪ; US ˈtuː-/ *n* [U, C] the third day of the week, next after Monday. (see examples of use at *Monday*).

tuft /tʌft/ *n* [C] bunch of hair, grass, etc.

tug /tʌg/ *v* (**-gg-**) [I, T] (*at*)) pull (sth) hard. **tug** *n* [C] 1 sudden hard pull. 2 (also **tugboat**) small powerful boat that pulls ships into harbours.

tuition /tjuːˈɪʃn; US tuː-/ *n* [U] (*fml*) (fee for) teaching: *have*

private ~.

tulip /ˈtjuːlɪp; US ˈtuː-/ *n* [C] garden plant with a large brightly-coloured cup-shaped flower on a tall stem.

tumble /ˈtʌmbl/ *v* 1 [I, T] (cause sb to) fall, esp helplessly. 2 [I] move in a disorderly way. 3 (*phr v*) **tumble down** fall to pieces; collapse. **tumble to sth** (*infml*) understand sth. **tumble** *n* [C, usu sing] fall. **tumbledown** *adj* falling to pieces. **tumble-drier** *n* [C] machine for drying washed clothes.

tumbler /ˈtʌmblə(r)/ *n* [C] straight-sided drinking glass.

tummy /ˈtʌmɪ/ *n* [C] (*pl* **-ies**) (*infml*) stomach.

tumour (*US* **-or**) /ˈtjuːmə(r); US ˈtuː-/ *n* [C] mass of diseased cells growing in the body.

tumult /ˈtjuːmʌlt; US ˈtuː-/ *n* [U, sing] (*fml*) 1 noisy disturbance caused by a large mass of people. 2 confused state. **tumultuous** /tjuːˈmʌltʃʊəs; US tuː-/ *adj* (*fml*) noisy; confused.

tuna /ˈtjuːnə/ *n* [C, U] (*pl* tuna or ~ s) large sea-fish eaten as food.

tune /tjuːn; US tuːn/ *n* 1 [C] (esp pleasant) series of musical notes. 2 (*idm*) **in/out of 'tune** (a) at/not at the correct musical pitch. (b) (*fig*) in/not in agreement or sympathy. **to the 'tune of sth** (*infml*) to the amount of: *fined to the ~ of £1000.* **tune** *v* [T] 1 adjust (a musical instrument) to the correct pitch. 2 adjust (an engine) so that it works well. 3 (*phr v*) **tune in (to sth)** adjust the controls of a radio so that it receives (a certain station). **tuneful** *adj* having a pleasant tune. **tunefully** *adv.* **tuner** *n* [C] person who tunes musical instruments, esp pianos. **'tuning-fork** *n* [C] small steel fork that produces a certain musical note when struck.

tunic /ˈtjuːnɪk; US ˈtuː-/ *n* [C] 1 close-fitting jacket as worn by police officers, soldiers, etc. 2 loose garment, usu worn with a belt round the waist, that reaches to the hips or knees.

tunnel /ˈtʌnl/ *n* [C] underground passage, eg for a road or railway. **tunnel** *v* (**-ll-**; *US* **-l-**) [I, T] make a tunnel (through, under, etc).

turban /ˈtɜːbən/ *n* [C] head covering worn by a Muslim or Sikh man, consisting of a long cloth wound round the head.

turbine /ˈtɜːbaɪn/ *n* [C] engine driven by a wheel that is turned by a current of water, steam, air or gas.

turbulent /'tɜːbjʊlənt/ adj confused; violent or uneven: ~ passions/waves. **turbulence** /-ləns/ n [U].

tureen /təˈriːn, tjʊˈriːn/ n [C] large deep dish from which soup or vegetables are served.

turf /tɜːf/ n (pl ~s or turves) 1 (a) [U] short grass and the soil just below the surface. (b) [C] piece of this. 2 the turf [sing] horse-racing. **turf** v [T] 1 cover with turf. 2 (phr v) **turf sb/sth out** (Brit infml) force sb to leave.

turkey /'tɜːkɪ/ n (a) [C] large bird, used for food. (b) [U] its meat.

turmoil /'tɜːmɔɪl/ n [C, usu sing, U] state of confusion or disorder.

turn¹ /tɜːn/ v 1 [I, T] (cause to) move round a central point: The earth ~ s round the sun. ○ ~ a key in a lock. 2 [I, T] (cause to) move so that a different side faces outwards or upwards: She ~ ed to look at me. 3 [I, T] (cause to) go in the direction that is mentioned: T~ left by the church. 4 [I, T] go round: The car ~ ed the corner. 5 (usu used with an adj) (cause to) become: The milk has ~ ed sour. ○ She's just ~ ed 50. 6 [I, T] (from) to/into) (cause to) pass from one state to another: Caterpillars ~ into butterflies. 7 [T] direct: ~ one's attention to the question of money. 8 (idm) **not turn a 'hair** not show fear, worry, etc in difficulty or danger. **turn one's back on sb/ sth** refuse to help sb; ignore sb/ sth. **turn a blind 'eye to sth** pretend not to notice sth. **turn the clock back** ⇒ CLOCK. **turn a deaf 'ear to sth** refuse to listen to sth. **turned 'out** dressed in a particular way: be elegantly ~ ed out. **turn one's hand to sth** begin to learn (a practical skill). **turn over a new 'leaf** start to improve one's behaviour. **turn the 'tables on sb** gain an advantage over sb who had an advantage over one. **turn 'tail** turn and run away. **turn up one's 'nose at sth/sb** (infml) consider sb/sth not good enough for one. **turn up trumps** ⇒ TRUMP. 9 (phr v) **turn (sb) against sb** (cause sb to) become unfriendly or opposed to sb. **turn sb away** refuse to allow sb to enter; refuse to help. **turn (sb) back** (cause sb to) return to his/her starting-place. **turn sb/sth down** refuse (sb, his/ her offer, etc). **turn sth down** adjust (a cooker, radio, etc) to reduce the heat, sound, etc. **turn 'in** (infml) go to bed. **turn sb 'in** (infml) take sb to the police to be arrested. **turn sb 'off** (infml)

cause sb to be bored or not (sexually) excited. **turn sth off** stop the flow or operation of sth: ~ off the tap. **turn sb on** attack sb suddenly. **turn sb 'on** (infml) cause sb to be interested or (sexually) excited. **turn sth on** start the flow or operation of sth: ~ on the radio. **turn 'out** (a) happen in the way that is mentioned; prove to be: Everything ~ ed out well. (b) be present at an event. **turn sth out** (a) switch (a light or fire) off. (b) empty sth: ~ out the cupboards. (c) produce sth. **turn sb out (of sth)** force sb to leave a place. **turn sth over** (a) think carefully about sth. (b) do business worth (the amount that is mentioned). **turn sth/sb over to sb** give control of sth/sb to sb: The thief was ~ ed over to the police. **turn to sb** go to sb for help, advice, etc. **turn up** arrive. **turn (sth) up** (cause sth to) be found: The book you've lost will probably ~ up somewhere. **turn sth up** adjust (a cooker, radio, etc)to increase the heat, sound, etc. 'turn-off n [C] road that leads away from a main road. 'turn-out n [C, usu sing] number of people who attend an event. 'turnover n [sing] amount of business done by a company: Their annual ~ over is £10 million. 'turn-up n [C] 1 [usu pl] folded-up end of a trouser leg. 2 (infml) surprising and unexpected event: a ~ -up for the book.

turn² /tɜːn/ n [C] 1 act of turning. 2 change of direction. 3 change in condition: Business has taken a ~ for the worse. 4 right or chance to do sth: It's your ~ to chose. 5 point in time when a new year or century starts. 6 short performance in a theatre. 7 attack of illness. 8 shock: You gave me a ~ coming in so suddenly! 9 (idm) **at every 'turn** everywhere; all the time. **done to a 'turn** (of food) cooked just long enough. **in 'turn** one after the other. **out of 'turn** at the wrong time. **take (it in) 'turns to do sth** do sth one after the other: The children took it in ~ s to play on the swing.

turning /'tɜːnɪŋ/ n [C] road that leads off another. 'turning-point n [C] time at which an important change happens.

turnip /'tɜːnɪp/ n [C, U] (plant with a) large round root used as a vegetable.

turnpike /'tɜːnpaɪk/ n [C] (US) very fast road which drivers have to pay to drive on.

turnstile /'tɜːnstaɪl/ n [C] small

entrance gate that turns round and allows one person through at a time.

turntable /'tɜːnteɪbl/ n [C] flat circular surface that turns round, on which a record is placed in a record-player.

turpentine /'tɜːpəntaɪn/ n [U] strong-smelling colourless liquid used for cleaning off or thinning paint.

turquoise /'tɜːkwɔɪz/ adj greenish-blue in colour. **turquoise** n [C, U] type of greenish-blue precious stone.

turret /'tʌrɪt/ n [C] 1 small tower on a building. 2 (on a tank, warship, etc) turning structure where the guns are fixed.

turtle /'tɜːtl/ n [C] large sea-animal with a hard shell.

tusk /tʌsk/ n [C] either of a pair of very long pointed teeth of an elephant, walrus or wild boar.

tussle /'tʌsl/ v [I] n [C] (have a) rough fight or argument.

tut /tʌt/ (also ,tut-'tut) interj (used for showing disapproval, annoyance, etc).

tutor /'tjuːtə(r); US 'tuː-/ n [C] 1 private teacher, esp of one pupil. 2 (Brit) university teacher who guides the studies of a student. **tutor** v [I, T] teach. **tutorial** /tjuː'tɔːrɪəl; US tuː-/ n [C] teaching period for a small group of students. **tutorial** adj of a tutor(2).

tuxedo /tʌk'siːdəʊ/ n [C] (pl ~s) (US) dinner-jacket.

TV /ˌtiː 'viː/ n [C, U] television.

twaddle /'twɒdl/ n [U] (infml) nonsense.

twang /twæŋ/ n [C] 1 sound of a tight wire being pulled and suddenly released. 2 sound of the human voice as if produced through the nose. **twang** v [I, T] (cause to) make a twang(1).

tweak /twiːk/ v [T] pinch and twist: ~ a child's nose. **tweak** n [sing].

tweed /twiːd/ n 1 [U] thick woven woollen cloth. 2 **tweeds** [pl] clothes, esp a suit, made of tweed.

tweet /twiːt/ v [I] n [C] (infml) (of a bird) (make a) short high cry.

tweezers /'twiːzəz/ n [pl] small two-piece jointed metal tool for pulling out or picking up very small things.

twelve /twelv/ pron, adj, n [C] 12. **twelfth** /twelfθ/ pron, adj 12th. **twelfth** n [C] ½.

twenty /'twentɪ/ pron, adj, n [C] (pl -ies) 20. **twentieth** /'twentɪəθ/ pron, adj 20th. **twentieth** pron, n [C] 1/20.

twice /twaɪs/ adv two times: I've read this book ~. ○ Your room is twice as big as mine.

twiddle /'twɪdl/ v [I, T] twist or turn (sth) with one's fingers, esp aimlessly.

twig[1] /twɪg/ n [C] small thin piece of a branch of a bush or tree.

twig[2] /twɪg/ v (-gg-) [I, T] (Brit infml) realize or understand (sth).

twilight /'twaɪlaɪt/ n [U] (time of) faint light after sunset.

twill /twɪl/ n [U] kind of strong woven cloth.

twin /twɪn/ n [C] either of two children born to the same mother at one time. **twin** adj similar, matching: ~ beds, ie two single beds.

twine /twaɪn/ n [U] strong string. **twine** v [I, T] twist or wind.

twinge /twɪndʒ/ n [C] sudden sharp pain: (fig) a ~ of guilt.

twinkle /'twɪŋkl/ v [I] 1 shine with an unsteady light: stars twinkling in the sky. 2 (of sb's eyes) look bright with happiness or amusement. **twinkle** n [sing]: a ~ in her eyes.

twirl /twɜːl/ v [I, T] turn round and round; spin. 2 [T] curl. **twirl** n [C] quick circular movement.

twist /twɪst/ v 1 [T] wind: ~ string round one's fingers. 2 [I, T] turn (sth) round: She ~ed (her head) round. 3 [I, T] (cause to) change into a strange shape by bending or turning: The car was a pile of ~ed metal. 4 [T] hurt (eg one's ankle) by turning it too sharply. 5 [T] turn: ~ the lid off the jar. 6 [I] (of a road or river) have many bends. 7 [T] change the meaning of: ~ sb's words. 8 (idm) ,twist sb's 'arm (infml) persuade or force sb to do sth. twist sb round one's little 'finger (infml) get sb to do anything one wants. **twist** n [C] 1 act of twisting. 2 twisted shape. 3 unexpected change or development: by a strange ~ of fate.

twit /twɪt/ n [C] (Brit infml) foolish person.

twitch /twɪtʃ/ n [C] small sudden uncontrollable repeated jerky movement of the muscles. **twitch** v [I] move with a twitch. 2 [I, T] pull (sth) quickly and suddenly.

twitter /'twɪtə(r)/ v [I] 1 (of a bird) make short high sounds. 2 talk quickly in an excited or nervous way. **twitter** n [sing].

two /tuː/ pron, adj, n [C] (pl ~s) 1 2. 2 (idm) put ,two and two to'gether guess the truth from what one sees and hears. ,two-'faced adj deceitful or insincere. 'twofold adj, adv (a) having two parts. (b) twice as many or as much. ,two-'way *adj* allowing movement or communication in two directions.

tycoon /taɪˈkuːn/ *n* [C] (*infml*) rich and powerful businessman or businesswoman.

tying ⇨ TIE¹.

type /taɪp/ *n* 1 [C] (one of a) group of things or people with certain features in common; kind or sort: *many different ~s of computers.* 2 [U] size, kind or style of printing: *italic ~.* type *v* [I, T] write (sth) with a typewriter or a word processor. type-cast /ˈtaɪpkɑːst/ *v* (*pt, pp* type-cast) [T] (esp passive) constantly give (an actor or actress) the same kind of part. 'typescript *n* [C] typed copy of sth. 'typewriter *n* [C] machine that prints letters on paper by means of keys that are pressed with the fingers. typing *n* [U] (skill at) using a typewriter or word processor. typist *n* [C] person whose job is to type letters, etc in an office.

typhoid /ˈtaɪfɔɪd/ *n* [U] serious infectious feverish disease, caused by bacteria in food or drink.

typhoon /taɪˈfuːn/ *n* [C] very violent tropical storm.

typhus /ˈtaɪfəs/ *n* [U] infectious disease causing fever and purple spots on the body.

typical /ˈtɪpɪkl/ *adj* having the usual qualities of a particular thing or person: *a ~ British home.* typically /-kli/ *adv*.

typify /ˈtɪpɪfaɪ/ *v* (*pt, pp* -ied) [T] be a typical feature or example of.

typist ⇨ TYPE.

tyrannical /tɪˈrænɪkl/ *adj* of or like a tyrant.

tyrannize /ˈtɪrənaɪz/ *v* [I, T] (*over*)// rule over (sb) cruelly and unjustly.

tyranny /ˈtɪrəni/ *n* [U] cruel and unjust use of power or authority.

tyrant /ˈtaɪərənt/ *n* [C] cruel unjust ruler.

tyre /ˈtaɪə(r)/ *n* [C] air-filled thick band of rubber round the wheel of a bicycle, car, etc.

U u

U, u /juː/ *n* [C] (*pl* U's, u's /juːz/) the twenty-first letter of the English alphabet. U-turn *n* [C] 1 turning movement of 180° (by a car) so as to point in the opposite direction. 2 (*infml*) complete change of

opinion.

ubiquitous /juːˈbɪkwɪtəs/ *adj* (*fml*) (seeming to be) present everywhere.

udder /ˈʌdə(r)/ *n* [C] part of a cow, goat, etc that produces milk.

UFO /juː ef ˈəʊ *or* ˈjuːfəʊ/ *n* [C] (*pl* ~s) unidentified flying object, esp a spacecraft believed to have come from another planet.

ugh /ʊh/ *interj* (used to suggest a sound like ɜː/ *interj* (used for expressing disgust): *Ugh! What a horrible smell!*

ugly /ˈʌɡli/ *adj* (-ier, -iest) 1 unpleasant to look at. 2 threatening, likely to be violent: *an ~ situation.* ugliness *n* [U].

UK /juː ˈkeɪ/ *abbr* the UK the United Kingdom.

ulcer /ˈʌlsə(r)/ *n* [C] open sore area on the skin or inside the body. ulcerate *v* [I, T] (cause to) become affected with ulcers. ulcerous *adj*.

ulterior /ʌlˈtɪəriə(r)/ *adj* hidden, not admitted: *an ~ motive.*

ultimate /ˈʌltɪmət/ *adj* last, final or furthest. ultimately *adv* in the end.

ultimatum /ˌʌltɪˈmeɪtəm/ *n* [C] (*pl* ~s *or* -ta /-tə/) final statement of conditions to be agreed to without discussion.

ultraviolet /ˌʌltrəˈvaɪələt/ *adj* (of the invisible rays of light) beyond the violet end of the range of colours.

umbilical cord /ʌmˈbɪlɪkl/ *n* [C] tube that joins an unborn baby to its mother.

umbrella /ʌmˈbrelə/ *n* [C] 1 folding frame covered with cloth, used as a protection from rain. 2 (*fig*) single central organization, etc.

umpire /ˈʌmpaɪə(r)/ *n* [C] (in tennis, cricket, etc) person who sees that rules are obeyed. umpire *v* [I, T] act as an umpire in (a game).

umpteen /ˌʌmptiːn/ *pron* (*infml*) a very large number (of): *read ~ books on the subject.* umpteenth /ˈʌmptiːnθ/ *pron: for the ~th time.*

UN /juː ˈen/ *abbr* the UN the United Nations.

unable /ʌnˈeɪbl/ *adj* not able.

unaccountable /ˌʌnəˈkaʊntəbl/ *adj* (*fml*) that cannot be explained. unaccountably *adv*.

unaccustomed /ˌʌnəˈkʌstəmd/ *adj* 1 *to*// not in the habit of doing sth: *~ to speaking in public.* 2 unusual.

unanimous /juːˈnænɪməs/ *adj* in or showing complete agreement: *a ~ decision.* unanimity /ˌjuːnəˈnɪməti/ *n* [U].

unanswerable /ˌʌnˈɑːnsərəbl/

US /ˌʌnˈæn-/ adj that cannot be answered or argued against.

unarmed /ˌʌnˈɑːmd/ adj without weapons.

unassuming /ˌʌnəˈsjuːmɪŋ; US -ˈsuː-/ adj not attracting attention to oneself; modest.

unattached /ˌʌnəˈtætʃt/ adj 1 not connected. 2 not married or having a regular boy-friend or girl-friend.

unattended /ˌʌnəˈtendɪd/ adj not looked after; alone: Never leave a baby ~.

unavoidable /ˌʌnəˈvɔɪdəbl/ adj that cannot be avoided.

unaware /ˌʌnəˈweə(r)/ adj (of) not knowing sth; not aware. **unawares** /-ˈweəz/ adv by surprise: catch/take sb ~ s, ie surprise sb.

unbalanced /ˌʌnˈbælənst/ adj slightly mad.

unbearable /ˌʌnˈbeərəbl/ adj that cannot be tolerated or endured. **unbearably** adv.

unbeatable /ˌʌnˈbiːtəbl/ adj that cannot be beaten: ~ value for money.

unbelievable /ˌʌnbɪˈliːvəbl/ adj that cannot be believed; astonishing. **unbelievably** adv.

unborn /ˌʌnˈbɔːn/ adj not yet born.

unbroken /ˌʌnˈbrəʊkən/ adj not interrupted or broken: ten hours of ~ sleep.

unbutton /ˌʌnˈbʌtn/ v [T] unfasten the buttons of.

uncalled-for /ʌnˈkɔːld fɔː(r)/ adj not needed or deserved, because unkind.

uncanny /ʌnˈkænɪ/ adj (-ier, -iest) not natural; strange or mysterious.

unceremonious /ˌʌnˌserɪ-ˈməʊnɪəs/ adj 1 informal. 2 rudely sudden. **unceremoniously** adv.

uncertain /ʌnˈsɜːtn/ adj 1 not sure; doubtful: Be ~ about what to do. 2 likely to change; not reliable: ~ weather. **uncertainly** adv. **uncertainty** n [C, U] (pl -ies).

uncharitable /ʌnˈtʃærɪtəbl/ adj unkind or unfair.

unchecked /ˌʌnˈtʃekt/ adj not stopped.

uncivilized /ʌnˈsɪvəlaɪzd/ adj (of behaviour, etc) rude.

uncle /ˈʌŋkl/ n [C] brother of one's father or mother; husband of one's aunt.

uncomfortable /ʌnˈkʌmftəbl/ US -fərt-/ adj 1 not comfortable. 2 embarrassed; not relaxed. **uncomfortably** adv.

uncommon /ʌnˈkɒmən/ adj unusual. **uncommonly** adv (fml)

unusually; very.

uncompromising /ʌnˈkɒmprəmaɪzɪŋ/ adj not ready to change one's opinions, decisions, etc.

unconcerned /ˌʌnkənˈsɜːnd/ adj not interested or worried.

unconditional /ˌʌnkənˈdɪʃənl/ adj not subject to conditions; complete: ~ surrender.

unconscious /ʌnˈkɒnʃəs/ adj not conscious; not aware: knocked ~ . ~ of danger. **unconsciously** adv.

uncountable /ʌnˈkaʊntəbl/ adj that cannot be counted: 'Butter' is an ~ noun.

uncouth /ʌnˈkuːθ/ adj (of a person or his/her behaviour) rough and rude.

uncover /ʌnˈkʌvə(r)/ v [T] 1 remove a cover from. 2 discover (sth secret).

undaunted /ʌnˈdɔːntɪd/ adj (fml) not discouraged or afraid.

undecided /ˌʌndɪˈsaɪdɪd/ adj not having decided sth; not certain.

undeniable /ˌʌndɪˈnaɪəbl/ adj certainly true. **undeniably** adv.

under /ˈʌndə(r)/ prep 1 below: Have you looked ~ the bed? 2 covered by: Most of the iceberg is ~ the water. 3 less than: ~ £50. 4 in a state of; being affected by: ~ construction ~ these circumstances. 5 ruled by: Britain ~ Thatcher. 6 according to: ~ the terms of the contract. 7 using (a particular name): She wrote ~ the name of George Eliot. **under** adv in or to a lower place, esp under water. **under-** prefix 1 below: ~current. 2 not enough: ~ripe.

underarm /ˈʌndərɑːm/ adj, adv (sport) with the hand kept below the shoulder.

undercarriage /ˈʌndəkærɪdʒ/ n [C] aircraft's wheels for landing and their supports.

undercharge /ˌʌndəˈtʃɑːdʒ/ v [I, T] charge (sb) too low a price.

underclothes /ˈʌndəkləʊðz/ n [pl] = UNDERWEAR.

undercover /ˌʌndəˈkʌvə(r)/ adj working or done secretly, esp as a spy.

undercurrent /ˈʌndəkʌrənt/ n [C] 1 current of water below the surface. 2 (fig) hidden thought or feeling: an ~ of bitterness.

undercut /ˌʌndəˈkʌt/ v (-tt-, pt, pp ~cut) [T] sell goods or services at a lower price than (a competitor).

underdeveloped /ˌʌndə-dɪˈveləpt/ adj (of a country) lacking modern industries and having a low standard of living.

underdog /'ʌndədɒg; US -dɔːg/ n [C] person, etc thought to be in a weaker position, and so unlikely to win a competition.

underdone /ˌʌndə'dʌn/ adj (esp of meat) not completely cooked.

underestimate /ˌʌndər'estɪmeɪt/ v [T] make too low an estimate of: ~ the enemy's strength.

underfed /ˌʌndə'fed/ adj having not enough food.

underfoot /ˌʌndə'fʊt/ adv under one's feet: The grass was wet ~.

undergo /ˌʌndə'gəʊ/ v (pt -went /-'went/, pp -gone /-'gɒn; US -'gɔːn/) [T] experience (esp sth unpleasant).

undergraduate /ˌʌndə-'grædʒʊət/ n [C] university or college student working for his/her first degree.

underground /'ʌndəgraʊnd/ adj 1 below the earth's surface. 2 (fig) secret, esp of an illegal political organization directed against the government. **the underground** n [sing] 1 city railway system where electric trains run under the ground in tunnels. 2 secret political organization. **underground** /ˌʌndə'graʊnd/ adv under the earth's surface.

undergrowth /'ʌndəgrəʊθ/ n [U] bushes and plants growing thickly under trees.

underhand /ˌʌndə'hænd/ adj done secretly and dishonestly.

underlie /ˌʌndə'laɪ/ v (pt -lay /-'leɪ/, pp -lain /-'leɪn/, pres p lying) [T] be the (hidden) cause or basis of.

underline /ˌʌndə'laɪn/ v [T] 1 draw a line under. 2 (fig) emphasize.

undermanned /ˌʌndə'mænd/ adj having fewer workers than are needed.

undermine /ˌʌndə'maɪn/ v [T] 1 weaken gradually: Repeated failure ~d his confidence. 2 make a hollow or tunnel under.

underneath /ˌʌndə'niːθ/ prep, adv under; below.

underpants /'ʌndəpænts/ n [pl] short underwear worn by men and boys for the lower part of the body.

underpass /'ʌndəpɑːs; US -pæs/ n [C] road or path that goes under a railway, another road, etc.

underprivileged /ˌʌndə-'prɪvɪlɪdʒd/ adj not having the standard of living, rights, etc enjoyed by others in society.

underrate /ˌʌndə'reɪt/ v [T] have too low an opinion of.

underside /'ʌndəsaɪd/ n [C] side or surface that is underneath.

undersigned /ˌʌndə'saɪnd/ n the **undersigned** [C] (pl the **undersigned**) (fml) whose signature(s) is/are below the writing: We, the ~ ....

understand /ˌʌndə'stænd/ v (pt, pp **-stood** /-'stʊd/) 1 [I, T] know the meaning of (sb, his/her words, etc): She can ~ French perfectly. ○ I don't ~ what the problem is. 2 [I, T] know well the character of (sb): No one ~s me. 3 [T] (fml) have been told: I ~ that you wish to leave. 4 (idm) **make oneself understood** make one's meaning clear. **understandable** adj that can be understood; natural. **understandably** adv. **understanding** n 1 [U] knowledge. 2 [U] sympathy. 3 [C] informal agreement. **understanding** adj sympathetic.

understate /ˌʌndə'steɪt/ v [T] fail to state fully or adequately: ~ the extent of the problem. **understatement** /ˌʌndə'steɪtmənt/ n [C, U].

understudy /'ʌndəstʌdɪ/ n [C] (pl **-ies**) person able to take the place of an actor if he/she is ill.

undertake /ˌʌndə'teɪk/ v (pt **-took** /-'tʊk/, pp **~n** /-'teɪkən/) [T] (fml) 1 (start to) make oneself responsible for. 2 to// promise to do sth. **undertaking** n [C] 1 work undertaken; task. 2 (fml) promise.

undertaker /'ʌndəteɪkə(r)/ n [C] person who arranges funerals.

undertone /'ʌndətəʊn/ n [C] 1 low, quiet voice: speak in ~s. 2 hidden meaning or feeling.

undervalue /ˌʌndə'væljuː/ v [T] put too low a value on.

underwater /ˌʌndə'wɔːtə(r)/ adj, adv situated, used or done below the surface of the water.

underwear /'ʌndəweə(r)/ n [U] clothing worn next to the skin under other clothes.

underworld /'ʌndəwɜːld/ n the **underworld** [sing] 1 (people involved in) organized crime. 2 (in mythology) home of the dead.

underwrite /ˌʌndə'raɪt/ v (pt **-wrote** /-'rəʊt/, pp **-written** /-'rɪtn/) [T] promise to pay money for, eg to cover possible losses.

undesirable /ˌʌndɪ'zaɪərəbl/ adj likely to be harmful; unwanted. **undesirable** n [C] undesirable person.

undeveloped /ˌʌndɪ'veləpt/ adj (of a place, land, etc) not yet used for agriculture, industry, building, etc.

undies /'ʌndɪz/ n [pl] (infml) women's underwear.

undo /ʌn'duː/ v (pt **-did** /-'dɪd/, pp **-done** /-'dʌn/) [T] 1 unfasten or untie (sth wrapped or tied). 2 destroy the effect of: *He undid all my good work.* **undoing** *n* [sing] (*fml*) cause of sb's failure.

undoubted /ʌn'daʊtɪd/ *adj* certain; accepted as true. **undoubtedly** *adv.*

undress /ʌn'dres/ *v* 1 [I] take off one's clothes. 2 [T] take the clothes off (sb). **undressed** *adj* wearing no clothes.

undue /ʌn'djuː; *US* -'duː/ *adj* (*fml*) too much: *with* ~ *haste.* **unduly** *adv.*

undulate /'ʌndjʊleɪt/ *v* [I] move up and down gently like a wave: *The road ~s through the hills.*

undying /ʌn'daɪɪŋ/ *adj* (*fml*) that will last for ever: ~ *love.*

unearth /ʌn'ɜːθ/ *v* [T] 1 find by digging. 2 discover: ~ *the truth.*

unearthly /ʌn'ɜːθlɪ/ *adj* 1 unnatural or mysterious. 2 (*infml*) unreasonable: *at this* ~ *hour.*

uneasy /ʌn'iːzɪ/ *adj* (*-ier, -iest*) worried or anxious. **uneasily** *adv.* **uneasiness** *n* [U].

uneconomic /ˌʌniːkə'nɒmɪk, ˌʌn,ek-/ *adj* not producing profit.

unemployed /ˌʌnɪm'plɔɪd/ *adj* not having a job. **the unemployed** *n* [pl] unemployed people. **unemployment** /-'plɔɪmənt/ *n* [U].

unequal /ʌn'iːkwəl/ *adj* 1 different (in size, amount, etc). 2 (eg of a pay agreement) treating people differently. 3 *to/i* (*fml*) not strong, clever enough to do sth. **unequally** *adv.*

unequivocal /ˌʌnɪ'kwɪvəkl/ *adj* (*fml*) having a completely clear meaning. **unequivocally** *adv.*

uneven /ʌn'iːvn/ *adj* 1 not level or smooth. 2 varying in quality.

unexpected /ˌʌnɪk'spektɪd/ *adj* causing surprise because not expected. **unexpectedly** *adv.*

unfailing /ʌn'feɪlɪŋ/ *adj* (*approv*) continuous.

unfair /ˌʌn'feə(r)/ *adj* not right or just: ~ *remarks/competition.* **unfairly** *adv.*

unfaithful /ˌʌn'feɪθfl/ *adj* having a sexual relationship with sb other than one's husband, wife or lover.

unfamiliar /ˌʌnfə'mɪlɪə(r)/ *adj* 1 not well known. 2 *with/i* not having knowledge of sth: *I'm* ~ *with this type of computer.*

unfasten /ʌn'fɑːsn; *US* ʌn'fæsn/ *v* [T] undo the buttons, clips, straps, etc of.

unfinished /ʌn'fɪnɪʃt/ *adj* not completed: ~ *business.*

unfit /ˌʌn'fɪt/ *adj* not fit or suitable.

unfold /ʌn'fəʊld/ *v* 1 [T] open

(sth folded). 2 [I, T] (*fig*) (cause to) be made known or clear: *as the story* ~ *ed.*

unforeseen /ˌʌnfɔː'siːn/ *adj* unexpected.

unforgettable /ˌʌnfə'getəbl/ *adj* that cannot be easily forgotten.

unfortunate /ʌn'fɔːtʃənət/ *adj* 1 unlucky. 2 that makes one feel sorry: *an* ~ *remark.* **unfortunately** *adv.*

unfounded /ˌʌn'faʊndɪd/ *adj* not based on facts.

unfriendly /ˌʌn'frendlɪ/ *adj* (*-ier, -iest*) not friendly.

unfurl /ʌn'fɜːl/ *v* [I, T] unroll or open (a sail, flag, etc).

unfurnished /ˌʌn'fɜːnɪʃt/ *adj* (of a rented room, etc) without furniture.

ungainly /ʌn'geɪnlɪ/ *adj* clumsy or awkward.

ungodly /ʌn'gɒdlɪ/ *adj* 1 not religious. 2 (*infml*) unreasonable: *at this* ~ *hour.*

ungrateful /ʌn'greɪtfl/ *adv* not thankful.

unguarded /ˌʌn'gɑːdɪd/ *adv* careless, esp in speech.

unhappy /ʌn'hæpɪ/ *adj* (*-ier, -iest*) not happy. **unhappily** *adv.* **unhappiness** *n* [U].

unhealthy /ʌn'helθɪ/ *adj* (*-ier, -iest*) 1 not having or showing good health. 2 harmful to health.

unheard-of /ʌn'hɜːd ɒv/ *adj* not previously known of or done; very surprising or shocking.

unicorn /'juːnɪkɔːn/ *n* [C] imaginary horse with a long straight horn growing from its head.

unidentified /ˌʌnaɪ'dentɪfaɪd/ *adj* that cannot be identified.

uniform /'juːnɪfɔːm/ *n* [C, U] special clothes worn by members of an organization or group, eg the army or schoolchildren. **uniform** *adj* not changing; regular. **uniformed** *adj*: ~ *ed police officers.* **uniformity** /ˌjuːnɪ'fɔːmətɪ/ *n* [U].

unify /'juːnɪfaɪ/ *v* (*pt, pp* **-ied**) [T] form into a single unit. **unification** /ˌjuːnɪfɪ'keɪʃn/ *n* [U].

unilateral /ˌjuːnɪ'lætrəl/ *adj* done by only one group, country, etc: ~ *disarmament.*

union /'juːnɪən/ *n* 1 [C] (**a**) = TRADE UNION (TRADE¹). (**b**) club or association. 2 [C] group of countries or states. 3 [U] (*fml*) joining. **the Union Jack** *n* [sing] national flag of the United Kingdom.

unique /juː'niːk/ *adj* 1 being the only one of its kind. 2 *to/i* concerning only one person, group or thing: *problems* ~ *to blind people.* 3 (*infml*) unusual or special: *a* ~ *singing voice.* **uniquely** *adv.*

unisex /'ju:nɪseks/ adj designed to be used by both men and women.

unison /'ju:nɪsn, -zn/ n (idm) **in unison** (a) sounding the same musical note. (b) (fig) exactly together.

unit /'ju:nɪt/ n [C] **1** single thing, person or group. **2** group of people with a specific job or function: the university research ~. **3** machine with a special function: the central processing ~ of a computer. **4** standard of measurement: The metre is a ~ of length.

unite /ju:'naɪt/ v [I, T] become or make one; join. **the U̱nited 'King̱dom** n [sing] Great Britain and Northern Ireland. **the U̱nited 'Nations** n [sing] international organization of many countries which works for peace, friendship, etc.

unity /'ju:nətɪ/ n [U] state of being united; agreement.

universal /ˌju:nɪ'vɜ:sl/ adj of or affecting all people or things in the world or in a particular group. **universally** adv.

universe /'ju:nɪvɜ:s/ n **the universe** [sing] everything that exists in space, including all the stars and planets.

university /ˌju:nɪ'vɜ:sətɪ/ n [C] (pl -ies) (a) institution for advanced teaching and research. (b) members of such an institution.

unkempt /ˌʌn'kempt/ adj not kept tidy: ~ hair.

unkind /ˌʌn'kaɪnd/ adj not kind; cruel or harsh.

unknown /ˌʌn'nəʊn/ adj not known or identified.

unleash /ʌn'li:ʃ/ v [T] (fml) release (a powerful force).

unless /ən'les/ conj if ... not: You will fail ~ you work harder.

unlike /ˌʌn'laɪk/ adj, prep not like; different (from).

unlikely /ʌn'laɪklɪ/ adj (a) not likely to happen or be true: He's ~ to get better. (b) not expected, improbable: an ~ candidate for the job.

unload /ˌʌn'ləʊd/ v [I, T] remove (a load) from (sth). **2** [T] (on/ on to))) pass (sth unwanted) to sb else.

unlock /ˌʌn'lɒk/ v [T] open (a door, etc) using a key.

unlucky /ʌn'lʌkɪ/ adj having or bringing bad luck.

unmanned /ˌʌn'mænd/ adj (esp of a spacecraft) without a crew.

unmask /ˌʌn'mɑːsk/ US -'mæsk/ v [T] show the true character of.

unmentionable /ʌn'menʃənəbl/ adj too shocking or embarrassing to be spoken about.

unmistakable /ˌʌnmɪ'steɪkəbl/ adj so obvious that it cannot be mistaken for sth else. **unmistakably** adv.

unmitigated /ʌn'mɪtɪgeɪtɪd/ adj (fml) completely bad: an ~ disaster.

unmoved /ˌʌn'mu:vd/ adj not affected: ~ by her tears.

unnatural /ʌn'nætʃrəl/ adj **1** not natural or normal: ~ silence. **2** not expected or acceptable: ~ behaviour.

unnecessary /ʌn'nesəsrɪ; US -seserɪ/ adj not necessary. **unnecessarily** adv.

unnerve /ˌʌn'nɜ:v/ v [T] cause to lose confidence or courage.

unnoticed /ˌʌn'nəʊtɪst/ adj not seen or noticed.

unobtrusive /ˌʌnəb'tru:sɪv/ adj (fml) not easily noticeable.

unofficial /ˌʌnə'fɪʃl/ adj not official.

unpalatable /ʌn'pælətəbl/ adj (fml) **1** not tasting pleasant. **2** (fig) difficult to accept: his ~ views.

unpleasant /ʌn'pleznt/ adj **1** not pleasant: an ~ smell. **2** very unfriendly. **unpleasantness** n [U].

unprecedented /ʌn'presɪdentɪd/ adj never having happened or been done before.

unpredictable /ˌʌnprɪ'dɪktəbl/ adj (of a person, behaviour, etc) not able to be predicted: I never know how she will react, she's so ~.

unprintable /ʌn'prɪntəbl/ adj (of words, etc) too rude or likely to offend to be printed.

unqualified /ˌʌn'kwɒlɪfaɪd/ adj **1** not qualified for a job: ~ to teach. **2** not limited; complete: an ~ disaster.

unquestionable /ˌʌn'kwestʃənəbl/ adj that cannot be doubted; certain. **unquestionably** adv.

unravel /ʌn'rævl/ v (-ll-; US -l-) **1** [I, T] (cause sth woven or knotted to) separate into threads. **2** [T] (fig) solve: ~ a mystery.

unreal /ˌʌn'rɪəl/ adj not seeming real; imaginary. **unreality** /ˌʌnrɪ'ælətɪ/ n [U].

unreasonable /ʌn'ri:znəbl/ adj not reasonable or fair.

unremitting /ˌʌnrɪ'mɪtɪŋ/ adj never relaxing or stopping.

unrest /ʌn'rest/ n [U] disturbed social conditions: political ~.

unrivalled (US -l-) /ʌn'raɪvld/ adj better than any others.

unroll /ˌʌn'rəʊl/ v [I, T] open from a rolled state.

unruffled /ˌʌn'rʌfld/ adj not upset; calm.

unruly /ʌn'ru:lɪ/ adj not easy to control.

unsavoury (US **-vory**) /ʌn'seɪvərɪ/ adj unpleasant, unacceptable.

unscathed /ʌn'skeɪðd/ adj not harmed.

unscrupulous /ʌn'skru:pjʊləs/ adj not caring about being dishonest; doing wrong.

unseat /ʌn'si:t/ v [T] **1** throw (sb) off a horse, etc. **2** remove (sb) from a position of power.

unseemly /ʌn'si:mlɪ/ adj (fml) not proper or suitable: ~ behaviour.

unsettle /ʌn'setl/ v [T] cause to be worried, dissatisfied or uncertain: ~d (ie changeable) weather.

unsightly /ʌn'saɪtlɪ/ adj not pleasant to look at.

unsound /ʌn'saʊnd/ adj **1** in poor condition; weak. **2** (idm) of **unsound 'mind** (law) mentally ill.

unspeakable /ʌn'spi:kəbl/ adj extreme; extremely bad: ~ sadness.

unstuck /ʌn'stʌk/ adj **1** not stuck or fastened. **2** (idm) **come un'stuck** (infml) be unsuccessful; fail.

unswerving /ʌn'swɜ:vɪŋ/ adj not changing; firm: ~ loyalty.

unthinkable /ʌn'θɪŋkəbl/ adj too bad to be considered or accepted.

untidy /ʌn'taɪdɪ/ adj (-ier, -iest) not neat or ordered.

untie /ʌn'taɪ/ v (pt, pp ~d, pres p **untying**) [T] remove a tied rope or string from; undo.

until /ən'tɪl/ (also **till** /tɪl/) prep, conj up to the (time that): Wait ~ the rain stops.

untold /ʌn'təʊld/ adj (fml) too great to be measured.

untoward /ˌʌntə'wɔ:d; US ʌn'tɔ:d/ adj (fml) unexpected or unfortunate.

unused[1] /ʌn'ju:zd/ adj never having been used.

unused[2] /ʌn'ju:st/ adj to// not in the habit of doing sth; not familiar with.

unusual /ʌn'ju:ʒl/ adj not usual; interesting because different. **unusually** adv.

unveil /ʌn'veɪl/ v [T] **1** remove a covering from. **2** make known publicly.

unwarranted /ʌn'wɒrəntɪd/ adj (fml) not deserved or justified.

unwieldy /ʌn'wi:ldɪ/ adj difficult to move or control, because large or heavy.

unwind /ʌn'waɪnd/ v (pt, pp -wound /-'waʊnd/) **1** [I, T] (cause to) become drawn out from a roll, ball, etc. **2** [I] (infml) relax.

unwitting /ʌn'wɪtɪŋ/ adj (fml) not intended or known. **unwittingly** adv.

unwrap /ʌn'ræp/ v (-pp-) [T] remove the wrapping or cover from.

up /ʌp/ adv **1** to or at a higher level: Lift your head up. **2** to a vertical position: stand up. **3** out of bed: Is Anne up yet? **4** to an important place; to the north: go up to London. **5** (to)// so as to be close to sb/sth: He came up (to me) and asked the time. **6** (showing an increase): Profits are up again. **7** completely: The stream has dried up. **8** into pieces: tear the paper up. **9** (infml) happening: What's up? **10** (idm) up against sth faced with (difficulties or problems). **up and 'down** (a) backwards and forwards: walk up and down. (b) so as to rise and fall: The boat bobbed up and down in the water. **up for sth** (a) being tried for (an offence). (b) being considered for sth; on offer. **up to sb** the responsibility of sb. **up to sth** (a) as a maximum number or amount: My car takes up to four people. (b) until sth: up to now. (c) capable of sth: I don't feel up to going to work. **up prep 1** at or to a higher level: go up the stairs. **2** (of flat places) along: There's another telephone-box up the road. **up adj 1** going upwards: the up escalator. **2** being repaired: The road is up. **up** v (-pp-) [T] (infml) increase. **ˌup-and-'coming** adj (of a person) likely to succeed. **ˌups and 'downs** n [pl] good and bad experiences.

upbringing /ˈʌpbrɪŋɪŋ/ n [U] treatment and education during childhood.

update /ˌʌp'deɪt/ v [T] make more modern; bring up to date.

upheaval /ʌp'hi:vl/ n [C, U] great violent change.

uphill /ˌʌp'hɪl/ adv up a slope. ‚uphill adj difficult: an ~ task.

uphold /ʌp'həʊld/ v (pt, pp -held /-'held/) [T] **1** support: ~ the law. **2** confirm (a legal decision).

upholster /ʌp'həʊlstə(r)/ v [T] provide (a seat) with padding, springs, covering material, etc. **upholsterer** n [C]. **upholstery** n [U] materials used in upholstering.

upkeep /ˈʌpki:p/ n [U] (cost of) keeping sth in good condition: the ~ of a house.

upland /ˈʌplənd/ n [C, esp pl] higher part of a country.

up-market /ˌʌp ˌmɑ:kɪt/ adj (infml) for or being used by people with expensive and sophisticated tastes: *an* ~ *restaurant*.

upon /ə'pɒn/ *prep* (*fml*) = ON² 1,2,6,11,12,14.

upper /'ʌpə(r)/ *adj* 1 higher in place or position; situated above: *the* ~ *lip*. 2 (idm) the **upper** 'hand advantage or control: *gain the* ~ *hand*. **upper** *n* [C] part of a shoe above the sole. the ,upper 'class *n* [C] social class above middle class. ,upper-'class *adj*. 'upper-most *adj*, *adv* (to a position or place) that is highest or most important: *thoughts* ~ *most in his mind*.

upright /'ʌpraɪt/ *adj* 1 placed vertically to the ground; straight up. 2 completely honest; honourable. **upright** *n* [C] upright supporting post.

uprising /'ʌpraɪzɪŋ/ *n* [C] fighting by ordinary people against those in power.

uproar /'ʌprɔː(r)/ *n* [U, sing] (outburst of) noise and excitement or anger. **uproarious** /ʌp'rɔːrɪəs/ *adj* very noisy.

uproot /,ʌp'ruːt/ *v* [T] 1 pull (a tree, etc) out of the ground. 2 (*fig*) force (oneself, etc) to leave one's home.

upset /,ʌp'set/ *v* (-tt-, *pt*, *pp* **upset**) [T] 1 make (sb) feel worried or unhappy: *be* ~ *by the bad news*. 2 make (sb) feel slightly ill: *Milk* ~ *s her*. 3 cause (sth) to go wrong: ~ *one's plans*. 4 turn (sth) over, esp accidentally: ~ *a glass of water*. **upset** /'ʌpset/ *n* 1 [U, C] upsetting. 2 [C] slight illness: *a stomach* ~.

upshot /'ʌpʃɒt/ *n* the upshot [sing] (*of*//) final result.

upside-down /,ʌpsaɪd 'daʊn/ *adj, adv* 1 with the top underneath. 2 (*fig*) in disorder: *Burglars had turned the house* ~.

upstage /,ʌp'steɪdʒ/ *v* [T] attract attention away from (sb) to oneself.

upstairs /,ʌp'steəz/ *adv, adj* to or on a higher floor.

upstanding /,ʌp'stændɪŋ/ *adj* (*fml*) 1 strong and healthy. 2 honest and decent.

upstart /'ʌpstɑːt/ *n* [C] (*derog*) person who has suddenly risen to a high or wealthy position.

upstream /,ʌp'striːm/ *adv* in the direction from which a river flows.

uptake /'ʌpteɪk/ (idm) ,quick/ ,slow on the 'uptake quick/slow to understand what is meant.

uptight /'ʌp'taɪt/ *adj* (*infml*) nervous and worried.

up-to-date /,ʌp tə 'deɪt/ *adj* 1 modern: ~ *equipment*. 2 having

all the most recent information: *an* ~ *report*.

upward /'ʌpwəd/ *adj* going up. **upwards** (also **upward**) *adv* going up.

uranium /ju'reɪnɪəm/ *n* [U] radioactive metal used in producing nuclear energy.

urban /'ɜːbən/ *adj* of a town or city.

urchin /'ɜːtʃɪn/ *n* [C] poor dirty child.

urge /ɜːdʒ/ *v* [T] 1 try strongly to persuade: *They* ~ *d her to come back soon*. 2 recommend strongly: ~ *caution*. 3 drive (an animal) forcefully. **urge** *n* [C] strong desire: *a sudden* ~ *to run away*.

urgent /'ɜːdʒənt/ *adj* needing immediate attention, action or decision. **urgency** /'ɜːdʒənsɪ/ *n* [U]. **urgently** *adv*.

urine /'jʊərɪn/ *n* [U] liquid waste that is passed from the body. **urinate** /'jʊərɪneɪt/ *v* [I] pass urine from the body.

urn /ɜːn/ *n* [C] 1 container for holding the ashes of a cremated person. 2 large metal container for serving tea or coffee.

US /,juː 'es/ *abbr* the US the United States (of America): *a US citizen*.

us /ʌs/; strong form /ʌs/ *pron* (used as the object of a *v* or *prep*) me and another or others; me and you.

USA /,juː es 'eɪ/ *abbr* the USA the United States of America: *visit the USA*.

usage /'juːsɪdʒ; *US* 'juːzɪdʒ/ *n* 1 [U, C] way in which words are used: *a guide to modern English* ~. 2 [U] manner of using sth.

use¹ /juːz/ *v* (*pt, pp* ~ *d* /juːzd/) [T] 1 employ (sth) for a purpose; do sth with: ~ *a pen to write*. 2 consume; finish: *The car* ~ *d 20 litres of petrol for the journey*. 3 take advantage of (sb) unfairly; exploit. 4 (phr v) use sth up finish sth completely. **usable** *adj*. **used** *adj* having been used, worn, etc before: ~ *d cars*. **user** *n* [C] person or thing that uses.

use² /juːs/ *n* 1 [U, sing] using or being used. 2 [C, U] purpose for which sth is used: *a tool with many* ~ *s*. 3 [U] (a) power of using sth: *lose the* ~ *of one's legs*. (b) right to use sth: *You can have the* ~ *of my car*. 4 [U] value or advantage: *It's no* ~ *worrying about it*. 5 (idm) ,come into/go out of 'use start/ stop being used. in 'use being used. make use of sth use sth. of use useful. **useful** /'juːsfl/ *adj* serving a purpose well; helpful. **usefully** *adv*. **usefulness** *n* [U].

useless adj 1 not useful. 2 (infml) not able to do anything well. **uselessly** adv.

used /ju:st/ adj used to|| familiar with sth; in the habit of (doing): You will soon be/get ~ to the weather.

used to /'ju:s tə; before vowels and finally 'ju:s tu:/ modal v (used to show a past habit or state): I ~ play football when I was a boy.

usher /'ʌʃə(r)/ n [C] person who shows people to their seats in a theatre, cinema, etc. **usher** v [T] 1 show (sb) where to go; lead. 2 (phr v) **usher sth in** (fml) mark the start of sth. **usherette** /ˌʌʃə'ret/ n [C] woman usher.

USSR /ˌju: es es ɑ:(r)/ abbr the USSR the Union of Soviet Socialist Rebublics.

usual /'ju:ʒl/ adj existing, done, happening, etc most often: We'll meet at the ~ place. **usually** /'ju:ʒəlɪ/ adv most often.

usurp /ju:'zɜ:p/ v [T] (fml) take (sb's power, right, etc) wrongfully. **usurper** n [C].

utensil /ju:'tensl/ n [C] (fml) tool or object for use, esp in the home.

uterus /'ju:tərəs/ n [C] (anatomy) = WOMB.

utility /ju:'tɪlətɪ/ n (pl -ies) 1 [U] quality of being useful. 2 [C] public service such as the supply of water or a rail service.

utilize /'ju:təlaɪz/ v [T] (fml) make use of. **utilization** /ˌju:təlaɪ'zeɪʃn/ n [U].

utmost /'ʌtməʊst/ adj greatest: of the ~ importance. **utmost** n [sing] the greatest amount or extent possible: I shall do my ~.

utter[1] /'ʌtə(r)/ adj complete; total: ~ darkness. **utterly** adv.

utter[2] /'ʌtə(r)/ v [T] make (a sound) with the mouth; say. **utterance** /'ʌtərəns/ n [C] (fml) spoken word or words.

U-turn ⇨ U, u.

V v

V, v /vi:/ n [C] (pl V's, v's /vi:z/) 1 the twenty-second letter of the English alphabet. 2 Roman numeral for 5.

v abbr 1 versus. 2 volt(s). 3 very.

vacancy /'veɪkənsɪ/ n [C] (pl -ies) 1 unfilled job. 2 unoccupied room.

vacant /'veɪkənt/ adj 1 not filled or occupied; empty. 2 without thought or interest: a ~ expression.

vacate /və'keɪt, veɪ'keɪt/ v [T] (fml) leave empty; make available for sb else.

vacation /və'keɪʃn; US veɪ-/ n [C] 1 period when universities are closed. 2 (esp US) holiday.

vaccinate /'væksɪneɪt/ v [T] protect (sb) against a disease by injecting a vaccine. **vaccination** /ˌvæksɪ'neɪʃn/ n [C, U].

vaccine /'væksi:n; US væk'si:n/ n [C, U] substance injected into the body to protect it against a disease.

vacuum /'vækjʊəm/ n [C] (pl ~s or, in scientific use vacua /-jʊə/) space that is completely empty of all matter or gases: (fig) a ~ (ie feeling of emptiness) in his life since his wife died. **vacuum** v [I, T] clean (sth) with a vacuum cleaner. '**vacuum cleaner** n [C] electrical apparatus that sucks up dirt and dust from floors. '**vacuum flask** n [C] container with a vacuum between its two walls, used for keeping liquids hot or cold.

vagabond /'vægəbɒnd/ n [C] (dated) person who has no fixed home or job; wanderer.

vagina /və'dʒaɪnə/ n [C] (anatomy) passage from the outer female sex organs to the womb.

vagrant /'veɪgrənt/ n [C] (fml or law) person without a settled home or regular work and who begs. **vagrancy** /-rənsɪ/ n [U].

vague /veɪg/ adj (~r, ~st) 1 not clearly expressed, described, etc. 2 not expressing oneself clearly. **vaguely** adv. **vagueness** n [U].

vain /veɪn/ adj 1 having too high an opinion of oneself. 2 unsuccessful: a ~ attempt. 3 (idm) in 'vain unsuccessfully. **vainly** adv.

vale /veɪl/ n [C] (in poetry or place names) valley.

valentine /'væləntaɪn/ n [C] (card sent on St Valentine's Day, 14th February, to a) lover.

valet /'væleɪ, 'vælɪt/ n [C] man's personal servant.

valiant /'vælɪənt/ adj very brave. **valiantly** adv.

valid /'vælɪd/ adj 1 that is legally acceptable and can be used: The ticket is ~ until 1st May. 2 (of arguments) well based; reasonable. **validate** v [T] (fml) make valid. **validity** /və'lɪdətɪ/ n [U].

valley /'vælɪ/ n [C] low land between hills or mountains, often with a river.

valour (US -or) /'vælə(r)/ n [U] (rhet) great bravery.

valuable /'væljʊəbl/ adj 1 worth a lot of money. 2 very useful: ~

advice. **valuables** *n* [pl] valuable(1) things, esp jewellery.

valuation /ˌvæljuˈeɪʃn/ *n* 1 [C, U] deciding the value of sth. 2 [C] value decided on.

value /ˈvæljuː/ *n* 1 (a) [C, U] amount of money sth is worth. (b) [U] worth of sth compared with its price: *This large packet is good ~ at 99p.* 2 [U] quality of being useful or important: *the ~ of regular exercise.* 3 **values** [pl] principles: *high moral ~s.* **value** *v* [T] 1 estimate the money value of. 2 have a high opinion of: *I ~ my secretary.* ,**value 'added tax** *n* [U] tax added to the price of goods or services. **valueless** *adj* without value. **val-uer** *n* [C] person whose job is to estimate the money value of property, etc.

valve /vælv/ *n* [C] (a) device for controlling the flow of air or liquid in one direction only. (b) similar structure in the heart.

vampire /ˈvæmpaɪə(r)/ *n* [C] (in stories) dead person who sucks the blood of living people.

van /væn/ *n* [C] covered vehicle with no side windows, used for carrying goods.

vandal /ˈvændl/ *n* [C] person who deliberately destroys property, etc. **vandalism** /-dəlɪzəm/ *n* [U] deliberate damaging of property, etc. **vandalize** /-dəlaɪz/ *v* [T] damage or destroy (property, etc) intentionally.

vanguard /ˈvænɡɑːd/ *n* the **vanguard** [sing] 1 leading part of an advancing army. 2 (*fig*) leaders of a movement, branch of scientific research, etc.

vanilla /vəˈnɪlə/ *n* [U] flavouring that comes from a plant and is used in ice-cream and other foods.

vanish /ˈvænɪʃ/ *v* [I] 1 disappear suddenly. 2 cease to exist: *Her hopes of finding a new job have ~ed.*

vanity /ˈvænəti/ *n* [U] 1 having too high an opinion of oneself. 2 (*fml*) quality of being worthless: *the ~ of pleasure.*

vanquish /ˈvæŋkwɪʃ/ *v* [T] (*fml*) defeat completely.

vaporize /ˈveɪpəraɪz/ *v* [I, T] change into vapour.

vapour (*US* **-or**) /ˈveɪpə(r)/ *n* [U] gas-like form, eg steam or mist, of a liquid: *water ~.*

variable /ˈveəriəbl/ *adj* likely to change; varying. **variable** *n* [C] variable thing or quantity. **variably** *adv*.

variant /ˈveəriənt/ *adj*, *n* [C] (being a) different form of sth: *~ spellings of a word.*

variation /ˌveəriˈeɪʃn/ *n* 1 [C, U] (instance or degree of) varying: *~(s) in temperature.* 2 [C] (*music*) repetition of a simple tune in a different form.

varicose vein /ˈværɪkəʊs veɪn/ *n* [C, usu pl] swollen painful vein in sb's leg.

varied /ˈveərɪd/ *adj* 1 of different kinds. 2 showing changes or variety: *a ~ life.*

variety /vəˈraɪəti/ *n* (*pl* **-ies**) 1 [U] quality of not being the same: *a life full of ~.* 2 [sing] number of different things: *a wide ~ of interests.* 3 [C] kind: *rare varieties of birds.* 4 [U] entertainment with singing, dancing, comedy, etc: *a ~ act.*

various /ˈveərɪəs/ *adj* 1 of several different things: *This dress comes in ~ colours.* 2 more than one: *at ~ times.* **variously** *adv*.

varnish /ˈvɑːnɪʃ/ *n* [C, U] (liquid used for giving a) hard shiny surface on wood, etc. **varnish** *v* [T] put varnish on.

vary /ˈveəri/ *v* (*pt, pp* **-ied**) 1 [I] be different in size, amount, etc: *Car prices ~ greatly.* 2 [I, T] change: *~ one's route.*

vase /vɑːz; *US* veɪs, veɪz/ *n* [C] tall glass or china jar, used esp for holding flowers.

vast /vɑːst; *US* væst/ *adj* extremely large: *a ~ desert.* **vastly** *adv*: *~ly improved.* **vastness** *n* [U].

VAT /ˌviː eɪ ˈtiː, also væt/ *abbr* value added tax.

vat /væt/ *n* [C] very large container for liquids, eg in brewing.

vault[1] /vɔːlt/ *n* [C] 1 room with thick walls, where valuable things are kept safe. 2 underground room, esp where people are buried. 3 arched roof.

vault[2] /vɔːlt/ *v* [I, T] (*over*)// jump over (sth) using one's hand(s) or a pole: *~ (over) a wall.* **vault** *v* [I] jump made in this way. **vaulter** *n* [C] person who vaults: *a pole-~er.*

VDU /ˌviː diː ˈjuː/ *abbr* visual display unit.

veal /viːl/ *n* [U] meat from a calf.

veer /vɪə(r)/ *v* [I] change direction.

vegetable /ˈvedʒtəbl/ *n* [C] plant, eg potato, bean or onion, eaten as food. **vegetable** *adj* of or from plants in general: *~ oils.*

vegetarian /ˌvedʒɪˈteərɪən/ *n* [C] person who eats no meat.

vegetate /ˈvedʒɪteɪt/ *v* [I] (*fig*) lead a dull life with little activity.

vegetation /ˌvedʒɪˈteɪʃn/ *n* [U] plants in general.

vehement /'viːəmənt/ *adj* showing or caused by strong feeling. **vehemence** /-məns/ *n* [U]. **vehemently** *adv*.

vehicle /'vɪəkl; *US* 'viːhɪkl/ *n* [C] 1 something such as a car, bus or lorry that carries people or goods from place to place. 2 (*fml*) means of expressing sth: *Art may be a ~ for propaganda.*

veil /veɪl/ *n* 1 [C] covering for a woman's face. 2 [sing] (*fml*) something that hides: *a ~ of mist.* veil *v* [T] 1 cover (as if) with a veil. 2 (*fig*) hide.

vein /veɪn/ *n* 1 [C] one of the tubes that carry blood from various parts of the body to the heart. 2 [C] thin line in a leaf or an insect's wing. 3 [C] layer of metal or mineral in rock: *a ~ of gold.* 4 [sing] manner or style: *in a comic ~.*

velocity /vɪ'lɒsətɪ/ *n* [U, C] (*pl -ies*) (*fml* or *physics*) speed.

velvet /'velvɪt/ *n* [U] cloth made of cotton, silk, etc with a thick soft surface on one side. **velvety** *adj* soft like velvet.

vendetta /ven'detə/ *n* [C] long bitter quarrel between families who try to harm or kill each other.

vending-machine /'vendɪŋ məˌʃiːn/ *n* [C] machine that provides food, cigarettes, etc when money is put in it.

vendor /'vendə(r)/ *n* [C] 1 person who sells food, sweets, newspapers, etc, esp from a small stall in the street. 2 (*law*) person selling a house, land, etc.

veneer /və'nɪə(r)/ *n* 1 [C, U] layer of wood or plastic glued to the surface of cheaper wood. 2 [sing] (*fig*) false surface appearance: *a ~ of kindness.* veneer *v* [T] put a veneer(1) on.

venerable /'venərəbl/ *adj* (*fml*) deserving respect because of age, etc.

venerate /'venəreɪt/ *v* [T] (*fml*) feel great respect for. **veneration** /ˌvenə'reɪʃn/ *n* [U].

venereal disease /vəˌnɪərɪəl dɪ'ziːz/ *n* [C, U] disease passed on by sexual intercourse.

vengeance /'vendʒəns/ *n* 1 [U] harming sb in return for the harm he/she has done to one. 2 (*idm*) **with a 'vengeance** (*infml*) to a greater extent than normal.

vengeful /'vendʒfl/ *adj* (*fml*) showing a desire for revenge.

venison /'venɪzn, -ɪsn/ *n* [U] meat from a deer.

venom /'venəm/ *n* [U] 1 poison of certain snakes, etc. 2 (*fig*) strong bitterness or hate. **venomous** *adj:*

a ~ous snake/glance.

vent /vent/ *n* 1 [C] hole for air, gas, liquid to pass through. 2 (idm) **give 'vent to sth** express sth freely: *give ~ to one's feelings.* vent *v* [T] (*on*) // express (one's feelings) by making sb/sth suffer: *He ~ed his anger on his brother.*

ventilate /'ventɪleɪt; *US* -təleɪt/ *v* [T] cause fresh air to enter and move freely through (a room, building, etc). **ventilation** /ˌventɪ'leɪʃn; *US* -tə'l-/ *n* [U]. **ventilator** *n* [C] device for ventilating.

ventriloquist /ven'trɪləkwɪst/ *n* [C] person who can make his/her voice appear to come from sb/sth else.

venture /'ventʃə(r)/ *n* [C] something new and different in which there is a risk of failure: *a business ~.* venture *v* (*fml*) 1 [I] dare to do sth difficult or go somewhere dangerous. 2 [T] dare to say.

venue /'venjuː/ *n* [C] place where sth has been arranged to happen: *a ~ for the football match.*

veranda (also **verandah**) /və'rændə/ *n* [C] open space with a floor and a roof along one side of a house.

verb /vɜːb/ *n* [C] word or phrase that shows what a person or thing does or is, eg *bring, happen* or *give up.*

verbal /'vɜːbl/ *adj* 1 of or in words. 2 spoken, not written. 3 (*grammar*) of verbs. **verbally** /'vɜːbəlɪ/ *adv* in spoken words. **verbal 'noun** *n* [C] noun derived from a verb, eg *swimming* in: *Swimming is a good form of exercise.*

verbose /vɜː'bəʊs/ *adj* (*fml*) using more words than are needed. **verbosity** /vɜː'bɒsətɪ/ *n* [U].

verdict /'vɜːdɪkt/ *n* [C] 1 decision reached by a jury in a law-court: *a ~ of guilty/not guilty.* 2 opinion or judgement.

verge /vɜːdʒ/ *n* [C] 1 edge of a path or road. 2 (idm) **on the 'verge of sth** very close to sth: *on the ~ of war.* verge *v* (phr *v*) **verge on sth** be very close or similar to sth.

verify /'verɪfaɪ/ *v* (*pt, pp -ied*) 1 make sure that (sth) is true. **verifiable** *adj.* **verification** /ˌverɪfɪ'keɪʃn/ *n* [U].

veritable /'verɪtəbl/ *adj* (*fml* or *joc*) rightly named; real: *a ~ liar.*

vermin /'vɜːmɪn/ *n* [U] (usu with *pl v*) 1 small animals or insects that are harmful to crops, birds and other animals. 2 (*fig*) people who are harmful to society.

vernacular /və'nækjʊlə(r)/,

n [C] (in or of the) language or dialect spoken in a particular country or region.

versatile /'vɜ:sətaɪl; *US* -tl/ *adj* having many different skills or uses. **versatility** /ˌvɜ:sə'tɪlətɪ/ *n* [U].

verse /vɜ:s/ *n* 1 [U] writing arranged in lines, each having a regular pattern. 2 [C] unit in a poem, etc. 3 [C] short numbered division of a chapter in the Bible.

versed /vɜ:st/ *adj in|| (fml)* knowledgeable about or skilled in sth.

version /'vɜ:ʃn; *US* -ʒn/ *n* [C] 1 particular form of sth: *the film ~ of the play.* 2 account of an event, etc in the opinion of one person: *There were three ~s of what happened.*

versus /'vɜ:səs/ *prep* against: *England ~ Brazil.*

vertebra /'vɜ:tɪbrə/ *n* [C] (*pl* -**brae** /-briː/) any one of the bones in the backbone. **vertebrate** /'vɜ:tɪbrət/ *n* [C], *adj* (animal) having a backbone.

vertical /'vɜ:tɪkl/ *adj* at an angle of 90° to the earth's surface or to another line. **vertical** *n* [sing] vertical line or position. **vertically** /-klɪ/ *adv*.

vertigo /'vɜ:tɪgəʊ/ *n* [U] feeling of dizziness caused by looking down from a great height.

very[1] /'verɪ/ *adv* 1 to a great degree: *~ little|quickly.* 2 in the fullest sense: *the ~ best quality.* 3 (idm) **very likely** ⇨ LIKELY.

very[2] /'verɪ/ *adj* 1 actual: *This is the ~ book I want!* 2 extreme: *at the ~ end.* 3 (used for emphasis): *The ~ thought of it upsets me.*

vessel /'vesl/ *n* [C] (*fml*) 1 ship or large boat. 2 container, esp for holding liquids.

vest[1] /vest/ *n* [C] 1 (*Brit*) garment worn on the upper part of the body next to the skin under a shirt, etc. 2 (*US*) waistcoat.

vest[2] /vest/ *v* 1 [T, with, in|| (*fml*) (usu passive) give (sth) to (sb) as a right or responsibility: *the authority ~ed in her* ○ *~ sb with authority.* 2 (idm) **have a vested interest in sth** have a strong reason for doing sth, esp because one personally benefits from it.

vestige /'vestɪdʒ/ *n* [C] (*fml*) small remaining part; trace or sign: *not a ~ of truth in the report.*

vet[1] /vet/ *n* [C] (*infml*) short for VETERINARY SURGEON (VETERINARY).

vet[2] /vet/ *v* (-**tt**-) [T] examine (eg sb's past record, qualifications, etc) carefully.

veteran /'vetərən/ *n* [C] person

with long experience, eg as a soldier. **veteran 'car** *n* [C] car built before 1916, esp before 1905.

veterinary /'vetrɪnrɪ; *US* 'vetərɪnerɪ/ *adj* concerned with the medical treatment of animals. **veterinary 'surgeon** *n* [C] (*fml*) doctor skilled in the treatment of animals.

veto /'viːtəʊ/ *n* (*pl* -**es**) (**a**) [C, U] official right to forbid or reject sth. (**b**) [C] statement that forbids or rejects sth. **veto** *v* [T] put a veto on: *~ a proposal.*

vex /veks/ *v* [T] (*fml*) annoy or trouble. **vexation** /vek'seɪʃn/ *n* [C, U]. **vexed** *adj* (of a problem) very difficult and causing a lot of discussion.

via /'vaɪə/ *prep* travelling through; by way of.

viable /'vaɪəbl/ *adj* (esp of a plan or business) capable of succeeding. **viability** /ˌvaɪə'bɪlətɪ/ *n* [U].

viaduct /'vaɪədʌkt/ *n* [C] long high bridge carrying a road or railway across a valley.

vibrate /vaɪ'breɪt; *US* 'vaɪbreɪt/ *v* [I, T] shake with a quick continuous movement: *The house ~s whenever a heavy lorry passes.* **vibration** /vaɪ'breɪʃn/ *n* [C, U].

vicar /'vɪkə(r)/ *n* [C] clergyman in charge of a parish. **vicarage** /'vɪkərɪdʒ/ *n* [C] vicar's house.

vice[1] /vaɪs/ *n* 1 [C, U] (kind of) evil, illegal or immoral behaviour. 2 [C] (*infml* or *joc*) fault or bad habit; weakness: *Chocolate is one of his ~s.*

vice[2] /vaɪs/ *n* [C] tool with two metal jaws that hold sth firmly.

vice- /vaɪs-/ *prefix* next in rank to; deputy: *vice-president.*

vice versa /ˌvaɪsə 'vɜ:sə/ *adv* the other way round: *We gossip about them and ~,* ie they gossip about us.

vicinity /vɪ'sɪnətɪ/ *n* (idm) **in the 'vicinity (of sth)** in the area near sth.

vicious /'vɪʃəs/ *adj* 1 acting or done with evil intentions; cruel and violent. 2 (idm) **a vicious 'circle** state in which a cause produces an effect that then produces the original cause again, and so on. **viciously** *adv*.

victim /'vɪktɪm/ *n* [C] person who suffers death, injury, hardship or loss: *~s of the flood.* **victimize** *v* [T] treat (sb) unfairly. **victimization** /ˌvɪktɪmaɪ'zeɪʃn; *US* -mɪ'z/ *n* [U].

victor /'vɪktə(r)/ *n* [C] (*fml*) winner.

victory /'vɪktərɪ/ *n* (*pl* -**ies**) success in a war, competition, etc;

winning. **victorious** /vɪk'tɔːrɪəs/ *adj* having won a victory.

video /'vɪdɪəʊ/ *n* (*pl* ~s) 1 [U, C] videotape recording. 2 [C] video recorder. **video** *v* [T] record (a television programme) on videotape. **'video recorder** (also **video ca'ssette recorder**) *n* [C] machine for recording and showing television programmes. **'videotape** *n* [U, C] magnetic tape used for recording moving pictures and sound.

vie /vaɪ/ *v* (*pres part* **vying** /'vaɪɪŋ/) [I] *with/* compete with sb.

view¹ /vjuː/ *n* 1 [U] being seen; field of vision: *The lake came into* ~. *in full* ~ *of the crowd.* 2 [C] what can be seen from a place: *a magnificent* ~ *from the top of the mountain.* 3 [C] personal opinion: *In my* ~, *nurses deserve better pay.* 4 (idm) **in view of** sth considering sth: *In* ~ *of the weather, we will cancel the outing.* **on 'view** being shown in public. **with a view to doing** sth with the intention of doing sth. **'viewfinder** *n* [C] device in a camera showing the area, etc that will be photographed. **'viewpoint** *n* [C] point of view ⇔ POINT¹.

view² /vjuː/ *v* (*fml*) 1 [T] consider: ~ *the problem with some concern.* 2 [I] look at carefully; examine. 3 [I, T] watch (television). **viewer** *n* [C] person who watches television.

vigil /'vɪdʒɪl/ *n* [C] staying awake to keep watch, eg to look after sb who is ill or to pray.

vigilant /'vɪdʒɪlənt/ *adj* (*fml*) trying to notice any possible danger or trouble. **vigilance** /-ləns/ *n* [U]. **vigilantly** *adv*.

vigour (*US* **-or**) /'vɪgə(r)/ *n* [U] physical strength or energy. **vigorous** *adj* strong or energetic. **vigorously** *adv*.

vile /vaɪl/ *adj* (~r, ~st) 1 shameful; disgusting. 2 (*infml*) very unpleasant: ~ *weather.* **vilely** /'vaɪllɪ/ *adv*.

villa /'vɪlə/ *n* [C] house for holiday-makers, eg in the countryside: *rent a* ~ *in Spain.*

village /'vɪlɪdʒ/ *n* [C] group of houses, shops, etc that is smaller than a town and is in a country area. **villager** *n* [C] person who lives in a village.

villain /'vɪlən/ *n* [C] 1 (*Brit sl*) criminal. 2 wicked person, esp in stories. 3 (idm) **the 'villain of the piece** (*joc*) person or thing to be blamed for a problem, damage, etc.

vindicate /'vɪndɪkeɪt/ *v* [T] (*fml*)

1 free from blame or suspicion. 2 show or prove the truth, justice or validity of. **vindication** /ˌvɪndɪ'keɪʃn/ *n* [C, U].

vindictive /vɪn'dɪktɪv/ *adj* wanting to harm sb who has harmed one. **vindictively** *adv*. **vindictiveness** *n* [U].

vine /vaɪn/ *n* [C] climbing plant, esp one that produces grapes as its fruit. **vineyard** /'vɪnjəd/ *n* [C] area of land planted with vines for making wine.

vinegar /'vɪnɪgə(r)/ *n* [U] acid liquid made from malt, wine, etc used in preparing food. **vinegary** *adj*.

vintage /'vɪntɪdʒ/ *n* [C] year in which a particular wine was made. **vintage** *adj* 1 old and of very high quality. 2 (of a car) made between 1917 and 1930.

vinyl /'vaɪnl/ *n* [U] kind of strong flexible plastic.

viola /vɪ'əʊlə/ *n* [C] stringed musical instrument slightly larger than a violin.

violate /'vaɪəleɪt/ *v* [T] 1 break (a promise, agreement, etc). 2 treat (a holy place) with disrespect. 3 (*fig*) interfere with or disturb (personal freedom). **violation** /ˌvaɪə'leɪʃn/ *n* [U, C].

violent /'vaɪələnt/ *adj* 1 using, showing or caused by strong (esp unlawful) force: *a* ~ *attack.* 2 using, showing or caused by very strong feeling: ~ *argument.* 3 severe or extreme: *a* ~ *thunderstorm.* **violence** /-ləns/ *n* [U] 1 great force. 2 violent behaviour. **violently** *adv*.

violet /'vaɪələt/ *n* 1 [C] small plant with sweet-smelling purple or white flowers. 2 [U] bluish-purple colour.

violin /ˌvaɪə'lɪn/ *n* [C] stringed musical instrument held under the chin and played with a bow. **violinist** *n* [C] violin player.

VIP /ˌviː aɪ 'piː/ *abbr*, *n* [C] very important person.

viper /'vaɪpə(r)/ *n* [C] poisonous snake.

viral ⇔ VIRUS.

virgin /'vɜːdʒɪn/ *n* [C] person, esp a girl or woman, who has not had sexual intercourse. **virgin** *adj* 1 pure and untouched: ~ *snow.* 2 unused: ~ *soil.* **virginity** /və'dʒɪnətɪ/ *n* [U] state of being a virgin.

virile /'vɪraɪl/; *US* /'vɪrəl/ *adj* having the qualities traditionally expected of a man, esp strength and powerful sexual feelings. **virility** /və'rɪlətɪ/ *n* [U].

virtual /'vɜːtʃʊəl/ *adj* being what

is described, but not accepted officially: *The deputy manager is the ~ head of the business.* **virtually** /'vɜːtʃʊəlɪ/ *adv* in every important respect; almost.

virtue /'vɜːtʃuː/ *n* 1 [U] moral goodness. 2 [C] good quality: *Patience is a ~.* 3 [C, U] advantage: *The great ~ of the plan is its cheapness.* 4 (idm) by **virtue of sth** (*fml*) because of sth. **virtuous** *adj* morally good.

virus /'vaɪrəs/ *n* [C] (a) tiny living thing that causes infection. (b) (*infml*) disease caused by one of these. **viral** /'vaɪrəl/ *adj* of, like or caused by a virus: *a viral infection.*

visa /'viːzə/ *n* [C] official mark put on a passport allowing the owner to visit or leave a country.

viscount /'vaɪkaʊnt/ *n* [C] (title of a) British nobleman with the rank between a baron and an earl. **viscountess** *n* [C] 1 wife or widow of a viscount. 2 woman with the same rank as a viscount.

vise (*US*) ⇨ **vice**².

visible /'vɪzəbl/ *adj* that can be seen. **visibility** /ˌvɪzə'bɪlətɪ/ *n* [U] condition of the light or weather for seeing things clearly over a distance. **visibly** *adv* clearly.

vision /'vɪʒn/ *n* 1 [U] power of seeing. 2 [U] wisdom in planning the future: *problems caused by lack of ~.* 3 [C] imaginary picture in the mind: *~ s of great wealth.* **visionary** /'vɪʒənrɪ; *US* -ʒənerɪ/ *adj* 1 having or showing vision(2). 2 too grand to be practical. **visionary** *n* [C] (*pl* **-ies**) visionary person.

visit /'vɪzɪt/ *v* 1 [I, T] go to see (a person or place): *~ a friend/Rome.* 2 [T] go to (a place) to inspect it officially. 3 [I] *with// (US)* visit sb, esp for an informal talk. **visit** *n* [C] act or time of visiting: *pay a ~ to a friend.* **visitor** *n* [C] person who visits.

visor /'vaɪzə(r)/ *n* [C] movable part of a helmet, covering the face.

vista /'vɪstə/ *n* [C] (*fml*) 1 distant view. 2 (*fig*) series of scenes or events: *scientific discoveries that open up a new ~ s of the future.*

visual /'vɪʒuəl/ *adj* of or concerning sight. **visual 'aid** *n* [C] picture, film, video, etc used eg in teaching. **visual dis'play unit** *n* [C] machine with a screen, on which information from a computer, etc is shown. **visualize** *v* [T] form a mental picture of. **visually** *adv*.

vital /'vaɪtl/ *adj* 1 necessary or very important: *a ~ part of the*

machine. 2 lively and exciting. 3 of or concerned with life. **vitality** /vaɪ'tælətɪ/ *n* [U] liveliness. **vitally** /-təlɪ/ *adv.* **vital sta'tistics** *n* [pl] (*infml*) measurements round a woman's bust, waist and hips.

vitamin /'vɪtəmɪn; *US* 'vaɪt-/ *n* [C] chemical substance present in certain foods and necessary for health.

vitriolic /ˌvɪtrɪ'ɒlɪk/ *adj* (*fml*) savagely bitter or hostile.

vivacious /vɪ'veɪʃəs/ *adj* lively and exciting. **vivaciously** *adv.* **vivacity** /vɪ'væsɪtɪ/ *n* [U].

vivid /'vɪvɪd/ *adj* 1 (of light or colour) strong and bright. 2 very clear and strong: *a ~ description.* **vividly** *adv.*

vivisection /ˌvɪvɪ'sekʃn/ *n* [U] experiments on living animals for scientific research.

vixen /'vɪksn/ *n* [C] female fox.

vocabulary /və'kæbjʊlərɪ; *US* -lerɪ/ (*pl* **-ies**) *n* 1 [C] total number of words in a language. 2 [C] words known to a person: *the ~ of a three-year-old.* 3 [C] list of words with their meanings, esp at the back of a book used for teaching a foreign language.

vocal /'vəʊkl/ *adj* 1 of, for or produced by the voice. 2 expressing one's opinions freely and loudly. **vocal** *n* [C, usu pl] singing in a pop song. **vocal 'cords** *n* [pl] voice-producing part of the larynx. **vocalist** /-kəlɪst/ *n* [C] singer. **vocally** /-kəlɪ/ *adv.*

vocation /vəʊ'keɪʃn/ *n* [C, U] 1 strong feeling that one is called to a certain kind of work: *She thinks nursing is her ~.* 2 (*fml*) person's job or profession. **vocational** /-ʃənl/ *adj* of or for a job: *~al training.*

vociferous /və'sɪfərəs/ *adj* expressing one's views in a loud insistent voice: *a ~ group of demonstrators.* **vociferously** *adv.*

vodka /'vɒdkə/ *n* [U] strong Russian alcoholic drink.

vogue /vəʊɡ/ *n* [C, U] popular fashion: *a new ~ for low-heeled shoes.*

voice /vɔɪs/ *n* 1 (a) [C] sounds made when speaking or singing: *recognize sb's ~.* (b) [U] ability to produce such sounds: *He's lost his ~, ie he cannot speak.* 2 [U, sing] (right to express) one's opinion: *They should be allowed a ~ in deciding their future.* **voice** *v* [T] express (feelings, etc) in words.

void /vɔɪd/ *n* [C, usu sing] empty space. **void** *adj* (*fml*) 1 empty. 2 *of// without sth.* 3 having no legal value. **void** v [T] (*law*) make void.

volatile /'vɒlətaɪl; US -tl/ *adj* likely to change (in mood or behaviour) suddenly and unexpectedly.

vol au vent /'vɒləvɒːŋ/ *n* [C] small light pastry case filled with meat, fish, etc in a rich sauce.

volcano /vɒl'keɪnəʊ/ *n* [C] (*pl* ~es) mountain with an opening (= CRATER) from which hot melted rock, gas, etc burst out. **volcanic** /-'kænɪk/ *adj*.

volition /və'lɪʃn; US vəʊ-/ *n* (*idm*) **of one's own volition** (*fml*) because one has decided to, without being forced.

volley /'vɒlɪ/ *n* [C] **1** many shots fired at the same time. **2** (in tennis, football, etc) shot or stroke in which the ball is hit before it touches the ground. **volley** v **1** [I] (of guns) fire in a volley. **2** [I, T] hit (a ball) in a volley(2). **'volley-ball** *n* [U] game in which a ball is thrown over a net.

volt /vəʊlt/ *n* [C] unit of electrical force. **voltage** *n* [U, C] electrical force measured in volts.

voluble /'vɒljʊbl/ *adj* (*fml*) talking a lot. **volubly** *adv*.

volume /'vɒljuːm; US -jəm/ *n* **1** [C] book, esp one of a set of books. **2** [U, C] amount of space occupied by a substance. **3** [U] amount: *the ~ of exports fell last month.* **4** [U] (control for the) amount of sound of a radio, television, etc.

voluminous /və'luːmɪnəs/ *adj* (*fml*) **1** (of clothes) using a lot of material: *the ~ folds of a blanket.* **2** (of writing) great in quantity.

voluntary /'vɒləntrɪ; US 'terɪ/ *adj* **1** acting, done or given willingly, without being forced: *Attendance is ~.* **2** working or done without payment: *a ~ organization.* **voluntarily** /-trəlɪ; US ˌvɒlən'terəlɪ/ *adv*.

volunteer /ˌvɒlən'tɪə(r)/ *n* [C] **1** person who offers to do sth without being forced or paid. **2** person who joins the armed forces voluntarily. **volunteer** v **1** [I, T] give or offer (sth) willingly or without being paid. **2** [I] *for/* join the armed forces voluntarily.

voluptuous /və'lʌptʃʊəs/ *adj* (*fml*) **1** (of a woman) having a full and sexually desirable figure. **2** giving rich pleasure to the senses. **voluptuously** *adv*.

vomit /'vɒmɪt/ v [I, T] bring back (food, etc from the stomach) through the mouth. **vomit** *n* [U] food, etc from the stomach that has been vomited.

vote /vəʊt/ *n* **1** [C] formal expression of one's opinion, esp by marking a piece of paper or raising one's hand. **2** the **vote** [sing] votes given by or for a certain group, eg at an election: *the Labour ~.* **3** the **vote** [sing] right to vote in political elections. **vote** v **1** [I, T] formally express an opinion by voting: *~ for/against sb ○ ~ on the suggestion.* **2** [T] decide to spend (money) on sth. **voter** *n* [C].

vouch /vaʊtʃ/ v [I] *for/* express confidence and take responsibility for sb, his/her good behaviour, etc.

voucher /'vaʊtʃə(r)/ *n* [C] piece of paper that can be exchanged for certain goods or services.

vow /vaʊ/ *n* [C] solemn promise. **vow** v [T] make a vow about (sth).

vowel /'vaʊəl/ *n* [C] (a) speech-sound made without stopping of the breath by the tongue, lips, etc. (b) letter used for representing one of these, eg *a, e, i, o* and *u*.

voyage /'vɔɪɪdʒ/ *n* [C] long journey on a ship or in a spacecraft. **voyage** v [I] (*fml*) go on a voyage. **voyager** *n* [C].

vs *abbr* versus.

vulgar /'vʌlgə(r)/ *adj* **1** very rude or offensive. **2** showing a lack of good quality in appearance, style, etc. **vulgarity** /vʌl'gærətɪ/ *n* [U].

vulnerable /'vʌlnərəbl/ *adj* **1** easily attacked. **2** (of a person) easily hurt or harmed; sensitive. **vulnerability** /ˌvʌlnərə'bɪlətɪ/ *n* [U].

vulture /'vʌltʃə(r)/ *n* [C] **1** large bird that eats the flesh of dead animals. **2** (*fig*) greedy person who makes a profit from the misfortunes of others.

vying ⇨ VIE.

W w

W, w /'dʌbljuː/ *n* [C] (*pl* **W's, w's** /'dʌbljuːz/) the twenty-third letter of the English alphabet.

W *abbr* **1** west(ern): *W Yorkshire.* **2** watt(s).

wad /wɒd/ *n* [C] **1** thick bundle of papers, banknotes, etc. **2** mass of soft loose material: *a ~ of cotton wool.*

waddle /'wɒdl/ v [I] walk with short swaying steps, as a duck does. **waddle** *n* [sing].

wade /weɪd/ v **1** [I] walk with an effort through water. **2** (phr v) **wade into sth** begin to deal with sth in a determined way. **wade through sth** read (a long book, report, etc) with a lot of effort. **wading-bird** (also **wader**) n [C] long-legged water-bird that wades in shallow water to find food.

wafer /'weɪfə(r)/ n [C] thin crisp sweet biscuit, eaten with ice-cream.

waffle[1] /'wɒfl/ v [I] (Brit infml) talk or write, esp a lot, without saying anything important or sensible. **waffle** n [U].

waffle[2] /'wɒfl/ n [C] small crisp pancake with a pattern of raised squares.

waft /wɒft; US wæft/ v [I, T] move lightly and smoothly through the air: The scent ~ed into the room. **waft** n [C].

wag /wæg/ v (**-gg-**) [I, T] shake from side to side: The dog ~ged its tail. **wag** n [C].

wage[1] /weɪdʒ/ n [C] (usu pl) regular (usu weekly or monthly) payment for work: fight for higher ~s ○ a ~ increase.

wage[2] /weɪdʒ/ v [T] (against/on)) start and carry on (a war, campaign, etc): ~ a war on poverty.

wager /'weɪdʒə(r)/ n [C], v [I, T] (dated or fml) = BET.

waggle /'wægl/ v [I, T] move with short movements from side to side or up and down.

wagon (Brit also **waggon**) /'wægən/ n [C] 1 four-wheeled vehicle for carrying heavy loads, pulled by horses. 2 open railway truck for carrying goods, eg coal.

wail /weɪl/ v (a) [I, T] cry in a loud voice: a ~ing child. (b) [I] make a similar sound, eg of a siren or the wind. **wail** n [C] wailing cry.

waist /weɪst/ n [C] 1 part of the body between the ribs and the hips. 2 narrow middle part of a garment or device. **waistcoat** /'weɪstkəʊt; US 'weskət/ n [C] sleeveless garment worn under a jacket. '**waistline** n [C] measurement of the body around the waist.

wait[1] /weɪt/ v 1 [I] stay where one is, not do anything, etc, until sth happens: We had to ~ an hour for the train. ○ I'm ~ing to see the manager. ○ I can't ~ (ie I am impatient with excitement) to tell her! 2 [T] be ready for: He is ~ing his opportunity. 3 [I] not be dealt with immediately: The matter isn't urgent; it can ~. 4 (idm) , **wait** and 'see wait and find out what will happen before acting. **wait on sb hand and 'foot** do everything that sb wants. 5 (phr v) **wait on sb** serve food to sb in a restaurant.

wait up (for sb) not go to bed until sb comes home. **waiter** (fem **waitress** /'weɪtrɪs/) n [C] person who serves food and drink in a restaurant. '**waiting-list** n [C] list of people who will be served, treated, etc later. '**waiting-room** n [C] room in a station, doctor's surgery, etc where people wait.

wait[2] /weɪt/ n [C, usu sing] act or time of waiting: We had a long ~ for the bus.

waive /weɪv/ v [T] (fml) not insist on (a rule or right) in a particular situation: ~ a fee.

wake[1] /weɪk/ v (pt **woke** /wəʊk/, pp **woken** /'wəʊkən/) 1 [I, T] (up)/ (cause sb to) stop sleeping: What time did you ~ up? 2 (idm) **one's 'waking hours** time when one is awake. 3 (phr v) **wake up to sth** become aware of (a problem, etc).

wake[2] /weɪk/ n [C] 1 track left by a moving ship. 2 (idm) **in the 'wake of sth** coming after or following sth.

waken /'weɪkən/ v [I, T] (fml) = WAKE[1].

walk[1] /wɔːk/ v 1 [I] move on foot, not having both feet off the ground at the same time. 2 [T] walk with (sb) somewhere: I'll ~ you home. 3 [T] take (one's dog) for a walk. 4 (phr v) **walk away/off with sth** (infml) (a) win (a prize) easily. (b) steal sth. **walk into sth** (infml) (a) become caught in (an unpleasant situation), esp because one is careless: ~ into a trap. (b) get (a job) very easily. **walk out** (infml) (of workers) go on strike. **walk out (of sth)** leave (a meeting, etc) suddenly and angrily. **walk out on sb** (infml) leave sb, ending one's relationship with him/her. **walk over sb** (infml) treat sb badly. '**walkabout** n [C] informal walk by an important person, eg a president, among a crowd. **walker** n [C]. '**walking-stick** n [C] long wooden stick used as a support when walking. '**Walkman** n [C] (pl ~**s**) (P) small cassette recorder that has very light headphones and on which people can listen to music as they walk, etc. ,**walk-'on** adj (of a part in a play) small and with no words to say. '**walk-out** n [C] sudden strike by workers. '**walk-over** n [C] easy victory.

walk[2] /wɔːk/ n 1 [C] journey on foot: My house is a five-minute ~ from the shops. 2 [sing] manner of walking: a slow ~. 3 [C] path for walking on. 4 (idm) **a walk of 'life** a job or profession.

walkie-talkie /,wɔːkɪ 'tɔːkɪ/

n [C] (*infml*) portable radio transmitter and receiver.

wall /wɔːl/ *n* [C] 1 vertical solid structure of stone, brick, etc that encloses, divides or protects sth. 2 vertical side of a room or building. 3 (*fig*) something like a wall in appearance or effect: *a ~ of fire* ○ *the abdominal ~*. 4 (idm) **go to the 'wall** be defeated or ruined, esp financially. **up the 'wall** (*infml*) very angry: *That noise is driving me up the ~!*, ie making me very angry. **wall** *v* 1 [T] surround with a wall: *a ~ed garden*. 2 (phr v) **wall sth in/off** separate (and enclose) with a wall. **wall sth up** block sth with a wall or bricks. '**wallflower** *n* [C] garden plant with sweet-smelling flowers. '**wallpaper** *n* [U] paper, usu with a coloured design, for covering the walls of a room. '**wallpaper** *v* [T] cover the walls of (a room) with wallpaper. **wall-to'wall** *adj* covering the whole floor of a room.

wallet /'wɒlɪt/ *n* [C] small flat case, esp for carrying banknotes and credit cards.

wallop /'wɒləp/ *v* [T] (*infml*) hit (sb) very hard.

wallow /'wɒləʊ/ *v* [I] (*in*)) 1 roll about in mud, etc. 2 (*fig*) take pleasure in sth: *~ in luxury/self-pity.*

Wall Street /'wɔːl striːt/ *n* [U] centre of American business and finance, in New York.

wally /'wɒlɪ/ *n* [C] (*pl* **-ies**) (*Brit infml*) fool.

walnut /'wɔːlnʌt/ *n* (a) [C] (tree producing a) large nut with a divided shell. (b) [U] wood of this tree, used for making furniture.

walrus /'wɔːlrəs/ *n* [C] large sea-animal with two long tusks.

waltz /wɔːls; *US* wɔːlts/ *n* [C] (music for a) slow ballroom dance. **waltz** *v* [I] dance a waltz.

wand /wɒnd/ *n* [C] long thin stick as used by a magician.

wander /'wɒndə(r)/ *v* 1 [I, T] move around with no special purpose: *~ round the town* ○ *~ the streets.* 2 [I] move away from the subject. **wanderer** *n* [C]. **wanderings** *n* [pl] journeys from place to place.

wane /weɪn/ *v* [I] 1 (of the moon) show a decreasing bright area. 2 become weaker. **wane** *n* (idm) **on the wane** becoming weaker.

wangle /'wæŋgl/ *v* [T] (*infml*) get (sth that one wants) by a trick or clever persuasion: *~ an extra week's holiday.*

want¹ /wɒnt; *US* wɔːnt/ *v* [T] 1

have a desire for: *They ~ a new car.* ○ *I ~ to go home.* 2 need or require: *The grass ~ s cutting.* 3 to// should: *You ~ to be more careful.* 4 (*fml*) lack. 5 search for; hunt: *He is ~ed by the police.* 6 (idm) **be found wanting** be shown to be not reliable or not able to do (sth). 7 (phr v) **want for** suffer because of a lack of sth: *They ~ for nothing*, ie they have everything they need.

want² /wɒnt; *US* wɔːnt/ *n* 1 [C, usu pl] something wanted. 2 [sing, U] (*fml*) lack of sth: *die from/for ~ of water.*

war /wɔː(r)/ *n* [C, U] 1 (instance or period of) armed fighting between countries: *the First World W~* ○ *at ~.* 2 (*fig*) struggle or competition: *a trade ~* ○ *the ~ on drugs.* 3 (idm) **have been in the 'wars** (*infml*) show signs of having been injured. **warfare** /'wɔːfeə(r)/ *n* [U] (fighting a) war. '**war-game** *n* [C] mock battle used as a training exercise. '**warhead** *n* [C] explosive front end of a missile. '**warring** *adj* fighting in a war: *~ring tribes.* '**warlike** *adj* 1 ready for war. 2 fond of war; aggressive. '**war-path** *n* (idm) **on the 'war-path** (*infml*) ready for a fight or quarrel. '**warship** *n* [C] ship for use in war. '**wartime** *n* [U] period of war.

warble /'wɔːbl/ *v* [I, T] (esp of a bird) sing with a gentle trilling note. **warbler** *n* [C] bird that warbles.

ward /wɔːd/ *n* [C] 1 separate room in a hospital. 2 division of a local government area. 3 person, usu a child, under the protection of a guardian. **ward** *v* (phr v) **ward sth off** keep away (sth dangerous or unpleasant).

warden /'wɔːdn/ *n* [C] person in charge of sth: *the ~ of a youth hostel.*

warder /'wɔːdə(r)/ *n* [C] (*fem* **wardress** /'wɔːdrɪs/) (*Brit*) guard in a prison.

wardrobe /'wɔːdrəʊb/ *n* [C] 1 tall cupboard for hanging clothes in. 2 [usu sing] person's collection of clothes. 3 costumes of a theatre company.

ware /weə(r)/ *n* 1 [U] (esp in compounds) manufactured goods of the kind that is mentioned: *'silver~.* 2 **wares** [pl] (*dated*) articles offered for sale. '**warehouse** *n* [C] large building for storing goods.

warm /wɔːm/ *adj* 1 fairly hot; between cool and hot: *~ water.* 2 (of clothes) keeping the body warm: *a ~ jumper.* 3 friendly and kind: *a ~ welcome*. 4 (of colours) pleasant and bright. **warm** *v* 1 [I, T] (cause to) become warm. 2 (phr v) **warm to sb/sth** (a) begin to like sb. (b) become more interested in sth. **warm up** practise before a game. **warm (sth) up** (cause sth to) become more lively. **ˌwarm-ˈblooded** *adj* (of animals) having a constant blood temperature. **ˌwarm-ˈhearted** *adj* kind. **warmly** *adv*. **warmth** *n* [U] state of being warm.

warn /wɔːn/ *v* [T] tell (sb) in advance about a possible danger or difficulty: *I ~ed her that it would cost a lot.* ○ *They were ~ed not to climb the mountain in bad weather.* **warning** *n* [C, U] statement that warns: *He didn't listen to my ~ing. warning signals.* **warning** *adj* that warns: *~ing signals.*

warp /wɔːp/ *v* 1 [I, T] (cause) to become bent or twisted: *Some wood ~s in hot weather.* 2 [T] (*fig*) have a bad influence on: *a ~ed mind.* **warp** *n* [C, usu sing] warped condition.

warrant /ˈwɒrənt; US ˈwɔːr-/ *n* [C] written order giving authority to do sth: *a ~ for his arrest.* **warrant** *v* [T] (*fml*) cause to seem unnecessary or right. **warranty** *n* [U, C] (*pl* **-ies**) (written or printed) guarantee.

warren /ˈwɒrən; US ˈwɔːrən/ *n* [C] 1 area of land with many holes, in which rabbits live and breed. 2 (*fig*) building or district in which it is easy to lose one's way.

warrior /ˈwɒrɪə(r); US ˈwɔːr-/ *n* [C] (*fml*) (esp formerly) soldier; fighter.

wart /wɔːt/ *n* [C] small hard lump on the skin.

wary /ˈweərɪ/ *adj* (**-ier**, **-iest**) looking out for possible danger or difficulty. **warily** *adv*.

was ⇨ BE.

wash¹ /wɒʃ/ *v* 1 [I] make clean with water or other liquid: *~ one's hands/clothes.* 2 [I] clean one's body: *I had to ~ and dress in a hurry.* 3 [I] (of materials) be able to be washed without damage: *Does this sweater ~ well?* 4 [I, T] move by flowing or carrying gently: *Pieces of the wrecked boat were ~ed to the shore.* 5 [I] (*infml*) be accepted or believed: *That argument/excuse just won't ~.* 6 (idm) **wash one's hands of sth** refuse to be involved with or responsible for sth any longer. 7 (phr v) **wash sth away** (of water) remove or carry sth away to another place. **wash sth down** (a) clean sth by using a lot of water. (b)

drink sth while or after eating food. **wash sth out** (a) wash (the inside of sth) to remove dirt. (b) (of rain) bring (a game) to an end or prevent it from starting. **wash (sth) up** wash (plates, cutlery, etc) after a meal. **washable** *adj* that can be washed without being damaged. **ˈwash-basin** *n* [C] fixed bowl for washing one's hands and face. **ˌwashed ˈout** *adj* 1 faded. 2 pale and tired. **ˌwashing-ˈup** *n* [U] washing of plates, cutlery, etc after a meal. **ˌwashing-ˈup liquid** *n* [U] thick soapy liquid used with hot water for washing dishes, etc. **ˈwash-out** *n* [C] (*infml*) complete failure. **ˈwashroom** *n* [C] (*US*) toilet.

wash² /wɒʃ/ *n* 1 [C, usu sing] act of washing: *give the car a good ~.* 2 **the wash** [sing] clothes (to be) washed. 3 [sing] movement of water caused by a passing boat.

washer /ˈwɒʃə(r); US ˈwɒʃ-/ *n* [C] 1 small flat ring of metal, plastic, etc for making a screw or joint tight. 2 (*infml*) machine that washes.

washing /ˈwɒʃɪŋ; US ˈwɔːʃ-/ *n* [U] 1 clothes (to be) washed. 2 act of washing. **ˈwashing-machine** *n* [C] machine for washing clothes. **ˈwashing-powder** *n* [U] soap in the form of powder for washing clothes.

wasn't /ˈwɒznt; US ˈwʌznt/ was not. ⇨ BE.

wasp /wɒsp/ *n* [C] flying insect with black and yellow stripes and a sting in its tail.

wastage /ˈweɪstɪdʒ/ *n* [U] 1 amount wasted. 2 reduction in numbers: *natural ~.*

waste¹ /weɪst/ *v* [T] 1 use too much (esp time or money) on sth that is not important or useful. 2 not make full use of: *~ an opportunity.* 3 (*fml*) make weaker and thinner.

waste² /weɪst/ *n* 1 [U, sing] (act of) wasting or being wasted: *a ~ of time.* 2 [U] material, food, etc that is no longer needed: *industrial ~.* 3 [U, C, usu pl] large area of unused or unusable land: *the ~s of the Sahara.* 4 (idm) **go/run to waste** be wasted. **waste** *adj* 1 (of land) not (fit to be) used: *~ ground.* 2 no longer useful and to be thrown away: *~ -paper.* **wasteful** *adj* causing waste: *~ful processes.* **wastefully** *adv*. **ˌwaste-ˈpaper basket** *n* [C] container for paper, etc to be thrown away.

watch¹ /wɒtʃ/ *v* 1 [I, T] look at (sb/sth) carefully for a period of time. 2 [T] (*infml*) be careful

about: ~ one's language/manners.
3 (idm) **watch one's step** ⇨ STEP¹.
4 (phr v) **watch 'out** be careful.
watch over sb/sth protect and
guard sb/sth; take care of. **watch-
er** n [C].

watch² /wɒtʃ/ n 1 [C] small clock
worn on the wrist. 2 [sing, U] act of
watching: *keep (a) close ~ on her.* 3
[sing] person or group whose job
is to watch sb/sth. 4 [C] period of
duty on a ship. **'watch-dog** n [C] 1
dog kept to guard property. 2 (*fig*)
person or committee that guards
people's rights. **watchful** adj
watching closely. **'watchman**
/-mən/ n [C] (*pl* **-men** /-mən/) person whose job is to guard a building, esp at night. **'watchword**
n [C] word or phrase that expresses a group's principle or
guide.

water¹ /'wɔːtə(r)/ n 1 (a) [U] clear
colourless liquid that falls as rain,
is found in rivers, etc and is used
for drinking. (b) [U] this liquid as
supplied to homes, etc in pipes. (c)
[sing] mass of this liquid; lake,
river, etc: *He fell in the ~ and
drowned.* (d) [sing] surface of a
sea, lake, etc: *swim under ~.* 2
waters [pl] (a) mass of water in a
lake, etc. (b) sea near a particular
country: *in British ~s.* 3 (idm) **under 'water** flooded. **'water-
cannon** n [C] machine that
produces a powerful jet of water,
used for breaking up crowds.
'water-closet n [C] (*dated*) toilet.
'water-colour (*US* **-color**) n (a)
water-colours [pl] paints mixed
with water, not oil. (b) [C] picture
painted with such paints. **'water-
cress** n [U] plant that grows in
running water, with leaves used
as food. **'waterfall** n [C] very steep
fall of water over a cliff. **'water-
front** n [C, usu sing] street or part
of a town next to a harbour, the
sea, etc. **'water-hole** n [C] pool in a
dry area to which animals go to
drink. **waterlogged** /-lɒgd; *US*
-lɔːgd/ adj 1 (of land) extremely
wet. 2 (of a boat) full of water.
'watermark n [C] design in some
kinds of paper that can be seen
when the paper is held up to the
light. **'water-melon** n [C] large
round green fruit with juicy pink
flesh. **'water-mill** n [C] mill powered by moving water. **'waterproof** n [C], adj (coat) that does
not let water through. **waterproof** v [T] make waterproof.
'watershed n [C] 1 high land
separating river systems. 2 (*fig*)
point at which very important
changes happen. **'waterside**

n [sing] edge of a river, lake, etc.
'water-ski v [I] ski on water while
being pulled along by a boat. **'wa-
ter-skiing** n [U]. **'water-table**
n [C] level below which the ground
is filled with water. **'watertight**
adj 1 not allowing water to pass
through. 2 (*fig*) (of an agreement,
etc) allowing no escape or misunderstanding. **'waterway** n [C]
route, eg a canal, that ships can
sail along. **'waterworks** n [also
sing with pl v] 1 building with
pumping machinery, etc for supplying water to an area. 2 (idm)
turn on the 'waterworks (*infml
derog*) begin to cry.

water² /'wɔːtə(r)/ v 1 [T] pour
water on: ~ *the lawn.* 2 [T] give
water to (an animal). 3 [I] (of the
eyes or mouth) fill with water. 4
(phr v) **water sth down** (a) make
(a liquid) weaker by adding water.
(b) (*fig*) weaken the effect of: ~
down a speech. **'watering-can**
n [C] container with a long spout,
used for watering plants.

watery /'wɔːtəri/ adj 1 containing too much water. 2 (of colours)
pale; weak.

watt /wɒt/ n [C] unit of electrical
power.

wave /weɪv/ v 1 [I, T] move (one's
hand) from side to side as a greeting. 2 [T] signal with one's hand to
(sb) to move in the direction that is
mentioned: *The guard ~d us on.* 3
[T] hold (sth) in one's hand,
moving it from side to side: ~ *a
flag.* 4 [I] move gently up and
down or from side to side: *branches ~ing in the wind.* 5 (phr v)
wave sth aside show that sth is
not at all important. **wave** n [C] 1
long ridge of water, esp on the sea.
2 waving movement: *with a ~ of
his hand.* 3 curve like a wave: *the
~s in her hair.* 4 sudden increase
(and spread): *a ~of panic.* 5 form
in which heat, light, etc is carried:
radio ~s. **'wavelength** n [C] 1 distance between corresponding
points on a series of waves(s)(5). 2
length of radio wave of a particular station. **wavy** adj (-ier,
-iest) having curves: *a wavy line*
wavy hair.

waver /'weɪvə(r)/ v [I] 1 be or become weak or unsteady. 2 hesitate
about making a decision. 3 move
unsteadily.

wax¹ /wæks/ n [U] soft easily
melted sticky or oily substance
used for making candles, polish,
etc. **wax** v [T] put wax on, esp as
polish: ~ *the floor.*

wax² /wæks/ v [I] 1 (of the moon)
show an increasing bright area. 2

(*rhet*) grow or become: ~ *eloquent*.

way¹ /weɪ/ *n* 1 [C] method of doing sth: *the best* ~ *to help people.* 2 [sing] manner: *the rude* ~ *in which he spoke to us.* 3 [C] particular aspect of sth; point: *In some* ~ *s, I agree with you.* 4 **ways** [pl] habits: *She is not going to change her* ~ *s.* 5 [C] road, path, etc. 6 [C] route to be taken to reach a place: *ask sb the* ~ *to the airport.* 7 [sing] direction: *He went the other* ~. 8 [sing] distance: *It's a long* ~ *to London.* 9 [sing] (after a *v*) movement or progress: *He made his* ~ (ie He went) *home.* 10 (idm) **by the 'way** (used for introducing a new subject when talking). **by way of sth** (*fml*) as a kind of sth: *say something by* ~ *of introduction.* **get/ have one's (own) 'way** get or do what one wants, often in spite of opposition. **give 'way** break or collapse. **give way to sb/sth (a)** allow sb/sth to go first. **(b)** be replaced by sth: *Sorrow gave* ~ *to smiles.* **(c)** allow sb to have sth that one does not want him/her to have: *give* ~ *to their demands.* **go out of one's way (to do sth)** take particular care and trouble to do sth. **go one's own 'way** do what one wants. **make 'way (for sb/ sth)** allow sb/sth to pass. **no 'way** (*infml*) certainly not; no. **on one's 'way** in the process of going or coming. **out of the 'way (a)** finished. **(b)** distant. **(c)** uncommon. **out of/in the 'way** not causing/ causing a blockage of space or inconvenience. **under 'way** having started and making progress. **way of 'life** typical beliefs, habits and behaviour of a person or group.

way² /weɪ/ *adv* (*infml*) very far: *She finished the race* ~ *ahead of the others.* **way-'out** *adj* (*infml*) unusual or strange.

waylay /ˌweɪˈleɪ/ *v* (*pt, pp* **-laid** /-ˈleɪd/) [T] wait for and stop (sb), esp in order to question or rob him/her.

wayward /ˈweɪwəd/ *adj* not easily controlled: *a* ~ *child.*

WC /ˌdʌbljuː ˈsiː/ *abbr* water-closet, toilet.

we /wiː/ *pron* (used as the subject of a *v*) I and another or others: *We are all going to visit him.*

weak /wiːk/ *adj* 1 lacking strength or power: *still* ~ *after his illness.* 2 easily bent, broken or defeated: *a* ~ *joint/seam.* 3 easily influenced by others; not strong: *a* ~ *leader.* 4 not convincing: *a* ~ *argument.* 5 not easily seen; faint: ~ *sound/light.* 6 not good: ~ *at mathematics.* 7 containing too

much water: ~ *tea.* **weaken** *v* [I, T] become or make weak. **weak-'kneed** *adj* (*fig*) lacking courage; unable to make decisions. **weakling** /ˈwiːklɪŋ/ *n* [C] (*derog*) weak person. **weakly** *adv.* **weakness** *n* 1 [U] state of being weak. 2 [C] fault or defect: *We all have our little* ~ *nesses.* 3 [C] strong liking: *a* ~ *for cream cakes.*

wealth /welθ/ *n* 1 [U] (possession of a) large amount of money, property, etc. 2 [sing] (*fml*) large amount: *a book with a* ~ *of illustrations.* **wealthy** *adj* (**-ier, -iest**) rich.

wean /wiːn/ *v* 1 [T] gradually stop feeding (a baby) with its mother's milk and start giving it solid food. 2 (phr *v*) **wean sb from sth** cause sb to stop doing sth gradually.

weapon /ˈwepən/ *n* [C] something, eg a gun, bomb or sword, used in fighting. **weaponry** *n* [U] weapons.

wear /weə(r)/ *v* (*pt* **wore** /wɔː(r)/, *pp* **worn** /wɔːn/) 1 [T] have (esp clothes) on the body: ~ *a dress.* 2 [T] have (a particular look) on one's face: ~ *a smile.* 3 [I, T] (cause to) become damaged or useless by being used: *The carpets are starting to* ~. 4 [I] be capable of lasting: *These shoes have worn well.* 5 [T] (*infml*) accept or tolerate. 6 (phr *v*) **wear (sth) away** (cause sth to) become thin, damaged, etc by constant use. **wear (sth) down** (cause sth to) become gradually smaller, thinner, etc. **wear sb down** weaken sb. **wear off** disappear gradually. **wear on** (of time) pass, esp slowly. **wear (sth) out** (cause sth to) become useless because of constant wear or use. **wear sb out** tire sb greatly.

wear² /weə(r)/ *n* [U] 1 wearing or being worn: *a dress for evening* ~. 2 clothes: *mens* ~. 3 damage or loss of quality from use: *The carpet is showing signs of* ~. 4 capacity for continuing to be used: *There's a lot of* ~ *in these shoes.* 5 (idm) **wear and 'tear** damage, etc caused by ordinary use.

weary /ˈwɪərɪ/ *adj* (**-ier, -iest**) very tired. **wearily** *adv.* **weariness** *n* [U]. **weary** *v* (*pt, pp* **-ied**) [I, T] (*of*) become or make weary.

weasel /ˈwiːzl/ *n* [C] small fierce animal with reddish-brown fur.

weather /ˈweðə(r)/ *n* 1 [U] condition of sun, wind, temperature, etc at a particular area and time. 2 (idm) **under the 'weather** (*infml*) slightly ill. **'weather-beaten** *adj* tanned, roughened, etc by the sun and the wind. **'weather forecast** *n* [C] statement of what the weather is expected to be. **'weatherman** *n* [C] (*pl* -**men** /-men/) (*infml*) person who forecasts the weather, esp on television or radio. **'weatherproof** *adj* that keeps out rain, wind, etc. **'weather-vane** *n* [C] pointer on the top of a building that turns round to show the direction of the wind.

weather² /'weðə(r)/ *v* 1 [I, T] (cause sth to) change shape or colour because of the sun, rain, etc. 2 [T] come safely through: ~ *a storm/crisis*.

weave /wi:v/ *v* (*pt* **wove** /wəʊv/ or in sense 4 ~**d**, *pp* **woven** /'wəʊvn/ or in sense 4 ~**d**) 1 [I, T] make (cloth) by passing threads over and under each other. 2 [T] twist (eg twigs or flowers) to form (sth): ~ *flowers into a wreath*. 3 [T] (*fig*) compose (a story). 4 [I, T] move along by twisting and turning to avoid obstructions: ~ *through the traffic*. **weave** *n* [C] way in which material is woven. **weaver** *n* [C].

web /web/ *n* [C] 1 net of fine threads made by a spider. 2 (*fig*) complicated structure. 3 skin joining the toes of ducks, frogs, etc. **webbed** *adj* having the toes joined by webs.

wed /wed/ *v* (*pt, pp* -**ded** or **wed**) [I, T] (*esp dated*) marry.

we'd /wi:d/ 1 we had. ⇨ HAVE. 2 we would. ⇨ WILL¹, WOULD¹.

wedding /'wedɪŋ/ *n* [C] marriage ceremony. **'wedding-ring** *n* [C] ring worn to show one is married.

wedge /wedʒ/ *n* [C] 1 V-shaped piece of wood, metal, etc used for splitting sth or to keep two things separate. 2 something shaped like a wedge: *a ~ of cake*. **wedge** *v* [T] fix firmly (as if) with a wedge: ~ *the door open*.

wedlock /'wedlɒk/ *n* [U] (*dated*) being married.

Wednesday /'wenzdɪ/ *n* [U, C] the fourth day of the week, next after Tuesday. (See examples of use at *Monday*).

wee /wi:/ *adj* (*Scot*) little.

weed /wi:d/ *n* [C] 1 unwanted wild plant. 2 (*infml*) thin weak person. **weed** *v* 1 [I, T] remove weeds from (the ground). 2 (*phr v*) **weed sth/sb out** get rid of sth/sb: ~ *out the lazy students*. **weedy** *adj* (-**ier**, -**iest**) 1 full of weeds. 2 (*infml*) thin and weak.

week /wi:k/ *n* [C] 1 period of seven days, esp from Sunday to Saturday. 2 period spent at work in a week: *a 35-hour week*. 3 (*idm*)

,**week after 'week, week in, week 'out** every week. **'weekday** *n* [C] any day except (Saturday and) Sunday. ,**week'end** *n* [C] Saturday and Sunday. **weekly** *adj, adv* happening or appearing every week or once a week. **weekly** *n* [C] (*pl* -**ies**) newspaper or magazine that is published once a week.

weep /wi:p/ *v* (*pt, pp* **wept** /wept/) [I, T] (*fml*) cry. **weeping** *adj* (of a tree) having branches that hang down.

weigh /wei/ *v* [T] 1 measure how heavy (sb/sth) is: *She ~ ed herself on the scales*. 2 have (a certain weight): ~ *10 kilograms*. 3 (*up*)// consider (sth) carefully. 4 compare carefully: ~ *one plan against another*. 5 (*idm*) **weigh 'anchor** raise the anchor at the start of a voyage. 6 (*phr v*) **weigh sb down** (a) make sb carry a heavy load. (b) make sb feel worried or depressed. **weigh in (with sth)** (*infml*) join a discussion, argument, etc by saying (sth important). **weigh on sb** make sb worried. **weigh sth out** measure a quantity of sth.

weight /wei/ *n* 1 [U] (measurement of the) heaviness of sb: *My ~ is 70 kilograms*. 2 [C] piece of metal of known weight: *a 100-gram weight*. 3 [C] heavy object. 4 [C, U] unit by which weight is measured. 5 [U] importance or influence: *opinions that carry ~*. 6 [sing] worry or problem: *feel a great ~ of responsibility*. 7 (*idm*) **be/take a weight off one's mind** ⇨ MIND¹. ,**over/under 'weight** weighing too much/too little. **put on/lose 'weight** (of a person) become heavier/lighter. **weight** *v* [T] 1 (*down*)// make (sth) heavy, esp by fixing weights. 2 (usu passive) organize (sth) so that one person or group has an advantage: *The law is ~ed towards rich people*. **weightless** *adj* having no weight. **'weight-lifting** *n* [U] sport of lifting heavy weights. **'weight-lifter** *n* [C]. **weighty** *adj* (-**ier**, -**iest**) 1 heavy. 2 (*fig*) important or serious.

weir /wɪə(r)/ *n* [C] wall across a river to control its flow.

weird /wɪəd/ *adj* 1 strange; unnatural: ~ *shrieks*. 2 (*infml*) unusual and unconventional. **weirdly** *adv*. **weirdness** *n* [U].

welcome /'welkəm/ *v* [T] 1 greet (sb) in a friendly way when he/she arrives. 2 accept gladly: *The decision has been ~ d by everyone*. **welcome** *interj* (greeting said to sb who has just arrived): *W ~ home!* **welcome** *n* [C] greeting or reception. **welcome** adj **1** received with or giving pleasure: a ~ change. **2** to// allowed freely to do sth: You're ~ to use my car. **3** (idm) **you're 'welcome** (used as a polite reply to thanks).

weld /weld/ v [T] join (pieces of metal) together, when the metal is hot. **weld** n [C] welded joint. **welder** n [C] person who welds.

welfare /'welfeə(r)/ n [U] health, comfort and happiness. the **,welfare 'state** n [sing] system of social services for people who are ill, unemployed, old, etc paid for by the State.

well[1] /wel/ interj (used for showing hesitation, surprise, acceptance, etc): W~, ... I don't know about that. ○ W~, ~, so you've come at last!

well[2] /wel/ adj (**better** /'betə(r)/, **best** /best/) **1** in good health: feel/ get ~. **2** in a satisfactory condition: All is not ~ at home. **3** advisable: It would be ~ to start early.

well[3] /wel/ adv (**better** /'betə(r)/, **best** /best/) **1** in a good, right or satisfactory manner: The children behaved ~. **2** completely or thoroughly: Shake the mixture ~. **3** reasonably: You may ~ be right. **4** to a considerable extent: drive at ~ over the speed limit. **5** (idm) **as well (as sb/sth)** in addition (to sb/ sth). **do 'well** succeed; make progress. **do well to do sth** act wisely in doing sth. **leave/let well a'lone** not interfere with sth satisfactory. **may/might (just) as well do sth** considering the situation, it is reasonable to do sth. **,very 'well** (used for showing agreement, often with some unwillingness). **,well and 'truly** completely. **,well done** (used for expressing praise and congratulations). **well in (with sb)** having a friendly relationship with sb. **well 'off** in a good position, esp financially. **,well 'out of sth** fortunate enough not to be involved with sth. **,well-ad'vised** adj sensible; wise. **,well-'being** n [U] state of being happy, healthy, etc. **,well-'bred** adj having good manners. **,well-con'nected** adj friendly with or related to important or influential people. **,well-'done** adj cooked thoroughly. **,well-'earned** adj fully deserved. **,well-'heeled** adj (infml) rich. **,well-in'formed** adj having wide knowledge. **,well-in'tentioned** adj showing good intentions, but often unsuccessful. **,well-'known** adj known by many people; famous. **,well-'meaning**

adj = WELL-INTENTIONED. **,well-nigh** /,welnaɪ/ adv (fml) almost. **,well-'read** adj having read many books; knowledgeable. **,well-'spoken** adj speaking correctly or in a socially acceptable way. **,well-'timed** adj done, said, etc at the most suitable time. **,well-to-'do** adj rich. **'well-wisher** n [C] person who wishes another success, happiness, etc.

well[4] /wel/ n [C] **1** deep hole dug or drilled to obtain water or oil from under ground. **2** space in a building for a staircase or lift. **well** v [I] (up)// flow or rise like water from a well(1): Tears ~ed up in his eyes.

we'll /wiːl/ **1** we shall. ⇨ SHALL. **2** we will. ⇨ WILL[1].

wellington (also **,wellington 'boot**) /'welɪŋtən/ n [C] waterproof rubber boot that reaches to the knee.

welter /'weltə(r)/ n [sing] confused mix: a ~ of details.

wend /wend/ v (idm) **wend one's way** (arch or poet) walk slowly.

went pt of GO[1].

wept pt, pp of WEEP.

were ⇨ BE.

we're /wɪə(r)/ we are. ⇨ BE.

weren't /wɜːnt/ were not. ⇨ BE.

werewolf /'wɪəwʊlf/ n [C] (pl -**wolves** /-wʊlvz/) (in stories) person who sometimes turns into a wolf.

west /west/ n [sing] **1** the west point on the horizon where the sun sets. **2** the West (a) non-Communist countries of Europe and America. (b) part of a particular country towards the west. **west** adj **1** in or towards the west. **2** (of winds) from the west. **west** adv towards the west. **'west-bound** /'westbaʊnd/ adj travelling towards the west. **westerly** adj, adv **1** in or towards the west. **2** (of winds) from the west. **westward** /'westwəd/ adj towards the west. **westward(s)** adv.

western /'westən/ adj of the west part of the world or of a particular country. **western** n [C] film or book about cowboys, etc in the western USA in the 19th century. **westerner** n [C] person who comes from or lives in the West. **westernize** v [T] introduce the ideas, institutions of the West(2a) into.

wet /wet/ adj (~**ter**, ~**test**) **1** covered or soaked with water or other liquid: ~ clothes/roads. **2** rainy: ~ weather. **3** (of paint, cement, etc) not dry or solid. **4** (infml derog) lacking purpose; weak. **5**

(idm) **a ˌwet ˈblanket** (*infml*) person who prevents others from enjoying themselves. **ˌwet ˈthrough** completely soaked. **wet** *n* 1 **the wet** [sing] wet weather. 2 [C] (*Brit infml*) moderate Conservative politician. **wet** *v* (-**tt**-, *pt*, *pp* **wet** or ~**ted**) [T] make (sth) wet. **ˈwet suit** *n* [C] rubber garment worn by underwater swimmers to keep warm.

we've /wiːv/ we have. ⇨ HAVE.

whack /wæk; *US* hwæk/ *v* [T] hit with a hard noisy blow. **whack** *n* [C] 1 (noise of a) hard blow. 2 (*infml*) share. **whacked** *adj* (*infml*) very tired. **whacking** *n* [C] (*dated infml*) beating. **whacking** *adj* (*infml*) very big.

whale /weɪl; *US* hweɪl/ *n* 1 [C] very large sea-animal hunted for its oil and meat. 2 (idm) **have a ˈwhale of a time** (*infml*) enjoy oneself very much. **whaler** *n* [C] 1 ship used for hunting whales. 2 person who hunts whales. **whaling** *n* [U] hunting whales.

wharf /wɔːf; *US* hwɔːrf/ *n* [C] (*pl* ~**s** or **wharves** /wɔːvz; *US* hwɔːrvz/) place where ships are tied up to load or unload goods.

what /wɒt; *US* hwɒt/ *adj*, *pron* 1 (used in questions for asking information about sb/sth): *W~ time is it?* *W~ are you reading?* 2 the thing(s) that: *Tell me* ~ *happened next.* 3 (used for showing surprise): *W~ a good idea!* 4 (idm) **what about ...?** ⇨ ABOUT¹. **what for** what purpose: *W~ is this tool used for?* *W~ did you do that for?* what if what would happen if. **what's more** what's more important. **what's ˈwhat** what things are useful, important, etc. **what with** sth (used in listing several, esp bad, causes).

whatever /wɒtˈevə(r); *US* hwɒt-/ *adj*, *pron* 1 any or every (thing): *You can eat* ~ *you like.* 2 no matter what: *Keep calm,* ~ *happens.* 3 (used in questions for showing surprise) what: *W~ do you mean?* **whatever, whatsoever** *adv* (used for emphasis): *no doubt* ~.

wheat /wiːt; *US* hwiːt/ *n* [U] (plant producing) grain from which flour is made.

wheedle /ˈwiːdl; *US* ˈhwiːdl/ *v* [I, T] (*derog*) try to obtain (sth) by flattering sb: *She* ~*d the money out of her brother.*

wheel /wiːl; *US* hwiːl/ *n* [C] 1 disc or circular frame that turns on an axle (as on cars, bicycles, etc). 2 = STEERING-WHEEL (STEER). 3 (idm) **at/behind the ˈwheel** (a) driving a car, etc. (b) (*fig*) in control.

wheel *v* 1 [T] push or pull (a vehicle with wheels). 2 [I] move in a curve or circle. 3 (idm) **ˌwheel and ˈdeal** (*infml esp US*) bargain, esp in business, in a clever, often dishonest, way. **ˈwheelbarrow** *n* [C] small cart with one wheel and two handles, pushed by hand. **ˈwheelchair** *n* [C] chair with wheels for sb who is unable to walk. **-wheeled** (forming compound adjectives) having the number of wheels mentioned: *a three-wheeled vehicle.*

wheeze /wiːz; *US* hwiːz/ *v* [I] breathe noisily, esp with a whistling sound in the chest. **wheeze** *n* [C] sound of wheezing. **wheezy** *adj* (-**ier**, -**iest**).

whelk /welk; *US* hwelk/ *n* [C] kind of sea-animal like a snail.

when /wen; *US* hwen/ *adv* 1 (used in questions) at what time; on what occasion: *W~ did you come?* 2 (used after words or phrases that refer to a time) at or on which: *Sunday is the day* ~ *few people work.* *Her last visit to the town was in May,* ~ *she saw the new hospital.* **when** *conj* 1 at or during the time that: *It was raining* ~ *we arrived.* 2 considering that; although: *Why buy a new car* ~ *your present one runs well?*

whence /wens; *US* hwens/ *adv* (*arch* or *fml*) from where.

whenever /wenˈevə(r); *US* hwen-/ *conj* 1 at any time; no matter when: *I'll discuss it* ~ *you like.* 2 every time that: *I go* ~ *I can.* **whenever** *adv* (used in questions for showing surprise) when.

where /weə(r); *US* hweə(r)/ *adv* 1 (used in questions) in or to what place or position: *W~ does he live?* 2 (used after words or phrases that refer to a place) at, in or to which (place): *the place* ~ *you last saw it* ○ *one of the few countries* ~ *people drive on the left* ○ *He then went to London,* ~ *he stayed for three days.* **where** *conj* (in) the place in which: *Put it* ~ *we can all see it.* **ˈwhereabouts** *adv* (used in questions) in or near what place: *W~ abouts did you find it?* **ˈwhereabouts** *n* [C, with *sing* or *pl v*] place where sb/sth is: *Her* ~ *abouts is/are unknown.* **whereˈas** *conj* but in contrast; while: *He gets to work late every day* ~ *she is always early.* **whereˈby** *adv* (*fml*) by which: *He thought of a plan* ~ *he might escape.* **whereuˈpon** *conj* (*fml*) after which; and then.

wherever /ˌweərˈevə(r); *US* ˌhweər-/ *conj* 1 in any place; no matter where: *I'll find him, ~ he is.* **2** in all places that; everywhere: *Crowds of people queue to see her ~ she goes.* **wherever** *adv* (used in questions for showing surprise) where.

wherewithal /'weəwɪðɔːl; US 'hwear-/ *n* **the wherewithal** [sing] (*fml*) the money needed for a purpose: *Does he have the ~ to buy a car?*

whet /wet; US hwet/ *v* (-tt-) (*idm*) **whet sb's appetite for sth** increase sb's desire for sth.

whether /'weðə(r); US 'hweðər/ *conj* (showing choice or doubt) *If: I don't know ~ to accept or refuse.*

which /wɪtʃ; US hwɪtʃ/ **1** *adj, pron* (used in questions when there is a choice): *W~ way shall we go - up the hill or along the road?* **2** *pron* (used for referring to sth previously mentioned): *This is the car ~ she drove.* ○ *His best film, ~ won many awards, was about Gandhi.* **3** *pron* (*fml*) (used for referring back to what has just been said): *He said he had lost the key, ~ was untrue.*

whichever /wɪtʃ'evə(r); US hwɪtʃ-/ *adj, pron* **1** the person or thing which: *Take ~ hat you like best.* **2** no matter which: *W~ way you travel, it is expensive.* **whichever** *adj, pron* (used in questions for showing surprise) which.

whiff /wɪf; US hwɪf/ *n* [C] **1** slight smell. **2** (*fig*) small amount.

while /waɪl; US hwaɪl/ *conj* **1** during the time that: *She fell asleep ~ watching television.* **2** (used for showing a contrast): *She likes tea, ~ I prefer coffee.* **3** (*fml*) although: *W~ I want to help, I do not think I can.* **while** *n* [sing] period of time: *for a long ~.* **while** *v* (*phr v*) **while sth away** pass (time) in a leisurely way.

whilst /waɪlst; US hwaɪlst/ *conj* = WHILE.

whim /wɪm; US hwɪm/ *n* [C, U] sudden (esp unreasonable) desire or idea.

whimper /'wɪmpə(r); US 'hwɪ-/ *v* [I] make weak crying sounds. **whimper** *n* [C].

whimsical /'wɪmzɪkl; US 'hwɪ-/ *adj* strangely fanciful or playful.

whine /waɪn; US hwaɪn/ *n* [C] long complaining cry or high-pitched sound. **whine** *v* [I] **1** make such cries: *The dog was whining to come in.* **2** complain: *a child that never stops whining.*

whinny /'wɪni; US 'hwɪ-/ *n* [C] (*pl* -ies) gentle cry of a horse. **whinny** *v* (*pt, pp* -ied) [I] make such a sound.

whip¹ /wɪp; US hwɪp/ *n* **1** [C] piece of leather or rope fastened to a handle, used for hitting people or animals. **2** [C] (member of a political party who gives an) order to members to attend and vote on an issue. **3** [C, U] dish of whipped cream, eggs, etc.

whip² /wɪp; US hwɪp/ *v* (-pp-) **1** [T] hit with a whip. **2** [I, T] move quickly and suddenly: *He ~ped out a knife.* **3** [T] stir (cream, eggs, etc) until thick or stiff. **4** (*phr v*) **whip sth up** cause (a strong feeling) in people. **whipping** *n* [C, U] beating with a whip. **'whip-round** *n* [C] (*Brit infml*) collection of money from a group of people.

whirl /wɜːl; US hwɜːl/ *v* **1** [I, T] move quickly round and round. **2** [I] spin; be confused: *Her mind was ~ing.* **whirl** *n* [sing] **1** whirling movement. **2** fast series of activities. **3** state of confusion. **4** (*idm*) **give sth a 'whirl** (*infml*) try sth. **'whirlpool** *n* [C] strong circular current of water. **'whirlwind** *n* [C] tall column of quickly circulating air: (*fig*) *a ~wind romance,* ie one that happens very quickly.

whirr (also esp *US* **whir**) /wɜː(r); US hwɜː-/ *n* [C, usu sing] low sound of a machine turning fast or a bird's wings moving quickly. **whirr** (also esp *US* **whir**) *v* [I] make such sounds.

whisk /wɪsk; US hwɪ-/ *v* [T] **1** move (sb/sth) quickly: *They ~ed him off to prison.* **2** beat (eggs, cream, etc) into froth. **whisk** *n* [C] small hand-held device for beating eggs, etc.

whisker /'wɪskə(r); US 'hwɪ-/ *n* **1** [C] long stiff hair near the mouth of a cat, etc. **2** **whiskers** [pl] hair on the side of a man's face.

whisky (*US* or *Irish* **whiskey**) /'wɪski; US 'hwɪ-/ *n* [C, U] (*pl* -ies) strong alcoholic drink made from grain.

whisper /'wɪspə(r); US 'hwɪ-/ *v* [I, T] **(a)** speak or say very quietly, using the breath but with no sound from one's vocal cords. **(b)** say (sth) secretly. **2** [I] (eg of the leaves or the wind) make soft sounds. **whisper** *n* [C] whispering sound.

whist /wɪst; US hwɪst/ *n* [U] card-game for two pairs of players.

whistle /'wɪsl; US 'hwɪ-/ *n* [C] **1** clear high sound made by forcing air through a small opening in the lips: (*fig*) *the ~ of the wind through the trees.* **2** instrument that produces a clear high sound, esp as a signal. **whistle** *v* **1** **(a)** [I] make the sound of a whistle. (b) [T] produce (a tune) in this way. 2 [I] move quickly with a whistling sound: *The bullets ~d past us.*

white /waɪt; *US* hwaɪt/ *adj* (~r, ~st) 1 of the colour of fresh snow. 2 of a pale-skinned race. 3 pale, eg because of shock. 4 (of coffee) containing milk or cream. 5 (idm) **a white elephant** something expensive but useless. **a white lie** small harmless lie. **white** *n* 1 [U] white colour. 2 [C] white-skinned person. 3 [C, U] part of an egg that surrounds the yellow part (= YOLK). 4 [C] white part of the eyeball. ˌwhite-'collar *adj* of office workers, not manual workers. **the 'White House** [sing] (official home of the) President of the USA. **whiten** *v* [I, T] become or make white or whiter. **whiteness** *n* [U]. ˌWhite 'Paper *n* [C] official government report of the government's plans on a matter. 'white-wash *n* 1 [U] mixture of lime or chalk and water, used for painting walls white. 2 [C, U] (*fig*) process of hiding errors. 'whitewash *v* [T] 1 put whitewash(1) on. 2 (*fig*) try to make (sb/sth bad) appear blameless by hiding errors.

Whitsun /'wɪtsn; *US* 'hwɪ-/ *n* [U, C] the seventh Sunday after Easter and the days close to it.

whittle /'wɪtl; *US* 'hwɪ-/ *v* 1 [I] cut thin slices or strips off (wood). 2 (phr v) **whittle sth down/away** reduce sth gradually: *The value of our savings is being slowly ~d down by inflation.*

whiz /wɪz; *US* hwɪz/ *v* (-zz-) [I] (*infml*) 1 move very fast. 2 make the sound of sth moving very fast through the air.

whiz-kid /'wɪzkɪd; *US* 'hwɪz-/ *n* [C] (*infml*) person who becomes successful very quickly.

who /huː/ *pron* 1 (used in questions as the subject of the verb to ask about the name, identity or function of sb): *W~ is the woman in the black hat?* 2 (*infml*) (used as the object of a verb or preposition) which person or people: *W~ are you phoning? W~ do you want to speak to?* 3 (used for referring to sb previously mentioned): *The people ~ called yesterday want to buy the house. My husband, ~ has been ill, hopes to see you soon.*

whoever /huː'evə(r)/ *pron* 1 the person who: *W~ says that is a liar. You must speak to ~ is the head of the department.* 2 no matter who: *W~ rings, I don't want to speak to them.* **whoever** *pron* (used in questions for showing

surprise) who.

whole /həʊl/ *adj* 1 complete; entire: *He told us the ~ story.* 2 not injured or damaged; unbroken: *She swallowed the sweet ~.* 3 (idm) **go the whole hog** (*infml*) do sth thoroughly. **whole** *n* 1 the whole [sing] *of/|* all of sth. 2 [C] thing that is complete. 3 (idm) **on the whole** generally. ˌwhole-'hearted *adj* with complete and enthusiastic support. ˌwhole-'heartedly *adv*. 'wholemeal *n* [U] flour from which no part of the grain has been removed. ˌwhole 'number *n* [C] number, eg 1, 3 or 27, with no fractions or decimals. **wholly** /'həʊlɪ; *adv* completely: *I'm not wholly convinced.*

wholesale /'həʊlseɪl/ *n* [U] selling of goods (esp in large quantities) to shopkeepers who then sell them to the public. **wholesale** *adj, adv* 1 of or by wholesale. 2 on a large scale: *the ~ slaughter of animals.* **wholesaler** *n* [C] trader who sells goods wholesale.

wholesome /'həʊlsəm/ *adj* 1 (of food) good for one's health. 2 (*approv*) morally acceptable; good.

whom /huːm/ *pron* (*fml*) 1 (used in questions as the object of a verb or preposition) which person or people: *W~ did she invite?* 2 (used as the object of a verb or preposition for referring to a person): *The person to ~ this letter is addressed died two years ago.*

whoop /huːp; *US* hwuːp/ *n* [C] loud cry of happiness or excitement. 2 gasping cough. **whoop** *v* [I] make a loud cry: *~ing with joy.* 'whooping cough *n* [U] children's disease which causes a gasping cough and breathing problems.

whore /hɔː(r)/ *n* [C] (*dated* or *derog*) prostitute.

whose /huːz/ *1 pron, adj* (used in questions) of whom: *W~ (house) is that?* 2 *pron* (used to refer back to sb previously mentioned) of whom; of which: *the children ~ mother is a doctor.*

why /waɪ; *US* hwaɪ/ *adv* 1 (used in questions) for what reason: *W~ are you late?* 2 for which (reason): *Nobody understands ~ she left him.* 3 (idm) **why not** (used in suggestions): *W~ not go now?*

wick /wɪk/ *n* 1 [C] burning piece of string, etc in a candle or oil-lamp. 2 (idm) **get on sb's wick** (*Brit infml*) annoy sb.

wicked /'wɪkɪd/ *adj* 1 morally bad. 2 intended to harm. 3 mischievous: *a ~ grin.* **wickedly** *adv*. **wickedness** *n* [U].

wicker /'wɪkə(r)/ n [U] twigs or canes woven together. **'wickerwork** n [U] baskets, furniture, etc made of wicker.

wicket /'wɪkɪt/ n [C] (a) (in cricket) set of three sticks (= STUMPS) at which the ball is bowled. (b) area of grass between the two wickets.

wide /waɪd/ adj (~r, ~st) 1 measuring a large amount from side to side: a ~ river. 2 measuring the amount that is stated from side to side: 12 metres ~. 3 including many different things: a ~ range of interests. 4 far from what is aimed at: His shot was ~. 5 (idm) **give sb a wide berth** avoid sb. **wide of the 'mark** far from being correct. **wide** adv fully: He was ~ awake. ○ ~ open. **,wide-'eyed** adj with eyes opened wide in (inexperience and) surprise. **widely** adv 1 to a large extent: Prices vary ~ly from shop to shop. 2 over a large area: travel ~ly. 3 by many people: It is ~ly known that . . . **widen** v [I, T] become or make wider. **widespread** adj existing or happening over a large area.

widow /'wɪdəʊ/ n [C] woman whose husband has died. **widow** v [T] (usu passive) cause to become a widow or widower. **widower** n [C] man whose wife has died.

width /wɪdθ, wɪtθ/ n [U, C] measurement from side to side.

wield /wiːld/ v [T] have and use: ~ an axe ○ ~ power.

wife /waɪf/ n [C] pl **wives** /waɪvz/) woman to whom a man is married.

wig /wɪg/ n [C] covering of false hair for the head.

wiggle /'wɪgl/ v [I, T] move with quick side-to-side movements: The baby was wiggling its toes. **wiggle** n [C].

wigwam /'wɪgwæm; US ˑwɑ:m/ n [C] North American Indian hut or tent.

wild /waɪld/ adj 1 (a) (of animals, birds, etc) that normally live in natural conditions; not tame. (b) (of plants) growing in natural conditions. (c) (of people) not civilized. 2 (of land) not cultivated and not lived in. 3 stormy: ~ weather. 5 very uncontrolled and excited. 6 made without much thought: a ~ guess. 7 about‖ (infml) very enthusiastic about sth. 8 (idm) **run 'wild** ⇨ RUN¹. **wild** n 1 **the wild** [sing] natural surroundings. 2 **the wilds** [pl] area far away from where most people live. **,wildcat 'strike** n [C] sudden unofficial strike by workers. **,wild-'goose**

chase n [C] (infml) search for sb/ sth that cannot be found. **'wildlife** n [U] wild animals, birds, etc. **wildly** adv 1 in a wild manner. 2 (infml) extremely. **wildness** n.

wilderness /'wɪldənɪs/ n [C, usu sing] 1 wild uncultivated land. 2 (idm) **in the 'wilderness** no longer in an important or influential (esp political) position.

wiles /waɪlz/ n [pl] tricks intended to deceive sb.

wilful (US also **willful**) /'wɪlfl/ adj 1 (of sth bad) done deliberately. 2 (of a person) determined to do sth he/she wants. **wilfully** adv.

will¹ /wɪl/ modal v (contracted form 'll /l/, neg will not, contracted form won't /wəʊnt/, pt would /wʊd/ strong form /wʊd/, contracted form 'd /d/, neg would not, contracted form wouldn't /'wʊdnt/) 1 (used to express the future tense): He ~/He'll be here tomorrow. 2 (used for expressing what is likely in the present): That ~ be the postman at the door. 3 (showing willingness or intention): We ~ not obey you. 4 (showing requests or invitations): W~ you come this way please? 5 (giving orders): You ~ carry out my instructions! 6 (describing general truths): Oil ~ float on water. 7 (describing habits): She would sit there, hour after hour, doing nothing. 8 (showing insistence): He '~ smoke between courses at dinner.

will² /wɪl/ v [T] 1 try to make (sth) happen by using one's mental powers. 2 (fml) leave (property, etc) to sb in a will¹(5).

will³ /wɪl/ n 1 [U, sing] mental power by which a person can direct his/her thoughts and actions. 2 [U, sing] (also **will-power** [U]) power to control one's mind: He has a strong/weak ~. 3 [U, C] determination: the ~ to live. 4 [U] what is desired by sb: the ~ of God. 5 [C] legal statement of what is to happen to sb's property and money after he/she dies. 6 (idm) **at will** whenever, wherever, etc one wishes.

willing /'wɪlɪŋ/ adj 1 (to) ready to do sth; prepared: ~ to learn. 2 doing sth enthusiastically and without being forced: a ~ helper. **willingly** adv. **willingness** n [U].

willow (also **'willow-tree**) /'wɪləʊ/ n [C] tree with thin flexible branches.

wilt /wɪlt/ v [I] 1 (of plants) bend, lose their freshness and begin to die. 2 (fig) (of people) become tired and weak.

wily /ˈwaɪlɪ/ adj (-ier, -iest) clever at getting what one wants, esp by deceiving people.

wimp /wɪmp/ n [C] (infml derog) weak and timid person, esp a man.

win /wɪn/ (-nn-, pt, pp won /wʌn/) v 1 [I, T] come first or defeat one's opponent in a game, competition, etc. 2 [T] get (sth) as a result of success in a competition. 3 [T] obtain: try to ~ support for one's ideas. 4 (idm) win (sth) hands 'down win (sth) easily. 5 (phr v) win sb over/round gain sb's support by persuasion. **winner** n [C] success; victory. **winning** adj 1 that wins. 2 attractive; pleasing: a ~ning smile. **winnings** n [pl] money won.

wince /wɪns/ v [I] show pain, distress, etc by a sudden slight movement of the face. **wince** n [C] wincing movement.

winch /wɪntʃ/ n [C] machine for lifting or pulling heavy weights. **winch** v [T] move by using a winch.

wind¹ /wɪnd/ n 1 [C, U] current of air moving as a result of natural forces. 2 [U] breath as needed for exercise. 3 [U] gas that forms in the stomach and causes discomfort. 4 (idm) get wind of sth (infml) hear about sth that others do not want one to know. put the wind up sb (infml) cause sb to be frightened. **wind** v [T] cause (sb) to be out of breath. **windfall** n [C] 1 fruit, eg an apple, blown off a tree by the wind. 2 (fig) unexpected piece of good fortune. **'wind instrument** n [C] musical instrument (eg an oboe) that one blows into to produce sounds. **'windmill** n [C] mill worked by the action of the wind. **'windpipe** n [C] passage for air from the throat to the lungs. **'windscreen** (US **'windshield**) n [C] glass window in the front of a motor vehicle. **'windscreen wiper** n [C] electrically operated blade with a rubber edge that clears a windscreen of rain. **'windsurfing** n [U] sport of surfing on a narrow board to which a sail is fixed. **'windsurfer** n [C]. **'wind-swept** adj (esp of a person's appearance, hair, etc) untidy because blown by the wind. **windy** adj (-ier, -iest): with a lot of wind ~ a ~y day.

wind² /waɪnd/ v (pt, pp wound /waʊnd/) 1 [I, T] (cause to) move in a curling twisting manner: The river ~s (its way) through the countryside. 2 [T] turn or wrap (sth) round and round sth else. 3 [T] (up)// cause (a clock, etc) to operate by turning a key to tighten the spring. 4 (phr v) **wind sth back, down, forward, in** etc cause sth to move backwards, down, etc, eg by turning a handle: ~ a window down. **wind down (a)** (of a clock, etc) go slow and then stop. **(b)** (infml) (of a person) relax. **wind (sth) down** gradually reduce the amount of work in (a business etc) before stopping. **wind up** (infml) be in the final state or place that is mentioned: We eventually wound up in a little cottage by the sea. **wind (sth) up** finish sth. **wind sb up** (infml) deliberately annoy sb in order to get him/her excited.

window /ˈwɪndəʊ/ n [C] opening (usu filled with glass) in a wall, vehicle, etc to let in light and air. **'window-box** n [C] box on a window-sill in which flowers are grown. **'window-dressing** n [U] act of arranging goods attractively in a shop window. **'window-pane** n [C] sheet of glass in a window. **'window-shopping** n [U] looking at goods in shop windows, usu without intending to buy. **'window-sill** n [C] flat shelf at the base of a window.

wine /waɪn/ n [C, U] alcoholic drink made from grapes or other fruit. **wine** v (idm) **,wine and 'dine** entertain (sb) or be entertained with a meal and wine.

wing /wɪŋ/ n 1 [C] one of the parts of the body of a bird or insect that is used in flying. 2 [C] one of the long flat surfaces that stick out from the sides of an aircraft and support it in flying. 3 [C] part of a building that extends from one side: add a new ~ to a hospital. 4 [C] part of a car around the wheel. 5 [C, usu sing] group in an organization, esp a political party, that has certain opinions or functions: the left/right ~. 6 [C] side part of the playing area in football, hockey, etc. 7 **the wings** [pl] sides of the stage hidden from the audience. 8 (idm) **take sb under one's 'wing** take care of sb and protect him/her. **wing** v [I, T] fly. 2 [T] wound slightly. **winged** adj having wings. **winger** n [C] (in football, hockey, etc) player who plays on the wing(6). **'wing-span** n [C] measurement across a bird's or aircraft's, etc wings when fully stretched out.

wink /wɪŋk/ v [I] 1 (at//) close one eye very briefly. 2 (of a star or light) shine or flash quickly. **wink**

n **1** [C] act of winking, esp as a signal. **2** [sing] very short period of sleep: *I didn't sleep a ~.* **3** (idm) **have forty 'winks** (*infml*) sleep for a short time, esp during the daytime.

winkle /'wɪŋkl/ *n* [C] small sea-snail used as food.

winner, winning *o* WIN.

winter /'wɪntə(r)/ *n* [U, C] coldest season of the year. **winter** *v* [I] (*fml*) spend the winter. ˌ**winter 'sports** *n* [pl] sports that take place on snow or ice. **wintry** /'wɪntrɪ/ *adj*.

wipe /waɪp/ *v* [T] **1** clean or dry (sth) in order to remove (dirt or liquid): ~ *the dishes with a cloth* ○ ~ *the writing off the blackboard.* **2** (phr v) **wipe sth out** (a) destroy sth completely: *War ~d out whole villages.* (b) cancel (a debt). **wipe sth up** remove dirt or liquid from sth with a cloth: ~ *up the milk you spilt* ○ ~ *up (ie dry) the cups.* **wipe** *n* [C] act of wiping.

wire /'waɪə(r)/ *n* **1** [C, U] (piece of) metal in thin thread-like form. **2** [C] (*infml* esp *US*) telegram. **wire** *v* [T] **1** fasten with wire. **2** connect to a supply of electricity, using wire. **3** (*US*) send a telegram to. **wiring** *n* [U] system of wires that supply electricity. **wiry** *adj* **1** strong and rough, like wire. **2** (of a person) thin but strong.

wireless /'waɪəlɪs/ *n* [C] (*dated*) radio.

wisdom /'wɪzdəm/ *n* [U] **1** quality of being wise. **2** (*fml*) wise thoughts, sayings, etc. ˌ**wisdom tooth** *n* [C] back tooth, usu appearing after 20 years of age.

wise /waɪz/ *adj* (~**r**, ~**st**) **1** having or showing experience, knowledge and good judgement. **2** (idm) **none the 'wiser** knowing no more than before. **wisely** *adv*.

wish /wɪʃ/ *v* **1** [T] *to/[I]* (*fml*) want to do sth: *He ~es to be alone.* **2** want (sth impossible or unlikely) to be true: *I ~ (that) I could be an astronaut.* **3** [T] say that one hopes (sb) will have (sth): ~ *sb good luck/happy birthday.* **4** [I] (*for*)// think what one would like to happen: *Blow out the candles (ie on a birthday cake) and wish!* **wish** *n* **1** [C] desire or longing for sth: *I have no ~ to interfere, but ....* **2** [C] something wished for. **3** **wishes** [pl] (expression of) hopes for sb's happiness, etc: *My father sends his best ~es.* **wishful 'thinking** *n* [U] belief that sth will come true simply because one wishes it.

wishy-washy /'wɪʃɪwɒʃɪ; *US* -wɔːʃɪ/ *adj* (*infml*) weak or feeble; not firm or clear.

wisp /wɪsp/ *n* [C] small separate bunch; small amount: *a ~ of hair/ smoke.* **wispy** *adj*.

wistful /'wɪstfl/ *adj* rather sad, as if wanting sth that is past or that one cannot have. **wistfully** /-fəlɪ/ *adv*.

wit /wɪt/ *n* **1** (a) [U] ability to express ideas in a clever amusing way. (b) [C] person well known for this ability. **2** (also **wits**) [U] quick understanding; intelligence. **3** (idm) **at one's wits' end** so worried by difficulties that one does not know what to do. **have/ keep one's wits about one** be alert and ready to act. **scare, frighten, etc sb out of his/her 'wits** frighten sb very much. **witticism** /'wɪtɪsɪzəm/ *n* [C] witty remark. **witty** *adj* (-**ier**, -**iest**) full of clever humour. **wittily** *adv*.

witch /wɪtʃ/ *n* [C] woman believed to have evil magic powers. **'witchcraft** *n* [U] use of magic (esp evil) powers. **'witch-doctor** *n* [C] person who is believed to have magic powers to cure illness. **'witch-hunt** *n* [C] search for people with ideas that are thought unacceptable, esp in order to punish them.

with /wɪð, wɪθ/ *prep* **1** (a) in the company or presence of: *live ~ one's parents* ○ *discuss sth ~ an expert.* (b) in the care of: *leave a child ~ a baby-sitter.* **2** having or carrying: *a coat ~ two pockets* ○ *a girl ~ blue eyes.* **3** (a) (showing a tool or object used): *cut it ~ a knife.* (b) (showing the material used): *Fill the bottle ~ water.* **4** supporting: *The managers are ~ us.* **5** against: *argue ~ Rosie.* **6** because of: *tremble ~ fear.* **7** (showing how sth is done): *look at one's daughter ~ pride.* **8** in the same direction as: *sail ~ the wind.* **9** concerning: *be patient ~ them.* **10** because of and at the same time as: *Skill comes ~ experience.* **11** in spite of: *W~ all her faults, we still like her.* **12** (idm) **be 'with sb** (*infml*) understand what sb is saying: *I'm not really ~ you, I'm afraid, so could you explain it again?* **'with it** (*dated sl*) (a) fashionable. (b) knowledgeable.

withdraw /wɪð'drɔː, also wɪθ'd-/ *v* (*pt* -**drew** /-'druː/, *pp* -**n** /-'drɔːn/) **1** [T] take (sth) away; remove: ~ *money from one's bank account.* **2** [I, T] (*fml*) move away: ~ *troops from the battle.* **3** [I, T] (cause sb) not to take part: ~ *from an argument.* **4** [T] take back (a promise, statement, etc): *If I don't* *have a reply by tonight I shall* ~ *my offer.* **withdrawal** /-'drɔːəl/ *n* [C, U] (act of) withdrawing. **withdrawal symptoms** *n* [pl] very unpleasant effects experienced by a person who has stopped taking a drug he/she is addicted to. **withdrawn** *adj* (of a person) unusually quiet and shy.

wither /'wɪðə(r)/ *v* [I, T] (cause to) become dry, faded and dead: *The hot summer had* ~ *the grass.* (fig) *Their hopes* ~ *ed.* **withering** *adj* making sb feel ashamed: *a* ~ *ing look.*

withhold /wɪð'həʊld, also wɪθ'h-/ *v* (*pt*, *pp* **-held** /-held/) [T] (*fml*) refuse to give: ~ *permission.*

within /wɪ'ðɪn/ *prep* not beyond; inside: ~ *the city walls* ~ *seven days.* **within** *adv* (*fml*) inside: *I could feel the anger rising* ~.

without /wɪ'ðaʊt/ *prep* 1 not having: *You can't buy things* ~ *money.* 2 (used with the *-ing* form to mean 'not'): *He can't speak German* ~ *making mistakes.*

withstand /wɪð'stænd, also wɪθ's-/ *v* (*pt*, *pp* **stood** /-'stʊd/) [T] (*fml*) endure (sth) without surrendering, collapsing, etc; resist: ~ *an attack* ~ *hard weather.*

witness /'wɪtnɪs/ *n* [C] 1 person who sees an event take place and is able to describe it. 2 person who gives information in a law-court. 3 person who signs a document to confirm that another person's signature is real. 4 (*fml*) sign or proof. **witness** *v* [T] 1 be present at and see: ~ *an accident.* 2 be a witness(3) to the signing of (a document). **'witness-box** *n* [C] enclosed area from which a witness(2) gives evidence.

witticism, witty ⇨ WIT.

wives *pl* of WIFE.

wizard /'wɪzəd/ *n* [C] 1 (esp in fairy stories) man believed to have magic powers. 2 person with very great ability: *a financial* ~.

wizened /'wɪznd/ *adj* having a dried-up wrinkled skin.

wobble /'wɒbl/ *v* [I, T] move from side to side unsteadily. **wobbly** *adj* (*infml*) wobbling: *a wobbly chair.*

woe /wəʊ/ *n* (dated or *fml*) 1 [U] great sorrow. 2 **woes** [pl] troubles. **woeful** *adj* (*fml*) 1 very sad. 2 very bad.

wok /wɒk/ *n* [C] large bowl-shaped Chinese cooking pan.

woke *pt* of WAKE[1].

woken *pp* of WAKE[1].

wolf /wʊlf/ *n* [C] (*pl* **wolves** /wʊlvz/) fierce wild animal of the dog family. **wolf** *v* [T] (*down*)//

(*infml*) eat quickly and greedily.

woman /'wʊmən/ *n* (*pl* **women** /'wɪmɪn/) 1 [C] adult female human being. 2 [U] women in general. 3 **the woman** [sing] feminine side of a woman's character. **womanhood** *n* [U] state or qualities of being a woman. **womanizer** *n* [C] man who tries to gain the friendship of many women, esp for sexual relationships. **'womankind** *n* [U] (*fml*) women in general. **womanly** *adj* (of a woman) having the qualities expected of a woman. **,Women's Libe'ration** *n* [U] freedom of women to have the same social and economic rights as men.

womb /wuːm/ *n* [C] organ in a woman's body in which a baby develops before it is born.

won *pt, pp* of WIN.

wonder /'wʌndə(r)/ *v* 1 [I, T] feel curious about (sth); ask oneself: *I* ~ *who she is.* 2 [I] (used to make polite requests): *I* ~ *if you could come earlier.* 3 [I] (*at*)// (*fml*) be surprised at sth: *I* ~ *that you weren't killed.* **wonder** *n* 1 (**a**) [U] feeling of surprise and admiration. (**b**) [C] thing or event that causes such a feeling: *the* ~*s of modern medicine* ~ *a* ~ *drug.* 2 (*idm*) **do/work wonders** have unexpectedly good results. **it's a wonder that ...** it is surprising that: *It's a* ~ *that they weren't all killed.* **no/little/small wonder** it is not surprising. **wonderful** *adj* extremely good; causing a feeling of wonder. **wonderfully** *adv.*

wonky /'wɒŋkɪ/ *adj* (*Brit infml*) unsteady; weak.

won't /wəʊnt/ will not. ⇨ WILL[1].

woo /wuː/ *v* [T] 1 try to obtain the support of: ~ *voters.* 2 (*dated*) try to persuade (a woman) to marry one.

wood /wʊd/ *n* 1 [U] hard substance of a tree under the bark. 2 [C, esp *pl*] area of land (smaller than a forest) where trees grow. 3 (*idm*) **out of the 'wood(s)** (*infml*) free from trouble, difficulties, etc. **wooded** *adj* covered with trees. **wooden** *adj* 1 made of wood. 2 stiff and awkward in one's manners. **'woodland** /-lənd/ *n* [U] land covered with trees. **woodpecker** *n* [C] bird with a long sharp beak that makes holes in tree trunks to find insects. **'woodwind** /-wɪnd/ *n* [sing] (with *sing* or *pl v*) (players of) wind instruments, eg the flute and the clarinet. **'woodwork** *n* [U] 1 parts of a building made of wood. 2 skill of making things from wood. **'woodworm** *n* [U, C] (dam-

age from a) wood-eating larva.
woody adj (-ier, -iest) 1 wooded: a
~y hillside. 2 of or like wood.
woof /wuf/ interj, n[C] (infml)
(used for showing the sound
made by a dog.
wool /wʊl/ n[U] (a) soft hair of
sheep and some other animals. (b)
thread or cloth made from this.
woollen (US -l-) adj made of wool.
woollens (US -l-) n[pl] clothes
made of wool. **woolly** (US also -l-)
adj (-ier, -iest) 1 made of or looking like wool. 2 (of people or their
ideas) confused; not clear. **woolly**
n[C] (pl -ies) (infml) woollen
sweater.
word /wɜːd/ n 1 [C] written or
spoken unit of language. 2 [C] remark or statement: Don't say a ~
about it. 3 [C] conversation: have a
~/a few ~s with sb. 4 [C] piece of
news; message: Please send me ~
of your arrival. 5 [sing] promise: I
give you my ~ that I will come
back. 6 (usu the word) [sing] command; order: The officer gave the
~ to fire. 7 (idm) by word of
'mouth in spoken, not written,
words. **have 'words with sb** quarrel with sb. **in 'other words** expressed in a different way. **in a
'word** briefly. **not in so many
'words** not using the exact words,
but suggested indirectly. **take
sb's 'word for it** believe that sb is
telling the truth. **too funny,
stupid, etc for 'words** (infml) extremely funny, etc. **word for
'word** in the exact words. **word**
v[T] express in words. **wording**
n[sing] words in which sth is expressed. **word-'perfect** adj able
to say sth from memory without
making any mistakes. **'word
processor** n[C] device that records typed words and shows
them on a visual display unit so
that they can be corrected, edited
and printed. **wordy** adj (-ier,
-iest) using too many words.
wore pt of WEAR¹.
work¹ /wɜːk/ n 1 [U] what sb does
as a job in order to earn money:
He's been looking for ~ for a year.
2 [U] use of one's body or mind to
do or make sth, in contrast to rest
or play: Do you like hard ~? 3 [U]
something to be done; task: I've
plenty of ~ to do. 4 [U] thing
produced as a result of work: the
~ of young sculptors. 5 [C] piece of
writing, art, music etc: the ~s of
Shakespeare. 6 **works** (with sing
or pl v) place where industrial
processes are carried on: a gas~.
7 **works** [pl] operations of building or repair; road-~. 8 the

works [pl] moving parts of a
machine. 9 (idm) **at 'work** (a) at
the place where one works. (b) operating: new technology at ~. **set
to 'work** begin. **have one's 'work
cut out** have sth difficult to do, esp
in the available time. **in 'work/
out of 'work** having/not having a
job. **'work-bench** n[C] table with
a hard surface at which a person
works with tools. **'workbook** n[C]
book with questions to be answered (in spaces provided).
'work-force n[C, also sing with pl
v] total number of workers in a
factory, industry, etc. **'work-load**
n[C] amount of work to be done by
sb. **'workman** n[C] man whose
job involves work with his hands.
'workmanlike adj done well;
skilful. **'workmanship** n[U] quality of skill in sth made. **,work of
'art** n[C] excellent painting, sculpture, etc. **'workshop** n[C] 1 room
or building where things are made
or repaired. 2 period of group discussion and practical work.
'work-shy adj not wanting to
work; lazy. **'work top** n[C] flat
surface in a kitchen, on which
food is prepared.
work² /wɜːk/ v 1 [I] do work, esp
as one's job: I've been ~ing hard
all day. 2 [I] function properly; operate: The lift is not ~ing. 3 [I]
have the desired result; be successful: Will your plan ~? 4 [T]
cause (sb/sth) to work. 5 [T] operate; manage: ~ a mine. 6 [T] cultivate (land). 7 [I] (against/for)//
make efforts to defeat/achieve sth:
a politician who ~ s for peace. 8 [T]
make or shape by pressing, hammering, etc: ~ clay/dough. 9 [I, T]
move into a new position, esp
gradually or with effort: ~ one's
way through a boring book. 10
(idm) **work loose** ⇨ LOOSE. **work
to 'rule** obey all the rules of one's
job very strictly in order to cause
delay, decrease output, etc, as a
protest. **work wonders** ⇨ WON-
DER. 11 (phr v) **work sth off** get rid
of sth by work or activity: He ~ed
off his anger by digging the garden. **work out** (a) develop in the
way that is mentioned: The situation ~ed out well. (b) do physical
exercises. **work out at sth** be equal to sth: The total ~s out at £180.
work sb out (infml) understand
sb. **work sth out** (a) calculate sth:
~ out the new price. (b) find the
answer to sth; solve: ~ out a problem. (c) plan sth: ~ out a new
scheme. **work sb/oneself up**
make sb/oneself very excited: He
gets very ~ed up about criticism.

work sth up develop or increase sth gradually: ~ *up business I can't* ~ *up much energy to go out*. **work up to** sth progress gradually to sth: *The music* ~ *ed up to a lively finish*. **worker** *n* [C] person who works. **'work-out** *n* [C] period of physical exercise. **,work-to-'rule** *n* [C] act or working strictly according to the rules to cause delay, etc, as a protest.

workable /'wɜːkəbl/ *adj* that will work well: *a* ~ *plan*.

workaholic /,wɜːkə'hɒlɪk/ *n* [C] (*infml*) person who finds it difficult to stop working.

working /'wɜːkɪŋ/ *adj* 1 doing work: *the* ~ *population*. 2 of or for work: ~ *hours/clothes*. 3 good enough, esp as a basis for further improvement: *a* ~ *knowledge of Russian*. 4 (idm) in **'working order** able to function properly. **working** *n* 1 **workings** [pl] way a machine, organization, etc operates. 2 [C] mine or quarry that has been dug in the ground. **the ,working 'class** *n* [C] social class of people who do manual work. **,working-'class** *adj*. **'working party** *n* [C] group of people that study and report on a subject.

world /wɜːld/ *n* 1 **the world** [sing] (a) the earth, its countries and people. (b) particular part of this: *the French-speaking* ~. 2 [C] planet: *life on other* ~ *s*. 3 [C] time or state of existence: *this* ~ *and the next*, ie life on earth and after death. 4 **the world** [sing] (a) human affairs: active life: *a man/ woman of the* ~, ie person with a great experience of life. (b) everybody: *I don't want the whole* ~ *to know about it*. 5 [C] people or things of a certain kind or activity: *the insect* ~ *the* ~ *of sport*. 6 (idm) **how, why, where, etc in the world** (used for emphasis): *How in the* ~ *did you manage to do it?* **out of this 'world** (*infml*) absolutely wonderful. **a/the 'world of difference/good**, etc (*infml*) a great deal of difference, etc: *My holiday did me a* ~ *of good*. **,world-'class** *adj* as good as the best in the world. **,world-'famous** *adj* known throughout the world. **worldly** *adj* 1 of material, not spiritual, things. 2 experienced in life. **worldliness** *n* [U]. **world 'power** *n* [C] nation with great influence on international politics. **,world 'war** *n* [C] war involving many important countries. **,world-'wide** *adj, adv* happening all over the world.

worm /wɜːm/ *n* [C] 1 (a) small

long thin creature with no bones or legs. (b) worm-like larva of an insect: *wood* ~. 2 (*infml derog*) weak worthless person. **worm** *v* [I, T] move slowly or with difficulty: *He* ~ *ed his way through the narrow tunnel*.

worn¹ *pp* of WEAR¹.

worn² /wɔːn/ *adj* damaged by use or wear. **,worn-'out** *adj* 1 very worn and no longer usable. 2 extremely tired.

worry /'wʌrɪ/ *v* (*pt, pp* **-ied**) 1 [I] (*about*)|| be anxious about sb/sth: *I'm worried about my son*. 2 [T] make (sb) anxious or troubled. 3 [T] seize with the teeth and shake: *The dog was* ~ *ing a rat*. **worried** *adj* anxious; troubled. **worry** *n* (*pl* **-ies**) 1 [U] feeling of anxiety. 2 [C] something that causes anxiety. **worrying** *adj* full of or causing worry.

worse /wɜːs/ *adj comparative* of BAD 1 not as good, less excellent: *Her work is bad, but his is* ~. 2 in or into less good health: *She got* ~ *in the night*. 3 (idm) **be none the 'worse (for sth)** be unharmed (by sth). **the ,worse for 'wear** worn, damaged or tired. **worse** *adv* 1 more badly: *She cooks badly, but I cook* ~. 2 more than before: *It's raining* ~ *than ever*. 3 (idm) **,worse 'off** poorer, unhappier or less healthy. **worse** *n* [U] worse thing(s). **worsen** *v* [I, T] (cause to) become worse.

worship /'wɜːʃɪp/ *n* [U] 1 reverence, respect or love for God or a god. 2 admiration or love for sb/ sth. **worship** *v* (**-pp-**; *US* **-p-**) [I, T] give worship (to). **worshipper** (*US* **-p-**) *n* [C].

worst /wɜːst/ *adj superlative* of BAD of the least good or least excellent least: *the* ~ *storm for years*. **worst** *adv* most badly. **worst** *n* 1 **the worst** [sing] the worst part, state, event, etc. 2 (idm) **at (the) 'worst** considering a situation in the most unfavourable way. **if the ,worst comes to the 'worst** if the worst possible thing happens.

worth /wɜːθ/ *adj* 1 having the value that is mentioned: *a car* ~ *£5000*. 2 giving a satisfactory or rewarding return for (doing sth): *The book is* ~ *reading*. 3 (idm) **for all one is 'worth** (*infml*) making every effort. **'worth it** very likely to give a good return for the money, effort or time spent. **,worth sb's 'while** useful, interesting or profitable to sb. **worth** *n* [U] 1 amount of sth that a certain sum of money will buy: *a pound's* ~ *of apples*. 2 value. **worthless** *adj* 1 having no value. **2** (of a person) having bad qualities. **worth-'while** adj useful or interesting, and worth the time, money or effort spent.

worthy /'wɜːðɪ/ adj (-ier, -iest) **1** (of)|| deserving sth: ~ of blame. **2** deserving respect.

would¹ /wəd/; strong form wʊd/ modal v (contracted form 'd /d/, neg **would not**, contracted form **wouldn't** /'wʊdnt/) **1** (a) (used for describing the result of sth imagined): If he shaved his beard off, he ~ look much younger. (b) (used for making polite requests): W~ you open a window, please? (c) (used in giving an opinion): I ~ think the film will last about 90 minutes. **3** (used in offers or invitations): W~ you like a sandwich? **4** (used for showing what sb wants or likes): I'd love a cup of coffee. **'would-be** adj that one wants to do or become: a ~-be artist.

would² pt of WILL¹.

wouldn't 1 would not. ⇨ WILL¹. **2** would not. ⇨ WOULD¹.

wound¹ /wuːnd/ n[C] injury to the body: a bullet ~. **wound** v[T] **1** give a wound to. **2** hurt (sb's feelings, etc).

wound² pt, pp of WIND².

wove pt of WEAVE.

woven pp of WEAVE.

wow /waʊ/ interj (infml) (used for expressing surprise or admiration).

wrangle /'ræŋgl/ v[I] n[C] (take part in) a noisy or angry argument.

wrap /ræp/ v (-pp-) [T] **1** cover (sth) in material; fold round: ~ (up) a parcel ○ W~ a cloth round your leg. **2** (idm) **be wrapped up in sb/sth** (infml) be deeply involved in sb/sth. **3** (phr v) **wrap (sb/ oneself) up** put warm clothes on sb/oneself. **wrap sth up** (infml) complete (a task, agreement, etc). **wrap** n[C] outer garment, eg a scarf. **wrapper** n[C] piece of paper wrapped round sth, eg a sweet or newspaper. **wrapping** n[C, U] something used for covering or packing.

wrath /rɒθ; US ræθ/ n[U] (fml or dated) extreme anger.

wreak /riːk/ v[T] (fml) cause or bring about (sth harmful).

wreath /riːθ/ n[C] (pl ~s /riːðz/) circle of flowers and leaves, eg put on a grave.

wreathe /riːð/ v[T] (in/with)|| (fml) (usu passive) cover or surround by sth: hills ~d in mist.

wreck /rek/ n[C] **1** car, aeroplane, etc that has been badly

damaged in an accident. **2** ship that has been badly damaged in a storm. **3** (infml) person whose health has been destroyed. **wreck** v[T] destroy or ruin: The train had been ~ed by vandals. ○ (fig) The weather ~ed all our plans. **wreckage** n[U] remains of sth that has been wrecked.

wren /ren/ n[C] kind of very small brown songbird.

wrench /rentʃ/ v[T] **1** twist or pull violently: ~ a door open. **2** injure (eg one's ankle) by twisting. **wrench** n[C] **1** sudden and violent twist or pull. **2** [C] (US) spanner. **3** [sing] sad and painful separation.

wrestle /'resl/ v[I] (with)|| fight with sb, trying to throw him/her to the ground. **2** with|| struggle to deal with (a problem). **wrestler** n[C] person who wrestles as a sport.

wretch /retʃ/ n[C] unfortunate or nasty person.

wretched /'retʃɪd/ adj **1** very unhappy: His stomach-ache made him feel ~. **2** causing great unhappiness. **3** (infml) annoying: That ~ dog! **wretchedly** adv. **wretchedness** n[U].

wriggle /'rɪgl/ v[I, T] move with quick short twists and turns: Stop wriggling and sit still! **2** (phr v) **wriggle out of doing sth** (infml) avoid doing sth unpleasant. **wriggle** n[C].

wring /rɪŋ/ v (pt, pp **wrung** /rʌŋ/) [T] **1** (out)|| twist and squeeze (sth wet) to remove liquid. **2** (fig) obtain (eg money or a confession) from sb with effort or force. **3** twist (a bird's neck) in order to kill it. **4** (idm) **wring one's 'hands** squeeze and twist one's hands in sorrow, worry, etc. **,wringing 'wet** very wet. **wringer** n[C] machine for wringing clothes that are wet.

wrinkle /'rɪŋkl/ n[C, usu pl] small fold or line in the skin, esp caused by age. **wrinkle** v[I, T] (cause to) form wrinkles. **wrinkly** adj.

wrist /rɪst/ n[C] joint between the hand and the arm. **'wrist-watch** n[C] watch with a strap that is worn round the wrist.

writ /rɪt/ n[C] formal legal paper ordering sb to do or not to do sth.

write /raɪt/ v (pt **wrote** /rəʊt/, pp **written** /'rɪtn/) **1** [I, T] mark (letters or other symbols) on a surface, esp with a pen or pencil. **2** [T] compose in writing: ~ a report/ book. **3** [I, T] write and send (a letter): She promised to ~ to me every week. **4** [T] complete (sth) by writ-

ing the correct information on it:
~ *a cheque*. 5 (idm) **be written all
over sb's 'face** be very obvious
from the expression on sb's face. 6
(phr v) **write sth down** put sth
down in words on paper. **write
off/away (to sb/sth)** write a letter
to (an organization, etc) to order
sth, ask for information, etc.
write sb/sth off (a) consider sb/
sth to be useless or a failure. (b)
damage sth so badly that it is not
worth repairing. (c) cancel (a
debt). **write sth out** write sth in
full. **write sth up** make a full written record of sth. **'write-off** *n* [C]
vehicle so badly damaged that it is
not worth repairing. **'write-up**
n [C] written report of an event.

writer /'raɪtə(r)/ *n* [C] 1 person
who writes. 2 author.

writhe /raɪð/ *v* [I] twist or roll
about, esp in pain.

writing /'raɪtɪŋ/ *n* 1 [U] activity
of writing; written or printed
words. 2 [U] handwriting. 3 **writings** [pl] written works of an auth-
or. **'writing-paper** *n* [U] (usu good
quality) paper for writing letters
on.

written *pp* of WRITE.

wrong /rɒŋ; *US* rɔːŋ/ *adj* 1 not
morally right: *It is ~ to steal*. 2 not
true or correct; mistaken: *a ~ answer   prove that sb is ~*. 3 not
suitable or the most desirable:
catch the ~ train. 4 in a bad condition: *What's ~ with the engine?*
wrong *adv* 1 in a wrong manner:
You've spelt my name ~. 2 (idm) **go
'wrong** (a) make a mistake. (b) (of
a machine) stop working properly. (c) have a bad result; fail.
wrong *n* 1 [U] what is wrong:
*know the difference between right
and ~*. 2 [C] (*fml*) unjust action. 3
(idm) in the **'wrong** responsible
for an error; guilty. **on the wrong
'track** ⇨ TRACK. **wrong** *v* [T] treat
unjustly. **'wrongdoer** *n* [C] person who does wrong. **'wrongdo-
ing** *n* [U]. **wrongful** *adj* not fair,
just or legal: *~ful dismissal (from
a job)*. **wrongfully** *adv*. **wrongly**
adv.

wrote *pt* of WRITE.

wrought iron /ˌrɔːt 'aɪən/ *n* [U]
tough form of iron made by forging.

wrung *pt, pp* of WRING.

wry /raɪ/ *adj* 1 slightly mocking:
a ~ smile. 2 twisted to show dislike: *a ~ face*. **wryly** *adv*.

X x

X, x /eks/ *n* [C] (*pl* **X's, x's**
/'eksɪz/) 1 the twenty-fourth letter of the English alphabet. 2 Roman numeral for 10. 3 (*mathematics*) unknown quantity.

xenophobia /ˌzenə'fəʊbɪə/ *n* [U]
great dislike or fear of foreigners.

Xerox /'zɪərɒks/ *n* [C] (*P*) (a)
machine that makes photographic
copies. (b) photocopy made on
such a machine. **xerox** *v* [T] make
a photocopy of, using a Xerox
machine.

Xmas /'krɪsməs, 'eksməs/ *n* [U, C]
(*infml*) Christmas.

X-ray /'eks reɪ/ *n* [C] (a) kind of
radiation that can pass through
solids and make it possible to see
into or through them. (b) photograph made by X-rays: *a chest ~*.
X-ray *v* [T] photograph or treat
(sb) using X-rays.

xylophone /'zaɪləfəʊn/ *n* [C]
musical instrument with a row of
wooden bars that are hit with
small wooden hammers.

Y y

Y, y /waɪ/ *n* [C] (*pl* **Y's, y's**
/waɪz/) the twenty-fifth letter of the English alphabet. **Y-fronts** *n* [pl] (*Brit
P*) men's underpants with seams
and an opening at the front in the
form of an inverted Y.

yacht /jɒt/ *n* [C] 1 light sailing-
boat, esp one used for racing. 2
large, usu motor-driven, pleasure-
boat. **yachting** *n* [U] skill or sport
of sailing yachts.

yam /jæm/ *n* [C] (edible white
tuber of a) kind of tropical climbing plant.

Yank /jæŋk/ *n* [C] (*Brit infml derog*) person from the United States
of America.

yank /jæŋk/ *v* [I, T] pull (sth) suddenly and forcefully.

yap /jæp/ *v* (-pp-) [I] 1 (of a dog)
make short sharp barks. 2 (*infml*)
talk noisily and foolishly.

yard¹ /jɑːd/ *n* [C] measure of
length; 3 feet (0.914 metre). **'yard-
stick** *n* [C] (*fig*) standard of comparison.

yard² /jɑːd/ *n* [C] 1 (usu enclosed)
area with a hard surface next to a
building. 2 enclosed area for a par-

ticular kind of activity: *a* ship-~.

yarn /jɑːn/ *n* 1 [U] fibres spun for knitting, weaving, etc. 2 [C] (*infml*) story.

yawn /jɔːn/ *v* [I] 1 open the mouth wide and breathe in, as when sleepy or bored. 2 be wide open: *a ~ ing gap*. **yawn** *n* [C] act of yawning(1).

yd *abbr* (*pl* ~s) yard(¹).

yeah /jeə/ *interj* (*infml*) yes.

year /jiə(r), also jɜː(r)/ *n* [C] 1 time taken by the earth in one orbit round the sun, about 365¼ days. 2 period of 365 days (or 366) from 1 January to 31 December. 3 period of about a year in business or an institution: *the financial/school ~*. 4 (idm) **all (the) year 'round** throughout the year. **year 'in, year ,out, year after 'year** for many years. **yearly** *adj, adv* (occurring) every year or once a year.

yearn /jɜːn/ *v* [I] *for; to*// want sth very much: *He ~ed for his home.* **yearning** *n* [C, U] strong desire.

yeast /jiːst/ *n* [C, U] substance used in making beer and wine and to make bread rise.

yell /jel/ *v* [I, T] shout loudly. **yell** *n* [C] loud shout.

yellow /'jeləʊ/ *adj* 1 of the colour of gold. 2 (*infml derog*) cowardly. **yellow** *v* [I, T] (cause to) become yellow: *The papers had ~ed with age.* **yellowish** *adj* slightly yellow. ,**yellow 'pages** *n* [sing or pl *v*] telephone directory listing companies, etc by the service they provide.

yelp /jelp/ *v* [I] *n* [C] (make a) short sharp cry, esp of pain.

yen¹ /jen/ *n* [C] (*pl* **yen**) unit of money in Japan.

yen² /jen/ *n* [usu sing] (*infml*) desire or longing: *a ~ to visit India.*

yes /jes/ *interj* (used when accepting, agreeing, etc): *Y~, I'll come with you.* **yes** *n* [C] word or answer of 'yes'.

yesterday /'jestədɪ, -deɪ/ *adv, n* [U] 1 (on) the day before today. 2 (in) the recent past.

yet /jet/ *adv* 1 up to now; to any time before then: *They haven't come ~.* 2 at some future time: *She may surprise us all ~.* 3 even: *~ another government report.* 4 still: *I have ~ to meet him,* ie I have still not met him. 5 (idm) **as 'yet** until now/then. **yet** *conj* but at the same time: *a clever ~ simple idea.*

yew (also **'yew-tree**) /juː/ *n* [C] tree with dark-green leaves and red berries.

Y-fronts ⇨ Y, s.

yield /jiːld/ *v* 1 [T] produce as a

natural product or profit: *The tax increase would ~ £10 million a year.* 2 [I] (*to*)// (*fml*) allow oneself to be defeated by sth: *~ to temptation.* 3 [T] (*fml*) surrender control of (sth). **yield** *n* [C] amount produced: *a ~ of three tonnes of wheat per hectare.* **yielding** *adj* 1 easily bending. 2 (*fig*) likely to accept others' wishes.

yippee /'jɪpiː/ *interj* (*infml*) (used to express pleasure or excitement).

yodel /'jəʊdl/ *v* (-ll-; *US* -l-) [I, T] sing with frequent changes from the normal voice to high notes.

yoga /'jəʊgə/ *n* [U] Hindu system of meditation and self-control.

yoghurt /'jɒgət; *US* 'jəʊgərt/ *n* [U, C] slightly sour thick liquid food made from fermented milk.

yoke /jəʊk/ *n* 1 [C] piece of wood placed across the necks of oxen pulling a cart, plough, etc. 2 [sing] (*fml fig*) harsh control: *freed from the ~ of slavery.*

yokel /'jəʊkl/ *n* [C] (*joc* or *derog*) simple country person.

yolk /jəʊk/ *n* [C, U] yellow part of an egg.

yonder /'jɒndə(r)/ *adj, adv* (*arch*) (that is) over there.

you /juː/ *pron* (used as the subject of a *v* or as the object of a *v* or prep) 1 person or people addressed. 2 (*infml*) everyone; anyone: *It's easier to cycle with the wind behind ~.*

you'd /juːd/ 1 you had. ⇨ HAVE. 2 you would. ⇨ WILL¹, WOULD¹.

you'll /juːl/ you will. ⇨ WILL¹.

young /jʌŋ/ *adj* (~**er** /-ŋgə(r)/, ~**est** /-ŋgɪst/) having lived or existed for a short time: *a ~ woman/ nation.* **young** *n* [pl] 1 young animals or birds; offspring. 2 **the young** young people as a group. **youngish** *adj* fairly young. **youngster** /-stə(r)/ *n* [C] young person.

your /jɔː(r); *US* jʊər/ *adj* belonging to you: *How old are ~ children?* **yours** /jɔːz; *US* jʊərz/ *pron* 1 of or belonging to you: *Is that book ~ s?* (in letter): *Y~ s/ Yours*) (used in ending a letter): *Y~ s faithfully/sincerely/ truly.*

you're /jʊə(r), also jɔː(r)/ you are. ⇨ BE.

yourself /jɔː'self, *US* jʊər'self/ *pron* (*pl* -**selves** /-'selvz/) 1 (used as a reflexive when the person or people doing sth are also the person or people affected by it): *Have you hurt ~ ?* 2 (used for emphasis): *You told me so ~.* 3 (idm) (**all) by your'self/your'selves** (a) alone. (b) without help.

youth /juːθ/ n (pl ~s /juːðz/) **1** [U] time or state of being young: in my ~. **2** [C] young man. **3** (also **the youth**) [also sing with pl v] young people considered as a group.
youthful adj young; seeming young: a ~ful appearance. **'youth hostel** n [C] building in which young people can stay cheaply while on walking or cycling holidays.
you've /juːv/ you have. ⇨ HAVE.
yuck /jʌk/ interj (infml) (used to express disgust).
yule /juːl/ n [U] (arch) Christmas.
yuppie /'jʌpɪ/ n [C] (infml) young professional person, esp one who is ambitious and earns a lot of money.

Z z

Z, z /zed; US ziː/ n [C] (pl Z's, z's /zedz; US ziːz/) the twenty-sixth letter of the English alphabet.
zany /'zeɪnɪ/ adj (-ier, -iest) (infml) amusing and foolish.
zeal /ziːl/ n [U] (fml) enthusiasm.
zealous /'zeləs/ adj full of zeal.
zealot /'zelət/ n [C] (sometimes derog) person who is very enthusiastic about sth, esp religion or politics.
zebra /'zebrə, 'ziːbrə/ n [C] African wild animal of the horse family with black and white stripes on its body. **zebra 'crossing** n [C] (in Britain) place on the road marked with black and white stripes where people may cross.
zenith /'zenɪθ/ n [C] highest point of one's fame, success, etc.
zero /'zɪərəʊ/ pron, adj, n [C] (pl ~s) **1** 0 0; nought. **2** lowest point; nothing. **3** point between + and − on a scale: The temperature was ten degrees below ~, ie -10°C. **zero** v (phr v) **zero in on sth** aim directly at sth. **'zero-hour** n [U] time at which sth, esp a military operation, is to begin.

zest /zest/ n **1** [U, sing] **(a)** great enjoyment or excitement. **(b)** quality of added interest or charm. **2** [U] outer skin of an orange or lemon.
zigzag /'zɪgzæg/ n [C] line that turns right and left at sharp angles. **zigzag** v (-gg-) [I] go in a zigzag: The path ~s up the cliff.
zinc /zɪŋk/ n [U] bluish-white metal.
zip (also **'zip-fastener**) /zɪp/ n [C] device for locking together two rows of metal or plastic teeth by means of a sliding tab, used for fastening clothing, bags, etc. **zip** v (-pp-) [T] open or close with a zip.
Zip code n [C] (US) postcode. **zipper** n [C] (esp US) zip.
zither /'zɪðə(r)/ n [C] flat musical instrument with many strings.
zodiac /'zəʊdɪæk/ n **the zodiac** [sing] imaginary band in the sky containing the positions of the sun, moon and planets, divided into twelve equal parts.
zombie /'zɒmbɪ/ n [C] (infml) person who seems to be completely unaware of what is happening around him/her and seems to act without thinking.
zone /zəʊn/ n [C] area or region with particular features or uses: a time ~ ○ a nuclear-free ~.
zoo /zuː/ n [C] (pl ~s) park where living animals are kept for people to look at.
zoology /zəʊ'ɒlədʒɪ/ n [U] study of the structure, form and distribution of animals. **zoological** /ˌzəʊə'lɒdʒɪkl/ adj. **zoologist** n [C] student of or expert in zoology.
zoom /zuːm/ v [I] **1** move very quickly, esp with a buzzing or humming noise. **2** (fig infml) increase suddenly and sharply. **3** (phr v) **zoom in/out** (of a camera) cause the object being photographed to appear nearer/further. **'zoom lens** n [C] camera lens that can make the object being photographed appear bigger or smaller.
zucchini /zʊ'kiːnɪ/ n [C] (pl zucchini or ~s) (esp US) courgette.

Common irregular verbs

Infinitive · Past Tense		Past Participle

(Where two forms are given, consult the dictionary to see if there is a difference of meaning.)

arise	arose	arisen
awake	awoke	awoken
be	was, were	been
bear	bore	borne
beat	beat	beaten
become	became	become
begin	began	begun
bend	bent	bent
beseech	besought, beseeched	besought, beseeched
beset	beset	beset
bet	bet, betted	bet, betted
bid	bid, bade	bid, bidden
bind	bound	bound
bite	bit	bitten
bleed	bled	bled
blow	blew	blown
break	broke	broken
breed	bred	bred
bring	brought	brought
broadcast	broadcast	broadcast
build	built	built
burn	burnt, burned	burnt, burned
burst	burst	burst
buy	bought	bought
cast	cast	cast
catch	caught	caught
choose	chose	chosen
cling	clung	clung
come	came	come
cost	cost, costed	cost, costed
creep	crept	crept
cut	cut	cut
deal	dealt	dealt
dig	dug	dug
do	did	done
draw	drew	drawn
dream	dreamt, dreamed	dreamt, dreamed
drink	drank	drunk
drive	drove	driven
dwell	dwelt	dwelt

Common irregular verbs

Infinitive	Past Tense	Past Participle

(Where two forms are given, consult the entry to see if there is a difference of meaning)

Infinitive	Past Tense	Past Participle
arise	arose	arisen
awake	awoke	awoken
be	was, were	been
bear	bore	borne
beat	beat	beaten
become	became	become
begin	began	begun
bend	bent	bent
beseech	besought, beseeched	besought, beseeched
beset	beset	beset
bet	bet, betted	bet, betted
bid	bid, bade	bid, bidden
bind	bound	bound
bite	bit	bitten
bleed	bled	bled
blow	blew	blown
break	broke	broken
breed	bred	bred
bring	brought	brought
broadcast	broadcast	broadcast
build	built	built
burn	burnt, burned	burnt, burned
burst	burst	burst
buy	bought	bought
cast	cast	cast
catch	caught	caught
choose	chose	chosen
cling	clung	clung
come	came	come
cost	cost, costed	cost, costed
creep	crept	crept
cut	cut	cut
deal	dealt	dealt
dig	dug	dug
do	did	done
draw	drew	drawn
dream	dreamt, dreamed	dreamt, dreamed
drink	drank	drunk
drive	drove	driven
dwell	dwelt	dwelt

Infinitive	Past Tense	Past Participle
eat	ate	eaten
fall	fell	fallen
feed	fed	fed
feel	felt	felt
fight	fought	fought
find	found	found
flee	fled	fled
fling	flung	flung
fly	flew	flown
forbid	forbad, forbade	forbidden
forecast	forecast, forecasted	forecast, forecasted
foresee	foresaw	foreseen
foretell	foretold	foretold
forget	forgot	forgotten
forgive	forgave	forgiven
forsake	forsook	forsaken
freeze	froze	frozen
get	got	got
give	gave	given
go	went	gone
grind	ground	ground
grow	grew	grown
hang	hung, hanged	hung, hanged
have	had	had
hear	heard	heard
hide	hid	hidden
hit	hit	hit
hold	held	held
hurt	hurt	hurt
keep	kept	kept
kneel	knelt	knelt
knit	knit, knitted	knit
know	knew	known
lay	laid	laid
lead	led	led
lean	leant, leaned	leant, leaned
leap	leapt, leaped	leapt, leaped
learn	learnt, learned	learnt, learned
leave	left	left
lend	lent	lent
let	let	let
lie²	lay	lain
light	lit, lighted	lit, lighted
lose	lost	lost
make	made	made
mean	meant	meant

Infinitive	Past Tense	Past Participle
meet	met	met
mislay	mislaid	mislaid
mislead	misled	misled
misspell	misspelt, misspelled	misspelt, misspelled
mistake	mistook	mistaken
misunderstand	misunderstood	misunderstood
mow	mowed	mown, mowed
outdo	outdid	outdone
outgrow	outgrew	outgrown
outshine	outshone	outshone
overcome	overcame	overcome
overdo	overdid	overdone
overhang	overhung	overhung
overhear	overheard	overheard
override	overrode	overridden
overrun	overran	overrun
oversee	oversaw	overseen
overshoot	overshot	overshot
oversleep	overslept	overslept
overtake	overtook	overtaken
overthrow	overthrew	overthrown
partake	partook	partaken
pay	paid	paid
put	put	put
read	read	read
repay	repaid	repaid
rewind	rewound	rewound
rid	rid	rid
ride	rode	ridden
ring	rang	rung
rise	rose	risen
run	ran	run
saw	sawed	sawn, sawed
say	said	said
see	saw	seen
seek	sought	sought
sell	sold	sold
send	sent	sent
set	set	set
sew	sewed	sewn
shake	shook	shaken
shear	sheared	shorn, sheared
shed	shed	shed
shine	shone, shined	shone, shined
shit	shat, shitted	shat, shitted
shoe	shod	shod

Infinitive	Past Tense	Past Participle
shoot	shot	shot
show	showed	shown, showed
shrink	shrank, shrunk	shrunk
shut	shut	shut
sing	sang	sung
sink	sank	sunk
sit	sat	sat
slay	slew	slain
sleep	slept	slept
slide	slid	slid
sling	slung	slung
slink	slunk	slunk
slit	slit	slit
smell	smelt, smelled	smelt, smelled
sow	sowed	sown, sowed
speak	spoke	spoken
speed	sped, speeded	sped, speeded
spell	spelt, spelled	spelt, spelled
spend	spent	spent
spill	spilt, spilled	spilt, spilled
spin	spun	spun
spit	spat	spat
split	split	split
spoil	spoilt, spoiled	spoilt, spoiled
spread	spread	spread
spring	sprang	sprung
stand	stood	stood
stave	stove, staved	stove, staved
steal	stole	stolen
stick	stuck	stuck
stink	stank, stunk	stunk
stride	strode	stridden
strike	struck	struck
string	strung	strung
strive	strove	striven
swear	swore	sworn
sweep	swept	swept
swell	swelled	swollen, swelled
swim	swam	swum
swing	swung	swung
take	took	taken
teach	taught	taught
tear	tore	torn
tell	told	told
think	thought	thought
thrive	throve, thrived	thriven, thrived

Infinitive	Past Tense	Past Participle
throw	threw	thrown
thrust	thrust	thrust
tread	trod	trodden
undercut	undercut	undercut
undergo	underwent	undergone
underlie	underlay	underlain
understand	understood	understood
undertake	undertook	undertaken
underwrite	underwrote	underwritten
undo	undid	undone
unwind	unwound	unwound
upset	upset	upset
wake	woke	woken
waylay	waylaid	waylaid
wear	wore	worn
weave	wove	woven
wed	wed, wedded	wed, wedded
weep	wept	wept
win	won	won
wind²	wound	wound
withdraw	withdrew	withdrawn
withhold	withheld	withheld
withstand	withstood	withstood
wring	wrung	wrung
write	wrote	written

Spelling

It is sometimes difficult to find a word in the dictionary if
you do not know how the first sound is written. Here are
the most common difficulties:

The first letter is silent

wh- is sometimes spoken as /h-/ as in *who, whole*.

wr- is spoken as /r-/ as in *write, wrist*.

kn- is spoken as /n-/ as in *knife, know*.

Also

ho- is sometimes spoken as /ɒ-/ as in *honest, honour*.

ps- is spoken as /s-/ as in *psychology*.

pn- is spoken as /n-/ as in *pneumonia*.

The second letter is silent

wh- is sometimes spoken as /w-/ as in *which, whether*.

gu- is sometimes spoken as /g-/ as in *guest, guess*.

gh- is spoken as /g/ as in *ghastly, ghost*.

Also

bu- is sometimes spoken as /b-/ as in *build, buoy*.

The first two letters have a special sound

ph- is spoken as /f-/ as in *photo*.

qu is nearly always spoken as /kw-/ as in *quick*.

ch- is sometimes spoken as /k-/ as in *chorus*.

Remember

c- can be /k-/ as in *call* or /s-/ as in *centre*.

g- can be /g-/ as in *good* or /dʒ-/ as in *general*.

If you have looked for a word in the dictionary and
cannot find it, here is a list for you to use as a guide:

If the sound is: look at this possible spelling:

f-	**ph-**	(as in *photo*)
g-	**gh-**	(as in *ghost*) or
	gu-	(as in *guest*)
h-	**wh-**	(as in *who, whole*)
k-	**ch-**	(as in *character*)
kw-	**qu-**	(as in *quick*)
n-	**kn-**	(as in *knife*) or
	pn-	(as in *pneumonia*)
r-	**wr-**	(as in *write*)
s-	**c-**	(as in *centre*) or
	ps-	(as in *psychology*)
dʒ-	**j-**	(as in *job*) or
	g-	(as in *general*)
ʃ-	**sh-**	(as in *shop*) or
	ch-	(as in *chalet*)
iː	**ea-**	(as in *each*)
ɪ	**e-**	(as in *enjoy*)
e	**a-**	(as in *any*)
ɑː	**au-**	(as in *aunt*)
ɒ	**ho-**	(as in *honest*)
ɔː	**au-**	(as in *author*) or
	oa-	(as in *oar*)
ə	**a-**	(as in *awake*) or
	o-	(as in *obey*)
ɜː	**ear-**	(as in *early*) or
	ir-	(as in *irk*)
eɪ	**ai-**	(as in *aim*) or
	ei-	(as in *eight*)
əʊ	**oa-**	(as in *oath*)
aɪ	**ei-**	(as in *either*)
juː	**eu-**	(as in *Europe*)